About the Editor

Ronald J. Manheimer is executive director of the North Carolina Center for Creative Retirement (NCCCR), a program of the University of North Carolina at Asheville, where he also holds an appointment as research associate professor of philosophy. Before becoming the NCCCR's first full-time director in 1988, Manheimer was director of older adult education at The National Council on the Aging (NCOA). He directed NCOA's national arts and humanities programs and its special collection in social gerontology, the Ollie A. Randall Library. Between 1984 and 1989, Manheimer was a member of the American Library Association's Library Services to an Aging Population Committee.

Trained in philosophy with a Ph.D. from the Board of Studies in History of Consciousness, University of California, Santa Cruz, Manheimer has combined theoretical and applied interests in aging by conducting research and developing educational programs for seniors in colleges, universities, libraries, senior centers, nursing homes, and retirement communities. Among published articles investigating philosophical issues of human development is his book, *Kierkegaard as Educator*. His entry to the field of aging came in 1977 when he volunteered to teach a humanities course at the Thurston County Senior Center in Olympia, Washington. Since then he has served as project director for seven public humanities programs for older adults, funded by the National Endowment for the Humanities. Manheimer conducts workshops and lectures on creativity, the humanities, and aging, and is the 1993–96 chairman of the American Society on Aging's Older Adult Education Network.

The North Carolina Center for Creative Retirement (NCCCR) was established in 1987 to promote opportunities for lifelong learning, leadership, and community service for retirement-age citizens of North Carolina. A program of the University of North Carolina at Asheville, the NCCCR serves as a laboratory for the state and the nation through the design, implementation, and evaluation of innovative educational programs in which seniors not only participate but exercise leadership and creativity.

The long-range mission of the NCCCR is to help foster an age-integrated society in which generations work together to improve the overall quality of life. The NCCCR has been featured in national publications such as the *New York Times*, *Parade* magazine, and the *Christian Science Monitor*. Volunteers of the center were honored when the White House designated the NCCCR as President George Bush's 360th Daily Point of Light.

The NCCCR conducts research and offers yearly workshops and seminars related to retirement lifestyles, older learners, public policy, and model programs.

OLDER AMERICANS ALMANAC

Highlights

Persons interested in a comprehensive reference providing information on all aspects on the subject of aging in the United States can turn to one accurate, convenient source: *Older Americans Almanac*. Arranged by 38 chapters that cover everything from the experiences of and attitudes toward aging in colonial times to aging in the 1990s and beyond, the *Almanac* integrates current and background information on a given subject and lists additional readings and resources to point the reader in the right direction for continued study. *Older Americans Almanac* covers a broad scope of topics, including:

- History, demography, and diversity of aging
- Physical, mental, and social processes of aging
- Government, politics, and law
- Employment and retirement
- Financial concerns
- Relationships and aging
- Health and wellness
- Health problems
- Elder care
- Social environments
- Lifestyles and choices

Arrangement Allows for Quick Information Access

Older Americans Almanac provides ample information, and its logical format makes it easy to use. The chapters contain subject-specific bibliographies and are enlivened by over 400 photographs, tables, and figures. Other value-added features include:

- Contents section, which details each chapter's coverage
- "Profiles of Productive Aging" and "Voices of Creative Aging" series, which highlight older Americans who have demonstrated innovation and determination while facing the challenges of aging
- Lists of organizations, including addresses, phone numbers, and fax numbers
- Suggestions for further reading and research
- General bibliography, which provides an alphabetical listing of classic literature in the field of aging
- Comprehensive keyword index, which lists primary and secondary locations of subjects

• • •

OLDER AMERICANS
ALMANAC

A Reference

Work on

Seniors in

the United

States

Ronald J. Manheimer, Ph.D., Editor

with

North Carolina Center for Creative Retirement,
University of North Carolina at Asheville

≡⊂ Gale Research Inc. • *DETROIT • WASHINGTON, D.C. • LONDON*

North Carolina Center for Creative Retirement Editorial Staff

Ronald J. Manheimer, *Managing Editor*
Carolyn Williams, *Contributing Editor*
Martin J. Ambrose, Eone G. Harger, Leah R. Karpen, Charles W. Parton, Lyn E. Teven, and Bettina H. Wolff, *Editorial Management Team*

Gale Research Inc. Staff

Lawrence W. Baker, *Senior Developmental Editor*
Jane Hoehner, *Contributing Developmental Editor*

Amy Marcaccio, *Acquisitions Editor*

Mary Beth Trimper, *Production Director*
Evi Seoud, *Assistant Production Manager*
Shanna P. Heilveil, *Production Assistant*

Cynthia Baldwin, *Art Director*
Barbara J. Yarrow, *Graphic Services Supervisor*
Mark C. Howell, *Cover Designer*
Sherrell Hobbs, *Page Designer*

Cover photographs (clockwise): © Alice A. Hardin (woman fishing); © Marianne Gontarz (ballerinas); and © Marianne Gontarz (man and boy).

Library of Congress Cataloging-in-Publication Data

Older Americans almanac / edited by R. Manheimer.
    p.   cm.
    Includes bibliographical references (p.   ) and index.
    ISBN 0-8103-8348-9 (acid-free paper) : $99.50
    1. Old age—United States—Encyclopedias. 2. Aged—United States—Encyclopedias. 3. Aging—United States—Encyclopedias. 4. Gerontology—United States—Encyclopedias.   I. Manheimer, Ronald J.
HQ1064.U50416   1994   94-9305
305.26′0973—dc20   CIP

♾ This book is printed on acid-free paper that meets the minimum requirements of American National Standard for Information Sciences—Permanence Paper for Printed Library Materials, ANSI Z39.48-1984.

♻ This book is printed on recycled paper that meets Environmental Protection Agency standards.

ISBN 0-8103-8348-9
Printed in the United States of America by Gale Research Inc.
Published simultaneously in the United Kingdom
by Gale Research International Limited
(An affiliated company of Gale Research Inc.)

The trademark ITP is used under license.

This book is dedicated to the memory and spirit of Jack Ossofsky (1925–92) who, in his service as director of The National Council on the Aging, strove to improve and empower the lives of older Americans.

Contents

Preface

Audience and Scope

Older Americans Almanac provides information on aging-related topics in the United States for older persons, their families and friends, those who provide services to seniors, individuals seeking to learn about aging and later life, students, and other concerned citizens.

The *Almanac* is more than a fact book since it provides explanatory information. In many places an effort has been made to alert users of the *Almanac* that certain facts and statistics about older adults are controversial and subject to numerous interpretations and sometimes opposing conclusions.

Self-help recommendations or how-to instruction are generally not prescribed within the context of *Almanac* chapters. The list of additional reading at the end of each chapter usually includes books of this type.

Perspectives on Aging

Attitudes toward aging and later life have undergone profound changes during the twentieth century. In the United States and other post-industrial countries with long-life expectancy rates and large percentages of older adults, one finds ambivalent views. Old age is alternately regarded as a burden on the individual and society, a time of decline and dependency, or is seen as a boon in which individuals spend their retirement years enjoying life while drawing on the strengths and wisdom of experience to serve the community.

Older Americans Almanac has the balanced viewpoint that both strengths and weaknesses accompany the aging process. Topics such as wellness, lifelong learning, spiritual development, and volunteerism are surveyed, while chronic health problems, caring for the elderly, and end-of-life issues are also carefully considered. This balanced coverage attempts to reflect contemporary experiences of later life—the gains and losses that come with aging.

The meaning of terms like old age, later life, or retirement are not static; they are continually being revised. Some people have discarded the stereotypical retiree-in-a-rocking-chair lifestyle in favor of taking educational trips through national parks, exploring full- or part-time careers, following the sun in their RVs, choosing to serve as volunteer tutors in public schools, or helping look after the grandchildren. Each new wave of retirement-age people brings different prior life experiences and, thus, different expectations to later lifestyles. There are few established role models to follow. Consequently, today's older persons are pathfinders in this new terrain of the life course. The *Almanac* reflects this dynamic process and diversity of choices.

Definition of "Older American"

The term older Americans, in this volume, generally refers to citizens of the United States over age 65. There are, however, many places in the *Almanac* where discussion also includes people 10 to 20 years younger. The reason: most federal legislation, such as the Older Americans Act, identifies the status of being older with reaching age 65, but some legislation, such as the Age Discrimination in Employment Act, regards "older workers" as those 45 and over. Similarly, economic and demographic data reported in the *Almanac* sometimes compare younger age groups with those 65 and over. Without a comparative context, some information loses its meaning. For example, it is important to compare poverty rates, income distribution, or population growth of older adults with younger age groups.

Information Pathways

Almanac users may follow several pathways to obtain information: the expanded contents section shows the main subjects discussed in each chapter—subjects that correspond to the bulleted headings at the beginning of each chapter; the detailed index shows primary and secondary locations of subjects.

The book begins with a chapter recounting the experiences of and attitudes toward aging from colonial times to the present day, and ends with a chapter on aging in the 1990s and future trends. *Almanac* sections that lie between these time-framing chapters offer readers information on demographic, legal, political, economic, social, health, and lifestyle issues affecting the elderly.

Topics have been placed in meaningful sections and chapter sequences that aid a reader's search for information. For example, the first section, "Aging in the United States: History, Demography and Diversity," contains three chapters that link interrelated issues: 1) how aging and old age have emerged in the second half of the twentieth century as issues of major importance in the United States; 2) how one should under-

stand the meaning of a demographically aging society and the various, often complicated, statistics that have been gathered; and 3) why diversity, influenced by factors of gender, race and ethnicity, is the hallmark of the U.S. aging population.

Another section, "The Process of Aging," provides an overview of three frameworks for understanding the process of growing older: the physical, mental, and social aspects of aging. This section is particularly appropriate for individuals seeking a general, comprehensive survey of how aging has been studied by biologists, psychologists, and sociologists. The three chapters found in this section function as a condensed version of gerontology, the science of aging.

Subsequent sections of the *Almanac* focus on more narrowly defined topics such as the new field of elder law, older Americans' participation in the political process, trends in work and retirement, and so on. The guiding strategy of each chapter is to lay out the subject according to its most important components—as indicated by the bulleted headings at each chapter's beginning—and then to direct the reader through the secondary and tertiary subcomponents. Chapter references and lists of additional reading and resources then point the reader to more in-depth sources.

A number of *Almanac* chapters have extensive citations of journal articles and specialized monographs. Many of these publications are only available through major university or urban libraries and through databases such as ERIC or the *Social Science Research Index*. Whether or not the *Almanac* user wishes to find these articles, he or she will at least be aware of the existence of supporting research and its currency.

Other Organizational Features

The *Almanac* attempts to place information in a meaningful context. Even if readers are uninterested in the research and policy dimensions of a subject, they should at least be aware that many subjects in aging are in a dynamic state of flux and that things as they are today may not have been that way yesterday and, indeed, may change tomorrow.

Unique to *Older Americans Almanac* is the integration of current and background information on a given subject with additional reference to the current state of research. For example, a discussion of Social Security, Medicare, and Medicaid not only includes descriptions of these benefit programs as we know them today, but historical background on when and how they originated, have evolved, and may change in the near future.

Perhaps more unusual is the *Almanac's* separation of health related topics into separate sections of "Health and Wellness" (Section VII) and "Health Problems" (Section VIII). A deliberate effort has been made to avoid discussing physical and mental well-being from a single clinical or medical perspective.

A contemporary trend is to view later life as a positive developmental stage rather than as a disease state. This is not to deny the inevitable illnesses and declines that come as one grows old, but it is to offset the biased perspective that regards later life as a one-way trip down a parabolic slope to the nadir of life. People do not get sick simply because they get older, nor do they stop growing psychologically and spiritually. Normal and optimal possibilities of health in later life deserve exploration.

Other Elements: "Voices of Creative Aging" and "Profiles of Productive Aging"

Two cameo series run through the *Almanac*. Public radio producer Connie Goldman provides excerpts from her audio interviews with people who have demonstrated innovation in coping with the challenges and limitations of later life. Her "Voices of Creative Aging" sketches help to put a face on the *Almanac's* abstract information about the elderly, reminding us of the diversity of responses to aging.

Lydia Brontë's "Profiles of Productive Aging" offer portraits of the energy, fortitude, and determination exhibited by over 40 people who created new careers after age 50 or remained vitally involved in their fields into later life. Most profiled individuals are well-known public figures.

Almanac Contributors: Aging Experts, Librarians, and Older Adults

Three groups of people collaborated to produce the *Older Americans Almanac*. Over 40 experts from the field of aging wrote the chap-

ters, several librarians (both employed and retired) helped shape the *Almanac's* informational form, and a team of retirees from the North Carolina Center for Creative Retirement critiqued the preliminary outlines and first drafts of chapters.

The experts represent a broad diversity of interests and specialties. For example, geriatric fellows (recently graduated doctors undergoing specialized training in geriatric medicine) and their faculty advisors from the Bowman Gray School of Medicine at Wake Forest University wrote many of the medical and health care chapters. Research gerontologists in sociology from the Duke University Center for Aging and Human Development and the University of North Carolina at Greensboro contributed information on relationships, social support, and caregiving. Other chapter contributors brought their knowledge of history, literature, politics, architecture, finance, and technology to the subject of aging.

The librarians provided ongoing evaluation of the *Almanac* as it developed by suggesting ways to balance factual information with explanatory text, providing recommendations for additional up-to-date readings, guiding user-friendly construction of the index and table of contents, and generally trying to insure the *Almanac's* usefulness to both librarians and patrons, as well as non-library users of reference books.

Editorial work on *Older Americans Almanac* was based in the offices of the University of North Carolina at Asheville's (UNCA's) North Carolina Center for Creative Retirement (NCCCR), an institute widely recognized for its innovative work promoting lifelong learning, leadership, and community service on the part of retirement-age citizens. UNCA's progressive belief that education knows no age limit and the university's support of a center where retirement-age people can pursue intellectual and artistic interests while benefitting the campus and community dramatically exemplifies the *Almanac's* approach to aging.

The team of editorial advisors, made up of volunteers from the NCCCR, functioned in two ways. Members of the team drew upon their own expertise in medicine, gerontology, librarianship, recreation, journalism, and other fields to evaluate the relevance of each chapter's content. They also approached the material as representative older adults, asking themselves whether each chapter was comprehensive, easily understood, well-documented, and interesting to read. Team members thought of their own information needs on a given subject and determined how well each chapter met those needs. A synthesis of their comments was reported to each contributor as part of the revision process.

The commitment of scholar-contributors, information specialists, additional consultants, and NCCCR members made assembling the *Almanac* a less arduous and more satisfying task.

Ronald J. Manheimer, Ph.D.
Editor

Acknowledgments

The editors are grateful to the following individuals who reviewed many of the chapters of this book and made suggestions related to content:

David A. Berkey, M.A. CCC-A
Alan Baumgarten, M.D.
Robert Douglas, C.P.A.
Ruth M. Katz, Ph.D.
Nancy Lesko, B.A.
Charles E. Lilien, M.A.
Harry R. Moody, Ph.D.

Staff members of Thoms Rehabilitation Hospital

Joan Chesick, CCC-A

William R. Neeriemer, CCC-SLP
Jenny Womack, MS, OTR-L

Special consultants

Mary Jo Brazil, M.L.S., Librarian, Vintage Health Library, Alta Bates Medical Center, Berkeley, California
Robert C. Atchley, Ph.D., Director, Scripps Gerontology Center, Miami University of Ohio

The editors also thank the following people for their contributions:

Beth Baker, for data entry and coding; Fran Locher Freiman, for copyediting; Theresa Murray, for indexing; and Linda Quigley, for proofreading.

Contributors

William A. Achenbaum is professor of history at the University of Michigan, Ann Arbor, and deputy director of its Institute of Gerontology. He holds a Ph.D. in history from the University of Michigan. He has written several books and articles on the history of old age in the United States, most notably *Old Age in the New Land, Shades of Gray,* and *Social Security: Visions and Revisions.* Achenbaum is currently a board member of the National Council on the Aging, Inc.

Rebecca G. Adams is associate professor of sociology at the University of North Carolina at Greensboro. She received a Ph.D. from the University of Chicago, with an emphasis on the sociology of aging. Her major research interest is friendship patterns, especially as they are affected by geographic separation and by cultural and structural context. She is co-editor of *Older Adult Friendship: Structure and Process,* co-author of *Adult Friendship,* and author of numerous articles.

Richard F. Afable is assistant professor with the Section on Internal Medicine and Gerontology at the Bowman Gray School of Medicine, Wake Forest University, Winston-Salem, North Carolina. He received his M.D. from Loyola-Stritch School of Medicine in Chicago and his master's degree in public health at the University of Illinois. He has

spent 12 years in the practice of internal medicine with particular emphasis on care of the elderly. His scholarly interests include preventive health issues and the use of exercise as a therapeutic measure in the treatment and prevention of chronic disability in older people.

Robert C. Atchley is director of the Scripps Gerontology Center and distinguished professor of gerontology at Miami University of Ohio. Joining Miami in 1966, Atchley quickly established a nationally known research program on adjustment to retirement. In 1972, he published the first widely used textbook in social gerontology. Now in its sixth edition, *Social Forces and Aging* has introduced more than 400,000 college students to this new field. Atchley has published more than a dozen other books, including *The Sociology of Retirement, Families in Later Life,* and *Aging: Continuity and Change.*

Lydia Brontë, a former research fellow at the Phelps-Stokes Institute in New York City, is director of The Long Careers Study, an exploration of longevity's affects on work and life. From 1982 to 1987 Brontë was director of The Aging Society Project, a study sponsored by Carnegie Corporation of New York, which led to a book she co-edited, *Our Aging Society: Paradox and Promise.* Her most recent publication is *The*

Longevity Factor. Brontë holds a Ph.D. in comparative literature from the University of North Carolina at Chapel Hill.

Nancy M. Coleman is director of the American Bar Association Commission on Legal Problems of the Elderly. She is responsible for all of the commission's activities with special emphasis on elder abuse, assisted housing, and protective services. She serves as the commission's advocate with the ABA as well as the aging and legal communities. Coleman received an A.B. from the University of California at Santa Cruz, and an M.S.W. and M.A. from the University of Michigan. She has published many articles related to legal planning for incapacity and advocacy in the Older Americans Act.

Christopher C. Colenda III is associate professor of psychiatry and behavioral sciences and an associate in the Department of Public Health Sciences at the Bowman Gray School of Medicine, Wake Forest University. He received his bachelor's degree in chemistry from Wittenburg University and his M.D. from the Medical College of Virginia. In addition, he received a master's degree in public health from the Johns Hopkins University. Colenda is also a member of the American Psychiatric Association's Council on Aging, where he serves on the Task Force of Practice Models in Geriatric Psychiatry and the Task Force of Geriatric Psychiatry in the Public Health Sector.

Christine L. Day is assistant professor of political science at the University of New Orleans. She is the author of *What Older Americans Think: Interest Groups and Aging Policy* and articles about public opinion and the politics of aging. Day received a Ph.D. in political science from the University of California at Berkeley.

Lilian Fischer is the principal of Fischer Financial Architects, an investment management firm in Asheville, North Carolina, serving individuals and institutions. Fischer has taught investment seminars for older adults. She earned master's and doctoral degrees from European universities and has held faculty positions at the University of Virginia and the University of Kentucky.

Lucy Rose Fischer is research scientist at Group Health Foundation in Minneapolis, Minnesota. Prior to joining Group Health, she directed the older volunteers project for the Wilder Research Center at the Amherst H. Wilder Foundation. Her most recent book is *Older Volunteers: A Guide to Research and Practice.* She is also the author of *Older Minnesotans: What Do They Need? How Do They Contribute?* and *Linked Lives: Adult Daughters and Their Mothers.* Her work has been cited in the popular press, and she has been interviewed on radio and television talk shows, including Minnesota Public Radio, *Donahue, Hour Magazine,* and *CBS Morning News.* She has been on the faculties of the University of Minnesota and St. Olaf College, and is a fellow of the Gerontological Society of America.

Lois Fuller is a freelance writer whose work has focused on economic development issues. She has worked as a correspondent for newspapers and has a background of experience in real estate sales and construction. Fuller received a bachelor's degree in university studies from the University of New Mexico.

George Gaberlavage is a senior analyst with the Public Policy Institute of the American Association of Retired Persons (AARP) where he specializes in housing and community planning issues. Prior to joining AARP, he was senior federal liaison with the National Association of Regional Councils where he worked with local government officials on the Older Americans Act and housing and environmental programs. A graduate of the State University of New York College at Fredonia, where he received a bachelor's degree in political science, he holds a master's degree in public administration in public policy from The American University in Washington, D.C.

Lawrence H. Geiger is a sociologist specializing in public opinion and marketing research. He has conducted public opinion surveys for a national news organization and has implemented marketing studies for a wide variety of consumer products and services. He graduated magna cum laude with a B.A. in philosophy from Brandeis University and received an M.A. in sociology from Columbia University. Geiger works as an independent consultant in applied social research.

Linda K. George is professor in the departments of Psychiatry and Sociology at Duke University. She received her Ph.D. from Duke University, and serves as the associate director for social and behavioral programs at the Duke

University Center for the Study of Aging and Human Development. George is the author of six books, including *Role Transition in Later Life* and *Quality of Life in Older Persons: Meaning and Measurement*, and is co-editor of the third edition of the *Handbook of Aging and the Social Sciences*. George is the 1994 president of the Gerontological Society of America.

Deborah T. Gold is assistant professor of medical sociology in the departments of Psychiatry and Sociology at the Duke University Medical Center, and a senior fellow in the Duke University Center for the Study of Aging. She received a Ph.D. in human development and social policy from Northwestern University. Her research has focused on changes in sibling relationships across the life course, with special emphasis on siblings in late life and coping with chronic disease in late life, specifically older adults with osteoporosis, Paget's disease of bone, cancer, and depression.

Connie Goldman is a public radio producer, writer, and speaker. For the past decade, all of her work has focused on issues and images of aging. Her nationally broadcast public radio programs include the award-winning series "Late Bloomer." She is co-author of *The Ageless Spirit* and *Secrets of How to Be a Late Bloomer*. Goldman holds an M.A. in communications from the University of Minnesota, and an M.A. in applied psychology from the University of Santa Monica.

William H. Haas III is associate professor of sociology at the University of North Carolina at Asheville. He received his Ph.D. in sociology, specializing in social and medical gerontology, from the University of Florida. Haas' publications have focused on health care issues and aging, particularly the impact of retirement migrants on their host local community. Recently he completed an extensive survey project on amenity migrant retirees' influence on local economic development.

Martha Holstein is currently completing her doctorate at the Institute for Medical Humanities at the University of Texas medical branch in Galveston after fourteen years as the associate director of the American Society on Aging. She has taught courses in ethics and aging at the University of California, Berkeley, and San Francisco State University, co-edited *A Good Old Age? The Paradox of Setting Limits*, covering the rationing of health care, and authored a number of articles and book chapters on aging.

Thomas D. Hughes is associated with the Foundation of Memorial Mission Medical Center in Asheville, North Carolina, where he serves as director of gift planning. He received a bachelor of arts from Ohio University. He has been granted the chartered financial consultant designation by The American College in Bryn Mawr, Pennsylvania, and has been awarded The American College's certificate in personal financial planning. Hughes has been on the faculty for conferences of the Association for Healthcare Philanthropy and the National Society of Fund Raising Executives.

Richard E. Johnson, a pychologist and psychotherapist, completed his doctorate at the University of Georgia in social psychology and did postdoctoral work in clinical psychology at Kent State University. He is in private practice at the Center for Change in Hendersonville, North Carolina. Johnson uses mythic stories in conducting workshops with adolescents and adults, and most recently with "elders" at the Center for Creative Retirement at the University of North Carolina in Asheville.

Robert J. Kastenbaum is professor of communications at Arizona State University. He served as director of adult development and aging at Arizona State University from 1981 to 1988. He received a Ph.D. in psychology from the University of Southern California in 1959, and did postdoctoral studies at the Institute of Human Development at Clark University. A past president of the American Association of Suicidology and the Division of Adult Development and Aging of the American Psychological Association, Kastenbaum continues to serve as editor of the *International Journal of Aging and Human Development* and *Omega: Journal of Death and Dying*. His writings include *The Psychology of Death* and *The Encyclopedia of Adult Development*.

Alice Lee and Fred Lee have co-authored *A Field Guide to Retirement* and are currently writing *The 50 Best Retirement Communities in America and 20 That Should Make Future Lists*. Since 1977 they have worked in partnership as retirement consultants, running retirement seminars. Fred Lee received a degree in business administration from Cleveland State University.

Steve Lee is a transportation program specialist with the American Association of Retired Persons (AARP) and is a nationally recognized expert on issues of public transit, older drivers, and transportation safety. Prior to joining AARP, he worked as a project manager with the National Association of Counties; as a government relations officer and senior planner with the regional government of metropolitan Portland, Oregon; and as administrator for the transportation and local government committees in the Oregon legislature. Currently, Lee is completing his master's degree in urban and regional planning degree at George Washington University in Washington, D.C.

Charles F. Longino, Jr., is Wake Forest University's distinguished professor of sociology and public health sciences. He is associate director of the J. Paul Sticht Center on Aging at the Bowman Gray School of Medicine and the director of the Reynolda Gerontology Program. Longino also taught at the universities of Miami, Kansas, Virginia, and North Carolina. He received a Ph.D. from the University of North Carolina at Chapel Hill and in the mid-1970s was a post doctoral fellow in the Midwest Council for Social Research in Aging. Longino's essays on aging and demography are found in numerous handbooks and encyclopedias, as well as in such publications as *American Demographics*. Since 1975, his research has been continuously funded by either the National Institute on Aging, the Social Security Administration, or the AARP-Andrus Foundation.

Mary Fennell Lyles is an associate professor of internal medicine in the Section on Internal Medicine and Gerontology at Bowman Gray School of Medicine of Wake Forest University, Winston-Salem, North Carolina. She received a bachelor of arts in biology from St. Louis University and an M.D. at the University of Mississippi. Her current professional interests are patient care, research in the teaching of geriatric medicine, medical direction of a long term care facility, and research on health promotion, notably smoking cessation. She has received American Board of Internal Medicine certification in internal medicine and geriatrics.

Kyriakos S. Markides is professor of preventive medicine and community health and is the director of the Division of Sociomedical Sciences at the University of Texas Medical Branch in Galveston. He received his Ph.D. in sociology from Louisiana State University. Markides is founding editor of the *Journal of Aging and Health* and has authored over 100 journal articles, chapters, and books, dealing mostly with aging, ethnicity, health, and family relations. He has served on the editorial boards of *Gerontologist*, the *Journal of Gerontology*, *Research on Aging*, *Abstracts in Social Gerontology*, *The Southwestern: The Journal of Aging in the Southwest*, and *Ethnicity and Disease*.

Olivia P. Maynard is the president and founder of the Michigan Prospect for Renewed Citizenship, a nonprofit policy institute committed to the development of a creative role for government and public institutions in shaping the future of the state. She received her B.A. in political science from George Washington University in Washington, D.C., and her master's in social work from the University of Michigan. Maynard served as director of the Michigan Office of Services to the Aging for eight years (1983–90) and more recently has taught at the University of Michigan School of Social Work and the Lansing Community College Center for Aging Education. In 1990 she ran for lieutenant governor with then-governor James J. Blanchard.

Catherine Messick is currently a fellow in the Section on Internal Medicine and Gerontology at the Bowman Gray School of Medicine of Wake Forest University in Winston-Salem, North Carolina. She graduated from the University of North Carolina School of Medicine and then completed a residency in internal medicine at the University of Rochester in New York. She left private practice in 1990 to pursue a master's degree in epidemiology. She is actively involved in the development and study of innovative health care delivery programs for the elderly. Messick is board-certified in internal medicine and has a certificate of added qualifications in geriatric medicine.

William P. Moran is assistant professor of medicine at the Bowman Gray School of Medicine of Wake Forest University where his research interests are applications of computer technology to preventive health care, disease screening, and primary care medical practice. He received his M.D. from the Georgetown University School of Medicine in Washington, D.C., where he subsequently took residency training in internal medicine. He practiced for four years at the Dorchester House Health Center under the auspices of the National Health Service Corps before completing fellowship training in Geriatric Medicine at the Bowman Gray School of Medicine and a master's degree in epidemiology at Wake Forest University.

Diane Moskow-McKenzie is a research associate with the North Carolina Center for Creative Retirement at the University of North Carolina at Asheville. She received a B.A. in psychology from Bellarmine College in Louisville, Kentucky, and a master's degree in public affairs/public administration from Boise State University in Idaho. She recently conducted a national study of the planning stages of 260 older adult educational programs in senior centers, Shepherd's Centers, OASIS (Older Adult Service and Information Systems), community colleges, four-year colleges, and universities. Her publications relating to older adult education include *Older Adults Education: A Guide to Research, Program, and Policies.*

Kani Louise Nicolls has a private practice in portable dentistry for homebound and nursing home individuals in Asheville, North Carolina. She completed her D.D.S. degree at the University of California at Los Angeles (UCLA) and moved east to complete a general practice residency at the University of North Carolina School of Dentistry and a fellowship in geriatrics through the university's School of Medicine, Program in Aging.

Barbara Pittard Payne is emerita professor of sociology and director of the Gerontology Center at Georgia State University in Atlanta. She holds a Ph.D. in sociology and a master's degree in philosophy from Emory University. Since 1963 her major research, writing, teaching, and professional interests have focused on religion and aging. Among her publications is a book she co-authored with Earl D.C. Brewer entitled *Gerontology in Theological Education.* She is currently head of Payne and Associates Aging Consultants, chair of the Georgia Council on Aging, and serves on state and national boards and committees of the United Methodist Church.

Donald L. Redfoot is a legislative representative on housing and transportation issues with the American Association of Retired Persons (AARP). Previously he served as a congressional

staff member to the House Aging Committee's Subcommittee on Housing and Consumer Interests where he wrote a committee report on the Congregate Housing Services Program. He received a Ph.D. in sociology from Rutgers University after receiving an M.A. in the philosophy and history of the social sciences from the University of Chicago and a B.A. in sociology from Westminster College. He spent three years as a post-doctoral fellow at the Aging Center at Duke University.

Harold L. Sheppard is professor of gerontology at the University of South Florida in Tampa. He received his Ph.D. in sociology and anthropology from the University of Wisconsin and his master's degree in sociology from the University of Chicago. Sheppard was the first research director, and, later, staff director for the Senate Special Committee on Aging. He has written and edited several works on the older worker issue and the challenges of population aging for American and international organizations.

Stanley Smith is assistant professor in the Department of Family and Community Medicine at the Milton S. Hershey Medical Center in Hershey, Pennsylvania. Previously he was a fellow in geriatrics at the Bowman Gray School of Medicine of Wake Forest University. He received his bachelor's degree in chemistry from Emory University in 1982 and his M.D. from the Medical College of Georgia. In 1991, he received a master's degree in epidemiology from Wake Forest University.

Gordon F. Streib, graduate research professor emeritus of the University of Florida, has conducted extensive research in the field of aging, focusing on retirement, the family, and special housing for older people, such as retirement communities, congregate housing, and small group homes. In 1989, he received the highest research award of the Gerontological Society of America—the Robert Kleemeier Award. Among his major works are *Retirement in American Society* and *Old Homes—New Families: Shared Living for the Elderly.*

Lyn E. Teven is a freelance writer and retired editor living in Asheville, North Carolina. She has written for newspapers, magazines, and public relations clients, and done freelance editing and writing for U.S. government agencies. As the wife of a foreign service officer, she lived abroad in five different countries over a twenty-year period. She received a bachelor's degree in English/journalism from Cornell College in Iowa.

David R. Thomas is associate professor of internal medicine in the Division of Gerontology/Geriatric Medicine at the University of Alabama at Birmingham (UAB), and a scientist at the UAB Center for Aging. He received his M.D. from the University of Mississippi School of Medicine and is board certified in internal medicine and geriatric medicine. He received additional training as a John Hartford faculty fellow in geriatrics at Johns Hopkins School of Medicine. He is medical director of the hospital-based Home Care Program in Birmingham, and attending physician in the Kirklin Geriatric Assessment Clinic. He serves on the regional Long-Term Care Task Force and the Jefferson County Ombudsman Committee. Thomas has been active in advocacy for older adults at the state level in North Carolina and Alabama. He is a member of the American Geriatrics Society, the Gerontological Society of America, the Alabama Gerontological Society, and is a fellow of the American College of Physicians.

Ramon Valez is professor of medicine and a member of the Division of General Medicine and Gerontology at the Bowman Gray School of Medicine of Wake Forest University. He received his M.D. from the New York University Medical School in 1970, and obtained a master of science in epidemiology from the London School of Tropical Medicine in 1981. His research interests are in preventive medicine and in issues of access to medical services for minority populations. He is principal investigator on a National Cancer Institute project to increase breast and cervical cancer screening among elderly African-American women living in low income housing communities in Winston-Salem, North Carolina.

Margaret A. Wylde is vice president of the Institute for Technology Development, Inc. (ITD), a private, non-profit corporation conducting research and development of products and environments that meet the needs of an aging populace. ITD, through the leadership of Wylde, has provided research to dozens of companies and has evaluated more than 100 different consumer and assistive products. Wylde holds a Ph.D. from the University of Oklahoma. She is author of an array of papers and publications, including *Building for a Lifetime.*

Editorial Management Team

Martin J. Ambrose parlayed his years of trailer-traveling into involvement with *Highways*, a national magazine for recreational vehicle owners. For five years he was a regional editor and feature writer, following his early retirement from AT&T. He has also contributed articles to North Carolina newspapers and is presently engaged in newsletter writing and editing. Ambrose has an M.S. in business administration from Columbia University in New York.

Eone Harger served as director of the New Jersey Division on Aging from 1958 to 1970. Following retirement from her state position, she was staff associate on aging in the Department of Community Affairs, Community Service Society of New York City from 1972 to 1973. Other positions held during those years were: member of the board of the Gerontological Society of America as chairman of the Section on Research, Planning and Practice; president of the National Association of State Units on Aging; consultant to the Senate Special Committee on Aging; and three-time delegate to White House Conferences on Aging. Harger received her B.A. in English, history, and psychology from Oberlin College in Ohio.

Leah R. Karpen has taught management and business writing at the graduate and undergraduate levels. Most recently she has taught courses in contemporary issues at the College for Seniors at the University of North Carolina at Asheville (UNCA). She founded and edited for seven years the quarterly *Journal of World Education*, which had worldwide distribution. Karpen has an M.A. in management from the Polytechnic Institute of New York and an M.A. in liberal arts from UNCA.

Charles William Parton has held positions at Hartford Hospical as pediatric surgeon and director of emergency services; at Mt. Sinai (CT) Hospital as chairman of the Department of Ambulatory and Community Medicine and vice president for medical affairs; at the University of Connecticut School of Medicine as associate professor of medicine in the Department of Community Health Care; and at the University of Hartford (CT) as adjunct professor of health care administration in the graduate school of public administration. Parton received his M.D. from Cornell University, his M.P.H. from Yale University, and his B.A. from Kenyon College.

Lyn E. Teven is a freelance writer and retired editor. Before moving to Asheville in 1989, she edited a journal of abstracts on underwater physiology for a professional medical society in Washington, D.C. She also compiled and indexed the abstracts for publication in book form and edited the society's bimonthly newsletter. Teven is co-contributor to the *Older Americans Almanac* chapter "The Meaning and Uses of Leisure."

Bettina H. Wolff has publishing, library, and graduate teaching experience and has written and edited numerous articles, papers, and reports. Major work-related experience with an aging population came as head of the New York State Library for the Blind and Visually Handicapped, which involved extensive work with nursing homes and institutions serving the elderly, as well as direct service to older readers. Wolff has a Ph.D. in public administration from the State University of New York, an M.A. in library science from the Drexel Institute of Technology, and an M.A. in English literature from Bryn Mawr.

Credits

Photographs and illustrations appearing in *Older Americans Almanac* were received from the following sources:

The American Association of Retired Persons 34, 74, 80, 116, 148, 159, 160, 402, 470, 514, 626, 630, 631, 758 (both), 763; **American Association of Retired Persons from *The Perfect Fit: Creative Ideas for a Safe and Livable Home*** 622, 623, 624, 625; **American Institute of Architects in cooperation with the American Association of Homes for the Aging/Gary Tarleton, photographer; Richard D. Nelson, Co., architect** 629; **American Public Transit Association** 645, 652, 653; **Bowman-Gray/Baptist Hospital Medical Center** 181, 377, 386, 422, 424, 427, 430, 432, 470, 471, 473, 487, 519, 520, 523, 530, 533, 534, 544, 546; **Chautauqua Institution** 61, 345, 728; **CompuMed** 665; **George Dzahristos** 440, 442; **Isabel Egglin** 41, 64, 118, 125, 189, 562, 793; **ETAC USA** 669; **Ferno Healthcare** 667; **Paul Gilmore** 57, 80, 329, 399, 704; **Givens Estates United Methodist Retirement Community, Asheville, North Carolina** 634; **Marianne Gontarz** 24, 26, 36, 51, 52, 91, 107, 114, 126, 169, 173, 174, 182, 195, 201, 209, 245, 320, 323, 326, 338, 347, 351, 352, 361, 365, 375, 382, 384, 392, 397, 399, 406, 410, 413, 420, 504, 507, 528, 545, 558, 561, 565, 567, 582, 584, 590, 618, 706, 784, 796; **Alex Gotfryd** 890; **Susan Granados** 777; **Michael Halsband** 459; **Alice A. Hardin** 93, 648; **Thomas Hardin** 644, 647; **Highland Farms Retirement Community, Black Mountain, North Carolina** 618, 637; **Donal F. Holway** 661; **Kohler Co.** 668; **Phil Kukelhan** 412, 796; **Library of Congress** 5, 7, 9, 11, 12 (both), 15 (both), 16 (both), 17; **Lifeline Systems Inc.** 682; **Love Lift** 674; **Lou Manna, Inc.** 170; **Med/West** 670; **Helaine Messer** 27; **The National Association for the Advancement of Colored People** 161; **The National Council on the Aging, Inc.** 127, 134, 137, 163, 199, 203, 217, 242, 760; **The National Council on the Aging, Inc./Lauren Fyfe, photographer** 530; **The National Council on the Aging, Inc./Jerry Hecht, photographer** 393, 563, 573, 637; **NobleMotion, Inc.** 675, 676; **Office of Senior Affairs, City of Albuquerque** 360; **J. C. Penney** 671; **Benjamin Porter** 34, 234, 489, 724, 726, 731, 736, 764, 769, 775, 790; **Recreation Vehicle Industry Association** 800; **ReSound Corp.** 679; **Anne Sager** 788; **Sanders-Brown Center on Aging, University of Kentucky/Tim Collins, photographer** 60, 96, 104, 214, 229, 448, 542, 611; **Tadder Photography/Courtesy of the Senate Special Committee on Aging** 136; **Ted Hoyer, Inc.** 684; **Wachter for the Chautauqua**

Institution 101; **Warman N.Y.** 425; **Wenzelite Corp.** 675; **William Nycum Architects Ltd./ David A. Steward Photography, photographer** 636; **Williams Sound** 679; **Winsford Products, Inc.** 672; and **Xerox Imaging Systems** 681.

Section I:

Aging in the United States: History, Demography, and Diversity

①

A History of Aging in America

● Old Age Across the Centuries ● Aging in the Settlement, Colonial, and Revolutionary Periods
● Old Age in the New Land, 1790 to 1900
● The Elderly in the New Urban-Industrial Order, 1870 to 1930
● The Great Depression as a Turning Point in the History of U.S. Aging
● The Elderly in an Age of Affluence

Historical demographers report that three-quarters of all gains in life expectancy at birth throughout world history have been registered since 1900. A child born ninety years ago could be expected to live about forty-seven years. Today, life expectancy at birth in the United States exceeds seventy-five years. Baby girls on average can expect to live about five years longer than baby boys. Most of the gains in life expectancy result from improvements in prenatal and postnatal care and from our success in conquering childhood diseases and epidemics. Illustrating the statistical differences dramatically, note that a child born in 1790 had as much probability of reaching his or her first birthday as a child born in 1970 is likely to reach age 65. Significant gains in adult life expectancy, especially for women, also occurred during the last half century. This demographic revolution affects all sorts of interpersonal relationships. More than ever before, most Americans can reasonably expect to live to see their grandchildren. For the first time in U.S. history, there are more people over age sixty-five than teenagers in the population. With increasing numbers of older men and women has come a growing awareness of the diversity of late-life experiences.

Older people are not all alike; they never have been. For example, gender differences have become critically important, especially in this

century. Prior to 1940 the U.S. Bureau of the Census reported that there were more older men than women. Many women died in early adulthood from complications of pregnancy or childbearing. Due mainly to improvements in obstetrics and gynecology, this pattern reversed. By 1987 nearly 60 percent of all people over 65 in the United States were females. The predominance of women is even more noticeable among those over 75: women constituted 51 percent of this group in 1890, 53 percent in 1940, and 65 percent in 1987. Race also affects the composition of the elderly. Life expectancy at birth for whites is considerably greater than for African Americans. The incidence of disability occurs earlier and more frequently in later life among African Americans than among whites. Cultural

Prior to 1940 the U.S. Bureau of the Census reported that there were more older men than women. Many women died in early adulthood from complications of pregnancy or childbearing. Due mainly to improvements in obstetrics and gynecology, this pattern reversed. By 1987 nearly 60 percent of all people over 65 in the United States were females.

3

as well as biological forces interact to create diversity and inequity in later years. More than 50 percent of all elderly African-American women subsist on incomes below the official U.S. poverty line, attesting to the effects of racism, sexism, and ageism throughout their lives.

While there is no question that being old in twentieth century America is very different from past conditions, it must be added that the aged's current circumstances also bear remarkable similarities to appearances and experiences in ancient times. Thus, in addition to describing changes over time, historians of aging must also take note of things that have not changed. History shows that the dissimilarity that characterizes the lives of older Americans today is hardly the hallmark of the modern era. The aged have always been a diverse group. They had no less dazzling an array of feelings, assets and liabilities, and attributes in earlier times as now. Accordingly, basic continuities in the human dimensions of aging figure in the unique experiences and meanings of old age that have emerged in twentieth century America.

● OLD AGE ACROSS THE CENTURIES

Scientists believe that the maximum life span of humans is roughly 120 years, the same amount of time cited in the Old Testament (Genesis 6:3) and by observers in ancient times and the Middle Ages. Modern-day experts validate the number's accuracy. This means that most of us will never attain our full potential longevity—despite enormous gains during this century in life expectancy at birth and modest gains in adult life expectancy. Nature has programmed a demographic gap. The causes of death for most Americans in the late twentieth century (various forms of cancer, cardiopulmonary diseases, accidents) differ from what killed earlier generations (influenza, pneumonia, epidemics, unsanitary conditions). But even if we were to find a cure for AIDS, heart attacks, and cancer, most Americans alive today will not become centenarians.

No single factor triggers the human aging process. Scientists suspect that the human body has built into it several systems designed to bring on death. Part of the aging process (possibly as much as 50 percent) is governed by genetics.

Long-lived people tend to have long-lived parents, grandparents, etc. Many theories for what causes aging have been proposed, but none are widely accepted; auto-immune, error, and wear-and-tear theories have gained popularity. Some scientists contend that cells self-destruct, or inadvertently create glitches in their message systems, or become frayed over the life cycle. Investigators suggest that older people may be vulnerable to diseases simply because they have been at risk longer than younger people. Alcoholism and drug abuse also take their toll.

Since ancient times people have been fascinated with extending the human life span, but it seems highly unlikely that lifetimes can be lengthened beyond 120 years. A question intriguing scientists in the late twentieth century is whether the gap between average life expectancy at birth and the maximum length of life can be narrowed. Some believe that this can happen: James Fries's concept of a compression of morbidity—that death occurs after a brief period of frailty or decline, before which the person has enjoyed a long and vigorous life—is a popular, recent version of this long-sought ideal.

Yet, as the number of people reaching old age increases, there is disturbing evidence that much remains to be done before such a compression of morbidity can be engineered. The fastest growing segment of the U.S. population is that over the age of 75. Recent studies of octogenarians and nonagenarians revealed hitherto unreported wide variations in this group's cognitive functioning, physical well-being, economic support, and household status. The incidence of disease clearly rises with advancing years. Chronic disabilities multiply over time. Americans presently 65 can expect to live another 16.9 years, but only part of this remaining life expectancy will be active. Members of this age-group on average are forecast to be functionally disabled for 6.9 years (U.S. Disability Commission, 1991). Living longer does not invariably enhance life quality.

The Hebrews expressed this reality in Psalm 90:9–10:

> For all our days pass away under your wrath;
> our years come to end like a sigh.
> The days of our life are seventy years,
> or perhaps eighty, if we are strong;
> Even then their span is only toil and trouble
> they are soon gone, and we fly away.

The psalmist offers two chronological benchmarks. Reaching 80 is seen as a sign of strength (it is called a reward in other scriptural passages), but the Ancients also knew that the blessing brought toil and trouble. So it is centuries later, according to Public Health statistics. The range in capacities among the nation's very oldest citizens suggests another dimension of diversity in late-life experiences that merits attention in the history of the science of aging, gerontology.

Americans presently 65 can expect to live another 16.9 years, but only part of this remaining life expectancy will be active.

Before elaborating on this diversity, however, it is worth commenting on the psalmist's use of chronological boundaries to mark the thresholds of old age. Given the startling gains in life expectancy at birth during this century, it is tempting to assume that old age began earlier once upon a time. Just three decades ago American youth shouted that they could not trust people over 30. Did the Romans look for gray hairs among those over the age of 21? Such was not the case. In the Bible, with exception of the lengthy years attributed to the patriarchs, the ages given for elders seem consistent with modern standards—from 60 to 90. In ancient Greece and Rome, age criteria for serving in a *gerusia* (literally the council of old men) or in the *senate* (a word derived from *senex*, meaning old) parallel present-day notions of how old a senior diplomat, professor, or actress should be.

The Boundaries of Old Age in America

In terms of U.S. experience, Americans have always recognized old age as a distinctive stage of life, beginning around age 65, though there is considerable (and, over time, consistent) variations around this mean. The American Association of Retired Persons (AARP) now accepts as members anyone over the age of 50 who can pay eight dollars for dues. In the early 1800s, the distinguished revolutionary physician, Benjamin Rush, began to keep a detailed diary on the health of his surviving patients, including only those who were at least 80. In his book *Medical Inquiries on Disease*, Rush wrote:

The moral faculties, when properly regulated and directed, never partake of the decay of intellectual faculties in old age, even in persons of uncultivated minds. It would seem as if they were placed beyond the influence, not only of time, but often of diseases, and accidents, from their exercises being so indispensably necessary to our happiness, more especially in the evening of our life.

Reasons for selecting certain ages vary with intellectual fashions and political calculations. Popular opinion holds that President Franklin D. Roosevelt made 65 the benchmark for receiving Social Security benefits because German chancellor Bismarck established that age for the German social insurance system in 1881 (the latter actually picked age 70, to keep costs down). Rather, New Deal policymakers chose 65 as a compromise: limiting eligibility to age 70 was too restrictive; providing benefits to people at age 60 was estimated to be too costly. So while certain chronological ages have long been used to designate the beginning of old age, the age-spread is

Revolutionary physician Benjamin Rush. (Courtesy of the Library of Congress)

Popular opinion holds that President Franklin D. Roosevelt made 65 the benchmark for receiving Social Security benefits because German chancellor Bismarck established that age for the German social insurance system in 1881 (the latter actually picked age 70, to keep costs down). Rather, New Deal policymakers chose 65 as a compromise: limiting eligibility to age 70 was too restrictive; providing benefits to people at age 60 was estimated to be too costly.

---

actually rather wide, especially when compared to the narrow parameters surrounding eligibility for kindergarten or the onset of puberty. The boundaries of old age in America can be bent fifteen years either way, because biological processes warrant such latitude. People begin to manifest the marks of age at varying rates. Some diseases appear age-specific in incidence, but most do not. Their duration varies from person to person. Nonetheless, growing older is not simply a biological phenomenon.

Culture clearly shapes old age. Many of the popular images held about the elderly result from older people's representations of themselves, ways they interact with different age groups, as well as the contributions they make and the demands they place on society. Across socio-economic and biological dimensions, the elderly have always been very diverse. While others of her generation have died or gone into retirement homes, actress Jessica Tandy is still acting in such films as *Fried Green Tomatoes* and *Cocoon*. Maggie Kuhn launched the Gray Panthers organization two years after being forced into retirement at age 65. Some people are more physically active at 80 than others at 60. And so it goes. The portion of the life span designated as old age is the longest stage of the human life cycle, and wide variations in wealth, power, kin ties, mobility, and personality traits have great impact on the aged.

Attitudes Toward Aging

Certain attitudes toward aging recur throughout world history since ancient times. Fear,

The portion of the life span designated as old age is the longest stage of the human life cycle, and wide variations in wealth, power, kin ties, mobility, and personality traits have great impact on the aged.

---

respect, despair, and defiance are all key elements characterizing younger people's images of their elders. But there have been shifts over time, despite biological and sociocultural continuities. The social, economic, political, and cultural dimensions of old age have altered at different rates, depending on the political economy and prevailing norms. Variations by race, class, gender, ethnicity, and sometimes even differences in age become significant. In the American experience there have not been any sudden changes in attitudes. Instead subtle modifications in work, sources of support, family relationships, and political options, among other things, have had a cumulative effect on meanings and experiences in the last stages of life.

● AGING IN THE SETTLEMENT, COLONIAL, AND REVOLUTIONARY PERIODS

U.S. historians probably know less about continuities and changes in the meanings and experiences of being old during the first decades of New World settlement than about any other era, and within that time frame, more is known about eighteenth- than sixteenth-century developments. (If U.S. history were to predate 1492, beginning with the arrival of the Asiatic migrants, then the historical record is extremely deficient. No ethnographic study of any tribe of Native-American elders yet exists.) Little is known about conditions during the seventeenth and eighteenth centuries in the South or in the middle colonies. As more historical information becomes available, some of the current observations will need modifying.

As in most Caribbean and Pacific outposts prior to 1800, youth dominated the Spanish, French, and British settlements dotting the Atlantic and Gulf coasts. According to the first U.S. census (1790), the median age of Americans was 16. Claims that the United States was a "young Republic" thus have a genuine demographic basis. There *were* older people in the New World. Two elderly couples came over on the *Mayflower* but it seems unlikely that senior citizens were among the founding patriarchs and matriarchs of Jamestown. If they were, they probably did not survive the first years, given the staggering mortality rates there. But many of the young and middle-aged people who figured that they would be better off if they crossed the Atlantic passage chose to stay in the New World. That is, they aged in place. In most seventeenth-century Massachusetts towns, 20-year-olds had roughly a 70 percent chance of surviving past their sixtieth birthday. So, once an area in New England had been occupied by Europeans persistently for about five decades, typically only one percent to three percent of its population was over 65.

The situation for older men in seventeenth and eighteenth century New England was sociologically advantageous but psychologically disadvantageous, and very little is known about older women during this period (Demos, 1978). Owner-

> According to the first U.S. census (1790), the median age of Americans was 16. Claims that the United States was a "young Republic" thus have a genuine demographic basis.

ship of land gave the aged power and control over their children and status in the local society. The old and the rich (with a high degree of correlation between the two) sat in the front of the meeting-house and were elected wardens, selectmen, officers of the militia, members of the town council, and representatives to the provincial assembly. Those who arrived first in the community typically acquired large tracts of land, which eventually would be divided among the children of each successive generation. Certain inequities, of course, arose from this arrangement. Those who held title early on to the choicest lots managed to gain wealth with minimal effort. Late-comers, even the

The Life and Age of Woman. Stages of a Woman's Life from the Cradle to the Grave. Hand colored lithograph by James Baille, 1848. (Courtesy of the Library of Congress)

shrewdest members of each successive generation, had to hustle if they hoped to do as well. Widows were only entitled to a third of their husbands' estates, which introduced a disparity in women's relative wealth and social standing compared to men.

Roles of Older Persons

Older people contributed to the well-being of fledgling communities by sharing their practical experience, which sometimes was painfully acquired. The aged, after all, were the ones most likely to remember how their own parents had survived Indian attacks, blizzards, and poor crop seasons. Having worked the land for decades, they were full of clever ideas for increasing productivity in a given vicinity. Older women often managed the domestic scene at advanced ages. Where else could the young acquire such insight? There were yet no *Farmer's Almanac*s for sale, nor were there agricultural extension bureaus or colleges. The aged were especially valued for their spiritual wisdom. Puritans honored gray hairs. Piety was expected, and virtue rewarded.

Older people were not always venerated, however. Many young men in colonial New England chafed under their fathers' rule. Without property, they could not marry. Neither could they take a fully adult role in society, nor act like independent agents. Sometimes waiting was costly: the more siblings who had a claim on the land, the smaller each share; the longer the land had been cultivated, the less fecund it was likely to be (especially if tobacco had been grown). Young women were bound by a different sort of patriarchal custom: they either lived with their parents or with their husbands. Living alone simply was not an option.

So many young people left, heading west or north, figuring that their chances for success were better if they started from scratch. This meant leaving their aging parents behind, at a stage of life in which the old wanted to be able to count on support from their offspring.

Because of such outmigration the percentage of 60-year-olds in Hampton, New Hampshire, rose from four percent to 6.3 percent from 1656 to 1680. There were 206 adults in Newbury, Massachusetts (population 420) in 1678; 28 were at least 60, which represented 6.7 percent of the total population and 13.5 percent of the adult popula-

tion. Thriving seaports like Boston or county seats like Northampton had smaller proportions of senior citizens in their midst, because of the steady flow of newcomers. In these places, the plight of the old was different. Surrounded by many people, the aged nonetheless were strangers to whom no obligations were due, effectively isolating them.

The vulnerabilities that economically secure, healthy men faced in late life were even more keenly felt by older women and minorities who lacked status. Though wives traditionally received a third of their husbands' estates, the number of husbands who stipulated in their wills just how much firewood their sons were to deliver to their widows suggested that this custom was not always observed. Aging spinsters moved from sibling to sibling before turning to their nieces and nephews. If there were no kin or neighbors to help, elderly women sought poor relief from the local community. In the colonial period, arrangements tended to be informal. Usually provisions were given to enable the elderly to stay at home. Occasionally they were boarded out to the person who assured the town that they could care for them for the least amount of money. African Americans were in a somewhat analogous situation; owners exploited their older slaves as long as possible. Most African Americans since 1619 were denied autonomy and power all of their lives; old age brought only additional pain.

Disability and dependence were their chief fears. Morbidity rates for that period do not exist; available evidence suggests, however, that failing health caused superannuation, a term used in colonial times to describe persons past their productive years. Hence blind, enfeebled Reverend Ebenezer Gay of Hingham reluctantly quit the pulpit after preaching on his eighty-fifth birthday (Smith, 1978). In the absence of modern medical and social services, older people unable to take care of their daily physical requirements had to count on the compassion of loved ones or those who lived nearby. Williamsburg opened an almshouse in 1683 to care for the sick of all ages. Philadelphia, Boston, and New York established similar facilities during the next century. But nowhere in the colonies was there an old-age home designed specifically to care for this segment of the population.

Aging and Political Life

After 1763, as British administrators sought to impose more taxes and regulations on the North American provinces, a call for independence increasingly was heard in many cities and villages. In *Growing Old in America* (1977), David Hackett Fischer contended that the liberating, egalitarian, intellectual, and social forces transforming the provinces in revolutionary ways also affected attitudes toward the elderly. He noted changes in terms used to refer to the elderly, shifts in seating patterns in meetinghouses, compositions of family portraits, and alterations in fashions, inheritances, and child-naming patterns. But other scholars disagree. David Troyansky analyzed of the French Revolution in *Old Age in the Ancien Regime*, he claimed the young radicals of France celebrated the aged's wisdom, loyalty to tradition, and stabilizing influence.

Other students of the American Revolution and the U.S. Constitution periodically note age differences among the various factions, but interpretations are disputed as well. About a third of the colonists sided with the rebels; a third remained Loyalists, some of whom moved to Canada; and the remainder were utterly indifferent, siding with whichever group had forces close by. Scholars of grassroots allegiances report a tendency for people to make "your enemy into my friend," but none of this is age-related. Eric McKitrick and Stanley Elkin maintained that the young men of the Revolution became Federalists, in opposition to an older cohort of Anti-Federalists, yet they based their conclusion on a small sample. Had they

---

Williamsburg opened an almshouse in 1683 to care for the sick of all ages. Philadelphia, Boston, and New York established similar facilities during the next century. But nowhere in the colonies was there an old-age home designed specifically to care for this segment of the population.

The Life and Age of Man. Stages of a Man's Life from the Cradle to the Grave. Hand colored lithograph by James Baille, 1848. (Courtesy of the Library of Congress)

examined the biographies of all of the participants, as Fischer did (1970), they would have discovered that the Federalists were on average a year or so older than the Anti-Federalists.

The truly important legacy of older Americans who had lived through the Revolutionary period is that many survived long enough to share their experiences and their values with a rising generation. Benjamin Franklin was the Grand Old Man (at the age of 81) at the Constitutional Convention. Many of his contemporaries also lived past their eightieth birthdays. The first five presidents of the United States, George Washington, John Adams, Thomas Jefferson, James Madison, and James Monroe, were old men when they left the White House. The sixth, John Quincy Adams, was 62 when he lost the election of 1828, but then he was elected to Congress two years later, where he served for the next seventeen years. Men and women of more modest fame—Revolutionary soldiers and women who had crossed enemy lines to relay information—were honored at July Fourth ceremonies, where their tales of valor and patriotism were admiringly heard.

These Revolutionary patriots tried (with mixed success) to instill what one writer in the *Niles Register* called "happy mediocrity" (1817). Mediocrity conveyed a sense of Jeffersonian balance —a recognition that many things are important for a good life, but moderation in all pleasures is desirable. The aspect of mediocrity that could be regarded as happy connotes a mature outlook on human existence. Older people, it was said, ranked among those most capable of putting life into perspective, to affirm its positive qualities over its negative features. Particularly at a time in which virtue counted as much as representation, freedom, and democracy, the elderly's efforts to embody the fundamentals of human dignity was an important contribution. The spirit of 1776 that animated aging Revolutionary survivors was worth passing on to generations who had not witnessed the epoch firsthand.

● **OLD AGE IN THE NEW LAND, 1790 TO 1900**

In the first monographs that surveyed the history of the elderly in the United States, considerable attention was paid to shifts in attitudes toward old age. D. H. Fischer thought that the period between 1770 and 1820 constituted a period of revolutionary change. During the first 150 years of the New England experience, he claimed, older people were venerated, while a cult of youth, which inspired Thoreau and others to debunk the supposed wisdom of age, flourished from 1820 to the 1970s. Another historical study, *Old Age in the New Land* (Achenbaum, 1978), questioned whether the shift from "gerontophilia" to "gerontophobia" was as extreme or as sudden as Fischer maintained. Achenbaum maintained that, prior to the Civil War, attitudes toward the elderly by and large were positive, because Americans perceived that the aged made valuable contributions to the well-being of others. During the latter third of the nineteenth century, however, changes in the political economy, in science, and in cultural norms caused Americans to reevaluate, in increasingly negative terms, the perceived status of the elderly. Carole Haber, author of *Beyond Sixty-five* (1983), offers evidence for yet a third position. She stressed that unflattering comments have been made about older people, especially widows and the poor, from the colonial period to the present day. While confirming that new ideas about aging were expressed by physicians and corporate managers after the Civil War, Haber nonetheless criticized earlier histories for depicting the elderly's conditions in unduly rosy terms. Historians concur that there never was a golden age in the history of old age.

Currently a consensus seems to have been reached on two counts. The origins of many contemporary negative assumptions about the elderly in the United States can be traced to Aristotle, the Bible, Chaucer, medieval iconography, Shakespeare, and numerous folk tales, while more positive notions sometimes rework ideas from the classics. Recent scholarship underscores the wide range of conflicting, ambivalent, and ambiguous emotions and ideas that are to be found in every period (Cole, 1992). Events, trends, legislation, and institutions that took shape after 1900 have caused the most noteworthy changes in the perceived and actual status of

---

Historians concur that there never was a golden age in the history of old age.

senior citizens over the course of U.S. history. Only with the institutionalization of twentieth-century policies like Social Security does the modern era of old-age history begin.

Effects of Industrialization on Older Adults

One reason for such continuity was that, prior to the closing of the frontier, the United States remained predominantly an agrarian society. More than 50 percent of all American men gainfully employed were engaged in agricultural pursuits before 1870. In absolute numbers, farming remained the single largest occupational category for males during the next fifty years—despite the fact that fewer and fewer farmers were needed to grow food for the country's burgeoning population.

Even as agriculture declined in importance in the U.S. economy, older people found work on the farm. The saga of Johnny Appleseed illustrates the importance of farming to older people and vice versa. Farming pursuits occupied 54 percent of all men over 65 who were gainfully employed in 1890; as late as 1960, elderly men who remained in the labor force were more likely to be reported to be farmers than any other occupation. Why? Farming tends to be less age-graded than other enterprises: an aging farmer can reduce his schedule and delegate heavy work to younger hands. On the other hand, it seems likely that many aged people could not afford to give up farming. This probably accounts for the high proportion of aged African-American tenant farmers and widowed farm managers listed in the federal censuses.

During the initial stages of industrialization, which began to transform the American landscape by the 1830s if not earlier, older men also found jobs in the non-agrarian sectors of the economy. Many worked as skilled craftsmen, taking on apprentices well into their eighth decade. The percentage of men over 65 working as carpenters and masons, boot and shoemen, and coopers and blacksmiths exceeded the average of younger men in these same positions. Compared to the population as a whole, elderly men were disproportionately employed as peddlers, merchants, agents, and collectors. A similar pattern obtains for older women of the time. While few were employed outside the home, women over 65 were more likely than middle-aged women to be seamstresses, tailors, milliners, and dressmakers; and it was socially acceptable for older widows to run saloons, manage hotels, or take in boarders.

Prior to the Civil War there were few instances of mandatory retirement. (Based on estimates from state and federal census data, it appears that

James Smillie's 1849 engraving *Voyage of Life: Old Age,* based on a painting by Thomas Cole, was popular during the pre-Civil War era when Americans respected older persons because of their age, wisdom, and experience. (Courtesy of the Library of Congress)

physical debility caused at least 20 percent of men over 65 to become superannuated.) Mandatory age ceilings were rare. Appointments to selected judicial offices were restricted by age only in New York (1777), New Hampshire (1792), Connecticut (1819), Alabama (1819), Missouri (1820), Maine (1820), and Maryland (1851). Embarrassed by the bad press surrounding its most distinguished jurist, James Kent, who revealed in his *Commentaries* that he was forced at age 60 off that state's highest bench, New York dropped the old-age restriction for justices in 1846. No other profession, trade, or industry made old age a criterion for employment—but the federal and state constitutions did argue whether *young* people were mature enough to vote and to hold public office. If there is a bias to be found, it operated against youth.

The elderly often assumed leadership positions in government and in local affairs. Consider their role in developing new religious orders. In their heyday (roughly between 1820 and 1880), Shaker communities from New England to the Midwest

Within some tribes, older Native Americans were accorded ceremonial honors and assured security. (Courtesy of the Library of Congress)

developed profitable seed and furniture businesses, attracted many visitors, and adopted thousands of children. The elders and eldresses, all over age 60, filled all central and local offices. And young men were founders of the Church of Jesus Christ of Latter-Day Saints, but once the Mormons reached Utah, older men generally took charge of matters. Reliance on the old was not unique to these sects. In mainstream Protestant denominations, bishops and other senior officials tended to be drawn from the ranks of the elderly clergy.

Yet few aged African Americans on the plantation possessed health, wealth, prestige, or power. Owners usually required aging slaves to help around the house, oversee younger field hands, and care for their children. Owners sometimes freed their slaves once they were well past their prime and incapable of doing much, thereby cutting their costs and avoiding the responsibility of caring for these slaves during their final illnesses. Members of the slave community saw things differently, however. To them, the aged were respected repositors of family histories and wisdom; some elders, said to possess magical powers and spiritual insights, were held in a mixture of fear and awe. Freed elderly African Americans routinely returned to the slave quarters every night, where they shared bread with their kin, biological or otherwise. Ethnographic evidence suggests that, at least within some tribes, older Native Americans also were accorded ceremonial honors and assured security very late in life.

Prior to 1900, most of the elderly lived, for better and for worse, in what might be characterized

The Four Seasons of Life: Old Age. The Season of Rest. Currier and Ives lithograph, 1868. (Courtesy of the Library of Congress)

as an age-integrated society. People were keenly aware of differences between young and old, but there was much less age-grading in the United States than exists in institutions and within social networks today (Chudacoff, 1990). Particularly in the early days of the Republic, older people, like all others, were to contribute to the well-being of all. As a Fourth of July orator put it in 1825, the nation needed "at once, all the vigor and firmness of youth, the strength and firmness of age. Great as is the undertaking, your powers are equal to its completion; be but united, firm, and persevering, and if heaven smile on your labors, success is sure" (*Niles Register*, 1825). The wisdom of age was no less essential than the resources of youth and middle age.

Yet when the aged needed assistance, there really was no safety net in place. Widows and the sick, as in colonial times, had to rely on family members and neighbors. Some states had enacted laws governing family relations, but none stipulated special provisions for the old. Enforcing poor laws, maintaining an almshouse, or erecting private institutions for aged indigents were local matters. Resources varied considerably from community to community. In the antebellum period Americans built special facilities for orphans, the deaf, the blind, the insane, and the criminal, but old-age homes were rare. Noisy and filthy, most almshouses provided disagreeable shelter for the elderly. Thus Will Carlton struck a raw nerve with his 1871 poem, "Over the Hill to the Poor-House":

> Over the hill to the poor-house I'm trudgin' my
>   weary way—
> I a woman of seventy, and only a trifle gray—
> I who am smart an' chipper, for all the years I've
>   told,
> As many another woman that's only half as old. . . .
>
> What is the use of heapin' on me a pauper's
>   shame?
> Am I lazy or crazy? am I blind or lame?
> True, I am not so supple, nor yet so awful stout;
> But charity ain't no favor, if one can live
>   without. . . .
>
> Over the hill to the poor-house—my child'rn
>   dear, good-by!
> Many a night I've watched you when only God
>   was nigh;
> And God'll judge between us; but I will al'ays
>   pray
> That you shall never suffer the half I do to-day.

For months after this poem first appeared, managers reported that children came to the almshouse to pick up their parents. Two years later, Carlton wrote another poem, "Over the Hill from the Poor-House," but it never commanded the attention of his earlier work. There were other options, equally limited and grim: older people unable to obtain refuge from family or neighbors or to make their way to poorhouses often ended up in insane asylums.

In the antebellum period Americans built special facilities for orphans, the deaf, the blind, the insane, and the criminal, but old-age homes were rare.

● THE ELDERLY IN THE NEW URBAN-INDUSTRIAL ORDER, 1870 TO 1930

By the end of the nineteenth century, magazine contributors, social critics, academics, scientists, and other observers of the American scene expressed worries about the status of the elderly. New social and cultural forces created circumstances more threatening than the traditional problems that affected individuals as they grew older. Old age, they felt, was beginning to be considered a *social problem.*

Earlier in the nineteenth century doctors considered old age a natural stage of the human life course, but in the latter years of the century a less positive interpretation of older people's maladies took shape. Translations of J. M. Charcot's *Clinical Lectures on the Diseases of the Aged and Their Chronic Illnesses* (1881) influenced scientific thinking at the research-oriented medical schools of Harvard, Johns Hopkins, Michigan, Pennsylvania, and elsewhere. Taking cues from Charcot's conviction that the pathological manifestations found in elderly patients merited attention, physicians probed elderly people's bodies for the cause of disease in late life. Senility, once a benign synonym for old age, became a technical term referring to the "weakness and decrepitude characteristic of old age." Case studies of senile gangrene, senile chorea, senile pneumonia, and senile bronchitis were published in medical journals. That no cures were found for old age heightened people's sense of dread. Pohl's Spermine

Preparations, a potion to restore sexual vigor, did not prove rejuvenating. Eating yogurt three times a day, as Nobel laureate Elie Metchnikoff recommended, did not prolong life. Decay seemed inevitable, a loathsome consequence of living (too) long.

While medical investigators cataloged the hazards of growing older, steel producers, railroad managers, and other captains of industry were independently concluding that older workers grew obsolete. As F. Spencer Baldwin, an economics professor, explained in *The Annals of the American Political and Social Sciences* (1911):

> It is well understood nowadays that the practice of retaining on the payroll aged workers who can no longer render a fair equivalent for their wages is wasteful and demoralizing. The loss is twofold. In the first place, payment of full wages to workers who are no longer reasonably efficient, and in the second place, there is the direct loss entailed by the slow pace by the presence of worn-out veterans, and the consequent demoralization of the service.

Entrepreneurs and capitalists calculated that it made more sense to invest in youth. Older workers were reassigned jobs as gatekeepers or watchmen. Supervisors sometimes permitted discharged workers to beg by the factory gates on paydays. In an economic world increasingly governed by the principle of "survival of the fittest," the prevailing view was that only the fittest deserved to survive. Those over 40 years old found it harder and harder to make the grade. Those over 60 faced even more barriers.

Early Versions of Retirement

Retirement became a way for large organizations to thrive and for superannuated workers to survive. President Abraham Lincoln established the precedent: in 1862 he pensioned his admirals (all of whom were over 60) so that he could promote younger men to fight the Civil War at sea. In 1875 the American Express Company permitted selected workers over 60 to receive compensation if they quit their jobs. The Baltimore and Ohio Railroad in 1884 inaugurated a more elaborate plan for workers over 65 with at least ten years of service to qualify for pensions. Only seven more companies offered retirement plans by 1900. By 1929, 140 companies, potentially cov-

ering nearly a million workers, paid out $6.7 million to 10,644 retiree beneficiaries. Even so, less than 20 percent of the labor force was protected by pension programs.

Life insurance companies experimented with retirement vehicles. Fraternal orders of workers gave members the option of buying annuities in addition to disability insurance and burial funds. Some union officials expressed slight interest in old-age benefits, but most of the leadership was far more interested in bolstering membership ranks by focusing on the bread-and-roses issues that appealed to younger men and women. Several states permitted savings banks to underwrite tontine insurance, a pooled account declared illegal in 1906. Retirement programs were established for various groups of public employees. By the turn of the century most of the nation's largest cities gave benefits to teachers, police, and fire personnel. County- and state-level bureaucrats gained protection during the Progressive era. The federal government inaugurated a Civil Service Retirement System in 1920 (Graebner, 1980).

Concerted efforts were made in the private sector to relieve the growing number of older people suffering from sickness or poverty. Benefactors left money to build old-age homes for their (upper) middle-class friends and servants. Philanthropists such as Benjamin Rose gave $3 million in 1911 to enable "respectable and deserving" residents in Cleveland to remain in their homes. Andrew Carnegie set aside $10 million to provide annuities for college professors. Religious and ethnic organizations in every metropolitan area erected old-age homes to which older members of their community might turn when necessary.

Decades after states had established school systems and earmarked funds to delinquents, orphans, and other needy youth, legislators reluc-

---

By 1929, 140 companies, potentially covering nearly a million workers, paid out $6.7 million to 10,644 retiree beneficiaries. Even so, less than 20 percent of the labor force was protected by pension programs.

tantly considered the merits of old-age assistance. Fearing costs and generally seeing no compelling need to act, some states tried to resist appeals by commissioning panels of experts to investigate the situation. The tack occasionally worked. A 1910 Massachusetts survey reported that conditions for the noninstitutionalized aged poor were "comparatively good." Besides being expensive, concluded the blue-ribbon panel, providing old-age relief might destroy thriftiness, weaken family ties, lower wages, and prove unconstitutional. Indeed, several of the first state programs—including Arizona (1914) and Pennsylvania (1925)—were declared invalid by their respective state supreme courts; hidden provisions or lack of funds rendered old-age assistance systems in four other states inoperative.

The Pension Debate

Ironically the executive and legislative branches of the federal government were even more adamant than state officials in opposing old-age pensions. President Franklin Pierce's 1854 case against initiating national welfare schemes deterred his successors from committing the federal government to provide welfare. Bills for old-age relief were routinely submitted to every session of Congress after 1909, but none passed. (Most considered Bismarck's 1881 landmark measure and Britain's 1908 old-age assistance policy too undemocratic.) Yet for decades Washington had been exceedingly generous to one segment of the elderly population—veterans. In 1818, Madison approved a plan to relieve indigent Revolutionary War soldiers, most of whom were

then at least 55. Congress so underestimated the number eligible for benefits that it imposed a means test a year later: applicants had to plead poverty to gain benefits. Similarly, veterans of the War of 1812 and the Mexican War were granted huge land bounties when they were old men. Thanks to successful lobbying from the Grand Army of the Republic, Union veterans and their spouses gained more and more financial and health benefits the older they got: Congress declared in 1907 that old age per se was a disability, thus opening the Treasury's coffers to more claimants. A decade later pensions were the costliest item in the federal budget (Quadagno, 1988). By 1929, veterans' pensions represented 80 percent of all the financial transfers being made to older Americans. For a select few, Washington was operating a de facto old-age welfare state.

Bills for old-age relief were routinely submitted to every session of Congress after 1909, but none passed.

Citing so many innovations in quick succession may give the misleading impression that old-age dependency and the diseases of old age had become major issues by the first years of the twentieth century. This is not the case. There was no massive exodus of older men from the marketplace. According to the census, nearly 70 percent of all men over 65 were gainfully employed in 1900. (Some historians argue that, if certain technical adjustments are made to the census data, labor-force rates actually remained constant, or possibly even rose slightly, between 1870 and

Ethnic organizations such as the Chinese Benevolent Association, shown here in 1936, offered assistance to its older members. (Courtesy of the Library of Congress)

Blacksmith at work, 1910. (Courtesy of the Library of Congress)

Labor-force participation rates dropped nearly 17 percent between 1930 and 1940 for workers over 65. (Courtesy of the Library of Congress)

1930.) In any case, due to deaths, disabilities, layoffs, strikes, and closings, most American workers never became eligible for corporate old-age pensions before 1929. Scientific interest in old age can likewise be exaggerated. Heart disease, epidemics, children's illnesses, and mental disorders attracted far more attention in the medical profession than did late-life maladies. Until his brother-in-law did him a favor and pulled a few strings, I. L. Nascher could not find a publisher for *Geriatrics* (1914). Nascher and a junior colleague constituted the entire membership of his geriatric society (the nation's first and only such organization) until his death.

● THE GREAT DEPRESSION AS A TURNING POINT IN THE HISTORY OF U.S. AGING

As the economic dislocations wrought by the Great Depression attained crisis proportions in the early 1930s, the patchwork quilt of economic and social services for the elderly became unstitched. With unemployment rates reaching 25 percent, thousands of young and middle-aged workers lost their jobs and had difficulty finding work. Grim as it was, younger people still fared better than the aged. Older workers were among the first to be fired; many never earned another dollar. Labor-force participation rates dropped more precipitously (nearly 17 percent between 1930 and 1940) for workers over 65 than for any other age group.

In addition to being unable to support themselves through gainful employment, few senior citizens could count on income from other sources. Hopes that former employers or unions would help the elderly in desperate straits were dashed. Under the law, corporate pensions were viewed as gratuities, which could be distributed or withheld as managers chose. Granting pensions seemed a less plausible strategy for keeping a business afloat than reinvesting in the firm or retaining valuable young workers on the payroll. In any case, many companies declared bankruptcy and had nothing to give. Earlier, in more prosperous years, many people tried to save as much as they could for their old age. But those precious funds were lost in the 1930s as banks went under. Most family members wanted to help the old, of course, but their sons and daughters had children of their own to feed. In many instances there simply was not enough of anything to go around.

Private sources of support dried up along with public ones. Charitable organizations anticipated a downturn of only three to four years, since that seemed to be the length of earlier recessions. But the longer the Great Depression dragged on, the less money there was available to distribute. By 1934, moreover, half the states were on the verge

The Great Depression made the plight of America's elderly a major priority. (Courtesy of the Library of Congress)

of bankruptcy. To maintain operations as long as possible, bureaucrats cut back and then discontinued benefits across the board. Old-age assistance plans were suspended. Experts at the time estimated that as many as two-thirds of all the nation's elderly were potentially dependent. Old age as a social problem was no longer a topic of passing academic interest; the Great Depression had made the plight of America's elderly a major priority.

The Coming of Social Security

For the first time in history older people began to mobilize politically to demand redress. In the 1930s a California-based physician and failed real estate agent, Francis Townsend, proposed that older Americans be granted $200 each per month, on the condition that they not work and that they spend the money in thirty days. Novelist and reformer Upton Sinclair inspired a pension scheme based on scrip, the Ham and Eggs movement. Two radicals—Louisiana senator Huey Long and Detroit radio activist Father Charles Coughlin—pledged to eliminate old-age poverty, hoping to rally the aged to their radical causes (Pratt, 1977).

President Roosevelt, however, waited until the third year of his presidency to take decisive action. Why the delay? It cannot be that he was insensitive to the issue, because in 1929, as governor of New York, he had signed into law the country's most progressive old-age assistance scheme. Nor was he the only national politician under pressure from elderly constituencies: the number of bills before Congress sharply increased; the American Federation of Labor, which had opposed federal old-age intervention, reversed its position in 1933. Apparently FDR felt that other measures aimed at institutional reforms, human relief, and national reconstruction merited higher priority; however, by the time he signed the Social Security Act in 1935, the Supreme Court had already invalidated many of his New Deal programs. Yet many scholars insist that the Social Security Act was FDR's greatest accomplishment.

The first title of the 1935 Social Security Act dealt with old-age assistance. The federal government promised to match (up to $15 a month) half the pension awarded to eligible persons in a given state. Those who were denied benefits were given the right to appeal a local official's decision. Sig-

nificantly, benefits could not go to the institutionalized aged, a regulation calculated to accelerate the demise of the almshouse. In order to keep the future costs of Title I in bounds, an old-age insurance plan was established under Title II. Employers and employees were to contribute up to one-half percent of the first $3,000 of the salary of workers in selected areas of the economy; once the old-age insurance trust fund was large enough, benefits would start being paid out beginning in 1942. Other provisions of the omnibus legislation allocated funds for the blind, for mothers with young children (which eventually became Assistance to Families with Dependent Children), for the unemployed, and for public-health services (Achenbaum, 1986).

Social Security under Fire

Because of its complexity, Social Security was misunderstood from the start. Polls at the time indicate that people trusted that they would get something back for their contributions, but few knew the first thing about how the system worked. Kansas senator Alf Landon derided the measure as socialistic, and his political advisers figured that attacking Social Security might win him the 1936 election. Even Supreme Court justices were ambivalent: *Helvering v. Davis* (1937) upheld the constitutionality—not necessarily the wisdom—of the act. The 1939 amendments, which greatly affected the scope and the philosophy of the original measure, added to the confusion. Before the first Title II benefit was ever paid, Congress increased the beneficiary pool to include the spouses and children of workers who

Uncle Sam introduced Social Security to American citizens in 1935, as interpreted in Clifford Berryman's 1937 drawing. (Courtesy of the Library of Congress)

contributed to the program, though it did not raise Social Security taxes so as not to impede economic recovery.

Historians, economists, and social scientists have long debated the original intent and eventual impact of the 1935 Social Security Act and its 1939 amendments. Compared to other New Deal measures, which straightforwardly regulated banking or promoted conservation, Social Security controlled people's options in murky, complicated language. Did Title II endorse the Townsendite strategy of insisting that older people stop working as a condition for receiving benefits? The evidence is very ambiguous. Did Title I reinforce racism? It may have. Southern legislatures claimed that they were too poor to enact old-age assistance plans, a tack that kept African Americans off pension roles (Gratton, 1985). Title II also worked against the interests of aged minorities: farmers were not covered under Social Security until 1954; older African Americans, most of whom had remained in agrarian pursuits, therefore did not earn Social Security retirement benefits for two decades because their employment was not covered. However, Social Security did not then incite intergenerational tensions, even though lawmakers had to decide whether to finance pensions for elders (who voted) with school taxes earmarked for children (who did not vote), but the generational-equity debate became a factor in national politics in the late 1970s. Nonetheless, the enactment of the Social Security Act is a clear turning point in the history of old age.

Because of its complexity, Social Security was misunderstood from the start. Polls at the time indicate that people trusted that they would get something back for their contributions, but few knew the first thing about how the system worked.

● THE ELDERLY IN AN AGE OF AFFLUENCE

Throughout most of U.S. history, major changes in the elderly's status occurred after transformations in younger people's conditions. The aged remained in farming longer. They organized politically later. Their values were tradition-al, at odds with the Roaring Twenties generation characterized by novelist F. Scott Fitzgerald as "the damned and the beautiful." Increasingly after the 1930s, however, dealing with the problems of the elderly required taking bold steps, innovating, making tough choices. By the middle of the twentieth century, older Americans were pioneers—and not just because large numbers were retiring to Sunbelt communities throughout the South. In numbers greater than any previous group, those coming of age after World War II experienced the blessings and banes of longer lives, of enjoying the rights (and rites) of retirement. More likely to live alone or at a distance from their children, they kept contact through phone calls and rapid transport, and while many of these issues will be amplified later in this almanac, their historical novelty is significant to mention.

Particularly since World War II, public and private institutions have coordinated efforts to achieve genuine economic security for senior citizens. Social Security became the single most important source of income; coverage gradually became universal; and benefits also increased, initially whenever Congress adjusted rates, and then, after 1972, through automatic cost-of-living adjustments (COLAs) pegged to inflation. In the late 1940s, the Supreme Court backed the rights of unions to negotiate pensions, which spurred a revival of private pension plans with eligibility and benefit structures typically complementary to those prevailing under Social Security. The Employee Retirement Income Security Act of 1974 (ERISA) offered financial and tax incentives to the self-employed, among others, to shelter money for use in later years.

As a result of this concerted interest in old-age security, the poverty rate among senior citizens dropped from 33 percent in the early 1960s to 12 percent in 1987. (Without Social Security, as many as two-thirds of all older Americans presently would have incomes below the poverty line.) Such a remarkable achievement demonstrates that social engineering through policymaking sometimes works as intended. Yet success has been uneven. Elderly women and minorities still tend to have less income at their disposal than retired white males. And for the first time in U.S. history, a greater percentage of the nation's children (20 percent) are likely to be poor than are the old.

In the late 1940s, the Supreme Court backed the rights of unions to negotiate pensions, which spurred a revival of private pension plans with eligibility and benefit structures typically complementary to those prevailing under Social Security.

Emergence of Organizations on Aging

Nor has government limited its concern to the economics of aging. Acquiring basic information about the elderly's needs early on became a high priority. In 1939, with support from the Josiah Macy Foundation, the Public Health Service established a Gerontological Research Center (GRC) in Baltimore. Under Nathan Shock's direction this became one of the country's premier training units for biomedical investigators. Thirty-five years later, a greatly expanded GRC became the internal wing of the National Institute on Aging (NIA), the eleventh branch of the National Institutes of Health (NIH). On the social science/policy side, the Federal Security Agency in 1950 began to gather data and a year later convened a group of experts in Washington to discuss a host of problems besetting senior citizens. Their mission was to propose ways of promoting

---

Profiles of Productive Aging

McGeorge Bundy
Foundation president

"I don't believe in retirement per se. It never occurred to me to retire at 65. I was half way through a job at Ford I intended to finish. I believe retirement age no longer works for most people; most people over 65 don't think of themselves as old."

Former Ford Foundation president McGeorge Bundy was born in 1919. His father was a lawyer; his mother had many charitable and educational interests, including family planning and the women's suffrage movement. Bundy attended the Groton School and Yale, where he received a bachelor's degree in mathematics, then served in Latin America during World War II. In 1946, shortly after returning to civilian status, he helped Henry Stimson, secretary of war during World War II, organize his papers and write his memoirs. After two years, he returned to Harvard, became an assistant professor of government, and was appointed dean at the age of 34. Bundy contended that being dean was the most excellent training he'd ever had. "If you like decisions, if you like helping a first-rate outfit stay first rate and get better, if you like the process of dealing with other human beings on a common enterprise or resisting the bad ideas that a few people will have from time to time," Bundy remarked, "Harvard then was a wonderful place."

Bundy left Harvard to become assistant for National Security Affairs in Washington, D.C., under President Kennedy. Working for the Kennedy administration "was very intense," Bundy recalled, "in the sense that you were doing one part of the daily business that mattered to the President of the United States.... You learned your job by doing it. And you learned simply from the contrast, that you have to know your man as well as your set of problems. You can only help a President the way he wants to be helped. You can't teach him to do it Ike's way."

Accepting an invitation to be president of the Ford Foundation in New York City in late 1966, Bundy was known for his quick wit and occasionally tart tongue, which won him a reputation as a formidable opponent. He hired a staff as energetic as he was and set out to tackle a whole range of social problems. Bundy achieved many of his objectives during his tenure at Ford, which many considered legendary.

In the 1970s Bundy taught history as a visiting professor at New York University. In 1979, when he reached the Ford Foundation's retirement age, he began teaching full time at New York University and started several writing projects. Currently on the staff of Carnegie Corporation of New York, Bundy is part of a three-man commission exploring the future of arms control. A student of the nuclear arms problem from a historical point of view for more than a decade, Bundy provides strictly "policy-making, recommendational" input.

Lydia Brontë

better social adjustment in late life. The success of this approach led to the 1961 White House Conference on Aging, which became a decennial affair.

Often taking cues from those interested in the well-being of children, scholars and advocates established private organizations directed at the mature population. In the 1930s Lillien Martin, a retired Stanford psychologist, opened an Old Age Center in San Francisco to help her peers "sweep out the cobwebs." William McKeever started a School for Maturates in Oklahoma City. Just as the Macy Foundation helped the government establish a unit devoted to aging research, so too it facilitated the first meetings of professionals who chartered the Gerontological Society in 1945 to advance research in aging, training, and policy making. Twelve years later, Ethel Percy Andrus, a retired Los Angeles high school principal, started the National Retired Teachers Association (NRTA). Her organization really flourished after she met Leonard Davis, who proposed a mutually beneficial insurance program for her members. Andrus's group is now called the American Association of Retired Persons. (AARP). It now boasts thirty-seven million members. After the Roman Catholic Church, it is the second largest social organization in the United States. The National Council on the Aging (NCOA) owes its origins to a grant from the Ford Foundation after the 1961 White House Conference on Aging. NCOA now depends heavily on federal funding under Title V of the Older Americans Act, which came out of President Lyndon B. Johnson's concept of a Great Society.

Most of the social policies developed during the 1960s were targeted for special groups—African Americans, youth, infants, people living in Appalachia, in cities or on farms. The needs of older citizens often were reserved—or relegated—for special consideration, because as a group the elderly were considered sicker and poorer than the population at large. The summer of 1965 proved a bonanza for the elderly. Medicare and Medicaid offered them hospital insurance and, if indigent, coverage for long-term care. The preamble to the Older Americans Act (OAA), moreover, envisioned seemingly boundless federal support as the nation's aged sought to pursue meaningful, secure, healthful lives (Achenbaum, 1983; Rich and Baum, 1984). Delegates to the 1971 White House Conference demanded—and received—a wide range of social services for senior citizens. OAA amendments enacted in the mid-1970s mandated that states provide social services for men and women over 60. State Offices of Aging became increasingly important. Networking became ever more complex.

The Paradox of Aging

During the past two decades there have been clear indications that prevailing ideas about aging and the aged are once again in flux. It is now regarded as questionable to characterize old age as a problem. If the experiences of late life are as diverse as experts document and ordinary people perceive, then it makes no sense any longer to talk about the elderly as a monolithic group. Media portrayals stereotyping the elderly as bumbling, sexless, foolish people do a disservice to the variety of personalities and performances acted out by the old. These realizations have profound policy implications. Programs targeted for the average older American do not reach the truly vulnerable subsets in the elderly population, such as women and minorities. Bernice Neugarten, one of the nation's preeminent gerontologists, thinks that the present confusion over the meanings of old age results from a paradox: categorical welfare programs have become even more age-specific during the very period that chronological age has been proven to be a poor predictor of health, social integration, income, and well-being. Neugarten (1983) suggested abolishing programs that require some arbitrary chronological age to be eligible for a program and instead design policies to help those truly in need.

During the past two decades there have been clear indications that prevailing ideas about aging and the aged are once again in flux. It is now regarded as questionable to characterize old age as a problem.

However, Neugarten's criticisms and suggestions were overshadowed by a different controversy: the assault from neo-conservatives and baby-boom critics who regarded current federal aging policies as leading to an old age welfare state (Myles, 1984). Senior-citizen discounts, special tax credits, and automatic increases in Social Security benefits to citizens just because they happen to be over 65 were caricatured as morally, fiscally, and politically irresponsible. Magazine covers featured "greedy geezers" enjoying golf as they lived off unearned perquisites. Meanwhile their children were born to pay and toil away, destined to be the first generation in U.S. history not to achieve the same standard of living their parents enjoyed, according to Philip Longman (1987). In academe, in journals, and in policy circles, pundits sparked a generational-equity debate. Critics exulted that the liberals' misguided aging enterprise was exhausted, intellectually and fiscally. But despite their attacks on Social Security and fears over the "graying" of the federal budget, conservatives in the 1980s and early 1990s were unwilling or unable to gore the very programs they denounced as sacred cows. Meanwhile, the elderly found their resources strained and economic fears mounting: In 1961 they spent on average 10.7 percent of their disposable income on health care; three decades later, despite enormous increases in the extent of Medicare coverage, they paid more than 17 percent. As the United States enters the twenty-first century, it faces a tremendous challenge regarding how to treat aging citizens, an issue that will require great maturity.

References

Achenbaum, W. A. *Old Age in the New Land.* Baltimore, MD: Johns Hopkins University Press, 1978.

———. *Shades of Gray.* Boston, MA: Little, Brown, 1983.

———. *Social Security: Visions and Revisions.* New York: Cambridge University Press, 1986.

Chudacoff, H. *How Old Are You?* Princeton, NJ: Princeton University Press, 1990.

Cole, T. R. *The Journey of Life.* New York: Cambridge University Press, 1992.

Demos, J. "Old Age in Early New England." *Turning Points.* Eds. S. S. Boocock and J. Demos. Chicago: University of Chicago Press, 1978.

Fischer, D. H. *Growing Old in America.* Expanded ed. New York: Oxford University Press, 1977.

———. *Historians' Fallacies.* New York: Harper & Row, 1970.

Graebner, W. *A History of Retirement.* New Haven, CT: Yale University Press, 1980.

Gratton, B. *Urban Elders.* Philadelphia, PA: Temple University Press, 1985.

Gruman, G. *A History of Ideas About the Prolongation of Life.* Philadelphia, PA: Transactions of the American Philosophical Society, 1966.

Haber, C. *Beyond Sixty-Five.* New York: Cambridge University Press, 1983.

Longman, P. *Born to Pay.* Boston, MA: Houghton Mifflin, 1978.

Myles, J. *Old Age in the Welfare State.* Boston, MA: Little, Brown, 1984.

Neugarten, B. L., ed. *Age or Need?* Beverly Hills, CA: Sage Publications, 1983.

Niles Register 28 (July 30, 1825): 346.

Pratt, H. J. *The Gray Lobby.* Chicago, IL: University of Chicago Press, 1977.

Quadagno, J. *The Transformation of Old Age Security.* Chicago, IL: University of Chicago Press, 1988.

Rich, B., and M. Baum. *The Aging.* Pittsburgh, PA: University of Pittsburgh Press, 1984.

Smith, D. S. "Old Age and the 'Great Transformation.'" In *Aging and the Elderly.* Eds. S. F. Spicker, D. D. Van Tassel, and K. M. Woodward. Atlantic Highlands, NJ: Humanities Press, 1978.

Troyansky, D. *Old Age in the Ancien Regime.* Ithaca, NY: Cornell University Press, 1989.

U.S. Disability Commission. *Disability in America.* Washington, DC: National Academy of Sciences, 1991.

Additional Reading

Laslett, P. *Household and Family in Past Time.* Cambridge, Eng.: Cambridge University Press, 1972.

Premo, T. *Winter Friends.* Urbana: University of Illinois, 1990.

Stearns, P. *Old Age in Preindustrial Society.* New York: Holmes and Meier, 1982.

W. A. Achenbaum, Ph. D.

②

Population Growth, Distribution, and Characteristics

- How Populations Age ● Population Aging in the United States
- U.S. Population Trends: Past and Future
- Distribution of Older Adult Population in the United States ● Retirement Migration
- Diversity Among the Aging Population ● Race, Gender, and Marital Status
- Household Composition and Housing ● Educational Attainment ● Labor Force Participation
- Income Distribution

Rapid growth and increasing diversity are the hallmarks of the older adult population in the United States. The United States is being transformed by a significant increase in the numbers of the elderly. In a matter of decades this nation has gone from the youth orientation of the post-World War II baby boom, with its crowded public school classrooms and burgeoning college campuses, to a society concerned with Social Security, long term care insurance, aging parents, and issues of generational equity. Recent attention to the implications of the United States' aging has led many to view those 65 years old and over as a unified group of people, rather than to understand the great variation within this elderly population. One of the tasks of demographers is to help identify these differences.

Populations are studied by the science of demography. As members of an interdisciplinary field, demographers come from a number of specialties such as sociology, economics, geography, biology, and statistics. Demographers are interested in the size, distribution, structure, *and* change *in* populations.

Size refers simply to the number of people in a population. Distribution of populations refers to geographic spread, along with issues of den- sity or concentration of people (i.e., rural versus urban). The structure of a population refers to characteristics of the group under study, such as the age mix, ratio of men to women, or marital status. Formal or pure demographers are only interested in those characteristics that would influence change within a population. Change within populations arises from the three demographic processes of mortality, fertility, and migration.

● HOW POPULATIONS AGE

One type of population change is a shift in the age structure of a society. To a demographer individuals grow older, but populations age. A population is said to be aging when its median age rises. Conversely a population can become younger if the age structure shifts in the other direction, and the median age declines. All three of the core demographic processes can contribute to the aging of a population.

Mortality Reduction

A population can age when there is a reduction in mortality and, consequently, more people grow older. *Life expectancy* is the average number of years of life remaining at a specified age.

23

Coming to Terms with Demography

Aging refers to the increase in the overall age of a population as measured by the median age.

Younging refers to a decrease in the median age of a population.

Cohort is a group with a common characteristic. The term is most commonly used in demography to identify a group of people born within a specified time period, as in birth cohort.

Dependency or support ratios are measures of the composition of a population supported by or dependent on other members of society.

Fertility refers to the actual birth performance of individuals or groups. *Fecundity* is the physiological capacity to reproduce and is frequently reported as women 15 to 44 years old, although the U.S. government reports birth from 10 to 49 years old. *Natality* refers to the role of births in population change.

Life expectancy is a synthetic measure based on current age- and sex-specific death rates, and it addresses the average number of years of life remaining. Typically it is reported at birth and at age 65.

Life span is the theoretical limit or maximum age a species could live under optimum conditions. It is typi-cally defined as the age beyond which less then 0.1 percent of the original cohort survives.

Migration is a form of spatial mobility involving a change of usual residence between clearly defined geo-graphical units. *Immigration* refers to migration into a nation, and *emigration* specifies the movement out of a country. Migration within a country's border is described by the terms *in-migration* and *out-migration*. *Donor* locales refer to the places people leave, and *host* locales refer to places that receive migrants. Items that promote people leaving a location are called *push factors*, and those items that attract people to a locale are called *pull factors*. A *move* is a residence change within a country.

Mortality refers to death as a component of popula-tion change.

Senescence is the biological process of aging by which the organism becomes less vital and more vul-nerable to changes in the environment.

Sex Ratio is a measure of sex composition of a pop-ulation. It is defined as the number of males per 100 females. *Old-old* is defined by Neugarten (1975) as those 75 years old and older. *Old-oldest* is defined by Riley and Suzman (1985) as those 85 years old and older. *Young-old* is defined by Neugarten (1975) as those 55 to 74 years old.

Typically it is reported at birth and at 65 years old. When a society reduces mortality, then life expectancy at birth or at 65 moves closer to the *life span*, the theoretical age limit a species can survive under optimal conditions. Demographers often define life span as the age at which one tenth of one percent (0.1%) of the original birth cohort survives. This appears to be approximate-ly 100 among humans (U.S. Bureau of the Census, 1975), although some suggest the life span could be as much as 115 (Kirkwood, 1985).

Among the developed nations the first major stage in mortality reduction came about within the younger age groups. An epidemiological tran-sition (Orman, 1977) occurred at the beginning of the industrial era. Improvements in public health, provision of sufficient and sanitary food supplies, and better housing constrained the spread and deleterious effects of acute infectious diseases (e.g., cholera, pneumonia, typhus, typhoid, tuber-culosis). Decrease of the acute self-limiting disor-ders allowed the young to live and grow older, and face the diseases of later life. The second and more difficult stage of mortality reduction comes in later life, when medical science combats the more complex chronic conditions (e.g., the three biggest killers in the United States: cardiovascu-lar disease, cancers, and stroke).

The structure of a population refers to characteristics of the group under study such as the age mix, ratio of men to women, or marital sta-tus. (Copyright © Marianne Gontarz)

Fertility Reduction

Another mechanism that ages a population is a reduction in fertility. When fewer people are being born, the proportion of younger members in the population decreases, and conversely the proportion of the older members increases. As a result, the smaller cohorts of females will in part reduce the future fertility when they become *fecund* (i.e., have the capacity to reproduce: 10–49 years of age). Even if fertility again increases, there will be fewer fecund females, and this will constrain the youthful trend in the society.

So-called replacement rate fertility is the projected number of births per 1,000 fecund women that a society needs to maintain a stable population size. Among the industrialized nations, the replacement rate is 2,100 per 1,000 women, or 2.1 per woman. Of 2,100 per 1,000, the 2,000 serves to replace the women and their mate(s), while 100 compensates for deaths among females before they come to reproductive age. When a nation falls below replacement rate fertility, an increasingly higher proportion of the population is older; hence, the nation ages.

Migration

Finally the aging of a population can be influenced by migration. Just as a reduction in fertility ages a population, so does out-migration of young adults from an area, and the corresponding loss of their fertility leaves behind an older population. In-migration of older adults can also create an aged population, even as normal fertility and mortality processes continue. Of course the converse of these migration processes, such as the immigration of the young, can make the age structure more youthful.

● POPULATION AGING IN THE UNITED STATES

Growing Numbers of Elderly

Numerically, the U.S. elderly population has grown in a dramatic fashion since the turn of the century (see Table 2.1). The 65-plus population in 1900 totaled just over 3 million, and as of the 1990 census it stood at 31.2 million, a 913 percent increase. An even more overwhelming increase of 2,024 percent is reported for the 85 years old and older age group, which went from 123,000 in 1900 to 3 million in the last census. A detailed break-

Table 2.1

United States Population 65 Years Old and Older and 85 Years Old and Older in Thousands: 1900 to 2050

Year	Number 65+	Number 85+
1900	3,084	123
1910	3,950	167
1920	4,933	210
1930	6,634	272
1940	9,019	365
1950	12,270	577
1960	16,560	929
1970	19,980	1,409
1980	25,544	2,240
1990	31,241	3,080
2000	35,036	5,136
2010	39,269	6,818
2020	51,386	7,337
2030	64,345	8,801
2040	66,643	12,946
2050	67,061	16,063

Sources: 1900 to 1990: U.S. Bureau of the Census. Census of the Population.

2000 to 2050: U.S. Bureau of the Census. "Projections of the Population of the United States, by Age, Sex, and Race: 1988 to 2050." Gregory Spencer. *Current Population Report* Series P-25, no. 1018 (January 1989).

down of the U.S. population's age structure in 1990 is found in Table 2.2. Projected increases between 1990 to 2050 are not as large, although the fastest growth is still in the 85-plus age group. Between 1990 and 2050 the 65 years old and over group will grow by 155 percent to about 67 million. Yet during the same period the 85 and older group will increase by 422 percent to over 16 million.

Measuring the Age of a Population

A population's age structure can be measured in several ways. Median age represents the value in the exact middle of an ordered distribution of ages in a population. When a population has a median age of under 20 years old it is said to be young. Those populations whose median age ranges between 20 and 29 are defined as intermediate. Finally a population that has a median age of 30 years old and older is said to be old.

The percent of a population 65 years old and

The 65-plus population in 1900 totaled just over 3 million, and as of the 1990 census it stood at 31.2 million, a 913 percent increase. (Copyright © Marianne Gontarz)

older is a second measure of the age structure. This figure is obtained by simply dividing the number of people 65-plus in a population by the total number of people in a population and multiplying the result by 100.

The dependency ratio is a more complex measure of the population's age, for it embraces the concept of economic dependency. This measure is based on the assumption that in each population some age groups (young adults and middle aged) are more likely to be engaged in actively generating the economic resources in a population, and other groups are more likely to be financially dependent on them. Youth are typically dependent on the economic transfers from their parents and the local taxes that support education. In contrast older adults in our society receive income from working adults via social insurance programs (Social Security and Medicare) or pensions, for which they are qualified through their own or their spouses' previous labor force participation, and their own investments. Three forms of the dependency ratio are shown in the following equations. Table 2.3 displays the dependency ratios for the population from 1900 to 2050.

Youthful Dependency Ratio

$$\frac{\# \ 0\text{--}17 \ \text{yrs. old}}{\# \ 18\text{--}64 \ \text{yrs. old}} \times 100$$

Old Age Dependency Ratio

$$\frac{\# \ 65+ \ \text{yrs. old}}{\# \ 18\text{--}64 \ \text{yrs. old}} \times 100$$

Total Dependency Ratio

$$\frac{\# \ 0\text{--}17 \ \& \ 65+ \ \text{yrs. old}}{\# \ 18\text{--}64 \ \text{yrs. old}} \times 100$$

Population pyramids are a graphic way of displaying the age and sex structure of a population. Figure 2.1 illustrates the structure of the U.S. population based on the 1990 census data. The right column displays different age groups. Across the bottom is the scale in millions of people. The bar graph indicates the numbers of women in various age groups on the right side; on the left side, the men are represented in a similar fashion.

Table 2.2
United States Population by Age: 1990

Age	Count	Percent
Total population	248,709,873	
Under 5 years	18,354,443	7.4
5 to 17 years	45,249,989	18.2
18 to 20 years	11,726,868	4.8
21 to 24 years	15,010,898	6.1
25 to 44 years	80,754,835	32.5
45 to 54 years	25,223,086	10.2
55 to 59 years	10,531,756	4.3
60 to 64 years	10,616,167	4.3
65 to 74 years	18,106,558	7.3
75 to 84 years	10,055,108	4.1
85 years and over	3,080,165	1.2

Source: U.S. Bureau of the Census. 1990 Census of the Population.

Profiles of Productive Aging

W. Edwards Deming
Statistical scientist

"I would say the best part of my life has come from the last 20 years. I'm having more fun, I understand better what I'm doing, I see more and more fields open that need to be explored and understood better. It's a great life."

The man who more than anyone else was responsible for the economic resurgence of Japan after World War II is W. Edwards Deming. Born in Iowa in 1900, Deming, the son of a lawyer, trained as an engineer at the University of Wyoming, the University of Colorado, and Yale University, where he received his Ph.D., and worked as a mathematical physicist at the U.S. Department of Agriculture for over a decade.

Then in his late thirties, he became interested in statistics, a new science "in the wind," as he said. When he received an offer from the Bureau of the Census in Washington, he jumped at the opportunity. Deming became deeply engaged in learning how statistical methods could be used for a variety of functions, ranging from monitoring intercity motor freight to consumer research. In 1947, the Japanese Census Bureau invited him to Japan to advise them on how to use statistical science to restructure their devastated agency. Fascinated by the question of how one rebuilds an economy as devastated as Japan's was immediately after the war, Deming thought that the use of statistical method in quality control would be extremely useful.

Many of his ideas struck home in the Japanese imagination. He devised the method the Japanese used to construct the most stunning economic recovery in the world, eventually wrestling superiority from the United States as a manufacturer and exporter. "I didn't have to teach the Japanese about cooperation,"

Deming remarked. "They already understood it; it was part of their culture." So successful were his concepts that the Japanese, in 1951, established an annual prize in his name, the W. Edwards Deming Prize. Over the next decade he returned to Japan every few years to meet with industry leaders and conduct seminars. In 1960 the emperor of Japan decorated him with the Second Order Medal of the Sacred Treasure.

Despite the brilliant success of Deming's method in Japan, the United States virtually ignored it. Only when the Japanese began to pull ahead of the United States economically did American business begin to pay attention to Deming's concepts. As a result, Deming felt that the past twenty years were his most productive period and his greatest career peak. Describing what made his recent years so fruitful, Deming stated: "I can see things in perspective. Time brings vision. I see where to put emphasis. What I've learned becomes clearer— week by week, day by day."

Deming was elected into the National Academy of Engineering and the Science and Technology Hall of Fame in Dayton in 1986, and President Reagan awarded him the National Medal of Technology in 1987. A year later he received the Distinguished Career in Science Award from the National Academy of Sciences.

Until his death from cancer on December 20, 1993, Deming remained busy consulting for major corporations, helping them revamp their methods and techniques so as to make their companies more productive. Deming claimed, "I spend half my time on public seminars, the other half with clients." His four-day seminars reached over 10,000 people per year and became more popular every year, a fact Deming relished. "Many people are interested," he said. "My seminars are overbooked months ahead!"

Lydia Brontë

● U.S. POPULATION TRENDS: PAST AND FUTURE

The nation's aging throughout this century and into the middle of the next century is charted in Table 2.3. Median age climbed steadily through the first half of this century from 23 in 1900 to 30 in 1950. The baby boom dropped the median age to 29 in 1960, and by 1970 it dipped to 28 years of age. By 1980 the median age had again risen to 30.

By 2020 the median age is projected to rise by ten years. As the baby boom ages out of the population, the median age will reach 43 in 2050.

With 12.6 percent of the population over 65, the United States is one of the oldest countries in the world. Only Northern Europe (16 percent) and Western Europe (14 percent) have more age dense populations. Exceptionally low fertility, in

Table 2.3
Median Age, Percent 65 Years Old and Older, Percent 85 Years Old and Over, and
Dependency Ratios: 1990 to 2050

	Median Age	Percent 65+	Percent 85+	Dependency Ratios		
				65+	0–17	Overall
1900	23	4.0	.2	7	76	84
1910	24	4.3	.2	–	–	–
1920	25	4.7	.2	8	68	76
1930	26	5.4	.2	–	–	–
1940	29	6.8	.3	11	52	63
1950	30	8.1	.4	–	–	–
1960	29	9.2	.5	17	65	82
1970	28	9.8	.7	–	–	–
1980	30	11.3	1.0	19	46	65
1990	33	12.6	1.2	20	41	62
2000	36	13.0	1.7	21	39	60
2010	39	13.9	2.2	22	35	57
2020	40	17.7	2.3	29	35	64
2030	42	21.8	2.7	38	36	74
2040	43	22.6	4.1	39	35	74
2050	43	22.9	5.1	40	35	75

Source: Statistical Abstract of the United States, 1985. U.S. Bureau of the Census. "Projections of the Population of the United States by Age, Sex, and Race: 1988 to 2050." By Gregory Spencer. Current Population Report Series P-25, No. 1018 (January 1989).

part, has aged Northern Europe (1,800 births per 1,000 women) and Western Europe (1,600 births per 1,000 women). Among the less developed nations, the percent of the population 65 years and over stands where the United States was in 1900, at 4 percent (Haub et al., 1991). As the baby boom generation ages, the elderly will be over one-fifth of the nation's population by 2025, and the oldest old (85 plus) will account for one in twenty of the population in 2050. Projections of the percent of the elderly and oldest-old found in Table 2.3 are based on replacement rate fertility, or 2,100 children per 1,000 women. Fertility below replacement rate would increase the proportion of the elderly population. As shown in Table 2.4, the United States has not experienced a total fertility rate over 2,100 since 1971 (2,267). Total fertility rates decreased through the early 1970s to a low of 1,738 in 1976; they recently increased to 2,081.

The percent of the population 65-plus also could be accentuated by a significant increase in life expectancy. This projection by the U.S. Bureau of the Census assumes male and female life expectancy at birth will rise to 76.4 and 83.3,

respectively, by 2050. Fries and Crapo (1981), using a demographic model called a survival curve, estimate that even in the absence of disease, the average life expectancy at birth will be 85, with a standard deviation of 4 years. Their calculations are in line with a life span of 100.

The Life Expectancy Controversy

Can life expectancy be extended further than Fries and Crapo suggest? Cellular biologist Leonard Hayflick (1980) contends that cells only replicate a limited number of times, the so called Hayflick Limit. This limit illustrates the concept of *senescence*, or the basic biological aging of an organism, by which it becomes less vital and more vulnerable to the environment. Finding the cures to various diseases, no doubt, will extend life expectancy to some degree. Yet such cures cannot extend human life indefinitely. The National Center for Health Statistics (1988) estimates a cure for all heart disease would extend life at birth by 5 years; another 3.7 years could be achieved with a cure for cancer, and 0.91 year for strokes. Yet the ultimate biological clock still

Figure 2.1
United States Population Pyramid: 1990

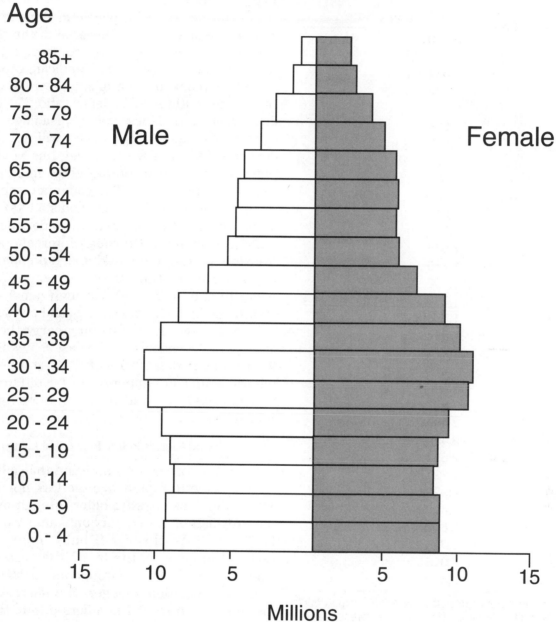

Source: Bureau of the Census.

ticks, even though various disease entities are conquered.

Unless a way is found to reverse the primary aging process, there is a limit to mortality reduction. Hayflick (1976) argues that the vast efforts and resources that go to cure cancer, stroke, and cardiovascular disease are shortsighted. Cures for the nation's three big killers still leave a biological limit on life. It also leaves an older and frailer population. Lobbying for his science,

Hayflick suggests more resources are needed for research on how to unlock the basic biological limit on longevity.

Immigration

Recent immigration into the United States rivals in size the great waves at the turn of the century. In part this counter-balances the rapid aging of the population caused by reduction in fertility and mortality. Over a quarter (28.4 per-

Table 2.4
Total Fertility Rates United States: 1940 to 1991

Year	Total Fertility Rate[1]
1991	2,073
1990	2,081
1989	2,014
1988	1,932
1987	1,871
1986	1,836
1985	1,843
1984	1,806
1983	1,803
1982	1,829
1981	1,815
1980	1,840
1979	1,808
1978	1,760
1977	1,790
1976	1,738
1975	1,774
1974	1,835
1973	1,879
1972	2,010
1971	2,267
1970	2,480
1969	2,456
1968	2,464
1967	2,558
1966	2,721
1965	2,931
1960–64	3,449
1955–59	3,690
1950–54	3,337
1945–49	2,985
1940–44	2,523

Note: 1. Projected number of births per 1,000 women during fecund years (10–49 years old) based on present age-specific fertility.

Source: U.S. Statistical Abstract (1988). Advance Report of Final Natality Statistics (1991).

cent) of the U.S. population growth arises from immigration. Immigrants are typically young individuals. In addition, Latin American immigrants, which comprise 35 percent of legal migrants, have a higher than average fertility. Among all women in the United States in 1980 between 35 and 49 years of age, the lifetime fertility rate was 2.6. In comparison, Latin American immigrant women in the same age group experience a lifetime fertility rate of 3.1 (Bouvier & Gardner 1986).

Dependency ratios displayed in Table 2.3 are a source of some debate. Increase in the old age dependency ratio has many concerned for the future of Social Security and Medicare programs, yet others point to the dramatic decrease occurring in the youthful dependency ratio. The overall dependency ratio is less volatile, leading some to suggest that aging of the nation will not be burdensome. Still it is worth noting that youth and older adults tend to obtain economic support from different sources. The young are supported by their families and by local and state taxes that subsidize education, whereas the older adult population is supported through intergenerational transfers (taxing the working age population to pay benefits to the retired by way of Social Security and Medicare), through pension programs, and by their own savings and investments. Hence the nation overall may carry the same amount of dependency in the past as it will in the future (comparing 1920 with 2030 and beyond), but the sources of support are far different and may not easily be transferred from one generation to another.

Recent Factors in U.S. Population Aging

Complex forces are unfolding that have and will continue to rapidly age the U.S. population. The nation was growing older through much of the early part of this century until after World War II. The post-World War II baby boom, which reached its peak in the late 1950s, turned the aging of the population around and helped make the U.S. population younger. The migrants coming to shore in record numbers during the first decade of this century were growing older and contributed to the aging of the nation after World War I. Fertility dropped during the 1920s, which some attribute to a surge of feminist perspectives in that decade; then, especially low birth rates occurred during the depression years; and with the mobilization of men, there were relatively few births during the war years. The post-World War II demobilization, the economic upswing during the 1950s, and a resurgence of traditional family values spurred the baby boom. At mid-century the aging of the U.S. population stalled for a decade and a half.

The aging of U.S. population has resumed and is being driven forward by a number of variables. The post-War World II baby boom has aged thirty years and is now moving into middle age. In two more decades (about 2010) the baby boom generation will start to retire. The aging of the baby boom generation is accented by the "birth dearth" that followed; if the 1950s saw a return to traditional family values, the women's movement of the 1960s had an effect on the life and fertility of the baby boom generation's leading edge.

As the nation moved through the 1970s and into the 1980s, baby boom women increasingly enrolled in college. In 1959 only 5.9 percent of women completed four years of college; by 1989 18.1 percent had obtained a bachelor's degree—an increase by a factor of 2.2. In comparison, males going to college increased by a factor of 1.5 (U.S. Bureau of the Census, 1991a and 1975a). Median age of marriage among females increased from 20.3 years old in 1960 to 23.7 years old by 1989 (U.S. Bureau of the Census, 1975a; National Center for Health Statistics, 1991a). A clear pattern is emerging of delayed fertility among college-educated women (National Center for Health Statistics, 1991c).

Another ten to fifteen years will tell if this deferred fertility will mean reduced fertility, further accentuating the aging of our population. Even women not motivated by career interest are sharing the labor force with their husbands in order to make ends meet and achieve the middle-class dream. Divorce also propels women into the work force, and divorce has doubled in the last three decades, moving from 9.2 per 1,000 married women 15 years and older in 1960, to 20.7 in 1988 (National Center for Health Statistics, 1991a). Hence far more women are working now than in the past, from 34.9 percent in 1960 to 57.4 percent in 1989 (U.S. Bureau of the Census, 1991a and 1975a). Not surprisingly, the fertility of women aged 35 to 44 in the work force (2,034 births per 1,000 women) is lower than that of women aged 35 to 44 who are not in the labor force (2,417 births per 1000 women) (U.S. Bureau of the Census, 1991b).

As the baby boom generation was marked by low fertility before it began, it was punctuated by even lower fertility after it ended. This gives the baby boom its characteristic imprint on the U.S. population pyramid (see Figure 2.1) as it moves through aging the nation.

Table 2.5
College-Educated Women by Age Groups: 1989

Age Group	% of First Births to College-Educated Women
20 to 24	7 Percent
25 to 29	33 Percent
30 to 34	46 Percent

Source: National Center on Health Statistics, 1991.

Along with decreased fertility, the reduction in mortality is aging the United States. The battle against acute infectious disease is about over, and so life expectancy at birth has not increased as fast in the second part of this century as it did in the first. Nevertheless, it is still growing and helps age the nation. Medical science now turns its attention to the reduction of chronic mortality, and at age 65 life expectancy is now being extended.

Changes in life expectancy in this century can be traced in Table 2.6. Note that the most significant changes in life expectancy at birth came about in the first half of the century (an increase of 0.42 years of life per year), compared to the next 41 years of this century (an increase of 0.18 years of life per year). At age 65 life expectancy grew more in the second part of the century with a 3.3 year increase from 1950 to 1989, compared to 2 years at the turn of the century to 1950.

More Life to Live: Some Differences in Life Expectancy

In 1991 the United States had the largest expenditures for health care in the world ($751.8 billion), with 3.2 percent being the greatest percent of the gross national product (GNP) devoted to health care, and at $2,868 the largest per capita expenditures on health care (National Center for Health Statistics, 1993). Yet compared to other industrialized nations the United States has a rather low life expectancy (see Table 2.7). At birth male life expectancy is 22d and female is 16th in the world. Life expectancy in the United States at age 65 ranks 25th for males and 10th for females in comparison to other countries. This disparity between the nation's output for health care and the outcome in terms of life expectancy is typically explained by the conjunction of three factors.

Table 2.6
Life Expectancy at Birth and at 65 Years Old by Sex and Race: 1900 to 1991

	All Races			White			African American		
Year	Both Sexes	Men	Women	Both Sexes	Men	Women	Both Sexes	Men	Women
At birth:									
1900[1]	47.3	46.3	48.3	47.6	46.6	48.7	33.0[3]	32.5	33.5
1950[2]	68.2	65.6	71.1	69.1	66.5	72.2	60.7	58.9	62.7
1960	69.7	66.6	73.1	70.6	67.4	74.1	63.2	60.7	65.9
1970	70.9	67.1	74.8	71.7	68.0	75.6	64.1	60.0	68.3
1980	73.7	70.0	77.4	74.4	70.7	78.1	68.1	63.8	72.5
1990	75.4	71.8	78.8	76.1	72.7	79.4	69.1	64.5	73.6
1991	75.5	72.0	78.9	76.3	72.9	79.6	69.3	64.6	73.8
At age 65:									
1900–02	11.9	11.5	12.2	—	11.5	12.2	—	10.4	11.4
1950	13.9	12.8	15.0	—	12.8	15.1	13.9	12.9	14.9
1960	14.3	12.8	15.8	14.4	12.9	15.9	13.9	12.7	15.1
1970	15.2	13.1	17.0	15.2	13.1	17.1	14.2	12.5	15.7
1980	16.4	14.1	18.3	16.5	14.2	18.4	15.1	13.0	16.8
1989[4]	17.2	15.2	18.8	17.3	15.2	18.9	15.8	13.8	17.4

Notes: 1. 10 states and the District of Columbia. 2. Includes the deaths of the nonresidents of the United States. 3. Figure is for the nonwhite population. 4. Provisional data.

Sources: 1900 to 1980 data: National Center for Health Statistics, Health, United States, 1988, DHHS Pub. No. (PHS)89-1232, Washington, DC: Department of Health and Human Services (March 1989).

First is the issue of life style, which encompasses such well known factors as smoking, drug abuse, malnutrition, lack of exercise, and the often unrecognized factor of violence. The U.S. homicide rate is ten times that of the Europeans and is the tenth biggest killer in the United States. Among our young, murder is one of the most significant causes of death, ranked third among 5–14 year olds and second among 15–24 year olds (National Center for Health Statistics, 1991c). Since these deaths occur so young in life, a reduction in violent deaths along with mortality from motor vehicle accidents would probably make the single largest contribution to life expectancy at birth. In addition, those in poverty typically lack knowledge about health care, often lead deleterious life styles, and cannot afford to purchase health care. Finally, most of the nations that have higher life expectancies than the United States have either a national health care system or national insurance plan. Such mechanisms insure universal access to health care. In 1989 some 15.7 percent of those under age 65 did not

have health care coverage in the United States (National Center for Health Statistics, 1993). And those who cannot gain access to health care are at greater risk of premature death.

Life expectancy is not shared equally by all in the United States (see Table 2.6). Life expectancy is greater for females than for males. In 1991, on the average, at birth a women could expect to live 6.9 years longer than her male counterpart. The differential in life expectancy is down from 7.7 years in 1970.

The degree to which nature or nurture influences this difference is not clear. The expansion of the difference in male to female mortality in this century (differential mortality in 1900 was two years) has been explained in part by the reduction of maternal mortality (death in childbirth). Preston (1976) and Retherford (1975) detailed the widening of the mortality differential between the sexes attributable to degenerative lung and cardiovascular diseases. Based on the prevalence of smoking among males and its link to those disorders, researchers consider smoking

Table 2.7
National Life Expectancy Comparisons: 1987

Country	MALE Life Expectancy in Years		Country	FEMALE Life Expectancy in Years	
	At Birth	At 65		At Birth	At 65
Japan	75.9	16.4	Japan	82.1	20.4
Sweden	74.2	15.1	France	81.1	20.2
Hong Kong	74.2	15.0	Switzerland	81.0	19.7
Greece	74.1	15.4	Sweden	80.4	19.1
Switzerland	74.0	15.4	Netherlands	80.3	19.3
Netherlands	73.6	15.4	Canada	80.2	19.6
Israel	73.4	14.9	Australia	79.8	19.0
Canada	73.3	15.1	Norway	79.8	18.8
Australia	73.2	14.9	Hong Kong	79.7	18.5
Spain	73.1	15.0	Spain	79.7	18.4
Cuba	73.0	16.2	Italy	79.2	18.2
Norway	72.8	14.4	Greece	78.9	17.7
Italy	72.7	14.3	Finland	78.9	17.7
England and Wales	72.6	13.9	Federal Republic of Germany	78.9	18.1
France	72.6	15.4	Puerto Rico	78.9	19.2
Kuwait	72.5	14.5	United States	78.4	18.7
Federal Republic of Germany	72.2	14.0	England and Wales	78.3	17.9
Costa Rica	72.1	14.0	Austria	78.2	17.6
Denmark	71.9	14.2	Belgium	78.2	17.8
Ireland	71.6	13.1	Denmark	78.0	18.2
Austria	71.6	14.3	Portugal	77.5	17.6
United States	71.5	14.8	New Zealand	77.3	17.6
Belgium	71.4	13.6	Ireland	77.3	16.6
Singapore	71.3	13.5	Northern Ireland	77.2	16.9
Northern Ireland	71.1	13.0	Israel	77.0	16.0
New Zealand	71.0	13.7	Costa Rica	76.9	16.8
Puerto Rico	70.7	16.3	Scotland	76.6	16.7
Finland	70.7	13.5	Singapore	76.5	16.6
Portugal	70.6	14.3	Cuba	76.5	17.9
Scotland	70.5	12.8	German Democratic Republic	76.0	15.6
Chile	70.0	13.7	Kuwait	75.8	16.2
German Democratic Republic	69.9	12.7	Chile	75.7	16.7
Yugoslavia	68.5	13.3	Czechoslovakia	75.3	15.5
Bulgaria	68.3	12.6	Poland	75.2	15.9
Czechoslovakia	67.7	11.9	Bulgaria	74.6	15.0
Romania	67.1	12.8	Yugoslavia	74.3	15.6
Poland	66.8	12.3	Hungary	73.9	15.4
Hungary	65.7	12.1	U.S.S.R	73.9	16.2
U.S.S.R.	65.1	12.5	Romania	72.7	14.7

Notes: Rankings are from highest to lowest life expectancy based on the latest available data for countries or geographic areas with at least 1 million population. This table is based on official mortality data from the country concerned, as submitted to the *United Nations Demographic Yearbook* or the *World Health Statistics Annual*.

In 1989, on the average, at birth a woman could expect to live 6.7 years longer than her male counterpart. (Copyright © Benjamin Porter)

an important external factor in the difference in life expectancy between the sexes. But this may now be changing based on the increased prevalence of cigarette smoking among females since World War II. Lung cancer recently became the number one cancer killer among females.

Madigan's (1956) classic study of a teaching order of nuns and monks with equivalent life styles offers some tantalizing evidence. He reported that the nuns and monks both showed better life expectancies than the general population. Still, the nuns lived longer than their male colleagues. While the control for life style in the study was not perfect, it came as close as may be found in the real world and supports the hypothesis that there is a biological component to longevity.

African Americans and whites display stark differences in life expectancy of over 7.0 years at birth in 1991. Since the differential mortality in 1900 was 14.6 years, the evidence over the course of this century indicates that the divergence has been reduced as the burden of the racial difference in society has decreased. Still, a report in the *Journal of the American Medical Association* (Otten et al., 1990) ascribes 38 percent of the differential mortality to the socio-economic difference between the races. An additional 31 percent of the mortality difference can be ascribed to six well known risk factors (smoking, systolic blood pressure, cholesterol level, body-mass

Life expectancy is not shared equally by all in the United States. Blacks and whites present a stark difference in life expectancy of over 7.0 years at birth. (Courtesy of the American Association of Retired Persons)

Table 2.8
Deaths Due to AIDS by Age Group

Age Group	Rank Order of Cause of Death	Death Rate per 100,000 Attributable to AIDS	Overall Mortality
15 to 24	Sixth	1.7	613
25 to 44	Third	26.5	21,747

Source: National Center for Health Statistics, 1993.

index, alcohol intake, and diabetes), some of which are certainly directly tied to lifestyle.

Much attention has been given to the Acquired Immune Deficiency Syndrome (AIDS) epidemic and the inevitable mortality associated with the disease. Since its recognition only a decade ago, AIDS has become the ninth largest cause of mortality in the United States. With a death rate of 11.7 per 100,000, it accounts for 1.4 percent of the mortality in the nation. Yet the overall death rate in the United States is 860.3 per 100,000, with disease of the heart (285.7 per 100,000) contributing 33.2 percent of the mortality. Cardiovascular disease is followed by neoplasms (i.e., cancers; 204.1 per 100,000) with 23.7 percent of the mortality, and cerebrovascular diseases (i.e., strokes; 56.9 per 100,000) at 6.6 percent of the nation's mortality. Compared to the big three chronic diseases, AIDS is a relatively small contributor to U.S. mortality, yet it is an infectious disease. Among the reproductive age groups, AIDS is a much more significant component of mortality.

No doubt AIDS will make a significant impact on the lives of millions of Americans, though it is too early to fully assess the impact of the disease on the aging of America. How fast the disease spreads through the population will be influenced by how quickly and to what degree changes in lifestyle occur, not to mention how soon a vaccination or cure for the disease is discovered.

● DISTRIBUTION OF OLDER ADULT POPULATION IN THE UNITED STATES

The nation's most populous states are also those with the most people age 65 and over (see Table 2.9). California has 3.1 million elderly, according to the 1990 census. Florida has the second most elderly persons by count (2,369,431), followed closely by New York (2,363,722). Another six states (Pennsylvania, Texas, Illinois,

Ohio, Michigan, New Jersey) have over one million older adults.

Florida is the oldest state, as measured by the percent of the population 65 years and older. The United States has 12.6 percent of its population who are 65 years and over, while Florida is at 18.3 percent. The United States will not achieve such an age density until the early 2020s, when the peak of the baby boom turns 65. Yet it would be a mistake to consider Florida a crystal ball in which to view the nation's aging. Florida has aged to such a degree by the in-migration of a select type of financially secure and educated elderly person who is seeking amenities (e.g., warm climate) in the locale.

A significant gap lies between Florida and the next most age-dense state, Pennsylvania, with 15.4 percent of its population 65 plus. Of the remaining top ten states, six are in the rural midwestern farm belt. These states have aged in part by the out-migration of the young, who seek economic opportunities in more urbanized settings. Alaska, the frontier state of the union, is the youngest, with only 4.1 percent of its population 65 and over, and its elderly population numbering only 22,369.

● RETIREMENT MIGRATION

Demography has tended traditionally to focus on youthful migration, and labor force migration in particular. Increasing attention, however, is being given to non-labor force motivated migration, particularly to the migration of retirement age persons. Interstate migration streams of the elderly are highly focused. Half of the interstate migrants, regardless of their origin, flow into only seven of the fifty states. Florida dominates the scene, having received about one-quarter of all interstate migrants aged 60 or over in the five years preceding the 1960, 1970, and 1980 census-

Table 2.9
Population 65 Years Old and Older and Percent Population 65 Years Old and Older by State: 1990

State	Population 65 Years and Over	Percent 65 Years and Over	State	Population 65 Years and Over	Percent 65 Years and Over
UNITED STATES	**31,241,831**	**12.6**	25 Kentucky	466,845	12.7
1 Florida	2,369,431	18.3	27 Illinois	1,436,545	12.6
2 Pennsylvania	1,829,106	15.4	27 Indiana	696,196	12.6
3 Iowa	426,106	15.3	29 Minnesota	546,934	12.5
4 Rhode Island	150,547	15.0	29 Mississippi	321,284	12.5
4 West Virginia	268,897	15.0	31 North Carolina	804,341	12.1
6 Arkansas	350,058	14.9	31 Delaware	80,735	12.1
7 South Dakota	102,331	14.7	33 Idaho	121,265	12.0
8 North Dakota	91,055	14.3	34 Michigan	1,108,461	11.9
9 Nebraska	223,068	14.1	35 Washington	575,288	11.8
10 Missouri	717,681	14.0	25 Vermont	66,163	11.8
11 Kansas	342,571	13.8	37 South Carolina	396,935	11.4
11 Oregon	391,324	13.8	38 Hawaii	125,005	11.3
13 Massachusetts	819,284	13.6	38 New Hampshire	125,029	11.3
13 Connecticut	445,907	13.6	40 Louisiana	468,991	11.1
15 Oklahoma	424,213	13.5	41 Maryland	517,482	10.8
16 New Jersey	1,032,025	13.4	41 New Mexico	163,062	10.8
17 Montana	106,497	13.3	43 Virginia	664,470	0.7
17 Wisconsin	651,221	13.3	44 Nevada	127,631	10.6
17 Maine	163,373	13.3	45 California	3,135,552	10.5
20 New York	2,363,722	13.1	46 Wyoming	47,195	10.4
20 Arizona	478,774	13.1	47 Texas	1,716,576	10.1
22 Ohio	1,406,961	13.0	47 Georgia	654,270	10.1
23 Alabama	522,989	12.9	49 Colorado	329,443	10.0
24 District of Columbia	77,847	12.8	50 Utah	149,958	8.7
25 Tennessee	618,818	12.7	51 Alaska	22,369	4.1

Source: U.S. Bureau of the Census. 1990 Census of Population.

So far, studies of elderly seasonal migrants have shown them to be relatively advantaged, attracted by nonlabor-force issues such as climate, cost of living, and the locations of family members and friends. (Copyright © Marianne Gontarz)

es (Table 2.10). Although Florida, California, and Arizona have different major recruitment areas, they are the only states that attract several unusually large streams from outside their regions. Florida's donor states are primarily from east of the Mississippi River, and Arizona's and California's are primarily from west of it. Among the elderly, the special characteristics of the host community, or *pull factors*, tend to be more important than the distance. Warm climate, economic growth, and lower cost of living are important in the location decision.

Permanence is an important but difficult dimension of migration to study. The census assumes that one's usual place of residence is not

Profiles of Productive Aging

Louis Harris
Pollster

"Go all out, flat out. That's the way to lead life. If you're wrong, so be it, but if you're right, at least you've done it. All out, flat out means going at 100% of your capacity. I really believe that."

Pollster Louis Harris was born in 1921 to a prosperous family who lost everything during a bank run in 1928, a week after his father died. Harris was 7 at the time. The family's only source of income during the Depression was the rent on a commercial garage, but the renter rarely paid; Harris resorted to selling magazine subscriptions to support his family and save money for college.

Initially Harris dreamed of becoming a lawyer: "I had a picture of myself as a Justice of the U.S. Supreme Court.... This was probably when I was eight or nine. I could see the door for some reason: Justice. Never Chief Justice, just Justice Louis Harris."

That aspiration evolved into a desire to be a journalist: "I had a yen to communicate. That's been a thread all through my life." Harris worked for his high school newspaper, then got a paying job as the Hill House High School correspondent for the *New Haven Register.* He used his earnings to buy himself a secondhand typewriter to teach himself to type; it cost $8.75, a small fortune in 1933. "That was blood money," Harris reflected. He later became editor of the school magazine and associate editor of the newspaper.

Harris studied at the University of North Carolina at Chapel Hill, where he got "a wild but very formative college education." He served in the Navy, for which he received a commendation, then worked briefly for the American Veterans Committee as its research and program director. One day he noticed an article in the *New York Herald Tribune* about a poll that had been done on veterans. Harris went to see the pollster, Elmo Roper, who offered Harris a job as his assistant.

Harris started his own polling firm in 1956, Louis Harris & Associates in New York "on a wing and a prayer." His clients had encouraged him to open his own office, and they supported his business in the early days of the firm. Soon he was doing extremely well, polling for a variety of political candidates and for the AFL-CIO. Eventually, as the accuracy of his polls made him famous, he became chief pollster for John F. Kennedy's presidential campaign in 1960.

Polling is his calling, Harris believes, and he works tirelessly at it to keep on top of all national trends and attitudes: "Data is always talking to me. I have a feel for what people are trying to say. I try to glean it out.... I always worked hard. I thought nothing of working until three in the morning and going to work in the morning and working hard all day. It's always been work, work, work for me."

Harris has advanced the field of polling dramatically by initiating such changes as using computers to assist the CBS Vote Profile Analysis. He is also the author of six books on contemporary American issues and has written a syndicated weekly column called "The Harris Poll" since 1963.

Lydia Brontë

temporary. In reality, however, much of the migration among older people may be temporary. So far studies of elderly seasonal migrants have shown them to be relatively advantaged and attracted by non-labor force issues such as climate, cost of living, and the locations of family members and friends.

The cycle of migration away for a job when one is young and then returning to one's hometown and roots after retirement is a famous literary theme. However Andrei Rogers (1990) recently demonstrated that elderly persons are no more likely to return home than are the nonelderly; the probabilities of return migration by the elderly are lower than those of the general population. There is wide state variability, however. The southeastern region is unusually attractive to older return migrants, and return migration is uncommonly high among older African Americans moving into that region.

Metropolitan-to-metropolitan migration predominates among the elderly. Of the one-third who were changing environmental types, no increase occurred between the 1960 and 1980 censuses in the proportion moving out of metropolitan areas in each decade. The movement in

Figure 2.2
Percent of Total State Population 65 Years and Over: 1990

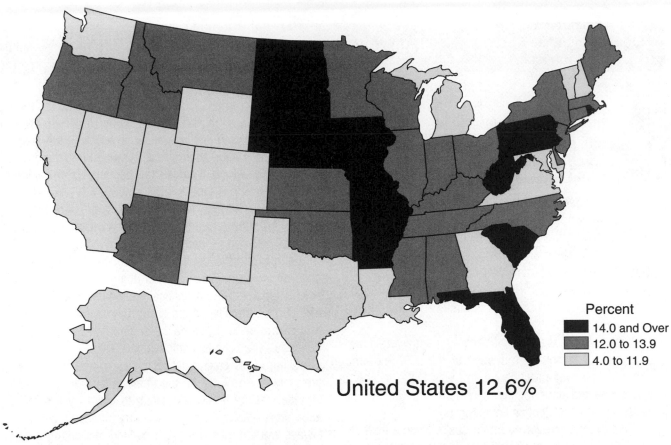

Percent

- 14.0 and Over
- 12.0 to 13.9
- 4.0 to 11.9

United States 12.6%

Source: U.S. Bureau of the Census, 1990 Census of Population.

Table 2.10
Ten States Receiving the Largest Share of In-Migrants Age 60+: 1960, 1970, and 1980

Rank	State	1960 Total	%	State	1970 Total	%	State	1980[1] Total	%
1	FL	208,072	22.3	FL	269,141	24.6	FL	437,000	26.3
2	CA	126,883	13.6	CA	109,342	10.0	CA	145,000	8.7
3	NJ	36,019	3.9	AZ	46,451	4.2	AZ	95,000	5.7
4	NY	33,794	3.6	NJ	43,597	4.0	TX	78,000	4.7
5	IL	30,355	3.3	TX	38,682	3.5	NJ	49,000	2.9
6	AZ	29,571	3.2	PA	34,006	3.1	PA	40,000	2.4
7	OH	27,759	3.0	OH	30,492	2.8	NC	39,000	2.3
8	TX	26,770	2.9	NY	30,388	2.8	WA	36,000	2.2
9	PA	25,738	2.8	IL	29,434	2.7	IL	36,000	2.2
10	MI	20,308	2.2	MO	24,395	2.2	NY	35,000	2.1
Total Interstate Migrants		931,012			1,094,014			1,654,000	
% of Total in Top 10 States			60.8			59.9			59.5

Note: 1. Estimated numbers are rounded to the nearest thousand.

Sources: U.S. Census of the Population, 1960. Detailed Population Characteristics.
U.S. Census of the Population, 1970. Detailed Population Characteristics.
U.S. Bureau of the Census, 1983. 1980 Public Use Microdata Sample A.

the opposite direction, up the metropolitan hierarchy, however, declined, both among older intrastate and interstate migrants. The net difference made it appear as though the flow from cities increased. Metropolitan-to-nonmetropolitan migrants, especially those moving longer distances, tend to have more income, to be married, and to live in their own homes. A higher proportion of nonmetro-to-metro migrants is older, widowed, and living dependently, especially with their children.

Litwak and Longino (1987) bring a significant refinement to the study of retirement migration with a developmental approach. They offer a model of young-old, relatively healthy and financially secure couples making a move primarily for amenity reasons. Onset of disabilities in later life and/or widowhood initiates a second type of move to a more supportive environment. A counter migration stream is found leaving Florida, containing migrants who tend to be widowed and who are

more often disabled (Longino et al., 1984). A final type of move, to an institutional setting, is brought on by severe and chronic disabilities. No types of moves are inevitable, but when they do occur, they tend to be patterned by relative age.

● DIVERSITY AMONG THE AGING POPULATION

A consideration of our aging society often leads to comparing the older age group to other age groups or strata. Focusing on the differences between age strata tends to obscure the variance among older adults. This section reviews some of the major variations within the older adult population in the United States.

Age

A common misconception about the elderly is that the one thing they all have in common is being old. Yet the amount of time from the artificially defined beginning of old age at 65 to the

Too Many Centenarians?

Those who watch the "Today" show cannot help but be struck by the fact that Willard Scott gives two or three birthday wishes to 100 year olds each morning. It is not unusual for him to give a birthday greeting to someone 105 or over. Life span is approximately 100 years, but it is defined as the age to which 0.1 percent of a birth cohort lives. So although Willard Scott's birthday people are not anomalies, they are certainly rare.

Recently, a question has been raised about the number of centenarians reported in the nation (Coale, 1991). The concern over the actual number of 100 year olds rest on two issues. First, some esteem and benefits are associated with reaching this venerable age, which provides an incentive to exaggerate one's age. Mazes and Forman (1979) reported on such systematic exaggeration in Vilcabamba, Ecuador; Leaf (1982) also agreed that claims of extreme longevity should be treated with suspicion. Second, the United States does not keep a national registry of vital events. This mechanism, used in many countries throughout the world, centralizes records of birth, marriage, children born, divorce, and death for each citizen. For geographically mobile Americans, their birth, marriage, and death certificates will be scattered across the United States. A national registry where birth and death registrations are kept together would make it easy to produce an exact count of centenarians and accurate age at time of death. In the United States, however, there is no easy way to tell if people are being accurate.

Coale (1991) reports that in countries with higher life expectancies than the United States the reported deaths of their oldest citizens are much closer to their assumed life span than in the United States. Among five European countries (France, Netherlands, Sweden, Switzerland, and Italy) and Japan, the oldest male and female death reports were 109 and 112, respectively. In the United States the oldest reported death for men and women is 124. The 1980 U.S. census indicates approximately 1,900 individuals reported being above 110 years old. And yet, in the same year, only 84 people of that age group died! A ratio of the reported census population to a demographic model of persons in different age groups revealed the following increasingly divergent ratios: 1.4:1 at 100 and over, 9.5:1 at 105 and over, and 119.1:1 at 110 and over, meaning that there is increasing divergence from the model with advancing age and suggesting that once a person reaches 100 years of age, he or she starts to gain more than a year or two of life expectancy at each birthday thereafter!

Table 2.11
Age Classifications of the Elderly

	Age Groups	Number	Percent of Population
Young-Old	55 to 74	39,254,481	15.8
Old-Old	75 to 84	10,055,108	4.0
Oldest-Old	85 and over	3,080,165	1.2

Source: U.S. Bureau of the Census, 1990.

maximum expectation of the life span encompasses over 35 years. Neugarten (1975) helped gerontologists think about the diversity among older adults by suggesting there are significant differences between the *young-old* (55 to 74 years old) and the *old-old* (75 years old and older). Considering the growing percent of the population over 85, Riley and Suzman (1985), added the concept of the *oldest-old* to gerontological jargon.

The oldest-old are intensive users of medical and social services. Those 85 and over have the highest rates of functional disability, physician visits, hospitalizations, length of stay in hospital, nursing home placement, and poverty rates. The compression of mortality into advanced old age has produced the fastest growing age group, whose members are frail and in great need of supportive services. This presents the nation with serious policy implications. High private and public cost of supporting this age group has caused some to suggest controversial solutions, such as altering the basic premise of Social Security and Medicare by requiring financial need rather than age as a criterion for benefits (Neugarten, 1982). Callahan, in *Setting Limits* (1987), suggests even more radically that there may come a time in an individual's life when all but simple comforting medical care is withheld, and nature is allowed to run its course.

Table 2.12
Older Population by Age, Race, and Sex: 1990

Age	Total Male	Total Female	Total White	White Male	White Female	Total African-American	African-American Male	African-American Female
50+	28,061,328	35,678,939	55,536,383	24,537,888	30,998,495	5,681,930	2,368,572	3,313,358
55+	22,546,590	29,843,164	46,031,512	19,880,504	26,151,008	4,502,919	1,836,596	2,666,323
60+	17,512,220	24,345,778	37,063,096	15,549,693	21,513,403	3,470,170	1,379,677	2,090,493
65+	12,565,173	18,676,658	27,851,973	11,214,909	16,637,064	2,508,551	965,432	1,543,119
85+	857,698	2,222,467	2,788,052	764,450	2,023,602	230,183	68,592	161,591

Age	American Indian, Eskimo, & Aleut (AIEA)	AIEA Male	AIEA Female	Asian & Pacific Islander (API)	API Male	API Female	Other Race	Other Male	Other Female
50+	304,375	138,523	165,852	1,235,259	564,180	671,079	982,320	452,165	530,155
55+	227,661	101,635	126,026	923,608	412,095	511,513	704,054	315,760	388,294
60+	165,842	72,281	93,561	672,975	298,586	374,389	485,915	211,983	273,932
65+	114,453	48,089	66,364	454,458	204,447	250,011	312,396	132,296	180,100
85+	9,205	3,274	5,931	29,738	12,399	17,339	22,987	8,983	14,004

Age	Hispanic (Any Race)	Hispanic Male	Hispanic Female	Total
50+	3,110,222	1,402,955	1,707,267	63,740,267
55+	2,354,233	1,038,736	1,315,497	52,389,754
60+	1,714,925	736,365	978,560	41,857,998
65+	1,161,283	481,409	679,874	31,241,831
85+	94,564	33,497	61,067	3,080,165

Source: U.S. Bureau of the Census. 1990 Census of the Population.

● RACE, GENDER, AND MARITAL STATUS

Older people today are predominately white, as demonstrated by the data from the 1990 census (see Tables 2.12 and 2.13). However, because migration streams into this country have shifted in this century from Europe to Latin America and Asia, and since minority groups traditionally have had higher fertility rates than white Americans, so literally the complexion of the country will change. And over the course of time additional color will be added to the aging of America. While

While today approximately 14 percent of our elderly population are from minority groups, that figure will double in fifty years, and by the year 2050, 32 percent of the older adult population will be from a minority group. (Copyright © Isabel Egglin)

Table 2.13
Racial and Hispanic Origin, General Population, 65 Years Old and Older, and 85 Years Old and Older: 1990

General Population	Number	Percent
White	199,686,070	80.3
African American	29,986,060	12.1
Asian & Pacific Islander	7,273,622	2.9
American Indian, Eskimo & Aleut	1,959,324	0.8
Other	9,804,847	3.9
Total	31,241,183	100.0[1]
Hispanic (Any Race)	22,354,059	9.0[2]
Age 65 and Over	**Number**	**Percent**
White	27,851,973	88.3
African American	2,508,551	8.0
Asian & Pacific Islander	454,458	1.5
American Indian, Eskimo & Aleut	114,453	0.4
Other	312,396	1.0
Total	31,241,183	100.0[1]
Hispanic (Any Race)	1,161,283	3.7[2]
Age 85 and Over	**Number**	**Percent**
White	2,788,052	90.5
African American	230,183	7.5
Asian & Pacific Islander	29,738	1.0
American Indian, Eskimo & Aleut	9,205	0.3
Other	22,987	0.8
Total	3,080,165	100.0[1]
Hispanic (Any Race)	94,564	3.1[2]

Source: U.S. Bureau of the Census. 1990 Census of the Population.

Notes: 1. Figures do not total to 100% exactly due to rounding; 2. Percentage of Hispanic out of total.

today approximately 14 percent of our elderly population are from minority groups, that figure will double in fifty years, and by the year 2050, 32 percent of the older adult population will be from minority groups. (See Chapter 3, **Gender and Ethnic Diversity in Aging,** for a further discussion of this topic.)

Sex/Gender

Throughout the entire life cycle, one's sex is an important variable influencing one's social experi-

Table 2.14
Sex Ratio 65 Years Old and Older and 85 Years Old and Older: 1990

Age 65 and Over	
Overall	67.3
White	67.4
African American	62.6
Hispanic	70.8
Asian & Pacific Islander	81.8
American Indian, Eskimo & Aleut	72.5
Age 85 and Over	
Overall	38.6
White	37.8
African American	42.5
Hispanic	54.9
Asian & Pacific Islander	71.5
American Indian, Eskimo & Aleut	55.2

Source: U.S. Bureau of the Census. 1990 Census of the Population.

Table 2.15
Marital Status of Older People by Age, Sex, Race, and Hispanic Origin: 1989

Marital Status	65+		65 to 74		75 to 84		85+	
	Men	Women	Men	Women	Men	Women	Men	Women
All races								
Total (thousands)	12,078	16,944	7,880	9,867	3,506	5,669	693	1,408
Percent	100.0	100.0	100.0	100.0	100.0	100.0	100.0	100.0
Never married	4.7	5.0	4.9	4.5	4.6	5.8	3.2	5.6
Married, spouse present	74.3	40.1	78.4	51.4	70.4	28.1	48.2	9.1
Married, spouse absent	2.7	1.6	2.7	1.8	2.3	1.5	4.4	0.9
Widowed	14.0	48.7	8.9	36.6	19.7	61.5	42.1	82.3
Divorced	4.3	4.5	5.1	5.7	2.9	3.0	2.1	2.1
White								
Total (thousands)	10,798	15,204	7,050	8,767	3,136	5,174	612	1,263
Percent	100.0	100.0	100.0	100.0	100.0	100.0	100.0	100.0
Never married	4.6	5.1	4.8	4.5	4.5	6.0	3.1	5.7
Married, spouse present	76.3	41.2	80.6	53.3	72.3	28.7	47.9	8.8
Married, spouse absent	2.1	1.2	2.0	1.3	1.6	1.1	4.8	0.6
Widowed	13.2	48.1	8.1	35.5	19.2	1.0	41.8	82.7
Divorced	3.8	4.4	4.5	5.4	2.4	3.2	2.4	2.2
African-American								
Total (thousands)	981	1,455	619	913	300	416	62	126
Percent	100.0	100.0	100.0	100.0	100.0	100.0	100.0	100.0
Never married	4.5	4.5	4.0	4.3	6.0	4.6	(B)	5.7
Married, spouse present	56.0	27.9	58.6	33.4	50.9	20.8	(B)	12.2
Married, spouse absent	8.3	5.8	8.6	6.0	9.2	5.9	(B)	4.2
Widowed	21.4	55.3	17.6	47.1	24.7	66.9	(B)	76.3
Divorced	9.8	6.5	11.1	9.2	9.2	1.9	(B)	1.6
Hispanic origin								
Total (thousands)	447	558	301	350	120	176	26	31
Percent	100.0	100.0	100.0	100.0	100.0	100.0	100.0	100.0
Never married	6.6	8.2	6.4	6.8	6.0	11.0	(B)	(B)
Married, spouse present	65.6	37.6	69.7	47.5	62.8	23.1	(B)	(B)
Married, spouse absent	7.7	2.5	8.5	2.4	6.6	2.9	(B)	(B)
Widowed	15.1	43.6	9.3	33.6	21.4	57.8	(B)	(B)
Divorced	5.0	8.1	6.1	9.7	3.2	5.2	(B)	(B)

Source: U.S. Bureau of the Census. "Marital Status and Living Arrangements: March 1989." *Current Population Reports* Series P-20, no. 445 (1990).

Note: Percentage distributions may not add to 100.0 due to rounding; * People of Hispanic origin may be of any race; (B) Base less than 75,000.

ence. Contemporary older adult women were raised at a time when gender was more of a dividing factor in the social world than it is currently. As people advance into late life, differential mor- tality makes growing old more and more often women's work. The number of males per 100 females (sex ratio) becomes ever more extreme moving from the young-old to the oldest-old (see

Table 2.14). Between 65 to 69 years old the sex ratio is 84; for those ten years older it declines to 65 males per 100 females, and at 85 and older the ratio plummets to 39 males for every 100 females.

Marital Status

As the sex ratio increasingly favors females in terms of longevity, it reflects a change in marital status. Table 2.15 reports that with advancing age, marriage gives way to widowhood; at all ages men are far more likely to be married. At ages 65 to 74, 80.6 percent of men and 53.3 percent of women are married, but by 85-plus only 47.9 percent of men and 8.8 percent of women live with their spouses. A further review of the data in the table points out that most of the elderly were once married (94 percent to 96 percent). Compared to present standards, few have divorced, an even rarer event among the oldest-old. Overall the patterns maintain, but clearly there is variation between whites, African Americans, and those of Hispanic origin.

Differential mortality is a significant force creating more widows in later life than widowers. At age 65 a female's life expectancy is 3.9 years longer than a male's. Compounding the differential mortality, women in this age group tended to marry men who were on the average 2.5 to 3.5 years older than themselves (U.S. Bureau of the Census, 1975a). Additionally women are less likely to remarry in later life. Data from 1988 report 12,567 widows 65-plus remarried at a rate of 1.8 per 1,000; whereas 20,653 widowers remarried at a rate of 15.0 per 1,000 (National Center for Health Statistics, 1991b). The fact that there are fewer eligible men than women in later life influences these remarriage rates. This disparity leads one author (Kassel, 1966) to suggest that polygamy should be legalized after age 60, but it is doubtful that many older Americans would flaunt cultural norms even if such a change in the law were to occur. Social norms, though, are more tolerant of a man remarrying under the assumption that a male is less likely to take care of himself. In fact, throughout the life cycle, norms support males marrying younger women, which further expands their pool of eligible mates. (See Chapter 16, **Family Relationships in Later Life,** for a further discussion of this topic.)

● HOUSEHOLD COMPOSITION AND HOUSING

Living arrangements of older adults (listed in Table 2.16) reflect marital status. Differential mortality heightens the chances of a woman living alone. Further analysis of the data in Table 2.16 indicates that a slightly higher percentage of women not living with their spouses tend to live alone rather than with other family members, compared to the men not living with their spouses. Men are slightly more likely than women to live with other family members in later life. It is also much more probable for members of the African-American and Hispanic communities to live with family members other than their spouses than their counterparts in the white community.

Of those older households in the community, 76 percent lived in owner-occupied units, and the rest were renters. There is diversity within the age groups. Those 75 years of age and older are more typically renters, compared to the 65 to 74 year group (31 percent versus 21 percent). Women were renters more frequently than were men (35 percent versus 17 percent). This, in part, is a reflection of widowhood, since among those living alone, 62 percent are renters, as compared to those living with spouses, where 88 percent are homeowners. Of the owner-occupied households, 83 percent were owned outright. Twenty-nine percent of elderly rental units benefited from some sort of housing subsidy or rent control (*Aging America*, 1991).

Approximately 5 percent of the population 65 and over is in nursing homes at any one moment. However, this seemingly low percentage is misleading—the so-called 4 or 5 percent fallacy (Kastenbaum and Candy, 1973)—and diminishes concern for issues of institutionalization in later life. At any given moment, only 5 percent of the 65 plus age group is institutionalized, but 22 percent of the age 85-plus group lives in nursing homes (*Aging America*, 1991). It has been estimated that of those 65-plus in 1990, 43 percent will live some portion of their remaining life in a nursing home (Murtaugh et al., 1990). This illustration underscores how deceptive statistics about the elderly (or 65-plus age group) can be. Growing old is not static; it is a dynamic process. Later life is a motion picture and not a snap shot of the average person 65-plus. (See Chapter 29,

Table 2.16
Living Arrangement of Older People by Age, Sex, Race, and Hispanic Origin: 1989

Living Arrangement	65+		65 to 74		75 to 84		85+	
	Men	Women	Men	Women	Men	Women	Men	Women
All Races								
Total (thousands)	12,078	16,944	7,880	9,867	3,506	5,669	693	1,408
Percent	100.0	100.0	100.0	100.0	100.0	100.0	100.0	100.0
Living with spouse	74.3	40.1	78.4	51.4	70.4	28.1	48.2	9.1
Living with other relatives	7.7	16.9	6.4	13.5	8.7	19.1	17.3	32.6
Living alone	15.9	40.9	13.3	33.5	18.4	50.5	32.6	54.0
Living with nonrelatives	2.1	2.0	2.0	1.5	2.5	2.3	1.7	4.3
White								
Total (thousands)	10,798	15,204	7,050	8,767	3,136	5,174	612	1,263
Percent	100.0	100.0	100.0	100.0	100.0	100.0	100.0	100.0
Living with spouse	76.3	41.2	80.6	53.3	72.3	28.7	47.9	8.8
Living with other relatives	6.6	15.4	5.3	11.8	7.7	17.5	16.8	31.1
Living alone	15.3	41.4	12.5	33.5	17.9	51.5	33.7	55.5
Living with nonrelatives	1.8	2.0	1.7	1.4	2.0	2.3	1.6	4.6
African-American								
Total (thousands)	981	1,455	619	913	300	416	62	126
Percent	100.0	100.0	100.0	100.0	100.0	100.0	100.0	100.0
Living with spouse	56.1	27.9	58.6	33.4	51.0	20.7	(B)	11.9
Living with other relatives	15.6	29.7	15.0	26.4	17.0	32.2	(B)	45.2
Living alone	23.9	39.8	22.8	37.7	24.7	43.5	(B)	42.9
Living with nonrelatives	4.6	2.6	3.7	2.5	7.3	3.6	(B)	0.0
Hispanic origin								
Total (thousands)	447	558	301	350	120	176	26	31
Percent	100.0	100.0	100.0	100.0	100.0	100.0	100.0	100.0
Living with spouse	65.5	37.7	69.8	47.4	62.5	23.3	(B)	(B)
Living with other relatives	15.2	35.5	12.6	30.0	18.3	43.2	(B)	(B)
Living alone	17.4	25.7	15.0	21.1	19.2	33.5	(B)	(B)
Living with nonrelatives	1.8	1.4	2.7	1.4	0.0	0.6	(B)	(B)

Source: U.S. Bureau of the Census. "Marital Status and Living Arrangements: March 1989." *Current Population Reports* Series P-20, No. 445 (1990).

Note: Percentage distributions may not add to 100.0 due to rounding; (B) Base less than 75,000; *People of Hispanic origin may be of any race.

Long-Term Care, for further discussion of this topic.)

● EDUCATIONAL ATTAINMENT

Successive cohorts both among the nation's younger and older adult populations are better educated (see Table 2.17.) The gap in median years of school widens from 1950 to 1970; since 1970 the gap has narrowed. A similar pattern is found for the percent completing high school, although that divergence peaks in 1980.

The initial difference in education between the two age groups is an interesting example of *cohort effect*. The divergence between the young and old arises not only because of biological or social maturation (*age effect*) but also from the influence of socio-historical events on different age cohorts. In this case the widening gap in education between the generations (1950 to 1980)

Table 2.17
Educational Attainment Age 25 Years Old and Older and 65 Years Old and Older: 1950 to 1989

Year and Age Group	High School Education	Four or More Years of College	Median Years of School
1989			
25+ years	76.9	21.1	12.7
65+ years	54.9	11.1	12.1
1980			
25+ years	66.5	16.2	12.5
65+ years	38.8	8.2	10.0
1970			
25+ years	52.3	10.7	12.1
65+ years	27.1	5.5	8.7
1960			
25+ years	41.1	7.7	10.5
65+ years	19.1	3.7	8.3
1950			
25+ years	33.4	6.0	9.3
65+ years	17.0	3.4	8.3

Sources: U.S. Bureau of the Census. Unpublished data from the March 1989 Current Population Survey.

U.S. Bureau of the Census. "Detailed Population Characteristics." 1980 Census of Population. PC80-1-D1, United States Summary (February 1973).

U.S. Bureau of the Census. "Characteristics of the Population." 1960 Census of Population. Volume 1, Part 1, United States Summary, Chapter D (1964).

arises from the contrasting experiences of childhood and adolescence for those 65 and over and the younger age groups. People born before the turn of this century and in its first two decades grew up in the transitional phase of late industrialization, when child labor laws were first enforced and mass education became compulsory. In comparison to the younger age groups, the earlier cohorts of today's elderly grew up at a time when education was a luxury, not a requirement.

Obtaining a college education continues to demonstrate increased divergence. This also is an artifact of cohort effect. In this case the younger generations benefited from the growth in recent decades of public higher education. The difference between the generations is further accented by the disruption of the life cycle in a whole

cohort of young adult caused by the Great Depression. Education and career plans of many young men and some women were radically altered in the 1930s as they and their families were forced to adapt to the economic downturn.

On an individual level, in part, the experiences of later life vary from cohort to cohort as each one is better educated. Each new cohort brings a different perspective to the challenges of later life arising from the abilities and expectations associated with education. Significant change can be expected from the impact of better educated older cohorts on society. Education is associated with increased participation in politics and the electoral process, more aggressive health-seeking behavior, different styles of consumerism, and the desire for lifelong learning.

● LABOR FORCE PARTICIPATION

Active involvement in the labor force decreases quickly after age 60, yet up to a quarter of males work after the traditional retirement age and 10 percent beyond 70 years old. Generally those who continue to work in later life either tend to have a professional and rewarding position or are in economic need. Women have lower labor force participation rates than men throughout the later portion of the life cycle. This trend may change as middle-aged women (45-64) become represented in the labor force. As of 1989 70.5 percent of all women between the ages of 45 and 54 were in the labor force.

● INCOME DISTRIBUTION

Households headed by persons over age 65 have median incomes ($22,806) that are 63 percent of the incomes of households headed by 25 to 64 years old ($36,058). Still within the elderly population there is a great diversity of income

Table 2.18
Labor Force Participation in Later Life

	50–54	55–59	60–64	65–69	70+
Male	89.3	79.5	54.8	26.1	10.9
Female	65.9	54.8	35.5	16.4	4.6

Source: U.S. Department of Labor, Bureau of Labor Statistics. *Employment and Earnings* 37, no. 1, January 1990.

Table 2.19
Median Income Among Older Age Groups: 1989

Age	Families	Unrelated Individuals	
65-plus	$22,806	$ 9,422	
65 to 74	$24,868	$10,821	
75 to 85	$19,520	$ 8,684	
85 plus	$17,600	$ 7,947	
Marital Status	**Male**	**Female**	
Married	$13,756	$ 5,984	
Single	$10,080	$10,048	
Widow	$11,200	$ 8,362	
Divorced	$10,709	$ 8,147	
Race	**65+**	**65 to 69**	**70+**
White	$ 9,838	$11,323	$9,305
Black	$ 5,772	$ 6,552	$5,517
Hispanic	$ 5,987	$ 6,664	$5,715

Source: U.S. Bureau of the Census. Unpublished data from the March 1990 Current Population Survey.

(see Table 2.19). Median income is highest among the white, younger elderly, and those who live within intact families. Regardless of the other characteristics such as age, race, or marital status, women always have lower economic resources than men have. Several of these variables do come together in a compounding effect and create extreme economic hardship for the oldest-old widowed women, and this is particularly true for African-American women.

Fewer older adults live in poverty today than in previous times. Most of the decline in poverty took place between 1966 (when 28.5 percent of our population 65 plus was in poverty) to 1978 (when the poverty rate dropped to 14 percent). Thereafter, it drifted upward to 15.7 percent in 1980, and then dropped to a 1989 low of 11 percent. In the same time period, poverty among 18 to 65 year olds was less volatile: 10.5 percent in 1966, reaching a high of 12.4 percent in 1983 and settling at 10.2 percent in 1989. The pattern of poverty in later life mirrors the income distribution: the oldest, the widowed, and minority women are most apt to experience poverty. This

Table 2.20
Age 65 Years Old and Older Below Poverty by Race, Hispanic Origin, Sex, and Living Arrangements: 1989

Race/Hispanic	Total	Alone	With Spouse	With Others
Overall				
Men	7.8	17.4	5.6	10.4
Women	14.0	23.3	5.2	12.7
Total	11.4	22.0	5.4	12.0
White				
Men	6.6	13.9	5.0	7.2
Women	11.8	20.0	4.6	8.5
Total	9.6	18.8	4.8	8.1
African-American				
Men	22.1	48.2	13.7	21.0
Women	36.7	60.6	13.0	29.6
Total	30.8	57.3	13.4	26.6
Hispanic				
Men	18.6	34.7	15.1	19.5
Women	22.4	41.9	12.4	20.4
Total	20.6	39.5	13.9	20.2

Source: U.S. Bureau of the Census. Unpublished Data from the March 1990 Current Population Survey.

leads some to suggest that there is a triple jeopardy status for being old, a woman (who is more likely to become a widow), and a person of minority status (see Table 2.20).

Older families are not as liable to be as far below the poverty line as those families headed by a 25 to 64 year old. The elderly are slightly better off than the general population in terms of living above the poverty line, yet they are far more likely to live within 124 percent of the poverty line (7.7 percent versus 4.1 percent) in what is called near poverty, or between 125 and 149 percent of poverty (8.1 percent versus 4.1 percent). The significance of near poverty is that, for a matter of a few hundred or thousand dollars a year, one is no longer eligible for certain federal government benefits such as Section VIII housing, food stamps, Medicaid, and Supplemental Security Income. Perhaps instead of a cut-off line, benefit levels should taper off between poverty line and the top end of near poverty. (See Chapter 11, **Retirement,** for a further discussion of this topic.) In 1989, these were poverty levels: family of four, $12,675; elderly couple, $7,501; elderly person, $5,947.

References

Bouvier, L. F., and R. W. Gardner. "Immigration to the U.S.: The Unfinished Story." *Population Bulletin* Vol. 41, no. 2 (1986).

Callahan, D. *Setting Limits: Medical Goals in an Aging Society.* New York: Simon & Schuster, 1987.

Coale, A. "People Over Age 100: Fewer than We Think." *Population Today* Vol. 19 (1991): 6–8.

Fries J. F., and L. M. Crapo. *Vitality and Aging.* San Francisco, CA: W.H. Freeman, 1981.

Haub, C., M. Kent, and M. Yanagishita. *World Population Data Sheet.* Washington, DC: Population Reference Bureau, 1991.

Hayflick, L. *Aging in Americans Future.* New Jersey: Hoechst-Rousel Pharmaceutical, 1976.

———. "The Cell Biology of Human Aging." *Scientific American* Vol. 242 (1980): 58–65.

Kassel. "Polygyny After 60?" *Geriatrics* (1966): 214–18.

Kastenbaum, R., and S. Candy. "The Four Percent Fallacy: A Methodological and Empirical Critique of Extended Care Facility Population Statistics." *International Journal of Aging and Human Development* Vol. 4 (1973): 15–21.

Kirkwood, T. "Comparative and Evolutionary Aspects of Longevity." *Handbook of the Biology of Aging.* Eds. C.E. Finch and E.L. Scheinders. 2d ed. New York: Van Nostrand Reinhold, 1985.

Leaf, A. "Long-lived Population: Extreme Old Age." *Journal of the American Geriatrics Society* Vol. 30 (1982): 485–87.

Litwak, E., and C. F. Longino, Jr. "Migration Patterns Among the Elderly: A Developmental Perspective." *The Gerontologist* Vol. 27 (1987): 266–72.

Longino, C. F., Jr., J. C. Biggar, C. B. Flynn, and R. E. Wiseman. *The Retirement Migration Project.* Coral Gables, FL: Center for Social Research in Aging, University of Miami, 1984.

Longino, C. F., Jr., B. J. Soldo, and K. G. Mauton. "Demography of Aging in the United States." *Gerontology Perspectives and Issues.* Ed. K. F. Ferraro. New York: Springer Publishing Company, 1990.

Madigan, F. C. "Are Sex Mortality Differentials Biologically Caused?" *Milbank Memorial Fund Quarterly* Vol. 35 (1956): 202–23.

Mazes, R. B., and S. H. Forman. "Longevity and Age: Exaggeration in Vilcabamba, Ecuador." *Journal of Gerontology* Vol. 34 (1979): 94–98.

Murtaugh, C., P. Kemper, and B. Spillman. "The Risk of Nursing Home Use in Later Life." *Medical Care* Vol. 28 (1990): 952–62.

National Center for Health Statistics. *Health, United States 1992.* Hyattsville, MD: Public Health Service, 1993.

National Center for Health Statistics. L. R. Curtin, and R. J. Armstrong. "United States Life Tables Eliminating Certain Causes of Death." *U.S. Decennial Life Tables for 1979–1981* Vol. 1, no. 2. DHHS Pub. No. (PHS)88-1150-2. Public Health Service. Washington, DC: U.S. Government Printing Office, 1988.

———. Advance Report of Final Divorce Statistics, 1988. *Monthly Vital Statistics Report* Vol. 39, no. 12, Sup. 2. Hyattsville, MD: Public Health Service, 1991a.

———. Advance Report of Final Marriage Statistics, 1988. *Monthly Vital Statistics Report* Vol. 40, no. 4, Sup. Hyattsville, MD: Public Health Service, 1991b.

———. Advance Report of Final Mortality Statistics; *Monthly Vital Statistics Report* Vol. 42, no. 2. Hyattsville, MD: Public Health Service, 1992.

———. Advance Report of Final Natality Statistics, 1973. *Monthly Vital Statistics Report* Vol. 42, no. 3, sup. Hyattsville, MD: Public Health Service, 1993.

Neugarten, B. L. *Age or Need in Public Policies for Older People.* Beverly Hills, CA: Sage, 1982.

———. "The Future of the Young-Old." *The Gerontologist* Vol. 15 (1975): 4–9.

Omran, A. "The Epidemiological Transition in the United States." *Population Bulletin* Vol. 32, no. 2, 1977.

Otten, M. W., S. M. Teutsch, D. F. Williamson, and V. S. Marks. "The Effect of Known Risk Factors on the Excess Mortality of Black Adults in the United States." *Journal of the American Medical Association* Vol. 263 (1990): 845–50.

Preston, S. *Mortality Pattern in National Population with Special Reference to Recorded Causes of Death.* New York: Academic Press, 1976.

Riley, M. W., and R. Suzman. "Introducing the Oldest Old." *Milbank Memorial Fund Quarterly* Vol. 63 (1985): 177–86.

Retherford, R. D. *The Changing Sex Differentials in Mortality.* Westport, CT: Greenwood Press, 1975.

Rogers, A. "Return Migration to Region of Birth Among Retirement-Age Persons in the United States." *Journal of Gerontology* Vol. 45 (1990): 128–34.

Serow, W. J., D. F. Sly, and J. M. Wrigley. *Population Aging in the United States.* New York: Greenwood Press, 1990.

Shryock, H. S., and J. S. Siegel and Associates. *The Materials and Methods of Demography.* 3d Printing, U.S. Bureau of the Census, Washington, DC: U.S. Government Printing Office, 1975b.

U.S. Bureau of the Census. *Current Population Reports, Series P-20, No. 454, Fertility of American Women: June 1990.* Washington, DC: U.S. Government Printing Office, 1991b.

——. *Historical Statistics of the United States, Colonial Times to 1970.* Bicentennial Edition. Washington, DC: U.S. Government Printing Office, 1975a.

——. *Statistical Abstract of the United States: 1991.* Washington, DC: U.S. Government Printing Office, 1991a.

U.S. Senate Special Committee on Aging, with the American Association of Retired Persons, the Federal Council on the Aging, and the U.S. Administration on Aging, U.S. Department of Health and Human Services. *Aging America: Trends and Projections.* 1991.

William H. Haas, III, Ph. D. and
Charles F. Longino, Jr., Ph. D.

❸

Gender and Ethnic Diversity in Aging

• Gender Diversity • Gender, Mortality, and Health • Economic Status
• Family Structure and Family Relationships • Interconnected Factors • Ethnic Diversity
• Studying Ethnic Diversity • Needed Research

A prevalent myth about old age in the United States is that being old takes a similar form in all older people—that most seniors think, feel, act, and look basically the same and that they have similar needs. While no one would speak of a "typical" thirty year old or middle-aged person, there is a tendency to lump together all 31 million Americans over 65 as "the elderly." This misconception of the homogeneity of older adults is held not only by the non-elderly, but even senior citizen groups at times pursue their interests as if they represented a constituency with one common agenda and set of values (Bass, Kutza, and Torres-Gil, 1990).

Older Americans have been portrayed in the popular media in two fundamental ways: as frail, sick, and dependent, or as greedy geezers racing around on golf course cartways. But neither of these generalizations is accurate, and since the United States as a whole society is growing older, with its average age rising dramatically, it is crucial to understand the diverse experiences and situations of people as they age and grow old. Among the most significant factors contributing to variations in the aging experience are those of race, ethnicity, and gender.

● GENDER DIVERSITY

While a person's sex—male or female—is fundamentally a biological factor, gender is a social

and cultural factor. Both sex and gender have long been of interest to gerontologists as ways of explaining differences (explanatory variables) in various aging-related phenomena, including social roles, health and mortality, economic status, retirement, and family relationships. In the instance of mortality, it has long been recognized that factors of sex and gender account for differences in life expectancy and result in considerably more older women than older men in the population. Figure 3.1 shows that the sex ratio (number of men per 100 women) decreases steadily in old age, reaching only 39 for persons aged 85 and over. This dramatic imbalance demonstrates that what is typically thought of as universal problems of old age are, in fact, more likely to be women's experience, such as widowhood, social isolation, poverty, and institutionalization.

Despite the fact that there are many recognized differences between men and women in old age and in the aging process, there is surprisingly limited literature documenting and explaining gender diversity in gerontology This is particularly evident in theoretical development in the field. For example, there is scant reference to gender differences in a recent important volume on theories of aging (Birren and Bergston, 1988). Moreover, the subfield of gender studies in aging remains undeveloped. The following section outlines the development of interest in gender issues

49

Figure 3.1
Men per 100 Women, by Age Group: 1989

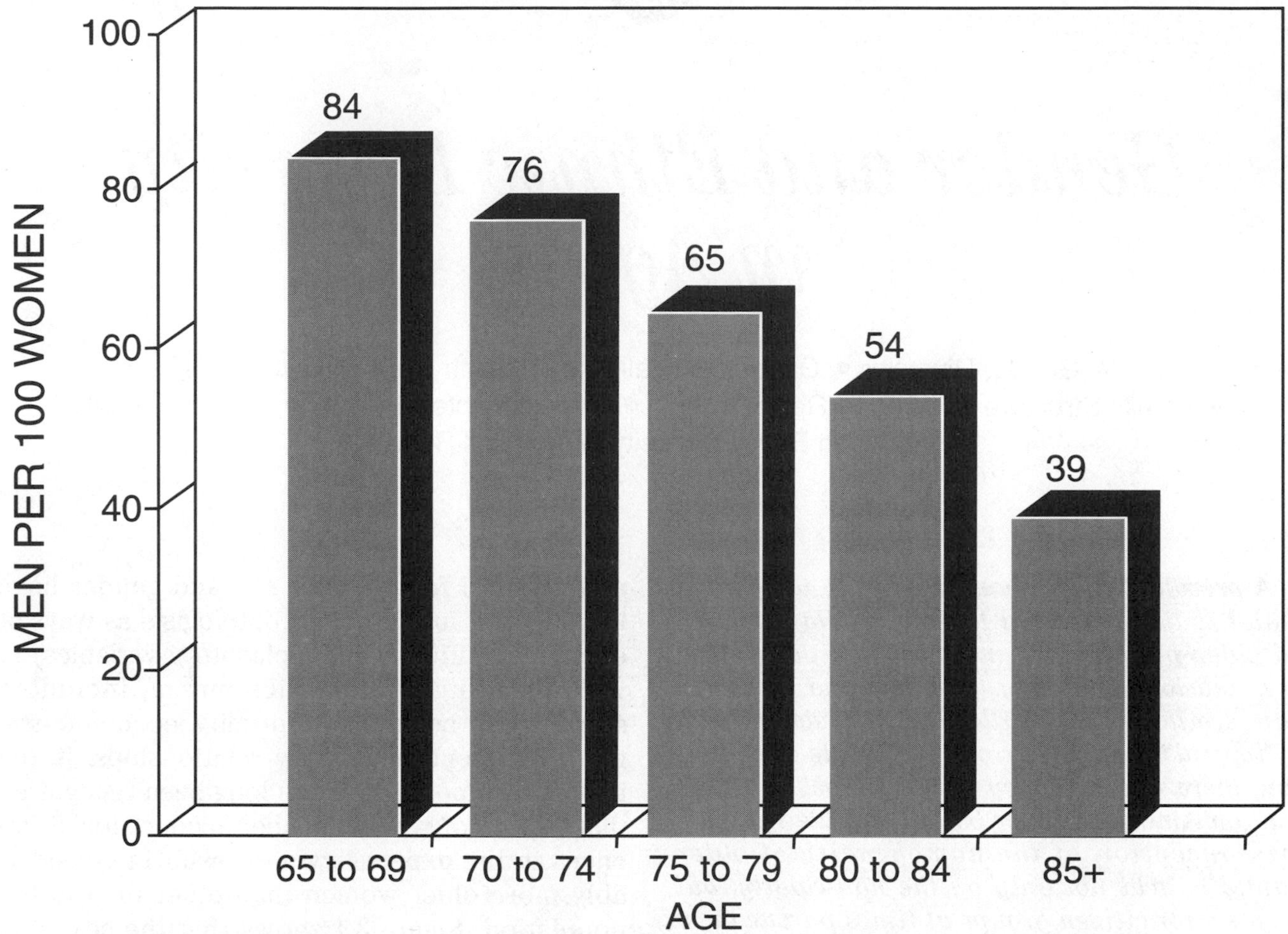

Source: U.S. Bureau of the Census. "U.S. Population Estimates, by Age, Sex, Race, and Hispanic Origin: 1989," by Frederick W. Hollman. *Current Population Reports* Series P-25, No. 1057 (March 1990).

by gerontologists; it also discusses gender differences in health and longevity, economic factors, and family relationships.

● **GENDER, MORTALITY, AND HEALTH**

One of the most established gender differences in modern society is the considerable gap in life expectancy between men and women. In the United States, for example, women are expected to live approximately seven years longer than men. In 1986, the life expectancy at birth of white women was 78.8 years compared to 72.0 for white men (Table 3.1). The corresponding figures for non-whites were 75.1 and 67.2 years. The gender gap in life expectancy at birth increased over much of this century and was at its highest around 1980, showing modest declines during the

Despite the fact that there are many recognized differences between men and women in old age and in the aging process, there is surprisingly limited literature documenting and explaining gender diversity in gerontology.

1980s. Recent declines are the result of relatively larger gains made by men.

The figures in Table 3.1 show that the gender gap in life expectancy declines steadily with age. In 1986, it was 3.9 years at age 65 for whites and only 1.4 years at age 85. Among non-whites, it was 3.6 years at age 65 and 1.1 years at age 85.

Race, ethnicity, and gender are significant factors influencing the variety of ways people age. (Copyright © Marianne Gontarz)

Comparable gaps at these older years were observed in 1980 and in 1970.

For some time, demographers have identified a reversal in the life expectancy of whites and non-whites at advanced ages referred to as the racial mortality crossover. It appears that non-whites have lower life expectancies at every age than whites until about ages 75 or 80 when a reversal is observed wherein the life expectancy of non-whites becomes greater. This reversal is thought to be associated with higher early mortality of non-whites that leads to the survival to advanced ages of only the hardiest people (Manton and others, 1979; Markides and Machalek, 1984). Implications of this cross-over and of selective survival in general are more fully addressed later when discussing ethnic diversity.

The gender gap in life expectancy, regardless of race or ethnic membership, is the result of gender differentials in leading causes of death, especially diseases of the heart. Among all ages taken together, the mortality rate from diseases of the

Table 3.1
Life Expectancy by Gender & Race at Selected Ages, United States, 1986, 1979–81, 1969–71

Age Males	1986 Whites	1986 Non-Whites	1979–81 Whites	1979–81 Non-Whites	1969–71 Whites	1969–71 Non-Whites
0	72.0	67.2	70.8	65.6	69.9	61.0
45	30.4	27.8	29.6	27.5	27.5	24.6
50	26.1	23.9	25.3	22.9	23.3	21.2
55	21.9	20.3	21.3	19.6	19.5	18.1
60	18.2	17.0	17.6	16.5	16.1	15.4
65	14.8	14.1	14.3	13.8	13.0	12.9
70	11.7	11.5	11.4	11.4	10.4	10.7
75	9.1	9.2	8.9	9.2	8.1	9.0
80	6.9	7.1	6.8	7.2	6.2	7.6
85	5.1	5.7	5.1	5.7	4.6	6.1
Females	**Whites**	**Non-Whites**	**Whites**	**Non-Whites**	**Whites**	**Non-Whites**
0	78.8	75.1	78.2	74.0	75.5	69.1
45	35.8	33.4	35.5	32.8	33.5	29.8
50	31.2	29.1	31.0	28.6	29.1	26.0
55	26.8	25.0	26.6	24.7	24.9	22.4
60	22.6	21.2	22.5	21.0	20.8	19.1
65	18.7	17.7	18.6	17.6	16.9	16.0
70	15.1	14.5	15.0	14.4	13.4	13.3
75	11.8	11.5	11.6	11.7	10.2	11.1
80	8.8	8.9	8.7	9.2	7.6	9.0
85	6.4	6.8	6.3	7.2	5.5	7.1

Source: National Center for Health Statistics, 1988.

heart for men was double that for women in 1985 (Verbrugge, 1989). The difference was greatest at ages 45 to 54 where the male rate was 3.21 times the female rate. This male excess declined to 2.6 times at ages 55 to 64, 2.02 times at ages 65 to 74, 1.56 at ages 75 to 84, and 1.17 times at ages 85 and older.

The second leading cause of death, malignant neoplasms or cancer, also shows a considerable gender gap in mortality. For all ages combined, men's mortality rate from cancer was 1.48 times greater than the rate for women in 1985. However, unlike the case of heart disease, the male excess in mortality from cancer increases somewhat with age. Women appear to enjoy an advantage in mortality from all other major causes of death except diabetes, where no significant gender differences are observed (Vergrugge, 1989).

Why do women live longer than men? This question has occupied the minds of scholars and researchers for some time. There is considerable debate in the literature regarding the relative importance of specific factors, but there is general agreement that both biological (genetic or hor-

A major factor in why women outlive men is their lower susceptibility to heart disease. (Copyright © Marianne Gontarz)

Profiles of Productive Aging

Elizabeth Janeway
Writer and social commentator

"I guess I always thought I'd like to be a writer... most of my family had a kind of capacity to write, the way some families can sing or have musical talents."

Elizabeth Janeway was a highly successful novelist for twenty years and then became even more successful writing nonfiction. Born in New York City to a large, slightly eccentric family, Janeway became accustomed to the idea of writing early in her life. Later, winning a short story contest at Barnard College "gave me a sense of assurance that I could get published, which was a valuable thing," Janeway recalled.

Janeway attended Swarthmore for a year before the Depression, then wrote advertising copy "for Abraham and Strauss' basement" and earned a degree in history at Barnard. Then she worked half time at Book-of-the-Month Club, devoting the rest of her time on her first novel, *The Walsh Girls.*

"I wrote it over seven years and I wrote it three times," Janeway recalled. "I didn't know how to write a novel; I had to figure out how to do it, and I am a rewriter by nature. I finally finished it because I was about to have a second child, and I sort of thought, you can have one child and still think of yourself as a writer, but if you have two children, you are a housewife, dear, and you'd better face up to it. And I didn't want to. So I finished it very fast the winter I was pregnant with Bill. I completed it about two weeks before he was born." *The Walsh Girls* was featured on the first page of the *New York Times Book Review,* and Janeway subsequently wrote six more novels and four children's books.

In the 1960s, Janeway began to take stock of the massive upheavals occurring in the society. "It came to me that it was going to be hard to write fiction, because so much in the world was changing," she said. "Not just the outer things, but the basic premises fiction takes for granted. So I decided to turn to nonfiction, and wrote *Man's World, Woman's Place,* which presented a view of the changes in those fundamental assumptions—what they had been, how they had affected men and women and how we looked at the world. Again, I had to write it three times—learning how to write nonfiction is very hard if you have been used to the advantages that fiction gives—characters and dialogue and suspense and narrative that hold people's attention. If you don't have those things and if you have to do it on your own flat feet, it's harder." She further reflected, *"Man's World, Woman's Place* did quite well, and I was able to make a lateral career change, from being a fiction writer to being a social commentator." She has written books on the women's movement and on other current issues, including *The Powers of the Weak,* which examined how subordinate groups in any society use their powerlessness.

Janeway and her husband, Eliot Janeway, have recently moved from their five-story house into an apartment, and now that the move is completed, Janeway is getting ready to start another book.

Lydia Brontë

monal) and psychosocial factors are involved (Waldron, 1983). With respect to the latter, it is agreed that men's greater rates of smoking and other negative health behaviors account for some of their excess mortality. However, increases in smoking rates among women after World War II have contributed to the fact that lung cancer mortality among women has become equal to (if not greater than) breast cancer mortality. Nevertheless, lung cancer mortality continues to be considerably higher among men than among women.

Other factors with psychosocial origins explaining men's lower life expectancy include considerably higher mortality rates from accidents, suicide, and other violent causes. A recent and emerging cause of death afflicting men at much higher rates than women is AIDS. Yet AIDS remains a relatively minor cause of death in the larger mortality picture of the United States and other developed societies.

Although there is agreement in the literature that psychosocial factors do not account for the total gender gap in life expectancy, biological factors are also involved, particularly with respect to mortality from heart disease. It has been found, for example, that an excess male mortality from

Figure 3.2
Gap in Life Expectancy for Men and Women: 1950–2050
(Female Life Expectancy Minus Male Life Expectancy)

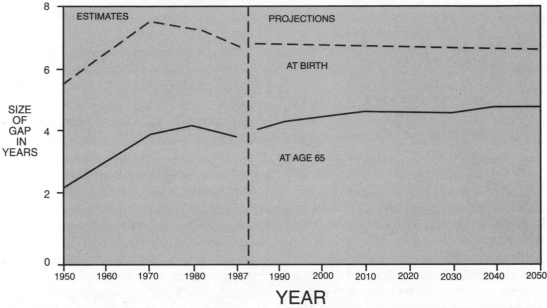

Note: Life expectancy estimates (1950–1987) are taken from National Center for Health Statistics data, while life expectancy projections (1990–2050) are drawn from Census Bureau data. The use of two different data bases accounts for the slight jump in the life expectancy differential between men and women at age 65 from 1987 to 1990.

Sources: U.S. Bureau of the Census. "Projections of the Population of the United States, by Age, Sex, and Race: 1988 to 2080." Gregory Spencer. *Current Population Reports* Series P-25, No. 1018 (January 1989).

National Center for Health Statistics. *Health, United States, 1988.* DHHS Pub. No. (PHS)89–1232, Washington: Department of Health and Human Services, March 1989.

National Center for Health Statistics. "Life Tables." *Vital Statistics of the United States.* 1987 Vol. II, Section 6 (February 1990).

diseases of the heart is observed among non-smokers (Waldron, 1983). It appears that the female advantage is related to the protective influences of sex hormones (Waldron, 1976).

While biological factors probably account for much of the female advantage in heart disease mortality, there is not sufficient convincing evidence that they also contribute to women's overall advantage in mortality from cancer (Waldron, 1983), where psychosocial factors are probably more important. As mentioned earlier, smoking rates appear to be the greatest contributor to gender differences in cancer mortality, and women's higher smoking rates after World War II have contributed to increases in women's lung cancer mortality in recent years.

Differences in mortality rates and life expectancy provide only a partial picture of gender differences in health in middle and old age.

Also important is the differential prevalence of chronic conditions, many of which are non-fatal but disabling nevertheless.

Prevalence rates of the five leading chronic conditions by gender for 1983–85 for three broad age groups are given in Table 3.2. The leading chronic condition among men aged 45 to 64 is high blood pressure, afflicting 254 of every 1,000 persons. It is followed by arthritis, hearing impairment, chronic sinusitis, and ischemic heart disease. Among women in this age group, the leading condition was arthritis, afflicting 339 of every 1,000 persons. It is followed by high blood pressure, chronic sinusitis, hearing impairment, and hay fever with asthma. The same conditions are generally involved for the age groups 64 to 74 and 75 and over. There are some notable gender differences, prominent among which is the consistently greater prevalence of arthritis among

Table 3.2
Five Leading Chronic Conditions by Age & Sex, United States,
1983–85 (Average Annual Rate per 1,000 Persons)

Men	Rate	Women	Rate
Ages 45–64			
High blood pressure	254	Arthritis	339
Arthritis	214	High blood pressure	274
Hearing impairment	196	Chronic sinusitis	198
Chronic sinusitis	163	Hearing impairment	106
Ischemic heart disease	87	Hay fever w/o asthma	98
Ages 65–74			
Arthritis	371	Arthritis	528
High blood pressure	349	High blood pressure	454
Hearing impairment	318	Hearing impairment	216
Ischemic heart disease	190	Chronic sinusitis	182
Chronic sinusitis	147	Cataracts	125
Ages 75 and over			
Hearing impairment	447	Arthritis	566
Arthritis	405	High blood pressure	459
High blood pressure	286	Hearing impairment	343
Cataracts	178	Cataracts	278
Ischemic heart disease	158	Chronic sinusitis	153

Source: Adapted from Verbrugge, 1989.

women. High blood pressure is also more prevalent among women, while heart disease is more prevalent among men.

Table 3.2 data present what appears to be a paradox: women live longer and suffer less from major fatal conditions, but at the same time they suffer more from a variety of non-fatal conditions, chief among which is arthritis. Women are also more likely to report the experience of physical symptoms in their daily lives. As Verbrugge notes, when people add it all up in their global evaluations of their health, no clear gender differences emerge, except that older men are a little more likely to rate their health as either excellent or poor, while women are more likely to choose the middle categories of good and fair (Verbrugge, 1989).

It also appears that older women are more limited in their ability to perform activities of daily living, such as using the toilet, dressing, and bathing (Dawson, 1987). Finally, while women can look forward to living more years free of disability, given their greater life expectancy, they are also more likely to live more years in a disabled status (Katz and others, 1983). Women's greater longevity and disability contribute to their greater likelihood of becoming institutionalized, as does the fact that considerably more older women than men are unmarried.

In summary, we know that women live longer than men, but the gender gap in life expectancy has declined somewhat in recent years. Women live longer because they are protected from major causes of death, particularly heart disease, the leading cause of death among both women and men. Although women live longer than men, they appear to have greater prevalence of non-fatal but nevertheless limiting conditions, chief of which is arthritis. In addition, women experience more physical symptoms and report greater disability in older age. Because of this, their low rates of marriage, and other factors, they have considerably higher rates of institutionalization than men.

Although women's greater longevity can be explained to a large extent by psychosocial factors, genetic and hormonal factors are also

Figure 3.3
Percent of Older Men and Women Widowed, by Age, Race, and Hispanic Origin: 1989

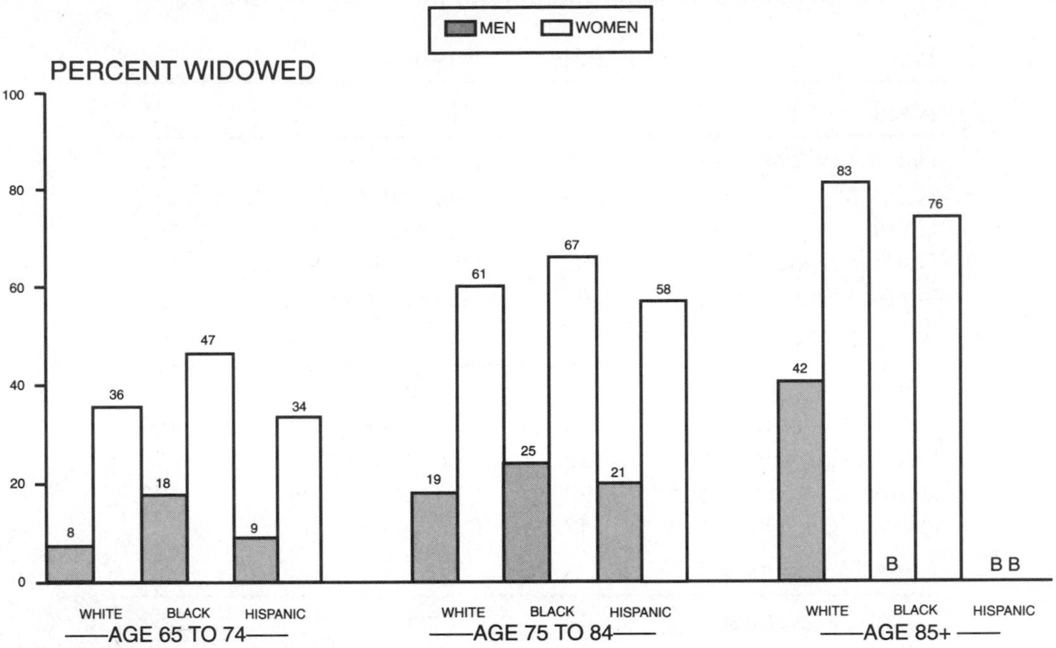

PERCENT WIDOWED

■ MEN   □ WOMEN

Note: B: base less than 75,000.

Source: U.S. Bureau of the Census. "Marital Status and Living Arrangements: March 1989." *Current Population Reports* Series P-20, no. 445 (June 1990).

important, especially with regard to their advantage in mortality from disease of the heart.

Women's greater suffering from non-fatal conditions is not easily understood. Perhaps their greater longevity is important. Recent gains in life expectancy appear to have been accompanied by more illness and disability in the older years and not by a compression of morbidity into fewer years just prior to death as Fries (1980) would suggest. In the years to come, it seems likely to predict that increases in life expectancy will be accompanied by a greater concentration of infirmities in old age, particularly among women. Medical professionals, as well as policy makers, need to be less concerned with lengthening life and more concerned with preventing disabilities and with improving or maintaining older people's quality of life.

● **ECONOMIC STATUS**

A conceptual framework that has relevance to the study of both gender and ethnicity is the *multiple hierarchy stratification* perspective, which

views gender as a source of inequality along with race/ethnicity, class, and age (Bengston, 1979). Although this formulation is relatively recent, social scientists have long recognized that gender stratifies societies according to such variables as power, prestige, and income. Unlike the case with life expectancy, in modern society women have generally been disadvantaged relative to men in these social and economic variables.

Women live longer because they are protected from major causes of death, particularly heart disease, the leading cause of death among both women and men. Although women live longer than men, they appear to have greater prevalence of non-fatal but nevertheless limiting conditions, chief of which is arthritis.

African-American elderly women face some of the most serious challenges of economic survival. (Copyright © Paul Gilmore)

Women's socioeconomic disadvantage in old age represents a continuation of disadvantages experienced throughout the life course. While the economic status of all elderly in the United States has risen both in absolute terms and in relation to younger persons (Holden, 1989), a significant gender gap clearly remains. The gender gap is particularly large with respect to women living alone. For example, in 1987 white married elderly couples had a median income of $21,000, while single white elderly women had an income of only $8,000. The situation was much worse for African-American elderly women who had a median income of only $5,000. Hess notes that approximately 80 percent of elderly women had yearly incomes under $13,000 in 1987 (Hess, 1992).

The sharp differences in income by marital status noted above are usually given as evidence that widowhood causes drastic declines in women's income, since after their husbands' deaths pension income ceases and income from other sources declines. While this is true to a large extent, this hypothesis is based on cross-sectional data taken at a given point in time. As Holden (1989) argues, however, such cross-sectional data probably overstate the impact of widowhood on income. She explains:

> Widows are on average older than married women. Even when married, their own and their husbands' retirement income on average will have been lower than those of younger cohorts. For example, in any single year, Social Security retired-worker benefits paid to men fall sharply

with increasing age. This is an expected result in an earnings-related retirement income program when real earnings of workers increase over time. Because older retired men would not have shared in the growth of real wages since their own retirement, their widows, even if their husbands had not died, would have been worse off than more recently retired couples (Holden, 1989).

Holden goes on to note that the incomes of elderly women are directly associated with their past and current occupational choices and market earnings. Thus the incomes of working widows are higher than those of non-working widows. Similarly, women with pension incomes other than Social Security are better off than women who do not have pension incomes (Holden, 1989). However, at the present time considerably fewer women than men receive pensions and of those who do, women receive considerably lower pensions. In addition, U.S. Social Security benefits, which are based on a person's work history, result in vast inequalities between men and women, since few women have worked as long as men and at similar wages. Similar inequalities are observed with regard to the status of ethnic minority populations.

These factors translate into considerably more women living in poverty than men. In 1987, 12.5 percent of older white females lived in poverty, compared to only 6.8 percent of older white men. The situation was much worse for African Americans with 40.2 percent of older women and 24.6 percent of older men living in poverty. Among women living alone, 25 percent of whites and 63 percent of African Americans lived in poverty (Hess, 1992). In fact, as Davis, Grant, and Rowland (1992) note: "Living arrangement, widowhood, and gender are strong indicators of poverty among elderly people." These authors also link poverty to ill health. It is well known that poverty leads to poor health, and the opposite is often true. At the same time, women live considerably longer than men, putting them at much greater risk for needing long-term care. The financing of long-term care remains a largely unaddressed issue by Medicare and private insurance programs, and although Medicaid does provide some coverage, it can only do so after personal resources have been almost depleted (Davis and others, 1992).

Table 3.3

Marital Status of Older People, by Age, Sex, Race, and Hispanic Origin: March 1989 (Excludes People in Institutions)

Marital Status	65+		65 to 74		75 to 84		85+	
	Men	Women	Men	Women	Men	Women	Men	Women
All races								
Total (thousands)	12,078	16,944	7,880	9,867	3,506	5,669	693	1,408
Percent	100.0	100.0	100.0	100.0	100.0	100.0	100.0	100.0
Never Married	4.7	5.0	4.9	4.5	4.6	5.8	3.2	5.6
Married, spouse present	74.3	40.1	78.4	51.4	70.4	28.1	48.2	9.1
Married, spouse absent	2.7	1.6	2.7	1.8	2.3	1.5	4.4	0.9
Widowed	14.0	48.7	8.9	36.6	19.7	61.5	42.1	82.3
Divorced	4.3	4.5	5.1	5.7	2.9	3.0	2.1	2.1
White								
Total (thousands)	10,798	15,204	7,050	8,767	3,136	5,174	612	1,263
Percent	100.0	100.0	100.0	100.0	100.0	100.0	100.0	100.0
Never Married	4.6	5.1	4.8	4.5	4.5	6.0	3.1	5.7
Married, spouse present	76.3	41.2	80.6	53.3	72.3	28.7	47.9	8.8
Married, spouse absent	2.1	1.2	2.0	1.3	1.6	1.1	4.8	0.6
Widowed	13.2	48.1	8.1	35.5	19.2	61.0	41.8	82.7
Divorced	3.8	4.4	4.5	5.4	2.4	3.2	2.4	2.2
Black								
Total (thousands)	981	1,455	619	913	300	416	62	1126
Percent	100.0	100.0	100.0	100.0	100.0	100.0	100.0	100.0
Never Married	4.5	4.5	4.0	4.3	6.0	4.6	(B)	5.7
Married, spouse present	56.0	27.9	58.6	33.4	50.9	20.8	(B)	12.2
Married, spouse absent	8.3	5.8	8.6	6.0	9.2	5.9	(B)	4.2
Widowed	21.4	55.3	17.6	47.1	24.7	66.9	(B)	76.3
Divorced	9.8	6.5	11.1	9.2	9.2	1.9	(B)	1.6
Hispanic origin								
Total (thousands)	981	1,455	619	913	300	416	62	126
Percent	100.0	100.0	100.0	100.0	100.0	100.0	100.0	100.0
Never married	447	558	301	350	120	176	26	31
Married, spouse present	65.6	37.6	69.7	47.5	62.8	23.1	(B)	(B)
Married, spouse absent	7.7	2.5	8.5	2.4	6.6	2.9	(B)	(B)
Widowed	15.1	43.6	9.3	33.6	21.4	57.8	(B)	(B)
Divorced	5.0	8.1	6.1	9.7	3.2	5.2	(B)	(B)

Notes: Percentage distributions may not add to 100.0 due to rounding; (B) Base less than 75,00; * People of Hispanic origin may be of any race.

Source: U.S. Bureau of the Census. "Marital Status and Living Arrangements: March 1989." *Current Population Reports* Series P-20, No. 445 (June 1990).

● FAMILY STRUCTURE AND FAMILY RELATIONSHIPS

As already noted, the low economic status of many elderly women is the result of their marital status and living arrangements. For many reasons, such as higher economic resources of males, Social Security programs that favor married couples, and savings from joint living arrangements, women who are married fare much better economically than women who are not, a matter that is complex and goes beyond marital status and living arrangements.

Yet the correlation between living arrangements and economic well-being is high. In 1987, 75.1 percent of all American men aged 65 and over were married and living with their spouses. The comparable figure for older women was only 29.8 percent. A total of 48.7 percent of all older women were widowed, with the comparable figure for men being only 13.9 percent (Hess, 1992). These differences are associated with women's greater life expectancy, their greater propensity to marry men older than themselves, and men's greater propensity to remarry (typically younger women) after they become widowed.

The greater likelihood of women living alone, coupled with their greater longevity, is a major factor behind their much greater rate of nursing-home institutionalization: approximately three out of four nursing home residents are women. While disabled and demented men are most likely to be cared for by their wives, disabled women are more likely to be cared for by an adult child or by another relative. Caregiving of elderly people in modern society is almost exclusively a task carried out by women, many of them elderly (Montgomery and Datwyler, 1992). Although some elderly disabled women are cared for by their husbands and some by their daughters or other relatives, many become institutionalized, particularly those who are single or without children.

The growth of the elderly population and its greater longevity with more disability concentrated in the older years means that the burden of caregiving is increasingly becoming greater. While institutional care is increasing, approximately 80 percent of long-term care is provided by family members, most of them women. Supporting this care and relieving its burden has not been a policy goal in the United States. Hooyman (1990) notes that health and social benefits are allocated on the basis of the older person's health and economic status and not on the basis of his or her family care situation. Thus, Medicare and Medicaid fund institutional care but

Figure 3.4
Living Arrangements of Elderly People, by Race and Hispanic Origin: 1989

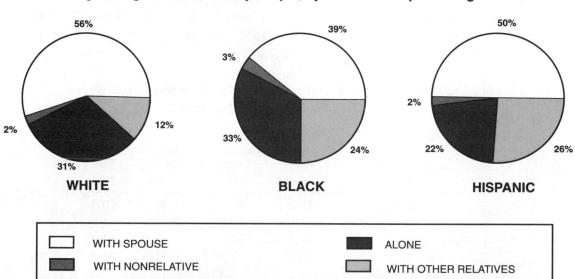

WHITE — 56%, 2%, 31%, 12%

BLACK — 39%, 3%, 33%, 24%

HISPANIC — 50%, 2%, 22%, 26%

| | WITH SPOUSE | | ALONE |
| | WITH NONRELATIVE | | WITH OTHER RELATIVES |

Note: May not add to 100 percent due to rounding.

Source: U.S. Bureau of the Census."Marital Status and Living Arrangements: March 1989". *Current Population Reports* Series P-20, No. 445 (June 1990).

In 1990, older men were nearly twice as likely to be married as older women—77 percent of men, 42 percent of women. (Courtesy of Sanders@Brown Center on Aging, University of Kentucky/Tim Collins, photographer)

not in-home care, day care, and other services that could relieve the burden on caregivers.

That women provide more care is, among other things, a sign of their greater involvement in social networks. It is well established that older women have more people in their support networks, they engage in more frequent contact with others, and give and receive greater support (Antonucci, 1990). Women's more extensive social networks are important in helping them adapt to declines in health and to losses such as widowhood (Ferraro, 1989). At the same time, men are more likely to remarry after widowhood.

As seen earlier in discussing caregiving, the advantage of older women in social networks and supports is not without costs. An emerging literature suggests that women's greater embedded-

> The greater likelihood of women living alone, coupled with their greater longevity, is a major factor behind their much greater rate of nursing-home institutionalization: approximately three out of four nursing home residents are women.

ness in social networks may take its toll on their physical and emotional well-being because of the greater reliance on them. This appears to be particularly the case in more family-oriented populations such as Mexican Americans (Markides and Mendes de Leon, 1987) and Italian Americans (Cohler, 1983).

The literature on family relationships of older people has given considerable attention to relationships with their children (and, to a lesser extent, grandchildren). An important concept describing such relationships is *intergenerational solidarity*. One dimension of intergenerational solidarity is *associational solidarity*, which "reflects the observable activities or encounters that characterize the interaction between family members" (Bengston, Rosenthal, and Burton, 1990). The literature generally shows a relatively high associational tendency for elderly parents to live in quarters independent from their children. The literature also shows that women, both older and middle-aged, are more likely than men to be in contact with family mem-

Table 3.4
Living Arrangements of Non-Institutionalized Persons Aged 65 and Over, United States, 1987 (Percents)

	Men		Women	
	Age 65–74	Age 75+	Age 65–74	Age 75+
Family householder	78.3	65.7	10.1	10.1
Non-family householder	1.2	0.7	0.7	1.1
Lives alone	12.3	21.8	33.5	51.1
Spouse of householder	3.6	2.5	48.3	21.2
With other relative(s)	3.3	7.3	6.4	13.9
With non-relative(s)	1.3	1.2	0.8	1.3
In group quarters	-	0.8	0.2	0.9

Source: United States Bureau of the Census, 1989.

Men are less likely than women to have social skills adaptive to retirement. However, many men turn to hobbies and the arts for personal fulfillment. (Courtesy of Chautauqua Institution)

bers in other generations (Bengtson and others, 1990). This holds also for African Americans (Mutran and Reitzes, 1984) and Mexican Americans, with the latter exhibiting the highest levels of associational solidarity among major ethnic groups (Markides, Boldt, and Ray, 1986).

Another dimension of intergenerational solidarity is *affectual solidarity,* or the "subjective judgments concerning the quality of family interaction—the perception of closeness, warmth, and satisfaction with interaction" (Bengston and others, 1990). The limited evidence available suggests rather high levels of affection between parents and children, particularly between elderly mothers and their daughters (Bengston and others, 1990; Markides and others, 1986).

● INTERCONNECTED FACTORS

This section has focused on three broad areas where research has shown great gender diversity:

> The literature generally shows a relatively high associational tendency for elderly parents to live in quarters independent from their children. The literature also shows that women, both older and middle-aged, are more likely than men to be in contact with family members in other generations.

longevity and health, economic status, and family relationships. As noted earlier, these conceptual perspectives have emphasized women's disadvantage.

The extent of disadvantage or advantage in these areas is not simple. There is no doubt, for example, that women live longer than men, but at the same time they do so with more disability. In the economic arena, it is clear that older women and women in general are severely disadvantaged. As for the area of family relationships, the picture is mixed: while women have more contact with family members, their greater embeddedness in social and family networks often takes its toll on their physical and psychological well-being. Moreover, because of their greater rates of widowhood, many more older women than men spend their later years institutionalized.

Health, economic, and family factors are interconnected. To understand gender differences in one arena, one needs to study gender differences in the other arena. Taken together, the picture that emerges is one in which older women occupy an inferior position in modern society. Social policies in place, at least in the United States, often discriminate against older women and further contribute to their low status in society. Older women and women in general are indeed a minority group in a sociological sense, much like many ethnic groups often are.

● ETHNIC DIVERSITY

The field of ethnicity and aging is a new one, but gerontology is itself a relatively new field. It was not until 1945 that the *Journal of Gerontology* was established, and the 1950s and 1960s before important studies and significant theoreti-

Figure 3.5
Growth of the Minority Elderly Population: 1990–2050

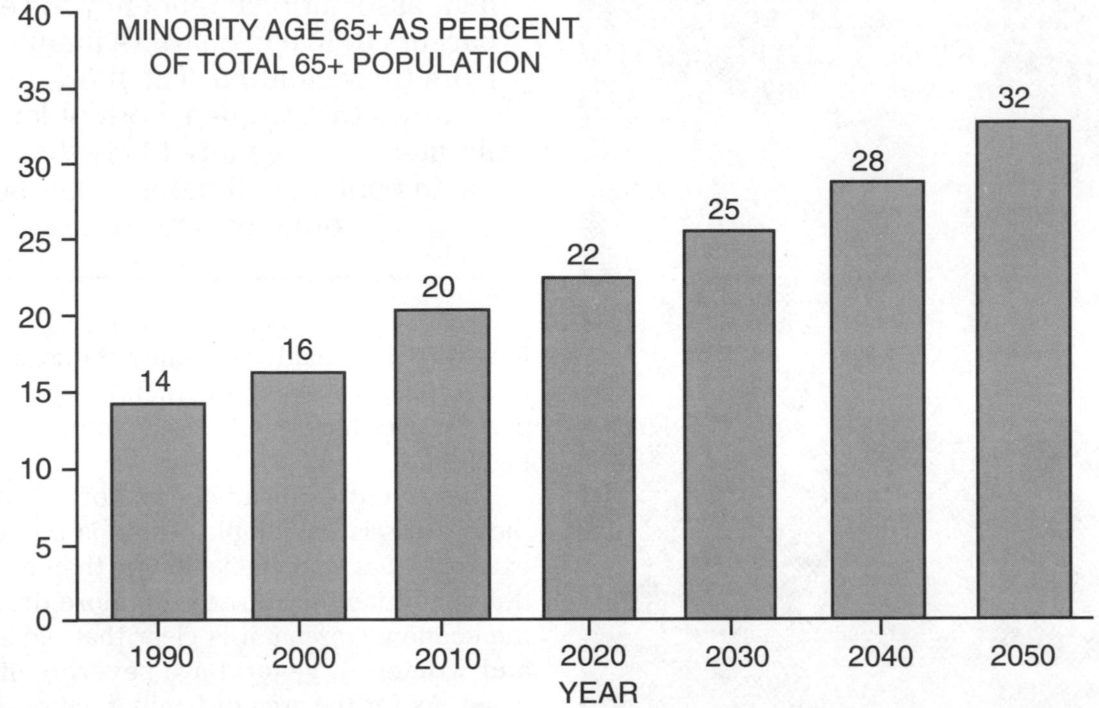

MINORITY AGE 65+ AS PERCENT
OF TOTAL 65+ POPULATION

Year	Value
1990	14
2000	16
2010	20
2020	22
2030	25
2040	28
2050	32

YEAR

Sources: Figures computed by Donald G. Fowles, U.S. Administration on Aging, from data in U.S. Bureau of the Census. "Projections of the Hispanic Population: 1983–2080," by Gregory Spencer. *Current Population Reports* Series P-25, No. 995 (November 1986) and in U.S. Bureau of the Census, "Projections of the Population of the United States, by Age, Sex, and Race: 1988 to 2080," by Gregory Spencer. *Current Population Reports* Series P-25, No. 1018 (January 1989).

cal debate took place. This early development of the field took place without special attention to ethnic and racial diversity. It was not until the 1960s when African Americans were given significant attention. Hispanics (mostly those of Mexican origin) were first studied systematically in the 1970s and it was the 1980s when Americans of Asian origin and Native Americans were given significant attention (Markides and Mindel, 1987).

By the early 1980s criticisms of this literature, both by American (e.g., Holzberg, 1981) and Canadian writers (e.g., Rosenthal, 1983), emerged. A call for studying cultural diversity among groups of European ethnic origin was made (see Gelfand, 1982), and some research on these groups appeared both in the United States and Canada. This research picked up some momentum in the early 1980s but appears to have stalled more recently.

Theories About Ethnicity and Aging

Conceptual development in the field of ethnicity and aging remains limited. Early efforts have

their origins not in an intellectual tradition, but in the efforts of certain advocacy groups to highlight the double disadvantage of being old and being African American. The well-known double-jeopardy hypothesis growing out of these efforts has been applied to a variety of ethnic groups and has been discussed extensively in the literature (Jackson, 1985; Markides, Liang, and Jackson, 1990). The double jeopardy hypothesis fits under a larger framework often referred to as the multiple hierarchy stratification model, which treats ethnicity as one source of inequality among other social structural variables—namely, social class, gender, and age. The bottom of the social hierarchy is thus occupied by poor, older, ethnic minority women, while the top is occupied by middle- and upper-class middle-aged (or younger) white men.

Another broad theoretical perspective grew out of the modernization theory of aging. This general theory of aging predicts that the status of the elderly declines in the historical transition from traditional agrarian, rural societies to more complex, industrialized modern ones (Cowgill, 1974). According to modernization theory, technology increases life expectancy, and consequently the numbers and proportions of older people who have to compete for a shrinking number of jobs. Older people are thrown out of the labor force and thus command less power in relation to younger generations. This kind of perspective can be applied to ethnic groups immigrating to a modern society from a simpler one. Thus, it may be predicted that the status of the elderly in such immigrant groups will decline in the modern society. The theory can also be applied to so-called traditional ethnic groups within a society who may be undergoing a process of assimilation into the larger society. An example would be Mexican Americans in the United States, most of whom are U.S.-born.

The Multiple Jeopardy Model

Both the multiple hierarchy stratification model and applications of modernization theory to ethnicity and aging have been criticized by American and Canadian writers. With regard to the former it has been suggested that evidence in support of the multiple hierarchy perspective can be found in objective indicators of social stratification such as income, power, and prestige. However, researchers' ability to examine all structural factors simultaneously has been hampered by a lack of sufficiently large samples and lack of longitudinal analyses that measure change over time. In addition, they have been unable to successfully translate objective inequalities into differences in psychological well-being, health, and family relationships, the three most popular social gerontological variables (Markides, Liang and Jackson, 1990).

A key problem is researchers' reliance on cross-sectional data. For example, differences between disadvantaged and advantaged groups do not seem to increase from middle-age to old age as the multiple jeopardy perspective predicts; instead they diminish. One important factor, which may explain this research finding, is the higher mortality rate in ethnic minority populations that leads to more selective survival of only the heartiest and most adaptive people compared to the majority populations. But, examination of cross-sectional differences by age may lead to misleading conclusions, since disadvantaged populations may appear to enjoy a diminishing disadvantage with aging, and older minority people may even appear advantaged on some indicators such as life expectancy and health. Examination of the situation longitudinally will indeed reveal the great disadvantage with aging of minority populations, a disproportionate number of whom are removed by premature aging and early death.

The multiple jeopardy model was applied to Canadian data by Penning (1983), who found support for the model with regard to income differences. However, no support was found with regard to subjective indicators of well-being (i.e., individuals' assessment of their own condition). Using data from the province of Manitoba, Havens and Chappell (1983), also examined whether a triple jeopardy exists in being old, female, and a member of a disadvantaged ethnic group. Again, no support was found for the hypothesis with regard to subjective well-being.

These findings replicate similar findings in the United States with various ethnic groups. Particularly important are data on psychological well-being. Double jeopardy predictions are not supported, because it is not clear whether ethnicity and minority group status are related to well-being over and above what might be expected from socioeconomic status differences between groups. Subjective evaluations of psychological well-being are made with important reference groups in mind. It is unrealistic to expect wide gaps in objective conditions to translate into wide gaps in subjective assessments. There is also the added problem that aging itself does not appear to be associated with lower psychological well-being when health, socioeconomic status, and marital status differences are taken into account. In fact, there is evidence that once these factors are accounted for, aging may very well be related to greater subjective well-being.

A very important indicator of well-being in social gerontological research is relations of the elderly with their families. And even though the supportive qualities in ethnic and minority families may have been overemphasized in the literature, there is agreement that ethnic minority elderly enjoy relatively good relationships with their children, particularly as seen objectively from the outside. Double jeopardy predictions with regard to family relationships have not been supported.

Modernization Theory

Modernization theory predictions have also been criticized by both U.S. and Canadian scholars. Although the unilinear prediction of decline in the status of the elderly with modernization has been criticized by many (e.g., Driedger and Chappell, 1987), some have argued that the theory is basically sound. For example, Dowd (1980) has suggested that there are exceptions to what the theory might predict because the theory is not sufficiently general.

In her critique of the application of modernization theory to the study of family relations, Rosenthal (1983) has argued that the evidence does not consistently support the view that there are better family relations and greater social supports in less modernized ethnic families in either Canada or the United States. She suggested that a more dynamic view of ethnicity and culture is necessary: "Change need not imply loss. Furthermore, ethnic culture may be viewed as not only a context of meaning, but a pool of meanings from which people may draw as they wish and as they need according to their situations. Ethnicity may change its salience to people at different periods in the life course. This is a view of culture which ... could prove most fruitful in the development of cultural gerontology" (Rosenthal, 1983).

> Aging itself does not appear to be associated with lower psychological well-being when health, socioeconomic status, and marital status differences are taken into account. In fact, there is evidence that once these factors are accounted for, aging may very well be related to greater subjective well-being.

Lack of support for modernization theory's predictions was found by a recent analysis of Canadian ethnic group variations in family support in late life by Payne and Strain (1990). They conclude that "for both research and practice, idealizing ethnic families as highly supportive of their elderly members and negatively stereotyping Anglo groups as nonsupportive is a mistake."

Acculturation Theory

A concept that is assuming some prominence in research on ethnicity and aging is the concept of acculturation, or the learning of a culture, "the sociocultural adjustment occurring when two or more 'cultures' interact" (Roberts, 1987). Great interest can be found in the importance of acculturation in the mental health literature, where "acculturative stress" is thought to have negative consequences. The mental health literature on ethnic groups has failed to yield consistent results about the role of acculturative stress. Problems identified relate to conceptualization and measurement of acculturation and at which point on the acculturation continuum stress is highest.

With regard to the effects of acculturation on mental health and other well-being outcomes, there appears little or no evidence of negative outcomes among the aged. A problem here is the assumption that acculturative stress should have the same effect on well-being regardless of one's

The ethnic elderly, especially Asians and Hispanics, expect more from their children than they believe their children are willing to provide. (Copyright © Isabel Egglin)

stage in the life course. It is true older people in immigrant ethnic groups often face linguistic and cultural barriers that prevent them from obtaining adequate services in modern society. However, there is not much evidence of the direct impact of these factors on their health, mental health, and psychological well-being. Published and unpublished studies of a variety of ethnic groups have not uncovered a direct influence of acculturation on the well-being of older people.

Although acculturation may not have a direct effect on the well-being of older people, accumulating evidence with various ethnic groups suggests that the acculturation of younger generations may have negative consequences on the well-being of the older parents. Researchers have found this with Hispanic populations in the Southwest and the Northeast as well as with Asian groups in the West. Older Hispanics and Asians perceive that their children are neglectful of them. The ethnic elderly appear to expect more from their children than they believe their children are willing to provide (Markides and Mindel, 1987).

When looking at family relationships from the outside, researchers generally find strong inter-generational bonds between ethnic group elders and their children. However, the objective reality seen by the investigator may be of less value than the subjective perception of that reality by the elderly themselves.

An important research question is the extent to which such unfulfilled expectations lead to inter-generational tensions and have negative consequences on the psychological well-being of the elderly. Written speculation about this hypothesis has not been confirmed by direct tests.

● STUDYING ETHNIC DIVERSITY

The theories previously discussed involve dynamic concepts of change over time, such as aging, modernization, and acculturation. Yet most research has employed cross-sectional data at one point in time. Looking at age differences in cross-sectional data may not be very informative about age changes as people get older. For example, the double jeopardy hypothesis predicts widening differences between disadvantaged and advantaged populations, but cross-sectional comparisons reveal narrowing disadvantages. Longi-

> Although acculturation may not have a direct effect on the well-being of older people, accumulating evidence with various ethnic groups suggests that the acculturation of younger generations may have negative consequences on the well-being of the older parents.

tudinal data will reveal that the narrowing differences result from greater early mortality in disadvantaged populations that lead to greater selective survival. Aging effects cannot be deduced by comparing survivors in advantaged and disadvantaged populations.

Researchers need to look at people earlier in life and follow them up into old age. They need to go beyond studying old people to study the aging process, employing a life course perspective that involves taking into account more than just the passage of time as captured by chronological age. A life course approach involves looking at people as they go through a variety of stages in the life course, an approach that ultimately demands longitudinal data. There is an increasing number of longitudinal studies in aging research but very few in the area of ethnicity and aging.

Research on the general population is revealing a great deal about life course transitions but little about such transitions in the various ethnic populations. For example, is the experience of widowhood or retirement different for minorities, and if so, why? Findings indicate that most older women seem to adjust to widowhood in the long-run; however, when widowhood is an unexpected or "unscheduled" event, as in middle-age (or earlier), the consequences are more severe. Is this true in different ethnic populations? What are the factors that might make the impact of widowhood (either early or late) different in different ethnic contexts? The same issues can be raised about retirement, the transition to the "empty nest," or about divorce. What about the impact of declining health of elderly parents on their middle-aged children? Are the stresses of caregiving different, and if so, how and why? Who does the caring, and is it shared by more people in certain populations where the number of offspring is larger?

Profiles of Productive Aging

Kenneth B. Clark
Psychologist

"I believe that people should go on with what they are doing as long as they want to. I never thought about retirement; I thought about changing focus."

Educator and psychologist Kenneth Clark was born in Panama in 1914, of Jamaican immigrants. Clark immigrated to the United States to join his mother and sister, and he still remembers coming through Ellis Island with his grandmother.

Clark went to public school in Harlem and then attended Columbia University where he switched from medicine to psychology in his sophomore year. He earned a master's degree at Howard University, then a Ph.D. in social psychology from Columbia in 1940. "I didn't think of my studies in terms of using an understanding of psychology to improve racial understanding." Clark reflected. "I thought at that point that I was using psychology to understand *human beings.*"

The first African American to teach at City College in New York, Clark subsequently taught at several other colleges and universities in the New York area before being assigned to the Office of War Information during World War II. His group at OWI studied the morale of civilian African Americans to find out whether racism and prejudice had a persistent negative affect on them. But a year later he left the office because he wasn't getting enough support and was being undermined by the FBI. "I never stayed in a situation where I had to adjust to racism or interference," he stated.

Clark returned to City College. He and his wife, Marine, whom he had married in 1938, received a fellowship to research self-image in children. Clark traveled around the country, using dolls to test children's self-image. Their research was published in 1940, generating concern that children were being conditioned into negative self-images by gender and racial prejudices.

Clark's findings of the effects of prejudice and dis-crimination on children came to the attention of NAACP attorney Thurgood Marshall, who later served on the U.S. Supreme Court. Marshall recruited Clark to work on *Brown v. the Board of Education,* the school segregation case, to develop a social science brief to be used as expert testimony during the trial. When school segregation was declared unconstitutional, Clark revealed: "I was jumping for joy ... we certainly didn't anticipate that our research was going to have any revolutionary impact."

Clark wrote a similar report on adolescents in Harlem, participated in the creation of Harlem Youth Opportunities, and wrote his 1965 prize-winning book, *Dark Ghetto,* on youths in Harlem. Later he and his wife co-founded the Northside Center for Child Development in Harlem.

When Clark retired from his teaching position at City College in 1975, he faced the protest of students, faculty, and administration. But he objected: "I never gave retirement a thought. I just wanted something different from teaching," Clark explained. "My definition of retirement was retirement from 31 years of teaching. I wanted an easier approach to looking at the world rather than the curriculum approach."

Since leaving City College, Clark started the Metropolitan Applied Research Center and Kenneth B. Clark & Associates, a consulting business with particular emphasis on race relations and affirmative action programs. The NAACP, the U.S. Department of State, AT&T, Chemical Bank, Con Edison, IBM, and NASA number among his clients. Clark received the Spingarn Medal and the 1986 Presidential Medal of Liberty, and is the author of several books and numerous articles, including *Prejudice and Your Child* (1955), *Dark Ghetto* (1965), and *Pathos of Power* (1975).

Lydia Brontë

Research needs to go beyond trying to find out whether people in certain ethnic groups are worse off or better off than people in other groups and examine how they are different. Is the life course experienced differently?

In addition to an absence of a life course perspective, research in the field of ethnicity and aging often lacks a historical perspective. For example, there is evidence of strengthening inter-generational relationships among Italian

Americans immigrating to the United States around the turn of the century from what was the case back in Italy (Cohler and Grunebaum, 1981). The challenges of the new land apparently led to strengthening family ties instead of weakening them, as modernization theory would predict.

The life course is, apparently, a cultural concept; its experience becomes altered with social and historical changes. What researchers know about the experience of the life course in a given group today may not resemble what is experienced a generation or two into the future. That does not mean that they should not study the life course. What they can do (and are increasingly doing) is to study aging and the life course in a variety of ethnic groups and social classes under different social and historical circumstances. This also means that researchers must engage in cross-cultural or cross-national research. Only through such comparative research can they hope to make significant contributions to knowledge in the form of theory that can guide both research and social policy.

Important special problems in this type of research relate to sampling, sample size, difficulties in collecting data, equivalence of measures in different cultural contexts, and issues of data analysis. However, appropriate techniques are becoming increasingly available (Markides, Liang, and Jackson, 1990).

With regard to more specific and more applied research areas, there are many opportunities for research, including on caregiving of disabled or demented elderly, bereavement, gender differentials in life expectancy, co-morbidity, diet and nutrition, doctor-patient relations, health services access and utilization, and rates of institutionalization.

● NEEDED RESEARCH

The study of ethnic diversity remains outside the gerontological mainstream. Large-scale studies that include adequate numbers of subjects from various ethnic groups are few. Theoretical approaches have been undeveloped. There is a need for research employing a life course perspective that is sensitive to historical circumstances. There is also a need for cross-cultural and cross-national studies. Studying diversity is important for both political and scientific reasons. Without adequate attention to ethnic diversity, the understanding of the process of aging in general remains incomplete.

Organizations

American Indian Law Center
117 Stanford, NE
Albuquerque, NM 87131
(505) 277-5462

American Jewish Congress
15 East 84th St.
New York, NY 10028
(212) 249-3672

Association for Gerontology and Human Development in Historically Black Colleges
1424 K St., NW, Ste. 601
Washington, DC 20005
(202) 628-5322

Center for Women Policy Studies
2000 P St., NW, Ste. 508
Washington, DC 20036
(202) 872-1770

Hispanic American Geriatrics Society
1 Cutts Rd.
Durham, NH 03824-3102
(508) 372-4302

Japanese-American Citizens League
1765 Sutter St.
San Francisco, CA 94115
(415) 921-5225

Minority Training and Development Program in Long-Term Care
1424 K. St., NW, Ste. 500
Washington, DC 20005
(202) 637-8400

National Association for Hispanic Elderly
3325 Wilshire Blvd., Ste. 800
Los Angeles, CA 90010-1724
(213) 487-1922

National Black Aging Network
1212 Broadway, Ste. 830
Oakland, CA 94612
(510) 208-5640

National Caucus and Center on Black Aged
1424 K. St., NW, Ste. 500
Washington, DC 20005
(202) 637-8400

National Resource Center on Minority Aging Populations
San Diego State University Center on Aging
College of Health and Human Services
San Diego, CA 92182-0273
(619) 594-6989

Organization of Chinese Americans
20252 Eye St., NW, Ste. 926
Washington, DC 20006
(202) 223-5500

References

Antonucci, T. C. "Social Supports and Social Relationships." *Handbook of Aging and the Social Sciences.* Eds. R. H. Binstock and L. K. George. 3d ed. San Diego, CA: Academic Press, 1990.

Bass, S. A., Elizabeth A. Kutza, and Fernando M. Torres-Gil, eds. *Diversity in Aging: Challenges Facing Planners and Policymakers in the 1990s,* Glenview, IL: Scott, Foresman, 1989.

Bengtson, V. L. "Ethnicity and Aging: Problems and Issues in Current Social Science Inquiry." In *Ethnicity and Aging: Theory, Research, and Policy.* Eds. D. E. Gelfand and A. J. Kutzik. New York: Springer, 1979.

Bengtson, V. L., C. Rosenthal, and L. Burton. "Families and Aging: Diversity and Heterogeneity." In *Handbook of Aging and the Social Sciences.* Eds. R. H. Binstock and L. K. George. 3d ed. San Diego, CA: Academic Press, 1990.

Cohler, B. J. "Autonomy and Interdependence in the Family of Adulthood: A Psychological Perspective." *The Gerontologist* Vol. 23 (1983): 33–39.

Cohler, B. J., and H. U. Grunebaum. *Mothers, Grandmothers, and Daughters: Personality and Childcare in Three-Generation Families.* New York: Wiley, 1981.

Cowgill, D. O. "Aging and Modernization: Our Vision of the Theory." In *Late Life Continuities in Environmental Policy.* Ed. J. F. Gurbrium. Springfield, IL: Thomas, 1974.

Davis, K., P. Grant, and D. Rowland. "Alone and Poor: The Plight of Older Women." In *Gender and Aging.* Eds. L. Glasse and J. Hendricks. Amityville, N.Y.: Baywood, 1992.

Dawson, D., G. Hendershot, and J. Fukon. "Aging in the Eighties: Functional Limitations of Individuals Age Sixty-Five Years and Over." *Advance Data No. 133.* Hyattsville, MD: National Center for Health Statistics, 1987.

Driedger, L., and N. Chappell. *Aging and Ethnicity: Towards an Interface.* Toronto, Ont.: Butterworths, 1987.

Ferraro, K. F. "Widowhood and Health." In *Aging, Stress, and Health.* Eds. K. S. Markides and C. L. Cooper. Chichester, England: Wiley, 1989.

Fries, J. F. "Aging, Natural Death, and the Compression of Morbidity." *New England Journal of Medicine* Vol. 303 (1980): 130–35.

Gelfand, Donald E., and Charles M. Barresi, eds. *Ethnic Dimensions of Aging.* New York: Springer, 1987.

Havens, B., and N. Chappell. "Triple Jeopardy: Age, Sex and Ethnic Variation." *Canadian Ethnic Studies* Vol. 15 (1983).

Hess, B. B. "Gender and Aging: The Demographic Parameters." In *Gender and Aging.* Eds. L. Glasse and J. Hendricks. Amityville, NY: Baywood, 1992.

Holden, K. C. "Economic Status of Older Women: A Summary of Selected Issues." In *Health and Economic Status of Older Women.* Eds. A. R. Hertzog, K. C. Holden, and M. M. Seltzer. Amityville, NY: Baywood, 1989.

Holzberg, C. S. "Ethnicity and Aging: Anthropological Perspectives on More Than Just the Minority Elderly." *The Gerontologist* Vol. 22 (1982): 249–57.

Hooyman, N. R. "Women as Caregivers of the Elderly: Implications for Social Welfare Policy and Practice." In *Aging and Caregiving: Theory, Research, and Policy.* Eds. D. E. Biegel and A. Blum. Newbury Park, CA: Sage, 1990.

Jackson, J. J. "Race, National Origin, Ethnicity, and Aging." In *Handbook of Aging and the Social Sciences.* Eds. R.H. Binstock and E. Shanas. 2d ed. New York: Van Nostrand Reinhold, 1985.

Katz, S., L. G. Branch, M. H. Branson, and others. "Active Life Expectancy." *New England Journal of Medicine* Vol. 309 (1983): 1218–24.

Manton, K. G., S. S. Poss, and S. Wing. "The Black/White Mortality Cross-Over: Investigation from the Perspective of the Components of Aging." *The Gerontologist* Vol. 19 (1979): 291–300.

Markides, K. S., J. S. Boldt, and L. A. Ray. "Sources of Helping and Intergenerational Solidarity: A Three-Generation Study of Mexican Americans." *The Journal of Gerontology* Vol. 41 (1986): 506–11.

Markides, K. S., J. S. Jackson, and J. Liang. "Race, Ethnicity, and Aging: Conceptual and Methodological Issues." In *Handbook of Aging and the Social Sciences.* Eds. R. H. Binstock and L. K. George. 3d ed. San Diego, CA: Academic Press, 1990.

Markides, K. S., and R. Machalek. "Selective Survival, Aging, and Society." *Archives of Gerontology and Geriatrics* Vol. 3 (1984): 207–22.

Markides, K. S., and C. F. Mendes de Leon. "Aging, Family Relations, and Mental Health: Selected Findings from a Three-Generation Study of Mexican Americans." In *Mental Health Issues of the Mexican Origin Population in Texas.* Eds. R. Rodriguez and M. T. Coleman. Austin, TX: Hogg Foundation, 1987.

Markides, K. S., and C. H. Mindel. *Aging and Ethnicity.* Newbury Park, CA: Sage, 1987.

Montgomery, R. J. V., and M. M. Datwyler. "Women and Men in the Caregiving Role." In *Gender and Aging.* Eds. L. Glasse and J. Hendricks. Amityville, NY: Baywood, 1992.

National Center for Health Statistics. *Vital Statistics of the United States, 1986.* Vol. II, Sec. 6; *Life Tables.* Public Health Service. Washington, DC: U.S. Government Printing Office, 1988.

Payne, B., and L. A. Strain. "Family Social Support in Later Life: Ethnic Variation." *Canadian Ethnic Studies* Vol. 22 (1990): 99–110.

Penning, M. "Multiple Jeopardy: Age, Sex and Ethnic Variations." *Canadian Ethnic Studies* Vol. 15 (1983): 81–105.

Roberts, R. E. "An Epidemiologic Perspective on the Mental Health of People of Mexican Origin." In *Mental Health*

Issues of the Mexican Origin Population of Texas. Eds. R. Rodriguez and M. T. Coleman. Austin, TX: Hogg Foundation, 1987.

Rosenthal, C. J. "Aging, Ethnicity, and the Family: Beyond the Modernization Thesis." *Canadian Ethnic Studies* Vol. 15 (1983): 1–16.

Verbrugge, L. M. "Gender, Aging, and Health." In *Aging and Health: Perspective on Gender, Race, Ethnicity, and Class.* Ed. K. S. Markides. Newbury Park, CA: Sage, 1989.

Waldron, I. "Sex Differences in Human Mortality: The Role of Genetic Factors." *Social Science and Medicine* Vol. 17 (1983): 321–33.

———. "Why Do Women Live Longer Than Men?" *Social Science and Medicine* Vol. 10 (1976): 349–62.

Kyriakos S. Markides, Ph.D.

Additional Reading

Alexander, Jo, Jr., et al., eds. *Women and Aging: An Anthology by Women.* Corvallis, OR: Calyx Books, 1986.

Becerra, Rosina M. *The Hispanic Elderly: A Research Reference Guide.* Lanham, MD: University Press of America, 1984.

Coyle, Jean M. *Women and Aging: A Selected Annotated Bibliography.* No. 9 of Bibliographies and Indexes in Gerontology. New York: Greenwood Press, 1989.

Doress, Paula Brown, et al. *Ourselves, Growing Older: Women Aging with Knowledge and Power.* New York: Simon and Schuster, 1987.

Gelfand, D. E. *Aging: The Ethnic Factor.* Boston, MA: Little, Brown, 1982.

Jones, Reginald L., ed. *Black Adult Development and Aging.* Berkeley, CA: Cobb & Henry, 1989.

Kanellos, Nicolás, ed. *The Hispanic-American Almanac.* Detroit, MI: Gale Research, 1993.

Kehoe, Monika. *Lesbians over 60 Speak for Themselves.* New York: Haworth Press, 1989.

Murguia, Edward, et al. *Ethnicity and Aging: A Bibliography.* San Antonio, TX: Trinity University Press, 1984.

Vacha, Keith. *Quiet Fire: Memoirs of Older Gay Men.* Trumansburg, NY: Crossing Press, 1985.

Section II

The Physical, Mental, and Social Processes of Aging

4

The Physical Process of Aging

- The Three Processes of Aging • The Nature of Physical Aging
- Physical Energy • Stature, Mobility, and Coordination • Physical Appearance
- Susceptibility to Physical and Mental Illness

Aging is a broad concept that includes physical *changes that occur in the body over adult life,* psychological *changes in the mind and in mental capacities, and* social *changes in how aging adults are viewed, what they can expect in the way of social treatment, or what is expected of them. The study of aging also includes the effects on societies or groups of having members who are aging.*

● THE THREE PROCESSES OF AGING

It is common to think of human life as having a period of maturation in which the person develops capabilities, a period of maturity in which the person exercises full capacity, and a period of aging in which the person experiences declining capacity. This view is based on the biological characteristics of life in both animals and plants, but it is too simplistic. Biological aging is the result of many processes that progress at different rates. For example, the kidneys typically show diminished functioning much sooner than the skin does. In addition, maturity occurs for different physical functions at different ages. For instance, people usually reach sexual maturity several years before they reach full height. To confuse matters further, most physical functions vary quite a bit among individuals at all stages of life.

Examining the effects of aging on mental functioning shows that some capabilities diminish with aging, others increase, and some remain relatively constant throughout adulthood. For example, accuracy of visual perception generally declines with age, vocabulary usually increases, and habits tend to remain relatively constant throughout adulthood. Variability for mental functions is as great as that for physical functions.

On the other hand, social aging is largely an arbitrary process of defining what is appropriate for or expected of people of various ages, based only very loosely on concrete information about the capabilities of people of various ages. Thus, airline pilots must retire at age 60 even though nearly all are still quite capable of effective performance. The age when young people are considered old enough to marry varies from age 13 to 16 in some subcultures to 25 or 30 in others. As a result social aging adds yet another dimension of variability to an already complex problem.

Dual Aspects of Aging

Aging is not one process but many, and it has both positive and negative outcomes. On the positive side, aging increases experience and thus brings opportunities to gain wisdom or to become quite skilled at subtle arts and crafts ranging from politics to music. Wisdom and experience can give an older person the kind of long-range perspective that is invaluable in an adviser or mentor. Older people can also be keepers of tradition. They have information about many unrecorded events that have happened over the years in families, workplaces, communities, and the nation. Aging can also bring personal peace and mellowing. Once the heavy responsibilities of employ-

For some aging is mainly positive, for others it is mainly negative, and for still others it is somewhere in between. (Courtesy of the American Association of Retired Persons)

ment and of child rearing are set aside, later life can be a time of freedom and opportunity. On the negative side, aging for some people is experienced as a series of losses. They may lose physical or mental capacities, their good looks, or the opportunity for employment and the income that goes with it; they may outlive their spouse and friends; or they may lose their positions in organizations. *Aging is not predictable.* For some it is mainly positive, for others it is mainly negative, and for still others it is somewhere in between.

How aging is viewed by society reflects its two-sided nature. In some quarters, such as politics, the advantages of age are stressed. In others, such as industrial employment, the disadvantages are emphasized. In still others, such as in the family, both sides are experienced.

The double-edged nature of aging is documented in the current literature on aging. Some researchers emphasize the negative aspects of aging. They focus on sickness, poverty, isolation, and demoralization. The theories they develop

seek to explain causes of these unwanted outcomes. They tend to see aging as a social problem. Other researchers emphasize the positive. They look at older people and see that most have good health, frequent contact with family members, modest but adequate incomes, and a high degree of satisfaction with life. They develop theories to explain how aging can have such positive outcomes. They see aging as a social problem applying to only a minority of elders. Certainly both kinds of outcomes exist, and understanding both kinds of outcomes is important. However, it is also important to acknowledge that *positive outcomes outnumber the negative by at least two to one.*

The dual nature of aging is reflected in the fact that aging is both a social problem and a tremendous social achievement. A significant minority of older Americans has difficulty securing adequate incomes, employment, social services, adequate health care, and adequate housing and transportation. That these difficulties recur regularly certainly represents a significant social problem. Yet a large majority of older Americans are in good health, have modest but adequate retirement income, own their own homes, drive their own cars, and need little in the way of social services. And the fact that most elderly people do not need assistance makes it possible to do something for those who do. For example, most states are resisting the costs of providing nursing home services to less than 3 percent of the older population. What would the response be if 60 percent of the older population needed publicly funded care?

Diverse Experiences of Aging

Variety is a key idea to remember about aging. A group of 1,000 ten-year-olds followed throughout their lives would become more unlike one another with each passing year. Some of these differences are created by differing physical attributes, such as athletic ability, or mental attributes, such as problem-solving ability or mechanical aptitude. Others are due to emerging personality factors such as dominance-submissiveness or need for achievement. Still other differences result from the different sex roles of males and females. People also vary widely in terms of their values, beliefs, or aptitudes, often according to the social class, race, ethnic group, size of community, or region of the country in

Profiles of Productive Aging

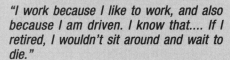

Eileen Ford
Business owner and writer

"I work because I like to work, and also because I am driven. I know that.... If I retired, I wouldn't sit around and wait to die."

Founder of the Ford Model Agency with her husband, Jerry, Eileen Ford was born in 1922 and grew up on Long Island. Ford always knew that she was going to work, because her mother told her that she would be a lawyer. Her own ambitions were more flamboyant. First she wanted to be a movie star with bleached hair, plucked eyebrows, and a white fox fur stole. Then she was going to be a show business agent. She tried out for the Billy Rose Aquacade, but her mother wouldn't let her accept.

While attending Barnard College, where she majored in psychology, she took summer jobs as a model. After graduation, she worked as a photographer's assistant, a fashion reporter, an advertising copywriter, and a stylist. Through a friend, she met Jerry Ford and fell instantly in love with him. When he graduated, he was sent to San Francisco for training before he and his unit were shipped out to the Pacific; Eileen borrowed money from everyone she knew for a train ticket, so they could get married.

When she returned to New York, Eileen worked as a stylist at the Constables' department store, where she got to know a number of models who worked there. After the war was over and Jerry returned, Eileen became pregnant and realized she would need to find work that could be done at home. Several of the Constables' models needed an appointments secretary, so she took them on. By the time the baby was born,

Eileen was managing eight models, and Jerry took over part of the work. The couple has headed the agency together for over forty years.

Neither Eileen nor Jerry Ford intended to start a model agency; it "just happened," and once established it "grew like Topsy," Eileen said. "You have to be in the right place at the right time to do what we did." They started a children's agency because Teri Shields wanted a new agent for her daughter Brooke, who at age 8 was getting too tall for the taste of her current agent. Their mens' agency was launched when they bought out a rival agency started by Huntington Hartford.

Ford became the largest modeling agency in the world and represented some of the most famous models. The firm was billed in *Life* magazine as a "Family-Style" model agency. Models had typically been considered fair game by every unscrupulous type in the book; Ford's was the first model agency that had truly professional standards and protected its models from unwanted advances.

Ford, who has also written five books on beauty and modeling and raised four children, continues to travel around the country and the world seeking new talent. She describes her work essentially as "helping people," and she is still as passionate about it as she was forty years ago. "I work because I like to work, and also because I am driven. I know that; I'm restless," she acknowledged. "If I retired, I wouldn't sit around and wait to die. I would write a book. I would work as a volunteer for the Humane Society. Even if I were just a surrogate grandparent at the New York Family Hospital, there are so many things you can do to help people."

Lydia Brontë

---

which they grew up. Of course some experiences may be shared—such as language, political orientation, or economic philosophy. In an extremely pluralistic society, aging is a highly variable set of processes that makes for a huge variety of possible experiences and outcomes.

The challenge is to identify those dimensions of aging that can best organize the vast chaos represented by the individual experiences of millions of people from all walks of life. Fortunately, although there is no denying the great variety in

the older population, certain processes, events, transitions, and outcomes are common to just about everyone. And there are areas of life where we can discover the *relative* proportions of people who have various kinds of essentially similar situations.

Some generalization is inevitable when developing an overview, but it may gloss over exceptions—sometimes important ones. However, it is not necessary that an individual's experiences match a particular generalization in order for it to be true *in general*. For example, it is true that a large majority of the elderly have children living nearby and are in frequent contact with them. But the 5 percent of older people who have no living children are important exceptions.

● THE NATURE OF PHYSICAL AGING

Ideas about physical aging are tied to the concept of the *life span*—the length of life that is *biologically possible* for a given species. Among animals there are wide variations in life span, and these variations are thought to be programmed into the genetic makeup of the species. The life span of human beings is about 120 years, the maximum genetically possible length of life. *Life expectancy* is the average length of life that would occur under current mortality rates. For example, under mortality conditions in 1900 in the United States, the average length of life that could be expected was 46 years. Under conditions prevailing in 1990, life expectancy had risen to 75 years. By the year 2000 life expectancy will no doubt be even higher. But even when life expectancy was short, *some* members of the population survived to old age. Life span and life expectancy both refer to a biological life cycle. As discussed later, *life course* is a culturally defined program suggesting what people should do and be during various socially defined stages of life.

Physical aging involves processes that reduce the viability of the body and increase its vulnerability to disease. Reduced viability occurs at all physiological levels—cells, molecules, tissues and organs, and control systems. The increase in vulnerability to disease results mainly from a decline in the functioning of the immune system.

Causes of Aging

The search for explanations of aging has produced numerous possibilities. Aging may result from:

- A hereditary genetic program that sets limits on growth, aging, and longevity
- Age related declines in the functioning of the genetic program that cause newly formed cells to be less effective than their predecessors
- Age-related lowered efficiency of the immune system in identifying and destroy-ing potentially harmful germs, viruses, or mutated cells such as cancer cells
- A decrease with age in the capacity of the endocrine system to control various vital functions such as respiration rate, temperature, or blood pressure
- Age-related decline in the capacity of the nervous system to speedily and efficiently maintain bodily integration and to prevent bodily deterioration

It will be some time before these various potential explanations are tested and sorted out. It is likely that they all play some part in aging and that no single key will unlock the mystery of physical aging.

The significance of physical aging is what happens to the human body *during* the life span. As mentioned, human bodies go through a period of maturation, during which the body grows and develops to its peak level of functioning; a period of maturity, during which physical functioning remains at peak levels; and a period of aging, during which the body gradually loses its capacity for peak performance. Each of the body's systems and organs is on a slightly different schedule for maturation, the duration of maturity, and the point of onset and rate of aging.

This framework is valid and useful for guiding the work of physiologists, but generalists are not as interested in aging's effects on *peak* physical performance as on its effects on the ability to perform physically in order to support a typical adult life-style. They also want to know how to compensate for the effects of aging, or the *ability to perform to a socially defined minimum* rather than to a physiologically defined maximum.

More useful to the general public is information on compensating mechanisms such as corrective lenses, hearing aids, or medication. To regard many of the age changes as compensable means there is a substantial reduction in the physical decrements due to aging. This is not to say that aging brings no decrements. It does. However, if a minimum level of functioning required of a typical adult is accepted, then social impairments resulting from aging do not become widespread until well after age 75.

What Are the Facts About Physical Aging?

There is a genetically determined maximum life span for the human species, but heredity and environment can substantially alter this species-wide maximum. Thus, as a group of age peers increases in age, so do physical and mental variations among the individuals, so even though physical aging is generally well described, no one can predict *when* it will occur for a particular function in a particular individual or the *rate* at which the change will occur.

Physical and mental aging affect human functioning in many ways. Physical aging alters energy levels; affects stature, mobility, and coordination; alters physical appearance; and increases susceptibility to physical and mental illness.

Three basic questions merit consideration:

1. What usually happens?
2. Can decrement be prevented, treated, reversed, or compensated for?
3. What are the *social* consequences of the typical change?

● PHYSICAL ENERGY

The amount of physical energy available to a person is a function of the body's capacity to deliver oxygen and nutrients throughout the body and to remove waste products. This process requires a vast amount of coordination among the various bodily systems. Because aging reduces both the body's capacity to coordinate its systems and the level of functioning of these systems, aging reduces the supply of physical energy that the body can mobilize.

For example, the ability to get oxygen into the blood peaks at about age 20, remains relatively high through about age 45, and then declines steadily. At age 80, the volume of oxygen that can be absorbed into the blood is only about half as much as at age 40 (Whitbourne, 1985). Masoro (1985) indicated that glucose (the basic fuel for cell metabolism) utilization is also impaired with age. Accordingly, although muscle strength remains relatively constant through age 70, maximum work output declines steadily after age 40 (Whitbourne, 1985).

However, the socially important issue is the extent to which this decline interferes with typical social functioning. Shock (1977) reported that at low to moderate levels of physical work, age does not affect ability to perform work, but does result in a somewhat longer time required to recover from work. Since most work preferred by

American adults is in the low to moderate range, it is thus well within the physical capacities of older adults who do *not* have disabling chronic conditions (at least 60 percent of the older population).

But availability of physical energy is more than simply the body's ability to perform work. It is also a function of drives. Drives frequently experienced as feelings of tension or restlessness are unlearned bodily states that make people want to act. When a person is hungry, for example, feelings of tension and restlessness do not have to be learned—they just appear. The sex drive is another important example.

One common myth about aging is that it causes the sex drive to disappear. Masters and Johnson (1966) concluded that with regard to sex, the old adage "use it or lose it" appears to be largely true. People who have sex often tend to maintain that pattern into late life. Women sometimes experience physical changes in their sex organs following menopause, and without treatment these changes can lead to painful coition and orgasm. This difficulty in turn can lead to a reluctance to engage in sex. However, this condition is treatable and is not a change in sex drive per se. For men, physical illness rather than a declining sex drive appears to be the most important biological factor influencing sexual behavior. For men who encounter a reduction in sexual behavior in later life, social factors, such as the death of a spouse or institutionalization, and psychological factors, such as fear of failure, play at least as important a part as physical aging.

● STATURE, MOBILITY, AND COORDINATION

Physical activity also depends on the structure of the body and the ability to move effectively. As people grow older, they get shorter, partly because bones that have become more porous develop curvature, and partly because some older people carry themselves with a slight bend at the hips and knees. A height loss of three inches is not uncommon. Height loss is currently more common among older women, but this may change in the future as more women take preventive steps to avoid osteoporosis. Older women are especially likely to find themselves too short to reach conveniently in environments where heights and widths are the common "adult standard." For example, standard kitchen cabinets, sinks, and counters tend to be too high and too deep.

Ability to move may also be influenced by aging, for with age the prevalence of arthritis increases and connective tissue in joints stiffens. However, how these changes influence ability to flex and extend arms, legs, or fingers is unknown and is a major area in need of research.

Much more is known about coordination. Physical coordination is a complex process that involves taking in sensory information, attaching meaning to it through perception, selecting appropriate action based on that perception, transmitting instructions to various parts of the body that need to act, and initiating action. Coordination depends on several bodily systems. Sensory systems provide information. Neurological systems transmit that information to the brain. Various parts of the brain handle perception and selection, initiation, and monitoring of action. Various muscle groups perform action under the control of the nervous system and the brain. In most cases, these separate functions occur in such rapid succession that the interval between sensation and responsive action is slight. This rapidity is especially true of practiced skills such as typing, playing a musical instrument, or operating familiar equipment.

One common myth about aging is that it causes the sex drive to disappear. Masters and Johnson (1966) concluded that with regard to sex, the old adage "use it or lose it" appears to be largely true.

Aging can influence coordination by influencing any of the systems that support physical activity. In fact, however, sensory systems and muscle groups are generally more than able to perform well into old age. Coordination and performance are much more likely to be influenced by age changes in brain-based functions (Spirduso and MacRae, 1990).

For example, suppose a 70-year-old man is just learning to play the piano. His eyesight and sense of touch would probably be quite adequate to the task, as would his muscle tone and strength in his arms and fingers. His progress would be much more likely to be limited by the speed with which he could interpret notes and decide which keys to play and when. Chances are that he would have to go very slowly until the translation process became habitual. On the other hand, a 70-year-old man who had been playing the piano with skill for 60 years would probably encounter very little difficulty in continuing to play, because his skills would be mainly automatic and would require very little conscious interpretation or decision making. The contrast between performance in practiced skills versus new skills is probably a primary reason why many older people find little pleasure in trying to learn new skills requiring intricate physical coordination. Young people also experience frustrations in trying to learn new skills, but they do not have a large, contrasting backlog of much less frustrating practiced skills.

When older people must learn new skills, particularly those required for employment, they are able to do so. Nevertheless, there are definite changes in observed physical coordination as individuals age. The most important differences from the point of view of social functioning are in reaction time, speed of response, and ability to make complex physical responses.

Reaction time increases with age. This increase is very slight for simple tasks, such as responding to traffic signals, but becomes greater as the tasks get more complex. The more choices involved in the task, the longer it takes older people to react compared to the young. Botwinick (1984) has suggested that more cautiousness among older people compared to the young may play a big part in slowed reaction, because older people are perceptibly slower only when they have time to be cautious.

The slowing of reactions in older people may also result partly from a tendency toward care and accuracy. Older people tend to spend more than an average amount of time checking their results; therefore, part of their slowness may be the difference between the time required for *accuracy* and the time required for *certainty*.

Botwinick (1984) also pointed out that exercise, increased motivation, and practice can reduce the age effects of slowed reaction time. Extended practice may eliminate slowing completely. Finally, individual differences in reaction time are so great that, even with age changes, many older people respond more quickly than many young adults.

Profiles of Productive Aging

Eleanor Lambert
Fashion publicist

Founder of the world famous "Best Dressed" lists, Eleanor Lambert has spent over fifty years promoting U.S. fashion. Born in Crawfordsville, Indiana, in 1903, Lambert attended the Chicago Art Institute and moved to New York in the early 1930s, hoping to get a job with fashion publication *Breath of the Avenue.* In the trough of the Depression, the firm's owner gave her only half-time work, so she found another half-time job at Franklin Spear, a firm doing publicity for book publishers.

Spear noticed Lambert's talent for calling people on the telephone and drumming up business, and suggested that she go into business for herself. Choosing the field of art, she became the first director of publicity for the Whitney Museum and represented such artists as Jackson Pollock and George Bellows. Lambert was so successful in promotion that several dress designers wanted her to handle their publicity.

Lambert's activities were noticed by Henri Bendel, who was interested in finding new ways to promote the U.S. fashion industry during World War II. Lambert decided to focus on personalities and stories rather than patriotic billboards. When the Paris "Best Dressed List" was discontinued, Lambert took it over and released her first "Best Dressed List" in 1940.

Released annually, the list contains a dozen men and women. Lambert and her office begin the process by mailing 1,200 ballots to fashion experts worldwide. The results are decided by a committee of eight people, whose membership varies from year to year. Lambert admitted that the keys to being nominated for the list are wealth and visibility, but the people who make the final list also must embody a remarkable sense of style.

Over the years the list has featured such new categories as "Best Dressed Women Fashion Professionals" (1947), "Best Dressed List" for men (1966), "Great Fashion Classicists" and "Most Imaginative Women in Current Fashion" (1968), "Best Dressed Women in Private Life," "All Time Fashion Greats," and "The Best Dressed Hall of Fame" (1970). Its definitions of style and fashion have moved away from conservative, slender, high society men and women to those with a more unusual look, such as rock star Madonna, opera diva Jessye Norman, former Britain prime minister Margaret Thatcher, and actor Kevin Kline. Overall, however, Lambert has concluded that people do not dress as well as they used to: "There's a fastidiousness missing, a lack of attention to grooming."

Lambert also founded the Coty awards, devised the fashion industry's Press Week Shows, organized the first American fashion show at the Palace of Versailles, and brought U.S. fashion shows to a number of countries around the world, including Russia. At 89, she still enjoys her work immensely.

Lydia Brontë

Speed of movement also tends to decline with increasing age. In fact, when older people try to hurry, their control capabilities are often so poor that their movements appear jerky in comparison with the more fluid motions of younger people. For simple movements such as sewing, the decline with age is very slight, whereas for complex movements such as typing, in which the same muscles must be more controlled, the slowing with age is generally more marked. However, people are quite variable with respect to this and all other physical functions. For example, in 1922, Mike Bachman, a 78-year-old printer, gained fame illustrating how fast the then-new Linotype machine for setting type could be operated. While Bachman sat at the Linotype, the foreman was kept busy providing trays fast enough to receive the set type from Bachman's machine (Graebner, 1980). Botwinick (1984) reported that over a wide range of studies of response speed, the median amount of variation predicted by age was only 20 percent, meaning that 80 percent of response speed differences between people result from factors other than age.

Although physical coordination generally declines with age, it is much less marked for *practiced* skills. Older people are apparently more effective in processing and coordinating responses over well-established networks than they are at establishing new ones. It is possible

Height loss is currently more common among older women, but this may change in the future as more women take preventive steps to avoid osteoporosis. (Courtesy of the American Association of Retired Persons)

for them to learn new skills, but it is easier to ply established ones. This tendency may be one important reason why older people seem to prefer "tried and true" methods rather than new ones.

● PHYSICAL APPEARANCE

Wrinkled skin, "age spots," gray hair, and midriff bulge are common examples of age-related changes in appearance. Yet these changes do not predictably influence physical attractiveness. If people are held to a narrow, idealistic view of physical beauty or attractiveness, then few would meet the standard. But in terms of *practical* attractiveness—the ability to draw positive attention through one's physical appearance—there are plenty of unattractive 25-year-olds. Many people find that they become *more* attractive as they grow older, yet many others fear what aging may do to their appearance, especially if they see it as one of their major assets. Some people in middle

age or later resort to surgically altering the effects of aging on their appearance, citing reasons of job security, marital security, and social attitudes about appearance (Wantz and Gay, 1981).

Most people tend to be preoccupied with physical aspects of attractiveness and ignore other aspects. Yet many of the most attractive people attract with their enthusiasm, attention, and personality. And these aspects of attractiveness can also improve with age. Nevertheless some people experience aging as a loss of attractiveness, and this change can be difficult to deal with. Far more grow older with mates and friends who affirm by their actions that changes in physical appearance are not nearly so important.

● SUSCEPTIBILITY TO PHYSICAL AND MENTAL ILLNESS

Health is a central factor in everyone's life, and most people can take good health for granted.

Health is a major determinant of ability to participate in the family, the job, the community, and in leisure pursuits. (Copyright © Paul Gilmore)

However, poor health affects people's life satisfaction, participation in most social roles, and even the way other people respond to them. In later life, declining health cuts across all social, political, and economic lines. However, disabling illness is more common and occurs at earlier ages among people at the lower socioeconomic levels. Health is a major determinant of ability to participate in the family, the job, the community, and in leisure pursuits. Health needs absorb a larger amount and proportion of older people's incomes.

Health is a continuum, with wellness on the positive end and illness and death at the negative. Wellness is not merely an absence of disease but is the positive vitality experienced by those who are optimally healthy. Health promotion programs take wellness as a positive goal to be pursued. Prevention of illness is an important part of wellness, but by no means all of it. The number of wellness programs tailored to the needs of elders has increased sharply in recent years. They focus on the roles that diet, stress reduction, and physical and mental exercise play in promoting wellness. Illnesses are malfunctions or disorders that have a negative effect on the organism's ability to function and can be classified either by their expected duration or by the magnitude of their effect on functioning. Acute illnesses or injuries are expected to be short-term or temporary. They include such conditions as the common cold or a sprained ankle. Chronic illnesses or injuries are expected to be long term or permanent. Examples include paralysis, amputation, diabetes, or emphysema.

Acute and Chronic Illnesses

Both acute and chronic illnesses can cause people to restrict their activities. Minor disabilities cause some restrictions, but not in major activities such as employment, child care, or housework. Minor disabilities interfere with some kinds of activities, but they do not interfere with major life roles. Major disabilities interfere with central life activities such as employment, going to school, or child rearing. People usually must have a major disability in order to qualify for disability benefits. For example, in order to qualify for Social Security disability benefits, a person must have a job-related disability that is expected to last at least a year. Disabilities can be mental as well as physical.

Aging affects both the kinds of illnesses people are likely to have and the degree of limitation that illnesses or injuries cause. Compared to the young, older people are less likely to have acute conditions such as colds or flu but are more likely to have chronic conditions such as diabetes or allergies. Regardless of the type of condition, older people are more likely to be disabled by them than young people.

Despite the high prevalence of chronic conditions among older people, only a small proportion are severely handicapped. Although in 1990 nearly 90 percent of the older population had one or more chronic conditions, 62 percent were not limited in any way by them, and only about 22 percent were severely limited by them. So although the expected increase in chronic conditions among older people does occur, the proportion who escape serious limitation by these factors is surprisingly large. For example, in 1990 over 20 million older Americans reported no serious limitations in activity caused by health problems (National Center for Health Statistics, 1991).

The major chronic physical illnesses that limit the activities of older people are heart conditions, arthritis, and visual impairment, and they affect 22 percent, 20 percent, and 9 percent of the older population, respectively. Diabetes, cancer, and allergies are the other main chronic illnesses among older people.

Older people are also much more susceptible to injury from falls, compared to younger people. Burnside (1981) found that falls were the leading cause of accidental death among people over 75. Older women are especially likely to fall. The most common cause of falls in the elderly is tripping or stumbling over something at home, often related to poor coordination or poor eyesight. However, many falls occur as a result of dizziness, a side effect of chronic illnesses such as high blood pressure (hypertension) and the medications used to treat them.

Many health care professionals assume that a certain amount of limiting illness is normal in an aging person. Physicians sometimes tell older patients that they must accept a certain amount of disability as a normal part of the aging process. This assumption is absolutely untrue. Although limiting chronic conditions are common among older people, many of them are preventable, most are treatable, and all can be compensated for to

Although in 1990 nearly 90 percent of the older population had one or more chronic conditions, 62 percent were not limited in any way by them, and only about 22 percent were severely limited by them.

some extent. And limiting physical illness is not *typical* of older people until after age 90.

The social consequences of chronic conditions fall into two major categories: functional limits imposed by the illness and social limits imposed by other people's perceptions of the illness. Social limits caused by people's assumptions about the effects of illness are often much more severe than the actual physical limits. The major functional limit caused by illness in later life is in the area of employment. Parnes and Nestel (1981) found that 51 percent of the 2,016 men's retirements they studied were caused by poor health. Poor health is also by far the greatest limitation on participation in the community and on leisure pursuits, but the proportion of older people affected in nonemployment areas is less than 20 percent.

Mental Disorders

Mental disorder is a noticeable dysfunction of behavioral or psychological patterns and its occurrence is associated with personal distress or impaired ability to function in everyday social roles. The incidence and seriousness of mental disorders is affected by age. Of the nonorganic disorders such as schizophrenia, paranoia, anxiety, and depression, depression is the most likely to have its onset in later life, usually in response to losses either in physical functioning or of social resources through death. Depression can also be a side effect of some medications used to treat diseases common to later life (LaRue, Dessonville, and Jarvik, 1985). Symptoms of depression include a depressed mood, loss of interest in almost all usual activities, loss of appetite, sleep disturbance, psychomotor retardation or agitation, feelings of worthlessness, guilt or self-reproach, or suicidal thoughts or behavior. As much as 30 percent of the elderly may exhibit mild depression, and 2 percent to 6 percent show signs of major (disabling) depression (LaRue,

Dessonville, and Jarvik, 1985). Fortunately, depression is the most treatable nonorganic mental disorder.

Organic mental disorders, also called dementias, are typified by mental confusion, loss of memory, incoherent speech, poor orientation to the environment—and sometimes poor motor coordination, agitated behavior, depression, or delirium as well. About 55 percent of dementias in the elderly are caused by Alzheimer's disease, a progressive and irreversible deterioration of brain tissue. The remainder are caused by strokes, brain tumors, nutritional deficiencies, alcoholism, adverse reactions to drugs, and a variety of other factors (Katzman, 1982). The prevalence of all types of dementia increases with age.

Some varieties of dementia can be treated, but because symptoms of all types are similar, diagnosis is problematic and must be inferred from laboratory tests such as computed tomographic scans (often called "cat" scans), electroencephalograms, blood tests, and metabolic screening as well as previous medical history. For example, if a physician sees a patient with symptoms of dementia, before settling on a diagnosis, he or she may check for malnutrition, find out what drugs the patient has been taking, and check for infections or diseases such as diabetes, hyperthyroidism, congestive heart failure, alcoholism, or stroke. If none of the possible causes of reversible dementia is present, then it is usually assumed that the patient has Alzheimer's disease, for which there is currently no effective treatment.

As the percentage of the older population that is very old increases, so will the prevalence of organic brain disorders. Estimates of the prevalence of dementia severe enough to limit ability to live independently have ranged from 2 percent at age 65 (Shanas and Maddox, 1976) to 36 percent at age 85 and over (Raskind and Peskind, 1992).

References

Botwinick, Jack. *Aging and Behavior.* 2d ed. New York: Springer, 1978.
———. *Aging and Behavior.* 3d ed. New York: Springer, 1984.
Burnside, Irene M. "Falls: A Common Problem in the Elderly." In *Nursing and the Aged.* Ed. Irene M. Burnside. New York: McGraw-Hill, 1981.

Graebner, William. *A History of Retirement*. New Haven, CT: Yale University Press, 1980.

Katzman, Robert. "The Complex Problem of Diagnosis." *Generations*. Vol. 7, no. 1 (1982): 8–10.

LaRue, Asenath, Connie Dessonville, and Lissy Jarvik. "Aging and Mental Disorders." In *Handbook of the Psychology of Aging*. Eds. James E. Birren and K. Warner Schaie. 2d ed. New York: Van Nostrand Reinhold 1985.

Masoro, E. J. "Metabolism." In *Handbook of the Biology of Aging*. Eds. Caleb E. Finch and Edward L. Schneider. New York: Van Nostrand Reinhold, 1985.

Masters, William H., and Virginia Johnson. *Human Sexual Response*. Boston: Little, Brown, 1966.

National Center for Health Statistics. *Health Statistics Series B*, no. 9. Washington, DC: National Center for Health Statistics, 1959.

———. "Nineteen Ninety–One Current Estimates From the Health Interview Survey." *Vital and Health Statistics Series 10*, no. 181, Washington, DC: U.S. Government Printing Office.

Parnes, Herbert S., and Gilbert Nestel. "The Retirement Experience." In *Work and Retirement*. Ed. Herbert S. Parnes. Cambridge, MA: MIT Press, 1981.

Raskind, Murray A., and Elaine R. Peskind. "Alzheimer's Disease and Other Dementing Disorders." In *Handbook of Mental Health and Aging*. Ed. J. E. Birren and others. New York: Academic Press, 1992.

Shanas, Ethel, and George L. Maddox. "Aging, Health, and the Organization of Health Resources." In *Handbook of Aging and the Social Sciences*. Eds. Robert H. Binstock and Ethel Shanas. New York: Van Nostrant Reinhold, 1976.

Shock, Nathan W. "Biological Theories of Aging." In *Handbook of the Psychology of Aging*. Eds. James E. Birren and K. Warner Schaie. New York: Van Nostrand Reinhold, 1977.

Shock, Nathan W., and A. H. Norris. "Neuromuscular Coordination as a Factor in Age Changes in Muscular Exercise." In *Physical Activity and Aging*. Eds. D. Brunner and E. Jokl. New York: Karger, 1970.

Spirduso, Waneen W., and Priscilla G. MacRae. "Motor Performance and Aging." In *Handbook of the Psychology of Aging*. Eds. J. E. Birren and K. W. Schaie. 3d ed. New York: Academic Press, 1990.

Wantz, Molly S., and John E. Gay. *The Aging Process: A Health Perspective*. Cambridge, MA: Winthrop, 1981.

Whitbourne, Susan K. *The Aging Body: Physiological Changes and Psychological Consequences*. New York: Springer Verlag, 1985.

Whitbourne, Susan K., and Comilda S. Weinstock. *Adult Development: The Differentiation of Experience*. 2d ed. New York: Praeger, 1986.

Robert C. Atchley, Ph. D.

5

The Mental Process of Aging

- Two Aspects of Mental Aging • Mental Functioning
- Aging and Adult Development

The study of mental aging is concerned with mental processes such as thinking, creativity, and problem-solving, as well as the nature and content of consciousness, and the role of consciousness in behavior. Additionally interchanges between the person and the physical or social environment are studied, as well as the person's adaptations to both internal experiences and external experiences of the world. This broad set of concerns—which is by no means complete—produces many views about the nature and results of mental aging, with two of the major perspectives of particular concern.

● TWO ASPECTS OF MENTAL AGING

The first involves the study of various separate mental dimensions such as perception or intelligence. This perspective is useful for developing a basic factual description of aging's effects on specific mental processes, such as hearing or problem solving. The second is a more global perspective, called human development, which looks at the mind and its various dimensions as an evolving whole. This second perspective is useful for gaining insights into aging's effects on the interaction between mental processes, subjective experiences, and adaptive strategies on the one hand and the individual's social environment on the other.

Processes such as perception, motor coordination, and reaction time have obvious ties to physical aging. They depend on sensory organs, neurological transmission, and muscular capacities to take in information, process it, and coordinate

action based on it. Research supports the maturation-maturity-aging model, which predicts general declines with age in psychophysiological functioning.

However, with "higher" mental processes, such as intelligence, learning, memory, creativity, thinking, and problem solving, the dependence on biological functioning is not as direct, and the effects of aging are much less clear-cut. For example, scientists used to think that intelligence declined with age, and the scoring formulas for standardized intelligence tests contained an "age credit" that allowed for the fact that older people usually scored lower on such tests. However, in the 1970s research began to appear based on studies of various aspects of intelligence in the same people over time. When mental abilities were divided into those that are based on neurological processes in the central nervous system, such as visual flexibility, versus those that are based on learned abilities to evaluate or diagnose or solve problems, an interesting difference appeared. Learned abilities increased over time for adults of all ages, while biologically based abilities declined for all adults over 40 (Nesselroade, Schaie, and Baltes, 1972). There was no decrement in learned abilities, and the decline in overall ability was due to declines in functioning within the central nervous system. Functions that were closely linked to biological functioning were negatively influenced by age, and those based on learning and experience were not. Thus, the maturation-maturity-aging view of aging is not appropriate for mental abilities that rest on prior learning and experience. In these areas, models based on stability or increment are more accurate (Woodruff-Pak, 1989).

The Senses and Aging

The *senses* are the means through which the human mind experiences the world both outside and inside the body. The sensory process is not particularly complex. Sensory organs pick up information about changes in the internal or external environment and pass this information on to the brain. All the input from the sensory organs is collected and organized in the brain. The subjective result is called sensory experience.

The minimum amount of stimulation a sensory organ must experience before sensory information is passed to the brain is called a *threshold*. All individuals have their own unique thresholds for each sense. The higher the threshold, the stronger the stimulus needed to get information to the brain. For example, some people require very little sound before they begin to hear, while others require a considerable amount. This chapter looks at the sensory processes as a function of age—both with changes in threshold that occur with increasing age and with the complete failure of a particular sensory process (Birren, Sloane, and Cohen, 1992).

Vision is usually affected dramatically by aging. Increasing age decreases the ability of the eye to change shape and therefore to focus on very near objects, which means that many older people find reading glasses necessary, for example. The tendency toward farsightedness increases about tenfold between age 10 and age 60, but does not appear to increase much thereafter. Close work of all kinds becomes more difficult without glasses, but many find adjusting to bifocal or trifocal lenses very aggravating.

Proper focusing of the eye on the image requires the proper quantity of light. The eye of the average 60-year-old admits only about one-third as much light as the eye of the average 20-year-old, which means that greater levels of illumination are required by older people. Older people seem to adapt to darkness about as fast as the young, but their level of adaptation is not nearly as good (Botwinick, 1984). This decline makes moving about in a dark house and night driving more dangerous for older people.

Color vision also changes as the individual grows older. The lens of the eye gradually yellows and filters out the violet, blue, and green colors toward the dark end of the spectrum. The threshold for these colors increases significantly as people grow older, and it is much easier for older people to see yellow, orange, and red than to see the darker colors. For older people to get the same satisfaction from looking at colors in their surroundings that young people get, their environment must present more yellow, orange, and red, and less violet, blue, and green.

About 25 percent of the people over 70 have cataracts, a condition in which clouding of the eye's lens diffuses light, heightens sensitivity to glare, and impairs vision. To people with cataracts the world looks darker, objects are less distinguishable from one another, and visual acuity is often quite poor. Treatment involves surgically removing the lens and replacing it with a contact lens. This treatment generally improves vision but requires a period of adjustment.

Only a small percentage of older people are blind. For example, 2.6 percent of Americans age 65 to 74 and 8.3 percent of those age 75 or over are legally blind (National Center for Health Statistics, 1959). Yet these people constitute a large proportion of the blind population. One California study found that 55 percent of the blindness in that state occurred after age 65 and that 85 percent occurred after age 45 (Birren, 1964). Thus, although blind people are a relatively small proportion, blindness is definitely related to age.

Hearing is the second major sense. It involves detecting the frequency (pitch) of sound, its intensity, and the time interval over which it occurs. As people grow older, their reactions to frequency and intensity change, but there is no evidence to indicate that ability to distinguish time intervals changes significantly with age. Why these changes occur is not clear.

Hearing loss begins about age 20. Very gradually, as they get older, people generally lose their ability to hear high frequencies and to discriminate among adjacent frequencies. Intensity threshold also changes with advancing age. Older people cannot hear some frequencies no matter how loud, but even within the range of pitch that they can hear, the intensity level necessary to produce hearing is greater, particularly for higher pitches. As a result, older people enjoy music with more low-pitched sounds and with uniform intensity. Older people must play radios and televisions louder in order to hear them. Background noise is more distracting to older listeners than to the young. Estimates of the proportion of elders having severe hearing loss range from 13 percent to 33 percent (Whitbourne, 1985). A consistent gender difference appears in hearing ability; after age 55 men show greater incidence of hearing loss compared to women. Botwinick (1978) suggested that greater exposure to noise pollution on the job may be a cause of this differential.

Hearing loss can have a major impact on speech communication. Age-related changes in ability to discriminate among sounds make speech more difficult to hear, especially when people talk fast, when there is background noise, and when there is sound distortion or reverberation (Fozard, 1990). Among older people, 30 percent of men and 25 percent of women have difficulty hearing faint speech, and 5 percent of both men and women cannot hear even amplified speech (Corso, 1977). Hearing aids often can help, but they also can be frustrating in the presence of background noise because they tend to amplify it, too.

As a sense, *taste* certainly can have a good deal to do with satisfaction. The evidence indicates that all four qualities—sweet, salt, bitter, and sour—show an increase in threshold after age 50. Nevertheless, it is unlikely that large changes in taste sensitivity occur before age 70. People in later life are apt to require more highly seasoned food to receive the same taste satisfactions they received when they were 20.

Engen (1977) pointed out that the senses of taste and smell are of greater importance than the research on them indicates. These senses are major components in one's capacity to enjoy. They also make important contributions to one's capacity to survive. For example, taste is important in detecting spoiled food, and smell can alert people to the presence of smoke or natural gas.

The senses provide the means for assembling and classifying information, but not for evaluating or remembering it. Perception and memory are our major means of processing information.

Perception

The process of evaluating information gathered by the senses and of giving it meaning is called *perception*. Most research shows an age decrement in perception. One possible reason for this loss is that aging affects the speed with which the nervous system can process one stimulus and make way for the next. The "trace" of the initial stimulus in the nervous system interferes with ability to perceive subsequent stimuli. Thus, older people can be confused or irritated by visual images that change too rapidly, or by auditory stimuli presented at a rapid pace.

Memory

There are three stages of *memory*. Registration is the "recording" of learning or perceptions. In concept, registration is analogous to the recording of sound on a tape recorder. Retention is the ability to sustain registration over time. Recall is retrieval of material that has been registered and retained. Obviously, in any type of memory, a failure at any of these stages will result in no measurable memory.

There is an age deficit in memory. However, some older people escape memory loss altogether. People who exercise their memories tend to maintain memory well into old age. As age increases, the retention of things heard becomes increasingly superior to the retention of things seen, and use of both gives better results than the use of either separately.

● MENTAL FUNCTIONING

Sensation, perception, and memory are all very important for the functioning of the individual, yet in human beings, as in no other animal, these processes take a back seat to mental functioning. The term *mental functioning* refers to a large group of complex processes, subdivided for convenience into intelligence, learning, thinking, problem solving, and creativity.

Intelligence

The concept of intelligence embraces both a potential and an actual ability, but in practice, researchers consider only measurable ability. As many as twenty basic abilities go together to make up intelligence. Troll (1982) reported that abilities that require quick thinking, such as timed matching tasks, decline steadily after about age 40. This decline is no doubt related to age changes in response speed. Tests of stored information such as vocabulary or general information may continue to increase to the end of life. Tests of logical abilities such as arithmetic reasoning often show a plateau throughout adulthood.

Baltes and Labouvie (1973) reviewed the literature on age and intelligence and concluded that individual differences are so great that age is of little predictive value. In addition, studies of intervention suggest that age changes can be altered, even in old age. They also concluded that although biological aging undoubtedly influences intellectual functioning, the impact of environment has been underestimated or ignored. If environment is not conducive to "intellectual acquisition and maintenance," functioning may also be impaired.

Learning

Learning is the acquisition of information or skills. When someone improves performance at a given intellectual or physical task, he or she has learned. All studies of performance indicate a decline in learning with age.

Clearly, however, factors other than learning ability affect performance. These factors include motivation, speed, intelligence, ill health, and physiological states. In practice, it is extremely difficult to separate the components of performance in order to examine the influence of learning ability, although a number of studies have attempted to do so. Because research to date has not been able to isolate learning ability from other causes of performance and because very little longitudinal research has been done on learning, it is not clear what effect age has on learning ability.

From a practical point of view, learning performance seems to decline as age increases, although the declines are not noticeable until past middle age. All age groups can learn. If given a bit more time, older people can usually learn anything other people can. Extra time is required both to learn information or skills and to demonstrate that learning has occurred. Tasks that involve manipulation of concrete objects or symbols, distinct and unambiguous responses, and low interference from prior learning are particularly conducive to good performance by older people.

Via intelligence, learning, and memory, human beings have at their disposal a great many separate mental images. Thinking, problem solving, and creativity all involve the manipulation of ideas and symbols.

Thinking

Thinking involves manipulating ideas. It helps bring order to the chaos of data brought into the mind by perception and learning because it differentiates and categorizes data into constructs called concepts.

Older people seem to be particularly poor at forming concepts. Concept formation often involves making logical inferences and generalizations. Older people have been found to resist forming a higher order generalization and to refuse choosing one when given the opportunity. All studies seem to agree that as age increases, ability at concept formation and its components declines.

Concept formation is not completely independent of other skills such as learning and intelligence, but at the same time it is not completely dependent on them either. A substantial part of the decline with age in measured ability to form concepts appears to be genuine.

Problem Solving

Problem solving is the development of decisions out of the processes of reason, logic, and thinking. Whereas thinking involves the differentiation and categorization of mental data, problem solving involves making logical deductions about these categories, their properties, and differences among them. Problem solving differs from learning in that learning is the acquisition of skills and perceptions, whereas problem solving is using these skills and perceptions to make choices.

In solving problems, older people are at a disadvantage if they must deal with many items of information simultaneously. They have more difficulty giving meaning to stimuli presented and have more trouble remembering this information later when it must be used to derive a solution. The number of errors made in solving problems rises steadily with age. This difficulty is why older people are often befuddled by forms they are asked to complete, particularly if the instructions are complex.

Compared to young adults, older people take a longer time to recognize the explicit goal of a par-

Profiles of Productive Aging

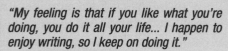

Isaac Asimov
Writer

"My feeling is that if you like what you're doing, you do it all your life... I happen to enjoy writing, so I keep on doing it."

The great science fiction writer Isaac Asimov was born in Petrovigy, U.S.S.R. in 1920. When he was three his parents moved to the United States, settling in Brooklyn, New York. Unable to read English, they encouraged Asimov to learn to read by taking him to a local library, since like many new immigrants they could not afford to buy books themselves. He would voraciously read the three books that he was allowed to borrow a week. His father insisted that he borrow two nonfiction books, and only one fiction. Asimov, of course, loved fiction and would finish the fiction book on the first day he borrowed it; then he had to wait six more days for another.

It was this scarcity of reading material that inspired him to write his first story, while still a young teenager. At first he had tried to copy the borrowed fiction books so as to reread them, but this proved to be a tedious task. Unperturbed, he hit upon an idea that would shape his life. "Why not make up my own book," he asked himself. So he went to work.

At first he wrote "endless sagas"—stories that he never finished. By age 17 he had another idea: "Why not write a short story and finish it?" His imagination had been fuelled by the science magazines he loved to read—*Science Wonder Stories* and *Astounding Science Fiction*. So Asimov wrote his first science fiction short story. On the advice of his father, he took it to *Astounding* magazine to see if they would buy it. Its editor, John W. Campbell, did not buy the story, but he became Asimov's friend and later played an important role in shaping his career.

It was several years and 13 short stories later before Campbell would buy a story. This story launched Asimov's writing career, and became an all-time classic: "Nightfall," developed from an Emerson quotation that Campbell liked and suggested to Asimov, is widely considered one of the best science fiction stories of all time, and is still in print over a half century later.

Between 21 and 30, Asimov continued the academic career he had begun earlier, when he gained his B.S from Columbia University at age 19. By his mid-20s he received a Ph.D. in physics. He pursued his academic career, taking a teaching job at Boston University's School of Medicine. A decade later he would quit teaching to write full-time.

At age 30, Asimov's first novel, *Pebble in the Sky*, was published. It was followed shortly by the famous *Foundation* trilogy—*Foundation, Foundation and Empire*, and *Second Foundation*—written between 1951 and 1953. The popularity of these books was such that in 1982 Asimov wrote another addition to the series, *Foundation's Edge*, his 262nd book, which remained on the *New York Times* bestseller list for six months and was the first straight science fiction novel ever to rise to the number three spot.

Asimov's fiction enthralled readers with its combination of imaginative storylines and a rationality of prose that was uniquely his own. "I started writing before I became a scientist, and I became a scientist because I had a tendency to rationality." His "Three Laws of Robotics," which like "Nightfall" was in part formulated by Campbell, would help create the science of psychohistory, the study of predicting human behavior. Asimov would discount the profundity of his early writing, saying "All I was trying to do in those days was to write interesting stories so I could pay my way through college."

Asimov's career was notable for his extreme productivity and his far-reaching expertise. In 1952, after his collaboration on a biochemistry textbook, he decided to seriously consider writing nonfiction. Before long it became the mainstay of his career. He would write on such wide-ranging topics as Shakespeare, the Bible, and even published *Isaac Asimov's Treasury of Humor*. "Writing novels is very hard work. And writing the other things I do is very easy," he explained in an interview in 1983.

Luckily for his many admiring readers he continued writing fiction simultaneously. At the time of his death in April 1992, at age 72, he had published 461 books, an immense number of short stories, and was the recipient of 14 honorary academic degrees and countless literary awards. In 1987 he was named the Grandmaster of Science Fiction by the Science Fiction Writers of America, a title which has since become synonymous with his name.

Lydia Brontë

ticular problem. Their search for information is thus characterized by haphazard questioning rather than by concentration on a single path to the goal. They attain information randomly, have trouble separating the relevant from the irrelevant, and thus tend to be overwhelmed by a multitude of irrelevant facts. They also tend toward repetitive behavior, a tendency that can be disruptive in situations where the nature of problems and their solutions is constantly or rapidly changing.

In general, the same trend of decline is observed with regard to problem solving that was observed in the other mental processes. However, Arenberg (1968) has shown that when abstract reasoning is required in relation to concrete tasks such as shopping, older people are in fact able to think at abstract levels. In addition, some data on the role of education indicate that older people whose jobs had trained them to perform deductions (for example, physicians) showed deductive ability comparable to younger colleagues (Cijfer, 1966). This finding suggests that sizable cultural and social factors may be operating in the data that have been the mainstay of our knowledge of the relationship between age and problem solving. Indeed, Kesler, Denney, and Whitely (1976) found that what had been presumed to be age effects in problem solving disappeared when education and nonverbal intelligence were controlled. Thus, those entering the older population now may be at less disadvantage compared to those who entered the older population thirty years ago.

Creativity

Creativity is often defined as unique, original, and inventive problem solving. Research based on this definition revealed that age was unrelated to the degree of creativity attributed to a specific contribution (Simonton, 1990). The age at which the volume of creative work is greatest depends on the field. For example, in pure mathematics, theoretical physics, or computer design, creative work tends to peak in early adulthood and drop off sharply in mid-life, whereas in novel writing, history, and philosophy creative work tends to peak in mid-life with little or no dropoff thereafter (Simonton, 1990). Those areas where peaks usually occur in early adulthood often involve being able to apply enormous amounts of mental

energy to concentrate on abstract problems within a system of abstract symbols. By contrast, areas that peak later are those based on a broad mental perspective and cumulative experience. Certainly individual exceptions are prevalent enough in every field and declines are gradual enough that no one should assume that older people automatically reach an end of their creativity, particularly at any given chronological age.

Mental aging is definitely not a unitary process. Some mental functions decline with age, some remain relatively constant over the entire adult life span, and others improve steadily with age. The closer the tie to physical functioning, the more likely a function will decline with age. Nevertheless, the variability in physical aging means that the results of mental aging are rarely predictable.

Getting information is a problem for only a small proportion of the elderly. Most can successfully compensate by using glasses or hearing aids. Age changes in the ability to process information can be minimized by continuing to practice skills such as thinking, problem solving, and creativity. Losses can be offset by compensating. For example, declining short-term memory can be offset by note taking. Learning can be improved by slowing down the pace of the material being presented.

Considering the various mental processes separately results in a piecemeal approach. The adult development approach to mental aging provides a more holistic alternative.

● AGING AND ADULT DEVELOPMENT

Adult development is concerned with the evolution of adaptive capacity over the adult lifespan. Adaptive capacity resides in the coping styles contained in the personality and in the self-concept. The self-concept contains ideas about the self that form the basis for initiative and self-confidence, or lack of them. The key questions for the developmentalist are how aging influences (1) what people must adapt to, (2) the approaches they take to realize adaptation, and (3) the way people see and react to themselves.

Erikson's Stage Theory

The idea that people go through stages of development has been around a long time. Perhaps the most influential stage theory of adult development was formulated by Erik Erikson

(Erikson, Erikson, and Kivnick, 1986). Erikson's theory is mainly concerned with how people develop an identity in childhood and adolescence, but he also considered development in old age. To Erikson, identity is formed on a foundation of trust, autonomy, initiative, and industry. These qualities develop in childhood and allow individuals to form a view of themselves as capable, worthwhile, and safe. People who do not develop these qualities have difficulty trusting others, have doubts about their abilities and feel guilt about their poor performance, feel inferior to others, and feel no basis for confidence in their ability to face the changes brought on by adulthood. Obviously, these two extremes are end points of a continuum, and individuals can vary considerably along it in terms of bringing a strong sense of positive identity into adulthood and later on into old age.

According to Erikson, in early adulthood the main issue in human growth and development is learning to establish *intimacy*—close personal relationships such as with a friend or mate. This process involves learning to unite one's own identity with that of another person. People who do not learn to develop intimacy remain isolated, relating to others but never having a sense of unity with them. In middle adulthood, the issue is *generativity* versus *stagnation*. Generativity is the ability to support others, particularly one's children and other members of younger generations. It involves caring and concern for younger people and also an interest in making a contribution to the world one lives in. Stagnation results when an individual does not learn to contribute to others. It is typified by a lack of interest in others, especially the young, a feeling of having contributed nothing, and the appearance of just going through the motions. In late adulthood, the issue is what Erikson calls *ego integrity* versus *despair*. Integrity involves being able to look at one's life as having been meaningful and being able to accept one's self as a whole being having both positive and negative dimensions, without being threatened by this acceptance.

Integrity provides the basis for approaching the end of life with a feeling of having lived completely. Despair is the result of rejecting one's life and oneself and the realization that there is not enough time left to alter this assessment. Such a person is prone to depression and fear of death.

Erikson's theory contends that life is a process of continuous growth, provided one adequately resolves the issues of life's successive stages. In order to develop intimacy, one must first have developed a positive identity. In order to develop generativity, one must have the capacity for intimacy. And in order to develop integrity, one must have the feelings of connectedness and contribution that come from intimacy and generativity. This progression of human growth is closely tied to chronological age in childhood by the expectations of home and school, but in adulthood the individual is freer to move at his or her own pace. Thus, although generativity may be typically something people are learning in middle adulthood and certainly something they are supposed to be learning, many people are still trying to learn to deal with identity or intimacy, and they may feel irritated by demands that they exhibit generativity.

Erikson's framework provides a tool for relating to people. By listening to them, one may get a sense of where they stand on the issues Erikson raised, which in turn promotes understanding not

Generativity is the ability to support others, particularly one's children and other members of younger generations. (Copyright © Marianne Gontarz)

Profiles of Productive Aging

Joan Erikson
Therapist and writer

"Discovering one's own capacities and power makes it possible to recreate yourself."

Dancer, artist, jewelry designer, and therapist Joan Erikson has managed her enormously varied career around her role as wife and mother. Raising four children, encouraging and helping her husband in his career, and still managing to create an identity of her own was, she emphasizes, a process that took place over time, often difficult, often bumpy. One of the subjects of Mary Catherine Bateson's book, *Composing a Life,* Joan Erikson is a model for both women and men on how to manage and adapt to change.

Born in 1903 in a tiny community in Canada where her father was the local Episcopal minister, Erikson had what she called a "chaotic and disorganized" childhood, which fueled her desire to have a strong and healthy family of her own one day. After two years of college without a clear career objective, Erikson, who loved studying dance, decided instead to become a teacher and enrolled in Columbia Teacher's College. There a wonderful dance teacher who, like Erikson, was tall, convinced her to consider dance again: "She was as big as me and she danced beautifully and I thought, 'To hell with it. I'm going to be a dancer.'" Erikson recounted. "So that's what I became. Suddenly I knew who I was, and what I was doing, and why I was doing it. It was grand. Of course, that brings success! You can't help it if you're that enthusiastic."

In 1928 she went to Europe to work on her dissertation for a year and ended up staying two and marrying a young psychologist she met there, Erik Erikson. The Eriksons returned to the United States and spent time at several universities, Philadelphia to Cambridge to Yale, finally settling at Berkeley where Joan became deeply involved with the schools.

After World War II, when the McCarthy period began, Erik Erikson was so profoundly offended by the university's practices of loyalty oaths and preferential treatment of senior professors that he resigned. Buoyed by the favorable reception of *Childhood and Society,* which had just been published, they returned to the East Coast, where Erikson accepted a position in psychiatry at Austen Riggs Hospital in Stockbridge, Massachusetts. Then Joan Erikson came into her own.

She received permission to organize structured activities for the hospital's young patients. For five years, Erikson generated programs and health-giving relationships among the patients and staff at Austin Riggs and encouraged better relations between the hospital and the townspeople. When her husband took a sabbatical to write *Young Man Luther,* Erikson gave up her position to be with him. For many years she had edited her husband's work—his English was still craggy enough that he needed editorial help in setting down and polishing his written work. By working as an invisible partner with her husband, she helped reshape and greatly expand psychological theory and practice.

Erikson herself became interested in beads and jewelry making, acquiring a high degree of skill and winning prizes for her work. When they returned to Stockbridge, she organized a half-way house for Riggs patients so they could "stretch out into the community when they got past Riggs." By that time she was also writing her own book, which was published several years later, launching her career as a writer.

Today she is working at the Erikson Center at Harvard, established in 1982 to promote intergenerational integration of lives around the life cycle principles, with the support of all the growth-enhancing and healing arts. "We teach and learn how to live and grow creatively," she explained. "Could anything be more challenging and engrossing?"

Lydia Brontë

only of their behavior but also their priorities and their aspirations.

Process Theory

For many psychologists, adult development does not involve discrete stages but instead results from the continuous operation of various processes of development. Riegel (1976) contended that human development arises out of contradictory ideas or actions produced by the constant changes occurring in the person and his or her environment. Riegel saw these contradictions not as deficiencies to be corrected but as invitations to a new level of integration. For example, a person might notice that at times she is cautious, and at other times she is adventuresome. Accepting both views as valid parts of herself is a higher level of integration than putting them in opposition to one another and trying to make herself be only one or the other. Thus, "developmental and historical tasks are never completed. At the very moment when completion seems to be achieved, new questions and doubts arise in the individual and in society" (Riegel, 1976).

Whitbourne and Weinstock (1986) addressed more specifically the dynamics of continuous development. They argued that adult identity is an integration based on a person's knowledge about his or her physical and mental assets and liabilities, ideas (motives, goals, and attitudes), and social roles. Identity serves to organize the interpretation of experiences—the assignment of subjective meaning to them. And identity can be modified by experience. The day-to-day contradictions that appear between the identities people bring to experience and the feedback they get from it can be responded to in numerous ways. People who are flexible about the content of their identities realize that identity is a theory of the self that is constantly being tested, modified, and refined through experience. To the extent that people's observations about themselves are honest, the theory gets better as time goes on. That is, the results people's identities lead them to expect are the results they get. A large measure of human growth involves living with doubts and fears while developing the knowledge and skills necessary to perform at a personally satisfying and socially successful level. Once skills are developed, they are *maintained* by practice.

Sometimes people develop an identity but refuse to test it. They use their identity to decide how to act, but they do not let the results modify their ideas about themselves. Other people never quite develop a firm identity that could be tested. They don't quite know what to expect of themselves in various situations, and the result is that they behave in inconsistent and confusing ways.

Identity

Aging affects the stability of identity in several important ways. First, the longer one has an adult identity, the more times one's theory of self can

Aging for most people means continuing familiar activities in familiar environments. (Copyright © Alice Hardin)

be tested across various situations. This experience usually results in a stable personal identity that stands up well to the demands of day-to-day living. Second, the reduction in social responsibilities associated with later adulthood can reduce the potential for conflict among various aspects of identity. Third, aging for most people means continuing familiar activities in familiar environments (Atchley, 1989). Most have long since developed skill and accumulated accomplishments in these arenas. All they need do now is maintain them.

The identity perspective also provides a basis for predicting when change might reach crisis proportions. When change in either the individual or the environment is so great that it cannot be integrated without a fundamental reorganization of one's theory of self, an identity crisis results. An identity crisis means reassessing the very foundations of one's identity. The changes that precipitate the crisis may occur in the individual or in the social situation.

Consider these examples:

Mr. F has learned that within six months to a year he will be totally blind.

Mrs. T's husband died six weeks ago. They had been married 47 years.

Mr. M retired from teaching after 41 years.

Mrs. B has become increasingly frail. After 16 years of living alone as a widow, she must move in with her divorced, middle-aged daughter.

None of these changes need automatically trigger an identity crisis. Whether an identity crisis occurs depends on how central the changed dimension is to the individual and whether the change was anticipated. Profound physical changes usually have less ambiguous outcomes than social changes. Going blind would be a profound adjustment for anyone. But how much Mrs. T is affected by her husband's death depends on how her relationship with him has fit into her identity. Whether they were inseparable companions whose selves were completely intertwined, or whether theirs had been a marriage of convenience that had endured mainly by force of habit, could make a substantial difference in whether or not his death brings on an identity crisis in his wife. Mr. M may well be able to give up teaching easily if he feels that he has completed what he set out to do as a teacher and that it is time to move on. He may not be able to leave easily if he is being forced to retire when he feels he still has something to contribute. How Mrs. B resolves her dilemma depends on how she feels about being dependent—what it implies for her identity—particularly in her relationship with her daughter. Identity crises are not produced by events alone—they stem from the interpretation of events in the context of a particular identity.

References

Arenberg, David. "Concept Problem Solving in Young and Old Adults." *Journal of Gerontology* Vol. 23 (1968): 279–82.

Atchley, Robert C. "Continuity Theory of Normal Aging." *The Gerontologist* Vol. 29 (1989): 183–90.

Baltes, Paul B., and G. Labouvie. "Adult Development of Intellectual Performance." In *The Psychology of Adult Development and Aging.* Eds. Carl Eisdorfer and M. Powell Lawtons. Washington, DC: American Psychological Association, 1973.

Birren, James E. *The Psychology of Aging.* Englewood Cliffs, NJ: Prentice-Hall, 1964.

Birren, James E., Bruce Sloane, and Gene D. Cohen. *Handbook of Aging and Mental Health.* 2d ed. New York: Academic Press, 1992.

Botwinick, Jack. *Aging and Behavior.* 2d ed. New York: Springer, 1978.

———. *Aging and Behavior.* 3d ed. New York: Springer, 1984.

Cijfer, E. "An Experiment on Some Differences in Logical Thinking Between Dutch Medical People, Under and Over the Age of 35." *Acta Psychologica* Vol. 25 (1966): 159–71.

Corso, John F. "Auditory Perception and Communication." In *Handbook of the Psychology of Aging.* Eds. James E. Birren and K. Warner Schaie. New York: Van Nostrand Reinhold, 1977.

Engen, Trygg. "Taste and Smell." In *Handbook of the Psychology of Aging.* Eds. James E. Birren and K. Warner Schaie, New York: Van Nostrand Reinhold, 1977.

Erikson, Erik H., Joan Erikson, and Helen Kivnick. *Vital Involvement in Old Age.* New York: Norton, 1986.

Fozard, James L. "Vision and Hearing in Aging." In *Handbook of the Psychology of Aging.* Eds. J. E. Birren and K. W. Schaie. 3d ed. New York: Academic Press, 1990.

Kesler, Mary S., Nancy W. Denney, and Susan E. Whitely. "Factors Influencing Problem Solving in Middle-Aged and Elderly Adults." *Human Development* Vol. 19 (1976): 310–20.

National Center for Health Statistics. *Health Statistics* Series B, no. 9. Washington, DC: National Center for Health Statistics, 1959.

Nesselroade, John R., K. Warner Schaie, and Paul B. Baltes. "Ontogenetic and Generational Components of Structural and Quantitative Change in Adult Cognitive Behavior." *Journal of Gerontology* Vol. 27 (1972): 222–28.

Riegel, Klaus F. "The Dialectics of Human Development." *The American Psychologist* Vol. 31 (1976): 689–700.

Simonton, Dean Keith. "Creativity and Wisdom." In *Handbook of the Psychology of Aging.* Eds. J. E. Birren and K. W. Schaie. 3d ed. New York: Academic Press, 1990.

Troll, Lillian E. *Continuations: Adult Development and Aging.* Monterey, CA: Brooks/Cole, 1982.

Whitbourne, Susan K. *The Aging Body: Physiological Changes and Psychological Consequences.* New York: Springer Verlag, 1985.

Whitbourne, Susan K., and Comilda S. Weinstock. *Adult Development: The Differentiation of Experience.* 2d ed. New York: Praeger, 1986.

Woodruff-Pak, Diana S. "Aging and Intelligence: Changing Perspectives in the Twentieth Century." *Journal of Aging Studies* Vol. 3 (1989): 91–118.

Robert C. Atchley, Ph. D.

6

The Social Process of Aging

• Aging and Social Roles • The Life Course • Social Response to Aging People
• Aging and Social Inequality • Aging and the Economy • Aging and Politics
• Aging and Government • Processes of Aging: Review

Individuals' lives are also structured by their social environments. People interact with one another not only as individuals but as role players. And the roles are organized sequentially into a life course tied to age or life stage. In addition, social processes such as socialization involve the individual with his or her social world. All these aspects of the social environment can be influenced by age.

● AGING AND SOCIAL ROLES

Social roles are important because individuals often define themselves in terms of these roles, and their places in society are determined by them. *Roles* are the expected or typical behavior associated with positions in the organization of a group. A large part of everyday life consists of human relationships that are structured at least partially by the social roles of the various actors. But in everyday life the action is much more like improvisational theater, for the characters and dialogue are made up right on stage, not scripted as with formal theater.

General role definitions serve as the background for initial interactions in new role relationships, but almost immediately role players begin to incorporate *personal* information into their expectations for their *specific* relationship. They each gradually modify and refine their expectations to take an increasing amount of personal information into account.

When life is filled with relatively new relationships, as in young adulthood, people are uncer-

tain about what to expect from others and what is expected from them. But when life is filled with long-term relationships, there is a large component of *security* in knowing what to expect—even if the relationship is not all it could be. In middle age and later life, most role relationships for most people are long-standing relationships that are highly personalized.

In adulthood, advanced age occasionally makes people eligible for valued roles such as *retired person*, but more often it makes them ineligible for roles they value. Whether one is merely *assigned* to roles, or whether one must have the opportunity to *achieve* them, or whether one *selects* them, one does not simply play or take over or retain roles. They are usually available as a result of having met certain criteria. In most societies, particular rights, duties, privileges, and obligations are set aside for children, adolescents, young adults, the middle-aged, and the old. In today's culture, the primary eligibility criteria are health, *age*, gender, social class, ethnicity, color, experience, and educational achievement. These criteria may be gradually modified and personalized in some cases, but overall these attributes govern role eligibility in predictable ways.

Throughout the life process, the field of roles people are eligible for keeps changing. Young boys can legitimately be members of a neighborhood peer group, pupils, and not employed—all things they cannot be as adults. As young men, they can be auto drivers, soldiers, and voters—all things they cannot be as children. As older adults,

When life is filled with long-standing relationships, there is a strong sense of security in knowing what to expect. (Courtesy of Sanders-Brown Center on Aging, University of Kentucky/Tim Collins, photographer)

they can be retired, be great-grandfathers, or act as family historians—all things they cannot do as young adults. Of course, age also works negatively, as when older people are prevented from holding jobs, even if they want to work.

Age also serves to *modify* what is expected of people in particular roles. Young people are often dealt with leniently in adult roles because of their inexperience. In old age, the standards may also be different. For example, an 86-year-old father is allowed to be more dependent in his relationships with his offspring than a 56-year-old father is.

Roles that adults play provide various degrees of access to advantages such as prestige, wealth, or influence. Highly rewarded roles can be obtained either through family background or individual initiative or both. But despite the rhetoric that an open class system exists in which one can rise from rags to riches, in reality only a small minority of people ever move out of the social class into which they were born.

Growing older in an advantaged social position generally means being able to accumulate personal wealth and prestige. People do not become wealthy, revered, or influential just by becoming old, but by playing an advantaged role for a number of years. A great many of the richest and most influential Americans are old, but their age is not the reason why they are rich or influential. In fact, their wealth and influence *discounts* their age in the sense that rich and powerful people are much less likely than others to be disqualified from participation purely on account of age. Age disqualification happens mainly to people who are already relatively disadvantaged.

One can also be advantaged by having *exceptional* skills. Great writers, musicians, artists, therapists, diplomats, and others can use their skills to offset their age and to avoid being disqualified. Pablo Picasso or Georgia O'Keefe never had to worry about age discrimination—their talents remained in demand. Other people find that presumptions about the effects of age often offset ordinary skills and lead to disqualification.

Some of the disqualifying character of age is related to erroneous beliefs about the predictability of age's effects on performance. But some is related to the scarcity of leadership positions, the desire of younger people to acquire them, and the willingness of older people to give up responsibilities.

● THE LIFE COURSE

The *life course* is an idealized and age-related progression or sequence of roles and group memberships that individuals are expected to follow as they mature and move through life. Thus, there is an age to go to school, an age to marry, an age to "settle down," and so forth. But the life course in reality is neither simple nor rigidly prescribed.

Figure 6.1
Various Dimensions of the Life Course. (Dotted lines mean that the timing is discretionary.)

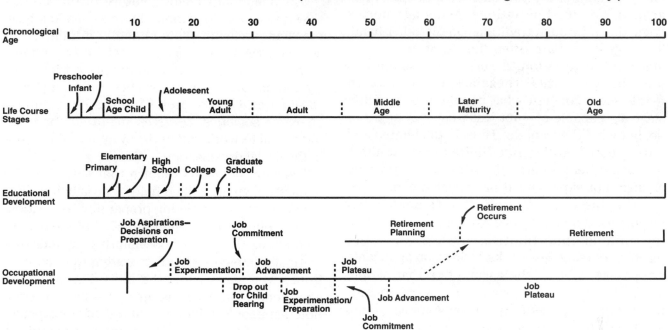

For example, various subcultures (whether based on gender, social class, ethnicity, race, or region of the country) tend to develop unique ideas concerning the timing of the life course. This leads male auto workers to favor retirement in the mid-fifties while physicians prefer the late sixties. In addition, even within subcultures, there are often several alternatives. Thus, like a road map, the abstract concept of the life course in reality is composed of a great many alternative routes to alternative destinations.

As people grow older, their accumulated decisions about various life course options produce increased differentiation among them. Although very-late-in-life options may diminish somewhat because of social and physical aging, the older population is considerably more differentiated than the young.

Yet even with the increased complexity of the life course with age, certain generally accepted standards serve as a sort of master timetable for the entire population. Even though there are many exceptions and variations, most Americans start school, finish school, get married, have children, experience the "empty nest," and retire—each within a span surrounding a particular chronological age, the age at which these events are *supposed* to happen for people of their social

class, ethnicity, and gender. Most people spend their lives reasonably on schedule, and when they get off schedule they are motivated to get back on again (Hagestad and Neugarten, 1985).

Life Course Stages

Figure 6.1 shows ways the life course stages are related to chronological age, education, and occupational careers. More dimensions could be added, but the important point is that various social institutions tend to prescribe their own development program related to the various life stages.

The various stages of the life course are made real for the individual in three ways. First, they are related to more specific patterns such as the occupational career. Second, specific expectations or age norms accompany various life stages. And finally, particular types of choices are forced during given phases of the life course.

Age Norms

Age norms dicate what people in a given life stage are allowed to do and be, and what they are required to do and be. Age norms sometimes operate very generally to specify dress, personal appearance, or demeanor in a wide variety of social roles. Other age norms govern approach, entry, incumbency, and exit from social roles, groups, or social situations. Many age norms come down through tradition. On the other hand, legal age norms are often the result of compromise and negotiation. A series of assumptions underlie age norms. These assumptions, often uninformed, concern what people in a given life stage are capable of—not just what they *ought* to do, but what they *can* do. Thus, both children and older people experience limited opportunities because others assume that they are not strong enough, not experienced or educated enough, or not capable of adequately mature adult judgments. For instance, older workers are passed by for training opportunities because "you can't teach an old dog new tricks." Older job applicants are passed over on the assumption that people aged 60 have too few years left to work to warrant investing in them. By the same token, young adults are passed over because they "don't have enough experience."

Sometimes age norms make useful and valid distinctions. For example, few people would want to share the road when 6-year-olds are behind the wheels of the other cars. But beginning with adolescence it becomes increasingly difficult to justify the essentially arbitrary nature of many age norms. And the greater the gap between the actual level of individual functioning and the level implied by the age norm, the more likely that age norms will be seen as unjust.

As people grow older, their accumulated decisions about various life course options produce increased differentiation among them.

Conformity to age norms is encouraged by several factors. People are taught early in life by their parents, teachers, and peers how to apply age norms to themselves. If they do not conform, friends, neighbors, and associates can be counted on to apply informal pressures. In the formal realm, regulations bring bureaucratic authority to bear. And finally, laws put the full power of the state behind age norms. For example, the idea that airline pilots should retire by age 60 is supported at every level along this continuum.

Decision Demands

The sometimes chaotic nature of the alternatives presented by various life courses has been mentioned earlier. This chaos is minimized to some degree by age, gender, social class, ethnicity, and so forth. But how do people get into *specific* situations? It is impossible to assign people to each and every niche in complex, rapidly changing societies. *Decision demands* force the individual to work within the system to find a slot in the social organization.

Decision demands require that selections be made from an age-linked field of possibilities. For example, after completing preparatory education, young adults usually enter a period of job experimentation. The field of possibilities expands dramatically immediately after graduation and continues to expand while the individual gains job experience. But there is an increasing expectation that people will find positions of employment into which they will settle; during this period the field of jobs for which they are eligible may slowly contract. Contraction also occurs as jobs are selected by others of similar age and experience. For many jobs, career tracks are difficult to begin after age 35.

Decision demands tend to be concentrated in the first half of the life course. That is, individuals are *required* to make choices and select their career tracks in all sorts of areas—education, employment, family, community, voluntary associations, and so on. Life-styles developed before or during middle age tend to persist as long as health and money hold out. Thus, middle-aged people who want to switch tracks or get involved in new areas sometimes confront the fact that the available slots were taken earlier by their age peers.

On the other hand, those middle-aged people who do retrain and switch careers often find that their new careers develop at an accelerated rate compared to those younger people starting at the same time. This acceleration is probably due to their greater maturity and general experience plus the underlying notion that a person's position in an organization should match his or her life stage. More research is needed on this phenomenon.

Social Processes

Socialization is a group of processes through which a group encourages and/or coerces its

Voices of Creative Aging

Helen S., a folksinger and clinical social worker who, at age 65, made a move from urban to rural life after years of careful planning. She offers her views on coming to terms with aging:

When I was 50 I began looking for a place where I might want to settle. I earned my living as a touring folksinger and clinical social worker and didn't want to change my clinical work, maybe just do less of it. I certainly didn't want to give up my music, so I had to find a community that held the kind of people that I mingle well with, and which offered me the opportunity to earn a moderate kind of living. I have always loved the woods, and as soon as I became eligible for Social Security, I sold my house and moved from the city.

I had to supplement my income from Social Security. Having been a single parent raising two children, I had only part-time jobs, leaving me with no pension. Fortunately I found a position as a therapist here in the local health clinic and can work as many hours as I like. That's how I earn enough to support my singing. This way I have the best of both worlds. I can't imagine not singing, whether I do it for an audience or not. I have a piano here in my house in the woods and sing every day for a little bit. I just need to.

I think what I have learned and what I would try to get across to anybody counseling on the subject of aging is that first of all, unless you cease to exit, old age is coming, so there's no sense pretending it isn't coming. After you digest that one—and a lot of people don't; they fight it until they are in a mess about it—you need something else that has nothing to do with aging: it has to do with living. That is, you need to have developed the capacity somewhere for making yourself happy. When you know that, then you can face most of what happens to you at any age.

Excerpt from Connie Goldman's "Late Bloomer"
public radio series

members to learn and conform to its culture. *Acculturation* is the actual learning of a culture. Much of what individuals seek to learn through acculturation is aimed at making them more effective role players. To the individual, socialization and acculturation are important prerequisites for getting whatever society has to offer. If people know and understand the social system, they can potentially put the system to use. If they do not understand the culture, their lives can be confusing and unpredictable.

Socialization produces a measure of continuity from one generation to another. Society needs new participants, and socialization is a major process through which society attracts, facilitates, and maintains participation. The efforts of the group to help individuals learn the system range from formal, structured programs in which the group is responsible for the outcome, to unstructured, informal processes in which the individual is responsible for the outcome. For example, families are expected to teach children to speak, and schools are expected to teach children to read and write. On the other hand, adults must generally find out on their own how to locate a library.

Age affects what the individual is expected to know and what he or she needs to know in order to be an effective participant in society. Early in life, the emphasis in socialization is on learning language and customs; then it shifts to preparing for adult social roles. In adulthood, expectations gradually shift toward self-initiated acculturation; that is, adults often recognize their need for knowledge and skills and seek them without waiting to be told. At the same time, fewer publicly supported, formal opportunities exist for socialization in adulthood compared to the opportunities that exist for young people.

Older people often have few required contacts with the general community. They associate primarily with people they know and who know them. In addition, most older people continue to function mainly in roles they have occupied for many years. The point is that most roles older people play are roles they have been socialized to for a long time. Aging often results primarily in adjusting the nuances of role playing rather than its basic structure.

Most societies pay little attention to their adult members' needs for maintenance or renewal of knowledge or skills. In this age of the computer, for example, where do middle-aged or older adults go to learn how to use this new way of dealing with information? This pattern seriously hampers the ability of some older members of society to remain integrated in the society, particularly in terms of the knowledge and skills required for employment. If older people need information and skills that are necessary for participation in society but are not readily available to them, then the socialization processes in the society are not adequate.

The process of *role anticipation* involves learning the rights, obligations, resources, and outlook of a position one will occupy in the future. To the extent that the future position is a general one, it need not represent an unknown. Through fantasies, it is possible to anticipate what the future will hold, identify potential problems, and to prepare in advance. The role changes common to later life can often be anticipated, thus smoothing the process of transition.

However, many roles taken up in later life have a degree of vagueness that allows some flexibility in playing them but at the same time hinders anticipation. Such roles are not "packaged," as roles that young people play often are. For example, the role of high school student is much more clearly defined than the role of retired person. As a result, older people must often negotiate new role definitions with significant other people in their environment. Thus, in late adulthood, acculturation—learning or relearning how to function in one's social milieu—depends heavily on the characteristics of others with whom the older person must negotiate. The attitudes of others concerning who the older person is becoming are probably crucial to the content of acculturation in later life. As images of aging become less stereotyped in American culture, the outcome of these negotiations can be expected to become more positive and individuated.

Social roles, even the specific ones such as mother or teacher, tend to be defined in terms that allow room for interpretation. *Adaptation* to roles is a process of fitting role demands to the individual's capabilities and vice versa. Negotiation—the interpersonal aspect of this adaptation—takes place between role players. This process of tailoring the role to fit the individual and the situation means that it is impossible to describe *the* role of *the* grandfather, but look-ing at how grandfathers play their roles reveals similarities and differences applied to the role by different people.

Thus, through socialization society tells its members that retirement is normal and that it should occur around age 65. Through acculturation, an individual comes to *believe* that retirement is normal and that it should occur around age 65. Through anticipation, the individual identifies potential problems associated with retirement and tries to solve them in advance. Once the individual retires, the process of adaptation involves tailoring the rather vague retirement role to fit the needs of the individual. Part of this process may involve negotiations between spouses about what the retirement role will consist of and how it will influence their life together.

● SOCIAL RESPONSE TO AGING PEOPLE

In addition to the social factors influencing individual aging directly through social roles, the well-being of aging and older people is also affected by society's response to aging and older people as a social category. There are various social responses to aging; how aging interacts with social class, ethnicity, and gender; and how aging people are responded to by the economy, politics and government, and health care and social service systems.

General Social Responses to Aging

General social responses to aging exist in the ideas of a culture, in the media and educational materials through which people learn these ideas, and in the attitudes and actions that result. Americans appear to be genuinely ambivalent about aging. While most people seem to want to think well of older people, aging poses both real and imagined threats to important social values. Family security, freedom of choice, and general happiness are all vulnerable to the ups and downs of one's own aging, the aging of family members for whom one may be responsible, and the aging of society in general. In addition, popular notions present aging as a threat to such social values as productivity and efficiency. Yet general beliefs and stereotypes about aging are not predictably negative or inaccurate; sometimes they are and sometimes they are not, though negative and inaccurate beliefs about older people as jobholders does underpin widespread age discrimination in employment.

People seem to dislike both the idea of aging and the people who experience it. This is true throughout the life cycle. And this dislike seems to result from the public's association of aging with unpleasant outcomes such as illness, unattractiveness, and inability. On the other hand, people also seem to like the idea that wisdom, warmth, and goodness increase with age. Such is the nature of ambivalence.

Contemporary children's books and adult novels generally portray aging in a positive and humanistic light. Children are presented with the ideal that older people are to be treated with respect. Older characters are depicted with a full range of human qualities. Even contemporary television drama recognizes multi-generational relationships as a natural and interesting part of life. There are more older characters in continuing series portraying well-developed, successful people in family or job situations. More than 90 percent of the older characters are portrayed positively. Nevertheless, older people in television news programming seem to be held to the inaccurate view of later life as a life stage beset with serious problems, and this reinforces the prevalent view of later life as an undesirable life stage.

Such ambivalent beliefs, attitudes, and perceptions about aging as a threat to important values translate into age prejudice, or ageism, and age discrimination. *Age discrimination* imposes negative outcomes on older people just because they

The well-being of aging and older people is affected by society's response to aging and older people as a social category. (Copyright © Curt Wachter for the Chautauqua Institution)

are older. Some of it is subtle, as when older people are ignored or avoided in interaction or social planning. It is more direct where people are denied participation because of their age. Direct age discrimination is especially prevalent in the occupational sphere but also appears to operate in volunteer work and other areas too. Age discrimination also occurs when public agencies fail to orient public programs meant for the general population as much toward older people as they do toward younger people.

Societal disengagement is the withdrawal of interest in the contributions or involvement of older people. It is *not* a mutually satisfying process but one that is imposed on older people by the withdrawal of opportunities to participate and by circumstances such as ill health. Like age discrimination, the more general process of societal disengagement rests not so much on the functional needs of society as on its prejudices.

The general social treatment of aging and older people reflects ambivalence. On the one hand, age prejudice institutionalized the removal of older adults from the labor force; on the other hand, retirement income systems transformed retirement into a reward. Society's treatment of the older age categories is softened by centuries-old family values of respect and caring for elders.

● AGING AND SOCIAL INEQUALITY

Social class affects aging by influencing the attitudes, beliefs, and values people use to make life course choices and by influencing life course opportunities, particularly in terms of education and jobs. People whose social-class backgrounds lead to middle-class jobs or higher approach aging with much greater resources—knowledge, good health, adequate retirement income—compared to the working class and the poor. The positive picture of individual aging presented earlier is primarily middle class because most older Americans are middle class. On the other hand, many of the problematic aspects of aging are concentrated among the working class and the poor.

Racial discrimination has concentrated African Americans disproportionately in low-paying jobs and in substandard housing; this fact applies more to older African Americans than to African

Profiles of Productive Aging

Maggie Kuhn
Activist

"My feeling is that in late life we are free to transcend our own history and to be progressive. To take a new view of ourselves and the world. And we are concerned about the tribe's survival, not our own. Let's get that across to people."

Philadelphia organizer and activist Maggie Kuhn, founder of the Gray Panthers, was born August 3, 1905, in Buffalo, New York. The family settled in Cleveland, where Kuhn attended the women's college of Western Reserve University. She planned to be a teacher, but when her creativity was not viewed favorably by her teaching supervisor, she accepted a job with the Young Women's Christian Association. A natural organizer, she was good at the job and loved it. She also pursued graduate study at Columbia University Teacher's College, taking the equivalent of a master's degree in a joint program with Union Theological Seminary, and then worked for the YWCA in Philadelphia. Kuhn's work was with business women, but quickly developed into supervising WPA workers and maintaining liaison with forty other agencies in the Greater Philadelphia area, including the Federal Job Corps and the Youth Conservation Corps.

During World War II Kuhn worked for the YWCA national staff in New York in the USO Division and helped reorganize the Unitarian general alliance. Kuhn's father, a Presbyterian, humorously described this as "doing missionary work among the Unitarians." Several years later Kuhn returned to Philadelphia to help care for her mother and work with a Presbyterian organization, editing the organization's journal and working on their program unit. She kept this job for twenty-two years, until she retired at the age of 65. During the last several years of her tenure, she was posted to the Interchurch Center in New York, near Riverside Church.

"They told me [retirement].... was mandatory on my 65th birthday," Kuhn recalled. "If I had been a man, I could have been negotiating for a year at a time; but this was not the case. There were six of us in the New York area, an interesting group of women who were confronted with the same difficulty." Kuhn remembered: "We got together and discussed it and we said: 'The question is, what do we do with the rest of our lives?' And we said, 'We can't answer that alone. We've got to deliberate it, and get some kind of a collective answer.' So we wrote that in a very simple manifesto, and called a meeting at the International House of Columbia. A hundred people showed! It was in June, 1970; a historical moment."

Kuhn and her friends had chosen Vietnam as their topic, and they decided to "stand with the kids" and demonstrate, calling themselves, the "Consultation of Older and Younger Adults for Social Change." They were invited to appear on a talk show at WBAI in New York, but the producer winced to hear their name and said: "That name will get you nowhere. You're the Gray Panthers!" The semantic link to the black civil rights movement delighted them, and they adopted the name.

In May 1972, Kuhn attended the General Assembly of the Presbyterian Church at its annual meeting in Denver, Colorado. When the featured VIP failed to appear at the press conference in the hotel, the press officer begged Kuhn to fill in and talk about her Gray Panthers. There was a huge media turnout for the conference—all the wire services as well as the *Denver Post,* the *Washington Post,* and the *New York Times.* "A month later I was on the Johnny Carson show," Kuhn recalled. "It was unbelievable."

Kuhn had a goal in mind, but she did not expect her path to develop as it has. "I didn't set out to start a movement," she said. "In many ways it was to answer this very odd question: What do you DO with the rest of your life, when you've been so involved with your work? You see, people who have work they love have a certain amount of privilege. And their personal and their professional lives are blended." But it isn't just those who are privileged to have work that they love who must worry about what to do after "retirement." Kuhn saw it is a universal problem: "Those who do not have work they love, hate what they do, and aren't affirmed by their jobs are glad to leave them. But *then* what do they do? They're miserable, too."

Kuhn sees a continuity linking the things she did earlier in her career with her activities over the past twenty years leading the Gray Panthers. "I'm building today on all the things that I learned when I was younger," she acknowledged.

Lydia Brontë

Americans in general. Compared to older whites, older African Americans have lower Social Security benefits, fewer private pensions, and greater incidence of illness and disability.

Older Native Americans face an even worse situation than older African Americans. Excluded from participation in American society and heavily concentrated in rural areas and on Indian reservations, older American Indians are much less likely than other older people to have access to services. Compared to older whites, older Native Americans are much less likely to have had middle-class jobs and much more likely to have inadequate incomes and poor health.

The picture for older Asian Americans is mixed, although all groups show some negative effects of racism. Japanese-American elders have had jobs that closely parallel those of whites and as a result have retirement incomes closer to those of whites than any other racial category. There is great diversity among older Chinese Americans in terms of jobs and retirement income. Filipino-American older people are more likely to have had low-paying jobs and thus low retirement incomes. Despite their lower incomes, older Asian Americans tend to be in better health than older whites.

The Hispanic population is quite diverse also. Older Hispanic Americans tend to be better off than older African Americans but not as well off as older non-Hispanic whites or older Asian Americans in terms of health and retirement income.

Of the categories of people who experience discrimination in American society, women experience the greatest inequality. Women who opt to be housewives are quite vulnerable economically to the breakup of their marriages through divorce or widowhood. Those who are employed are concentrated in "women's work," which tends to be low paying and not covered by private pensions. As a result, retirement incomes of women are only about 55 percent as high as those for men.

Multiple jeopardy increases the probability of having poor health and inadequate income. Being a woman is the greatest disadvantage, followed by having less than high school education (being working-class) and by being African American. Social inequality has a great influence on aging through its effect on jobs and lifetime earnings

and their consequent impact on health and retirement income in later life.

● AGING AND THE ECONOMY

The economy is a very complex social institution, one that affects middle-aged and older people by governing their access to jobs, by providing the economic surplus needed to finance retirement income, and by its approach to aging people as consumers. The U.S. economy is influenced by a long-standing free market ideology that seeks to increase the wealth of private individuals and sees the operation of this accumulated wealth in the private market as the most appropriate way to meet people's needs.

However, access to wealth is not equal in American society. A core private sector of the economy, comprised of the largest business and financial corporations, has relatively plentiful opportunities to earn high incomes, amass substantial investments, and generate entitlement to high retirement incomes. Workers in this sector are predominantly white males; and at the upper echelons, where opportunities are greatest, they tend to be from the most well-to-do families. The peripheral private sector is made up of smaller, more competitive businesses that operate on lower profit margins in which wages tend to be low and fringe benefits and private pension coverage inadequate or nonexistent. Most American workers are employed in the peripheral private sector. The government sector of the economy employs about 17 percent of the labor force. Some government workers fare nearly as well as those in the core private sector in terms of wages, fringe benefits, and pension adequacy, but most are somewhere between the core and peripheral private sectors. Thus access to fully adequate retirement income is not available to all Americans, only those in about the top 30 percent of jobs. The incomes that support older people are overwhelmingly *earned* income from wages, accumulated assets, and pension credits. Less than 5 percent of the incomes of elders comes from "unearned" sources such as Supplemental Security Income (public welfare) or Medicaid.

The income inequalities among people increase as they move into later maturity, as a result of inequities in access to retirement pensions and

Social inequality has a great influence on aging through its effect on jobs and lifetime earnings and their consequent impact on health and retirement income in later life. (Courtesy of Sanders-Brown Center on Aging, University of Kentucky/Tim Collins, photographer)

assets and also of a tax structure that concentrates tax breaks for older people among the most well-to-do. There is a large minority of older people for whom the American economy does not deliver adequate retirement income.

For many older people, the private economy is effective in delivering food, clothing, housing, transportation, recreation, and the like. But the private economy has not responded to many elders' needs, particularly housing, health care, and transportation, because meeting those needs is not profitable enough.

Retirement is not only a life stage that must be financed but also an important tool of employment policy. It helps society keep unemployment within acceptable bounds, helps reduce labor mobility in highly skilled jobs, gives workers incentive to endure undesirable or overly demanding jobs by limiting their duration, provides a graceful means of phasing out ineffective workers, and creates opportunities for younger

workers. Accordingly, retirement benefits the entire society, not just currently retired individuals.

The need to provide retirement income has played an important role in capital formation since World War II. Pension funds now own substantial interests in the corporations of America.

Older people have customarily been treated as a trivial market for consumer goods. However, with the declining numbers of young people, the slowing of population growth, and the improvement of retirement incomes for the middle class, business is beginning to show an interest in older markets. Indeed, population age 55 and over is currently spending more discretionary money than any other age category in the population, particularly on luxury goods and services. In the future, businesses will likely develop more products and services aimed directly at the older population.

● AGING AND POLITICS

Politics is the route to political power, and political power means control over the machinery of government. Older people are concerned with politics and government, as they prove when they participate in politics through voting, working in political organizations, and holding office. Older people are also the object of governmental programs.

Older people seek to remain informed about and interested in politics, particularly if they are well educated or involved in local affairs. Older people vote in about the same proportions as when they were middle-aged. Each age cohort apparently develops its own level of participation, which stays relatively stable throughout the life course, but differential mortality and the tendency for women to vote less both reduce the actual proportion voting.

Older people have stronger party identification than the young only if they have been associated with a party over many years. It is number of years of affiliation, not age itself, that produces a strong party identification. In politics, youth apparently still bows to experience, and experience rather than age is the crucial variable. Older people have equal opportunities in politics, but only if they have been lifelong participants; there is little room for the inexperienced retired person who suddenly decides to get into politics.

In terms of political power, early pressure groups of older people suffered from lack of leadership, regional segregation, heterogeneity of interests among older people, and lack of funds. Action on behalf of older people has almost always depended on the political support of organizations not based on age, such as unions or political parties. The role of modern old age interest groups such as the American Association of Retired Persons is to make the need for action highly visible and to lobby for the interests of older people within existing programs. In more recent years, older Americans have gradually increased their share of benefits from general government programs. In the 1980s, based on inaccurate assumptions about the actual situation of the older population, severe cuts were made in Social Security, Medicare, and Medicaid.

● AGING AND GOVERNMENT

Governmental programs for older people meet some of their needs at various levels of government. The federal government operates programs in income and health care financing. But efforts to address other needs usually require involvement on the part of state and local governments. The 1973 reorganization of the Older Americans Act, which gave states and local areas authority, funds, and responsibility, took a large step toward creating local advocates for older Americans.

The need to provide retirement income has played an important role in capital formation since World War II. Pension funds now own substantial interests in the corporations of America.

The biggest problem in creating governmental programs for older people is deciding how these programs should be organized and coordinated, particularly in terms of intergovernmental relations. Older people have benefited a great deal from being the first target for large-scale social programs in the United States. It is unlikely that Supplemental Security Income, Medicare, or many of the other supports to older Americans would be there if such supports had to be provided to everyone. American politics is still very sensitive to government intervention on too large a scale. In recent years the legitimacy of federal programs for elders has been called into question, but public support for programs such as Social Security remains strong.

Aging, Health Care, and Social Services

Health care and social services to older people have increased dramatically in scope and amount since the early 1960s, but the size of the older population has increased even faster. As a result, there are substantial gaps in national programs to finance health care and social services, and continued inflation, especially in health care costs, has prevented these gaps from closing.

When individuals have difficulty in getting adequate services, they may think theirs is an isolated case and ask, "Why me?" But in the case of health care and social services to elders, the problems are greatly influenced by the haphazard nature of the social structures that provide these services. In health care, although all models of care delivery have their appropriate applications, the medical model has tended to dominate definitions of who could get services, what services they could get, and who could provide them. In addition, national programs for financing health care for older people have emphasized funding for institutionally provided medical services and discouraged less expensive institutional services such as personal care and noninstitutional services such as home care. The dominance of the medical model is in large part due to an imbalance of resources and credibility between physician-directed advocates and advocates for the social and holistic models of care, which call for a greater variety of care alternatives and involvement of a wider variety of types of caregivers.

Medicare, a major financier of hospital care for older people, is much less effective in its coverage of physicians' fees, home health care, and long-term care. It completely ignores the needs for eyeglasses, hearing aids, dental care, and immunizations.

Medicaid is a major source of funding for long-term care, but to qualify for it, older people must deplete their resources until they become eligible for welfare. Medicaid is not available to most middle-class older Americans.

Because inflation in health care costs has been substantially higher than in other areas of the economy over the past several years, severe problems have developed in financing Medicare and Medicaid and private health insurance as well. A large portion of the federally supported effort originally intended to address enforcement of care quality and accomplish planning has instead gone into trying to contain increasing costs. There has been a resulting reduction in the number of people being served and an increase in the financial burden borne by older people and their families, but there has been little effect on the rate of inflation in health care costs.

Social services are provided to elders through a network of federal, state, and local agencies created by the Older Americans Act and funded through the Older Americans Act, Social Services Block Grants, local United Way agencies, local foundations, and a variety of other minor sources. The Older Americans Act has encouraged the development of an array of services that is similar in most communities, including information and referral, transportation, outreach, both congregate and home-delivered meals, homemaker and home health services, telephone reassurance, and legal services. However, funding levels for these services have been at spartan levels, especially when compared with the sums spent on health care.

As a result of the increased number of older people and the increasing costs of health and social services, a debate has emerged over whether age or need is the more appropriate criterion to use in establishing eligibility for services. This debate is likely to remain spirited.

● PROCESSES OF AGING: REVIEW

There are three basic ways to look at aging. It can be viewed as a biological phenomenon involving maturation, maturity, and decline of the body and its various functions. Aging can also be viewed as a process of mental development that involves a great deal of continuity in functioning, some declines in functioning, and some increases in functioning. Or aging can be viewed as a social phenomenon in which chronological age is used to define people's capabilities and opportunities. All these approaches are true, and all are limited. In combination, they provide concepts that can be used to better understand aging.

The physical model of aging as a process of maturation, maturity, and decline is useful for

guiding the work of physiologists, and it tends to accurately describe what happens to various bodily functions in general over the life span. But for most purposes the maturation-maturity-aging model has two serious limitations. First, because there is so much variability among people and between functions even within the same person, the model is not very useful for deciding what to expect in specific cases. Second, because many declines in physical functions can be completely or partially compensated for, the model very greatly overestimates the effects of aging on social functioning. Social impairments due to aging do not become widespread until well after age 75.

Mental aging can be viewed either as a process of change in specific mental factors such as memory or motor coordination, or as a more global process of evolution in the mind and its various dimensions. From the perspective of specific traits, aging has variable results. Functions such as vision, reaction time, or memory that have a strong dependence on the body and its level of functioning are much more likely to decline with age than are learned functions such as vocabulary, creativity, or problem solving that depend more on the mind and are more easily maintained by practice. Some mental functions increase steadily with age, some remain relatively constant, and some decline. Therefore, the effects of aging on mental capacities cannot be assumed to follow any single pattern.

From the adult development perspective, aging can be viewed either as a process of moving through several discrete stages or as a continuous process of unfolding. Process theories of adult development concern identity and how it evolves over the life span. Aging can solidify identity by providing a large amount of experience about the self. The reduction in job and parenting responsibilities that often accompanies aging can reduce the potential for conflict among the various aspects of identity. Aging is more a process of identity maintenance than a process of identity formation. Identity crises result from age changes in the individual or the environment that cannot be accommodated without a large-scale reorganization of the person's self-concept. No life change predictably causes identity crises. Identity crises result from the individual's interpretation of life events.

Self-concept relates to ideas about ourselves that form the basis for initiative and self-confidence, or lack of them. (Copyright © Marianne Gontarz)

Social aging involves the use of age by society to assign people to roles based on their chronological age or life stage. Age is used to determine eligibility, evaluate appropriateness, and modify expectations with respect to various roles in society. Roles largely define the participation of people in their society. At the beginning, people tend to play roles rather formally, but the longer they have been in a role the more personalized the role tends to become and the more comfortable they are in it. Aging is a socially satisfying process to many people because it increases the duration and therefore the security of their role relationships. Holding an advantaged social position for a long time can also result in an accumulation of advantages such as wealth, prestige, and influence. Holding a position for a long time can also lead to the development of exceptional skills that can be used to offset the disqualifying character of older age as an eligibility criterion.

The life course is an ideal sequence of roles a person is expected to play as he or she moves through life. There are many versions of the life course, depending on the gender, ethnicity, or social class of the individual. The time schedule implied by the life course can also change over historical time, so that, for example, the ideal time to marry in one era may be much older than the ideal time to marry in another. As people grow older, their accumulated decisions about various life course options result in increased differentiation among them.

The age norms used to allocate people to positions and roles are based loosely on ideas about what people of various ages are capable of as

well as about what is appropriate for them. The greater the gap between the assumptions about functioning implied by the age norm and the actual level of functioning of the individual to whom the norm is applied, the more likely that the age norm will be seen as unjust.

Society conveys age norms through socialization, and individuals learn them through acculturation. As age increases, opportunities for formal socialization decrease. Role anticipation allows people to prepare for and to smooth life transitions. Adaptation and negotiation processes allow people to fit themselves to new roles and vice versa.

Aging can have both positive and negative outcomes; it is mainly positive for most people; and it is unpredictable for any given individual. Variety among people increases with age as a result of biological, psychological, and social processes that operate differentially. No single model or set of assumptions about the effects of aging can capture the reality of aging.

References

Atchley, Robert C. *Aging: Continuity and Change.* 2d ed. Belmont, CA: Wadsworth, 1987.

———. *Social Forces and Aging.* 6th ed. Belmont, CA: Wadsworth, 1991.

Hagestad, Gunhild O., and Bernice L. Neugarten. "Age and the Life Course." In *Handbook of Aging and the Social Sciences.* Eds. R. H. Binstock and E. Shanas. 2d ed. New York: Van Nostrand Reinhold, 1985.

"Late Bloomer" audio cassette. Available from Connie Goldman Productions, 926 Second Street, Suite 201, Santa Monica, CA 90403. (310) 393-6801.

Additional Reading

Beauvoir, Simone de. *The Coming of Age.* New York: Warner, 1973.

Butler, Robert N. *Why Survive? Being Old in America.* New York: Harper & Row, 1975.

Chinen, Allan B. *In the Ever After: Fairy Tales and the Second Half of Life.* Wilmette, IL: Chiron Publications, 1989.

Cunningham, Imogene. *After Ninety.* Seattle, WA: University of Washington Press, 1977.

Scott-Maxwell, Florida. *The Measure of My Days.* New York: Knopf, 1968.

Sexon, Sue V., and Mary Jean Etten. *Physical Change and Aging: A Guide for the Helping Professions.* New York: Tiresias Press, 1987.

Robert C. Atchley, Ph. D.

The material in Chapters 4, 5, and 6 is adapted from *Aging: Continuity and Change* and *Social Forces and Aging* (see Atchley, 1977 and 1991).

Section III:

Government, Politics, and Law

7

Government and the Aging Network

- Historical Overview of Aging Legislation ● The Older Americans Act of 1965
- Older Americans Act Amendments: 1967–92 ● Administrative Leadership
- State and Community Programs on Aging: Title III ● Volunteer Programs Through the Aging Network
- Legislative Process as It Relates to Aging Policy ● Role of National Aging Interest Groups
- Leadership Council of Aging Organizations
- National Association of State Units on Aging Membership Directory

The 1965 Older Americans Act (OAA) was the most important piece of legislation affecting older adults and their families in U.S. history. But the act, like all policy development, had historical precedents and was part of a dynamic process. Its passage was the result of people interacting with policy and decision makers in and out of government. Aging policy was developed in an arena filled with many pressures as individuals and groups worked to find the resources to fulfill the expectations for the elderly in American society.

The number and percentage of elderly in the United States have risen dramatically since the turn of the century. In 1900, only 2.9 percent of the population was 65 and older. By the 1920s, that percentage had increased to 7.5 percent. By 1960, the percentage 65 and over had grown to 11 percent. But it was not only the numerical increase that brought about the aging legislation of the 1960s and subsequent decades, but new ideas about later life also were emerging. To understand how the network of aging services and organizations came about, it is helpful to begin with a brief historical overview of aging legislation in the United States.

● HISTORICAL OVERVIEW OF AGING LEGISLATION

Concern about the economic and social conditions of the elderly began to surface in the aftermath of the United States' participation in World War I. A small number of social activists and government leaders contended that conditions prevailing in the country were rapidly making the plight of the older people more visible and acute (Achenbaum, 1978). Not surprisingly, some of the first actions to deal with the economic difficulties following retirement came through federal and state government legislation.

Civil Service Retirement Act

The Civil Service Retirement Act of 1920 was an early example of government's increased role in recognizing and working to alleviate the economic burden of older Americans. The act established retirement benefits for the first time for federal employees. It provided pensions for workers over age 70 who had fifteen years of service; in fact, different retirement criteria were established for several categories of workers. (Smith, 1928) Even earlier in the century some major city governments had established pensions for firemen and police. In at least thirty-three states retirement provisions had been enacted for elementary and secondary school teachers (Achenbaum, 1986).

Social Security Act

The Social Security Act of 1935 was landmark federal legislation recognizing the economic needs of older Americans. Through Social Security President Franklin Roosevelt and the Congress sought to provide a supplemental income base for the elderly in retirement. President Roosevelt called it "a law that will take care of human needs and at the same time provide for the United States an economic structure of vastly greater soundness" (Bowen, 1968).

Title I of the Social Security Act provided federal dollars to each state, which, in turn, with state criteria and benefit levels, furnished financial assistance to its elderly citizens. Title II of the act established a one-percent tax on employees' wages (up to $3,000) and on employers (contribution-based social insurance). At the inception of the act only 60 percent of the workers were covered, leaving uncovered the poorest of the work force. The Social Security Act has been amended a number of times, beginning in 1939. It was not until the 1962 amendments, however, that services for the elderly were provided in several titles of the act (Achenbaum, 1986).

Additional Activity

From the end of World War II to the 1960s a number of factors impacted the elderly: demographics, an improvement in retirement income, earlier retirement ages, and attempts to improve the general condition of the elderly (Atchley, 1985). A National Labor Relations Board (NLRB) ruling in 1948 was an example of the latter. That

---

The Social Security Act has been amended a number of times, beginning in 1939. It was not until the 1962 amendments, however, that services for the elderly were provided in several titles of the act.

---

ruling granted labor the right to bargain for employee benefit programs such as pensions (*Inland Steel Co. v. NLRB* [CA 7; 1948]).

States also began to look at the issue of elderly services. Connecticut established a State Commission on the Care and Treatment of the Chronically Ill, Aged, and Infirm in 1945. Other states such as Rhode Island, New Jersey, Minnesota, and Massachusetts soon followed with state-supported aging organizations. In 1950 the Truman Administration recognized the needs of the vulnerable elderly through the Federal Security Agency's sponsorship of the first National Conference on Aging. The recommendations of this Conference led to the establishment of the first Federal Committee on Aging and Geriatrics, housed in the Department of Health, Education, and Welfare (established in 1953 to replace the Federal Security Agency). The committee's primary responsibility was to bring to the nation's attention older Americans' need for social and health services (Ficke, 1985).

Development of the National Commitment

Momentum gathered in the 1950s for an aging "focal point." In 1956 President Dwight Eisenhower created the Federal Council on Aging to coordinate the aging activities of various government units (House Select Committee on Aging, August 1988). Also in that year Congressman John E. Fogarty (D-RI) introduced a bill calling for the first White House Conference on Aging (WHC). After state conferences were held around the country, the first White House Conference was convened by the Eisenhower administration in 1961 (Ficke, 1985).

In a period of great prosperity—the gross national product had more than doubled from 1945 to 1960—the White House Conference on Aging drew attention to the fact that in the midst of this prosperity "60 percent of older people . . . had incomes below, at, or very near the poverty level and [that] 80 percent of them had no income whatever apart from Social Security" (Atchley, 1985). Statistics were even worse for minority populations, especially African Americans. In addition to the economic situation, a key issue raised at the conference was health care. Upon the conference's conclusion, the Committee on Aging staff began work on resolutions that by 1965 would bring about Medicare legislation (to

Key Aging Network Legislation and Events

1920 Civil Service Retirement Act

1935 Social Security Act

1950 First National Conference on Aging

1956 Creation of the Federal Council on Aging

1961 First White House Conference on Aging

1965 The Older Americans Act, July 14, 1965. It established the Administration on Aging (AoA) within the Department of Health, Education, and Welfare (HEW) and created State Units on Aging (SUA)

1965 Medicare, Title XVIII, a health insurance program for the elderly, established as part of the Social Security Act

1965 Medicare, Title XIX, a health insurance program for low-income persons, added to the Social Security Act

1967 Older Americans Act extended for two years

1967 Age Discrimination Act

1969 Older Americans Act amendments. "National Older Americans Volunteer Program" authorizing the Foster Grandparent Program

1971 Second White House Conference on Aging

1972 "Nutrition Program for the Elderly Act"

1973 Older Americans Act comprehensive services amendments. Establishment of Area Agencies on Aging (AAA). Grants to local community agencies for multi-purpose senior centers and creation of the Community Service Employment grant program for low-income persons age 55 and older

1974 Older Americans Act minor amendments

1975 Older Americans Act amendments extended existing programs and establishment of four national priority services (transportation, home services, legal/other counseling services, and residential repair/renovation programs). Services to Native-American elders

1977 Older Americans Act amendments. Surplus commodities through the U.S. Department of Agriculture (USDA)

1978 Older Americans Act comprehensive amendments. Strengthen SUA and AAA advocacy through three distinct mandated priority services: access, in-home, legal. New title for grants to Indian tribes

1981 Third White House Conference on Aging. Older Americans Act amendments to give flexibility to programs

1984 Older Americans Act amendments. Programs to prevent elder abuse and for health and nutrition education programs. Supportive services to older persons with Alzheimer's disease and their families

1987 Older Americans Act amendments. Services for the frail elderly living at home; persons at risk of abuse, neglect, or exploitation; and low-income minority elderly. Elevation of Administration on Aging

1990 Age Discrimination in Employment Act

1992 Reauthorization of the Older Americans Act

improve health care) and the Older Americans Act (which would impact the quality of life).

In 1962 Senator Patrick McNamara (D-MI), chairman of the Senate Special Committee on Aging, and Congressman Fogarty each introduced bills to create a permanent and independent three-member federal Commission on Aging. However no action was taken on either bill until 1965. In fact, in 1962 160 bills affecting older people were introduced. Eight of them were enacted, covering areas such as rehabilitation, pension planning, and medical and dental care deductibility (Ficke, 1985).

Passage of the Older Americans Act

As pressure grew within the Congress for public policy that would eventually establish both the Medicare system and the Older Americans Act, two conflicting viewpoints concerning social services for the elderly manifested themselves. The first viewpoint was articulated by the traditional public welfare advocates who argued that "the *existing* system, if it were better *funded* [author's emphasis], was more than adequate to meet the needs of the elderly." The second viewpoint was that the aging population "could expect to receive the attention they deserved only if their needs and problems were treated separately from those of other population segments" (D. Quirk in Ficke, 1985).

Although the actual introduction and passage of the Older Americans Act brought little debate, the document was a compromise that recognized that while it is a public responsibility to alleviate the complex needs of the elderly, it is also essential for the "aging network" to reach out and be part of the larger human service systems.

On July 14, 1965, President Lyndon B. Johnson signed the Older Americans Act introduced by Congressman John Fogarty and Senator Patrick McNamara. The president's statement at the signing included the following expression of commitment: "[This Act] clearly affirms our nation's high sense of responsibility toward the well-being of older citizens. . . . Under this program, every state and every community can move toward a coordinated program of both services and opportunities for older citizens" (Ficke, 1985).

Medicare was also signed into law in 1965, thus recognizing older Americans' need for improved health services.

● THE OLDER AMERICANS ACT OF 1965

Written in the spirit of the Johnson administration's efforts to create the "Great Society," Title I of the Older Americans Act reflected a commitment and promise to all older Americans. This took the form of ten objectives for improving and maintaining the quality of life for older Americans:

- an adequate income in retirement in accordance with the American standard of living
- the best possible physical and mental health that science can make available, without regard to economic status
- suitable housing, independently selected, designed and located with reference to special needs and available at costs that older citizens can afford
- full restorative services for those who require institutional care
- opportunity for employment with no discriminatory personnel practices because of age
- retirement in health, honor, and dignity after years of contribution to the economy

Title I of the Older Americans Act promotes equal opportunity for participation in and contribution to society. (Copyright © Marianne Gontarz)

- pursuit of meaningful activity within the widest range of civic, cultural, and recreational opportunities
- efficient community services that provide social assistance in a coordinated manner and that are readily available when needed
- immediate benefit from proven research knowledge that can sustain and improve health and happiness
- freedom, independence and the free-exercise of individual initiative in planning and managing their own lives (Public Law [PL] 89–73)

Title II

Under Title II the Administration on Aging (AoA) was created as an agency in the Department of Health, Education, and Welfare (HEW). The AoA was to be headed by a commissioner, appointed by the president and confirmed by the Senate. The responsibilities of the agency included serving as a clearinghouse for information "related to the problems of the aged and aging," assisting the secretary in "all matters pertaining to the problems of the aged and aging," administering grants provided by the Act, and "stimulat[ing] more effective use of existing resources and available services" (PL 89–73).

Title III

Title III was the cornerstone of the Older Americans Act of 1965. Although amended many times since, its essence endures. The Title provided grants for community planning, services, and

The Older Americans Act of 1965 (As Amended 1992)

Title I Declaration of objectives: definitions
Title II Administration on Aging
Title III Grants for state and community programs on aging
    Part A - General provisions
    Part B - Supportive services and senior centers
    Part C - Nutrition services
        Subpart 1 - Congregate nutrition services
        Subpart 2 - Home-delivered nutrition services
        Subpart 3 - School-based meals for volunteer older individuals and multigenerational programs
        Subpart 4 - General provisions
    Part D - In-home services for frail older individuals
    Part E - Additional assistance for special needs of older individuals
    Part F - Preventive health services
    Part G - Supportive activities for caregivers who provide in-home services to frail older individuals
Title IV Training, research, and discretionary projects and programs
    Part A - Education and training
    Part B - Research, demonstrations and other activities

    Part C - General provisions
Title V Older Americans community service employment program
Title VI Grants for Native Americans
    Part A - Indian program
    Part B - Native Hawaiian program
    Part C - General provisions
Title VII Vulnerable elder rights protection activities
    Part A - State provisions
        Subpart 1 - General state provisions
        Subpart 2 - Ombudsman programs
        Subpart 3 - Programs for prevention of elder abuse, neglect, and exploitation
        Subpart 4 - State elder rights and legal assistance development program
        Subpart 5 - Outreach, counseling, and assistance program
    Part B - Native-American organization provisions
    Part C - General provisions
Title VIII Amendments to other laws: related matters
    Part A - Long-term care workers
    Part B - National school lunch act
    Part C - Native-American programs
    Part D - White House Conference on Aging
Title IX General provisions

training. To qualify for state formula grants, each state was required to designate a single State Unit on Aging (SUA) and to write a plan for developing and implementing a statewide aging program. Grants were for three years and required state cost sharing. The State Units on Aging were given principal responsibility for administering the state plan (PL 89–73).

Title IV

Title IV provided for discretionary grants (through the secretary of the Department of Health, Education, and Welfare) to address issues of national concern about the aged and aging. Grants were made to public and private nonprofit organizations.

Title V

This title provided grants for training and academic curricula to aid people employed or preparing to work in the field of aging. These grants, too, were made to public and private nonprofit organizations.

Title VI

Title VI was a general title that discussed the advisory committees, as well as administration and authorization levels for Titles IV and V (PL 89–73).

The Older Americans Act of 1965 provided for the first time a legislative basis by which older citizens shared the benefits of American society through services.

● **OLDER AMERICANS ACT AMENDMENTS: 1967–92**

The Older Americans Act of 1965 has been amended thirteen times since its original adoption—including the 1991–92 amendments.

1967 Amendments

The original OAA authorization was for two years. In 1967 Congress overwhelmingly supported an additional two-year authorization with a few minor amendments. Authorized funds for Title III (state grant programs), Title IV (discretionary grants), and Title V (training grants) were slightly increased. The Commissioner on Aging was required to assess the needs, present and future, for qualified aging services personnel (Ficke, 1985).

1969 Amendments

The 1969 Amendments created a new Title VI called the "National Older Americans Volunteer Program," authorizing the Foster Grandparent Program. (Authority was later repealed and reauthorized under the Domestic Volunteer Service Act of 1973.) The rest of the 1969 amendments assisted state units to coordinate a social service system more effectively. New language gave state units the authority for "statewide planning, coordination and evaluation of programs and activities related to the purposes of the Act." Minimum state administration and planning funds were increased and a new area-wide model project initiative was created (Ficke, 1985).

The White House Conference of 1971

The second White House Conference on Aging in 1971 called for increased services within the OAA "to meet definite and identifiable nutritional needs of the elderly." President Richard Nixon supported the conference position and in March 1972 signed the "Nutrition Program for the Elderly Act," authorizing $100 million for a national elderly nutritional services program. Nutritional demonstration projects had first been funded under OAA in 1968. The 1972 Act specified that greatest priority be given to those in greatest need of nutrition and social services. State units were assigned as the principal organizations responsible for program administration (O'Shaughnessy, January 19, 1990).

1973 Amendments

The 1973 amendments were comprehensive, greatly expanding the scope of the Older Americans Act.

The concept of regional planning and service

In 1971, the second White House Conference on Aging led to expanding the scope of the Older Americans Act—for example, establishment of the "Nutrition Program of the Elderly Act." (Courtesy of the American Association of Retired Persons)

areas (PSAs) administered by Area Agencies on Aging (AAA) reflected President Nixon's "New Federalism," more control to local governments within states. Under an enlarged Title III, State Units were required to divide their states into PSAs and designate AAAs to be responsible for "planning, coordinating, developing, and pooling resources to assure the availability and provision of a comprehensive range of services at the substate level. At the same time, greater emphasis was placed on state units' planning and administration responsibility (Ficke, 1985).

Congress in its 1973 reauthorization provided appropriations for the 1972 nutrition program, granting up to 90 percent of the funding needed to establish and operate the numerous nutrition projects. The goal for congregate nutrition programs went beyond the meal provided. Programs were to "foster social interaction," "facilitate social service delivery," and "provide health promotion" along with a range of supportive services (O'Shaughnessy, January 19, 1990).

Regulations promulgated after the 1973 reauthorization clarified what types of services were to be provided in addition to congregate meals: transportation, information and referral (I & R), health and welfare counseling, nutrition education, shopping assistance, and recreation (Ficke, 1985).

The Older American Community Service Employment Act, Title IX (modeled after an earlier program in the Economic Opportunity Act) converted older workers pilot projects into a permanent OAA program. Funding was provided through the U.S. Department of Labor for low income, unemployed persons, 55 and older, to qualify for job retraining through positions in community service organizations.

The 1973 amendments included grants for model projects, senior centers, and multidisciplinary centers of gerontology. Discretionary grant subject areas were: housing, continuing education, pre-retirement education, and services for handicapped elders.

Title IV was expanded to create demonstration projects to meet the transportation needs of elderly Americans. As in 1967, the commissioner was directed to assess aging services personnel needs (Ficke, 1985).

1974 Amendments

The 1974 amendments were minor. A special transportation program in Title III was added, though no appropriation was ever made and the nutrition program was extended for three years.

1975 Amendments

The 1975 amendments recognized for the first time that Native-American elders were not receiving adequate services and authorized the Commissioner on Aging to fund directly a proportionate sum of a state's allotment to tribal organizations if it were determined Indian tribe members "were not receiving benefits equivalent to the older persons in their state or area."

Priority services were mandated for the first time. Both state and area agencies were to develop programs in:

1. transportation
2. home services (e.g., homemaker, home health, shopping escort, reader, letter writing)
3. legal, tax, and financial aid
4. residential repair and renovation

Reauthorization language that encouraged coordination of transportation services was official recognition that such services were fragmented and difficult for the elderly to utilize.

Added to 1975 priorities were model projects for ombudsman services for nursing home residents, services or programs to meet the needs of those "not receiving adequate services" from OAA and "ambulatory day-care services to assist in the maintenance of independent living."

Training grants were expanded to include training programs of less than a year in duration and at a post-secondary education level. Training was expanded as well to lawyers, paralegals, and to personnel in aging administration and service delivery (Ficke, 1985).

1977 Amendments

Under the 1977 amendments nutrition projects could take advantage of the surplus commodities program of the U.S. Department of Agriculture.

1978 Amendments

The emphasis of the 1978 major changes was coordination. Before this time Titles III, V, and VII separately provided grants to social services, senior centers, and nutrition, but now were consolidated into a single Title III grant program. Each state still received four allocations: administration and social services (Part B) and congregate and home-delivered meals (Part C). The intent was to improve state and area agencies' coordination (House Select Committee on Aging, August 1988).

Significant amendatory language required the U.S. commissioner, state units, and area agencies to serve as "visible advocates for the elderly." This language strengthened the original intent of the Older Americans Act. In addition, state units were mandated to provide state-wide ombudsman services (from their Title III-B funds).

An amendment that expanded the discretionary grants programs was also of importance. Areas for possible funding included: long-term care, legal services, national projects for expanding service delivery, and energy assistance demonstrations.

Mandated priority services were separated into

three distinct categories: 1) access services (transportation, outreach, information, and referral); 2) in-home services (homemaker, home health aid, visiting, telephone reassurance, and chore maintenance); and 3) legal services.

At least 50 percent of Area Agencies on Aging III-B funds were to be allocated to these services with some dollars in each category. AAAs were required to "assure" that preference be given to older persons in "greatest economic or social need" (Ficke, 1985).

The Older Americans Community Service Employment Program was changed from Title IX to Title V (where it remains today).

Of great importance was the creation of a new Title VI. The new title provided separate fund authorization and programs for Indian tribal organizations. Grants were to be awarded directly by AoA to tribal organizations for the provision of nutrition and social services to Native Americans 60 years and older (House Select Committee on Aging, August 1988).

1981 Amendments

Flexibility described the 1981 amendments. According to the late Senator John Heinz (R-PA), Congress's intent was to "streamline and improve the efficiency of programs, increase flexibility to meet local needs, and increase the participation of older persons in the operation of programs intended to serve them."

Flexibility meant the elimination of the 50 percent spending requirement for Title III priority services. (Required instead was an "adequate proportion.") State units and area agencies were permitted planning cycles ranging from two to four years. Indian tribal organizations also were provided increased flexibility in the administration of their Title VI grants. Finally, the Title IV discretionary grants program was consolidated (Parts A through E) in order to make that program more flexible (Ficke, 1985).

White House Conference of 1981

The theme of the 1981 White House Conference on Aging was "The Aging Society: Challenge and Opportunities." The Leadership Council of Aging Organizations played a major advocacy role during and after the conference.

The messages from the conference were:

A 1978 amendment to the Older Americans Act established a separate fund authorization and programs for Native-American tribal organizations. (Copyright © Isabel Egglin)

"don't cut Social Security," "expand community options," and "reinstate the cuts to human services" (*Aging Alert*, December 15, 1981). The conference brought immediate impact on reauthorization of the Older Americans Act. President Ronald Reagan did establish a special bipartisan National Commission on Social Security Reform to develop a rescue plan for the Social Security system. The commission's plan was signed into law in 1983 (Jehle, 1987).

1984 Amendments

The 1984 amendments continued the flexibility of the 1981 amendments. Within Title III transfer authority between B and C increased from 25 percent to 29 percent, giving greater flexibility to the AAAs in the administration of regional supportive services and nutrition programs.

The amendments also provided a new Title VII, the Older Americans Personal Health Education and Training Program (Title VII was never funded by Congress). Alzheimer's disease services were added to the list of possible demonstration projects for the first time. Minor changes were made at the federal level in modifying the appointment procedures for the Federal Council on Aging as well as adding responsibilities for the Administration on Aging (House Select Committee on Aging, August 1988).

Language in the 1984 Conference Report on Reauthorization was significant to the issue of the voluntary nature of the Older Americans Act programs: "Any method which has as its motive transformation of the contribution from voluntary to involuntary is totally violative of the intent of

Congress, as reflected in this legislation" (House Select Committee on Aging, August 1988).

1987 Amendments

The 1987 amendments were both a reaffirmation of the act and recognition of special group needs. The language of Title II required that the commissioner be directly responsible to the secretary, elevating the commissioner to the same level of authority as other assistant secretaries.

The 1987 language established for the first time an office for American Indian, Alaska Native, and Native Hawaiian programs, along with a permanent task force. Additional service dollars were made available to individual Native Americans by the removal of previous prohibition for an individual to receive both Title III and Title IV funds.

The reauthorization recognized the needs of vulnerable community-based elderly, either because of frailty or by reason of abuse, neglect, or exploitation. Institutional elderly needs were positively impacted by the expansion of the ombudsman programs.

State units, area agencies, and service providers were required to identify persons with greatest economic or special need, particularly low-income minority older persons. Once they were identified, methods to provide targeted services were required. Congressional intent remained that services under Title III were to be available to *all* older persons with no income restrictions. At the same time Congress emphasized that services must be focused on those with special needs because of income, racial, ethnic status, or "social need for services offered" (Select Committee, August 1988).

Flexibility increased for funds spent on Title III, B and C with the percentage allowable being raised to 30 percent. USDA was modified. Long-term care became a mandatory area for Title IV-funded gerontology centers. Title VII, never funded, was deleted. Finally, the 1987 reauthorized Older Americans Act called for a White House Conference on Aging to be held in 1991.

1991/1992 Reauthorization Process

The issue of mandatory cost sharing for Title III programs was raised again in the 1991 reauthorization process. State units and area agencies advocated mandatory contributions for certain services and under certain conditions. The Bush administration proposed that states have the flexibility to require or permit fee for service. (Forty states have mandatory/volunteer cost sharing under state supported services.) The General Accounting Office (GAO) report also concluded that Congress should consider amending the OAA to permit state units and area agencies to establish charges for in-home care. There were, however, a number of advocates in opposition to a means-tested program, arguing that such charges did not reflect the original legislative intent for the Older Americans Act nor its intent when area agencies on aging were created in 1973. Congress reiterated its opposition to mandatory cost sharing (O'Shaughnessy, November 27, 1991).

Both the House and the Senate bills had provisions to strengthen targeting to low income older minority persons, and the bills required better Administration on Aging data collection. Although a 1989 Administration on Aging report stated that "participation rates have remained stable over time (for low income minority elders)," both the American Association for Retired Persons (AARP) and the GAO criticized the accuracy of the data (O'Shaughnessy, November 27, 1991).

Two recent court cases, *Meek v. Martinez* in Florida and *Appalachian Agency for Senior Citizens v. Ferguson* in Virginia, raised the issue of the role the intrastate formula plays in the targeting of services to those in greatest economic or social need. A GAO report indicated that if Congress wanted AoA to be more directly involved in each state's intrastate funding formula, it needed to amend OAA language. Both House and Senate vehicles required the commissioner to approve each state's intrastate formula, which had to take into account the geographic distribution of older people, "individuals with greatest economic and special need, with particular attention to low-income minority older persons" (O'Shaughnessy, November 27, 1991).

The recent variety of arrangements that state units and area agencies have with for-profit corporations, particularly "workplace elder-care programs," drew a lot of attention. Concern had been raised by some as to the impact such relationship would have on the public mission of Title III agencies. On the other hand, some asked for even more flexibility. In 1990 AoA commissioner Joyce

Berry had instructed state units to develop guidelines. Both House and Senate amendments required Title III agencies to disclose the nature of their relationship with for-profit corporations and assure such activities are consistent with the "public purpose mission" of the Act. The House bill went further and prohibited Title III fund use to subsidize "contractual arrangements that do not implement the Title III program" (O'Shaughnessy, November 27, 1991).

The long-term care ombudsman, services to prevent abuse, neglect, or exploitation of older individuals, and legal assistance are all programs that protect the rights and independence of older people. All these services were funded through Title III grants. The Title III program to provide outreach to those who might be eligible for Medicaid, Food Stamps, or SSI had not been funded.

The Senate's reauthorization bill created a new Title VII and placed under that title all programs that protect the rights of the elderly. The House version strengthened the ombudsman program but retained all programs within Title III. Both proposals created an office for the ombudsman program in AoA, a National Ombudsman Resource Center, and a National Center on Elder Abuse (O'Shaughnessy, November 27, 1991).

The nutrition issue related to the transfer of funds between Title III Part B and C, nutrition and supportive services. The transfer allowance had been 30 percent. The House bill would have decreased the transfer amount from 30 percent to 25 percent in Fiscal Year (FY) 1993 and to 20 percent in FY 1995. The Senate version would not have changed the past policy (O'Shaughnessy, November 27, 1991).

A perpetual issue for the Congress and aging network has been status of the Aging commissioner within the Department of Health and Human Services (HHS). The 1987 amendments required the commissioner to report directly to the secretary of the Department of HHS. Nonetheless, as a result of reorganization within the department, the commissioner had been reporting to the secretary only on "policy matters" and received "administrative and logistics services" from the Office of the Secretary. The House bill required that AoA be under the direct authority and supervision of the secretary and report directly to the secretary on all matters relating to

the Act. In addition, language in the House version guaranteed appropriate staffing levels for AoA (O'Shaughnessy, November 27, 1991).

Language in both Senate and House bills contained provisions to assure that Indian tribal organizations were as fairly funded as Native Hawaiian organizations (O'Shaughnessy, November 27, 1991).

In September 1992, Senator John McCain (R-AZ) withdrew the Older Americans' Freedom to Work Act (S. 194), an amendment to the Older Americans Act reauthorization that repealed the Social Security earnings test for retired persons. The other roadblock for the OAA had been Senator Connie Mack's (R-FL) proposal for the Administration on Aging to use annually updated Census Bureau data to allocate state funds. His proposal was included in the final bill. On September 15, 1992, the Senate unanimously passed S. 3008, the Old Americans Act reauthorization. The House concurred unanimously on September 22. President George Bush signed the $1.7 billion reauthorization bill on September 30, 1992 (PL 102–375).

1991/1992 Amendments

Here are the many highlights of the 1991/1992 amendments to the Older Americans Act.

- Strengthened language on targeting services to those with "greatest economic need and individuals with the greatest social need . . . particular attention to low-income minority individuals." Outreach efforts are to include other specified vulnerable populations like frail, rural, non-English speaking. Technical assistance to be provided to minority service providers. An advisory group to facilitate increased access of Native Americans to Title III programs.
- Required the state units to develop the state formula "in consultation with AAA's and in accordance with the Commissioner's guidelines." The formula must take into account individuals 60+ within the state and individuals "with the greatest economic need . . . with particular attention to the low-income minority individuals. The SUA must submit its formula to the Commissioner for approval." If the

commissioner disapproves the formula, the state's allotment will be withheld.

- Commissioner is to monitor state compliance with a prohibition on conflicts of interest, requiring area agencies "to disclose . . . information regarding public/private partnerships."
- State plans will make assurances that AAAs will not give preference to individuals as a result of contract or commercial relationships not related to Title III.
- Specification that AAAs should provide case-management offered through nonprofit organizations, not "non-public" agencies.
- Creation of a new Title VII: Vulnerable Elder Rights Protection Activities which consolidates and expands "state responsibility for the development, coordination and management of statewide programs and services . . . ensuring that older individuals have access to, and assistance in securing and maintaining, benefits and rights." Title VII will expand state responsibility to assist in the utilization of public benefit programs and services, "protection from abuse, neglect and exploitation" and require states to provide "programs and systems of individual representation, advocacy, protection, counseling and assistance from older individuals." The ombudsman program is placed in Title VII (with an associate commissioner for ombudsman services heading an office of Long Term Care Ombudsman). A National Center on Elder Abuse is also in Title VII.
- Limitation of the transfer of funds between nutrition and supportive services. For FY 1993 a 30 percent cap between Title III B and III C. Reduction to 25 percent in FY 1994 and to 20 percent in FY 1996. A waiver request is permitted. Limitation of funds transfer between Title III C 1 and 2 (congregate and home-delivered meals) to 30 percent with a waiver request permitted.
- Clarification of the commissioner's status within the HHS by describing the role as "assisting the Secretary (HHS) *directly* in aging matters" [author's emphasis].
- Reemphasis of the coordination of services

between Title III and Title VI (Indian Tribal and Native Hawaiian organizations). Stipulation that all FY 1991 Title VI grantees must be funded at FY 1991 levels before funding new Title VI grantees. (does not preclude participation of new tribal organizations).

Some additional amendments included:

- Amendment of the Title I objectives to include "support to family members and others who provide voluntary long-term care services"
- Establishment of a National Aging Information Center to "annually compile, publish and disseminate data regarding older individuals"
- Establishment of state mechanisms to "ensure quality in the provision of in-home services"
- Availability of an advance of up to 75 percent of a state's total disaster relief reimbursement within five working days of request
- Permission for State Units to withhold AAAs funds with the establishment of due process procedure
- Continuation of the waiver procedure for those AAAs requesting direct provision of services
- Increased emphasis on the importance of dietary issues
- Increased per-meal USDA rate reimbursement to .61 with future increase tied to the Consumer Price Index (CPI)
- Permission for rural areas to serve fewer than five meals a week
- Establishment of a new nutrition program: "school based meals for volunteer older individuals and multigenerational programs"
- Priority to certain legal problems, including age discrimination
- Requirement for states to designate a state legal assistance developer
- Provision for a state volunteer coordinator if more than half of the AAAs have area volunteer coordinators
- Addition of possible supportive services: information and assistance, language

Older Americans Act and Amendments

PL 89–73	Older Americans Act of 1965, July 14, 1965
PL 90–42	Older Americans Act Amendments of 1967, July 1, 1967
PL 91–69	Older Americans Act Amendments of 1969, September 17, 1969
PL 92–258	Nutrition Program for the Elderly Act, March 22, 1972
PL 93–29	Older Americans Act Comprehensive Services Amendments of 1973, May 3, 1973
PL 93–351	Amendments to the Nutrition Program for the Elderly Act, July 12, 1974
PL 94–135	Older Americans Act Amendments of 1975, November 28, 1975
PL 95–65	Older Americans Act Amendments of 1977, July 11, 1977
PL 95–478	Comprehensive Older Americans Act Amendments of 1978, October 18, 1978
PL 97–115	Older Americans Act Amendments of 1981, December 29, 1981
PL 98–459	Older Americans Act Amendments of 1984, October 9, 1984
PL 100–175	Older Americans Act Amendments of 1987, November 29, 1987
PL 102–375	Older Americans Act Amendments of 1992, September 30, 1992

translation, housing advice, information on elder rights, planning for adults with "adult children with disabilities," second career counseling, guardianship, representative payee support, multigenerational activities

- Some of the areas that training, research, and discretionary projects and programs will focus on: training and attracting minority personnel, demonstration projects in multigenerational services, caregivers of disabled adult children, music, art and dance therapy, volunteer service credit programs, ombudsman and advocacy, housing, neighborhood senior care, information and assistance systems, career preparation, private resource enhance-

ment projects (*Congressional Report,* September 15, 1992)

● ADMINISTRATIVE LEADERSHIP

U.S. Commissioners on Aging

The Administration on Aging, housed in the office of the secretary of the Department of Health and Human Services, is headed by a commissioner on aging appointed by the president. The leadership direction and skills of the commissioner can and should have a major impact on the aging network. The commissioner works to establish priorities and develop systems through which services are delivered. The commissioner's ability to work within and outside the executive and legislative branches of government are key to the success or failure to establish priorities and reach committed goals.

The first Aging commissioner, appointed by President Johnson, was William D. Bechill. Prior to his appointment Bechill worked as both a public administrator and a university professor. His major challenge while in office was the establishment of the State Units on Aging as well as the development of new program systems for older people.

John Martin was appointed by President Nixon. His previous experience had been in state level administrative and elective offices. Like his predecessor, Martin worked on "the vertical development of the aging network," enlarging the capacity of grass roots organizations. During Martin's tenure the national aging advocacy organizations began to grow in number and strength (Ficke, 1985).

U.S. Commissioners on Aging

1965–69	William D. Bechill
1969–73	John B. Martin
1973–78	Arthur S. Flemming
1978–81	Robert C. Benedict
1981–84	Lennie-Marie P. Tolliver
1984–89	Carol Fraser Fisk
1989–93	Joyce T. Berry
1993–	Fernando M. Torres-Gil

In 1973 President Nixon appointed the third Aging commissioner, Arthur S. Flemming. Flemming had previously served as secretary of Health, Education, and Welfare, in 1971 was director of the White House Conference on Aging, and had numerous other achievements. Susan Ficke observed that Flemming's "high energy level, commanding and expansive personality, and penchant for involvement all served to propel him and AoA into many more advocacy activities than ... in the past" (1985).

As commissioner, Flemming's goal was to bring groups and individuals together to work on common goals. He was often successful.

Robert C. Benedict served as the fourth commissioner of aging during President Jimmy Carter's four years in the White House. Benedict had previously worked in state aging administration. In his tenure major changes were made in the Older Americans Act (1978 amendments). A top priority of his administration was the development of long-term care alternatives.

Commissioners Lennie-Marie P. Tolliver and Carol Fraser Fisk, appointed to serve under President Reagan, developed policy in a period of fewer government resources. Often this meant an even greater emphasis on the private, voluntary sector. Commissioner Joyce T. Berry, who began her career in the Administration on Aging under Arthur Flemming, was appointed by President Bush as acting commissioner in 1989 and commissioner in 1990. She, too, had to develop programs and policies for an aging society in an era of fewer resources. Her major initiative was the National Eldercare Campaign, a campaign targeted to reach and assist that group of elders at risk of losing their independence.

In 1993 President Bill Clinton appointed Fernando M. Torres-Gil as assistant secretary for aging. Torres-Gil brings Washington, D.C. legislative experience and academic experience from UCLA. He is the first Aging commissioner to hold the rank of assistant secretary.

Administrative Rulemaking

The Congress, through the passage and reauthorizations of the Older Americans Act, establishes its legislative intent. The Aging commissioner puts that intent into action through administrative rule making. Thus the commissioner plays a major role in how the act becomes a functioning public law.

Through Title II, Administration on Aging, the commissioner is given the authority to interpret, develop, and transmit policies and procedures. Specifically, in Title II Section 205 (c) and (d) the commissioner [through the secretary] must "issue and publish in the Federal Register proposed regulations for the administration of [the] Act." These regulations must be published within 120 days of enactment and after a reasonable period for public comment. "Not later than 90 days after such publication," final regulations are to be published. In addition, each fiscal year the commissioner makes public the "proposed specific goals to be achieved by the network."

Although the regulations do leave considerable flexibility to the state units and through them to the area agencies on aging, regulations clarify OAA direction and assure that grant programs adhere to the national objectives. Even though the OAA requires a specific timetable for the promulgation of rules, the process is often long and drawn out. On occasion the network functions with interim regulations rather than final regulations between reauthorization dates.

Individuals and groups who are concerned about the direction of the aging network must pay careful attention not just to the reauthorization of the Older Americans Act but also equal attention to the publication of the regulations that follow. Administrative regulations can direct the manner in which the act is fulfilled. Examples of this include the Internal Revenue Service's (IRS) regulations on lobbying which impacted the nonprofits within the network, the regulations for carrying out services to those in "greatest economic or social need" or the elimination of public hearing requirements replacing that requirement with "whatever methods . . . determine[d] appropriate" (Ficke, 1985).

● STATE AND COMMUNITY PROGRAMS ON AGING: TITLE III

Programs and Policies under Title III

While other titles provide for programs and policies, Title III remains the underlying subdivision of the Older Americans Act. What is significant for Title III, Grants for State and Community Programs on Aging, is its provision of the contin-

Figure 7.1
The National Aging Network

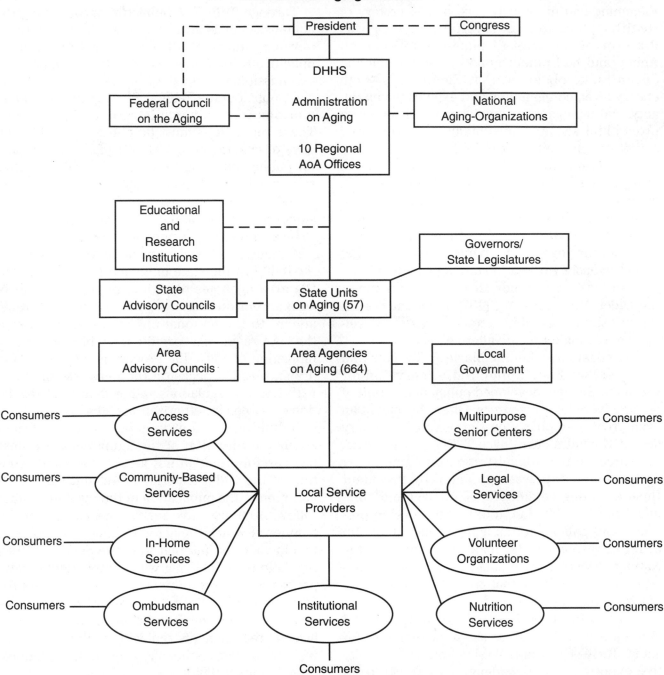

Source: National Association of State Units on Aging.

uum of community-based services supporting older individuals with dignity and with maximum possible independence. Title III provides the framework within which the Administration on Aging, the State Units on Aging, and Area Agencies on Aging work in a coordinated fashion to provide such services. Figure 7.1 shows how federal, state, local, and private agencies com-

prise what is called the "Aging Network." The flexibility of the act encourages both state units and area agencies to respond to the needs of their communities efficiently and effectively while carrying out specific grant programs (Ficke, 1985). The language states that state and area agencies are encouraged "to concentrate resources in order to develop greater capacity and foster the development and implementation of comprehensive and coordinated service systems to serve older individuals" (OAA Title III Sec. 301(a) PL 100–175).

Organizations That Implement the Programs and Policies of Title III

State Units on Aging (SUA)

A State Unit on Aging (SUA) is each governor's designated focal point for the state's elderly, their needs, and their programs. The responsibility of SUA is to keep older people in their own homes through supportive services. State units work to "remove individual and social barriers to economic and personal independence" and "provide a continuum of care for the vulnerable elderly." The vulnerable elderly include those in long-term care facilities. State units are to be effective and visible advocates for and with the elderly. They are to work cooperatively with area agencies and others in their state to provide aging network programs

Providing support services enabling older people to live in their homes has been a major emphasis of the Older Americans Act. (Copyright © Isabel Egglin)

> A State Unit on Aging (SUA) is each governor's designated focal point for the state's elderly, their needs, and their programs. The responsibility of SUA is to keep older people in their own homes through supportive services.

and service (OAA Title III Sec. 301(a)(2) and (3) PL 100–175).

Organization. A State Unit on Aging may have one of a variety of designations: office, board, bureau, commission, department. In many states it is an independent, single purpose agency. In many others it is housed in a multipurpose agency or department. In a few it is placed in the governor's office. In all cases the state unit must "be primarily responsible for the coordination of all state activities related to the purposes of this Act." (OAA Title III Sec. 305(a)(1)(c) PL 100–175).

Functions and Responsibilities. Since any state activity that affects an older person can in reality fall within a SUA's review, the functions that a state unit is expected to carry out often go beyond the resources it has to carry out those responsibilities.

Management and Administration. SUA is responsible for the efficient management of its office as well as for the correct and efficient operation of all other activities under the auspices of the Older Americans Act in its state. Its prime function is the development, expansion, and maintenance of a comprehensive service system. The state plan is the major tool for SUA in providing management and oversight. The state plan contains specific programmatic and financial commitments and reflects both citizens' input and area agencies' plans. SUA is responsible for dividing the state into planning and service areas (PSAs) and designating a public or private agency as the area agency. It must establish an intrastate funding formula (since 1978) for issuing grants (Ficke, 1985). The 1991–92 reauthorized language requires that state units develop this formula "in consultation with AAA's and in accordance with the commissioner's guidelines." The formula must take into account individuals 60+ within the state and individuals "with the greatest economic need … with particular attention to low income minority individuals. The SUA must submit its formula to the Commissioner for approval." If the commissioner disapproves the formula, the state's allotment will be withheld (*Congressional Record*, September 15, 1992).

Title III programs do not carry an income restriction for participation (this original legislative intent was reiterated in 1973, 1984, and 1987 [House Select Committee on Aging, August, 1988; O'Shaughnessy, November 27, 1991]). Within this context state units must provide assurances that they will require outreach efforts to identify and have assistance available to "older individuals with greatest economic need (with particular attention to low-income minority individuals), older individuals with greatest social need (with particular attention to low-income minority individuals), and older individuals who reside in rural areas" (OAA Title III Sec. 307(a)(24)(A) and(B) PL 100–175).

Assurances must also be provided "with respect to the needs of older individuals with severe disabilities" (OAA Title III Sec. 307(a)(25) PL 100–175).

Management activities vary from state to state, but much of SUA's management is accomplished through fiscal and program monitoring and review. The goal is to improve the overall system of delivering services to older persons by maximizing the use of federal and state grants, by making sure of consistency of federal, state, area, and local plans, and by assuring grantee/contractor compliance to rules and regulations. Review is accomplished either by paper (desk review) or by on-site visits. Such review may lead to corrective action or to technical assistance and training (Ficke, 1985).

With a multitude of service and nutrition providers and many area agencies, system building for the state unit means coordination and cooperation between state, area, and local agencies. SUAs and AAAs need to work together. The SUAs must build liaisons as well at both the state and federal levels. The relationship to the state governor's office is crucial.

Systems Development Including Services. The services that the state units look for the AAAs to develop, expand, and coordinate include:

Advocacy means building a more responsive service delivery system by persuading other agencies to change policies or funding decisions. (Copyright © Marianne Gontarz)

access services	transportation, information and referral case management
in-home services	home health homemaker home-delivered meals chore service respite case management personal care services
community services	day care/respite congregate meals continuing education
LTC facilities	ombudsman (specifics guiding this program are, in the 1991–92 provisions, now under Title VII, Vulnerable Elder Rights Protection Activities) case management case work placement or relocation assistance

The three mandated areas are access, in-home, and legal assistance.

The SUA looks for ways to maximize program continuity, improve the quality of service, build on the informal family network, and build on other systems in existence. In particular, over the last decade SUAs have been working to develop community-based long-term care systems within their states. Some of the tools utilized are statewide needs assessments and model projects, helping to identify needs and to research those programs that work best (Ficke, 1985).

Advocacy. Advocacy strategies are significant to the development of new service systems or the strengthening and expanding of present systems. Although strategies may vary from state to state, the key is total involvement of the elderly, individually, through formal advisory boards, and through informal coalitions.

The Older Americans Act became law in the spirit of empowerment of the 1960s. Today the language of the act emphasizes advocacy. Each state unit is to be an "effective and visible advocate for the elderly" (OAA Title III Sec. 305(a)(1)(D) PL 100–175). Advocacy activity may include budget development, seeking influence within the executive branch, working with the legislature, reviewing and commenting on all state plans that impact the elderly, seeking input from the elderly and those who work with the elderly, working to build coalitions, and expanding services and systems.

Advocacy also includes the training of other advocates, the elderly, or those who work with them. It includes communication, that is, sharing information with the network and aging coali-

tions (Ficke, 1985). Advocacy is an important challenge for every state unit on aging.

Area Agencies on Aging (AAA)

Organization. An Area Agency on Aging (AAA) is a public or private nonprofit agency or office that has been designated by the state unit to carry out the mandates of the Older Americans Act at the Planning and Service Area level (substate level). At this level the AAA is both an advocate for the elderly and responsible to work toward the development of a more comprehensive and coordinated service system for the elderly.

Most OAA services are funded through AAAs. Through AAAs these services are implemented, coordinated, and enlarged. The goals and timetables by which AAA will accomplish these challenges is established in their area plan.

Currently there are 664 Area Agencies on Aging in 44 of the 57 state jurisdictions. Thirteen states and U.S. territories function as single PSAs: Alaska, Delaware, District of Columbia, Nevada, New Hampshire, North Dakota, Rhode Island, South Dakota, Wyoming, American Samoa, Guam, Republic of Palau (formerly Trust Territory), and the Virgin Islands. In these circumstances the state unit functions as both state unit and area agency.

Area agencies are quite diverse. Their organizational structures may vary from a private nonprofit, to a section of city government, or a unit of county government. Some AAAs are a consortium of county governments or part of a community action agency. (There are other varieties not listed.) An area agency does not always use the name "area agency." No matter the appellation, such as "Senior Alliance," "Northwest Senior Resources," "San Francisco City/County Commission on Aging," or "Region VII Area Agency on Aging," each functions as an area agency on aging.

Management and Administration. In order to receive the Older Americans Act grants each AAA must prepare an area plan (two-, three-, or four-year cycle). Each plan "shall be based upon a uniform format for area plans within the state" (OAA Title III, Sec. 306(a) PL 100–175). Plan formats vary from state to state. Most plans contain:

Some 664 Area Agencies on Aging (AAA) have been designated to provide planning and services as well as advocacy for older adults at the local level. (Courtesy of the National Council on Aging, Inc.)

1. An agency organization that describes its organization and operating system, including assurances required under the act.

2. A program plan that establishes program priorities related to the ascertained needs of the elderly in the area. It lays out specific goals and timetables with units of service and numbers of elderly to be served. A program plan also includes future program development goals and timetables.

3. An advocacy plan that elaborates on advocacy strategies for the PSA. At minimum these strategies need to include the involvement of the AAA's advisory council.

4. A financial plan that lists AAA resources and the budget established to utilize these resources (Ficke, 1985).

Systems Development Including Services. The development, expansion, and coordination of services and service systems is the prime responsibility of area agencies on aging. Because there are never enough OAA funds allocated to AAAs, an area agency's success in developing services is often tied to that AAA's ability to bring additional resources to expand aging programs. Outside resources might be public, like local government funds or local tax dollars. They might be private resources from fundraisers, foundations, corporations, or volunteer workers.

In addition, the AAA needs to coordinate effectively with any services already offered. Coordination can be accomplished by training agency personnel, by organizing coordinating councils, or by becoming involved in joint planning endeavors. The OAA requires each AAA to designate (where feasible) a focal point in each community "for comprehensive service delivery—giving special consideration to designating multipurpose senior centers" (OAA Title III Sec. 306(a)(3) PL 100–175). Under the 1991–92 OAA reauthorization, focal points are to be specified in grants, contracts, and agreements (*Congressional Record,* September 15, 1992).

Currently, two areas receive a great deal of service system development: community-based long-term care and the needs and the rights of elders, community-based and institutionalized.

Area agencies must provide services in the three mandated priority areas: access, in-home, and legal (with maintenance of attorney/client privilege). Ombudsman services, now moved to Title VII,

must also be provided (*Congressional Record,* September 15, 1992). AAAs provide services for information and referral, outreach, education, transportation, congregate meals, home-delivered meals, employment, counseling, and senior centers (Ficke, 1985). The OAA also authorizes AAAs to provide services in:

Day care

Respite

Coordination with providers of veterans' health care

Coordination or service provision with entities involved in the prevention, identification, and treatment of the abuse, neglect, and exploitation of older individuals

Mental health services coordination

Outreach for older Indians (if significant population)

Provisions of information on institutions of higher education

Activities to identify elder individuals who are eligible for supplemental security income (SSI) benefits, Qualified Medical Benefits (QMB), and food stamps

In-home services for frail older individuals

Additional assistance for special needs of older individuals

Preventive health services

Source: OAA Title III Sec. 306 PL 100–175.

The 1991–92 reauthorized act allows AAAs to provide "an area volunteer services coordinator," requires "specific service objectives for minority targeting," requires "grievance procedures for individuals who are dissatisfied or denied service" (denial is legitimate if insufficient resources), specifies coordination between Title III and Title VI services, and specifies that case/management services may not be offered by "non-public" agencies (*Congressional Record,* September 15, 1992).

An AAA's decision as to which services are best suited to the needs of the elderly in its PSA is determined by public input forums, public hearings, task forces, and ad hoc study committees. Data from the census is utilized as well as formalized needs surveys.

Advocacy. Advocacy is crucial to an area agency's success or failure. Regionally an AAA represents older persons' views and needs. Advocacy means building a more responsive service delivery system by persuading other agencies to change policies or funding decisions. It includes representing elder interests at legislative hearings or in task forces. Advocacy is the development of a favorable public climate through public relations, through informing the larger public, and through informing public officials who make key policy decisions. It means building liaisons with these key decision makers.

Important in all advocacy is the training and empowerment of the elderly themselves so they can participate in the decisions that advance their dignity and maintain their independence through needed programs and services.

● VOLUNTEER PROGRAMS THROUGH THE AGING NETWORK

Title I of the Older Americans Act declares that one of its objectives is to assist older people to secure equal opportunity to the full and free enjoyment of "participating in and contributing to meaningful activity within the widest range of civic, cultural, educational, training, and recreational activities" (OAA Title I).

The Older Americans Act has opened new vistas and activities for senior volunteers. The three most significant national volunteer programs are the Foster Grandparents, Senior Companions, and Retired Senior Volunteers. Although each has a different legislative history, each provides volunteer service opportunities for older persons within their communities.

Foster Grandparents Program (FGP)

The oldest of the three programs is the Foster Grandparents Program (FGP), initiated in August 1965 as a national demonstration project. The demonstration (under the auspices of the Office of Economic Opportunity [OEO]) showed that low-income persons 60 years and older had "the maturity and experience to establish a personal relationship with children having either exceptional or special needs." Following the 1965 demonstration, an agreement between OEO and the Administration on Aging resulted in twenty-one funded Foster Grandparent programs. Foster Grandparents was originally an employment program.

Funding authority was transferred to AoA in 1969 through then-Title VI. At this time the Foster Grandparents Program became a "stipended" (receiving a minimal hourly stipend) volunteer program for low-income elderly (60+) serving special needs children up through 17 years of age.

In 1971 Foster Grandparents Program authority was transferred to a newly created federal agency, ACTION. The Domestic Volunteer Service Act (DVSA) of 1973 (PL 93–113) was ACTION's enabling legislation. (In addition to senior volunteer programs, ACTION houses the VISTA program [Volunteers in Service to America]. VISTA is a full-time "stipended" program, not limited to low-income individuals but targeted in service to low-income communities.) The 1976 amendments to DVSA raised the age of children from 17 to 21 years of age with the ability under certain circumstances to work with mentally retarded children beyond 21.

Currently the Foster Grandparents Program is administered by separate staff within the office of Older American Volunteer Programs (OAVP) within ACTION. The mission of FGP continues to be low-income elderly who contribute to their communities while enhancing their self-esteem and the self-esteem of the children whom they assist. These exceptional needs and special needs children can be in private institutions; in special public, private, and alternative schools; in correctional facilities; or be status offenders, neglected, or abused. The programs can work to prevent juvenile delinquency as well as work with parents of special needs children.

Exceptional needs include developmentally disabled (mentally retarded, autistic, cerebral palsy, epilepsy); visually handicapped; speech impaired; hearing impaired; orthopedically impaired; multi-handicapped, emotionally disturbed; language disorder; specific learning disability; and a significant health impairment. Special needs include abused or neglected; in need of foster care; status offenders; juvenile delinquents; runaway youth; certain teenage parents; and children in need of protective intervention in their home.

Since the end of the 1980s Foster Grandparent Programs may locally establish non-stipended Foster Grandparents if there is no Retired Senior Volunteer Program (RSVP) in the area (DVSA PL 102–73, July 25, 1991; *ACTION Handbook 4405.90*, January 1989).

Profiles of Productive Aging

Millicent Fenwick
Congresswoman

"Do justly. Love mercy. And walk with God. I believe that if you haven't got a God, you must walk with the evidence of truth. Submit yourself and your prejudices and your biases to the evidence of truth. To my mind that is the best prescription for life that I know."

Walter Cronkite called her "The Conscience of Congress." Morley Safer dubbed her "Thoroughly Modern Millicent." The Honorable Millicent Fenwick of New Jersey took her first seat in the U.S. House of Representatives at the age when most people retire.

Born in Bernardsville, New Jersey, in 1910 to a well-to-do family, Millicent Fenwick never intended to have a career. She married, had children, and planned to settle into domestic life. However, the Depression dried up the young family's income, and her marriage split apart. Forced to find work, she moved into New York City, but without a high school diploma, "they wouldn't even talk to me," Fenwick recalled. Even a job as a salesgirl in Bonwit Teller required a college degree.

She worked briefly as a model, and then a friend, who knew of her interest in writing, suggested that she apply for the position of associate editor at *Vogue* magazine. Fenwick landed her first job at age 28, was later made war editor, and remained at *Vogue* for fourteen years. She wrote *The Vogue Book of Etiquette*, a perennial best seller.

In 1952, Fenwick left *Vogue* and moved back to her home town. "I decided I was going to retire. I was 42. I had worked very hard for 14 years." But she was asked to serve on the Bernardsville Recreation Commission and soon became chairperson. Her first achievement was to get a swimming pool installed for the townspeople without using tax money; she raised it all through contributions.

Soon Fenwick became active in local and state party politics, serving in various roles until, at the age of 64, she ran for Congress from New Jersey's Fifth District and was elected to four consecutive terms. When her 1982 bid for a seat in the Senate failed, President Reagan offered her a post in Rome for the United Nations Agency for Food and Agriculture (FAO), which she held from August 1983 until March 1987.

When asked about aging in 1989, at age 79, Fenwick said she saw aging as a "highly individual" process. "I don't think you can prepare for old age," she explained. "Nobody has any idea what it's like. It's impossible to describe what it is like—each person's old age is a little different, the circumstances are different. The main thing is: Are you interested in something besides yourself?"

Fenwick died on September 16th, 1992, at her New Jersey home, after a short illness.

Lydia Brontë

Senior Companion Program (SCP)

Congressional interest in a Senior Companion kind of program originated in 1968. Although efforts to establish a program targeting services by and for older persons failed in the 1968 OAA reauthorization process, the Administration on Aging funded two Senior Companion demonstrations in Tampa, Florida, and Cincinnati, Ohio, from 1968 to 1971. No SCPs were funded from 1971 to 1974.

In early 1973 President Nixon asked Congress to authorize ACTION "to expand the role of low-income older volunteers to provide person-to-person service helping more older Americans . . . work with older persons."

By the end of 1973 the Domestic Volunteer Service Act was amended and eighteen model SCPs were funded by August the following year. Senior Companions serve institutional elderly; but from its beginning over 60 percent of the assignments were in private homes. Major expansion of the programs occurred in 1976–77. The end of the 1980s saw the development of a number of non-ACTION funded Senior Companion Programs and the development of local non-stipended Senior Companions (if no RSVP in the area). The Senior Companion Program is administered by a separate staff within the office of OAVP.

The SCP, like FGP's, is a stipended program for

low-income older persons. While enhancing their own self-esteem SC participants contribute to their communities, providing "supportive services to adults, especially older persons, in an effort to maintain independent living." In-home settings continue to dominate volunteer placement. Senior Companions work with both physically and mentally frail older persons. A number of recent projects have provided assistance to families of Alzheimer's victims (*ACTION Handbook 4405.91*, January 1989).

Retired Senior Volunteer Program (RSVP)

In 1965 the Community Service Society of New York developed a pilot project called SERVE (Serve and Enrich Retirement by Volunteer Experience). This Staten Island program involved a small group of older volunteers and demonstrated their value to community service. The project's success led to a 1969 OAA amendment establishing the Retired Senior Volunteer Program (RSVP).

RSVP began in 1971 with a $500,000 grant from the Administration on Aging. In July of that year, RSVP was transferred to ACTION and eleven projects were started. Today RSVP operates with separate staff within OAVP.

ACTION grants in 1972 and 1973 gave State Units on Aging RSVP resource specialists to assist the development of local RSVP projects. The early 1970s was the greatest period of growth. In the 1980s some non-ACTION local projects were developed.

RSVP "promotes the use of older persons as community resources in planning for community improvement and in delivery of volunteer services." Their goal is reached through a variety of opportunities both with the elderly and with the community as a whole. Locally controlled agencies manifest great diversity. Included are such programs as preschool substance-abuse education, work with the handicapped, home repairs, transportation, and visiting the home bound. Unlike the FGP and SCP, RSVP is a non-stipended volunteer program (*ACTION Handbook 4405.92*, January 1989).

The key to each of these programs is the older volunteer who, while manifesting the "inherent dignity of the individual in our democratic society" (OAA Title I), contributes to the quality of life for many individuals and for the entire local community.

● LEGISLATIVE PROCESS AS IT RELATES TO AGING POLICY

The role of Congress in the development of the Older Americans Act is significant to every older citizen. Congress works on issues of importance to the elderly at the same time it is faced with many other issues and crises. Thus congressional members are always mediating between conflicting interests. Since the 1980s they have also been faced with an ever-increasing federal deficit. Because congressional activity has such a significant impact on the lives of older Americans, it is important to understand that process.

The United States Congress

The Congress is composed of two houses, the Senate and the House of Representatives. The Senate has one hundred voting members, two from each state. Every two years one-third of the membership is up for election, a term being six years. Serving without a vote but with all other rights and privileges is one senator from the District of Columbia. The presiding officer of the Senate is the vice-president, who may vote in case of a tie.

The House of Representatives has 435 members with every seat being up for election every

Table 7.1
Fourteen Critical Points in the Legislative Process

- Bill filing
- Referral of bill to committee with specific jurisdiction and then to subcommittee
- Subcommittee hearings, deliberation, and mark-up
- Report out of subcommittee
- Referral back to full committee for consideration and amendment
- Report out of full committee
- Floor action and message to other house for concurrence
- Report out of committee(s) of other house
- Conference committee action between two houses to work out differences (if any)
- Report out of conference committee
- Final floor action
- Bill adoption and enrollment
- Action by president
- Publication

Source: Ficke, 1985.

two years. Although every state has at least one representative, the rest of the seats of the House are reapportioned by state after the census every ten years. Serving without a vote but with all other rights and privileges are representatives from Puerto Rico, American Samoa, the District of Columbia, Guam, and the Virgin Islands. The Speaker of the House is elected by the full House membership.

The primary responsibility of the Congress is to make laws and to adopt the budget originally presented by the president. Each house is of equal status. However, only the House may originate revenue bills. Only the Senate may give advice and consent to the president on nominations and international treaties. The Commissioner on Aging is an appointment needing Senate approval.

Each congressional session lasts two years. Each new session begins January 3 (unless another date is designated). All proceedings are published in the *Congressional Record*.

Because the federal legislative process is often complex and confusing (even to those who operate within the process), the "Fourteen Critical Points in the Legislative Process" listed below may assist advocates in understanding those points where input might be effective.

Input early in the process is often the most effective. For this reason, the activities and decisions of congressional committees and subcommittees are of great importance. The House has twenty-two standing (permanent) committees; the Senate, fifteen. Most committees are divided

into subcommittees to deal with complicated legislative issues. Congressional members tend to specialize in particular areas and rely a great deal on staff expertise and colleagues for information on other subjects.

Written and/or oral testimony before subcommittee hearings provides input opportunity for advocates. "Mark-up" takes place after hearings are completed. (The revised bill language may even become a new bill with a new number.)

The next step in the process is the committee vote on whether to vote the bill out favorably, unfavorably, or let it die without action. Committee reports contain both legislative intent and fiscal impact.

Once out of committee the entire body (House or Senate) debates and usually amends the bill. When all amendments are completed, the bill is put in final copy (engrossed) and put to final vote. Majority vote carries. A bill passed by one house is reported to the second chamber where the same procedure occurs. If the second chamber concurs with the first, it is signed first by the Speaker of the House, then by the president of the Senate, then the enrolled bill is sent to the president.

If there is disagreement between the two bodies a conference committee is appointed. A conference committee can deal only with the issues of disagreement. It can recommend that either house withdraw all or some of its amendments. It can advise an inability to reach agreement totally or in part. Both houses must agree on the conference committee report or the process begins

Table 7.2
Budget Process Timetable

January 3	Congress convenes
1st Monday in February	President submits budget
February 15	Congressional Budget Office (CBO) submits report to budget committees
February 25	Committees submit views and estimates
April 1	Senate Budget Committee reports concurrent resolution on the budget
April 15	Congress completes action on concurrent resolution on the budget
May 15	Annual appropriations bills may be considered in the House
June 10	House Appropriations Committee reports last annual appropriations bill
June 15	Congress completes action on reconciliation
June 30	House completes action on annual appropriations bill
October 1	Fiscal year begins

Sources: The Offices of U.S. senator Donald W. Riegle (D-MI) and U.S. congressman Dale E. Kildee (D-MI).

Table 7.3
Major Phases of the Federal Budget Process

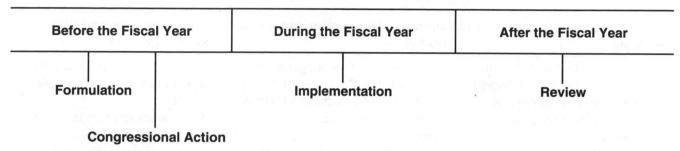

Before the Fiscal Year	During the Fiscal Year	After the Fiscal Year
Formulation	Implementation	Review

Congressional Action

Formulation of the President's Budget: The President submits his budget to Congress in early February, about eight months before the fiscal year starts on October 1. Budget guidelines are developed in the preceding spring, and agencies prepare their requests during the summer. In the fall, the President and the Office of Management and Budget (OMB) review the agency requests.

Congressional Action on the Budget: Congress adopts the budget resolution in the spring and then considers spending, revenue, and debt-limit legislation in the summer and fall (sometimes not completing action on important budgetary legislation until after the fiscal year has begun).

Implementation of the Budget: OMB apportions funds to agencies; agencies make allotments, obligate funds and conduct activities, and request supplemental appropriations; and the President proposes impoundments.

Review: Post-auditing and program evaluation occur and final budget data are made available.

Source: Congressional Research Service.

again. By law, the president has ten days (excepting Sunday) to sign or veto the enrolled bill, unless Congress is in adjournment. Then nonsignature is the same as a veto (known as a "pocket veto"). To overcome a presidential veto, a bill must receive a two-thirds majority vote in both houses.

Budget Process

Because any implemented policy must also be funded, the budget process is a major part of the legislative process. The federal budget is both a basic economic and policy document. Decisions made on funding priorities are essentially policy decisions. In a number of reauthorizations of the Older Americans Act, for example, new programs have been introduced, yet are never implemented because they fail to receive funding.

Appropriations legislation grants actual dollar amounts. The amount is often below what has been *authorized*. For example, in 1991 the authorization level for the OAA was $1,749,550 billion. The appropriated amount was $1,333,924 billion (O'Shaughnessy, November 27, 1991).

The congressional budget process has three distinct parts:

1. Budget resolution, also called the "congressional budget process"

2. Passage of the annual appropriations bills

3. Passage of other legislation that has impact on the federal budget, such as, authorizing legislation, reconciliation bills, or other measures that change tax law or entitlement programs (Schick, December 24, 1991)

The Older Americans Act is authorizing legislation. Its language establishes programs and places the upper limit on the amount of funds that can be obligated in a given fiscal year. It does not, however, operate as an appropriations bill.

The president submits his budget to Congress by early February. Then the Congress, working through appropriations and budget committees, adopts a budget resolution. This document (to be adopted by April 15) serves as a guideline for subsequent action on budget-related measurers. Parallel House and Senate appropriations subcommittees recommend spending levels to their full committees and hold budget hearings from February through June. When Congress fails to enact all regular appropriations bills by the start of the new fiscal year (October 1) it can provide interim funding in "continuing resolutions." These

Table 7.4
Principal Budgetary Functions of the Executive Branch

President	Office of Management and Budget	Federal Agencies
Establishes executive budget policy and submits budget to Congress.	Operates executive budget system and advises President on issues.	Submit budget requests to OMB; appeal to President for more funds.
Submits supplemental requests, budget amendments, and updates to Congress.	Issues planning targets and budget "marks" to agencies.	Justify President's budget recommendations before congressional committees.
Signs (or vetoes) revenue, appropriations, and other budget-related measures passed by Congress.	Prepares budget options and recommendations for President.	Request apportionment from OMB and allot funds among subunits.
Notifies Congress of proposed rescissions and deferrals.	Issues sequestration reports under the Gramm-Rudman-Hollings Act.	Maintain accounting systems and systems of internal control.
Issues sequestration orders to cancel budgetary resources.	Reviews proposed legislation and testimony to determine whether it conforms to the President's budget.	Obligate funds and pre-audit expenditures.
	Appropriations funds and oversees execution of the budget.	Carry out the activities for which funds were provided.
	Conducts management activities to improve efficiency of federal expenditures.	

Source: Congressional Research Service.

can provide appropriations from a few months to a full fiscal year. The budget, passed by the Congress and signed by the president, is implemented by federal agencies once the Office of Management and Budget (OMB) apportions the appropriated funds.

The final phase of the budget process is review

The 102nd Congress House Select Committee on Aging focused particular attention on the special needs of the vulnerable, low income, frail and ethnic/racial minority elderly. Courtesy of The National Council on the Aging, Inc.)

and audit. The standards for review and audit are established by the General Accounting Office (GAO).

Congressional Committees on Aging

The Senate has a special committee to oversee and study matters pertaining to older people. Since 1993 that responsibility in the House has been given to an Older Americans Caucus.

Although these committees/caucuses do not deal with specific legislation, they do serve as focal points for aging issues and can have great influence within Congress on aging policy.

A review of the first session of the 102d Congress House Select Committee on Aging activities will give an idea of the kinds of issues covered. The full committee looked at issues relating to health, employment, Social Security, housing, and human services.

Health. Health issues included national health plan legislation; Alzheimer's legislation; federal budget cuts; the Gramm-Rudman-Hollings Act and subsequent budget process changes; the rising Medicare Part B premium; out-of-pocket health care costs for the elderly and nonelderly; the financial risk of long-term care; long-term

Table 7.5
Principal Budgetary Functions of Congressional Committees

Authorizing Committees	Appropriations Committees	Revenue Committees	Budget Committees
Report authorizing and entitlement legislation.	Report regular and supplemental appropriations bills.	Report revenue legislation.	Report budget resolutions.
Oversee executive agencies.	Review proposed rescissions and deferrals.	Report legislation on public debt, Social Security, and certain other entitlement.	Draft reconciliation instructions and compile reconciliation bills.
Submit views and estimates to budget committees on matters in their jurisdiction.	Submit views and estimates to budget committees on Federal spending.	Submit views and estimates to budget committees on matters in their jurisdiction.	Allocate new budget authority, outlays, and new entitlement and credit authority to committees.
Recommend changes in laws pursuant to reconciliation instructions.	Include limits on credit programs in appropriations bills.	Recommend changes in laws pursuant to reconciliation instructions.	Monitor budget and advise Congress on its status.
Include CBO cost estimates in reports on their legislation.	Establish rules for reprogramming.		Senate reports resolutions waiving certain budget procedures.
	Establish account structure for federal agencies.		

Source: Congressional Research Service.

care financing legislation; care management; nursing reimbursement; the cost versus quality debate; impact of Medicare cost-containment on hospital care and access to post-hospital care; health and long-term care quality (especially home; nursing home, HMO, and ambulatory care); accessibility and quality of mental health care; central city and rural health care access; the rights of the terminally ill; health care needs of special populations; multi-generational equity; retiree health benefits; and health and aging research.

Employment. Employment issues included policies providing the elderly with the flexibility to choose between employment, training, or retirement without experiencing financial hardship; the lack of employment and job training opportunities for older workers; disincentives to continued employment; age discrimination in employment (the enforcement of the federal law protecting older workers from discrimination, the Age Discrimination in Employment Act); the problems experienced by displaced and disadvantaged older workers, employment problems faced by the elderly poor, minorities, and women; alter-

native work opportunities; federal employment and training programs such as the Job Training Partnership Act and the Senior Community Service Employment Program; public and private pension systems; and the relationship between labor market forces and employment/retirement decisions.

Social Security. Social Security issues included work to insure the financial integrity and viability of the Social Security system, the Social Security Administration (SSA), and the programs administered under the Social Security Act; efforts to improve the SSA's operations; and reform of the Old-Age and Survivors Insurance program (OASI), the Disability Insurance program (DI), and the Supplemental Security Income program (SSI).

Housing. Housing issues included housing regulations as well as safe, affordable, appropriate housing for the elderly, for older Americans with diverse socio-economic, cultural, and health needs. Primary areas of examination were: low income housing needs; alternative living arrangements for the frail and semi-independent elderly, such as congregate housing, shared housing, life care communities, and home equity conversions; rural housing needs; and the needs of special populations such as elderly farm workers.

Human services. Human services issues included appropriate community-based services that can assist older individuals to remain independent and self-sufficient, including Older Americans Act (OAA) programs; food stamp and nutrition assistance; low income energy and weatherization assistance; legal services; Community Development, Community Service, and Social Service Block Grants; the Older American Volunteer Programs; crimes against the elderly; intergenerational assistance issues; and issues affecting disenfranchised subpopulations of older Americans; particular attention was focused on the special needs of the vulnerable, low-income, frail, and ethnic/racial minority elderly.

Various subcommittees also studied and held hearings on such issues as Social Security, Supplemental Security Income (SSI) program, private pensions, employment issues, retirement

Senator David Pryor (D-Arkansas) became chairman of the U.S. Senate Special Committee on Aging in 1989. (Copyright © Tadder Photography; courtesy of the Senate Special Committee on Aging)

planning, the Medicare Catastrophic Coverage Act, long-term care, board and care facilities, private long-term care insurance, elder abuse, breast cancer, quality of care outside hospitals, and preventive health care (House Select Committee on Aging, August 1991).

Members of the Senate Special Committee on Aging can be reached at: Special Committee on Aging (there are no subcommittees), SD-G31, Washington, D.C. 20510-6400, (202) 224-5364.

In 1993 the House let authorization for the Select Committee expire. The House now has an Older Americans Caucus chaired by William J. Hughes (D-NJ) and Ralph Regula (R-OH). It can be reached at (202) 225-6572.

Key authorizing committees like the House Committee on Education and Labor and the Senate Committee on Labor and Human Resources and key appropriations and budget committees play a major role in aging policy, as well as committees that oversee such areas as Social Security, health care, food stamps, and nutrition.

● ROLE OF NATIONAL AGING INTEREST GROUPS

The advocacy of a number of individuals and groups played an important role in the passage of the 1965 Older Americans Act. Coalitions among these individuals and groups grew stronger during Aging Commissioner John Martin's tenure (1969–73). Individual advocates and coalitions of interest groups have been essential to the effectiveness of the White House Conferences of 1961, 1971, and 1981. Many of these coalitions were part of the pressure on the Bush administration to hold a White House Conference in 1993. The 1991–92 Reauthorized OAA calls for the next White House Conference on Aging to be held no later than December 31, 1994. In the context of the "relationship between the generations," the conference is to assess "the most appropriate public policies to meet the needs to enhance the contributions of older Americans." It will include a conference on the needs of older Indians and will look at the impact of the Social Security earnings test (*Congressional Record*, September 15, 1992).

Interest groups are individuals and organizations that share one or more common goals and together create support for that goal. National

The Kennedy campaign in 1960 was the first presidential campaign to pay attention to issues of older citizens with "Senior Citizens for Kennedy." (Courtesy of The National Council on the Aging, Inc.)

interest groups develop support for their goals through research, through policy positions, through information shared with Congress and the executive branch, and through the education of and communication with their members (Ficke, 1985).

There are three kinds of national groups: mass membership organizations like the American Association of Retired Persons (AARP) with 33 million members, professional organizations like the Association for Gerontology in Higher Education (AGHE), and those groups who represent public administrative agencies like the National Association of State Units on Aging (NASUA).

The earliest national interest group was established in the 1920s, the National Association of Retired Federal Employees (NARFE). Today it represents over 500,000 retired federal employees. In the 1950s both the National Council on the Aging (NCOA) and the American Association of Retired Persons (AARP) were founded. That decade also brought more labor union interest in the concerns of their retirees (Ficke, 1985). It was a time as well for more viable senior centers; the first center was developed in New York City in 1943 (Gelfand, 1988).

"Senior Citizens for Kennedy," formed during the Kennedy campaign in 1960, was the first presidential campaign to pay attention to issues of older citizens. The focus on older voters continues to this day in presidential campaign activities.

In 1961 the first White House Conference on Aging brought together people from all over the country. While developing policy positions for what was to become Medicare and the OAA, it also led to the establishment of the National Council of Senior Citizens (NCSC), made up mostly of retired union members, and indirectly to the National Association of State Units on Aging (NASUA), through training meetings and through states' establishment of state units to participate in the conference.

National aging organizations played major roles in both the 1971 and 1981 White House Conferences on Aging. Although their members were less than a majority of the delegates, they were more focused and could influence outcomes. Through the seventies, eighties, and into the nineties, aging organizations have strengthened their relationships with both Congress and the executive branch of government and have developed relationships with a number of state governments. While national interest groups receive the most media attention, numerous state and local interest groups work in coalition on elderly issues at the state and local levels. Such groups have different names, such as Senior Senate, Senior Power Day, Gray Haired Legislature.

In the 1970s, as a result of both the White House Conference and a fear of federal spending reduction, an Ad Hoc Coalition of Leadership Organizations was formed. Three years later, in May 1980, the Ad Hoc Coalition reorganized and became the Leadership Council of Aging Organizations (the current membership follows), an institutionalized framework enabling aging organizations to work together. The Leadership Council played a major role both during and after the 1981 White House Conference, developing "Aid for the Eighties" to advocate for important conference recommendations (*Aging Alert*, December 15, 1981). With some exceptions, most organizations who belong have aging as their primary focus. The aging community has greater strength when it can speak through this unified voice. The council's decisions are made by consensus and its chairmanship rotates between the three largest organizations, NCOA, NCSC, and AARP (Ficke, 1985). Obviously there are issues on which aging interest groups disagree. The differences are often apparent at reauthorization time. Yet, with increasing needs and ever-increasing competition for resources, it is important for interest groups within the aging community to work together to communicate the needs of the elderly, always understanding that American society is interdependent by nature.

● LEADERSHIP COUNCIL OF AGING ORGANIZATIONS (AS OF 11/4/93)

AFL-CIO Department of Employee Benefits
815 16th St., NW
Washington, DC 20006
(202) 637-5000
(202) 637-5058 (fax)

AFSCME Retiree Program
1625 L St., NW
Washington, DC 20036
(202) 429-1274
(202) 429-1293 (fax)

Alliance for Aging Research
2021 K St., NW, Ste. 305
Washington, DC 20006
(202) 293-2856
(202) 785-8574 (fax)

Alzheimer's Disease and Related Disorders Association
1334 G St., NW, Ste. 500
Washington, DC 20005
(202) 393-7737
(202) 393-2109 (fax)

American Association for International Aging
1133 20th St., NW, Ste. 330
Washington, DC 20036
(202) 833-8893
(202) 883-8762 (fax)

American Association of Homes for the Aging
901 E St., NW, Ste. 500
Washington, DC 20004-2037
(202) 783-2242
(202) 783-2255 (fax)

American Association of Retired Persons
601 E St., NW
Washington, DC 20049
(202) 434-2300
(202) 434-2320 (fax)

American Society on Aging
833 Market St., Room 516
San Francisco, CA 94103
(415) 974-9600
(415) 974-0300 (fax)

Asociacion Nacional pro Personas Mayores
3325 Wilshire Blvd., Ste. 800
Los Angeles, CA 90010-1784
(213) 487-1922
(213) 385-3014 (fax)

Association for Gerontology and Human Development in Historically Black Colleges and Universities
Washington Office
1424 K St., NW, Ste. 601
Washington, DC 20005
(202) 628-5322
(202) 347-0895 (fax)

Association for Gerontology in Higher Education
1001 Connecticut Ave., NW, Ste. 410
Washington, DC 20036-5504
(202) 429-9277
(202) 429-6097 (fax)

Catholic Golden Age
1255 23rd St., NW, Ste. 285
Washington, DC 20005
(202) 775-4557
(202) 775-4391 (fax)

Eldercare America, Inc.
1141 Loxford Terrace
Silver Spring, MA 20901
(301) 593-1621

Families USA
1334 G St., NW
Washington, DC 20005
(202) 737-6340
(202) 347-2417 (fax)

Gerontological Society of America
1275 K St., NW, Ste. 350
Washington, DC 20005-40006
(202) 842-1275
(202) 842-1150 (fax)

Gray Panthers
2025 Pennsylvania Ave., NW, Ste. 821
Washington, DC 20006
(202) 466-3132
(202) 466-3133(fax)

Green Thumb Inc.
2000 N. 14th St., Ste. 800
Arlington, VA 22201
(703) 522-7272
(703) 522-0141 (fax)

National Asian Pacific Center on Aging
Melbourne Tower, Ste. 914
1511 Third Ave.
Seattle, WA 98101
(206) 624-1221
(206) 624-1023 (fax)

National Association for Home Care
519 C St., NE
Stanton Park
Washington, DC 20002
(202) 547-7424
(202) 547-9559 (fax)

National Association of Area Agencies on Aging
1112 16th St., NW, Ste. 100
Washington, DC 20036
(202) 296-8130
(202) 296-8134 (fax)

National Association of Foster Grandparents Program Directors
(*See* National Senior Volunteer Corps Directors Associations)

National Association of Meal Programs
101 N. Alfred St., Ste. 202
Alexandria, VA 22314
(703) 548-5558
(703) 548-8024 (fax)

National Association of Nutrition and Aging Services Programs
2675 44th St., SW, Ste. 305
Grand Rapids, MI 49509
(616) 531-8700
(616) 531-3103 (fax)

National Association of Retired Federal Employees
1533 New Hampshire Ave., NW
Washington, DC 20036
(202) 234-0832
(202) 797-9697 (fax)

National Association of RSVP Directors
(*See* National Senior Volunteer Corps Directors Associations)

National Association of State Units on Aging
1225 I St., NW, Ste. 725
Washington, DC 20005
(202) 898-2578
(202) 898-2583 (fax)

National Association of Senior Companion Project Directors
(*See* National Senior Volunteer Corps Directors Associations)

National Caucus and Center on Black Aged
1424 K St., NW, Ste. 500
Washington, DC 20005
(202) 637-8400
(202) 347-0895 (fax)

National Council of Senior Citizens
1331 F St., NW
Washington, DC 20004-1171
(202) 347-8800
(202) 624-9595 (fax)

National Council on the Aging
409 3rd St., SW, 2nd Fl.
Washington, DC 20024
(202) 479-1200
(202) 479-0735 (fax)

National Hispanic Council on Aging
2713 Ontario Rd., NW, Ste. 200
Washington, DC 20009
(202) 745-2521
(202) 745-2522 (fax)

National Senior Citizens Law Center
1815 H St., NW, Ste. 700
Washington, DC 20006
(202) 887-5280
(202) 785-6792 (fax)

National Senior Volunteer Corps Directors Associations
11481 Bingham Terrace
Reston, VA 22091
(703) 860-9570 (phone and fax)

Older Women's League
666 Eleventh St., Ste. 700
Washington, DC 20001
(202) 783-6686
(202) 638-2356 (fax)

United Auto Workers Retired Members Department
8731 East Jefferson Ave.
Detroit, MI 48214
(313) 926-5231
(313) 824-5750 (fax)

● **NATIONAL ASSOCIATION OF STATE UNITS ON AGING MEMBERSHIP DIRECTORY**

Alabama

Commission on Aging
RSA Plaza, Ste. 470
770 Washington Ave.
Montgomery, AL 36130
(205) 242-5743

Alaska

Older Alaskans Commission
Department of Administration
Pouch C-Mail Station 0209
Juneau, AK 99811-0209
(907) 465-3250

American Samoa

Territorial Administration on Aging
American Samoa Government
Pago Pago, American Samoa 96799
011 (684) 633-1252

Arizona

Aging and Adult Administration
Department of Economic Security
1789 W. Jefferson, #950A
Phoenix, AZ 85007
(602) 542-4446

Arkansas

Division of Aging and Adult Services
Arkansas Department of Human Services
P.O. Box 1437, Slot 1412
7th and Main Streets
Little Rock, AR 72201
(501) 682-2441

California

Department of Aging
1600 K St.
Sacramento, CA 95814
(916) 322-5290

Colorado

Aging and Adult Service
Department of Social Services
1575 Sherman St., 4th fl.
Denver, CO 80203-3851
(303) 866-3851

Connecticut

Department on Social Services, Elderly Services Division
175 Main St.
Hartford, CT 06106
(203) 566-3238

Delaware

Division on Aging
Department of Health and Social Services
1901 N. DuPont Highway
New Castle, DE 19720
(302) 577-4791

District of Columbia

Office on Aging
One Judiciary Sq.
441 4th St., 9th fl.
Washington, DC 20001
(202) 724-5622

Florida

Department of Elder Affairs
Building I-Room 317
1317 Winewood Blvd.
Tallahassee, FL 32399-0700
(904) 922-5297

Georgia

Office of Aging
2 Peachtree St., NE, 18th fl.
Atlanta, GA 30303
(404) 657-5258

Guam

Division of Senior Citizens
Department of Public Health and Social Services
Government of Guam
P.O. Box 2816
Agana, Guam 96910
011 (671) 734-4361

Hawaii

Executive Office on Aging
Office of the Governor
335 Merchant St.
Room 241
Honolulu, HI 96813
(808) 586-0100

Idaho

Office on Aging
Statehouse, Rm. 108
Boise, ID 83720
(208) 334-3833

Illinois

Department on Aging
421 East Capitol Ave.
Springfield, IL 62701
(217) 785-2870

Indiana

Bureau of Aging/In Home Services
402 W. Washington St., #E-431
Indianapolis, IN 46207-7083
(317) 232-7020

Iowa

Department of Elder Affairs
914 Grand Ave.
Ste. 236, Jewett Bldg.
Des Moines, IA 50319
(515) 281-5187

Kansas

Department on Aging
Docking State Office Bldg., 122-S
915 SW Harrison
Topeka, KS 66612-1500
(913) 296-4986

Kentucky

Division of Aging Services
Cabinet for Human Resources
CHR Building, 6th West
275 East Main St., 6 West
Frankfort, KY 40621
(502) 564-6930

Louisiana

Office of Elderly Affairs
4550 N. Boulevard, 2d fl.
P.O. Box 80374
Baton Rouge, LA 70806
(504) 925-1700

Maine

Bureau of Elder and Adult Services
Department of Human Services
State House, Station #11
Augusta, ME 04333
(207) 624-5335

Maryland

Office on Aging
State Office Building
301 West Preston St., Rm. 1004
Baltimore, MD 21201
(301) 225-1100

Massachusetts

Executive Office of Elder Affairs
1 Ashburton Place, 5th fl.
Boston, MA 02108
(617) 727-7750

Michigan

Office of Services to the Aging
P.O. Box 30026
Lansing, MI 48909
(517) 373-8230

Minnesota

Board on Aging
444 Lafayette Rd.
St. Paul, MN 55155-3843
(612) 296-2770

Mississippi

Council on Aging
Division of Aging and Adult Services
750 N. State St.
Jackson, MS 39202
(601) 359-4929

Missouri

Division on Aging
Department of Social Services
P.O. Box 1337, 615 Howerton Ct.
Jefferson City, MO 65102-1337
(314) 751-3082

Montana

The Governor's Office on Aging
State Capitol Bldg.
Capitol Station, Room 219
Helena, MT 59620
(406) 444-3111

Nebraska

Department on Aging
P.O. Box 95044
301 Centennial Mall-South
Lincoln, NE 68509
(402) 471-2306

Nevada

Division for Aging Services
Department of Human Resources
445 Apple St., Ste. 104
Reno, NV 89502
(702) 688-2964

New Hampshire

Division of Elderly and Adult Services
State Office Park S
115 Pleasant St.,
Annex Bldg. #1
Concord, NH 03301-3843
(603) 271-4680

New Jersey

Division on Aging
Department of Community Affairs
CN 807
South Broad and Front Streets
Trenton, NJ 08625-0807
(609) 292-4833

New Mexico

State Agency on Aging
224 E. Palace Ave., 4th fl.
La Villa Rivera Bldg.
Santa Fe, NM 87501
(505) 827-7640

New York

Office for the Aging
New York State Plaza
Agency Bldg. #2
Albany, NY 12223
(518) 474-4425

North Carolina

Division of Aging
CB 29531
693 Palmer Dr.
Raleigh, NC 27626-0531
(919) 733-3983

North Dakota

Aging Services Division
Department of Human Services
P.O. Box 7070
Northbrook Shopping Center (NSC)
N. Washington St.
Bismarck, ND 58507-7070
(701) 224-2577

Northern Mariana Islands

Office of Aging
Division of Veterans Affairs—DC and CA
Off the Governor's Commonwealth of the
    Northern Mariana Islands
Saipan, MP 96950
Tel. Nos. 9411 or 9732

Ohio

Department of Aging
50 W. Broad St., 9th fl.
Columbus, OH 43266-0501
(614) 466-5500

Oklahoma

Aging Services Division
Department of Human Services
P.O. Box 25352
312 NE 28th St.
Oklahoma City, OK 73125
(405) 512-2327

Oregon

Senior and Disabled Services Division
500 Summer St., NE 2d fl. N
Salem, OR 97310
(503) 378-4728

Pennsylvania

Department of Aging
MSS Office Bldg.
400 Market, 7th fl.
Harrisburg, PA 17101-2301
(717) 783-1550

Puerto Rico

Governors Office for Elderly Affairs
Corbian Plaza Stop 23
Ponce De Leon Ave. #1603
U.M. Office C
San Ture, PR 00908
(809) 721-5710

Republic of Palau

Agency on Aging
P.O. Box 100
Koror, PW 96940

Rhode Island

Department of Elderly Affairs
160 Pine St.
Providence, RI 02903-3708
(401) 277-2858

South Carolina

Division on Aging
S. C. Retirement Systems Bldg.
202 Arbor Lake Dr., #302
Columbia, SC 29223
(803) 737-7500

South Dakota

Office of Adult Services and Aging
700 Governors Dr.
Pierre, SD 57501
(605) 773-3656

Tennessee

Commission on Aging
706 Church St., Ste. 201
Nashville, TN 37243-0860
(615) 741-2056

Texas

Department on Aging
P.O. Box 12786 Capitol Station
1949 IH 35, South
Austin, TX 78741-3702
(512) 444-2727

United States

Administration on Aging
U.S. Department of Health and Human
　Services
Washington, DC 20201
(202) 619-0724

Utah

Division of Aging and Adult Services
Department of Social Services
120 North, 200 West
Box 45500
Salt Lake City, UT 84145-0500
(801) 538-3910

Vermont

Aging and Disabilities
103 S. Main St.
Waterbury, VT 05676
(802) 241-2400

Virgin Islands

Senior Citizen Affairs
Department of Human Services
#19 Estate Diamond Fredericksted
St. Croix, VI 00840
(809) 772-4950 Ext. 46

Virginia

Department for the Aging
700 Centre, 10th fl.
700 E. Franklin St.
Richmond, VA 23219-2327
(804) 225-2271

Washington

Aging and Adult Services Administration
Department of Social and Health Services
P.O. Box 45050
Olympia, WA 98504-5050
(206) 586-3768

West Virginia

Commission on Aging
Holly Grove, State Capitol
Charleston, WV 25305
(304) 558-3317

Wisconsin

Bureau of Aging
Division of Community Services
217 S. Hamilton St., Ste. 300
Madison, WI 53707
(608) 266-2536

Wyoming

Commission on Aging
Hathaway Bldg., Rm. 139
Cheyenne, WY 82002-0710
(307) 777-7986

References

Achenbaum, W. Andrew. *Old Age in the New Land: The American Experience Since 1790.* Baltimore and London: Johns Hopkins University Press, 1978.

———. *Social Security Visions and Revisions: A 20th Century Fund Study.* New York: Cambridge University Press, 1985.

Aging Alert. Vol. 6, no. 19 (December 15, 1981). Lansing, MI: Michigan Area Agencies on Aging Association.

Altmeyer, Arthur J. *The Formative Years of Social Security.* Madison: University of Wisconsin Press, 1966.

Atchley, Robert C. *Social Forces and Aging.* 4th Ed. Belmont, CA: Wadsworth, 1985.

Bowen, William G., Frederick H. Harbison, Richard A. Lester, and Herman M. Somers. *The American System of Social Insurance: The Princeton Symposium Held June 1967 in Honor of J. Douglas Brown.* New York: McGraw-Hill, 1968.

Ficke, Susan Coombs. *An Orientation to the Older Americans Act.* Washington, DC: National Association of State Units on Aging, 1985.

Gelfand, Donald E. *The Aging Network, Programs & Services.* 3d ed. New York: Springer Publishing Co., 1988.

Inland Steel Co v. NLRB (CA-7; 1948) 15 LC pp. 64, 737, 170 F 2d 247 Enf'g 77 NLRB 1.

Jehle, Faustin F. *The Complete and Easy Guide to Social Security and Medicare.* Madison, CT: Fraser Publishing Co., 1987.

Melone, Joseph J., and Everett T. Allen, Jr. *Pension Planning.* Homewood, IL: Richard D. Irwin, Inc., 1972.

O'Shaughnessy, Carol. "Older Americans Act: 1991 Reauthorization and FY 1992 Budget Issues." Congressional Research Service, Order Code 1391002. Washington, DC: The Library of Congress, November 27, 1991.

———. "Older Americans Act Amendments of 1987: PL 100–175; A Summary of Provisions." Congressional Research Service, 88-233 EPW. Washington, DC: The Library of Congress, March 14, 1988.

———. "Older Americans Act Nutrition Program." Congressional Research Service, Order Code 90-115 EPW. Washington, DC: The Library of Congress, January 19, 1990.

———. "Older Americans Act Programs: Brief Summary and Funding Levels; FY 1988-FY 1991." Updated ed. Congressional Research Service, 90-200 EPW. Washington, DC: The Library of Congress, November 21, 1990.

O'Shaughnessy, Carol, and Richard J. Price. "Long-Term Care for the Elderly." Congressional Research Service, Order Code 1B88098. Washington, DC: The Library of Congress, October 28, 1991.

———. "The Role of the Older Americans Act in Long-Term Care." Congressional Research Service. Washington, DC: The Library of Congress, April 19, 1991.

Schick, Allen, Robert Keith, and Edward Davis. "Manual on the Federal Budget Process." Congressional Research Service 91-902 GOV. Washington, DC: The Library of Congress, December 24, 1991.

Smith, Darrell Hevenor. *The United States Civil Service Commission: Its History, Activities and Organization.* Baltimore: The John Hopkins Press, 1928.

U.S. Code Service 3001 et seq., as Amended.

U.S. Congress. House. Committee on Education and Labor, Subcommittee on Human Resources. *Compilation of the Older Americans Act of 1965 as Amended through December 31, 1988.* 101st Congress, March 2, 1989. (Serial No. 101-A and Senate Special Committee on Aging Serial No. 101-B).

U.S. Congress. House. Select Committee on Aging. *Publications List 1975 to the Present.*

———. *A Report by the Chairman. Activities of the Committee.* 102d Congress, 1st session. August 1991. (Pub. No. 102-815).

———. *Report Presented by the Chairman: Proposed Activities.* 102d Congress, 1st session.

U.S. Congress. House. Select Committee on Aging, Subcommittee on Human Services. *Staff Summary of Older Americans Act.* 4th Revision, August 1988 (Pub. No. 100-683).

U.S. Congress. Senate. *Congressional Record.* September 15, 1992.

U.S. Government. *Congressional Directory 1991–1992.* 102d Congress. (S. Pub. 102–4).

———. *The Domestic Volunteer Service Act of 1973, Amended July 25, 1991.* Washington, DC: U.S. Government Printing Office (P.S. 102–73).

———. "Foster Grandparents." *ACTION Handbook 4405.90.* Washington, DC: U.S. Government Printing Office, January 1989.

———. "Retired Senior Volunteers." *ACTION Handbook 4405.92.* Washington, DC: U.S. Government Printing Office, January 1989.

———. "Senior Companions." *ACTION Handbook 4405.91.* Washington, DC: U.S. Government Printing Office, January 1989.

The World Almanac. New York: New York World-Telegram, 1962.

Additional Reading

Franco, Celinda M., and Kathleen M. King. "Medicare: FY 1992 Budget." Updated ed. archived. Congressional Research Service (1B91032). Washington, DC: The Library of Congress, December 13, 1991.

Generations: Aging Policy and the OAA. Summer/fall 1991.

Hamilton, Dana. "Selected Legislation Affecting the Elderly in the 102nd Congress." Congressional Research Service 91–624 EPW. Washington, DC: The Library of Congress, August 9, 1991.

Kollman, Geoffrey. "Social Security: Proposed Modifications to the Earnings/Test." Congressional Research Service Order Code 1B89114. Washington, DC: The Library of Congress, December 18, 1991.

———. "Social Security: The Earnings Test." Congressional Research Service 88–89 EPW. Washington, DC: The Library of Congress, January 22, 1988.

———. "Summary of Major Changes in the Social Security Cash Benefit Program: 1935–1990." Congressional Research Service 90–582 EPW. Washington, DC: The Library of Congress, February 28, 1985, updated December 12, 1990.

Merrill, Samuel, Jr. "Aging: Health Effects and Behavior." Congressional Research Service 87–404SPR. Washington, DC: The Library of Congress, 1987.

Neuschler, Edward. "Medicaid Eligibility for the Elderly in Need of Long Term Care." Congressional Research Service 87–986 EPW. Washington, DC: The Library of Congress, September 1990.

U.S. Congress. House. Committee on the Budget. *Staff Summary and Analysis of President Bush's Fiscal Year 1993 Budget.* February 1992. (Ser. No. CP-6).

Olivia Maynard, M.S.W.

8

The Older American Voter

- Political Interest and Voter Turnout ● Ideology and Issue Attitudes
- Generational Issues: Attitudes Toward Old-Age and Children's Benefits
- Attitudes Toward the Medicare Catastrophic Coverage Act of 1988
- Partisanship and Electoral Choice ● Old-Age Political Organizations
- Coalitions and Social Movements in Old-Age Advocacy

When Congress passed the Medicare Catastrophic Coverage Act in 1988—expanding Medicare benefits and taxing Medicare beneficiaries to pay for them—older people across the nation protested through pickets, demonstrations, letters, and phone calls. Seventeen months later, in an unprecedented move, Congress repealed the act. Observers heralded the political power wielded by the elderly, who forced Congress to reverse itself. This was "the first time Congress had rescinded major social benefits it had created" (Congressional Quarterly, 1989).

The catastrophic coverage incident illustrated not only the collective power of older U.S. citizens, but also their diversity. Older Americans were deeply divided in their opinions toward the legislation, and so were the organizations representing them. While many senior adults benefited from the catastrophic coverage program, others claimed to lose more than they gained. Thus it becomes difficult if not impossible to define what is in the interest of the elderly, and what is not.

Older people in the United States are increasingly active and influential in politics. Old-age political organizations have expanded tremendously in number, size, and influence during the last few decades. Older people share a number of political concerns, and collectively they benefit from government programs based on old age or retirement status. At the same time, the elderly are a heterogeneous group, and their economic and social diversity has increased along with their political visibility. Group identities based on social status, religion, partisanship, occupation, gender, or ethnicity, for example, may be more politically significant than age.

Misconceptions that have guided some of the previous research on older people's political attitudes include the notion that the elderly comprise a monolithic bloc with similar interests and opinions. Findings about the diversity of their opinions—even on aging-related issues—dispel that fallacy. Some other incorrect assumptions about the political behavior of the elderly include: (1) older people tend to withdraw from political activity as they retire from work; (2) older people are inherently more conservative than younger people and more resistant to change; and (3) older people's self-interested political attitudes promote generational conflict.

● POLITICAL INTEREST AND VOTER TURNOUT

Political interest and activity do not subside in old age; if anything, they grow. Decades of research have shown political interest to increase steadily throughout a person's life (Hudson and Strate, 1985). Most political activities, ranging from voting to campaign work to organization membership, remain stable or increase beyond the age of sixty-five (see, for example, Cutler,

Table 8.1
Interest in 1990 Political Campaigns, by Age (Percent)

	Age				
	17–35	36–49	50–64	65–74	75+
Very interested	11	21	31	35	27
Somewhat interested	49	48	39	38	44
Not very interested	40	31	30	27	29
Total	100	100	100	100	100

Source: American National Election Study, 1990.

1977, and Wolfinger and Rosenstone, 1980). Thus, while many researchers half a century ago supported the "disengagement theory"—the view that older people tend to withdraw from political and other prior activities—most researchers today reject that theory.

There is, of course, no particular age at which one can be said to turn "old." Age 65 is used as the boundary between "old" and "not old" in this chapter, as it is often used elsewhere, because 65 marks the age at which people are eligible for full retirement benefits and many other benefits as well. Thus people 65 years of age and over have many political interests in common. It should be noted, however, that many gerontologists distinguish between the "young-old" and the "old-old," noting that the latter are much more likely to need health and social services. Nor is 65 necessarily the most politically relevant lower boundary; age eligibility for joining the American Association of Retired Persons, for example, begins at 50.

Older people's high level of attention to politics and current events can be seen in the 1990 survey data displayed in Tables 8.1 and 8.2. Asked about their interest in the current political campaigns, more older than young or middle-aged adults said they were very interested. Interest in the campaigns increases steadily with age, falling off slightly after the age of 75 as seen in Table 8.1.

Older people are also more likely to follow the news daily, as noted in Table 8.2. More older than younger and middle-aged people reported reading a daily newspaper and watching the news on television every day during the previous week. Like political interest, attention to the news media rises steadily with age, dropping off only slightly—but still not down to the middle-age level—among the oldest old.

Some other incorrect assumptions about the political behavior of the elderly include: (1) older people tend to withdraw from political activity as they retire from work; (2) older people are inherently more conservative than younger people and more resistant to change; and (3) older people's self-interested political attitudes promote generational conflict.

Not only do older people pay close attention to politics, they also vote more than younger adults. Historically, voter turnout has tended to increase with age and then decline somewhat in old age, largely due to the lower level of education among the elderly (Wolfinger and Rosenstone, 1980). Since the mid- to late-1980s, however, voter turnout in national elections has been even higher

People over age 65 exhibit the highest rate of voter turnout of any age group. (Courtesy of the American Association of Retired Persons.)

Table 8.2
Use of News Media During Past Week, by Age, 1990 (Percent)

	Age				
	17–35	36–49	50–64	65–74	75+
Read newspaper					
Every day	28	42	54	67	55
4–6 days	14	10	7	5	5
1–3 days	37	29	19	13	14
No days	22	19	20	15	26
Total	101	100	100	100	100
Watched TV news					
Every day	39	47	68	82	80
4–6 days	18	22	10	7	4
1–3 days	33	20	15	6	6
No days	10	12	8	5	10
Total	100	101	101	100	100

Note: Due to rounding, total percentages may not add to 100.

Source: American National Election Study, 1990.

among those 65 and over than among middle-aged voters, as can be seen in Table 8.3. During the last few decades, while turnout has been rising among the elderly, it has been declining, for the most part, among all other age groups. Combined with the growing proportion of older people in the U.S. population, this high turnout rate makes the elderly an increasingly important group of voters.

People's interest in politics may increase with age for several reasons. As people move from young adulthood to middle age and then to old age, they tend to become less distracted from pol-

itics by such personal concerns as going to school, establishing a career, and caring for small children. At the same time, they become more established and settled in their communities, leading to more involvement in public and political affairs (Hudson and Strate, 1985).

Older Americans' high rate of political interest and activity is likely to rise even further. Higher education, good health, and a comfortable standard of living are all linked to political participation. These conditions have all improved significantly in recent decades for the elderly as a group. Longer and more comfortable periods of

Table 8.3
Percentage of People Who Reported Voting in National Elections, by Age

	Presidential Elections							Congressional Elections			
	1988	1984	1980	1976	1972	1968	1964	1986	1982	1978	1974
Age:											
18–24	36	41	40	42	50	50	51	22	25	24	24
25–44	54	58	59	59	63	67	69	41	45	43	42
45–64	68	70	69	69	71	75	76	59	62	59	57
65+	69	68	65	62	64	66	66	51	60	56	51

Note: Prior to 1972, persons 18 to 20 years old could vote in Georgia and Kentucky; those 19 to 20 could vote in Alaska; 20-year-olds could vote in Hawaii.

Source: U.S. Bureau of the Census, 1989.

retirement allow older people more leisure time for political activity. Furthermore, as government programs and benefits have expanded for the elderly, so has their stake in government. Thus, they have good reason to mobilize as a group and defend their gains, particularly in an era of large deficits and fiscal austerity.

At the same time, the diversity of older Americans hinders their development as a cohesive bloc of voters. Crosscutting loyalties, conflicting needs, and different experiences throughout their lives ensure that older people will vary widely in their political views.

● IDEOLOGY AND ISSUE ATTITUDES

Though Americans are divided in their ideological and policy preferences, those divisions seldom pit older against younger people. The distribution of attitudes is generally quite similar among young, middle-aged, and older adults. When differences do occur between age groups, two possible explanations arise. One explanation is that people's attitudes tend to change in a certain direction as they grow older; that is, their attitudes are subject to life-cycle effects. The other explanation is that people's attitudes are influenced by the historical trends and events of their time, producing similarities in experience and outlook among people in the same generation. Age group differences in this case are attributable to generational or cohort effects (Bengtson and others, 1985; Riley, 1973).

The idea that people become more conservative as they move through the life cycle and into old age has been linked to the notion that older people are more set in their ways and resistant to change. This common stereotype receives limited support, however, in the examination of ideological self-placement and political attitudes.

Data from a 1990 survey question on ideological self-placement—whether people perceived themselves as liberal, moderate, or conservative—appear in Table 8.4. No clear pattern emerges toward conservatism in moving from youth to old age. People in the 50- to 64-year-old age group are the most conservative and least liberal by this measure; those between the ages of 36 and 49 are the most liberal; and those 75 years of age and over are the least conservative. If any trend is apparent across the age groups, it is a trend toward ideological moderation in old age. The most obvious conclusion to be drawn from Table 8.4, however, is that all age groups are deeply divided on this measure, with only minor differences **between** age groups (see also Campbell, 1971, and Campbell and Strate, 1981).

Self-placement on the ideological scale, however, is not the best measure of ideology, since many people have vague and varying conceptions of what "liberal" and "conservative" mean. A more complete picture requires looking at attitudes on three types of political issues: social issues, domestic economic issues, and national defense.

Older people tend to be somewhat more conservative on social issues, or issues concerning lifestyle, social change, and government policies to control them. This tendency is evident in survey data presented by earlier researchers (e.g., Campbell and Strate, 1981; Hudson and Strate, 1985) and in Table 8.5. Older people surveyed in 1988 and 1990 were less likely to favor women

Table 8.4
Self-Described Ideology, by Age, 1990 (Percent)

	Age				
	17–35	36–49	50–64	65–74	75+
Liberal	28	30	16	18	20
Moderate	37	31	40	42	51
Conservative	36	40	44	40	29
Total	101	101	100	100	100

Note: Due to rounding, total percentages may not add to 100.

Source: American National Election Study, 1990.

Table 8.5
Attitudes Toward Social Issues: Percentage of Persons in Each Age Group Who Agree

	Age			
	17–35	36–49	50–64	65+
Women and men should be equal (1990)	72	74	60	47
Abortion should not be restricted (1990)	41	48	33	34
School prayer should be permitted (1988)	31	30	43	46
Gays should be protected from discrimination (1988)	56	54	49	47

Source: American National Election Studies, 1988 and 1990.

having "an equal role with men in running business, industry, and government." People over 50 were also more likely than younger adults to favor restrictions on abortion, to favor allowing prayer in the public schools, and to oppose government protection against job discrimination for gays and lesbians.

No clear pattern emerges toward conservatism in moving from youth to old age. People in the 50- to 64-year-old age group are the most conservative and least liberal by this measure; those between the ages of 36 and 49 are the most liberal; and those 75 years of age and over are the least conservative.

Older people's relative conservatism on social issues is likely the result of cohort effects rather than life-cycle effects. This conservatism, in other words, does not stem from increasing rigidity and resistance to change in old age. Social changes such as women's equality, access to abortion, and alternative lifestyles were not prominent on the political agenda when today's older people were young adults. Younger people may be more comfortable with such changes because they were socialized in an era when these changes were becoming more widely accepted. Studies following various age cohorts over time have found that older cohorts and younger cohorts alike change their views with the times; thus rigidity in old age is not a likely explanation for age differences in social attitudes (Hudson and Strate, 1985).

Voices of Creative Aging

Franklin F., a writer who walked from Los Angeles to Washington, DC, at age 79 with a peace march for global nuclear disarmament. He speaks to the advantages of old age:

None of us knew whether we could walk across the United States. We had never done it! Older people generally could do much more, I believe, than they do if they just felt encouraged to try some of these things. It is quite possible, as I saw in this march, for older people to be exceedingly vigorous right through. We understand what our bodies can do. We know we can't conquer the world, but we can do a lot of things. I walked most of the way, although there were periods when I couldn't because of a sore leg from tendinitis.

I was elected one of the five board of directors of this peace march, and the press sought me out. I have been able to state our point of view regarding the march and get it to a larger audience than perhaps a younger person would be able to, because they didn't have the distinction of being old.

The march was a high point of my life. Now that it is over, I have returned to Colorado to teach and write. Being older, I think, is more fun than being younger, because we have more points of reference and more experiences through our own past lives and the lives of those around us. So, younger people have something to look forward to; they ought to hurry up and get old.

Excerpt from Connie Goldman's "Late Bloomer" public radio series

Table 8.6
Attitudes Toward Defense Spending, by Age (Percent)

	Age			
	17–35	36–49	50–64	65+
Federal Spending on Defense (1990)				
Increase	23	23	26	18
Leave the same	31	30	38	42
Decrease	46	47	36	40
Total	100	100	100	100
Federal Spending on Star Wars (1988)				
Increase	19	23	16	14
Leave the same	35	34	39	39
Decrease	46	44	45	47
Total	100	101	100	100

Note: Due to rounding, total percentages may not add to 100.

Source: American National Election Studies, 1988 and 1990.

Previous studies have also found older people to be more conservative than younger people on foreign policy issues, and more likely to support higher defense spending (Campbell and Strate, 1981). Hudson and Strate (1985) attribute this, as well, to cohort effects. The generations who lived through one or both World Wars may feel more anxious about national security than succeeding generations. More recent data indicate that these age differences on defense issues have largely disappeared, as shown in Table 8.6. Older people in 1988 and 1990 were no more supportive of increased defense spending and spending on the

Strategic Defensive Initiative, or "Star Wars," than younger people. If anything, older people were slightly less supportive of increased defense spending. World War II ended just around the time today's 65-year-olds reached adulthood, which may explain the decline in age differences on defense attitudes since then.

On domestic social welfare and economic issues, evidence of attitudinal differences among age groups is mixed. When age differences do appear, they are generally in a conservative direction. Older people tend to oppose government spending on social welfare programs more than younger people. Age differences vary according to the specific issue, however, as can be seen in Table 8.7. When asked whether "government should provide fewer services, even in areas such as health and education, in order to reduce spending," more older people said "yes." Similarly, older people were less supportive of the notion that the government "should see to it that every person has a job and a good standard of living," and less favorable toward government efforts "to improve the social and economic position of blacks." On the other hand, all age groups were nearly identical in their attitudes toward government-funded medical insurance, as well as in their opinions toward a tax increase to reduce the federal budget deficit.

Older Americans, in sum, are not much different from younger and middle-aged Americans in their ideological preferences and issue attitudes. If older people are any more conservative than younger people, the differences are slight and issue-specific. "Knowing that someone is old will not help very much in predicting how conservative he or she is," as Campbell and Strate note:

Table 8.7
Attitudes Toward Economic and Social Welfare Issues: Percentage of Each Age Group in Favor

	Age			
	17–35	36–49	50–64	65+
Provide more government services (1990)	52	42	42	38
Government provide jobs, standard of living (1990)	43	33	32	28
Government provide aid to African Americans (1990)	29	26	24	23
Government provide health insurance (1988)	44	41	40	44
Support higher taxes to reduce deficit (1990)	40	44	40	42

Source: American National Election Studies, 1988 and 1990.

"The elderly are very much in the mainstream of American political opinions."

A measure of mainstream voting patterns is found in the 1992 national election. Among voters sixty and older, fifty percent voted for Bill Clinton, thirty-eight percent for President Bush, and twelve percent for H. Ross Perot. Economic factors were the biggest issues, with thirty percent of older voters saying their top concern was the economy and the lack of jobs. According to a study by Voter Research Surveys, twenty-eight percent of older voters said health care was the issue that mattered most.

The data indicate that there are deep divisions and little consensus on social, economic, and defense policies. The divisions are not along age lines; they cut across the generations so that there are much larger attitudinal differences within age groups than between them.

● GENERATIONAL ISSUES: ATTITUDES TOWARD OLD-AGE AND CHILDREN'S BENEFITS

The specter of generational conflict has begun to draw the attention of journalists, politicians, and academic researchers, as some people have claimed that the elderly are receiving more than their fair share of government benefits (e.g., Fairlie, 1988; Longman, 1985). Thus, during the last decade or two, there has been a shift in the major research questions asked about older people's attitudes. Today, the focus is less on older people's relative conservatism and more on their group-oriented attitudes. Now the major question is: Do older people support increased old-age benefits and oppose the growth of programs that benefit young people?

Such generational conflict does not appear to be a major driving force in older people's attitudes toward aging policy issues. Support for old-age benefits and programs remains high among all age groups and is no higher among the elderly than among young or middle-aged adults. On children's issues—government funded child care and public schools—people fifty years and older are less favorable toward government action. Overall, however, the generational conflict scenario, pitting older against younger people in a battle over government benefits, receives scant support in contemporary surveys.

Some earlier researchers did detect an element of elderly group interest when they studied attitudes toward government medical insurance in the 1950s through the early 1970s. Older people seemed to support government health benefits more than younger people, and since older people may feel a greater need for such benefits, they exhibited a coherence on this issue that "transcend[ed] previous ideological and partisan attitudes, opinions, and loyalties" (Weaver, 1976; see also Bengtson and others, 1985; Campbell, 1971; Schreiber and Marsden, 1972). Age differences on the health insurance question seemed to disappear after the mid-1970s, however (Day, 1990). Americans are still divided on the national health insurance issue, but not along age group lines.

As public debate over changes in Social Security, Medicare, and other aging policies has escalated since the late 1970s, surveys gauging people's attitudes toward these issues have become common. Researchers have therefore been able to study these attitudes more systematically, and few have uncovered any sign of generational conflict. Support is high among people of all ages for Social Security, Medicare, and other old-age benefits. Older people are, if anything, slightly less supportive of increases in these programs than are younger people (Day, 1990; Dobson and St. Angelo, 1980; Klemmack and Roff, 1980). Older people were also found to be slightly more supportive of aid to poor families with children and less supportive of aid to the elderly poor than younger people (Ponza and others, 1988).

Widespread popular support for increases in Social Security and other old-age benefits is evident in Table 8.8. Older people are even less likely than younger and middle-aged adults to favor increasing those benefits; they are more likely to be satisfied with current levels of spending. Almost no one of any age favors cutting back on those benefits. The numbers in Table 8.8 are consistent with findings in virtually all surveys published during the 1980s.

On programs that benefit primarily families with children—government provision of child care and aid to public schools—much the same pattern is evident (see Table 8.9). Here, too, younger adults are generally more favorable toward these benefits. More specifically, the younger age groups—those under 50 years of age—favor increasing these children's benefits by

Table 8.8
Attitudes Toward Government Benefits for Older People, by Age (Percent)

	Age				
	17–35	36–49	50–64	65–74	75+
Spending on the elderly (1982)					
Increase	78	71	62	53	44
Leave the same	18	23	30	39	44
Decrease	4	6	8	8	12
Total	100	100	100	100	100
Spending on elderly care (1988)					
Increase	81	81	75	68	59
Leave the same	18	19	24	31	41
Decrease	1	1	1	1	0
Total	100	101	100	100	100
Spending on Social Security (1990)					
Increase	64	64	65	60	53
Leave the same	33	32	33	37	44
Decrease	3	4	2	3	3
Total	100	100	100	100	100

Note: Due to rounding, total percentages may not add to 100.

Source: ABC News/*Washington Post* Poll of Public Opinion on Aging, 1982; American National Election Studies, 1988 and 1990.

large margins, while those over 50 are rather evenly divided.

The elderly's comparatively lower support for government funded child care and aid to the public schools may be a sign of underlying generational conflict. More likely, however, it simply reflects a general pattern: older people are somewhat more reluctant to support expanded social welfare expenditures, even those that benefit the elderly as a group. They do not oppose children's benefits in an effort to secure a larger piece of the pie for themselves. Studies of local referenda on public school funding, for example, conclude that older people are no more resistant to new school taxes than younger adults (Binstock, 1990; Chomitz, 1987). Button and Rosenbaum (1989)

Table 8.9
Attitudes Toward Government Benefits for Families With Children, by Age, 1990 (Percent)

	Age				
	17–35	36–49	50–64	65–74	75+
Government provide child care					
Yes	71	60	47	45	43
No	29	40	53	55	57
Total	100	100	100	100	100
Spending on public schools					
Increase	75	65	50	55	52
Leave the same	23	30	43	40	46
Decrease	2	5	7	5	2
Total	100	100	100	100	100

Source: American National Election Study, 1990.

even concluded in their Florida study that "the presence of an organized, relatively affluent, and educated aging population can lead to increased support for local educational referenda."

Generational issues, like the more general political issues discussed earlier, generate controversy among Americans, but not much controversy between generations. The major divisions on aging policies and children's benefits fall along income and partisan lines, with Democrats and lower-income people of all ages preferring higher levels of government support, and Republicans and wealthier people of all ages preferring lower benefit levels. Once again, the political, social, and economic diversity of older Americans frustrates any attempt to unite them around aging policy issues.

The income and partisan divisions among older people are illustrated in Table 8.10. This poll is particularly amenable to an examination of divisions among older people, because it includes an oversample of elderly persons. The total number of respondents age 65 and over is 680. Older Democrats are much more likely to favor higher government spending on the elderly than older Republicans; older people on lower incomes are also more likely than their wealthier counterparts to support increased spending on the elderly. Older people's subjective financial situation is also critical. Those who claim that "not having enough money to live on" is a serious problem are much more likely to support increased benefits than those who feel they have no financial problems. Other variables such as ideology, educational level, retirement status, race, gender, and marital status are also related to support for old-age benefits; however, when income and political party are held constant, these variables are no longer significant. The economic and partisan divisions are the ones that remain after other variables have been taken into account (Day, 1990).

Thus the lines dividing Americans on aging policy issues seem to be more economic and partisan than generational. Nevertheless, the elderly could unite to defend the benefits they have if those benefits were seriously threatened. With the repeal of the Medicare Catastrophic Coverage Act, following nationwide protests by angry Medicare recipients, many saw the potential for an effective age-based mass movement.

Table 8.10

Percent Support for Increased U.S. Government Spending on the Elderly, Persons 65 Years and Over, 1982

Democrats	63
Independents	46
Republicans	29
Money very serious problem	88
Money serious problem	79
Money minor problem	57
Money no problem	35
Income below the median	53
Income above the median	30

Source: ABC News/*Washington Post* Poll of Public Opinion on Aging, 1982.

● **ATTITUDES TOWARD THE MEDICARE CATASTROPHIC COVERAGE ACT OF 1988**

When older people mobilized in protest against the new Medicare Catastrophic Coverage Act (MCCA) of 1988, they won. Their actions were perceived as selfish by many, creating generational tensions fed by media images of "greedy geezers" (Torres-Gil, 1992). Older people's attitudes toward the MCCA, however, further illustrate the diversity of the elderly, and the economic and partisan differences that divide them.

The catastrophic health care program laid out in the MCCA was clearly meant to benefit the elderly, and some of the old-age advocacy organizations were among its most prominent supporters. Designed to help Medicare beneficiaries who were saddled with sudden astronomical medical expenses, the coverage included unlimited hospital and doctor bills beyond the deductible, prescription drugs, mammography, and extended nursing home, hospice, respite, and home health care. Although it did not cover long-term care for chronic illness, MCCA provided a partial substitute for private "medigap" insurance, affecting 70 percent to 80 percent of Medicare beneficiaries. Most who pay for medigap insurance themselves would have been better off financially under the new program (Rovner, 1990).

Some beneficiaries objected to the program on two grounds: the funding mechanism, and the duplication of benefits that some older people already had. The program duplicated insurance coverage that was fully or partially paid for by former employers of about 23 percent of retired beneficiaries. Many of these people were angry about paying higher taxes for benefits they felt they did not need (Rovner, 1989).

The new benefits were to be financed solely by Medicare beneficiaries themselves; the more affluent among them were to pay the most. Funding was to come from two sources: an increase of $4.00 in the flat monthly Part B premium to be paid by all but the poorest, and a progressive income tax surcharge paid for by the 40 percent of beneficiaries who owed more than $150.00 in federal income tax. In order to build up a financial reserve, benefits were to be phased in slowly while premium and surtax collection began immediately. This move was fiscally prudent but politically unpopular, as middle- and upper-income beneficiaries began to protest the cost, while few felt compelled to defend benefits they were not yet receiving (Haas, 1989).

While wealthier Medicare recipients paid a larger share of the new benefits' cost, poorer recipients stood to gain the most from the benefits. The Congressional Budget Office estimated that the 30 percent wealthiest enrollees might have paid more than they saved in insurance premiums, while the remaining 70 percent would have enjoyed a net gain (Moon, 1991). Furthermore, on the private medigap insurance market, the oldest and poorest policy holders are most often the victims of fraudulent sales tactics (Kosterlitz, 1989). Overall, therefore, the catastrophic coverage program was generally a better deal for lower- and middle-income older people.

Given the amount of media attention received by the MCCA and the protests against it, it is no surprise that 85 percent of Medicare recipients surveyed in August 1989—just three months before the repeal—said they were aware of the program. Fully two-thirds, however, said they had no opinion when asked whether they liked or disliked the catastrophic coverage program. (In the ABC News/*Washington Post* National Survey, August 1989, only respondents who said they were Medicare recipients—216 in all—were asked the questions about the Medicare Catastrophic Coverage Act.) On another question, nearly three-fourths said they would choose to remain in the catastrophic coverage program if it were made optional. Thus, despite the widespread protests against the program, most

Medicare beneficiaries perceived it as neither a hot issue nor a terrible burden (Day, 1993).

As with other aging policy issues, older people divided along economic and partisan lines in their attitudes toward the MCCA. Republicans and those with higher incomes, as well as those who thought they had to pay higher taxes under the legislation, were less willing than others to choose the program if it were optional (see Table 8.11). Those who had previous medigap coverage and those who did not were evenly divided on this question; however, the survey did not ask whether their previous coverage was paid for by employers or by the policy holders themselves. The divisions along income lines are logical, given the differential costs and benefits of the program for higher- and lower-income recipients. The partisan divisions are somewhat less rational, since the MCCA received bipartisan support in Congress. However, they fit the general pattern for other aging policy issues, with Democrats more supportive of expanded benefits than Republicans.

With high support for old-age programs and benefits among people of all ages, and with the

Table 8.11
Percentage of Medicare Recipients Who Would Choose Government Catastrophic Coverage if Optional, 1989

Total	71
Democrat	74
Independent	69
Republican	67
Must pay higher taxes	62
No higher taxes	76
Income under $8,000	89
$8,000–$12,000	79
$12,000–$20,000	68
$20,000–$30,000	66
Above $30,000	67
Have other coverage	70
No other coverage	71

Note: The question is worded as follows: "Right now participation in the new Medicare catastrophic health care program is required for Medicare recipients. If it were made optional, would you choose to remain in the program or not?"

Source: ABC News/*Washington Post* National Survey, August 1989.

elderly themselves divided in their support for increased benefits, the potential for generational conflict seems negligible. Nevertheless, with slow economic growth and huge budget deficits limiting the national government, competition among beneficiary groups—including older people and families with children—may rise. It is more difficult than ever for the government to expand benefits without also raising additional revenue; yet there are strong public pressures for expanded health coverage, long-term care, public education, and other programs. Under these conditions, the question of who pays for new benefits may—as in the case of the MCCA—promote discord among previously harmonious constituencies (Torres-Gil, 1992).

● PARTISANSHIP AND ELECTORAL CHOICE

Partisanship is an important factor in older people's issue positions, and older people are as divided in their partisan loyalties as younger people are. Compared to younger and middle-aged people, older people are slightly more Democratic and less Republican, as noted in the 1990 data displayed in Table 8.12. Older people are also more likely to be partisans, and less inclined to claim independence from partisan ties.

Older people in earlier decades tended to identify more with the Republican party and less with the Democrats, compared to younger people. The direction of this difference was so consistent that some earlier researchers concluded that people naturally become more Republican as they age, due to life-cycle effects. Other researchers who

traced the partisan preferences of cohorts over time, however, concluded that there was no general movement toward Republicanism as people aged. They attributed the Republican tendencies of older people, therefore, to cohort or generational effects, with partisan loyalties reflecting people's early socialization (Bengtson and others, 1985; Campbell and Strate, 1981).

Compared to younger and middle-aged people, older people are slightly more Democratic and less Republican, as noted in the 1990 data displayed in Table 8.12. Older people are also more likely to be partisans, and less inclined to claim independence from partisan ties.

By the mid-1980s, older people were comparatively more Democratic, lending further support to the cohort-effect theory. Rather than becoming more Republican, older people of the 1980s and early 1990s retained their ties to the Democratic party, forged during the era of the Great Depression and Franklin D. Roosevelt's New Deal. Many of today's older people came of age during that era, when distress over the Depression and the subsequent popularity of the New Deal contributed to a mass realignment toward the Democratic party (Bengtson and others, 1985).

The age-related trend toward partisanship and away from independence, on the other hand, is a trend commonly attributed to life-cycle effects. Younger people are more likely than older people to claim partisan independence; as they age, their political ideas come into clearer focus, and so do their party attachments. The strength of partisan loyalties also tends to increase with age (Hudson and Strate, 1985).

Voting behavior in national elections among the elderly, like party identification, differs little from that of younger and middle-aged adults. Tracing presidential elections from 1952 through 1980, Campbell and Strate (1981) note that the elderly vote and the middle-aged vote never diverge by more than a few percentage points. The largest difference occurred in 1960, when older people were about 10 percent more favor-

Table 8.12
Party Identification by Age, 1990 (Percent)

	Age				
	17–35	36–49	50–64	65–74	75+
Democrat	47	55	53	61	59
Independent	15	10	9	7	5
Republican	39	35	38	33	36
Total	101	100	100	101	100

Note: Due to rounding, total percentages may not add to 100.

Source: American National Election Study, 1990.

Profiles of Productive Aging

Margaret Chase Smith
Former U.S. senator

"Age never meant anything to me. I never think of myself in connection with years. I ran always on my record, and my phrase was 'Don't change a record.'"

Margaret Chase Smith was born in 1897 in Skowhegan, Maine. By 1930, when she was business manager of a major textile mill in Skowhegan, she married Clyde H. Smith, a prominent local and state politician, and campaigned for her husband's 1936 bid for Congress. In 1940 Clyde Smith suffered a fatal heart attack while campaigning for re-election, and Margaret Chase Smith ran in his place, eventually serving four terms in the House of Representatives. Her greatest legislative achievement was obtaining permanent status for women in the military, which directly affected military nurses serving in World War II.

In 1948 Smith ran for the Senate. In the Republican primary she defeated her opponents by a margin of victory exceeding her opponents' total votes combined, then defeated her Democratic opponent to become the first woman elected to the U.S. Senate on her own

merit. Smith held her Senate seat through six administrations, from Franklin Roosevelt to Richard Nixon's first term, for a total of four six-year terms. She held the all-time roll call voting record in the Senate until 1981, with 2,941 consecutive role calls. Her most important contribution to American history was her opposition to "McCarthyism" in the early 1950s, denouncing Senator Joseph McCarthy in a Senate speech called "the Declaration of Conscience." In recognition of her support of the space program, the director of NASA said, "If it were not for a woman—Margaret Chase Smith—we would not have put a man on the moon."

Smith sought the Republican nomination for the presidency, in 1963, and was the first woman in U.S. history to have her name placed in nomination for the presidency at a convention by a major political party. She left politics in 1973 at the age of 76, and then became a visiting professor and lecturer, roles that continue to occupy her. In 1989 Smith received the highest national honor, the Presidential Medal of Freedom.

Lydia Brontë

able than middle-aged people toward Richard Nixon over John F. Kennedy. The distribution of presidential votes among all age groups was similar throughout the 1980s as well (Binstock, 1990). Table 8.13 displays the 1988 presidential vote. All age groups are closely divided between the candidates, and the difference between age groups is small.

Voting behavior in congressional elections exhibits much the same pattern: sharp divisions within age groups, small differences on average between age groups (Binstock, 1990). In the 1990 congressional elections, as noted in Table 8.14, the youngest and the oldest voters were the most Democratic and least Republican in their choices. But the differences from one age group to the next never vary by more than a few percentage points.

Older Americans clearly do not vote as a monolithic bloc, nor do they distinguish themselves in their electoral choices from younger voters.

Politicians nevertheless act sometimes as though elderly voters might exact retribution at the polls for any action taken against old-age benefits. The repeal of the Medicare Catastrophic Coverage Act illustrates this concern for appeasing older constituencies, as does President Reagan's hasty withdrawal of a proposal to cut Social Security benefits in 1981. Among federal programs funded

Table 8.13
1988 Presidential Vote, by Age (Percent of Two-Party Vote)

	Age				
	18–35	36–49	50–64	65–74	75+
Bush	51	53	56	52	52
Dukakis	49	47	44	48	48
Total	100	100	100	100	100

Source: American National Election Study, 1988.

Table 8.14
Partisan Vote for Congress, by Age, 1990 (Percent of Two-Party Vote)

	Age				
	18–35	36–49	50–64	65–74	75+
House					
Democrat	68	62	61	64	70
Republican	32	38	39	36	30
Total	100	100	100	100	100
Senate					
Democrat	59	57	56	59	68
Republican	41	43	44	41	32
Total	100	100	100	100	100

Source: American National Election Study, 1990.

by discretionary domestic spending, social services for the aging suffered the least from the budget cuts of the early Reagan administration (Day, 1990).

Older people have yet to demonstrate their ability to unite in national elections and swing the vote. However, they are very well organized politically in a multitude of advocacy groups. These organizations may employ what Binstock (1990) calls "the electoral bluff," convincing elected officials of the potential for collective action—including at the polls—on the part of the elderly.

● OLD-AGE POLITICAL ORGANIZATIONS

Old-age interest groups represent one of the great political success stories of the later twentieth century. The last three decades have wit-

Organizations advocating for the elderly have empowered many seniors to speak out at public hearings. (Courtesy of the American Association of Retired Persons)

nessed a tremendous expansion in the number, the memberships, the visibility, and the political activity of these groups. Some of them contribute money to political campaigns; however, their main sources of strength are their large memberships, which they can mobilize in massive letter-writing campaigns and other activities, and their lobbying expertise, which has gained them Washington insider status (Day, 1990).

These groups rarely present a united front. While many of them coalesce periodically around certain issues, they differ in their outlooks and goals in several ways. The range and variety of groups, in fact, reflect the diversity of the older Americans they represent (see Day, 1990; Lammers, 1983; Pratt, 1983, 1976).

The American Association of Retired Persons (AARP), with over 30 million members, is the largest and most visible of the organizations today. It is, in fact, one of the largest voluntary organizations of any type. Founded in 1947, AARP was originally a service organization concerned with older people's status, self-esteem, and access to insurance. By the 1970s AARP had evolved into a political organization as well, and its membership recruitment and political efforts expanded dramatically throughout the 1980s. Today AARP has a moderate-to-liberal stance, actively lobbying to expand old-age and other social welfare benefits. Its staff of 1,300 includes an active legislative staff of over 100; its annual budget exceeds $200 million; it even has its own zip code in Washington.

AARP's 30 million members range widely in their political views. The organization attracts such a large and diverse membership by offering a multitude of benefits for a low membership fee, including insurance and health aid discounts, mail-order pharmaceuticals, travel services, investment opportunities, tax assistance, magazines, and newsletters. In addition, members can meet socially and get involved politically through thousands of local chapters.

The National Council of Senior Citizens (NCSC) is an organization of over 4,000 state and local clubs with more than 5 million members. Founded with the support of labor unions and the Democratic National Committee, NCSC arose out of the campaign to establish Medicare and still retains its liberal stance and its union ties. Contributions from its political action committee,

The American Association of Retired Persons (AARP) is the largest and most visible senior (50+) interest group in the United States. (Courtesy of the American Association of Retired Persons)

formed in the 1980s, go primarily to Democratic candidates. Most of its leaders are retired union members, and its members are largely retired blue-collar workers; but it has been working to expand its appeal beyond its union base. NCSC, like AARP, offers an array of membership benefits, although not on the same grand scale.

With a staff of over 100, NCSC, like AARP, actively lobbies the government; it also holds mass rallies and demonstrations to attract government and media attention. Both organizations can mobilize large letter-writing campaigns. While they often work together on aging policy issues, NCSC, with its retired blue-collar membership, and AARP, with a larger white-collar and professional contingent, sometimes clash on such issues as mandatory retirement.

The Gray Panthers was founded as a radical coalition of "age and youth in action" by 67-year-old activist Maggie Kuhn in 1970. The Panthers' goals emphasize radical social change, and the issues pushed by the organization extend beyond old-age benefits and age discrimination to include anti-poverty and nuclear arms reduction programs. The Gray Panthers is loosely organized with over 6,000 members in 80 local chapters, or networks. While the Panthers do lobby at the national level, they engage more often in local grassroots organizing and street demonstrations.

At the conservative end of the ideological scale is the National Alliance of Senior Citizens (NASC), founded in 1974. NASC calls itself the organization for "responsible" senior citizens, and opposes most federal spending for old-age programs on the grounds that such spending will bankrupt the government and prove detrimental to older people in the long run. NASC has no local chapters; instead, it has recruited its 375,000 members through a computerized direct-mail operation, offering health insurance and other services to those who join. NASC restricts its lobbying to the national level.

The newcomer among elderly mass membership organizations is the National Committee to Preserve Social Security and Medicare (NCPSSM), founded in 1982 by Franklin D. Roosevelt's son James. Like NASC, NCPSSM has no local chapters, and it recruits members through computerized direct mail. With more than five million members, NCPSSM also operates a large grassroots lobbying network through its direct mail system. Its massive letter-writing and petition drives have become highly visible on Capitol Hill, and its staff lobbies the government directly as well. Some legislators have denounced its grassroots lobbying techniques for using "scare tactics" in its mass mailings—warning members of immediate crises in the Social Security fund, for example. However, the millions of letters to Congress produced in such campaigns are difficult for government officials to ignore. NCPSSM also has a large political action committee.

Some old-age mass membership organizations with a narrower occupational focus also have a strong presence in Washington. The National Association of Retired Federal Employees (NARFE) is one of the oldest and most visible. Founded in 1921, NARFE has about a half million members, 1,700 local chapters, a small legislative staff, and a large political action committee. NARFE maintains high visibility and respect among policy makers. Its members are, after all, retired federal employees, and they know their way around the national government.

Several groups with a more narrowly defined demographic and policy focus were formed during the 1970s, most of which consist mainly of policy professionals and academics. The exception is the Older Women's League (OWL), a grassroots organization with over 10,000 members. Other advocacy organizations for particular groups of older people include the National Caucus and Center on Black Aged, the Asociacion Nacional pro Personas Mayores, the National Indian Council on Aging, and the National Asian/Pacific Center on Aging.

The Families U.S.A. Foundation is the most visible organization focusing exclusively on the problems of the elderly poor. The foundation donates funds to other persons and groups for research and advocacy on low-income elderly issues. Families U.S.A. is not a membership organization, nor does it have a political action committee, but it engages a small staff of well-connected lobbyists and policy specialists.

Organizations of professionals and service providers studying and serving the elderly are also active on the national political scene. The largest of these is the National Council on the Aging (NCOA), a loose confederation of some seven thousand public and private social welfare agencies and specialists in gerontology and geriatrics founded in 1950. NCOA and other professional and service provider associations add prominence to aging policy issues through expert research and testimony.

This array of organizations advocating on

The National Caucus and Center on Black Aged has supported advocacy for African-American elderly. (Courtesy of the National Association for the Advancement of Colored People)

behalf of older Americans is formidable. But it is also a diverse range of groups, sometimes with conflicting strategies and goals. The Medicare Catastrophic Coverage Act is one example of an issue that generated conflicts among the old-age organizations.

The American Association of Retired Persons and the National Council of Senior Citizens both supported the bill, reluctantly accepting the seniors-only tax on the grounds that overall benefits outweighed the costs to the elderly. Both organizations continued to support the program after it was passed, despite complaints from many of their own members about the progressive income surtax.

Other old-age interest groups opposed the bill. The absence of long-term care coverage was the source of much organized opposition, including that of the Gray Panthers and the National Committee to Preserve Social Security and Medicare. After the bill's passage in 1988, the most visible opposition focused on the financing scheme. NCPSSM was among the groups that prompted an outpouring of letters and phone calls demanding repeal, along with the National Association of Retired Federal Employees and the Retired Officers Association. The latter two organizations objected to their members having to pay for benefits they already enjoyed under federal retirement health insurance programs, and they led a coalition of forty-four groups opposed to the new law (Day, 1990; Haas, 1989; Torres-Gil, 1989).

Such disarray among old-age advocacy groups, on this and other issues, does not mean that older people are not being well represented. On the contrary, as Freeman (1975) has observed, "American movements have thrived best when they were highly pluralistic, with each group within them having a solid identity and sense of purpose rather than trying to be everything to everyone." Old-age organizations have been effective in attaining—or at least in defending—government programs and benefits for older Americans, even if they do not always work in perfect harmony.

● COALITIONS AND SOCIAL MOVEMENTS IN OLD-AGE ADVOCACY

The success of old-age organizations, both in building their memberships and in gaining visibility and access to policy makers, has increased their popularity as coalition partners. Interest groups promoting various social welfare programs, concerned about cutbacks in the domestic budget, have enlisted the aid of elderly groups. Until just a decade or two ago, however, it was the old-age groups who were depending more upon other organizations for advocacy and support (Day, 1990; Pratt, 1976; Williamson, Evans, and Powell, 1982).

Old-age membership organizations played a small part, at best, in the pension movement of the 1920s and 1930s that finally resulted in the enactment of Social Security. Other social insurance advocacy groups, industrial managers, and government officials were much more instrumental. In the 1960s and 1970s, an era of impressive political gains for older Americans, organized labor was critical to the passage of Medicare, the Employee Retirement Insurance Security Act, and expanded Social Security benefits. In addition, consumer groups pushed for more nursing home and prescription drug regulation; the blind and disabled supported higher Supplemental Security Income benefits; and other social welfare lobbies aided the elderly on a number of issues. All of these actions contributed to a general social movement promoting improvements in the lives of older Americans.

By 1980 the movement had evolved into well-defined and established old-age interest groups with a power base of their own. Yet the power they exercise, like that of many interest groups, is often defensive—more effective in defending old-age benefits than in program expansion or innovation. Nor have old-age advocacy groups done much to change the vast inequalities among the elderly. Older people have become increasingly diverse and the gap between the richest and the poorest has widened. While the elderly as a group have achieved many gains, the needs of the most disadvantaged elderly remain unfulfilled (Binstock, 1990).

Horizontal alliances among old-age organizations were popular and effective in the late 1970s and early 1980s, as exemplified by the Leadership Council of Aging Organizations, which helped fight Social Security reductions. Today, vertical alliances among aging and nonaging groups have become more common, in response to various factors: (1) the increasing diversity within each

age group, (2) the need to defend domestic programs in the face of ongoing deficits and a burdensome national debt, (3) the push to expand the welfare state to include such universal benefits as long-term care and medical insurance for people of all ages, and (4) the backlash among some political elites against the elderly who, opponents claim, enjoy a disproportionate share of government benefits paid for by younger taxpayers (Torres-Gil, 1992).

Old-age membership organizations played a small part, at best, in the pension movement of the 1920s and 1930s that finally resulted in the enactment of Social Security. Other social insurance advocacy groups, industrial managers, and government officials were much more instrumental. In the 1960s and 1970s, an era of impressive political gains for older Americans, organized labor was critical to the passage of Medicare, the Employee Retirement Insurance Security Act, and expanded Social Security benefits.

Generations United, a coalition of over one hundred organizations representing children and the elderly, is a prominent example. The National Council on the Aging and the Child Welfare League of America led the coalition formation in 1986. Today, the American Association of Retired Persons and the Children's Defense Fund serve with them as coalition co-chairs. Generations United members respond to charges of generational conflict by asserting that one age group's gain is not necessarily another's loss. Expansion of benefits for all age groups, they suggest, may be funded through such means as defense cuts, energy taxes, and taxes on millionaires (Dumas, 1991).

No coalition, horizontal or vertical, is easy to maintain in the face of fiscal austerity. One development causing friction in both types of alliances is the government's trend toward differential treatment of poorer and wealthier older people. Not only did the Medicare Catastrophic Coverage Act contain a progressive surtax, but the 1983 Social Security amendments also began taxing a

A well known aging advocate until his death in 1989, Congressman (and former Senator) Claude Pepper addresses a national conference of the National Council on the Aging. (Courtesy of the National Council on the Aging, Inc.)

portion of the benefits of higher income recipients. These taxes have helped to finance benefit increases for the elderly poor. The 1986 Tax Reform Act eliminated the general personal exemption for all older people while providing tax credits to those with low incomes, and Older Americans Act programs are moving toward the use of sliding scale fees (Binstock, 1990; Haas, 1987).

There are two possible reactions to this trend: older people may unite to defend their universal age-based benefits, or relatively disadvantaged people of all ages may unite to expand the social welfare state. One type of conflict or another is probably inevitable, as long as the national government remains in debt, economic growth remains slow, and resistance to higher taxes remains strong. Although there is little sign of generational conflict in Americans' attitudes today, the complex interaction of age, class, and partisan divisions makes it difficult to predict the shape of future conflicts.

NOTE: 1. The survey data analyzed in this chapter come from the following studies: American National Election Study, 1988 (number of cases = 2,040); American National Election Study, 1990 (number of cases = 2,000); ABC News/*Washington Post* Poll of Public Opinion on Aging, 1982 (number of cases = 1,672); and ABC News/*Washington Post* National Survey, August 1989 (number of cases = 1,509). Data for the first two studies were originally collected by Warren E. Miller and the National Election Studies; data for the other two were originally collected by ABC News and *The Washington Post*. The first three were made available by the Inter-University Consortium for Political and Social Research; the fourth was made available by The Roper Center for Public Opinion Research. Neither the collectors nor the distributors of the data bear any responsibility for the analyses or interpretations presented here.

Organizations

American Association of Homes for the Aging
901 E St., NW, Ste. 500
Washington, DC 20004-2037
(202) 783-2242
(202) 783-2255 (fax)

American Association of Retired Persons (AARP)
601 E St., NW
Washington, DC 20049
(202) 434-2277
(202) 785-8524

American Society on Aging
833 Market St., Room 516
San Francisco, CA 94103
(415) 974-9600
(415) 974-0300 (fax)

Asociacion Nacional pro Personas Mayores
3325 Wilshire Blvd., Ste. 800
Los Angeles, CA 90010-1784
(213) 487-1922
(213) 385-3014 (fax)

Catholic Golden Age
1255 23rd St., NW, Ste. 285
Washington, DC 20005
(202) 775-4557
(202) 775-4391 (fax)

Families USA
1334 G St., NW
Washington, DC 20005
(202) 737-6340
(202) 347-2417 (fax)

Gray Panthers
2025 Pennsylvania Ave., NW, Ste. 821
Washington, DC 20006
(202) 466-3132
(202) 466-3133 (fax)

National Alliance of Senior Citizens
1700 18th St., NW, Ste. 401
Washington, DC 20009
(202) 986-0117

National Asian/Pacific Center on Aging
Melbourne Tower, Ste. 914
1511 Third Ave.
Seattle, WA 98101
(206) 624-1221
(206) 624-1023 (fax)

National Association of Area Agencies on Aging
1112 16th St., NW, Ste. 100
Washington, DC 20036
(202) 296-8130
(202) 296-8134 (fax)

National Association of Retired Federal Employees
1533 New Hampshire Ave., NW
Washington, DC 20036
(202) 234-0832
(202) 797-9697 (fax)

National Association of State Units on Aging
1225 I St., NW, Ste. 725
Washington, DC 20005
(202) 898-2578
(202) 898-2583 (fax)

National Caucus and Center on Black Aged
1424 K St., NW, Ste. 500
Washington, DC 20005
(202) 637-8400
(202) 347-0895 (fax)

National Committee to Preserve Social Security and Medicare
2000 K St., NW, Ste. 800
Washington, DC 20006
(202) 822-9459
(202) 822-9612 (fax)

National Council of Senior Citizens
1331 F St., NW
Washington, DC 20004-1171
(202) 347-8800
(202) 624-9595 (fax)

National Council on the Aging
409 Third St., SW, 2d Fl.
Washington, DC 20024
(202) 479-1200
(202) 479-0735 (fax)

National Hispanic Council on Aging
2713 Ontario Rd. NW, Ste. 200
Washington, DC 20009
(202) 745-2521
(202) 745-2522 (fax)

National Senior Citizens Law Center
1815 H St., NW, Ste. 700
Washington, DC 20006
(202) 887-5280
(202) 785-6792 (fax)

Older Women's League
666 11th St., Ste. 700
Washington, DC 20001
(202) 783-6686
(202) 638-2356 (fax)

References

Bengtson, Vern L., Neal E. Cutler, David J. Mangen, and Victor W. Marshall. "Generations, Cohorts, and Relations Between Age Groups." In *Handbook of Aging and the Social Sciences*. 2d ed. Eds. Robert H. Binstock and Ethel Shanas. New York: Van Nostrand Reinhold, 1985.

Binstock, Robert H. "The Politics and Economics of Aging and Diversity." In *Diversity in Aging: Challenges Facing Planners and Policymakers in the 1990s*. Eds. Scott A. Bass, Elizabeth Ann Kutza, and Fernando M. Torres-Gil. Glenview, IL: Scott, Foresman, 1990.

Button, James W., and Walter A. Rosenbaum. "Seeing Gray: School Bond Issues and the Aging in Florida." *Research on Aging* Vol. 11 (1989): 158–73.

Campbell, Angus. "Politics Through the Life Cycle." *Gerontologist* Vol. 11 (1971): 112–17.

Campbell, John Creighton, and John Strate. "Are Old People Conservative?" *Gerontologist* Vol. 21 (1981): 580–91.

Chomitz, Kenneth M. "Demographic Influences on Local Public Education Expenditures: A Review of Econometric Evidence." In *Demographic Change and the Well-Being of Children and the Elderly*. Ed. Committee on Population, Commission on Behavioral and Social Sciences and Education, National Research Council. Washington, DC: National Academy Press, 1987.

Congressional Quarterly. "Catastrophic-Coverage Law Is Repealed." *Congressional Quarterly Almanac, 1989*. Washington, DC: *Congressional Quarterly*, 1989.

Cutler, Stephen J. "Aging and Voluntary Association Participation." *Journal of Gerontology* Vol. 32 (1977): 470–79.

Day, Christine L. *What Older Americans Think: Interest Groups and Aging Policy.* Princeton, NJ: Princeton University Press, 1990.

———. "Older Americans' Attitudes Toward the Medicare Catastrophic Coverage Act of 1988." *Journal of Politics* Vol. 55 (1993): 167–77.

Dobson, Douglas, and Douglas St. Angelo. *Politics and Senior Citizens: Advocacy and Policy Formation in a Local Context.* Washington, DC: U.S. Administration on Aging, 1980.

Dumas, Kitty. "Focus on Children May Curtail Funding Plans for Elderly." *Congressional Quarterly Weekly Report* (May 11, 1991): 1206–07.

Fairlie, Henry. "Talkin' 'bout My Generation." *New Republic* (March 28, 1988): 18–22.

Freeman, Jo. *The Politics of Women's Liberation.* New York: Longman, 1975.

Haas, Lawrence J. "Big-Ticket Restrictions." *National Journal* (September 26, 1987): 2413–18.

———. "Fiscal Catastrophe." *National Journal* (October 7, 1989): 2453–56.

Hudson, Robert B., and John Strate. "Aging and Political Systems." In *Handbook of Aging and the Social Sciences.* 2d ed. Eds. Robert H. Binstock and Ethel Shanas. New York: Van Nostrand Reinhold, 1985.

Klemmack, David L., and Lucinda L. Roff. "Public Support for Age as an Eligibility Criterion for Programs for Older Persons." *Gerontologist* Vol. 20 (1980): 148–53.

Kosterlitz, Julie. "States Bracing for 'Medigap' Abuses." *National Journal* (December 16, 1989): 3056–57.

Lammers, William W. *Public Policy and the Aging.* Washington, DC: Congressional Quarterly Press, 1983.

"Late Bloomer" audio cassette. Available from Connie Goldman Productions, 926 Second Street, Suite 201, Santa Monica, CA 90403. (310) 393-6801.

Longman, Phillip. "Justice Between the Generations." *Atlantic Monthly* (June 1985): 73–81.

Moon, Marilyn. "The Rise and Fall of the Medicare Catastrophic Coverage Act." *National Tax Journal* Vol. 43 (1991): 371–81.

Ponza, Michael, Greg J. Duncan, Mary Corcoran, and Fred Groskind. "The Guns of Autumn? Age Differences in Support for Income Transfers to the Young and Old." *Public Opinion Quarterly* Vol. 52 (1988): 441–66.

Pratt, Henry J. *The Gray Lobby.* Chicago, IL: University of Chicago Press, 1976.

———. "National Interest Groups Among the Elderly: Consolidation and Constraint." In *Aging and Public Policy: The Politics of Growing Old in America.* Eds. William P. Browne and Laura Katz Olson. Westport, CT: Greenwood Press, 1983.

Riley, Matilda White. "Aging and Cohort Succession: Interpretations and Misinterpretations." *Public Opinion Quarterly* Vol. 37 (1973): 35–49.

Rovner, Julie. "The Catastrophic-Costs Law: A Massive Miscalculation." *Congressional Quarterly Weekly Report* (October 14, 1989): 2712–15.

———. "Climbing Medigap Premiums Draw Attention on Hill." *Congressional Quarterly Weekly Report* (February 17, 1990): 527–31.

Schreiber, E. M., and Lorna R. Marsden. "Age and Opinions on a Government Program of Medical Aid." *Journal of Gerontology* Vol. 27 (1972): 95–101.

Torres-Gil, Fernando M. *The New Aging: Politics and Change in America.* New York: Auburn House, 1992.

———. "The Politics of Catastrophic and Long-Term Care Coverage." *Journal of Aging and Social Policy* Vol. 1 (1989): 61–86.

U.S. Bureau of the Census. "Voting and Registration in the Election of November 1988." *Current Population Reports,* Series P-20, no. 440. Washington, DC: U.S. Government Printing Office, 1989.

Weaver, Jerry L. "The Elderly as a Political Community." *Western Political Quarterly* Vol. 29 (1976): 610–19.

Williamson, John B., Linda Evans, and Lawrence A. Powell. *The Politics of Aging: Power and Policy.* Springfield, IL: C. C. Thomas, 1982.

Wolfinger, Raymond E., and Stephen J. Rosenstone. *Who Votes?* New Haven, CT: Yale University Press, 1980.

Christine L. Day, Ph.D

9

Legal Issues

- Problems Faced by the Elderly • Emergence of Elder Law • Resources for Legal Services
- Specialized Practice • The Private Bar • Finding an Elder Law Attorney
- Legal Issues That Increase with Aging • Legal Planning for Incapacity
- Protective Services • Durable Power of Attorney • Health Care Power of Attorney
- Living Wills/Natural Death Acts
- The Social Security System • Administrative Law • Summary

Issues are raised here to alert readers to a number of the legal problems faced by the nation's elderly. This should not be considered as offering legal advice. It is always wise to check with local legal services programs, state bar associations, and specialized community legal services programs or hotlines.

One of the most significant demographic facts affecting America's present and future direction is the aging of its population. In fact, the older population as a proportion of the total population has tripled in this century. In 1900 fewer than one in ten Americans was age 55, and only one in twenty-five was age 65 and over. No Social Security and few retirement plans existed.

By 1990 one in five Americans was at least 55 years old (52.6 million) and one in eight was at least 65 (31 million). Of these, 18.1 million were 65 to 74, 10.1 million were 75 to 84, and 3.1 million were 85+ (often referred to as the old-old). This "graying of America" has contributed to a host of complex law-related problems for society at large and the elderly in particular. What are these problems? What are some of the consequences of these problems? This chapter presents an overview of legal issues that concern the elderly, the legal resources available, and information that older persons and their families should know.

● PROBLEMS FACED BY THE ELDERLY

The elderly are often dependent on programs and services provided by large governmental bureaucracies that are implemented through complex, rapidly changing regulations. They commonly face Social Security, (Supplemental Security Income, SSI), Medicare, Medicaid, pension, tax, will and probate, nursing homes, consumer rights, housing, guardianship, and age discrimination problems. Also, because of increased longevity, there is a realistic likelihood that many elderly will become frail and need assistance with activities of daily living (ADLs).

The demand for long term care is expected to increase primarily because of the growth in the proportion of people age 85+, many of whom will require nursing home care. In 1990, approximately seven million older people needed long term care. By 2005, the number is expected to increase to about nine million. Advances in medical technology that provide the means to prolong life such as respirators, increased use of antibiotics, and artificial nutrition and hydration create new choices that many older people may want to discuss with attorneys before an emergency situation arises. Questions about the right-to-die controversy, how to maintain one's dignity when confronting the end of life, and other health care decision-making may need to be documented through legal instruments. When such instruments become effective has to do with another legal concept, that of a person's mental capacity to make decisions in a health care context.

The President's Commission on Bioethical Decision-Making and the Office of Technology Assessment's Life-Sustaining Technology studies differentiate the individual's capacity to make different types of decisions. For example, the capacity to sign a will may be different from the decision to consent to take medicine or refuse surgery. Moreover, if there is a question about the capacity of an individual to make such decisions, the court, through guardianship, will need to intervene. However, the two studies mentioned above suggest that the capacity to make decisions may differ based on the complexity of the decisions, the person's ability to understand the consequences, and even the time of the day. For someone whose mental faculties may be decreasing because of a disease and/or old age, the person may demonstrate greater ability to make important decisions in the morning when most alert. All these factors taken into account demonstrate how complex the plight of the elderly can be.

● EMERGENCE OF ELDER LAW

Elder law is now an emerging area of the law. Just as American companies and organizations are increasingly gearing their products and services to an older audience, the legal profession now claims a small but growing group of specialists known as "elder law" attorneys.

Today, elder law attorneys champion a movement they claim will challenge long-held notions both about their own profession and about the aging process. Generally, there are two groups of attorneys who serve older clients: private attorneys and publicly funded legal services attorneys.

Just as American companies and organizations are increasingly gearing their products and services to an older audience, the legal profession now claims a small but growing group of specialists known as "elder law" attorneys.

Not long ago, lawyers who provided traditional services to seniors were expert at either poverty issues (attorneys employed by legal services organizations) or planning for death (attorneys in private practice). The publicly funded attorneys

---

Voices of Creative Aging

Jacob L., a retired public school administrator who earned a law degree at age 67, tells his experience of meeting the challenge of changing one's career in later life:

I was having Thanksgiving dinner at my home with my son, my daughter, and four grandchildren. My daughter was telling us about her experiences going to law school, and I was very envious of her. I said, "I wish I could do that!" She said, "Why don't you?" I replied, "How can I? Here I am; I'm old and decrepit and aged. And anyway, no one would want to accept an old man in his dotage." My daughter told me I didn't know that and if I really wanted to do it, I could.

That weekend I made a commitment to my daughter and my son that I really would find out. The very next Monday I telephoned New York University and asked point blank whether it was possible for me to go to law school. The response was that they couldn't turn me down solely because I was too old and I was invited to go and take the exam that upcoming Saturday. I hustled over to a bookstore and got some exam practice materials. I took that exam, and to my surprise I did very well. So, I went to law school.

The proudest moment of my life was at graduation. The dean cautioned the audience not to applaud and disrupt the proceeding but to wait until all the names were announced. But when they called my name, everybody in the place got up and applauded. If I had won all the medals at graduation, it would not have meant as much as that moment to me. Society must come to understand that growing older doesn't diminish a person's individual worth.

I framed my diploma and prepared to hit the pavement in search of a job. A foundation, which had read about me in the local newspaper, offered me a position concerned with legal issues for the aging. I accepted the position and have devoted my energy to working for the economic benefits for the elderly poor in this community.

Excerpt from Connie Goldman's "Late Bloomer"
public radio series

still concentrate on administrative law, income maintenance, and problems created by institutionalization. Private attorneys now focus more broadly on legal planning. They work with other professionals to concentrate on meeting all of a client's legal needs.

Whether they were publicly funded legal services attorneys previously or were always private attorneys, those specializing in elder law agree that the range of issues they must understand demands a holistic approach to practicing law and serving their clients. The National Academy of Elder Law Attorneys (NAELA), a national organization of attorneys serving older clients, was founded in 1987 in order that "elder law attorneys focus on the legal needs of the elderly, and work with a variety of legal tools, techniques, and professionals to meet the goals and objectives of the older client" (NAELA brochure). According to NAELA, under this holistic approach the elder law practitioner handles general estate planning issues and counsels clients about planning for incapacity with alternative decision-making documents. The attorney also assists the client in planning for possible long-term care needs, including nursing home care. In addition, the elder care attorney may locate the appropriate type of care, coordinate private and public resources to finance the cost of care, and work to ensure the client's right to quality care. To add to the complexity, consider the case of a husband who has Alzheimer's disease and whose condition is gradually degenerating. What is the attorney's responsibility to the surviving spouse? How does the attorney look after the husband's needs and at the same time protect the interests of the wife? Such a holistic approach might also be appropriate for physicians, social workers, and other service providers so that the older person can be provided with the appropriate type of care and services.

Since most Americans rarely plan for possible scenarios such as the case noted above, the elder law attorney advises his or her clients about the options or alternatives for action. These options may vary from family to family depending upon finances, insurance, housing opportunities, and so forth. A holistic approach provides greater opportunity for planning and meeting the special needs of the couple, together and individually.

This holistic strategy of working with a variety of professionals has its advantages in attempting to resolve complex issues. However, there are also potential disadvantages.

Confidentiality

Attorneys have specific rules of professional conduct that provide for confidential communication with the client as well as how to conduct exchanges of information with other professionals. The attorney must have the client's permission to communicate with physicians, stock brokers, financial planners, social workers, and others.

Identifying the Client and Non-Clients

When a family or a couple approach an attorney, there may be a question as to who is the client. For social workers, the client could very easily be the family. Ethically speaking, therefore, the attorney needs to determine whom he or she is representing. When, for example, a daughter calls an attorney for an appointment for her mother and says that she will be paying the attorney's fee for her mother's will, a durable power of attorney, and guidance on transferring her mother's assets so that when the mother needs to go to a nursing home she will be eligible for Medicaid—who is the client? Many elder law attorneys consider the older person as the client, but the above situation is very common and creates a potential conflict for the attorney. This is especially problematic if, for example, the daughter will be the beneficiary.

Moral and Ethical Considerations

Elder law attorneys frequently find themselves having to make moral and ethical judgments that

Elder law attorneys must deal with the potential conflict arising when an adult child seeks legal advice for an aged parent. Who is the client? (Copyright © Marianne Gontarz)

fall outside the purview of the law. They may need to determine, for example, the motivation of family members, the quality of the family's relationships, and what the older person would want if he or she could express his or her wishes.

● RESOURCES FOR LEGAL SERVICES

There are several potential sources for providing legal services to the public. The Legal Services Corporation and the Older Americans Act are two publicly financed federal sources. An ever increasing number of private attorneys and bar association services also are oriented toward serving the elderly.

The Legal Services Corporation

In 1975 the Legal Services Corporation (LSC) was established because of concerns that the poor in the United States were not being served by the private bar and that the poor did not have adequate resources to beneficially access the justice system. The Legal Services Corporation actually was an outgrowth of the War on Poverty Program started by President Lyndon Johnson in the 1960s. A quasi-governmental entity, LSC annually receives an appropriation from Congress, but has a presidentially appointed board of directors who oversee the program. The board and a central staff monitor and fund local programs throughout the country.

The LSC programs do not necessarily specialize in serving older clients, but do attempt to meet the legal needs of the poor, of which the elderly are a large proportion. LSC attorneys provide legal services to people based on financial need. Persons are eligible for the LSC if their income is no higher than 125 percent of the yearly established poverty level. LSC programs have had difficulties in reaching the isolated and vulnerable elderly who do not find their way to the LSC offices. Many elderly who are legally underserved do not know about the LSC. And if they are aware of available services, elderly in nursing homes cannot get out of their beds to see attorneys. One of the major differences between the LSC programs and those funded under the Older Americans Act is the mandatory nature of outreach.

At its height, before President Reagan cut its budget and tried to abolish it, the LSC had more than 700 offices throughout the country and was staffed by over 3,000 attorneys, in addition to paralegals, volunteers, and support staff. Despite the cutbacks, many elderly poor continue to be served by the LSC programs. The predominate method of service delivery used by LSC projects is the staff-attorney model. Attorneys are trained in poverty law issues and advocate for their clients through direct representation.

LSC attorneys primarily represent the elderly in government benefit cases such as Medicare, Social Security, food stamps, and public housing. LSC attorneys also may represent the elderly in housing, consumer issues such as enforcing home improvement contracts or credit issues, and health care issues.

Older Americans Act

The second federal program funding the delivery of legal assistance to the elderly is the Older Americans Act (OAA), originally adopted in 1965. In 1971 the White House Conference on Aging recommended that legal services be provided under the OAA, and this provision was included in the 1975 OAA reauthorization.

The structure of the Older Americans Act differs greatly from that of the LSC. Funded by Congress, the Administration on Aging (AoA) is a sub-unit of the Department of Health and Human Services, a large federal bureaucracy. It allocates funding to state entities which in turn fund local entities, which then fund legal services. However, legal services are only one of many service areas competing for funding. Nutrition programs, transportation, health care, recreation, and many others are all major services that impact the elderly and compete for funds. The services that are ultimately funded at a local level are determined annually by the local political decision-makers, the area agencies on aging (AAA). Despite an OAA mandate requiring legal representation as a required service, neither a specific dollar amount nor a percentage has been designated for this purpose. Those organizations that want to provide legal assistance must apply annually for the OAA funding.

Despite the barriers created by the legislation and the local political process, over 600 legal programs funded by OAA throughout the country attempt to meet the legal needs of those elderly who are in the greatest social and economic need. This targeting of services is needed since the allocation of OAA money to legal services is so small. The theory behind the OAA has been that, despite differing income levels, most older people are isolated, and all should be served. For services offered under the Act there is no means test. Many of the legal programs which receive OAA funding, perhaps as high as 50 percent, are also the local LSC grantees. The remainder are free-standing programs or programs providing services by contracts with private attorneys.

OAA funded programs are often different from LSC projects in the degree of outreach to the elderly community. OAA funded attorneys often spend as much as 50 percent of their time speaking at senior centers or nutrition sites and visiting persons either in nursing homes or in their own homes. OAA funds and programs specialize in government benefits as well as surrogate decision-making (guardianship, health care powers of attorney, durable powers of attorney for financial issues, and living wills) and health care access.

Many of the local agencies that fund legal services with OAA monies require programs to prepare wills and to provide community education. These are two areas where local private attorneys are encouraged to join the program on a pro bono (free of charge) basis. The role of the private bar in an OAA program may lead to greater clout. When, for example, the funding agency limits the type of representation, the private bar may be able to tackle law reform or class action cases through its pro bono representation. The private bar also may be able to act as a political factor in changing the nature of the OAA funded legal services future contracts by being involved. For instance, area agencies on aging are often part of county governments and may react as county governments to be protective of their own interests. These may be contrary to the interests of the elderly. Private attorneys can play an advocate's role as outsiders instead of the subcontractor who does not have political influence. Also, attorneys generally have influence in the communities in which they practice. But if the funding agency wants the legal assistance program to provide only wills and community education rather than public benefits, the elderly will suffer. In fact, under such conditions the current provider may lose interest in these issues and may not seek funding for the next year. A change in the provider may result in a loss of services to the elderly.

The Older Americans Act also requires that each state fund a legal services developer (LSD) to assure that the legal needs of the elderly are being met. The LSD is an employee of the state aging department or another agency who has a contract with the state agency. In some states the LSD will act as a general counsel to the state's department for the elderly, while in others he or she may encourage continuing legal education programs or work with the local agencies to ensure that enough funding is being provided for programs to meet the legal needs of the state's elderly population.

In addition, as in the case of the LSC Act, the OAA requires that national support be provided. To meet this requirement, the Administration on Aging (AoA) contracts with three national entities to provide this support. These entities are the National Senior Citizens Law Center (also the LSC national support center); Legal Counsel for the Elderly, a part of the American Association for Retired Persons (AARP, the largest older persons organization in the United States with 34 million members); and the American Bar Association's Commission on Legal Problems of the Elderly. AoA also funds other national and local legal assistance demonstration projects.

A recent development in the delivery of legal services has been the establishment of legal hotlines for the elderly. The Administration on Aging (AoA) and AARP's Legal Counsel for the Elderly have worked to fund and develop nine hotlines around the country. These legal hotlines provide free legal advice and referrals by toll-free telephone to those in a particular state. Each hotline is staffed by private attorneys who have been trained, and who are supervised by the legal services provider. If the hotline receives a problem that cannot be resolved over the phone, then the staff either matches the caller with a member of the statewide lawyer referral panel set up for the hotline or refers the caller to one of the in-house staff attorneys. The in-house or legal services referrals depend on the nature of the particular delivery system in the state. It might include several staff offices as well as pro bono attorneys. Hotlines currently exist in the District of Columbia, Pennsylvania, Maine, Florida, Michigan, Ohio, Texas, New Mexico, and Arizona. While only nine exist now, more are planned in the near future.

Profiles of Productive Aging

Eleanor Jackson Piel
Attorney

"I didn't follow the rules. If you work by yourself you're not used to the rules.... It just never occurred to me that I couldn't do anything that I wanted."

At 73 Eleanor Jackson Piel continues to practice law, motivated by nothing other than the sheer enjoyment that it brings her. Born in 1920 into an upper middle class family in Santa Monica, California, she wanted to be a journalist and worked for the paper when she attended University of California, Los Angeles. Regarding journalism as "sort of an entrance point to the events of the world," she became disillusioned when she realized that the journalist was a spectator and wasn't really making things happen.

After she began to study law, Piel discovered law was "a kind of lever on the world," with the power to make things happen in a way that journalism could not. She graduated from the University of Southern California Law School in 1943 and worked for a federal judge, as a deputy for the California state attorney general, for a senator in Washington, D.C., then transferred to the Justice Department, where she joined a U.S. attorney and his team of lawyers on their way to Japan to prosecute war criminals. From 1945 to 1948 she concentrated on writing the international prosecution section of the group's pamphlets and advising Japanese government emissaries. Piel is credited with singlehandedly helping Japanese government-run corporations distribute goods in short supply in order to get their industry going again.

After her return to Los Angeles in 1948, she worked for L.A. Bloom for two years, then, in 1950, she opened her own practice, specializing in criminal law. Marriage in 1955 to Gerard Piel meant a move to New York, leaving behind her successful practice in Los Angeles, but she was admitted to the New York bar and continued her emphasis on criminal law, adding gender and race discrimination litigation to her practice over the years. Of her victories, Piel noted that she represented a man in Florida wrongfully convicted of murder and secured a stay of execution for him sixteen hours before he was to be executed.

Lydia Brontë

A recent development in the delivery of legal services has been the establishment of legal hotlines for the elderly. The Administration on Aging (AoA) and AARP's Legal Counsel for the Elderly have worked to fund and develop nine hotlines around the country.

● SPECIALIZED PRACTICE

Older persons who have adequate financial resources have always had access to the legal profession, but not all lawyers have expertise in all areas of concern. The recently established National Academy of Elder Law Attorneys may be better able to meet the legal needs of these elderly because of their expertise and specialization in elder law. Although close to 40 percent of those in the United States die having made no valid will (intestate), the majority of the elderly seek out legal representation to write wills. To get one's life in order and to be able to designate the beneficiary of one's few possessions is a goal of most older persons. The elderly generally have access to will drafting through LSC or OAA funded attorneys, the wills panels sponsored by bar associations, and other private practitioners.

Another specialized bar has evolved to serve older and disabled individuals with their Social Security problems. The National Association of Social Security Claimants Representatives (NOSSCR) exists to provide training for attorneys interested in this area. Since attorneys' fees are allowed in Social Security cases, a segment of the bar has a primary practice in this area. The attorneys' fees paid in this area are deducted from the back-award that a claimant receives. Most persons prefer to lose some of an award by being represented rather than being denied eligibility and risk losing benefits. However, when legal services or pro bono attorneys represent clients in

Although close to 40 percent of individuals in the United States die having made no valid will, the majority of the elderly seek out legal representation to write wills. (Copyright © Marianne Gontarz)

such cases, the client receives the entire back-award. Legal representation in Social Security cases improves a client's chance of receiving a back-award or on-going benefits.

The National Academy of Elder Law Attorneys (NAELA)

In late 1987 a new attorney group, the National Academy of Elder Law Attorneys (NAELA), was incorporated to ensure delivery of quality legal services for the elderly and advocate for their rights. Generally they serve the needs of the elderly whose financial resources exceed the eligibility requirement of publicly financed legal assistance programs. The NAELA has become a specialty group similar to matrimonial attorneys, where those who seek services know that they will be served by experts in the field. Well over 1,500 attorneys nationwide belong to this organization and have a largely elderly clientele. These attorneys come predominantly from either legal services or estate planning backgrounds. The attorneys typically do comprehensive financial, legal, and health care planning with the families of Alzheimer's victims. The interplay between government benefit programs and estate planning is a major focus of this specialty. Additionally, a sensitivity to the aging process and knowledge of community services and resources are critical to the success of the elder law specialist.

● THE PRIVATE BAR

American Bar Association (ABA)

The American Bar Association (ABA) is the largest voluntary professional organization in the United States. Since the early 1970s the ABA's 370,000 members have taken policy positions to encourage the delivery of legal services to the poor and the elderly through active support of the Legal Services Corporation and the Older Americans Act. Entities within the ABA monitor the actions of the LSC and work to support congressional actions which increase funding in order to assure that adequate numbers of attorneys are available to meet the legal needs of the poor.

The ABA has many sections and entities whose substantive law concerns touch the lives of the elderly. The Real Property, Probate and Trust Law, Administrative Law, Individual Rights and Responsibilities, Senior Lawyers, Young Lawyers, Tort and Insurance Practice, Judicial Administration Division, and Science and Technology Sections have jurisdictions which address issues affecting the elderly.

The Commission on Legal Problems of the Elderly was formed in 1978 to act as an advocate for older persons within the association. It is composed of a fifteen-member interdisciplinary group appointed annually by the president of the ABA. The focus of the commission is to educate the members of the bar and the aging community about legal issues affecting the elderly. The staff and members of the commission participate in research on policy issues affecting older persons.

Committees of State and Local Bar Associations

There are over thirty-five state and twelve local bar association committees on the elderly. Some of these are free-standing, while others are subcommittees of other state or local bar entities. These entities usually have been established through the staff efforts of the ABA's Commission on Legal Problems of the Elderly. Since they are voluntary activities of the committee members, the programs and projects vary with the initiative and commitment of the leadership. The state bars of Arizona, Connecticut, Florida, Maine, Minnesota, New Hampshire, New York, Oregon, Virginia, Wisconsin, and Wyoming have established Sections on the Elderly because they considered that a committee was limited to just a few active members, yet the problems of the elderly were a growing issue.

Bar committee membership is usually limited to members of the bar. In some jurisdictions committees have followed the structure of the ABA commission and have an interdisciplinary membership. Some committees have budgets allowing them to travel to meetings (allowing for regular meetings), present seminars, and/or write and produce monographs. Activities vary from year to year as the leadership changes. Types of projects that might be undertaken are the provision of legal services, community education, continuing legal education, legislation, and substantive law issues.

Pro Bono Programs

Since the early 1980s there has been tremendous growth in the development of large scale pro bono programs. This has come about largely because of Legal Services Corporation's requirement that each of their programs spend 12.5 percent of their funds on private bar involvement and the Older Americans Act requirement that the local area agencies on aging work with the private bar. In addition, the canons of professional responsibility require that each attorney meet an obligation to provide service to the public.

All of the LSC-funded projects have sought a working relationship with state and local bar associations to jointly sponsor pro bono programs. The legal service grantee usually trains attorneys, screens clients, and acts as a resource for the private attorney in the area of public benefits law. In return, private attorneys generally take two to four free cases a year, depending on the nature of the cases. The programs and the bar associations work out the types of cases given to pro bono attorneys. Some cases may be simple wills, while others may involve major litigation that seeks to reform the law. The City Bar of New York has asked that each attorney, whether in a law firm, a corporation, or working for the government, spend at least thirty hours each year doing pro bono representation. The general counsel for Exxon and former secretary of state Cyrus Vance spearheaded the recruitment drive to assure a high level of participation. The ABA recommends that attorneys do fifty hours per year of pro bono legal services.

One can always tell when a program has become institutionalized; it is when a national association is formed. In 1991 the National Association of Pro Bono Coordinators formalized

its existence and now holds regular meetings. The ABA helped foster the development of pro bono by providing technical assistance to bar associations, by providing seed grants to programs in their infancy, and by providing political clout to the development of such projects. When state or local bar associations may have been skeptical about the idea, or when portions of the bar may have thought that their livelihoods might be in jeopardy, national leaders of the ABA would appear on the local level to provide reassurance.

Reduced-Fee Programs

Under a great number of lawyer referral programs in the United States, one can receive the names of attorneys by calling a bar association. There was an attempt a few years ago to develop sophisticated referral systems to refer only attorneys with experience in very circumscribed areas of the law. The notion was that a person would call a referral number, be screened to determine the nature of the legal problems, and then be given the names of lawyers who had also been screened to assure that they knew about the legal issues. This referral system has been proved to work only in very large bar associations where people specialize in specific areas of the law.

Attempting to have an overlay specifically to provide reduced fees for the elderly has been a difficult proposition. The problem of screening fees is impossible unless a fee structure is set up ahead of time to assure that attorneys are simply not reducing the cost of writing a will from $100 to $95, for example.

A person should choose an attorney as he or she would choose a doctor, dentist, accountant, or anyone providing professional services. (Copyright © Marianne Gontarz)

● FINDING AN ELDER LAW ATTORNEY

A person should choose an attorney as he or she would choose a doctor, dentist, accountant, or anyone providing professional services. However, before making the effort a person should determine whether he or she actually has a legal problem in which an attorney needs to be involved. If unsure, one may ask a social worker, a financial adviser, or a trusted friend to help decide whether this is a legal issue rather than a medical, social services, or financial issue. In many cases there will not be a clear distinction.

To find an attorney who specializes in problems of the elderly, individuals should check with local agencies to obtain good quality local referrals. Some of the agencies to call include Alzheimer's Association, American Association of Retired Persons, the local legal services program serving the elderly, the Area Agency (or Council) on Aging, state or local bar associations, and/or support groups for specific diseases.

However, the National Academy of Elder Law Attorneys does not make its membership list available to the general public. Most of the other agencies can be found in the yellow pages of the telephone book under the heading "Associations." Many attorneys give community talks or write columns for local newspapers about elder law issues. These lawyers may be very good resources for identifying other attorneys. In addition, many attorneys may be on the boards of local aging agencies or groups like the Alzheimer's Association and may be known to members of these groups.

To find an attorney who specializes in problems of the elderly, individuals should check with local agencies to obtain good quality local referrals. Some of the agencies to call include Alzheimer's Association, American Association of Retired Persons, the local legal services program serving the elderly, the Area Agency (or Council) on Aging, state or local bar associations, and/or support groups for specific diseases.

Members may have used the attorneys for their own legal needs and thus may know how effective the individual may be as an attorney. Attorneys can also give a referral to an elder law attorney. Often an attorney is aware of someone who handles such issues and whether that person is an effective attorney. Such persons are often the best and safest sources of referrals.

Potential clients should ask a lot of questions before selecting an elder law attorney. This should start with an initial phone call, since one does not want to end up paying an attorney who is unable to help. Questions such as the following should be asked:

1. How long has the attorney been in practice?
2. Does the attorney's practice emphasize a particular area of the law?
3. How long has the attorney been in this field?
4. What percentage of the attorney's practice is devoted to elder law?
5. Is there a fee for the first consultation, and if so, how much is it?
6. Given the nature of the problem, what information should be brought to the initial consultation?

The answers to these questions will help determine whether a particular attorney has the qualifications important for a successful attorney/client relationship. If a specific legal issue requires immediate attention, one should be sure to inform the office of this during the initial telephone conversation.

When an appropriate attorney is found, the client makes an appointment to see him or her. During the initial consultation, the attorney will usually ask the client to explain the reason that he or she is seeking assistance; so it is important for the older person to be prepared, to be organized, and to bring all the information pertinent to the situation.

After the prospective client has explained the situation, he or she should ask:

1. What will it take to resolve it?
2. Are there any alternative courses of action?
3. What are the advantages and disadvantages of each possibility?
4. How many attorneys are in the office?
5. Who will handle the case?

6. Has that attorney handled matters of this kind in the past?

7. If a trial may be involved, does the attorney do trial work? If not, who does the trial work? If so, how many trials of this nature has the attorney handled?

8. Is the attorney a member of the local bar association, its health advocacy committee, elder law committee, or trusts and estates committee?

9. Is the attorney a member of the National Academy of Elder Law Attorneys?

10. How are fees computed?

11. What is the attorney's estimate of the cost to resolve the problem, and how long will it take?

Regarding fees, there are many different ways of charging fees, and each attorney may choose to work differently. One should be aware of how the attorney charges. One should find out how often the attorney bills. It is a good idea to ask about these matters at the initial conference, so that there will be no surprises.

Some attorneys charge by the hour, with different hourly rates for work performed by attorneys, paralegals, and secretaries. If this is the case, the client should find out what the rates are. Other attorneys charge a flat fee for all or parts of the services. This is not unusual if, for example, one is having documents prepared. The attorney might use a combination of these billing methods.

In addition to fees, most attorneys will charge for their out-of-pocket expenses. Out-of-pocket expenses typically include charges for copies (and these may be very high, so check in advance), postage, messenger fees, court fees, deposition fees, long distance telephone calls, and other such costs. The client should find out if there will be any other incidental costs. The attorney may ask for a retainer (money paid before the attorney starts working on the case), which is usually placed in a trust account. Each time the attorney bills a client, the attorney pays himself or herself out of that account. The size of the retainer may range from a small percentage of the estimated cost to the full amount.

Once a person decides to hire the attorney, the older person should ask that the arrangement be put in writing in a letter or a formal contract. It should spell out what services the attorney will perform and what the fee and expense arrangement will be. Even if the agreement remains oral and is not put into writing, it still constitutes a contract; and the client is responsible for all charges for work done by the attorney and his or her staff.

● LEGAL ISSUES THAT INCREASE WITH AGING

The elderly share many of the legal problems of the rest of the population, but also have concerns that are expected to increase with age. As people age, they experience a unique set of physical, psychological, financial, and social changes such as retirement, loss of friends and family, change in residence, possible chronic medical conditions and sensory losses, and perhaps changes in self-perception and in orientation as the end of life draws near.

These changes generate a vast array of legal issues enmeshed in a complex of federal, state, and local laws, regulations, and programs. In particular, the elderly face problems in the following areas, some more than once, and often more than one problem at a time:

1. **Housing**: landlord-tenant, conversion of apartment to condominium, home ownership, mobile home, continuing care retirement communities

2. **Government benefits**: Social Security and Supplemental Security Income, Medicare and Medicaid, Qualified Medical Benefits, food stamps, veterans benefits, and other federal retirement programs

3. **Consumer**: collections, fraud and other scams, bankruptcy, hearing aids, eyeglasses, funeral arrangements, health quackery

4. **Health care**: access to health care, health insurance

5. **Employment**: pensions and age discrimination

6. **Personal decision-making**: health and financial planning, durable powers of attorney for financial and health care, living wills

7. **Guardianship and conservatorship**

8. **Nursing home**, home care, and other long term care services

9. **Family**: divorce, grandparent visitation, custody

To a non-lawyer, the legal system can be quite forbidding. People think of it as a costly, time-consuming means to resolve a problem and usually do not seek legal advice until the need arises. Although some problems certainly arise unexpectedly and must be handled promptly at that point, crises may at times be averted if they are anticipated and handled earlier. Legal action can help an individual gain access to or retain essential services, such as income, food, shelter, or health care, and through advance planning and preparation, it may enable a person to preserve his or her independence and decision-making authority.

Many resource materials are available at the state and local levels to help identify legal issues. Many of these are available through state and local bar associations, area agencies on aging, and legal services providers. For example, the State Bar of California has produced the book *Senior Citizens Handbook: Laws and Programs Affecting Older Californians*, and a brochure on nursing home rights was published by the Bet Tzedek Legal Services in Los Angeles. There is no complete list available of such publications, but such references are at the state or local bar associations, the legal services provider in the local community, or the local library.

● LEGAL PLANNING FOR INCAPACITY

This section examines alternative decision-making tools used by the elderly, the increasingly frail population, and persons with disabilities, and also describes protective services, guardianship, and the tools used for "advance planning." These tools include durable powers of attorney, living wills, and health care powers or proxies. Through guardianship and protective proceedings, the courts have been used when advance planning has not been anticipated. Without advance planning directives, persons who are unable to make their own decisions have, in essence, forfeited their autonomy, and the state has the authority to intervene and make those decisions on their behalf.

Without advance planning directives, the state will primarily intervene through guardianship or the use of protective services. Guardianships are generally involuntary, while protective services may be either voluntary or involuntary. Before any formal intervention is put into effect, the state assesses the individual's ability to make decisions.

The key question in doing any planning or intervention is determining whether the individual is no longer able to take care of his or her own affairs or person. The language as well as the legal concepts have changed in recent years. Previously, because of statutory language and practice, courts either found an individual incompetent or competent, without regard to the person's ability to make some types of decisions but not others. Reforms in this area have replaced the notion of total incompetency with partial capacity to perform some functions. Upon finding limited capacity, the court will fashion a decision based on the individual's ability. For example, a person may be able to balance a checkbook but may not be able to handle selling a house. The same is true for consent to health care. A person may have the ability to consent to routine medical care, but not to invasive surgery. More recently the terminology has shifted the emphasis away from examining the person's mental status and toward measuring the person's ability to function in society. The term incapacity may eradicate the negative and all-encompassing connotation of the term *incompetency* (Anderer, 1990). The use of the term incapacity also lends itself to the assessment of partial incapacity and partial disability. The term also reflects the emerging trend in the state statutes towards limited powers in guardianship.

● PROTECTIVE SERVICES

Since 1985 the area of adult protective services has radically changed. Previously, state and local governments sought to protect children; then, at the end of the 1970s, they began to apply some of the same principles to protect the elderly. The presumption is that if the state has an interest in protecting its vulnerable children based on its *Parens Patriae* role (Regan, 1981), then it has the same responsibility towards the vulnerable elderly.

Intervention can be provided through voluntary and involuntary methods. The latter is an action taken through either an administrative or a court procedure that is contrary to what the person needing help wants. The term "protective services" encompasses an interdisciplinary program of assistance to people with mental or physical disabilities who are not able to provide for their own basic needs. These services are often labeled preventive, supportive, and surrogate. The preventive role is based on early recognition of a need and the provision of information and encouragement for independent living. The supportive function is based upon the provision of assistance and support so the individual can maintain self-direction and attain the highest possible level of functioning.

Services are coordinated by a case worker who assesses each person's needs and arranges for appropriate services. In many instances these services assist persons in need who cannot identify or acquire necessary services and who might otherwise be unable to protect themselves from abuse, neglect, or exploitation.

Protective services are distinguished by the surrogate function, that is, the legal authorization to act in the person's behalf. This is accomplished through the appointment of a surrogate decision-maker and/or the provision of services with or without the individual's consent. These forms of involuntary services include civil commitment, representative payee and guardianship. Historically, civil commitment meant the involuntary placement of a mentally ill or developmentally disabled person in a hospital or other institution for protection and/or treatment. Currently, the term describes loss of liberty to a state authority, which may result in hospitalization, placement in a group home, or out-patient status that follows a course of treatment. Representative payee relates to a person or organization designated by a government agency to receive a public benefit payment on behalf of someone else (Legal Counsel for the Elderly, 1987).

Guardianship

Interest in guardianship matters was catapulted into the forefront when numerous stories of abuses by the system appeared in the press and led to an Associated Press (AP) study of the nation's guardianship system, which culminated in the report *Guardians of the Elderly: An Ailing System* (Associated Press, 1987). State legislatures, as well as the U.S. Congress, have responded by holding hearings on guardianship and introducing major legislative changes since the AP report was issued.

Guardianship can be defined broadly as the process by which a court finds a person's ability to make decisions so impaired that the court gives the right to make decisions to another person. The standards for defining what incapacity is and the process to impose a substitute decision-maker are generally left up to state statutes and procedures.

Each state jurisdiction has statutes for some form of guardianship of adult persons and conservatorship of their property if they are not able to care for themselves without assistance. Many states have combined these aspects into a single statute.

The 1987 AP study stressed that major problems existed in the administration of the various state guardianship statutes. The intent of guardianship is to assure care for incapacitated people.

Each state jurisdiction has statutes for some form of guardianship of adult persons and conservatorship of their property if they are not able to care for themselves without assistance. Many states have combined these aspects into a single statute.

For some time the major problems of the traditional guardianship statutes and their implementation have been documented (Hortsman, 1975; Mitchell, 1979; Regan, 1977 and 1981). All commentators raised similar concerns about: (1) the standards for determining incapacity; (2) court procedures failing to provide for adequate notice, the presence of the person at the hearing, and trial by jury; (3) representation by counsel; and (4) protection against conflicts of interest by guardian. Another very important concern raised by the early guardianship studies was the lack of alternatives and limited orders. In recent years, state statutes have been drafted that consider more limited scope of both orders and alternatives. For example, there has been a movement toward statutes providing for, and courts recommending, more limited intervention over a person's life, as opposed to full plenary guardianships (of all aspects of a person's life). Additional problems result from the lack of due process in the initial proceedings as well as the lack of court supervision of the guardian following his or her appointment (American Bar Association, 1989; Hurme, 1991).

Several states also have changed their statutes to consider additional alternatives, either through limited guardianship orders or other less restrictive planning tools. Some of these changes are discussed throughout the remainder of the chapter. A number of social service organizations have developed money management programs (Zuckerman, 1988) to provide for less intrusive intervention. Volunteer programs for people to be representative payees for Social Security or Veterans Administration beneficiaries have spread throughout the country. A movement exists nationwide to develop alternatives to guardianship, all of which have their advantages and disadvantages.

Voluntary Guardianship as an Alternative

Some states allow individuals to ask courts to appoint guardians over their property voluntarily. This option is generally known as a voluntary guardianship, and these laws enable an individual who is aware of, or concerned about, the impending loss or risk of incapacity to plan for property management prior to becoming incapacitated. A voluntary guardianship may be seen as an alternative to a full (plenary), involuntary guardianship (Stiegel, 1992).

Depending on an individual's circumstances, a voluntary guardianship may have advantages over other alternative measures such as durable powers of attorney, living trusts, or joint property management. These advantages include: (1) avoiding the stigma of being involuntarily declared legally incompetent, (2) possibly having more control over the selection of the guardian, and (3) allowing court oversight and monitoring of the guardian's actions. This alternative could be particularly useful if the individual does not have anyone he or she trusts to act as a surrogate or to add as a joint owner of property or bank accounts.

Several alternatives exist to assure maintenance of an individual's autonomy. In general, these legal tools assure decision-making on health and financial issues. Such planning can be incorporated into the estate planning process. Several legal instruments that may be used include the durable powers of attorney, the durable health care power, and the living will.

● DURABLE POWER OF ATTORNEY

What Is a Durable Power of Attorney?

A traditional power of attorney is a written document in which one person grants authority to another to act on the person's behalf. For instance, the person may be planning an extended trip and may appoint a surrogate power of attorney to pay bills in his or her absence. To execute such a document the person must have capacity when the power of attorney is made. The person must remain legally competent for the power to stay valid, because by law the power is automatically invalidated when the person becomes incompetent. Although the law protects an incompetent person from being taken advantage of by a surrogate, a traditional power of attorney does not serve a person who wants to plan in advance to authorize another to act if incompetency does occur.

In response to this problem, all fifty states and the District of Columbia passed laws allowing durable powers of attorney (DPOA). The difference between a traditional and durable power of attorney is that a durable power of attorney generally remains valid if the principal becomes incompetent.

This distinction is very important because it means that by using a durable power of attorney a person can designate a surrogate to make decisions and act for the person if he or she becomes incapacitated at some later date. Because of this advance planning tool, a court may never need to appoint a legal guardian to make decisions and act for the person who is protected by a durable power of attorney (Collin, 1991).

What Powers Are Conferred by a Durable Power of Attorney?

A durable power of attorney may have a number of different characteristics and confer various powers upon the surrogate.

Depending on state law, those powers may be general or specific, may address money and property matters or health care matters or both, and may become effective immediately or, in some states, after some certain event. These options allow a person greater flexibility to prepare a durable power of attorney that meets his or her specific needs.

The difference between a traditional and durable power of attorney is that a durable power of attorney generally remains valid if the principal becomes incompetent.

A general durable power of attorney authorizes the surrogate to manage all of the person's monetary and property affairs. Alternatively, a special durable power of attorney gives the surrogate authority to act only in specified matters.

The authority potentially granted under a DPOA includes such things as managing the person's bank accounts, selling or buying real estate or personal belongings, borrowing money, hiring and firing employees, bringing legal actions, operating the person's business, giving gifts, and creating or modifying a trust. A person may want to make a durable power of attorney to authorize others to make health care or other personal decisions on his or her behalf. Because the law regarding powers of attorney developed to handle property and financial concerns, the DPOA is clear on such decisions; however, state laws are less clear about the types of personal decisions that can be made by an attorney-in-fact on behalf of a surrogate. Generally, controversy arises over decisions on health care and placement of the principal in an institution (Collin, 1991).

With few exceptions (e.g., California, Pennsylvania, Florida, the District of Columbia), state statutes do not expressly authorize use of a durable power to delegate health care decision-making. There is uncertainty over whether a DPOA may be used to delegate such powers without such a specific provision in the law. Some argue that no law or court decision restricts the use of DPOA to property matters, and that the power may be used for any purpose not contrary to a state's law or public policy (Stiegel, 1991). Others believe that the issue of whether a DPOA may be used for health care decisions is, at best, unsettled and depends largely upon the scope of powers laid out in the statute. They argue that the more specifically the statute addresses the authority that may be delegated, the less likely it is that the power may be used to delegate the authority to make health care decisions (Collin, 1991).

A DPOA may be effective immediately or it may "spring" into effect at some later date. The latter form, known as a "springing" power, does not take effect until the person becomes incapacitated. The document should explain how incapacity is to be determined—whether, for example, by certification of incapacity by two physicians or upon the occurrence of a specific event stated in the power (e.g., hospitalization, placement in a nursing home). Some states, however, do not allow "springing" powers (Collin, 1991).

Who May Make a Durable Power of Attorney?

A durable power of attorney must be made while the person is legally competent to execute the DPOA. By virtue of their age, minors are not legally competent to execute documents. No standards exist on whether an adult is legally competent to make and sign a DPOA. The applicable legal standard is that the person making a DPOA must have the requisite capacity to understand the nature and significance of his or her act at the time the document is signed.

State laws vary regarding requirements for witnessing and notarizing durable powers. A person who moves to another state or owns property in another state may need to re-execute the DPOA to comply with different legal requirements.

May a Durable Power of Attorney Be Revoked?

A durable power of attorney may be revoked in four ways: (1) a competent person may revoke the power at any time; (2) the power is automatically revoked upon the principal's death or, in some states, when the surrogate is notified of the person's death; (3) in some states the DPOA may be automatically revoked if a guardian is appointed for the person who made the power; (4) the DPOA may expire according to its own terms, e.g., when a specified event occurs (Stiegel, 1992).

What Are the Advantages of Using a Durable Power of Attorney?

A durable power of attorney offers many advantages as a tool allowing an individual to maintain control over his or her affairs even after incompetency occurs: (1) The delegation of authority can be tailored to the person's current and anticipated needs. (2) At any time the person may revoke the grant of authority, as long as he or she remains competent. (3) The person is able personally to choose those who will have authority over his or her affairs. (4) There is no need to have the person declared incompetent or to have a guardian appointed for the purpose of making health or property decisions, and the advance selection of a decision maker may expedite decisions. (5) Little expense is involved in executing a durable DPOA, there is no court involvement in creating or revoking the power, and court supervision is not required. (6) The DPOA may be particularly attractive in jurisdictions that allow "springing" powers of attorney.

What Are the Disadvantages of Using a Durable Power of Attorney?

Despite its many advantages as a tool for maintaining control after one becomes incompetent, a durable power of attorney has shortcomings: (1) It becomes effective immediately upon execution, unless it has "springing" power. (2) The lack of court supervision over the decisions of the attorney-in-fact may prove to be a disadvantage if that person is not trustworthy and acts contrary to the intent of the principal. However, oversight provisions may be included (e.g., allowing a family member to challenge certain actions of a surrogate). (3) Third parties such as banks, stockbrokers, and government agencies with which the surrogates may have to deal may not recognize durable powers. (4) If the person's incapacity is the triggering event in a "springing" power, the event may have to be established conclusively to a third party before the power will be honored (Stiegel, 1991).

● HEALTH CARE POWER OF ATTORNEY

The Difference Between a Health Care Power of Attorney and a Living Will

A living will is a written statement of an individual's wishes regarding the use of any medical treatments specified. The statement is to be followed if the person is unable to provide instructions at the time the medical decision must be made. Living wills have been recognized by law in most states, but they are commonly limited to

decisions about life-sustaining procedures in the event of terminal illness.

In three important ways the health care power of attorney is different from and more flexible than the living will:

1. A health care power of attorney *authorizes an agent to act as a surrogate* if the person cannot act, but a living will does not. The advantage of appointing a surrogate is that, at the time a decision needs to be made, the agent can participate in discussions and weigh the pros and cons of treatment decisions in accordance with the person's wishes.

2. The health care power of attorney *applies to all medical decisions*, unless the person decides to include limitations. The living will normally applies only to particular decisions near the end of life.

3. The health care power of attorney *can include specific instructions* to the surrogate about preferred treatment, or refusal of treatment, or whatever issues are most important.

A health care power of attorney *authorizes an agent to act as a surrogate if the person cannot act, but a living will does not.*

In theory, a living will could be combined with a health care power of attorney (Sabatino, 1989). However, state laws regarding the contents or formalities for signing the two documents must be compatible (Sabatino, 1991).

A critical part of a health care power of attorney is the designation of a surrogate to make health care decisions for the person. (Courtesy of the Bowman-Gray/Baptist Hospital Medical Center)

A health care power of attorney (sometimes called a medical power of attorney or health care proxy) is a document in which someone (called the "person") authorizes another person to make health care decisions on the person's behalf in the event he or she becomes unable to do so. Because of the dispute about whether durable powers of attorney can be used for health care decision-making, if the state law does not specify that purpose, an increasing number of states have passed laws that clearly recognize health care powers of attorney. As of June 1992, forty-four jurisdictions had such laws.

Why Are Health Care Powers of Attorney Useful?

Health care powers of attorney are useful for several reasons: (1) They allow a person to designate in advance of illness or disability another person who can make health care decisions on his or her behalf. A person who loses the capacity to make or communicate decisions will be able to control who makes important health care decisions. (2) If a health care agent has not been appointed, the health care provider may make critical health care decisions alone on behalf of the sick person. Those decisions might conflict with the person's wishes. (3) In some situations they may permit a person to avoid a guardianship proceeding. Where there is no health care power of attorney, the health care provider might ask a court to appoint a guardian to make decisions for the sick person. (4) A health care power of attorney that includes a statement of preferences regarding specific medical decisions may relieve family or friends of some of the stress and conflicts that may arise if they have to make decisions on behalf of the sick person without any guidance as to what he or she wants.

What Should a Health Care Power of Attorney Say?

The critical part of a health care power of attorney is the designation of a surrogate to make health care decisions for the person. Nothing else has to be included; the person can choose to rely completely on the judgment of the appointed agent. However, the principal may want to be more specific to ensure that his or her wishes regarding health care are followed. To accomplish this purpose, generally a health care power may also include statements that define or limit the scope of the surrogate's powers and guidelines for decision-making that the surrogate should follow. The person may also want to name successor surrogates in case the primary surrogate becomes unwilling or unable to act. A person should not name co-agents; however, if they cannot agree on a decision, a guardianship may then become necessary.

If a person opts to include guidelines for decision-making in the health care power, the level of specificity is a matter of choice. Specific preferences about the provision or withholding of certain medical treatments, including the artificial provision of food and water, may be included in the document.

What Should Be Considered Before Making a Health Care Power of Attorney?

Before making a health care power of attorney, a person should consider values and thoughts about life and death. The person's values will shape the decision-making guidelines set forth in the health care power, which in turn will shape how the principal may experience a period of illness or disability and possibly the end of life. To determine those guidelines and to communicate them to an agent or family and friends, a principal may wish to develop a "values history" for medical decisions. A values history is an attempt to record a person's attitudes, beliefs, feelings, and thoughts about a myriad of issues. The reader of the values history can then, if needed, make a substituted judgment about what a person would have wanted, based on what is known about him or her. The University of New Mexico has developed the values history (Gibson, 1990).

Some people write down a "values history" to provide guidelines to the person who may have to make health care decisions for them. (Copyright © Marianne Gontarz)

Someone interested in making a health care power needs to select the surrogate carefully, as the surrogate will have great authority over the person's health and personal care if he or she becomes incapacitated. Since no formal oversight or monitoring exist for an agent's decisions, one should name a surrogate who can be trusted to make the same decisions a person would make if capable of doing so. A person who wants to make a health care power of attorney should explain his or her intentions to the potential agent and make sure that person is willing to serve as the surrogate and follow the principal's wishes.

Are There Special Requirements for Making Health Care Powers of Attorney?

Special health care power laws have imposed various procedural protections to reduce abuse and ensure that the individuals voluntarily delegate decision-making authority. Some of the health care power of attorney laws contain restrictions on who may be appointed as a surrogate or who may witness the person's signatures. Some state laws mandate use of special forms and signing procedures; others provide forms but allow their use at the person's option. Some statutes limit the authority of the named surrogate by providing that the person cannot make certain decisions, often relating to issues such as abortion, sterilization, and commitment, and sometimes concerning life-sustaining treatment and withholding or withdrawal of artificial nutrition and hydration.

Some states allow the living will declaration and health care power of attorney to be combined into one document; others require two documents. Some states limit the effective duration of a health care power, thus requiring a principal to make a new power after a certain number of years. A state's procedural requirements must be followed carefully to ensure the validity and effectiveness of the health care power of attorney.

● LIVING WILLS/NATURAL DEATH ACTS

Definition

A living will is the popular name for a document in which an individual expresses directions about the health care he or she wishes to receive in the event that he or she has a terminal illness or is near death and is unable to make or communicate those health care decisions. Forty states and the District of Columbia have natural death or living will laws establishing requirements and guidelines for the use of living wills. Generally those laws restrict the health care decisions that can be directed through a living will to those concerning the use, withdrawal, or withholding of life-sustaining or life-prolonging procedures. Some states exclude artificial hydration and nutrition from the purview of a living will; other states leave that decision up to the individual or simply do not address the issue.

What Do State Living Will Laws Usually Address?

Although state living will and natural death statutes vary, they generally share several common provisions that provide guidelines and conditions for the use of living wills. (1) By recognizing written advance instructions to physicians, living wills extend an adult's right to control medical treatment decisions to use, withhold, or withdraw life-sustaining procedures in the event of a terminal condition. (2) They immunize from civil and criminal liability physicians and other health care providers who comply with a patient's advance directive according to the statute's requirements. (3) They specify the requirements necessary to "qualify" the patient for implementation of an advance directive (usually a certified terminal diagnosis based upon personal examination by the attending and one other physician). (4) They define "life-sustaining procedures" (often those that are "artificial" and that only "prolong the dying process"). (5) They generally provide that if a qualified patient's attending physician is unwilling to carry out the declaration, the physician must facilitate the patient's transfer to another doctor who will honor it. (6) They usually invalidate the declaration of a qualified patient during pregnancy. (7) They provide that the individual's current wishes supersede the wishes expressed in the living will. (8) They contain penalties for forging or intentionally destroying a living will and for concealing knowledge of its revocation. (9) They provide that the living will has no effect upon the individual's life insurance or health care benefits, and that implementation of a qualified individual's living will does not constitute suicide or assisted suicide.

● THE SOCIAL SECURITY SYSTEM

Social Security comprises programs administered by the Social Security Administration (National Senior Citizen Law Center [NSCLC], 1990; Commerce Clearing House, 1992). These provide benefits to eligible workers and their families when the worker retires, becomes severely disabled, or dies.

General Eligibility

For older persons, their spouses, and their dependents to qualify for Social Security benefits, the person must have worked in employment covered by Social Security and must have accumulated a certain number of quarters of coverage. The exact number of quarters needed to attain "insured" status and become eligible for benefits depends on the age of the person and the type of benefits sought. The maximum number of quarters required to be fully insured is forty, or ten years of coverage (NSCLC, 1990). If the worker has not attained insured status, he or she and spouse or dependent will not be eligible for benefits (NSCLC, 1990).

Retirement Benefits

To receive retirement benefits the person must be at least 62 years of age, fully insured, and retired. The spouse, if 62 years of age or over, or if under 62 years of age and caring for a child, can also be eligible based on the older person's earnings record. The unmarried children under 18 are eligible, if they are dependent on the person. Limited benefits for full-time, dependent students may also be available.

Reduced Benefits. If the person retires before the age of 65, the retirement benefits will be reduced permanently. Payments to a spouse, widow, or widower are also reduced if they start receiving benefits before 65. The amount of reduction depends on the number of months prior to age 65 years the person starts receiving such benefits.

Disability Benefits. Disability benefits may be available if the person is disabled, fully insured, and has sufficient quarters of coverage. As a general rule, the person must have worked for five out of the last ten years prior to becoming disabled. The dependent children and spouse, if aged 62 or over or under 62 and caring for a child, are also entitled to disability benefits.

Disability, for the purposes of Social Security, means the inability to engage in any substantial gainful employment due to a physical or mental impairment that is expected to result in death or has lasted, or is expected to last, for at least twelve months.

Survivor's Benefits. If a fully insured worker or retired person dies, survivor's checks can go to certain members of the worker's family. A widow or widower who is over 60, or between 50 and 60 if disabled, will receive monthly benefits. A surviving divorced spouse who meets these requirements may draw benefits also if he or she was married to the deceased worker for at least ten years. Younger surviving spouses may be eligible if they are unmarried and are caring for the deceased worker's child. Unmarried dependent children receive survivor's benefits if the parent died or became disabled while fully or currently insured. A parent of a deceased worker who died while the worker was currently insured may receive benefits if the parent is 62 or older *and* was dependent on the deceased worker for half of their support.

A lump sum death benefit payment can also be made when a worker dies. This payment will be made only to an eligible surviving widow, widower, or entitled child.

Earnings after Retirement. If the person is under age 70 and returns to work, the earnings will affect the Social Security benefits. In 1992 the earnings amount is $10,200, under which one is exempt from the earnings limitation. The amount is indexed and increases each year.

There is a great deal of discussion in Congress and among aging advocates to have the earnings test eliminated or liberalized. Unless this change occurs in the near future, the current test will remain.

The current earnings limitation applies only to those under 70 years. Over age 70, a person can earn unlimited income and not lose any Social Security benefits.

If an individual earns more than the annual exempt amount in any year, Report of Earnings must be filed with the Social Security office by April 15th of the following year.

How to Apply. Application for Social Security benefits should be made at the local or district

Social Security offices. It is necessary to document the claims with a Social Security card or record of the correct Social Security number, proof of age, and a marriage certificate if the application is for widow or widower's benefits.

Appeal Rights

If an application for Social Security benefits is denied, if any of the benefits are reduced or terminated, or if there is a charge or an overpayment, a person has the right to appeal the decision. The appeals process for Social Security benefits is the same as for Supplemental Security Income and Social Security Disability Payments and includes the following steps:

1. Reconsideration: If a decision is incorrect, a request for reconsideration should be filed within sixty days of receipt of the notice of the initial decision. This request should be in writing and copies of all the correspondence should be kept.

2. Hearing: If the reconsideration is denied, a request for a hearing before an administrative law judge may be made within sixty days of receipt of the reconsideration decision.

3. Appeals Council Review: A request to the Social Security Administration's Appeal Council to review an adverse hearing decision may be made within sixty days of receipt of the hearing decision.

4. Judicial Review: An individual may appeal a case to the United States District Court, if he or she is still not satisfied with the decision.

5. Attorney Representation: It is not absolutely necessary to be represented by an attorney or a paralegal as one goes through the appeals process. However, meeting all of the requirements is difficult; many of the standards employed by the vast array of laws and regulations used by Social Security are impossible to understand even by many attorneys. For instance, the standard used to determine disability uses "the lack of ability to engage in gainful activity by reason of any medically determinable physical or mental impairments which can be expected to last not less than 12 months" (NSCLC, 1990). Social Security uses a test to determine whether a person's impairments are severe enough to meet the standard. These are complicated determinations that require a sophisticated knowledge of the system.

Statements on the initial notice from the Social Security Administration indicate that a person may be represented by an attorney. Many Social Security district offices post notices as to how to find an attorney. These may include local legal services offices, bar associations, and the National Organization of Social Security Claimants Representatives (NOSSCR). NOSSCR is a membership organization of attorneys who specialize in Social Security representation and may be reached at 1-800-431-2804, 6 Prospect St., Midland Park, NJ 02432.

The Social Security Act provides for the payment of attorneys' fees out of back-awards due applicants. Extensive rules and procedures have been developed to protect the claimants against attorneys who may attempt to take an unwarranted share. However, claimants who are represented by counsel have a greater chance of obtaining awards. That is, there is a greater likelihood that a claimant will win an award if he or she is represented by an attorney. Therefore, it is usually worthwhile for a claimant to pay a portion to the attorney. Few jurisdictions have adequate free legal services or pro bono representation for all Social Security claimants.

Paralegals often represent people in administrative hearings. Paralegals work under the direct supervision of attorneys. For Social Security and other public benefits where the government is the payor, such hearings are the initial or the secondary level of appeal. Although a person does not have to have an attorney or paralegal at these types of hearings, representation is advisable. In general, the government, or agency, is not represented by an attorney; the role of the hearing officer is to represent the government as well as be the decision-maker.

Supplemental Security Income

Supplemental Security Income (SSI) is a federal program that was established to provide a basic level of income to persons age 65 and over as well as to blind and disabled persons of any age who have limited income and resources. SSI may be the sole source of income for some people; for others it supplements their monthly income from other sources. In recent years there has been an effort to inform people about the SSI program so that more people who are eligible will apply. It is estimated that less than half of those eligible have applied.

SSI is administered by the Social Security Administration; however, one can be eligible for SSI even if one never worked. SSI is funded through general tax revenues, not Social Security taxes withheld from payroll checks. People can be eligible for both Social Security and SSI.

SSI is not only a cash program. In most states a person who is eligible for SSI is also eligible for Medicaid (the state/federal health program). Thus, it is extremely important to apply for SSI even if the countable income is just below the eligibility level, as outlined below.

Who Is Eligible? To be eligible for SSI a person must meet the following basic requirements:

- A person must be either age 65 or older, disabled, or blind;
- A person must be a resident of the United States;
- A person must be either a citizen or a permanent resident of the United States under color of law (color of law is that which appears to be the fact without the written documentation);
- A person must have a limited income and limited resources.

To be eligible as a disabled person, one must have a physical or mental impairment that prevents one from doing any work for at least twelve months or is expected to result in death. Proving eligibility is more difficult than it sounds. As discussed above, the criteria and standards are confusing and often difficult to prove to the satisfaction of the Social Security Administration.

To be eligible as a blind person, one must have vision no better than 20/200 or a limited visual field of 20 degrees or less with the best corrective eyeglasses. Even if a person's visual impairment is not severe enough to be considered blindness, one might still qualify as a disabled person. Again the caution is that the standard is clear, but how one proves it is not.

If a person qualifies under more than one category, the person will receive SSI payments under the category that is the most advantageous. For example, if the person is 65 and blind, he or she receives a higher payment as a blind person.

Payment Levels. Not everyone in the same eligibility category will receive the same amount of payment. Some persons will receive more or less depending on their incomes or their living situations. For example: the allotment for a single person or a couple living in the household of another and receiving room and board in-kind will be different than that of persons living in a place where they cannot prepare their own meals. However, states in turn may supplement the SSI amount depending either on income and resources or on the type of living arrangement.

Income and Resource Limitations. Income and resources that limit the eligibility of potential SSI beneficiaries is subject to both those items that can be considered to be counted and those that cannot, as explained below. The program is a very complex one and attempts to limit the number of federal dollars that will be spent on any given individual.

Any money received in a calendar month, whether cash or check, whether earned or unearned, is considered income. Income that is counted for purposes of SSI includes pensions, rent from property, gifts, royalties, income from investments, and interest on bank accounts. Social Security payments and benefits are also counted as income.

Not all income is counted, however. There are a number of income exclusions—income not counted in determining eligibility and payment. The following are the most commonly applied exclusions:

- The first $20 of income in a month is not counted.
- The first $65 a month in regular earnings is disregarded. For each $2 in earnings over $65, the SSI payment is reduced by $1.
- Infrequent or irregularly received income is also "exempt" income. It exempts no more than $20 per month if the income is unearned (a gift, for example, or dividends from an investment), and no more than $10 per month if the income is earned. Loans received are not considered income if they must be paid back.

The limits on resources are also quite restrictive. At the present time, to be eligible one cannot have more than $1,500 in total countable resources or $2,250 for a couple. The most common resources that are excluded are as follows:

- A home, with no limit on the value.
- Household goods and personal belongs with an maximum equity value of $2,000.
- An automobile with a market value of $4,500 or less. A car will not be counted at all if used for transportation to work or regular medical treatment, or if modified for transportation or use by a disabled person.
- Burial plot with no limit on the value.
- Burial expenses (earmarked and set aside) and face value of life insurance totaling no more than $1,500.

Resources are a very complicated issue that can make some people ineligible for a period of time. If the resources are above the limits, one can spend down to the $1,500 level and then become eligible. However, giving away resources to become eligible may make the person ineligible for SSI and even Medicaid, when what one needs is help with medical expenses. Selling property below a fair price is counted as giving away. If one gives away or transfers property for less than fair value within twenty-four months prior to applying for SSI, one may not be eligible. Because accounting for resources is an elaborate issue, one should check with an attorney or other advocate familiar with the issues.

How to Apply. Applications are made with the Social Security office, preferably in person. When an application is made, people should insist on filing a formal written application. This establishes the right to the correct grant from the day of the original application. One should not be satisfied with an informal oral denial. A disabled or blind applicant might be able to receive presumptive eligibility payments for up to three months while the application is pending.

Right to Appeal. The appeals process is the same as for the rest of the Social Security system. See the earlier discussion on Social Security appeal rights.

Overpayments

Another issue in Social Security payments is that of overpayments. An overpayment is the amount a person receives that is more than the amount for which he or she is eligible. Generally the Social Security Administration (SSA) sends a notice of overpayment, and the money will have to be paid back or it will be withheld from a future payment. Overpayments may have a number of reasons, such as duplicate checks, excess resources, increased earnings, Social Security miscalculations, and, in some instances, misstatement or concealments. Overpayments can occur in both the regular Social Security retirement program and in the SSI program.

In general, one is obliged to pay the SSA back for overpayments. However, there are exceptions, and an individual probably needs some help in determining the best strategy to assure the proper outcome. Several areas need to be explored. A person may not have to pay back Social Security if the SSA made a mistake, and really no overpayment occurred. One may receive a waiver, so that one does not have to pay back even if there was an overpayment. That happens if one is without fault in causing the overpayment and if paying it back would create a serious hardship. If a person is not going to pay back SSA, then one must file for a waiver and ask for a reconsideration. This appeals process is similar to that described above.

A waiver is a request that SSA not recover the overpayment even if one agrees that there was an overpayment. A reconsideration is a request that SSA look at the overpayment decision again to determine whether SSA made a mistake in either deciding there was an overpayment or in the amount of the overpayment. This issue is complicated and not easily deciphered. It is best to obtain some sort of representation from either a local legal services office or a private attorney with knowledge of the Social Security system.

The following requests should be made of SSA when requesting a reconsideration or waiver because of an overpayment:

1. Waiver of Repayment: Because one is not at fault in causing the overpayment, and it would create a serious hardship to repay the money.

2. Reconsideration of Overpayment: Because no overpayment ever occurred or because the amount Social Security claims is overpaid is wrong.

It is essential to take both of these actions immediately when one hears from Social Security, because of the peculiarities of the SSA procedures. It is essential to act within the time limits.

    1. A waiver request within thirty days from the date of the notice of overpayment; SSA will not start to withhold any part of the benefits.

    2. A request after thirty days; SSA will stop withholding while the request is considered.

    3. While the waiver request is pending, no repayments will have to be made.

The Social Security Administration and its programs provide an income stream to the elderly, the blind, the disabled, and the poor. Although many of the programs are set up through different statutes and regulations, they are all administered through the SSA. The appeals process is generally the same and administered through the same levels and by the same people. A cautionary note needs to be made and bears repeating: The SSA programs are complicated, and one should approach any level of the appeals process with an advocate. The advocate may be an attorney, a paralegal, a representative from an advocacy organization, or a friend. The message is, do not try to do this alone.

● ADMINISTRATIVE LAW

Older persons are eligible for a myriad of services because of both age and income. These include food stamps, Medicare, Social Security, home equity loans, and tax refunds. Many of these involve the filing of applications and follow-up to see that the administrative or government agency is aware of the application and has acted on it. In many cases, to assure that the desired outcome is achieved, a hearing or letter requesting a reconsideration may have to be filed. Although it is not essential to have an attorney do this, all of the appropriate steps must be followed. Where necessary one should check with an advocate. Identification of a problem as a legal one is probably the most difficult. For example, a Medicare claim that is turned down or one for which not enough of the doctor's charges are paid creates a legal problem, because a course of action can be followed to create a due process consideration for further determination of the outcome.

Applications for administrative benefits are made at a variety of sources. These include offices on aging, welfare offices, city and county tax offices, and others. In most jurisdictions an Area Agency on Aging (AAA) is a good source for programs and resources to advocate for older persons in any given community. The AAA will also maintain lists of possible benefit programs for seniors in the particular community. In addition, many local legal services programs for the elderly maintain checklists of benefit programs to help assure that the seniors in their communities are getting all of the benefits for which they may be eligible. The legal services program will also help those who are eligible apply for the benefits.

● SUMMARY

Increasing numbers and percentages of the older persons in our society, by virtue of their age and increasingly failing health, are in need of legal assistance. There are well over 800,000 attorneys in the United States, but only a small percentage are aware of the legal needs of the elderly. Proportionately, the elderly are the greatest beneficiaries of administrative services and government benefit programs. All of these have eligibility rules and regulations that are more easily accessed with the help of advocates or lawyers.

In many cases, the elderly are experiencing an increased frailty. Often this is mistaken for "diminished capacity." As a consequence, the elderly may become vulnerable to potential abuse as some individuals may take advantage, for example, of an older person's financial holdings. However, legal tools such as powers of attorney or joint bank accounts allow the elderly person to designate alternative decision-makers and preclude either abuse or their total loss of autonomy through court intervention. Attorneys should be able to help older persons plan for incapacity before involuntary actions are necessary.

The delivery of legal services to older persons is in an emerging stage of development. Several years ago the majority of legal services were provided by the publicly funded programs with the private bar doing mostly estate planning. With the growing numbers of older persons and the complications of planning for incapacity and not just death, the private practice of elder law has emerged. In addition, there is a growing sense that new and innovative types of delivery systems must be developed. The legal hotline for older

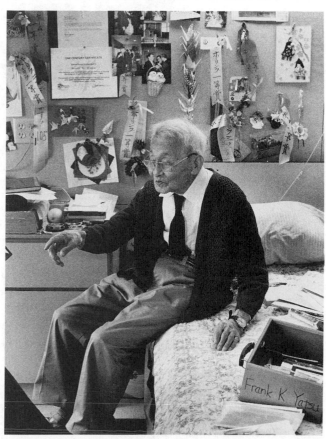

Only a small percentage of the nation's 800,000 attorneys are aware of the legal needs of the elderly. (Copyright © Isabel Egglin)

adults is an example of this type of innovation. Self-help materials and resources now are available for older persons to assist them to begin the diagnosis of legal problems. However, one should seek legal advice when the standards for decision-making, such as in Social Security, are confusing and difficult to meet. This is an ever increasingly complicated society that makes it impossible in many cases for an individual to self-diagnose and solve all of life's problems.

Organizations

American Bar Association Commission on Legal Problems of the Elderly
1800 M St., NW
Washington, DC 20036
(202) 331-2299

American Council of the Blind
1155 15th St., NW, Ste. 720
Washington, DC 20005
(202) 467-5081

American Indian Law Center
1117 Stanford, NE
Albuquerque, NM 87131
(505) 277-5462

Choice in Dying
250 West 57th St.
New York, NY 10107
(212) 246-6973

Cooperative Services
25900 Greenfield Rd., Ste. 326
Oak Park, MI 48237
(810) 967-4000

Equal Employment Opportunity Commission
1801 L St., NW, Suite 9024
Washington, DC 20507
(202) 663-4900

Mental Health Law Project
1101 15th St., NW, Ste. 1212
Washington, DC 20005-5002
(202) 467-5730

National Academy of Elder Law Attorneys
655 N. Alvernon Way, Ste. 108
Tucson, AZ 85711
(602) 881-4005

National Clearinghouse for Legal Services
407 S. Dearborn, Ste 400
Chicago, IL 60605
(312) 939-3830

National Consumer Law Center
11 Beacon St.
Boston, MA 02108
(617) 523-8010

National Organization of Social Security Claimants Representatives
19 E. Central Ave.
Pearl River, NY 10965
(914) 735-8812

National Senior Citizens Law Center
1815 H St., NW, Ste. 700
Washington, DC 20006
(202) 877-5280

Native American Rights Fund
1506 Broadway
Boulder, CO 80302
(303) 447-8760

References

American Bar Association Commissions on Legal Problems of the Elderly and the Mentally Disabled. *An Agenda for Reform*. Washington, DC: American Bar Association, 1989.

———. *Court Related Needs of Elderly Persons with Disabilities*. Washington, DC: American Bar Association, 1991.

Anderer, S. *Determining Competency in Guardianship Proceedings*. Washington, DC: American Bar Association, 1990.

Associated Press. *Guardians of the Elderly: An Ailing System*. New York: Associated Press, 1987.

Brown, R. N. *The Rights of Older Persons*. Washington, DC: Legal Council for the Elderly, 1989.

Collin, F. J., J. Lombard, Jr., A. L. Moses, and H. J. Spitler. *Drafting the Durable Power of Attorney: A Systems Approach*. 2d ed. New York: Shepard's McGraw-Hill, 1991.

Commerce Clearing House, Inc. *Social Security Benefits*. Chicago: Commerce Clearing House, 1992.

Fairbanks, J. E. "Home Equity Conversion Programs." *Clearinghouse Review* Vol. 23 (1989): 481–87.

Gibson, J. "National Values History." *Generations* Vol. 14 (1990): 51–64.

Hogue, K., C. Jensen, and K. M. Urban. *The Complete Guide to Health Insurance*. New York: Walker, 1988.

Horstman, P. "Protective Services for the Elderly: The Limits of Parens Patriae." *Missouri Law Review* Vol. 40 (1975): 215.

Hurme, S. *Steps to Enhance Guardianship Monitoring*. Washington, DC: American Bar Association, 1991.

Karp, N., and B. Brewer. "Medigap Insurance." *Clearinghouse Review* Vol. 25 (1991): 670–77.

"Late Bloomer" audio cassette. Available from Connie Goldman Productions, 926 Second Street, Suite 201, Santa Monica, CA 90403. (310) 393-6801.

Legal Counsel for the Elderly. *Decision-Making, Incapacity, and the Elderly*. Washington, DC: Legal Counsel for the Elderly, 1987.

———. *Life Changes and Their Effects on Public Benefits*. Washington, DC: Legal Counsel for the Elderly, 1990.

———. *Medicare Practice Manual*. Washington, DC: Legal Counsel for the Elderly, 1991.

———. *Organizing Your Future: A Guide to Decision-Making in Your Later Years*. Washington, DC: Legal Counsel for the Elderly, 1991.

Mitchell, A. "The Objects of Our Wisdom and Our Coercion: Involuntary Guardianship for Incompetents." *Southern California Law Review* Vol. 52 (1979): 1405.

National Senior Citizens Law Center. *Representing Older Persons: An Advocates Manual*. Washington, DC: National Senior Citizens Law Center, 1990.

Polniaszek, S., and J. Firman. *Long-Term Care Insurance*. Washington, DC: United Seniors Health Cooperative, 1991.

President's Commission for the Study of Ethical Problems in Medicine and Biomedical and Behavioral Research. *Deciding to Forego Life-Sustaining Treatment*. Washington, DC: U.S. Government Printing Office, March 1983.

Regan, J. J. "Protecting the Elderly: The New Paternalism." *Hasting Law Journal* Vol. 32 (1981): 1111–32.

———. *Your Legal Rights in Later Life*. Washington, DC: Legal Counsel for the Elderly, 1989.

Regan, J. J., and G. Springer. *Protective Services for the Elderly: A Working Paper*. Report prepared for the U.S. Congress, Senate Special Committee on Aging. 95th Cong., 1st sess, 1977.

Sabatino, C. *Health Care Powers of Attorney*. Washington, DC: American Bar Association, 1990.

———. "Surrogate Decision-Making in Health Care." In *Health Care and Financial Planning Issues for the Elderly*. Washington, DC: American Bar Association, 1991.

Savage, K., and S. Edelstein. "Housing Rights of Older Persons." *Clearinghouse Review* Vol. 25 (1991): 648–53.

State Bar of California. *Senior Citizens Handbook: Laws and Programs Affecting Older Californians*. San Francisco: State Bar of California, 1991.

Stiegel, L. *Alternatives to Guardianship*. Washington, DC: American Bar Association, 1992.

U.S. Congress. Office of Technology Assessment. *Life-Sustaining Technologies and the Elderly*. OTA-BA-306. Washington, DC: Office of Technology Assessment, July 1987.

U.S. Congress. Senate Special Committee on Aging, the American Association of Retired Persons, the Federal Council on Aging, and the U.S. Administration on Aging. *Aging America: Trends and Projections*. Washington, DC: U.S. Government Printing Office, 1991.

Wood, E. F., and R. Hoffman. "Mediation: New Path to Problem Solving for Older Americans." *AARP Consumer Alert* (Winter 1991–92).

Zuckerman, D. *Life Services Planning*. Washington, DC: American Bar Association, 1988.

Additional Reading

Aday, Ron H. *Crime and the Elderly: An Annotated Bibliography*. Westport, CT: Greenwood Press, 1988.

Bernstein, Merton C., and Joan B. Bernstein. *Social Security: The System that Works*. New York: Basic Books, 1988.

Douglass, Richard L. *Domestic Mistreatment of the Elderly—Towards Prevention*. Washington, DC: American Association of Retired Persons, 1987.

Gelfand, Donald E. *The Aging Network: Programs and Services*. 3rd ed. New York: Springer, 1988.

Johnson, Tanya F., et al. *Elder Neglect & Abuse: An Annotated Bibliography*. Westport, CT: Greenwood Press, 1985.

Matthews, Joseph L. *Social Security, Medicare and Pensions: A Sourcebook for Older Americans*. 3rd ed. Berkeley, CA: Nolo Press, 1990.

Millman, Linda J. *Legal Issues and Older Adults*. Santa Barbara, CA: ABC-CLIO, 1992.

Soled, Alex J. *The Essential Guide to Wills, Estates, Trusts and Death Taxes*. Glenview, IL: Scott, Foresman, 1987.

Nancy M. Coleman, A.B.

Section IV

Employment and Retirement

10

Issues of Older Workers

- Labor Force Participation • Employment and Unemployment
- Myths and Realities About Older Workers • Policies and Programs for Older Workers
- Alternative Work Arrangements • Older Women Workers • Future Trends

In mid-1992, two separate front-page articles appeared in the New York Times *related to aging and work. The first reported revised estimates of the older population in the next century, with some researchers predicting three times the conventional population projections of more conservative demographers at the Census Bureau. The second article detailed the unexpectedly high costs incurred by some state governments due to their policies of encouraging early retirement.*

These examinations of future older populations and the public cost of early retirement dramatize the importance of the "older worker" topic. Whether a society offers inducements to encourage or force early retirement, or to attract people to stay in the workforce becomes especially crucial in a country like the United States with its burgeoning middle-aged and older adult population. Interest in, and concern about, the older worker issue over the past several years has emerged because of a number of trends and events.

- *The average age of a U.S. worker will reach 40 in the 1990s.*
- *Passage of the Age Discrimination in Employment Act (ADEA) has prohibited hiring or firing based on age and eliminated mandatory retirement.*
- *The public has been more aware about aging due to dissemination of gerontological knowledge beyond the research and academic community.*

- *The ratio of retirees to workers, the "dependency ratio," has changed significantly during the past thirty years.*

● LABOR FORCE PARTICIPATION

Earlier in the twentieth century, the prevailing view was that people, usually men, would remain in the labor force as long as possible. Older workers would retire only because they were forced to. The number of persons aged 65 and older has increased tenfold since 1900, and the number potentially available for work has correspondingly grown, but since 1950 the number of older people in the workforce has remained almost steadily at around three million. Greater economic security and changing attitudes have led to the current average age of withdrawal from the workforce at 63.

A simple comparison of age groups in the workforce in 1972 and 1992 vividly illustrates the effects of aging on the workforce. Table 10.1 reveals the following: (1) for men, the percentage in the workforce has declined between 1972 and 1992 in all age categories; (2) the older the age group in any one of the two years indicated, the lower its rate of participation in the labor force; (3) after the age group 55 to 59 there is a marked drop in participation rates; and (4) there is a dramatic contrast between men and women in changes in labor force participation rates.

The first item is quite well known: participation in the labor force declines in accordance with

Table 10.1
Labor Force Participation Rates by Age and Gender, 1972–92

	1972	1992
Men		
All Ages	79	76
20–24	85	83
25–54	95	93
55–59	87	80
60–64	71	56
65–69	35	27
70 & over	16	11
Women		
All Ages	44	58
20–24	60	70
25–54	48	56
60–64	35	36
65–69	17	16
70 & over	5	1

Source: U.S. Department of Labor, Employment and Earnings, for December 1972 and May 1992. Figures are rounded percentages.

age. But the pronounced drop in the rate after ages 55 to 59 (for both years, but especially in 1992) is explainable primarily by the availability of "early" retirement at age 62, under the Social Security system. This helps to account for the drop from the 1972 rate for men 60 to 64 (71 percent) to that of 1992 (56 percent), a decrease of 15 percent.

While the twenty-year period saw declining rates for men of all ages, the very opposite applied to women under the age of 65. Even for women 65 to 69, the difference between 1972 and 1992 shows only a tiny decline—from 17 to 16 percent. While older men are taking advantage of early retirement opportunities, older women working outside the home are remaining in the workforce longer. There are many reasons for this, the primary one of which is financial need. Working women may be waiting for their husbands to retire. They also may be seeking to add years toward higher pension coverage—especially if they have taken time out for child-rearing.

The overall participation rate of women 45 to 64 has climbed dramatically since the 1940s when, due to the wartime effort, many women entered the labor force (see Figure 10-1). Until recently, women were not expected to work out-side the home, particularly middle-aged and older women. But that trend has changed as gender roles have undergone a transformation. Middle-aged women, in contrast to men, have been streaming into the labor force. As of 1989, 70.5 percent of all women 45 to 54 were in the labor force, nearly double the percentage of 1950 (Rix, 1990).

The number of persons aged 65 and older has increased tenfold since 1900, and the number potentially available for work has correspondingly grown, but since 1950 the number of older people in the workforce has remained almost steadily at around three million.

It should be noted that these percentages do not differentiate between full-time and part-time participants in the workforce. Furthermore, rates of "labor force participation" are essentially average annual percentages of persons working or looking for work, as a proportion of the total working-age population (or of specific age groups). But such averages referring to "participation rates" are not the same as figures that show how many persons in any given year have had any degree of "work experience." This is especially important when dealing with older workers because the Department of Labor's statistics on persons of any given age who have worked in any past year show that there are many more older workers who have had such work experience than statistics on their participation rates would indicate. For example, among men 60 to 64, the participation rate in 1991 was 56 percent, but in fact the Bureau of Labor Statistics shows, for that same year, more than 3.1 million men 60 to 64 (64 percent) actually had some degree of work experience (Bureau of Labor Statistics, unpublished tables for 1991 work experience). In other words, participation rate statistics tend to underestimate the numbers of persons with actual work experience—and such discrepancies are greatest in the case of older persons, starting at about age 55.

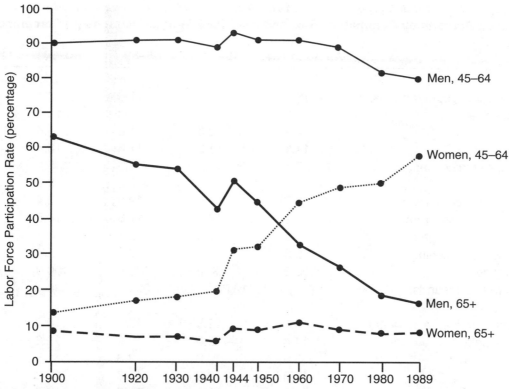

Figure 10.1 Labor Force Participation Rates of Midlife and Older Men and Women, 1900–1989

Sources: *U.S. Bureau of the Census, 1965; U.S. Department of Labor, 1985 and January 1990.*

As of 1989, 70.5 percent of all women 45 to 54 were in the labor force, nearly double the percentage of 1950.

● EMPLOYMENT AND UNEMPLOYMENT

Employment

Older employed workers can be found in nearly every industry and occupation, a fact that contradicts a widespread image or stereotype. However, their proportions in selected industries and occupations may differ from those of younger persons. Furthermore, gender makes a difference. One should not talk about "older workers" as if they were one homogeneous population. For example, older women are disproportionately employed in service and clerical jobs, compared to men. And among men, the older ones have the highest self-employed percent-

age—higher than younger men and older women. Men age 60 to 64 and 65+ also are relatively well represented in executive and managerial occupations (see Table 10.2). This type of contrast also applies to the occupation designated as "operators, fabricators, and laborers" (i.e., semi- and unskilled laborers); older men have the highest percentage, compared to younger men and older women.

Older men have the highest self-employed percentage—higher than younger men and older women.(Copyright © Marianne Gontarz)

Table 10.2
Employed Persons by Occupation, Sex, and Age, 1988 Annual Averages (in Percentages)

Occupation	All Ages 16+	45–54	55–59	60–64	65+
Men					
Executive, administrative, managerial	13.6	18.6	17.6	17.4	16.4
Professional specialty	11.9	14.0	13.3	13.1	13.1
Technicians	2.9	2.5	1.8	1.4	0.9
Sales	11.1	11.2	11.6	12.4	16.1
Admin. support, including clerical	5.7	4.7	5.3	5.2	5.8
Service	9.6	7.0	7.8	9.9	11.8
Precision production, craft, repair	19.7	20.0	19.6	17.4	10.7
Operators, fabricators, laborers	20.9	18.2	17.8	16.8	10.9
Farm operators and managers	1.7	1.9	3.1	4.1	10.1
Farm workers, forestry, fishing	2.8	1.8	2.1	2.4	4.2
Total percentage	100.0	100.0	100.0	100.0	100.0
Total number (in thousands)	63,273	10,201	3,954	2,638	1,911
Women					
Executive, administrative, managerial	10.8	12.5	10.7	10.3	8.6
Professional specialty	14.4	15.6	13.8	10.2	10.6
Technicians and related	3.3	2.8	2.3	1.5	1.2
Sales	13.0	10.6	11.8	13.2	14.5
Admin. support, including clerical	28.3	28.6	27.5	29.6	24.6
Service	17.9	16.1	19.8	20.6	27.6
Precision production, craft, repair	2.3	2.7	2.4	2.6	2.9
Operators, fabricators, laborers	8.8	9.9	10.1	10.3	7.2
Farm operators and managers	0.4	0.6	0.9	0.8	1.8
Farm workers, forestry, fishing	0.7	0.6	0.7	0.8	1.0
Total percentage	100.0	100.0	100.0	100.0	100.0
Total number (in thousands)	51,696	8,246	2,938	1,904	1,286

Source: U.S. Department of Labor, Bureau of Labor Statistics, unpublished data.

Unemployment

Many of the problems of older workers (defined by some legislation as persons over 40 or 45) surface during times of widespread, general unemployment when such workers seek reemployment; when companies go out of business (or relocate); and also in situations involving opportunities for retention, promotion, and/or training in an enterprise.

Looking only at unemployment rates among different age groups reveals that older workers tend to have lower jobless rates when compared to younger workers. This is true especially when unemployment rates of teenagers (15 percent in 1989) are compared to those of the older workers (3 percent in 1989 for those over 65). Indeed,

workers 62 and older typically have the lowest unemployment rates.

A more comprehensive picture of unemployment and age, however, reveals such points as the following:

1. When older workers do become unemployed, they tend to stay unemployed much longer than do younger unemployed workers.

2. Once they become unemployed, many workers 62 and older leave the labor force completely because at that age they became eligible for retired worker benefits under the Social Security system, and possibly for private pensions. In fact, many private pension plans make it possible for workers under 62 to leave the paid work force.

Profiles of Productive Aging

Studs Terkel
Radio interviewer, author

"The lifespan is increasing, and we've got the least to lose. Make some trouble. Let's do it."

Eighty-two-year-old Studs Terkel is America's foremost oral historian and chronicler of the American working class. He was born in New York City in 1912 to working class parents; his father was a tailor with poor health. When Terkel was 8, his father became ill, and the family moved to Chicago. His mother ran a rooming house and later a small hotel to support the family. His childhood experiences stimulated his intense interest in people, primarily those of a lower middle working class.

Terkel attended the University of Chicago, earned his law degree, and passed the bar exam. But the minutely detailed aspect of legal practice bored him completely. To this day he considers his three years of law school a "waste of time." His next job was to count "baby bonds" with the Treasury Department in Washington, D.C. "It drove me nuts, of course," Terkel gave as his reason for quitting.

Back in Chicago, he joined a WPA-sponsored labor theater group performing in such controversial plays as Clifford Odets's socialistic "Waiting For Lefty." He also played the role of a gangster in the radio soap opera "Ma Perkins."

Other radio jobs included disc jockey, sportscaster, and commentator. This latter role proved to be a perfect vehicle for expressing his liberal pro-Roosevelt leanings. Since most of his colleagues were anti-Roosevelt, he "got kicked off the air a lot." Always outspoken, Terkel built his career on his willingness to stir up debate and controversy.

In the 1950s, he was part of the "Chicago Style TV" group with Dave Garroway and "Kukla, Fran, and Ollie." Terkel's show, "Studs' Place," was taken off the air because of his "big mouth," so to speak. Terkel recalled, "I used to lose jobs one after the other. I used to be fired all the time."

By the early 1950s he landed a job with WFMT in Chicago, then a small classical music station. Terkel, who has been with WFMT now for over forty years, developed the author interviews for which he is famous. "I work like an old-time craftsman," he recounted. "In other words, what I do isn't an art, it's a craft. Either I'm a good craftsman or I'm not. I have to do my homework." As for his current motivation, Terkel declared: "The thing I live for now is to make trouble. I like the idea of making trouble. The young seem to have lost that, at least for the moment. So it's got to be some other group ... the most unexpected group. And the most logical group."

Lydia Brontë

3. The government does not count as unemployed any worker who is not looking for employment. But when they lose jobs, a large proportion of them eventually become discouraged in their job search and stop looking completely. These workers—typically in the older age groups—are classified as "discouraged" workers, and the official jobless measures do not include them.

4. Contrary to popular belief, most older job-losing workers (until they reach age 65) are looking for full-time jobs, not part-time ones. Unemployed persons in their late fifties and early sixties (or older, in some instances) have a high degree of commitment to being in the labor force.

5. Among older unemployed workers, very

few voluntarily leave their previous jobs. That is, the vast majority (except for those 65 and older) have lost their previous jobs. Even among those 65 and older, as of 1987, 45 percent of the men and 39 percent of the women were "job losers." Actually, among older unemployed persons, very large percentages of those 65+ tend to be re-entering the labor force, or entering for the first time (e.g., housewives), to look for employment. In 1987, the percentage for men was 48 percent; for women of the same age group, it was 55 percent.

To repeat, very few of the unemployed older workers—fewer than those 25 to 54 years old—are voluntary job leavers. While it is true that most persons 65 and older are retired and remain retired, large numbers nevertheless are looking for employment. Their job search is motivated by both psychological and financial-need reasons.

The reasons for the unemployment of older workers have to do not only with the ups and downs of the economy but also with such factors as "structural changes"—for example, increased foreign competition, the movement of companies to other countries and regions of the United States, changes in the population structure, and changes in the industrial/occupational make-up of the total U.S. employment. Factory and office closings, reduced need for products and services, "downsizing," and the abolition of occupations are among the factors that produce "displaced workers."

Contrary to popular belief, most older job-losing workers (until they reach age 65) are looking for full-time jobs, not part-time ones.

A 1986 report by the Department of Labor, based on Census Bureau surveys (Bureau of Labor Statistics, January 1986) found that older workers (55 and older) had the highest percentages of displaced workers because companies had closed or moved. Many people believe that older workers tend to be protected by "seniority" rules, but in fact companies going out of business or moving away are more likely to be in declining industries, industries from which workers have a higher chance of being displaced. Such industries, including manufacturing, tend to have an older age profile than growing new industries.

As stated earlier, the problems of older work-ers are highlighted or dramatized by data about what happens to them once they become unemployed. Among workers with at least three years in the labor force who then lost their jobs in a previous five-year period, the Department of Labor reported in 1990 that only 53 percent of the group 55 to 64 years old and 28 percent of those 65 and older found new jobs—percentages far below those for the younger age groups. Table 10.3 shows the rates by age for (1) re-employment, (2) continued joblessness, and (3) exit from the labor force.

While many in the youngest age group, once unemployed, enter or re-enter the education system, older workers in the same situation—especially those 65 and older—are more likely to take advantage of their eligibility for retirement benefits under Social Security and/or their private pensions. Leaving the labor force is one explanation for the 65+ group having a lower "still-unemployed" percentage than nearly all the other, younger age groups. If the job-losers who have left the labor force were excluded from the category, then the rates of job-losers still jobless would rise to 23 percent of the 55 to 64 year-olds and 26 percent of the 65+ group. In other words, even after eliminating job losers who left the work force, older workers still had the highest rate of unemployment, compared to those job losers under the age of 55. Some of this difference may be due to differences in job skills, but earlier research analyses show that even when "non-age" factors are accounted for, age by itself still is a factor in the job-finding success rates of older workers.

Furthermore, in 1991, a year characterized by high general unemployment, the labor force participation rates of men 55 to 64 and 65+ declined

Table 10.3
Labor Market Experience of Job Losers by Age

Age	Re-employed	Still unemployed	Left labor force
20–24	76%	10%	14%
25–54	78%	14%	8%
55–64	53%	16%	31%
65 & older	28%	10%	62%

Source: U.S. Department of Labor, 1990 data. Percentages rounded.

from previous years. In addition, the "discouraged worker" numbers—those who gave up the job search—rose by 33 percent from 1990 to 1991, which was a higher rate of increase than for younger workers seeking employment. Finally, the same period witnessed an increase in older workers employed only on part-time basis, even though they wanted full-time jobs (AARP Public Policy Institute, 1992).

In summary, older workers tend to have lower jobless rates than younger ones, but once they do become unemployed, they stay unemployed longer and/or become discouraged and give up altogether (and therefore are no longer counted as unemployed). Furthermore, if they do find new employment, most if not all research indicates that older men re-employed on a full-time basis tend to find jobs that pay less than did their previous full-time jobs.

Loss of a job in one's midlife and in older years can have a severely negative effect on a longer-term (or permanent) basis, when comparisons are made with younger job losers. Compared to younger workers, older job losers have "few tomorrows," or opportunities for second chances.

● MYTHS AND REALITIES ABOUT OLDER WORKERS

Contrary to what was believed around the turn of the twentieth century, even by eminent authorities, the work capacity of older persons is of such a quality as to warrant continued employment in a variety of occupations. But consider the 1905 declarations of the famous physician William Osler: "I have two fixed ideas.... The first is the comparative uselessness of men above forty years of age.... My second fixed idea is the uselessness of men above sixty years of age, and the incalculable benefit it would be ... if, as a matter of course, men stopped work at this age" (Rix, 1990).

Contrary to what was believed around the turn of the 20th century, the work capacity of older persons is of such a quality as to warrant continued employment in a variety of occupations. (Courtesy of The National Council on the Aging, Inc.)

Nearly a century later, however, in 1991, Dr. T. Franklin Williams, former director of the National Institute on Aging (NIA), testified to Congress, "Contrary to earlier views that aging is associated with inevitable declines in physical and mental functioning, we now know with great confidence that there are few inevitable declines, and that most people can, and many do, continue to function into their seventies and eighties and even longer at much the same levels as they have functioned in earlier years" (House Select Committee on Aging, 1991).

When there was a widespread call for special performance tests to determine the work capacity and qualifications of older workers, experts in the field of industrial gerontology maintained that since testing and evaluation of persons of younger ages are conducted, there is no reason not to use the same standards and criteria for all ages. Data already disclose that younger persons in workplaces frequently develop some level of disabling symptoms or conditions, and that—after treatment or rehabilitation—they can return to their previous jobs. In other cases, work modifications accommodate a wide range of disabled employees of all ages.

Regarding the impact of such chronic ailments as coronary disease, studies by the National Institute on Aging have shown that it is possible to predict the capabilities of persons in their sixties and seventies, not only those in their forties and fifties, over several years after diagnosis. NIA former director Williams maintained that if individuals pass such tests (no signs of heart disease), then the risk of having some sort of heart attack over the following four or five years is only about 3 percent for both the 40 to 59 age group *and* the 60 to 69 age group.

Williams and other experts (going as far back as the famous Ross McFarland of Harvard University, in the 1950s and 1960s) believe there is no scientific, medical reason for determining the eligibility for hiring and for continued employment on the basis of chronological age—"in any profession or job." Rather eligibility should be determined through the testing and evaluation of individuals—regardless of the year of their birth.

Another finding is the concept of heterogeneity: individual variability within any age group, and the overlap of work capacity measures between different age groups. For example, one

milestone longitudinal study (Schaie, 1989) reported that not only were there no changes over several years in cognitive abilities of persons in their sixties and early seventies, but there were no differences for those in their forties and fifties. More than half of the oldest groups had very similar scores to persons in their twenties.

It is possible to measure the capacity (both physical and mental) of any specific individual for performing a given job. This is being done all the time for younger workers, and again, there is no reason to construct special measurements or tests for older persons. However, variability in measures is so great *within* any one age category, and the overlap between age groups on these measures so great, that age by itself is not a useful criterion for determining work capacity.

The passage of the Americans with Disabilities Act in 1992 points up the need for greater information about the range of abilities affecting the employability and re-employability of older persons. In a study of ten items involving mobility, endurance for confined movement, lower and upper body strength, fine motor skills (e.g., grasping with fingers), etc., among working persons 55 to 74 years old, the National Center on Health Statistics (1987) found, for example, that:

- Only 5 percent were unable to walk a quarter mile
- Only four percent were unable to walk up ten steps
- Only six percent were unable to stand on feet for two hours
- Only ten percent were unable to stoop, crouch, or kneel
- Only five percent were unable to lift or carry twenty-five pounds

Among persons who had retired for nonhealth reasons, the percentages were only slightly higher. The full report (National Center for Health Statistics, 1987) provides greater details by specific age groups within the general 55 to 74 population. Overall, the study found that 73 percent of those still working had no difficulty with any of the ten work-related activities, compared to 60 percent of those retiring because of nonhealth reasons and only 14 percent of those retiring because of health reasons. According to the report, "potentially, many of the people who had retired for reasons other than their health could

More than 65 percent of the employers in one study considered workers 55 and older to be "more reliable, punctual, or loyal." (Copyright © Marianne Gontarz)

have remained in the labor force." Workplace adaptations, as well as accommodations by workers themselves who might be labeled "disabled," along with monitoring of possible discrimination on the basis of both age and "disabilities," are necessary requirements for meeting this problem.

According to a 1991 report for the Small Business Administration (Thalheimer and others), small businesses generally rated the labor market experience and skills-accumulations of older workers as superior to those of younger workers. More than 65 percent of the employers in the study considered workers 55 and older to be "more reliable, punctual, or loyal," while less than 5 percent rated them as being less so.

Absenteeism and Tardiness

The rate of absenteeism among older workers tends to be lower than that among younger ones, but the evidence indicates that once absent, they may be away from the job longer. Injuries—as an important cause of absenteeism—may be fewer, but the severity of the older workers' injuries tends to be greater. These kinds of measures need to be viewed with a comprehensive perspective as women become an increasing part of the total labor force. Middle-aged women, for example, may tend to have longer work-interruptions than men, largely because they still have to bear the bulk of family caregiving. Any useful analysis of such measures as absenteeism and tardiness needs to take into account gender, marital status, age, and the extent to which middle-aged and older workers have older family members who may constitute a "risk factor" for such workers.

As women swell the ranks of the middle-aged and older worker population, it is possible for the statistics on absenteeism and tardiness to increase—even if age per se is not the explanation.

According to a 1991 report for the Small Business Administration small businesses generally rated the labor market experience and skills-accumulations of older workers as superior to those of younger workers.

Concerning accidents as a cause of absenteeism, the frequency of type of accident can differ according to the age of the worker. For example, accidents involving falls tend to increase with age, but the opposite is true for accidents such as getting caught in a machine, or being injured when starting a machine. The latter example suggests that accidents that are preventable through using good judgment based on previous experience tend to go down by age, while accidents involving a quick, "evasive response" to unexpected sudden incidents tend to increase by age (Birren, 1964; Welford, 1958).

Finally, according to Dr. Leon Koyl, an expert in the field of industrial gerontology, the vast majority of workplace accidents take place during the first two years of employment. If that is the case, it means that recently hired employees are at most risk of incurring industrial injuries—and such employees are typically younger (Koyl, 1983).

● POLICIES AND PROGRAMS FOR OLDER WORKERS

In recent years, policy discussions have included an interest in deferring retirement beyond the typical retirement age. Work continuity, training and retraining, alternative work arrangements, and "second careers" have been among the specific topics explored in such discussions. Emerging challenges are associated with the employment experiences of older women. In terms of history, retirement is a relatively new achievement—a mark of a civilized industrial society. For some time, early retirement has been

For some older persons, retirement means a reduced income, and they need to work for that reason. (Copyright © Susan Granados)

viewed as an even stronger measure of such a society. But another view accompanies such sentiments: men and women need to feel useful, and one medium of that usefulness is participation in the paid labor force. For some older persons, retirement means a reduced income, and they need to work for that reason. Also, the "unused" or "wasted" contributions that otherwise could be made to the economy, as a result of premature or (in previous years) compulsory retirement, have been bemoaned.

Work Continuity

Despite the many reasons, or incentives, for older workers to retire—or the disincentives to remain in the labor force—there nevertheless are workers who do continue in the paid labor force. How do they differ from those who have retired?

One obvious difference is that "work continuers" need to remain in the work force for financial reasons; their personal and household incomes tend to be lower than those of retirees (of the same ages). Continuers are less likely to be eligible for, or to be receiving, an employer's pension (private or public).

While the evidence is not too well established, the fear of eroding real income (purchasing power) may be influencing today's workers to remain longer in the labor force. As a general rule, the greater the years in retirement, the lower one's personal and/or household income; conversely the older one is at the time of his or her retirement, the greater is that person's income.

As another confirmation of people's financial reasons to continue working, the "continuers" are more likely to be still paying on a mortgage for

their homes and also more likely to be renters, which is typically an indication of their lower socio-economic status. To be sure, the general rule indicated earlier requires some modification: middle-aged and relatively "young-old" workers who can expect a relatively high retirement income and who have negative attitudes toward their work (or have some attraction toward retirement activities) may be able to and want to leave the labor force. They tend to retire at an early age. But generally speaking, the longer a person waits to leave the labor force, the greater will be his or her income at retirement time.

The significance of these relationships is that, to the extent that a worker can time his or her age of retirement and becomes aware of the financial advantage of delayed retirement (depending on type of pensions, etc.), the odds are increased that he or she will continue to stay in the labor force. One qualification to such a statement has to do with the feelings a worker has about the job.

The propositions above are confirmed by the fact, for example, that persons in professional occupations tend to remain in the labor force longer than workers in unskilled jobs—despite their higher retirement-income potentials, compared to the potentials of nonprofessionals. Again, one of the primary reasons is that the job satisfaction levels of professionals are higher than those of lesser-skilled workers. Just as important, if not more so, is that the odds for poor health conditions are lower among professionals, thus removing one of the most important reasons for relatively "young-age" retirement. In addition, a far lower proportion of retired professionals cite income from work as the one thing they missed most about not working any longer, compared to retirees from other occupational levels.

Work continuers in the older ages also retained a level of work commitment (measured by negative preferences for retiring completely) almost the same as the younger adults. This applies to those 65 and older as well as to those 55 to 64 years old (Sheppard, 1988). Whether for financial or social-psychological reasons, more than 80 percent of the 65+ continuers claimed they did not look forward to leaving the labor force completely—compared to only 45 percent of those 55 to 64. But much of this wide difference is due to the fact that the very oldest workers in this study (Sheppard, 1988) had no private pension coverage.

Training and Retraining

Given the fact that in the 1990s the average age of American workers is about 40, and the further reality that the economy, industrial/occupational structure, and technology are changing, the need for continuous education and training/retraining may become greater than in the past few decades. One advantage of this "aging of the workforce" is that it could mean a more experienced group of middle-aged and older workers whose background makes them prepared to meet changing labor demands and technologies. Employers and their representatives (as well as policy makers) will have to change their images about the capacity and the willingness of middle-aged and older workers to learn new skills, and adapt to the changes cited above. Any reluctance or failure to provide for and encourage training for such workers could contribute negatively to the nation's levels of productivity in a world of global competition.

Organizations need to conduct current and expected skill needs surveys, assess their personnel's age and skill profiles, and plan accordingly. This type of planning involves recognition of, and preparation for, such career events as plateauing, "burn-out," and skill obsolescence. This perspective and strategy are the subject not only of organizations and government agencies in the United States, but also in most of the industrialized and industrializing countries in the world (Plett and Lester, 1991).

One frequently overlooked feature of training and the older worker is the possibility of using older persons themselves as trainers—"an untapped reserve in the workplace or in the community" (Plett and Lester, 1991). Many experts claim that the processes of learning among older persons are essentially the same as among younger men and women, but there can still be the problem of persuading middle-aged and older workers to volunteer for training programs more than they do now. Some of them may be con-

Worker training programs exist in most industries. (Courtesy of the National Council on the Aging, Inc.)

cerned about their capacities or pace of learning in the midst of younger trainees. For some skills, it might require longer learning time, with more instructor assistance, compared to their younger peers. But for many others, there are no such fears. They might resent having to be the victims of age segregation in the classroom or workplace.

The major point, however, is that while older trainees might need (depending on the skills to be learned) more time to learn the skills, they tend to perform on the job no differently from younger trainees. "There is no evidence to show that cognitive functioning and learning ability decline with age.... There is abundant evidence to show that people can continue to learn at any age" (Plett and Lester, 1991). In the environment of technological dynamics, frequent and continuous training or retraining can make older workers even more ready and capable of adjusting to changing skill demands.

One frequently overlooked feature of training and the older worker is the possibility of using older persons themselves as trainers—"an untapped reserve in the workplace or in the community".

Some specific research and demonstration results regarding this topic include the following: (1) differences in output per hour among age groups in given occupations tend to be insignificant; (2) there is a great deal of variation *within* age groups, which means that large percentages of older workers can exceed the average performance of the younger ones; and (3) older workers tend to have less variation in their rates of work performance. Such findings, once again, confirm the principle of evaluating workers on an individual-by-individual basis, and not on the basis of year of birth.

Private Sector Training Programs

Worker training programs exist in most industries. Some are conducted in-house while others are offered through trade schools, community colleges, four-year colleges, and universities.

These adult education courses are often supported by companies through tuition assistance, when employees' training is deemed job related. Employers are more likely to provide or pay for men ages 45 to 54 to take adult education courses than other age groups. Courses taken by women are less likely to be subsidized by employers, yet they provide or subsidize more than half of such courses taken by middle-aged women (Rix, 1990).

Public Sector Training Programs

In addition to private sector training programs, the federal government also plays a role in training older workers. Two programs, the Senior Community Service Employment Program (SCSEP) and the Job Training Partnership Act (JTPA), offer training opportunities to those who meet fairly restrictive eligibility requirements.

SCSEP (based on Title V of the Older Americans Act) was established to promote part-time opportunities in community services for low-income persons. SCSEP participants must be at least 55 years old and have incomes not exceeding 125 percent of the poverty level. Qualifying older workers are placed in part-time (twenty to twenty-five hours per week) public service jobs in such settings as day-care centers, schools, hospitals, and senior centers. Federal funds may be used to compensate participants for up to 1,300 hours of work per year, including orientation and training. SCSEP is designed to help older workers transition to private sector jobs once on-the-job training has been accomplished. The program has been criticized because it reaches so few older workers (65,000 in 1990), offers limited (usually low-tech) retraining, and does not offer preplacement training.

The SCSEP gives grants to national nonprofit sponsoring organizations, such as The National Council on the Aging and the National Council of Senior Citizens, and state agencies that receive federal funds to manage employment programs. These agencies, in turn, administer the program.

The largest government-sponsored training program is the Job Training Partnership Act (JTPA), which was enacted in 1982 as a replacement to CETA, the "War on Poverty" era's Comprehensive Employment and Training Act. JTPA primarily serves youth, but through its Title

II-A it channels funds to persons 55 and older. JTPA programs, sponsored by local governments and private sector planning agencies, involve classroom training, job search assistance, and on-the-job training.

SCSEP (based on Title V of the Older Americans Act) was established to promote part-time opportunities in community services for low-income persons. SCSEP participants must be at least 55 years old and have incomes not exceeding 125 percent of the poverty level.

● ALTERNATIVE WORK ARRANGEMENTS

The concept "alternative work arrangements" refers to the scheduling of workers of any age to engage in employment on terms that differ from conventional patterns, particularly the typical five-days-a-week, seven or eight hours per day, year-round model. All of these different forms of work-time allocation (including job-sharing) can be subsumed for practical purposes under the category of part-time work.

From 1960 to 1982, the percentage of middle-aged and older workers employed on a part-time basis (in a variety of models for the distribution of their time) had been increasing, but it has apparently leveled off since. According to Department of Labor data, this was especially the case among both men and women 65 and older.

There are many persons 55 and older who want to—and actually do—work on a part-time basis, for financial and/or other reasons. Some of these workers would like to retire, but probably will continue in the labor force on a part-time basis—some as long as they can. Generally they prefer to stay in the same kind of work as before. The Commonwealth Fund (McNaught and others, 1989) study found that 83 percent of persons 50 to 64 years old said that they would prefer part-time work. Even though interest in working part time is higher among older workers, evidence suggests that among *unemployed* older workers, more than three out of every four (78 percent in

Table 10.4
Percent Part-Time of Workers 65+ in Nonagriculture, 1960 to 1989

	1960	1970	1982	1989
Men	30	38	48	48
Women	44	50	60	59

Source: *U.S. Senate Special Committee on Aging, U.S. Administration on Aging, and American Association of Retired Persons,* Aging America: Trends and Projections, *1991 edition, Table 3-9, p. 102.*

1991) were looking for full-time jobs. Also, while nearly one-half of workers 65 or older are working part-time voluntarily, only 14 percent of workers of *all* ages work on such a basis out of choice.

One barrier to part-time opportunities—with one's previous employer especially—can be an employer's pension rules, which prohibit receipt of their retirees' private pensions if they work for that employer more than a certain number of hours per year (but still less than on a full-time basis). Travelers Insurance, in need of qualified personnel who knew that company's work culture, found that it made more sense to bring back on a part-time basis their recent retirees, instead of recruiting other workers through private employment agencies. But the company had to liberalize its limits on hours worked per year for continued pension eligibility in order to utilize successfully their well-trained, experienced "former" employees.

The Commonwealth Fund study found that 83 percent of persons 50 to 64 years old said that they would prefer part-time work. Even though interest in working part time is higher among older workers, evidence suggests that among *unemployed* older workers, more than three out of every four (78 percent in 1991) were looking for full-time jobs.

One of the problems concerning part-time jobs for older workers, some observers point out, is that they too often are jobs that pay very little and provide few, if any, fringe benefits. While there are some obstacles that may prevent older persons from seeking and finding full-time employment after having retired from another employer, some advocates feel that efforts should be made to provide opportunities that do include higher wages and nonwage benefits. Such jobs may be hard to find in the current economy. But Hilda Kahne (1985) believes that "new concept" part-time work should be developed in a wider range of occupations that could pay wages and benefits on a pro-rata basis, that is, on less than a full-time basis. "New concept" part-time jobs could expand if and when shortages of workers in the younger age groups are felt, and employers seek alternative solutions. Many older workers—especially those 62 and older—have financial reasons for not working on more than a part-time basis. If they were to earn beyond a certain level (about $10,000 in 1992), they would lose $1.00 in Social Security retired worker benefits for every $3.00 over that limit. But from the public policy point of view, such retired worker benefits are available only to men and women 62 and older who—as the benefit implies—are "retired." For administrative convenience, a dollar threshold is used to differentiate fully retired from partially retired and fully employed persons. "Retired worker" benefits are not available to workers at a certain age *regardless* of their labor force status.

One of the other problems associated with part-time work for older persons is that for many employers, part-time workers tend to be more costly and not as productive as their full-time employees, according to a study for the National Commission for Employment Policy (Jondrow and others, 1983). This partly explains why workers are offered a lower hourly wage if they work on a part-time basis. Another problem is that employers tend to completely lay off their workers during a period of declining product or service demand, instead of reducing hours of work.

In addition to the possibility that employers find it less expensive to hire on a full-time basis, part-time jobs tend to be concentrated in industries that typically pay low wages, to begin with. Careful statistical analyses (Jondrow and others, 1983) indicate that compensation "increases sharply with hours per week." Besides such arrangements, job redesign and other "organic" principles can be used to facilitate the perfor-

mance of older workers—indeed, all workers, for that matter (Czaja, 1990; Garag, 1986).

Second Careers

Working in the same occupation after many years is becoming less frequent today than in the past. The "candidates" for second (or third) careers may be persons whose organizations conventionally have early retirement options, as young as 45, 50, or 55, and who feel they are "too young" for full-time retirement. They may also include persons whose retirement income is felt to be too low for full-time retirement. The candidates also are made up of men and women who undergo the loss of employment due to company shutdowns, reductions-in-force, and/or company relocations. Once in such a position, they move on to occupations other than their previous ones. Finally, research has also found that there are workers who become dissatisfied and "unfulfilled" in their jobs and seek a marked change in their work lives in the form of new careers in their middle and later years.

Vast Unused Human Resources

According to the most recently completed and comprehensive analysis of the question about just how many older persons not working now are ready and able to work, and how many have sufficient skills and education, there are approximately 1.1 million men (ages 55 to 64) and women (50 to 59) who meet these criteria (McNaught and others, 1989). The labor force economists who directed the study for the Commonwealth Fund found that most of these 1.1 million men and women deemed available for employment did not view themselves as "early retirees" and wanted to continue full-time jobs when they did leave the labor force. They were the ones who had lost their jobs and, by and large, had retired involuntarily. Others who had retired for other reasons (because of poor health or having to care for relatives) wanted to return to work, when the original circumstances no longer prevailed.

The figure of 1.1 million men and women not in the labor force but who nevertheless are available for employment is a conservative estimate. First, the figures are restricted to men 55 to 64 years old and women 50 to 59. Second, and more important, the 1.1 million estimate was arrived at only after a series of screening questions aimed at a sample representing more than 7 million. Answers to those questions eliminated more than 6 million people in the above age groups who were not working at the time of the survey.

Just as important is the fact that official government estimates of the size of an available older worker pool are roughly only half the 1.1 million determined by the Commonwealth Fund study reported on here. The labor force econo-mists directing the Commonwealth Fund study feel that the questions used by the government are not appropriately worded and/or are not complete.

If the expected demographic changes do lead to a shortage of younger and qualified labor force entrants and job applicants, it should be clear from these and other research findings that there are at least 1 million persons in the 50 to 59 age group (women) and 55 to 64 group (men) quite adequately prepared, able, and willing to meet any employer demand for labor.

Profiles of Productive Aging

Liz Carpenter
Journalist

"I was born at a time when your life expectancy was only 63 years. But today, thanks to God, Shirley MacLaine or medical science, we've been given 15 to 20 more years."

Liz Carpenter has become the unofficial advocate of the aging American population since her book *Getting Better All the Time* was published in 1986. "No one remains the same person after meeting Liz," raved humorist Erma Bombeck. "She makes Auntie Mame look like a shut-in."

Born in Salado, Texas in 1920, Liz Carpenter later moved to Austin with her family. She has always expressed herself, arguing politics around the kitchen table with her outspoken family members. Strongly opposed to the rampant corruption of the big tycoons of the day and the promise offered by Roosevelt's New Deal, Carpenter became a "true Southern liberal."

After graduating from the University of Texas Journalism School, she went to Washington, D.C. with a scrapbook full of clippings and knocked on doors at the National Press Building. Esther Van Wagner Tufty, who represented the Michigan League of Home Dailies, hired the young reporter, giving Carpenter the opportunity to attend several of Franklin and Eleanor Roosevelt's famous press conferences. She married Leslie Carpenter in 1944, then worked for United Press. In 1952 the Carpenters formed their own news bureau in Washington through the *Arkansas Gazette* and the *Tulsa Tribune,* and represented up to twenty newspapers. Carpenter served as the president of the Women's National Press Club in 1954, and in 1960 her career took a major turn.

After attending the Democratic Convention that nominated Kennedy and Johnson, Carpenter joined the election campaign as Lady Bird's press liaison. Soon she was flying all over the country with the Johnsons and the Kennedys, concentrating her special efforts on Texas. "Although I loved working in the press building, I found that being a participant was so much more fun that just being a critic," Carpenter reflected. After the election, Johnson appointed her as his executive assistant, the first woman to hold the position. From 1963 to 1969, she served as Lady Bird's press secretary and chief of staff. Carpenter wrote a book about that era, *Ruffles and Flourishes: The Warm and Tender Story of a Simple Girl Who Found Adventure in the White House.*

Then public relations firm Hill & Knowlton sought her out to serve as vice-president, and in 1971 she helped found the National Women's Political Caucus. President Ford appointed Carpenter to the International Women's Year Commission, and President Carter named her assistant secretary of education for public affairs. *Ladies Home Journal* honored Carpenter as 1977 Woman of the Year in the field of politics and public affairs.

"I think one of the most aging things is to have no sense of purpose," Carpenter expressed. "When you work, you have a sense of purpose." Carpenter lives in Austin, Texas, where she writes and lectures frequently.

Lydia Brontë

● OLDER WOMEN WORKERS

Women began their greater participation in the paid labor force in the United States and other Western countries, as a result of factors associated with urbanization and a variety of other reasons and conditions, including:

- World War II opened up jobs that were previously the domain of men.
- The possibility of lower fertility released many women from childrearing, allowing them to seek and obtain jobs.
- Increased education made women more eligible for job openings.
- Families found it more advantageous to work for paid employment once a wide range of goods and services produced outside the household were available, rather than having to produce them within the household.

Possibly the increase in part-time jobs—especially for women still needed at home—also raised the level of their general participation. Over a period of time, young and middle-aged women in such situations eventually grew older, and their attachments to the paid work force was greater than what characterized women of previous generations. Thirty or more years ago, there was very little attention paid to older female workers. One major reason was that few women, certainly compared to the 1990s, were in the labor force on a full-time basis with a long-term commitment to the labor market. In the 1950s, furthermore, the tendency was for women who lost their jobs to remain out of the labor force. The participation of women in the work force—and on a relatively steady basis—has increased tremendously, as reported above. Today, women out of the labor force are also more likely to seek new jobs than in past decades.

Many women return to the workforce after first having "retired" and already receiving their retired-worker benefits, according to the data from the Social Security Administration. These returning women tended to be persons who did not have a private pension to augment their Social Security benefits, especially if their health permitted the return. In particular, unmarried women were more likely to return to work because of their low unearned incomes. Wives were much more likely to be working if their husbands were working than if their husbands were no longer working. It is also worth noting that retired-worker women were more likely to be at work again if:

- they had been in their longest-held job at least 10 years
- they had been working in a nonprofit organization
- they were in self-employed jobs, or
- they were in service occupations in such longest-held jobs

Except for women who had worked for state governments, unmarried women were clearly more likely to be working than married ones. Finally, the research results from the Social Security Administration's New Beneficiary Survey indicated that "the factors associated with employment appear to be similar for men and women." These new trends and phenomena mean that there are increased numbers of women in the labor force who continue to be in (or to re-enter) the labor force, into their middle and upper ages. Furthermore, the increase in the numbers and percentages of never-married, divorced or separated, and widowed women in recent decades makes the problem of older women workers even more urgent than in the past. Many of them, especially in the oldest groups of the old, might have few, no skills, or the wrong skills, when seeking employment for the first time, or when re-entering the labor force after many years of not working in the paid labor force.

Their problems are made even more severe (especially for those not married) when it comes to such things as coverage by private pensions and/or the adequacy of such pensions—as well as the amount of retired worker benefits they can expect from the Social Security system. A good part of these problems stems from such facts as their lower wage and occupational levels (compared to men in general), and fewer constant, uninterrupted years in the work force. Our public and private retirement income programs require work experience. Since women are out of the labor force for many years—typically for childrearing or care for spouses and elderly parents and relatives—they do not benefit from such programs as much as men do.

It remains to be seen whether future generations of women workers will have more continuous, uninterrupted work experience than today's women. Unlike other countries (e.g., in Western Europe), American women receive no pension credits for the time they are temporarily out of the labor force.

American women receive no pension credits for the time they are temporarily out of the labor force. (Copyright © Marianne Gontarz)

> Except for women who had worked for state governments, unmarried women were clearly more likely to be working than married ones.

● FUTURE TRENDS

The status of older workers in the short- and long-term future will depend on a number of factors and trends, as well as on retirement-and-work policies determined by our major institutions—government, employers, and employee organizations. Those factors and trends include the following: an expected shortage of young entrants into the labor force, which could put a premium on the retention and employment of older workers; the legislated increases in age-of-retirement for full benefits under Social Security over the next several years; the possible leveling off (or even decrease) of private pension coverage and benefit levels; and a more vigorous imple-

---

Voices of Creative Aging

Michelle C., a 68-year-old talent agent in the world of rock and roll, tells how she uses her years of experience in the entertainment industry to help young talent:

I began my career at age 15, making radio commercials for women's cosmetics. I became a talk show host and a radio and television writer. When I married, I gave up my on-air career to write copy for advertising. Several years ago a young man asked my help in getting a job at a radio station. That was the start of my new career in helping young people get a foothold in the entertainment industry.

I meet a lot of 20-year-old disc jockeys who play hard rock, and I think that's funny. Since I was a performer myself, I think I am a pretty good judge of talent, and if the way they present their music amuses me at my age, then it must be good! I think what I understand is the music's rhythmic noise—it makes me want to dance. I also know a good voice when I hear one. When I think a voice is good, I work hard to sell it to radio and television stations all across the country. For years I helped people find jobs. The big difference now is that I get paid for it.

I don't just get a person a job and take the money and run. I'm interested in careers, and as long as they are with me they get career guidance. The thing they don't know how to do is to handle themselves in political situations in the entertainment business, and I'm an old and practiced warrior at that.

I think when I go in to see station managers and owners, they are a little surprised by my age and that I am a woman. I just come in and sit down and talk about the talent I represent and what they have to offer. The only time that I get really rough is when the contract that I have negotiated is violated. I just don't allow that.

As I grow older, I would like to feel that a number of people young enough to carry on would make me a part of their lives.

Excerpt from Connie Goldman's "Late Bloomer" public radio series

mentation of the Age Discrimination in Employment Act.

Partly related to the above is the much-discussed issue of an increasing "burden" of non-working older persons that could be imposed on the working population: that alleged burden could be reduced by increasing the working population side of the ledger through the retention of older workers in the labor force. Incentives and disincentives to remain in the labor force and/or against retiring are already in process.

As for the youth labor shortage, there is no question that the rate of increase in young labor force entrants is extremely low over the next several decades. But some experts doubt that such a shortage will be as great as others have projected, especially if and when increases in productivity occur. In fact, from a historical viewpoint, productivity increases due to automation, for example, have frequently been the result of labor shortages.

But there does remain the issue of the quality of that future work force. Many employers are concerned about the skill and attitudinal competencies of entry-level applicants and employees, especially when compared to those of older adult employees.

Besides increasing their own training programs to meet these deficiencies of new employees, some companies plan on keeping their existing workers longer than otherwise. This could have a substantial influence on the "early retirement" trends.

A survey by the Conference Board (Johnson and Fabian, 1992) found that in comparing their older workers with "average age" workers, the older ones were reported as being better in turnover, absenteeism, and overall job skills. Older workers were evaluated as better in motivation, production, and cost effectiveness—even when some "high-cost" factors such as health care costs were taken into account.

On the other hand, that very same survey found that despite these overall positive ratings, three-fifths of the employers were using early retirement incentives if they were engaged in "downsizing" their labor forces. If this is the case, there looms the high risk of losing the actual and potential skills of these experienced workers: "Employers are faced with the ironic possibility that they will be remediating large numbers of unqualified job entrants while simultaneously encouraging the early exit of many highly trained employees."

At the individual, organizational, governmental, and societal levels, the next several years will be characterized by extensive discussions and debates surrounding the issue of "early retirement." Here that term applies to exiting from the labor force (not merely a given organization) typically before the youngest age at which retired worker benefits under Social Security are available (now age 62), or exactly at that age despite the gradual increase in the "full-benefit" age.

Many employers are concerned about the skill and attitudinal competencies of entry-level applicants and employees, especially when compared to those of older adult employees.

Any examination of the benefits and costs of early retirement should include evaluations from the standpoint of the potential retiree; the worker who replaces such retirees; the employer; and the government (Mirkin, 1987). For example, from the potential retiree's angle, the benefits could include the value of increased leisure, while the costs could include how much is lost in no longer having a salary or wages exceeding the level of the pension. From the viewpoint of the employer, the costs include those factors already cited above, while the benefits include, for example, the value of having to pay lower wages and salaries (and perhaps less costly fringe benefits).

The government benefits from having a reduction in expenditures for unemployment compensation (if the older worker becomes unemployed and does not leave the labor force), and other income transfer costs; and even an increase in income tax revenues, assuming the retiree is replaced by another worker not previously working. On the other hand, on the cost side, the government faces a loss of Social Security contributions and income taxes, assuming the retiree is not replaced by another worker.

As a closing observation, Mirkin's general evaluation of early retirement policies (especially when used to disguise employment among older persons) expresses a valid argument: "From a long-term perspective, the advisability of encouraging premature retirement seems highly questionable. Given falling birth rates and subsequent future contractions in the working-age population, labor force growth will come to a virtual standstill in developed countries by the turn of the century."

The social, psychological, and financial implications of a longer than expected period of retirement may be a reality now dawning on individual workers and their families, as well as on American communities and government.

References

American Association of Retired Persons. *Public Policy Institute Data Digest* (August 1992).

Birren, James. *The Psychology of Aging.* Englewood Cliffs, NJ: Prentice Hall, 1964.

Czaja, Sara. *Human Factors Research Needs for an Aging Population.* National Research Council. Washington, DC: National Academy Press, 1990.

Garag, Arun. "Ergonomics and the Older Worker: An Overview." *Experimental Aging Research* Vol. 17 (Autumn 1991): 143–55.

Iams, Howard Mark. "Employment of Retired Worker Women." *Social Security Bulletin* (1986).

Johnson, Arlene, and Fabian Linden. *Availability of a Quality Work Force.* New York: Conference Board, 1992.

Jondrow, James M., and others. *Older Workers in the Market for Part-Time Employment.* Washington, DC: National Commission for Employment Policy, 1983.

Kahne, Hilda. *Reconceiving Part-Time Work: New Perspectives for Older Workers and Women.* Totowa, NJ: Rowman & Allanheld, 1985.

Koyl, Leon. In *Policy Issues in Work and Retirement.* Ed. Hervert Parnes. Kalamazoo, MI: Upjohn Institute for Employment Research. 1983.

McNaught, William, M. C. Barth, and P. H. Henderson. "The Human Resource Potential of Americans over 50." *Human Resource Management* Vol. 28, no. 4 (1989).

Mirkin, Barry. "Early Retirement as a Labor Force Policy: An International Overview." *Monthly Labor Review* (March 1987): 19–33.

National Center for Health Statistics, U.S. Department of Health and Human Services. "Aging in the Eighties: Ability to Perform Work-Relate Activities." *NCHS Advanced Data Report, No. 136.* Washington, DC: Government Printing Office, May 8, 1987.

Plett, Peter, and Brenda Lester. *Training for Older People.* Geneva: International Labor Office, 1991.

Rix, Sara E. *Older Workers: Choices and Challenges.* Santa Barbara, CA: ABC-CLIO, 1990.

Schaie, Warner. "Perceptual Speed in Adulthood: Cross-Sectional and Longitudinal Studies." *Psychology and Aging* (1989).

Sheppard, Harold L. "Work Continuity Versus Retirement: Reasons for Continuing Work." In *Retirement Reconsidered.* Eds. Robert Morrison and S. A. Bass. New York: Springer, 1988.

Thalheimer Research Associates. *Older Workers in the Labor Market.* Springfield, VA: National Technical Information Service, 1991.

U.S. Department of Labor. *Labor Market Problems of Older Workers,* January 1989.

U.S. Department of Labor. Bureau of Labor Statistics. *Current Population Surveys: Displaced Worker Supplement,* January 1986.

———. Unpublished tables on 1991 work experience. 1992.

U.S. House of Representatives Select Committee on Aging. *Older Workers in the Labor Market,* 1992.

Welford, A. T. "Psychomotor Performance" In *Handbook of Aging and the Individual.* Ed. James Birren. Chicago: University of Chicago Press, 1958.

Additional Reading

Achenbaum, W. Andrew. *Social Security: Visions and Revisions.* Cambridge: Cambridge University Press, 1986.

American Association of Retired Persons (AARP). *Business and Older Workers: Current Perceptions and New Directions for the 1990s.* Washington, DC: AARP, 1989.

———. *Work and Retirement: Employees over 40 and Their Views.* Washington, DC: AARP, 1986.

———. *Workers Over 50: Old Myths, New Realities.* Washington, DC: AARP, n.d.

Axel, Helen. "Job Banks for Retirees." *Research Report No. 929.* New York: Conference Board, 1989.

Bird, Carolina. *Second Careers. New Ways to Work After 50.* Boston, MA: Little, Brown, 1992.

Bureau of National Affairs. *Older Americans in the Workforce: Challenges and Solutions.* Washington, DC: Bureau of National Affairs, 1987.

———. "Part-Time Employment: Crosscurrents of Change." In *Flexible Workstyles: A Look at Contingent Labor.* Washington, DC: U.S. Department of Labor, Women's Bureau, 1988.

Connor, J. Robert. *Cracking the Over-50 Job Market.* New York: Plume, 1992.

Coyle, Jean M. *Women and Aging: A Selected, Annotated Bibliography.* Westport, CT: Greenwood, 1989.

Crown, William H., Phyllis H. Mutschler, and Thomas D. Leavitt. *Beyond Retirement: Characteristics of Older Workers and the Implications for Employment Policy.* Waltham, MA: Policy Center on Aging, Heller School, Brandeis University, 1987.

Fyock, Catherine D., and Greg Newton. *Making the Older Worker Connection.* Louisville, KY: Innovative Management Concepts, 1988.

Harris, Louis, & Associates. "Older Americans: Ready and Able to Work." *Report No. 1, Study No. 884030.* New York: Louis Harris and Associates, n.d.

ICF. *The Impact of Increased Employment of Older Workers on the National Economy* (report prepared for the Commonwealth Fund). Fairfax, VA: ICF Inc., 1989.

———. *Why Workers Retire Early* (report prepared for the Commonwealth Fund). Fairfax, VA: ICF Inc., 1989.

Knowles, Daniel E. "Dispelling Myths about Older Workers." In *Employing Older Americans: Opportunities and Constraints.* Ed. Helen Axel. New York: Conference Board, 1988.

"Late Bloomer" audio cassette. Available from Connie Goldman Production, 926 Second Street, Suite 201, Santa Barbara, CA 90403. (310) 393-6801.

Levitan, Sara A., and Elizabeth A. Conway. *Part-Time Employment: Living on Half Rations.* Washington, DC: George Washington University, Center for Social Policy Studies, 1988.

Miller, Jill. "Displaced Homemakers in the Employment and Training System." In *Job Training for Women: The Promise and Limits of Public Policies.* Ed. Sharon L. Harlan and Ronnie J. Steinberg. Philadelphia, PA: Temple University Press, 1989.

Moloney, Thomas W., and Barbara Paul. "Enabling Older Americans to Work." In *The Commonwealth Fund 1989 Annual Report.* New York: Commonwealth Fund, 1989.

Morgan, John S. *Getting a Job After 50.* Princeton, NJ: Petrocelli, 1987.

Myers, Albert, and Christopher P. Anderson. *Success over Sixty.* New York: Summit, 1984.

Olmsted, Barney, and Suzanne Smith. *Creating a Flexible Workplace: How to Select and Manage Alternative Work Options.* New York: AMACOM, 1989.

Opinion Research Corporation (ORC). *Report of a National Survey of Women 45 and Older Who Work Part-Time.* Princeton, NJ: ORC, 1989.

Peterson, David, and Sally Coberly. "The Older Worker: Myths and Realities." In *Retirement Reconsidered.* Eds. Robert Morris and Scott A. Bass. New York: Springer, 1988.

Rosen, Benson, and Thomas H. Jerdee. *Older Employees: New Roles for Valued Resources.* Homewood, IL: Dow Jones-Irwin, 1985.

Selden, Ina Lee. *Going into Business for Yourself: New Beginnings after 50.* Glenview, IL: Scott, Foresman, 1989.

Stagner, Ross. "Aging in Industry." In *Handbook of the Psychology of Aging.* Eds. James E. Birren and K. Warner Schaie. New York: Van Nostrand Reinhold, 1985.

Sterns, Harvey L., and Dennis Doverspike. "Training and Developing the Older Worker: Implications for Human Resource Management." In *Fourteen Steps in Managing an Older Workforce.* Ed. Helen Dennis. Lexington, MA: Lexington, 1988.

Sum, Andrew, Christopher Ruhm, and Peter Doeringer. *Work, Earnings, and Retirement.* Boston: Boston University Center for Applied Social Science/Institute for Employment Policy, 1988.

Treas, Judith. "The Historical Decline in Late-Life Labor Force Participation in the United States." In *Age, Health, and Employment.* Eds. James E. Birren, Pauline K. Robinson, and Judy E. Livingston. Englewood Cliffs, NJ: Prentice-Hall, 1986.

U.S. Bureau of Census. *Employment Discrimination Against Older Women: A Handbook on Litigating Age and Sex Discrimination Cases.* Washington, DC: Older Women's League, 1989.

———. *Labor Market Problems of Older Workers.* Report of the Secretary of Labor, prepared by Philip L. Rones and Diane E. Herz. Washington, DC: Department of Labor, 1989.

U.S. Bureau of Labor Statistics. *Occupational Outlook Handbook.* Washington, DC: U.S. Government Printing Office, 1990–91.

U.S. Department of Labor. *Older Worker Task Force: Key Policy Issues for the Future.* Report of the Secretary of Labor. Washington, DC: U.S. Department of Labor, January 1989.

———. *Opportunity 2000: Creative Affirmative Action Strategies for a Changing Workforce.* Prepared by the Hudson Institute for the Department of Labor. Washington, DC: U.S. Government Printing Office, September 1988.

Pamphlets

All available from the American Association of Retired Persons (AARP) at no charge.

The Age Discrimination in Employment Act Guarantees You Certain Rights: Here's How . . . . Washington, DC: AARP, 1987.

How to Manage Older Workers. Washington, DC: AARP, Worker Equity Department, 1988.

How to Recruit Older Workers. Washington, DC: AARP, Worker Equity Department, 1988.

How to Train Older Persons. Washington, DC: AARP, Worker Equity Department, n.d.

Look Before You Leap: A Guide to Early Retirement Incentive Programs. Washington, DC: AARP Worker Equity, 1988.

Using the Experience of a Lifetime. Washington, DC: AARP, Worker Equity Department, 1988.

Working Options: How To Plan Your Job Search, Your Work Life. Washington, DC: AARP, 1985.

Harold L. Sheppard, Ph. D.

11

Retirement

- What Is Retirement? ● Labor Force Participation in Later Life ● Retirement as a Social Institution
- Planning for Retirement ● Social Security ● Pensions ● Other Types of Retirement Income
- Health Issues ● Legal Issues ● Housing ● Migration and Lifestyle
- Factors Affecting the Timing of Retirement ● Adjustment to Retirement
- Retirement as a Process ● Retirement and Disengagement

Late nineteenth and early twentieth century industrialization altered the structure of the U.S. economy and influenced development of the new portion of the life cycle called retirement. In the United States, retirement has gradually become accepted as a natural part of the life course. It marks the ending of one's work life and entry into a continuing life process, and signifies an emergent social institution with rules, roles, and often new responsibilities. Retirement as a broad social institution is influenced by government policy on matters such as Social Security and health care, by business, banking, and industry, in matters varying from pensions, investments, retirement planning, and production, by the housing and real estate sectors, and by the growth of the leisure and travel industry.

The experience of retirement has become more common since the turn of the century. As a proportion of the life cycle, retirement has increased dramatically for men (see Table 11.1). While most Americans do not plan extensively for retirement and relatively few take part in formal retirement planning programs, the majority find retirement a positive and rewarding time of life. On an individual level retirement is not just an event or a static portion of life, rather it can be considered a dynamic and evolving process with stages or phases.

● WHAT IS RETIREMENT?

To many people, retirement denotes an older person leaving the work force to enjoy leisure activities while receiving Social Security checks and other pension income. Yet leaving the work force, receiving a retirement income, or following leisure pursuits do not necessarily occur in a fixed order. For example, should a displaced 60 year old worker living off his or her savings and seeking continued employment be considered retired? Similarly, what is the status of a 55 year old receiving monthly pension checks after thirty years service with an employer, but also holding a full-time position with another employer?

Retirement is difficult to define since it may not always be associated with a single event such as turning 62 or 65. Nor is retirement tied to withdrawal from the labor force, or the pursuit of leisure activities, or obtaining retirement income based on former employment. Two sets of findings illustrate the variety: Erdman Palmore (1967) found that among men who were 65 years old, some 64 percent had not worked in the previous year, another 13 percent had worked less than full time year around, while 80 percent had received income based on former employment. A more recent study (Parnes and Less, 1985) found that among men at least 60 years old, a significant majority (70 percent) were receiving a pension check, yet 43 percent of the overall group were

While most Americans do not plan extensively for retirement, the majority find retirement a positive and rewarding time of life. (Courtesy of Sanders-Brown Center on Aging, University of Kentucky/Tim Collins, photographer)

obtaining retirement income and still working more than 20 hours a week.

In the United States, retirement has gradually become accepted as a natural part of the life course. It marks the ending of one's work life and entry into a continuing life process, and signifies an emergent social institution with rules, roles, and often new responsibilities.

Difficulty in coming to terms with the meaning of retirement is reflected in studies conducted by the gerontological community. Quinn and Burkhauser (1990) note that several different criteria have been used in the study of retirement: (1) subjective appraisal of one's retirement status (Parnes and Less, 1985; Hausman and Wise, 1985); (2) the receipt of retirement income or

income based on previous work status such as Social Security or employer pension plan (Burkhauser, 1980); and (3) degree of labor force participation such as complete labor force withdrawal (Quinn, 1977; Gordon and Blinder, 1980; Sickles and Taubman, 1986), quarter time or less work (Boskin, 1977), a rapid reduction in work hours (Burtless and Moffitt, 1985), or a departure from a primary job (Fields and Mitchell, 1984).

Atchley (1991) also notes the difficulty of operationally defining retirement, and he stresses the importance of two major dimensions: (1) the receipt of pension income, whether from Social Security or from an employer program, based on previous work history; and (2) a reduction in or a cessation of labor force participation. Merging these two concepts together Atchley suggests another criterion for retirement: when the major source of a household's income shifts from wage earnings to pension income. Thus, retirement may be defined as that stage in life marked by a distinct decline in labor force participation, combined with an increase in household income derived from past work history.

● LABOR FORCE PARTICIPATION IN LATER LIFE

If defining retirement is difficult, measuring the prevalence of retirement is an equally challenging task. Gerontologists use the Labor Force Participation Rate to measure withdrawal from the civilian labor force by the elderly. Yet labor force participation includes both the employed and those unemployed who are still seeking work. In addition, workers reporting themselves as not in the labor force are classified by the U. S. Department of Labor as keeping house, going to school, unable to work because of long-term physical or mental illness, or retired. A final "other category" of non-labor force participants includes people who are too old, temporarily unable to work, voluntarily idle, seasonal workers in the off season, and discouraged workers (i.e., people who have given up hope of finding employment). Thus the opposite of labor force participation is not necessarily retirement.

Table 11.2 clearly shows the cross-sectional decline in labor force participation among older age groups. Overall, only two-thirds of the 55- to 59-year-old civilian population remain in the labor

Table 11.1
Life Cycle Distribution of Education, Labor Force Participation, Retirement, and Work in the Home: 1900–80

Subject	Year					
	1900	1940	1950	1960	1970	1980
	Number of years spent in activity					
Men						
Average life expectancy	46.3	60.8	65.6	66.6	67.1	70.0
Retirement/work at home	1.2	9.1	10.1	10.2	12.1	13.6
Labor force participation	32.1	38.1	41.5	41.1	37.8	38.8
Education	8.0	8.6	9.0	10.3	12.2	12.6
Pre-school	5.0	5.0	5.0	5.0	5.0	5.0
Women						
Average life expectancy	48.3	65.2	71.1	73.1	74.7	77.4
Retirement/work at home	29.0	39.4	41.4	37.1	35.3	30.6
Labor force participation	6.3	12.1	15.1	20.1	22.3	29.4
Education	8.0	8.7	9.6	10.9	12.1	12.4
Pre-school	5.0	5.0	5.0	5.0	5.0	5.0
	Percent distribution by activity type					
Men						
Average life expectancy	100	100	100	100	100	100
Retirement/work at home	3	15	15	15	18	19
Labor force participation	69	63	63	62	56	55
Education	17	14	14	15	18	18
Pre-school	11	8	8	8	7	8
Women						
Average life expectancy	100	100	100	100	100	100
Retirement/work at home	60	60	58	51	47	40
Labor force participation	13	19	21	27	30	38
Education	17	13	14	15	16	16
Pre-school	10	8	7	7	7	6

Sources: U.S. Bureau of the Census, "Educational Attainment in the United States: March 1981 and 1980." *Current Population Reports* Series P-20, no. 390 (August 1984) (median years of school for persons 25 years or older, 1940–80).

Best, Fred. *Work Sharing: Issues, Policy Options, and Prospects.* Upjohn Institute for Employment Research (1981), page 8 (1900 estimates of median years of school for persons 25 years or older).

National Center for Health Statistics. "Life Tables." *Vital Statistics of the United States 1987* Vol. 2, Section 6 (February 1990) (life expectancy data).

U.S. Department of Labor, Bureau of Labor Statistics. "Worklife Estimates: Effects of Race and Education." *Bulletin* 2254 (February 1986).

force. A steady decline in labor force participation is found in each of the five-year incremental periods. Only one-fifth of the 65 to 69 age group remains in the labor force. A decline in labor force participation in each advancing age group holds true for both males and females, and for African Americans and whites.

Females demonstrate lower labor force participation rate than their male counterparts (56.8 percent, versus 78.9 percent at ages 55 to 59).

Still, female and male rates decline steadily, and among older age groups, the discrepancy between the sexes narrows (16.0 percent for men, versus 8.3 percent for women, among those 65 years and older).

Table 11.3 displays the two forces at work that narrow the gender difference in labor force participation rates. Men are leaving the labor force

Retirement may be defined as that stage in life marked by a distinct decline in labor force participation, combined with an increase in household income derived from past work history.

Table 11.2
Labor Force Participation and Percent Unemployment of Older Adults by Age, Sex, Race: 1992 (Annual Averages)

| | Age of Respondent | | | | | |
	55-59	60-64	65-69	70-75	75+	65+
Total						
Labor force						
Participation rate	67.4	45.0	20.7	11.2	4.5	11.6
Percent unemployed	5.1	4.9	4.2	3.5	2.9	3.3
Male						
Labor force						
Participation rate	78.9	54.7	25.9	15.0	7.3	16.1
Percent unemployed	5.7	6.0	4.0	2.3	2.4	3.3
Female						
Labor force						
Participation rate	56.8	36.5	16.2	8.2	2.8	8.3
Percent unemployed	4.0	4.4	4.3	5.2	3.6	4.5
White						
Male						
Labor force						
Participation rate	80.1	55.2	26.4	15.3	7.3	16.3
Percent unemployed	5.3	5.7	4.0	1.9	2.3	3.1
Female						
Labor force						
Participation rate	57.3	36.8	16.3	8.2	2.8	8.3
Percent unemployed	3.9	4.3	4.3	5.1	3.9	4.5
African American						
Male						
Labor force						
Participation rate	66.7	50.8	21.7	10.9	6.4	13.7
Percent unemployed	7.9	8.3	4.8	6.9	2.4	4.9
Female						
Labor force						
Participation rate	54.5	35.2	15.3	8.8	3.2	8.6
Percent unemployed	4.2	4.4	4.8	7.0	NR	4.9

Note: NR: Data "not reported," as the base is too small (*n* < 35,000).

Source: U.S. Department of Labor, Bureau of Labor Statistics, Employment and Earnings Vol. 40, no. 1 (January 1993).

earlier in life, shown by the presence of 86.9 percent of men 55 to 59 years old in the labor force in 1950, but only 67.0 percent were part of the labor force by 1992. Meanwhile, women's labor force participation rose from 27.0 percent in 1950 to 46.6 percent in 1992 for the 55 to 59 year old age group. More women are entering the labor force, and they are staying in it till later in life.

At age 65 and up a different pattern is found, showing little variation in women's labor force participation rates since mid-century (9.7 in 1950, versus 8.3 in 1992). In contrast, the steady decline in the male labor force participation rates found in the younger age group (i.e., 55 to 59 years old) is also reflected in the 65+ group, with 45.8 percent in the labor force in 1950, but only 16.1 percent in 1992.

Table 11.2 reveals a difference between white and African-American male labor force participation in the 55 to 59 age group (white at 80.1 percent, versus African American at 66.7 percent). The divergence narrows quickly with the advance of years to a point at age 65+ where the white

A greater proportion of African-American males considered to be in the labor force are among the ranks of the unemployed. (Courtesy of The National Council on the Aging, Inc.)

rate is 16.3 percent, and the African-American rate is 13.7 percent. A greater proportion of African-American males considered to be in the labor force are among the ranks of the unemployed. Among females there is not as large a spread between white and African-American labor force participation (i.e., 55 to 59 years old: white at 57.3 percent, versus African American at 54.8 percent).

For men and women 45 to 64 years old, the proportion of full-time employed has held steady for the past three decades (see Table 11.4). Approximately 95 percent of employed men in the aforementioned age group are working full time, while the percentage of full-time working women has remained about twenty points lower. Greater change is reflected in the 65+ age group: the percent of employed males working full time has decreased from 70 percent in 1960, to approximately 52 percent by 1982, where it has remained virtually unchanged. Women have experienced less of a decline in full-time employment in the 65+ age group, moving from 56 percent to 39 percent in those two decades. As with men, the rate has remained at the same level during the past decade.

The vast majority of men and women in the 65+ age group who work part time have chosen a reduced work schedule. About 90 percent (females at 89 percent, versus males at 91 percent) report they have voluntarily chosen to work reduced hours rather than reporting an inability to find full-time employment. This choice is far less likely to be the reason for part-time employment among the younger age groups. Here 51 per-

Table 11.3
Civilian Labor Force Participation Rates for Older People, by Age and Sex: 1950–92 (Annual Averages)

Year	Men 55–64	Men 65+	Women 55–64	Women 65+
1950	86.9	45.8	27.0	9.7
1955	87.9	39.6	32.5	10.6
1960	86.8	33.1	37.2	10.8
1965	84.6	27.9	41.1	10.0
1970	83.0	26.8	43.0	9.7
1975	75.6	21.6	40.9	8.2
1980	72.1	19.0	41.3	8.1
1985	67.9	15.8	42.0	7.3
1990	68.8	15.7	46.0	8.4
1992	67.0	16.1	46.6	8.3

Sources: 1950–80 data: U.S. Department of Labor, Bureau of Labor Statistics, *Handbook of Labor Statistics Bulletin* 2217 (June 1985).

1985 data: U.S. Department of Labor, Bureau of Labor Statistics, *Employment and Earnings* Vol. 33, no. 1 (January 1986).

1990 data: U.S. Department of Labor, Bureau of Labor Statistics, *Employment and Earnings* Vol. 38, no. 1 (January 1991).

1992 data: U.S. Department of Labor, Bureau of Labor Statistics, *1991 Employment and Earnings* Vol. 40, no. 1 (January 1992).

Table 11.4

**Full- Or Part-Time Status of Workers 45+ in Nonagricultural Industries, Percentages by Sex and Age:
Selected Years, 1960–92**

Sex & Age	1960		1970		1982		1992	
	Full-time	Part-time	Full-time	Part-time	Full-time	Part-time	Full-time	Part-time
Men:								
45–64	94	6	96	4	93	7	93	7
65+	70	30	62	38	52	48	52	48
Women:								
45–64	78	22	77	23	74	26	77	23
65+	56	44	50	50	40	60	39	61

Sources: U.S. Department of Labor, Bureau of Labor Statistics. *Employment and Earnings* Vol. 40, no. 1 (January 1993); Vol. 30, no. 1 (January 1983); Vol. 17, no. 7 (January 1971).

U.S. Department of Labor, Bureau of Labor Statistics. *Labor Force and Employment in 1960,* Special Labor Force Report no. 14 (April 1961).

cent of the males and 75 percent of the females voluntarily chose part time employment.

Not only has there been a decline in the 65+ portion of the labor force since mid-century, but among those who have remained working at that age, one finds a decline in the percent who are employed full time. There has been a general disengagement from the work force by older adults based on the growth of a system of retirement income and changes in the nature of work in a modern industrialized society.

● **RETIREMENT AS A SOCIAL INSTITUTION**

A constellation of complex forces has come together with industrialization to create the social institution of retirement. On an economic level the mechanization of production and the shift from human and animal energy to fossil fuels increased the productivity of society, which affects the development of retirement in two ways. First, increased productivity means that the average worker produces more than he or she needs for mere survival. This excess can be channeled into benefits for a later time in life when the worker withdraws from the labor force. An example of how this surplus is transformed monetarily is the 7.05 percent FICA tax paid to the federal government by both employees and employers, which is transferred to the retired population through Social Security and Medicare.

A second way this productivity influences retirement is through the reduced need for labor in a society. Industrial modes of production require fewer labor force participants. Retirement, like adolescence and young adulthood, is a stage of the life cycle that arose after industrialization. By extending the requirements for time spent in education for youths and young adults, and by encouraging labor force withdrawal in the later years, the size of the labor force is controlled. Retirement and the financial means to support retirees reduce unemployment among younger people and the possibility of social unrest, which may be associated with large-scale unemployment.

On a demographic level, the increase in life expectancy, which coincides with industrialization, further increases the retirement stage of the life cycle. As a society moves through industrialization, there is an increase not only in the standard of living but also in scientific knowledge, in medical applications, and in public health technology. These changes bring about an increase in life expectancy at birth (47.3 years in 1990, versus 75.5 years in 1991), hence allowing more individuals to live to retirement age. In the more advanced industrial societies, medicine is able to make inroads at extending life expectancy at age 65 (the extension was 13.9 years in 1950, versus 17.4 years in 1991), further increasing the retirement age population.

Bureaucratic organization is a form of social

Profiles of Productive Aging

Celeste Holm
Actress

"Being an actress is being everything. You can do anything. I teach, I lecture, I write. It's a wonderful springboard for almost anything."

Celeste Holm was born in Brooklyn, New York and fell in love with the theater after seeing Anna Pavlova perform. At first she trained to be a dancer, but after attending boarding school in Paris, where the language difference proved unnerving, she concentrated on acting because of its "universal" appeal.

Holm played leads in all her school plays, and recalled that even then people treated her as a "professional." After graduating she found work in New York, where she said at first she "took anything," but it was not long before she got her first role in the successful Broadway play *The Women*. Roles such as Ado Annie in the smash *Oklahoma!* soon followed. Holm recalled her audition for the Rodgers and Hammerstein musical *Green Grow the Lilacs,* where she fell flat on her face while getting on stage. "Because I had fallen on my face I was no longer nervous. I mean after that happens there's nowhere to go but up," remembered Holm, who got the part.

During World War II Holm worked at the Stage-door Canteen, where she "waited on tables and danced with the soldiers." The atmosphere at the canteen heightened Holm's desire to contribute to the war effort; she embarked on a tour of France and Germany to entertain the American troops abroad. After the war, Holm launched her film career in Hollywood. War-torn Europe made the glittering world of show biz seem overwhelmingly artificial, so throughout her Hollywood career Holm, like many actors, developed a healthy disrespect for the studio system. "There was a whole process arranged to make you feel like two cents worth of dirty ice," she explained.

Holm refused to play the role of the naive young starlet, and while she did her share of "stupid musicals," she also enjoyed worthy material. Over five decades Holm worked in films, plays, and television. Accolades include an Academy Award for her work in *The Gentlemen's Agreement.* She is currently president of the Creative Arts Rehabilitation Center and even finds time to study semiotics at Claremont College. When asked why she never retired, Holm said: "If actors retired there'd never be a John Gielgud, or Katherine Hepburn or Jessica Tandy. Actors never retire."

Lydia Brontë

technology, which is more frequently found in an industrial society, allowing for the handling of a large number of units (applications, checks, etc.) in a standardized way. Such organization enables intergenerational transfers of money, such as Social Security, to support the retired population. During 1992, Social Security collected $307.1 billion from 132 million workers (94 percent of the work force). In turn, approximately $254.8 billion in benefits were paid out to 25.7 million retired workers and 7.6 million survivors during the same year. This transfer was completed at an administrative cost of only .7 percent (U.S. Social Security Administration, 1993). The Health Care Financing Administration paid out $83.9 billion in hospital insurance and $49.2 billion in supplemental medical insurance to 35 million enrollees at an administrative cost of 1.3 percent and 3.2 percent respectively (U.S. Social Security Administration,

1993). In addition to the federal government's social insurance programs, there are 729,922 private pension plans, 201 state pension programs, and 2,213 locally administered programs. State and local plans pay benefits to 920,515 and 1,985,284 people, respectively. Private plans hold assets of $1.5 billion and pay benefits to 12.5 million Americans (U.S. Bureau of Labor Statistics, 1992). These are all examples of the complex bureaucratic structures that help sustain a large retirement population.

● PLANNING FOR RETIREMENT

As with other stages of the life cycle, the greatest amount of preparation for retirement is informal. Some individuals start to read pertinent literature and talk with their spouses, other relatives, and friends as early as fifteen years ahead of their planned retirement. The prevalence of this pattern and the intensity of this style of informal planning does increase with age (Evans and others, 1985).

Formal planning programs are not very common. An American Association of Retired Persons (AARP) survey (1986) revealed that among workers 40 years old and older, only 23 percent report that their employers offered retirement planning. Such programs were typically benefits provided by large corporate employers. Organizations such as AARP and The National Council on the Aging (NCOA) have developed retirement planning programs that are widely used by businesses, clubs, trade, and other types of organizations.

While accessibility of these programs is limited, their utilization is even more limited. Campione (1988) found only 10 percent of those persons who had access to retirement planning actually enrolled in the programs. Apparently self-selection is at work among the small group who attend such programs. Individuals who attend retirement planning programs tend to be careful planners. They have made their lists, and by attending the program they are checking them twice, and often report satisfaction with the program.

Economic planners and other experts recommend that before middle age, at least partial planning for retirement should be considered. Whether through formal planning programs, consultation with a financial planner, a tax accountant, or more informal means, consideration of the most important financial requisites for facing the retirement years should be undertaken as early as possible.

Financial planning is one important element for a comfortable retirement. While it is never too late to take steps to secure a retirement income, advance planning may allow for more options. The 1981 President's Commission on Pension Policy concluded that a household would need to receive 75 percent of preretirement income in retirement to maintain its standard of living. However, this high a replacement income in retirement would require a high rate of savings every year. There are several forms of retirement income to replace income from work in retirement. The most significant is based on Social Security.

> An American Association of Retired Persons (AARP) survey (1986) revealed that among workers 40 years old and older, only 23 percent report that their employers offered retirement planning.

● SOCIAL SECURITY

The Social Security act was signed into law in August 1935 and was designed to help those who in later life found it difficult to continue to work. It also served the economic function of reducing the labor force participation of older workers during the Great Depression, thereby opening up jobs for younger workers.

Amendments to the act have been made throughout the years. After Title 2 retirement and survivors benefits (1939), permanent disability benefits (1957) and Medicare Title 18 (1965) have been added. The amended act also includes other programs: black lung disease, Supplemental Security Income (SSI), unemployment insurance, Aid to Families with Dependent Children (AFDC), Medicaid, maternal and child benefits, Food Stamps, worker's compensation, Railroad Retirement, and energy assistance. While technically all of these other programs are part of the Social Security Act, it is important to note that they are funded by general tax revenues, not by Social Security taxes, and are not administered by the Social Security Administration. What most people think of as Social Security is what the federal government calls OASDHI or Old Age, Survivors, Disability, and Hospital Insurance, which is funded by the Federal Insurance Contributions Act (FICA).

Social Security is the primary source of income in later life. Some 38 percent of all income received by those 65 years old and older comes from the retirement and survivors benefit. Practically all older adult households (94 percent) receive Social Security benefits. A sizable minority of these households depend significantly on Social Security. Some 13 percent receive no income other than Social Security, and 3 percent receive four-fifths of their income from Social Security (U.S. Senate Special Committee on Aging, 1991b).

● A PRIMER ON SOCIAL SECURITY

Financing Social Security

Old Age Survivors Disability and Hospital Insurance (OASDHI) is financed by the Federal Insurance Contributions Act (FICA). What is typically thought of as Social Security OAI or Title II of the Social Security Act is a pay-as-you-go system. Intergenerational transfers are made from the working age population via the FICA taxes to the retired generation receiving the benefits of this social insurance system. Employees pay one-half of the rate, and employers the other half of the tax.

Employers can deduct their portion of the tax as a cost of doing business. Employees pay federal income tax on their contributions. Self-employed individuals pay both portions of contributions, although there is a special deduction, which can be taken when filing the federal tax return. More information can be obtained from Social Security Administration Publication no. 05-10022 entitled "If You're Self Employed."

Deductions for the employed individual in 1994 up to the first $60,600 earned in a year are as follows: OASI, 5.60 percent; DI, 0.60 percent; and HI, 1.45 percent on all earned income. The initial rate for OASI in 1937 was 1.0 percent, for DI in 1957 was 0.25 percent, and for HI in 1966 was 0.35 percent. As of September 1991 approximately 132 million workers contributed to the system.

As of September 30, 1992, the OASI trust fund had receipts of $307.1 billion, and disbursements of $256.2 billion, and assets of $306.2 billion. The administrative cost of the program amounted to 0.7 percent.

More details about the financing of the Social Security system can be obtained from Social Security Administration Publication no. 05-10094 entitled "Financing Social Security."

Benefit Calculation

A. Eligibility is based on forty quarters of payment to FICA.
B. Primary Insurance Amount (PIA) is based on Average Indexed Monthly Earnings (AIME). AIME is calculated in this manner:
  1. Calculate number of covered months between age 22 or 1951 and when the beneficiary becomes 62 years old, dies, or is permanently disabled.
  2. Translate number of months into years and exclude the five lowest years of earnings.
  3. Index the AIME earnings.
    a. Calculate how many times greater the average wage in each year considered for computation is versus indexing year.

Rate difference	Average Wage earnings year		Average Index year	
2.5 times greater	1950	$3,000	1980	$7,500
2.1 times greater	1951	$3,500	1980	$7,500
1.9 times greater	1952	$4,000	1980	$7,500
	etc. ...			

  b. Multiply the beneficiary's wages in each year considered for computation by the corresponding rate difference between earning year and indexing year.
  4. Sum the average yearly earnings translated into index year's dollar amounts.
  5. Divide the total of the indexed wages by the total number of months in the computation years not including five lowest earning years. This is the AIME.
  6. The PIA is based on replacing with Social Security an individual's wages by giving:
    a. 90 percent of the first x dollars of AIME. 1994 x = $422.
    b. 32 percent of the dollar amount of AIME between x and y. 1994 y = $2,545.
    c. 15 percent of AIME above y.
    d. These dollar amounts (x and y) are changed each year and are called bend points.
  7. Sum the products of the replacement rate formula to find the PIA.
C. Full retirement age is presently 65 years old. This age was changed in 1983 legislation. It is being increased to deal with changes in longevity.

Year of birth	Full retirement age
1937 or earlier	65
1938	65 and 2 months
1939	65 and 4 months

→

Year of birth	Full retirement age
1940	65 and 6 months
1941	65 and 8 months
1942	65 and 10 months
1943–54	66
1955	66 and 2 months
1956	66 and 4 months
1957	66 and 6 months
1958	66 and 8 months
1960	66 and 10 months
1961 and later	67

D. Early retirement benefits can be obtained at age 62. Yet benefits are reduced by 20 percent at age 62; by 13.33 percent at age 63; and 6.66 percent at age 64.

E. Delayed retirement credit is added to the full retirement age benefit. A percentage is added for each year benefit is delayed up to age 70.

Year of Birth	Yearly Percentage Increase
1916 or earlier	1.0 %
1917–24	3.0 %
1925–26	3.5 %
1927–28	4.0 %
1929–30	4.5 %
1931–32	5.0 %
1933–34	5.5 %
1935–36	6.0 %
1937–38	6.5 %
1939–40	7.0 %
1941–42	7.5 %
1943 and later	8.0 %

F. Earnings influence Social Security benefits. Between ages 62 to 64, for every $2 earned above the limit (1992—$7,740), $1 in benefits is withheld. Between ages 65 to 69, for every $3 earned above the limit (1992—$10,200), $1 in benefits is withheld. Earnings in or after the month one becomes 70 years old do not influence Social Security benefits. Social Security Administration offers free of charge *Publication no. 05-10069:* "How Work Affects Your Social Security Benefits."

G. Taxes are paid on one-half of Social Security benefits by a small number of beneficiaries: those filing *individual* federal tax returns with a combined income exceeding $25,000 and those filing *joint* federal tax return with a "combined income" exceeding $32,000.

Combined income means you and your spouse's adjusted gross income *plus* nontaxable interest, *plus* one-half of your Social Security benefit. Note taxes were paid on the employee contributions, but employer or self-employed portion is deducted as a cost of doing business.

Internal Revenue Service offers free of charge: *Publication 554:* "Tax Benefits for Older Americans" and *Publication 915:* "Tax Information on Social Security"

Coverage

A. Those who have been in covered employment for ten quarters and their survivors.

B. Old Age Survivors Insurance (OASI)

1. Retired Worker (see Benefit Calculation):

a. Early benefit at age 62.

b. Full Retirement Age benefit presently at 65; although increasing to age 67 in the next century.

c. Delayed benefit (up to 70); delayed retirement credit moving up to 8 percent.

2. Retired Worker's spouse and children:

a. Spouse 62 years and over.

b. Spouse of any age if caring for a child under 16 years old or disabled.

c. Unmarried children who are:

(1) Under 18 years old; or

(2) Under 19 years old if still in elementary or secondary school as a full-time student; or

(3) Over 18 years old and severely disabled (the disability must have started before age 22).

Note: Full benefit for spouse is 50 percent of retired worker. If spouse's benefit is taken before age 65, it is reduced to low of 37.5 percent at age 62. No reduction exists if spouse is taking care of a child under the age of 16 or disabled. Of course spouse may claim a benefit on his or her own work history if it is higher than the spouse benefit.

Family member benefits are usually 50 percent of worker's benefit. There is a maximum benefit for the family, usually 150 to 180 percent of the worker's benefit.

3. Worker's divorced spouse:

a. Married to worker for ten years; or

b. Ex-spouse of worker is 62 years old or older; or

c. Not eligible for an equal or higher benefit on own or other's Social Security record.

Note: Ex-spouse benefit will not affect workers' or their family benefit. Ex-spouse can receive a benefit even if worker is not receiving a benefit.

4. Survivors of worker:
   a. Widow or widower 60 years old and over.
   b. Widow or widower 50 years old and over and disabled.
   c. Widow or widower at any age if they are caring for a child under 16 or disabled.
   d. Unmarried children and:
      (1) Under 18 years old; or
      (2) Under 19 years old if still in elementary or secondary school as a full-time student; or
      (3) Over 18 years old and severely disabled (the disability must have started before age 22).
   e. Parents of worker, if they were dependent on them for at least half of their support.
   f. Divorced widows or widowers:
      (1) 60 years old and older (50 if disabled) and was married for ten years to worker; or
      (2) At any age if caring for a child who is eligible for benefits from worker, yet not eligible for an equal or higher benefit on their own record;
      (3) Not currently married, unless the remarriage occurred after age 60 (50 if disabled). In cases of remarriage, the ex-spouse if eligible for the higher benefit from either previous spouse's or present spouse's work history.

Note: A one-time death benefit of $225 may be available to certain family members. Survivor's benefit is typically 75 percent to 100 percent of the worker's benefit.

The Social Security Administration offers free of charge *Publication no. 05-10084:* "Survivors."

A decision on a Social Security claim can be appealed. See these publications of the Social Security Administration: *Publication no. 05-10041:* "The Appeals Process" and *Publication no. 05-10075:* "Social Security and Your Right to Representation."

History

An outline history is provided by a record of important dates, how OASI benefits have increased, and the changes in covered employment.

A. Important Dates
   1. August 1935—OAI Title II of the Social Security Act becomes law.
   2. 1939—legislation to create survivors benefits.
   3. First benefits paid out in 1940.
   4. Women granted early retirement option (age 62) in 1956.
   5. Disability benefits added 1957.
   6. Men granted early retirement (age 62) option in 1962.
   7. Medicare becomes law 1965.
   8. Indexing of benefits to the Consumer Price Index.
   9. 1983—solvency plan for OASI and prospective payment (DRG) for HI.

B. OASI Benefit Increases
   1. September 1950—77%
   2. September 1952—12.5%
   3. September 1954—13%
   4. January 1959—7%
   5. January 1965—7%
   6. February 1968—13%
   7. January 1970—15%
   8. January 1971—10%
   9. September 1972—20%
   10. After 1972, benefits increases tied to the Consumer Price Index (CPI).
   11. 1983 Social Security Amendment halts indexing if CPI 3% or less (unless Congress acts otherwise) and goes to wage indexing under adverse funding conditions.

C. Covered Employment
   1. Manufacturing and commerce: 39 percent of the labor force.
   2. Agriculture: 1951, farm workers; 1955, self-employed farmer.
   3. Professions: 1955, all except below; 1956, lawyers, dentists, other health care workers; 1965, doctors of medicine; 1968, compulsory participation by clergy.
   4. Government workers:
      1951   Federal civilian not under civil service
      1957   Military
      1951   State and local not covered
      1955   Covers state and local
      1983   All new federal employees
   5. Miscellaneous:
      1951   Domestics
      1966   Waiters and waitresses

Answers to questions about Social Security or requests for the Social Security Administration's booklets mentioned here can be obtained by calling 1-800-772-1213 between 7 A.M. to 7 P.M. any business day.

The sidebar "A Primer on Social Security" illustrates how a Social Security benefit is calculated. A statement of individual earnings and an estimate of one's benefits can be obtained by submitting form SSA-7004-PC-OPI, "Request for Earning and Benefit Estimate Statement," which is available from any Social Security Administration Office. Full retirement benefits can be secured at age 65. As of current legislation, the qualifying age for full retirement benefits slowly rises starting in 2003, ending in the year 2027 with an age of 67. Early retirement benefits can start as early as age 62, but at a reduced amount. Those who take early benefits will collect on the average about the same total amount of benefits, but in smaller installments. For each year benefits are delayed after normal retirement age (65), benefits are increased until 70 years of age. Additionally, Social Security benefits can be reduced before age 70 if one's earnings rise above a yearly preset limit.

A small number of individual benefits are subject to income tax. This tax is paid back into the OASI Trust Fund. The 1990 receipts from this tax were $5.8 billion, or 1.8 percent of the system's receipts and 2.3 percent of the benefits paid in that year.

Concerns about Social Security

Two concerns about Social Security are frequently heard. First, some believe the system will not be able to support the retirement payments to the generation born between 1947 and 1963 (the "baby boomers"). When the baby boomers reach retirement age, it is often said that only three workers will be paying into the system for each retired beneficiary. Yet between now and their retirement, the baby boom generation is paying large amounts into the system, which is accumulating a sizable reserve. Yearly reports from the Board of Trustees of the Federal Old-Age and Survivors Insurance and Disability Insurance Trust Fund indicate the trust fund is adequately growing in size in order to help subsidize workers' payments during the retirement of the baby boomers.

The most recent Board of Trustees, Federal Old-Age and Survivors Insurance and Disability Insurance Trust Funds report (1992) shows that Old-Age and Survivors Insurance (OASI) is projected to be healthy for the next fifty years; however, assuming a worst-case scenario, the Disability Insurance (DI) portion is projected to be in financial trouble by 1995 and Hospital Insurance (HI) by the year 1998. Changes legislated in 1983, which went unnoticed by most taxpayers, took the bankrupt OASI trust fund to its present level of $306.2 billion in assets and prevented Medicare from bankrupting as projected in the early 1990s.

A second concern is that the system has diverted its assets to other government programs. The trust funds are invested in U.S. Treasury bonds, and in this respect the Social Security system is "investing" in the national debt. Still, it must be noted that none of the money designated on a pay stub as FICA (Social Security) has ever been directly spent outside of the system. Once, during the early 1980s, Congress permitted a portion of the Social Security taxes designated for Disability Insurance and Medicare to be used to pay the retirement benefits. That inter-trust fund borrowing stopped on June 30, 1983, and the trust fund for the retirement benefits (OASI) has since paid back the money it borrowed to the Disability Insurance (DI) and Medicare (HI) trust funds.

The inter-trust fund borrowing occurred because of unusual economic circumstances, when high inflation was accompanied by high unemployment. In the late 1970s and early 1980s, the soaring cost of oil and other economic factors pushed the yearly inflation rate above 10 percent. Because of automatic cost-of-living adjustment (COLA) based on the inflation rate, retirees' Social Security benefits increased, and the payout of the system rose quickly. At the same time, unemployment was high, and real wages lagged behind inflation. Therefore, the system's income, or the collection of Social Security taxes, did not keep up with inflationary demands on the system. Changes in the Social Security Act legislated in 1983 put in place a fail-safe mechanism to protect the system. If the financial health of the system is endangered, the cost-of-living increase would be indexed to the lower rise in wages or prices.

In all likelihood, Social Security will be available to all who read this and will be an important aspect of their retirement income. Those in the lowest income groups find Social Security a very important part of their income (see Table

11.5). Railroad Retirement pension or Social Security makes up 79 percent of the income of those who fall below the poverty level. Social Security or Railroad Retirement income decreases in the percentage it comprises of a household's income as one rises above poverty. For those who live at three to four times the poverty level, Social Security makes up only 37 percent of their income. Conversely, other sources of retirement income become more important with rising income levels. Both pensions, interest, and dividends rise from 3.7 percent of income for those in poverty to 23.8 percent for pensions and 21.7 percent (interest and dividends) of income in the group whose incomes is three to four times the poverty level. While Social Security is an important aspect of financial maintenance in later life, secure financial well-being requires additional sources of retirement income. Most retirees need a three-legged stool: Social Security, pension, and some form of savings and/or investments.

● PENSIONS

Pensions are an important source of retirement income. Employer-based pensions account for about 18 percent of all the income for the 65 years old and older age group. Those in higher income brackets receive a larger portion of their retirement income from pensions.

Pension coverage has grown rapidly: only 17 percent of the full-time workers were covered in 1940, versus 52 percent in 1970. The quick rise, in part, resulted from a Supreme Court decision (*Inland Steel Company v. NLRB*, 1949) over collective bargaining on issues of deferred compensation like pension programs. Coverage has remained static since the 1970s because of the decline of unionized industry and the growth of the service sector of the economy, which typically does not provide this benefit to employees (Beller and Lawrence, 1992). Coverage varies widely, with larger employers and particular industries more likely to offer coverage (see Table 11.6). Over 39 percent of covered workers are enrolled in an additional supplemental plan (U.S. Bureau of Labor Statistics, 1992).

Approximately two-thirds of covered employees are vested in their plans; that is, they are entitled to a pension benefit even if they leave their employer before retirement (U.S. Bureau of Labor Statistics, 1992). A third of the private sector retirees over 55 years old are now receiving pension income (Beller and McCarthy, 1992). In

Table 11.5

Percent of Total Unit Income[1] from Various Sources, by the Ratio of Total Income to the Poverty Threshold[2], for Units Age 65+: 1989

Source of income	Ratio of total unit income to poverty threshold						
	0–0.99	1.00–1.24	1.25–1.49	1.50–1.99	2.00–2.99	3.00–4.99	Total
Total	100.0	100.0	100.0	100.0	100.0	100.0	100.0
Earnings	0.1	1.8	3.2	3.9	7.1	12.7	15.4
OASDI, railroad retirement	79.3	79.9	76.4	67.8	53.1	37.0	37.8
Pensions	3.7	5.1	7.1	12.8	20.1	23.8	18.5
Unemployment compensation, veterans payments	1.2	2.9	1.3	1.4	1.2	1.1	1.0
AFDC, SSI, general assistance	11.6	4.5	3.8	1.6	0.5	0.2	0.9
Child support, alimony	0.1	0.1	0.0	0.1	0.1	0.1	0.1
Interest, dividends	3.7	4.6	6.7	10.0	14.8	21.7	22.5
Other income	0.3	1.1	1.5	2.4	3.1	3.4	3.8

Notes: Units are married couples living together—at least one of whom is 65+—and unmarried people 65+. Income of aged units does not include income from other household members. 1. Only for units with non-negative income. 2. Based on Bureau of Census poverty levels.

Source: U.S. Bureau of the Census, unpublished data from the March 1990 *Current Population Survey.*

the inflationary period from 1978 to 1982, postretirement benefit increases were noted in 51 percent of all retirement plans. In the more stable period from 1984 to 1988, however, only 22 percent of plans had such benefit increases (Allen and others, 1992). Public employees have the highest level of pension coverage. All federal employees are covered (U. S. Senate, Special Committee on Aging, 1991a) as well as 85 percent of state and local public employees. Seventy percent of the state and local employees are vested in their plans. Over a third of the beneficiaries have received postretirement benefit increases (Phillips, 1992).

Pension coverage has grown rapidly: only 17 percent of the full-time workers were covered in 1940, versus 52 percent in 1970.

Types of Pension Plans

Pensions come in two basic varieties: defined benefit plans and defined contribution plans. The former type usually offers benefits as a function of the employee's years of service or based on years of service and rate of pay. The large plans tend to be funded by the employer, with only about 3 percent of the contributions to such plans coming from employees (U. S. Senate, Special Committee on Aging, 1991a). Defined benefit plans make up about 27 percent of the pension plans in 1985 (U.S. Bureau of the Census, 1991).

Defined contribution plans specify the amount of employee contributions. Benefits are determined by the amount of contributions and the accrued interest in the accounts. These types of plans are growing as a proportion of all pension plans. In the ten-year period from 1975 to 1985, these plans increased from 69 percent to 73 percent of all pension plans. Not only has the number of such plans grown, but also the number of participants involved has increased enormously. In 1975 there were 11.5 million participants in defined contribution plans, and by 1985 there were 35 million participants. This represents a growth rate of 204 percent, compared to a growth rate of 20 percent in the defined benefit plans (U.S. Bureau of the Census, 1991).

Both types of plans receive special tax treatment from the federal government. Employers do not pay a tax on their contributions to the plan, and the earnings of the trust funds are not taxed. Employees do not pay tax on the contributions made by their employers or the earnings until benefits are paid out (U.S. Senate, Special Committee on Aging, 1991a).

Regulating Pension Plans

The Employee Retirement Income Security Act (ERISA) of 1974 established standards for financing and administrating private pension programs; the 2,414 state and local government programs are not regulated by federal laws. ERISA established the employer-funded Pension Benefit Guaranty Corporation (PBGC), to insure the solvency of pension plans, as it also stipulated vesting, or ownership of pension rights. The 1986 Tax Reform Act enhanced previous vesting rules. Full vesture will occur after five years of employment if no benefits are previously vested, or full vesture will occur at seven years if the employer offers some percent of vesting before five years of service. The Retirement Equity Act (REA) of 1984 took an important step in pension coverage when it specified that spouses can obtain survivors benefits and that divorced spouses also have certain rights (U.S. Senate, Special Committee on Aging, 1991a).

Pension Plan Portability

Portability is the last important, unresolved issue associated with pension coverage. Workers in private pension plans are not allowed to transfer or accrue benefits from one plan to another as the worker moves from job to job. Many workers are allowed to take lump sum distributions upon leaving employment. Yet only 5 percent of lump sum payments are put into retirement accounts and only 32 percent are put aside in any form of savings. Even among older or highly educated workers, only about one-half put the lump sum distribution into a retirement savings account (U. S. Senate, Special Committee on Aging, 1991a). A commission set up by President Carter offered a solution to the issue of portability through the so-called Minimum Universal Pension System (MUPS) (President's Commission on Pension Policy, 1981). This program would require all employers to offer a minimum pension program, funded by a 3 percent employee payroll

Table 11.6

Employees with Employer- or Union-Provided Pension Plans, by Occupation, 1989, and Industry, 1987

Occupation, 1989	Number (thousands)	Percent of work force
Total[1]	52,074	39.2
Executive, admin., managerial	8,041	51.6
Prof. specialty	9,726	58.1
Tech./related support	2,217	53.4
Sales workers	4,138	24.9
Admin. support, inc. clerical	9,602	46.2
Precision prod., craft/repair	6,137	41.0
Mach. operators, assemblers	3,832	43.2
Transportation/material moving	2,104	39.2
Handlers, equip. cleaners	1,642	26.9
Service workers	4,170	21.9
Pvt. households	10	0.9
Other	4,160	23.1
Farming, forestry and fishing	364	8.6
Armed forces	102	43.6

Industry, 1987	Number (thousands)	Percent of work force
Total[1]	48,195	40.8
Agriculture, forestry, fisheries	210	8.5
Mining	473	61.2
Construction	2,104	30.4
Manufacturing	12,289	54.2
Transportation, public utilities	4,900	59.9
Wholesale trade	1,811	39.7
Retail trade	3,934	18.3
Finance, insurance, real estate	3,637	45.9
Business services	1,485	23.7
Personal services	440	9.5
Entertainment and recreation	292	17.9
Professional and related	12,047	49.2
Public administration	4,490	76.4

Notes: For civilian wage and salary workers 15 years old and over as of March 1988 and 1990. 1. Includes civilians whose longest job was in the Armed Forces, not shown separately; includes inspectors; includes helpers and laborers.

Source: U.S. Bureau of the Census, based on Current Population Survey (March 1990).

contribution, and a portability clearinghouse would allow transfer of pension investiture from job to job, but President Carter's proposal was not enacted into law.

401K Plans

A recent innovation in pensions and retirement savings are 401K plans, which can take the form of a defined contribution pension plan or a supplemental pension savings plan. Named after the section of the IRS code that set up their tax deferred status in 1978, such plans have grown rapidly in the 1980s (see Table 11.7). Approximately 41 percent of employers offer such plans now.

These plans allow for sole employer contributions, employer one-to-one matching contribu-

Table 11.7
Growth of 401K Plans

	No. of plans	No. of participants	Amount of contributions
1983	1,703	4.4 million	$16.3 billion
1987	45,054	13.1 million	$33.2 billion

Source: Andrews, Emily S. "The Growth and Distribution of 401(K) Plans." In *Trends in Pensions, 1992.* Eds. John A. Turner and Daniel J. Beller. Washington, DC: Government Printing Office, 1992: 146–76.

tions, or employee salary reductions. Tax deferments on the plans are limited to yearly ceilings of $30,000 for profit sharing programs and $8,475 for salary reduction programs. Distribution is based on retirement or termination of employment. Early withdrawal of funds can occur under "immediate and heavy financial needs," although there is typically a penalty associated with it. As with all ERISA covered plans, guidelines are in place to keep highly compensated staff (top management or professionals in a practice) from unique or disproportionately extended benefits (Andrews, 1992).

● OTHER TYPES OF RETIREMENT INCOME

Individual Retirement Accounts (IRAs)

An IRA is a special form of savings put aside during working years to provide income in later life. The money deposited into an IRA is tax deductible, although there are penalties (10 percent) on withdrawal from the accounts before the age of 59½. Heavy penalties are also leveled if withdrawals are not begun by age 70½. At the end of 1989 an estimated $465 billion were held in IRAs. Mutual funds held the largest percent of these funds (24 percent), followed by commercial banks (21.3 percent), and savings institutions (21 percent) (U.S. Bureau of the Census, 1991).

In the recent past it was clear that those taking advantage of IRAs were less likely to be financially needy in later life. The participation rate of those making less then $20,000 yearly was 60 percent less than those in the $20,000 to $50,000 yearly income group, and 80 percent less than the over $50,000 a year group. Additionally, the tax deferral of the deposits represented a tax loss to

the federal government of approximately $16.8 billion a year (U.S. Senate, Special Committee on Aging, 1991a). Hence, the 1986 Tax Reform Act reduced the IRAs tax incentives for those with higher incomes. Those who do not have pensions, or those who have pensions whose adjusted gross income falls below $25,000 (individual) or $40,000 (family), can make up to a $2,000 a year IRA deposit, which is tax deferred. For workers covered by a pension earning them between $25,000 to $35,000 (individual) or $40,000 to $50,000 (family), the tax deferred deposit is reduced as a function of income. No tax deferral is allowed for those covered by pensions over the aforementioned income limit (U.S. Senate, Special Committee on Aging, 1991a).

Supplemental Security Income (SSI)

SSI is a program designed to augment the income of people who are over the age of 65, blind, or disabled. To be eligible for the program, households must fall below federal poverty standards. In 1992 eligibility was based on monthly income below $422 for an individual or $633 for a couple. However the first $20 of existing monthly income is excluded from the above figures, along with the first $65 dollars of earned monthly income and one-half of remaining earned income. The value of social services provide by federal, state, or local programs are not considered for eligibility (U.S. Senate, Special Committee on Aging, 1991a).

Along with the income test, there is also an asset test: an individual may have $2,000 or less and a couple may have $3,000. The exclusions from these assets are homes, household goods, and personal effects with a limit of $2,000 in equity value; $4,500 in the market value of a car, unless used as transportation for medical treatments or employment; burial plots; $1,500 in burial funds per individual; and $1,500 in cash values of insurance policies.

Benefits are designed to supplement income, but not to lift the household out of poverty. The 1991 maximum benefit for an individual ($407) left the person at 75 percent of the poverty level; couples fare a bit better at 89 percent of the poverty level with a maximum benefit of $610. All but eight states will add to the federal benefits. Three states (Alaska, California, and Connecticut) provide supplements designed to bring benefits up to the poverty level. Those eligible for the program are also eligible for food stamps and Medicaid. It should be noted that about one half of older adults who are eligible for SSI do not participate. (U.S. Senate, Special Committee on Aging, 1991a). More information about SSI can be obtained from the Social Security Administration's booklet *SSI Publication no. 05-11000.*

Women's Retirement Income

Women's retirement income is likely to be less adequate than that of retired males. O'Rand and Henretta (1982) report women have a more unstable work history and work in lower-paying positions. Both factors adversely influence pension benefits and also Social Security benefits. The income differential between men and women in the work place is repeated in later life, when females' pension benefits are about 60 percent that of males (Belgrave, 1988). This differential should decrease as women are more fully integrated into the labor force. A recent study indicated women's pattern of job changes and early age of retirement is becoming more similar to men's experience (Hayward and others, 1988).

The disparity between the pension coverage of women and men has decreased overall. Women's pension coverage has increased between 1972 to 1988 from 38 percent to 48 percent of the full-time worker force, while men's coverage decreased from 54 percent to 49 percent. Yet in the age group closest to retirement (55 to 59 years old) the disparity in coverage was far wider,

with female coverage at 49 percent and male coverage at 60 percent (Korczyk, 1992). Progress has been made in coverage,which in time will translate into receipt of benefits, but progress here is slow. Men were 2.8 times likelier to receive benefits in 1976 than women; by 1988 the figure had dropped to 2.1 (Chen, 1992).

African Americans' Retirement Income

African Americans' retirement incomes reflect discrimination, which has constrained labor force participation and earnings. The white median monthly retired worker Social Security benefit in 1990 was $612.60, versus the African-American benefit of $505.80. There is a small disparity in pension coverage between African Americans at 43 percent, and whites at 49 percent (U.S. Department of Labor, 1992). During 1971, 18 percent of whites were receiving benefits, and only 7 percent of African Americans had pension income. Pension income increased for both groups by 1988, with African Americans experiencing a 143 percent increase, up to 17 percent; and a 72 percent increase for whites, up to 31 percent level (Chen, 1992).

The income differential between men and women in the work place is repeated in later life, when females' pension benefits are about 60 percent that of males. This differential should decrease as women are more fully integrated into the labor force.

● HEALTH ISSUES

Health is probably the second most important issue (after income) considered in retirement planning. Good health can make retirement a pleasurable experience, while health care costs can be a significant drain on a retirement budget. The first principle of good health, like financial planning, is that one should start early in life to learn about and to adopt a healthy lifestyle. In conjunction with a physician's advice, a dietary and exercise regime should be developed and followed. Generally people are encouraged to avoid the use of tobacco and to use alcohol in modera-

A recent study indicated women's pattern of job changes and early age of retirement is becoming more similar to men's experience. (Courtesy of Sanders-Brown Center on Aging, University of Kentucky/Tim Collins, photographer)

MEDICARE AT A GLANCE

Medicare Title XVIII of the Social Security Act was passed into law in 1965. The program is operated by the Health Care Finance Administration (HCFA) in the Department of Health and Human Services. Social Security Administration offices take applications for the program and also provide general information. Medicare is split into two basic parts, Hospital Insurance (HI, or Part A) and Supplemental Medical Insurance (SMI, or Part B).

Hospital Insurance (HI)

A. Part A coverage, Hospital Insurance (HI), is practically universal for those age 65 and older. Those eligible (workers and spouses) for Social Security and railroad retirement benefits, along with some federal government employees who are 65 years old and over, can obtain benefits. Some disabled individuals are also covered.

Note: Those 65 years old and older not eligible for free coverage may purchase coverage (in 1994, the monthly premium is $245).

B. What is covered:
1. Inpatient hospital care
2. Skilled nursing facility (SNF)
3. Home health services
4. Hospice
C. Finances for the system arise from the 2.9 percent FICA tax (1.45 percent employee, and 1.45 percent employer) on all earned 1994 income. The most recent report of the Board of Trustees of the Federal Hospital Insurance Trust Fund (1993) projects, under the most optimistic conditions, the trust fund will be exhausted in 2000, while most pessimistic assumptions have the fund depleted by 1998.

D. Cost-sharing mechanisms:
1. Benefit period: Begins upon entering hospital and ends 60 days after leaving hospital or skilled nursing facility (SNF).
2. Deductible: Upon each benefit period an initial amount is paid by the beneficiary ($696 in 1994); deductible rises each year and reflects average per diem rate for inpatient hospital services.
3. Copayment: A daily fee paid by the beneficiary after 60 days and up to 90 days of hospitalization ($174 in 1994). A lifetime reserve of 60 days can be drawn upon if the patient stays beyond 90 days. These days are subject to a copayment of $348 in 1994.

Skilled nursing facility (SNF) service is covered for 100 days in a benefit period, but after 21 days a copayment of $87 per day in 1994 is required of the beneficiary. After 100 days, the beneficiary pays all cost.

Copayments and deductibles change each January.
4. A 20-percent coinsurance deductible is to be paid by the beneficiary on durable medical goods provided by home health care.
5. Limited cost-sharing of outpatient drugs and inpatient respite care for hospice.
6. First 3 pints of blood in a calendar year.

→

tion. Most people require seven to eight hours of sleep a night, and they should start the day with breakfast. These recommendations may seem elementary, but they are important requisites for a healthy and vigorous later life.

A second aspect of health in retirement planning is how to pay for health care. These costs continue to rise at a rate faster than inflation, and older adults are the most intensive users of all health care services. The elderly comprise almost 13 percent of the U.S. population, but utilize over one-third of the nation's health care dollars. In a ten-year span starting in 1977, the average annual growth rate in health care spending on the elderly was 14 percent. By 1987, the per capita expenditure for the older adult population reached $5,360 (U.S. Senate, Special Committee on Aging, 1991b).

Medicare

Medicare, while almost universal in its coverage of the population 65 and older, is not universal in its coverage of health care costs. Medicare covers 45 percent of the health care costs of the elderly. Out-of-pocket and private insurance funds cover 37.4 percent of the health care costs of the population 65 and older. Medicaid (for the financially impoverished) covers 12 percent of health costs for older adults.

Supplemental Medical Insurance (SMI)

A. Any person enrolled in Part A, Hospital Insurance (HI), is eligible for Part B, Supplemental Medical Insurance (SMI). Additionally most any resident of the United States 65 years and over can obtain coverage.

B. What is covered:
   1. Practitioners services:

   Medical doctors and doctors of osteopathy services are covered. Chiropractors, dentists, optometrists, and podiatrist services are given limited coverage.

   Note: Medicare does not pay for routine physical examinations and associated tests; routine foot or dental care; examinations for prescribing and fitting eyeglasses and hearing aids; or diagnostic or therapeutic service provided by a chiropractor, other than manual manipulation of spinal subluxation demonstrated by an X-ray (the X-ray itself is not covered).

   2. Outpatient lab, diagnostic, and treatment
   3. Durable medical equipment
   4. Ambulance
   5. Physical and speech therapy
   6. Home health care

C. Financing Supplemental Medical Insurance (SMI) comes from approximately 75 percent general tax revenues and 25 percent monthly premiums. In 1994 the premiums amount to $41.10. The original premium in 1966 was three dollars. Premiums can change each January.

D. Cost-sharing mechanisms:

1. Deductible: Patient pays the first $100 (1994) of charges in a year.
2. Coinsurance: Patient pays 20 percent of the approved charge after the deductible is paid.
3. Approved charges are set by Medicare taking into account regional variations.
4. Assignment is a mechanism by which the provider directly bills Medicare and receives payment directly from Medicare. The patient is still responsible for the $100 yearly deductible and the 20 percent coinsurance.

Some doctors and suppliers display emblems or certificates indicating they participate in Medicare's assignment program.

A directory of participating doctors or suppliers can be obtained from the carrier or the company that processes Medicare claims in a region. The directory is also open for inspection at local Social Security Administration offices.

Even if not a participating doctor or supplier, the provider can take a patient on assignment.

Patients not taken on assignment are billed directly and must pay the provider directly. The claim submitted to the Medicare carrier will be paid based on the approved charge.

Patients are responsible for the $100 yearly deductible, 20 percent coinsurance, and the full amount of the charge above the approved amount. The fee charged to the patient can be no more than 120 percent of the approved charge.

A detailed explanation of Medicare is offered in the *Medicare 1992 Handbook Publication* no. HCFA 10050.

Medicare is divided into two parts. Hospital Insurance (Part A) is financed through the Social Security tax (FICA). This part covers inpatient hospital care, skilled nursing facility care after hospitalization, home health care, and hospice care. If a person is one of the few not eligible for Medicare, then Part A coverage, in 1994, can be purchased for $245 a month. Part B of Medicare or Supplemental Medical Insurance is paid for in part (approximately 75 percent) by general tax revenue, and the balance in premiums is paid by beneficiaries; the 1994 monthly premium is $41.40. Part B covers physician services, outpatient hospital care, diagnostic tests, durable medical equipment, and ambulance services.

Both parts A and B have cost-sharing mechanisms. These include deductibles, coinsurance, and allowable charges. Medicare also does not cover routine examinations, most out-patient pharmaceuticals, dentistry, corrective lens, private duty nursing, and much nursing home care.

If possible, older persons should obtain so-called "medigap," or supplemental, insurance to cover the cost and services Medicare does not cover. A booklet on how to shop for compatible health insurance for Medicare, entitled *Guide to Health Insurance for People with Medicare*

(518-Y), is available through the Consumer Information Center, Department 59, Pueblo, CO 81009.

Medicaid

Medicaid is the federal-state partnership to provide health care for those who are impoverished. Long-term care frequently causes a financial burden in later life and requires many elderly to turn to Medicaid. The elderly in 1991 were 11.9 percent of the program recipients; and 33 percent of the vendor payments were made on behalf of the elderly (National Center for Health Statistics, 1993), with most of the payments going to long-term care (Waldo and others, 1989).

The Consolidated Omnibus Budget Reconciliation Act (COBRA) of 1985 mandated that former employees be able to purchase health insurance for up to eighteen months at the rate the employer pays after leaving a job. Such coverage is extended to retirees. It is especially helpful to those who retire before they are eligible for Medicare at age 65. An extension of this coverage was part of the Omnibus Budget Reconciliation Act (OBRA) of 1986. Employees can purchase continuing coverage, until death, if the previous employer files forbankruptcy. Spouses can only purchase thirty-six months of continuing coverage (U.S. Senate, Special Committee on Aging, 1991a).

Other Health Care Benefit Programs

After the passage of Medicare, employers started to offer retiree health care benefit programs as a form of deferred compensation. Growth has been significant but, as with pensions, this benefit has been instituted only among larger employers. Approximately 84 percent of firms with over 2,500 employees offer such a program, but only 47 percent of firms with 100 to 250 employees offer this form of deferred compensation (U.S. Senate, Special Committee on Aging, 1986). About 7 million former employees and their spouses were covered in 1983 (U.S. Department of Labor, 1986). Typically, the employee must pay some part of the cost of this benefit.

Rising medical costs, longevity, and a growing number of pensioners has led some employers to alter or even attempt to abolish health care benefit programs. In general the courts have ruled the elimination of such plans illegal if they were in place when the retiree became vested, unless the employer explicitly reserved the right to do so. Many employers have altered the plans though, by raising co-insurance and premiums (Clark, 1990).

● LEGAL ISSUES

Legal issues such as power of attorney, guardianship, wishes for kinds of medical treatment, disposition of estate, and burial wishes become more important with advancing age. While poor health, disability, and death can occur at any stage in life, likelihood of these events increases in later life. Thus, putting one's legal house in order provides security that one's wishes will be respected. In addition, family members are supported in difficult decisions by knowing their loved one's wishes.

Wills and Estate Planning

Wills and estate planning should be reviewed and updated on a regular basis. Less frequently considered by most persons are the steps to be taken in case one becomes incapacitated. Among intact married couples, one's spouse may act for the benefit of the other person in most matters. Difficulty arises for widows and widowers who, when they cannot act on their own, need to have a guardian appointed to act in their place in legal and financial matters, such as the disposition of their homes.

Medical Decisions

Finally, consideration needs to be given to the control of medical treatment. Living wills can indicate that individuals do not want life prolonged by extraordinary means, if the hope for recovery is small. A second document, an Advance Medical Directive, allows individuals to express their wishes about a number of categories of medical procedures, if they become incapacitated and are unable to act on their own behalf. These documents need only be signed in front of a witness and notarized. It is advisable to discuss one's intentions with the attorney handling one's estate. It is very important that a person's wishes be made known to family members and to physicians.

● HOUSING

Housing needs will alter as circumstances in later life change. It is advisable to plan and to explore options early on rather than to be forced to react quickly to changed circumstances. Most older adults (76 percent) own their residences (U.S. Bureau of the Census, 1990a). Yet, there are still costs associated with ownership (e.g., taxes, insurance, utilities, repairs, and maintenance). Excluding repairs and maintenance, housing costs as a percent of income in 1989 were 17.1 percent for homeowners without a mortgage, 26 percent for homeowners with a mortgage, and 36.5 percent for renters 65 years old and older (U.S. Bureau of the Census, 1990b).

Home Ownership

Home ownership may mean increased costs for taxes, insurance, maintenance, and repairs. Changes in family patterns (e.g., children moving out) and lifestyle (e.g., decrease in formal entertaining) may mean that a larger home purchased earlier in life is no longer required. A smaller home, where maintenance costs may be lower, needs to be weighed against the sentimental value of the home.

A house is the most valuable asset owned by most older adults. Some 68 percent of elderly households' net worth is in the form of home ownership (U.S. Bureau of the Census and U.S. Department of Housing and Urban Development, 1989). The U.S. Senate Special Committee on Aging (1991a) reports some $700 billion to $1 trillion is tied up in the home equity of older adult households. This asset can be tapped by the sale of a home. The sale requires that either a less expensive home is purchased or the household rents property. A one-time exclusion from taxation of $125,000 worth of capital gains from the sale of a home after the age 55 allows the owner to invest that capital and use it as a source of income.

Another way a house can be used as an asset is through Reverse Annuity Mortgages (RAMs). The homeowner obtains what amounts to a home equity loan from a financial institution. The homeowner can receive regular payments while living in the house; a line of credit or a lump sum distribution principle and payment comes due upon the death of homeowner or the sale of the property. Further information can be obtained by writing: AARP Home Equity Information Center, American Association of Retired Persons, 601 E St. NW, Washington, DC 20049.

Excluding repairs and maintenance, housing costs as a percent of income in 1989 were 17.1 percent for homeowners without a mortgage, 26 percent for homeowners with a mortgage, and 36.5 percent for renters 65 years old and older.

Changes in health are as important as financial considerations in later life housing. Encroaching physical restrictions may become a concern related to housing. Single-level living or placement of bath facilities can become important considerations. Decreased physical ability does not always require a change in residence. Fixtures like door knobs and short flights of stairs can be retro-fitted with easy to grasp handles and ramps.

Retirement Communities

A small number of people move into planned or naturally occurring retirement communities. Some people have attitudes against age-segregated communities. They believe it is better for all ages to be integrated (Mumford, 1956). Yet research clearly demonstrates that individuals who voluntarily choose age-segregated communities have high levels of morale and life satisfaction. This high morale arises, in part, from living in a community that offers a rich social network with interesting activities. One should note that people in such communities tend to be in good health and are financially secure (Bultena and Wood, 1969), hence they might be expected to express higher life satisfaction.

● MIGRATION AND LIFESTYLE

A minority (about 5 percent) of retirees move from one state to another. One-quarter of these migratory retirees move to Florida. California, Arizona, New Mexico, Texas, New Jersey, and North Carolina are also among the most popular retirement states. Western states are the more popular retirement sites for those who live west

Whether before or after retirement, a range of activities should be considered, such as education, recreation, self-improvement, volunteer, and civic involvement. (Copyright © Benjamin Porter)

of the Mississippi river. Those living in the Northeast or in the industrial states surrounding the Great Lakes tend to choose Florida (Longino and others, 1984). Some individuals use vacations to visit new locations each year in order to choose a retirement location, while others retire to the place that has been their summer vacation spot for years.

Migration shortly after retirement is usually a search for pleasant environmental conditions (e.g., climate and terrain) and/or recreational opportunities (e.g., lakes, seashore, ski slopes). After time, the loss of a spouse or the onset of disabilities may bring a second migration in search of supportive services or residence closer to family or relocation to a life care community (Litwak and Longino, 1987).

Lifestyle

Activities that expand into the life space opened by retirement also should be considered.

Some observers suggest middle age is a time to develop the recreation and leisure interests one will pursue in retirement. Whether before or after retirement a range of activities should be considered, such as education, recreation, self-improvement, and volunteer and civic involvement. A range of activities allows continuing involvement, even if health problems force one to give up the more physically demanding interests. Both physically and mentally engaging tasks help to keep one vital and alert.

● FACTORS AFFECTING THE TIMING OF RETIREMENT

Mandatory Retirement

Mandatory retirement has been virtually eliminated by the Age Discrimination in Employment Act (ADEA). The Department of Labor, in 1965, reported that 50 percent of job openings were restricted to individuals under 55 years of age, and an additional 25 percent of employers had such a policy addressed to those under age 45 (Schulz, 1988). Initially, ADEA as enacted in 1967 prevented discrimination in employment only for those between 40 to 65 years of age. Among those who started to draw Social Security benefits in 1968, over half (57 percent) indicated that their retirement was employer initiated, but by 1982 that figure dropped to 20 percent (Reno and Grad, 1985). Employers may have initiated many retirements before ADEA, but this does not mean workers were reluctant to retire. Schulz (1974) estimates that among Social Security beneficiaries between 1968 and 1970 only 10 percent of the males were unwilling to retire at age 65 and were still able to work.

A 1978 amendment to ADEA raised the age for mandatory retirement to 70 years of age, but this did not affect many workers. A survey of ninety-six employers covering over a million employees demonstrated no trend toward working longer (LaRock, 1987). Mandatory retirement age has been essentially abolished since the 1986 amendment to ADEA. Some occupations (tenured faculty members at institutions of higher education, state and local police officers, prison guards, and fire fighters) were exempted from the protection of the law until the end of 1993. In addition, employees of businesses with fewer than twelve employees are not protected by ADEA (U.S. Senate, Special Committee on Aging, 1991a).

Voluntary Retirement

Voluntary retirement is a complex process involving several decisions that are influenced by a constellation of factors (Atchley, 1991). The process begins with preretirement attitudes or specific events that alert a person to consider the option of retirement. People generally have positive attitudes about retirement, for over 90 percent express a desire to retire (Atchley, 1974 and 1982). The small number of older persons who wish to remain employed tend to have careers that allow for a great deal of autonomy, such as self-employed professionals (e.g., physicians, attorneys, accountants, engineers) and college professors.

Health Problems

Health problems play an important role in the decision to retire. Health has declined somewhat as a reason for retirement. Approximately, one third (34 percent) of Social Security beneficiaries age 65 years old surveyed in 1968 reported that retirement was initiated by health problems. By 1982 health problems initiated retirement in 29 percent of a similar survey population (Sherman, 1985). This decline is attributed to changes in physical demands at the work place and better health care. Poor health is the primary reason given by some persons who withdraw from the labor force, particularly among those who retire before age 65 (Sammartino, 1987).

Among younger retirees 62 to 64 years old, Parnes and Less (1981) found 28 percent left the labor force because of poor health. It has been noted that health may be overstated as a reason for retirement. Young retirees may use illness as a socially legitimate explanation for withdrawal from the work force before the age of 65. Among the participants in the national Retirement History Study, 18 percent of women and 11 percent of men, who reported no health limitation and considered themselves to be in better health than others of their age, also stated that health was the primary reason for retirement (Quinn, 1977).

The relationship between health, retirement, and occupation is complex. Blue collar occupations typically require greater physical exertion in more adverse settings. Such workers with even moderate amounts of impairment are less likely to remain in the labor force (Parnes, 1981). Streib and Schneider (1971) reported that some of their working class subjects' health improved after retirement. Ekerdt and his colleagues (1983a) found 38 percent of men from various social backgrounds reported improved health in retirement. Hence, when workers withdraw from the rigors of the daily regime on the job, some may discover that their health improves. This may explain, in part, the seemingly paradoxical data reported by Quinn (1977).

A decline in health may be a consideration for retirement in three distinct ways. First, poor health may reduce an individual's earning potential. Next, the preference for leisure activity may increase. Finally, the individual may perceive that his or her life expectancy will be shortened by continued employment (Sammartino, 1987).

Loss of Employment

Loss of employment may also move people to consider retirement. Table 11.2 indicated that the unemployment rate among the 65+ age group was 3.3 percent. The U.S. Department of Labor (1989a) reported in 1987 that in the 65+ age group, discouraged workers, those who would like to work but cannot find employment and hence give up job-seeking, were more prevalent than unemployed workers. Displaced workers, those who lost employment because of plant closings or moves, slack work, or abolishment of their positions or shifts, are less likely to become reemployed and more likely to leave the labor force (see Table 11.8).

Many who cannot find work may become retirees by starting to draw upon their retirement benefits. The U.S. Department of Labor (1989a) indicates 40 percent of unemployed males 62 to 64 years old were drawing Social Security benefits, 9 percent were drawing pension benefits and 4 percent were drawing benefits from both sources of retirement income.

Employers Incentives

Employers may raise the possibility of retirement with workers (Scott and Brundy, 1987). Some employers use the carrot approach by holding out special pension benefits (Beck, 1985) and thus encourage employees to think about early retirement. If early pension benefits are available based on years of service and/or reaching a certain age, an individual may find it attractive to retire (Rhine, 1984). Bell and Marclay (1987) found in 1983 that 79 percent of pension plans provide for full benefits by age 62, up from 55 percent in the 1974 Bureau of Labor Statistics survey. Additionally, full benefits could be obtained as early as age 55, typically with 30 years service, by 37 percent of the reporting firms. The attractiveness is enhanced if the pension benefits remain constant or diminish in value after a certain age or years of service.

The incentives in employer pension plans can be especially attractive if the individual is eligible for or close to early Social Security benefits. The cash value of a life insurance policy or other financial resources can help individuals bridge their income needs until they are eligible for Social Security benefits.

Early Retirement Incentive Plans (ERIP) may be offered when an employer wishes to downsize its labor force or reduce labor costs. Such bonuses are frequently offered during a window of

Table 11.8
Displaced Workers

Age	Employed	Unemployed	Left Labor Force
25–54	72.5%	18.1%	9.4%
55–64	47.4%	17.6%	35.0%
65 & Over	23.4%	4.3%	72.4%

Source: U.S. Department of Labor, 1989a.

opportunity (between a month to a year). If accepted, new retirees may have their pension benefits enhanced or receive special severance pay (Leavitt, 1983). Approximately a third of employees accept such an opportunity (Hewitt Associates, 1986). Some persons feel these programs are beneficial to all involved (Mutschler and others, 1984), while others perceive them as "older worker termination programs" (Meier, 1986).

The "stick" approach may also be used to get employees to start thinking about retirement. Working conditions may be altered negatively, or the individual may be reassigned to a less rewarding position or downgraded in responsibilities. The U.S. Department of Labor (1979) reported that 75 percent of the age discrimination complaints lodged were associated with working conditions, not with hiring or firing practices.

Influence of Family and Friends

Family and friends may be influential in how a person thinks about retirement. Atchley (1976) pointed out that wives and children may influence a man's retirement decision. And in turn, women are more likely to retire early to share retirement with their slightly older husbands (Atchley, 1982).

While one's neighbors and friends are still in the labor force, retirement is not considered, but as more of a person's associates retire, more thought is given to the possibility of leaving the labor force. Occupational norms may also set a "proper" time to retire (Scott and Brudney, 1987). Barfield and Morgan's study (1969) of early retirement showed clearly that a normative retirement age among assembly line workers is earlier than 60. Foner and Schwab (1983) and Ekerdt (1987) point out that certain profession-

Profiles of Productive Aging

Hugh Downs
Broadcast journalist

"Though I love my work, I have never regarded it as anything but a means to an end, my job must enhance my life."

With fifty years in broadcasting, Hugh Downs is one of the most familiar figures in American television. Born in Akron, Ohio, in 1921, he began his broadcasting career as a teenager on a hot summer day in 1939. His family had suffered financially in the Depression. Downs was a freshman at nearby Bluffton College, and his father thought that he should quit college and get a job to help the family survive. Downs had won his college scholarship in a public speaking contest, so on a whim he stopped in at the town's 100-watt radio station to see if he could get work as a radio announcer. He auditioned, and even though the program director announced cheerfully that his performance was "really quite bad," the station needed someone immediately, and Downs was hired as a staff announcer for $12.50 a week.

But his father was not impressed: he did not consider radio broadcasting a real job. "Keep looking for a job for a week," Downs's father advised; "if you don't find a job, go with the radio station." Downs reported years later that "even after I'd put decades in broadcasting behind me, my father refused to believe I had found a real job."

By the 1950s Downs worked in Detroit, hosting broadcasts for various radio stations. After serving in the infantry during World War II and several other jobs, Downs helped launch *The Tonight Show*—the first real television talk show—with Jack Paar. When Paar quit *The Tonight Show* five years later, Downs became host of the fledgling *Today* show, in 1962.

Downs stayed at the *Today* show for nine years, and also reported for and narrated for a number of NBC news documentaries and specials, including the Emmy Award-winning *The Everglades* (1971). Then, on October 11, 1971, Downs took early retirement at age 50 to pursue other interests: writing, consulting, and hobbies, particularly flying gliders and doing aerobatics, and established his retirement home in Carefree, Arizona.

Though he expected "retirement" to be more leisurely than his hectic work life, his energy level was high, and he kept adding to his list of things to do. Downs admitted: "I took on such a load that Jean Ferrara, my secretary, said at one point, 'I wish you'd go back to work; you'd have more free time!' Which was true. When I went back to work I had more free time. I had safeguarded vacations when I had contracts with the networks. So in a way, when I went back to work it was a sort of relief. I jokingly said more than once that every time I retired I got busier than before."

In 1976 Downs was called by the producers of the pilot show *20/20*. The premiere had been a disaster, but the network thought the concept was worthwhile and decided to change the format and the people involved. "I was lucky they called on me for the second show," Downs noted. "Even then, for some months, they felt a need to grab the viewer by the lapels and say, 'Don't go away, because we are going to be interesting.'"

Downs's return to broadcasting was one of the most successful comebacks in media history. The *20/20* program has the reputation for covering issues and providing information its viewers want and need, tackling cultural features, investigative reports, and stories on science, space, medical issues, childrens' problems, aging, and exploration. Downs holds the Guinness record for the most hours on network commercial television; when he celebrated his fiftieth year in broadcasting in May 1989, a commemorative segment on his career was aired on *20/20*. Of his future with *20/20*, Downs declared: "There is nothing I want to do in the business other than this. I'm going to stick where I am until the audience is sick of me."

Lydia Brontë

---

als, such as professors and physicians, tend to delay retirement, since they find work more rewarding and they have more control over their environment.

Financial Considerations

Financial considerations are an important part of the retirement decision. Economists Quinn and Burkhauser (1990) view future retirement income as a form of delayed compensation, or as a form of wealth or assets. Vested rights in future Social Security or pension payments can be a significant portion of an older person's wealth (Quinn, 1985; Wolff, 1987). Typically, each year a person works adds to one's retirement wealth. Additional years of earnings may increase the base upon which a person's retirement benefit is calculated. Some plans increase the percentage of preretirement income paid in the pension for each year worked.

Employers may offer disincentives for additional years of work: a percent of preretirement pay may not automatically increase after a certain age or years of service. Older workers also may find themselves at the top end of a pay range for their job description and have little hope of promotion. They are not able to increase their retirement base. There also may be a limited offer of increased benefits for retiring in a specified time period.

Once an individual is eligible for disbursement of retirement income, whether by age, service requirement, or a combination of both, a new factor enters into the equation. While pension income may be increased by the additional year of service, it is at the cost of giving up a year of retirement benefits. Overall pension wealth increases if working another year increases benefits in future years over the value of this year's foregone retirement benefit.

Quinn and Burkhauser (1990) indicate employer pension wealth loss is frequent after age 65. Out of ten pension plans studied (Fields and Mitchell, 1987) five provided best benefits by age 60 and four by age 62. The Kotlikoff and Wise (1987) study of 2,000 pension programs reported accrual of pension wealth until 62 or in some plans to 65. Thereafter, loss of pension wealth provides a financial disincentive for further years of employment. Moore (1988) points out that pension accrual over age 65 cannot be denied. Yet, years of service and total benefit levels can be capped.

The age of retirement has decreased sharply over the last several years, and recently may be leveling out. Age 65 has become the artificial marker of entry into later life and is considered by some as the "normal" age of retirement. Full Social Security benefits presently can be obtained at age 65. This age is always used when the federal government and other agencies break down data by age groups. Hence age 65 is probably most frequently thought of as the age of retirement. Yet clearly the vast majority in the United States are retiring earlier.

The Kotlikoff and Wise (1987) study of 2,000 pension programs reported accrual of pension wealth until 62 or in some plans to 65. Thereafter, loss of pension wealth provides a financial disincentive for further years of employment.

The average age to start Social Security benefits is now 63.7. In 1990 some 66.1 percent of men and 72.9 percent of women received their initial retirement benefit awards from Social Security at between 62 and 64 years of age (U.S. Social Security Administration, 1991).

Two factors combine to encourage an early withdrawal from the labor force. Social Security's early retirement benefits (age 62) for women and men were established in 1956 and 1962 respectively. Private pension plans, which encouraged retirement before the age of 65, also have had a significant effect in early retirement.

The trend toward earlier ages of retirement has abated and is unlikely to change significantly. In fact, the age of full Social Security benefits will start a slow movement to 67 after the turn of the century. Social Security, as the largest source of retirement income for all but the most affluent older adults (see Table 11.5), has probably restricted retirement age to the early sixties for most individuals. Unless significant changes occur in the way retirement is financed, only minor fluctuations in the age individuals retire should occur in the future.

There may even be a slight rise in the average age of retirement in the coming years. The baby boom generation will reach retirement age after the turn of the century. The "birth dearth generation," which followed the baby boom, might not provide enough workers for the needs of our economy. Hence incentives to retain older workers may replace the incentives for early retirement. Such speculation is based on the notion that the nation's economy will need the same size or a larger work force (U.S. Department of Labor, 1989b).

Fullerton (1991) illustrates rather large

decreases in labor force participation rates among older men between 1970 and 1975 (see Table 11.9). Smaller decreases in labor force participation rates followed during the next ten years. Between 1985 and 1990, even smaller decreases in labor force participation were found in the 60 to 64 year group, while slight increases were found in the 55 to 59, 65 to 69, and 70 to 74 year groups. Fullerton projects a slight decline in labor force participation among 55 to 64 year old men over the next fifteen years. At the same time, the 65 year old and over group will experience slight increases in labor force activity.

Phased Retirement

Degree of labor force withdrawal is another consideration relating to retirement. Between 60 percent and 80 percent of workers said they would like to have phased withdrawal from the labor force (Jondrow and others, 1987). Yet phased employment to retirement is not the typical pattern (Quinn and Burkhauser, 1990). About one-third of the respondents in the Retirement History Study reported themselves as partially retired at some time during their retirement (Gustman and Steinmeier, 1984a and b; 1985b). Among study participants 58 to 63 years old, some 5 percent of those working for an employer and 12 percent self-employed workers referred to themselves as employed part time (Quinn, 1980). One study reported that many of the those who are self-employed became so after the age of 58 (Fuchs,

1982). A shift to self-employment in later life may be one mechanism to control the hours worked and to withdraw gradually from the labor market.

The lack of phased retirement has at least two explanations. First, opportunities for reduced work-time at an employer are not common. The Gustman and Steinmeier (1983, 1985a) survey of employers (1979) found only 15 percent offer such programs and only 7 percent offer these opportunities to all employees. A more recent survey found only 3 percent of 350 large firms offer such programs (Rhine, 1984). Pension benefits can only be obtained in many firms by leaving the company's employment. Hence part-time employment with their former firm is not available to many employees if they wish to draw pension benefits.

Another reason for the lack of phased employment programs is that part-time employment means lower compensation. It was reported in the Retirement History Study that part-time retirees lose up to 10 percent in hourly wages if they remain with a previous employer, and as much as 30 percent if they find part-time employment with another employer (Gustman and Steinmeier, 1985a).

Until age 70, Social Security benefits are reduced if earnings from employment rise above a prescribed amount. This restriction can constrain phased retirement if Social Security benefits are needed to augment income in phased retirement. This earnings test as part of Social

Table 11.9
Percent Change in Labor Force Participation of Men 55 Years and Over, by Age: 1970–2005

Period	55+ years	55–59 years	60–64 years	65–69 years	70–74 years
Historical					
1970–75	-6.4	-5.1	-9.5	-9.9	-5.9
1975–80	-3.7	-2.7	-4.7	-3.2	-2.9
1980–85	-4.6	-2.1	-5.2	-4.1	-3.3
1985–90	-1.7	0.2	-0.1	1.6	0.6
Projected					
1990–95	-0.9	-0.3	-0.8	0.6	0.0
1995–2000	1.2	-0.3	-0.5	0.7	0.2
2000–05	2.2	-0.4	-0.9	0.6	0.1

Source: Fullerton, Howard, Jr., Bureau of Labor Statistics. "Labor Force Projections: The Baby Boom Moves On." *Monthly Labor Review*, Vol. 114, no. 11 (November 1991):37–38.

A shift to self-employment in later life
may be one mechanism to control the
hours worked and to withdraw gradually
from the labor market.

Security requirements reduces the interest in returning to work after retirement before age 70.

Labor force reentry upon retirement is not very common. Beck (1985) indicates few older men seek reentry employment, even when they have low pension benefits. Iams (1987) reports only 25 percent of Social Security beneficiaries have been employed within two years of obtaining benefits. The Social Security system report only 3.2 percent of beneficiaries have benefits withheld due to earnings. Early retirees have a low rate of withheld benefits (between 1.2 percent and 1.4 percent). Those who retire at age 65 and beyond have a slightly higher rate of benefits withheld, starting with 4.8 percent at age 65 and declining to 3.1 percent at age 69 (at age 70 no benefits are withheld because of earnings) (U.S. Social Security Administration, 1991).

Retirement trajectories are graphic mechanisms to display possible combinations of age of retirement, rate of withdrawal from the labor force, and possible reentry into the work force. Abrupt retirement patterns take three forms. The traditional pattern is retiring at age 65 and permanently leaving the work force. The newer early retirement patterns are the more common style of retirement between 62 and 65 years old, or the very early retirement pattern when a person leaves the work force before early Social Security benefits can be obtained. The least common of the abrupt retirement patterns is that of leaving the workforce after age 65.

Phased retirement may involve a single step or have several incremental steps before withdrawal from the work force. Phased withdrawal may take place before, after, or at the traditional retirement age of 65.

Finally, either phased or abrupt retirement can be followed by reentry into the labor force. Reentry may be phased, be part time or full time, followed by a phased reduction or a complete cessation to a second retirement, or death.

The most common pattern of these trajectories

is the abrupt early retirement without labor market reentry. Another common pattern is abrupt retirement at age 65. Some of the other trajectories occur less often. The multiple trajectories shown in Figure 11.1 provide insight into the varied styles of labor force exit in later life.

● ADJUSTMENT TO RETIREMENT

The traditional work ethic is still held by some persons in society, but this emphasis is eroding. Popular beliefs live beyond the reality of social experience. The work ethic and a strong self identity with their jobs are identified as the reasons some persons have difficulty adjusting to retirement. This is a mistaken generalization for most Americans, for the evidence from a number of national studies presents a different picture. The National Council on the Aging (1981) reported 90 percent of those participating in a national sample felt they made the right decision about retirement. Only 6 percent of those polled said they retired too early; 1 percent reported they retired too late, and 3 percent were not sure. Longitudinal research finds neither life satisfaction nor morale (Palmore and others, 1985), nor self esteem (Atchley, 1982) are adversely influenced by retirement. Parnes (1985) has summarized the situation clearly and succinctly: "If one is compelled to make a single generalization about retirement, perhaps the most valid would be that it is generally entered into voluntarily, found to be pleasant, and not regretted even after many years." Neither males nor females report any decrease in life satisfaction, and in fact women tend to have a bit more positive view toward retirement (Atchley, 1982).

An increase in suicide rates starts to occur approximately around retirement age among elderly white males and continues into advanced old age. Keep in perspective suicide accounts for about 1 percent of deaths among older males. Yet, Stenback (1980) does not find evidence that retirement increases the risk of suicide.

Health

Health is frequently mentioned as deteriorating because of retirement, but evidence indicates this is not the case. There is neither a decline in physical health (Ekerdt and others, 1983b; Kasl, 1980;

Figure 11.1
Retirement Trajectories

Abrupt retirement patterns: Two variations at age 65 or 70

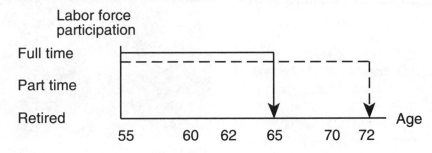

Phased retirement patterns: Two variations on transitions to part-time employment

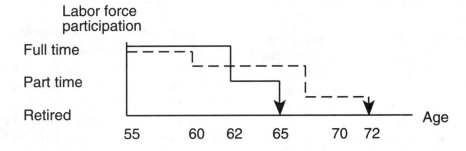

Reentry retirement patterns: Transition to retirement at age 60 and 65, and part-time reentry at age 65 and 68.

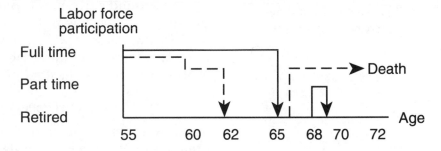

Streib and Schneider, 1971) nor mental health (Crowley, 1985). In fact some (typically unskilled workers) report improvement in their physical

---

The work ethic and a strong self identity with their jobs are identified as the reasons some persons have difficulty adjusting to retirement. This is a mistaken generalization for most Americans, for the evidence from a number of national studies presents a different picture.

---

health associated with retirement (Streib and Schneider, 1971). Men with type A behavior before retirement often lose these traits in retirement (Howard and others, 1986).

There is a potential for the casual observer to fall victim to spurious reasoning. Both retirement and health status are related to advanced age. So while it may appear that retirement is causing poor health, in actuality growing older not only increases the likelihood of retiring but also succumbing to illness. It is not unusual for those in their sixties to have health problems and even die, whether they are retired or still in the work force. Additionally, since health problems may select individuals out of the work force, it is not

Voices of Creative Aging

Carl R., *an 83-year-old poet, reflects on the joys of retirement and creativity:*

I couldn't wait to retire. I never looked back. I never gave it a moment's thought. Social work was in the past; it was buried. I had reawakened creatively. I wrote and published poems when I was young, but having family obligations, I gave up writing and developed a career in social work. Several weeks before my retirement, I received a letter from someone who had admired those earlier poems. That letter inspired me and I couldn't wait to begin writing.

As I grow older I really have not detected any loss of imagination. The only change I've seen in myself is some slowing up and having to stop writing because I feel a little sleepy. I take a nap right after lunch. I don't spend as much time on writing as I did before and the work is slower, but in no other ways are there differences. In fact, there may be some benefits in that slowness—it improves thought.

People talk about creativity as if it were some kind of a mystery, something to be achieved. Creativity is something that is part of our nature. People just need the time and opportunity to express themselves. . . . It's there.

Excerpt from Connie Goldman's "Late Bloomer"
public radio series

Some individuals associate retirement with improvement in their physical health. (Courtesy of The National Council on the Aging, Inc.)

family, and former work associates. Streib (1983) points out that even physicians, who are more likely to see those who do not feel well, collect these stories of patients who upon retirement become ill. He notes the select sample of clinical practice versus the experience of the elderly in the community. Second, the visibility of retirement as a life event makes it a handy reference point. Declines in health associated with age observed in others can be viewed as having crystallized around retirement, particularly if the retired individual has not been seen for some time. Finally, persons who revere the work ethic may use as a rationalization the belief that retirement is "bad for one's health."

Marital Issues

Marital satisfaction, as in the case of health, often has been suggested to decrease in retirement. Typically the notion is offered that wives are not accustomed to increased contact with their husbands. This perspective was supported by research in the 1950s (Kerckhoff, 1966). Anecdotal stories are sometimes heard of the middle or upper-middle class husband redirecting his instrumental role from the office to the domestic aspect of household management to the annoyance of the wife. Retirement has less of an impact on shared domestic activities than had been previously thought. Males tend to stay within their sex roles (Brubaker and Henon, 1982). However, companionship in leisure activities does increase and is important in the appraisal of marital satisfaction (Vinick and Ekerdt, 1989).

Overall, the research on marital satisfaction in

unusual to find these people reporting health problems in retirement. Yet retirement is not the causal agent; conversely, poor health caused retirement.

Ekerdt (1987) offers three reasons gerontologists have a hard time convincing the public that retirement does not create health problems. First, there is a storehouse of anecdotes in the popular culture of the ill effects of retirement on friends,

---

Health is frequently mentioned as deteriorating because of retirement, but evidence indicates this is not the case.

---

retirement indicates that couples adjust well. Atchley and Miller (1983) report no difference in marital satisfaction between retired and nonretired couples of similar ages. Some 70 percent of retired couples reported they were extremely satisfied with their marriage, 27 percent satisfied, and only 3 percent dissatisfied. No change in couples' marital satisfaction was reported over six years, moving from preretirement to retirement. One study did report change in marital satisfaction associated with retirement: Vinck and Ekerdt (1989) found that 60 percent of couples indicated marital satisfaction increased, and 10 percent said it decreased. And a Canadian study (Keating and Cole, 1980) reported that wives tend to plan activities to keep husbands busy, despite the husbands' objections.

Social Isolation

Social isolation has been suggested to occur because of retirement, as work is frequently an important means for building social ties. Atchley (1991) reported only a small percent of retirees decrease their social participation and felt an increase in isolation and loneliness. Women do report slightly lower activity levels in retirement than their male counterparts (Atchley, 1991). Part of this drop in social life is related to widowhood. Some observers have suggested that isolation in retirement is more prevalent among the working class (Rosenberg, 1970), with lower social participation in later life the result of both the nature of the work, which did not provide as much social integration, and a lower income, which constrains social activity (Simpson and others, 1966). Over all, Parnes (1985) indicated retirement is rarely the cause of lower social involvement.

● RETIREMENT AS A PROCESS

Robert C. Atchley, author of one of the most widely used texts in social gerontology, points out that retirement is not a single event but rather a process. Atchley's research on retirement (Atchley, 1967, 1974, 1982) describes eight phases of retirement, though he cautions that "phases are not inevitable responses to retirement" (Atchley, 1991). Individuals reflecting upon their own retirement or practitioners working with older clients should not be concerned about mov-

> Overall, the research on marital satisfaction in retirement indicates that couples adjust well. Atchley and Miller (1983) report no difference in marital satisfaction between retired and nonretired couples of similar ages.

ing through all these stages in an orderly and timely fashion.

Retirement Phases

The preretirement phase is divided into a remote and near stage. A remote stage is filled with vague thoughts of the pleasant possibilities associated with separation from the work force.

The near stage serves two functions. First, people start to seriously define themselves as leaving the work force and in so doing start to modify their sense of identity as based primarily on their occupation. They may develop a "short timer's" attitude. Second, individuals engage in serious daydreaming about their life in retirement. This anticipatory socialization allows people to mentally rehearse retirement.

The retirement event has not been the focus of systematic social research. It is unknown whether ceremonies marking retirement are common or not. And as Atchley (1991) indicates, what is remarkable about the retirement event is the lack of a commonly accepted tradition surrounding this rite of passage. Employer-sponsored events range from lavish all-day functions given for CEOs to award ceremonies in which a number of individuals are recognized. Retirement may also be marked by celebrations hosted by family and friends. In fact, the greeting card industry has a marketing strategy to invent traditions by means of retirement greeting cards and party favors. Upon retirement the new retiree may take one of three paths: honeymoon, rest and relaxation, or an immediate routine.

The honeymoon phase for the new retiree engaging in a variety of new pursuits is an upbeat, happy, and carefree time of activity. The hallmark of this stage is keeping busy. Retirees moving through this stage frequently mark their retirement with an extended vacation. This temporary phase requires financial resources and good health. Ekerdt and his colleagues (1985) studied life satisfaction among recent retirees and found the highest level reported was within the first six months of retirement. This evidence has been interpreted as support for the honeymoon phase.

A rest and relaxation (R & R) phase contrasts to the active euphoric honeymoon stage. R & R offers some retirees a brief respite from their previously demanding and busy work schedule. Yet, following this hiatus, retirees tend to become reengaged in activities, obligations, and commitments. Atchley (1982) offered proof from a longitudinal study of retirees that showed a decrease in activity upon retirement with a return to preretirement levels of activity after three years.

Immediate retirement routine is another path recent retirees may follow. Those with an active life before retirement can often readjust their schedules to establish a rewarding life style. Here people readjust their activity schedules to find fulfilling retirement routines, which fill the temporal and social void left by leaving the world of work.

Disenchantment occurs among a small number of retirees. The letdown after the honeymoon phase may cause a mild disenchantment, similar to the experience after the holiday season or after returning home from an extended vacation. Others may notice the gap between unrealistic, preretirement daydreams and life in retirement. This disparity between the daydream and reality may result from difficulties in financial planning or by those who make a retirement move without thoroughly evaluating their new community. Circumstances beyond individual control may also bring about disenchantment, such as the death of a spouse or disabling health problems. One cross-sectional study (Atchley, 1976) found less than 10 percent experience this phase, and a later longitudinal study (Atchley, 1982) suggested a disenchantment stage is extremely rare.

Reorientation occurs as people adjust to the realities of retirement and explore and discover a comfortable lifestyle.

Many make this realignment on their own, while others may take part in age-based groups (e.g., senior centers or AARP chapters) and take advantage of informal peer socialization or role modeling. Still others may need more professional help, as in the case of grief counseling, or from rehabilitative professions for changes brought about by disabling illness.

Retirement routine is that phase in which a stable and satisfying pattern of activities develops, providing meaning and structure to life. In this stage, pragmatic adjustments are made in response to changes in health or financial circumstances.

Termination of the retirement role occurs if and when a person becomes permanently disabled and dependent to a significant degree. Here the individual moves from the retirement role to that of the invalid or disabled role. Constraints on autonomy and an increase of dependency are the hallmark of this stage.

● RETIREMENT AND DISENGAGEMENT

The theory that social disengagement is a natural part of the aging process was promoted by some gerontologists (Cumming and Henry, 1961). Disengagement theorists suggested that later life is characterized by a mutual withdrawal between the individual and other persons. This gradual withdrawal limits disruptive effects when it is completed. The individual and his or her social world has a new form of social equilibrium and sets of relationships. Retirement, like other major role transitions in later life, is considered a part of this inevitable disengagement process occurring between the individual, other persons, and society. Hochschild (1975) raised some important criticisms against disengagement theory. As an example, she questioned both the inevitability and mutuality of the process. Disengagement may be the result of socially held stereotypes of older people and others and by the social policies that make retirees feel superfluous.

Other theories of social engagement in later life have more optimistic overtones. Activity theory (Havinghurst and others, 1968) argued that levels of activity in mid-life should be retained in order to maintain a healthy self-image. Active engagement in the social world insulates oneself from the negative stereotypes of old age such as being ineffectual, incompetent, and useless. Activity theorists suggested if one social role is relinquished, another should be assumed. Withdrawal was considered a sign of "failure." However, this perspective does not adequately address how individuals might cope with the inevitable decline in later life or the idea of death.

Differential disengagement was a theoretical perspective offered by Streib and Schneider (1971) as a mechanism to bridge the gap between disengagement theory and activity theory. Their work was based on a study following a large group of individuals from preretirement, through the retirement event, and several years beyond. Their conceptualization of differential disengagement accepted that there is a physical and psychological slowing down in later life and hence a corresponding degree of disengagement from activities that are not meaningful or rewarding. But this disengagement is not sudden and across the board. Rather there exists variety in the nature and depth of one's social engagement. Retirement may mean disengagement from the work force, but it can be balanced by an increased engagement in social or in leisure activities or in civic involvement, such as volunteering in a community service agency. Thus new roles of "activity within disengagement" are possible and are fulfilled by many persons in retirement.

The "busy ethic," as Ekerdt (1986) suggests, shields the retiree from a "moral" conflict arising from the pursuit of leisure activities in retirement and dropping the work role. A job, a career, and financial goals are replaced in retirement by other acceptable goals and activities, demonstrating active physical and mental social engagement, which are consistent with a work ethic. Through recreational activities, late-life learning, artistic endeavors, civic action, hobbies, or even an increase in domestic activities (e.g., gardening and minor home repair) a person demonstrates that the day is full of worthwhile pursuits and gives a positive definition to the retirement role. A cross-cultural insight to this busy ethic is found in the comprehensive study *Older Adults in Three Industrialized Nations*. Shanas and her colleagues (1968) pointed out that unlike retired counterparts in England and the Netherlands, retirees in the United States approach their leisure as if it were work.

There is little doubt that retirement involves degrees of disengagement, but it may not signal a unilinear decreasing engagement in the social world. In retirement individuals develop routines that fill their lives and offer many satisfactions. Some retirees are busier than others. Some people engage and reengage in diverse social pur-

There is little doubt that retirement involves degrees of disengagement, but it may not signal a unilinear decreasing engagement in the social world. (Copyright © Marianne Gontarz)

suits. Over the course of time there are necessary individual adjustments as people encounter the physical and psychological difficulties associated with later life.

The development of the institution of retirement has been accompanied by a supportive culture milieu involving national pensions and a public health program for older persons. There is broad acceptance that individuals deserve retirement as a reward for years of effort in the work force and for their contributions to society. The reward notion is linked to the expectation among the working public they too will obtain that reward in the future.

For many persons, the traditional work ethic is perhaps more accurately described as the remuneration ethic. These people work until their pension benefits and savings will support their desired lifestyle, and then may say, "It's not worth it to work any more." Furthermore, many persons have embraced a "choice ethic"—that the good life is one that permits the individual the greatest amount of choices. Certainly retirement gives people a greater range of choices as to how they will spend their time than if they remained in the work force.

Multiple meanings and complex social practices encompass the social institution we label retirement. Whether American society can develop and adapt its social organizations and cultural practices to the demands of an aging society in the future is a challenge for the ongoing cohorts of workers and retirees. The Social Security and health care systems will change to meet new needs. It is a hope the people and institutions of the United States will adapt positively in the longer term.

Organizations

American Association of Retired Persons (AARP)
Work Force Education
601 E St., NW
Washington, DC 20049
(202) 434-2100

International Society for Retirement Planning
11312 Old Club Rd.
Rockville, MD 20852
1 (800) 327-4777

National Council on the Aging
Retirement Planning Program
409 Third St., SW
Washington, DC 20024
(202) 479-1200, Ext. 6971

Social Security Administration
Department of Health and Human Services
Altmeyer Bldg., Room 900
6401 Security Blvd.
Baltimore, MD 21235
(301) 594-1234

Newsletters

Retirement Advisory Insights
RAI
919 Third Ave.
New York, NY 10022
  Quarterly.

United Retirement Bulletin
United Business Service
Babson-United Bldg.
101 Prescott St.
Wellesley Hills, MA 02181-3319
  Monthly.

References

Allen, Steven G., Robert L. Clark, and Ann A. McDermed. "Post-Retirement Benefits Increases in the 1980s." In *Trends in Pensions, 1992*. Eds. John A. Turner and Daniel J. Beller. Washington, DC: U.S. Government Printing Office, 1992.

American Association of Retired Persons. *Work and Retirement: Employees Over Forty and Their Views.* Washington, DC: American Association of Retired Persons, 1986.

Andrews, Emily S. "The Growth and Distribution of 401(k) Plans." In *Trends in Pensions, 1992*. Eds. John A. Turner and Daniel J. Beller. Washington, DC: U.S. Government Printing Office, 1992.

Atchley, Robert C. "The Meaning of Retirement." *Journal of Communications* Vol. 24 (1974): 97–101.

———. "The Process of Retirement: Comparing Women and Men." In *Women's Retirement.* Ed. M. Szinovacz. Beverly Hills, CA: Sage, 1982.

———. "Retired Women: A Study of Self and Role." Unpublished doctoral dissertation. Ann Arbor, MI: University Microfilms, 1967.

———. *Social Forces and Aging.* 6th ed. Belmont, CA: Wadsworth, 1991.

———. *The Sociology of Retirement.* Cambridge, MA: Schenkman, 1976.

Atchley, Robert C., and Sheila J. Miller. "Types of Elderly Couples." In *Family Relationships in Later Life.* Ed. T. H. Brubaker. Beverly Hills, CA: Sage, 1983.

Barfield, Richard E., and James Morgan. *Early Retirement: The Decision and the Experience.* Ann Arbor, MI: University of Michigan, Institute of Social Research, 1969.

Beck, Scott H. "Determinants of Labor Force Activity Among Retired Men." *Research on Aging* Vol. 7, no. 2 (1985): 251–80.

Belgrave, Linda Liska. "The Effects of Race Differences in Work History, Work Attitudes, Economic Resources, and Health in Women's Retirement." *Research on Aging* Vol. 10, no. 3 (1988): 383–98.

Bell, Donald, and William Marclay. "Trends in Retirement Eligibility and Pension Benefits, 1974–1983." *Monthly Labor Review* Vol. 4 (1987): 18–25.

Beller, Daniel J., and Helen H. Lawrence. "Trends in Private Pension Plan Coverage." In *Trends in Pensions, 1992*. Eds. John A. Turner and Daniel J. Beller. Washington, DC: U.S. Government Printing Office, 1992.

Beller, Daniel J., and David D. McCarthy. "Private Pension Benefits." In *Trends in Pensions, 1992*. Eds. John A. Turner and Daniel J. Beller. Washington, DC: U.S. Government Printing Office, 1992.

Board of Trustees, Federal Hospital Insurance Trust Fund.

Annual Report of the Board of Trustees of the Federal Hospital Insurance Trust Fund, 1993. Washington, DC: U.S. Government Printing Office, April 1993.

Board of Trustees, Federal Old-Age and Survivors Insurance and Disability Insurance Trust Funds. *Annual Report of the Board of Trustees of the Federal Old-Age and Survivors Insurance and Disability Insurance Trust Funds, 1993.* Washington, DC: U.S. Government Printing Office, April 1993.

Board of Trustees, Federal Supplementary Medical Insurance Trust Fund. *Annual Report of the Board of Trustees of the Federal Supplementary Medical Insurance Trust Fund, 1993.* Washington, DC: U.S. Government Printing Office, April 1993.

Boskin, M. J. "Social Security and Retirement Decisions." *Economic Inquiry* Vol. 15 (1977): 1–25.

Brubaker, Timothy H., and Charles B. Hennon. "Responsibility for Household Tasks: Comparing Dual-Earner and Dual-Retired Marriages." In *Women's Retirement.* Ed. M. Szinocacz. Beverly Hills, CA: Sage, 1982.

Brubaker, Timothy H., and Edward A. Powers. "The Stereotype of Old: A Review and Alternative Approach." *Journal of Gerontology* Vol. 31 (1976): 441–47.

Bultena, Gordon L., and Vivian Wood. "The American Retirement Community: Bane or Blessing?" *Journal of Gerontology* Vol. 24 (1969): 209–17.

Burkhauser, R. V. "The Early Acceptance of Social Security: An Asset Maximization Approach." *Industrial and Labor Relations Review* Vol. 33 (1980): 484–92.

———. "The Pension Acceptance Decisions of Older Workers." *Journal of Human Resources* Vol. 14 (1979): 63–75.

Burtless, G., and R. A. Moffitt. "The Joint Choice of Retirement Age and Postretirement Hours of Work." *Journal of Labor Economics* Vol. 3 (1985): 209–36.

Campione, Wendy A. "Predicting Participation in Retirement Preparation Programs." *Journal of Gerontology: Social Sciences* Vol. 43, no. 3 (1988): S91–95.

Chen, Yung-Ping. "The Role of Private Pensions in the Income of Older Americans." In *Trends in Pensions, 1992.* Eds. John A. Turner and Daniel J. Beller. Washington, DC: U.S. Government Printing Office, 1992

Clark, Robert L. "Income Maintenance Policies in the United States." In *Handbook of Aging and the Social Sciences.* Eds. R. H. Binstock and L. K. George. 3d ed. San Diego, CA: Academic Press, 1990.

Crowley, Joan E. "Longitudinal Effects of Retirement on Men's Psychological and Physical Well-Being." In *Retirement Among American Men.* Ed. Herbert S. Parnes. Lexington, MA: Heath, 1985.

Cumming, E., and W. H. Henry. *Growing Old: The Process of Disengagement.* New York: Basic Books, 1961.

Ekerdt, David J. "The Busy Ethic: Moral Continuity Between Work and Retirement." *Gerontologist* Vol. 26 (1986): 239–44.

———. "Why the Notion Persists that Retirement Harms Health." *Gerontologist* Vol. 27 (1987): 454–57.

Ekerdt, David J., L. Baden, R. Bossé, and E. Dibbs. "The Effect of Retirement on Physical Health." *American Journal of Public Health* Vol. 73 (1983): 779–83.

Ekerdt, David J., Raymond Bossé, and Sue Levkoff. "An Empirical Test for Phases of Retirement: Findings From the Normative Aging Study." *Journal of Gerontology* Vol. 40 (1985): 95–101.

Ekerdt, David J., R. Bossé, and J. S. LoCastro. "Claims That Retirement Improves Health." *Journal of Gerontology* Vol. 38 (1983): 231–36.

Evans, Linda, David J. Ekerdt, and Raymond Bossé. "Proximity to Retirement and Anticipatory Involvement: Findings From the Normative Aging Study." *Journal of Gerontology* Vol. 40 (1985): 368–74.

Fields, G. S., and O. S. Mitchell. "Restructuring Social Security: How Will Retirement Ages Respond?" In *The Problem Isn't Age.* Ed. Stephen H. Sandell. New York: Praeger, 1987.

———. *Retirement, Pensions, and Social Security.* Cambridge, MA: MIT Press, 1984.

Foner, Anne, and Karen Schwab. "Work and Retirement in a Changing Society." In *Aging in Society: Selected Reviews of Recent Research.* Eds. Matilda White Riley, Beth B. Hess, and K. Bond. Hillsdale, NJ: Lawrence Erlbaum Associates, 1983.

Fuchs, V. "Self-Employment and Labor Force Participation of Older Males." *Journal of Human Resources* Vol. 17 (1982): 339–57.

Fullerton, Howard. "Labor Force Projections: The Baby Boom Moves On." *Monthly Labor Review* Vol. 114 (1991): 37–38.

Gordon, R. H., and A. S. Blinder. "Market Wages, Reservation Wages, and Retirement Decision." *Journal of Public Economics* Vol. 14 (1980): 277–308.

Gustman, A. L., and T. L. Steinmeier. "The Effects of Partial Retirement on Wage Profiles of Older Workers." *Industrial Relations* Vol. 24 (1985a): 257–65.

———. "Minimum Hours Constraint and Retirement Behavior." *Contemporary Policy Issues* Vol. 3 (1983): 77–91.

———. "Modeling the Retirement Process for Policy Evaluation and Research." *Monthly Labor Review* Vol. 107, no. 7 (1984b): 26–33.

———. "The 1983 Social Security Reforms and Labor Supply Adjustments of Older Individuals in the Long Run." *Journal of Labor Economics* Vol. 3 (1985b): 237–53.

———. "Partial Retirement and the Analysis of Retirement Behavior." *Industrial and Labor Relations Review* Vol. 37 (1984a): 403–15.

Hausman, J. A., and D. A. Wise. "Social Security Health Status and Retirement." In *Pensions, Labor, and Individual Choice.* Ed. D. Wise. Chicago: University of Chicago Press, 1985.

Havinghurst, R. J., B. L. Neugarten, and S. S. Tobin. "Disengagement and Patterns of Aging." In *Middle Age and Aging: A Reader in Social Psychology.* Ed. B. L. Neugarten. Chicago: University of Chicago Press, 1968.

Hayward, Mark D., William R. Grady, and Steven D. McLaughlin. "The Retirement Process Among Older Women in the United States." *Research on Aging* Vol. 10, no. 3 (1988): 358–82.

Hewitt Associates. *Plan Design and Experience in Early Retirement Windows and in Other Voluntary Separation Plans.* Lincolnshire, IL: Hewitt Associates, 1986.

Hochschild, Arlie R. "Disengagement Theory: A Critique and Proposal." *American Sociological Review* Vol. 4 (1975): 553–69.

Howard, John H., Peter A. Rechnitzer, David A. Cunningham, and Allan P. Donner. "Change in Type A Behavior a Year After Retirement." *Gerontologist* Vol. 26 (1986): 643–49.

Iams, Howard M. "Jobs of Persons Working After Receiving Retired-Worker Benefits." *Social Security Bulletin* Vol. 11 (1987): 4–19.

Jondrow, J., F. Breehling, and A. Marcus. "Older Workers in the Market for Part-Time Employment." In *The Problem Isn't Age: Work and Older Americans*. Ed. S. H. Sandell. New York: Praeger, 1987.

Kasl, S. V. "The Impact of Retirement." In *Current Concerns in Occupational Stress*. Eds. C. L. Cooper and R. Payne. New York: John Wiley, 1980.

Keating, Norah C., and Priscilla Cole. "What Do I Do with Him 24 Hours a Day? Changes in Housewife Role after Retirement." *Gerontologist* Vol. 20 (1980): 84–89.

Kerckhoff, Alan C. "Norm-Value Clusters and the Strain Toward Consistency Among Older Married Couples." In *Social Aspects of Aging*. Eds. Ida H. Simpson and John C. McKinney. Durham, NC: Duke University Press, 1966.

Korczyk, Sophie M. "Gender and Pension Coverage." In *Trends in Pensions, 1992*. Eds. John A. Turner and Daniel J. Beller. Washington, DC: U.S. Government Printing Office, 1992.

Kotlikoff, Lawrence, and D. A. Wise. "The Incentive Effects of Private Pension Plans." In *Issues in Pension Economics*. Eds. Z. Bodie, J. Shoven, and D. Wise. Chicago, IL: University of Chicago Press, 1987.

LaRock, Seymour. "Retirement Patterns, 1978–86: ADEA Protection Has Little Effect on Employee Decision." *Employee Benefit Review* (April 1987): 30–34.

"Late Bloomer" audio cassette. Available from Connie Goldman Productions, 926 Second Street, Suite 201, Santa Barbara, CA 90403. (310) 393-6801.

Leavitt, Thomas D. *Early Retirement Incentive Programs*. Waltham, MA: Policy Center on Aging, Brandeis University, 1983.

Litwak, Eugene, and Charles F. Longino, Jr. "Migration Patterns Among the Elderly: A Developmental Perspective. *Gerontologist* Vol. 27, no. 3 (1987): 266–72.

Longino, Charles F., Jeanne C. Biggar, Cynthia B. Flynn, and Robert F. Wiseman. *The Retirement Migration Project: A Final Report for the National Institute on Aging*. Coral Gables, FL: Center for Social Research in Aging, University of Miami, 1984.

Meier, Elizabeth L. *Early Retirement Incentive Programs: Trends and Implications*. Washington, DC: American Associationof Retired Persons, Public Policy Institute, 1986.

Moore, Patricia M. "Age-Related Changes in Retirement Policies and Plans." *Compensation and Benefits Management* (Spring 1988): 217–20.

Mumford, Lewis. "For Older People: Not Segregation But Integration." *Architectural Record* (May 1956): 191–94.

Mutschler, Phyllis H., James H. Schultz, and Thomas D. Leavitt. *What Price Retirement? A Study of Early Retirement Incentive Programs*. Washington, DC: American Association of Retired Persons, Andrus Foundation, December 1984.

National Center for Health Statistics. *Health United States, 1991*. Hyattsville, MD: Public Health Service, 1992.

National Council on the Aging (NCOA). *Aging in the Eighties*. Washington, DC: NCOA, 1981.

O'Rand, Angela M., and John C. Henretta. "Midlife Work History and Retirement Income." In *Women's Retirement*. Ed. M. Szinovacz. Beverly Hills, CA: Sage, 1982.

Palmore, Erdman. "Employment and Retirement." In *The Aged Population of the United States*. Ed. Lenore Epstein. Washington, DC: U.S. Government Printing Office, 1967.

Palmore, Erdman, B. M. Burchett, G. G. Fillenbaum, L. K. George, and L. M. Wallman. *Retirement: Causes and Consequences*. New York: Springer, 1985.

Parnes, H. S. "Conclusion." In *Retirement Among American Men*. Ed. Herbert S. Parnes. Lexington, MA: Heath, 1985.

———. "From the Middle to the Later Years." *Research on Aging* Vol. 3 (December 1981): 387–402.

Parnes, H. S., and Lawrence J. Less. *From Work to Retirement: The Experience of a National Sample of Men*. Columbus, OH: Ohio State University Center for Human Resource Research, 1983.

———. "The Volume and Pattern of Retirements, 1966–1981." In *Retirement Among American Men*. Eds. H. S. Parnes, J. E. Crowley, R. J. Haurin, L. J. Less, W. R. Morgan, F. L. Mott, and F. Nestel. Lexington, MA: Lexington Books, 1985.

Phillips, Kristen. "State and Local Government Pension Benefits." In *Trends in Pensions, 1992*. Eds. John A. Turner and Daniel J. Beller. Washington, DC: U.S. Government Printing Office, 1992.

President's Commission on Pension Policy. *Coming of Age: Toward a National Retirement Income Policy: Report of the Commission*. Washington, DC: President's Commission on Pension Policy, 1981.

Quinn, Joseph F. "The Extent and Correlates of Partial Retirement." *Gerontologist* Vol. 21 (1981): 634–43.

———. "Labor Force Participation Patterns of Older Self-Employed Workers." *Social Security Bulletin* Vol. 43, no. 4 (1980): 17–28.

———. "Microeconomic Determinants of Early Retirement: A Cross Sectional View of White Married Men." *Journal of Human Resources* Vol. 12 (1977): 329–47.

———. "Retirement Income Rights as a Component of Wealth in the United States." *Review of Income and Wealth* Vol. 31 (1985): 223–36.

Quinn, Joseph F., and Richard V. Burkhauser. "Work and Retirement." In *Handbook of Aging and the Social Sciences*. Eds. R. H. Binstock and L. K. George. 3d ed. San Diego: Academic Press, 1990.

Reno, Virginia, and Susan Grad. "Economic Security, 1935–1985." *Social Security Bulletin* Vol. 48 (December, 1985): Table 20.

Rhine, S. H. *Managing Older Workers: Company Policies and Attitudes*. New York: Conference Board, 1984.

Rosenberg, George S. *The Worker Grows Old*. San Francisco, CA: Jossey-Bass, 1970.

Sammartino, F. J. "The Effect of Health on Retirement." *Social Security Bulletin* Vol. 50, no. 2 (1987): 31–47.

Schulz, James H. *The Economics of Aging.* 4th ed. Dover, MA: Auburn House, 1988.

———. "The Economics of Mandatory Retirement." *Industrial Gerontology* Vol. 1 (New Series, 1974): 1–10.

Scott, Hilda, and Juliet F. Brudney. *Forced Out.* New York: Simon & Schuster, 1987.

Shanas, Ethel, P. Townsend, D. Wedderburn, H. Friis, P. Milhoj, and J. Stehouwer. *Older People in Three Industrial Societies.* New York: Atherton Press, 1968.

Sherman, S. R. "Reported Reasons Retired Workers Left Their Last Job: Findings From the New Beneficiary Study." *Social Security Bulletin* Vol. 48, no. 11 (1985): 22–30.

Sickles, R. C., and P. Taubman. "An Analysis of Health and Retirement Status of the Elderly." *Econometrica* Vol. 54 (1986): 1339–56.

Simpson, Ida H., Kurt W. Back, and John C. McKinney. "Continuity of Work and Retirement Activities, and Self-Evaluation." In *Social Aspects of Aging.* Eds. Ida H. Simpson, and John C. McKinney. Durham, NC: Duke University Press, 1966.

Streib, Gordon F. "Two Views of Retirement: In the Clinic and in the Community." In *Clinical Aspects of Aging.* Ed. W. Reichel. 2d ed. Baltimore, MD: Williams & Wilkins, 1983.

Streib, Gordon F., and C. J. Schneider. *Retirement in American Society: Impact and Process.* Ithaca, NY: Cornell University Press, 1971.

Stenback, Aser. "Depression and Suicidal Behavior in Old Age." In *Handbook of Mental Health and Aging.* Eds. James E. Birren and R. Bruce Sloane. Englewood Cliffs, NJ: Prentice-Hall, 1980.

Turner, John A., and Daniel J. Beller, eds. *Trends in Pensions, 1992.* U.S. Department of Labor, Pensions and Welfare Benefits Administration. Washington, D.C.: U.S. Government Printing Office, 1992.

U.S. Bureau of Labor Statistics. *Employer-Sponsored Retiree Health Insurance.* Washington, DC: U.S. Government Printing Office, 1986.

———. *Employment and Earnings.* Washington, DC: U.S. Government Printing Office, January 1993.

U.S. Bureau of the Census. "Home Ownership Trends in the 1980s." *Current Housing Reports Series H-121, no. 2.* Washington, DC: U.S. Government Printing Office, December 1990a.

———. "Money Income and Poverty in the United States: 1989." *Current Population Reports Series P-60, no. 168.* Washington, DC: U.S. Government Printing Office, September 1990b.

———. *Statistical Abstract of the United States: 1991.* 111th ed. Washington, DC: U.S. Government Printing Office, 1991.

U.S. Bureau of the Census, and U.S. Department of Housing and Urban Development. "American Housing Survey for the United States in 1987." *Current Housing Reports Series H-150 no. 87.* Washington, DC: U.S. Government Printing Office, December 1989.

U.S. Department of Labor. *Age Discrimination in Employment Act of 1967: Activities Under the Act During 1978.* Washington, DC: U.S. Department of Labor, 1979.

———. *Labor Market Problems of Older Workers: Report to the Secretary of Labor.* Washington, DC: U. S. Department of Labor, 1989a.

———. *Older Worker Task Force: Key Policy Issues for the Future; Report to the Secretary of Labor.* Washington, DC: U.S. Department of Labor, 1989b.

U.S. Senate. Special Committee on Aging. *Aging America: Trends and Projections.* Washington, DC: U.S. Department of Health and Human Services, 1991b.

———. *Developments in Aging, 1991* Vol. 1. Washington, DC: U.S. Government Printing Office, March 1991a.

———. *Retiree Health Benefits: The Fair Weather Promise?* Washington, DC: U.S. Government Printing Office, 1986.

U.S. Social Security Administration. *Annual Statistical Supplement to the Social Security Bulletin.* Washington, DC: U.S. Government Printing Office, 1993.

Vinick, Barbara H., and David J. Ekerdt. "Retirement and the Family." *Generations* Vol. 13, no. 2 (1989): 53–56.

Waldo, Daniel R., Sally T. Sonnefeld, David R. McKusick, and Ross H. Arnett III. "Health Expenditures by Age Group, 1977 and 1987." *Health Care Financing Review* Vol. 10, no. 4 (Summer 1989).

Wolff, E. N. "The Effects of Pensions and Social Security on the Distribution of Wealth in the U.S." In *International Comparisons of the Distribution of Household Wealth.* Ed. E. N. Wolff. Oxford, England: Clarendon, 1987.

Additional Reading

Biracree, Tom, and Nancy Biracree. *Over Fifty: The Resource Book for the Better Half of Your Life.* New York: HarperCollins, 1991.

Chapman, Elwood N. *Comfort Zones: A Practical Guide for Retirement Planning.* Los Altos, CA: Crisp Publications, 1987.

Gaudio, Peter, and Virginia Nicols. *Your Retirement Benefits.* New York: Wiley, 1992.

Rix, Sara E. *Older Workers: Choices and Challenges.* Santa Barbara, CA: ABC-CLIO, 1990.

Ross, Marilyn, and Tom Ross. *Country Bound! Trade Your Business Suit Blues for Blue Jean Dreams.* Buena Vista, CO: Communication Creativity, 1992.

Snyder, Harry. *Medicare/Medigap: The Essential Guide for Older Americans and Their Families.* New York: Consumer Report Books, 1990.

Solomon, David H., Elyse Salend, Anna Nolen Rahman, Marie Bolduc Liston, and David B. Reuben. *A Consumer's Guide to Aging.* Baltimore, MD: Johns Hopkins Press, 1992.

William H. Haas, III, Ph.D. and Gordon F. Streib, Ph.D.

Section V

Financial Concerns

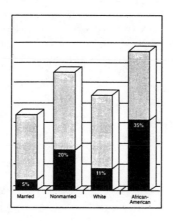

12

The Economic Status of Older Adults

- The Income of the Elderly • Income Diversity Among the Elderly
- Taxes, Assets, Non-Cash Benefits, Gifts, and Loans • Maintaining Standard of Living
- Impact of Inflation • Future Trends

At least since passage of the Social Security Act of 1935, concern for the economic well-being of older adults has been expressed in Congress, industry, the media, and through advocacy organizations. While earlier there was little question that a large percentage of older U.S. citizens were among the poor (one out of three in 1959), in more recent decades that percentage has declined (one in eight in 1990) and led to a debate as to whether older adults are at least as well off, or in relatively better economic circumstances, than the general population of adults.

Contrary views of seniors' economic condition abound. For example, one hears of testimony before Congress of older people whose life savings have been depleted due to devastating health care costs, or of elderly women living on the streets because they are not able to obtain a minimal income through Social Security benefits. In contrast, the Consumer Research Center reported in 1985 that people 50 and over represented half the discretionary spending dollars ($130 billion) of the U.S. economy (Vierck, 1990). Others see a contest for economic well-being between the young and old generations. The headline in a Sunday "Outlook" section of the Washington Post *read, "The Coming Conflict—As We Soak the Young to Enrich the Old." Popular for awhile in the 1980s on recreational vehicles driven by snowbirds—nomadic retirees who follow the sun around the coun-*try—*were bumper stickers that read "We're Spending Our Children's Inheritance."*

Are older Americans primarily among the downtrodden poor, or are they "greedy geezers?" Are older people already receiving too many entitlements from the government, not enough, or just the right amount? Moreover, how does one go about evaluating economic well-being, comparing one age group to another, determining who is and who is not getting enough? How do factors such as retirement, illness, and loss of one's spouse effect an older person's economic status?

Investigation of the economic status of the elderly will reveal the same wide spectrum of diversity that one finds concerning health, life style, social and psychological functioning, and housing conditions. Research findings clearly document that the diverse circumstances of people over 55 or 65 are not reducible to simple generalizations. However, this diversity does reveal patterns and trends. For example, married couples are generally better off than single elders, men better off than women, whites better off economically than African and Hispanic Americans, the young old (65 to 74) better off than the old-old (85 and over). And one should keep in mind that many of these categories overlap. As a general rule, widowhood is closely linked with lower income status. Being a widow, in advanced old age, combined with minority status, places one among the most economically vulnerable.

The economic status of older adults has improved over the years, while exhibiting more variation than any other age group (see Figure 12.1). But reviewers of statistics on the elderly need to be cautious. By relying on comparisons of average statistics, they may miss the simple fact that more than a fourth of the elderly are near or below the poverty level (U.S. Congress, 1991).

● THE INCOME OF THE ELDERLY

Since poverty among older people is probably the most controversial issue, and since it provides a basis for understanding the meaning and measures of economic well-being, it forms the point of departure for the ensuing discussion of the income of the elderly.

Poverty Rates

The "poverty index" is a measure of how adequate a person, couple, or family's income is in relation to a minimal level of consumption. Poverty definitions in the United States were developed in the 1960s and based on the cost of a minimally adequate household food budget. Since the average family spent about one-third of its income on food, the U.S. Department of Agriculture (USDA) deduced that three times that amount would yield a minimum income requirement. A set figure is established but adjusted for size of family and other characteristics, and is indexed to the inflation rate. In 1989 the poverty threshold for a family of four was $12,675; for an elderly couple, $7,501; and for an elderly individual, $5,947. However, a less recognized and possibly biased factor is that the poverty threshold is different for people under 65, based on the assumption that the cost of living will be higher for the nonelderly who have dependent children and labor force participation expenses. Accordingly, in 1985 the poverty line was set at an amount 8.5 percent higher for nonelderly individuals and 11.2 percent higher for couples under 65. Whether, in fact, older people have lower economic needs is questionable and is discussed later.

Figure 12.1
Annual Income of Older Adult Households, 1990

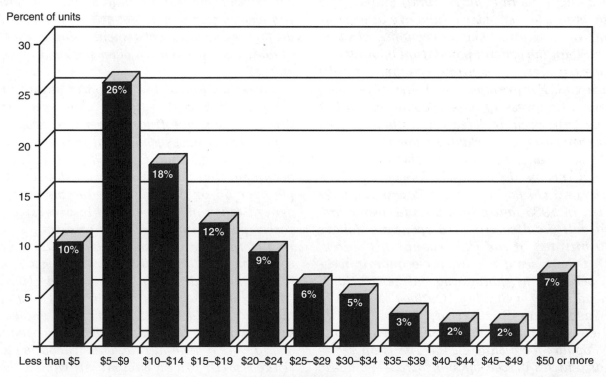

Source: Social Security Administration. *Income of the Aged Chartbook, 1990.* Washington, DC: Government Printing Office, 1992.

Figure 12.2
Trends in Official Poverty Rates Among Children, All Persons, the Aged, and Adults

Percent in poverty

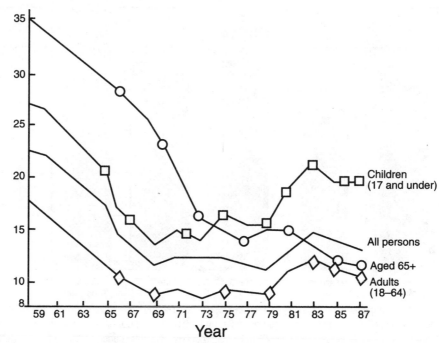

Source: U.S. Bureau of the Census. *"Money Income and Poverty Status in the United States."* Current *Populations Reports Series* P-60, no. 16 (Washington, DC: Government Printing Office, August 1988).

When compared to other adults, the elderly are slightly more likely to be poor. In 1989, 11.4 percent of people over 65 were below the poverty line, compared with 10.2 percent age 18 to 64. However, when children (17 and under) are included in the average, because of their overall higher numbers (about twice the 65+ population) and poverty rate, the rate of all those 64 and under rises to 13 percent in poverty (U.S. Bureau of the Census, 1990). In 1990, the poverty rate for children 17 and under was 20.6 percent (Tauber, 1992).

Figure 12.2 shows changes in poverty rates for children, all persons, the aged, and adults (18 to 64). Around 1974, the trend lines for the elderly poor and poor children cross, moving in opposite directions. Some interpret these facts and figures as evidence of intergenerational conflict and justification for sweeping reductions in public benefit to the elderly. It would be ironic to blame elderly victims of poverty for improvements in their economic status and quality of life.

Moreover, poverty among children is attributed, in part, to rising numbers of single-parent families, due to marital disruption and unmarried child-bearing. According to the Congressional Research Service (1989), 57 percent of all poor children lived in fatherless families, compared with 24 percent of their counterparts in 1959. Children are poor because their parents are poor—a serious issue, though separate from that of the elderly.

The major reasons for decline in percentage of the elderly poor are federal subsidies in the form of health care benefits (Medicare or Medicaid) and income security (Social Security). Figure 12.3 shows that the proportion of older adults, by marital status and race, kept out of poverty by Social Security benefits is close to one-third for all groups.

Moreover, keeping older people out of poverty lessens the economic burden on younger family members on whom their elders might otherwise be more financially dependent. Further, the

Figure 12.3
Role of Social Security in Reducing Poverty, by Marital Status and Race, 1990

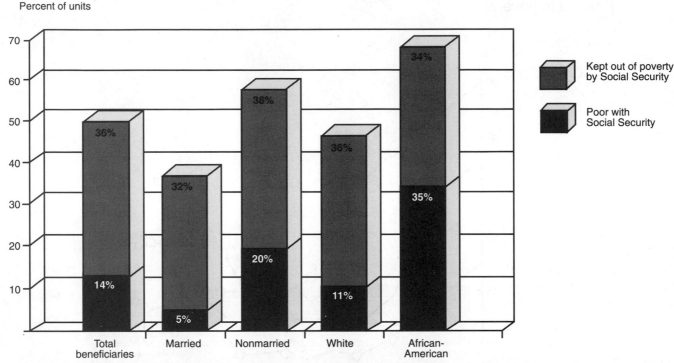

Percent of units

Legend:
- Kept out of poverty by Social Security
- Poor with Social Security

Values: Total beneficiaries: 36% / 14%; Married: 32% / 5%; Nonmarried: 38% / 20%; White: 36% / 11%; African-American: 34% / 35%

Although there are aged beneficiaries with family income below the poverty line,* the poverty rate would be much higher if they did not have their Social Security benefits. Fourteen percent of the aged are poor, and 36% are kept out of poverty by their Social Security benefits—so that the total poverty rate without Social Security would be about 50%. Although poverty rates vary considerably by marital status and race, the proportion kept out of poverty by their Social Security benefits is close to one-third for all groups.

Note: *Based on family income rather than aged unit income to conform with official measures of poverty.

Source: *Income of the Aged Chartbook, 1990.* Washington, DC: U.S. Department of Health and Human Services, Social Security Administration, September 1992.

progress of lessening older persons' economic hardship was not made at the expense of children and other age groups (Villers Foundation, 1987). Nevertheless, the poverty of children in the United States remains a national scandal.

A 1990 Census Bureau report (see Table 12.1) compares poverty rates for elderly and nonelderly people based on 1989 data. Differences between poverty and near poverty (125 percent of

Table 12.1
Elderly and Nonelderly People, by Ratio of Income to Poverty, 1989

Ratio of income to poverty level	Number (in thousands)		Percent	
	Under 65	65+	Under 65	65+
Below poverty	28,165	3,369	13.0	11.4
100%–124% of poverty level	8,845	2,280	4.1	7.7
125%–149% of poverty level	8,979	2,404	4.1	8.1
Total below 150% of poverty level	45,989	8,053	21.2	27.2

Source: "Money Income and Poverty Status in the United States: 1989." *Current Population Reports* Series P–60, no. 168 (U.S. Bureau of the Census, September 1990).

Table 12.2
Poverty Rates Among Subgroups of the Elderly, 1986
(Estimates show percentage of persons poor in each age group.)

Category of elderly	All 65+	65–74	75–84	85+
Total	12.6	10.6	15.5	18.8
Male	8.5	7.5	9.2	16.6
Male, married	5.9	5.5	6.1	9.7
Female	15.6	13.0	19.2	19.7
Female, widowed	21.3	19.8	20.3	23.4
Female, married	6.1	5.5	7.6	10.7

Source: House Ways and Means Committee (1988).

poverty) may amount to only a few thousand dollars or less.

The poverty rate among the elderly increases significantly with age (see Table 12.2). In 1986, for example, only 10.6 percent of those 65 to 74 compared to 15.5 percent of those 75 to 84, and 18.8 percent of those 85 and older were below the poverty line. While this progression holds true regardless of marital status, the poverty rates for the married are considerably lower than for the widowed. Even in the 85+ category, the married had poverty rates lower than the aggregate 12.6 percent level reported for all elderly in 1986.

Another measure policy makers and economists take into account is proximity to poverty. As shown in Table 12.1, 7.7 percent of people 65+ are in the 100 percent to 124 percent of poverty level, compared with only 4 percent of those under 65. Correspondingly, 8.1 percent of those over 65 are in the 125 percent to 149 percent of poverty level, compared to 4.1 percent of those under 65.

Lumping millions of older people into simple categories—poverty, near poverty, married, single, white, Hispanic, and so forth—provides bold headlines for the news about their economic status, but it fails to tell a complete or detailed story. What, for example, of the middle-income elderly or the wealthy? Are income levels of certain segments of the elderly rising or falling with the decades? Are older people in the 1990s generally better off than their age-peers in the 1960s, 1970s or 1980s? How have social policies changed the economic well-being of older people? The answer to some of these questions can be answered by looking at the income distribution of the elderly.

Income Distribution

According to the U.S. Bureau of the Census, in 1990, households of families headed by persons over 65 and related by blood or marriage reported a median income of $25,049. About one of every ten family households with an elderly head had incomes less than $10,000, and 40 percent had incomes of $30,000 or more. By contrast, for

Figure 12.4
Percent Distribution by Income, 1990*

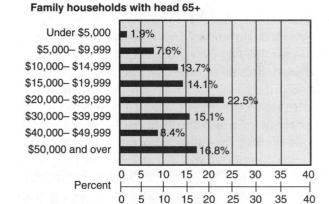

$25,105 median for 10.9 million family households 65+
$10,244 median for 9.6 million nonfamily households 65+

Source: Based on data from U.S. Bureau of the Census.

Figure 12.5
Distribution of Money Income of Elderly and Nonelderly Families, 1987

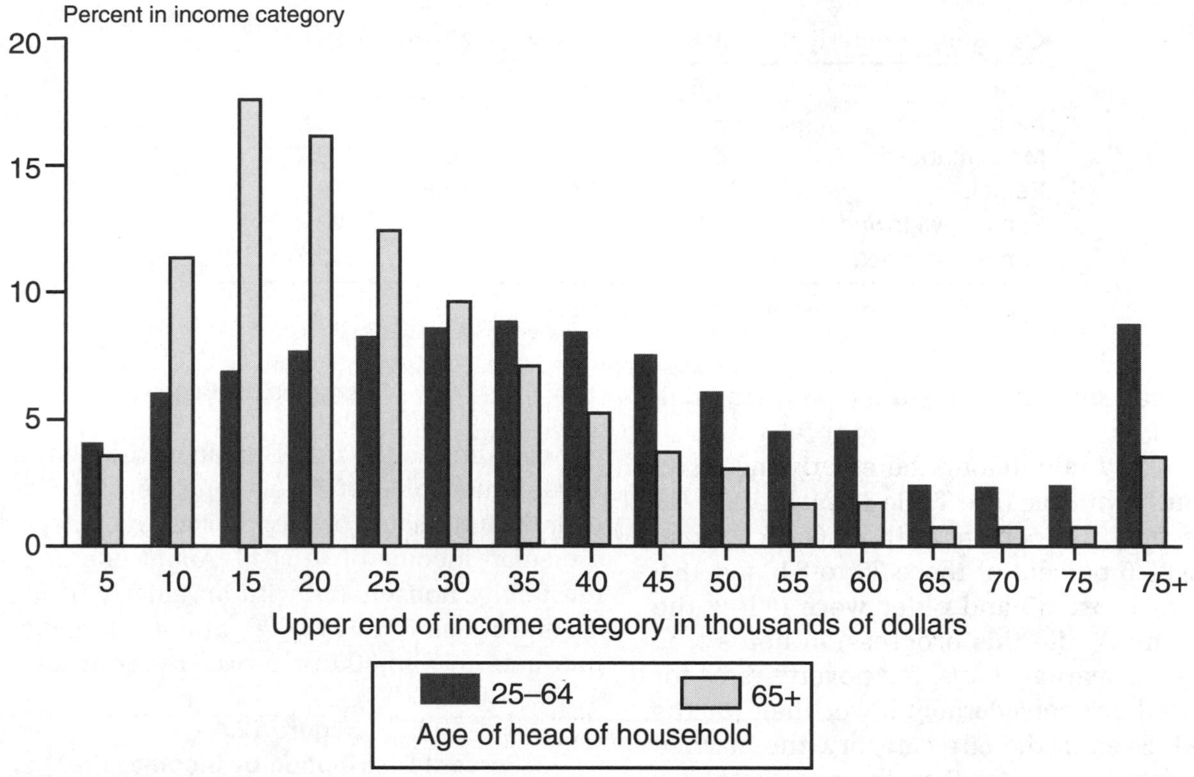

Percent in income category

Upper end of income category in thousands of dollars

■ 25–64　　□ 65+
Age of head of household

Source: Congressional Research Service. Current Population Survey (March 1988).

households headed by people over 65 who are not related, three times as many have income levels under $15,000 (see Figure 12.4).

How does the income distribution of older people compare with that of the nonelderly? According to the 1988 Current Population Survey, 70 percent of nonrelated households headed by people 65 and over had monetary incomes below $15,000, compared with 37 percent of people age 45 to 54. But as Figure 12.5 indicates, comparative income of the over and under 65 age groups changes according to amounts. For example, while the elderly far outweigh younger age groups in the under $25,000 income category, they are about equal in representing incomes in the $30,000 to $39,000 income category, and decline sharply in the over $40,000 income categories.

In 1990, the median income for households headed by an elderly person (but including widowed and unrelated household members) was about half the median income of households headed by someone under 65 ($16,855 versus $33,920). This difference was even greater for households headed by someone 75 and over,

where the median income was only $13,150 (U.S. Bureau of Census, 1991). Since households headed by an elderly person generally have fewer members, the per capita income differences are not as great as it would seem by comparing only the median incomes (Tauber, 1992).

There is a significant difference in income level between married and nonmarried elderly. Thus, as Table 12.3 shows, the median income of married couples with at least one person over 65 is almost three times that of nonmarried persons. The nonmarried are heavily represented in the low income categories, while married couples predominate in the middle and upper income categories.

A major reason for this difference is that nonmarried elderly are largely surviving female spouses whose net worth may have been depleted during the illness of a husband and who, because of fewer years in the work force and at generally lower wages than men, have lower Social Security benefit rates.

The measure of income for older persons is not static. Rates of poverty and median income have changed dramatically. For example, in 1962 mar-

Table 12.3
Distribution of Total Money Income of Aged Families[1] in 1988
Percentages in Each Income Category

Total Money Income	Married Couples	Nonmarried Persons
Less than $5,000	2	22
$5000–9,999	11	39
$10,000–14,999	18	16
$15,000–19,999	17	9
$20,000–29,999	22	8
$30,000–49,999	18	4
$50,000 and over	11	2
Median Income	$20,305	$7,928
Total Percent	100%[2]	100%

Notes: 1. Tabulation is for units where at least one person is age 65 or older. It includes aged persons living with a younger relative who is considered the "Householder"; such units are classified in Bureau of the Census tabs as members of nonaged families. 2. Does not add to 100% due to rounding.

Source: Grad, S. *Income of the Population 55 or Older,* 1988. Washington, DC: U.S. Department of Health and Human Services, June 1990, Table 12.

ried elderly couples had a median income (in 1990 dollars) of $12,401, while similar couples in 1990 had an income 88 percent higher ($23,352) even adjusting for inflation (U.S. Department of Health and Human Services, 1992).

Individual preferences and social policies also affect the picture of income distribution. For instance, a tendency for older persons, especially widows, to choose to live separately from children and other family members has also colored household income statistics. The choice to live independently results in more household units, many with low incomes, but not necessarily any worse off than if they were living within a family household. Policy-wise, the legislated principle linking cost-of-living-adjustments (COLAs) to Social Security has helped to push many elderly above the poverty level. When Social Security income is combined with other income sources such as pensions and assets, the effect is to make older adults generally better off.

Sources of Income

What are older persons' sources of income? For 13 percent of persons over 65, Social Security checks represent their only source of income. As an aggregate, 38 percent of all income received by the elderly came from Social Security. But for households with incomes over $20,000, Social Security represented only 23 percent of income.

The pie chart in Figure 12.6 provides a general view of income sources for all people over 65. However, one should keep in mind the wide variation in percentages from different income sources depending on income level. For example, 32 percent of older people reported they had no income from assets. Moreover, the pie chart includes both elderly still in the labor force and those retired. This difference in income source is not reflected in the chart.

Placing income sources in the historical perspective of the last few decades, earnings (see Figure 12.7) have declined as a portion of income, probably because of the trend toward early departures from the labor force, while assets and pension sources have risen slightly. Social Security, while the highest percentage of income source, has remained about the same.

Pensions, which once were thought of as the boon to retirement economic security, have not fulfilled the promise. In recent years, many employers have increased the employee's portion of contribution to private pension plans, and have implemented more stringent requirement for years of service and minimum retirement age. While the number and percentage of people covered by a private pension plan has risen from 18 percent in 1962 to 44 percent in 1990, the impact or share of the total income has only increased by two percent since 1976 (see Table 12.4).

Figure 12.6
Income Sources of Persons Over 65, 1990

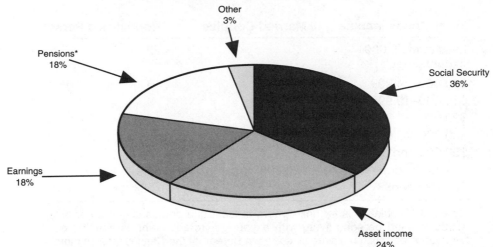

Money income for the population 65 or older comes largely from four sources. Social Security provides the largest portion—36%. Asset income provides the next largest proportion—24%. These two sources together account for 60% of the aged units' total income. Smaller, but still important, shares come from earnings and from pensions other than Social Security. Only 3% of the aged units' income comes from other sources.

Note: *Includes private pensions, government employee pensions, and Railroad Retirement.

Source: Income of the Aged Chartbook, 1990. U.S. Department of Health and Human Services, Social Security Administration, September 1992.

Figure 12.7
Change in Income Sources Since 1962

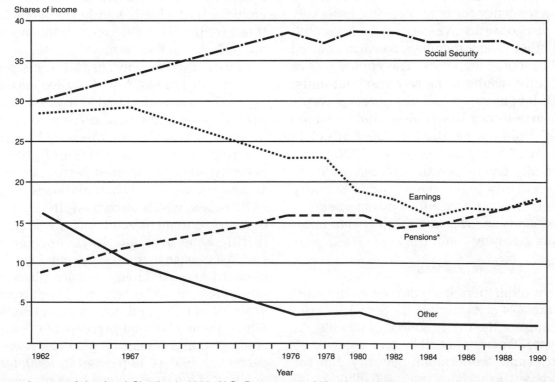

Source: Income of the Aged Chartbook, 1990. U.S. Department of Health and Human Services, Office of Research and Statistics, September 1992.

Table 12.4
Changes in Income Sources Since 1962

In 1962, Social Security was received by 69% of the aged; in 1990, by 92%. As shown in Table 12.4 and Figure 12.7, most of the increase occurred in the 1960s. Receipt of other pension income more than doubled since 1962, with most of the increase occurring since the early 1970s. The proportion of aged units with asset income grew from just over one-half to more than two-thirds, and the proportion with earnings declined from less than two-fifths to about one-fifth. The proportion receiving public assistance also declined substantially to only half its 1962 level.

Sources of income, selected years

Year	Social Security	Asset income	Pensions*	Earnings	Public assistance
1962	69%	54%	18%	36%	14%
1967	86	50	22	27	12
1971	87	49	23	31	10
1976	89	56	31	25	11
1978	90	62	32	25	9
1980	90	66	34	23	10
1982	90	68	35	22	8
1984	91	68	38	21	9
1986	91	67	40	20	7
1988	92	68	42	22	7
1990	92	69	44	22	7

Note: *Includes private pensions, government employee pensions, and Railroad Retirement.

Source: *Income of the Aged Chartbook, 1990* U.S. Department of Health and Human Services, Office of Research and Statistics, September 1992.

How accurate are reports of income on which these statistics depend? According to the experts, not completely reliable. For example, a 1977 Census Bureau study showed that people over 65 underreport their income by as much as 41 percent, with the largest reporting discrepancies being among the higher income groups (Schulz, 1992).

● INCOME DIVERSITY AMONG THE ELDERLY

The Effects of Retirement

Information collected on the economic status of the elderly frequently ignores whether individuals are retired or still working. Hence, data that combines the two groups tends to produce an impression of lower income levels, since retirees, on the whole, have less income. For example, comparing married couples still working and drawing earnings versus those that have retired, reveals that the former have incomes twice that of the retired (Schulz, 1992).

Expenditure Patterns and Aging

As mentioned earlier, the assumption that the elderly have lower consumption needs—and hence should be assigned a lower poverty index level—may not be justified. Rising health care costs, for which the elderly are the major users, combined with lower percentages of Medicare coverage and rising costs of medicines are factors that need to be taken into account. The elderly generally consume fewer goods and services than others and spend slightly higher proportions of their total budgets on essentials. People age 65 and over spent 59 percent of their 1989 consumption dollars on housing, utilities, food, and medical care, compared with only 50 percent spent by younger households on these items. Health care expenditures make up the major difference between the age groups (U.S. Congress, 1991).

A comparison of age categories does show a decline in the overall amount that people spend as they age. For example, in 1989, those 65 to 74

Figure 12.8
Distribution of Expenditures, by Type of Expenditure and Age of Reference Person, 1989

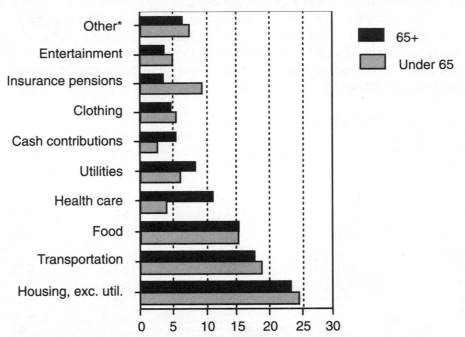

Note: *Includes tobacco products, alcoholic beverages, personal care products and services, reading, education, and miscellaneous expenditures.

Source: "Consumer Expenditures in 1989." Press Release USDL 90–616. U.S. Department of Labor, Bureau of Labor Statistics, November 30, 1990.

had a total average expenditure of $21,152, while those over 75 spent $15,919. The decline in expenditures may be accounted for by decline in income rather than need, fewer household members on whom to spend, mortgage-free home ownership, and changing patterns of need (e.g., less for transportation, food, and entertainment).

Effects of Race and Gender on Income

A person's race and gender may have a profound influence on the quality of their later life and for most represents a continuation or magnification of how things were before they turned 65. For example, the median income in 1989 of African-American men over age 65 was 61 per-

Table 12.5
Median Income of People Age 65+, by Age, Race, Hispanic Origin, and Sex: 1989 Current Dollars

| Race and Hispanic Origin | Both sexes 65 to | | | Men 65 to | | | Women 65 to | | |
	65+	69	70+	65+	69	70+	65+	69	70+
All races	9,420	10,722	8,936	13,024	15,273	12,022	7,508	7,584	7,476
White	9,838	11,323	9,305	13,391	15,680	12,410	7,816	7,977	7,756
Black	5,772	6,552	5,517	8,192	10,464	7,224	5,059	5,235	5,032
Hispanic*	5,978	6,664	5,715	8,469	10,240	6,816	4,992	4,640	5,112

Notes: *Hispanic people may be of any race.

Source: Unpublished data from Current Population Survey (March 1990).

cent that of white men, and for Hispanic men the figure was 63 percent. Similar differences are found in comparing African-American and Hispanic women to white women (see Table 12.5).

Combinations of factors such as race, gender, and whether or not one lives alone can be seen to magnify one's financial vulnerability. For example, Figure 12.9 shows the dramatic increase in poverty level among African-American women living alone.

In 1989, elderly women outnumbered elderly men by a ratio of three to two. With age the ratio increases—39 men for every 100 women in the 85 and over category. Growing old intensifies the economic vulnerability of women. Women predominate among the elderly poor and, in 1988, represented 72 percent of the aged poor. Several reasons can be given for this condition.

As women outlive men, they are most often left with depleted incomes due to long-term care expenses. Since it was the pattern among women in earlier generations not to be employed outside the home (with the exception of the World War II years), most women lack pensions and receive lower Social Security benefits. Even if they did

work, because of time taken off for pregnancies and child rearing, they likely accumulated fewer pension credits.

The effects of divorce on women also contrast sharply with men, since women tend to lose access to a spouse's pension and other benefits. In 1989, divorced women 65+ had a median annual income of $8,147, compared to $10,709 for divorced men.

● **TAXES, ASSETS, NON-CASH BENEFITS, GIFTS, AND LOANS**

Examining poverty levels, marital status, workforce participation, gender, and race issues as they affect older people reveals that the elderly are not a homogeneous group and that their economic situations may vary widely. Added to these are four other factors that determine how much of older people's income will be available to them for use. Tax breaks, assets, in-kind income, and gifts and loans made within families may influence older persons' purchasing power. They also constitute less easily measured components of economic well-being. For example, an older person may report a modest or low annual cash

Figure 12.9
Percent of Elderly Below the Poverty Level, by Selected Characteristics, 1989

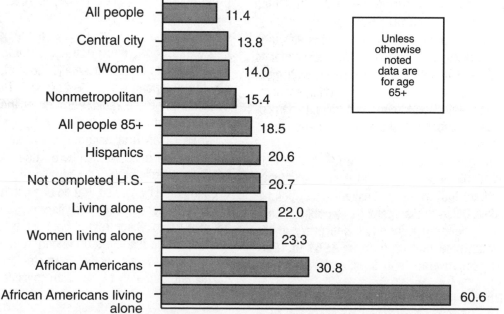

Source: U.S. Bureau of the Census. "Money Income and Poverty Status in the United States, 1989." *Current Population Reports* Series P-60, no. 168 (September 1990) and unpublished data from the March 1990 Current Population Survey.

income, yet be in possession of a mortgage-free home that, when compared with others, puts them well ahead financially, since they do not pay anything for use of their dwelling except property taxes (which also may be reduced for the elderly) and maintenance. However, their financial advantage may go unrecognized. Similarly, special tax advantages may mean lower federal, state, and local payments to governments for older persons.

Their advantage when compared to other age groups is difficult to evaluate.

Taxation

In recognition of the elderly's generally disadvantageous financial position, federal and state governments have legislated special tax advantages. As a result, in 1980 households headed up by nonelderly persons paid taxes averaging about

---

Profiles of Productive Aging

C. Douglas Dillon
Art museum chairman

"The Metropolitan just became more and more engrossing."

Vocations as investment banker, diplomat, and public servant occupied C. Douglas Dillon until he was 60, at which time he began a particularly brilliant period as president and later chairman of the Metropolitan Museum of Art in New York City.

Dillon was born in August 1909, and his father was the head of the New York banking firm Dillon, Read & Company. After graduating from Harvard in 1931, Dillon went to work for his father's company, but he was not exclusively fixed on banking as a career. When he returned from the Navy during World War II, Dillon worked in New Jersey State Republican politics. President Eisenhower awarded Dillon for his efforts in the election campaign by naming him ambassador to France from 1953 to 1957, a post he held with great flair and distinction. Afterwards he ran foreign economic policy for the State Department, becoming undersecretary of state for economic affairs in 1958 and undersecretary of state in 1959.

Dillon earned such widespread respect in Washington for his understanding of finance and international markets that in 1960 President-elect John F. Kennedy asked Dillon to disregard his Republican party affiliation and become Kennedy's secretary of the Treasury. Dillon held that office from 1961 to 1965, drafting many improvements in fiscal policy during his term.

When Dillon returned to New York in 1965, he became increasingly involved in not-for-profit activities, serving on the boards of the Rockefeller Foundation and the Brookings Institute, later becoming chairman of each, as well as the Harvard Board of Overseers and the Board of Groton School.

When he contemplated retiring from the financial world, Dillon thought he would spend most of his time on the Brookings Institute, since he was already very involved at Brookings, and policy research interested him. But Brookings never became a major focus for him, and, in contrast, "the Metropolitan just became more and more engrossing." In 1970, at the age of 60, he was elected president of the board at the Metropolitan Museum of Art. Working "more or less full time," Dillon focused his efforts on expanding the museum's Asian collection, which resulted in construction of the Astor Court and Dillon Gallery to house a growing Chinese art collection. After 1976 Dillon became chairman. The Museum doubled its gallery space during Dillon's tenure, with many new collections and exhibition areas added, including the famous Temple of Dendur, the Rockefeller Collection of Primitive Art, the American wing, the European Decorative Arts Collection, and the radical growth of the collection of twentieth century art.

When Dillon first became chairman, the museum had a number of board members who no longer had the energy to function fully. One of Dillon's first actions was to change the bylaws so that no one could be elected to the board after reaching 72 years of age. To abide by his own ruling, Dillon retired voluntarily from his chairmanship when his last term ended in 1983, at the age of 74. Yet he remains active as trustee emeritus, devoting his efforts mainly to the Asian collection.

Lydia Brontë

25 percent of their annual income, while persons over 65 paid only 13 percent on the average. However, this situation has changed somewhat in more recent years. Starting in 1984, Social Security benefits became taxable. While this did not have a major impact on low-income elderly, it contributed to increases in tax obligations for those with household incomes of over $25,000. Households in the high-income brackets continue to approach paying the same tax rate as the nonelderly. They narrow dramatically at around $40,000 and become undifferentiated at income levels of about $100,000. Social Security income is tax-free for recipients whose adjusted gross income plus one-half of their Social Security benefit is less than $25,000 ($32,000 for couples).

Property tax reductions for older persons are found in all states. The reductions are determined by a sliding-scale relative to the taxpayer's income. In most states the property tax is capped at 3 percent to 5 percent of household income. Homeowners are not the only ones to receive special tax breaks. Elderly renters, in some states, may receive tax credits or rebates based on a percentage of their rental payments under what are called "homestead" regulations. Also, there is a one-time capital gains exemption for individuals 55 and over that waives taxes on up to $125,000 profit from home sale.

Assets

As mentioned earlier, some 25 percent of older persons' average annual income is derived from assets. These potential income sources may include savings, investments, home ownership, insurance policies, and personal possessions such as automobiles, jewelry, paintings, furniture, and other valuables. Generally, assets are divided into two groups: liquid and nonliquid. Liquid assets are those that can readily be converted into cash, while nonliquid assets take longer to convert to cash—equity in a home or business are two primary examples.

People often try to accumulate assets as a safety barrier in case of serious problems such as unexpected illness or the need for long-term care. Others tap their assets in more positive situations: to take a long-postponed trip, or to make a major gift to one's children or a charitable organization.

Subtracting a person's debts and other financial obligations from his or her assets yields what is called net worth. Generally, net worth increases with age up to 74, when it begins to decrease. In 1988, the median net worth of persons 65 and over was $73,471, as compared with a net worth of $6,078 for people under 35. Equity in a home accounts for 40 percent of older persons' net worth, though the percentage is actually higher for younger age groups and is highest for those 35 to 44 (49 percent).

Table 12.6
Median Net Worth and Monthly Household Income, by Age of Householder, 1988

Age of householder	Number of Households (thousands)	Median monthly household income	Median net worth	
			Total	Excluding home equity
Total	91,554	$1,983	$35,752	$9,840
Less than 35 years	25,379	2,000	6,078	3,258
35–44 years	19,916	2,500	33,183	8,993
45–54 years	13,613	2,604	57,466	15,542
55–64 years	13,090	2,071	80,032	26,396
65+	19,556	1,211	73,471	23,856
65–69 years	6,331	1,497	83,478	27,482
70–74 years	5,184	1,330	82,111	28,172
75+	8,041	977	61,491	18,819

Source: U.S. Bureau of the Census. "Household Wealth and Asset Ownership: 1988." *Current Population Reports* Series P-70, no. 22 (December 1990).

Table 12.7
Distribution of Net Worth, by Age of Householder and Type of Asset, 1988
Percentage by Asset Types

Type of asset	All households	Less than 35 years	35–44 years	45–54 years	55–64 years	65+ years
Total net worth	100.0	100.0	100.0	100.0	100.0	100.0
Own home	43.1	45.1	49.2	43.2	41.0	40.4
Savings and checking accounts	18.9	14.8	12.1	12.6	16.2	29.7
Interest-earning assets at financial institutions[1]	14.1	10.8	9.0	9.4	12.0	22.4
Other interest-earning assets[2]	4.2	2.8	2.5	2.7	3.7	6.8
Checking accounts	0.6	1.2	0.6	0.5	0.5	0.5
Financial investments	11.3	8.2	9.9	9.8	14.2	11.6
Stocks and mutual fund shares	6.5	4.3	5.3	5.2	7.0	8.2
U.S. savings bonds	0.6	0.5	0.4	0.4	0.8	0.6
IRA and KEOGH accounts	4.2	3.4	4.2	4.2	6.4	2.8
Real estate (except own home)	12.2	12.0	11.9	16.2	13.0	9.3
Rental property	7.9	6.8	6.7	11.3	8.0	6.7
Other real estate	4.3	5.2	5.2	4.9	5.0	2.6
Business or profession	8.8	14.6	12.0	11.9	9.4	3.0
Other	5.9	5.3	5.0	6.4	6.1	6.1
Motor vehicles	5.8	15.6	7.6	5.7	4.7	3.1
Other investments[3]	3.0	1.5	1.7	3.9	3.1	3.5
Unsecured liabilities	-2.9	-11.8	-4.3	-3.2	-1.7	-0.5

Notes: 1. Passbook savings accounts, money market deposit accounts, certificates of deposit, and interest-earning checking accounts. 2. Money market funds, U.S. Government securities, municipal and corporate bonds, and other assets. 3. Mortgages held from sale of real estate, amount due from sale of business, unit trusts, and other financial investments.

Source: U.S. Bureau of the Census. "Household Wealth and Asset Ownership: 1988." *Current Population Reports* Series P-70, no. 22 (December 1990).

Table 12.8
In-Kind Federal Benefits for Low-Income Households, 1984
Persons 65 and Over

Participation and type of program	Total	Married couples	Nonmarried Men	Nonmarried Women
None of the programs	85%	94%	84%	78%
One program	11	5	13	16
Two or more programs	4	1	3	6
Energy assistance	7	3	7	10
Food stamps	6	3	7	8
Public housing	4	1	4	6
Rental assistance	2	1	2	3

Source: U.S. Social Security Administration. Income and Resources of the Population 65 and Over. Washington, DC: U.S. Government Printing Office, 1986.

Hence, home equity, while significant, is not the main source of difference in net worth. After home ownership, savings and checking accounts make up the largest source of net worth (29.7 percent for those 65 and over, compared to 14.8 for householders under 35).

While these statistics may give the impression that the elderly are an advantaged group, it must be kept in mind that their accumulated net worth is a lifetime accomplishment. Once retired, they begin depleting their financial resources and, usually, begin to draw down the principal portion of saving and investments. Serious illnesses and other costly emergencies can quickly eliminate even significant assets that the person cannot replace through employment income.

In-Kind Income

Goods and services that are available to older people without expenditure of money or available at costs below market value are considered in-kind income. Examples include such things as food stamps, subsidized housing, government-sponsored health care insurance, and energy assistance. While it is nonmonetary, in-kind income can have a profound affect on the economic condition of older people. For example, in 1984, 15 percent of the elderly participated in one or more of the following noncash, government-sponsored programs: energy assistance, food stamps, public housing, and rental assistance.

The most important in-kind benefit, Medicare Insurance, was received in 1989 by 95 percent of the elderly not living in institutions. Adding the market value of Medicare and the other noncash benefits to the income distribution of the elderly causes a significant upward shift. The proportion of this increase is largest among the low-income elderly.

Home ownership, as mentioned earlier, provides another type of in-kind benefit, especially if the home is owned mortgage-free. Seventy-five percent of older householders own their own homes, and of these, 83 percent are owned mortgage-free. The dollar value of the rent that would otherwise be paid was calculated at an average of $3120 per year for 1986 (Smeeding, 1990). Home owners are faced with maintenance costs and property taxes, which may counterbalance some of the advantage of not paying rents. They are, however, less susceptible to the kind of vulnerability of renters whose monthly payments can suddenly rise.

Cash and Non-Cash Support within Families

Informal support within families takes many forms: loans and gifts, food and shelter, childcare or eldercare. Within families, transfers of money most often take place with older family members giving to younger ones. Only about 3 percent of older persons in 1985 received money from their children. Gifts of money are, however, less frequent than the giving of time and service. Potential family help, even if not actually needed, seems to provide comfort and security to both old and young. Information about loans and gifts among family members is elusive.

While fewer and fewer older people live with their children (12.6 percent in 1990, compared to 16.1 percent in 1980), for those who do there are clear financial advantages in savings of rents, utilities, and food costs. Among certain minorities, especially Hispanics, there is a higher incidence of aged parents living in the same household as their children.

● MAINTAINING STANDARD OF LIVING

Two of the chief difficulties older people face is that of maintaining their standard of living at a level comparable to that before they retired and, for those remaining in the work force, the challenges of declining health or diminishing energy. Retirement planners advise that retirees should plan on needing about 75 percent of their preretirement income after retirement. Savings and investments are a hedge against inflation as long as financially debilitating illnesses are not encountered. Yet, as people live longer, the struggle to maintain or modify one's living standards remains problematic.

A 1990 study of how well retirees in the early 1980s fared financially revealed that over 90 percent received funds from Social Security and private pension benefits that were less than the amount of income needed to maintain their previous standard of living (Grad, 1990).

Retirement planning programs can be especially helpful for determining retirement income needs and modifications of existing lifestyles that can close the gap between cost of living and available income. However, few participate in these programs and, of those that do, participation often takes place just a year or two before retirement. This leaves the person with little time to modify or establish an investment, pension, or saving plan. Those who decide to retire early or are forced to through corporate layoffs face additional problems, since they lose a number of years of financial accumulation needed to cover added years of retirement costs.

How much do people need in retirement? While the meaning of standard of living varies from one person or couple to another, the U.S. Bureau of Labor Statistics (BLS) has attempted to devise a budget reflecting what is necessary and desirable in meeting social and physical needs. BLS estimates in 1981 for retired couples established three levels of comfort or expectation: low, intermediate, and high. The low budget was $7,226, intermediate, was $10,226, and the high was $15,078. Ironically, the study of BLS budget estimates was curtailed due to budget cutbacks at the bureau itself.

It is commonly assumed that people living below the poverty index are the worst off economically. But Smeeding (1990) has identified the group whose income is between 100 percent and 200 percent of the poverty index (the lower middle-class elderly) as being more economically vulnerable than those below the poverty index. There are two reasons for this: the group falls outside the "safety net" of public programs for which they do not qualify, and yet they are not well enough off to provide for their own needs. Smeeding called this group the "'tweeners," for being caught in the middle. In 1984, he estimated that 4.5 million people fell into this category.

The major factors of financial vulnerability for "'tweeners" include lack of Supplemental Security Income (SSI) protection, supplemental medical insurance beyond Medicare (Medicaid), inability to cover costs of long-term care, higher housing costs, and problems of disability.

● IMPACT OF INFLATION

Discussion of the economic status of the elderly cannot ignore the phenomenon of inflation. In the United States it is the Consumer Price Index that is used to measure the changes in the prices of goods and services from year to year. Obviously, as costs rise and one's income fails to rise, increasing financial limits are encountered. Inflation is particularly hard on income from interest-bearing assets, which do not increase in value with inflation. Fixed pensions and annuities suffer the same consequences.

For this reason, Social Security benefits are linked to inflation rates through the so-called Cost of Living Adjustments (COLAs). The COLA is the chief reason that poverty rates among the elderly have declined.

Inflation rates are not consistent for all goods and services. In recent years, health care costs have far exceeded the inflation rate of other services. Since older people are primary users of health care services, they are especially hard hit by these increases.

In recent years there has been much discussion of the economic clout of older persons, the so-called "gold in grey" phenomenon. Statistics about the vast discretionary wealth of Americans over 50 presents the image of a wealthy, untapped market. Businesses are advised not to ignore older consumers and to learn more about their needs, values, and expenditure patterns. "They buy the steak, not the sizzle," goes one adage about older consumers. The problem with taking the over-50 as an aggregate is similar to that of taking people over 65 as a single homogeneous group. They aren't! Hence, a literal reading of the statistics can lead to highly misleading conclusions.

Older people do accumulate some range of wealth with age. A small percentage of the elderly do hold substantial financial assets such as stocks, bonds, saving accounts, and insurance policies. A large portion of older people hold tangible assets such as homes, cars, and boats. The monetary value of some tangible assets keeps pace with inflation, while financial assets may adjust in various (positive, negative, or neutral) ways with changes in the general level of prices.

● FUTURE TRENDS

Several decades of census information and numerous surveys indicate that the next generation of older people (i.e., those born between 1925 and 1935 who will become 65 during the 1990s) will continue in the trend of improved economic well being. This age group has been dubbed the "good times" generation by demographer Carl Harter, because its members had the good fortune to be in their prime working years during the period of maximum earning growth during the 1960s, saw the value of their homes soar during the inflationary 1970s, and were well positioned to benefit from the stock market boom of the 1980s. Also, among this age group one finds the beginning of a rise in two-earner families, launching the now prevalent trend of women entering or reentering the workforce. A 1983 Federal Reserve Board study found that the mean net worth of those 55 to 64 years old was 84 percent above the national mean net worth.

Poverty among the elderly is likely to continue to fall. However, those near poverty will fare about the same. With about one quarter of elderly family households receiving under $15,000 a year income and one quarter receiving over $40,000, the spectrum of diversity and economic disparity is evident.

Generalization about the economic status of the elderly should provoke skepticism, given the diversity revealed through closer analysis. Indeed, referring to the "over 50 market" among those promoting the "gold in grey" market place opportunities is an idea that should be greeted with raised eyebrows. True, as a group, those over 50 do have larger disposable or discretionary incomes, yet the over-50 are hardly a group in any sense. But these people do belong to communities—racial, geographic, generational—and to situations of gender, widowhood, health condition, and so on. The truth of the economic status of the elderly can be found in the details.

References

Congressional Research Service. "Progress Against Poverty in the United States, 1959–1987." *EPW Publications Report 89–211*. Washington, DC: U.S. Government Printing Office, March 24, 1989.

Grad, Susan. "Earnings Replacement Rates of New Retired Workers." *Social Security Bulletin 53*. Washington, DC: U.S. Social Security Administration, October 1990.

Schulz, James H. *The Economics of Aging*. 5th ed. Westport, CT: Auburn House, 1992.

Smeeding, Timothy M. "Economic Status of the Elderly." In *Handbook of Aging and the Social Sciences*. 3d ed. Eds. Robert H. Benstock and Linda K. George. San Diego, CA: Academic Press, 1990.

Tauber, Cynthia M. "Income and Poverty Trends for the Elderly." Testimony March 26, 1992, to Subcommittee on Retirement Income and Employment. Washington, DC: U.S. House of Representatives, Select Committee on Aging, 1992.

U.S. Bureau of the Census. "Money, Income, and Poverty Status in the United States, 1989." *Current Population Reports* Series P-60, no. 168. Washington, DC: U.S. Government Printing Office. September, 1990.

———. "Money Income of Households, Families in the United States, 1990." *Current Population Reports* Series P-60, no. 174. Washington, DC: U.S. Government Printing Office, 1991.

U.S. Congress. Senate. Special Committee on Aging. *Aging America: Trends and Projections, 1991*. Washington, DC: U.S. Department of Health and Human Services.

U.S. Department of Health and Human Services. Social Security Administration, ed. Office of Research and Statistics. *Income of the Aged Chart Book, 1990*. Rev. Washington, DC: U.S. Government Printing Office. September, 1992.

Vierck, Elizabeth. *Fact Book on Aging*. Santa Barbara, CA: ABC-CLIO, Inc., 1990.

Villers Foundation. *On the Other Side of Easy Street: Myths and Facts About the Economics of Old Age*. Washington, DC: Villers Foundation, 1987.

Additional Reading

Binstock, Robert H. "Perspectives on Measuring Hardship: Concepts, Dimensions, and Implications." *Gerontologist* Vol. 26, no. 1 (1986): 60–62.

Brown, Arnold S. "The Extent of Economic Dependency Among the Aged." *The Social Processes of Aging and Old Age*. Englewood Cliffs, NJ: Prentice-Hall, 1990.

Clark, Robert L. "Economic Well-Being of the Elderly: Theory and Measurement." *Journal of Cross-Cultural Gerontology* Vol. 4, no. 1 (1989): 19–34.

Coyle, Jean M. *Women and Aging: A Selected, Annotated Bibliography*. Bibliographies and Indexes in Gerontology Series; No. 9. New York: Greenwood Press, 1989.

Crooks, Louise. "Women and Pensions: Inequities for Older Women." *Vital Speeches of the Day* Vol. 57, no. 9 (1991): 283–85.

Crown, William H., Daniel Mazur, Phyllis Mutschler, Margaret Stubbs, and Rebecca Loew. *Pension and Healthy Benefits for State, Local, and Teacher Retirees: Coping With Inflation, 1982–1987*. Walthams, MA: Policy Center on Aging, Heller School, Brandeis University, 1990.

Crystal, Stephen. *Economic Resources of the Elderly: Distribution and Policy Indicators, Final Report*. New Brunswick, NJ: Rutgers State University of New Jersey, Division of Aging/AIDS Research Group, Institute for Health Care Policy and Aging Research, 1991.

Harris, Richard J. "Recent Trends in the Relative Economic Status of Older Adults." *Journal of Gerontology* Vol. 41, no. 3 (1986): 401–7.

Hatch, Laurie Russell. "Effects of Work and Family on Women's Later-Life Resources." *Research on Aging* Vol. 12, no. 3 (1990): 311–38.

———. "Gender and Work: At Midlife and Beyond." *Generations* Vol. 14, no. 3 (1990): 48–50+.

Holder, Karen. "The Economic Status of Older Women: A Summary of Selected Research Issues." In *Health and Economic Status of Older Women: Research Issues and*

Data Sources. Society and Aging Series. Vol. 1. Eds. Herzog and others. Amityville, NY: Baywood, 1989.

Hurd, Michael D. "Research on the Elderly: Economic Status, Retirement, and Consumption and Saving." *Journal of Economic Literature* Vol. 28 (1990): 565–637. (Note: Extensive bibliography, pp. 633–37).

Kilty, Keith M. "Social Security, Private Resources, and the Economic Security of Older Americans." *Journal of Aging Studies* Vol. 4, no. 1 (1990): 97–109.

Kirk, Juanda. *Multiple Family Responsibilities, Caregiving, and Related Concerns: An Annotated Bibliography.* Washington, DC: American Association of Retired Persons, 1991.

Longino, Charles F., Jr., and William H. Crown. "Older Americans: Rich or Poor?" *American Demographics* Vol. 13, no. 8 (1991): 48–52.

Moon, Marilyn. "Impact of the Reagan Years on the Distribution of Income of the Elderly." *Gerontologist* Vol. 26, no. 1 (1986): 32–37.

O'Bryant, Shirley, and Leslie A. Morgan. "Financial Experience and Well-Being Among Mature Widowed Women." *Gerontologist* Vol. 29, no. 2 (1989): 245–51.

Radner, Daniel B. "Assessing the Economic Status of the Aged and Non-aged Using Alternative Income-Wealthy Measures." *Social Security Bulletin* Vol. 53, no. 3 (1990): 2–14.

Schwenk, F. N. "Women Sixty-five Years or Older: A Comparison of Economic Well-Being by Living Arrangement." *Family Economic Review* Vol. 4, no. 3 (1991): 2–8.

Sheppard, Harold L., and Larry C. Mullins. "Comparative Examination of Perceived Income Adequacy Among Young and Old in Sweden and the United States." *Aging and Society* Vol. 9, no. 3 (1989): 223–39.

Stone, Michael E. "Shelter, Poverty, and the Elderly." *Journal of Aging and Social Policy* Vol. 2, no. 3–4 (1990): 61–83.

U.S. Bureau of the Census. "Measuring the Effect of Benefits and Taxes on Income and Property, 1979 to 1991." *Current Population Reports* Series P-60, no. 182 RD. Washington, DC: U.S. Government Printing Office, 1992.

———. "Money Income of Households, Families and Persons in the United States, 1991." *Current Population Reports* Series P-60, no. 180, Washington DC: U.S. Government Printing Office, 1992.

———. "Poverty in the United States, 1991." *Current Population Reports* Series P-60, no. 181. Washington, DC: Government Printing Office, 1992.

Uhlenberg, Peter, and Mary Anne P. Salmon. "Change in Relative Income of Older Women, 1960–1980." *Gerontologist* Vol. 26, no. 2 (1986): 164–70.

Walker, Alan. "Economic Burden of Aging and the Prospect of Intergenerational Conflict." *Aging and Society* Vol. 10, Part 4 (1990): 377–96.

Wise, David A. *The Economics of Aging.* Chicago, IL: University of Chicago Press, 1989.

Lawrence H. Geiger, M.A.

13

Major Financial Issues of Retirement Planning

- Financing Retirement: The Basic Steps • Determining Net Worth
- Projecting Expenses and Required Income • Income Profiles
- Sources of Retirement Income • Insurance Decisions

The famous parable of the blind men and the elephant is a useful analogy to the challenge of financial planning for retirement. Each man touches a separate part of the animal and reports such different impressions that no complete and accurate picture of the whole animal can be formed. Likewise, planning for one's retirement years involves examining many aspects of personal finances: Social Security benefits, projected savings and pension income, tax obligations, interest on investments, mortgage payments (if any), estimated effect of inflation over fifteen to thirty years, and other related factors. If these elements are left as unrelated fragments of information, it will be difficult if not impossible to understand future needs and present options and choices. While financial planning tends to make many people anxious to the point of inaction, a reasonably simple and systematic approach can prove more valuable than guessing in the dark. The objective, then, is seeing more clearly how all the pieces go together to make a whole.

Nevertheless, this chapter is not a complete how-to-do-it guide to retirement financial planning. It is more of a summary of basic steps that are frequently recommended in retirement planning workshops, seminars, and in books on retirement planning. Some people, especially

employees in larger corporations, may be offered one- or two-day retirement planning seminars. Others will seek out assistance of a tax expert, accountant, financial planner, insurance agent, or someone else familiar with the steps of organizing such a plan. This chapter presents basic issues and principles, provides additional printed information, and suggests next step.

While financial planning tends to make many people anxious to the point of inaction, a reasonably simple and systematic approach can prove more valuable than guessing in the dark.

Financial planning for retirement is important for the average person, perhaps even more so than for someone with considerable wealth. The average person has to stretch his or her income to cover many needs. When employment income stops due to retirement, it will be all the more necessary that a plan be put in place to ensure at least a modest degree of financial security and stability. Even the decision when to retire will be influenced by a financial plan.

271

Financial planning for retirement can help in a number of ways:

- increase the benefits of present income and savings
- combat the effects of inflation on savings
- enable a person to make certain financial choices that are only effective if decided long in advance
- help one identify expected sources and amounts of retirement income
- achieve a realistic picture of financial needs and how these match goals and expectations for the future

The following discussion of financial issues of retirement planning concerns three major activities: (1) developing a retirement plan; (2) reviewing the many options for saving and investing (such as tax-deferred savings plans, stocks and bonds, real estate, etc.); and (3) becoming aware of the best financial information available.

Because of the complexity of these topics, the reader is encouraged to consult the books and publications listed at the end of this chapter. Even with a good financial planner or investment broker, a future or current retiree is wise to become acquainted with the key financial planning issues of later life.

● FINANCING RETIREMENT: THE BASIC STEPS

Constructing an individual financial retirement plan involves the commitment of time and study, but the benefits overwhelmingly favor the effort. A plan involves defining the existing situation, specifying the desired destination, and then determining the best path to arrive at that destination. Getting a clear picture of the present informs the future, gives awareness to the past, and increases consciousness of the consequences of daily actions. A heightened sense of security, self-esteem, and direction should result from a good financial plan.

Ideally, a financial retirement plan should also increase enjoyment of the retirement years by providing extra resources to spend when there's time to enjoy experiences that were put off during the working years. This should also be an opportunity for self-recognition and reward for years of hard work.

Developing a retirement plan requires five basic steps: (1) making the list of dreams, (2) list-ing all assets and debts to determine one's net worth, (3) defining the future needs and dreams in terms of income and expenses, (4) planning and investing to create the needed future income, and (5) implementing and managing the plan on a monthly and/or yearly basis.

Financing Retirement Possibilities

A financial plan first involves preparing a list of expectations for the future—both the necessary and the possible. Although the list may contain items beyond one's current resources, this is not sufficient reason to exclude them. A wish, no matter how sincerely desired, is merely a fantasy, but attaching a time frame and a plan may turn the fantasy into an achievable goal. Numerous studies have shown that setting clear definite goals greatly increases the chances of reaching them. Realistic, practical planning (and a few sacrifices along the way) can create actuality from sheer fancy. A first planning step for couples is to talk over the separate hopes and common vision of what retirement might mean.

● DETERMINING NET WORTH

One's net worth is the total value of assets (savings, property, investments, and so on) minus the total dollar amount of all liabilities (what is owed). In other words, it is the amount that would be left over if all of one's possessions were turned into cash and all debts were paid off. The net worth figure is crucial in the planning process because it reveals one's current financial status. By examining net worth, individuals can determine whether they are building wealth and have options for investing disposable income, or whether changes in spending and saving patterns need to be made if plans for the future are to be carried out successfully.

Determining one's net worth many also involve collecting in one place (perhaps a file cabinet) a variety of important documents such as bank statements, mortgages, stock certificates, and so on. Organizing and possibly setting up a computerized database of assets, liabilities, and locations of documents are other options some people choose. All too often, one spouse will have primary responsibility for these matters. In the event of death or divorce, the other partner is suddenly at a loss for information.

Table 13.1
Net Worth Balance Sheet

Current assets	Value
Cash in checking and savings accounts	$_____
CDs and money market accounts	_____
Money market mutual funds	_____
Stock mutual funds	_____
Stocks	_____
Bonds	_____
Life insurance cash value	_____
Mortgages held	_____
Bond or mortgage mutual funds	_____
Automobiles	_____
Jewelry, silver	_____
Retirement accounts	_____
Pension accounts	_____
Profit sharing accounts	_____
Home residence	_____
Other real estate	_____
Art and antiques	_____
Other personal property	_____
Total assets	$_____

Current liabilities	
Bills outstanding	$_____
Personal loans	_____
Credit card debt	_____
Revolving credit	_____
Auto loans	_____
Life insurance loans	_____
Home mortgage	_____
Other mortgages	_____
Home equity loan	_____
Student loans	_____
Taxes due	_____
Total liabilities	$_____
Net worth (assets minus liabilities)	$_____

Assets

The first step in determining one's net worth is to prepare a list of all major assets. This task takes a bit of research and organization. Documents and information that should be prepared or collected are bank statements, brokerage account statements, estimated market value of household items, business records, mutual fund statements, current mortgage principal, and any other data that will indicate the value of assets. Taking the time to be thorough and accurate is important, but if an exact figure just cannot be derived, then a good estimate should be used.

By examining net worth, individuals can determine whether they are building wealth and have options for investing disposable income, or whether changes in spending and saving patterns need to be made if plans for the future are to be carried out successfully.

Table 13.1 represents a sample form for preparing a net worth balance sheet. There are several good computer software programs that can be of help, such as Andrew Tobias's "Managing Your Money" and Intuit's "Quicken." Included as assets will be real estate, stocks, bonds, the cash value of whole life insurance policies, and any other holdings that have or can be converted into monetary value. Each asset listing should include the original purchase price of investment, the current market value, and any information concerning right of survivorship or other important details.

Market values on real estate can be derived from sales of similar residences in the neighborhood or by adjusting the original purchase price by a factor for inflation or deflation. In some cases it may be wise to hire an independent appraiser to prepare an unbiased appraisal. A good appraisal is important when the time comes to sell the property.

Liabilities

Following the asset list comes a list of all secured debts (mortgages, auto loans, and other debts for which collateral has been given), then a list of all unsecured debts. Unsecured debts are unpaid bills, credit card balances, unsecured loans, loans from family members, and any other indebtedness not tied to a particular asset. On both types of debts, one should write down the balance on the account and the interest rate. After completing the inventory of assets and lia-

Table 13.2
Sample Approach to Returns on Assets, Costs of Liabilities

Asset	Returns on assets		
	Amount	Percentage	Yearly income or increase
Short-term assets			
Checking account	$600	2.5%	$15
Money market	5,000	3.5	175
CDs	10,000	6.0	600
Mutual funds	10,000	9.0	900
Bonds	10,000	8.0	800
Annual return on short-term assets			$2,490
Long-term assets			
Pension plan	$80,000	7.0%	$5,600
IRAs	20,000	9.0	1,800
Mutual funds	25,000	12.0	3,000
Real estate	120,000	6.0	7,200
Annual return on long-terms assets			$17,600
Total annual return on assets			$20,090

bilities, one subtracts the debts from the value of assets. This figure is one's net worth.

Evaluating Net Worth

The net worth balance sheet can be used to analyze a variety of aspects of the financial picture. By comparing the net worth amount from year to year one can see whether debts are too large, or are growing faster than savings, and how well one's investments are growing. Since the goal is to increase the net worth figure, one must continue to look for ways to increase earnings on assets and to decrease and limit liabilities. Table 13.2 is an example of a method that can be used for this purpose and to project future net worth.

Short-Term and Long-Term Assets and Liabilities

The net worth amount also indicates which assets are more accessible and which would take longer to liquidate. For example, cash, mutual funds, stocks and bonds, and life insurance cash values can be sold quickly to confront a financial emergency. Conventional wisdom says that emergency savings and short-term assets should amount to approximately three to six months of income. Real estate is a long-term asset, because property could take months to sell. Short-term liabilities are generally those that are unsecured,

while the home mortgage is a good example of a liability that will be a part of the budget picture for the long term.

By listing all assets and liabilities according to short-term and long-term categories, one can then project the annual return (income) from each entry in the list of income-producing assets and the yearly expenses from liabilities. If one extends the projection five years, a future prediction of net worth will emerge. This exercise will indicate which investments are doing the best and which liabilities are the greatest burden.

The short- and long-term balance sheet will also be a guide for deciding on a good balance between quick assets, which may have low yields, and long-term assets invested for higher yields. Detailed information on asset allocation—deciding how much to put where for how long—can be found in Chapter 14.

A Spending Plan: The Best Way to Decrease Liabilities

The retirement financial planning process is a good time to create a good spending plan in order to increase assets and decrease liabilities. Short-term debts often take the heaviest toll on financial power, and in the 1990s these are likely to appear in the form of credit card debt. By assessing debts and interest rates one can see exactly

Table 13.3
Interest Costs on Liabilities

Short-term liabilities	Amount	Interest rate charged (%)	Yearly expense
Personal loans	$6,000	13.0	$780
Revolving credit	3,000	18.0	540
Credit cards	5,000	18.0	900
Annual expense on short-term liabilities			$2,220
Long-term liabilities			0
Personal loans	$8,000	12.0	$960
Mortgages	40,000	8.5	3,400
Life insurance loan	5,000	7.0	350
Annual expense on long-term liabilities			$4,710
Total annual expense on long-term liabilities			$6,930

where a household paycheck really goes. If debt reduction is a problem, there are a number of useful books that can be helpful. Some give very specific plans for getting out of debt (Mundis, 1990).

Paying off all short-term obligations will require making a plan and sticking to it. After they are paid, funds previously spent on debt reduction can now be placed in an investment account each month, and this will dramatically enhance tomorrow's options.

● PROJECTING EXPENSES AND REQUIRED INCOME

Although it may be continually revised, fulfilling one's list of dreams and of financial security is the goal. The step of projecting future expenses involves predicting future difficulties, costs, and surpluses that can be realistically secured. Relatively few people will retire wealthy, but most people can maintain a modest reserve to minimize retirement financial difficulty and vulnerability. Depending, in part, on current resources, planned retirement income may fall somewhere between financing life's basic necessities to supporting an affluent lifestyle. Each person must, as the saying goes, "do what you can where you are with what you have."

Inflation and the Monthly Retirement Budget

The experience of coming across an old magazine or newspaper and laughing at the prices of goods from ten or twenty years ago is familiar to most people. The dollar just doesn't buy what it

did then. Inflation, the erosion of buying power of the dollar, must be accounted for in making projections of future expenses. In recent years, the annual inflation rate has been about 3.5 percent, while in the early 1980s it was at least 7 percent. Five, ten, or fifteen years from now the rate could be quite different. For simplicity, an annual inflation rate of 5 percent can be used to translate current expenses into future projected expenses. However, some goods and services have experienced a historically greater rate of inflation. Prescriptions and medical care in general have increased by 15 percent to 20 percent annually, far outpacing an average annual inflation rate of 5 percent.

Future Housing and Medical Care Costs

Housing expenses may go up or down, depending on choices made by the person or couple at the time of retirement. For many, housing expenses will decrease, because the mortgage loan on the family home has been paid. Others may move to a smaller, less expensive house or to a condominium. Retirement planners will want to realistically assess what the expected housing situation and costs will be at the time of retirement and later when housing needs may change due to increased care needs.

As health care costs continue to escalate, legislation is coming before Congress for major reforms that may limit cost increases in the health care industry. The Clinton administration has made health care reform a major goal. In the meantime, the consumer must keep abreast of changes in health care options and in costs.

In order to maximize health care benefits, consumers should strive to associate with companies or government units that offer group health care coverage. Maintaining group coverage throughout retirement is a tremendous advantage as opposed to purchasing an individual policy. Many group plans will retain the policyholder as long as the premiums are paid. Individual plans are less likely to have this protection. However, many companies are dropping or reneging on promises for covering full or partial group and individual health care insurance policies.

Prescriptions and medical care in general have increased by 15 percent to 20 percent annually, far outpacing an average annual inflation rate of 5 percent.

It is wise to read the annual reports of health care insurance companies to keep in touch with their financial condition. Also, local libraries carry A. M. Best's *Review of Insurance Companies*, which gives ratings of the financial strength of most insurance companies.

Medicare is available to individuals aged 65 and over. In 1992, this coverage generally provides for hospital stays of up to 60 days, 80 percent of doctor's fees, and up to 100 days in nursing homes. It may be best to buy supplemental Medigap insurance for expenses not covered by Medicare. For example, after the first 100 days in a nursing home, individuals must pay the entire cost themselves. A nursing home can easily cost as much as $30,000 per year. Most health care insurance plans do not cover nursing home care, but a separate policy can be purchased to help cover the nursing home charges. Generally, these policies are available to individuals aged 45 and over.

The Expense Budget

An expense budget also will include costs of groceries and restaurant meals, clothing, entertainment, utilities, laundry, gifts, newspapers, magazines and books, car payments and auto insurance or other transportation, travel, income tax, and any other expenditures that will be a part of the retirement budget.

Table 13.4
Example of Monthly Estimated Expenses in Retirement

Auto and/or other transportation	$200
Cash and miscellaneous expenses	100
Clothing and appearance	50
Dining out	70
Entertainment	30
Gifts, contributions	25
Groceries	240
Home mortgage or rent, property taxes	700
Home repair and improvement	100
Household and furniture	150
Income taxes	670
Insurance:	
Auto	40
Home and/or household contents	60
Health	130
Life	80
Legal and professional fees	25
Medical and dental	150
Telephone	80
Travel	150
Utilities	150
Total	$3,200

The result of the future expense plan might look like Table 13.4. It is easy to use today's dollar cost estimates and then project them into the future. The expense estimates are examples only.

Using this current projection of $3,200 monthly expenses, future costs can be computed by adding a 5 percent inflation factor for each year until retirement. This gives a figure that should be reasonable for future cost of living increases. For example, if a person or couple were retiring in five years, then multiplying 1.05 times $3,200 and 1.05 times that total (compounding the yearly inflation rate) would yield a figure of $4,084 as the monthly expense rate for the fifth year. Clearly, the compounded inflation rate is a significant factor that must be taken into account.

Each person or household must decide on a reasonable cost of living rate for future projections. A low estimate may lead some to run out of money earlier than anticipated. Some retirement planners believe that a couple can maintain their pre-retirement lifestyle on about 75 percent of their pre-retirement income. Others estimate the percentage at about two-thirds, assuming that the couple has no mortgage loan payments to make. Added to these projections are state and federal income taxes, which can take between one-fourth and one-third of one's income. In Table 13.4 the monthly expenditure need is projected five years to retirement. But what of the extended time of one's retirement until death? This is where a life expectancy calculation must be factored in. This is especially critical as people are generally living well into their seventies and eighties.

One planning guide, *Managing Your Money* (Tobias, 1992), estimates an individual's life expectancy based on criteria such as gender, smoking habits, occupation, seat belt use, and general health. Financial planners frequently use an assumption of a ninety-year life expectancy. This is a conservative, safe projection—better that the end comes before the money runs out, rather than vice-versa.

Table 13.5 assumes a couple is five years away from retirement at age 65. They currently spend $3,200 (including income taxes) per month. Using the 5 percent per year inflation rate, they can project their $3,200 monthly expenses into the future as follows (amounts are rounded to the nearest $50).

Table 13.5
Cost of Living Effects to End of Life

Age	Income needed per month
60	$3,200
65 (retirement begins)	4,100
75	6,650
90	13,850

Savings Goal

Income during the retirement years typically comes from Social Security, a company pension, and earnings from investments. Table 13.5 shows the couple need $4,100 monthly income. If their Social Security benefit is $1,000 and their pension is $800, they would require $2,300 monthly income from investments. If their investments earned 7 percent, they would need approximately $394,000 savings.

But each year their expenses are increasing 5 percent, and by the time they are age 75 they need $6,650 a month. Most company pensions do not provide for cost-of-living increases. Social Security benefits do increase with inflation, and in this scenario would be about $1,625 in ten years. Required earnings from investments at age 75 would be $4,225 (that is, $6,650 – $800 – $1,625). Savings at age 75 would have to be over $724,000 to produce $4,225 income at a 7 percent rate. Monthly savings is the answer. After determining the total amount of money necessary to retire at age 65, one can compute the monthly savings amount needed to realize the retirement nest egg. A quick look at Table 13.6 shows how essential it is to begin saving as early as possible. The top figures are the desired monthly income at age 65. The side figures indicate the age at which consistent monthly savings begin.

Retirees who do not invade their principal for living expenses are usually the most comfortable. All of the savings projections in Table 13.4 and in Table 13.6 assume the savings principal is left intact and is not spent. For most retirees this conservative approach is not feasible. If they are to live comfortable lives they must use some or all of their investment principal during their retirement.

● INCOME PROFILES

One helpful way to visualize the timing and amount of retirement income and to relate it to estimated monthly expenses or income needs is to use an income profile. This is a graph with vertical and horizontal axes—one demarcating time (years) and the other monthly income (dollars). Four sample income profiles, reprinted from the retirement planning program of The National Council on the Aging (NCOA), illustrate the situations of two couples, a single woman, and a widow (NCOA, 1993).

Financial planners frequently use an assumption of ninety-year life expectancy. This is a conservative, safe projection— better that the end comes before the money runs out, rather than vice-versa.

Figure 13.1

Income Profile: Husband Plans to Retire in 2002 at Age 65; Wife Plans to Retire in 2002 at Age 62

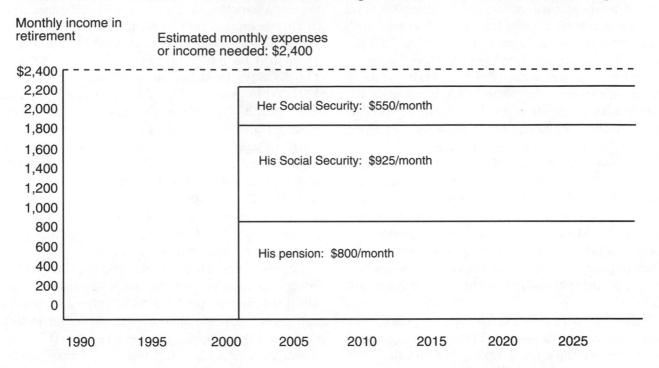

Husband's Age: 65

Wife's Age: 62

Explanation: The Greys estimate that they will require about $2,400 a month in retirement. They find that if the husband works until 65, his pension will be $800 a month. His Social Security will be $925 a month and hers will be $550 a month. This comes to $2,275 a month, or $125 a month less than they feel they need. The Greys are now considering possible ways of increasing their retirement income (e.g., through a new savings plan, some work in retirement, and other possibilities). Regarding taxes, although income from work can cause deductions in Social Security retirement benefits, income from other sources does not cause such deductions. Also for 1988, a couple age 65 or over needed to have more than $9,400 in income other than Social Security before having to pay any federal income taxes. Beginning in 1989, this amount (based on standard deductions) will increase with inflation.

Source: The National Council on the Aging, Inc., © 1993.

Figure 13.2
Income Profile: Husband Plans to Retire in 1995 at Age 60; Wife Plans to Retire in 2000 at Age 60

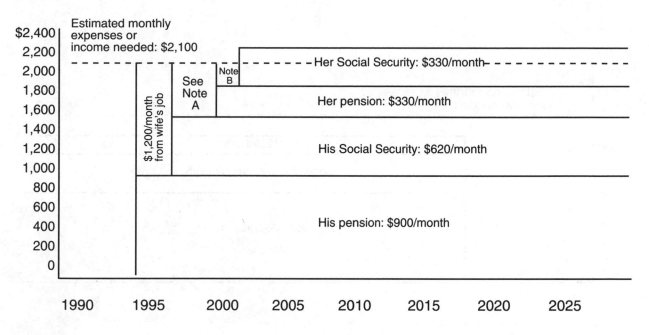

Husband's age: 60

Wife's age: 60

Explanation: Mr. Brown plans to retire at age 60 with a company pension of $900 a month. His wife will continue her job, and they will use $1,200 a month from her earnings to meet living expenses. When he is 62 and his wife is 57 his Social Security will start, adding $620 a month. When she reaches age 60, the wife will quit her job and begin to receive a pension of $330 a month from her employer. When she reaches age 62, she will begin to receive Social Security benefits of $330 a month.

Notes: A. From 1997 to 2000, they plan to save approximately 50 percent of the wife's income for their retirement years together. B. During the two years from 2000 to 2002, they will need a "supplementary fund" to provide approximately $250 per month.

Source: The National Council on the Aging, Inc., © 1993.

Figure 13.3
Income Profile: Single Woman Plans to Retire in 1997 at Age 65

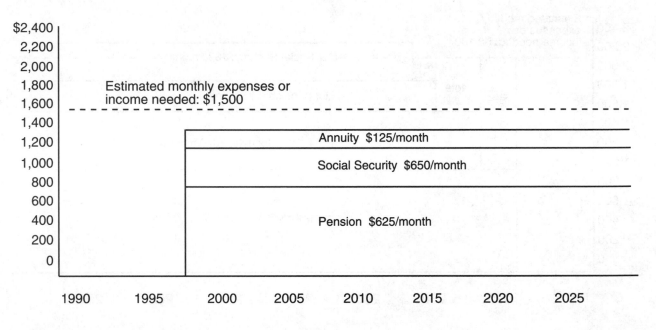

Age: 65

Explanation: Ellen Johnson plans to retire in 1997 at age 65. She will receive a company pension of $625 a month, a Social Security benefit of $650 a month, and income from an annuity of $125 a month. She estimates she will need $1,500 a month, or $18,000 a year, when she retires. She is now exploring ways of increasing her retirement income by $100 a month.

Source: The National Council on the Aging, Inc., © 1993.

Figure 13.4
A Survivor's Income Profile

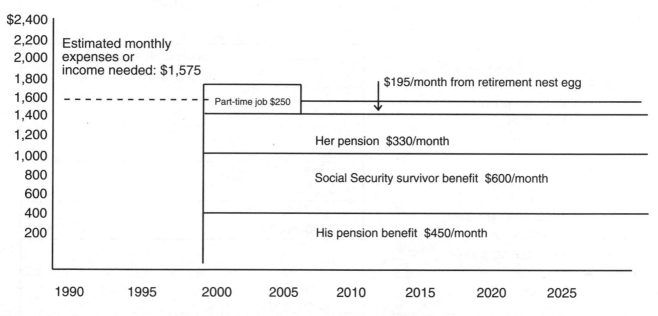

Generally, wives outlive their husbands. Not only do they tend to be younger than their husbands, but in general, women have a longer lifespan than men. Since the chances are that a wife will spend some years as a widow, it is very important that a separate income profile be prepared to display her currently expected retirement income as a survivor. Actually, since no one has a crystal ball, either spouse could end up being the survivor. It is therefore valuable to prepare a Survivor Income Profile for both husband and wife.

Explanation: Mr. and Mrs. Brown have considered what would happen to their finances if Mrs. Brown becomes widowed at age 60. They decided she will need $1,575 a month to cover her expenses. She will qualify for a survivor benefit under both Mr. Brown's pension plan and Social Security; and she will receive a $330 pension from her own previous full-time job, providing her with $1,380 a month income. To supplement this she could take a part-time job in order to provide another $250 a month. She will not lose any Social Security benefits, because her total annual earnings are not high enough to cause this. With all of this she will have $1,630 a month.

She plans to stop her part-time job at age 68 and supplement her monthly benefits by drawing about $195 a month from her savings. This will give her the $1,575 a month income she will need.

Source: The National Council on the Aging, Inc., © 1993.

Figure 13.5
Decline in Purchasing Power of a $400 a Month Pension Over 20 Years if Inflation Is 7% a Year

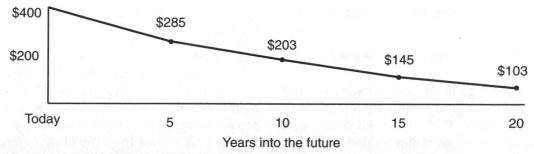

Source: The National Council on the Aging, Inc., © 1993.

Figure 13.6
Loss of Purchasing Power With 7% Rate of Inflation

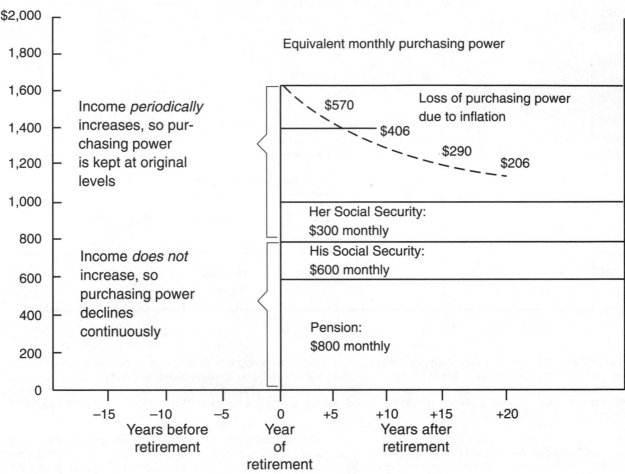

Husband's age: 65

Wife's age: 62

Explanation: John R. and his wife, Eve, expect to have a retirement income of $1,700 a month. About $800 of this will come from a private pension plan and $900 from Social Security. The pension is not "variable" with living costs, but it is in the form of a fixed-income annuity.

The Problem: How can John and Eve maintain $1,700 a month purchasing power over the twenty years they expect to be retired?

Analysis: If John and Eve wish to put aside enough to make up for the loss in the pension's purchasing power over twenty years, it will be a sizable amount. The figure above shows that in ten years, about one-half of the pension's purchasing power will be lost to inflation, if inflation is 7 percent a year. John and Eve will need to figure out how much money they need invested to compensate for inflation. Clearly, some forms of savings and investments will be needed to offset the effects of inflation.

Source: The National Council on the Aging, Inc., © 1993.

The Effect of Inflation on Income Profiles

What the income profiles have not shown is the effect of inflation on purchasing power: the projected income needs (Table 13.5) when inflation was figured at 5 percent compounded annually, and that amount calculated from retirement at age 65 to the age of 90. While some forms of income, such as Social Security benefits, may also rise with inflation (cost of living adjustments, or COLAs), other income sources such as private pension plans and annuities will not rise. Figure 13.5 shows the effects of 7 percent inflation on a $400 monthly pension; Figure 13.6

Table 13.6
Monthly Savings Needed to Reach Desired Monthly Income at Age 65

Monthly Income Goal

	$1,000	$2,000	$3,000	$4,000	$5,000	$6,000	$7,000	$8,000	$9,000	$10,000
Age 30	61	122	184	245	306	368	429	491	552	613
Age 35	94	189	283	378	472	567	661	756	850	945
Age 40	148	296	444	592	740	888	1,036	1,184	1,332	1,480
Age 45	239	478	717	956	1,195	1,434	1,673	1,912	2,151	2,390
Age 50	407	814	1,221	1,627	2,034	2,441	2,848	3,255	3,662	4,068
Age 55	770	1,539	2,309	3,078	3,848	4,618	5,387	6,157	6,926	7,696
Age 60	1,916	3,832	5,748	7,665	9,581	11,497	13,413	15,329	17,245	19,161

Explanation: Find age at beginning of monthly savings in first column and read across to find minimum monthly savings required to yield desired monthly income at age 65. Example: At 40, monthly savings of $740 must be made in order to yield a monthly income at age 65 of $5,000 per month. This figure assumes that savings earn 8% annual interest and the principal is not spent.

examines an income profile that includes the factor of inflation.

● SOURCES OF RETIREMENT INCOME

Becoming Educated

This section introduces some of the more common methods of increasing the asset side of the net worth balance sheet. The kinds of investments are defined, and their strengths and weaknesses are discussed.

Since everyone's situation is different, each retirement plan and investment strategy must be unique as well. No one can possibly design a future better than the individual who plans to live it. Thus it is important for individuals to gain much more information on the innumerable options for creating wealth before establishing the definitive plan.

Continued Full- or Part-Time Employment

About half of the 25 percent of retirees who become re-employed or choose self-employment do so for financial reasons, the other half for emotional compensation. Since 33 percent of AARP members wish they were working (Petras, 1991), it seems wise not to anticipate that a job will necessarily be available when retirement age arives. On the other hand, self-employment may be more of an option. Those over 65 years of age need to consider that earning an income can reduce Social Security benefits and will mean paying into FICA even if Social Security benefits are being drawn. Part-time work may be a good way to avoid these problems while striking a balance between work and leisure. Changing careers is often done at retirement age, and there are many sources of job-hunting and career advice for the older worker. In terms of employment, the main issue when planning retirement income is not to count too heavily on income from wages.

Social Security

Social Security benefits are based on the amount of one's earned income. The higher the level of income on which Social Security taxes were paid, the more the retiree will collect in Social Security payments. The Social Security Administration provides a Personal Earnings and Benefit Estimate Statement to anyone who requests it. This statement will indicate the amount of Social Security earnings to date and the anticipated monthly retirement benefit. The report can also be used to make sure that the

> About half of the 25 percent of retirees who become re-employed or choose self-employment do so for financial reasons, the other half for emotional compensation.

amount of reported income recorded by Social Security agrees with the worker's own records. In case of a discrepancy, copies of tax returns or W-2s can be used to justify the corrections.

Currently Social Security benefits can begin anytime between ages 62 and 70. During this period, the longer one waits to begin collecting, the higher the monthly check. (For a detailed discussion of Social Security, see Chapters 9 and 11.)

Employer Pension Plans

These retirement plans are set up by an employer who helps provide for employees' retirement by creating a pool of money, investing it, and specifying rules and procedures for dispensing the proceeds. Self-employed people can set up their own pension plans through the Simplified Employee Pension, a Keogh, or an Individual Retirement Account (IRA).

In the past pension plans have been considered a major source of retirement income. Although they are still successfully used, serious shortfalls have occurred in some company pension plan coffers. Pension plan problems include the following (Petras, 1991):

- Some companies are cutting into employee pension funds in order to reduce costs.
- Some plans are discontinued altogether.
- Others are replaced by new less expensive ones, less beneficial to the employees.
- The company goes bankrupt.
- The company's pension plan falls victim to changes made through merger, acquisition, or take-over.
- More people are changing jobs and careers, which means shorter stays with any one company.
- Layoffs have increased, as companies tighten their belts in the 1990s.
- Some layoff decisions are made to save the company from pension payments.
- According to recent government data, many pensions haven't kept up with inflation.

It is important to understand how one's own pension plan works, what money will be available, and how the money will be disbursed at retirement. The company is required to provide a Summary Plan Description and an Individual Benefit Statement. Also the company's employee benefits office can help estimate what the retirement amount or annuity will be.

The retiree may be permitted to receive the pension as an annuity or in a lump sum. Annuity options are discussed later in this chapter. A lump sum distribution can be rolled into an Individual Retirement Account (IRA) or an annuity of the retiree's choice. When changing jobs, it is imperative to roll over any company pension lump-sum into an IRA or into a pension of the new employer. Spending this money will mean the loss of many years of tax-deferred compounding returns, paying income tax on the sum, and the IRS penalty of 10 percent if the employee is under age 59½.

Some questions to ask about pension plans are:

- Is the plan a defined benefit or defined contribution plan (see Annuities for definitions of these types of plans)?
- How has the pension fund been keeping up with inflation? How is the money in the pension fund invested? May the employees choose the investment vehicle in which their account will be invested?
- What happens if an employee works past retirement age?
- What happens if the employee leaves before retirement?

Employees should also seek out other profitable long-term investment vehicles to be assured of retirement security. Since many pension funds don't keep up with inflation and are vulnerable to recent changes in the company and job markets, this source of retirement income is not the sure thing that it was twenty years ago.

Keogh Plans

For those who are self-employed or work for unincorporated companies, Keogh plans offer an excellent vehicle for tax deferred retirement savings, since yearly contributions can exceed the maximum IRA amount of $2,000. For people whose only income is through self-employment, this type of pension plan is critical. Employed people who work for themselves on the side can also participate. An employer who starts a plan for herself or himself must also set up a Keogh plan for all of her/his employees. Up to 20 percent (with a ceiling of $30,000) of the year's net earnings from the business may be contributed to a Keogh account for self-employed people. The two main types of Keoghs are defined benefit plans, which provide set benefit amounts with contributions to the plan based on actuarial assumptions, and defined contribution plans, where benefits are based only on the amount contributed to the account and contributions are a stated amount or are based on a stated formula. It is wise to discuss the practicalities of setting up a Keogh plan with a qualified accountant, actuary, or lawyer.

IRAs

Funding an Individual Retirement Account is another way for individuals to save for retirement. The Internal Revenue code allows up to $2,000 a year per wage earner to be invested through a savings institution, brokerage firm, mutual fund company, or insurance company, which becomes the custodian of the IRA account. The advantages of IRAs are: they are easy to open; the contribution can be tax deductible, and the earnings are tax-deferred; a wide variety of investment vehicles are available.

IRAs were first created as fully deductible to all wage earners. Now, however, assured deductibility is limited to those who are self-employed or whose firms do not provide a pension plan. Also, if individual adjusted gross income (AGI) is under $25,000 ($40,000 for married couples), the IRA contribution is tax deductible. Partial tax deductibility occurs in the income range of $25,000 to $35,000 for individuals and $40,000 to $50,000 for couples. In all cases, IRA earnings are not taxable until the funds are withdrawn.

Withdrawals prior to age 59½ carry a 10 percent penalty along with income tax on the earnings and the deductible contributions. After the age of 59½, no penalties apply. However, distributions from the account must begin by the age of 70½ and, to be free of penalties, must not fall below a certain amount. IRS calculates this minimum yearly distribution (based on actuarial tables) so that all IRA contributions will be distributed during one's lifetime.

401(k) Savings Plan

Jane Bryant Quinn says, "Compounding interest is a perpetual money machine." A machine that should be working throughout one's life. The 401(k) plan is an easy, lucrative, and relatively painless way to begin building a nest egg. This do-it-yourself pension plan uses an investment account set up by employers. Participating in a 401(k) plan is one of the easiest and quickest ways to accumulate a retirement fund because:

- contributions are drawn before the paycheck is issued, making it a more painless way to save
- contributions are tax deductible
- earnings build up also on a tax-deferred basis
- the maximum yearly contribution is much larger than the IRA maximum
- an employer may match up to 100 percent of the employee's contribution (this is an invisible salary—like free money!)
- the employee can borrow against the account (under certain conditions)
- employers usually offer a variety of investment options
- in certain cases, large amounts can be rolled over into IRAs

The investment options may include employer company stock, mutual funds, common stocks, bonds, money-market investments, and combinations of these. The yearly ceiling set by the IRS in 1991 was $8,475.

Some possible drawbacks with 401(k)s are:

- the employer determines the formula and maximum amounts for contributions
- the employer determines the available investment vehicle (not necessarily the most lucrative investments)
- some difficulty and loss can occur when changing jobs

A new tax law, which took effect in January 1993, requires that upon a change of employment, the employer must transfer 401(k) funds directly into the employee's IRA or the new company's 401(k) plan. Previously the employee could have use of the money for up to sixty days before reinvesting. Now, if the employee touches the money himself, the government will withhold 20 percent in income tax. The employee must replace the 20 percent before reinvesting or the IRS will impose its 10 percent prepayment penalty as well, if the taxpayer is under age 59½.

A new tax law, which took effect in January 1993, requires that upon a change of employment, the employer must transfer 401(k) funds directly into the employee's IRA or the new company's 401(k) plan.

Annuities

Annuities are investments sold by insurance companies and are designed to provide a guaranteed monthly income primarily in the retirement years. One can invest a large sum and get an immediate annuity, receiving a guaranteed monthly income, often for life. Generally, however, the investor contributes a set amount monthly for a period of years and then, at a given age, he or she begins to receive guaranteed, fixed monthly withdrawals. Again, annuities are tax-deferred investments; most withdrawals before age 59½ will be penalized ten percent by the IRS. Annuities can be variable or fixed. If variable, the company promises to try to get the best return, but it is not required to meet a specific earning rate. Variable annuities invest in common stock. The benefit received at maturity by the annuitant depends on the investment experience of the account.

The amount of the monthly benefit depends on:

- age when monthly withdrawals begin
- the withdrawal option selected
- amount invested
- amount of return on investment

The withdrawal options for annuities are:

- *Life annuity:* A monthly income that terminates at the insured's death
- *Fixed period annuity:* Rather than terminating at death, in this plan the payments end after a predetermined number of years or at death
- *Joint life and survivor annuity:* Provides income over the lifetimes of two individuals with benefits continuing in full or in a

reduced amount to the survivor after the first death
- *Life annuity with period certain:* A preset number of years of payments; if the insured dies before all the payments have been made, the beneficiary receives the rest of the payments

CDs and Money Market Funds

Certificates of Deposit (CDs) are convenient and flexible bank deposits through which funds are committed for a period of time—usually six months to ten years—for a fixed rate of interest. Some banks will waive the early withdrawal penalty in return for offering lower interest. It is generally better to take the higher interest CD and pay the penalty if forced to break it early. CDs are often established for cautionary purposes: rainy day funds, unexpected health care costs, family emergencies, and so on. Since CD rates are low, they generally don't keep up with inflation but are much better than not saving at all. The highest rates possible are generally on the longest term CDs. High-yield CDs pay around one percentage point more than the average. Some high paying CDs can be obtained because the borrowing institution is strong, has lent too much money, and needs to attract more deposits. Other institutions are insolvent and may soon be taken over by the government. If they are taken over, the CD rates will go down. To receive a free list of the S&Ls and savings and other banks already under government supervision, write Resolution Trust Corp., 801 17th St. NW, Washington, DC 20429, and ask for their Conservatorship List. Higher rates may also be found through major stockbrokerage houses.

Money market accounts are another type of bank deposit savings account. Money market account interest rates fluctuate during the investment period, generally paying more than savings account interest during high interest periods, and paying similar to savings accounts during low rate periods. Unlimited deposits and withdrawals are allowed.

Money market accounts are good short-term investments for money that may be used for emergencies or more lucrative investment. They are convenient and return a bit more than savings accounts. They are not generally a good vehicle for long-term savings since there are much higher returns in other vehicles. The same can be said of money market mutual funds. In this instrument, the investor buys shares of a privately managed mutual fund that invests in short-term money market securities. This type of mutual fund tends to be a bit riskier (with resulting higher yields) than savings or money market deposit accounts, although both risk level and yield levels vary. Some money market mutual funds are free of either state or federal income taxes, but none are federally insured.

Treasury Bills, Notes, and Bonds

"Treasuries" are U.S. government debts and as such are federally guaranteed. On a regular basis, the Treasury Department determines how much money it needs and sells these instruments to banks, brokers, and individuals. Treasury interest is exempt from state and local income taxes. T-Bills, or Treasury Bills, are the shortest term investment, maturing in one year or less with a minimum $10,000 purchase. Treasury notes mature in one to ten years and carry a minimum investment of $1,000 to $5,000, depending on the length of time to maturity. U. S. Treasury bonds mature in ten to thirty years. As with other bonds, interest is paid to the investor twice a year. The principal is paid at maturity. Since the effect of interest rate changes in price increases with the time to maturity, the price of long term Treasury bonds can fluctuate much more than the price of shorter term bonds. By selling before maturity, losses may be incurred. When interest rates rise, bond prices fall, and vice-versa.

U.S. Savings Bonds

Once disparaged as an investment, Series EE Savings Bonds now pay a respectable return if held to maturity in about twelve years. Series EE bonds pay current interest; instead they are sold at a discount, $25 for a $50 bond to $5,000 for a $10,000 bond. Interest on EE Bonds is never taxed by state and local authorities, and federal income tax is deferred until the bonds are cashed. The bonds are redeemable after two months, but early redemption can reduce the yield. The interest rate is variable and is adjusted every six months, but cannot fall below 6 percent, unless the law is changed by Congress.

U.S. Government Securities—Non Treasury

GNMAs, or Ginnie Maes as they are called, are mortgage-backed securities issued by the Government National Mortgage Association, a U.S. government agency. The term Ginnie Mae is also used to refer to a family of related income securities: bonds made up of real estate mortgages. A bank sells large pools of homeowner mortgages to the government or another financial institution, which then sells them to investors in individually sized securities. The investor receives monthly payments of principal and interest just as a bank receives mortgage payments. The minimum size is $25,000, unless a major part of the principal has been paid off. Then they can be bought for less. Ginnie Maes and her relatives are investments that yield higher rates than Treasury Bonds.

Freddie Macs, backed by the Federal Home Loan Mortgage Association, and Fannie Maes, backed by the Federal National Mortgage Association, are similar types of bonds to Ginnie Maes but are not considered as safe, since they are backed by quasi-governmental agencies. Their yields are therefore often higher.

One potential disadvantage of the Ginnie Mae family is that when interest rates fall, homeowners often refinance their mortgages, and the investor with a Ginnie Mae holding will be repaid earlier than the stated maturity of fifteen or thirty years. The investor then must reinvest the money at lower prevailing rates. To deal with early repayment, a spin-off type of security was created by Wall Street called Collateralized Mortgage Obligations, or CMOs. These are more predictable in terms of principal and early repayment but are not backed by government agencies.

Stocks

Buying stocks means actually buying shares of ownership in a corporation. Investors make money two ways: through dividends, which are profits of the corporation; or through profits from selling the stock for more than the purchase amount. This latter profit (or loss) is called a capital gain (or capital loss) and is taxed differently from regular income. Dividends are not always paid; some companies don't make a profit and some reinvest corporate profits in the company. The two ways to buy stocks are by picking individual ones or by selecting a mutual fund, which consists of a group of stocks. For a closer examination of stock investments see the chapter on Asset Allocations. Here, a few general comments can be made.

The best place for long-term money growth is the stock market. The numbers say it all: Over the past fifty years the stock market has earned on average 9 percent compounded, more than any other investment. And although there have been downturns, crashes, and minicrashes, if an average investor had stayed invested in the market, buying and holding stocks, those stocks would have come out ahead of any major investment (Quinn, 1991).

The downside is that investing in the stock market is a complex mission. There are so many indicators of good and bad ventures that without some expertise and familiarity, this type of investment is really a gamble. Only by studying and becoming educated can a person become proficient enough to make profitable investment decisions. Experts encourage following these guidelines and strategies:

- Don't buy and sell too often; a long-term strategy usually works best.
- Construct a carefully planned portfolio that reflects your long-range investment goals.
- A strong portfolio is a diversified one with some money kept out of the market altogether.
- Cut losses early; the longer and further a stock is allowed to fall in price, the greater gain that must be made elsewhere just to break even.
- Buy stocks with good value: those underpriced relative to their potential or quality.
- Use corporate ratios (such as P/E, or price-earnings, ratios) with awareness that they can only report the past, not predict the future.
- Buy what you know; in an industry the investor understands, he or she has an inside advantage.
- Buy stocks in sound and flourishing industries and those that can withstand recessions and bull markets.
- Keep informed with good sources of market information.
- Avoid investing on emotional motives.

Most stocks are traded on exchanges such as the New York Stock Exchange (NYSE), the American Exchange, small regional exchanges, the National Association of Securities Dealers Automated Quotations System (NASDAQ), and the National Association of Security Dealers Exchange for over-the-counter stocks.

Mutual Funds

A mutual fund receives money from many investors and invests that money in stocks, bonds, and/or other types of securities. There are stock funds, bond funds, gold funds, money market funds, and Ginnie Mae funds. Mutual funds are excellent vehicles for owning stocks mainly because the diversification and portfolio management are built-in, making it easy for novice investor and expert alike. Stock mutual funds are considered by many to be the absolute best buy for long-term financial investment (Quinn, 1991). Jane Bryant Quinn is adamantly enthusiastic about mutual funds; her list of reasons is so definitive that it is summarized here.

1. You get full-time money management from the person or committee who runs the fund. Brokers ... don't have time to worry about the overall shape of your investment.

2. You can pick exactly the level of risk you want to take. By contrast, when you buy your own stocks, you generally have no idea how risky your total investment position is.

3. You share in the fortunes of a large number of securities rather than owning just a few.

4. You can check a fund's past performance record.

5. You can buy and hold for the long term. There's no need to switch from one stock to another as market conditions change. Your mutual-fund manager does that for you.

6. You don't have to spend a lot of time doing stock research and following market conditions.

7. You avoid all the costly risks of falling into the hands of a bad broker—churning, bad recommendations, high sales commissions, and so on.

8. You can automatically reinvest your dividends and capital gains. Steady compounding doubles and redoubles the returns that you would get from stocks alone.

9. Mutual funds are easy to understand. You can pick good funds yourself, without having to pay for advice.

Profits from mutual funds come from three sources: a share of stock dividends; a share of interest on bonds or other holdings of the fund; and a share of the capital gains when assets in the portfolio are sold.

Some funds charge a sales commission (or load) at the time of purchase. Others may charge an exit fee. Most independent advisers recommend saving the commission expense by buying no-load mutual funds, since numerous load and no-load funds perform equally well.

Bonds

Buying stocks means buying a piece of a company. Bonds, on the other hand, are debt investments; that is, owning a bond means lending money to a company or some other entity. Bonds are issued by a corporation that wants to borrow money. Typically, federal, state, and local governments, corporations, and other organizations sell bonds, often in blocks of $1,000, to finance multi-million-dollar projects or other initiatives. The face amount, say $1,000 or $5,000, is the amount the issuer promises to pay back at the date of maturity. In the meantime, the issuer pays interest to the holder, usually twice a year. The risk is in the possibility that the issuer will default. To determine a bond's safety rating, refer to a rating organization such as Fitch Investors Service, Moody's Investors Service, or Standard & Poor's. These services publish their ratings, which are available in public libraries and brokerage houses. Retirement investors should stay with high-grade bonds or invest in high quality bond mutual funds.

The interest rate is set at the time the bond is issued. Another risk in bond investments is that interest rates may rise, leaving the bond holder with a low interest bond. The bond will still yield its face value at maturity, but if it is sold before maturing, its value would be discounted to compensate the new buyer for its lower interest pay out.

Real Estate

The primary home. Even though the dominant choice for a home is based on many non-financial criteria, such as architectural style, location, and proximity to family, any real estate holding is an investment. The growth of the retirement market has spawned increasing alternatives in housing opportunities. One growing area for retired people is the retirement community. Many of these are planned communities in which restrictive covenants are placed on the unit, limiting its use, occupancy, and other features. Many appear to be attractive but should be carefully investigated.

One of the largest real estate scams ever involved retirement communities that were built in the South and marketed to retirees in other states. The prices were greatly inflated, and the promoters took great pains to isolate the potential buyers and prevent them from obtaining independent information on competitive prices in the area. The scams included fraudulent, certified appraisals that corroborated the inflated values of the proposed units. Most retirement communities are not scams, but one should consider the following. Be wary of:

1. Overly slick promotional materials
2. Developments that are in the very early stages of construction
3. Requirements for large deposits on yet-to-be-built units
4. Inflated prices, compared to competing developments
5. High pressure sales tactics that require an immediate commitment or deposit
6. Projects that market to out-of-state buyers; developers know that local buyers will be more familiar with market prices and therefore less easy to deceive
7. Retirement communities that are far removed from other developed areas; costs of bringing in power, roads, and water may be prohibitive

Home equity. Considering the family home as a source of retirement income works if the home is to be sold with the proceeds turned into an annuity or other income-producing investment. If the owners plan to stay in the home, they can benefit from income in the form of a reverse equity mortgage. The Federal National Mortgage Association (Fannie Mae) program is known as the Home Equity Conversion Mortgage. Under this program, the home owners receive monthly payments or a line of credit secured by the equity in their home. Payments to the owners can be made until the credit limit is reached, and the owner is not required to repay the loan during his or her lifetime. The bank cannot foreclose on the property until the borrower moves out or dies. The unpaid balance accrues interest until repaid. In addition, Fannie Mae insures that the balance on the loan will not exceed the value of the home. If it does, Fannie Mae pays the difference to the lender. This protects the borrower and his or her estate from any deficiency judgment and guarantees that the lender will be repaid for the full balance on the loan. There may be an additional monthly servicing fee. This program is relatively new, strictly regulated, and may be difficult to qualify for.

For more information on Home Equity Conversion Mortgages, one can obtain, "Money From Home" from Fannie Mae (see Additional Reading).

To figure the equity in a home, figure the difference between the fair market value (less selling expenses such as commissions) and the balance on any existing mortgages.

Protecting the home investment. Elderly people are increasingly the targets for con artists. One recent scam involving elderly home owners is the home improvement and hidden mortgage trick. In this con a "home improvement expert" agrees to do certain repairs on the home. Typically there is a barrage of paperwork for the home owner to sign, and one of the documents will be a mortgage on the owner's property that gives the holder the right to foreclose if payments are not made. The estimated amount of the repairs is highly exaggerated, the repairs may never be made or are done partially or poorly, and the scammer ends up with the house when the owner cannot or refuses to pay.

A consumer should never sign a contract unless all blanks are filled in and the contract is fully understood. Reading the fine print, taking extra care to understand legal jargon, and having a legal adviser go over the contract will prevent many scams. It is also a good idea to look into the history and credentials of anyone with whom one does business.

Investing in Real Estate for Retirement

Real estate has been the source for more millionaire fortunes in the United States than any other type of investment vehicle. It is also risky, requiring more sophistication and management than other more passive investments such as CDs, mutual funds, or bonds. A cardinal rule is that an investor should never invest in anything he or she does not understand. With this in mind, much care should be exercised before proceeding. Many investors have suffered serious losses in limited partnership real estate ventures and other complex investments, some of which are heavily promoted by brokerage houses and other financial service providers. Prudently scrutinizing the prospectus and the projects will help, but one must be very familiar with the markets as well.

An excellent resource on commercial real estate investing is J. K. Lasser's *Real Estate Investment Guide* (Barr and McGee, 1989). Many other books and seminars abound on this subject, too complex and extensive to go into here.

For investors who are willing to educate themselves, take some risk, and commit time and energy to active management, there are many opportunities for hands-on real estate investing. Meeting with a local real estate investment association may provide excellent opportunities to learn from experienced investors. Meetings are often advertised under commercial real estate investing in the classified ads of local newspapers.

Real estate has been the source for more millionaire fortunes in the United States than any other type of investment vehicle. It is also risky, requiring more sophistication and management than other more passive investments such as CDs, mutual funds, or bonds.

Investments to Avoid

Limited partnerships allow an investor to share the profits or losses from a passive investment in large businesses such as cable TV, oil, or real estate. The investment is passive, in that none of the business decisions are made by the investor. In general, limited partnerships have been proved over the years to be extremely risky. Over 50 percent of limited partnerships in film, theater, agricultural equipment, agriculture, and oil and gas lose money (Petras, 1991). About $130 billion was taken from limited partners in the 1980s, and much of that money vanished due to failure or was pocketed by sharks (Quinn, 1991). Limited partnerships are also highly non-liquid, carry high commissions (often 20 percent to 30 percent), and are ordinarily not tax deductible. The common advice is that only rich and truly adept business people should venture into these precarious waters.

Over-the-phone, television, and high-pressure solicitation for investment should be avoided. Choosing a broker or an investment is a task involving careful research and scrutiny, not a choice to be made on the whim of a pushy telephone call. Commodities, buying on margin, and collectibles are also much too volatile and risky to be worthwhile for most investors. When considering any investment, read the fine print and do in-depth research. A. M. Best (a rating service whose reference books are available in the public library) and other authorities should be well employed when making important investment decisions.

Working with Brokers

No agent or adviser can possibly know enough about any investor's present circumstances and future needs to provide a comprehensive investment plan. Trusting a broker or salesperson with one's life savings and future security is risky if not foolish. There is a vital difference in motivation, attention, and even perception when dealing with another's assets than when one's own fortune is at stake. A stockbroker can make you or—quite literally—break you. The less you know about investing, the more breakable you are (Quinn, 1991).

Much investing and earning can be accomplished without a broker—through no-load mutual funds and Treasury securities. It is best to choose a stockbroker based on how one invests. Dedicated stock traders and serious long-term investors use discount brokers. Anyone who picks his or her own stocks and knows how to get the scoop on Wall Street can save money with discount brokers.

When looking for advice, ideas, research on the companies, and explanations for the market dipping (or soaring), a full-service broker is needed.

It is important to remember, however, that these people receive substantial commissions on customers' buying and selling. Their income is not dependent on the client's success.

Choosing a stockbroker involves gathering information from friends and associates, especially those who share investment objectives with the investor. Those brokers who have been in the business for fifteen years or so have the experience of a variety of different market conditions. Interviewing prospective brokers for experience, honesty, success, and a good fit with one's goals is paramount, as well as interviewing some of his or her clients. Another criterion is the amount and frequency with which a broker sends information on owned and recommended stocks. One cannot spend too much time or be too thorough in this research. The investor should check all information the prospective broker gives and never allow himself or herself to be intimidated for asking in-depth questions. Any broker who resists, who is inexperienced, or has any questionable background should be crossed off the list.

Keeping good communication with the broker will help him or her to become well acquainted with the investor's goals and plans. After working with the broker to decide on a plan that balances income, growth, and risk, a letter documenting the plan should be signed by both parties and saved for reference. Each purchase and sale will be confirmed in writing so that what was advised can be proved later. Keeping notes on all conversations will help keep the broker on track, especially if he or she knows the notes are carefully written and saved. Finally, for any buy or sell advice, the broker should be asked how the suggestions he or she makes will fit into the overall plan of investment.

After choosing a broker, one must continue to do research on stocks, companies, and all the data that go into picking and winning with stocks. The faster one learns to make good choices, the sooner the commissions can be saved by using a discount broker.

Many experienced investors have accounts with more than one broker. They might use a full-service broker for transactions when they need advice or research. If they are doing their own research and making their own decisions, the trades will be made with a discount broker. If one is going to invest in bonds, a broker that specializes in that area should be sought, since bond investing requires unique expertise, just as real estate investing is unique.

● INSURANCE DECISIONS

There are essentially two types of life insurance, term and cash value. Whereas they both afford protection, the rates for cash value are higher, because a portion of the premium is an investment.

The benefits of a life insurance policy are usually not paid to the person who is insured. It is the surviving beneficiaries who normally receive the proceeds to replace the income loss resulting from the death of the insured. In forgetting that it is the beneficiaries who profit from the policy can cause a misplaced emphasis on the potential to accumulate savings in a cash-value policy. Measured by the cost of coverage per year, it is term insurance that provides more protection per premium dollar than cash-value life insurance.

One needs life insurance only if he or she has dependents who would not be able to replace lost income resulting from premature death. If both husband and wife earn an income, each probably should have insurance. Business owners may need life insurance to cover business debts and taxes that might otherwise become the obligation of survivors.

To determine the amount of coverage that will meet the dependents' needs, one should calculate the expected Social Security benefits, surviving spouse's earnings, and any other income sources. The gap between the family's total projected cost of living and the total expected income is the amount of coverage that will be adequate in the case of a wage earner's premature death. By repeating the calculation every few years, one can evaluate the policy relative to the prevailing rate of inflation, life-style changes, and shifts in the family's income, expenditures, assets, and liabilities.

Term Insurance

The sole purpose of term insurance is protection. The goal is to replace lost wages and meet anticipated expenses. While the cost of a premium rises each year, the policy probably will not be needed after retirement. By then, other sav-

> There are essentially two types of life insurance, term and cash value. Whereas they both afford protection, the rates for cash value are higher, because a portion of the premium is an investment.

ings, pensions, and Social Security payments will be available.

The fact that term rates are lower than cash-value rates in the early years means that a higher amount of coverage can be bought for the same premium dollar. The money saved by buying term insurance can then be put into some investment vehicle with a higher yield than can be achieved in a cash-value policy. Since life insurance agents earn higher commissions selling cash-value policies, some agents may steer consumers to buying insurance with less coverage per premium dollar.

Life insurance is needed after retirement only if it is expected that the spouse and dependent children will need income other than pensions, Social Security, and investment income. Over a period of twenty or thirty years, most other investment vehicles will outperform cash-value accumulations as a hedge against inflation.

Any term insurance policy should be renewable as long as it may be needed. If it is convertible, it can be exchanged for a cash value policy without a health examination. Information on finding the lowest cost term insurance is available from the National Insurance Consumer Organization, 121 North Payne St., Alexandria, VA 22314.

Cash-Value Life Insurance

After age 65, cash-value policy rates become more affordable than term insurance. Term policies are prohibitive in later years and are sometimes not available at any price.

There are five major types of cash-value life insurance:

1. *Traditional Whole Life.* A good policy usually earns a yield in the neighborhood of 4 percent to 6 percent, although some may go as high as 8 percent. This is comparable to other conservative investments. The option is avail-

able to buy a smaller paid-up policy by applying the cash value to paying off the premiums for a specified number of years. For example, if $1,000 in cash value has been accumulated at a certain point, that $1,000 might be applied to the purchase of future coverage.

2. *Interest Sensitive Whole Life Insurance.* This is a good type to buy if one wants to use life insurance as an investment vehicle. The cash values in this kind of policy may increase faster than they do with Traditional Whole Life, thus probably producing a higher investment yield.

3. *Mixed Whole Life and Term.* Different ratios of Whole Life and Term are available. It is good for people who will need coverage after age 65 but still want to benefit from lower premiums in the earlier years.

4. *Universal Life Insurance.* These policies can be maintained by a variable premium each year, which adjusts the coverage and the investment yield. Yield rates are guaranteed at only 4 percent to 6 percent. It is hard to keep track of the variations in the yield, which is a disadvantage resulting from the option to vary the size of the premium.

5. *Universal Variable Life Insurance.* In this type the death benefit and cash values vary with the performance of the investments. If the performance is less than adequate, it may be necessary to increase the premium just to keep the policy in force. The investment side of these policies is more important to the insurance company than the benefits side. It must be remembered that they carry high overhead and administrative expenses before interest is applied.

When to Choose Cash-Value Policies

One could well conclude that an uninformed layman cannot evaluate and select cash-value policies in any reliable way. Computer-generated policy value projections will most certainly prove overly generous in time, and cost indexes adjusted for inflation may be no more accurate. Yet there are circumstances when cash-value policies can have some advantages. If all tax-deductible, tax-deferred savings plans are being used to their legal limit, and if one has secured all the term insurance he or she needs but still wants more coverage, and if one finds a policy

with relatively low commission and sales expenses, then a cash-value policy may be advisable.

The National Insurance Consumer Organization publishes a guide to buying both term and cash-value policies: *Taking the Bite Out of Insurance: How to Save Money on Life Insurance.*

Living-Benefits Life Insurance

Some life insurance policies allow the owner to withdraw a part of the coverage, if struck by certain major diseases like cancer and Alzheimer's. And some offer a monthly payment, if the policyholder enters a nursing home for the rest of his or her life. For now, these living benefits are available only with cash-value, not term, policies.

In summary, it is best to build up investment equity in a vehicle other than life insurance. Life insurance should be bought for pure protection. Employer-sponsored life insurance should be seen as a welcome extra but not totally relied upon, because it probably will be terminated if the employee leaves the company. Getting sufficient and dependable coverage means having one's own policy.

Organizations

Federal National Mortgage Association (FNMA)
Customer Education Group
3900 Wisconsin Ave., NW
Washington, DC 20016-2899

Institute for Certified Financial Planners
2 Denver Highlands
10065 East Harvard Ave.
Suite 320
Denver, CO 80231
(303) 751-7600

Internal Revenue Service
Call toll free 800-424-1040 or check the government section of your local phone book. Request free publications.

National Council on the Aging, Inc.
Retirement Planning Program
409 Third St., SW
Washington, DC 20024
(202) 479-6971

Pension Rights Center

918 16th St., NW
Suite 704
Washington, DC 20006
(202) 296-3776

References

Barr, Gary, and Judith Headington McGee. *J. K. Lasser's Real Estate Investment Guide*. New York: Simon & Schuster, 1989.

FannieMae Customer Education Group. *Money from Home: A Consumer's Guide to Home Equity Conversion Mortgages*. Washington, DC: Federal Publications, 1992.

Mundis, Jerrold. *How to Get Out of Debt, Stay Out of Debt, and Live Prosperously*. New York: Bantam Books, 1990.

Petras, Kathryn, and Ross Petras. *The Only Retirement Guide You'll Ever Need*. New York: Poseidon Press, 1991.

Quinn, Jane Bryant. *Making the Most of Your Money*. New York: Simon & Schuster, 1991.

Tobias, Andrew. "Managing Your Money" (computer software). Fairfield, CT: Mecca Software, 1992.

Additional Reading

American Association of Retired Persons (AARP). *A Guide to Understanding Your Pension Plan*. Single copies are available free from AARP, 601 E St., NW, Washington, DC 20049, (202) 434-2277.

American Bar Association. *Attorney's Guide to Home Equity Conversion*. Washington, DC: American Bar Association Commission on Legal Problems for the Elderly, 1992.

Bamford, Janet, and others. *Complete Guide to Managing Your Money*. Mount Vernon: Consumers Union, 1989.

Bernstein, Peter W., ed. *The Arthur Young Tax Guide*. New York: Ballantine Books, 1992.

Breitbard, Stanley, and Donna Sammons Carpenter. *The Price Waterhouse Book of Personal Financial Planning*. New York: Henry Holt, 1988.

Brown, Judith N., and Christina Baldwin. *A Second Start: A Widow's Guide to Financial Survival at a Time of Emotional Crisis*. New York: Simon & Schuster, 1987.

Callahan, David P., and Peter J. Strauss. *Estate and Financial Planning for the Aging or Incapacitated Client*. New York: Practicing Law Institute, 1990.

CCH Tax Law Editors. *1992 U.S. Master Tax Guide*. Chicago: Commerce Clearing House, 1991.

Cooper's and Lybrand. *The Cooper's & Lybrand Guide to Business Tax Strategies Planning*. New York: Simon & Schuster, 1990.

Dowd, Merle E. *A Consumer's Guide to Financial Planning*. New York: Franklin Watts, 1987.

Esperti, Robert A., and Renno L. Peterson. *Loving Trust: The Right Way to Provide for Yourself and Guarantee the Future of Your Loved Ones*. New York: Viking, 1988.

Federal Trade Commission. *The Law and Us*. Washington, DC: Federal Publications, 1989.

Givens, Charles J. *Financial Self-Denfense: How to Win the Fight for Financial Freedom*. New York: Simon & Schuster, 1990.

Gordon, Harley. *How to Protect Your Life Savings from Catastrophic Illness and Nursing Homes*. Boston: Financial Planning Institute, 1991.

Hardy, Dorcas R., and C. Colburn Hardy. *Social Insecurity: The Crisis in America's Social Security System and How to Plan Now for Your Own Financial Survival*. New York: Villare Books, 1991.

Institute of Certified Financial Planners. *Avoiding Investment and Financial Scams: Seeking Full Disclosure Is the Key*. Denver, CO: Institute of Certified Financial Planners, 1991.

Jacobs, Sheldon. *The Handbook for No-Load Fund Investors*. The No-Load Fund Investor, Inc., P.O. Box 283, Hastings-on-Hudson, NY, 10706. Published annually.

Mercer, William M. *1993 Guide to Social Security and Medicare*. Louisville, KY: William M. Mercer, Inc., 1992.

Miller, Theodore J. *Invest Your Way to Wealth*. Washington, DC: The Kiplinger Washington Editors, Inc., 1992.

National Council on the Aging. *Retirement Planning Program* (workbook). Washington, DC: The National Council on the Aging, 1993.

Porter, Sylvia. *Sylvia Porter's Your Finances in the 1990s*. New York: Simon & Schuster, 1987.

Raphaelson, Elliot, and Debra Raphaelson West. *How to Be Your Own Financial Planner*. Glenview, IL: Scott, Foresman, 1990.

Regan, John J. *Your Legal Rights in Later Life*. Washington, DC: American Association of Retired Persons, 1989.

Sayles, Jennie Polo. *How to Marry the Rich*. Little Rock, AR: GEMar Publications, 1989.

Shane, Dorlene V., and the United Seniors Health Cooperative. *Finances After Fifty*. New York: Harper & Row, 1989.

Shilling, Dana, and John Hancock Financial Services. *Real Life, Real Answers*. New York: John Hancock Financial Services, 1988.

South Carolina National Bank. *The Book of Loans*. 1992.

TimeValue Software. "T-Value" (computer software). Irvine, CA: TimeValue Software, 1992.

Updegrave, Walter L. *How to Keep Your Savings Safe: Protecting the Money You Can't Afford to Lose*. New York: Crown, 1992.

Weaver, Peter, and Annette Buchanan. *What to Do With What You've Got: The Practical Guide to Money Management in Retirement*. Washington, DC: American Association of Retired Persons, and Scott, Foresman, 1984.

Weinstein, Grace W. *The Lifetime Book of Money Management*. Detroit: Gale Research, 1993.

Lois Fuller, B.A., with assistance from Paul King

14

Asset Management: Preserving the Retiree's Standard of Living

● Risks and Returns of Investing ● Risk Management ● Asset Allocation

All older Americans desire to maintain or even improve their standard of living after retirement. During the retirement years, money has to work for the retiree, instead of the person working for money. The moneys now working were set aside in retirement plans and private savings vehicles or contributed to Social Security. This chapter focuses on the funds under the retiree's direct control—personal assets. These funds are very important for two main reasons. First, asset income accounts for an ever-increasing share of the funds available to retirees. Whereas only 54 percent of households headed by those 65 and over had asset income in 1962, 69 percent received asset income in 1990. Furthermore, asset income is the second largest source of funds for the 65-plus population, after Social Security. In 1990 Social Security provided the largest portion of money income—36 percent; asset income provided 24 percent. The remainder is mostly attributable to pensions and earnings.

During the retirement years, money has to work for the retiree, instead of the person working for money.

There is a second reason for paying particular attention to the retiree's asset income. Not only has the role of asset income grown—with more retirees deriving asset income, and asset income constituting a growing portion of overall earnings—but asset income also tends to play a pivotal role in maintaining a retiree's standard of living. In many cases pension income takes the form of an annuity, providing equal payments that do not rise with inflation. Social Security, though currently indexed to inflation, may lag behind or even, at some point, lose that feature. Furthermore, even current indexation typically does not keep up with the cost increases actually experienced by retirees. Thus retirees face the difficult task of managing their self-controlled financial assets in such fashion that this portion of their wealth remains particularly responsive to inflation. Yet retirees tend to be conservative in their attitude toward investments, with primary emphasis on preservation of principal. This dilemma typically lies at the root of most retirees' fear of outliving their financial resources. It is the purpose of this chapter to explore asset management techniques that allow retirees to stay ahead of inflation, while barely overstepping the limits set by their typical cautiousness.

● RISKS AND RETURNS OF INVESTING

All investments establish a relationship between a person with disposable money and an entity in need of money. Contractually this relationship assumes one of two basic forms. The investor (i.e., the person with disposable money)

uses his or her funds to buy into a viable enterprise and assume the position of part owner, or lends money to the organization and becomes a creditor. In the first case the investor receives a certificate of ownership (stock) and the right to receive dividends. In the second case the investor receives a negotiable promissory note (bond) stating the exact terms of compensation during the term of the note and the date when the note will be redeemed. In the first case the new owner of an ongoing enterprise hopes for growth and change; his or her returns will move with the fortunes of his company. By contrast, the creditor to a company expects and hopes for high levels of stability, to safeguard the promises received in exchange for his or her money. The consequences from these two types of relationships are quite obvious. The investor-turned-owner assumes the risk inherent in the ownership of any undertaking, and he or she participates in all future growth. The investor turned creditor assumes little risk, if any, but he or she also does not participate in the company's growth. Investment performance data demonstrate the difference.

Investment Return

After subjecting the returns obtained through ownership of U.S. stocks to the ravages of inflation, Table 14.1 shows the average annual compound returns for the period from 1926 to 1991 (Ibbotson Associates Inc., 1992).

Table 14.1
Stock Owners Average Annual Compound Returns, 1926–91

Type of Stock	Rate of Return (adjusted for inflation)
Common stocks	7.0%
Small stocks	8.7%

On the other hand, bond holders, that is, lenders to the U.S. government and to U.S. corporations, obtained the results in Table 14.2.

The retiree who holds only bonds and uses the income from these bonds actually uses up principal. If the owner of corporate bonds withdraws income of, say, 6 percent annually, and the inflation adjusted total return on these bonds is only

Table 14.2
Bond Holders Average Annual Compound Returns, 1926–91

Type of Bond	Rate of Return (inflation adjusted)
Long-term corporate bonds	2.2%
Long-term government bonds	1.6%
Intermediate government bonds	1.9%
U.S. Treasury bills	0.05%

2.2 percent (see Table 14.2), then the retiree has used 3.8 percent of his or her principal on an inflation-adjusted basis in order to cover his or her income needs. This simple computation does not even take taxes on bond income into consideration. Thus the entire notion of preservation of principal has to be rethought. Instead of considering principal in nominal terms, it is imperative that the retiree think of preservation of principal in "real," that is, inflation-adjusted terms. The data in the tables demonstrate convincingly that the ownership of stocks is more likely to keep the retiree's money whole. Thus some ownership of stocks is essential to the financial well-being of every retiree.

There is another consideration. To maintain one's standard of living, the retiree needs to be able to fund his or her purchases and expenses. The retiree may want or need a new car, new clothes, food, medicine, etc. The prices of these goods and services are subject to inflation. As the retiree is inevitably a consumer of goods and services, he or she should just as inevitably be the owner of companies providing these goods and services. Instead of being merely at the mercy of the companies charging ever higher prices, the retiree can also participate in the profits generated by such increasing prices. Through ownership of these companies, the retiree reassumes some of the control over the living expenses that he or she has ceded to inflation.

Investment Risks

Now the other side of the coin: As most retirees are painfully aware, the ownership of stocks in U.S. or foreign companies requires a different mind-set than does the ownership of bonds and other fixed investments. The word "risk" immediately comes to mind. Whenever retirees discuss the ownership of stocks, they will talk about the risk involved and will describe themselves as conservative and risk-averse. Most retirees neither fully understand the nature of risk nor the techniques to manage such risk.

First of all, investment returns are directly linked to the amount of risk assumed. The inflation-adjusted investment data shown in Tables 14.1 and 14.2 make the point. Statistically, risk is measured through standard deviations. A standard deviation measures the likely range of investment returns, in deviation from an average annual return. U.S. stocks, over long periods of time, provide an average annual return of 10 to 12 percent. This average annual return is a mere benchmark. Actual returns will deviate from the average return. An asset's standard deviation measures the likely amplitude of the swings away from its average return. The wider the amplitude, the less predictable an investment return, the higher the risk; and vice versa.

About 68 percent of the time investment returns will fall within plus or minus one standard deviation of the expected return, and about 96 percent of the time the returns will fall within plus or minus two standard deviations of the expected return. Table 14.3 shows the compound annual return and standard deviation for U.S. common stocks between 1926 and 1991. The mean one-year return for stocks has been 12.4 percent. The standard deviation has been 20.8 percent. These data allow the following conclusion: During any one-year period, there is a 68 percent likelihood that U.S. common stocks will provide returns ranging between 12.4 percent plus 20.8 percent, and 12.4 percent minus 20.8

percent. In other words, returns are likely to be somewhere between positive 33.2 and negative 8.4 percent. It is this rather wide range of likely returns that frightens investors. However, financial markets will reward the investor in exact proportion to the amount of risk he or she is willing to assume, that is, in exact proportion to the range of returns that an investor can tolerate. An investor who cannot assume any risk at all and must have entirely predictable returns will want to consider Treasury bills (see Chapter 13). The standard deviation on Treasury bills is only 3.4 percent, thus about one-sixth the risk of that assumed by the stock owner. The return is, of course, equally low. In contrast to stocks' mean return of 12.4 percent, Treasury bills' mean return is 3.8 percent.

Figure 14.1 tells the same story using a different "language." It charts the growth of a hypothetical $1 investment made on December 31, 1925, in five different asset classes. Stocks obviously provided the largest increase in wealth by a huge margin. The $1 investment in the Standard & Poor's 500 (an index of the stock performance of 500 leading U.S. companies) increased by over 600 times to $675.59. The small stock investment grew to an even more impressive $1,847.63. By contrast, fixed income investments provided only a fraction of this growth. Cash equivalents basically kept up with inflation, but no more. From a purely visual standpoint, Figure 14.1 understates the difference in total returns. The graph uses a logarithmic scale, where equal percentage changes show up as equal vertical distances, in contrast to a linear scale where equal percentage changes show up as different vertical distances.

Table 14.3
Summary Statistics, 1926–91

	Compound return	Arithmetic mean	Risk (Standard deviation)
Small stocks	12.1%	17.5%	35.3%
Common stocks	10.4	12.4	20.8
Municipal bonds	3.8	4.2	10.9
Corporate bonds	5.4	5.7	8.5
Long-term government bonds	4.8	5.1	8.6
Treasury bills	3.7	3.8	3.4
Inflation	3.1	3.2	4.7

Source: Ibbotson Associates. *The Asset Allocation Decision.*

Figure 14.1
66 Years of Investment Performance

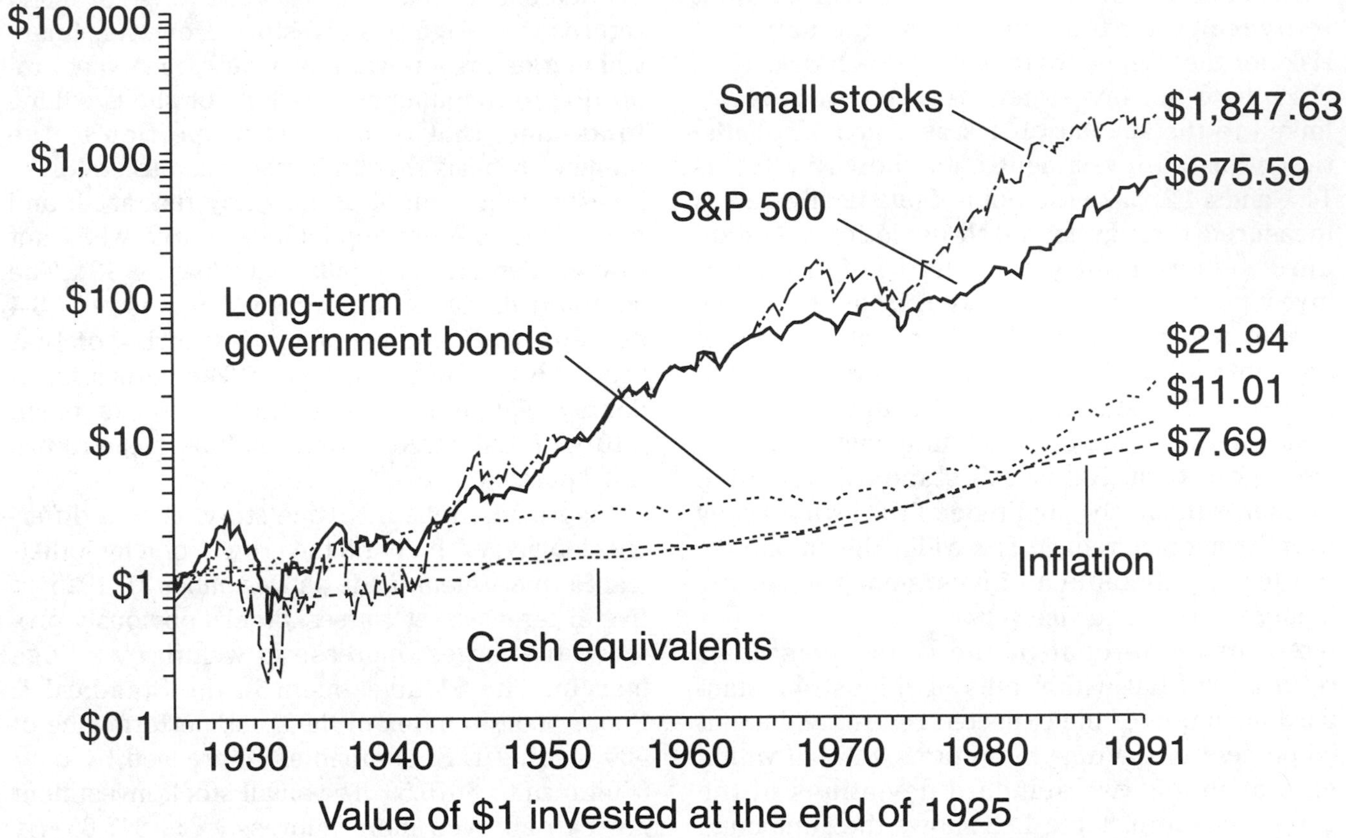

Value of $1 invested at the end of 1925

Source: "The Asset Allocation Decision." Ibbotson Associates, Chicago. Used with permission. All rights reserved.

The figure also demonstrates the price paid for higher returns. Both stock indices show relatively steep peaks and valleys, indicative of high levels of volatility on a month-to-month and year-to-year basis, giving a clear picture of the relationship between higher returns and higher risk (standard deviation), and vice versa.

● **RISK MANAGEMENT**

Retired investors must make sure that their investment assets keep growing with the economy and stay ahead of inflation. Growth is absolutely necessary, and growth is inexorably linked to risk. Once this direct correlation is fully understood, the question is no longer whether or not to assume risk but how to manage it. Or, in other words, the investor will ask how he or she can be sure to assume no more than the risk necessary to obtain a competitive return.

In order to better understand and manage risk, several basic techniques for risk reduction should

be explored. The significance of different time horizons should be considered and the concept of asset allocation should be closely analyzed.

Retired investors must make sure that their investment assets keep growing with the economy and stay ahead of inflation. Growth is absolutely necessary, and growth is inexorably linked to risk.

Time Horizons

Time is the first important consideration. Whereas investment returns and investment risk are typically measured for one-year periods, it is important to consider longer time periods—for example, five years. When an investor looks at five-year returns, a very different picture emerges, and with currently longer life expectancies, five-year time periods are also appropriate for retired investors.

In considering five-year rolling returns for stocks beginning in 1926, the first such period runs from 1926 through 1930, the second from 1927 through 1931. Within this five-year context, the mean return on the S&P 500 is 10 percent, and the standard deviation is a low 8.4 percent. The risk has been reduced to less than half the risk assumed over one-year periods, while the return decreased only 2 percent (see Figure 14.2). A focus on longer time horizons thus provides a very different perspective. Short-term price fluctuations, when seen within a context of longer periods, become less troublesome. Thinking within longer time periods has another benefit: The individual is less likely to commit the cardinal sin of all investors, the sin of buying high and selling low. The investor with a short time horizon is likely to be frightened by volatility and sell a stock investment at a low point. Similarly, a short-term oriented investor tends to get caught up in the excitement of an upward move and is likely to buy at the top. Equipped with a longer-term perspective, the investor will not give in to the temptation to dump an investment that is temporarily depressed nor to buy an investment temporarily overpriced.

Risk Management Techniques

Certain strategies can support the investor in his or her longer time horizon, including two frequently recommended, simple, and effective risk management techniques.

The first strategy combines the purchase of common stocks with the purchase of U.S. Treasury zero coupon bonds. Zero coupon bonds are stripped of all interest payments and are sold at a discount to their value at maturity. Such a bond, maturing at $1,000 five years hence, for example, could be bought today for $750. A very cautious investor may want to buy a number of discounted zero coupon bonds to mature five or ten years later at a value identical to the total amount invested today in common stocks and in zero coupon bonds. For example, one may want to put $7,500 into zeros and $2,500 into stocks. The five years in zeros will be worth $10,000, thus reconstituting the entire original capital outlay of $10,000. The inclusion of these bonds will help to manage the most significant risk factor in the

entire portfolio equation, namely the investor himself. If the investor knows that his or her capital will definitely be reconstituted at a certain point in time, regardless of stock market performance, he or she will be more likely to accept or ignore stock market volatility in the interim.

A second strategy not only helps reduce uncertainty and allay the fear of investment volatility but actually enhances the likeliness of strong long-term returns. Instead of investing a large sum of money in stocks all at once, fixed amounts can be invested at certain intervals of time, regardless of the direction of stock prices. As stock prices fluctuate, a fixed dollar amount will buy sometimes more and sometimes fewer shares. This process, called dollar-cost-averaging, brings a definite discipline to bear on the investment process. The investor automatically buys fewer shares when the prices are high and more shares when the prices are low, resulting in an average purchase price that is lower than the average market price over the same period of time. The investor who purchases shares wisely may actually come to regard stock market volatility as an ally, rather than an adversary. After all, lower stock market prices enable the investor to buy more shares.

Many mutual fund companies have developed automatic dollar-cost-averaging programs. Money is placed into a money market account and then transferred to stock accounts at periodic intervals. Except for authorizing the strategy initially, the investor need not be concerned with the process as it unfolds.

● ASSET ALLOCATION

Owning stocks in combination with other assets diminishes the problem of risk even further. To combine different types of stocks with different types of bonds, all with their own characteristics, is to practice the process of asset allocation.

Examples of different asset classes are large company stocks, small company stocks, and foreign stocks; corporate bonds, government bonds, and Treasury bills. When measuring the risk inherent in a portfolio holding several different asset classes, the portfolio's standard deviation is not a simple weighted average of the standard deviation for each included asset class. The actu-

Figure 14.2
Performance Data, 1926–1991

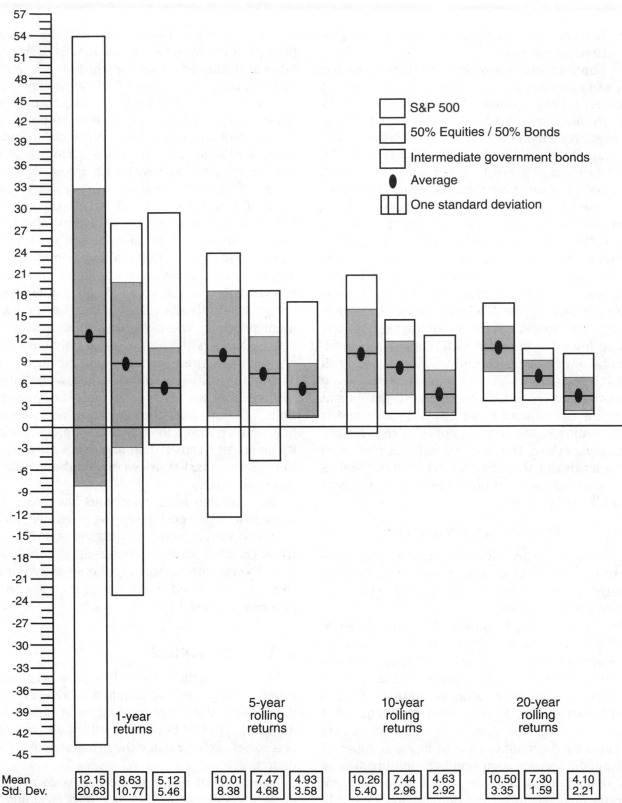

	1-year returns			5-year rolling returns			10-year rolling returns			20-year rolling returns		
Mean	12.15	8.63	5.12	10.01	7.47	4.93	10.26	7.44	4.63	10.50	7.30	4.10
Std. Dev.	20.63	10.77	5.46	8.38	4.68	3.58	5.40	2.96	2.92	3.35	1.59	2.21

Note: This information was derived from historical data taken from Ibbotson's *1992 Yearbook*. Figures shown here represent performance of the S&P 500 Index and Ibbotson's Intermediate Government Bond Index from 1926 through 1991. No implication or inference should be drawn by present or prospective clients that similar investment performance will occur in the future.

Source: Ibbotson Associates. *Stocks, Bonds, Bills, and Inflation: 1992 Yearbook*. Chicago: Ibbotson Associates, 1992.

al portfolio standard deviation will be lower than a weighted average. Such risk reduction is due to the simple fact that different investment classes react differently to identical economic circumstances. For example, stocks and Treasury bills react differently to high levels of inflation.

By choosing economically diverse asset classes, the investor chooses assets whose total returns are poorly correlated. Such poor correlation is highly desirable. Simultaneous moves by different asset classes, in different directions, will partially offset each other and thus reduce the overall volatility and risk of the portfolio. Diversification among asset classes ensures that at least part of the portfolio will always be in the right place at the right time. The result is a series of base hits rather than home runs, thereby increasing stability while achieving good results.

Figure 14.2 demonstrates two different types of factor relationships through a series of vertical bars. One set of relationships concerns the combination of different asset classes; the second concerns different time horizons.

Risk and return data are provided for two different asset classes: the S&P 500, standing for a U.S. common stock portfolio, and intermediate government bonds. In addition, a portfolio consisting of equal portions of these two asset classes is shown. The risk/return data for these three portfolios are shown for one-year, five-year, ten-year, and twenty-year periods. The vertical bars demonstrate volatility, by graphing standard deviations. In each case the shaded area represents one standard deviation, while the entire vertical bar shows the entire range of returns, the highest ever and the lowest. A mere glance at this graph reveals decreasing risk levels as time horizons lengthen. The risk characteristics for the portfolio containing 50 percent equities and 50 percent bonds are increasingly favorable as time horizons lengthen. Over five-year periods, the risk is barely higher than that of the portfolio holding only intermediate bonds. By contrast, the mean annual rate of return is approximately 2.5 percent higher. Even though most retirees are not willing to think in terms of twenty-year returns, it is still interesting to note that the risk relationship between these two portfolios is reversed with 20-year figures. The return on the mixed portfolio is not only 3.2 percent higher than that of the bond portfolio, but the risk is actually lower.

Asset Allocation Decision Making

All investors, and particularly retired investors, should actively engage themselves in the asset allocation decision underlying any portfolio construction. Approximately 92 percent of the total returns generated by any portfolio are due to the asset allocation decision, that is, to the particular asset classes included in a portfolio. Security selection, on the other hand, accounts for a mere 5 percent to 6 percent of the results obtained. For example, the choice of U.S. common stocks is all important; once the asset class is chosen, it is of very little significance which particular stocks (such as Kodak, General Electric, etc.) are chosen to represent that asset class. The only requirement is that the asset class be represented by a sufficiently large number of individual securities. If, for example, an insufficient number of securities (e.g., fewer than fifteen stocks) are chosen to represent a particular asset class, then an extra element of risk is added. The principles of asset allocation presuppose appropriate diversification within each asset class. Many investment advisers believe that diversification is best achieved through the use of mutual funds. For example, a mutual fund holding large company stocks would represent the asset class of large stocks.

While the asset allocation decision accounts for 92 percent of portfolio returns obtained, and security selection accounts for 5 percent to 6 percent, the remaining 2 percent to 3 percent are due to market timing. Market timing refers to the decision to buy or sell an asset class because of anticipated market moves. An investor may decide to sell stocks because he or she expects the stock market to decline. Market timing, even when practiced by experienced professionals, has frequently proven ineffective. A market timer needs to be accurate in his or her moves at least 70 percent of the time in order to match the returns obtained by someone simply holding an asset.

It is also important to remember that, within stock market cycles, most of the returns are obtained during the early part of an upswing, that is, at a time when most investors do not yet trust the new upward move. A study conducted by Ibbotson demonstrated that, whereas common stocks provided an average annual return of 10.3 percent during the thirty-year period of 1962 through 1991, a common stock investor who missed the 12 best months had an average annual return of only 5.4 percent. In other words, the investor who missed the 12 best months out of all 360 one-month periods saw his or her return cut in half. Furthermore, inflation averaged 5.2 percent over the same period. The unlucky investor who made only 5.4 percent thus barely broke even on an inflation-adjusted basis. Here is one more reason to stick with asset class allocations, once they have been determined and implemented.

When stressing asset allocation over security selection and market timing, the retired investor frequently acts counter to his or her natural instincts. The retiree's thinking about financial matters was probably formed in the 1960s and 1970s, when the primary focus of individual and institutional investors was on individual securities and possibly market timing. Most people still enjoy looking for a "hot stock" and are tempted to follow some wizard's pronouncement on the stock market's likely next move. Every investor is well advised to resist such hot tips and stay with his or her long-term asset allocation decision. The investor who takes advantage of modern research results no longer attempts to "beat the market" but rides with the market and takes advantage of differential moves among various asset classes.

Because the information and suggestions pro-

Figure 14.3
Portfolio Allocation Scoring System Version 3

	Strongly Agree	Agree	Neutral	Disagree	Strongly Disagree
1. Earning a high long-term total return that will allow my capital to grow faster than the inflation rate is one of my most important objectives.	5	4	3	2	1
2. I would like an investment that provides me with an opportunity to defer taxation of capital gains and/or interest to future years.	5	4	3	2	1
3. I do not require a high level of current income from my investments.	5	4	3	2	1
4. My major investment goals are relatively long-term.	5	4	3	2	1
5. I am willing to tolerate sharp up and down swings in the return on my investments in order to seek a potentially higher return than would normally be expected from more stable investments.	5	4	3	2	1
6. I am willing to risk a short-term loss in return for a potentially higher long-run rate of return.	5	4	3	2	1
7. I am financially able to accept a low level of liquidity in my investment portfolio.	5	4	3	2	1

Portfolio Allocation Models

Total Score	Money Market	Fixed Income	Equities
30–35	10%	10%	80%
22–29	20%	20%	60%
14–21	30%	30%	40%
7–13	40%	40%	20%

Source: Droms, William G., *Portfolio Allocation Scoring System, Version 3 (August 1988).*

It is also important to remember that, within stock market cycles, most of the returns are obtained during the early part of an upswing, that is, at a time when most investors do not yet trust the new upward move.

vided in this chapter are, of necessity, generic in nature, the retiree should talk to a trusted financial adviser about his specific situation. Every person's case is unique and should be considered carefully. In order to start the individual decision-making process, the questionnaire in Figure 14.3 may be helpful. A simple but effective Portfolio Allocation Scoring System was developed by William G. Droms, professor of finance at Georgetown University. The questions address the major issues encountered by retirees, including the need for capital growth, the investor's sensitivity to taxes, the need for current income and easy access to capital, the investor's time horizon, and risk tolerance levels. Many retirees who use this scoring system find that the results suggest a larger allocation to equities. Obviously, this scoring system is incomplete and should be regarded merely as a starting point, but it does provide a sense of the questions to be asked and of the individual's likely appropriate direction.

Example of Asset Allocation

Figure 14.4 first shows a portfolio containing only long-term government bonds. The risk is 11.7 percent, while the expected return is 5 percent. Such a portfolio is inherently "inefficient," since risk and return are not in equilibrium. Modern research has shown that certain levels of risk and certain levels of return go together. Every increment in risk taken by an investor should be rewarded with a commensurate increase in return. Conversely, a desired level of return should be obtained while incurring no more than the absolutely necessary amount of risk. Portfolios with risk and return in equilibrium are "effi-

Figure 14.4
Diversification and the Risk/Return Tradeoff

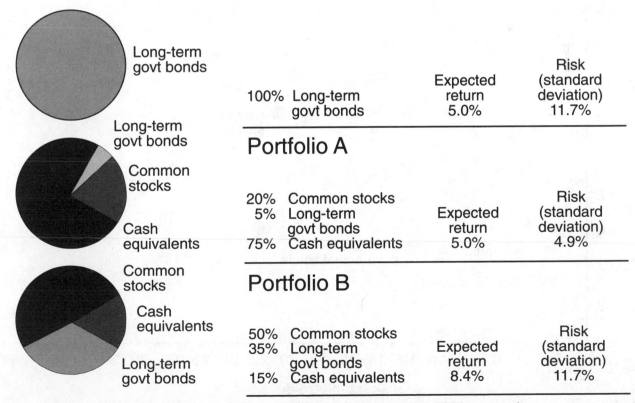

		Expected return	Risk (standard deviation)
100%	Long-term govt bonds	5.0%	11.7%

Portfolio A

		Expected return	Risk (standard deviation)
20%	Common stocks		
5%	Long-term govt bonds	5.0%	4.9%
75%	Cash equivalents		

Portfolio B

		Expected return	Risk (standard deviation)
50%	Common stocks		
35%	Long-term govt bonds	8.4%	11.7%
15%	Cash equivalents		

cient," while portfolios with non-aligned risk and return numbers are "inefficient." Just as efficiency in the modern workplace refers to an optimal relationship between effort and output, efficiency with regard to financial portfolios refers to an optimal relationship between risk (effort) and return (output).

Portfolio A in Figure 14.4 is based on the assumption that an expected return of 5 percent, obtained through ownership of long-term government bonds, is the desired result. Portfolio A achieves the desired return of 5 percent with less than half the risk. It does so by adding common stocks and cash to long-term government bonds. The risk-averse owner of Portfolio A, satisfied with a 5 percent return, has reduced his or her long-term government bond holdings to 5 percent, invested 75 percent in cash, and put 20 percent in common stocks. Interestingly, the inclusion of 20 percent common stocks reduces risk. Whereas the earlier emphasis was on the need to assume the risk inherent in stock ownership, the investment results shown in Figure 14.4 demonstrate that the inclusion of stocks in a conservative portfolio can actually reduce risk. Risk reduction in this case is largely due to the poor correlation between stocks and cash equivalents. For example, cash equivalents respond to inflation positively, with rates on cash increasing rapidly during inflationary times, whereas stocks tend to do poorly during highly inflationary times.

Portfolio B has been constructed for the investor willing to live with the 11.7 percent standard deviation of long-term government bonds. In order to achieve the return appropriate for this risk level, the long-term government bond position, originally 100 percent, has been reduced to 35 percent. The remainder of the portfolio consists of 15 percent cash equivalents and 50 percent common stocks. The resultant expected rate of return is 8.4 percent. When applying the portfolio's standard deviation, the returns are likely to

Figure 14.5
The Efficient Frontier

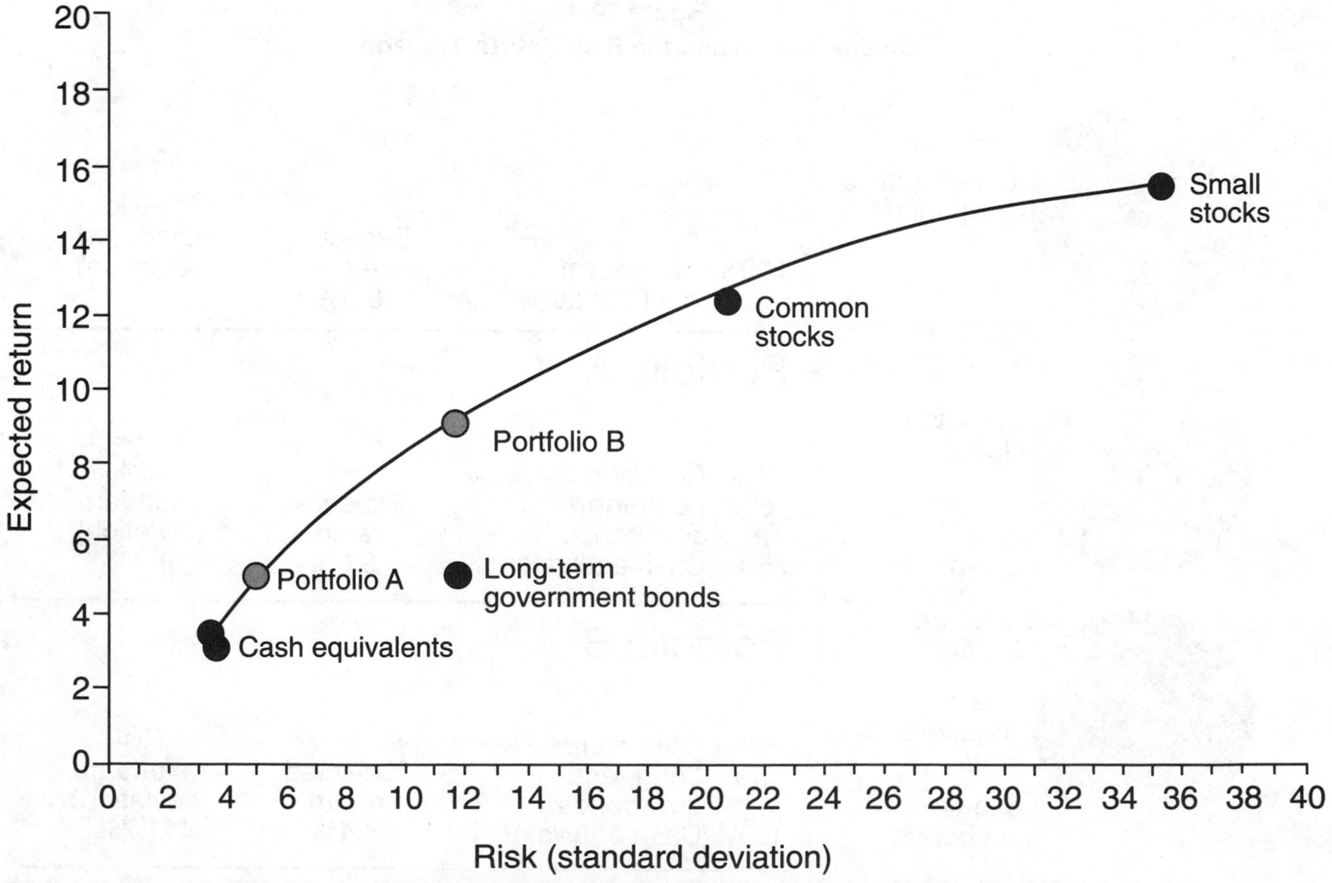

Source: Ibbotson Associates. *The Asset Allocation Decision.* Chicago. Used with permission. All rights reserved.

range from positive 20.1 percent to negative 3.3 percent. Instead of common stocks' normal 20.6 percent standard deviation, the combination of 50 percent common stocks with a mixture of short- and long-term bonds results in a standard deviation of less than half.

The Efficient Frontier

Figure 14.5 plots the risk/return relationships for various asset classes and for portfolios A and B. The graph's horizontal axis measures standard deviations, while the vertical axis measures expected returns. Of course, cash equivalents are in the southwest quadrant of the resultant graph, given the low risk and low return characteristics of this asset class. At the other end of the spectrum, small stocks are in the northeast quadrant, demonstrating high risk and high return. Each of the three asset classes (cash equivalents, common stocks, and small stocks) have optimal risk/return characteristics, with risk and return in equilibrium. They are efficient. A line connecting

these asset classes is called the efficient frontier. By contrast, a portfolio holding only long-term government bonds is inefficient. The graph demonstrates this with a location off the efficient frontier. Portfolios A and B, both located on the efficient frontier, improve upon a long-term government bond portfolio. Portfolio A is located west of the long-term government position, with risk substantially reduced. Portfolio B, on the other hand, is located due north, demonstrating increased return.

Balancing Risk and Returns

Figure 14.6 plots additional asset classes in risk/return space. The real estate portfolio shown here holds an equally weighted combination of business, farm, and residential real estate. Judging from this graph, it would appear that real estate has had higher returns and lower risks than either corporate or government bonds. However, the risk of real estate is understated by these data. Real estate return data are based on

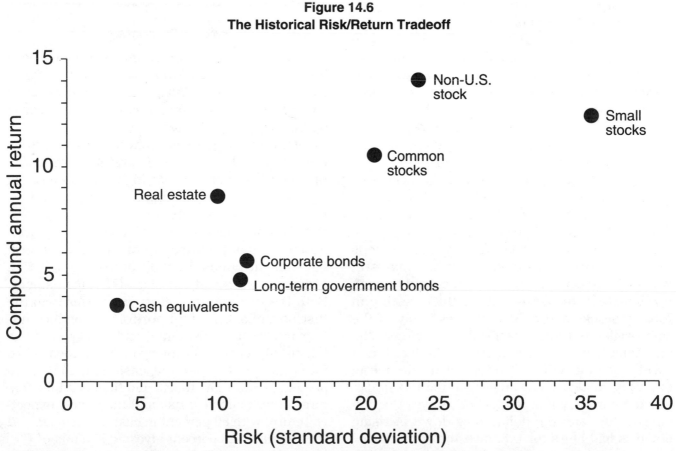

Figure 14.6
The Historical Risk/Return Tradeoff

appraisal values rather than actual prices. This method artificially smoothes the data and results in a standard deviation lower than that found in actual markets. On the other hand, the position plotted for non-U.S. stocks in risk/return space should be considered with great interest. Non-U.S. stocks and, incidentally, non-U.S. bonds offer very attractive risk/return characteristics. As the graph demonstrates, non-U.S. stocks have had a considerably lower standard deviation and a higher return than U.S. small stocks. Over the last twenty years, non-U.S. stocks have had a standard deviation of 24 percent and an annual compound rate of return of 14 percent. Similarly, non-U.S. bonds have had a standard deviation of 12 percent, the same as long-term U.S. government and U.S. corporate bonds, with a considerably higher 11 percent average rate of return .

Investing in Non-U.S. Stocks

Those investors who find it difficult to consider U.S. stocks may really balk at the mention of non-U.S. stocks. But since every retiree's desire to maintain his or her standard of living necessitates the ownership of some U.S. stocks, the same argument applies to foreign stock ownership. All of us are global consumers, because today it is extremely difficult to restrict our purchases to only domestic products. Currently, Honda (a Japanese company) builds its Accords in Ohio, but Chevrolet builds its Luminas in Canada. Products that may seem foreign to us actually have U.S. ties. Many U.S. companies rely on overseas sales to make their profits. Coca Cola now gets 75 percent of its earnings by selling its products around the world. General Motors may be losing money on its U.S. car sales but is profitable selling cars in Europe.

Even if the retiree concedes that he or she is indeed a global consumer, he or she may still worry about any additional risk assumed through foreign-stock ownership. Actually, investing in foreign stocks and bonds involves many of the same risks as buying domestic securities. The additional currency risk is due to the fact that a foreign stock will be traded on its domestic exchange in a currency other than the U.S. dollar. But the currency risk works both ways. The dollar goes up, and the dollar goes down. A rising dollar is bad news for U.S. investors with money overseas. A falling dollar is good news. If the dol-

lar falls, the same number of pounds (marks, francs, yen, etc.) will buy more dollars. It should also be noted that currency risk contributes to the additional diversification effect achieved through foreign-stock ownership. The correlation between non-U.S. stocks and U.S. common stocks is considerably lower than the correlation between U.S. small stocks and U.S. common stocks. Such lower correlation is highly desirable. Furthermore, over the last ten years (through the end of 1991) the U.S. stock market was never the best performer; rather, its best finish was second place in 1982. Of the eleven largest stock markets in the world, the U.S. market ranks at the bottom for average annual return.

All of us are global consumers, because today it is extremely difficult to restrict our purchases to only domestic products. Currently, Honda (a Japanese company) builds its Accords in Ohio, but Chevrolet builds its Luminas in Canada.

Portfolio Performance

Figure 14.7 incorporates international stocks into its highest risk/highest return portfolio. Every one of the shown portfolios is diversified and efficient, with different asset classes utilized optimally.

Again, an investor can choose from various portfolios with different risk/return levels. The first portfolio achieves its high returns entirely through stocks, approximately two-thirds U.S. common stocks, one-sixth U.S. small stocks, and one-sixth international stocks. The second portfolio includes approximately one-third long-term government bonds, in addition to one-half U.S. common stocks and one-sixth U.S. small stocks. Both the risk and the return are lower than the first portfolio. The third portfolio diversifies further into cash equivalents, and equity holdings fall to 40 percent; 60 percent are allocated to fixed income (40 percent cash equivalents, 20 percent bonds). The fourth and final portfolio features both the lowest risk and the lowest expected return, with 80 percent in cash equivalents and the remaining 20 percent invested in a mix of U.S. common stocks, U.S. small stocks, and govern-

Figure 14.7
Expected Portfolio Performance

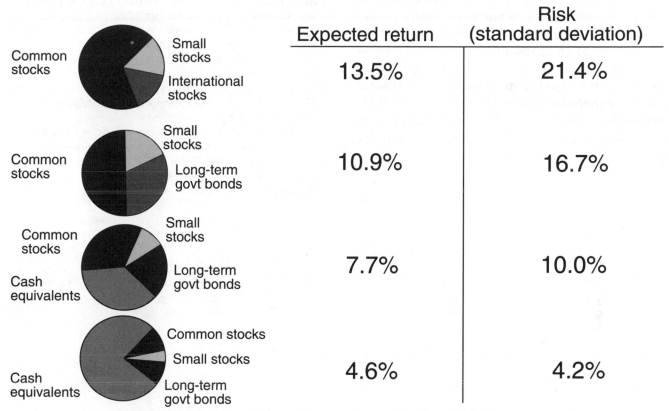

	Expected return	Risk (standard deviation)
Common stocks / Small stocks / International stocks	13.5%	21.4%
Common stocks / Small stocks / Long-term govt bonds	10.9%	16.7%
Common stocks / Cash equivalents / Small stocks / Long-term govt bonds	7.7%	10.0%
Cash equivalents / Common stocks / Small stocks / Long-term govt bonds	4.6%	4.2%

ment bonds. This four-part chart establishes a clear relationship between risk and return and provides a guideline for achieving specific investment objectives "efficiently." Investors should note that even the lowest-risk portfolio contains stocks.

Since all these efficient portfolios hold some stocks, the retired investor used to living off his or her bond interest may wonder how he or she can take income out of a portfolio diversified into stocks. Here the retiree should be prepared to use not only bond income but also growth generated through stock holdings in order to satisfy income needs. If a retiree's stocks and bonds are owned through mutual funds, one preferred method reinvests all income and capital gains distributions during the course of a year. Once or twice a year, an appropriate number of shares from all parts of the portfolio are redeemed. Such redemption could come proportionately from every different part of the portfolio, or the retiree could sell shares from those sectors of his portfolio that

appreciated the most during the preceding twelve months. The latter method is preferable, since it stresses the process of selling high. The funds obtained through such share sales could be placed in a cash account to satisfy income needs during the course of the year. The retiree "harvests" part of his or her portfolio's entire appreciated value, by accessing both interest income and capital growth.

Again, it behooves all investors, retired or not, to keep their focus on longer time horizons and proper diversification. Once a retiree establishes an appropriate asset allocation, implements this asset allocation through purchase of fitting investments, and focuses on the longer term, he or she should be well set to contemplate the financial future with a high level of confidence. It is very advisable to put the asset allocation decision in writing. Hopefully the retired investor will read through and be reacquainted with his or her investment policy" whenever he or she is suffering from a knee-jerk reaction to current market moves. At such a point in time, the retiree should remember that U.S. common stocks have been giving negative returns three out of every ten calendar years from 1926 through 1991. Consequently, one year's negative return should not lead to the abandonment of a well-conceived investment policy. The process of initial policy construction and subsequent policy reaffirmation will allow the retired investor to calmly meet the slings and arrows of periodically outrageous markets and maintain his or her focus on the goal: a level or improving standard of living.

Further Reading

Arnott, Robert D., and Frank J. Fabozzi. *Active Asset Allocation: State-of-the-Art Portfolio Policies, Strategies and Tactics*. Chicago, IL: Probus, 1992.

Dunnan, Nancy. *Dun & Bradstreet Guide to $Your Investments$*. New York: Harper Collins, 1991.

Gibson, Roger C. *Asset Allocation: Balancing Financial Risk*. Homewood, IL: Dow Jones-Irwin, 1990.

Ibbotson, Roger G., and Gary P. Brinson, *Investment Markets: Gaining the Performance Advantage*. New York: McGraw-Hill, 1987.

Ibbotson Associates. *Stocks, Bonds, Bills, and Inflation: 1992 Yearbook*. Chicago, IL: Ibbotson Associates, 1992.

Maginn, John L., and Donald L. Tuttle, eds. *Managing Investment Portfolios: A Dynamic Process*. Boston, MA: Warren, Gorham & Lamont, 1990.

Lilian Fischer, Ph.D.

⑮

Estate Planning

- The Purpose of Wills • Making a Will • Substitutes for Wills: Joint Ownership and Living Trusts
- Tax Planning • Charitable Planning

In the minds of some, the word "estate" conjures up the vision of acres of meticulously cared for lawns, an enormous mansion, and all the trappings of a life of luxury. To others, "estate" means only property left behind by a deceased person. These assumptions may lead some into thinking that "I don't own enough to bother with estate planning," while others view estate planning as only something done "so I can leave my property to my heirs when I die" (usually thought of as an occurrence in the distant future).

More accurately, a person's estate consists of whatever he or she has—much or little—at any time throughout the lifespan. Consequently estate planning is concerned with financial planning during life and at death. It involves estate creation and conservation as well as the disposition of property. The goal is to save money and to plan for the care of oneself and one's family for the rest of a person's life and in the event of his or her death.

However, even when people know why estate planning should be done, many never get beyond good intentions and some very general ideas concerning the subject. Two common reasons for their procrastination are not knowing where to begin and the concern that situations or circumstances will change, thus making their plans mistaken or incomplete.

Happily almost every public library includes in its holdings at least one of the more popular personal finance magazines as well as books on estate planning aimed at the general reader.

These articles and books help readers understand the steps, tools, and techniques of the estate planning process, including where to begin and how to deal with changing situations and circumstances. Their readers learn, for example, that estate planning consists of three constituent elements: preparing a will, planning to minimize taxes, and planning for contingencies during life for oneself and one's family.

● THE PURPOSE OF WILLS

Why should a person make a will? Perhaps the biggest reason is that a will enables one to have control over his or her property—the power to choose where the person's property will go. Without a will, that decision will be made by officials of the individual's state of legal residence. The "intestacy" laws (laws governing the property of one who dies "intestate," that is, without a last will and testament) vary from state to state; but it is not likely that any state will distribute people's property in just the way they themselves would choose.

This matter is of more importance than many realize. Broadly speaking, one's estate may be distributed upon death to three places only: (1) to family and/or other persons; (2) to charity; (3) to federal and state governments in the form of death taxes and other costs. While the intestacy laws of the several states do distribute property to family members, the proportionate shares are not distributed in view of one's intimate knowledge of the persons involved, together with their needs and circumstances. The state's distribution is arbitrary and inflexible. No charitable distribution is made under the laws of intestacy, even though one would want to remember the institutions and organizations that have meant so much to the individual. Furthermore, the most effective means of saving death taxes and costs are not elements of the laws of intestacy. A will is vital!

Even younger people need wills. In the event of the death of one or both parents with minor children, the parents' will may designate the surviving children's legal guardian. In the absence of such a designation, the court will appoint the guardian. Not only could this be someone other than the person the parents would have chosen, the property inherited by the children will also be subject to costly court jurisdiction. Furthermore, the children will receive full control of their inheritance upon reaching age 18. A will can provide for a trust to manage the children's affairs until they have reached an age, perhaps 25 or 30, when they are more likely to be ready for this responsibility.

A will also allows the choice of one's personal representative/executor. If such a nomination is not made in a will, the court will appoint someone to oversee the administration of the estate, someone who may not be at all familiar with the survivors' needs or the deceased person's wishes.

Many people have been closely involved with a college, church, social service agency, hospital, or other charitable cause. As a student, member, contributor, or volunteer, a close bond has been created over the years. Many people find that a final bequest to benefit these organizations is a source of gratification and satisfaction. In addition, making a charitable bequest is a way of making a final demonstration of their values to their families. Without a will, no such bequest is possible.

A will can make provisions for special situations, such as the management or transfer of ownership of a closely held business or farm. In many cases, particularly in the event of a sudden and unexpected death, lack of such provisions has led to chaos and the ultimate ruin of both business and survivors.

An incompetent family member presents another reason for having a will. Financial inexperience or physical or mental handicaps may require the establishment of trusts to provide for good estate management and the special needs of some heirs, while advanced age may make trusts desirable for others. Such trusts can be established by direction of a will.

Finally, a will may save one's estate a great deal of money in several ways. By using certain will provisions, estate and inheritance taxes may be greatly reduced (e.g., by using a "credit shelter trust," $600,000 that would otherwise be subject to tax may be made exempt from tax). Costs of probating the estate can likewise be reduced by will provisions that reduce court, accounting, bonding, and attorney fees.

The various guardianships, trusts, and other will provisions mentioned are standard techniques and will usually be discussed as part of any estate planning interview or process conducted by an attorney practicing in the field of estate planning.

Who can make a will? Each state has its own rules governing this, but all require that a certain minimum age must have been attained (usually 18, but there are exceptions). A person making a will must also be of "sound mind," meaning that one knows the nature and extent of one's property and also knows who one's natural beneficiaries are.

● MAKING A WILL

The process of actually making the will involves a number of parts and decisions. For most people, the process can be viewed as consisting of five steps.

The first step is to review one's assets. "What do I own, how do I own it, and what is it worth?" Taking an inventory of assets and committing it to paper can be of enormous help to survivors. It lets everyone know just exactly what the person has. It also saves time (and, therefore, money) in the attorney's office, because it indicates to the attorney just which property will be controlled by the will to be written and which property falls outside the control of the will. It also indicates whether or not one would benefit from tax-saving trusts or other devices. Not all property is controlled by a will. Named beneficiaries of life insurance policies, employee benefits, or Individual Retirement Accounts (IRAs) will receive the proceeds of these contractual arrangements quite apart from the will. Such contracts take precedence and cannot be altered by a will provision.

Likewise, real estate, autos, bank accounts, or other property held in some form of "joint tenancy with right of survivorship" will pass to the surviving owners. "Community property" states (Arizona, California, Idaho, Louisiana, Nevada, New Mexico, Texas, Washington, and Wisconsin) generally take the view that all property acquired by spouses during their marriage is one total "community" of property, belonging to a 50-50 marital partnership. Upon the death of one spouse, this property becomes entirely the property of the surviving marital partner.

The next step in will-making is to determine who will be the beneficiaries of the will. "If I die today, to whom do I want my property to go?" It is good planning to include secondary or contingency beneficiaries, in the event that the primary beneficiaries are not living at the time of one's death. The names of primary and contingency beneficiaries should be reviewed from time to time, making certain that all are still alive and that one is satisfied with the order in which they are mentioned.

This may also be an occasion to review the status of one's spouse's inheritance. With some second marriages entered into later in life, a person may not intend that the surviving spouse will inherit the deceased spouse's estate but that it will go instead to the children of the first marriage. However, unless this is planned for with a pre-nuptial agreement, the surviving spouse can dissent from the will and receive as much inheritance as would have been received under the laws of intestacy. If no pre-nuptial agreement exists, certain trust arrangements may be considered to remedy this potential problem.

The third step in the will-making process is to select the executor. Sometimes called a "personal representative," this person is the one who represents the interests of one's estate and actually carries out the provisions of the will. This is the one who presents the will to the court to be "proven" (the literal meaning of the word "probate") as the person's bona fide last will and testament. Once the will is admitted into the probate process, the executor inventories all of one's assets, collects them together, pays all debts that may exist, files any tax returns that may be required, and, finally, distributes the assets to the named beneficiaries. All this is done under the supervision of the court, to which a final accounting must be made to ensure that all was done in accordance with one's wishes and the law.

Some work is required to be an executor, so it is advisable to secure the nominee's agreement to serve and to have an alternate in the event the nominee is unable to serve when the time comes. The executor (and perhaps a co-executor) is customarily chosen from among the surviving spouse, other family members, and friends. However, if the estate is large or complex, the amount of work may be more than a private individual may be willing or able to assume. In that case, a bank or trust company may be selected as the executor or co-executor. Settling the estate will take anywhere from three months to two years or more, depending on size and complexity.

Fourth, if trusts are established by the terms of the will, trustees will need to be selected from among family members, friends, or banks and trust companies. The trustee(s) will manage trust assets until trust termination.

The fifth and final step in will-making is to select, if necessary, guardians for minor children. Once again, it is advisable to secure prospective guardians' agreement to serve and to provide for alternates.

When all of this is complete, it is time to have an attorney draft the person's will. While the laws of one's state may allow handwritten or oral wills under certain circumstances, these can be extremely dangerous! It is too easy for an amateur draftsman to neglect to include some important provisions or to make drafting errors, either of which can lead to unhappy and unwanted consequences. Too many people overestimate the cost of having a will drawn professionally and do not realize that a well-constructed will can actually save much more than it costs.

Executing the Will

Once the will is prepared, it is time to execute it. There are certain formalities required by law. One is required to have two or three witnesses (the number varies from state to state) who must be both "competent" and "disinterested"—that is, they must fully understand what they are doing and must not be beneficiaries or their spouses. In addition, it is wise to have the will notarized. This makes the will "self-proving," meaning that witnesses do not need to be located and brought to court when the will is entered into probate.

Louis Hector
Attorney

"A lawyer's life consists of taking up new problems constantly, problems that often involve a new type of business or subject matter, new people; it's that variety which is one of the most attractive features of the practice of law."

Louis Hector was born in 1915 in Florida, where he has lived for most of his life. His father, "a very active businessman," encouraged Hector to do whatever he wanted, while his mother steeped him in the Midwestern ideals of self-education and self-improvement and stimulated his intellectual curiosity. He reported that his first career aspiration, at the age of 12, was to be an architect, because "I like planning things."

Hector received his A.B. from Harvard University and Williams College and then attended Oxford University in England as a Rhodes Scholar, where he began to study law. Hector completed his legal studies at Yale Law School in 1942. He served as an attorney in the Department of Justice and the State Department in 1944 as assistant to the undersecretary, then transferred in 1945 to the Office of Strategic Services, Southeast Asia and China Command, to see out the end of World War II. In 1946 he returned to Miami to work for the law firm Scott, McCarthy & Preston.

In 1947, at age 33, Hector stopped practicing law to run a family business, Hector Supply Company of Miami. When eight years later he returned to the practice of law, he formed his own firm, then served a two-year term on the Civil Aeronautics Board.

Hector attributes his career flexibility to his legal background. "Your career trains you to change from one subject matter to another," he said. "I think lawyers are particularly flexible." He served as the trustee of Northeast Airlines for Howard Hughes and arranged for its sale, was chairman of the executive committee of the Southeast Banking Corporation, and, since 1983, has been the chairman of the Lucille P. Markey Charitable Trust and a board member of various institutions, such as the American Academy of Arts and Sciences, and the Chamber Music Society of Lincoln Center. Hector believes that law firms generally value the presence of older lawyers. "They encourage the older, retired lawyers to come down and have lunch with the younger lawyers, and they encourage the younger lawyers to ask the older lawyers for advice. I don't think that corporations operate that way. When you're out, you're out."

He never thought about retiring at 65, and insists that today he continues to be much too busy to consider retirement. "If you're part of an institution or if you're practicing law or administering a big estate, you have to keep busy." This impetus to remain working, Hector feels, is unique to the legal profession. "If you've been an officer of a corporation and you retire there's no institution that keeps you involved in new, fresh problems and in contact with younger, busy people. I find I get the greatest pleasure out of the younger lawyers because they are so active and they're so interesting. They're enthusiatic and that's contagious."

Lydia Brontë

Once the will is signed and notarized, it should be kept in a safe place. Ease of accessibility to safe deposit boxes after death varies from place to place. A person's attorney can advise him or her of the situation in the local area. Other alternatives may be one's attorney's vault, the Clerk of Court's vault, or, if a person's bank is to serve as executor of the estate, the will may be placed in the bank's vault for safekeeping.

Updating the Will

Having done all this, one should remember to review the will from time to time to determine if it still makes sense if one were to die now. At the very least, it is a good idea to review one's will if one or more of the beneficiaries dies or is born; if minor children reach the age of legal adulthood; if one marries or divorces; if the tax law changes (one's attorney or bank trust department will be able to provide this information, if it is requested); if one's net worth goes up or down, requiring some tax planning or a change in how beneficiaries will share in one's estate; or if one moves to another state.

If a person does move to another state, it may be a good idea simply to write a new will. The old will is probably valid, but the individual's new state of residence may interpret things a little differently from the former state. Since an attorney in the new state may need to spend valuable time in reviewing the old will to determine its effect under new rules, it may be less costly to do a new will.

In the process of the periodic review of a will, the person may need or desire to make some changes to it. This may be done either by attaching an amendment, known as a codicil, to the existing will, or by doing an entirely new will. If the changes are few and of a minor nature, a codicil may suffice. Even a codicil, however, must have the full formalities of signing in the presence of witnesses, etc., so some simply prefer to do an entirely new will. This is especially true if the reason for the codicil is to change a beneficiary's share, since the change can be seen by any who read the will. This may be an unhappy disclosure, causing hurt feelings and resentment.

Wills can be revoked simply by the execution of a new will or by destroying the will. The latter method is not advisable, because it places a person's estate at the mercy of either the laws of intestacy or a previous, unrevised will.

No matter how many good reasons there are for making a will, some people seem determined to find a "will substitute," hoping to avoid probate. Two of the more common are joint ownership and living trusts.

● SUBSTITUTES FOR WILLS: JOINT OWNERSHIP AND LIVING TRUSTS

Joint ownership avoids probate because the deceased person's interest in jointly owned property passes immediately upon death to the surviving joint owner, in accordance with the property's title, thus avoiding the probate process. While this is effective in most situations, it does not work in the event of simultaneous deaths. Yet another consideration is that the entire property is now in the hands of the survivor, which may create a future tax problem. For example, a survivor with $400,000 worth of assets that are growing at the rate of 4 percent per year, who lives for 18 more years, will have an estate of $800,000. Since $600,000 is the maximum amount that an individual can leave to heirs without incurring federal estate tax, the estate would be taxable. In

short, while joint ownership may seem attractive, it easily turns into a trap.

Living trusts also avoid the probate process for the property in the trust. It is probably impossible and impractical to place all property in the trust, however. Jewelry and cars, for example, may cause title and insurance problems when placed in a living trust. In addition, living trusts will not meet the need to appoint a guardian for minor children or save taxes.

A living trust can be beneficial for someone who owns real property in more than one state, because it makes it possible to avoid dealing with the probate process in two states, thus decreasing settlement time and costs.

Another good use of living trusts is for the benefit of individuals who have no one available to manage their financial affairs in the event of their absence or incapacity. A long trip or serious illness could result in considerable chaos unless a trustee is waiting in the wings to assume management when asked or when certain pre-arranged events occur.

● TAX PLANNING

For an ever-growing number of individuals, tax planning is an important part of the estate planning process. If one's estate—individually, or combined with one's spouse's estate—is over $600,000 or might possibly grow to that amount (if only as the result of inflation) during the life of either partner, one needs to think about tax planning. Federal estate tax rates begin at 37 percent and can go as high as 55 percent. Clearly, this is not a tax to be ignored!

Many people, however, do manage to overlook the ways in which this tax creeps up on them. Life insurance, for example, is often thought of as being "tax free." It is tax free to a named beneficiary who receives the policy's death benefit. However, it will be included in the deceased's estate if the deceased was the "owner" of the policy—that is, if the deceased retained any rights to the policy during life, such as the right to borrow from it or even the right to change the names of the beneficiaries. Likewise, for those who have a pension plan, it may be included in their estate. One's house, or interest in it if it is jointly owned, will also be included.

Just these three items—life insurance, pension

plans, and real estate—may very well add up to enough to put a person's estate in danger of tax, now or in the surviving spouse's lifetime. The vast majority of those whose estates are or may become taxable, however, can avoid the tax by using two relatively simple devices: the unified credit and the unlimited marital deduction.

Unified Credit

The unified credit is a tax credit that can be applied against taxes due on transfers made from an individual to anyone he or she chooses. It is "unified" because it applies to all transfers made, whether during life or at death, "unifying" them together as though they were one unified whole. For transfers made during life, the unified credit may be applied against gift tax. For transfers at death, it is applied against estate tax. Both gift and estate taxes use the same "unified" rates. The effect of the unified credit is that most individuals, during life and at death, may pass a combined, "unified" total of $600,000 free of tax. But the credit is phased out for estates larger than $10 million, so that no credit is available for very large estates.

Unlimited Marital Deduction

The second commonly used estate tax planning device is the unlimited marital deduction. As its name implies, the effect of this provision of the law is that an individual may give an unlimited amount to his or her spouse, during life or at death, and no tax will be paid. The transfer to the spouse may be either an outright transfer or a transfer via certain kinds of trusts. Usually the income from the trust is paid to the surviving spouse for life. When the surviving spouse dies, the property remaining in the trust passes in one of three ways. With a "general power of appointment" trust, the surviving spouse has the "power" to "appoint" those who will receive the trust's property upon that spouse's death. This is useful if it is desirable to keep open the surviving spouse's future options to deal with heirs' future situations and circumstances.

Another type of trust is the "Q-TIP" trust. "Q-TIP" stands for "Qualified Terminable Interest Property." It is "qualified" because it qualifies for the unlimited marital deduction in the estate of the deceased spouse. But the surviving spouse's

"interest" in the trust's "property" is "terminable"; that is, the surviving spouse's power over the property terminates at death, with no power to appoint those who will receive the property at death. That power is retained by the first spouse to die. This is useful in the event of second marriages, with children from a first marriage. It assures the first spouse to die that his or her children will receive their intended inheritance.

A variation on this "Q-TIP" theme is a trust for the surviving spouse's lifetime benefit, but with the first spouse designating one or more charities to receive the remainder upon the second spouse's death.

Thirdly, the surviving spouse may simply have the right to pass the property on to heirs as part of his or her estate. Note that there is no marital deduction if one's spouse is not a U.S. citizen. In that event, there are some other options one may wish to discuss with an attorney.

Tax Advantages

The net result of the combined effect of the unified credit and the unlimited marital deduction is that a married couple can leave $1,200,000 to their heirs, absolutely free of federal estate taxes. How is this accomplished?

Each spouse takes full advantage of the unified credit by establishing a "credit shelter trust." These trusts, created under the terms of an individual's will, can hold up to $600,000 at the time of their creation (the death of the first spouse)—the amount that can be "sheltered" by the unified credit. This trust's property will pass ultimately to heirs, pausing along the way to benefit the surviving spouse. When used by both spouses, a total of $1,200,000 can pass without tax. It may be necessary, if one spouse owns a disproportionate share of the property, to shift ownership of some of the assets to the other spouse, using the unlimited marital deduction to avoid any gift tax liability. This will balance the ownership, allowing both to make full use of their individual credit shelter amount.

This simple credit shelter trust technique can save $235,000 in taxes for a married couple with a combined estate of $1,200,000. Without credit shelter trusts, although there would be no tax at the first death (because of the unlimited marital deduction), only the surviving spouse would be able to make use of the unified credit. This would expose everything over $600,000 to federal estate tax—a tax of $235,000 in an estate of $1,200,000. The benefit of having wills that create these trusts for husband and wife is an obvious one.

For estates above the $1,200,000 level, other tax-planning techniques may be brought into play. A "generation-skipping" trust, which transfers property to grandchildren, is one tool that may be suggested by one's advisers.

Still other tax-planning methods are available for use by persons whose estates are on either side of the $600,000-if-single/$1,200,000-if-married line. Perhaps the most popular is the ability of an individual to give $10,000 per year, tax free, to as many other individuals as desired. If the donor's spouse joins in, the gift can be $20,000 per donee. Thus, if a husband and wife joined in making these kinds of annual gifts to a child and the child's spouse, $40,000 could be given to a child and the child's spouse per year. If the donor-couple has more than one child, or if grandchildren are involved in this kind of annual gifting program, the amount of the tax-free transfers can mount dramatically and have an equally dramatic effect on reducing the potential estate tax liability in the donor-couple's estate.

Many grandparents choose to make such gifts not only to lower their own estate tax liability but simply to help their families. Other methods of using the $10,000-per-donee "annual exclusion" are available as well. For example, gifts can be made to a Uniform Transfers to Minors Account, which can hold assets until the child reaches 21—instead of making those assets available instantly or at 18, the age of legal adulthood. Other methods are available also.

In considering the various tools and techniques available in the planning of one's estate, one should always keep in mind that not only do situations and circumstances change, but so do federal and state laws. Today's best solution to a problem may be no solution tomorrow. This is not a reason not to plan one's estate now, however, for there will almost certainly never be a time when the laws are finally fixed and unchanging. It is only a warning to remember that things do change. When using published materials, one should be sure to check for current publication dates (federal laws underwent major changes in 1981 and 1986, for example, and may change

again). Above all, obtain legal advice or other expert assistance from advisers who keep current in their field of expertise. There is no substitute for the services of a competent professional person.

● CHARITABLE PLANNING

One area of the law that continues to remain favorable for estate planners governs charitable planning. Despite many revisions of the relevant sections of the Internal Revenue Code, the basic aspects have remained intact. Perhaps the most significant changes occurred as long ago as 1969. It is an area with which every estate owner/planner should be familiar.

There are many reasons for making charitable gifts. However, a desire on the part of the donor to support the work of an institution or organization is paramount. People simply want to help. But how can one support charity in the most cost-effective way, enabling the person to make the largest possible gift while doing no harm to one's own financial well-being? Many donors want to do more for their favorite charities but do not know how it may be possible.

Charitable Contribution Deductions

This is where the tax laws are very friendly. They not only allow for charitable giving, but they positively support it. This support is given by providing charitable contribution deductions for income, gift, and estate tax purposes and by providing other benefits, such as the by-pass of the tax on capital gains. Indeed, in a few situations, where charitable gifts have been carefully planned, it is possible for a donor and/or the donor's heirs to be financially better off than if the gift had not been made.

Since there can be a number of tax and other technicalities involved with a charitable contribution, it is a good idea to contact a charitable organization for some assistance. Most colleges, many hospitals, and other large charitable organizations have charitable giving specialists on staff who can advise individuals concerning such things as the valuation and appraisal rules for donating real property or tangible personal property (a little trickier than cash donations), deduction limitations on various kinds of property, alternative minimum tax implications, etc.

Because this is a highly specialized area of knowledge, it is not familiar territory even to a great many tax advisers. The gift planning officer of an individual's favorite charity can be helpful in saving the donor's adviser costly research time by giving quick and accurate information, which can then be verified in the relevant section of the law.

Individuals may want to consider some of the ways in which they may be able to do more for their favorite causes. Take the example of a businessman and owner of a closely held corporation. In good times, the company may be able to accumulate a substantial amount of earnings. But if it accumulates too much, there will be an "accumulated earnings tax." If some of the cash is taken out as a dividend, both owner and corporation will pay a tax. However, if some of the closely held stock is given to charity, the corporation can redeem it with some of the accumulated earnings, retiring it as treasury stock. The owner gets a personal income tax charitable contribution deduction, the corporation avoids the accumulated earnings tax, and the owner still maintains control of the corporation. Other techniques allow one to pass control and ownership of a corporation to the next generation, avoiding the burdensome costs of transfer taxes.

Wealth Replacement

One of the most popular techniques of charitable estate planning uses the "wealth replacement" concept. Many people own real estate or securities that have grown greatly in value. At or near retirement, they would like to sell this property and reinvest it for greater income. The difficulty is that the very growth that made it such a wonderful investment in earlier years will now trigger a capital gain tax. After paying the tax, the amount available for reinvestment will not produce the income desired—unless a highly risky and undesirable investment is used. At this point, many people feel "locked in," unable to get out of the low-yielding investment.

However, by creating a charitable remainder trust, the property can be sold inside the trust without paying any capital gain tax, then reinvested for the desired higher yield. The donor (and the donor's spouse) can receive an income from the trust for life. In addition to bypassing the capital gain tax and increasing current income, an income tax charitable contribution deduction (based on the donor's age and the rate of annual income received) is generated, thus reducing current income tax. In addition, probate costs and estate taxes can be reduced or eliminated.

The creator of such a plan can also provide for his or her family. By using the tax savings and perhaps some of the increased income, life insurance (to replace the asset inside the charitable remainder trust) can be purchased. At death, when the charity receives the proceeds from the trust, the life insurance passes—tax free—to the family heirs.

This technique makes it possible to better one's circumstances during life as well as the circumstances of one's heirs at death. With its many benefits, this kind of charitable plan is one of the most powerful financial, tax, and estate planning tools available today.

Many other charitable gift planning arrangements are available. Not all require large contributions (some can be entered into for under $1,000, depending on the individual charity's requirements). Many do not require trust agreements.

Of course, the old standby of charitable estate planning is the bequest by will. Of all the deferred giving arrangements, this is the most universally used. Which brings us back to the beginning. To make a bequest, you need a will.

Further Reading

Brosterman, Robert, and Thomas Brosterman. *The Complete Estate Planning Guide.* New York: McGraw-Hill, 1987.

Soled, Alex J. *The Essential Guide to Wills, Estates, Trusts, and Death Taxes.* Glenview, IL: Scott, Foresman, 1987.

Thomas D. Hughes, B.A., ChFC

Section VI:

Relationships and Aging

⑯

Family Relationships in Later Life

- Family Roles in an Aging Society ● Marriage, Social Support, and Adult Children in Later Life
- Grandparents and Grandchildren ● Sibling Relationships in Later Life
- Extended Kin Relationships ● Never-Married Older Adults
- Gay and Lesbian Relationships in Later Life ● Divorce and Widowhood in Old Age
- Adapting to Changing Family Patterns

During the past fifty years, the American family has experienced many changes. Some of these changes result from increased geographic mobility; others are caused by changing population characteristics. However, regardless of the reason, the American family is different now than it was fifty years ago in terms of longevity and structure. The differences in families are especially evident to older people who were raised in two- and three-generation families living under the same roof and typically unaffected by divorce. During the past fifty years, older adults have witnessed radical alterations in their own family forms and in the generations within their families.

One of the causes of changing family composition is the aging of American society. The population is aging in large part because people are living longer. Table 16.1 compares adults in 1900 with those in 1990 in terms of average life expectancy, the proportion of the population that is 65 years and older, the number of people 85 years old and older, and life expectancy for people at age 65 (U.S. Bureau of the Census, 1992).

Four out of five people born in the 1990s can expect to live at least to age 65, and 50 percent of the people who reach age 65 will live past age 80 (Hooyman and Kiyak, 1988). These demographic changes have had a powerful effect on the age distribution of the population and have

resulted in a greater number and higher proportion of older people in the U.S. population than ever before.

● FAMILY ROLES IN AN AGING SOCIETY

As individuals live longer, they spend more time in their family roles and may experience different family roles than their parents did. For example, one of the most rapidly changing trends is that of the multigenerational family. The increasing numbers of older people in the population combined with earlier marital and childbearing patterns of many people age 65 and older have resulted in families that span three, four, and even five generations frequently living in separate households. Of people age 65 and older who have adult children, 40 percent live in four-generation families. Ninety-four percent of the people who head these families have grandchildren, and 46 percent have great-grandchildren (Brody, 1990). As the number of living generations per family increases, so too does the number of family roles available to older adults. More older people are currently grandparents and great-grandparents than ever before.

However, older people are not the only ones to experience changes in their family roles. Adults have living parents for a much longer time than ever before as shown in Table 16.2.

These proportions are remarkable, especially

The rise of multigenerational families has extended the time people spend as grandparents. (Copyright © Marianne Gontarz)

Table 16.2
Adults and Their Living Parents, 1984

Adult	Proportion with at least one living parent
Age 50–59	40%
Age 60–69	10%
Age 70–79	3%

Source: Brody, E. "Parent Care as a Normative Family Stress." *Gerontologist* Vol. 25 (1985): 19–30.

The increasing numbers of older people in the population combined with earlier marital and childbearing patterns of many people age 65 and older have resulted in families that span three, four, and even five generations frequently living in separate households.

to older people who themselves may not have had a single living grandparent during childhood. These changes in family patterns are highlighted even more considering that 10 percent of all people age 65 and older also have a child who is 65 years of age or older (Brody, 1985).

The Rise of Multigenerational Families

Multigenerational families result in an increase in the number of years that most older people spend as grandparents or great-grandparents. The possibility of multigenerational family interactions is quite high for most elderly. But longevity also means that older adults have the potential for experiencing long periods of dependency during which they may need support from other family members. Extended life expectancy is a wonderful gift when the added years are healthy and happy, but it can be a burden for older people with chronic, debilitating illness. Whether an older person is healthy or not, the family plays a critical role for a much longer period of time than was true in the past.

Increasing life expectancy is not the only change affecting the population of the United States. Family size is another demographic trend that continues to influence family structure. Although parents during the late 1940s through the mid-1960s had large families, their children

Table 16.1
Differences in Aging, 1900–90

	Average Life Expectancy at Birth	% of the Population Age 65+	Number of People Age 85+	Life Expectancy at Age 65
1900	47.3 years	4	122,000	11.9
1990	75.3 years	12.5	3,021,000	17.2

Source: U.S. Bureau of the Census. *Current Population Reports,* Special Studies, P23-178, *Sixty-Five Plus in America.*

(known as the baby boomers) are having, on average, substantially smaller families. This trend cuts across all social, economic, and race categories in this country. Bengtson and his colleagues (1990) call this consequence of declining birth rate the "verticalization" of the family. Instead of families with successively more members in younger generations, verticalization results in more living generations per family but fewer members within each of those generations.

Verticalization has an impact on family life of older people in several ways. First, verticalization affects patterns of family interaction. Instead of interacting within generations (with siblings or cousins), family members typically interact between generations. Because fewer members exist in any single generation, family members must look up and down the family tree rather than just within generations to find people with whom they can share family bonds and establish important family relationships. Older adults will have fewer brothers and sisters, nieces and nephews, cousins, uncles, and aunts as the vertical families increase in number. This pattern may affect family members negatively as they search for potential family ties. For example, young children in smaller families may have few or no siblings; they may have no cousins either. These children might then rely only on grandparents and great-grandparents for family relationships.

Second, verticalization can affect patterns of support within the multigenerational family. The smaller number of members in any one generation may mean that dependent family members, especially older adults, cannot simply look to the next generation for support. For example, an older widowed man with serious chronic illness who has only one son and no daughters might have to ask his granddaughters or great-granddaughters to cook his meals or help him with personal care. Of course, these family members will be available only if his son has had children. Choices for support providers within the family are diminishing as generations become smaller.

Finally, verticalization has affected the length of time women spend in different family roles across their lives. Men and women have different life expectancies, with women expecting at birth to live on average 7.6 years longer than men. Women continue to have an advantage in life expectancy at age 65 when they can expect to live

4.5 years longer than men. These differences, combined with the fact that men in older cohorts tended to marry younger women, result in the feminization of the oldest age groups (Hooyman and Lustbaden, 1986). It is quite possible in a five-generation family to have the two or three oldest generations comprised entirely of widowed females. Advanced age and widowhood can result in inevitable dependency for these women, with aging daughters caring for even older mothers. The younger generations in families like this are often too small to meet the dependency needs of older family members. If current trends of extending life expectancy continue, the multigenerational family headed by a generation or generations of females may become even more prevalent.

> Instead of families with successively more members in younger generations, "verticalization" results in more living generations per family but fewer members within each of those generations.

Declining Birth Rate and Delayed Childbearing

Patterns of family establishment also have been altered because of the declining birth rate in this country. Delayed childbearing is one way in which individual families are affected by these demographic changes. Instead of marrying and having children in their early twenties, many young adults currently wait until their late thirties or early forties to start a family. This delay gives young adults opportunities to establish themselves in their careers and their marriages. But later parenthood means later grandparenthood as well, and older people find themselves waiting much longer before making the transition to grandparenting.

When delayed childbearing occurs in multiple generations in the same family, the result is called an age-gapped family (Bengtson, Rosenthal, and Burton, 1990). First, age differences between family generations increase. Instead of twenty or twenty-five years between parent and child, the age-gapped family can have up to forty or forty-five years between generations. Eventually, this pattern will limit the number of generations living concurrently. But, more importantly, the age-gapped family has a potentially negative impact for older family members who need family support. In the age-gapped family, the pool of support providers for older adults is quite small at any given time. Some older adults who find themselves in an age-gapped family may have to explore community services or institutional care because of a shortage of family caregivers.

On the other hand, some families experience timing and sequencing between generations differently. According to Linda Burton, a researcher at Pennsylvania State University, sequential teenage pregnancy in multiple generations in a family causes an age-condensed family (Bengtson, Rosenthal, and Burton, 1990). Unlike the age-gapped family in which generations are spaced many years apart, the age-condensed family can have as little as 15 years between generations, with a consequent blurring of generational lines or boundaries within a family. For example, a 30-year-old mother and her 15-year-old pregnant daughter may relate to each other as members of the same generation (i.e., as two mothers) rather than in an intergenerational relationship. The age-condensed family bestows the role of grandmother on very young people. With 15 year intervals between generations, a woman could become a grandmother at age 45. The probability of four- and five-generation families is extremely high under these conditions.

Diversity of Family Forms

Several other social trends also have affected the family lives of older adults. The increase in women in the labor force has had a striking effect on traditional marriages and family forms, resulting in such phenomena as latch-key children. Often, grandparents find themselves with responsibility for raising or providing daycare for their grandchildren. Further, divorce is at an all-time high in this country, with about 50 percent of all marriages ending in divorce. Older adults usually find divorce of their adult children difficult, in part because the divorce may affect relationships with grandchildren. This is especially problematic for parents of the non-custodial spouse.

Divorce and remarriage can result in a blended or reconstituted family—that is, a marriage between two previously married spouses with children from the previous marriages. This combining of families is another way in which traditional family forms have been modified. It is difficult to maintain relationships with grandchildren and great-grandchildren when families remain intact for only short periods of time. Keeping family members emotionally invested in each other when they are no longer bound by legal ties is difficult. Further, integrating step-children and step-grandchildren into a family can be complex and can result in anger and rivalry. Family decisions, including divorce and remarriage, have consequences for all generations.

Reconstituted families have become more common as divorces and remarriages increase. Other family forms include increased cohabitation by unmarried couples as well as gay and lesbian relationships. Non-traditional families introduce many levels of complexity into multigenerational relationships within the family. Yet the impact of these changes is not well understood or well documented. Further research will be needed to measure the ways in which these changes affect family feelings of obligation, commitment, caring, and the ways in which older adults react to these changes. Most social scientists agree that this diversity is unlikely to be replaced by more homogeneous marriage and family patterns.

● MARRIAGE, SOCIAL SUPPORT, AND ADULT CHILDREN IN LATER LIFE

Regardless of its type or generational structure, the family is—and always has been—extremely important to older adults. In the eighteenth and nineteenth centuries, family ties were often economic in nature; for example, children in rural areas were expected to provide labor on farms. Today's families are bonded together more by emotional than by financial ties. Further, the intensity of bonds between multiple generations appears to have increased in the last fifty years. Although families are often far from agreement on politics, religion, and gender roles, many family ties are considered inviolate by multiple generations.

The Role of Spouse in Late Life

Of all family relationships of older adults, marriage is the most important in terms of physical

Marital satisfaction in the post-parental years is often higher than at any other time in the life course. (Copyright © Marianne Gontarz)

health, mental health, and overall well-being. Marriage provides crucial support for most older people; a spouse is a ready-made confidant and companion. Once responsibilities of parenting and employment decline, older people often turn to their life-long companions for social interaction and intimacy. Not surprisingly, marital satisfaction in the post-parental years is often higher than at any other time in the life course. According to Bengtson, Rosenthal, and Burton (1990), most older adults rate their marriages as either happy or very happy. A much larger proportion of older men are married than older women, partially reflecting differences in marital satisfaction. Men tend to report higher marital satisfaction than women; they also report having their emotional needs more fulfilled within the marriage than women do (Gilford, 1984). On the other hand Holahan (1984), in her longitudinal study of marital attitudes over forty years, found that older women often report a decrease in marital satisfaction. However, satisfaction of older

women still tends to be higher than that of younger, more recently married women.

Holahan (1984) also suggests that there have been multiple changes in attitudes of older adults toward marriage during the last forty to fifty years. For example, contemporary men appear to be far more involved in family life and child care than married men were in the past. Further, men appear to recognize more equality in marriage than they did in the past. Yet Holahan still found some enduring sex differences about marital attitudes in her study. For example, women favored a wife's being fully informed about family finances, while men were less certain that this was important. Holahan notes that both aging and historical change contribute to these attitudinal changes.

Increased marital satisfaction in later life may result in part from children leaving home; the empty nest gives parents freedom and opportunity that are not available during childrearing. Further, many investigators have found that a gender crossover occurs in late life in which men become more affectionate and less achievement oriented while women turn their interests and efforts outside the home (Livson, 1981; Gutmann, 1989, 1987). This crossover may bring spouses closer together in old age and appears to strengthen most late-life marriages. In one longitudinal study, Erikson and his colleagues found that most older spouses described their marriages as compassionate, companionate, affectionate, and supportive; they also saw these relationships as lifelong commitments (Erikson, Erikson, and Kivnick, 1986).

Research has found that marriage is not only perceived as positive and satisfying but actually appears to improve quality of life as well. When married older adults are compared with their unmarried peers, married people seem happier, healthier, and longer lived (Brubaker, 1985). There is substantial evidence to show that married older adults report greater life satisfaction, morale, and social integration (Depner and Ingersoll-Dayton, 1985). Married people are also less vulnerable to health problems than are unmarried people, with widowed and divorced people less protected than the never married (Kohen, 1983).

Marital satisfaction is the most important factor predicting life satisfaction for older women—more important than health, age, education, or

Profiles of Productive Aging

Hume Cronyn
Actor

"There is a quotation I'm very fond of by I. J. Singer. He was changing careers, giving up journalism and becoming a professor of Classical Languages. He learned to speak both Latin and Greek. And somebody said, 'Mr. Singer, what do you have to look forward to?' And he said, 'I hope to die young, as late as possible.' Isn't that marvelous?"

For over sixty years, Hume Cronyn has successfully conducted simultaneous careers on stage, screen, and television. He has contributed his talents not only as an actor but also as a producer, director, playwright, screenwriter, and lecturer.

Cronyn was born in 1911 in London, Ontario, Canada in what he calls an "Edwardian" family. Though he never planned on becoming a professional actor when he was growing up, he spent his childhood days in "some sort of mad fantasy world," where he played the cowboys *and* the Indians—*and* even the horses.

He graduated from Ridley College in 1930 and entered pre-law studies at McGill University. "I went through my first two years and found I was doing absolutely nothing about law, but I was in every amateur theatrical project that was offered to the community." With his family's support, he left his legal studies and went to New York City. The first casting director he met told him frankly that "you don't look like anything"—he couldn't easily be typecast. This quality turned out to be an enormous advantage for Cronyn, allowing him to play a broad spectrum of roles.

In New York, Cronyn enrolled at the American Academy of Dramatic Arts, graduating in 1934. He made his professional stage debut in *Up Pops the Devil* at the National Theatre in Washington, D.C. in 1931. His Broadway debut soon followed in 1934 in *Hipper's Holiday.* Since then Cronyn has appeared in more than 80 plays. He made his stage directorial debut in Los Angeles with *Portrait of a Madonna,* followed by his Broadway directorial debut in 1950 with *Now I Lay Me Down to Sleep.* He has since directed many successful stage productions.

In 1942 he married actress Jessica Tandy. Tandy and Cronyn have enjoyed performing together throughout their careers and have become one of America's favorite entertainment duos. They have worked together in hit plays, including *Foxfire* and *The Gin Game* (which he also coproduced with Mike Nichols), and on screen in the landmark film about aging, *Cocoon.* The couple even had their own television series in 1953 called *The Marriage.*

Cronyn made his screen debut in Alfred Hitchcock's *Shadow of a Doubt* and has appeared in 32 major motion pictures. He made his television debut in 1939 in *Her Master's Voice* and has always remained involved with high quality television productions as an actor, producer and director. He coauthored (with Susan Cooper) *The Dollmaker* and *Foxfire,* both award-winning teleplays.

Cronyn has received numerous honors from the theatrical community. He has been nominated for a Tony award four times, winning in 1964 for his performance as Polonius in *Hamlet.* He was also nominated for an Academy Award for his performance in *The Seventh Cross.* He won an Emmy for the television special *Age-Old Friends* (1989) and an Obie for *Krapp's Last Tape* (1973). In 1986 he and Tandy were honored together by the Kennedy Center for the Performing Arts for their lifetime achievement.

His recent autobiography, *A Terrible Liar,* was an instant best-seller.

Cronyn describes the actor's life: "To go on being an actor, you need sheer animal energy. If you can't restock your energy, you have to hide your lack of it." As he continues to be involved in several projects at once, Cronyn exhibits no lack of energy, finding sufficient fuel in his work.

Lydia Brontë

retirement; for men, marital satisfaction is second only to good health in predicting overall life satisfaction (Guilford, 1985–86). According to Atchley (1991), marriage encourages three major functions for older adults: intimacy, interdependence, and a sense of belonging. These functions enhance the possibility of positive health and well-being among married older people.

Married older adults have other advantages over the unmarried as well. The social support and social integration of married older adults is reportedly higher than those of unmarried people.

Marriage leads to increased social status and economic security, especially for women of current older cohorts who may not have qualified for pensions in their own rights. As compared to married couples, widows and widowers both experience a decline in financial well-being (Zick and Smith, 1986). Little is known about the economic impact of spousal death on widows and widowers in rural areas or on minority widows and widowers.

Increased marital satisfaction in later life may result in part from children leaving home; the empty nest gives parents freedom and opportunity that is not available during childrearing. Further, many investigators have found that a gender crossover occurs in late life in which men become more affectionate and less achievement oriented while women turn their interests and efforts outside the home.

Spouses and Social Support

Although marriage seems to protect older adults from some negative consequences of aging, that protection cannot continue indefinitely. Sadly, one spouse usually begins to experience physical, cognitive, or emotional declines as he or she ages. Unlike unmarried people who rarely have an identified support provider, married older adults can turn to spouses as a first line of defense against the dependence created by physical or mental illness. Provision of support can continue for long periods of time, even though the supportive spouse may also experience problems. Yet older spouses who are providing support must continue to contend with their own problems of illness, financial limitations, or legal burdens. Thus, although spouses are always there to provide support, the role is not without its own expensive costs.

Not only does the spouse as an individual provide support, but being married also appears to have an impact on the number of people available to give assistance. Women tend to have larger social networks than men; further, married people have larger networks than do nonmarrieds.

Thus, being married not only insures the provision of support from the spouse but also from larger support networks and more possible sources of support outside the nuclear family.

The impact of differential life expectancies is seen once again as many more older wives provide support to their disabled or ill husbands than husbands providing support for dependent wives. These women are the hidden victims of family illness, for they often experience the loneliness, isolation, and overload of providing support (Brody, 1990). Stressful for all older spouses, supporting an ill or demented spouse may be especially difficult for those older adults who are recently married. Spouses in those circumstances do not have a lifetime of shared experience upon which they can call. But regardless of length of marriage, providing support for a physically or mentally ill older adult can take a tremendous toll on older spouses. This topic is covered in greater depth in the section on caregiving.

Adult Children and Their Relationships with Aging Parents

One persistent social myth suggests that older people spend most of their time alone and lonely. Yet research shows that this is not true, that older adults—even those without spouses—find that their adult children are important sources of contact and support. Although the popular press delights in reporting that bonds between generations have gotten weaker in the 1980s and 1990s, on the whole the relationships between older adults and their adult children are extremely positive. About four out of five older adults have living children, but it is interesting to note that having children does not appear to increase happiness in old age (Johnson and Troll, 1992). It does increase the likelihood of older people having support providers.

Although older adults have frequent contact with many of their adult children, most older people choose to live independently. The American ethic cherishes autonomy and self-care, and many older adults feel that living with children might compromise their own and their children's privacy (Rosenthal, 1986). Less than 20 percent of older adults reside in their children's households; however, as parents grow older and become widowed, separated, or divorced, shared living arrangements become more common (U.S.

Fewer than 20 percent of older adults reside in their children's household. (Copyright © Marianne Gontarz)

Senate, 1985). Further, adult children who themselves become separated or divorced are more and more likely to return to their parental home for support and assistance. This may be especially true for single parents with children who find live-in baby sitters and housekeepers beneficial. Older parents like living near their adult children, but just as they do not want to move into their children's households, older parents prefer not having adult children return to their homes.

Even if they do not share a home, older adults and their adult children engage in frequent and positive contact. Older people and their children experience close relationships, even at a distance (Moss, Moss, and Moles, 1985). According to one classic study by Ethel Shanas at the University of Illinois (1980), approximately 80 percent of all older people with children live less than an hour from at least one child; 50 percent have at least one child living within ten minutes of their home; and 84 percent see an adult child at least once a week.

Are there race differences in the frequency with which older adults see, talk to, or write their adult children? Mitchell and Register (1984) hypothesized that older African Americans would see and receive help from their children and grandchildren more frequently than whites. Although their study showed that older African Americans were more likely to receive assistance from children and grandchildren, older whites were more likely to see their children and grandchildren. This finding contradicts findings of some earlier studies and indicates that additional research in this area is needed.

Most research on contact between older adults and their adult children has focused on relationships in which older adults are geographically proximate to their children. Relations with children living at a distance have been ignored, despite the fact that one study showed that over 50 percent of older people had at least one adult child living more than five hundred miles away (Schooler, 1979). Emotional support might be one area in which distant children could provide help, yet no one has yet examined how that kind of assistance affects the lives of older people. Relationships between older adults and both nearby and distant adult children are important for the elderly and need additional investigation as employment opportunities drive families geographically further apart.

According to one classic study by Ethel Shanas at the University of Illinois (1980), approximately 80 percent of all older people with children live less than an hour from at least one child; 50 percent have at least one child living within ten minutes of their home; and 84 percent see an adult child at least once a week.

Although geographic distance affects the frequency with which older people and adult children have contact with each other, it does not affect the quality of relationships between parents and their adult children (Lee and Ellithorpe, 1982). Even when they live far apart, most adult children report feeling close to their older parents (Litwak, 1981). As noted above, long distances between family members usually result from children's mobility in searching for employment opportunities. Differences in socioeconomic status appear far more powerful in creating barriers to close parent-child relationships than does geographic distance (Shanas, 1979). Lower- and working-class families tend to remain geographically and emotionally close, while middle- and upper-class families may experience greater geographic and emotional distance. Parents and adult children with different socioeconomic statuses tend to drift apart; many feel that they have nothing in common. Given that the parent-child relationship is one of inherent inequality (i.e., one in which one member has a clear advantage in power over the other), some researchers suggest that contact within that relationship is driven by obligation rather than by volition (Leigh, 1982). Yet the number of studies that have found consistently that adult children feel close toward their parents makes the obligational expectation difficult to believe (Cicirelli, 1981).

Social Support From Adult Children

After spouses, adult children are the single most important source of social support for older people. Even though most adult children work, care for their own families, and try to save for their own old age, they willingly provide support for their parents. As adult children improve their own financial positions, they may have access to more resources than their parents do; often later in life, support from child to parent becomes a normative and expected exchange.

Adult children provide three distinct types of support to their parents. First, they provide emotional support that includes listening to problems, providing advice, and giving comfort. Second, they provide instrumental or tangible support that includes goods and services, especially around the home. Additional instrumental support might be given in the form of transportation, home repairs, housework, or assistance with personal care. Third, adult children provide financial support, although many older people continue to give financial assistance to their children and grandchildren despite their own needs (Gatz, Bengtson, and Blum, 1990). Social class strongly affects patterns of intergenerational support, with lower- and working-class families giving more instrumental support, and middle- and upper-class families giving emotional and financial support. Women from blue-collar families become care providers themselves; women from white-collar families become care managers, identifying needed services and locating quality providers. Adult children with higher incomes have more options about how to provide support.

One consistent research finding relates to gender differences in support from adult children. Without question, women provide substantially more support to their parents than do men; daughters are the primary support providers in almost every situation, and when daughters are unavailable, daughters-in-law or granddaughters frequently take over support responsibilities. Brody (1985) found in her Philadelphia sample that about 80 percent of support providers to chronically ill older adults are women. Of that 80 percent, daughters represent approximately 30 percent of primary and secondary caregiving. When sons provide support, they tend to give money and supervision; daughters provide personal care and emotional support. Studies have consistently shown that men rarely provide the personal, day-to-day care given by wives and daughters. On average, men take part in personal care or instrumental tasks only when no female relative (i.e., wife, daughter, daughter-in-law, sister, granddaughter) is available (Brody and Schoonover, 1986). Interestingly, sons appear to feel less stress when they provide support to parents than daughters do, even when they provide the same kinds of assistance (Horowitz, 1985).

Little is known about racial and ethnic differences in the provision of support to aging parents. Being both old and a member of a minority group creates a double disadvantage, according to Jackson (1988). The family plays an important role in African-American and Hispanic culture, but how that role translates into actual support is not clear (Becerra, 1988). Markides and Mindel (1987) suggest that older members of ethnic or racial minority families enjoy close relationships with younger family members and that support is mutual.

It appears, however, that African-American families and their elderly members are diverse (Stanford, 1990). Many older African-American adults utilize their extended families as critical sources of support (Taylor, 1985). Mutran (1985) suggests that both socioeconomic status and race have an influence on family support, but the way in which support is given and received in minority families has not been well documented. There is the need to learn a great deal more about the effects of minority status on the provision of social support.

Most families, regardless of minority status or socioeconomic class, make efforts to care for an aging parent in preference to institutionalizing that parent. Typically, adult children begin to consider placing a parent in a nursing home when the needs of that parent exceed the support capabilities of the children (Soldo and Manton, 1985). Most adult children view nursing homes as negative environments. Therefore, the placement of a parent in a long-term care facility can be stressful for parent and child. Although institutionalization may provide relief from providing support on a daily basis, it does not necessarily relieve the stress that may be experienced by adult children. Many decisions to institutionalize are precipitated by a life event or crisis of the family member providing support (e.g., widowhood, serious illness). Therefore, these decisions are often made under pressure, and careful selection of facilities may not be possible.

On average, men take part in personal care or instrumental tasks only when no female relative (i.e., wife, daughter, daughter-in-law, sister, granddaughter) is available. Interestingly, sons appear to feel less stress when they provide support to parents than daughters do, even when they provide the same kinds of assistance.

Becoming a grandparent is one of the most positive changes in late life. (Copyright © Phil Kukelhan)

● GRANDPARENTS AND GRANDCHILDREN

Most older adults view becoming a grandparent as one of the most positive changes in late life (Thomas, 1986). Adults often become grandparents for the first time while they are in their middle to late forties and fifties. At that time they are still occupationally and socially engaged and often are enjoying the freedoms of having had their own children leave home and establish themselves as independent adults. The appearance of grandchildren often gives an older adult tremendous pleasure (Strom and Strom, 1987). The birth of that next generation assures that the family name will continue beyond the older adult's lifetime.

Increasing life expectancy frequently means that grandparents are not necessarily the generation closest to death in a family. In an ever-growing number of families, at least one older generation remains alive. Great-grandparenthood, once an extremely rare phenomenon, is occurring more frequently as people live longer (Doka and Mertz, 1988). Of older adults who have children, 94 percent are grandparents and 46 percent are great-grandparents. Nearly three-quarters of all grandparents see at least one grandchild on a weekly or biweekly basis. This pattern of contact is quite different from the one experienced by older adults and their grandparents. Many of today's children have four living grandparents and may have multiple great-grandparents still alive. In contrast, many older adults never met their own grandparents. As life expectancy continues to increase, more and more older adults will become both grandparents and great-grandparents.

Research in grandparent-grandchild relations has been inconsistent. Several different investigators have examined the perspective of grandparents (e.g., Bengtson and Robertson, 1985), and some investigators have studied relations between children and their grandparents (Hartshorne and Manaster, 1982; Matthews and Sprey, 1985). But the role of grandparents in their grandchildren's lives is still not clear, especially when the grandchildren are adults. Although it might be assumed that grandparents who live with their grandchildren exert more influence on them, there is little empirical evidence to support this belief.

The classic study on grandparenthood was done by Neugarten and Weinstein (1964) at the University of Chicago. In it, the authors identified five different styles of grandparenting: the formal, the fun-seeking, the distant, the surrogate parent, and the reservoir of family wisdom. The names of these types characterize the kinds of relationships between grandparents and their grandchildren. Older grandparents tended to fall into the formal or distant styles, never establishing a close, interactive relationship with their grandchildren. Younger grandparents emphasized the closeness of their relationships, often looking to grandchildren as sources of interest and pleasure. The grandparent who became a surrogate parent had more of a parent-child relationship with grandchildren than a grandparental one. And the reservoir of family wisdom was seen as a person who could provide family history and personal knowledge for grandchildren.

Of older adults who have children, 94 percent are grandparents and 46 percent are great-grandparents. Nearly three-quarters of all grandparents see at least one grandchild on a weekly or biweekly basis.

Another study by Kivnick (1982) suggested that grandchildren provide immortality to grandparents and that older adults live vicariously through this generation. It is credible that grandparents might see their grandchildren as the bearers of the family name and family reputation. Although evidence of vicarious living through grandchildren is limited, only rarely has research indicated that the role of grandparent is not central to older people's lives and that the status of being a grandparent does not contribute to life satisfaction (Wood and Robertson, 1976). For the most part, grandparenting is an important activity for older adults, one that provides ongoing pleasure. Instead of being a parent and having total responsibility for young children, older people can anticipate their interactions with their grandchildren, concentrating on sharing enjoyment rather than imposing discipline.

Grandparents can act as role models for their grandchildren. Grandmothers tend to have more influence than grandfathers. (Copyright © Paul Gilmore)

Relationships between grandparents and grandchildren appear to be influenced by gender. Grandfathers are more closely linked to sons of sons while grandmothers develop a greater closeness with daughters of daughters (Hooyman and Kiyak, 1988). If grandchildren are carriers of family tradition and symbols of immortality and family unity, it is understandable for grandfathers to feel emotionally closer to male grandchildren and grandmothers to female grandchildren. Grandparents also can act as role models for their grandchildren, and the gender links here make sense as well.

One important correlate of the grandparent-grandchild relationship has not been examined closely: the importance of the middle generation, the children of grandparents and the parents of grandchildren. It is not yet known whether grandmothers with close relationships with daughters also have close relationships with their granddaughters. It is also unclear whether grandfathers who rarely interact with their sons also remain aloof from their grandsons. Additional studies will be necessary before these questions can be answered with any confidence.

Studies on grandparenting reveal that grandmothers have more influence over their grandchildren than do grandfathers (Kivnick, 1982). In part, this may result from the parenting experiences of today's older adults. In other words, fathers who took no active part in parenting may also distance themselves from their grandchildren. For whatever reasons, it appears that current grandparents have differential influence on their grandchildren by gender. The longer life

Profiles of Productive Aging

Bernice Neugarten
Gerontologist

"Development is like a fan. It opens as we age. People become more different from each other the older they become. If we want to look for similarities, we do best to look at people toward the beginning of the life span. There they are likely to be more alike."

Bernice Neugarten, one of the nation's leading authorities on aging, was born in rural Nebraska in 1916. She had what she terms "an odd childhood," where her above-average intelligence saw her skip grade after grade. While this proved helpful academically, Neugarten found it an isolating experience. "I was a child and everybody else was an adolescent," she explains.

Upon graduating from high school she swiftly moved to Chicago, where she attended the University of Chicago, gaining a B.A. in English literature in 1936. Not sure what to do after graduation, she became interested in the field of educational psychology and gained her Masters in education the following year. She then entered a newly formed program called the Committee on Human Development to work towards her Ph.D.

When she gained her degree in 1943 she was the first person to do so under the Committee.

Neugarten married in 1940 and decided to take time off to raise a family. She returned to the University of Chicago a decade later to work part time as a counsellor. "I wanted something to do out of the house," she explains. "I had no motivation about building a fancy career. I needed something that was interesting intellectually and I wanted it on my terms."

In 1952 Neugarten was asked to teach the course "Maturity and Old Age." "I was invited to join the research team that was beginning a study of middle-aged and aging persons in the metropolitan area of Kansas City," she recalls. "Had it been a course in child development that needed an instructor, I might well have wound up today as a child psychologist."

Neugarten's pioneering work in the then fledgling field of human development saw the committee "boom in size" over the following years. By 1960 she was named associate professor and in 1964 she became a professor. From 1969 to 1973, she served as chairperson of human development, and from 1969 to 1970 she chaired the first Committee on University Women.

During these years she also became a prolific

expectancy of grandmothers may contribute to this phenomenon as well. The changing patterns of parenting for today's fathers may alter their experiences as grandfathers as well.

On the subject of the relationships between adult grandchildren and their grandparents, a recent study by Hodgson (1992) of a national

---

Grandfathers are more closely linked to sons of sons while grandmothers develop a greater closeness with daughters of daughters. If grandchildren are carriers of family tradition and symbols of immortality and family unity, it is understandable for grandfathers to feel emotionally closer to male grandchildren and grandmothers to female grandchildren.

---

sample of adult children age 18 and older explored the relationships of these young adults with their grandparents. Hodgson found that the strength of grandparent-adult grandchild relations depended in part on the ages of grandchild and grandparent, their geographical proximity, the parent-child relationship, and the parent-grandparent relationship. But much is still poorly understood about grandparenting in general and grandparents and adult grandchildren in particular.

Finally, grandparenting can be disrupted by marital discord of young-adult or middle-aged sons and daughters. Divorce can upset the lives of young children and render their relationships with their grandparents ambiguous. Colleen Johnson (1985; 1988) in California interviewed older adults and their adult children on the topic of divorce. She found that grandmothers were often integral parts of their children's and grandchildren's lives, even after divorce. This was espe-

Profiles of Productive Aging (contd.)

researcher. She sought to challenge psychologists of the time who believed that personality ended when a person completed adolescence. She also challenged other traditional ideas such as the notion that nearly all people experience a midlife crisis or regularly timed transitions. Her major publications began with a monograph that she coauthored in 1957 and later turned into a book cowritten with colleagues. That work, *Personality in Middle and Late Life* (1964), became a classic in the field of aging. In it she discusses her findings that personality continues to develop and change throughout the life span.

She then went on to work in the study of grandparenting and retirement, coauthoring *Adjustment to Retirement* (1969) and *Social Status in the City* (1971) and editing *Age or Need? Public Policies for Older People* (1982), a book that reflected her growing interest in public policy issues.

Neugarten contends that because of the wide variety of differences in the way people grow old, age is a poor predictor of an adult's needs and physical, social, or intellectual competence. For this reason, public policy should be based on people's needs and not their ages, she says.

She also identified distinctions within the elderly population, defining "young-old" as people who, though technically senior citizens, retain an active, involved lifestyle, and "old-old" as those who behave as if they are elderly.

In 1981, Neugarten was named deputy chairperson of the White House Conference on Aging, a position she says accelerated her interest in the relationship between scholarship and public policy. That interest also led her in 1980 to accept an appointment at Northwestern University as a professor in the School of Education and Social Policy.

Throughout her long career Neugarten gained many honorary degrees from universities around the world. In 1992 she was one of 100 women featured in the Women's Heritage Exhibit at the American Psychological Association's centennial conference in Washington, D.C.

While she planned to retire in her mid-60s, Neugarten found herself "talked into" joining the Center on Aging, Health and Society at the University of Chicago. She continues to work there as a Rothschild Distinguished Scholar.

Lydia Brontë

cially true when the middle generation—the adult children—were committed to facilitating grandparent-grandchild relations. Grandparents who respond to the divorce situation with compassion and assistance helped sustain family relationships on all levels (Matthews and Sprey, 1984; Gladstone, 1988). Without question, grandparents who were judgmental about their children's divorce were included less often in family activities and decisions.

The status of grandparents after a divorce is unclear as well (Wilson and DeShane, 1982). In many instances, relations between grandparents and grandchildren are stronger after a divorce. This is especially true when grandparents help the custodial parent with emotional or instrumental support. However, parents of the non-custodial child may be denied access to their grandchildren. The custodial parent can remove the grandchild geographically from grandparents or simply refuse to allow grandparents to visit. The legal sta-

tus of grandparents in this situation is still unclear. In a few states, grandparents can have legal visitation rights with grandchildren; in most states, however, parents control visitation. These barriers to grandparent-grandchild relations may have a long-term impact on the grandchild, and grandchildren raised in these circumstances may find it difficult to establish relationships with their own grandchildren many years later.

Reconstituted families after divorce can also create problems for grandparents. This phenomenon occurs when two adults who have both been married before and have children from previous marriages decide to form a new family. In this instance, young children have "old" and "new" grandparents, the old from the first marriage and the new from the second. Grandparent relations with old and new grandchildren in this situation are unclear, and further research is vital to understanding the changes that occur when families are blended and reconstituted. However, the potential for conflict in this situation is high, especially for the non-custodial parent's parents.

● SIBLING RELATIONSHIPS IN LATER LIFE

Of all family interactions of older adults, those with siblings can be both the most rewarding and the most annoying simultaneously. Siblings share the most durable of family bonds, potentially lasting from shared childhood experiences through the death of one sibling. Sisters and brothers often share more with each other than with anyone else, including family heritage, cultural background, and life-long experiences. Ambivalence about siblings often may be generated in childhood and sustained throughout adulthood. Siblings may be viewed as concurrent allies and competitors throughout the life course. Despite feelings of sibling rivalry, childhood typically signals closeness and sharing with siblings. Older adults reminiscing about their sibling relationships classify childhood as a time of close and positive relations. Because only 10 percent of older adults are only children, the vast majority of older people have experienced the social role of sibling.

Adolescence is a time during which most sibling relationships become less involved. Traditional developmental theory states that adolescence is focused on independence and autonomy, and the need to find an individual identity affects sibling relationships strongly. Many siblings have little or no contact during these years and may continue to diverge in young adulthood, a time traditionally reserved for establishing a career, getting married, and starting a family. These major changes often leave little time for nurturing sibling bonds. The exception to this weakening of sibling bonds occurs between sisters who have children at approximately the same time. These sisters use each other as mentors and sounding boards, asking advice and providing suggestions when crises over children occur.

If young adulthood is the time of establishing family and career, middle age is the time of peak responsibilities in these areas. Career demands may be strongest at this time; family may be equally demanding. In early middle age, siblings often continue the separation of earlier years. If older parents need care, middle-aged siblings may be brought together to solve this problem.

However, this area is rife with the potential for serious conflict among siblings if they disagree on major decisions about parent care (e.g., institutionalization). Concern over aging parents can be either a positive or negative influence on mid-life sibling relations.

In late middle age, sibling bonds begin to be reforged. The first parental death can be a strong stimulus for sibling closeness; an even greater closeness may occur when the second parent dies. These incidents may bring siblings together as they realize they now belong to the generation in the family that is closest to death. Other major life transitions such as the empty nest (children leaving home) and retirement often stimulate interest in sibling relationships.

Like childhood, old age is a time of positive sibling relations and strong sibling bonds (Gold, 1989a). Over 80 percent of older adults have positive relations with brothers and sisters, and many have some contact with siblings at least once a week. Throughout life, the sibling relationship is based on equality and reciprocity. Unlike the parent and child relationship in which one person clearly has authority and power, siblings share a balance of power and operate from norms of equity. Further, the sibling relationship is more voluntary than are other family relationships. Nothing forces adults to interact with their sisters and brothers except their own wishes, and it is rare that the ties between siblings are those of obligation. These feelings of choice and free will often result in more positive and supportive interactions.

According to Deborah T. Gold (1989b) of Duke University Medical Center, the sibling bond is central to well-being in later life for a large proportion of older adults. Her studies of siblings across the life course suggest that five different types of late-life sibling relationships exist. The first is the *intimate* relationship, categorized by intense closeness and total sharing. These siblings are best friends and feel that their sibling bond is stronger than that with their spouses or children. *Congenial* siblings are friends rather than best friends but still share a tremendous amount of time and support with sisters and brothers. Although confidences might first be shared with a spouse, congenial siblings confide both positive and negative feelings to each other.

Loyal siblings are always there when needed. They attend family weddings and family funerals with equal regularity and can be counted on to provide emotional and instrumental support in times of difficulty. Although loyal siblings may not see or talk to each other on a regular basis, each sibling knows that the other is there and available when necessary.

In late middle age, sibling bonds begin to be reforged. The first parental death can be a strong stimulus for sibling closeness; an even greater closeness may occur when the second parent dies. These incidents may bring siblings together as they realize they now belong to the generation in the family that is closest to death.

Unfortunately, not all sibling relationships in late life are positive and supportive. *Apathetic* siblings have little or no contact, not even at special occasions. They are not angry with each other; they are simply indifferent. These siblings report that their lives took different directions in adolescence and young adulthood; further, there appears to be no interest in reviving the sibling bond later in life. The most negative relationships of all are the *hostile* sibling relationships that are filled with hatred and disgust. These siblings feel betrayed or misled by the other and would not, under any circumstances, provide support for each other. It is interesting to realize that hostile and intimate siblings spend about the same amount of time thinking about each other. The difference is that intimate siblings empathize with and support each other while hostile siblings focus on negative aspects of their relationships.

Shared reminiscence is something that late-life siblings engage in frequently. Robert Butler (1980–81) identified the life review as an important part of the aging process. He defines the life review as the process of sorting through the memories of life and putting them together into a coherent whole. For most older adults, siblings are the only living people who knew them during childhood and adolescence. Brothers and sisters are valuable links to the past and validate each other's life review by mutual remembering. This assistance is invaluable in completing this major psychological task in late life.

Do different gender pairs of siblings have different kinds of relationships? Study after study has shown that sisters are the closest of all sibling pairs, and that this distinction holds true across the life course (Gold, 1989a). Sisters frequently report deepest intimacy and closeness, sharing all aspects of life. Many brothers of brothers, on the other hand, report feelings of animosity and competition, especially when parental comparisons were made frequently in childhood. Somehow, the fact that parents held one brother up as a model to another is never forgotten, and issues such as family size, income, prestige in employment, and children's education perpetuate rivalry through adulthood.

Brother-sister sibling pairs are more like pairs of sisters than brothers. Researchers suggest that it is the presence of a woman in the sibling pair, rather than having two sisters, that leads to closeness and sharing in sibling relationships. Brothers report that they can confide in sisters more than in brothers; they also report greater interest in hearing the confidences of sisters than of brothers. However, some pairs of brothers capitalize on the increased emotionality of men in late life and are able to establish relationships of intimacy and caring.

Older adults who are widowed, divorced, or never married find that siblings are especially important sources of emotional support. For childless elderly, nieces and nephews often provide contact with the next generation and may also provide needed instrumental support. Researchers predict that those born between 1945 and 1960 (the baby boomers) will find siblings more important in late life than have other older people. As older adults, the baby boomers will have more siblings than children. Therefore, when they need support or care, they may have to find a sibling rather than a child to help.

But what of the children of the baby boomers? Many will be only children and will not learn sharing and cooperation from brothers and sisters; others will have only one sibling. The lack of sibling relationships may encourage this generation to have slightly larger families so that their children can have sisters and brothers.

> Study after study has shown that sisters are the closest of all sibling pairs, and that this distinction holds true across the life course. Sisters frequently report deepest intimacy and closeness, sharing all aspects of life.

● EXTENDED KIN RELATIONSHIPS

Primary family relationships are of greatest importance in American culture. These relationships include those with parents, children, spouses, and siblings. But most older adults also have active relationships that extend beyond the nuclear family. Feelings of family solidarity (Bengtson, Rosenthal, and Burton, 1990) or family unity can be promoted by keeping a network of extended kin relationships invested in family interactions. Of all family relations, those with extended kin are most dependent on geographic proximity and family tradition for continuing closeness. Parents who interact with their own cousins, aunts, uncles, nieces, and nephews will influence their children to do the same. Older adults without spouses or children often turn to extended family members for social contact and support. Extended kin engage in family rituals, reunions, remembering holidays or birthdays, and reminiscing about past family events (Bengtson, Rosenthal, and Burton, 1990). Cousins, nephews, and nieces take the place of primary family members in family traditions.

Often, one person in the extended family network is identified as the kinkeeper, who keeps in touch with all family members and organizes family activities. Typically, the kinkeeper is female and responds to suggestions about potential family interactions from different network members. At some point, the older generation will not be able to continue this monumental effort, and kinkeeping responsibilities are passed down to the next generation. In this way, the extended family is kept alive and connected.

Alternatively, there may be an identified head of the extended family who can be male or female. If the head of the family is male, the task of keeping in touch with family members may be delegated to someone else. Many families adopt a bureaucratic structure, especially as the size of the network increases. As with the kinkeeper, the head of the family will, at some point, need to step down and may identify his or her successor prior to doing so.

● NEVER-MARRIED OLDER ADULTS

About 5 percent of current older adults have never been married and therefore will experience aging with a unique set of needs. Future groups of older people will have higher proportions of never-married members. Two different kinds of never-married adults exist: those for whom being single is a choice, and those who wanted to get married but never did. It is as yet unclear whether those types of single older adults age differently.

The vast majority of never-married older adults are not lonely (Bengtson, Rosenthal, and Burton, 1990), although they may feel socially isolated (Burnley, 1987). The emphasis in our culture is on the nuclear family, and key roles associated with that family (i.e., parent, spouse) are never available to single people. Extended kin relationships can be very important to those who have not married, and family ties with siblings, aunts and uncles, and nieces and nephews tend to be strong. Because never-married older adults have spent all of adulthood independently, they report much less loneliness than do widows. Further, they establish relationships with *fictive* (fictional) kin to replace missing family relationships. For example, a single woman without a sister may develop a close friendship with someone near her own age who acts like a sister and meets many of the needs ordinarily met by sisters. This fictive kin can help maintain stability in the never-married person's life and provide a family with whom single people can spend holidays and celebrate important events.

Those older adults who never married are also typically childless. Although this, too, may change as people become more accepting of single parents, the lack of children can be problematic for older adults who need care. Beckman and Houser (1982) found that childless older adults tended to have fewer social contacts than older people with children; however, this held true for both the married and unmarried childless. In addition, childless older adults with health problems are more likely to become socially isolated. These people turn to siblings, nieces, and nephews for support when needed. The childless, never-married older adult is, in some ways, in double jeopardy; he or she has neither a spouse nor children to provide assistance. Johnson and Catalano (1981) found that childless unmarried elderly were much more likely to use nursing homes and other social services than married childless elderly. And the unmarried childless elderly are at higher risk of institutionalization than either married older adults or older parents.

However, many never-married older people realize that their independence may create future difficulties and that support is essential. These single older people establish strong social support systems to assume responsibilities for care ordinarily taken by a spouse or adult child. In these networks, extended kin can play an important part. However, support networks can also be comprised of friends, neighbors, members of the same church, or other informal contacts. These non-family support networks appear less viable as older people become impaired or disabled and have increasing instrumental support needs. At that point, unmarried older people may need to utilize many more community services in order to meet their support needs.

The proportion of each generation that remains unmarried seems to be slowly increasing; further, current young adults appear to be marrying later. But if that trend continues, strong informal networks and accessible community services will be a necessity for independent living.

● GAY AND LESBIAN RELATIONSHIPS IN LATER LIFE

Little research has focused on homosexuality in late life, but research shows that relationships between gay and lesbian older adults are diverse

---

Because never-married older adults have spent all of adulthood independently, they report much less loneliness than do widows. Further, they establish relationships with *fictive* (fictional) kin to replace missing family relationships.

(Lee, 1987a). Existing research also suggests that about 10 percent of people age 65 years and older are gay or lesbian, the same proportion that is found in the adult population at large (Berger, 1984). Many of these people have strong, committed relationships with members of the same sex. But gay and lesbian relationships are not identical, and it is important to examine patterns of family relations among gay men and lesbians separately (Quam and Whitford, 1992).

Typically, older lesbians have had either one or a series of intimate relationships throughout their adult lives (Kehoe, 1986; Friend, 1987). Older lesbians without partners continue to hope to find a new mate (Kehoe, 1989). Despite the importance of sex in the relationships of older lesbians, it is not the factor that keeps lesbian couples together (Wolf, 1982). Shared interests and long-term commitments are much more important to lesbian couples. Although lesbians remain sexually active, frequency of sexual interaction declines in later life (Deevey, 1990; Peplau and Gordon, 1982).

Patterns of relationships of gay men in later life are somewhat different from those of lesbians. During middle age (i.e., 46 to 55 years old), the number of monogamous partnerships between gay men peaks at approximately 59 percent; however, gay couplehood decreases after age 60 because of death of one partner or because some older men may reject monogamy in late life (Gee, 1987). Berger (1984) found that the majority of older gay men reported satisfaction with their partners and indicated a greater sense of well-being and life satisfaction than did younger gay men. Although older lesbians generally do not fear the physical changes that result from aging, many older gay men show great concern about physical appearance in late life (Lee, 1987b). Like older lesbians, gay male couples continue to report sexuality as important in their relationships despite reduced frequency of sexual interactions (Berger and Kelly, 1986).

The gay community may function for gay men and lesbians in the same way that extended kin networks function for heterosexual older adults (Gray and Dressel, 1985). If this is true, the support networks of gay men and lesbians can provide as much help in times of crisis as do spouses or adult children. Society's increasing acceptance of homosexuality over the last twenty years may suggest that future older homosexuals will be more socially accepted than they have been in the past.

During middle age (i.e., 46 to 55 years old), the number of monogamous partnerships between gay men peaks at approximately 59 percent; however, gay couplehood decreases after age 60 because of death of one partner or because some older men may reject monogamy in late life.

● DIVORCE AND WIDOWHOOD IN OLD AGE

A variety of changes in late life can result in the end of marital relationships. From separation and divorce to death of a spouse, circumstances may require older people to establish independence in all walks of life. Sometimes this independence is not possible, and nursing homes or other institutional care is essential. But those elderly who find themselves without a spouse in later life for one reason or another face a difficult adjustment. Although divorce and widowhood both have the same ultimate outcome—that is, the end of a marriage—adjustments may be quite different for those who face these two transitions.

Divorce and the Elderly

Most married older adults report having high marital satisfaction in late life. However, there are some late-life marriages that simply do not work. Today, divorce is considered an acceptable means of ending an unhappy marriage, and more older adults are choosing divorce than ever before. In 1960, 1 percent of divorces involved someone age 65 and older; in 1980, this proportion had increased to 3.4 percent (Brubaker, 1985). Although the number of late-life marriages ending in divorce is still relatively low compared to other age groups, between 10 percent and 13 percent of older adults have been divorced at some point in the life course (Uhlenberg and Myers, 1981). This rate was slightly higher for males than females and declined as age increased.

In the future, both the number and proportion of

older people experiencing divorce will increase. Brubaker (1985) predicts that one-third of those reaching age 65 between 2010 and 2014 will have been divorced at least once during their lives. For those born between 1950 and 1954, Cherlin (1981) estimates that 45 percent will have been divorced from at least one spouse. One contributing factor may be the increasing economic independence of women. Further, because people are living longer, and death is not terminating as many marriages before the participants reach old age, the divorce rate will continue to rise for the elderly.

One reason for increasing numbers of divorced older adults may be the social acceptance of divorce as an alternative to an unhappy marriage. Further, the number of people who remarry after divorce is also increasing; this trend may make divorce more acceptable to those who still believe in marriage and want a marital relationship. However, remarriages are more likely to end in divorce than are first marriages. Thus remarrying does not necessarily increase the likelihood of success in marriage.

People who are divorced in late life often suffer serious economic and social consequences. Women are more likely to have these problems than men, especially if they have not qualified for Social Security or pensions on their own (Uhlenberg and Myers, 1981). Furthermore, the loss of a spouse to divorce is also the loss of a potential source of support. There is also evidence that late-life divorce may also weaken relationships between older parents and their adult children. If some or all children take sides in a divorce between older people, children may be lost as a potential sources of support as well. Divorce may also compromise the quality of relationships between older people and their grandchildren and great-grandchildren (Johnson, 1985); legal guidelines for grandparent-grandchild contact are unclear.

Those older adults who readjust successfully from divorce have greater resources including money, education, and strong social support networks (Smyer and Hofland, 1982). But older people have fewer alternatives than do young people after the end of a marriage. This is especially true for older women for whom remarriage may be an impossibility. Thus late-life divorce results in unhappiness and loss of family and social networks for some divorcing couples.

In 1960, 1 percent of divorces involved someone age 65 and older; in 1980, this proportion had increased to 3.4 percent.

Widowhood in Late Life

Throughout late life, older adults face major changes. Of all the role changes older people experience, moving from spouse to widow is perhaps the most difficult. Widowhood requires greater readjustment by an older adult than does any other stressful life event in old age (Silverman, 1986). Yet by age 70, most women have been widowed already. Men, on the other hand, may not experience widowhood at all because their life expectancy is typically shorter than that of their wives. The differences in widowhood rates for men and women are shown in Table 16.3.

The trend of men marrying younger women also makes it less likely that men will be widowed. If widowhood does occur for older men, it is likely to happen at age 85 or older. However, as is evident from Table 16.3, men's widowhood rates never come close to those of women. Race plays an important part in timing and frequency of widowhood as well. Twice as many nonwhite women experience widowhood as do white women, and those nonwhite women are likely to be widowed at an younger age. Further, while Hispanic and Asian widows frequently move in with others, African-American and white widows remain alone. This living pattern may have implications for support as widows continue to age.

Widows are more likely to cope successfully with spousal death if that death occurs "on time"—that is, late enough in life that one might expect to be widowed. "Off-time" deaths of spouses are substantially more difficult to manage because there has been no time for emotional preparation either for the death or for the widowhood that follows. The widow who is often best prepared is the one who has cared for a chroni-

Table 16.3

Percentage of Persons 65 Years and Over, by Marital Status, Age, Sex, Race, and Hispanic Origin, 1990
(Nonstitutional population)

Age, race, and Hispanic origin[1]	Married, spouse present		Widowed	
	Male	Female	Male	Female
65 years and over	74.2	39.7	14.2	48.6
White	76.3	41.1	13.3	48.1
Black	54.2	25.3	23.4	53.7
Hispanic origin[1]	73.3	40.0	12.6	42.2
65 to 74 years	78.2	51.1	9.2	36.1
White	80.3	53.2	8.2	35.1
Black	55.5	29.6	19.8	45.1
Hispanic origin[1]	77.4	48.2	7.9	31.5
75 to 84 years	71.2	27.7	19.5	62.0
White	72.8	28.3	19.0	62.1
Black	56.1	22.0	23.6	61.0
Hispanic origin[1]	67.2	26.3	18.8	60.9
85 years and over	46.9	10.1	43.4	79.8
White	48.7	10.3	42.0	79.1
Black	(B)	8.6	(B)	85.6
Hispanic origin[1]	(B)	(B)	(B)	(B)

Notes: B: Base is less than 75,000. 1. Hispanic origin may be of any race.

Source: Saluter, Arlene F., U.S. Bureau of the Census, "Marital Status and Living Arrangements." *Current Population Reports,* Series P-20, no. 450 (March 1990). Washington, DC: U.S. Government Printing Office, May 1991.

Twice as many nonwhite women experience widowhood as do white women. (Copyright © Marianne Gontarz)

cally or terminally ill spouse. In this instance, the widow has had ample time to accept the idea of the death of the spouse, to mentally rehearse widowhood and changing roles with family members, and may have even begun the grieving process prior to the death itself (Marshall and Levy, 1990).

Other factors influence how great an impact widowhood has on older adults. In addition to gender, age, race, and "on time" or "off time" widowhood, social class, health, and living situation also affect the individual's response to this major life transition. Because there are five widows to every widower in American society, most research on widowhood has focused on women and their adaptation.

Do women cope with widowhood more effectively than men? The answer to that question is complex. For example, income and socioeconomic status help widows cope and encourage independence and continuing social participation; however, male widows are more likely to have higher incomes than are women and there-

fore might cope better. Some older women may have great difficulty in facing the economic consequences of widowhood. Financial repercussions may be especially problematic if the deceased spouse has been chronically ill and the widow has been serving as caregiver. Health services and long-term care can erode any family's resources, and widows in this situation may be left with little or no financial security. Nearly 40 percent of widowed women live in or near poverty (Hill and others, 1988), and the needs of these women have not yet been addressed by public policy.

In terms of health following bereavement, Thompson and his colleagues (1984) reported that recently widowed older people were more likely to report new illness or exacerbation of an existing condition than were non-widowed peers. The widows also reported more new medication use than did non-widows. Earlier studies had shown that men were more likely to experience illness after bereavement than women (Murrell, Himmelfarb, and Phifer, 1988).

Ferraro (1985) compared widows and widowers and found that bereaved men visited doctors more frequently and used more medications than bereaved women. Some studies (e.g., Feinson, 1986) found that widowers have worse physical health, greater isolation and loneliness, less social support, and fewer confidants than widows. Thus the negative consequences of widowhood can be damaging regardless of gender.

Although the financial arena of widowhood appears to favor men, women are better off in terms of friendship and support. Older women tend to have much larger and more supportive social networks than men, and women are more likely to accept both emotional support and instrumental help from network members (Lopata and Brehm, 1986). Because these networks can and do provide companionship and assistance for widows, widowed women often have little interest in remarriage. As noted, the differing life expectancies of men and women make the available group of older men very small, and almost 60 percent of all older women who are widowed remain unmarried and live alone. In one large study, 36 percent of widows reportedly liked being single and the independence that was part of the single life (Gentry and Shulman, 1988). Some widows chose not to remarry because they idealized their late husbands; others said that they did not want additional caregiving responsibilities. In all, the combination of few potential partners and preferences for independence means many widows remain unmarried for the rest of their lives.

In contrast, most older widowed men are not only interested in remarriage but are likely to remarry relatively soon after bereavement. Widowers complain much more about loneliness than widows, often a reflection of their lack of social networks (Diamond, Lund, and Caserta, 1987). For a man whose confidante is his wife, widowhood can be especially devastating. Furthermore, because men are socialized not to betray their emotions, they may have difficulty in expressing feelings of grief and bereavement. When a wife dies, her husband has not only lost his best friend and confidante, but he may have lost his housekeeper and support provider as well. However, men's social networks may not be able to provide eligible candidates for remarriage quickly. As a result, widowers often report greater isolation and experience difficulty with simple survival tasks such as cooking, cleaning, and caring for the household.

Widowhood has well-documented mental health effects for both men and women. In a large study, researchers found that all widowed persons reported higher levels of mental impairment than did age-matched married people (Goldberg and others, 1988). In California, Gallagher and her colleagues (1981–82) report equal levels of difficulty in adjustment to widowhood for men and women. In particular, Gallagher reports that the mental health consequences of widowhood are high for both men and women. Suicide rates, incidence and prevalence of chronic illness, and other negative events can accompany widowhood. However, widows who have supportive family members can adapt more effectively to life changes.

As noted, widows with strong social support networks are more likely to experience bereavement successfully and to restructure their lives to meet current needs than are isolated widows. Adult children can play an important role during this process, providing emotional support and tangible help when necessary; they can also provide entertainment and distraction for their widowed parent. It is equally important, however, for

---

As noted, the differing life expectancies of men and women make the available group of older men very small, and almost 60 percent of all older women who are widowed remain unmarried and live alone. In one large study, 36 percent of widows reportedly liked being single and the independence that was part of the single life.

---

widowed people to have social contact with people their own age. For widows, becoming socially involved with other widows is extremely important. Rather than try to interact in a couple-based social network, groups of widows often gather and share social and recreational activities. One widow is usually more able to accept help from another widow than from married couples or professionals. Of course the most likely people to participate in groups like this are women; widowers, even when groups are available, tend to remain isolated.

● ADAPTING TO CHANGING FAMILY PATTERNS

Family support throughout late life is extremely important to the physical and mental well-being of older adults; widowhood can make this assistance even more valuable. However, the changing American family often leaves older adults unclear about sources of emotional and instrumental assistance. Families that remain intact have well demarcated lines of assistance for older adults; this help can come from adult children, sisters and brothers, grandchildren, extended family or fictive kin. Families no longer intact because of geographical mobility, divorce, remarriage, or death have greater difficulty in identifying who will help and in what way. Just as some older adults need to rearrange their lives in order to accommodate the divorce of one of their children, others have to face their own losses through divorce or widowhood. Throughout this era of rapid social change and individual differences, however, it is important to remember that the family in American society remains the central source of love and support for the elderly.

Organizations

Children of Aging Parents
2761 Trenton Rd.
Levittown, PA 19056
(215) 945-6900

Older Women's League
730 11th St., NW, Ste. 300
Washington, DC 20001-4512
(202) 783-6686

References

Atchley, R. *Social Forces and Aging.* 6th ed. Belmont, CA: Wadsworth, 1991.

Becerra, R. M. "The Mexican-American Family." In *Ethnic Families in America: Patterns and Variations.* Eds. C. H. Mindel, R. W. Habenstein, and R. Wright, Jr., 3d ed. New York: Elsevier, 1988.

Beckman, L. J., and B. B. Jauser. "The Consequences of Childlessness on the Social-Psychological Well-Being of Older Women." *Journal of Gerontology* Vol. 37 (1982): 243–50.

Bengtson, V. L., and J. F. Robertson eds. *Grandparenthood.* Beverly Hills, CA: Sage, 1985.

Bengtson, V. L., C. Rosenthal, and L. Burton. "Families and Aging: Diversity and Heterogeneity." In *Handbook of Aging and the Social Sciences.* Eds. R. H. Binstock and L. K. George. 3d ed. San Diego: Academic Press, 1990.

Berger, R. M. "Realities of Gay and Lesbian Aging." *Social Work* Vol. 29 (1984): 57–62.

Berger, R. M., and J. Kelley. "Working with Homosexuals of the Older Population." *Social Casework* Vol. 67 (1986): 203–10.

Brody, E. "Parent Care as a Normative Family Stress." *Gerontologist* Vol. 25 (1985): 19–30.

——. *Women in the Middle: Their Parent-Care Years.* New York: Springer, 1990.

Brody, E., and C. Schoonover. "Patterns of Parent-Care When Adult Children Work and When They Do Not." *Gerontologist* Vol. 26 (1986): 372–81.

Brubaker, T. H. *Later Life Families.* Beverly Hills, CA: Sage, 1985.

Burnley, C. S., "The Impact of Emotional Support for Single Women." *Journal of Aging Studies* Vol. 1 (1987): 253–64.

Butler, R. N. "The Life Review: An Unrecognized Bonanza." *International Journal of Aging and Human Development* Vol. 12 (1980–81): 35–38.

Cherlin, A. J. *Marriage, Divorce, Remarriage: Changing Patterns in the Postwar United States.* Cambridge, MA: Harvard University Press, 1981.

Cicirelli, V. G. *Helping Elderly Parents: The Role of Adult Children.* Boston, MA: Auburn House, 1981.

Deevey, S. "Older Lesbian Women: An Invisible Minority." *Journal of Gerontological Nursing* Vol. 16 (1990): 35–39.

Depner, C. E., and B. Ingersoll-Dayton. "Conjugal Social Support: Patterns in Late Life." *Journal of Gerontology* Vol. 40 (1985): 761–66.

Diamond, M., D. A. Lund, and M. S. Caserta. "The Role of Social Support in the First Two Years of Bereavement in an Elderly Sample." *Gerontologist* Vol. 13 (1987): 79–84.

Doka, K. J., and M. E. Mertz. "The Meaning and Significance of Great-Grandparenthood." *Gerontologist* Vol. 28 (1988): 192–97.

Erikson, E. H., J. M. Erikson, and H. Q. Kivnick. *Vital Involvement in Old Age.* New York: Norton, 1987.

Feinson, M. J. "Aging Widows and Widowers: Are there Mental Health Differences?" *International Journal of Aging and Human Development* Vol. 23 (1986): 241–55.

Ferraro, K. F. "The Effect of Widowhood on the Health Status of Older Persons." *International Journal of Aging and Human Development* Vol. 21 (1985): 9–25.

Friend, R. A. "The Individual and Social Psychology of Aging: Clinical Implications for Lesbians and Gay Men." *Journal of Homosexuality* Vol. 4 (1987): 307–31.

Gallagher, D., L. Thompson, and J. Peterson. "Psychosocial Factors Affecting Adaptation to Bereavement in the Elderly." *International Journal of Aging and Human Development* Vol. 14 (1981–82): 79–95.

Gatz, M., V. L. Bengtson, and M. J. Blum. "Caregiving Families." In *Handbook of Psychology and Aging.* Eds. J. E. Birren and K. W. Schaie. 3d ed. San Diego, CA: Academic Press, 1990.

Gee, E. M. "Historical Change in the Family Life Course." In *Aging in Canada.* Ed. V. Marshall. 2d ed. Markham, Ontario: Fitzhenry & Whiteside, 1987.

Gentry, M., and A. D. Shulman. "Remarriage as a Coping Response for Widowhood." *Psychology and Aging* Vol. 3 (1988): 191–96.

Gilford, R. "Contrasts in Marital Satisfaction Throughout Old Age: An Exchange Theory Analysis." *Journal of Gerontology* Vol. 39 (1974): 325–33.

Gladstone, J. W. "Perceived Changes in Grandmother-Grandchild Relations Following a Child's Separation or Divorce." *Gerontologist* Vol. 28 (1988): 66–72.

Gold, D. T. "Generational Solidarity: Conceptual Antecedents and Consequences." *American Behavioral Scientist* Vol. 33 (1989a): 19–32.

——. "Sibling Relationships in Old Age: A Typology." *International Journal of Aging and Human Development* Vol. 28 (1989b): 37–51.

Goldberg, E. L., G. W. Comstock, and S. D. Harlow. "Emotional Problems and Widowhood." *Journal of Gerontology* Vol. 43 (1988): S206–S208.

Gray, H., and P. Dressel. "Alternative Interpretations of Aging Among Gay Males." *Gerontologist* Vol. 25 (1985): 83–87.

Guilford, R. "Marriages in Later Life." *Generations* Vol. 10 (1985–86): 16–20.

Gutmann, D. L. "Psychoanalysis and Aging: A Developmental View." In *The Course of Life: Psychoanalytic Contributions Toward Understanding Personality Development. Vol. 3: Adulthood and the Aging Process.* Eds. S. I. Greenspan and G. H. Pollack. Washington, DC: United States Government Printing Office, 1980.

——. *Reclaimed Powers: Toward a New Psychology of Men and Women in Later Life.* New York: Basic Books, 1987.

Hartshorne, T. A., and G. J. Manaster. "The Relationship with Grandparents: Contact, Importance, Role Congestion."

International Journal of Aging and Human Development Vol. 15 (1982): 233–45.

Hill, C. D., L. W. Thompson, and D. Gallagher. "The Role of Anticipatory Bereavement in Older Women's Adjustment to Widowhood." *Gerontologist* Vol. 28 (1988): 792–96.

Hodgson, L. G. "Adult Grandchildren and Their Grandparents: The Enduring Bond." *International Journal of Aging and Human Development* Vol. 34 (1992): 209–25.

Holahan, C. K. "Marital Attitudes Over Forty Years: A Longitudinal and Cohort Analysis." *Journal of Gerontology* Vol. 39 (1984): 49–57.

Hooyman, N. R., and H. A. Kiyak. *Social Gerontology: A Multidisciplinary Perspective*. Boston, MA: Allyn & Bacon, 1988.

Hooyman, N. R., and W. Lustbaden. *Taking Care: Supporting Older People and Their Families*. New York: Free Press, 1986.

Horowitz, A. "Sons and Daughters as Caregivers to Older Parents: Differences in Role Performance and Consequences." *Gerontologist* Vol. 25 (1985): 612–23.

Jackson, J. S., ed. *The Black American Elderly: Research on Physical and Psychosocial Health*. New York: Springer, 1988.

Johnson, C. L. "Active and Latent Functions of Grandparenting During the Divorce Process." *Gerontologist* Vol. 28 (1988): 185–91.

———. "Grandparenting Options in Divorcing Families: An Anthropological Perspective." In *Grandparenthood*. Eds. V. L. Bengtson and Joan F. Robertson. Beverly Hills, CA: Sage, 1985.

Johnson, C. L., and D. J. Catalano. "Childless Elderly and Their Family Supports." *Gerontologist* Vol. 21 (1981): 610–18.

Johnson, C. L., and L. Troll. "Family Functioning in Late Late Life." *Journal of Gerontology* Vol. 47 (1992): S66–S72.

Kehoe, M. *Lesbians Over Sixty Speak for Themselves*. New York: Harrington Park Press, 1989.

———. "Lesbians Over Sixty-Five: A Triply Invisible Minority." *Journal of Homosexuality* Vol. 12 (1986): 139–52.

Kivnick, H. Q. *The Meaning of Grandparenthood*. Ann Arbor, MI: University of Michigan Press, 1982.

Kohen, J. A. "Old But Not Alone: Informal Social Supports Among the Elderly by Marital Status and Sex." *Gerontologist* Vol. 27 (1983): 66–71.

Lee, G. R., and E. Ellithorpe. "Intergenerational Exchange and Subjective Well-Being Among the Elderly." *Journal of Marriage and the Family* Vol. 44 (1982): 217–24.

Lee, J. A. "The Invisible Lives of Canada's Gray Gays." In *Aging in Canada*. Ed. V. Marshall. 2d ed. Markham, Ontario: Fitzhenry & Whiteside, 1987a.

———. "What Can Homosexual Aging Studies Contribute to Theories of Aging." *Journal of Homosexuality* Vol. 13 (1987b): 43–71.

Leigh, G. "Kinship Interaction Over the Family Life Span." *Journal of Marriage and the Family* Vol. 44 (1982): 197–208.

Litwak, E. *The Modified Extended Family, Social Networks, and Research Continuities in Aging*. New York: Columbia University, Center for Social Sciences, 1981.

Livson, F. B. "Paths to Psychological Health in the Middle Years: Sex Differences." In *Present and Past in Middle Life*. Eds. D. H. Eichorn, J. A. Clausen, N. Haan, M. P. Honzik, and P. H. Mussen. New York: Academic Press, 1981.

Lopata, H. Z., and H. P. Brehm. *Widows and Dependent Wives: From Social Problem to Federal Program*. New York: Praeger, 1986.

Markides, K. S., and C. H. Mindel. *Aging and Ethnicity*. Beverly Hills, CA: Sage, 1987.

Marshall, V. W., and J. A. Levy. "Aging and Dying." In *Handbook of Aging and the Social Sciences*. Eds. R. H. Binstock and L. K. George. 3d ed. San Diego, CA: Academic Press, 1990.

Matthews, S. H., and J. Sprey. "Adolescents' Relationships with Grandparents: An Empirical Contribution to Conceptual Clarification." *Journal of Gerontology* Vol. 40 (1985): 621–26.

———. "The Impact of Divorce on Grandparenthood: An Exploratory Study." *Gerontologist* Vol. 24 (1984): 41–47.

Mitchell, J., and J. C. Register. "An Exploration of Family Interaction with the Elderly by Race, Socioeconomic Status, and Residence." *Gerontologist* Vol. 24 (1984): 48–54.

Moss, M. A., S. Z. Moss, and E. L. Moles. "The Quality of Relationships Between Elderly Parents and Their Out-of-Town Children." *Gerontologist* Vol. 25 (1985): 134–40.

Murrell, S. A., S. Himmelfarb, and J. F. Phifer. "Effects of Bereavement/Loss and Pre-Event Status on Subsequent Physical Health in Older Adults." *International Journal of Aging and Human Development* Vol. 27 (1988): 89–107.

Mutran, E. "Intergenerational Family Support Among Blacks and Whites: Response to Culture or to Socioeconomic Differences." *Journal of Gerontology* Vol. 40 (1985): 382–89.

Neugarten, B. L., and K. K. Weinstein. "The Changing American Grandparent." *Journal of Marriage and the Family* Vol. 26 (1964): 199–204.

O'Bryant, S. L., and L. A. Morgan. "Financial Experience and Well-Being Among Mature Widowed Women." *Gerontologist* Vol. 29 (1989): 245–51.

Peplau, L. A., and S. L. Gordon. "The Intimate Relationships of Lesbians and Gay Men." In *Gender Roles and Sexual Behavior*. Eds. E. R. Allgeirer and N. B. McCormick. Palo Alto, CA: Mayfield, 1982.

Perlmutter, M., and E. Hall. *Adult Development and Aging*. 2d ed. New York: John Wiley and Sons, 1992.

Quam, J. K., and G. S. Whitford. "Adaptation and Age-Related Expectations of Older Gay and Lesbian Adults." *Gerontologist* Vol. 32 (1992): 367–74.

Rosenthal, C. J. "Family Supports in Later Life: Does Ethnicity Make a Difference?" *Gerontologist* Vol. 26 (1986): 19–24.

Schooler, K. K. *National Senior Citizens Survey, 1968*. Ann Arbor, MI: Inter-University Consortium for Political and Social Research, 1979.

Shanas, E. "The Family as Social Support in Old Age." *Gerontologist* Vol. 19 (1979): 169–74.

———. "Older People and Their Families: The New Pioneers." *Journal of Marriage and the Family* Vol. 42 (1980): 9–14.

Silverman, P. R. *Widow to Widow.* New York: Springer, 1986.

Smyer, M., and B. F. Hofland. "Divorce and Family Support in Later Life." *Journal of Family Issues* Vol. 3 (1982): 61–77.

Soldo, B. J., and K. G. Manton. "Health Status and Service Needs of the Oldest Old: Current Patterns and Future Trends." *Milbank Memorial Fund Quarterly* Vol. 63 (1985): 286–319.

Stanford, E. P. "Diverse Black Aged." In *Black Aged: Understanding Diversity and Service Needs.* Eds. Z. Harel, E. A. McKinney, and M. Williams. Newbury Park, CA: Sage, 1990.

Strom, R., and S. Strom. "Preparing Grandparents for a New Role." *Journal of Applied Gerontology* Vol. 6 (1987): 476–86.

Taylor, R. J. "The Extended Family as a Source of Support to Elderly Blacks." *Gerontologist* Vol. 25 (1985): 488–95.

Thomas, J. L. "Gender Differences in Satisfaction with Grandparenting." *Psychology and Aging* Vol. 1 (1986): 215–19.

Thompson, L. W., J. N. Breckenridge, D. Gallagher, and J. Peterson. "Effects of Bereavement on Self-Perceptions of Physical Health in Elderly Widows and Widowers." *Journal of Gerontology* Vol. 39 (1984): 309–14.

Troll, L. E., ed. *Family Issues in Current Gerontology.* New York: Springer, 1986.

Uhlenberg, P., and M. A. Myers. "Divorce and the Elderly." *Gerontologist* Vol. 21 (1981): 276–82.

U.S. Bureau of the Census. Current Population Reports, Special Studies, 23–178, *Sixty-Five Plus in America.* Washington, DC: United States Government Printing Office, 1992.

U.S. Senate Special Committee on Aging. *Aging America: Trends and Projections.* Washington, DC: United States Government Printing Office, 1986.

———. *America in Transition: An Aging Society, 1984-1985 Edition.* Washington, DC: United States Government Printing Office, 1985.

Wilson, K. B., and M. R. DeShane. "The Legal Rights of Grandparents: A Preliminary Discussion." *Gerontologist* Vol. 22 (1982): 67–71.

Wolf, D. C. *Growing Older: Lesbians and Gay Men.* Berkeley, CA: University of California Press, 1982.

Wood, V., and J. F. Robertson. "Friendship and Kinship Interaction: Differential Effect on the Morale of the Elderly." *Journal of Marriage and the Family* Vol. 38 (1976): 367–75.

Zick, C. D., and K. R. Smith. "Immediate and Delayed Effects of Widowhood on Poverty: Patterns from the 1970s." *Gerontologist* Vol. 26 (1986): 669–75.

Additional Reading

Brazelton, T. Berry. *Families: Crisis and Caring.* Reading, MA: Addison-Wesley, 1989.

Brubaker, Timothy H. *Family Relationships in Later Life.* Newbury Park, CA: Sage Publications, 1990.

Campbell, Scott, and Phyllis R. Silverman. *Widower.* New York: Prentice-Hall, 1987.

Cherlin, Andrew J., and Frank F. Furstenberg. *The New American Grandparent: A Place in the Family, A Life Apart.* New York: Basic Books, 1986.

Fisher, Lucy Rose. *Linked Lives: Adult Daughters and Their Mothers.* New York: Harper & Row, 1986.

Halpern, James. *Helping Your Aging Parents: A Practical Guide for Adult Children.* New York: Crown, 1988.

Silverstone, Barbara, and Helen Kandel Hyman. *You and Your Aging Parent: The Modern Family's Guide to Emotional, Physical, and Financial Problems.* New York: Pantheon Books, 1989.

Deborah T. Gold, Ph.D.

Friendship and Aging

● Aging and Friendship Patterns ● How Active Are Older Adults as Friends?
● Values in Friendships ● Older People's Friends ● Activities of Friends
● Benefits of Friendships ● Strain in Older Adult Friendship
● Types of Beneficial Friendship Patterns ● Improving Older Adult Friendships ● Research Trends

For many years researchers accepted the common perception that as people age their friendship circles gradually become smaller. Certainly aging can contribute to social losses. Almost every elderly person lives to witness the death of life-long friends. When elderly people relocate to be near family members or to live in a warmer climate, they leave friends behind. Upon retirement, work-related friendships sometimes dissipate. The departure of children from the home makes contact with the parents of the children's friends less likely. Becoming a widow or widower can make it difficult to socialize with couples. Failing health or inadequate financial resources sometimes make it difficult to accept or to reciprocate invitations. Those who live dependently often receive very few visitors.

Thus, it is not surprising that many younger people hold the erroneous view that older people have few or no friends. However, the social losses and constraints on friendship that accompany the aging process are only part of the story. Each role change associated with aging creates opportunities for friendship as well as constraints on it (Allan and Adams, 1989). Retirement, the departure of children from the home, and even widowhood often mean that older people have more time for friendship. In addition, they often feel less bound by social expectations and exercise their newfound freedom by developing different types of friendships than they had previously (Adams, 1987).

● AGING AND FRIENDSHIP PATTERNS

Each role transition affects the social lives of older adults differently, depending on their specific circumstances. The effects of widowhood are different for young women than for older ones, mainly because when widows are older, they are in the majority (Blau, 1973). Among middle-aged people, socializing tends to be couple-centered. Women who are widowed relatively early in life are often excluded from social gatherings, perhaps because a single woman is perceived as a threat or because a widow is a reminder to married women of what is to come (Loewinsohn, 1984).

In contrast, widowhood can be a liberating experience for an older woman (Adams, 1983, 1987). Husbands, especially chronically ill ones, often interfere with their wives' social lives. This situation can be frustrating for the older woman whose widowed friends are free to socialize whenever they want. Older women are often embarrassed by the sense of relief they experience when their husbands die. They enter the society of widows expectantly, establishing new friendships and reestablishing old ones.

Very little research has been done on the effects of retirement on friendship. Scant evidence shows that the effects of retirement are different depending on the social class of the retiree and on what proportion of the retiree's friends were work-based (Allan and Adams, 1989).

Retirement does not appear to affect the friendships of middle-class men, but it does reduce contact for women and working-class men. People who depend on work as a primary source of identity and of friendship experience declines in social life upon retirement (Atchley, 1991). People with interests and networks outside of the work place often experience the same feeling of libera-

---

Profiles of Productive Aging

David Brown
Film producer

"I became more productive in my 70's than I ever had been before in my whole life."

David Brown achieved his greatest successes in the last ten years. With careers in journalism and publishing behind him, Brown produced hit movies and Broadway smashes, including *Tru, A Few Good Men* and *The Cemetary Club,* and the award-winning television program *Women and Men.* He has also published several best-selling books and is currently working on one about the 1930s.

Born in New York City in 1916, Brown was interested in journalism before he could even read. He loved to listen to radio broadcasters Lowell Thomas and Edmund C. Hill, and from the age of 5 he pored over newspapers—"I looked at the advertising and the drawing and the pictures," he recalled; "I was interested in the world outside and I was interested in how it would impact on me."

He studied social sciences and psychology, graduated from Stanford, and received a master of science degree from Columbia University; his first job was at Fairchild Publications for $25 a week. Over the next few years he worked for *Women's Wear Daily* as a drama critic and copyeditor, wrote horoscopes, and did some freelance writing. In 1940, newly married, he decided he had to get a "real" job.

He worked for his father, doing public relations for the milk industry, but his father fired him in short order. "I couldn't keep regular hours," Brown admitted. He next became the nightclub editor of one of the burgeoning picture magazines, *Pic.* "I covered nightclubs, cabaret and theatre. That's how I got interested in show business," he recalled.

Brown began writing skits for comedian Eddie Cantor, which led to a job with the weekly magazine *Liberty.* After the army, Brown returned to *Liberty* and then became managing editor of *Cosmopolitan,* until Darryl F. Zanuck called him to Hollywood in 1951.

At Twentieth Century-Fox, Brown rose from story editor to producer to head of the scenario department. When the studio went bankrupt in 1963, Brown returned to New York and fell into yet another profession: book publishing. He founded New American Library, which boasted Ian Fleming's James Bond books on its list. But two years later he was back in the movie business.

In 1964 Brown purchased the film rights to the popular play *The Sound of Music,* which put Twentieth Century Fox back on the map. In six years, he became executive vice-president of creative operations, but in 1970, in a political coup against Darryl Zanuck, Brown and Richard Zanuck were fired. Brown learned from this experience: "It convinced me that I was never going to let a company control my destiny again—except my own company, which controls my destiny on a daily basis."

Brown and the younger Zanuck formed their own company on July 28, 1972. The Zanuck-Brown Company produced such successful films as *Jaws, The Sting, The Verdict,* and *Cocoon,* a landmark film that examined attitudes about aging. Brown was also executive producer for the Academy Award-winner *Driving Miss Daisy* which proved that a story about an aging person could garner critical acclaim. After a long and fruitful partnership, Brown started his own development and production company, the Manhattan Project.

In 1991 the Academy of Motion Picture Arts and Sciences presented Brown and Zanuck with the Irving G. Thalberg Award, the highest honor for a film producer.

At 78, Brown attributes his physical, mental, and emotional well-being to the fact that he has never stopped working. "I'm healthy and energetic because I work. I take pleasure in my work. I still work seven days a week, and I enjoy it. As Tennessee Williams said, 'Make voyages. Attempt them. That's all there is.'"

Lydia Brontë

While a painful loss, the experience of widowhood can be a liberating experience for some older women. (Courtesy of Chautauqua Institution)

tion when they retire that many women experience when they become widows.

Although relocation means leaving old friends behind, it can also provide an opportunity to make new friends (Shea and others, 1988). This is especially true when the older person moves into a neighborhood or apartment complex mainly or exclusively occupied by his or her age peers (Rosow, 1967). Some recent research shows that older adults even establish new relationships in nursing homes (Bear, 1990).

Declining health can make it difficult for the older adult to maintain contact with friends (Brown, 1990), but it does not necessarily lead to the termination of relationships. In close relationships, the inability to reciprocate is not an important factor (Roberto and Scott, 1986). Furthermore, one must view reciprocity over the entire life course. Sometimes, even though a friendship seems one-sided at a given moment, an examination of its history might reveal that an accumulated debt is being paid. In addition to the continuation of long-term friendships, older peo-

ple in poor health who live among their age peers often attract good Samaritans as friends, people who enjoy helping those less fortunate than themselves (Adams, 1983).

More research is needed on why people respond to these age-related role changes in different ways. We know very little, for example, about how gender, ethnicity, race, and class background affect friendship. Beth Hess (1972) argues that older women probably fare better in friendships than older men, because women are more numerous among the elderly, because they have better developed interpersonal skills, and because their friendships are less likely to be work-based and activity-oriented. Researchers have not yet designed studies to test this hypothesis.

Maintaining Friendships

Certainly making and maintaining friendships comes more naturally to some people than to others, regardless of their gender, ethnic group, race, or class background. Not everyone is good at maintaining old friendships across long distances by writing letters, keeping in touch by telephone, and occasional visiting. Some people have never developed the relevant social skills or habits; they have relied on others or on routine interaction to make friends and maintain relationships.

For other people, their ability to keep in touch is determined by their access to resources. Older adults who have adequate finances for entertainment, travel, and telephone bills, who have access to transportation, or who have someone who can help them with correspondence often have an advantage.

The immediate circumstances in which older people live also affect their ability to make friends and maintain friendships as they age. Such factors as how isolated their home is, whether they live independently, how dangerous they perceive their neighborhood to be, how available support services are, and how easy it is to keep their home presentable for visitors can all affect the way people's friendships evolve as they age.

Beth Hess (1972) argues that older women probably fare better in friendships than older men, because women are more numerous among the elderly, because they have better developed interpersonal skills, and because their friendships are less likely to be work-based and activity-oriented.

Common sense suggests that broader societal and cultural circumstances also influence older adult friendship patterns, but very little information is available about this topic. When the people who are currently old were young, they learned different friendship styles and abided by different social rules than young people do today. What they learned in their youths surely affects the friendships they have today. Given recent trends, the next generation of older women may be more likely to name men as friends than the current age cohort.

The opportunities for and constraints on older adults' friendships today differ from those of even just a generation ago. Since more people survive into old age now than in the past, they have a greater number of age peers from whom to select their friends. Cultural and social changes also influence friendships. The growth of senior centers, improved attitude toward aging, relatively better health of today's older adults, and the tendency of people to retire younger have affected older adult friendship patterns.

● HOW ACTIVE ARE OLDER ADULTS AS FRIENDS?

Contrary to the stereotypical image of older adults as lonely and friendless, almost all older people do have friends. Estimates of the average number of friends older people have range from 0 to 12, depending on their circumstances. Retsinas and Garrity (1985) observed nursing home residents interacting with from 0 to 6 friends. Those who had greater lucidity and better vision and speech had more friends. In another study, widows reported an average of 1.25 friends (Lopata, 1979). Elderly female residents of a middle-class suburb named an average of 12 friends (Adams, 1987). Participation in social activities (Spakes, 1979) and employment (Babchuk and Anderson, 1989) both lead to larger social circles.

Comparing the findings of studies of adult friendships of various ages suggests that older people tend to have approximately the same number of friends as younger people (Blieszner and Adams, 1992). This evidence is not conclusive, though, because almost all of these studies were of a specific age group, took place in distinctive settings, or were of people who were socially similar to one another. No one has ever done a study of friendship in which a representative sampling of people of all adult ages, from all over the country, and from all walks of life were interviewed. For this reason, any statements comparing older adult friendship to friendship during the earlier stages of adulthood are tentative.

Not only do older people have friends, they see them quite frequently. Some researchers have found that older people see each of their friends an average of several times a month (Adams, 1985–86; Blieszner, 1982), and others have found that they tend to see them more frequently than that (Dykstra, 1990; Jones and Vaughan, 1990). They tend to see their close friends more frequently than their more casual ones (Adams,

1985–86) and to spend more time with these close friends than with their casual ones when they do see them (Blieszner, 1982).

● VALUES IN FRIENDSHIPS

Members of our culture, regardless of their ages, define friendship in a variety of ways. Although social conventions and circumstances influence our understanding of "friendship," we are allowed a great deal of freedom in interpreting the meaning of the word. Some people use the term "friend" to refer to mere acquaintances, and others reserve it for intimates. Each older adult thus has a slightly different concept of what friendship is and has developed a distinctive friendship style during his or her life. Furthermore, most older individuals have a variety of types of friendships, ranging from intimate to casual and from activity-oriented to helping relationships. Because of this variation, it is difficult to describe in general terms what friendship means to older adults. Nonetheless, despite this individual variation, some general statements are relevant.

Older women, for example, tend to define "friendship" affectively. In one study (Adams, 1983), they mentioned feelings of concern, caring, kindness, warmth, love, liking, compatibility, intimacy, acceptance, openness, sincerity, honesty, or closeness. The friend's willingness to help was mentioned by almost half of the women, and about a quarter of them referred to the length of time they had known the person. No one has conducted a similar study of older men's perceptions of friendship, though research on younger men suggests that they would emphasize shared activities and time spent together more than older women do (Caldwell and Peplau, 1982).

In her retrospective study of friendships across the life course, Sarah Matthews (1986) discovered that people had one of three conceptions of friendship that were related to whether they were able to acquire new friendships as they aged. The *independents* are people who have such an idealized concept of friendship that almost no one qualifies. They associate with people who happen to be available, without expectations that the relationships will continue. The *discerning* have a small circle of close friends and emphasize their friends' specific qualities. Their friendships are

Older women tend to define friendship in terms of emotions, such as concern, care, kindness, warmth, and love. (Copyright © Marianne Gontarz)

mainly long-term and thus impossible to replace when friends relocate or pass away. *Acquisitive* people, on the other hand, are likely to have made and committed themselves to friendships throughout their lives, in whatever circumstances they found themselves. Although they do not necessarily maintain these relationships when circumstances change, they consider them important at the time. The acquisitive thus hope their current friendships will continue and are open to forming new ones as opportunities present themselves.

One can find compelling examples of friendship types among older people in film and literature. Examples drawn from the contemporary short story, the novel, and children's literature are offered in this section.

Clearly some types of relationships are more satisfying to older adults than are others. In general, the closer friends feel to one another, the more satisfied they are with the relationship (Adams, 1983; Blieszner, 1982). Several researchers have found that reciprocity, giving

Friendships in Literature

Richard Bausch's 1984 novel *The Last Good Time* provides portraits of people with three distinct friendship styles (Matthews, 1986). Edward Cakes, a widower in his seventies who lives alone, has a discerning friendship style. His best friend, Arthur Hagood, lives in a nursing home. Edward visits him often, spending whole afternoons. When Arthur appears to be dying, Edward utters "not now." It would not be possible to replace Arthur, his life-long friend. Mary, a young woman who abruptly enters Edward's life, leaves just as abruptly when her circumstances change, with no apparent regrets. She illustrates the independent friendship style. Ida Warren, Edward's new elderly neighbor, pursues a friendship with him despite his reluctance. Her acquisitive style is effective; the book ends when Arthur dies, and Edward puts on a clean shirt and his good wing-tip shoes to visit Ida.

and taking equally, is important for satisfaction in more casual relationships, but not important in close ones (e.g., Roberto and Scott, 1986). When older people feel very close to a friend, they do not keep track of who owes whom what. They do what they can for their friend and do not feel imposed upon if the friend does not repay them.

On the other hand, if willingness to help is part of an older woman's definition of friendship and if her network is relatively nonsupportive, she is less satisfied with her relationships as a whole (Adams, 1983). This finding is not inconsistent with a lack of concern about reciprocity in specific close relationships. The same woman might feel very satisfied with a specific close relationship in which she helps the friend more than the friend helps her, but dissatisfied with her friendships in general because of the lack of support she receives from her circle of friends as a whole. Some research has shown that this general perception of lack of support of friends leads to feelings of loneliness among older adults (Rook, 1987).

● OLDER PEOPLE'S FRIENDS

Older people have accumulated their friends over their life times. Research has shown that older adults have known their closest friends for an average of 23 to 39 years and their less close friends for an average of 19 to 24 years (Blieszner and Adams, 1992). Because their oldest friends tend to be their closest friends and their newest friends tend to live nearest to them, older people's closest friends tend to live further away from them than do their more casual friends (Adams, 1985–86). The need to maintain important relationships across great distances is a common artifact of a long life.

Not all of the friendships of older adults have endured for decades, however. The authors of

Friendships in Literature

The lack of need for close friends to reciprocate favors is aptly illustrated in William Stegner's 1987 novel *Crossing to Safety*. On the evening of Charity's death, her husband, Sid, their best friends, Larry and Sally, and the rest of the family gather at their summer home. Larry reflects on the life-long friendship of the two couples. Charity and Sid met Larry and Sally when the two men were both young faculty members at the University of Wisconsin. When Larry's contract was not renewed and Sally became ill, Charity and Sid came to their aid. Sally and the baby spent the summer with them in Vermont at Charity's family's home. Larry would remain in Wisconsin to work on his novel while house-sitting for Charity and Sid. When Sally and Larry protested that they would never be able to repay the kindness, Charity clearly stated that "friends don't *have* to repay anything."

Although life led the two couples down different paths, Larry and Sally and Sid and Charity remained close, often spending summers together. Larry's account of their friendship makes it clear that much of the credit for its endurance belonged to Charity. Charity was better equipped to maintain friendships than others, because of her personality, characteristics, social skills, and financial circumstances.

Friendships in Literature

Most close friends tend to age at a distance. In contrast to this typical situation, Alice Adams's 1988 novel *Second Chances* describes a group of life-long friends who relocate to the same town when they become older. One of the central relationships in the story is the friendship between Dudley Venable and Edward Crane, which is based on a lifetime of shared experiences. They first met at summer camp as adolescents. During their old age, the old friends often walk and talk. Dudley supports Edward when Edward's gay lover leaves town. Edward provides Dudley comfort upon the death of her husband. On one occasion, Dudley exclaims, "Darling Edward, whatever in the world would I do without you?"

one study (Shea and others, 1988) reported that within a period of ten months, some of the friendships between older adults who had moved simultaneously into a newly constructed retirement community involved more liking, loving, and commitment than others. Another study (Adams, 1987) showed that women who previously worked most of their lives took advantage of opportunities during retirement to become active in senior centers and social clubs and, for the first time in their lives, to supplement their enduring close relationships with casual ones. Other women who previously had community-based and family-centered friendships expanded their networks to include people outside of their neighborhood.

Research has shown that older adults have known their closest friends for an average of 23 to 39 years and their less close friends for an average of 19 to 24 years.

People tend to accumulate friends who are socially similar to themselves. Most middle-aged adults tend to have friends who are similar to themselves in terms of level of education, occupational status, ethnicity, age, marital status, income, gender, and religion (Fischer, 1982; Verbrugge, 1977). Although elderly people also

Friendships in Literature

Fictional accounts of intergenerational relationships are plentiful. Fannie Flagg's 1987 novel *Fried Green Tomatoes at the Whistle Stop Cafe* describes the friendship between Evelyn and Mrs. Threadgoode. Through conversations with Mrs. Threadgoode, Evelyn gains perspective on her own life. She learns to be more assertive and not to fear death. Mrs. Threadgoode, a nursing home resident, looks forward to regular visits from her young friend, who often brings her sweet treats.

Clyde Edgerton's *Walking Across Egypt* (1987) tells the story of the friendship between Mattie Rigsbee, an independent, strong-minded senior citizen who is slowing down just a bit, and Wesley Benfield, a young delinquent. Mattie decides that Wesley is one of "the least of these my brethren" and that in doing something for him, she will be doing something for Jesus. She cleans him up, takes him to church, and decides to adopt him. He thinks that she must be his grandmother and submits to her affection, lured by her mouth-watering pound cake. The consequence for Mattie is that she no longer lives alone and no longer has to depend on her biological son and chance visitors to do the chores that have become difficult for her.

In the children's book *The Treasure Hunt,* about intergenerational friendship, Christopher Wilson (1980) describes a treasure hunt designed by the older adults in a community to bring them together with the local children. The children realize they have much to learn from senior citizens, and the older adults experience pleasure while teaching them.

Profiles of Productive Aging

"Mother" Clara Hale
Childcare pioneer

"You can have anything you want if you work at it. But you have to do it yourself. No one is going to give it to you. That's what I told all my children and it made life nice. They teach their children the same thing and they have happy children."

Clara McBride Hale, the founder of the Hale House center for child care in New York City, was born in 1905 and grew up in Philadelphia. Extremely fragile as an infant, Hale recalled her mother often said she didn't believe that she would be able to raise Clara to adulthood. When Hale was four, however, her health suddenly changed for the better. Hale's father died when she was two, and she had no memory of him; she was extremely close to her mother, who supported the family, and as Clara got older she helped her mother care for the children. When she was sixteen, her mother died at the age of 44, which was a great loss to her.

At twenty-two, she married Thomas Hale. By the time they had two children, Hale was disenchanted with Philadelphia; she packed up the children and moved to New York, leaving a note for her husband to join them as soon as he could. In need of work, Hale learned of the advantages of being a building superintendent and found a position on the Upper East Side.

Once settled, Hale decided to start taking in children. "I didn't want my children alone, so I took care of other people's children," she said. "And the kids got so they didn't want to go home at night. Oh, did we have a time! They wanted to spend the night. Then they'd go home on the weekends with their mothers. I had six or seven kids I took care of every night." The number grew and grew. Sometimes Hale had to persuade the children to go back to their homes, because they had so much more fun with her.

Within the first ten years in New York, Hale's husband became ill and died of cancer at the age of 37.

Hale simply kept going: she took in more children to make more money, and continued raising her own. Her daughter Lorraine grew up and received a Ph.D. in early childhood development, an interest stimulated by her mother's vocation.

One day in 1969, Lorraine saw a woman with a baby sleeping on the stoop of a neighboring house. The woman was high on drugs, and Lorraine, afraid that she might drop and injure the baby, gave her Hale's address and telephone number. The next day the woman showed up, handed the baby to Mother Hale, and left. Three weeks later, she returned, told Hale the baby's name, and left again. Eventually Hale said the woman returned and brought her other two children, boys who were "real housewreckers." Hale helped the woman get her life together, and as a result she was able to remarry and take the children back.

Word spread, and soon Hale had a new vocation: taking care of the children of women who were addicts. By this time Lorraine had completed her doctorate and had begun to work with her mother. She incorporated their work as a not-for-profit agency and applied for government funding to support their work, and Hale House was born. Since it opened in 1969, over 800 children have come through its program.

"Mother" Clara Hale genuinely loved her calling. Even when her lifelong devotion to the children of Hale House won her international recognition and acclaim as an "American heroine" when she was saluted by President Ronald Reagan in his 1985 State of the Union address, the always matter-of-fact Hale responded, "I'm not an American hero—I'm simply a person who loves children."

When she died of a stroke, on December 18, 1992, her funeral was attended by her own four children, sixty foster children, and hundreds of other people, all paying tribute to the woman who loved children.

Lydia Brontë

tend to have friends of similar social status to themselves, they are less socially similar to their friends than their younger counterparts are in terms of marital status, education, and age (Usui, 1984). Friendships people establish in old age are more likely to be with people who are socially different from themselves than are those they establish earlier in life.

Why might this be? Older people are more likely to be widowed and less likely to be high school or college graduates than younger adults. Because there are fewer people with the same

Friendships in Literature

Interracial relationships, such as the one described by Hennie Aucamp (1991) in her short story "Soup for the Sick," are relatively rare among people of all ages. Tant Rensie had health problems. The only help she received was from her life-long nurse and friend, Sofietjie. Sofietjie continued to care for her, even though she too had heart problems. Tant could not reciprocate, both because of her own health and because of the racial status differences between them. Sofietjie died before her friend did. Tant Rensie requested that Sofietjie be buried in her garden. When the town council would not allow it, she was buried in a cemetery near the "colored" location. When Tant Rensie died, she left the town money to build a hospital on the condition that she be buried near her friend. She wanted to be near the woman who had helped her selflessly throughout her life.

marital status and level of education available to be friends with them, widows, widowers, and older people with relatively little formal education are less likely than those in majority statuses to have friends who are socially similar to themselves. Furthermore, the older someone is, the fewer age peers are available. This lack of peers provides older adults with motivation to establish relationships with people junior to themselves. Though people exercise a great deal of freedom in selecting their friends, the characteristics of the people in the social context in which friendships are formed may limit the extent of choice.

Researchers have not closely examined older people's relationships with people having different levels of education or different marital statuses than theirs, and they have only examined intergenerational friendships in passing (e.g., Adams, 1985). The scant evidence suggests that the older person is often a mentor to the younger person. The younger person, in return, helps the older person with everyday tasks. Other times intergenerational friendships are not reciprocal. Older people sometimes report friendships with professional helpers who consider the older adult as a client rather than as a friend or with a member of their church or a neighbor who visits them out of a sense of duty rather than as a result of affection.

Older people and younger adults are equally unlikely to have friends who differ from them in terms of race and gender (Usui, 1984). Although researchers have not examined the cross-race friendships of older adults, they have begun to study their cross-sex relationships. Men are more likely to report friendships with women than women are to report them with men (Usui, 1984). This finding can be interpreted in two different ways. On the one hand, it provides further support for the notion that types of people in the minority are more likely to have friends who are socially different from themselves than types of people in the majority. Due to the greater longevity of women, during old age they have more gender peers of their age to choose as friends than men and thus a higher proportion of their friendships are with members of the same sex. On the other hand, the difference could be attributable

Friendships in Literature

Mr. Silver and Mrs. Gold, Dale Fink's 1980 children's story about the friendship between Mr. Silver and Mrs. Gold, accurately depicts the type of companionship involved in many older adult courting relationships. When they are together, Mr. Silver and Mrs. Gold play music, take walks in the park, share conversation, garden, bake, and drink tea and coffee.

Men are more likely to report friendships with women than women are to report them with men. (Copyright © Marianne Gontarz)

to a gender difference in the informal social rules regarding cross-sex relationships. Because members of the older cohort were taught to view cross-sex relationships as romantic, older women who have friendships with men are sometimes stigmatized as being improper (Adams, 1985). Older women may thus be more hesitant than older men to report cross-sex friendships.

Very few of older women's cross-sex friendships are actually courting relationships, however. One study (Adams, 1985) showed that most of their cross-sex friendships are actually friendships with couples or with younger people who help them in a professional capacity or as a favor to someone else. About an eighth of the older women studied did have courting relationships. Although some of these courting relationships were sexually intimate, the women emphasized that companionship was more important.

● ACTIVITIES OF FRIENDS

To date, researchers have not systematically examined what older people do with their friends. Ethnographers have observed groups of older people participating in activities together. For example, Arlie Hochschild (1973) reported that the older women she observed talked about age-related concerns and tended to fill their leisure time with productive activities, such as crafting presents for their families or mailing packages to members of the armed services. Such reports suggest how aging affects friendship activity, although surely different types of people have different experiences.

Since the 1950s, survey researchers have found that spending time with friends and participation in various types of leisure activities contributes positively to the older person's happiness, morale, and adjustment (Larson, 1978). The problem is that researchers have asked separate questions about the older adults' activities and their friendships and have not asked what they do while they are with their friends. A few researchers specifically interested in friendship have included questions in their research instruments about what older people do with their friends, but they have reported findings in ways that obscure details. For example, Dykstra (1990) reported that the more emotionally close the friendship, the more likely the pair was to partake of food and drink together and the more likely they were to share activities and conversation.

Studies of younger adults suggest that men and women do very different things with their friends; women talk and confide in one another, and men participate in specific activities (Caldwell and Peplau, 1982). This conclusion overgeneralizes, however. The women who participated in one study (Adams, 1993) did mention talking as their most frequent friendship activity—but, in order of decreasing frequency, they also mentioned eating meals, recreational activities, participation in clubs, outings, cultural events, helping one another, social gatherings, and even exercising and participating in sports.

● BENEFITS OF FRIENDSHIPS

Gerontologists have repeatedly found that having companions and confidants is important for the mental health of older adults (e.g., Strain and Chappell, 1982). In fact, they have found friends to be more important than family members to the

Close friendships are an important part of mental health in later life. (Copyright © Marianne Gontarz)

psychological well-being of older adults (Larson, 1978). Researchers have suggested many explanations for this finding (see Crohan and Antonucci, 1989). Because the elderly have no rigid expectations of friendship, they are grateful for signs of affection and small favors. They expect more from their family members; therefore, they evaluate them more harshly. Helping friends can also protect the elderly from negative self-evaluation by making them feel needed. Also, because friends often have more in common with older adults than their family members, they are more likely to involve the older adult in activities that keep them engaged with the larger community and society. Furthermore, the freedom of choice in selecting friends is important for feelings of autonomy during old age.

Although friends are not as likely to be full-time caregivers as family members are, they do help older adults in many practical ways. Friends are more likely to help some older adults than they are to help others (Blieszner and Adams, 1992). Elderly people who have no family members living near them are most likely to name friends as helpers. Widowed elderly women receive more help from friends than married elderly women do. Retired people report more confidants and are more likely to have someone to rely on in emergencies than employed people are.

Friends are more likely to help elderly people with certain types of tasks than with others. The most common type of help friends give older adults is emotional support and companionship (Crohan and Antonucci, 1989). Litwak (1985) argued that because of demographic similarities, older adults are likely to consult friends during role transitions such as retirement or becoming a widow. Because their age peers are likely to have gone through similar adjustments, they are the preferred source of support in these instances.

He argued further that friends are likely to be asked for help with tasks that do not take too long, require only intermittent help, and are not too personal. Adams (1983) found that older women asked friends for help when it was convenient for the friend to help them or when they had an emergency.

Close friends are more likely to help older adults than casual friends (Adams, 1983). Intimate relationships that involve confiding are more likely to involve material and service resource exchanges than less intimate ones (Blieszner, 1982).

The amount of help provided to older adults by friends may be underestimated in the research literature. In studies of the support older adults receive from friends, kin, neighbors, and others, researchers have usually asked hypothetical questions ("Who would you turn to for help if . . . ") rather than questions about actual behavior. Hypothetical questions tend to elicit socially acceptable responses. Possibly because people typically turn to their families for help rather than to their friends, responses to hypothetical questions lead researchers to underestimate the amount of help that is actually provided by friends. Researchers also tend to ask older adults to name only the person who gives them the most help with a given task. In many cases, the help friends give older adults supplements more extensive help from family members.

Elderly people who have no family members living near them are most likely to name friends as helpers. Widowed elderly women receive more help from friends than married elderly women do.

Friendships in Literature

Fictional accounts of problematic friendships are ample. Ida Warren irritated Edward Cakes (see first "Friendships in Literature") with her persistence and her failure to realize that he wanted to be alone (Bausch, 1984). Larry was upset with Charity's (see second "Friendships in Literature") tendency to exert control over other people and situations (Stegner, 1987). Celeste, one of Edward and Dudley's friends (see third "Friendships in Literature"), suspected that yet another member of their circle previously had an affair with her husband and that they had never told her (Adams, 1988).

● STRAIN IN OLDER ADULT FRIENDSHIP

Although friendship is mainly a positive experience for older adults, it is not without its problems. Researchers have studied the problematic aspects of family relationships more than they have studied the problematic aspects of friendships. Karen Rook (1989) argues that neglecting to recognize the existence of strain in friendship is unfortunate, because problematic exchanges between friends become more frequent as relationships progress, can be extremely potent, and are potentially critical to the elderly because of the importance of friendships in their lives.

Older people sometimes get irritated or feel betrayed by their friends just like younger people do. One study (Adams, 1983) reported that older women were occasionally irritated by a tenth of their friends and often by another tenth. They criticized their friends for having ideas different than theirs and for being temperamental, snobbish, sloppy, bossy, plainspoken, too reserved, too talkative, hard of hearing, too heavy a drinker, too nosey, unfriendly, senile, unreliable, a complainer, and impossible to change.

In a review of the limited research literature on the negative aspects of older adult friendship, Rook (1989) concluded that strains have numerous origins. Possible sources of strain include: being expected to divulge personal information as the relationship deepens, failing to communicate or to interpret expectations accurately, deficient social skills, problematic personality characteristics, failure of family to meet their obligations and subsequent inappropriate impositions on friends, competition with other network members, and disruptive external events, such as age-related role transitions. These strains can change the course of the friendship, lead to the dissolution of the relationship, affect other relationships, and have an adverse effect on psychological well-being.

● TYPES OF BENEFICIAL FRIENDSHIP PATTERNS

Most of the research on the consequences of friendship has been relatively superficial. Researchers have examined the effects of number of friendships, frequency of interactions with friends, and of emotional and practical support from friends. Very little attention has been paid to the effects of patterns of friendship, of the constellation of characteristics of the friendships, and the interconnections among the friends in a person's entire network.

Studies examining types of friendship patterns are sorely needed, because different types of friendship patterns might have very different consequences. For example, one study (Litwak, 1985) showed that older people should cultivate a wide variety of types of friends because then they will have a broader, more diffuse resource base. He also suggested that older people should establish friendships with their juniors to ensure having people capable of helping them out in their later years.

Another study (Adams, 1983) demonstrated that older people who have tightly knit friendship circles are probably better prepared for emergencies than are those with loosely knit networks. If, for example, an older person becomes bedridden, the information can be quickly transmitted from friend to friend, and they can organize support. If, however, the friends in the network do not know one another, the older adult would have to contact each friend individually and would not likely be the recipient of coordinated efforts to help. On the other hand, a tightly knit network might not be the best type when the older adult needs to confide. Gossip flows more readily in such networks; if the older adult wants to ensure secrecy, it is less risky to confide in friends who do not know one another.

Consequences of friendship may also vary depending on the degree of similarity between the social characteristics of the older adult and his or her friends. If an older adult is seeking information or needs help with a specific problem, having a large number of friends from a variety of backgrounds is beneficial. Different types of people have access to different types of information; having a large and diverse friendship network increases the probability that the needed information or help will be obtained. On the other hand, if the older adult wants to confide in friends who have had similar life experiences, having a small circle of intimate friends who are similar to the older adult is advantageous.

● IMPROVING OLDER ADULT FRIENDSHIPS

Older people's social lives are influenced every day by institutions, family, service providers, and policy makers. For example, they may attend

Organizations such as churches and synagogues often provide informal, supportive friendship networks. (Copyright © Paul Gilmore)

senior recreation centers and meetings of organizations to make new acquaintances. Their children or spouses may influence or even control the visitors they receive. For some, therapists help them develop interpersonal skills and to overcome personality problems. Architects design age-segregated housing to facilitate social interaction. Policy makers sometimes pass laws that encourage older adults to rely on their friends and relatives for help rather than on formal agencies.

Whether or not these interventions are intentionally designed to change an older adult's friendship patterns, they might have myriad consequences. They might increase or decrease their satisfaction with their friendships. Other, less direct consequences might be changing the older adult's behavior, resources, attitudes, values, health, or mental health.

Interventions can be designed to affect the social life of one individual, to alter the relationship of a pair of friends, or to transform interaction in an entire social circle, building, community, or society (see Blieszner and Adams, 1992).

If an older adult is seeking information or needs help with a specific problem, having a large number of friends from a variety of backgrounds is beneficial. Different types of people have access to different types of information; having a large and diverse friendship network increases the probability that the needed information or help will be obtained.

Before such interventions can be designed and implemented effectively and responsibly, however, researchers need to study the consequences of different types of friendship patterns much more extensively. In other words, they need to know what needs to be changed and why before they implement strategies that affect elderly people's social lives.

● RESEARCH TRENDS

Many chapters of the story of older adult friendship remain unwritten. The written media has contributed virtually nothing to public knowledge of the topic. In the last five years, *The Reader's Guide to Periodical Literature* lists only two articles that appeared in the popular press about older people's friendships. Novelists, short story authors, and people who write scripts for television and films have only begun to explore a few of many possible friendship and aging themes.

Although philosophers have pondered the meaning of friendship for centuries, researchers have just recently begun to examine the phenomenon. At first, scholars discussed older people's friendships only in passing, mainly in the context of discussions of retirement and widowhood. Since the early 1970s, however, many research projects have focused specifically on friendship in later life. In fact, researchers have paid more attention to older adult friendship than they have to friendship during earlier stages of adulthood.

Researchers are only beginning to be able to answer questions posed in this chapter about the friendships of older adults. They still know very little about what older people value in friends, do with friends, and dislike about friends. Older people from different ethnic, racial, and class backgrounds, of different genders, living in different periods of history, and raised in different cultural contexts probably all have different friendship experiences, but this is not known for sure. While people understand on a basic level that friendship is psychologically and practically beneficial to older adults, researchers have neither identified what types of friendship patterns are most rewarding nor examined the full range of possible consequences. Attempts to change the friendship patterns of older adults, however well intentioned, are thus risky.

References

Adams, R. G. "Activity as Structure and Process: Friendships of Older Adults." In *Activity and Aging*. Ed. J. R. Kelly. Newbury Park, CA: Sage, 1993.

———. "Emotional Closeness and Physical Distance Between Friends." *International Journal of Aging and Human Development* Vol. 22 (1985–86): 55–75.

———. *Friendship and Its Role in the Lives of Elderly Women*. Ph.D. dissertation, University of Chicago, 1983.

———. "Patterns of Network Change: A Longitudinal Study of Friendships of Elderly Women." *The Gerontologist* Vol. 27 (1987): 222–27.

———. "People Would Talk: Normative Barriers to Cross-Sex Friendship for Elderly Women." *The Gerontologist* Vol. 25 (1985): 605–11.

Adams, R. G., and R. Blieszner, eds. *Older Adult Friendship: Structure and Process*. Newbury Park, CA: Sage, 1989.

Allan, G., and R. G. Adams. "Aging and the Structure of Friendship." In *Older Adult Friendship*. Eds. R. G. Adams and R. Blieszner. Newbury Park, CA: Sage, 1989.

American Association of Retired Persons (AARP). *Ideas for Helping a Friend in Crisis*. Washington, DC: AARP, Social Outreach and Support Program Department, 1989a.

———. *Reflections and Suggestions on Making New Friends*. Washington, DC: AARP, Social Outreach and Support Program Department, 1989b.

Atchley, R. *Social Forces and Aging*. Belmont, CA: Wadsworth, 1991.

Aucamp, H. "Soup for the Sick." In *Vital Signs: International Stories on Aging*. Eds. D. Sennett and A. Czarniecki. Saint Paul, MN: Graywolf Press, 1991.

Babchuk, N., and T. B. Anderson. "Older Widows and Married Women: Their Intimates and Confidants." *International Journal of Aging and Human Development* Vol. 28 (1989): 21–35.

Bausch, R. *The Last Good Time*. Garden City, NY: Doubleday, 1984.

Bear, M. "Social Network Characteristics and the Duration of Primary Relationships after Entry into Long-Term Care."

Journal of Gerontology: Social Sciences Vol. 45 (1990): S156–62.

Blau, Z. S. *Old Age in a Changing Society*. New York: New Viewpoints, 1973.

Blieszner, R. *Social Relationships and Life Satisfaction in Late Adulthood*. University Microfilms, No. 82-28863, 1982.

Blieszner, R., and R. G. Adams. *Adult Friendship*. Newbury Park, CA: Sage, 1992.

Brown, B. B. "A Life-Span Approach to Friendship." In *Friendship in Context*. Eds. H. Lopata and D. R. Maines. Greenwich, CT: JAI Press, 1990.

Caldwell, M. A., and L. A. Peplau. "Sex Differences in Same-Sex Friendship." *Sex Roles* Vol. 8 (1982): 721–32.

Crohan, S. E., and T. C. Antonucci. "Friends as a Source of Social Support in Old Age." In *Older Adult Friendship: Structure and Process*. Eds. R. G. Adams and R. Blieszner. Newbury Park, CA: Sage, 1989.

Dykstra, P. A. *Next of (Non)Kin*. Amsterdam: Swets & Zeitlinger, 1990.

Edgerton, C. *Walking Across Egypt*. New York: Ballantine, 1987.

Fink, D. B. *Mr. Silver and Mrs. Gold* (children's book). New York: Human Sciences Press, 1980.

Fischer, C. S. *To Dwell Among Friends*. Chicago: University of Chicago Press, 1982.

Flagg, F. *Fried Green Tomatoes at the Whistle Stop Cafe*. New York: Random House, 1987.

Hess, B. B. "Friendship." In *Aging and Society*, Vol. 3: *A Sociology of Age Stratification*. Eds. M. W. Riley, M. Johnson, and A. Foner. New York: Russell Sage, 1972.

Hochschild, A. R. *The Unexpected Community*. Englewood Cliffs, NJ: Prentice-Hall, 1973.

Jones, D. C., and K. Vaughan. "Close Friendships Among Senior Adults." *Psychology and Aging* Vol. 5 (1990): 451–57.

Larson, R. "Thirty Years of Research on the Subjective Well-Being of Older Americans." *Journal of Gerontology* Vol. 33 (1978): 109–25.

Litwak, E. *Helping the Elderly*. New York: Guilford, 1985.

Loewinsohn, R. J. *Survival Handbook for Widows (and for Relatives and Friends Who Want to Understand)*. Glenview, IL: Scott, Foresman, 1984.

Lopata, H. Z. *Women as Widows*. New York: Elsevier North Holland, 1979.

Matthews, S. *Friendships Through the Life Course*. Beverly Hills, CA: Sage, 1983.

Pogrebin, L. C. *Among Friends*. New York: McGraw-Hill, 1987.

Retsinas, J., and P. Garrity. "Nursing Home Friendships." *The Gerontologist* Vol. 25 (1985): 376–81.

Roberto, K. A., and J. P. Scott. "Friendships of Older Men and Women: Exchange Patterns and Satisfaction." *Psychology and Aging* Vol. 1 (1986): 103–9.

Rook, K. "Reciprocity of Social Exchange and Social Satisfaction among Older Women." *Journal of Personality and Social Psychology* Vol. 62 (1987): 145–54.

———. "Strains in Older Adults' Friendships." In *Older Adult Friendship: Structure and Process*. Eds. R. Adams and R. Blieszner. Newbury Park, CA: Sage, 1989.

Rosow, I. *The Social Integration of the Aged*. New York: Free Press, 1967.

Shea, L., L. Thompson, and R. Blieszner. "Resources in Older Adults' Old and New Friendships." *Journal of Social and Personal Relationships* Vol. 5 (1988): 83–96.

Spakes, P. R. "Family, Friendship, and Community Interaction as Related to Life Satisfaction of the Elderly." *Journal of Gerontological Social Work* Vol. 1 (1979): 279–93.

Stegner, W. S. *Crossing to Safety*. New York: Random House, 1987.

Strain, L. A., and N. L. Chappell. "Confidants: Do They Make a Difference in Quality of Life?" *Research on Aging* Vol. 4 (1982): 479–502.

Usui, W. M. "Homogeneity of Friendship Networks of Elderly Blacks and Whites." *Journal of Gerontology* Vol. 39 (1984): 35–56.

Verbrugge, L. M. "The Structure of Adult Friendship Choices." *Social Forces* Vol. 56 (1977): 576–97.

Wilson, C. *A Treasure Hunt*. Washington, DC: National Institute on Aging, 1980.

Rebecca G. Adams, Ph. D.

18

Social Support in Later Life

- Informal Social Support • Spouse as Support Provider • Social Support From Adult Children
- Characteristics of Adult Children Who Provide Support • Support From Extended Family
- Social Support From Friends and Neighbors • Formal Support Services

Many of the changes that occur during late life alter the ways in which older people interact with family and friends. Some of these changes are positive; retirement, for example, allows older people to pursue interests other than their careers. Having grandchildren is another positive change for older adults. However, some of the changes associated with late life may have a negative impact on social interactions. For example, widowhood and chronic health problems may limit opportunities for social exchanges and interpersonal involvement. One irony associated with late life is that even as negative changes occur that may limit sources of assistance, older adults may be in greater need of social support than ever before. Given that various problems may increase older people's need for assistance, older people often find themselves in an incongruous situation: opportunities for social support diminish while needs for support grow.

● INFORMAL SOCIAL SUPPORT

Informal social support includes assistance provided by family, friends, and neighbors for which older adults do not pay. Unlike formal services, such as those offered by health care providers or transportation and housekeeping services, informal social support focuses first on emotional reassurance and second on the provision of specific kinds of support. The vast majority of older adults have some kind of informal support network upon which they can call in

times of real difficulty (Callahan and others, 1990). For the most part, this network is one of reciprocity, with older adults exchanging support with network members. Although support given and received are not necessarily balanced, older people need to be able to provide whatever they can to others in their network. For example, if an older widow's grandson mows her lawn, she may bake him a pie in return. The efforts of mowing a lawn and baking a pie are quite different, yet they become a social exchange in this instance. Informal support can help older adults with tasks from the simplest to the most complex. Knowing that this support network exists provides peace of mind for many older adults.

Countless studies have examined the ways in which family members of older people function as an informal support system (Antonucci, 1990). According to the classic study on family interactions in old age done by Ethel Shanas at the University of Illinois (1979), family (i.e., individuals related by blood or marriage) is the first resource of both young and old for emotional and instrumental (i.e., tangible) support. Ninety-four percent of older adults have regular and frequent contact with family and friends; therefore, these individuals are present and available when support becomes necessary. Despite geographic mobility that may result in adult children moving some distance from their parents' home, most older people have multiple family members or close friends for whom they can provide support and from whom they can expect support in times of difficulty (Brubaker, 1991).

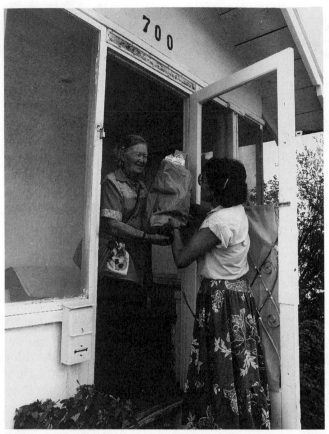

Family members are an important part of older people's informal social support network. (Courtesy of the Office of Senior Affairs, City of Albuquerque)

As money for federal programs grows tighter and formal services are cut back, informal support plays an even more critical role in the lives of older adults (Chappell, 1990). Neighbors, relatives, friends, and acquaintances can help older adults manage some of the negative consequences of chronic illness and loss. We know that those older people who have no informal social networks can experience problems with chronic illness (Dean, Kolody, and Wood, 1990), stressful life events (Wethington and Kessler, 1986), and bereavement or widowhood (Vachon and Staglianos, 1988). Further, those older people without informal networks rely much more on formal services for assistance; these individuals are at higher risk of institutionalization as well (Riter and Fries, 1992).

● **SPOUSE AS SUPPORT PROVIDER**

If an older person in need of support is married, the primary support provider for that per-

son will most likely be the spouse (Penning, 1990). As life expectancy continues to increase, more elderly spouses will need to provide support for each other. Support needs can range from a few days or weeks during the course of an acute problem to many years when dementia or serious physical illness occurs. Stone, Cafferata, and Sangl (1986) found in their national survey that wives of older and disabled husbands provided 60 percent of the support they needed.

> Ninety-four percent of older adults have regular and frequent contact with family and friends; therefore, these individuals are present and available when support becomes necessary.

Although family sociologists knew that many older women were providing support for their physically ill or demented husbands, no one really knew the serious consequences that some of these wives were experiencing. Of the spouses interviewed in Stone and colleagues' study, over 70 percent were themselves age 65 or older. These women are the "hidden victims" of serious illness; they experience stress, isolation, and loneliness as they provide support for their spouses (Borden, 1991).

The spouse who provides all or most of the social support to an ill older adult may experience overload (Miller, McFall, and Montgomery, 1991). Wives like those described above have twenty-four-hour responsibility for providing support to their husbands. In addition, they must manage difficulties with their own aging and physical limitations, emotional adjustments, and financial burdens. These same burdens exist when older men provide support for their wives. Long-term spousal support rests on a life-long commitment and marriage; those who marry in late life may not have a strong enough foundation for continuing support. Most spouse providers could benefit from services like case management, respite care, and education, yet little has been done at the federal, state, or local level to provide such help (Sommers, 1982).

Because men and women have different life expectancies, wives will more likely provide support for their husbands instead of the opposite. In general, women are more often support providers than support receivers. Seventy-seven percent of men over age 65 are married and thus have access to a spouse as a potential source of emotional and concrete support. In contrast, only 37 percent of women over age 65 are married, and many of them provide support not only for spouses but for adult children, grandchildren, and other members of their social networks as well. However, when spouses do provide support, there appear to be no gender differences in the quality or type of support given.

Research on aging reveals that older adults learn to adapt to changes in multiple dimensions of their lives; often, one of these changes is a shift from a marriage based on equality and reciprocity to one of dependence. As soon as a husband or wife can no longer engage in equitable social exchange, marital expectations and roles must be renegotiated. This is equally true whether the shift results from a physical or mental illness. If either spouse is unable to readjust in a marriage because of dependence problems, depression and feelings of injustice can result (Holahan, 1984). Both the dependent spouse and the support provider must accept the changes, or the marriage cannot survive the stress associated with support provision.

● SOCIAL SUPPORT FROM ADULT CHILDREN

Adult children are second only to spouses in providing important emotional and instrumental support and social contact to their parents in late life. Most people age 65 and older live near at least some of their adult children and have substantial social contact with them (Rosenthal, 1986). Although older adults express the clear

Adult children are second only to spouses in providing forms of support to their parents. (Copyright © Marianne Gontarz)

> Seventy-seven percent of men over age 65 are married and thus have access to a spouse as a potential source of emotional and concrete support. In contrast, only 37 percent of women over age 65 are married, and many of them provide support not only for spouses but for adult children, grandchildren, and other members of their social networks as well.

preference for living independently if possible, they value the time shared with their children as well as the informal support provided in this relationship.

Shanas (1979), in her important study of family interactions, found that contact between older people and their adult children was frequent. Patterns of contact between these groups are represented in Table 18.1.

Table 18.1
Interactions Between Older Adults and Their Children

	Those who have an adult child living an hour away	Those who see an adult child at least once a week	Those who have an adult child within 10 minutes of home
Older adults with children	80%	84%	50%

Source: Shanas, 1979.

Those children who live reasonably close to their aging parents enjoy this contact and make efforts to have interactions with their parents and to insure interactions with grandchildren when they are available. However, some adult children are not at all geographically proximate to their aging parents. Yet almost no research has examined the quality of relationships between older adults and their distant children. Schooler (1979) found that approximately half of all older adults with children had at least one child living more than 150 miles away, and 33 percent had at least one child living more than 500 miles away. Because geographic mobility continues to increase and families may become more dispersed than they are now, it is critical to discover the different kinds of support that can be provided by near and distant children.

Most families establish patterns of support in which those who have more give to those who have less. When children are young or in adolescence, parents almost always are the givers and children the receivers of support. Not until children enter young adulthood do they begin to have resources of their own. Yet in this life period when young adults are finding their first jobs, getting married, and starting their families, they usually have no excess resources that can be given to others; in fact, parents frequently continue to provide monetary support to their young adult children. But as parents grow older, retire, and perhaps become ill, they are no longer able to subsidize their children. At this point, adult children often become the givers and the parents the receivers of financial assistance as well as emotional support (Donow, 1990). Despite this overall shift in resources, most older parents continue to provide some level of support to children and

grandchildren, even after their own support needs have increased.

Chronic health problems frequently cause older adults to need assistance. As disease worsens, older people often become more frail and disabled; these changes in functional status may make them dependent on their adult children. Elaine Brody (1990), one of the leading researchers on family support, says that the American culture teaches norms of family responsibility early in life, and that these norms demand that daughters and sons provide support to their aging parents. This contradicts the social myth that insists that today's families do not assume responsibility for aging parents and prefer to institutionalize them. Substantial research evidence shows that this is not true, that adult children provide more support over longer periods of time now than they did earlier in this century. Brody (1990) estimates that five million adult children provide regular and needed support to aging parents; this number is expected to increase in the twenty-first century. As life expectancy continues to rise and disability increases in prevalence, provision of social support to older parents is becoming an expectation in early and middle adulthood. Despite this normative change, most adults do little in the way of preparation for the eventuality of dependent parents. Without some preparation, adult children can be caught without the resources to provide necessary support to parents.

Even when pre-planning has not occurred, the vast majority of American adults find ways in which to help their aging parents. What are the most frequent kinds of support provided by adult children? Types of support are influenced by parents' cognitive functioning, functional status, and proximity to other support services. A wide variety of support can be provided by adult children from identifying needed community services to helping a parent with the activities of daily living and self-care. In almost every family with aging parents, adult children provide some emotional support. This assistance can range from listening to problems to offering sympathetic counsel.

But children's support is not limited to the emotional domain; adult children also help their parents financially when necessary. Whether children can provide financial support depends in large part on their own expenses. It is difficult for many families, for example, to bear both the costs of putting a child through college and maintaining a parent in a private-pay nursing home. Often, financial support does not occur until parents become almost entirely dependent.

Brody (1990) estimates that five million adult children provide regular and needed support to aging parents; this number is expected to increase in the twenty-first century. As life expectancy continues to rise and disability increases in prevalence, provision of social support to older parents is becoming an expectation in early and middle adulthood.

Tangible acts of support both at home and in managing society at large are also part of the support repertoire of many adult children. These activities may include shopping, housework, transportation, and cooking. Adult children may use their own educations and experience to help parents negotiate the bureaucratic nightmares of insurance or Medicare claims, paperwork for institutional placement, or durable power of attorney. These kinds of assistance seem distant from personal care such as helping with bathing, feeding, toileting, and dressing. Yet children can be called upon to provide support in both areas, sometimes simultaneously.

● CHARACTERISTICS OF ADULT CHILDREN WHO PROVIDE SUPPORT

In support provision between spouses, wives are more likely than husbands to provide all

kinds of support. This gender distinction appears to hold true for adult children as well (Abel, 1989). Many studies have examined the effect of gender on the kind and amount of social support provided for parents by children, and one finding appears consistently. Daughters are far more likely than sons to provide parental support. In fact, the vast majority of informal support providers are women, regardless of their relationship to the person receiving help (Brody, 1990; Spitze and Logan, 1989). After a spouse, a daughter is most likely to assist dependent parents.

Although sons can and do provide some support for their parents, they are less likely to provide support at all and unlikely to offer personal care or emotional support (Stoller, 1990; Spitze and Logan, 1990). Instead, sons often prefer to give support indirectly. For example, instead of helping to dress or bathe parents, sons are more likely to hire someone to complete those tasks. It is only when no female relative exists (including daughter, daughter-in-law, niece, and granddaughter) that sons engage in ongoing personal support.

Support of parents by adult children varies by social class as well as by gender. For example, working-class children are more likely to provide personal care and active support for their parents themselves (Archbold, 1983). Middle-class children, on the other hand, are more apt to puchase such services for their parents (Lieberman, 1978). They investigate services needed by their parents and adopt the role of case manager, hiring and paying for necessary services. Middle-class children provide more emotional support than do working-class children; they also provide more financial assistance to their parents than do their working-class counterparts (Rosenthal, 1986).

Social class may explain some variation in the provision of social support to aging parents, and race/ethnic group membership may also account for differences. Researchers have often assumed that minority families universally provide extensive support to aging family members. Substantial evidence shows that older African-American men and women receive support from their children (Chatters, Taylor, and Neighbors, 1989) and from other relatives as well (Taylor, 1988; Taylor and Chatters, 1991). However, African-American older men received many fewer telephone contacts and visits than did African-American women, especially from daughters (Spitze and Miner, 1992).

Not all minority groups should be expected to have identical patterns of family support. These differences need to be examined closely. Comparing specific minority groups, McAdoo (1982) found that older African Americans and Hispanics were more likely to enjoy advantageous positions in their families; this advantage might enable them to obtain necessary support. It is not known with certainty, however, that greater respect or admiration of elders in minority families translates into increased support from adult children. In another minority culture, the traditional value system of Asian Americans emphasizes the wisdom and honor of older people. However, this value has not translated well into the capitalistic and competitive American culture and may hinder support provision in this cultural context (Levkoff and others, 1979). Further, Hispanic families find that their traditional norms of behavior toward older adults may inhibit individual achievement. Instead of putting the family and family elders first as they would have in their original cultures, there is evidence that it may be more profitable to put themselves ahead of the family system (Hanson, Sauer, and Seelbach, 1983). These differences make it clear that additional research on minority and ethnic provision of family support is essential.

Daughters are far more likely than sons to provide parental support. In fact, the vast majority of informal support providers are women, regardless of their relationship to the person receiving help.

● SUPPORT FROM EXTENDED FAMILY

The nuclear family has always served as the centerpiece of American culture, and the extended family has often been ignored. However, many older adults are finding that extended family members can and do provide important support services, especially when traditional sources of support (including spouses and adult children) are not available. One of the most obvious poten-

tial sources of support for the elderly are their siblings. Research evidence indicates that the majority of sisters and brothers become substantially closer during late life and depend on one another for some assistance (Gold, 1989a).

Because siblings are approximately the same age and may have many of the same needs, they tend not to exchange tangible support (Gold, 1989b). For example, a sister whose chronic illness prevents her from doing her own housework will not be able to help her brother with his. However, sisters and brothers are important sources of emotional support. Siblings are the only kin who have the potential for life-long relationships and who fill dual roles of family members and age peers. This combination makes brothers and sisters exceptionally qualified to provide emotional support.

One psychological task of late life is called the life review, a process by which older adults examine their past and reconstruct their lives into orderly and complete memories (Butler, 1980–81; Wallace, 1992). Siblings are uniquely equipped to assist each other in the life review, pulling together shared memories from childhood onward. This support, and other forms of emotional support as well, can be provided as easily at a distance as it can be in person via telephone calls or letters. Therefore siblings need not be geographically close to help each other.

Other extended family members, including cousins, nieces, and nephews, can provide support for older adults as well. If older people live near younger extended family, certain instrumental support (e.g., mowing the lawn) may be provided by them. More likely, however, more kin will be distant both in degree of relationship and in geography. In this case, extended family members can best provide emotional support through regular contact by telephone or letter. Extended family can also be supportive by commemorating important family days. Family reunions, previ-

---

Research evidence indicates that the majority of sisters and brothers become substantially closer during late life and depend on one another for some assistance.

---

ously arranged by older adults, can be managed by younger extended kin. Birthdays and holidays can also be celebrated, with distant family members coming together to share important family achievements.

● SOCIAL SUPPORT FROM FRIENDS AND NEIGHBORS

As noted above, the majority of older people have some relatives living close enough to provide social support. An even greater percentage of older adults have friends available to help them in times of need. For older people whose relatives live at a distance, friends and neighbors are the front line of support provision. When families are far away, friends and neighbors can provide assistance quickly in an emergency. Friends can also help older people in routine ways. For example, if an older individual needs help getting on the bus to go shopping, a friend who is going as well may be able to provide assistance.

Friends are willing to help when it is most convenient for them to do so and when the need for help is predictable. Unlike most family relationships, friendship is based on norms of equity and reciprocity. As long as an older person can reciprocate in some way for services rendered, the exchange of support continues. However, when an older adult becomes almost totally dependent, family members usually take over.

Several studies have found that relationships with friends are more likely to lead to increased life satisfaction and higher morale than are relations with adult children (Wright, 1989). Because

people usually have more in common with friends than with family members, friendship interactions may help older adults feel increased self-esteem. Further, because friendship is volitional instead of obligatory and because friends are often more able to bring older people into contact with the larger society than are adult children, friends play extremely important roles in the lives of older adults.

Also, friends often provide more intimacy than do family members other than spouses (Simons, 1983–84). Widows in particular find contact with friends extremely important after their transition to widowhood. Friendship provides continuing alternatives to other traditional roles (e.g., spouse, parent), and older adults can function effectively as friends long after roles such as worker, spouse, and child rearer are gone. In discussing the importance of friends, most older adults say that the quality of friendship is extremely important. For those older people who have only limited contacts with society at large, friends provide companionship and links to the outside community. Friends may be particularly hard to replace in late life because situations in which friendships frequently originate and blossom (e.g., at work, at voluntary organization meetings, in school) often are not part of the lives of most older adults.

Friends and Gender

Older people tend to choose friends who are similar in age, race, religion, marital status, and income. Although younger people believe that older adults prefer friends of different ages, many studies have found that older people really prefer age-similar friends (Hochschild, 1973). Age-homogeneous residential settings such as life-care communities provide older adults with a large population of potential friends. Age-similar friends can act as each other's confidants, roles that for many men are often met only by their wives. Few older men have the strong, complex, and dense social networks developed by most older women, and few men benefit from friendships in the same ways women do (Chapman, 1989). Men, for example, may be devastated by widowhood because their confidante and support source has died, and friends are not easily accessed to fill these roles.

For older people whose relatives live at a distance, friends and neighbors are the front line of support provision. (Copyright © Mariane Gontarz)

Voices of Creative Aging

Magna S., age 66, received her master's in social work from Fordham University with a goal to ease life transitions for women in midlife and later year crises.

I see a tremendous hope for older women, and I hope to convey that to my patients, to my surroundings, and to myself. I wanted to be in the social work field because I have lent broad shoulders for many, many years to many people in my long years of volunteer work with the elderly. I've seen many places where they are getting excellent physical care; however, there is absolutely no support system, nothing to make their lives even tolerable emotionally. That disturbed me. When I decided to go into this field, I decided to work with the elderly and try to give as much as I can and do what I can for them.

My focus is on working with women facing turning points in their lives. So much more is expected of women today. In reaction to this societal expectation, many women from the older generation suffer low self-esteem, because they see their lives as unproductive. They don't need to go out and develop a career, or get a job, or do something very meaningful to society. They have to do something meaningful for themselves. When I faced my own problem of low self-image, I chose college as a way to improve my self-confidence. But we all need to find our own path.

I am aware of my mortality and am anxious to have a productive career as long as possible. In the back of my mind is the fear of how long I am going to be able to do it. Until I am unable, I would like to do what I feel will bring me pleasure. I have that luxury. You can't just vegetate; you've go to do something. I love helping those I come in contact with. There is life after 50, 60, 70, or even 80!

Excerpt from Connie Goldman's "Late Bloomer" public radio series

Unlike men, most women have close friends throughout their lives. These ongoing relationships satisfy important intimacy needs even during marriage and child rearing (Riley and Riley, 1986). As women grow older, networks may become closer and are certainly available for support during marital separation, divorce, and widowhood. This provision of support among female friends is extremely important to the well-being of older women and may contribute to their relative resilience after major life stresses such as widowhood. Widowed older women may receive more support from friends than married older women, perhaps because widows are more likely to be able to provide reciprocal support (Litwak, 1989). The intimate friendships of older women are critical to their self-concept and morale.

Friendship provides continuing alternatives to other traditional roles (e.g., spouse, parent), and older adults can function effectively as friends long after roles such as worker, spouse, and child rearer are gone.

● FORMAL SUPPORT SERVICES

Most older people will experience times in their lives when use of formal support services becomes almost mandatory (Maslow, 1990). Although assistance to older adults can be provided by families, friends, and neighbors, a continuum of long-term care services must include relevant formal services to impaired older adults (Montgomery and Borgatta, 1989). In these instances, family members may have to act as ombudsmen and assist older adults in contacting providers of formal care or arranging for necessary services. Bureaucracies of federal, state, and local governments may be too complex for older adults to negotiate alone. Thus, some combination of informal support and formal services may best meet older people's support needs.

Access services allow older adults to contact providers of necessary services. Access services include information and referral services as well as case managers who provide overall supervision and organization of the entire service community. Additional access services include transportation to help older adults travel to services that cannot be brought to the home.

For older people with serious physical problems, the *health care system* is one essential source of formal support. In addition to support received from physicians, many other health care professionals can contribute to the quality of life of older adults. Visiting nurses and home health aides may provide enough assistance to allow a partially disabled or dysfunctional older adult to remain in the community instead of being institutionalized. Physical and occupational therapists offer services which may be necessary for reha-

bilitation after serious acute problems or in ongoing management of chronic diseases. For those older adults who have had strokes or other health problems that disrupt their abilities to carry out activities of daily living, rehabilitation can assist them in returning to as near-normal a life as possible.

Nutrition services can be provided in multiple ways to the elderly. Meals on Wheels and other food delivery systems bring hot meals to those

Relaxation and leisure are necessary components of an older adult's life. Social and recreational services are of great importance. (Courtesy of The National Council on the Aging, Inc.)

older adults who cannot cook for themselves. Hot lunch programs at senior centers or congregate meal sites also insure that those more mobile adults who utilize these services get balanced meals. Many older adults with serious physical or mental handicaps rely on these services to provide their basic nutrition.

Relaxation and leisure are necessary components of an older adult's life, and *social and recreational services* are of great importance. Currently, senior centers provide probably the most consistent recreational and educational programming for older people. Programs such as adult day care and respite services for the cognitively impaired provide activities for older adults who cannot remain under 24-hour supervision by family members. These programs allow many older people to remain in the community who would otherwise be consigned to nursing homes or assisted living programs.

Personal support services such as companions, choreworkers, and telephone reassurance programs help older adults who can remain independent but who may need assistance in an emergency. These services enable older adults who otherwise might need institutional placement to remain in the community. Older people who have short-term illnesses, who are recovering from surgery, or who may be exceptionally frail can benefit tremendously from these services.

Finally, formal support can be provided in an *institution* such as a nursing home. At any given time, approximately 5 percent of all older adults live in institutions; this small percentage results from families providing support to their older members whenever possible. However, 25 percent of all older adults will at some time utilize institutional care. Nursing homes are the most typical providers of this formal service and may be an appropriate choice for those older adults who can no longer function independently even with some informal support or community services (Kane and Kane, 1990). Also, an older person is much more likely to need nursing home placement if there are few or no family members available in a support network; the unmarried and childless are most likely to find themselves in this situation.

The majority of nursing home residents are functionally impaired in some way, through physical illness, cognitive decline, or a combination of multiple problems. However, for every impaired older adult living in a long-term care facility, there are as few as two and as many as five equally impaired older adults living in the community. What makes some impaired older people able to continue community living while others need institutional care? Strong social support systems are the most important factor in determining who can survive in the community and who must rely totally on formal services (Braun and Rose, 1987). Therefore, cognitive and physical impairment *alone* do not explain institutional placement; available support is an equally important explanation.

Most older adults living in nursing homes are white, female, and widowed (or never married) who were placed in the institution after exhausting their informal support system's resources (National Center for Health Statistics, 1987). Three types of patients typically require institutional support: (1) the short-stay patients recuperating from acute problems (e.g., hip fracture), (2) the short-stay patients who die quickly in the nursing home, and (3) longer-stay patients with serious physical and cognitive limitations. The cost of formal institutional support is quite high, and Medicare covers these costs only under certain specific circumstances (when nursing home placement follows hospitalization) and for a limited amount of time (a maximum of 180 days). The vast majority of patients in nursing homes receive Medicaid assistance after having spent their own resources (Vladeck, 1980).

In the past, formal support services were primarily limited to nursing homes, and few community support services were available to older adults. In the present environment, a broad range of community support services provide assistance to older individuals. These services have helped older adults to retain their independence in the community as long as possible. Further, community support services provide assistance not only for the older adult but for family members as well. Respite care can provide important relief to informal support providers, allowing them to continue to care for their older family members. For the most part, programs that provide formal support to older people have been extremely successful in delaying permanent institutional placement and maximizing community living for older adults (Arling and others, 1984).

Twenty-five percent of all older adults will at some time utilize institutional care. Nursing homes are the most typical providers of this formal service and may be an appropriate choice for those older adults who can no longer function independently even with some informal support or community services.

However, not all parts of this country have access to the same level and quality of formal care. Urban areas are much more likely to have these services available to older adults and their families than rural areas. People with financial independence are more likely to be able to afford them as well. A major goal of policy makers in the future should be to bring such support services to all older adults at costs that can be met on a fixed income. Money must be made available to test innovative new support programs and to make them available to the majority of older adults.

Organization

Children of Aging Parents
2761 Trenton Road
Levittown, PA 19056
(215) 945-6900

Gray Panther Project Fund
3700 Chestnut St.
Philadelphia, PA 19104

Older Women's League
730 11th Street NW, Suite 300
Washington, DC 20001-4512
(202) 783-6686

References

Abel, E. K. "The Ambiguities of Social Support: Adult Daughters Caring for Frail Elderly Parents." *Journal of Aging Studies* Vol. 3 (1989): 211–30.

Antonucci, T. C. "Social Supports and Social Relationships." In *Handbook of Aging and the Social Sciences*. Eds. R. H. Binstock and L. K. George. 3d ed. San Diego, CA: Academic Press, 1990.

Archbold, P. G. "The Impact of Parent-Caring on Women." *Family Relations* Vol. 32 (1983): 39–45.

Arling, G., E. B. Harkins, and M. Romaniuk. "Adult Day Care and the Nursing Home." *Research on Aging* Vol. 6 (1984): 225–42.

Borden, W. "Stress, Coping, and Adaptation in Spouses of Older Adults with Chronic Dementia." *Social Work Research and Abstracts* Vol. 27 (1991): 14–21.

Braun, K. L., and C. L. Rose. "Geriatric Patient Outcomes and Costs in Three Settings: Nursing Home, Foster Family, and Own Home." *Journal of the American Geriatrics Society* Vol. 35 (1987): 387–97.

Brody, E. *Women in the Middle: Their Parent-Care Years.* New York: Springer, 1990.

Brubaker, T. H. "Families in Later Life." In *Contemporary Families: Looking Forward, Looking Back.* Ed. A. Booth. Minneapolis, MN: National Council on Family Relations, 1991.

Butler, R. N. "The Life Review: An Unrecognized Bonanza." *International Journal of Aging and Human Development* Vol. 12 (1980–81): 35–38.

Callahan, J., L. Diamond, J. Giele, and R. Morris. "Responsibilities of Families for Their Severely Disabled Elders." *Health Care Financing Review* Vol. 1 (1990): 29–44.

Chapman, N. J. "Gender, Marital Status, and Childlessness of Older Persons and the Availability of Informal Assistance." In *Health Care for the Elderly: An Information Source Book.* Eds. M. D. Petersen and D. L. White. Newbury Park, CA: Sage, 1989.

Chappell, N. L. "Aging and Social Care." In *Handbook of Aging and the Social Sciences.* Eds. R. H. Binstock and L. K. George. 3d ed. San Diego, CA: Academic Press, 1990.

Chatters, L. M., J. R. Taylor, and H. W. Neighbors. "Size of Informal Helper Network Mobilized During a Serious Personal Problem Among Black Americans." *Journal of Marriage and the Family* Vol. 51 (1989): 667–76.

Dean, A., B. Kolody, and P. Wood. "Effects of Social Support From Various Sources on Depression in Elderly Persons." *Journal of Health and Social Behavior* Vol. 31 (1990): 215–23.

Donow, H. S. "Two Approaches to the Care of an Elder Parent." *Gerontologist* Vol. 30 (1990): 486–90.

Gold, D. T. "Generational Solidarity: Conceptual Antecedants and Consequences." *American Behavioral Scientist* Vol. 33 (1989b): 19–32.

———. "Sibling Relations in Old Age: A Typology." *International Journal of Aging and Human Development* Vol. 28, no. 1 (1989a): 37–51.

Hanson, S., W. Sauer, and W. Seelback. "Racial and Cohort Variations in Filial Responsibility Norms." *Gerontologist* Vol. 23 (1983): 626–31.

Hochschild, A. *The Unexpected Community.* Berkeley, CA: University of California Press, 1973.

Holahan, C. "Marital Attitudes Over Forty Years: A Longitudinal and Cohort Analysis." *Journal of Gerontology* Vol. 39 (1984): 49–57.

Kane, R. L., and R. A. Kane. "Health Care for Older People: Organizational and Policy Issues." In *Handbook of Aging and the Social Sciences.* 3d ed. Eds. R. H. Binstock and L. K. George. San Diego, CA: Academic Press, 1990.

"Late Bloomer" audio cassette. Available from Connie Goldman Productions, 926 Second Street, Suite 201, Santa Barbara, CA 90403. (310) 393-6801.

Levkoff, S., C. Pratt, R. Esperanza, and S. Tomine. *Minority Elderly: A Historical and Cultural Perspective.* Corvallis, OR: Oregon State University, 1979.

Lieberman, G. L. "Children of the Elderly as Natural Helpers: Some Demographic Differences." *American Journal of Community Psychology* Vol. 6 (1978): 489–98.

Litwak, E. "Forms of Friendship Among Older People in an Industrial Society." In *Older Adult Friendship.* Eds. R. G. Adams and R. Blieszner. Newbury Park, CA: Sage, 1989.

McAdoo, H. P. "Stress-Absorbing Systems in Black Families." *Family Relations* Vol. 31 (1982): 479–88.

Maslow, K. "Formal Long-Term Care Services and Settings." In *Dementia Care: Patient, Family, and Community.* Ed. N. Mace. Baltimore, MD: Johns Hopkins University Press, 1990.

Miller, B., S. McFall, and A. Montgomery. "The Effect of Elder's Health, Involvement, and Stress on Two Dimensions of Burden." *Journal of Gerontology* Vol. 46 (1991): S9–S19.

Montgomery, R., and E. Borgatta. "The Effects of Alternative Support Strategies on Family Caregiving." *Gerontologist* Vol. 29 (1989): 457–64.

National Center for Health Statistics. "Use of Nursing Homes by the Elderly: Preliminary Data From the 1985 National Nursing Home Survey." *Advance Data: Vital and Health Statistics No. 135.* Washington, DC: U.S. Government Printing Office, 1987.

Penning, M. "Receipt of Assistance by Elderly People: Hierarchical Selection and Task Specificity." *Gerontologist* Vol. 30 (1990): 220–27.

Riley, M. W., and J. Riley. "Longevity and Social Structure: The Potential of the Adult Years." In *Our Aging Society.* Eds. A. Pifer and L. Bronte. New York: W. W. Norton, 1986.

Riter, R. N., and B. E. Fries. "Predictors of the Placement of Cognitively Impaired Residents on Special Care Units." *Gerontologist* Vol. 32 (1992): 184–90.

Rosenthal, C. J. "Family Supports in Later Life: Does Ethnicity Make a Difference?" *Gerontologist* Vol. 26 (1986): 19–24.

Schooler, K. K. *National Senior Citizens Survey, 1968.* Ann Arbor, MI: Inter-University Consortium for Political Social Research, 1979.

Shanas, E. "The Family as Social Support in Old Age." *Gerontologist* Vol. 19 (1979): 169–74.

Simons, R. L. "Specificity and Substitution in the Social Networks of the Elderly." *International Journal of Aging and Human Development* Vol. 18 (1983–84): 121–39.

Sommers, T. *Til Death Do Us Part: Caregiving Wives of Disabled Husbands.* Washington, DC: Older Women's League, 1982.

Spitze, G., and J. Logan. "Gender Differences in Family Support: Is There a Payoff?" *Gerontologist* Vol. 29 (1989): 108–13.

———. "Sons, Daughters, and Intergenerational Social Support." *Journal of Marriage and the Family* Vol. 52 (1990): 420–30.

Spitze, G., and S. Miner. "Gender Differences in Adult Child Contact Among Black Elderly Parents." *Gerontologist* Vol. 32 (1992): 213–18.

Stoller, E. P. "Males as Helpers: The Role of Sons, Relatives, and Friends." *Gerontologist* Vol. 30 (1990): 228–35.

Stone, R., G. Cafferata, and J. Sangl. *Caregivers of the Frail Elderly: A National Profile.* Washington, DC: U.S. Department of Health and Human Services, 1986.

Taylor, R. J. "Aging and Supportive Relationships Among Black Americans." In *The Black American Elderly.* Ed. J. S. Jackson. New York: Springer, 1988.

Taylor, R. J., and L. M. Chatters. "Extended Family Networks of Older Black Adults." *Journal of Gerontology* Vol. 46 (1991): S210–S217.

Vachon, M. L. S., and S. K. Staglianos. "The Role of Social Support in Bereavement." *Journal of Social Issues* Vol. 44 (1988): 175–90.

Vladek, B. C. *Unloving Care: The Nursing Home Tragedy.* New York: Basic Books, 1980.

Wallace, J. B. "Reconsidering the Life Review: The Social Construction of Talk About the Past." *Gerontologist* Vol. 32 (1992): 120–25.

Wethington, E., and R. Kessler. "Perceived Support, Received Support, and Adjustment to Stressful Life Events." *Journal of Health and Social Behavior* Vol. 27 (1986): 78–89.

Wright, P. "Gender Differences in Adults' Same- and Cross-Gender Friendships." In *Older Adult Friendship.* Eds. R. S. Adams and R. Blieszner. Newbury Park, CA: Sage, 1989.

Additional Reading

Loewinsohn, Ruth Jean. *Survival Handbook for Widows (and for Relatives and Friends Who Want to Understand).* Washington, DC: American Association of Retired Persons, 1984.

Ruberstein, Robert L. *Singular Paths: Old Men Living Alone.* New York: Columbia University Press, 1986.

Silverman, Phyllis. *Widow-to-Widow.* Vol. 7 of the Springer Series on Social Work. New York: Springer, 1986.

Deborah T. Gold, Ph. D.

Section VII:

Health and Wellness

Physical Wellness in the Elderly

- Changing Attitudes Toward Wellness • Healthy Behavior • Aging and Sexuality
- Emotional Health • Prevention and Wellness • Routine Check-ups and Physicals

Wellness is a term that describes a positive state of being, that is, a condition in which an individual is without illness, feels well both physically and emotionally, is functionally independent, and is generally in good health. Health has been defined as a state of complete physical, mental, and social well-being (World Health Organization, 1946). Physical wellness is a state of bodily well-being in which diseases and physical impairments are absent or their effects kept to a minimum, and where the person has the best possible functional capability, given the variables of normal aging. Physical wellness, however, implies more than the state of one's condition at a specific time. The activities of health promotion, preventive and healthy behaviors, and preservation of function are all involved. Wellness conveys the understanding that quality of life has top priority and that longevity is desirable as long as it is accompanied by good health and personal satisfaction.

The concepts of physical wellness and good health in the elderly can seem contradictory. People tend to experience bodily losses as they grow older and are commonly afflicted by multiple illnesses and disabilities. The question arises, therefore, can health and wellness be promoted in elderly people? Recent thinking indicates that this is not only possible, for many if not all older persons, but highly desirable. This is the philosophy of the wellness movement.

From a historical perspective, aging has been accepted as a biological process in which physical changes take a predictably downhill course, *ultimately resulting in illness and death. One is perceived as aged when physical features typical of the older person appear (such as gray hair or wrinkled skin) or age-related illness occurs (such as osteoarthritis, dementia, or many cancers). Consistent features of aging are the inevitable losses: physical ability, mental capacity, socialization, and ultimately life. While the process is universal, it varies dramatically from one person to another.*

Although aging is a predictable process of losses and change, the rate and expression of these losses are variable and unique to the individual. The health status of older people varies greatly, and age may be best measured by physical and psychological characteristics rather than in years. This variability in aging is determined by disease, hereditary factors, environmental influences, and individual characteristics. For example, an aged person who has few medical problems could be considered healthy with a greater potential for quality life than a younger person who suffers from acute or chronic illness and is frail and dependent. Functional markers such as independence in daily activities and socialization are generally better predictors of longevity than age.

● CHANGING ATTITUDES TOWARD WELLNESS

Health and health maintenance are important topics in the discussion of wellness and aging. Up until the 1970s, physicians and other caregivers in the United States approached older people in

373

much the same way as they did younger individuals: they defined health as the absence of disease. Health care meant diagnosing disease and recommending cures (surgery, medications, and so on). Since the elderly were commonly affected by chronic diseases normally not curable (e.g., osteoarthritis, dementia), caregivers often used to forego treatment in older people, assuming these chronic afflictions to be part of normal aging and that intervening was thus futile. Preventive measures and health promotion were considered inappropriate.

The shift in thinking during the last half century acknowledges the variability of health in older people. Greater value is placed on quality of life and functional capacity. Although disease-fighting is still important to health care, current thinking puts greater emphasis on preventive measures and health promotion. For example, billions of dollars have been spent in the treatment of hip fractures but until recently very little has been done in the way of prevention. Recent research recommends preventive measures such as exercise and hormone therapy to prevent osteoporosis; the improvement in capability and increased bone strength may ultimately help prevent hip fractures.

The other important component of the shift in philosophy is the belief that quality of life is more valuable than quantity of life. Compression of morbidity is a popular concept that highlights the goal of confining or compressing disability and physical illness into the shortest possible time period. Ideally, these undesirable but expected events would occur just prior to death, as close as possible to the finite maximum life expectancy (estimated at about 85 years for most of the population).

The concepts of physical wellness and health must respect the individual goals and wishes of older people. One goal may be to achieve a reasonable life expectancy. For example, a woman of age 70 may wish to live an additional decade or more; this is a reasonable goal considering that the average 70-year-old woman can expect to live an additional eight to twelve years. Another goal of older people is to remain independent and self-sufficient. Currently, a woman who reaches age 70 can expect to live six of the next twelve years with some degree of dependency, often so significant that long-term care in a nursing home or similar facility may be required. An obvious goal is to prevent this from occurring. Therefore, the concept of physical wellness for the elderly must take account of the changes inherent to older people and use individual life goals as a measure of good health and a positive state of being.

Although disease-fighting is still important to health care, current thinking puts greater emphasis on preventive measures and health promotion.

That it is sound and practical to advocate health and physical wellness for the elderly can now be affirmed, based upon a greater understanding of the aging process, the value placed on quality of life with less emphasis upon longevity alone, and on the individual and collective goals of older people.

The basic goals of physical wellness are as follows:

1. to prevent disease
2. to prevent or limit disability
3. to maintain optimum health and function
4. to minimize the duration and manifestations of disease and disability when they occur

The activities to achieve these goals are carried out by the individual and his or her health care providers (physician, nurse, therapist, counselor, family, friend, etc.). These activities include healthy behavior and specific preventive measures.

● HEALTHY BEHAVIOR

Healthy behavior is generally considered the most consistent and effective method for promoting good health. While this is true in all age groups, it applies particularly to the elderly considering that late life is usually the time when the negative effects of negligent behavior become most evident. For example, smoking is unhealthy behavior which, started at a younger age, can and often does result in cancer and/or chronic disease in later life. In contrast, favorable behavior such as regular aerobic exercise and maintenance of ideal body weight might be more valuable to older people than younger people in terms of actual benefit and the impact on quality of life.

Healthy behavior such as regular aerobic exercise and maintenance of ideal body weight might be more valuable to older people than younger people in terms of actual benefit and the impact on quality of life. (Copyright © Marianne Gontarz)

Healthy behavior as it pertains to the elderly can be categorized as (1) activities in early and middle years to prevent disease and disability later, and (2) activities by older persons to maintain health and prevent or lessen the manifestations of disease and disability. A summary of healthful life behavior is shown in Table 19.1.

Exercise

There is increasing evidence that the benefits of exercise extend into advanced age. Regular aerobic exercise (walking, biking, swimming, etc.) can improve bodily functions and prevent or forestall some illnesses. Exercise is a key component of fitness—a notion very popular today that can apply to all ages. Fitness is comprised of five elements: cardiovascular endurance, muscular strength, muscular endurance, flexibility, and body composition. Exercise can also improve self-image and emotional well-being. Graded exercise that is tailored to individual abilities can be advocated as an important part of health promotion and maintenance in the elderly.

But not many older people exercise. Data from 1985 show that fewer than 10 percent of those over the age of 65 jog, swim, cycle, or do calisthenics on a regular basis. This contrasts with up to 40 percent of those under age 65 who exercise regularly and vigorously. Only one-third of older people do *any* type of regular physical exercise, and most of these do casual walking only.

Table 19.1
Healthy Life Behavior

Younger Persons	Older Persons
Diet	Diet
low fat, low cholesterol	adequate calories
high fiber	high fiber
low or moderate salt	low or moderate salt
Aerobic exercise	Exercise
Tobacco cessation	aerobic
Limit alcohol consumption	strength, range of motion
Safe driving, seat belts	Tobacco cessation
Dental hygiene (prophylaxis)	Limit alcohol consumption
Avoid direct sunlight	Dental hygiene (treatment)
	Accident and fall prevention
	Avoid multiple drugs, especially over-the-counter drugs
	Socialization

Voices of Creative Aging

Bernice K., age 65, participates along with her husband, Ralph, in the Senior Olympics, a series of thirty-four sports competitions throughout the United States that emphasizes the social and recreational aspects of sports as much as competition. She relates how taking part in this program has enhanced the couple's quality of life in many ways:

After Ralph retired and our four daughters completed their education, we began to do some things with our lives that we hadn't had an opportunity to do before. We both started to participate in local Senior Olympics. Ralph suffered a heart attack a few years ago, and our life changed. He gained a lot of weight. I dedicated myself to help him to bring it down.

As a result of our walking exercise and change of diet, I lost forty-two pounds. I became interested in race-walking and qualified for the national competition. My six events are horseshoe, archery, one-mile race walk, discus, shotput, and high jump. Ralph does quite well in horseshoes. We travel to meets and are away from our home for up to three months at a time. The number of people in the games is growing rapidly. In on California meet, there were over 3,000 entries.

The Senior Olympic movement is composed of an inspiring group of people. They are all young at heart. Things happen to everybody; they have all sorts of physical handicaps, but it really doesn't stop them. They know their limitations and go for it. You should never do things that are beyond you, or push yourself too much at our age. Get physically fit first, get healthy, and then compete if that is an interest.

Excerpt from Connie Goldman's "Late Bloomer" public radio series

These data may reflect an age bias towards exercise as healthy behavior; exercise was not considered a social norm in years past and many older people are fearful of injury or potential for disease. Thus, in order to recommend regular exercise for the elderly, a caregiver must consider individual capabilities, weigh the risks of injury, and attempt to qualify and quantify individual benefits.

The physical benefits of exercise in older persons range from maintenance of ideal body weight to possible prevention of such conditions as diabetes, heart disease, and osteoporosis. Regular exercise can also improve functional capabilities such as gait, balance, transfer from chair and bed, and many activities of daily living such as toileting and bathing that require physical strength, as shown in Table 19.2.

Recent data have shown that elderly people can exercise effectively. Aerobic ability as measured by oxygen consumption can increase with physical training. Weight lifting is an exercise elderly people rarely perform, but studies have shown that even persons in their nineties can increase strength and muscle mass through weight training. Most exercise data report the result of short-term training programs (four to twelve weeks); whether older people will exercise for longer periods of time and whether the benefits are long-lasting remains to be seen.

A longer study of 200 men and women from 56 to 87 (at the Andrus Gerontology Center at the University of Southern California) produced encouraging findings. The group took part in regular exercise three to five times a week over a five-year period and showed distinct improvement not only in cardiovascular health, flexibility,

Table 19.2
Benefits of a Consistent Exercise Program

1. Increased flexibility and range of motion in joints resulting in better agility and coordination
2. Increased strength and endurance
3. Greater stamina and less chronic fatigue
4. Prevention of bone deterioration
5. Increased efficiency of cardiovascular and respiratory systems
6. Decreased digestive problems and constipation
7. Decreased chronic stress, tension, and mental fatigue
8. Decreased cholesterol levels
9. Better weight control
10. Improved sense of overall well-being

and muscle tone, but in condition of teeth, gums, and skin tone.

Exercise in the elderly should be prescribed by physicians or therapists in much the same way medications are prescribed. A physical examination and assessment of physical ability must be done to screen for cardiac and respiratory problems before any older person begins an exercise program. The prescription should be individualized, providing maximum benefit while keeping in mind the needs and goals of the older persons. For example, a progressive walking program may be best for an older person who is overweight and wishes to lose weight and suppress appetite (eg., brisk walk 30 minutes, three times per week). On the other hand, a very old person having trouble with housework may do well with a focused weight training program to improve upper body strength and stamina. As with younger people, the older person should be encouraged to exercise regularly.

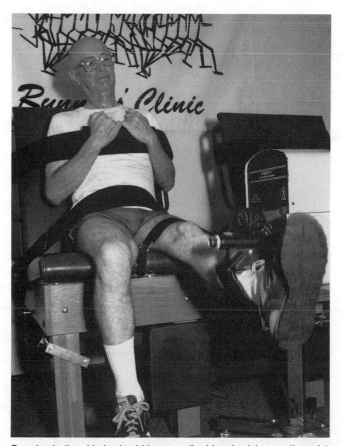

Exercise in the elderly should be prescribed by physicians or therapists in much the same way medications are prescribed. (Courtesy of Bowman Gray/Baptist Hospital Medical Center)

Diet and Nutrition

Good nutrition is a key component of wellness. It means a proper intake of foods (type and amount) to provide for normal bodily function. Dietary excesses or deficiencies can lead to disease conditions, especially in older persons who lack the nutritional reserves needed to avoid illness during times of physical stress. A proper balance of the major food groups is important: carbohydrates, proteins, fat, and grains and fiber.

Most Americans take in excess fat, many eating 50 percent or more of their diet in the form of fat (30 percent or less is desirable for the average adult person). Also, as energy needs tend to be lower in older people (because of decreased activity and lower body weight), fat intake as low as 10 percent of total intake may be more appropriate. This can be achieved by limiting red meat, removing skin from chicken, eating more fish, avoiding cooking in fats (especially animal fats), and eliminating fat condiments such as butter and mayonnaise. Replace fat in the diet with an increase in complex carbohydrates: cereals, fruits, vegetables, bread, rice, and pasta. Many dieticians urge 55 percent or more of your diet as carbohydrates.

Protein needs are diminished in older persons due to a decrease in muscle mass, but the percentage of protein intake (30 percent to 50 percent) is similar to that of younger people. Carbohydrates in the form of complex sugars and starches (e.g., bread, potatoes, etc.) are preferred to simple sugars (e.g., table sugar, candy, etc.). Simple sugars are high in calories while providing little nutritional value, other than as a rapid source of energy in those elderly who are very active physically. High caloric foods such as these should be avoided by older people who are prone to overweight.

Recent studies endorse diets plentiful in fiber. High fiber diets may reduce the risk of certain intestinal cancers and promote regular intestinal function. (Whether this is as true for all age groups is as yet unknown.) Sodium restriction can lower blood pressure and reduce the risk of illnesses associated with hypertension, such as stroke and kidney disease. As most Americans consume far more sodium than is needed, a reduction in very salty foods can be recommended for all age groups.

Vitamin supplementation remains a controver-

Table 19.3
American College of Sports Medicine Guidelines

In order to achieve benefits from exercise, the American College of Sports Medicine (ACSM) issues guidelines based on the latest research. They suggest an individual perform aerobic exercise using large muscle groups 15–60 minutes, 3–5 days per week. Having strong muscles, tendons, and ligaments may prevent injury, low back pain, faster recovery from injury, more strength to do everyday chores, and more muscle tone. To get the most from this aerobic exercise, you should exercise at an intensity level called your training heart rate zone, used to gauge how hard you are exercising. Ask your doctor to work with you in determining this level, using the following gauge.

Training Heart Rate Zone

Objective: To determine your personal training heart rate zone.

Note: To determine your resting heart rate, take your pulse while resting for 10 seconds and multiply by six. This is your resting heart rate per minute.

Intensity of Exercise

1. Estimate your own maximal heart rate (MHR)
    MHR = 220 minus age (220 – age)
    MHR = 220– _____ = _____ bpm (beats per minute)
2. Resting Heart Rate (RHR) = _____ bpm
3. Heart Rate Reserve (HRR) = MHR – RHR
    HRR = _____ – _____ = bpm
4. Training Intensities (TI) = HRR x TI + RHR
    50 Percent TI = _____ x .50 + _____ = _____ bpm
    75 Percent TI = _____ x .75 + _____ = _____ bpm
5. Training Heart Rate Zone. The optimum training heart rate zone as determined by the ACSM is between 60–90 percent. However, individuals who have been physically inactive or are in the poor or fair cardiovascular fitness categories should use 50 percent training intensity during the first few weeks of the exercise program.

Training Heart Rate Zone: _____ (50 percent TI) to _____ (75 percent TI).

If your heart rate falls below the optimum zone, you are not working hard enough to achieve aerobic benefits. If your heart rate is above this zone, slow down; overworking increases risk of injury and overexertion. Exercise heart rates for individuals on certain types of medications, such as beta blockers and high blood pressure medication, will be much lower.

---

sial topic. While vitamin deficiencies should definitely be treated, the use of supplementary vitamins in healthy older persons without vitamin deficiency has inconsistent support. Certain vitamins have particular appeal to older persons because of their effects on the aging process. Vitamin E is an antioxidant and may have value in slowing down the aging process; oxidation of body cells is one of the theoretical mechanisms of aging. Vitamin E's reported ability to enhance certain body functions such as memory and sexual function has as yet not been proven. The long-term effects of high doses of vitamin E are unknown. High doses of vitamin C have long been reported to prevent viral infections and may also improve the quality of skin and bone. Vitamin C has little or no adverse effects and therefore can be supported for general use in most older persons. Vitamin D deficiency is common in older

---

Protein needs are diminished in older persons due to a decrease in muscle mass, but the percentage of protein intake (30 percent to 50 percent) is similar to that of younger people.

Profiles of Productive Aging

Julia Child
Cookbook author, television personality

"I never thought of retirement; it would never occur to me. Because I like my work, I continue to go on and on. I think young people should realize that they have to have a passionate occupation."

Julia Child's career might be described as an odyssey. Born Julia McWilliams in Pasadena, California, in 1912 she graduated from Smith College in 1934 and went to work in advertising and publicity. When World War II broke out, she joined the Office of Strategic Services (OSS), which later became the CIA. In Ceylon, her first overseas assignment, she met Paul Child, served with him in China, and married him in 1946, after returning to the United States.

In those days, Child explained, if two people in government service got married, one of them was expected to quit—and it wasn't the man. She resigned and moved with her husband to France, where the U.S. Information Agency sent him after the war. Child discovered her true vocation in France. "I stepped off the boat," she remarked, "took one mouthful of French food, and I was hooked for life."

She studied at the Cordon Bleu and made two friends who became important collaborators: Simone Beck and Louise Bertholle. Post-World War II Paris housed many Americans, but few could speak French, making it difficult for women to take classes at any of the existing French cooking schools. In 1949 Child and her friends opened their own English-speaking cooking school, Le Club des Gourmettes, and began writing a book on French cuisine for an American audience. This book, the all-time bestseller, *Mastering the Art of French Cooking*, was published by Knopf in 1961, after the Childs returned to the United States.

Nervous about their prospects for selling 5,000 French cookbooks, Knopf arranged to feature Child in an hour-long TV book review show at WGBH in Boston. Child was momentarily stumped: "What was I going to do?" she wondered, "Read recipes for an hour?" Then she hit upon the notion of taking along something she could "whip up" on camera, as a demonstration. Since television studios in those days were not equipped with cooking facilities, Child thought of doing an omelette: All it required was a dozen eggs, a wire whip, a copper mixing bowl, an omelette pan, and a hot plate.

The omelette was a tremendous success and occasioned so many enthusiastic calls and letters from viewers the station asked Child to do her own cooking show, five days a week. Thus *The French Chef* was launched, and Americans, until then disdainful and suspicious of "foreign" food, embraced the cuisine. With her engaging and lighthearted manner, Child made French cooking fun and accessible.

After taping some 200 episodes of *The French Chef,* Child developed a new television series featuring a more contemporary cuisine, *Julia Child and Company,* and in 1984, with WGBH, she produced six one-hour teaching videos, "The Way to Cook." Child also published companion books for these series, *Julia Child and Company* (1974), *Julia Child and More Company* (1980), and *The Way to Cook.*

Today Child is still going strong at the age of 80, with new books, a new TV series, *Dinner With Julia,* and appearances on ABC's "Good Morning, America." She has had a career peak lasting thirty years—and it began at age 50!

Lydia Brontë

persons who have little exposure to sunlight; vitamin D is produced in the skin when exposed to the sun. This deficiency is especially common in older people who reside in nursing homes or are unable to go outdoors because of illness or disability. Oral vitamin D supplementation is appropriate for these individuals.

Minerals such as calcium, magnesium, and other trace metals are commonly used as dietary supplements, but only calcium has been shown to be of proven benefit. Calcium supplementation in postmenopausal women can help maintain or improve bone density, and doses of 1 gram to 1.5 grams per day combined with estrogens may prevent osteoporosis (a condition of weakened bones) and fractures. Adequate water intake is very important for the elderly. Extra liquids should be taken to replace fluids lost during exercise.

Abuses

Smoking. Giving up smoking is beneficial at any age. The long-term risks of tobacco use are well known: cancer (lung, breast, bladder, and probably others), chronic lung disease, and heart disease. Quitting or never starting will decrease the risk of these problems in later years. The older person who stops smoking will also benefit in more immediate ways. Twenty percent of older adults are current smokers and are at increased risk for lung infections such as pneumonia and influenza. Because respiratory infections are the fourth leading cause of death in persons over age 65, giving up smoking can reduce the likelihood of these serious and often fatal conditions.

Smoking is also associated with lower food intake and may contribute to weight loss in older people. Low body weight is an important marker

Profiles of Productive Aging

Dr. William Cahan
Surgeon

"I think that from the point of view of being physically and mentally able, I'm quite equipped and refuse to obey the numbers. Nothing bores me more than the chronological listing of peoples' ages as indications of their inability and ability."

Still a practicing surgeon at the age of 78, Dr. William Cahan has been at the forefront of several major advances in cancer surgery and treatment, while crusading for years against cigarette smoking. Born in New York City on August 2, 1914, the first day of World War I, Cahan was the only child of artistic parents: his father was an artist with *New York World*; his mother was an interior decorator. Cahan graduated from Harvard in 1935 with a bachelor of science degree, then earned his M.D. at Columbia Medical School. After interning at the Hospital of Joint Diseases, Cahan "walked into (Sloan-Kettering) Memorial Hospital January 1, 1942—24 days after Pearl Harbor—and, except for the three years I went to war, I've been there ever since."

Sloan-Kettering was an ideal place for Cahan to conduct his cancer research, because of the wide variety of patients and conditions and the supportive research environment of the hospital. Cahan proved that radiation, used to treat diseases like tuberculosis, was cancer-causing, and he developed treatments for various types of cancer, including cryogenics in the early 1960s. Using liquid nitrogen to freeze and "kill" tumor tissue, Cahan and Dr. Irving Cooper proved cryogenics to be very effective in treating bone cancer, skin cancers, benign and malignant tumors, removing cataracts and reattaching retinas.

His crusade against cigarette smoking also began in the 1960s. In the belief that smoking is the number one cause of rapid aging and early death in America, Cahan devised experiments that proved conclusively that cigarette smoking causes lung cancer. Responsible in large part for getting cigarette advertising off television and radio, Cahan testified before Congress as the representative of the American Cancer Society to change the labels on cigarettes in order to alert the public, the society awarded him their distinguished service award in recognition of his contributions.

Cahan has been active as a teacher at Cornell University Medical College, and he has been affiliated with many hospitals in New York and around the country. When he reached 70, Cahan fought Sloan-Kettering's attempt to retire him, because he had always dreamed of operating with his son, who was then a surgeon at New York Hospital, and he considered irrational any by-law that required retirement solely for chronological age: "I would quit in two seconds' if I thought I was technically unable to do it."

"I wrote a paper called 'Age and Cancer Surgery' in which I point out that the chronological age of people, if you take it without its context of the individual personality, is ridiculous. It's unscientific, first of all. Second, the people who are becoming septuagenarians and octogenarians are a different breed than they were a generation or two ago. I assure you, in another generation it will not be unique for nonagenarians to do remarkable things."

Cahan recently completed his autobiography, *No Stranger to Tears: A Surgeon's Story.* With many interests in addition to his medical pursuits, Cahan remains extremely active, needing only four hours of sleep a night.

Lydia Brontë

for frailty and eventual death in the elderly. In addition, quitting smoking will save money. This money could be used to purchase food or medication, which would have an even greater impact on the older person's health than quitting by itself.

Alcohol. Approximately 1 percent to 6 percent of older people have a problem with alcohol overuse, abuse, and dependency. While small amounts of alcohol (1–2 oz. per day) might prevent some cardiac and vascular conditions, larger amounts are associated with liver disease and neurological problems. Alcohol can also predispose to falls and is associated with suicide. Overuse of all forms of alcoholic beverage should be discouraged in older people to decrease their risk of encountering alcohol-related problems. Reasonable advice is to limit alcohol consumption to no more than 12 ounces of alcohol (1 oz. liquor = 12 oz. beer = 6 oz. wine) in any twenty-four hour period, and to avoid drinking daily.

Improper use of medication. The average older American uses 4.5 prescription drugs and 3.5 over-the-counter drugs annually. The frail elderly use medications even more often. The adverse effects of drug use are numerous and varied. Older persons are more susceptible because of body changes associated with normal aging, such as decreased kidney function, which in turn causes difficulty in the elimination of certain drugs from the bloodstream. Avoiding unnecessary medications and using the lowest possible dose can provide some protection for the older person. Physicians often contribute to adverse drug reactions by prescribing excessive and unnecessary amounts. Health promotion for the elderly must emphasize proper use of drugs, with the understanding that medications can improve health in the best of circumstances, but can cause serious and life-threatening problems when used inappropriately.

Obesity. Obesity in the elderly is a common problem. Approximately 30 percent of persons above the age of 65 are overweight (which is defined as weighing more than 30 percent above one's ideal). Obesity is associated with hypertension, stroke, heart disease, high cholesterol, diabetes mellitus, and osteoarthritis. Maintenance of ideal body weight is important in the prevention of these disorders and is an important facet of health promotion. Calories should not be restricted to less than 1,000 calories per day,

however, as this energy requirement is usually needed by the older person to maintain proper body function and prevent illness. Exercise will have an additive effect on weight loss when combined with proper nutrition.

Abnormally low body weight and malnutrition are problems as significant in the elderly as overweight; they predispose to disease states and can predict poor health and premature death. For example, overly thin elderly women are at greater risk of fractures and falls, both serious and threatening events. Excessive underweight may indicate underlying illnesses or functional disturbance; social difficulties such as poverty or inability to obtain food may result in weight loss as well.

**Table 19.4
Metabolism**

- As you get older, your bones become weaker especially if you are inactive. Osteoporosis (brittle bone disease) has been improved by participating in a regular weight-bearing exercise program and by resistance training.
- Chronic low back pain is most often caused by an imbalance of muscle strength. Abdominal muscles become weak and your hamstring muscles become tight. By increasing the strength of your abdominal muscles and stretching your hamstring muscles you can alleviate some pressure on your lower back.
- When your metabolism is in high gear, it gobbles up calories—when it's lazy it nibbles and yawns. Why? Because muscle is active tissue and fat is inactive.
- In one study, two groups of obese women exercised. One group combined aerobics and weight training, the other just aerobics. Both groups exercised four times a week. In the aerobic and weight training group, 86 percent of the body weight lost was fat. In the aerobic group, only 76 percent. Another study at West Virginia University followed 25 men who weight-trained three times a week for 45–60 min. In eight weeks, their HDL (good cholesterol) levels climbed from 38.3mg/dl to 44.1 mg/dl, their LDL (bad cholesterol) dropped from 132mg/dl to 121 mg/dl.

Sudden weight loss (defined as losing more than 5–10 percent body weight in six months or less) is a problem that may have multiple causes. The most common in older persons is inadequate intake of calories for any of a multitude of reasons: depression, unavailability of food, chewing problems, or difficulties with meal preparation. Cancer causes weight loss in no more than 20 percent of cases. The assumption that an older person who loses weight must have a malignancy is incorrect. Other causes of weight loss include diabetes and thyroid disease, common at this age. The effects of digitalis on appetite and intestinal function must always be considered in case of malnourishment or weight loss.

● AGING AND SEXUALITY

Fears and myths abound concerning changes in older person's sexual activity and experience. As a general rule, sexual interest and need continue into the later part of one's life. As with many other patterns of activity, frequency of sexual activity in earlier decades is the greatest determinant in later life.

One key limiting factor of sexual activity for many older people is the lack of a partner. Since widowers tend to remarry within two years of the death of a spouse, and older men have the availability of the large population of widows, divorced, and single older women, women are statistically disadvantaged. Also, their greater numbers means fewer men to go around.

Researchers (Brecher, 1984) have found that older people have the desire for sexual contact and that couples remain sexually active quite late into life—especially if there are no complicating illnesses. Sexual experience is clearly important for physical and psychological well-being, and achieving orgasm remains an important part of sexual satisfaction. For some older people, sexual experience actually improves with age. More flexible schedules, greater privacy from children, no fear of pregnancy, a more relaxing lifestyle, and increased appreciation of and knowledge about sexuality contribute to this enhancement.

Despite the diversity of personal attitudes and experiences, there are some generalizations that can be made about sexual changes that occur with age.

Researchers have found that older people have the desire for sexual contact and that couples remain sexually active quite late into life—especially if there are no complicating illnesses. (Copyright © Marianne Gontarz)

For men, the most common changes include the following:

- a longer period of direct stimulation may be necessary for full arousal and more time may be needed to complete an erection
- an erection may not be as firm or large as in earlier years
- there may be a reduction in lubrication before ejaculation
- a decrease in the force of ejaculation may occur but an ability to delay and make love longer may also occur
- the time it takes to achieve another erection after orgasm may increase

Men who have continued a satisfying sex life over the years will likely experience less dramatic changes in their sexual functioning unless certain illnesses (such as those affecting the prostate gland) are encountered. A pattern of regular sexual activity helps to preserve sexual ability. Periods of impotence are not unique to older men since they may be triggered at any age by fatigue, stress, illness, or excessive use of alcohol.

Occasional impotence in males is more readily overcome if partners are aware of the normality of occurrence and the woman is understanding and supportive. Periods of impotence are generally not considered a medical problem unless they occur in more than 25 percent of sexual intercourse with the same partner (Butler and Lewis, 1988). Where impotence is more frequent, medical evaluation is recommended.

Some of the physical causes of impotence are connected with certain diseases, surgery, or accidental damage to certain blood vessels or nerves which, in turn, upset hormonal balance. Other possible causes include excessive use of alcohol (a depressant), tobacco (nicotine constricts blood vessels), and some medications such as those used to treat high blood pressure and depression. Among diseases, diabetes and vascular (heart) disease are prominent causes of physical impotence.

In many cases, impotence caused by the identified factors can be alleviated through medical treatment or counselling. A variety of mechanisms are available for men unable to achieve erection. These include vacuum or suction devices that are placed around the penis to aid erection, and penile implants such as rod, inflatable, and self-contained prostheses.

While males reach a peak of sexual response in adolescence, and thereafter experience a gradual decline, females reach a peak of sexual response in their mid-thirties and generally stay at that level throughout the rest of their lives. Age alone generally does not trigger a reduction in sexual capacity for women. Changes that do occur are usually noticed many years after menopause. The most common changes in sexual functioning affecting older women are as follows:

- reduction in vaginal lubrication and longer lengths of time required for lubrication
- thinning of the vaginal lining
- narrowing and shortening of the vaginal canal and reduced elasticity of vaginal tissue
- increased possibility of infection in the vagina and bladder
- possible irritation of the bladder and urethra during intercourse

Vaginal dryness is a common experience for some postmenopausal women. As with men, sexual discomfort or difficulty can often be remedied through an understanding and supportive male partner and with the use of simple aids. For example, many women find that use of a water-soluble lubricant helps remove discomfort during sexual intercourse. Women experiencing severe vaginal atrophy may be treated with estrogen-replacement therapy (ERT) once a physician has determined that there are no pre-cancerous conditions present. Benefits of ERT include reduction in heart disease and osteoporosis (thinning of bones).

● EMOTIONAL HEALTH

It may seem awkward to categorize healthy mental activities as healthy life behavior. However, it is appropriate when one considers the benefits derived from socialization and stress reduction. Lack of social contact has been linked to depression and can be a marker for underlying medical illness. While a high degree of socialization may indicate a healthier individual, increasing one's social contacts will not definitively improve physical health. It does, however, directly improve emotional health and can relieve symptoms such as anxiety and improve or prevent reactive depression. It is appropriate to encourage greater socialization among older persons to maintain emotional well being, prevent psychological illness, and possibly improve overall health.

Stress is a response to physical and emotional demands often resulting in ill feelings and anxiety. Everyone experiences stress at one time or another; the ability to cope with the demand is what determines the intensity of the stress response. Common reactions to stress, both physical and psychological, are listed in Table 19.5. Methods to relieve stress include exercise, relaxation techniques, meditation, recreation, and other more personal actions. Table 19.6 shows some common relaxation techniques.

Undesirable responses to stress which nevertheless are all too common include substance abuse (alcohol, drugs, tobacco) and eating disorders. Maladaptive responses can lead to mental illness in susceptible persons.

Greater socialization among older persons is encouraged to maintain emotional well being, prevent psychological illness, and possibly improve overall health. (Copyright © Marianne Gontarz)

Table 19.5
Reactions to Stress

Physical reactions to stress

increased heart rate, blood pressure, respiration
decrease in efficiency of immune system
sweaty palms
cold hands and feet
headaches
backaches
constipation
diarrhea

Psychological reactions to stress

anxiety
panic
restlessness
memory loss
poor concentration
irrational behavior
poor self-esteem
fatigue

Health problems which may result from too much negative or chronic stress

high blood pressure
insomnia
ulcers and other disturbances in the digestive tract
headaches
poor circulation and restriction in breathing

● PREVENTION AND WELLNESS

Prevention as it pertains to health refers to a process or activity that is specifically intended to prevent disease/disability or detect early disease so that it can be treated before it causes serious problems. Conditions or diseases that may be preventable generally meet the following criteria: (1) there is a known cause or associated circumstance, (2) and beneficial interventions are available, acceptable to the person, and have reasonable risk and cost.

Preventive measures for conditions common in the elderly can be divided into three categories:

1. Primary prevention: measures to prevent the occurrence of disease (e.g., influenza vaccine).

2. Secondary prevention: measures to find hidden disease for early treatment. The benefit may be prolongation of life or relief of pain and suffering (e.g., screening mammogram for early breast cancer).

3. Tertiary prevention: measures to identify symptomatic disease or disability and use a treatment to improve the overall condition of the person (e.g., rehabilitation after a stroke).

Many conditions are amenable to preventive health measures (Table 19.7). The following preventive measures are discussed because of their particular importance to the elderly.

Immunization

Immunizations of known benefit to the elderly include influenza vaccine, pneumococcal vaccine, and tetanus. During epidemics of influenza A and B, the elderly are the most frequently affected and are more likely to be hospitalized or die from the illness. Eighty percent of influenza-related deaths occur in persons over the age of 65. Vaccination against influenza is recommended above age 65,

Table 19.6
Relaxation Techniques

Neck and Facial Massage

Seated in a comfortable position, breathe in and out, close eyes. Place your fingers behind your neck. Make five large circles on the back of your neck by moving your hands in an outward direction. Repeat this sequence with your chin, cheeks, temples, and forehead. Repeat the massage three times.

Clock Technique

While lying down, close eyes; breathe in and out. Imagine that you see a clock in front of you, hand pointed at 12 o'clock. Inhale through the nose and imagine the clock's hand moves toward 1 o'clock, exhale as it reaches 1 o'clock. Repeat all the way around the numbers of a clock.

---

especially to the very old and those with chronic illness. Influenza vaccine is 60 percent to 70 percent effective in reducing mortality and can prevent hospitalization. However, older Americans are not routinely vaccinated; surveys have shown that only 30 percent to 40 percent of eligible elders are vaccinated in any given year. Predictably, older people of lower socioeconomic classes and minorities are the least likely to receive the vaccine, possibly because of limited access, cost, or insufficient knowledge of its benefit.

Pneumococcal vaccine is a once-per-life time vaccination which helps to protect against pneumonia due to certain common bacteria. It is recommended for all persons over the age of 65, especially those with underlying lung disease or those who have problems fighting infections. It is 60 percent to 70 percent effective, relatively safe, and inexpensive.

Tetanus vaccination prevents tetanus, an infectious disease due to bacterial contamination of skin wounds. Primary immunization is given in childhood and a booster injection every ten years, every five years if a tetanus-prone wound occurs. Many older persons have never been vaccinated, since this vaccination was not mandatory in years past. Older people are also commonly behind on the timing of the tetanus booster and physicians rarely offer the booster unless a skin wound occurs. Greater efforts are necessary by public health organizations and the medical community

Table 19.7
Conditions Amenable to Prevention in the Elderly

Primary prevention

Influenza (vaccination)
Stroke (aspirin)
Osteoporosis (estrogen therapy)

Secondary prevention

Malnutrition
Dental disease
Alcohol abuse
Breast cancer
Falls
Heart disease
Hypertension
Prostate cancer
Obesity
Depression
Sensory deficits
Abuse or neglect
Colon cancer
Tuberculosis
Thyroid disease
Cholesterol elevation
Diabetes

Tertiary prevention

Stroke (rehabilitation)
Deconditioning (rehabilitation)
Sensory deficits: vision, hearing
Malnutrition
Multiple drug use
Osteoarthritis
Oral disease

---

to insure adequate protection against tetanus through routine and properly timed vaccination.

● ROUTINE CHECK-UPS AND PHYSICALS

There is inconsistent data to support routine check-ups for older persons. While seeing a physician regularly might serve to detect disease, it is unclear whether this practice will prolong life or improve outcome except in a few conditions. The traditional visit to the doctor is probably less valuable than a personalized functional health assessment. This assessment typically includes a survey of daily living activities and an inventory of social supports, along with more traditional assessments of health and function. Using this approach, health counseling may have much more impact on quality of life than mere advice on physical health.

An innovative approach to health care suggests that telephone "visits" with a physician can improve function and reduce hospitalization in elderly persons when compared to traditional office visits. Thus, the regular checkup for older people may be replaced by addressing functional health issues as a priority. The encounter could be in the office or clinic but may also be effectively carried out by telephone or by family conference. It is not yet known whether regular assessments of this type are cost effective or beneficial in the absence of specific illness or functional problem. Of course, periodic physical examinations and health assessments (e.g., an annual physical) remain an important component of health care but may not be needed as routinely as previously thought. The timing of health surveillance should be based upon the older person's individual needs and wishes.

Cancer

The majority of cancers are age-specific diseases; that is, they are more prevalent in older persons, and most new cases occur in older age groups. Because of this tendency, preventive measures should be directed towards this group. Healthful behavior in young and middle years are actually the best way to prevent cancer in later years. Eating a low fat diet helps prevent colon

Periodic physical examinations and health assessments remain an important component of health care but may not be needed as routinely (e.g. the annual physical) as previously thought. (Courtesy of Bowman Gray/Baptist Hospital Medical Center)

Table 19.8
Cancers for which Specific Screening is Available

Definite Benefit
Breast
Uterine cervix
Skin

Probable/Possible Benefit
Colon
Prostate
Oral
Ovarian

cancer; stopping smoking or never starting helps ward off lung, breast, and bladder cancer; and avoiding exposure to direct sunlight helps prevent skin cancer.

There are several cancers in the elderly amenable to preventive measures. These conditions are shown in Table 19.8.

Breast cancer. Breast cancer is more likely to occur as a woman ages; it is the most common cause of cancer death in older females. Mammography can detect early disease and improve the rate of survival when appropriately treated. Mammography is safe, well tolerated, and relatively inexpensive, so it is an important tool in improving health and prolonging life. Women over age 50 should be screened for early, treatable breast cancer.

Cancer of the prostate. Cancer of the prostate occurs almost exclusively in older men and has replaced lung cancer as the most common cancer in adult males. The increasing occurrence of prostate cancer in recent years may reflect improved ability to detect the cancer rather than an actual increase in the number of cases. Two screening tests are available to detect prostate cancer: the digital rectal examination (feeling for nodules or tumors) and a blood test for a prostate-specific antigen (PSA, a protein produced by cancerous prostate cells). Together these tests can detect asymptomatic cancer in as many as 85 percent of cases. Prostate cancer that is detected early will probably respond better to treatment, although this remains a somewhat controversial opinion. Nevertheless, digital examination and measurement of PSA should be done annually for men over age 50.

Cancer of the cervix. Screening for cancer of the cervix with a pap smear is no longer recommended for women over age 65 provided they have been previously properly screened. The number of new cases of cervical cancer decreases markedly after age 50, and the yield of screening women 65 and older who have had previously normal serial pap smears is low. Pelvic examination remains valuable and should be used to detect abnormalities of the female organs when appropriate.

Colon cancer. Colon cancer is a uniformly fatal disease when allowed to advance unchecked. The only reasonable chance for cure is surgical treatment of early lesions before the disease has spread outside the colon. Screening tests are available to find early disease: the digital rectal examination, testing stool for occult (hidden) blood, radiographs of the colon, and looking directly at the colon and rectum with an endoscope. While these tests can detect early, asymptomatic disease, there is no good evidence to show that early detection by these methods prolongs life. Drawbacks to routine use of screening tests for colon cancer include cost, risks of the procedure (including perforation of the intestine for endoscopy and radiographs), and possible patient discomfort. Thus it is appropriate to individualize decisions to conduct colon cancer screening in older persons. The risks and cost of the procedures must be weighed against the potential benefits (prolongation of life and relief of pain and suffering).

Heart disease and cholesterol. The most common form of heart disease in our society is blockage of the blood vessels of the heart due to fat deposits. The condition is called coronary heart disease and the process is called atherosclerosis. The elderly are affected by this condition in epidemic proportions; it is the most common cause of death and disability in Americans today. However, there are no good preventive measures once atherosclerosis has been established. Coronary artery bypass, angioplasty, and other surgical procedures improve symptoms but do not prolong life except in very few specific situations. The key to treatment of coronary heart disease, therefore, is prevention.

Risk factors for atherosclerosis include smoking, diabetes, hypertension, high cholesterol, and a family history of atherosclerosis. Healthful behavior such as low fat diet, smoking cessation, and exercise are appropriate preventive measures. Treatment of hypertension, high cholesterol, and diabetes are additional methods to prevent coronary heart disease. Hereditary factors pose a very significant risk.

There is controversy on how to approach these risk factors in older people. Conflicting data exists as to the benefit of lowering abnormal cholesterol levels in the elderly, especially those over age 70. No clinical trial has yet to show a clear advantage to aggressive treatment. In addition, dietary restrictions and the use of cholesterol-lowering drugs may be of greater risk to an older person than their potential benefits against heart disease. Decisions on treatment must be individualized, using known data on the benefits and judgment regarding the risks. There should also be agreement on the goals of therapy between the caregiver and the subject. Aggressively treating high cholesterol in persons over age 75 in order to prolong life or prevent atherosclerosis is probably inappropriate, though simple methods to improve blood cholesterol can be encouraged and advocated.

Smoking cessation in later years will likely have little if any effect in preventing heart disease; it is strongly recommended because of the potential benefit to respiratory function and prevention of lung infections. Treating hypertension in older persons is effective in preventing stroke and aggressive control of blood pressure is appropriate. In summary, coronary heart disease is a common condition in all age groups and is the most common cause of death and serious illness in our society. Preventive measures should be directed against behavior and conditions which predispose to atherosclerosis. Unfortunately, there are no definitive methods to prevent heart attack, heart failure, or death in those who have established coronary heart disease.

Osteoporosis. Loss of bone density is a uniform process after age 30. The rate of bone loss remains steady in men throughout life, but increases dramatically in women after menopause. Bone strength and density in women is dependent on the female hormone, estrogen; as estrogen levels decrease during and after menopause, bone density cannot be maintained. Early on, this bone loss causes few problems. But with time (fifteen to twenty-years on average) the cumulative losses can severely weaken certain bones (especially the hip, wrist, and spine) and make them vulnerable to fractures. The condition in which bones become weakened with age and subject to fracture is known as osteoporosis.

Osteoporosis is the leading cause of fractures in older women. Risk factors for osteoporosis include female gender, post-menopausal status, cigarette smoking, sedentary life style, caucasian race, small body build, and a family history of osteoporosis. Fractures of the hip, spine, and extremities are the most serious complications of osteoporosis and are significant causes of pain and disability. Hip fracture is associated with an increased risk of early death and commonly leads to nursing home placement.

Techniques to prevent osteoporosis includes exercise, calcium supplementation with vitamin D, and the use of estrogen replacement therapy. Studies show that osteoporosis can be improved by taking part in a regular weight-bearing exercise program and by resistance training (Singleton, 1992). Estrogen given in oral or topical form at the time of menopause will slow or stabilize the accelerated bone loss which would otherwise occur. It is generally accepted that women should be given estrogen replacement therapy for at least five to fifteen years after menopause, and possibly lifelong. Estrogen should be combined with calcium to give maximum benefit. It is not known whether women who are ten or more years past menopause will benefit from estrogen replacement therapy. Preliminary studies show some benefit, but conclusive evidence is as yet not available.

The most significant complication of estrogen therapy is an increased risk of uterine cancer. The risk is relatively small, and data have shown that there is no increased risk of death in women who develop uterine cancer while receiving estrogen therapy. The addition of a hormonal agent, progesterone, can nullify the risk of uterine cancer when added to estrogen therapy. Despite past concerns, there has been no convincing evidence that estrogen therapy causes breast cancer. An additional benefit is a statistical decrease in heart disease by 50 percent in women taking estrogen; this is likely due to estrogen's beneficial effect on cholesterol levels. All women at risk for osteoporosis should be considered for estrogen therapy at the time of menopause unless there are strong contraindications. Routine use in women more than ten years past menopause cannot as yet be recommended.

Sensory deficits. The elderly are universally affected by progressive losses in vision and hearing. Sensory loss is part of normal aging and will manifest to differing degrees in each older person. Vision will be commonly altered by presbyopia (loss of near vision due to changes in the lens of the eye). Hearing is altered by presbycusis (loss of hearing high tones due to dysfunction of the nerves to the ear). Prevention in the context of normal sensory impairment is tertiary in nature; that is, it consists of finding the condition and designing adaptive measure to improve function and prevent disability.

Eyeglasses are the obvious corrective measure for presbyopia. However, many older persons with vision impairment go undiagnosed, especially in nursing homes. Other common causes of visual impairment in older people include cataracts and macular degeneration (a degenerative process of the retina of unknown cause). Cataracts cannot be prevented, but the resulting impairment can be cured by surgical removal with artificial lens implantation. There is no treatment for macular degeneration, so it is a common cause of blindness in the elderly. Finding the visually impaired elderly is the most important step in preventing and treating the disabilities associated with this condition.

A hearing aid can greatly improve the functional capacity of older people with hearing impairment. It may allow independent living for persons who might otherwise require a more sheltered setting due to an inability to communicate. Hearing aids are very expensive and most health insurance (including Medicare) does not provide payment coverage. Finding and providing for elderly people who could benefit from a hearing aid is the preventive measure of choice. Besides presbycusis, the only additional cause which commonly occurs is ear wax impaction. The preventive measure is to detect the problem before it causes serious impairment, and to remove the wax obstruction as the definitive cure. Unfortunately, this condition is frequently overlooked, especially in nursing homes and among older people who cannot communicate their problems to caregivers.

Physical wellness, health promotion, and disease prevention have been neglected in the elderly and now deserve greater attention. The life expectancy of Americans has increased steadily throughout this century. As the largest portion of our population ages, there will be great need for maintenance of health and function into advanced age. This is necessary to avoid a tremendous manpower shortage, as well as expense, if frailty and dependency are the rule within this expanding group, rather than the exception. The goal is to increase the life expectancy of *healthy* Americans who can live and work in the community with a sense of contribution rather than a mere existence. The priority is quality of life.

References

Berg, R. L., and J. J. Cassells, eds. *The Second Fifty Years: Promoting Health and Preventing Disability*. Washington, DC: Institute of Medicine, National Academy Press, 1990.

Bierman, E. L., and W. R. Hazzard. "Preventive Gerontology." In *Principles of Geriatric Medicine*. Eds. W. R. Hazzard and others. New York: McGraw-Hill, 1991, pp. 167–75.

Brecher, Edward M., and the editors of Consumer Reports Books. *Love, Sex and Aging*. Boston, MA: Little, Brown, 1984.

Butler, Robert N., and Myrna I. Lewis. *Love and Sex after 60*. New York: Harper and Row, 1988.

Conrad, K. A., and R. Bressler, eds. *Drug Therapy in the Elderly*. St. Louis, MO: Mosby, 1982.

Constitution. Vol. 2. Geneva: World Health Organization, 1946.

Fried, L. P. "Health Promotion and Disease Prevention." In *Principles of Geriatric Medicine*. Eds. W. R. Hazzard and others. New York: McGraw-Hill, 1991, pp. 192–200.

"Health Promotion and Disease Prevention." In *Clinics of Geriatric Medicine*. Eds. G. S. Omenn, E. B. Larson, E. H. Wagner, and I. Abrass. Vol. 8, no. 1 (1992).

Kane R. L., and R. A. Kane. "Prevention in the Elderly." *Health Services Research* Vol. 19, no. 6 (1985): 945–1006.

Kane, R. L., J. G. Ouslander, I. B. Abrass. "Developing Clinical Expectation." In *Essentials of Clinical Geriatrics*. New York: McGraw-Hill, 1989.

"Late Bloomer" audio cassette. Available from Connie Goldman Productions, 926 Second Street, Suite 201, Santa Barbara, CA 90403. (310) 393-6801.

Shepard, R. J. "Scientific Basis of Exercise Prescribing for the Very Old." *Journal of the American Geriatrics Society* Vol. 38 (1990): 62–70.

Williams, M. "Outpatient Geriatric Evaluation." *Clinics of Geriatric Medicine* Vol. 3 (1987): 175–84.

Additional Reading

American Heart Association. *Sex and Heart Disease*. Single copies available free from your local chapter of the AHA, or write to 7320 Greenville Avenue, Dallas, TX 75231.

Arthritis Foundation. *Living and Loving: Information about Sex*. Single copies available free from your local chapter, or write to the Arthritis Foundation, P.O. Box 19000, Atlanta, GA 30326.

Christensen, Alice, and David Rankins. *Easy Does It Yoga for Older People*. San Francisco, CA: Harper & Row, 1979.

Clark, Etta. *Growing Old Is Not For Sissies: Portraits of Senior Athletes*. Corte Madera, CA: Pomegranate Books, 1986.

Comfort, Alex. *The Joy of Sex*. New York: Simon and Schuster, 1987.

Doress, Paula Brown, Diana Laskin Siegal, and the Midlife and Older Women's Book Project. *Ourselves Growing Older*. New York: Simon and Schuster, 1987.

Fries, James. *Aging Well*. Menlo Park, CA: Addison-Wesley, 1989.

Humphrey, James H. *Health and Fitness for Older Persons*. New York: AMS Press, 1992.

Kemper, Donald, and Molly Mettler. *Growing Wiser: The Older Person's Guide to Mental Wellness*. Boise, ID: Healthwise, 1986.

———. *Healthwise for Life: Medical Self-Care for Healthy Aging*. Boise, ID: Healthwise, 1992.

LaLanne, Elaine. *Fitness After 50*. Hauppauge, NY: Barron's, 1991.

Mockenhaupt, Robin, and Kathleen Boyle. *Healthy Aging*. Santa Barbara, CA: ABC-CLIO, 1992.

Pitzele, Sefra K. *We Are Not Alone: Learning to Live with Chronic Illness*. New York:Workman, 1985.

Schmerl, E. Fritz. *Challenge of Aging: A Guide to Growing Older in Health and Happiness*. New York: Continuum, 1991.

Scott, Hugh A. *The New Medicine Man*. Santa Barbara, CA: Fithian Press, 1992.

Shea, Edward J. *Swimming for Seniors*. Champaign, IL: Leisure Press, 1986.

Siegel, Bernie S. *Love, Medicine, and Miracles: Lessons Learned About Self-Healing from a Surgeon's Experience with Exceptional Patients*. New York: Harper & Row, 1986.

Starr, Bernard D., and Marcella Bakur Weiner. *The Starr-Weiner Report on Sex and Sexuality in the Mature Years*. New York: McGraw-Hill, 1981.

Ways, Peter, M.D. *Take Charge of Your Health: The Guide to Personal Health Competence*. Lexington, MA: Stephen Greene Press, 1985.

Weil, Andrew, M.D. *Natural Health, Natural Medicine. A Comprehensive Manual for Wellness and Self-Cure*. Boston, MA: Houghton-Mifflin, 1990.

Westheimer, Ruth. *Dr. Ruth's Guide to Good Sex*. New York: Warner Books, 1983.

White, Evelyn C. *The Black Woman's Health Book: Speaking for Ourselves*. Seattle, WA: Seal Press, 1990.

Newsletters

Johns Hopkins Medical Letter, Health After 50. Taking Control of Your Own Health and Medical Care. 550 North Broadway, Suite 1100, Johns Hopkins University, Baltimore, MD 21205-2111.

Perspectives in Health Promotion and Aging. Quarterly. National Eldercare Institute on Health and Aging, AARP, 601 E Street N.W., 5th Floor-B, Washington, DC 20049.

Richard F. Afable, M.D., M.P.H.

⓴

Mental Wellness

- The Meaning of Psychological Wellness • Loss and Mental Wellness
- Adaptation and Transformation • Developmental Models of Transformation
- The Transformation Process and Aging • The Grief Process • Facilitating Mental Wellness

Recent generations of retirees in the United States are probably the first to have expectations that well-being in later life may include more than avoidance of disabling physical diseases or mental impairments. The proliferation of health newsletters, magazines, and health promotion programs for seniors testify to dramatic increases in older persons' awareness of their health potential. Conceiving of wellness as more than just the opposite or absence of illness is a relatively new idea. Until recently, health in all its forms has been the domain of the medical establishment. But wellness and health promotion need to be viewed as extending beyond the medical model that emphasizes healing and disease prevention (Caplan, 1990). This is also true of mental health.

One can illustrate the difference between avoiding disease and pursuing optimal health. While older people can expect to avoid certain respiratory diseases by abstaining from the use of tobacco, they may also seek the respiratory capability of walking or running many miles. Hence, while not smoking is a disease preventative measure, aerobic activity is a health promotion endeavor. Optimal health, within individual limits, is a realistic goal for most older people.

The following discussion of mental wellness draws from the expertise of mental health practitioners and researchers who attempt to go beyond an illness or clinical orientation. This view focuses on growth, change, and attainment

of new ways of experiencing and relating to one's world in later life.

Conceiving of wellness as more than just the opposite or absence of illness is a relatively new idea.

The discussion takes into account a central theme of aging, namely the experience of loss in later life. How individuals cope with, adjust to, and learn from experiences of loss—whether of a job, spouse, physical capability—is a critical feature of mental wellness. Responses to loss are examined from the viewpoint of several human development theories about later life. Also presented is a list of activities and programs which may foster psychological wellness. In short, the challenges and possibilities of psychological growth form the main topic of this exploration.

● THE MEANING OF PSYCHOLOGICAL WELLNESS

How should psychological wellness be defined? One way is to say what it is not. Clearly, psychological wellness is not identical to happiness, normalcy, or freedom from worries and problems. Although a healthy person may experience happiness, it is also possible that to be happy in the context of real human problems may be little more than denial of reality. Psychological wellness may differ from normalcy or typicalness, since these terms assume certain norms as the standards of behavior. A certain maladaptive or dysfunctional style can become so typical in a society that it may appear to represent health. For example, disengagement from social participation and passive withdrawal into reminiscing were once considered to be normal and appropriate behaviors for older people. The rocking chair was synonymous with old age. Today, these attributes may be viewed as symptoms associated with depression, a reaction to forced retirement, or lack of social opportunities.

Psychological wellness is not identical with an absence of emotional distress. Mental illness is clinically recognized when an individual seeks help from a mental health practitioner and is diagnosed as having a specific disorder. The label and diagnostic category describe a person in a state of distress, wishing to make changes in his or her life. From this view, the individual could be regarded as demonstrating psychological wellness by seeking help as compared to the individual who needs it but fails to seek appropriate

Psychological wellness is not identical to happiness, normalcy, and freedom from worries and problems. (Copyright © Marianne Gontarz)

treatment. Sometimes the sense of felt distress is a result of another family member who creates stress as a result of destructive behavior patterns. Frequently, those who create stress fail to acknowledge their behavior. Thus, the person officially receiving the diagnostic label of mental illness may in fact turn out to be the healthier family member.

The concept of psychological wellness describes a process rather than a static way of being. It describes a manner of relating to a complicated changing world and how the individual and the world interact in this dynamic process. Mental well-being is influenced but not necessarily determined by economic and social status, intellectual capacity, and other individual factors limiting attainment of optimal psychological well-being.

Positive mental health in later life refers to successful encounters with challenging conditions and situations in which the person gains insight and expands his or her capability for relationships. Positive mental health includes ideals of growth, realization of personal potential (self-actualization), and integration of personality. These set standards of what is possible—even though complete attainment of the ideal may be statistically rare (Lebowitz and Niederehe, 1992).

Psychological wellness describes a process that is likely to change as an individual becomes older. The issues facing the adolescent and young adult differ from the issues of the older adult moving into the latter stages of life. Adaptations and transformations representing psychological wellness are also correspondingly different.

Within the field of psychology, humanistic psychologists have articulated a concept suggesting a non-illness orientation toward psychological wellness. Carl Rogers (1961), for example, uses the phrase "fully functioning person" to describe an active process rather than a static form of being. Rogers identified three main characteris-

---

Positive mental health in later life refers to successful encounters with challenging conditions and situations in which the person gains insight and expands his or her capability for relationships.

Rogers's characterization may help define wellness in any particular age group of the population, but this definition is especially useful when applied to how older individuals relate to a significant characteristic of old age: loss. More specifically, when encountering loss, does the older individual come to the experience with an attitude of openness? Is there an effort to respond to the loss in the present moment? Is there trust in the individual's experience of making decisions about the loss? When an older person embodies the three attributes, he or she may be described as exhibiting psychological wellness.

● LOSS AND MENTAL WELLNESS

Although individuals at any age may experience loss, individuals in the second half of their lives will be faced with multiple losses. George Minois (1989) indicates that losses in old age have long been a matter of concern. He quotes an Egyptian scribe who lived 4500 years ago:

> O sovereign my Lord! Oldness has come; old age has descended. Feebleness has arrived; dotage is here anew. The heart sleeps wearily every day. The eyes are weak, the ears are deaf, the strength is disappearing because of weariness of heart, and the mouth is silent and cannot speak. The heart is forgetful and cannot recall yesterday. The bone suffers old age. God becomes evil. All taste is gone. What old age does to men is evil in every respect.

Minois reviews concepts of old age from antiquity through the sixteenth century. His research

Although individuals at any age must necessarily cope with change, individuals in the second half of their lives will be faced with multiple losses. (Courtesy of The National Council on the Aging, Inc./Jerry Hecht, photographer)

tics: first, the fully functioning person manifests increasing openness to experience rather than defensiveness; second, such a person lives fully in the moment; finally, this person places a basic trust in his or her own "organism as a means of arriving at the most satisfying behavior" for each situation.

shows that with few exceptions, the plight of older adults has been difficult at best. In contemporary North American and European societies, there is increasing economic and social support for individuals during their elder years. Social awareness and public policy have contributed to improved support of certain kinds of personal losses as reflected in bereavement support groups, transferability of pensions to surviving spouses, retirement adjustment seminars, and Social Security and health care benefits.

Nonetheless, Silverstone and Hyman (1989) state that "if any word can sum up the varied catalogue of problems that do appear in old age, it is the word loss." Those commonly encountered in old age include: (1) physical losses—changes in the sense organs, nervous system, internal organs, bone structure, and depletion of the resources to cope with physical illness; (2) relationship losses—reduction of social contact after retirement from employment, reduced contact with friends due to death or limitations resulting from illness or injury, and changes in the nature of friendships resulting from illness, pain, and death; (3) loss of a stable environment as the world continues to change (4) loss of familiar roles—parent, breadwinner, homemaker, spouse, church member, athlete, householder; (5) loss of financial security in the context of inflation and rising medical costs; (6) loss of a sense of independence and personal power; and (7) loss of mental ability and mental stability. In addition to these actual losses, the older adult often becomes keenly aware of the ultimate loss, which is the approach of death.

The older adult who is psychologically well will suffer these losses just as surely as the elder who is psychologically unhealthy. The ability to respond effectively to these losses is perhaps the primary factor that separates psychological well-being from other states.

● ADAPTATION AND TRANSFORMATION

Adaptation is a concept used in the field of aging to describe the manner in which older individuals respond to changing circumstances, especially losses. Kastenbaum (1980–81) has categorized three main styles of adaptation: habituation, continuity, and conflict management.

Habituation is a process through which individ-

uals gradually pay less and less conscious attention to ways of acting and thinking—they do them automatically. A person coping with intense loss may distract him- or herself from the experience by becoming absorbed in day-to-day routines. Continuity refers to the way that new life experiences are absorbed into a context of familiar and relatively persistent patterns of self-activity and interaction with the environment. Kastenbaum suggests that older individuals have a stronger sense of this continuity than younger people. As a result, a significant loss will be accommodated into larger patterns of experience and cause a smaller disruption in day-to-day functioning.

Conflict management is the process by which perception of impasses is changed from negative to neutral or positive. Examples of conflict management include the use of humor (defusing angry elements of conflict by focusing on resolutions), altruism (viewing one's own needs as secondary to other people's), sublimation (channeling energy resulting from a conflict into socially acceptable activities), and suppression (coping by putting the conflict out of one's consciousness).

Atchley (1988) has described patterns of adaptation for specific problem areas. For example, loss of income in old age typically results in an adaptation pattern of doing with less. For individuals used to having a surplus of resources, this loss is more psychological than physical. For those who are at or below the minimal level of economic survival, doing with less can result in inadequate care of basic needs. Loss of roles and activities is common for older individuals in retirement. They can respond by substituting new roles for earlier ones. As people move into their late seventies, it may become increasingly difficult for them to find substitutive roles because of limited mobility and declining energy.

Another strategy is to redistribute one's energy in the remaining roles. Thus, one who discontinues employment may spend increasing time with friends, in activities around the house, or in hobbies. No new roles are added, but increased time is spent in remaining roles. Still other individuals gradually disengage from activities as they get older. While, for some there is a tendency to withdraw from the outside world and turn toward issues of a more inward spiritual nature, research indicates that some forms of disengagement are more likely to be a result of diminished opportunities rather than as a part of a natural process.

A form of coping that represents a less functional pattern than the adaptational styles above is escape. With escape, the problem remains but the individual chooses a reduced sense of self rather than a diminished sense of the problem.

Forms of escape include isolation, in which the person withdraws from life as a way of coping with problems; the use of drugs and alcohol as a strategy for reducing the experience of loss; and suicide.

The concept of adaptation is based on a biological model of how plants and animals modify themselves in order to survive. Similarly, human

---

Profiles of Productive Aging

Robert McNamara
Businessman, author

"I am over 75, but I don't feel physically or mentally old. I have an intense interest in the learning environment; it is fun for me. I don't feel any desire to retire to Palm Beach or go to the baseball games."

Former secretary of defense (1961–68) and Ford Motor Company director and president (1957–61), Robert McNamara was born in San Francisco in 1916. Neither parent had gone beyond high school, but they encouraged their children to achieve at school from an early age. "My earliest recollection of childhood is of the home environment that was focused on providing for the children opportunities which my parents hadn't had," recalled McNamara. "And they expected the children to take advantage of those opportunites."

McNamara graduated Phi Beta Kappa from the University of California in 1937 where he developed a passionate interest in economics, and enrolled at the Harvard Graduate School of Business in 1938. At this time McNamara married former Berkeley classmate Margaret Craig. The marriage lasted forty years, until her death in 1978. McNamara worked as an instructor at Harvard until the outbreak of World War II, when he was asked to go to Europe as a civilian consultant to the War Department.

When discharged in 1945, he and his wife fell sick with polio, stationed at Wright Field on inactive service. McNamara suffered only a light illness, but his wife became seriously ill and remained hospitalized for eight months. McNamara soon realized that his teaching job at Harvard, to which he hoped to return with the war over, would not cover the hospital debts. A colleague had an idea to save Ford Motor Co. (which had been experiencing large financial losses at the time) by sending a group of ten ecomomists to help run the company.

McNamara began work at Ford in 1946, where he had a distinguished career, working there for almost fifteen years. In 1957 he was elected director, and by 1960 he became the first non-family member in the history of the company to be elected president. Five weeks later, McNamara was appointed secretary of defense by President Kennedy. He said it was not easy to leave Ford: "I recognized my responsiblility to the Ford family and to the company, but it was very difficult to put personal or corporate considerations above those of the national interest." He served as secretary of defense from January 1961 to March 1968, when he became president of the World Bank Group of Institutions, where he worked until June 1981.

Since then McNamara has served on the board of numerous corporations and is associated with a number of nonprofit associations. He is the author of *The Essence of Security,* written while serving as defense secretary, and has written four other books. He engages in public speaking on such global issues as world peace and the environment and is the recipient of numerous honorary degrees and prizes worldwide, including the Albert Einstein Peace Prize.

Now in his seventies, McNamara is not phased by the aging process, and instead sees it as "a function of the mind." He explained: "I think the mind is a muscle. Therefore, the exercising of the mind is a way to maintain the strength of the muscle." Outside of his mental pursuits, he is an avid skier, tennis player, mountain climber, and runner. "I enjoy physical exercise," he admitted. "Exercising the mind and the body is important to maintain both physical strength and mental capability."

Lydia Brontë

adaptation in response to loss suggests self-modification or compensatory behavior rather than making changes to the environment or achieving personal new growth. Adaptation represents a higher form of psychological wellness when compared with escape, which attempts to ignore or deny the loss through activities that cannot actually diminish it.

Adaptation thus implies a continuum of change ranging from escape and denial at one end, stability in the middle, and positive growth or transformation in the quality of one's life experience at the other end.

Personal transformation is often discussed in the context of crises—identifiable with losses in later life. Crises may serve as a catalyst for development, leading to favorable outcomes rather than arrested growth or deficits. While no one consciously wishes to invite loss and crisis, such events may bring the person across a threshold to new experience, meanings, and psychological states (Lieberman and Peskin, 1992). For example, the loss of a spouse may challenge the individual to reevaluate beliefs and assumptions about the world, to renegotiate an established social network, and to shift one's sense of self from "we" to "I." In a study of the bereavement process, Yalom and Lieberman (1991) found that 27 percent of those recovering from the death of a spouse showed clear evidence of growth—"new behaviors, new ways of doing things, restructuring of the self in relationship to others...." What is critical to these positive outcomes of loss is having a supportive, nurturing environment: friends, support groups, educational resources, and so on.

Transformations in later life are more often identified through subjective self-reporting as collected in interviews or reflected in books and articles written in testimony to experience. Often illusive, transformations do not readily lend themselves to scientific examination in ways that adaptational approaches can be studied. Nonetheless, important questions must be asked about the nature of transformation: What are the conditions under which it may occur? What are the probable outcomes? In what ways does transformation for older adults differ from transformations at other ages? The following section details some current thinking about the kinds of transformations that are likely in the life of an adult who exhibits psychological wellness. In addition,

> A study of the bereavement process found that 27 percent of those recovering from the death of a spouse showed clear evidence of growth—"new behaviors, new ways of doing things, restructuring of the self in relationship to others...."

an attempt is made to explain the nature of transformation and why it applies particularly to older adults.

● DEVELOPMENTAL MODELS OF TRANSFORMATION

A developmental approach to transformation has been a useful tool for examining transitions through life. Theorists and researchers including Havighurst (1972), Peck (1956), Levinson (1978), and others have applied a developmental model to describe the aging process and to understand the ways mental wellness can be manifested as a result of changes in age. Erik Erikson has developed the most widely known conception of transformational stages (1950, 1982, 1986), and he has continued to revise and incorporate information into this schema. Erikson proposed an eight-stage theory, of which the later three stages are specifically related to mid-life and old age. In each of these stages he posits psychological tasks presented as opposing possibilities (e.g., trust versus mistrust, stagnation versus generativity). Under conditions of growth, the individual is able to accomplish the task, build on, and then move to the next developmental stage. Under conditions that do not favor growth, the individual is psychologically paralyzed at that stage.

Even as individuals age chronologically, they may respond to current situations from the unresolved viewpoint of an earlier developmental stage. As a result, older individuals may find themselves working through earlier stages. Although most of Erikson's work focused on childhood and adolescent stages, he believed that the later stages from young to older adulthood are the critical ones that encompass the "evolutionary development which has made man the teaching and instituting animal."

Erikson asserted that during childhood,

healthy development would involve a child's acquiring a sense of basic trust in the reliability of his or her world, control over behavior, confidence in undertaking tasks, recognition of competencies, and a firm sense of identity. Assuming adequate accomplishment in these areas, Erikson believed that the main task of early adulthood is acquiring the capacity for intimacy. Healthy intimacy assumes that the person has a clear sense of self that allows him or her to enter into relationships with a capacity for commitment and the ethical strength of character to maintain closeness. The mentally well adult would be able to maintain intimacy without fear of losing his or her identity or without engaging in behavior that would be consciously or unconsciously destructive to the relationship.

Even as individuals age chronologically, they may respond to current situations from the unresolved viewpoint of an earlier developmental stage. As a result, older individuals may find themselves working through earlier stages.

The developmental task for middle adulthood Erikson terms "generativity," which he defines as the commitment to establish and provide guidance for the next generation. Generativity for Erikson implies energy, mental growth, and absorption in others. Failure to achieve generativity is represented by stagnation—boredom, mental decline, obsessive pseudo-intimacy, and narcissistic self-indulgence. In the mode of generativity, older adults' relationships are characterized by growth, selflessness, giving, and involvement in the community. Their mental activity is open, flexible, and creative. Generativity brings about a realistic body image and a sense of being needed.

The contest of integrity or wisdom versus despair forms the basis for Erikson's last stage of development. He regards the healthy elder as able to perceive and accept a pattern of necessity in his or her life that enables the individual to embrace the past as the only history that one could have lived—in a sense, the destiny that one has fulfilled. Failure leads to despair, which is characterized by anxiety, social withdrawal, disappointment, bitterness, and the sense that one's life lacks overall coherence and inner meaning.

Integrity in relationships is evidenced in the form of autonomy, rather than dependency, and an ability to provide solutions to problems presented by others. Mental activity implies continuing study, artistic expression, and service to others. Such older individuals will have realistic evaluations and acceptance of their losses and a satisfactory resolution of the illness experience.

Another approach to late-life development has been formulated by Allan Chinen in two recent books (1989, 1992). Chinen expands upon his psychiatric training by drawing insights from over 5,000 fairy tales from throughout the world. He notes that about 10 percent of the fairy tales focus on characters who can be identified as "middle aged." Another 5 percent of the stories focus on characters who can be described as "elders" or people in their later years.

These stories, Chinen believes, convey psychological truths that can be helpful to individuals interested in psychological transformation. He claims that in preliterate societies, stories were told in small groups for the benefit of adults, who would recognize the symbolic or allegorical meanings of the tales. Chinen believes that these stories had the power to bypass rational thinking and touch the deeper aspects of consciousness. As a result, the telling of these stories provided a means for helping adults make necessary transformations in their lives.

Chinen's analysis shows that developmental tasks for youth differ from the tasks of adults in mid- and later life. The task of youth is to leave home. Almost all fairy tales about youth involve

Mental activity implies continuing study, artistic expression, and service to others. (Copyright © Marianne Gontarz)

departing from home and going into a difficult and frightening world. The hero of the story seeks true love and great adventure. Frightening adversaries are met and defeated. Finally, the youth acknowledges the power that comes from having passed through these experiences.

Fairy tales involving middle-aged adults are quite different. In these stories, the main character is forced to give up the dreams and ideals of an earlier time. As these earlier visions are given up, the middle-ager takes on a pragmatism and responsibility that was previously absent. In these middle-age tales, women acknowledge their talent and power and break out of their restricted social roles. Male characters begin to explore their feminine natures and recognize the importance of relationships. Having accomplished these important reversals, adults in middle age can tolerate ambiguity and no longer need to rely on arbitrary distinctions between good and evil. Middle-age tales show that a confrontation with death is a necessary developmental task at this time. Unlike the youthful hero, the middle-aged adult can face these fears. Often humor is the vehicle allowing for middle-aged adults to maintain their responsibilities, carry the burdens, and move toward their elder years without despair and cynicism.

Chinen identifies the task that defines the transformation from middle age to elder as the gaining of wisdom. Wisdom is often attributed to elders simply on the basis of being old, yet Chinen believes that wisdom is acquired through often painful experiences, and elders who have been unable or unwilling to face this pain may have no more wisdom than persons at any other age. When an individual undergoes an experience of pain and suffering and is simultaneously able to remain conscious of the choices that are being made, then wisdom is the likely result.

Fairy tales involving middle-aged adults are quite different. In these stories, the main character is forced to give up the dreams and ideals of an earlier time. As these earlier visions are given up, the middle-ager takes on a pragmatism and responsibility that was previously absent.

But wisdom is more than the accumulation of facts and the feeling of pain. Wisdom comes through an examination of the more recessive, less developed side of personality, which Carl Jung calls the "shadow" of the self. Jung described exploration of the shadow as a deepening process of development beginning in mid-life. In Jung's view, individuals in their early years take on roles and responsibilities that become "masks" of the self. With the achievement of adulthood, there may be more freedom to take off the masks to discover or remember the fuller picture of one's inner life and to affirm the full range of experiences, positive and negative. This is the basis for wisdom.

A second major task for elders identified by Chinen is transcendence of self, which is a moving beyond immediate personal needs similar to Erikson's notion of generativity. Chinen notes that elder tales provide three forms of transcendence of self: (1) moving beyond self by turning one's focus toward family, community, and society; (2) moving beyond self through spiritual discipline toward a direct experience of God; and (3) moving beyond our limited egocentric sense of "self" to the larger "Self." Carl Jung contends that this higher Self is the experience of the fully developed personality. The person who has moved fully into the experience of Self is able to view the realistic limits of his or her capacity and at the same time see the potential that exists in mankind. As these two experiences are held simultaneously, the individual is able to recognize the full potential of mankind that exists in him or herself. In this way the person transcends the smaller experience of self. Each of these three forms of transcendence requires the wisdom accumulated through earlier stages.

A third task for elders is a return to innocence and wonder. At this point of life, the elder has given up any notion of personal perfection. This allows for a return to childlike zest, spontaneity, and innocence. The elder takes delight in nature. In this stage the elder moves beyond social convention and is able to integrate the judgment and skill acquired in midlife with the newfound spontaneous experience of life.

Chinen maintains that the final task for the healthy elder is to bring the fullness of experience to bear on practical solutions to the world's dilemmas. Unlike earlier efforts, the elder does

The healthy elder has been described as being able to cope with loss in a transformational manner. (Copyright © Marianne Gontarz)

In Chinen's view, the healthy older person will have gained a unified view of the life cycle. (Copyright © Paul Gilmore)

not need to force solutions on others. The elder provides a model of groundedness, knowledge, discipline, and patience. As a result of these skills the elder is able to provide transitions for younger individuals attempting to achieve their own transformations, to mediate between two viewpoints that appear to be entirely oppositional, or to bridge the gap between intergenerational conflicts.

For Chinen, the healthy elder will be able to cope with loss in a transformational manner because the elder will have acquired wisdom, will have moved beyond the egocentric self, will

---

Chinen maintains that the final task for the healthy elder is to bring the fullness of experience to bear on practical solutions to the world's dilemmas. Unlike earlier efforts, the elder does not need to force solutions on others.

---

possess innocence and wonder, and will have the capacity to mediate between opposing views. In sum, the older person will have gained a unified view of the life cycle. The portrait of the wise older person is an ideal of the possible but should be tempered with modesty and humility to avoid creating new, over-idealized stereotypes to replace earlier negative ones. In today's Western societies, old age implies a loss of social status. But the ideal of older people contributing to a culture of wisdom may help point toward the future.

● THE TRANSFORMATION PROCESS AND AGING

While transformation can occur at any age, the potential for transformational change in older individuals is increased by several factors. First, like all individuals, elders have accumulated a lifetime of inevitable scars and wounds. Many of these wounds occurred at a very early age and resulted in unsophisticated strategies for coping with pain. While the aging process provides opportunities for personal growth, some individuals nonetheless arrive at old age with wounds that have not yet healed. The potential for transformation for healthy elders is heightened because there is less reason for them to hide from these wounds or to deny the scars or the ineffectual coping mechanisms.

A second factor increasing the possibility for transformation in the elderly is that the magnitude of stress can be quite large as a result of the number and intensity of losses so likely at this time of life. Not only are these losses inevitable, but there is also an attitude of anticipating future losses, notably the final loss of death and the accompanying apprehension that becomes increasingly prominent as one becomes older.

Significant transformation occurs in ways that ease the stress of existing wounds. Just as an earthquake is likely to relieve existing stresses in the earth's structure, the psychological earthquakes also relieve stress. If individuals are able to tolerate the conscious experience of pain, then they will be in the best position to choose the manner in which the stress can be resolved. As a result, the transformation is likely to be in a positive way rather than a regression to earlier stages of development.

Jean Houston (1982, 1987) asserts that positive transformations are most likely to occur when an individual is able to move from the small personal story to a larger mythological one, which helps the individual understand the nature of loss and provide a pattern for living out the loss in a heroic manner. However, in our society there are few opportunities to learn about mythological potential. Joseph Campbell (1968, 1973, 1990), Jean Shinoda Bolin (1985, 1989), Carol Pearson (1986, 1991), Robert Moore (1990), Robert Bly (1990), and Allan Chinen (1989, 1992) are at the forefront of those reintroducing this powerful perspective to our society. When elders have devoted themselves to enhancing their mythological world, the earthquakes are more likely to result in positive experiences.

Even if an older person devotes time to the mythological world, it does not mean that earthquake experiences can be avoided. Loss is a natural part of the life process. The manner in which a person responds to loss is the grief process.

● THE GRIEF PROCESS

Elisabeth Kubler-Ross (1969) was the first to detail the way individuals respond to their own process of dying. She identified five stages: denial, anger, bargaining, depression, and acceptance. Although initially identified in individuals who knew they had a terminal illness, the stages have also been extrapolated to anyone who is experiencing a significant loss. Not everyone experiences each of these stages, nor does each individual pass through them in a linear, sequential way, but the stages help validate reactions that are a normal part of the grief process. Although loss often produces the reactions char-

acterized by Kubler-Ross, this process does not always involve only negative reactions. Individuals may also respond to loss with (1) relief and hope that the future will be improved; (2) curiosity about the nature of loss as a new kind of experience; (3) apathy about the loss; and (4) relief resulting from the end of negative experiences (Kalish, 1985).

Each of these response styles can be a natural part of the grief process likely to occur with any significant loss. As an individual ages, there will be increasing opportunities to experiment with coping styles. Stephen Levine (1982, 1987) observes that some individuals approaching their death begin to live in a different way, closely resembling Rogers' concept of the fully functioning person. This way of being seems to capture the essence of psychological wellness.

Levine notes that individuals who are dying often view pain and death as the enemy. Resisting their pain, they become disconnected from the fullness and entirety of their being. They are not open to experience, because they fear pain; and they are unable to stay in the moment, because the present seems so overwhelming. They have difficulty trusting that they can move through the experience in a satisfying way.

In contrast, some individuals are able to experience spiritual growth by opening their hearts to the conscious experience of pain and dying. Through meditation it becomes possible to stay in the moment and to notice the subtle and exquisite changes that occur even in the face of death. As a result, it becomes possible to once again place trust in one's basic organism.

Levine describes a series of meditations designed to assist the individual to move beyond the denial, bargaining, anger, and depression that are associated with intense loss. These exercises involve forgiveness, loving kindness, and mindfulness, in response to the experience of dying. Ultimately the person comes to a place where death can be experienced fully, and it is at this moment that life is also experienced fully.

● FACILITATING MENTAL WELLNESS

Psychotherapy may be regarded as a vehicle for facilitating transformational shifts. Psychotherapies vary as to what experiences or capacities they emphasize. Traditional psychoanalysis, for example, puts great emphasis on the unconscious, dreams, fantasies, and sex drives. Behavioral therapies focus more on patterns of actual response to conflicts and fears and on how these can be changed through a process of relearning. Very generally, psychotherapies can be classified into two groups: ego-oriented psychotherapies, which focus attention on the ego's ability to adapt to pain and stress; and soul-oriented psychotherapies, which focus on more philosophical and sometimes cosmic issues relating individual meanings to broader, perennial meanings of life. Psychotherapists trained in Jungian thought and its archetypal or mythological perspectives are more likely to encourage a therapeutic experience which seeks these deeper forms.

Another approach to facilitating positive change in the mental health of older adults can be found in the work of Mary Baird Carlsen (1991), a therapist who works with and writes about creative potential in aging. Baird is influenced by schools of psychotherapy that emphasize ways that people make up or "construct" their realities. By helping people discover how they construct their world of values and perceptions, Baird is able to help them take responsibility for themselves, enabling them to tap their creativity as a process of "meaning-making." Carlsen recognizes that older adults may be especially inclined to explore their meaning-making potential, since they are able to perceive repeating and evolving patterns of experience in their lives.

Carlsen describes the goals and process of psychotherapy as a relationship formed between therapist and client, through which information is gathered and then reshaped into new patterns that validate the client's knowledge and sophistication. The final phase is a closure to the therapy relationship.

Psychotherapy may be regarded as a vehicle for facilitating transformational shifts. Psychotherapies vary as to what experiences or capacities they emphasize.

Carlsen believes that successful therapy introduces new possibilities, provides a model for cog-

nitive flexibility and openness, and stimulates clients to arrive at new insights. These insights are instances of new meaning-making. This process is accomplished when the client is able to "go meta," which means to stand away from the problem and to view it from above. This is the transformational aspect of psychotherapy. Carlsen details a variety of particularly helpful techniques for elders, including use of early recollections, representations of the family "tree," memory exercises, visualizing new patterns, meditation, family therapy, and "pet and gardening" therapies.

A similar program has been developed in a workshop format and companion workbook entitled *Growing Wiser: The Older Person's Guide to Mental Wellness* (Kemper, Mettler, Giuffre, Matzek, 1986). This program is organized in six parts: (1) strategies for creating positive expectations and becoming a "sage," (2) strategies for dealing with problems of memory, (3) strategies for maintaining mental alertness, (4) exercises for coping with personal grief and the grief of others, (5) techniques for establishing and maintaining communication with others, and (6) fostering relationships in the larger world.

Individuals interested in increasing their knowledge of mythology generally and of transformational mythology in particular can attend workshops regularly available in large cities by many of the authors mentioned in this section. Some of these workshops are primarily informational, but many of them require active participation by the attendees. For example, a mythological story may be told and explained; then the participants begin to enact the major roles of the story as a way of deepening the connection between the story and themselves.

Psychotherapy and growth-oriented workshops are expensive and beyond the budget or inclination of most elders. Many individuals continue to associate a stigma with seeking treatment in psychotherapy. Although there is a strong movement away from the mental illness concept toward a personal growth orientation, it is likely that this narrower view of psychotherapy will persist. Regardless of the reasons for not electing psychotherapy, it is important to remember that there are other options.

Support groups in many formats have developed to facilitate the change process. The twelve-step movement that began as Alcoholics Anonymous has been expanded and adapted to deal with issues including substance abuse, emotional excesses, sexual disorders, and relationship problems. In addition there are increasing numbers of consciousness-raising groups for men and women. These types of groups vary in orientation, style, and effectiveness from community to community and even within one group over a period of time. When one chooses to work on personal issues in a support group (or with any therapist, mentor, or friend), it is important that the helper be more focused on the best interest of the helpee rather than in fostering a particular type of change.

The church has often been associated with the kinds of changes discussed in this paper. Bible study, meditation groups, and focused discussion about spiritual matters is another prominent vehicle for transformational change. Increased interest in spirituality is reflected by the large number of spirituality-related courses listed in the Elderhostel catalog—an international learning and travel program attracting over 300,000 seniors each year. Also, the spiritual disciplines found within or derived from Eastern religions have provided opportunities for spiritual growth. These approaches provide a cognitive framework as well as a variety of disciplines, such as mindfulness meditation described by Levine and others.

Art has often been used as a vehicle for transformational growth. Poetry, creative writing, drawing and painting, sculpture, and music can all be used as a way of developing a connection with the inner Self. In fact, one now sees these forms as a regular part of curricula at community colleges. Further, therapists also use forms such as art therapy and music therapy as ways to further spiritual and psychological growth.

Elders may also look for help through community agencies. Even small community agencies such as community mental health centers, hospitals, and hospice centers may provide opportunities for personal growth. In addition, colleges and universities provide an increasing number of educational options for elders.

Organizations

National Eldercare Institute on Health Promotion
Program Department
601 E. St., NW
Washington, DC 20049
(202) 434-2220

National Institute of Mental Health
Public Inquiries Branch, Room 15C-05
Office of Scientific Information
5600 Fishers Lane
Rockville, MD 20857
(301) 443-4513

National Mental Health Association
1021 Prince St.
Alexandria, VA 22314-2971
(703) 684-7722

References

Atchley, Robert C. "Personal Adaptation to Aging." In *Social Forces in Aging*. 5th ed. Belmont, CA: Wadsworth, 1988.

Baird, Carlsen, M. *Creative Aging: A Meaning-Making Perspective*. New York: Norton, 1991.

Campbell, J. *The Hero with a Thousand Faces*. Princeton, NJ: Princeton University Press, 1968.

———. *Myths to Live By*. New York: Bantam Books, 1973.

———. *Transformations of Myth Through Time*. New York: Harper & Row, 1990.

Caplan, Arthur. "Can Philosophy Cure What Ails the Medical Model?" In *The Second Fifty Years*. Eds. Robert L. Berg and Joseph S. Cassells. Institute of Medicine. Washington, DC: National Academy Press, 1990.

Chinen, A. B. *In the Ever After: Fairy Tales and the Second Half of Life*. Wilmette, IL: Chiron Publications, 1989.

———. *Once Upon a Midlife: Classic Stories and Mythic Tales to Illuminate the Middle Years*. Los Angeles, CA: Jeremy P. Tarcher, 1992.

Erikson, E. H. *Childhood and Society*. New York: Norton, 1950.

Some individuals are able to experience spiritual growth by opening their hearts to the conscious experience of pain and dying. (Courtesy of the American Association for Retired Persons.)

———. *The Life Cycle Completed: A Review.* New York: Norton, 1982.

Erikson, E. H., J. M. Erikson, and H. Q. Kivnick. *Vital Involvement in Old Age.* New York: Norton, 1986.

Havighurst, R. J. *Developmental Tasks and Education.* New York: David McKay, 1972.

Houston, J. *The Possible Human.* Los Angeles, CA: J.P. Tarcher, 1982.

———. *The Search for the Beloved.* Los Angeles, CA: J. P. Tarcher, 1987.

Kalish, R. A. *Death, Grief, and Caring Relationships.* Monterey, CA: Brooks/Cole, 1985.

Kastenbaum, R. J. "Habituation as a Model of Human Aging." *The International Journal of Aging and Human Development* Vol. 12 (1980–81): 159–70.

Kemper, D. W., M. Mettler, J. Giuffre, and B. Matzek. *Growing Wiser: The Older Person's Guide to Mental Wellness.* Boise, ID: Healthwise, 1986.

Kubler-Ross, Elisabeth. *On Death and Dying.* New York: Macmillan, 1969.

"Late Bloomer" audio cassette. Available from Connie Goldman Productions, 926 Second Street, Suite 201, Santa Barbara, CA 90403. (310) 393-6801.

Levine, S. *Healing into Life and Death.* New York: Doubleday, 1987.

———. *Who Dies? An Investigation of Conscious Living and Conscious Dying.* New York: Doubleday, 1982.

Levinson, D. J. *The Seasons of a Man's Life.* New York: Knopf, 1978.

Libowitz, Barry D., and George Niederehe. "Concepts and Issues in Mental Health and Aging." In *Handbook of Mental Health and Aging.* 2d ed. Eds. James E. Birren, R. Bruce Sloane, and Gene D. Cohen. San Diego, CA: Academic Press, 1992.

Lieberman, Morton A., and Harvey Peskin. "Adult Life Crises." In *Handbook of Mental Health and Aging.* 2d ed. Eds. James E. Birren, R. Bruce Sloane, and Gene D. Cohen. San Diego, CA: Academic Press, 1992.

Minois, G. *History of Old Age From Antiquity to the Renaissance.* Trans. by S. H. Tenison. Chicago, IL: University of Chicago Press, 1989.

Moore, R., and D. Gillette. *King, Warrior, Magician, Lover.* San Francisco, CA: Harper, 1990.

Pearson, C. *Awakening the Heros Within.* San Francisco, CA: Harper, 1991.

———. *The Hero Within.* San Francisco: Harper, 1986.

Peck, R. "Psychological Developments in the Second Half of Life." In *Psychological Aspects of Aging.* Ed. E.I. Anderson. Washington, DC: American Psychological Association, 1956.

Rogers, C. R. *On Becoming a Person.* Boston, MA: Houghton Mifflin, 1961.

Shinoda Bolen, J. *Goddesses in Every Woman.* New York: Harper, 1985.

———. *Gods in Everyman.* San Francisco: Harper, 1989.

Silverstone, B., and H. Kandel Hyman. *You and Your Aging Parent.* New York: Pantheon, 1989.

Additional Reading

American Society on Aging. "Progress and Prospects in Mental Health." *Generations* Vol. XVII, No. 1, San Francisco, CA: American Society on Aging, Winter/Spring 1993.

Birren, James E., and K. Warner Schaie, eds. *Handbook of the Psychology of Aging.* 3d ed. New York: Harcourt Brace, 1989.

Butler, Robert N., and Myrna L. Lewis. *Aging and Mental Health: Positive Psychosocial and Biomedical Approaches.* New York: Merrill, 1991.

Campbell, Scott, and Phyllis R. Silverman. *Widower.* New York: Prentice-Hall, 1987.

Diamond, M. S. *Enriching Heredity.* New York: Free Press, 1988.

Doress, Paula Brown, Diana L. Siegal, and the Midlife and Older Women Book Project. *Ourselves, Growing Older.* New York: Simon and Schuster, 1987.

Foehner, Charlotte, and Carol Cozart. *The Widow's Handbook: A Guide for Living.* Golden, CO: Fulcrum, 1988.

Jacobs, Ruth. *Be An Outrageous Older Woman.* Available through Knowledge, Ideas, and Trends, Inc., 1131-0 Tolland Turnpike, Suite 175, Manchester, CT 06040, (203)643-7831.

Kaufman, S. R. *The Ageless Self.* New York: New American Library, 1986.

Kenyon, G. M., J. E. Birren, and J. Schroots, eds. *Metaphors of Aging in Science and the Humanities.* New York: Springer, 1991.

Markides, K., and C. Mindel. *Aging and Ethnicity.* Newbury Park, CA: Sage, 1987.

Scott-Maxwell, Florida. *The Measure of My Days.* New York: Knopf, 1968.

Seskin, Jane. *Alone—Not Lonely: Independent Living for Women Over Fifty.* Washington, DC: American Association of Retired Persons and Scott, Foresman, 1985.

Sherman, E. *Reminiscence and the Self in Old Age.* New York: Springer, 1991.

Skinner, B. F., and Margaret E. Vaughan. *Enjoying Old Age: A Program of Self-Management.* New York: Norton, 1983.

Richard Johnson, Ph.D.

㉑

Health Status of Older Americans

● Studying Health Status ● Chronic Conditions and Health Problems
● Health Status, Gender, and Race ● Activity Limitation
● Personal Health Habits in Disease Prevention ● Mortality ● Causes of Death

American culture sustains stereotypic myths about the health status of older adults. Typically, aging is caricatured by progressive illness, infirmity, or sickness. This myth persists not only among the public but also among health care professionals. Defining the health status of older adults depends first on perspective.

Does an inevitable decline in health status accompany aging? Describing the health status of older adults requires a unique approach. It is misleading to speak of older Americans as a homogeneous group. When 2-year-olds or 30-year-olds are discussed, certain general descriptions apply. The striking characteristic of young children or young adults is how similar they are. These groups can be characterized quite well by their similarities. Indeed, one of the hallmarks of these groups is their striving to be similar. With the elderly, no single pattern emerges. A 70-year-old may be ill and in a nursing home or may be healthy and active. Older Americans are the most heterogeneous group of the population. Older Americans are characterized by their differences.

● STUDYING HEALTH STATUS

The investigation of older Americans' health status depends upon the methods used to study the population. Two basic methods have been used to characterize health status: cross-sectional and longitudinal. One type of study takes a snapshot of a large group of people. A sample of peo-

ple from both young and old age groups is obtained. Information about health status is derived from each group. This cross-sectional type of study reveals that many more older people are ill at any one time compared to younger people. More disease conditions are present in the elderly than in younger persons. From this perspective, older persons represent the largest reservoir of disease in our population. Most studies of aging have used this methodology. From this type of study, a picture of poor health status among older adults emerges.

Older Americans are the most heterogeneous group of the population.

Another type of study follows a large group of people as they age. The same individuals are followed for a considerable time and observed for changes in health status. This longitudinal type of study shows a different picture. Many older people do not show a decline in health status with aging. Most of the decline in health status results from specific illnesses that people acquire as they age. When an individual contracts a chronic disease that does not result in death, the disease continues to be present. When persons who acquire a specific chronic disease are excluded, there is little difference in health status attributable to aging itself. From this type of study, a picture emerges of preserved health except in individuals with spe-

Many older people do not show a decline in health status with aging. (Copyright © Marianne Gontarz)

cific diseases. Careful longitudinal research suggests that loss of health is not a certain result of aging. The accumulated effects of chronic disease define the health status of an older American.

Certain changes in organ function do occur as people grow older. The net effect of these changes may or may not influence health status. Changes that occur in everyone in the absence of disease can be termed normal aging. Changes that occur as a result of disease can be termed pathological aging. Changes that were once felt to be inevitable consequences of aging are in reality due to the presence of chronic disease. This results in a higher prevalence of chronic disease in the older population (Rowe, 1990). Distinguishing between changes that are normal or pathological can be difficult.

Reviewing aging changes in specific organ systems can illustrate this difficulty. For example, changes in the cardiovascular system are subtle. In disease-free individuals, systolic, or contractile, function of the heart does not change with age. Diastolic, or resting, function of the heart may show mild decreases. The heart rate at rest does not change, but maximum heart rate with exercise declines by about one beat per year (Hossack, 1982). Maximum cardiovascular exercise capacity falls only slightly with aging. Age-related changes in the vascular bed are more prominent. There is loss of elasticity of larger arteries, with calcification of the media, or middle layer. This leads to an increase in work load on the left ventricle. At the level of individual cells, no morphological changes occur that are visible microscopically. Overall, these findings suggest there is little change in heart function that occurs

as otherwise healthy adults age. These types of changes represent normal aging.

Careful longitudinal research suggests that loss of health is not a certain result of aging. The accumulated effects of chronic disease define the health status of an older American.

On the other hand, individuals who develop heart disease may show large declines in function. This type of change represents pathological aging. In a cross-sectional study of elderly persons, which may include individuals who have heart disease, the findings may suggest that progressive decline in heart function accompanies age. In a longitudinal study of persons who do not have specific heart disease, one finds little difference as persons age.

For many medical conditions, changes that reflect normal aging as opposed to pathological aging have not been clearly worked out. As more is learned about normal aging, it is clear that individual variations are more important than group changes.

● CHRONIC CONDITIONS AND HEALTH PROBLEMS

Because chronic conditions tend to accumulate with age in survivors, elderly people have multiple problems. Eighty-five percent of persons over the age of 65 have one or more medical diseases. In community dwelling (non-institutionalized) elderly populations, the average number of chronic conditions ranges from three to seven (Williamson, 1964). Since most chronic conditions by definition are not life-threatening, older persons who are ill accumulate diseases. This complex interaction of several illnesses is called the burden of illness. This burden of illness greatly interferes with normal functioning and with quality of life.

The best way to examine the chronic conditions of aging is to observe the self-reported conditions that elderly adults experience.

The survey data shows that thirty to forty percent of chronic conditions affecting the elderly are due to sensory impairment. Sensory impairment accounts for the largest burden of illness.

Table 21.1
Top Ten Chronic Conditions Listed by Age and by Sex

Men 65–74	Women 65–74
1. Arthritis	1. Arthritis
2. High blood pressure	2. High blood pressure
3. Hearing impairment	3. Hearing impairment
4. Ischemic heart disease	4. Cataracts
5. Tinnitus	5. Ischemic heart disease
6. Diabetes	6. Varicose veins
7. Hardening of the arteries	7. Tinnitus
8. Cataracts	8. Diabetes
9. Cerebrovascular disease	9. Visual impairment
10. Varicose veins	10. Hardening of the arteries

Men 75–84	Women 75–84
1. Arthritis	1. Arthritis
2. Hearing impairment	2. High blood pressure
3. High blood pressure	3. Hearing impairment
4. Cataracts	4. Cataracts
5. Ischemic heart disease	5. Ischemic heart disease
6. Other visual impairment	6. Other visual impairment
7. Tinnitus	7. Hardening of the arteries
8. Hardening of the arteries	8. Tinnitus
9. Malignant neoplasms	9. Varicose veins
10. Diabetes	10. Diabetes

Men 85+	Women 85+
1. Hearing impairment	1. Arthritis
2. Arthritis	2. High blood pressure
3. High blood pressure	3. Hearing impairment
4. Cataracts	4. Cataracts
5. Visual impairment	5. Visual impairment
6. Hardening of the arteries	6. Hardening of the arteries
7. Ischemic heart disease	7. Ischemic heart disease
8. Deaf in both ears	8. Lower extremity orthopedic impairment
9. Lower extremity orthopedic impairment	9. Tinnitus
10. Malignant neoplasms	10. Varicose veins

Source: Olshansky, 1985.

Both hearing and visual impairments have profound effect on socialization and functional aspects of living. Most of these conditions are not life-threatening, yet limit the ability to be inde-

---

Sensory impairment accounts for the largest burden of illness.

---

pendent and enjoy living. The burden of these conditions primarily affects the quality of life experienced by the aged.

At all ages and for both sexes, arthritis is the most common chronic condition. In the very old, orthopedic problems in the lower extremity are common. These factors contribute to functional limitation in the old, or the ability to be independently mobile (see Table 21.1).

High blood pressure and ischemic heart dis-

Both hearing and visual impairments have a profound effect on socialization and functional aspects of living. (Copyright © Marianne Gontarz)

ease are among the most common cardiovascular conditions. Together these two conditions account for most routine medical care visits to physicians. In both these conditions the necessity for continued medications and health-related expenses further impair quality of life.

● HEALTH STATUS, GENDER, AND RACE

At all ages, men die at a greater rate than women. At all ages, women have a greater life expectancy than men. Average life expectancy can be used to estimate the number of years of life expected for most members of the population. The differences in average life expectancy for men and women can be seen in Table 21.2.

This sex differential in life expectancy has important demographic and social implications. Simply put, the effect of the sex-related difference in mortality means that more older women will be alive than older men. In social terms, the effect of this differential means that women experience more widowhood, loss of companionship, and loss of breadwinners with aging.

The types of illness that affect women, as seen in Table 21.1, are different from men. This sex differential is poorly understood. The responsible factor may be due to build-up of fats on artery walls, atherosclerosis, which affects men more often than women. Before menopause, women rarely develop narrowing of the arteries, arteriosclerosis, perhaps due to the protective effect of estrogen on blood lipids. The rate of development of arteriosclerosis increases in women after menopause.

Simply put, the effect of the sex-related difference in mortality means that more older women will be alive than older men.

Race also differentially affects survival. The mortality rates for African Americans exceed that of whites for every cause from birth to age 65 years. Therefore more whites reach old age than non-whites. However, after the age of 65 years, whites do not live longer. At age 75 years, the

Table 21.2
Life Expectancy at Birth and at 65 Years of Age, by Race and Sex: Selected Years 1900 to 1989

Specified age and year	All races			White		Black	
	Both sexes	Male	Female	Male	Female	Male	Female
At Birth							
1900[1,2]	47.3	46.3	48.3	46.6	48.7	32.5[3]	33.5[3]
1950[2]	68.2	65.6	71.1	66.5	72.2	58.9	62.7
1960[2]	69.7	66.6	73.1	67.4	74.1	60.7	65.9
1970	70.9	67.1	74.8	68.0	75.6	60.0	68.3
1980	73.7	70.0	77.4	70.7	78.1	63.8	72.5
1989	75.3	71.8	78.6	72.7	79.2	64.8	73.5
At 65 Years							
1900–1902[1,2]	11.9	11.5	12.2	11.5	12.2	10.4	11.4
1950[2]	13.9	12.8	15.0	12.8	15.1	12.9	14.9
1960[2]	14.3	12.8	15.8	12.9	15.9	12.7	15.1
1970	15.2	13.1	17.0	13.1	17.1	12.5	15.7
1980	16.4	14.1	18.3	14.2	18.4	13.0	16.8
1989	17.2	15.2	18.8	15.2	19.0	13.6	17.0

Notes: 1. Death registration area only. The death registration area increased from 10 States and the District of Columbia in 1900 to the conterminous United States in 1933. 2. Includes deaths of nonresidents of the United States. 3. Figure is for all other population.

Source: U.S. Bureau of the Census. *Current Population Reports, Special Studies,* pp. 23–178, *Sixty-Five Plus in America.* U.S. Government Printing Office, Washington, DC, 1992.

death rate of whites and African Americans is roughly the same. By 85 years, African Americans can expect to outlive whites (Department of Health and Human Services, 1980).

The causes of death among African Americans that account for this differential in survival may relate to income, education, and access to health care. The racial differential in survival may be caused by reversible environmental factors rather than genetic factors.

● ACTIVITY LIMITATION

Limitation of activity in elderly persons is critical to quality of life. Loss of functional ability results in dependence on others to carry out basic activities of daily living. Seventeen percent of persons over the age of 65 cannot carry out daily activities such as housework or jobs. Forty-five percent of those over the age of 65 have some activity limitation, increasing to 60 percent of those over 75. In contrast, only 8 percent of the population under 65 has activity limitations (Department of Health and Human Services, 1978).

When persons who are confined to institutions are excluded, the picture changes slightly. Limits in physical mobility occur in about 14 percent of non-institutionalized elderly. Two percent are bed-bound, 5 percent are housebound, and 7 percent go outdoors only with difficulty. These factors greatly impede the ability of elders to care for themselves, interact with friends and community, and maintain independence.

The reverse of this picture is that most older Americans do age successfully. Fully 85 percent of the elderly do *not* need aid with mobility or social services. Ninety percent report no unmet social needs. Only five in one hundred elderly persons need help with transportation or shopping (Branch, 1980).

Fully 85 percent of the elderly do *not* need aid with mobility or social services.

Age is the predominate factor in predicting activity limitations. While 9 percent of persons aged 70 to 74 have significant limitations in activity, 29 percent of persons over 85 years old do.

At all ages, men die at a greater rate than women. (Copyright © Marianne Gontarz)

The accumulation of chronic non-life-threatening illness, chiefly arthritis and sensory impairment, is the major factor in limiting physical activity.

● PERSONAL HEALTH HABITS IN DISEASE PREVENTION

Most of the limitations of aging are directly related to disease states. What can be done to decrease the burden of disease? The inevitable changes that occur with aging, or the genetic factors predisposing to disease, may be unmodifiable. However, certain environmental factors that lead to disease are well researched and are modifiable. These personal health habits directly influence the development of some diseases.

The single most important modifiable environmental factor is cigarette smoking. Cigarette smoking is the most important cause of obstructive lung disease in adults. Diseases causally related to smoking include arteriosclerotic cardiovascular disease, peripheral vascular disease, bronchogenic cancers, oral cancers, and other cancers.

When body weight exceeds 30 percent of age- and sex-specific norms, obesity is a cause of multiple chronic conditions. At least six risk factors are associated with obesity: hypertension, diabetes, hyperinsulinemia, hypercholesterolemia, hypertriglyceridemia, and reduced high-density lipoprotein (good cholesterol). Decreased calorie intake and increased calorie expenditure through exercise may contribute to risk reduction.

Cholesterol, especially the low-density lipoprotein (bad cholesterol), is a definite risk factor for the development of atherosclerotic heart disease. Evidence is accumulating that reduction in dietary fat (especially saturated fat and cholesterol) to less than 30 percent of total calories can reduce risk of atherosclerosis.

Some forms of cancer, particularly colon cancer, may be prevented by change in diet. Reduction in dietary fat to less than 30 percent of total calories, increase in total fiber content (whole grain cereal, fruits, and vegetables), and increase in beta-carotene and vitamin C may prevent development of some cancers. Intake of foods that are salt-cured, salt-pickled, or smoked should be reduced.

Osteoporosis, or thinning of the bones, depends in women upon the degree of skeletal calcification before menopause. Dietary intake of calcium, particularly during pregnancy and lactation, is important to maintain skeletal integrity. Dietary intake of calcium is most important in teenage and early adult years. Modeling of bone that strengthens with regular exercise is an important preventive measure for osteoporosis.

Reducing these modifiable factors represent the largest opportunity to modify the burden of illness with aging. Cessation of cigarette smoking, control of obesity, a prudent diet low in saturated fats and high in fiber, and adequate intake of calcium may result in important reductions in risk of disease.

● MORTALITY

Human beings are the longest lived of all mammalian species. Simple demographics show that more older persons are now alive than at any time in history. Within the next few years the number of older Americans is projected to grow substantially. Does this mean that humans are living longer?

Profiles of Productive Aging

Dr. Lewis Thomas
Physician

"The worst of all things to contemplate in one's sixties is boredom or loss of zest. The only way you get around that is to change jobs or quit. Quit working and start learning. Yes, learn something. That's the best thing."

The celebrated president of Memorial Sloan Kettering Cancer Center in New York, Dr. Lewis Thomas became known worldwide for his brilliant meditative essays on biology: *The Lives of a Cell, The Medusa and the Snail,* and *Late Night Thoughts on Listening to Mahler's Night Music.*

Thomas was born in Flushing, New York, on November 25, 1913. He thought of being a writer in his youth, although his real desire, as far back as he can remember, was to be a physician like his father. Thomas entered college at 15; after medical school at Harvard and an internship at Boston City Hospital, he launched a career as a researcher and administrator that took him to six cities over a period of thirty years, working in virus and bacteriological research, teaching, and heading several departments, ultimately becoming head of Memorial Sloan Kettering. ("I never could hold a job," Thomas joked about the string of distinguished appointments he has held.)

His research yielded several valuable discoveries. First, he found that papaya enzyme (papain) would selectively digest cartilage in the human body, a discovery that has since become a standard treatment for herniated discs, (when papain is injected into a disc it causes the cartilage inside the disc to collapse so that the disc can more easily resume its normal position.) Second, he found that vitamin A, when injected in large doses, has the same effect (but for a different scientific reason.) He also proposed, in 1958, that there was a connection between the mechanism through which the body rejects skin grafts, and the mechanism through which the body is protected from cancer, a concept which to date has not yet been proven but which looks as if it will be validated.

Thomas' career as a physician, researcher, and administrator was extremely distinguished, although it did not make him world famous. Then in 1970, something unpredictable happened, a tiny pulse within the framework of his life which ultimately led to a totally new direction in his work. "I was asked to give an after-dinner talk at an immunology meeting in Brooklodge, outside of Kalamazoo," he said. "I gave a light talk—I guess it was about inflammation, inflammatory reactions. I didn't realize it, but it was recorded. The company printed it up in a little folder and sent it around to a lot of people. It fell into the hands of Franz Inglefinger, who was then the editor of the *New England Journal of Medicine.* He wrote me a letter and said he'd like essays like that for the journal once a month, and they must not be any longer than one page, which would have been about eleven hundred words. In return for that, there would of course be no payment, but he would guarantee that nobody would ever be allowed to edit whatever I wrote. That was irresistible, so I started writing essays for the *New England Journal of Medicine.*"

After about three years, Thomas got a "very nice letter from Joyce Carol Oates, who said that her doctor up in Windsor, Ontario had been collecting these things and giving copies to her. She thought they'd make a good book." Eventually, Thomas recalls, he got a nice telephone call from Elizabeth Sifton, an editor at Viking, who had seen the essays through *her* doctor. She told him that Viking would like to publish the essays as they stood—no changes. "Viking wouldn't even lay a finger on them," Thomas commented with satisfaction. "I said all right." Viking printed about five thousand copies; neither the author nor the publisher expected that very many copies would sell. They did sell, of course, as Thomas remarks in his typical understated manner, "quite a lot."

Thomas was 57 when he began writing essays, and 61 at the publication of *Lives of a Cell* in 1974. Now almost 80, he is still writing, though he has had several bouts with illness which slowed him down temporarily. In 1988 he retired from active work at Sloan Kettering, where he is now a Scholar in Residence, devoting as much time as he wishes to his writing.

Lydia Brontë

Regular exercise strengthens bones and is an important preventive measure for osteoporosis. (Copyright © Phil Kukelhan)

Table 21.3
Estimates of Historical Life Expectancy and Maximum Life Span

Time	Approximate Age at 50% Survival	Approximate Maximum Span Potential
30,000 years ago	29	69–77
12,000 years ago	32	95
10,000 years ago	31	95
8,000 years ago	38	95
Classical Greece	35	95
Classical Rome	32	95
England, 1276	48	95
England, 1400	38	95
United States, 1900	61	95
United States, 1950	70	95
United States, 1970	73	95

Source: Deevy, 1960.

During the last several thousand years the proportion of older persons in society has increased. To understand this increase, measures of length of life must be understood. The first measure is life expectancy. This is the age at which half of those born remain alive. Past this age, fewer and fewer people of those born remain alive. The potential length of an individual life is the maximum life span. This is the maximum age that any one individual can expect to live without disease.

Not all individuals in the population can expect to live to maximum life span, but some do. A child can expect to live about seventy-three years at birth in present society.

This data confirms that life expectancy has progressively increased with time. The age at which half those born are still living is increasing. In classical Rome, for example, half the population died by age 32. Some persons lived to old age, but this group was a minority. During most of history, however, maximum life span has not increased at all. The age by which nearly everyone dies has remained the same.

Why has there been an increase in life expectancy? Most of the deaths in ancient populations occurred among the young. Modern health improvements have resulted in fewer deaths from infectious diseases and major epidemics. Life expectancy increases are largely due to a decline in early childhood death. When fewer young persons die, the age when half of the population remains alive increases. The conquering of measles, mumps, and diphtheria have eliminated childhood causes of death. Thus, eliminating early or acute causes of death has resulted in a shift to an increasingly older population. Persons are living longer than in the past but are not living *younger* longer. The conquering of acute illness has led to an increase in chronic illness.

Tuberculosis serves as an example of this shift in mortality. In 1900, tuberculosis was the leading cause of death in the United States. Most of the cases occurred in children and young adults. Today tuberculosis does not even make the top ten list as a cause of mortality. Drug treatment has drastically reduced the death rate for this disease. At the same time, tuberculosis has become a major problem in nursing homes. The largest reservoir of tuberculosis cases is now among the elderly.

The maximum potential life span of an individual has been remarkably constant in spite of large differences in life expectancy. Persons who have lower-than-normal life spans generally die from specific diseases. Persons who are fortunate enough to avoid specific diseases tend to live to maximum life span. Yet the age at which most persons die seems to be fixed.

Persons who are fortunate enough to avoid specific diseases tend to live to maximum life span. (Copyright © Marianne Gontarz)

at a fixed point in years. Death may not occur as a by-product of modifiable factors. Aging may be a passive characteristic, the ticking of a biological clock.

> The maximum potential life span of an individual has been remarkably constant in spite of large differences in life expectancy.

This survival curve has important implications. It means that the maximum length of life of humans may be a characteristic of the species. In the absence of specific factors, death may occur

● CAUSES OF DEATH

Heart disease, cancer, and cerebrovascular disease (stroke) are the three leading causes of death in persons over the 65 years of age. Table 21.4 identifies the mortality rates for older adults.

The rates for heart disease, cancer, and cerebrovascular disease increase in each decade past the age of 65. By age 85, pneumonia and influenza become the fourth leading cause of death. The mortality rates for most other conditions pale in comparison to the rates for the top three cause of

Table 21.4
Death Rates for Ten Leading Causes of Death Among Older People, by Age: 1988 (Rates per 100,000 Population in Age Group)

Cause of Death	65+	65 to 74	75 to 84	85+
All Causes	5,105	2,730	6,321	15,594
Diseases of the heart	2,066	984	2,543	7,098
Malignant neoplasms	1,068	843	1,313	1,639
Cerebrovascular diseases	431	155	554	1,707
Chronic obstructive pulmonary disease	226	152	313	394
Pneumonia and influenza	225	60	257	1,125
Diabetes	97	62	125	222
Accidents	89	50	107	267
Atherosclerosis	69	15	70	396
Nephritis, nephrotic syndrome, nephrosis	61	26	78	217
Septicemia	56	24	71	199

Source: National Center for Health Statistics, 1990.

Figure 21.1
Death Rates for Leading Causes of Death for People Age 75 to 84: 1950–89

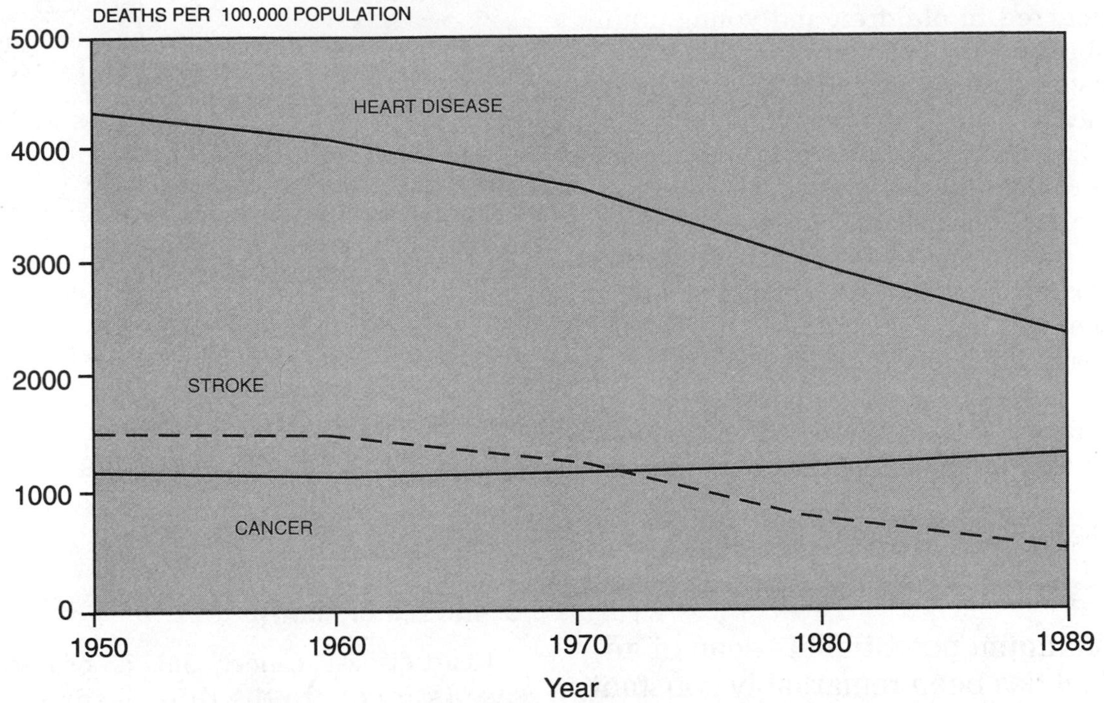

Sources: National Center for Health Statistics. "Health, United States, 1989." *DHHS Pub. No.* (PHS)90–1232. Washington: Department of Health and Human Services, March 1990.

National Center for Health Statistics. "Annual Summary of Births, Marriages, Divorces, and Deaths: United States, 1989." *Monthly Vital Statistics Report* Vol. 38, no. 13 (August 30, 1990).

National Center for Health Statistics. "Advance Report of Final Mortality Statistics, 1988." *Monthly Vital Statistics Report* Vol. 39, no. 7, supplement (November 28, 1990).

death. For this reason, research has focused on reversing these conditions. Nevertheless, diseases that are treatable with improved access to health care and health promotion continue to account for excess mortality among older adults.

Yet eliminating causes of death may not result in people living longer. For example, the effect of eliminating cancer completely would result in only an additional 1.4 years of life expectancy at age 65 (Keyfitz, 1977). Life expectancy and maximum life span may be only marginally improved by the elimination of disease. The improvement of quality of life, however, would be enormous.

As the aging process continues, any deterioration that accompanies aging steadily increases. Therefore, as acute life-threatening diseases decline in frequency, chronic conditions that do not result in death become more frequent in the population. This increase in chronic conditions

dramatically affects the quality of an individual's life. Thus, modifying the accumulation of chronic conditions has more potential for improving the health status of older Americans than eliminating causes of death.

References

Branch, L. G. "Functional Abilities of the Elderly: An Update on the Massachusetts Health Care Panel Study." *NIH Publication No. 80–969*. Washington, DC: Government Printing Office, July 1980.

Deevy, E. S. "The Human Population." *Scientific American* Vol. 203 (1960): 195.

Hossack, K. R. "Maximal Cardiac Function in Sedentary Normal Men and Women: Comparison of Age-Related Changes. *Journal of Applied Physiology* Vol. 53 (1982): 799.

Keyfitz, N. "What Difference Would it Make if Cancer Were Eradicated? An Examination of the Taeuber Paradox." *Demography* Vol. 14 (1977): 411–18.

Olshansky, S. J. "Pursing Longevity: Delay vs. Elimination of Degenerative Diseases." *American Journal of Public Health* Vol. 75 (1985): 754–56.

Rowe, J. W. "Toward Successful Aging: Limitation of Morbidity Associated with 'Normal' Aging." In *Principles of Geriatric Medicine and Gerontology*. 2d ed. New York: McGraw-Hill, 1990.

U.S. Department of Health and Human Services. "Current Estimates from the Health Interview Survey: United States, 1978." *Vital and Health Statistics*. Series 10, No. 130. Publication No. 80-1551 (November, 1978). Washington, DC: Government Printing Office.

U.S. Department of Health and Human Services. *National Center for Health Statistics*. Publication No. 80-1232 (November, 1980). Washington, DC: Government Printing Office.

Williamson, J., I. H. Stokoe, S. Gray, M. Fisher, A. Smith, A. McGehee, and E. Stemhenson. "Old People at Home: Their Unreported Needs." *Lancet* Vol. 1 (1964): 1117–20.

Additional Reading

Gordon, Michael. *Old Enough to Feel Better: A Medical Guide for Seniors*. Rev. ed. Baltimore, MD: John Hopkins University Press, 1989.

Journal of Nutrition for the Elderly. New York: Haworth Press.

Kane, Rosalie A., and Robert L. Kane. *Assessing the Elderly: A Practical Guide to Measurement*. Lexington, MA: Lexington Books, 1981.

Palmore, Erdman, and others, eds. *Normal Aging: Report From the Duke Longitudinal Studies*. 3 vols. Durham, NC: Duke University Press, 1970–85.

Resource Directory for Older People. Bethesda, MD: National Institute on Aging, 1989.

Roe, Daphne A. *Geriatric Nutrition*. 2d ed. Englewood Cliffs, NJ: Prentice-Hall, 1987.

Saxon, Sue V., and Mary Jean Etten. *Physical Change and Aging: A Guide for the Helping Professions*. 2d ed. New York: Tiresias Press, 1987.

Schneider, Edward L., and John W. Rowe, eds. *Handbook of the Biology of Aging*. 3d ed. New York: Harcourt Brace, 1989.

Strong, Maggie. *Mainstay: For the Well Spouse of the Chronically Ill*. Boston, MA: Little Brown, 1988.

Tideiksaar, Rein. *Falling in Old Age: Its Prevention and Treatment*. New York: Springer, 1989.

David R. Thomas, M.D.

Section VIII:

Health Problems

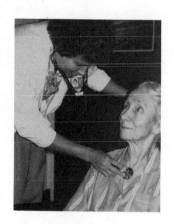

22

Diseases and Conditions

• Arthritis • High Blood Pressure • Hearing Loss • Tinnitus • Heart Disease • Vision Problems • Diabetes • Hardening of the Arteries • Cerebrovascular Disease • Varicose Veins • Cancer • Osteoporosis • Urinary Incontinence • Disorders of Bowel Function and Constipation

Specific diseases and conditions contribute to the burden of illness and functional limitations in older Americans. The ten most common chronic disease states of elderly persons aged 65 to 74 years are addressed in this section in approximate order of their frequency. For succeeding decades, the list is similar (see Table 21.1 in Chapter 21, Health Status of Older Americans).

● ARTHRITIS

Arthritis is the most common disease condition afflicting the elderly in both men and women. In 1984, the National Center for Health Statistics ranked arthritis first among the top ten chronic health problems. Forty-seven percent of persons over the age of 65 years are affected by arthritis. Continuing pain and functional limitation associated with arthritis critically affect enjoyment of life.

Arthritis literally means inflammation in the joint. Several different types of arthritis exist, each with a distinct cause and rate of progression.

Osteoarthritis

Among the types of arthritis, osteoarthritis is the most common. Normal aging produces observable changes in the articular cartilage and bone. These changes are distinct from the changes that occur in osteoarthritis. The theory that osteoarthritis is a normal result of aging has

been abandoned. Normal aging may somehow predispose a person to the development of osteoarthritis, but osteoarthritis is now clearly recognized as a disease.

Arthritis is the most common disease condition afflicting the elderly in both men and women.

Osteoarthritis typically involves the last and next to last joints of the hands, the base of the thumb and great toe, the hips, the knees, and the spine. The wrist, elbow, shoulder, and ankle are spared, for reasons that are not clear. Trauma in these joints may predispose a person to the development of osteoarthritis.

Symptoms include stiffness, particularly in the early morning or after inactivity. Pain is present with active movement and with passive motion. Effusion, or swelling in the joint, is common. With time, joint deformities occur. Disease in the joints can lead to pinching of the nerves passing close to the joint. Nerve compression may lead to pain, numbness, and tingling in the hands or legs.

There are no characteristic laboratory abnormalities in osteoarthritis. Radiographs (e.g. X-rays) do show characteristic degenerative changes in the bones. Treatment must be individualized. Physical therapy such as exercise or splints and anti-inflammatory or analgesic drugs help alleviate the symptoms.

Physical therapy such as exercise or splints combined with anti-inflammatory or analgesic drugs help alleviate the symptoms of osteoarthritis. (Copyright © Marianne Gontarz)

Rheumatoid Arthritis

Rheumatoid arthritis is the most common chronic inflammatory type of arthritis, affecting about 3 percent of the adult population. The peak onset is between ages 35 and 45. Few new cases occur in elderly populations. However, since the disease is chronic, the number of persons suffering from rheumatoid arthritis steadily increases with age. Many persons who develop this progressive disease carry the burden of disability into geriatric age.

The cause of rheumatoid arthritis is unknown. Some unidentified initiating agent induces an immunological reaction in the joints. The disease develops only in the presence of a certain individual genetic makeup. Apparently only individuals with this certain type of genetic makeup respond to the initiating agent. The result is a symmetrical inflammation, or synovitis, of the small joints of the hands, feet, wrists, and knees. Painful swelling occurs in these joints. Prolonged early

morning stiffness is prominent. Joint deformity and destruction may follow.

The course of rheumatoid arthritis can be roughly divided into thirds. One-third develop an acute illness with severe short-term symptoms but a benign course. One-third will develop a chronic, indolent arthritis. In one-third the disease proceeds to an inactive state. Rheumatoid arthritis that first begins in elderly persons tends to be a milder type.

Specific laboratory abnormalities and characteristic radiological findings help diagnose the illness. Treatment options depend on the severity of the disease. In addition to physical measures, several drug treatment options exist. Therapy begins with simple analgesics and progresses through anti-inflammatory drugs, heavy metals, and immunological suppressant drugs. There is evidence that early treatment with several agents may prevent later joint deformities.

Crystal Deposition Arthritis

Deposition of crystals in the joint space can result in arthritis. Two common types of crystals are associated with arthritis. The most common is urate crystals, the cause of gout. Deposition of calcium pyrophosphate crystals produces a more uncommon type of crystal disease.

Gout results from the deposition of urate crystals in the lining of the joint. This results in severe inflammation with abrupt onset of symptoms. In the elderly, the disease is common but is not typical in clinical symptoms. More than one joint tends to be involved, and the pattern may differ from that in younger persons.

The diagnosis of gout is established by finding crystals in the joint fluid by microscopy. A typical presentation of disease may not require joint aspiration (draining the fluid). The uric acid level in the blood is a poor guide to diagnosis in the elderly. Treatment is aimed at control of inflammation. In chronic or frequently occurring cases, treatment aimed at blocking the production or increasing excretion of uric acid may be used.

Polymyalgia Rheumatica

Several other arthritic conditions are much rarer, but still important in their impact. One of these is polymyalgia rheumatica. This condition occurs almost exclusively in individuals over age

Profiles of Productive Aging

Jonas Salk
Physician and scientist

"My job at the moment is to help people see what I see. If it's of value, fine. And if it's not of value, then at least I've done what I can do."

Dr. Jonas Salk, the world-renowned physician and scientist, was born on October 28, 1914, in New York City. As a child, Salk wanted to be a lawyer, but his mother was determined that her cherished eldest son would become a schoolteacher. Salk, however, had no interest in that profession; deprived of his first choice, he decided to become a medical research scientist. His mother opposed that too—but she had lost her veto power when Salk gave up his legal aspirations. After receiving a bachelor of science degree at the City College of New York in 1934, Salk enrolled in medical school at New York University and went on to become one of the century's greatest medical research scientists.

Salk says he chose medical science because similar principles are involved in law and science. In addition, scientific research in the 1930s, when he was in college and medical school, was still in its formative stages, and Salk wanted to help bring order and coherence to medical research, enabling the products of research to be better used for the relief of human suffering. Although he was extremely bright, learned quickly, and retained everything he learned, he did not know that he had an exceptional gift for medicine until he discovered to his surprise that he was a phenomenally talented diagnostician and exceptional researcher.

Salk spent the first twenty years of his professional life as an immunologist, creating vaccines. After the success of the polio vaccine in 1955, Salk decided that the nation needed a biomedical research institute where basic research could be cultivated and nourished. With the backing of the March of Dimes Foundation, he set about finding a site and gathering support for the Salk Institute for Biological Studies. Once the site was selected—in the San Diego suburb of La Jolla—and the city of San Diego had passed a referendum donating the land, Salk engaged the famous architect Louis Kahn to design the institute buildings. Their relationship developed into a close collaboration, with the two working together as coarchitects of a structure so contemporary in its striking beauty that it is a monument instead of a simple building complex.

When the institute was up and running, Salk turned his attention to writing. He published three or four books over a period of several years, focusing mainly on his concept of humans being the only biological form that can consciously participate in and change the course of their own evolution. Meanwhile, he was tapped for the board of trustees of the newly organized MacArthur Foundation in Chicago, concentrating particularly on research programs in health, the sciences, and medical research.

After a few years of intense work with the MacArthur Foundation, Salk began to take note of another new development: the appearance of AIDS. It was perhaps inevitable that the man who created the vaccine for the most feared disease of the 1940s and 1950s would become deeply fascinated by the AIDS virus and its devastating impact on human life. Because of his many French contacts through his wife, artist Françoise Gilot, Salk became acquainted with the major figures in a transatlantic quarrel over whether French or American researchers first isolated the virus. He played a key role in mediating that quarrel, which had threatened to disrupt research on both sides of the Atlantic for years to come.

Meanwhile Salk's own work on the AIDS virus appeared more promising. In September 1987 the State Legislature of California passed a bill allowing California physicians to test experimental substances on state residents, with permission only from the California Food and Drug Board—rather than from the national Food and Drug Agency. Part of the motivation for the passage of the law was the hope that it would speed Salk's ability to test his immunotherapeutic preparation more quickly—and the bill did just that. Already, Salk's preparation has gone through the early phases of testing in both chimpanzees and in a number of human subjects, with good results to date.

Salk has received many honors and awards, including the Congressional Gold Medal and the Presidential Medal of Freedom. He has received honorary degrees from universities in the United States, England, Israel, Italy, and the Philippines. He is author of four books and more than 135 scientific papers. Currently, Salk and his wife live in San Diego.

Lydia Brontë

fifty. Women are affected more than men. Symptoms include aching in the large muscles of the shoulders, thigh, and upper arms. About half the patients affected with polymyalgia rheumatica develop inflammation in large arteries, termed giant cell arteritis. This inflammation may lead to occlusion of blood vessels, particularly in the eye, causing sudden blindness.

Diagnosis is confirmed by biopsy and suggested by striking elevation in the sedimentation rate of blood cells. Treatment with corticosteroids is very successful, resulting in resolution of symptoms within twenty-four to forty-eight hours.

● HIGH BLOOD PRESSURE

High blood pressure is the second most common chronic condition affecting both men and women. Estimates of the number of persons with hypertension vary. About 30 percent of persons 60 to 65 years old have elevated blood pressure, and 40 percent of persons older than 65 years have hypertension. Hypertension occurs in two forms. In the first, systolic-diastolic hypertension, the systolic (or contractile) pressure is greater than 140–160 millimeters of mercury (mm Hg), and diastolic (or resting) pressure is greater than 90 mm Hg. In the second, isolated systolic hypertension, the systolic pressure is greater than 160 mm Hg, and diastolic pressure is less than 90 mm Hg.

Both systolic and diastolic blood pressure rise with aging. The rise in diastolic blood pressure levels off at about age 60. Therefore, the number of persons with combined systolic-diastolic hypertension (SDH) shows little increase after age 60. Systolic blood pressure continues to rise with aging. Isolated systolic hypertension (ISH) thus accounts for most of the increase in hypertension with aging.

High blood pressure is the second most common chronic condition affecting both men and women.

Using these definitions, the prevalence of SDH is about 15 percent in white elderly persons and 25 percent in African-American elderly persons. The prevalence of ISH is about 15 percent (JAMA,

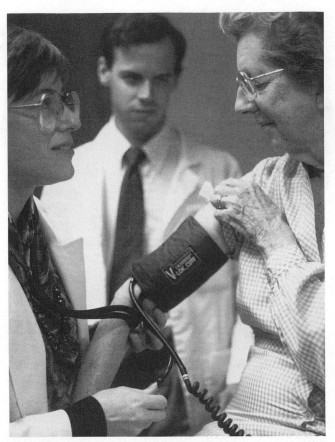

About thirty percent of persons 60–65 years old have elevated blood pressure, and forty percent of persons older than 65 years have hypertension. (Courtesy of Bowman Gray/Baptist Hospital Medical Center)

1986). Systolic hypertension is the single most important risk factor in the elderly for developing cardiovascular and cerebrovascular diseases after age itself.

Treatment of hypertension has been shown to reduce risk for both cardiovascular and cerebrovascular disease. Reduction of blood pressure to normal ranges is the goal of therapy. Both pharmacological and non-pharmacological treatments have been successful. Weight loss, exercise, and cessation of cigarette smoking have been shown to reduce blood pressure. When these methods result in normal blood pressure, no other treatment is required. When the blood pressure continues to be abnormal, the use of drugs becomes necessary. The effects and side-effects of many drugs differ substantially in elderly persons, making the choices of therapy highly individualized. Preserving quality of life is the single most important consideration when selecting drug therapy for elderly persons.

Preserving quality of life is the single most important consideration when selecting drug therapy for elderly persons.

● HEARING LOSS

Hearing loss is the third most common condition of elderly Americans of both sexes. The number of persons with hearing loss rises with age. In persons 65 to 74 years old, 24 percent have hearing loss. In persons older than 75 years old, 39 percent have hearing loss. Special populations of elderly persons, such as nursing home patients, have higher prevalence of hearing problems, rising to 70 percent (Health Interview Survey, 1981).

Although hearing loss is not life-threatening, profound disability results from poor hearing. The two most common consequences of hearing loss are depression (Jones, 1984) and social isolation (Norris, 1981). Loss of hearing impairs the person's ability to communicate. This may hinder education, social interaction, and opportunities for recreation, entertainment, and worship.

Hearing loss associated with aging is called *presbycusis*. This condition seems to be a true result of normal aging. Aging in the hearing apparatus results in most persons over the age of 40 years having some degree of hearing loss (Anderson, 1982). Several factors have been examined to explain age-related hearing loss. These include poor nutrition, high cholesterol levels, genetic factors, noise exposure, high blood pressure, and arteriosclerotic vascular disease. No single explanation emerges from these studies. Among these, genetic factors seem to be important. African-American men seem to have better preservation of hearing with age than white men (Royster, 1979).

Anatomical changes occur in the ear with aging. Changes in the external ear include a decrease in sebaceous (oil) and cerumen (wax) gland production in the skin. The resulting dryness leads to increased risk of infection. Hair follicles of the pinna begin to grow around age 40 years. In the middle ear, changes in bone structure may occur. None of the changes in the external or middle ear produce a clinically important change in hearing. Aging effects in the ear seem to be important only in the inner ear.

In the inner ear, four patterns of change occur. Degeneration in the organ of Corti results in high-frequency hearing loss. Degeneration of neurons produces loss of speech discrimination. Changes in the vascular and endolymph structure produce a flat frequency hearing loss with preservation of speech discrimination. Finally, changes in the cochlear conductive mechanism produce pure tone hearing loss. Clinical hearing loss results from a combination of one or more of these patterns.

Many elderly persons with hearing loss can be helped by hearing aid devices. Several misconceptions exist about hearing aids. It was once popular to "wait until hearing gets bad" before considering a hearing device. However, adaptation to the device is more difficult in severely impaired persons. Improvements in technology of hearing aids now allow significant help in speech discrimination. The prescription of an aid can be more individualized. The importance of early intervention when adaptation to a hearing device is easier cannot be overemphasized.

● TINNITUS

Tinnitus, or ringing in the ears, can be grouped with hearing disorders. Ringing in the ears is the fifth most common complaint in men and the seventh most common condition reported by women. This medical condition is poorly understood but is greatly annoying to patients.

Tinnitus may be a combination of several noises, described as ringing, buzzing, hissing, or chirping. Presbycusis, the changes that accompany aging, is associated with tinnitus. Hearing loss may be present or absent. Unfortunately, the precise cause is unknown and the condition is not reversible.

Treatment includes disguising the noise with "white noise." Random patterns of noise, such as that produced by radio static, help obscure the sound, particularly at night. Noise generators that produce wave or rain sounds often are helpful. Alternatively, a hearing aid to correct hearing loss may obliterate the annoying tinnitus.

● HEART DISEASE

Heart disease can take many forms. When vascular blood supply to the heart muscle is compro-

A cardiovascular health study begins with a baseline ultrasound of the carotid arteries. (Courtesy of Bowman Gray/Baptist Hospital Medical Center)

mised the muscle becomes deprived of oxygen. Decreases in blood flow in the coronary vessels leads to chest pain and impaired pumping of the heart. The result of ischemia and later muscle damage leads to congestive heart failure. Diseases in the valves of the heart can result in ischemia. Valvular disease can narrow the valve (stenosis) or cause backflow through the valve (insufficiency) and lead to heart failure. Blood vessel blockage outside of the heart leads to peripheral vascular disease.

Ischemic heart disease is by far the most common type of heart disease. Sudden occlusion in coronary blood flow causes myocardial infarction, or heart muscle death. Chronic decrease in blood flow causes heart failure.

Myocardial Infarction

Ischemic heart disease ranks fourth in chronic conditions reported by men and fifth in women. Heart disease is the most common cause of mortality in the United States at all ages. It is the most common cause of death over the age of 65 years. Seventy-two percent of all deaths from heart disease occur in persons over the age of 65 years. One out of five persons admitted to coronary care units is over the age of 70 years

---

Heart disease is the most common cause of mortality in the United States at all ages. It is the most common cause of death over the age of 65 years.

(Berman, 1979). The mortality rate from myocardial infarction in older persons is about twice that of younger persons (Kincaid, 1973).

Atherosclerosis, due to cholesterol deposition in coronary arteries, occurs more frequently than is diagnosed in life. Coronary arteriosclerosis has been found at autopsy in 46 percent of persons over the age of 60 years, and in 84 percent of persons over the age of 80 years (Medalia, 1952). Obviously, more disease is present at autopsy than is diagnosed while the person is living. Thus, a large amount of myocardial disease is "silent," that is, without apparent symptoms. Silent heart disease in older adults may be underdiagnosed.

Compounding the problem of underdiagnosis is misdiagnosis. The symptoms of heart disease differ substantially in older persons. While chest pain is still a common presenting symptom, fewer older patients experience chest pain with myocardial infarction. Shortness of breath, confusion, and gastrointestinal complaints are more common initial symptoms of myocardial infarction in the elderly. Altered perceptions of pain and atypical symptoms result in a confusing symptom presentation. Despite underestimates of the true frequency of myocardial infarction, this disease accounts for more deaths in the geriatric population than any other condition.

Congestive Heart Failure

The ability of the heart to pump blood follows the principle of supply and demand. At rest, the demand placed upon the heart is minimal. With exercise, the demand is increased. The heart has a reserve capacity available to increase work and to supply increased demand. When disease interferes with the ability of the heart to increase work, this reserve capacity is lost. Symptoms first appear with increased demand, as with exercise. As reserve capacity is lost, symptoms may appear with minimal increases in demand or at rest.

Failure of the heart to pump blood adequately is a major cause of morbidity and mortality in older Americans. Symptoms include shortness of breath, fatigue, poor exercise tolerance, and chest pain.

Three-quarters of all patients with congestive heart failure are over the age of 60 years (Smith, 1985). The rate of development of heart failure increases exponentially with age. Yet few changes

Profiles of Productive Aging

Irving Wright
Physician

"I did not want to retire altogether. Life would have been too boring and it would have been a waste of my life's experience."

Born in New York City in 1901, Irving Wright graduated from Cornell University Medical School in 1926. He taught clinical medicine at Columbia University, and became clinical professor of medicine and attending physician at New York Hospital-Cornell Medical Center in 1946, where he now serves as emeritus since 1968.

Wright's most significant contribution has been in treating heart disease with anticoagulants, a therapy that has been credited with saving or improving the lives of millions of people around the world. Anticoagulant therapy has also made possible a whole range of modern surgical techniques including organ transplants, microsurgery, and heart bypasses. Wright treated the first patient with an anticoagulant in 1938, and that patient has had an extra fifty years of life.

Wright has also made outstanding contributions in medical research, geriatrics, and the organization of the international medical community. He was instrumental in the formation of the American Heart Disease Association and was a founder of the American Federation for Aging Research. The recipient of many national and international honors, Wright also earned the Lasker award, the most prestigious prize in American medicine, and Cornell Medical School established the Irving S. Wright Professorship of Geriatrics in his honor.

Wright continued seeing patients until age 78. He now spends more time on his archeological pursuits, which have taken him to sites around the world to investigate ancient cultures, and he is tape-recording his recollections of twentieth–century medicine for Cornell Medical School. Wright's energy and curiosity are unflagging, even at age 91: "I would like to have a very comfortable chair facing a very large screen where I could see all of the things that the human race will do in the next 25 years. And just think about the direction in which the world is going."

He also marveled at the lengthened span of human life: "Looking back I wonder how I was able to accomplish so many interesting aspects of life. I suppose in part it is because I have been granted so many extra years. When I started to practice medicine, the average life expectancy was 47 years. Now it's 74 years."

Lydia Brontë

---

occur in the heart that can be directly attributed to aging. When specific diseases are excluded, congestive heart failure does not occur as a result of age alone. Accumulated damage to the heart from myocardial infarction, valvular heart disease, hypertension, and diabetes accounts for the morbidity of congestive heart failure associated with aging.

Treatment consists of aiding the heart to become more effective as a pump. Control of the blood volume through diuretics and relief of ischemia are important. Several drugs are available to aid the heart muscle directly or to reduce the resistance to heart pumping action.

Peripheral Vascular Disease

As a result of arteriosclerosis, disease of the peripheral vessels increases in frequency with age. Peripheral vessels are those vessels in the limbs. The prevalence of peripheral vascular disease is about 12 percent of individuals over the age of 65 years, rising to 20 percent of persons over the age of 75 years (Criqui, 1985).

The net effect of peripheral vascular disease is a reduction in blood delivery to the legs and arms. Symptoms include pain with walking or exercise. When blood flow is severely curtailed, tissue death and gangrene in the extremities may occur. Narrowing of the arteries facilitates the sudden occlusion of blood vessels, one of the chief causes of amputation of extremities. When accessible blockages are present, surgical bypass may be effective in preserving the limb.

● VISION PROBLEMS

The impact of visual impairment and blindness on society is tremendous, both socially and economically. Over half of all blind persons in the

United States are 65 years of age or older. Legal blindness, defined as persons whose corrected vision is less than 20/200 or whose field of vision is less than 20 degrees, occurs in 225 of every 100,000 persons. By age 85, 3,000 of every 100,000 persons are blind.

Chronic conditions cause most blindness. Blindness results from senile cataracts, glaucoma, macular degeneration, and diabetic retinopathy. Macular degeneration causes most new cases of blindness diagnosed in elderly persons.

The impact of visual impairment and blindness on society is tremendous, both socially and economically. Over half of all blind persons in the United States are 65 years of age or older.

Cataract

Cataract is the fourth most common self-reported chronic condition in women and ranks eighth in men. Not all cataracts interfere with vision. In the United States, 50 percent of the population over the age of 40 has some form of cataract. Yet cataract is a cause of legal blindness in only one of twelve cases.

Any opacity in the lens of the eye is called a cataract. Most cataracts result from changes in the protein structure of the lens. Trauma, chemical injury, or radiation injury may also cause opacities. Some types of cataracts due to specific diseases (diabetes, galactosemia, hypoparathyroidism) may be arrested by control of the underlying disease. No opacity of the lens can be reversed once it develops.

The most common form of cataract in the elderly is senile cataract, a slowly progressive opacification of the lens. Vision is lost slowly over time. There is no effective nonsurgical therapy. Surgical therapy is very effective, improving vision in 95 percent of cases.

Misconceptions about cataract surgery are common. One concerns the timing of the operation. There are only rare emergency reasons for a cataract to be removed. In the majority of cases, the only reason to remove a cataract is to help the person see better. The degree of interference

---

Voices of Creative Aging

Helen B., age 81, meets the challenge to maintain independence and cope with blindness.

At age 77 I was diagnosed with macular degeneration of the retina, a disease for which there is currently no cure.

Keeping my dignity while losing my vision was not an easy transition. It was one of the most difficult things I ever had to do. There was anger and disappointment. And I thought: "What is there for me?" My daughter got me interested in the Society for the Blind. I went there for training every day for about three months. The one thing I feel I gained more than anything was confidence. I live alone in the house my husband and I shared. It is large, but I am comfortable here and know where everything is. Living by myself and being independent give me a sense of accomplishment I find so important.

I would be in lots of trouble if I did not have a machine called the Voyager, which magnifies and projects a document. Before I got it I had to have a neighbor or my daughter read all my mail to me. It was very frustrating. Now, thanks to the machine, I can read everything—except the letters I get from people whose handwriting is really bad. If anything went wrong with this machine, I would be calling the repair people even in the middle of the night. That's how important it is in my life.

I do volunteer work for the Retired Senior Volunteer Program and the Society for the Blind. People bring work to my home—much of it to do on the telephone. I enjoy that a lot. I have people call everyday. I like to think that I am of some service. It is very difficult when you have been a person on the go, helping and doing, and then all of a sudden you can't. I won't crawl in my little shell and stay there and not be a part of the things going on around me. That's all there is to it.

Excerpt from Connie Goldman's "Late Bloomer" public radio series

with vision is the most important factor in planning surgery. Visual loss that may be acceptable for one person may be unacceptable for another. The timing of the operation is dependent on how well the person is functioning.

A second misconception is that cataracts must be "ripe" before surgical therapy. The results of surgery are the same whenever the cataract is removed. The success of postsurgical vision depends on the degree of visual impairment preoperatively. Vision after cataract surgery is always poorer than natural vision. In a severely impaired person, visual improvement may be remarkable. In mildly impaired persons, the result may be less satisfying.

When the natural lens is removed, another lens must be used to restore vision. Lenses may take the form of eyeglasses, contact lenses, or lenses implanted in the eye itself. Each of these has its benefits and disadvantages. The most natural vision results from the implantable lens. The decision to use any of these options is dependent on individual considerations.

Glaucoma

Glaucoma is a disease of increased pressure in the eye. There are two types of glaucoma: open-angle and closed-angle glaucoma. Closed-angle glaucoma occurs when the iris occludes the opening for the drainage of eye fluid. Often acute, painful symptoms are produced when the occlusion occurs. Closed-angle glaucoma may be correctable by surgery.

Over 95 percent of glaucoma is the open-angle type, the cause of which is unknown. Open-angle glaucoma is insidious and usually produces no symptoms until vision is impaired. The only means of detection is a measurement of eye pressure at eye examinations. The slow increase of eye pressure damages the retinal tissue, first causing a loss of peripheral vision and finally resulting in blindness. The damaged tissue cannot be restored, but further damage may be prevented.

Treatment is designed to reduce eye pressure. For the majority of patients, this involves the use of topical eye drugs. Surgical therapy may be useful in certain cases.

Macular Degeneration

The macula is the region of the retina where the highest degree of visual resolution occurs.

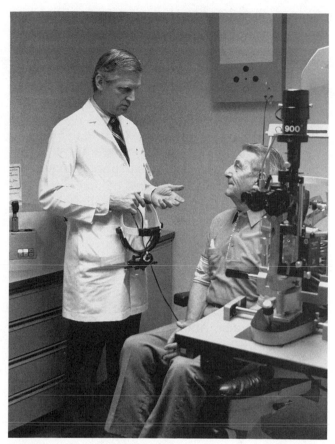

The only means of glaucoma detection is a measurement of eye pressure at eye examinations. (Courtesy of Bowman Gray/Baptist Hospital Medical Center)

This area is very small and is located centrally in the retina. Detailed vision results when the lens focuses on this region. Small amounts of damage in this area lead to profound loss of vision.

The causes of macular degeneration are not fully understood, but may be related to the choroidal vascular blood supply. Macular degeneration is the second leading cause of blindness. Most patients who experience this degeneration are 65 years of age or older.

Treatment with laser photocoagulation can be useful. For some specific causes, drug therapy is available.

Diabetic Retinopathy

The third leading cause of blindness is diabetic retinopathy. Diabetes produces changes in the blood supply to the retina. Often the first damage produces macular degeneration. Leakage of blood from the retinal arteries causes hemorrhages and exudates in the retina, progressively interfering with vision.

Since the changes that occur with diabetes take time, it is often ten years or more after the onset of diabetes before visual loss begins. For persons who develop diabetes in middle years, visual problems are often first seen as the person ages.

Control of diabetes may slow or prevent the changes that occur in the retina over time. Control of blood sugar is the single most important preventive measure. Laser photocoagulation can treat the vascular changes of diabetes, often restoring vision. Careful annual evaluation of the retina in diabetics is essential to preserve vision.

● DIABETES

Diabetes is common in the elderly, reported as the sixth most common condition in men and eighth in women. About one in five persons over the age of 70 have diabetes. Diabetes occurs six to eight times more frequently in the elderly than in younger adults (Wilson, 1986).

As a person ages, tolerance to carbohydrates declines. Two factors, physical inactivity and obesity, affect carbohydrate intolerance. About 20 percent of elderly persons show intolerance to carbohydrates, but this increases to 50 percent of those who are inactive or obese. Fasting blood glucose changes little with aging, but postprandial (after eating) glucose levels are higher with aging. Insulin secretion and hepatic production of glucose seem to be unaffected by aging. However, decreased clearance of insulin and defective transport of glucose into muscle and fat cells do occur. This leads to higher blood glucose levels in aging populations. The relationship of diabetes to glucose intolerance of aging is unclear.

When the blood sugar exceeds a fasting value of 140 milligrams per deciliter, or a two hour post-prandial level of 160 milligrams per deciliter, diabetes is present. A blood sugar level of 200 milligrams percent at any time also defines diabetes. Diabetes mellitus can be grouped into two types, depending on the relative amount of insulin.

The most common type of diabetes at all ages is Type II, or non-insulin dependent diabetes. Insulin levels may be normal or high. Diabetes seems to result from a failure of the cell to respond properly to insulin. Non-insulin dependent diabetes has hereditary associations and is aggravated by obesity. Type I diabetes, or insulin dependent diabetes, is more common in younger persons. In insulin dependent diabetes there is an absolute reduction in insulin levels.

The consequences of diabetes result from damage of organ systems. Elderly persons with diabetes have more coronary artery disease, peripheral vascular disease, blindness, neuropathy, and kidney disease than non-diabetic persons.

Dietary therapy is the cornerstone of management of both types of diabetes. Thus, timing meals and tailoring the amount of calories is essential to control of blood sugar. Type I diabetics have an absolute lack of insulin and require insulin injections. Type II diabetics have normal or increased amounts of insulin. When the diet is stabilized, the use of hypoglycemic drugs is often successful in controlling the blood sugar. If oral drugs are not successful, insulin injections are necessary to achieve glucose control in Type II diabetes.

Elderly persons with diabetes have more coronary artery disease, peripheral vascular disease, blindness, neuropathy, and kidney disease than non-diabetic persons.

● HARDENING OF THE ARTERIES

The term "hardening of the arteries" has been used to describe effects attributed to arteriosclerosis. Plaques of cholesterol and calcium in vessel walls reduce the diameter of arteries. The affected vessels may narrow to a point at which decreased amounts of blood are delivered to various organs. The results of the decrease in blood flow, termed ischemia, results in symptoms unique to each organ. In the heart, chest pain may appear. In the legs, pain with walking occurs.

At one time, decrease in brain blood flow was felt to be the cause of memory impairment in aged persons. Hardening of the arteries became synonymous with dementia. Authorities now feel that these effects are the result of specific disease, rather than a generalized decrease in blood flow. There is no evidence that cerebral blood flow declines with age without specific occlusion in blood vessels. Impairment of memory and dementia are due to specific diseases in the brain substance (see Chapter 24, **Mental Disorders**).

● CEREBROVASCULAR DISEASE

Cerebrovascular disease is the third most common cause of death in persons over the age of 65. While cerebrovascular disease, or stroke, is a prominent cause of death, disability from stroke is far more common. About 140,000 persons die of stroke annually, but 1,830,000 survivors of stroke were counted in 1984 (Posner, 1984). Stroke ranks ninth in the top ten list of chronic conditions in men. The neurological damage from stroke results in major disability in survivors.

Stroke occurs when a part of the brain is suddenly damaged and the effects last for longer than twenty-four hours. Damage that resolves in less than twenty-four hours is called a transient ischemic attack (TIA). Different kinds of vascular damage lead to stroke. The most common cause is atherosclerosis, although hypertensive vascular disease, arteritis, or inflammation in the arterial walls may also cause stroke.

Stroke ranks ninth in the top ten list of chronic conditions in men. The neurological damage from stroke results in major disability in survivors.

Damage to the brain can occur in two forms: infarction or stroke. Infarction, or cessation of blood flow, leads to death of brain tissue. Infarction can occur when an artery is occluded by atherosclerosis or hypertensive vascular disease. Infarction may also occur when a piece of clot, or embolus, breaks off from the heart or larger vessel and travels to the brain. Hemorrhage, resulting from the rupture of a blood vessel, may also cause brain tissue death. Hemorrhage usually occurs in vessels weakened by aneurysm, by hypertensive vascular disease, or bleeding disorders.

The clinical results of stroke are dependent on the area of the brain affected. Large infarctions of brain areas can lead to paralysis of half of the body, or lesser paralysis in smaller infarctions. About one in five cases of dementia are caused by small infarctions in the deep white matter of the brain.

Treatment of strokes once the brain is damaged is supportive. Rehabilitation aimed at recovery of function is paramount. Preventive measures, such as control of blood pressure, are much more important than treatment modalities.

Transient ischemic attacks may be considered warning signs of potential stroke. Search for a cause of embolus must be made. Daily long-term aspirin use, or anticoagulation with other drugs, is effective in reducing the risk of stroke.

● VARICOSE VEINS

Varicose veins represent the sixth most common chronic condition in women and the tenth most common condition in men. Varicose means "worm-like" and aptly describes cords of veins that appear in the lower extremities.

The lower extremities are drained by two venous systems, the deep veins and the superficial veins. Multiple connections occur between the systems. Because of upright posture, blood tends to pool in the lower extremities and must be assisted back up towards the heart. This assist occurs because of valves inside the venous system. When blood is pushed or pumped by muscular activity towards the heart, the valves prevent blood from flowing downwards with the force of gravity. When these valves become incompetent, blood tends to pool in the lower extremities. This venous hypertension leads to edema, or swelling, and to chronic skin changes including ulcerations.

Incompetent veins in the superficial system lead to venous hypertension. Since these veins are just under the surface, the skin is easily expanded outward, producing dilated, tortuous, worm-like cords of veins. Early on, these changes are merely cosmetic. Complications from superficial varicosities are rare.

Incompetent veins in the deep system are not as readily apparent, but are far more serious. Sludging of blood in the deep system may lead to the formation of blood clots. These clots further shunt the blood to the superficial system and increase venous hypertension. The major complication occurs when pieces of the clot break off and travel towards the heart.

Venous thromboembolism, the traveling of a

clot through the venous system, usually results in the clot being filtered in the lungs. Symptoms produced by this clot depend on the size of the piece. When large pieces are filtered in the lungs, pulmonary embolization occurs. This sudden blockage in blood supply to the lungs may produce profound symptoms, including death. Pulmonary embolism is estimated to occur about 650,000 times annually, with 38 percent of cases being fatal (Freiman, 1965). Only about half the cases are recognized before death in autopsy series. Conditions that lead to pulmonary embolus are more common in elderly persons, including immobilization, prolonged bed rest, hip fractures, obesity, congestive heart failure, and malignancy.

Factors that predispose to the development of varicose veins are more common in elderly persons, including obesity, previous thrombophlebitis, multiple pregnancies, and genetic history. The skin may become dusky in response to venous hypertension, and spontaneous ulcerations may develop. Relieving edema of the lower extremities by elastic support hose and elevation of the feet may help promote healing.

● CANCER

Malignant neoplasms, or cancer, do not appear in the top ten lists in the first two decades of aging. By ages above 85 years, cancer is a common problem. There is clear evidence that rates for certain cancers increase with aging. In autopsy studies, almost one-third of persons dying over the age of 65 years have one or more forms of cancer (Suen, 1979). Not all types of cancer are associated with aging. The incidence of certain types of cancer declines with age. For example, risk of cervical cancer declines after age 65. Several types of cancer do seem to increase with aging, including cancers of the prostate, breast, colon, lung, and endometrium, and certain types of leukemia.

Prostatic Carcinoma

Prostatic carcinoma is the most common form of cancer in men over the age of 80 years. This type of cancer is rare in men under the age of 40 years. In men, cancer of the prostate is the third leading cause of cancer death. Detection in an asymptomatic stage is important. By the time

A patient undergoes a test to determine lung capacity by blowing into a machine that electronically determines output. (Courtesy of Bowman Gray/Baptist Hospital Medical Center)

symptoms occur, only half of all persons will have disease in a potentially curable stage.

Breast Cancer

Breast cancer is the most common form of cancer in women. Breast cancer in women begins to increase in frequency at about age 40 years. The number of cases of breast cancer continues to increase up to age 80 years. Since early detection may result in a cure, a mammogram is important for every woman as she ages. Beginning at age 50 years, a mammogram should be done every one to two years.

Colon Cancer

Cancer of the colon in both men and women increases in frequency beginning at about age 60 years. Change in character of stool or bleeding in the stool are important symptoms. Detection of early colon cancer is possible by annual examination of the stool for occult bleeding. Additional studies by radiological or visual inspection of the colon can increase detection of early cancers, but may not be cost-effective or acceptable to patients.

Cancer of the Lung

Lung cancer increases with age in smokers, due to longer exposure to the carcinogens in cigarette smoke. Early detection of lung cancer is almost impossible. Treatment for large-cell carcinoma of the lung is currently inadequate. Considerable improvement in treatment for small-cell carcinoma of the lung has been made.

Endometrial Carcinoma

Endometrial carcinoma increases in women with aging. Usual symptoms are bleeding after menopause. Surgical therapy is often curative.

Hematological Neoplasia

Malignancies of the bone marrow and lymphoid cells are much less common than the cancers listed above, but some tend to occur more frequently in the elderly. The most common form of leukemia in elderly persons is chronic lymphocytic leukemia. The frequency of this leukemia increases after the age of 50 years. More than half of the cases of multiple myeloma occur in persons over the age of 70 years. Macroglobulinemia is similar to chronic lymphocytic leukemia and follows an indolent course. Certain malignancies of the myeloid cells also increase with age. Over half the cases of acute myelocytic leukemia occur in persons over the age of 60 years. Polycythemia vera increases markedly after the age of 50 years.

● OSTEOPOROSIS

Lower extremity orthopedic impairment, due to hip fracture or osteoarthritis of the knees, does not appear in the top ten listing until the eighth decade of life. Most of the disability that occurs in this condition is due to osteoporosis.

Osteoporosis and osteopenia are the most common conditions associated with fracture of the hip. It has been estimated that 33 percent of women and 17 percent of men may experience a hip fracture by age 90.

Osteoporosis and osteopenia are the most common conditions associated with fracture of the hip. It has been estimated that 33 percent of women and 17 percent of men may experience a hip fracture by age 90 (Melton, 1987). Other fractures are common with osteoporotic bones. Fracture of the vertebrae occurs in about one-half of women (JAMA, 1984). These vertebral fractures result in loss of height and spinal curvature. Fracture of the forearm is the next most common fracture seen in osteoporotic persons. The mor-

bidity and pain that accompany fractures is considerable.

Thinning of the bones, or osteoporosis, is one of the most common bone conditions of the geriatric population. A definition of osteoporosis is the loss of sufficient calcium from bone so that fractures occur. The presence of spontaneous fractures or fractures from minimal trauma is easy to detect. However, predicting which patients will suffer from fractures or the degree of bone loss in an individual person is much more difficult. About one-third of bone minerals must be lost before changes are apparent on radiographs. Bone loss that is apparent on X-rays or other tests is called osteopenia. Not all persons who have osteopenia will develop fractures. Only a small proportion of osteopenic persons ultimately develop a bone fracture.

Osteoporosis is a silent disease. Loss of bone mineralization occurs without symptoms. Detection in the late stages of the disease is not difficult. The skeleton is composed of two different types of bone: cortical and trabecular. Cortical bone is found in the bones of the wrist and hip. Trabecular bone makes up the vertebral column. Radiographs of the bone detect thinning of the bones when about 50 percent of bone is lost.

Other tests can detect early signs of osteoporosis. Single photon densitometry can detect loss of cortical bone at the wrist. Dual photon densitometry can detect osteopenia in trabecular bone. Quantitative computed tomography can detect osteopenia in the trabecular vertebral skeleton. The drawback with any of these methods is that a single low reading is difficult to interpret. Only when measurements are taken over time can the progression of bone loss be seen.

Osteoporosis must be distinguished from a similar condition, osteomalacia. Osteomalacia is a disease of bone matrix formation and mineralization. Osteomalacia and osteoporosis may coexist. Diseases such as malabsorption, malnutrition, renal disease, and hyperparathyroidism may cause osteomalacia. Deficiencies of calcium or phosphorous and certain drugs may lead to osteomalacia.

Bone loss in women begins at about age 30. From that age the skeleton begins progressively to lose minerals. Thus the amount of bone mass in the skeleton at age 30 determines the amount

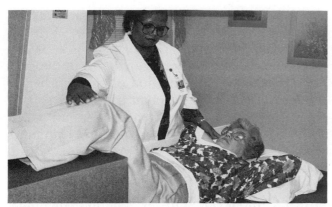

A bone densitometer is being used in a women's study on osteoporosis. The study is called F.I.T. for Fracture Intervention Trial. (Courtesy of Bowman Gray/Baptist Hospital Medical Center)

of bone remaining in the geriatric age. Exercise, race, adequate calcium intake, and adequate vitamin D intake determine the amount of calcification in skeletal bone. Intake of 1,500 milligrams of elemental calcium is recommended by the National Institute of Health for postmenopausal women.

At menopause bone loss accelerates. The loss of estrogen results in further bone loss in women. Estrogen replacement, if started soon after menopause, can prevent postmenopausal bone loss (Lindsay, 1987). How estrogens act to prevent bone loss is not known. Fracture rates in cortical bone are lower in women taking estrogens than in women who do not take estrogens.

Treatment of osteoporosis after fractures have occurred is more difficult. Several drugs have been tried, but data suggesting that future fracture rates are improved is scarce.

● URINARY INCONTINENCE

Urinary incontinence is more common in elderly persons. Surprisingly, this chronic condition does not make the top ten list in any decade. Underreporting of incontinence is common, perhaps due to embarrassment or failure to accept incontinence as a treatable condition. Urinary incontinence affects between 15 percent and 30 percent of community-dwelling elderly persons (Mohide, 1986; Diokno, 1986). In hospital settings about one-third of elderly persons are affected (Seir, 1987) and in nursing homes roughly half of all persons (Ouslander, 1982).

The impact of urinary incontinence is tremen-

dous. In community settings, embarrassment leads to social isolation and stress on caregivers. Urinary incontinence is among the chief precipitators for admission to nursing homes. Devices for the management of incontinence represent a large health-care cost in economic terms in this country. Complications of incontinence include skin breakdown, rashes, and urinary infections.

Urinary incontinence is among the chief precipitators for admission to nursing homes.

Under normal circumstances, the bladder fills with urine and serves as a reservoir between voiding. Pressure and urge to urinate increases with bladder filling. The urge to urinate can be suppressed by voluntary control in the frontal cortex of the brain. Normally, this is under voluntary control. Voiding occurs when the bladder muscle, the detrusor, contracts and squeezes out urine. Whenever bladder pressure increases above the opposing urethral pressure, urine flow occurs. Voiding is prevented by opposing pressure from the bladder outlet, the urethra.

Urinary incontinence is a heterogeneous condition with many different causes. The differing types can be classified into stress incontinence, urge incontinence, mixed incontinence, and functional incontinence. The management of incontinence depends on proper classification.

Urge Incontinence

The most common type of geriatric incontinence, urge incontinence, occurs when the bladder muscle, the detrusor, spontaneously contracts and the bladder is suddenly emptied. Causes of urge incontinence are not always clear. Spontaneous contraction of the bladder muscle may occur without obvious disease. Lack of frontal lobe voluntary inhibition of urination, as occurs in Alzheimer's disease or other dementias, is a common reason for this type of incontinence. Damage to the frontal lobes or connecting tracts, as occurs in stroke or Parkinson's disease, may result in urge incontinence. Irritations in the bladder itself, with urinary tract infections, stones, or tumors, may cause spontaneous voiding.

Stress Incontinence

The second most common type of urinary incontinence is stress incontinence. This occurs when the urethra or supporting pelvic muscles fail to provide resistance to voiding. The most common reason for this in women is pelvic muscle weakness. Pelvic muscle weakness is associated with multiple pregnancies and with obesity. Increase in bladder pressure, such as occurs with a cough or a sneeze, overcomes resistance to voiding, resulting in leakage of small amounts of urine.

Urinary incontinence can result from combinations of overactive detrusor muscles and weakness in the bladder outlet. When there is outlet obstruction, as in men with prostatic hypertrophy, the bladder may fail to empty completely. Bladder contractions increase in strength until the outlet obstruction is overwhelmed, and urine flow occurs.

Functional Incontinence

Functional incontinence comprises a wide range of problems with mobility, dexterity, and motivation. An awareness of the need to void may be present, but the person is unable to get to the toilet before spontaneous voiding occurs.

When the cause of urinary incontinence is understood, specific therapy may be planned. Detrusor overactivity, leading to urge incontinence, may be suppressed by drugs that inhibit bladder contraction. Unfortunately, these methods are not uniformly effective. Stress incontinence may be improved by weight loss, the use of pelvic floor exercises, or alpha-adrenergic drugs that increase sphincter tone. Outlet obstruction may be amenable to surgical correction.

Specific therapy for urinary incontinence is seldom perfect. A timed schedule of prompted voiding is often the best method of keeping the person dry. Pads and special undergarments are valuable if other measures fail.

● DISORDERS OF BOWEL FUNCTION AND CONSTIPATION

Constipation is a major problem for elderly persons. About one-third of women and one-fourth of men self-reported constipation in a health survey (Hale, 1986). The definition of constipation is unclear. Physicians define constipation by the frequency of bowel movements and the consistency of the stool. Patients tend to use different definitions of constipation, particularly if defecation is difficult or associated with straining. One-half of men and two-thirds of women who reported constipation had daily bowel movements (Whitehead, 1989).

Whether or not bowel function changes with aging is difficult to determine. Frequency of stooling may not be different among elderly and younger populations (Connell, 1965). A working definition of fewer than three bowel movements per week may be used for constipation. However, even one bowel movement per week may be normal if not associated with abnormal stool consistency or painful defecation.

> Constipation is a major problem for elderly persons. About one-third of women and one-fourth of men self-reported constipation in a health survey.

Differing definitions of constipation among elderly persons and healthcare providers may in part be cultural. Fifty years ago, the medical profession promulgated a theory of autotoxicity. Many diseases were felt to be due to the accumulation of toxins in fecal material. Frequent purging to remove these toxins was commonly recommended, both to treat illness and to maintain health. Annual doses of sulfur and molasses were recommended for both humans and farm animals. This belief in the need to cleanse the body of fecal material has led to frequent laxative use in the American population. Overuse is particularly common among the elderly who were taught that this was good health maintenance.

Almost all laxatives in this country are available without prescription. Over 700 products are sold at a cost of $400 million dollars. One-fourth of elderly persons surveyed had used laxatives in the month preceding the survey (Whitehead, 1989). This generous use of laxatives makes the true frequency of constipation difficult to determine.

The natural urge to defecate comes from muscle and nerve complexes in the gut wall. The stimulus for bowel movement is easily suppressed and may be affected by several disease states and drugs. Many drugs, including narcotics, antacids, antihypertensive drugs, neuroleptic drugs, anti-parkinsonian drugs, and central nervous system active drugs exacerbate constipation. Diseases of the bowel and central nervous system also are associated with constipation.

Infrequent use of stimulant laxatives is highly effective in relieving constipation and carries very little risk. Chronic use of stimulant laxatives such as phenothalein, senna, cascara, anthroquinones, and bisacodyl results in the abolition of the natural urge to defecate. Chronic use of these laxatives alters colonic motility, leading to dependency on laxatives for any defecation. Intractable constipation, or "laxative abuse colon," is treatable only by surgical diverting procedures on the colon.

The first step in dealing with chronic constipation is to exclude functional or mechanical disease. The most common remaining cause of constipation is a fiber-poor diet. The addition of fiber to the diet alone may alleviate constipation. Two additional steps may be helpful. Since the colon serves to conserve body water, the provision of at least two liters of fluid daily acts to prevent dry stool. Finally, bowel function is in part a trained stimulus. Observing a daily routine for bowel elimination, particularly soon after a meal, assists in daily function. The effect of exercise on colonic motility is poorly understood. Observation suggests that active elderly persons rarely experience constipation, while bed-bound persons have high frequencies of constipation.

Organizations

American Cancer Society
1599 Clifford Rd., NE
Atlanta, GA 30329
(800) 227-2345
(404) 320-3333

American Chronic Pain Association
257 Old Haymaker Rd.
Monroeville, PA 15146
(916) 632-0922
(412) 856-9676

The Arthritis Foundation
1314 Spring St., NW
Atlanta, GA 30309

American Heart Association
7320 Greenville Ave.
Dallas, TX 75231
(214) 750-5300

Hearing Helpline
The Better Hearing Institute
5021-B Backlick Rd.
Annandale, VA 22003
(800) 327-9355 (outside VA)
(800) 424-8576 (VA)

National Arthritis and Musculoskeletal and Skin Diseases Information
Box AMS
Bethesda, MD 20892
(301) 468-3235

National Association for Hearing and Speech Action
10801 Rockville Pike
Rockville, MD 20852
(800) 638-8255

National Center for Vision and Aging
111 East 59th St.
New York, NY 10022
(800) 334-5497
(212) 355-2200

National Digestive Diseases Clearinghouse
Box NDDIC
Bethesda, MD 20892
(301) 468-6344

National Health Information Center
P.O. Box 1133
Washington, DC 20013
(800) 336-4797 (outside MD)
(301) 565-4167

National Heart, Lung, and Blood Institute
Building 31, Room 4A21
Bethesda, MD 20892
(301) 496-4236

National Institute on Deafness and Other Communication Disorders
Information Office
9000 Rockville Pike
Bethesda, MD 20892
(301) 496-5751

National Kidney Foundation
30 East 33rd St.
New York, NY 10016
(212) 889-2210

**National Kidney and Urologic Diseases
   Clearinghouse**
Box NKUDIC
Bethesda, MD 20892
(301) 468-6345

National Stroke Association
300 East Hampden Ave. Suite 240
Englewood, CO 80110
(303) 762-9922

References

Anderson, R. G., and W. L. Meyerhoff. "Otological Manifestations of Aging." *Otolaryngeal Clinics of North America* Vol. 15 (1982): 353–70.

Berman, N. D. "The Elderly Patient in the Coronary Care Unit; I: Acute Myocardial Infarction." *Journal of the American Geriatric Society* Vol. 27 (1979): 145–51.

Connell, A. M., and others. "Variations in Bowel Habit in Two Population Samples." *British Medical Journal* Vol. 1 (1965): 1095.

"Consensus Conference: Osteoporosis 1984." *Journal of the American Medical Association (JAMA)* Vol. 252 (1984): 799.

Criqui, M. H., A. Fronek, E. Barrett-Conner, and others. "The Prevalence of Peripheral Arterial Disease in a Defined Population." *Circulation* Vol. 71 (1985): 510.

Diokno, A. C., B. M. Brock, M. B. Brown, and A. R. Herzog. "Prevalence of Urinary Incontinence and Other Urological Symptoms in the Non-Institutionalized Elderly." *Journal of Urology* Vol. 136 (1986): 1022.

Freiman, D. G., J. Suyemoto, and S. Wessler. "Frequency of Pulmonary Embolism in Man." *New England Journal of Medicine* Vol. 272 (1965): 1278–80.

Hale, W. E., and others. "Symptom Prevalence in the Elderly: An Evaluation of Age, Sex, Disease, and Medication Use." *Journal of the American Geriatrics Society* Vol. 34 (1986): 333.

"Health Interview Survey, 1981." U.S. Department of Health and Human Services, National Center of Health Statistics, unpublished.

Jones, D. A., and others. "Hearing Difficulty and Its Psychological Implications for the Elderly." *Journal of Epidemiological and Community Health* Vol. 38 (1984): 75.

Kincaid, D. T., and R. E. Botti. "Acute Myocardial Infarction in the Elderly." *Chest* Vol. 64 (1973): 170.

"Late Bloomer" audio cassette. Available from Connie Goldman Productions, 926 Second Street, Suite 201, Santa Barbara, CA 90403. (310) 393-6801.

Lindsay, R. "Estrogens in Prevention and Treatment of Osteoporosis." In *The Osteoporotic Syndrome.* Ed. L. V. Avioli. Orlando, FL: Grune & Stratton, 1987.

Medalia, L. S., and P. D. White. "Disease of the Aged: Analysis of Pathological Observations in 1,251 Autopsy Protocols in Old Persons." *Journal of the American Medical Association (JAMA)* Vol. 149 (1952): 1433.

Melton, L. J. III, and B. L. Riggs. "Epidemiology of Age-Related Factors." In *The Osteoporotic Syndrome.* Ed. L. V. Avioli. Orlando, FL: Grune & Stratton, 1987.

Modhide, E. A. "The Prevalence and Scope of Urinary Incontinence." *Clinics in Geriatric Medicine* Vol. 2 (1986): 639.

Norris, M. L., and D. R. Cunningham. "Social Impact of Hearing Loss in the Aged." *Journal of Gerontology* Vol. 36 (1981): 727.

Ouslander, J. G., R. L. Kane, and I. B. Abrass. "Urinary Incontinence in Elderly Nursing Home Patients." *Journal of the American Medical Association (JAMA)* Vol. 248 (1982): 1194–98.

Posner, J. D., K. M. Gorman, and A. Woldow. "Stroke in the Elderly; I: Epidemiology." *Journal of the American Geriatrics Society* Vol. 32 (1984): 95.

"Report of the Working Group on Hypertension in the Elderly." *Journal of the American Medical Association (JAMA)* Vol. 256 (1986): 70.

Royster, L. H., and W. G. Thomas. "Age Effect Hearing Levels for a White Nonindustrial Noise Exposed Population and Their Use in Evaluating Industrial Hearing Conservation Programs." *Annals of Industrial Hygiene Association Journal* Vol. 40 (1979): 504–11.

Sier, H., J. Ouslander, and S. Orzeck. "Urinary Incontinence Among Geriatric Patients in an Acute-Care Hospital." *Journal of the American Medical Association (JAMA)* Vol. 257 (1987): 1767–71.

Smith, W. M. "Epidemiology of Congestive Heart Failure." *American Journal of Cardiology* Vol. 55 (1985): 3A.

Suen, K. C., L. L. Law, and V. Yermakov. "Cancer and Old Age: An Autopsy Study of 3,535 Patients Over 65 Years Old." *Cancer* Vol. 33 (1979): 1164–68.

Whitehead, W. E., and others. "Constipation in the Elderly Living at Home. Definition, Prevalence and Relationship to Lifestyle and Health Status." *Journal of the American Geriatrics Society* Vol. 37 (1989): 423–29.

Wilson, P. W. F., K. M. Anderson, and W. B. Kannel. "Epidemiology of Diabetes in the Elderly." *American Journal of Medicine* Vol. 80, no. 5A (1986): 3–9.

Additional Reading

The American Cancer Society Cancer Book: Prevention, Detection, Diagnosis, Treatment, Rehabilitation, Cure. New York: Doubleday, 1986.

Becker, Gaylene. *Growing Old in Silence.* Berkeley, CA: University of California Press, 1980.

Burgio, Kathryn, and others. *Staying Dry: A Practical Guide to Bladder Control.* Johns Hopkins University Press, 1989.

Chalker, Rebecca, and Kristene Whitmore, M.D. *Overcoming Bladder Disorders.* New York: Harper & Row, 1990.

The Complete Book of Cancer Prevention: Food, Lifestyles and Medical Care to Keep You Healthy. Emmaus, PA: Rodale Press, 1988.

Foley, Conn, M.D., and H. F. Pizer. *The Stroke Fact Book: Everything You Want and Need to Know About Stroke—From Prevention to Rehabilitation.* Golden Valley, MN: Courage Press, 1990.

Fries, James F. *Arthritis: A Comprehensive Guide to Understanding Your Arthritis.* Reading, MA: Addison-Wesley, 1986.

Gach, Michael R. *Arthritis Relief at Your Fingertips: The Complete Self-Care Guide to Easing Aches and Pains Without Drugs.* New York: Warner Books, 1989.

Himber, Charlotte. *How to Survive Hearing Loss.* Washington, DC: Gallaudet University Press, 1989.

Janowitz, Henry, M.D. *Your Gut Feelings: A Complete Guide to Living Better with Intestinal Problems.* New York: Oxford University Press, 1987.

The Johns Hopkins Medical Handbook: The 100 Major Medical Disorders of People Over 50. Eds. Simeon Margolis, M.D., and Hamilton Moses, M.D. New York: Rebus, 1992.

Klieman, Charles, M.D. *Save Your Arteries. Save Your Life.* New York: Warner Books, 1987.

Kushner, Irving, ed. *Understanding Arthritis.* New York: Charles Scribner's Sons, 1984.

Kwiterovich, Peter O. *Beyond Cholesterol: The Johns Hopkins Guide to Avoiding Heart Diseases.* Baltimore, MD: Johns Hopkins University Press, 1989.

Learning to Live Well With Diabetes. Eds. Neysa C. Jensen and Michael P. Moore. Minnetonka, MN: International Diabetes Center, 1987.

Lesser, Gershon M., M.D. and Larry Strauss. *When You Have Chest Pains: A Guide to Cardiac and Noncardiac Causes and What You Can Do About Them.* Los Angeles, CA: Lowell House, 1989.

Lorig, Kate, and James F. Fries. *The Arthritis Handbook: A Tested Self-Management Program for Coping with Your Arthritis.* Reading, MA: Addison-Wesley, 1986.

Mayes, Kathleen. *Osteoporosis: Brittle Bones and the Calcium Crisis.* Santa Barbara, CA: Pennant Books, 1986.

Moskowitz, Roland W., and Marie R. Haug, eds. *Arthritis and the Elderly.* New York: Springer, 1986.

Notelovitz, Morris, and Marsha Ware. *Stand Tall! The Informed Woman's Guide to Preventing Osteoporosis.* Gainesville, FL: Triad, 1982.

Peck, William A., and Louis V. Avioli. *Osteoporosis: The Silent Thief.* Glenview, IL: Scott, Foresman, 1987.

The Physician's Guide to Cataracts, Glaucoma, and Other Eye Problems. Ed. John Eden, M.D. New York: Consumer Reports Books, 1992.

Thompson, W. Grant, M.D. *Gut Reactions: Understanding Symptoms of the Digestive Tract.* New York: Plenum Press, 1989.

Trieschmann, Roberta B. *Aging with a Disability.* New York: Demon Publications, 1987.

Newsletter

The HIP Report (Help for Incontinent People). Quarterly. HIP, Inc., P.O. Box 544, Union, SC 29379.

David R. Thomas, M.D.

Oral Health and Aging

• Oral Health Issues Facing Older Adults • Oral Anatomy, Physiology, and Changes Due to Aging
• Oral Conditions Commonly Associated with Aging • Interactions Between Systemic Diseases and Oral Health
• Nutrition and Oral Health • Special Problems of the Disabled or Frail Elderly • Preventive Strategies

Oral health is an important component of overall well-being. It includes the health of salivary glands, soft tissues of the mouth, as well as teeth. Oral diseases can cause pain and discomfort, interfere with chewing and nutrition, compromise speech, decrease self-esteem, and contribute to general health problems (Smith, 1979; Ettinger, 1987). Additionally, with the emergence of chronic systemic disorders, it is especially important that good oral health be attained and then maintained through effective preventive regimens.

With age, changes in teeth and mouth may occur. Some of the changes are due to natural aging processes, but many of the changes attributed to aging are actually due to systemic disease, the consequences of chronic oral disease, or medications.

There is a myth that losing teeth is a normal part of aging. In fact, tooth loss is not a normal part of aging. Teeth are most commonly lost because of oral disease or traumatic accidents. Oral and dental disease can usually be prevented or halted with appropriate dental treatment and good preventive programs, including regu-

---

Oral health is an important component of overall well-being. It includes the health of salivary glands, soft tissues of the mouth, as well as teeth.

---

lar teeth cleaning. The single most important preventive strategy for avoiding oral disease is daily plaque removal (brushing and flossing).

● ORAL HEALTH ISSUES FACING OLDER ADULTS

As people grow older they are at greater risk of experiencing oral diseases. Some changes in oral disease risk factors include:

- Increased risk of oral cancer associated with age; 95 percent of all oral cancers occur in persons over 40 years of age, and the average age at time of diagnosis is about 60 (Silverman, 1985).
- Susceptiblity to cavities (dental caries); the risk of developing cavities is actually greater for some older persons than for children (Beck, 1985) (see attrition, abrasion, recession, and xerostomia under **Oral Conditions Commonly Associated With Aging**).
- Decreased dexterity and ability to maneuver a toothbrush and dental floss may result in higher plaque levels and increase the risk for caries and periodontal disease.
- Termination of dental insurance benefits as well as lower retirement income may result in fewer dental appointments with less preventive care or treatment of early disease.
- Over-the-counter or prescription drugs can reduce salivary flow (xerostomia), profoundly effecting oral health.

Common Terms in Dental Treatment

Scaling and root planing: Removal of calculus from the crowns and the roots of the teeth

Amalgam (silver filling): Used to replace missing tooth structure and seal the tooth against bacterial entry

Composite: A tooth-colored filling usually used for fillings in the front teeth

Crown: Covers the coronal aspect (or crown) of the tooth; it replaces tooth structure lost to caries or trauma and provides strength to the tooth; it may be fabricated out of gold, nonprecious metals, or porcelain

Bridge: An appliance to replace one or several missing teeth; a dental bridge spans a void (like a highway bridge) and is anchored solidly at each end; an artificial tooth replaces the missing one and is held in place by connections to crowns on the adjacent teeth; a bridge cannot be removed and requires special techniques for proper cleaning

Partial denture: Used to replace one or many missing teeth when some natural teeth are present; the partial denture is held in place by the remaining natural teeth but is removed for cleaning and at night to let the oral tissues rest

Complete denture: Used to replace either all of the upper or all of the lower teeth or both; like the partial denture, it is removed for cleaning and at night

Implant: A biocompatible screw-like fixture inserted into the alveolar bone, which can then be used to anchor missing teeth or dentures

Veneer: A covering of composite or porcelain over the front surface of the tooth to cover discoloration, rebuild chips or cracks in the tooth, or to close gaps between teeth

Root canal: Removal of an infected or necrotic (dead) tooth pulp and filling the remaining pulp chamber with an inert, biocompatible material to seal the chamber from bacterial invasion

In addition to these risk factors, oral health can affect a person's general well being. For example, many oral diseases can adversely affect systemic disease, and many systemic diseases or treatments may profoundly affect oral health adversely. Disabled older people or those whose functions are compromised need special preventive care to maintain their teeth and oral function.

Access to care can be difficult for physical or financial reasons. A dental office may not be wheelchair accessible or transportation may be difficult to arrange. Since Medicare does not pay for dental treatment (except repair of fractured jaws in a hospital setting), older persons with limited income may be unable to afford routine dental treatment. Medicaid may cover basic dental treatment, but this coverage varies from state to state. The use of dental care may be affected by age, gender, race, income, education, perceived need, presence of teeth, and insurance coverage (Jones, 1990).

● ORAL ANATOMY, PHYSIOLOGY, AND CHANGES DUE TO AGING

Salivary Glands

There are three major pairs of salivary glands (parotid, submandibular, sublingual) and several minor glands in the lips, palate, and cheek. The primary function of these glands is to produce saliva. Saliva contains immunoglobulins, calcium salts, and other proteins that play a critical role in the preservation of oral health. The importance of these salivary components can be exemplified in salivary IgA, an immunoglobulin that inhibits bacterial adherence to mucosal surfaces and neutralizes viruses and toxins. Salivary secretion is controlled primarily by the autonomic nervous system through parasympathetic and sympathetic innervation.

In the past, salivary secretion was believed to be reduced as age increased. Atrophy of some secretory cells and degenerative changes occur in both major and minor salivary glands over time. However, recent studies show that salivary output and composition are not consistently altered in older, essentially healthy persons (Baum, 1991). On the other hand, older adults with systemic disease requiring medication face the greatest risk of developing salivary gland dysfunction and related oral problems.

Oral Mucosa

Oral mucosa is the name of the mucous membrane lining the oral cavity. The oral mucosa performs two essential protective functions that markedly affect a person's general health and well-being. First, the mucosa acts as a barrier to environmental insults (microbes, chemicals), shielding the systemic defense. Second, its sensory detectors warn of spoiled foodstuffs, temperature extremes, and sharp objects. The layer of saliva on the mucosal surface retains moisture, lubricates, protects against abrupt osmotic changes, and prevents adhesion of microbes to the mucosal surface.

A decline in the protective-barrier function of the oral mucosa could expose the aging person to multitudes of disease-causing organisms and chemicals entering the oral cavity during daily activities (Baum, 1991). Although some research has shown age-related changes in oral mucosa, these studies were not performed on healthy, nonmedicated persons, nor did the studies record the use of dentures or partial dentures, which can alter mucosal integrity.

To date, no well-designed studies have linked changes in oral mucosa to aging. In a recent study of the clinical oral mucosal condition of 182 healthy adults between 20 and 95 years of age, the oral mucosae were found to remain relatively unchanged with age (Wolff, 1991). It appears that there are no significant changes in the oral mucosa related to aging as long as the individual is in good health. Disorders of the oral mucosa in the older population are probably related to disease, malnutrition, drug usage, or ill-fitting dentures (Baum, 1991).

Chewing, Swallowing, and Speech

Chewing, swallowing, and talking involve some of the most intricate, complex, and sophisticated of all human movements. While each of these activities involves the mouth and associated oral structures, each activity is affected differently by the normal aging process.

Chewing ability has been shown to decrease with age. Recent well-designed studies have found that older persons with all of their teeth remaining were less able to adequately chew food when compared to younger subjects. This resulted in the older persons swallowing larger-sized food particles than did the younger subjects (Feldman, 1980). Missing or loose teeth result in even poorer chewing ability.

Swallowing behavior may also be affected by the normal aging process. Several aspects of swallowing, even in persons with good dental status, have been specifically shown to differ between people of different ages. These include the duration of the swallow and the presence of unusual or unnecessary structural movement. The swallowing mechanism appears to have a limited ability to successfully compensate for other age-related changes (such as decreased chewing ability) (Sonies, 1990).

Speech production is the function of the mouth that appears most resistant to aging. Scant data exist associating the aging process with speech-related movements of the lips, tongue, or jaw. It appears that healthy, older persons are quite capable of normal-sounding speech (Sonies, 1984).

Taste and Smell

Taste buds are sensory nerve endings found on the tongue, soft palate, and throat structures (pharynx, larynx, and epiglottis). Taste buds recognize chemicals from food dissolved in saliva. There is no reduction in the number of taste buds with age (Baum, 1991). Studies have shown that there is no general decrease in the taste function of older persons (Bartoshuk, 1986).

When we smell, olfactory nerve endings recognize volatile chemicals as stimuli. Clinical studies generally agree that the ability to smell declines with increasing age (Weiffenbach, 1986). Because the ability to smell is related to flavor perception, food recognition, food preference, and overall taste enjoyment, it appears that among healthy, older persons, decreased ability to smell may be the cause of complaints associated with lessened food enjoyment (Baum, 1991).

Teeth

Teeth, along with the jawbones, comprise the hard tissues of the mouth. Teeth have three layers (see accompanying illustration). The outer layer, called enamel, surrounds the crown of the tooth. Enamel is the hardest tissue of the body because it is highly mineralized; however, it is not a living tissue. Once enamel formation is completed during youth, the enamel forming cells die. Therefore enamel cannot grow back or be replaced, and the enamel layer, like fingernails, has no feeling.

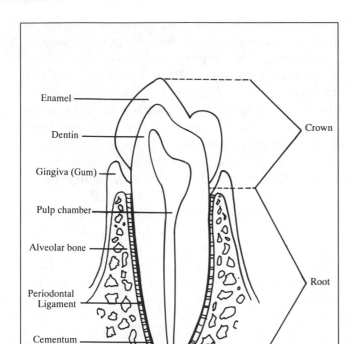

Normal dental anatomy. (Illustration by George Dzahristos)

The dentin layer makes up most of the root structure of the tooth and also supports the enamel of the crown. Dentin is less mineralized and thus is softer than enamel. It is yellow in color. Dentin is a living hard tissue that can transmit pain and has the ability to keep growing and heal itself. Dentin formed after the completion of tooth formation is called secondary dentin.

The thin layer surrounding the root is cementum, which is slightly harder than dentin but much softer than enamel. Cementum helps anchor the tooth to the alveolar bone (jawbone).

The center of the tooth is the pulp chamber, containing primarily nerves and blood vessels that enter and exit the hard structure of the tooth through an opening at the tip of the root.

The following changes occur over time:

1. Secondary dentin continues to form; this may result in decreased tooth sensitivity and a decrease in the size of the pulp chamber and root canals; this change in the thickness and type of dentin may also result in teeth becoming more yellow and less translucent.

2. The ridges and grooves on the surface of the tooth enamel are lost, resulting in altered light reflection of enamel and resultant tooth color changes.

3. The enamel becomes less permeable but more brittle and subject to fracture.

4. Superficial cracks in teeth may appear associated with years of temperature changes or chewing on hard objects.

Periodontium

The periodontium consists of the structures which support the tooth. These structures include alveolar bone surrounding the roots of the teeth, cementum, gingiva, and periodontal ligament. The teeth are anchored firmly in place by the periodontal ligament, running from the cementum surface to the alveolar bone. The gingiva is the soft tissue surrounding the teeth, also known as the gum.

With age, there are cellular and structural changes in the periodontium, as when the periodontal ligament becomes thicker and more fragile and the cementum is thicker but more susceptible to injury. Yet these changes do not clinically affect the function of the periodontium (to support the tooth).

● ORAL CONDITIONS COMMONLY ASSOCIATED WITH AGING

The most common oral diseases are caries and periodontal disease. Both caries and periodontal disease are infectious disease processes caused by bacterial plaque. Plaque is a sticky, adherent film on the teeth or dentures that consists of bacteria and their by-products. Plaque that is not removed daily is hardened by the minerals in our saliva into calculus (tartar). Calculus is not removed by toothbrushing but can be removed by the dental hygienist or dentist.

Caries and Root Caries

Dental caries is an infectious process that results in the destruction of the mineralized tooth tissues. *Caries* is a Latin word meaning "rottenness" or "decay." After eating a meal with sugar in it, the bacteria in plaque produce acids, which dissolve tooth enamel, for about twenty minutes. Therefore, it is most advantageous to brush as soon as possible after eating. After hundreds of exposures to the acid, a cavity is formed, which slowly progresses from the surface of the tooth toward the pulp. Initially the decay is only in the enamel layer and may go unnoticed, with no symptoms. When it reaches the dentin layer, sensitivity to hot, cold, or sweets may occur. In severe caries, the dental pulp can be infected, which can result in an abscess. Caries may occur on the crown of the tooth (coronal caries) or on the root surfaces (root caries). Root caries can progress rapidly, because there is no protective enamel layer on the root.

Periodontal Diseases

The two most common periodontal diseases are gingivitis and periodontitis. While both are caused by bacterial plaque, each disease is caused by a specific type of bacteria in plaque.

Gingivitis means inflammation of the gingiva (gums). Gingivitis may occur around only a few or all of the teeth. Gingivitis is usually the cause of bleeding gums and is an indication of inadequate plaque removal.

Periodontitis is an inflammation of the structures of the periodontium that are deeper than the gingiva, including the periodontal ligaments and alveolar bone. In periodontitis, bacteria create toxins, which irritate the gums and break down the attachment of gum tissues to the teeth. Over a period of time the infection can progress to the underlying bone. This process can be asymptomatic, and without dental check-ups, it may go unnoticed until teeth become loose or shift positions. Eventually, tooth loss occurs.

Several epidemiologic studies have noted an increase in the prevalence and severity of periodontal disease in older adults (Hunt, 1985). However, this phenomenon does not appear to be due to aging per se, but rather the cumulative effects of long-standing chronic periodontal disease.

Attrition

Attrition is the wearing away of tooth structure as the result of frictional tooth-to-tooth contact. This process can result in flattened tooth surfaces. Sometimes attrition is severe enough that the pulp chamber is exposed and the tooth becomes infected, but most of the time there is enough secondary dentin to cover and protect the pulp chamber. Severe attrition can also result in difficulty chewing or abnormal jaw relationships which may cause temporomandibular joint (TMJ) pain. Bruxism (grinding of teeth) can greatly accelerate the process of attrition.

Abrasion

Abrasion is the frictional wearing away of tooth structure usually caused by hard toothbrushes, excessive brushing pressures, or abrasive dentifrices. Abrasion generally occurs at the gingival area (gumline) of the teeth, where the dentin may be exposed. Severe cases may expose the dental pulp.

Recession

When the gums have receded or "shrunk" from the crowns of the teeth, it is called recession (see Figure 2). Recession results from long-standing, chronic periodontal disease. As the underlying periodontal structures, including the alveolar bone, are destroyed by bacterial toxins, the gum tissue may follow. Recession exposes the root of the tooth to oral bacteria and is a risk factor for root caries. Note that recession does not always occur in periodontal disease. There may be severe bone loss and loosening of teeth without recession.

Mucosal Lesions

Common lesions of oral mucosa are denture sores caused by ill-fitting dentures or partial dentures, fungal infections, tooth associated infections, or oral cancer. Because of the increased risk of oral cancer with age, all sores or growths in the mouth and throat should be examined at once by a professional. The risk of oral cancer also increases dramatically with tobacco and alcohol use.

Xerostomia

Xerostomia is dry mouth caused by lack of saliva. It is not a direct consequence of the aging process but may result from systemic causes or medications. Many types of drugs produce xerostomia as a side effect. Xerostomia, in turn, is one of the important risk factors for caries formation in older persons. The importance of saliva for antibacterial, remineralizing, and oral-cleansing purposes cannot be overemphasized.

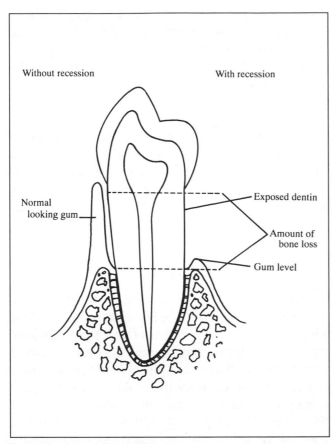

Without recession

With recession

Normal looking gum

Exposed dentin

Amount of bone loss

Gum level

Periodontal disease. (Illustration by George Dzahristos)

● INTERACTIONS BETWEEN SYSTEMIC DISEASES AND ORAL HEALTH

Systemic diseases can and do affect oral health either directly or indirectly. Oral disease can negatively affect some systemic disease states as well. Some of the more common medical conditions and their oral complications are discussed below.

Sjogren's Syndrome

Sjogren's syndrome is an autoimmune disease occurring predominantly in postmenopausal women. It is the single most common disease affecting salivary glands and can cause xerostomia (see **Xerostomia**).

Diabetes

Diabetes decreases resistance to all infections including oral infection. Uncontrolled diabetes may result in uncontrolled periodontal disease, periodontal abscesses, dry mouth, or fungal infection. Conversely, chronic infection in the mouth

can make diabetes more difficult to control. Therefore it is essential to maintain excellent oral hygiene and maintenance of oral health for optimal control of diabetes.

Hypertension

Hypertension is often treated with medications that cause dry mouth. The significance of dry mouth is discussed above. Some of the antihypertensive medications can cause an overgrowth of the gum tissue.

Organ Transplantation

Organ transplantation necessitates thorough dental treatment to eliminate potential sources of infection prior to the surgery. Following transplantation, medications are given that suppress the immune system in order to prevent rejection of the new organ. Suppression of the immune sys-

Functions of Saliva

Aids in preparation of food for swallowing

Lubricates and moistens oral tissues for protection and comfort

Preserves microbial ecologic balance to prevent fungal infections

Sustains antibacterial, antifungal, and antiviral activities

Neutralizes acids produced by decay forming bacteria

Acts as reservoir for minerals to aid in remineralization of teeth

Aids in washing plaque from tooth surfaces

Augments taste acuity

Most Common Causes of Dry Mouth

Medications (including antidepressants, antianxiety drugs, anti-parkinsonian drugs, antihistamines, antihypertensives, antispasmodics and anticholinergics, antipsychotics, appetite suppressants, cold medications, decongestants)

Head and neck radiation therapy

Sjogren's Syndrome

Diabetes

Anxiety

tem increases susceptibility to oral infection, which can be life threatening. Besides immuno-suppression, some of the medications can cause enlargement of the gums and decreased ability to tolerate stress.

Oral Cancer

Oral cancer includes cancer of the lips, tongue, salivary glands, floor of the mouth (under the tongue), gums, or anywhere else in the mouth. In early stages oral cancer is not painful or symptomatic. Early detection is essential to prevent increased morbidity or death. It is recommended that all persons age 55 and over be screened for oral cancer annually. Treatment with radiation or chemotherapy commonly results in infections of the mouth, and even a mild source of oral infection can become life threatening. Therefore, dental treatment eliminating all detectable sites of infection should be completed prior to treatment with radiation or chemotherapy. Regular check ups and cleanings should be obtained thereafter.

Stroke

A stroke can affect nerves on the side of the face. When this occurs, the cheek or tongue can be bitten repeatedly and not felt. Ulcers caused by dentures may not be detected on the affected side of the mouth. If face muscles are affected, an individual can have difficulty cleaning inside the cheeks. Collection of food between the cheek and gums or teeth can occur resulting in decay and gum disease progressing rapidly in that area. Tooth loss can follow. If the dominant hand is affected, toothbrushing and flossing may need to be relearned with the other hand. Toothbrushes can be modified, or reciprocating-type electric toothbrushes may be helpful.

Bleeding Disorders

Bleeding disorders or medications that prolong bleeding (such as coumadin) may result in bleeding gums or bruising of the oral mucosa. Acute oral infection can result in uncontrolled bleeding.

Arthritis

Arthritis resulting in limited movements may alter a person's ability to effectively use a tooth-brush or dental floss. Oral hygiene aids or tooth-brush modification can be of assistance.

Visual Impairment

Visual impairment can alter a person's ability to see oral debris, and this can indirectly affect oral hygiene.

Depression

Depression can cause a person to become uninterested in personal well-being, including oral health. Neglect of oral hygiene may result in periodontal disease and caries progressing rapidly and uncontrolled.

Anxiety

Anxiety about dental treatment prevents many persons from seeking necessary dental care, but dentistry has made many advances in recent years to better manage pain and anxiety. Severe chronic anxiety may result in xerostomia, with associated dental consequences.

● NUTRITION AND ORAL HEALTH

There are important relationships between nutrition and oral health. Oral conditions such as loose, painful teeth or ill-fitting dentures can result in a diminished desire or ability to eat. Persons who have difficulty chewing or have missing teeth often are embarrassed to eat with others and isolate themselves. This may lead to depression and poor eating patterns (Smith, 1979). Poor nutrition can in turn decrease resistance to oral disease or result in mucosal disorders.

Nutritional intake affects the maintenance and repair of the oral tissues and results in visible changes.

Many studies have established an association between diet and dental caries. This association results from certain oral bacteria producing an acid which dissolves the tooth structure when exposed to sugar (see **caries and root caries**). A diet high in sugars will certainly increase the risk of dental caries, but the increase will depend on such factors as the amount, concentration, retentiveness (stickiness), frequency, and sequence of sugar consumption. For example, associated with an increased risk of caries are:

Table 23.1
Nutritional Deficiencies and Their Possible Oral Consequences

Deficiency	Possible Oral Changes
Water	Xerostomia, tissue dehydration, burning sensation
Vitamin A	Decrease salivary flow, thickened gum tissue
Vitamin B_{12}	Paleness, inflamed tongue, cheilosis (sores at corners of mouth)
Folate	Smooth tongue, mouth ulcerations
Niacin	Inflamed tongue, burning tongue, cheilosis
Riboflavin	Pebbly tongue, magenta colored tongue, cheilosis
Vitamin C	Spongy, bleeding gums
Protein	Tissue fragility, burning sensation
Iron	Paleness, cheilosis, glossitis, burning tongue, smooth tongue
Zinc	Altered taste

- A high total amount of sugars consumed throughout day
- Specific food items with high sugar concentration
- Food that is highly retentive (sticks to the teeth as opposed to liquid form)
- Eating sugar more frequently (e.g., between meal snacks)
- Sequence of food consumption (e.g., eating cheese after sugar reduces the bacterial acid effect)

The precise role of nutritional factors in the cause, progression, and prevention of periodontal diseases is not known. However, nutritional factors can affect both susceptibility to this disease and its progression. Although malnutrition does not cause chronic inflammatory periodontal disease, a malnourished person has increased susceptibility to infection because of lowered immune defense.

● **SPECIAL PROBLEMS OF THE DISABLED OR FRAIL ELDERLY**

Disabilities can prevent the practice of effective daily oral hygiene. For example, partial paral-ysis from a stroke can affect use of the dominant hand, visual field problems can affect the ability to see half the mouth, dementia can affect the ability to practice or remember to practice effective daily oral hygiene, and depression can affect the motivation or interest in maintaining oral health. Poor oral hygiene is a risk factor for periodontal disease and caries, both of which can lead to pain, tooth loss, and impaired chewing function (another type of disability). Persons with disabilities who function well independently may need only simple modification of toothbrushes or other assistive devices or merely a reminder and encouragement to practice good oral hygiene. A dentist or occupational therapist can assist in making or obtaining appropriate devices. The new reciprocating electric toothbrushes can be very helpful and effective for plaque control.

Persons with disabilities who cannot provide effective oral hygiene on their own will need assistance with their daily oral hygiene regimen to prevent oral disability. This may include assistance with daily brushing of teeth, tongue, dentures or partial dentures, daily application of fluoride, wiping mouth of extraneous food particles after meals, and lubricating lips.

Persons in nursing homes are often unable to practice daily oral hygiene and instead rely on the nursing staff to assist them. Nurses receive minimal training in oral health and disease and, as a result, may not realize the importance of cleaning a denture or brushing a patient's teeth. Insistence by family or friends on a daily oral hygiene regimen may be needed.

> Persons with disabilities who function well independently may need only simple modification of toothbrushes or other assistive devices or merely a reminder and encouragement to practice good oral hygiene.

Persons who are homebound because of severe disabilities or in nursing homes may be unable to get to a dental office for treatment. A few dentists across the nation have portable dental practices, in which they bring portable dental equipment to the patient's home or the nursing home. Comprehensive care can usually be provided.

Alzheimer's disease can eventually render a person unable to maintain their oral hygiene. It is essential that a thorough dental examination and treatment be provided in the early stage of Alzheimer's disease while it can still be tolerated. Also, a person with advanced Alzheimer's disease will more likely tolerate aggressive preventive treatments such as fluoride gels if these preventive regimens are begun in the early stages of the disease. In the later stages of the disease, the person may be unable to communicate dental pain or tolerate dental treatment except under general anesthesia. Attention to daily mouth care can allow the person to remain free of pain and disease and able to chew food more effectively.

A few dentists across the nation have portable dental practices, in which they bring portable dental equipment to the patient's home or the nursing home. Comprehensive care can usually be provided.

● PREVENTIVE STRATEGIES

Because over 90 percent of oral cancers occur in persons over age 45 and the average age of persons diagnosed with oral cancer is 60 (Silverman, 1985), all older adults should receive annual oral exams. Many oral cancers are treatable if they are discovered early. Alert your dentist to any sores, swellings, or discolorations that you find on your tongue, lips, cheek, throat, jaw, or salivary glands.

Persons with Natural Teeth

Removal of plaque is of utmost importance for the preservation of the teeth and maintenance of a healthy mouth. Thorough brushing and flossing, at least once a day, removes plaque. Use of dental floss can help remove plaque from between teeth and under the gumline where a toothbrush cannot reach. Dental professionals can teach proper and effective preventive techniques. Plaque can also form on the tongue, so that brushing the tongue is necessary to prevent irritation of tongue mucosa and resultant fungal infection. Regular

teeth cleanings are needed to remove built up deposits of plaque and calculus.

Fluoride is highly effective in preventing caries. Fluoride works by making teeth more resistant to bacterial acids and may also inhibit bacterial plaque. Persons with any remaining teeth should use fluoride dentifrices and fluoride mouth rinses daily. Persons at especially high risk of dental caries may require a high concentration fluoride gel available by prescription from a dentist. The combination of fluoride and plaque removal constitutes a powerful preventive regimen.

Wearing a partial denture that attaches to natural teeth necessitates meticulous oral hygiene. A partial denture can trap dental plaque beneath the clasps and increase the risk of caries and periodontal disease. Special attention must be given to plaque removal and daily fluoride application. In addition, the partial denture must be brushed daily.

If a person is hospitalized, insist that the caretakers assist with or provide daily oral hygiene. While no studies have addressed this issue, older adults, with gingival recession, multiple fillings, and possible dry mouth from medications or mouth breathing may be at extreme risk for rampant caries while hospitalized.

In addition to regular oral exams and teeth cleaning, seeking prompt professional treatment can typically prevent further problems. Initial treatment is simpler and less expensive since problems usually progress and complications can develop. Bleeding gums and sensitivity to hot, cold, or sweets can indicate more serious, underlying oral disease and are best assessed by a dentist.

Wearing a partial denture that attaches to natural teeth necessitates meticulous oral hygiene.

Persons with Dentures

Besides on teeth, dental plaque can form on dentures and the tongue so they should be brushed daily. Plaque and calculus on dentures or tongue can irritate mucosal tissue and harbor microorganisms that cause fungal infection.

Dentures should be removed nightly to allow oral tissues to recover from the pressure of daily wear.

To prevent the loss of dentures and partial dentures in hospital or nursing homes, they should be labeled with the wearers name and social security number. Some states require that dentures be labeled when made. Dentists can provide labelling service when needed.

Organizations

At this time there is no central resource on dentistry for older adults available to the general public, as most literature on the subject is directed to dentists. However, the local dental society may be contacted for information on publications or services available, and local dental schools often offer special programs for treating older adults.

Organizations concerned with oral health and aging:

Adminstration on Aging
330 Independence Ave., Sw
Washington, DC 20201
(202) 619-0724

American Association of Retired Persons (AARP)
601 E St., NW
Washington, DC 20049
(202) 434-2277

American Dental Association
211 East Chicago Ave.
Chicago, IL 60601
(312) 440-2593

American Society for Geriatric Dentistry (ASGD)
211 East Chicago Ave.
Chicago, IL 60601
(312) 440-2660

Healthy Older People Program
Office of Disease Prevention and Health
  Promotion
330 C St., SW, Room 2132
Washington, DC 20201
(202) 205-8611

National Council on the Aging
409 Third St., SW
Washington, DC 20024
(202) 479-1200

National Voluntary Organization for the Independent Living for the Aging
600 Maryland Ave., SW
Washington, DC 20024

References

Bartoshuk, L. and others. "Taste and Aging." *Journal of Gerontology* Vol. 41 (1986): 51.

Baum, B. J., and others. "Aging and Oral Health." In *Geriatric Dentistry.* Ed. A. S. Papas. St. Louis, MO: Mosby Year Book, 1991.

Beck, J. D., R. J. Hunt, and others. "Prevalence of Root and Coronal Caries in a Non-Institutionalized Older Population." *Journal of the American Dental Association* Vol. 111 (1985): 964–67.

Ettinger, R. L. "Oral Disease and Its Effect on the Quality of Life." *Gerodontics* Vol. 3 (1987): 103–6.

Feldman, R. S., and others. "Aging and Mastication: Changes in Performance and in the Swallowing Threshold with Natural Dentition." *Journal of the American Geriatric Society* Vol. 28 (1980): 97–103.

Jones, J. A., and others. "Issues in Financing Dental Care for the Elderly." *Journal of Public Health Dentistry* Vol. 50 (1990): 268–75.

Silverman, S., Jr. *Oral Cancer.* New York: American Cancer Society, 1985.

Smith, J. M., and A. Sheiham. "How Dental Conditions Handicap the Elderly." *Community Dentistry and Oral Epidemiology* Vol. 7 (1979): 305–10.

Sonies, B. C., and A. J. Caruso. "The Aging Process and Its Potential Impact on Measures of Oral Sensorimotor Function." *American Speech-Language-Hearing Association Report* Vol. 19 (1990): 114.

Sonies, B. C., and others. "Tongue Motion in Elderly Adults: Initial In Situ Observations." *Journal of Gerontology* Vol. 39 (1984): 279–81.

Weiffenbach, J. M. "Taste and Smell Perception in Aging." *Gerodontology* Vol. 3 (1984): 137.

Wolff, A., and others. "Oral Mucosal Status in Healthy, Different Aged Adults." *Oral Surgery, Oral Medicine, Oral Pathology* Vol. 71 (1991): 569–72.

Kani L. Nicolls, D.D.S.

24

Mental Disorders

● Distinguishing Psychiatric Illness from Normal Aging ● Disorders of Cognition ● Dementia
● Delirium ● Depression ● Anxiety ● Sleep Disorders ● Alcohol and Drug Dependence
● Alcohol Abuse ● Drug Abuse and Misuse

Older people fear losing their mental abilities more than any other disability associated with aging. Anxieties concerning memory loss and, at the extreme, fear of Alzheimer's disease are commonly expressed among seniors. Many of these fears are unfounded. In the case of minor memory impairments, techniques exist, such as memory retention courses, to offset normal forgetfulness. However, mental health problems of the elderly are significant in frequency, in their impact on mental status in later life, and in their potential influence on the course of physical illness.

Estimates of mental illness in later life vary widely. Some studies (Roth, 1976) report that between 15 percent and 25 percent of older people have serious symptoms due to mental disorders. A large survey of the incidence, distribution, and control of diseases in populations conducted in the early 1980s (the Epidemiological Catchment Area [ECA] survey), reported that 7.8 percent of persons aged 65 and over were in need of mental health services. These were individuals living in the community (community dwelling elderly), not in institutions. By projecting this need to the population of the elderly in the Unites States, an estimated 1.9 million older persons are thought to be in need of mental health care. Yet, mental health services are generally underutilized by the community dwelling elderly.

In institutions, such as nursing homes, the overall rate of significant mental distress is 65

percent (U.S. Senate Special Committee on Aging, 1990), of which significant decline in mental abilities, dementia, is the most common problem (47 percent). Researchers estimate that the combined incidence of community and institutional mental illness is approximately 10.7 percent of older U.S. citizens.

Another measure of the severity of mental illness related to older adults is suicide. Suicide is a more frequent cause of death among older adults than among any other age group. The highest rate of suicide is among older white men—46 deaths per 100,000 population, which is 2½ times the rate for older black men (18 deaths). While the suicide rate for the general population is 12 per 100,000, for persons age 65–74 it is 20; for those 75–84 it is 25, and for persons over 85 it is 21 (National Center for Health Statistics, 1986).

● DISTINGUISHING PSYCHIATRIC ILLNESS FROM NORMAL AGING

Distinguishing psychiatric illness from aging is important, otherwise significant symptoms of disease may be overlooked. This is well illustrated by the increased understanding and proper diagnosis of Alzheimer's disease. In the past and even today, physicians and families often view senility as the inevitable fate of aging. Data from studies that have followed subjects over time (longitudinal studies) have shown that many older individuals maintain high levels of cognitive function into

Mental health problems of the elderly are significant in frequency, in their impact on mental status in later life, and in their potential influence on the course of physical illness. (Courtesy of Sanders-Brown Center on Aging, University of Kentucky/Tim Collins, photographer)

illness in declining mental health in late life, research efforts began to reveal the positive influence of medication management (psychopharmacology) and psychotherapy for modifying mental illness. This is nowhere more apparent than in advances in the evaluation and treatment of late-life depression. Depression is not a normal part of aging. Older individuals are able to cope with most stressful events with an amazing degree of resilience. Depressed older adults have been shown to respond to both pharmacologic treatment and psychotherapy. When left untreated, depression can contribute to an acceleration of decline in functional status.

Mental illnesses and behavioral disturbances in late life are often difficult to detect. Psychiatric illnesses can occur in concert with physical and social problems. Chronic physical illness can confound the detection of mental illness because symptoms can overlap. In this context, elderly patients often seek medical advice, either knowingly or unknowingly, for mental health problems under the guise of a physical ailment. Since symptoms can overlap and be applied to a diversity of illnesses, primary care physicians often neglect to

late life. Thus they are able to gain, absorb, and process new information. Although the speed with which new information is learned decreases and intellectual activities may slow, the great majority of the elderly remain mentally active and competent. Evidence indicates one can "teach an old dog new tricks."

Once physicians began to recognize the role of

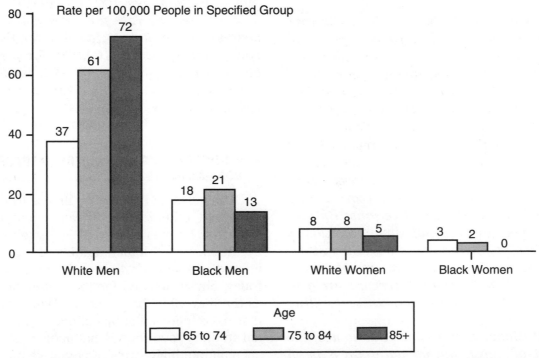

Figure 24.1
Suicide Rates for People 65+, by Age and Race: 1987

Rate per 100,000 People in Specified Group

	White Men	Black Men	White Women	Black Women
65 to 74	37	18	8	3
75 to 84	61	21	8	2
85+	72	13	5	0

Age
65 to 74   75 to 84   85+

Source: National Center for Health Statistics. *Health, United States, 1989.* DHHS Pub. No. (PHS)90-1232. Washington: Department of Health and Human Services (March 1990).

consider emotional illness as a primary problem. Expressing emotional distress in terms of a physical ailment places the older person at increased risk for unnecessary diagnostic evaluations, complications resulting from therapy (iatrogenic complications), and debilitating side effects caused by taking multiple medications (polypharmacy). Medications commonly used in treating various medical illnesses further compound this diagnostic problem because they can cause psychiatric symptoms, such as cognitive impairment, depression, and anxiety.

Depression is not a normal part of aging. Older individuals are able to cope with most stressful events with an amazing degree of resilience.

Physicians have long observed that mental health can influence physical illness and in turn, physical illness can influence mental health. Depression may impede recovery from medical conditions such as stroke or heart attack. Personality types have been associated with increased risk for certain medical conditions. For example, chronic stress and worry is associated with increased risk for stomach ulcers, and relentless striving for success has been associated with increased risk for heart disease. People with seemingly similar diseases may have vastly different expressions of impairment and/or disability that seem to be related to social, environmental, and personal factors.

Interestingly, personality traits have been shown to be relatively stable over one's life. Hence, negative attitudes and behaviors, once attributed to old age, are more likely to have been present as lifelong personality traits. In other words, people do not become fixed and rigid with age. For some people, it is more likely that they have been that way their entire lives. This information may be encouraging to those who feared old age as a time of rigidity, irritability, intolerance, and depression. However, for those who are unhappy with themselves or their lot in life, it is unlikely that time will result in an improvement in their condition without self-initiated positive steps toward change.

Recognition of the fact that mental illness in late life is not due to aging has lead to major advances in the care of mental illness in the elderly. The remainder of this chapter discusses the diagnosis and treatment of mental disorders of particular relevance to the elderly.

● DISORDERS OF COGNITION

Cognitive decline is the decreasing ability to learn new information and recall old information. One of the most feared and experienced concerns expressed by older people, it is becoming a prominent health concern for many aging Americans and their spouses or children. Two million to three million Americans were estimated to be cognitively impaired in 1986, and by the year 2000 the number of cognitively impaired elderly may well reach five million to six million. Of those people reaching age 80, one out of three will have significant cognitive impairment, resulting in dementia. Of those elderly in nursing homes, 40 percent to 60 percent are cognitively impaired.

Complaints of abnormal attention, impaired ability to calculate, and/or memory impairment pose a diagnostic challenge to primary care physicians. The lack of consistency in the terminology used to refer to these disorders (including delirium, dementia, presenile dementia, organic brain syndrome, acute brain failure, acute organic syndrome, exogenous psychosis, metabolic encephalopathy, toxic psychosis, and others) reflects the difficulty which the different disciplines of medicine have had in defining these disorders. Cognitive impairment is a decline from a previously attained level of intellectual function, characterized by demonstrable impairment in short- and long-term memory, abstract thought, judgment, language, spatial or temporal orientation, and/or adaptive behaviors. It may be overlooked because of the tendency of the elderly, as well as their families and physician, to attribute cognitive decline to normal aging. Dementia and delirium are two important forms of cognitive impairment in late life.

Cognitive decline is the decreasing ability to learn new information and recall old information.

● DEMENTIA

Dementia is defined as a significant decline from an individual's previously attained level of intellectual function. It is caused by a variety of diseases, such as Alzheimer's disease or cerebral vascular diseases. Dementia is characterized by brain dysfunction, particularly in those areas of the brain which integrate perception, thought, and purposeful action. As such, dementia usually involves a decline in cognitive capacity, adaptive behavior, and functional ability. Dementia is an insidious process. Symptoms usually do not rapidly accelerate over days or weeks, but by measuring mental functioning over a longer period of time, months to years, decline can be shown. To qualify as true dementia, memory impairment must be significant enough to cause difficulty at work or with social activities, and/or inability to live independently.

Symptoms

Dementia is characterized by demonstrable impairment in short- and long-term memory, abstract thought, judgment, or other higher level brain function such as impaired ability to communicate (aphasia), difficulty executing purposeful movement (apraxia), lack of ability to recognize familiar objects (agnosia), and decline in ability to interpret the visual environment (visuo-spatial integration). A person may experience decline or loss of insight or perception, leading to poor judgment demonstrated by the lack of ability to recognize situations that are dangerous, such as going outside in extremely cold weather with little or no clothing.

Older individuals often express concern over forgetfulness. This is, however, a normal part of everyday life. Locking one's keys in the car or forgetting names or remote events is not uncommon at any age, especially for those with busy lives. However, one should be cautious in attributing memory decline to normal aging. Where one crosses the line between normal forgetfulness and dementia is often hard to determine and should be left to a competent physician. Symptoms of memory loss, difficulty finding words or completing thoughts, inability to handle simple daily tasks, or getting lost in familiar surroundings should prompt a medical evaluation.

Table 24.1
Causes of Disorders of Cognition in the Elderly

Potentially reversible causes	Irreversible or progressive causes
Infections of the central nervous system	Alzheimer's disease
Metabolic disorders	Multi-infarct dementia
Intoxication	Parkinson's disease
Depression	Huntington's disease
Brain tumors	Pick's disease
Nutritional deficiencies	Progressive supranuclear palsy
Normal pressure hydrocephalus	

Psychiatric symptoms accompany dementing illnesses in over 75 percent of cases. They are often the most difficult aspect of the syndrome with which families have to cope. Psychiatric symptoms include agitation, depression, hallucinations, delusions, paranoid behavior, combativeness, wandering, excessive vocal behavior, and disrupted sleep patterns.

Diagnosis

Dementia is a clinical syndrome caused by specific illnesses that affect the brain (see Table 24.1). No specific diagnostic test for dementia is available. It is a group of findings as described above. The most important diagnostic tool is the history obtained from the affected persons and their family members. Many interview evaluation tests have been developed to help the physician numerically measure (quantify) memory impairment. Once significant memory impairment is found, reversible causes of dementia are first sought by the physician (listed in Table 24.1). However, research has shown that only about 10 percent or less of dementias are reversible. Alzheimer's disease is the leading cause of cognitive impairment in later life (see Figure 24.2). The second most common cause of cognitive decline is cerebral vascular disease. Together these two conditions account for 80 percent of the dementias found in late life. Other causes of dementia are listed in Table 24.1, accounting for the remaining 20 percent of dementing illness.

Figure 24.2
Percent of People 65+ with Probable Alzheimer's Disease, by Age Group

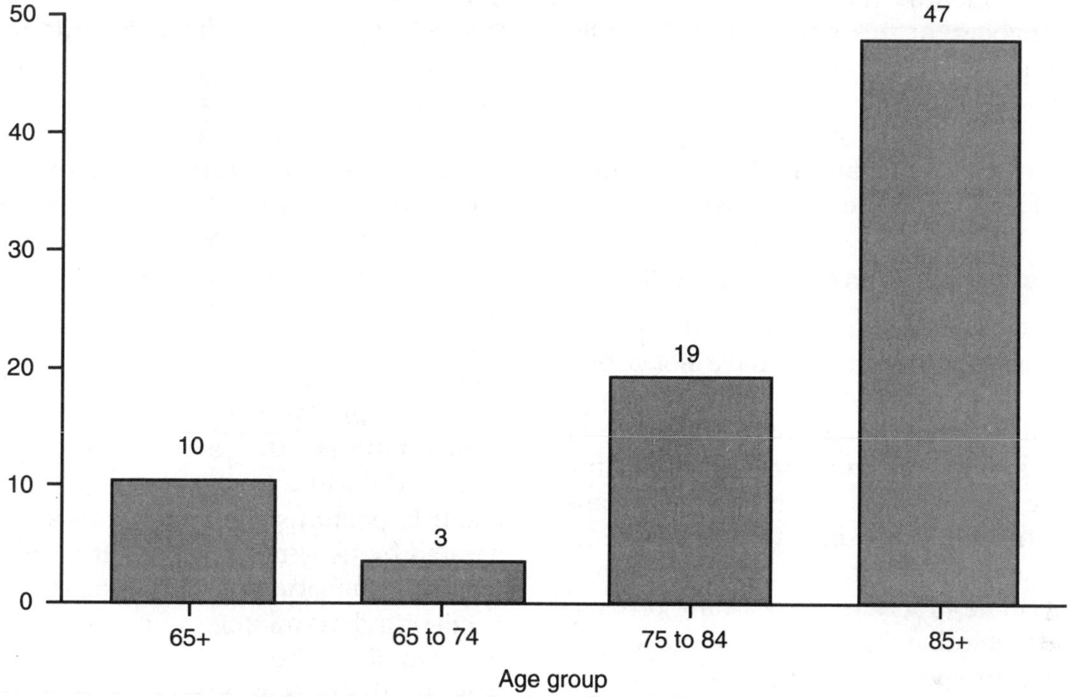

Note: Excludes people in nursing homes and other institutions.

Source: Evans, Denis A., M.D., et al. "Prevalence of Alzheimer's Disease in a Community Population of Older Persons." *Journal of the American Medical Association* Vol. 262, no. 18 (November 10, 1989).

Psychiatric symptoms accompany dementing illnesses in over 75 percent of cases.

Alzheimer's Disease

Alzheimer's disease was first described by Alois Alzheimer in 1907. At one time Alzheimer's disease was considered a rare disease. However, as the number of individuals reaching old age has increased, the disease has become increasingly more common. At present this progressive and irreversible degenerative brain disease is the fourth-leading killer in the United States. Approximately four million people over the age of 65 in the United States are afflicted by the disease. This is 14 percent of the elderly population (U.S. Senate Special Committee on Aging, 1990). The presence of Alzheimer's disease increases with age. The highest prevalence is among those over age 85 (47.2 percent).

The symptoms of Alzheimer's disease are the same as the symptoms caused by other dementing illnesses. A slowly progressive decline in cognitive ability followed by a decline in functional ability is the hallmark of the disease. The rate of decline is extremely variable from one individual to the next. However, the end result of the disease is consistently the same. In the end, the affected individuals are left in a childlike or vegetative (noncommunicative) state, unable to care for themselves.

No single diagnostic test is available to identify the patient with Alzheimer's disease. The evaluation for Alzheimer's disease is the same as that for cognitive impairment of any cause, and should include a complete medical history, cognitive testing, blood chemistry tests, and in certain situations, specialized X-ray examinations. If cognitive impairment is evident with formal testing, and no other cause can be identified (see Table 24.1), one is left with the diagnosis of Alzheimer's disease. Confirmation of the diagnosis can be made after death by microscopic examination of brain tissue, looking for characteristic cellular changes associated with the disease.

Research to identify the cause of Alzheimer's disease is ongoing. At this time, research studies suggest that there may be multiple causes, including genetic factors, environmental toxins, viral illness, and that what is currently known as Alzheimer's disease may, in fact, be the common end result of several different illnesses.

Medications Used to Improve Memory Function

Medications designed to enhance memory or slow the progression of disease have not proven successful to date. This includes vitamin preparations available at health food stores. Clinical trials of various agents are ongoing at this time. Medications that inhibit certain chemical transmitter substances in the brain (cholinesterase inhibitors) such as physostigmine and tetrahydroaminoacridine (Tacrine) show some promise. Tacrine hydrochloride (Cognex) may prove helpful in slowing progression of the disease but has not been shown to reverse the dementing process. Currently these drugs are not available except as part of experimental drug trials. Above all else, people should avoid gimmicks promising "miracle" results that are too good to be true, since they may do more harm than good.

Behavioral Management

Management of dementia is based on managing of the various behavioral problems that arise as a result of the cognitive impairment. Behavioral therapy should be the initial approach applied to behavioral problems. The primary aim of behavioral therapy is to help the person maintain self-control through modifying his or her environment and by changing patterns of social interaction. The behavioral problems associated with cognitive impairment can be divided into the categories of intellectual impairment, insomnia, immobility, instability, incontinence, and iatrogenesis.

The intellectual impairment may vary from day to day, and during the course of the day. It is not uncommon for demented people to be the most impaired in the evening. This is thought to be due to the lack of environmental stimuli as it gets dark. The demented elderly person will perform best in nonthreatening, familiar, and constant surroundings. Behavioral techniques to improve cognitive function include: prominent display of clocks and calendars, night-lights, daily schedules that might include checklists, written directions, and labels on commonly used items. Useful activities might include listening to music, watching television, and reading the newspaper. Encouragement to do things for oneself, such as household and outdoor chores, is necessary in order to avoid fostering dependency, although this may require additional supervisory efforts on the part of the caregiver. Physical exercise, structured social events (e.g., participating in an adult day-care program), and one-on-one reminiscence may be helpful as well.

Insomnia is often a major problem for caregivers. First-line therapy is behavioral management. Expected sleep changes in aging are exaggerated by dementia, and result in more frequent nighttime wakefulness. A physician's help may be needed in determining the presence of pain, fear, or drug side effects that disturb sleep, and in treating them appropriately. Restriction of late evening fluids, particularly beverages containing alcohol or caffeine, may prove helpful. Increased physical activity during the day should be encouraged as well as decreased frequency of naps. A glass of warm milk before sleep may be helpful because of the presence of a naturally occurring compound that promotes sleep. When these measures fail, medications under the direction of a physician may be helpful but should be used only on a limited basis.

Wandering, at night or day, is bothersome for the caregiver and potentially dangerous for the patient. The environment should be structured so the patient can pace or walk safely, such as in a well-lit room or fenced-in yard. Installation of complex locks requiring thoughtful action to open doors can effectively limit access to outside areas; disguising doors by covering with a sheet or a full length mirror will often limit access as well. Medi-alert bracelets or necklaces that cannot be easily removed may help if the person wanders and gets lost. If wandering is associated with psychiatric symptoms, such as paranoia or hallucinations, medications may prove helpful.

Inability to move (immobility) and walking (gait) instability may become a problem as the disease progresses. Acute onset of instability often signals an underlying illness and should be evalu-

> It is not uncommon for demented people to be the most impaired in the evening. This is thought to be due to the lack of environmental stimuli as it gets dark.

ated. Gait instability is common to the elderly population in general, and only made worse by a dementing process. Attention to environmental hazards is essential. An occupational therapist can be helpful by evaluating the environment for safety hazards and recommending aids to improve stability. Otherwise, the decline in function can be slowed by keeping the person active, out of bed, walking, or sitting up whenever feasible.

Urinary and fecal incontinence usually occur late in the course of dementia. Acute incontinence may represent underlying illness, such as infection, and should be evaluated by a physician. If evaluation fails to yield any treatable cause, behavioral measures again are first-line therapy. More frequent toileting at regular intervals may control the problem. An incontinence chart may help to identify a pattern of incontinence which can then be managed by scheduled toileting prior to times of expected incontinence. Bedside toilets and avoidance of impediments to the toilet may prove useful. When these measures do not resolve the problem, adult diapers are useful; however, catheters to drain the bladder, either indwelling or condom type, should be avoided because of increased risk of urinary tract infection.

In addition to the above, problems or complications arise resulting from the diagnostic evaluations or treatment directed by physicians. These are called iatrogenic problems. Hospitalization, diagnostic procedures, and medications should be considered carefully and the benefits weighed against the potential risk. The very old, demented, and incontinent are those who often fair worst in the hospital setting. Diagnostic procedures, especially those requiring some degree of cooperation, are difficult for the demented patient and often carry a higher risk of complications.

Medication Management (Pharmacotherapy)

If the elder's behavior cannot be adequately modified by behavioral intervention and the

behavior warrants correction, the use of medications (pharmacotherapy) under the direction of a competent physician (family physician, internist, or psychiatrist) may be required for treatment. First, it is important to classify the disruptive behavior (see Table 24.2). Physicians can improve their treatment success with systematic treatment of specific behaviors. Wandering and excessive vocal and nuisance behaviors are, in general, not amenable to medical therapy alone. However, in patients also manifesting anxiety, sleep disturbance, depression, or psychotic behavior together with the problem behavior, treatment of these conditions may result in reduced problem behavior. Treatment of anxiety, depression, and sleep disturbance are discussed later in this chapter.

Psychotic behaviors (hallucinations, delusions, and paranoia) and combative or violent behaviors in the demented elderly are most commonly treated with a class of medications called neuroleptics (Thorazine, Haldol, Moban, and others). These medications cause significant side effects, such as muscle stiffness and slow movement, rigidity, shuffling gait, and increased confusion. Long-term administration of these medications may cause a permanent movement disorder called tardive dyskinesia. Tardive dyskinesia consists of excessive uncontrolled muscular movements, particularly of the tongue and mouth muscles. For each year an individual is on one of these medications, there is a 1 percent chance of developing tardive dyskinesia. In some cases, the movement disorder reverses when the medication is stopped. These medications may help decrease uncontrollable speech and improve sleep. Other side effects commonly associated

Table 24.2
Noxious Behaviors in Demented Patients

Most likely to respond to medical therapy	Less likely to respond to medical therapy
Anxiety	Wandering
Depression	Excessive vocal behavior
Psychotic delusions	Hoarding
Paranoid behavior	Willful intrusive behavior
Sleep disturbance behaviors	Noxious repetitive
Delirium	

with these medications include sedation, dry mouth, blurred vision, urinary retention, and lowering of blood pressure.

Family Involvement

Foremost in the care of the demented elderly is the involvement of the family. Education and encouragement may be provided by local support groups and associations, such as the Alzheimer's Association. A number of publications for the lay audience provide further practical information on living and caring for the demented elderly person (see **Additional Reading**). Support groups can strengthen emotional well-being and allow an emotional outlet for stressed-out caregivers. The family physician should be able to help with ethical issues regarding medical interventions as they arise. It is very important for patients and families to make plans early on in anticipation of expected cognitive decline. For issues of "living wills" and power of attorney, the family will likely need the assistance of a lawyer. These legal instruments are particularly important for future estate management and health-care decisions. Although the disease process itself can not be altered, many aspects of how the disease effects patients and families can be altered.

● DELIRIUM

Delirium is a mental disturbance marked by rapid onset and characterized by abnormal attention, perception, cognition, and behavioral disturbances. Delirium characteristically develops over a short period of time, sometimes abruptly. In some instances delirium takes from only hours to a few days to develop. Like dementia, delirium has a number of synonyms, including acute confusional state, metabolic encephalopathy, acute organic brain syndrome, toxic psychosis, and confusion. Delirium is one of the most commonly encountered mental disorders, affecting 10 percent to 15 percent of hospitalized patients and 40 percent of hospitalized geriatric patients. Defective hearing or vision, chronic illness, lack of social support, social isolation, immobilization, sleep disturbance, and other factors put individuals at increased risk to develop delirium.

Symptoms

Delirium is often preceded by an initial phase, marked by uneasiness, anxiety, restlessness, insomnia, and diminished concentration. The full-blown syndrome is marked by hyperactive, hypoactive, mixed, or violent behavior. The flow, content, and form of a person's thoughts are dis-

---

Table 24.3
Potential Causes of Delirium

Primary cerebral disease	Intoxication
Meningitis	Alcohol
Brain tumor	Prescription drugs
Physical trauma	Recreational drugs
Cerebral vascular accident	Poisons
Systemic illness	Withdrawal
Infection	Recreational drugs
Metabolic abnormalities	Prescription drugs
Low oxygenation	Narcotic analgesics
Low or high blood sugar	Sedative-Hypnotics
Acid-base disturbance	Alcohol
Electrolyte disturbance	Vitamin deficiency
Organ failure	
Heart failure	
Heart attack	
Kidney failure	
Liver failure	

turbed. Reduced ability to discriminate may cause the person to misinterpret environmental stimuli and experience illusions. For example, a delirious person may mistake shadows for people, or flowers for insects. Actual false perceptions, such as hallucinations, may occur as well (e.g., seeing animals or hearing voices when no one is present). The person may experience disorientation to time and/or place. Other features include reduced level of consciousness and memory impairment that may fluctuate during the course of the day.

Diagnosis

Like dementia, delirium is a syndrome with many causes (see Table 24.3), which generally fall into four categories: primary cerebral disease (infection, cancer, trauma, or stroke), systemic illness (metabolic disturbances), intoxication (prescription medications, over-the-counter [OTC] medications, recreational drugs, or poisons), and withdrawal from substances, most commonly sedative-hypnotic medications and/or alcohol. Table 24.4 is a list of medications known to cause delirium.

Management

In general, delirium is secondary to an underlying organic cause and improves when the underlying cause is treated appropriately. Hospitalization is often necessary to determine the cause of delirium. Delirium occuring in the hospital setting is most often due to medication or a combination of medications and is alleviated once the offending drug is removed. Appropriate treatment requires that delirium be distinguished from dementia, although this may be difficult, because the two syndromes may at times coexist.

● DEPRESSION

Introduction

Depression and depressive symptoms have been coined the "common cold" of late life. Depressive symptoms are a normal and expected part of the human experience. But when symp-

---

Table 24.4
Selected Drugs That May Cause Delirium

Psychotropic and hypnotic agents	Analgesics
Barbiturates	Ibuprofen
Neuroleptics	Indomethacin
Benzodiazepines	Sulindac
Antidepressants	Narcotics
Chloral hydrate	Antihypertensives
Antacid medications	β-Blockers
Ranitidine	Clonidine
Cimetidine	Methyldopa
Famotidine	Reserpine
Nizatidine	Asthma medications
Antihistamines	Albuterol
Diphenhydramine	Metaproterenol
Hydroxyzine	Other common drugs
Diabetic medications	Acyclovir
Insulin	Corticosteriods
Sulfonylureas	Digitalis
Antiparkinson drugs	Metoclopramide
Amantidine	Metronidazole
Bromocriptine	OTC nasal decongestants
Carbidopa	
L-Dopa	

toms are persistent and accompany social, interpersonal, and biologic changes, depressive symptoms are no longer just expected but in fact constitute the illness called depression. Not all depressive illnesses have the same severity. Some illnesses are brief and clearly related to stressful events. Other depressive illnesses are more severe and life threatening, and are considered major depression. There are also individuals who have been "depressed" all their lives. These people suffer from a chronic form of the illness that is as much a part of their personality as it is due to outside factors such as stress or loss.

The prevalence of depression in late life is less than that for younger adults and does not increase with age. It is the increased prevalence of medical disorders, physical illness, functional disability, and cognitive impairment that places the elderly individual at higher risk of experiencing depressive symptoms. Rates of depressive illness are higher in women than in men across the life span. In surveys of community dwelling elderly, major depression is found in 1 percent to 2 percent of individuals over age 65. However, about 15 percent of the elderly have a significant degree of depressive symptoms or anguish (dysphoria) to the extent that it impairs function and/or ability to enjoy life. Institutionalized elderly have higher rates of depression. Major depression in institutionalized elderly is estimated at 12 percent. The most serious consequence of depression is suicide. Suicide rates increase with age, with the highest rates, as noted earlier, occurring in elderly white males.

Depression and depressive symptoms have been coined the "common cold" of late life. Depressive symptoms are a normal and expected part of the human experience.

There are many late-life psychological stressors that contribute to depression. One general theme of late life is how individuals cope with loss. Loss takes many forms. For example, physical illness and resulting functional disabilities are believed to be the most significant stressors in late life. Functional disabilities include limited mobility; inability to feed, dress, and bathe oneself; and sensory deprivation secondary to deafness or blindness, all of which may lead to social isolation. For many, economic deprivation and poor living conditions are a major problem. Social deprivation may take the form of loss of friends and family, immobility caused by inability to drive, loss of being "needed" by children, and the loss of achievement in business that follows with retirement. Although an important stressor, loss of a spouse or close friend may not result in life crises unless the loss is unexpected, since anticipation of the loss may cause grief work to be completed prior to the loss. Those depressive syndromes of particular interest to geriatrics will be discussed in the following sections.

Definition

As a generic term, depression encompasses a number of psychiatric disorders that all have altered mood as a common factor. Depression is a multidimensional concept. Mood varies normally throughout the day with periods of sadness and elation. Depression has both a cognitive and physical component. Depressed mood may be experienced as loss of interest or pleasure in previously fulfilling activities, difficulty concentrating, hopelessness, and feelings of worthlessness. Physical symptoms may also constitute symptoms of depression. They include appetite disturbance, weight loss or gain, loss of energy, and lack of sleep or excessive sleepiness.

The term *depression* is used by physicians to describe a variety of psychiatric disorders consisting of symptoms forming recognizable patterns. The most severe form of depression is major depression. The following discussion presents several different ways in which major depression appears in late life.

Melancholic Depression

Melancholic depression is that type of depression most commonly associated with the elderly. The symptoms include depressed mood or loss of interest in life's activities, preoccupation with guilt, lack of energy, poor appetite, poor concentration, feelings of hopelessness, and suicidal thoughts or ideas.

Psychotic Depression

Psychotic depression includes the above symptoms of depression as well as hallucinations or delusions (false beliefs that the person holds to be true despite all evidence to the contrary). These persons often become agitated, paranoid, hostile, and disruptive.

Manic-Depressive Illness

Manic-depressive (bipolar) illness is characterized by episodes of abnormally elevated mood (mania) and depression. Mood disturbance during a manic episode may include inflated self-esteem or grandiosity, pressured speech or excessive talkativeness, decreased need for sleep, excessive involvement in pleasurable activities with potential unfortunate consequences, poor attention span, and increase in goal-directed activity. The manic episodes may be followed by episodes of major depression. In the elderly, manic-depressive illness is not as frequent as in younger age groups. The course of illness may vary in that the person may have had episodes of mania during adulthood, but in late life develops the first major depressive episode.

Masked Depression

Masked depression is particularly common to the elderly. While younger patients may complain of feeling sad, older depressed individuals may instead have numerous physical complaints that do not fit any particular pattern of illness. Even though the complaints may be unfounded or unexplained, they may truly be disabling to the depressed person. In this case, the depression is "masked," or hidden. Careful observation on the part of the caregiver and/or family is necessary to detect signs of depression. Elderly persons with feelings of anxiety, agitation, or irritability may also be experiencing a masked depression. Finally, memory loss or change in mental functioning, resembling dementia, may occur with depression. This memory impairment associated with depression is referred to as pseudo-dementia.

Anxious Depression

Some patients demonstrate excessive symptoms of anxiety accompanying depressive mood disturbance. These symptoms include tenseness, anticipatory thoughts, panic reactions, foreboding, and restlessness. Often physicians may misinterpret these symptoms as representing just anxi-

ety disorder. This may cause them to treat these patients with antianxiety medications alone, but with little success. When correctly identified, these patients respond best to antidepressants.

Post-Stroke Depression

Post-stroke depression occurs in up to 50 percent of elderly stroke victims in the year following the stroke. There is widespread misconception that this reaction is appropriate, given the circumstances, and is untreatable. This is not true. Many post-stroke patients respond well to antidepressant therapy, leading to improved quality of life and ability to participate in rehabilitation efforts.

Bereavement

Feelings of depressed mood are a normal reaction to loss of a loved one and generally occur within the first two to three months of the loss. However, preoccupation with self-worthlessness, prolonged and significant functional impairment, loss of interest in activities, poor appetite, weight loss, and insomnia suggest that the grieving process has become complicated by the development of a major depression. Professional help should be sought if these symptoms persist.

Management

In the hands of skilled psychotherapists, cognitive behavioral therapy is effective for mild to moderate forms of depression without the need for medication. For more serious forms of depression, a combined psychotherapeutic and psychopharmacologic approach is needed. The pharmacologic intervention helps normalize the biological changes in the brain that occur in depressed patients, and psychotherapy helps clarify the psychological and cognitive distortions that arise as a result of the illness. Psychotherapy and pharmacologic therapies in tandem ensure a holistic, healing approach to treatment.

Post-stroke depression occurs in up to 50 percent of elderly stroke victims in the year following the stroke.

The choice of antidepressant medication is based on the type of depression, desired side effects of the medication (e.g., drowsiness versus excitation), and avoidance of undesired side effects. The most commonly used antidepressant medications are the cyclic antidepressants, the related drug Trazodone (Desyrel), monamine oxidase inhibitors (MAOIs), and the newer antidepressants fluoxetine (Prozac), and buproprion (Wellbutrin). Some cyclic antidepressants can cause sedation. This may be advantageous for depressed elderly suffering insomnia, but less useful for those who would like to be more alert during the day. A second side effect of both is postural hypotension, a sudden drop in blood pressure when arising, which can result in dizziness and falls. Symptoms of dizziness or unsteadiness should be reported to the physician responsible for prescribing the medication. Finally, cyclic antidepressants have anticholinergic effects (central nervous system effects), resulting in dry mouth, blurred vision, constipation, urinary retention, agitation, or sedation. Of the older antidepressants, nortriptyline (Pamelor) and desipramine (Norpramin) have been shown to have lower anticholinergic side effects and therefore are better tolerated by the elderly. Newer antidepressants promise better side-effect profiles but are often significantly more expensive than the older antidepressant drugs.

Because of the increased risk of undesirable side effects from antidepressant medications, electroconvulsive therapy (ECT) is becoming an increasingly popular form of treatment for severe forms of major depression in the elderly. Despite the fears and misconceptions of the general public, research studies have shown ECT to be a safe and effective means of treating depression. In practice, 80 percent to 90 percent of patients with major depression and melancholia will show marked improvement with ECT. Confusion and memory loss following ECT have been reported, but in fact treatment of depression more often results in improved memory.

When to Seek Help

Despite reluctance of the elderly to seek help for mental illness, the threshold for making contact with a physician should be low. Older persons and their families should seek professional help when depressive symptoms are exhibited that:

1. exceed one month
2. interfere with normal activities and cause a decline in function
3. compromise recovery from a medical illness
4. increase marital or family discord
5. result in increased or new sleep or appetite disturbance
6. and/or are associated with memory and concentration difficulties

● ANXIETY

Anxiety is a subjective psychological state of apprehension, tension, or uneasiness experienced by an individual in response to a generalized or indefinite sense of danger. Anxiety can be a temporary experience, or, for some individuals with a predisposition to anxiety, it can be a chronic problem. Anxiety can be a normal and expected human emotion in certain situations, but when anxiety crosses a threshold of severity and interferes with effective living or interpersonal relationships, it becomes pathological and can be considered a clinical disorder.

Descriptive research of anxiety in the elderly has been devoted largely to examining anxiety symptoms, not specific diagnostic disorders such as panic disorder. It is estimated that 10 percent of the elderly show measurable symptoms of chronic anxiety, and nearly 20 percent may be expected to take prescribed antianxiety drugs within a given year. Depending on age and gender, clinical studies have found that anxiety symptoms in primary care patient populations range from 5 percent to 30 percent.

The most detailed study of anxiety disorders in the elderly is drawn from data collected in the Epidemiologic Catchment Area (ECA) survey. The ECA survey found a decrease in anxiety disorders with age. The estimated prevalence of anxiety disorders for individuals age 65 and older was 5.5 percent, compared to 7.7 percent for those age 18 to 24, 8.3 percent for those age 25 to 44, and 6.6 percent for those age 45 to 64. Gender differences in the anxiety disorders were found as well. For those subjects over 65, the prevalence of anxiety disorders in males was 3.6 per-

Profiles of Productive Aging

Evelyn Nef
Psychotherapist

"I think it was an advantage for me to start very late."

Evelyn Nef's life took a dramatic new direction when she was in her early sixties and decided to train as a psychotherapist.

Born in 1913, she grew up in Brooklyn, the daughter of Hungarian immigrants. Her father, a successful designer of furs discovered that twelve year old Evelyn had a real talent for drawing. He sent her to study at a fashion design school. But two years later, he suddenly died of a heart attack; as Nef puts it, "his business died with him." Almost overnight the family went from being well-off to struggling for survival.

To help support the family, Nef along with all her siblings went to work. She worked in a dress shop, and later sang in a nightclub and became a photographer's assistant. She eventually escaped the struggle by developing her interest in marionettes; in this profession she met a gifted young marionette-maker whom she married when she was 19.

The marriage lasted three years. Subsequently she met and married a polar explorer, Vilhjalmur Stefansson, who had discovered large land masses in the Canadian Artic and written 27 books on his explorations. Nef was 27, Stefansson was 60; he became not only her husband but her mentor, encouraging her to write, and sending her to make speeches when he was unable. She considers her first real job to be her position as the librarian for Stefansson's library, which was the largest polar library in the world.

Nef wrote her own book, *Here is Alaska,* when she was 29, and the book has stayed in print for over 40 years. Her next book, *Within the Circle,* written when she was 31, profiled six Artic communities. Both books were widely popular.

Stefansson died at 82 when Nef was 49. They had spent the previous dozen years at Dartmouth where both Stefansson and Nef had been teaching (although she had not attended college) since the Stefansson library and collection had been given to Dartmouth. When the head of the Sociology Department at Dartmouth moved to Washington to set up the American

Sociological Association's national office, he asked Nef to be his personal assistant, even though she was not a sociologist or an administrator. Nef, encouraged by the president of Dartmouth who told her she could return in a year if it didn't work out, decided to go to Washington. Nef stepped right into her new administrative position, and was highly successful. During this time, while visiting friends in New York, she met her third husband, John Nef, a history professor at the University of Chicago, who was working in Washington.

After they were married, the Nefs returned to Washington where Nef spent her time furnishing her new home and organizing charity events. She began volunteering at the NIMH, working with Dr. Paul McClain, the inventor of the concept of the triune brain. But soon she hungered for a more professional career and decided that she needed to "study something." Nef was concerned that at age 60, institutions would be less enthusiastic about admitting her as a student. However, she secured an interview in New York with the director of the Institute for the Study of Psychotherapy, and was admitted to the program, although she did not have the required masters degree in social work.

While pursuing her degree, she became involved in a study of psoriasis; she raised $45,000 from the Milbank Foundation to examine the psychosomatic aspects of this disease. Once licensed she set up her own practice as a therapist in Washington, D.C.

Nef is very pleased with her choice to become a psychotherapist: "I am happy as a therapist ... I think it was an advantage for me to start very late," she said, "because I have the feeling I don't have seven years on the couch to give to somebody. If I'm going to do this, I have to do this quickly."

Because of this Nef finds her work energizing. "At the end of a day when people say, 'Aren't you exhausted and depressed when you had six or eight patients? ... I'm exhilarated because I've resolved, because I've helped, because the feedback is very good when you are successful as a therapist. Somebody who was unable to face something suddenly says, 'Ah, I found a way.'"

Lydia Brontë

cent while the prevalence in females was 6.8 percent. These findings confirm previous reports that anxiety disorders occur more frequently in women than in men. As with other epidemiologic studies, the ECA study did not partition the sample beyond 65 and over, and thus provided little further knowledge about the prevalence of anxiety disorders in late life.

Anxiety disorders can be classified into specific illnesses based on groups of specific signs and symptoms. Types of anxiety disorders that are particularly relevant to the geriatric population include generalized anxiety disorder, characterized by unrealistic or excessive worry for long periods (six months or longer) accompanied by motor tension, autonomic hyperactivity, and vigilance; panic disorder, involving discrete periods of intense anxiety and fear characterized by shortness of breath, trembling, sweating, and chest pain; and somatoform disorder, a preoccupation with physical dysfunction or symptoms not confirmed by physical or laboratory findings.

The reasons for anxiety in late life are multiple. For some, later life is a time of increased leisure, opportunities for travel and learning, volunteering, and pursuing neglected hobbies. For others, aging is a time of intense anxiety resulting from feelings of loneliness, fear of isolation, chronic ill health, financial limitations, diminished sensory and general functional capacities, and fear of death. These real life problems confront an elderly individual's sense of security, self-esteem, and equanimity and thereby increase the risk of experiencing subjective anxiety symptoms.

Anxiety disorders not only have specified diagnostic criteria, but recent advances in the neurophysiology of anxiety have found specific neurophysiologic markers in the brain, as well as demonstrable changes in neurotransmission and receptor site physiology, that influence the perception and modulation of anxiety. Though detailed explanation of the specific neurotransmitter deficits, disregulation of complementary systems, and alteration of receptor site function in the brain is beyond the scope of this discussion, it is important to acknowledge that alterations of these neurotransmitter systems directly contribute to an individual's perception and modulation of anxiety state.

Generalized Anxiety Disorder

Generalized anxiety disorder is a chronic (lifelong) condition that generally begins in young adulthood and is characterized by excessive worrying, along with other symptoms of anxiety (including motor tension, excessive sweating, muscle tremors, apprehension, and vigilance). Common everyday problems cause undue concern. Eventually, the person begins to exaggerate the problem itself. Something that is only mildly difficult or inconvenient for most people would be seen as overwhelming for these individuals. Whenever a problem occurs, the tendency is to develop strong feelings of fear or dread about potential negative consequences. The older individual is more likely to focus these feelings of dread on bodily dysfunction.

Panic Disorder

Panic disorder is characterized by episodes of sudden and severe anxiety that are generally short lived. These episodes may be accompanied by shortness of breath, trembling, sweating, chest pain, tingling fingers, choking sensations, or nausea. These attacks do not result from any medical condition. A trigger event or a specific stressful situation can sometimes precipitate these episodes, or they can occur without any apparent reason or cause.

Somatoform Disorders

Somatoform disorders are a group of disorders involving preoccupation with some imagined defect in physical function or physical appearance that is not confirmed by physical or laboratory findings. There are two forms of somatoform disorder of particular importance to the elderly: hypochondriasis and somatization. Hypochondriasis is the preoccupation or fear that one has a serious disease based on the person's interpreting physical problems or sensations as indicative of physical illness. The fear of disease persists after reassurance by the physician that examination has revealed no physical signs of illness. The fear may be associated with bodily functions, such as sweating, bowel function, digestion, or heartbeat, or physical abnormalities, such as skin discoloration or sores.

Somatization disorder is characterized by recurrent or multiple physical complaints (e.g., vomiting, nausea, dizziness, chest pain) of several years duration apparently not due to any true physical disorder. Complaints are often exaggerated, involving multiple organ systems. These patients are at high risk for polypharmacy (incompatible drug interactions) and/or complications from multiple diagnostic evaluations. Notably these disorders most commonly begin in early adulthood and when seen in late life represent lifelong personality traits. Depression often exaggerates the presentation of symptoms in these disorders.

Management of Anxiety: Practice Patterns and Problems

The first and foremost aspect of managing anxiety in late life is to make an accurate diagnosis. Patients with generalized anxiety disorder, panic disorder, and somatoform disorder in late life will probably exhibit symptoms recognizable to their primary care physician. Many elderly patients consider it more acceptable to see a primary care physician for emotional disorders such as anxiety. The elderly are often unable or unwilling to verbally express disturbance with their emotions and find it easier to complain of changes in behavior in terms of bodily dysfunction, such as shakiness, restlessness, dizziness, shortness of breath, upset stomach, frequent urination, and so forth. These patients pose subtle but important diagnostic dilemmas for physicians.

Somatic symptoms of anxiety may be misconstrued as symptoms of medical illness, and thus the general physician might order excessive diagnostic testing in order not to miss recognizing a "medical illness." The elderly confound the diagnostic process further, since they often have legitimate medical problems that could explain their somatic symptoms and are less likely to discuss their personal problems than younger patients, frustrating the physician who attempts to investigate the psychosocial aspects of their complaints.

Anxiety symptoms and syndromes in late life not only cause significant distress and disability, but may also contribute to excess medication use that may lead to addiction, dependence, and morbidity. Anxiety symptoms and legitimate anxiety disorders predispose elderly patients to receive medications from physicians, even though a patient's symptoms do not meet the criteria for a specific anxiety disorder. Further compounding the problem is the fact that elders may continue to receive the medication long after their symptoms subside.

In most instances the primary care physician chooses benzodiazepines (Xanax, Ativan, and others) or antidepressants (Tofranil) as a first-line treatment for anxiety. The excessive reliance on pharmacologic management is driven in part by the dramatic reduction of symptoms in the short term, but long-term administration of medication, particularly the benzodiazepines (Valium), may lead to drug dependence. Among those taking such medications, many elders reported persistence of symptoms as well as signs of psychological dependence.

It should be stressed that medications for anxiety symptoms or disorders in the elderly are not without complication. Compared to younger patients, the elderly are reported to have twice the number of adverse side effects and drug interactions. Medications are not cleared from the systems of elders as efficiently as they are in young adults. As such, some medications, like the long-acting benzodiazepines will accumulate in the system and cause excess sedation, diminished sexual desire, worsening of intellectual function, and reduction in the general level of energy. A recent study revealed the use of sedatives to be a significant risk factor for falls in the elderly.

Anxiety symptoms and syndromes in late life not only cause significant distress and disability, but may also contribute to excess medication use that may lead to addiction, dependence, and morbidity.

Psychotherapeutic Management of Anxiety

Psychotherapy offers an alternative to drug therapy. For anxiety disorders, cognitive and behavioral approaches appear to work, but the current generation of elderly individuals were raised in an era when use of mental health services was plagued by stigma.

Psychotherapy is a form of treatment that uses suggestion, persuasion, re-education, re-assurance, and support to effect a change in mental health, avoiding the potential complications of medical therapy. Through a variety of forms that include psychoanalysis, behavior therapy, cognitive therapy, group therapy, and family therapy, psychotherapy attempts to correct unsuccessful adaptation. Specific goals of psychotherapy might include redirecting of energy and creativity to new sources of fulfillment, accepting realistic levels of function, and reestablishing adaptive defenses used to promote feelings of control. When individuals feel they have some control over life events, stressful life events are less likely to adversely affect them. Complete discussion of psychotherapeutic methods is beyond the scope of this discussion, and one should refer to the many texts on the subject for further information.

● SLEEP DISORDERS

The elderly commonly complain of spending more time in bed but failing to feel rested. They complain of difficulty falling asleep, difficulty staying asleep, and needing frequent naps during the day. Of persons 65 years of age and older, 25 percent to 40 percent complain of disturbed sleep. Yet studies have found that, over one's lifetime, the total amount of sleep for a twenty-four-hour period is relatively constant. However, older individuals do not sleep with the same efficiency as younger individuals because of age dependent changes in sleep, chronic medical and neuropsychiatric disorders, and psychosocial and environmental changes. This section will review current knowledge of sleep disorders that are particularly important to the elderly and review approaches to treatment of these disorders.

Reasons for Sleep Disturbance in Late Life

Alterations in sleep occur with age and result in less efficient or restorative sleep. The natural circadian rhythm (twenty-four-hour cycles) changes with age, and elderly individuals find themselves retiring to bed earlier. Major sleep periods tend to occur early in the night's course of sleep. Some individuals develop shorter, more frequent sleep-wake periods similar to that of an infant. The elderly experience decreased continuity of sleep, marked by increased number of brief arousals (from three to fifteen). Daytime napping is another feature of sleep in late life. Sleep studies reveal that older subjects are more susceptible to being aroused by external stimuli during sleep. Studies reporting change in rapid

eye movement (REM) sleep are numerous, with mixed results. REM sleep has been shown to be that phase of sleep where dreaming is likely to occur. Reduction in REM sleep is reported in extreme old age and in individuals with Alzheimer's disease. Gender differences in sleep efficiency with age have not been well documented, but physicians hear more complaints of insomnia from women, and sleep medications are prescribed more often to women.

Of persons 65 years of age and older, 25 percent to 40 percent complain of disturbed sleep.

Poor sleep habits are a common cause of sleep disturbance. Poor sleep habits are conditions affecting the ability to sleep, such as environmental problems, including excessive heat, cold, or noise; evening use of alcohol, nicotine, or caffeinated beverages; or use of the sleep setting for activities not conducive to sleep, such as excessive worry or working in bed.

Beyond age-dependent changes in sleep and poor sleep habits, sleep changes may also be related to specific sleep disorders (see Table 24.5). For example, transient situational sleep disorder occurs in individuals who develop insomnia as a result of a stressful situation, such as the death of a spouse, and it resolves once the stressor is removed.

Medical disorders such as chronic pain, pulmonary disease, gastric disease, congestive heart failure, or diabetes may contribute to sleep problems. Any one or a combination of these problems may lead to difficulty falling asleep or staying asleep. In addition a number of medications for chronic illness may interfere with the sleep-wake cycle. Patients with dementia commonly have fragmented sleep, nighttime wakefulness, confusion, and wandering, which present major problems to families. Disturbances of sleep, poor sleep continuity, and inability to fall asleep often figure in depression as well.

Sleep apnea as a cause of sleep disturbance in the elderly is a relatively new finding. Recent research has found that 25 percent to 40 percent of the elderly experience sleep-disordered breathing. What is commonly called sleep apnea refers

Table 24.5
Causes of Disrupted Sleep in the Elderly

Age related changes
Poor sleep hygiene
Transient situational sleep disturbance
Miscellaneous medical and/or psychological
   conditions
Central sleep apnea
Periodic leg movements

to brief periods of breathing cessation that occur through the course of the night without the awareness of the individual. These periods of apnea result in reports of excessive daytime sleepiness.

Periodic leg movements during sleep, or nocturnal myoclonus, has been reported in as high as 44 percent of persons over 65 with disordered sleep. The leg twitches occur every twenty to forty seconds and may last five minutes to two hours; they are often reported by the bed partner, as the individual is seldom aware of the leg movements. These movements may result in fragmented and non-refreshing sleep.

Treatment Considerations

Since sleep disturbance in late life has multiple potential causes, those elderly with insomnia or excessive daytime sleepiness should seek the aid of a physician, who will explore sleep habits, adverse conditions, medications, and indicators of sleep apnea (nocturnal myoclonus). Information from the bed partner is helpful, as well as a sleep-wake log, which helps to determine the distribution and quality of sleep. If a specific underlying cause of insomnia is identified, such as congestive heart failure or sleep apnea, then appropriate medication therapy is indicated, but it should be supervised by a physician familiar with the nuances of sleep in late life.

Nonpharmacologic Treatment Options

In addressing sleep disturbance, it is important to understand that some sleep disturbance may be an unavoidable consequence of aging. Nonpharmacologic treatment relies on improving sleep hygiene. Sleep hygiene and thus quality of sleep may be improved through a variety of meth-

ods. The following sleep-promoting routine may help:

1. avoid caffeine intake after 2 P.M.
2. increase exercise and mobility as possible
3. reduce daytime napping
4. keep bedtimes regular (note that for an 85-year-old who needs only six hours of sleep, going to bed at 9:00 P.M. will result in awakening at 3:00 A.M.)
5. have realistic expectations about sleep
6. analgesics (e.g., acetaminophen or aspirin) at bedtime may be helpful.

Periodic leg movements during sleep, or nocturnal myoclonus, has been reported in as high as 44 percent of persons over 65 with disordered sleep.

● ALCOHOL AND DRUG DEPENDENCE

Alcohol and drug abuse is no longer thought to be limited to young or middle-age adults. It is estimated that as many as 10 percent of adult alcoholics are over the age of 60. Alcoholism is the most common form of substance abuse in late life. However, this may be due to the fact that the prevalence of drug dependence in the elderly is less clearly documented for various reasons. Appropriate versus inappropriate use of prescription and over-the-counter medications may be hard to determine in the geriatric population where chronic medical illness abounds. Use of recreational drugs by the elderly is not very common.

● ALCOHOL ABUSE

Alcohol dependence is a progressive disorder that peaks in early to mid-adulthood, yet can occur as a late-onset phenomenon in people 60 years and older. However, the majority of elderly alcoholics abused alcohol as young adults and thus have had a life-long problem that has persisted as they have aged. Heavy alcohol intake as a rule drops as people age, especially after age 75. This downward trend begins for most somewhere in the fifth or sixth decade of life. Gender differences in rates of alcoholism exist. The rates of alcohol abuse in men are four to six times that of women.

Elderly alcoholics commonly go undetected. Elderly alcohol abusers are commonly middle class and as such do not fit the common stereotype of the street corner alcoholic. Physicians often do not think of alcohol as a problem in the elderly and thus have a low index of suspicion and low detection rates. As the elderly are no longer working and may be living alone, they are not as closely observed in their daily life, and excessive alcohol intake may go unnoticed.

The reduced prevalence of alcoholism in late life may be due to a variety of factors. With age, there is an increased tendency for alcohol to induce cognitive impairment, unpleasant mood, or physical symptoms. These negative effects may play some role in the decline of alcohol use with age. Low economic or fixed incomes may limit consumption. Also, heavy alcohol abusers tend to die young and thus do not live to experience old age.

It is estimated that as many as 10 percent of adult alcoholics are over the age of 60.

Changes in Metabolism

Normal aging alters the metabolism of alcohol. With age, body water decreases, lean body mass is reduced, and body fat increases. Because ethanol is distributed primarily in body water, blood alcohol levels in elders will be higher for any given dose of alcohol compared to young adults. In other words, the elderly may get intoxicated after consuming lower quantities of alcohol than younger adults.

Cognitive impairment is well documented with alcohol use. Subtle deficits in memory, abstract reasoning, and ability to adapt to novel situations have been reported in alcohol abusers and more moderate drinkers as well, particularly social drinkers. It is not clear whether avoidance of alcohol intake will cause cognitive impairments to reverse.

Treatment Considerations

The treatment of older alcoholics is similar to that for younger alcoholics. Treatment begins with recognition of the problem. Hospitalization for detoxification may be required to avoid potentially serious complications of alcohol withdrawal (i.e., those symptoms associated with abrupt discontinuation of alcohol after prolonged intake). Withdrawal symptoms are characterized by muscle tension and tremor, hyperactivity agitation, sleeplessness, and, in severe cases, hallucinations and potential seizures.

Long-term abstinence may be improved with participation in groups such as Alcoholics Anonymous (AA). Research has found that antisocial personality, cognitive impairment, low socioeconomic status, and family drinking partners are indicators of poor prognosis for continued abstinence.

Family involvement and the guidance of skilled alcohol counselors is critical for successful treatment of those individuals with severe alcohol dependence. Drug and alcohol abuse involves complicated patterns of behaviors in patients and their families. Families can be well meaning, but in point of fact are actually "enablers" of alcohol dependence. Transgenerational conflicts and attitudes often fuel the dysfunction and dependent behavior. It is critical that skilled professionals help sort out the problems and offer direction for successful rehabilitation.

● DRUG ABUSE AND MISUSE

Compared to alcohol abuse, much less is known about drug abuse in late life. Across the life-span, drug abuse primarily focuses on the use of sedative hypnotics and mind altering drugs, such as marijuana, cocaine, LSD, and narcotic analgesics (such as morphine). Drug abuse is associated with a conscious and manipulative drive to obtain medications. This form of behavior leads to important decline in social, interpersonal, and recreational activities. There is little evidence to demonstrate that these patterns of behavior constitute major problems for the elderly at this time. However, prescription drug misuse is common. Doctors have recognized drug dependent behavior in some patients that can best be described as drug misuse.

Drug misuse is different from drug abuse. Drug misuse can occur with prescription and non-prescription medications. Drug misuse by the elderly may be subtle, concealed, and missed, even by the best of physicians and families. Detection is difficult because geriatric patients have chronic medical and psychiatric problems that predispose them to a higher risk of receiving legitimate medications.

The elderly may medicate themselves in an attempt to relieve suffering from chronic medical illness, insomnia, or feelings of anxiety and/or depression. Prominent symptoms of drug abuse occur when the patient is either unable or unwilling to "give up" a prescribed medication or over-the-counter (OTC) medication, or when the physician unthinkingly and repeatedly renews the patient's prescription. The symbolic act of prescribing a medication gets sanctioned when the patient represents the medication as necessary. Over the long term, the patient abdicates personal responsibility for the drug use. Often families and physicians will hear statements such as "it's okay to take this because the *doctor* prescribed it" or "I am not drug dependent because the *doctor* prescribed it." These types of statement indicate that the patient has abdicated personal responsibility for the consuming behavior and is using the physician to justify such actions.

Prescription Drug Use

~ Prescription drug abuse by the elderly has not been well studied. Of the geriatric patients admitted to the hospital, about 20 percent have a drug-induced reason for admission. Analgesics and psychoactive medications, such as the sedative hypnotics and minor tranquilizers, are the most frequently prescribed drugs for the elderly. However, recent data has shown encouraging downward trends in the use of these medications by elders.

The elderly are particularly vulnerable to excessive medication management because they often have complex and confusing symptoms as well as multiple chronic medical problems. Since primary care physicians are the major prescribers of minor tranquilizers and antidepressants in this country, they can inadvertently contribute to the excessive and prolonged use of these medication classes. Interestingly, research has shown that of those elderly taking antianxiety medications, many report that they continue to have the same symptoms that they had when they started the drug, yet they feel that they cannot do without the medication.

Over-the-Counter (OTC) Medication Use

Chronic OTC medication use is the other form of drug misuse by the elderly. Over-the-counter medications are non-prescription medications that may be obtained at pharmacies or health food stores, such as laxatives, cold preparations, aspirin, and so forth. The elderly are seven times more likely to use OTC medications, compared to the general population. One study found that 69 percent of those over the age of 60 took OTC medications, and 40 percent took them on a daily basis. The most commonly used OTC medications include analgesics, antihistamines, sedatives, laxatives, and cold preparations. Although perceived as safe, the side effects of OTC medications are potentially dangerous and increase with age. Complications of aspirin therapy are reported to be the most commonly cited cause of hospitalizations related to medication use. Chronic aspirin use may cause symptoms that mimic neurologic disorders (such as ringing in the ears). Aspirin commonly causes gastrointestinal disorders such as gastric ulcer, which can lead to blood loss. Chronic laxative use is present in at least 10 percent of the elderly and may cause chronic diarrhea, adverse changes in the lining of the large intestine, blood chemistry abnormalities, or malabsorption syndromes. Many cough and cold preparations contain medications (active ingredients) that can cause dry mouth, urinary retention, constipation, and confusion. Some OTC preparations contain antihistamines that cause excessive sedation, further increasing the risk of confusion for some patients. Nasal decongestant sprays can produce rebound symptoms even after short-term use. However the elderly commonly use OTC medications because they view them as a safe and less expensive alternative to visiting a physician.

Complications of aspirin therapy are reported to be the most commonly cited cause of hospitalizations related to medication use.

Treatment Considerations

Once drug dependent behavior is identified, treatment is similar to that of other substance abuse behaviors. Hospitalization may be required to manage the withdrawal symptoms. This will depend on the type of medication being abused, the dosage amount being taken, and the length of use. Educating the person to the potential risk of abusing medications may resolve the situation. Correction of underlying psychological problems, such as anxiety, depression, fears of isolation, or grief, may prove helpful. Emotional support and strengthening of the person's social support system is particularly useful in the elderly. The physician should set limits to access, and to use of addictive drugs, as well as discourage negative behaviors that promote dependence. As with alcohol dependence, family involvement is very important to the long-term success of rehabilitation and change in drug consuming behavior.

Organizations

Alzheimer's Association
National Headquarters
919 North Michigan Ave., Ste. 1000
Chicago, IL 60611
(800) 272-3900

Alzheimer's Disease and Related Disorders Association
70 East Lake St., Ste. 600
Chicago, IL 60601
(312) 853-3060

Alzheimer's Disease Research Center
225 Dickinson St.
San Diego, CA 92103-8204

American Association for Geriatric Psychiatry
P.O. Box 376A
Greenbelt, MD 20768
(301) 220-0952

National Alliance for the Mentally Ill
2101 Wilson Blvd., Ste. 302
Arlington, VA 22201
(703) 524-7600

References

American Psychiatric Association. *Diagnostic and Statistical Manual of Mental Disorders*. 3d ed., rev. Washington, DC: American Psychiatric Association, 1987.
Fogel, B. S., A. Furino, and G. L. Gottlieb. *Mental Health Policies for Older Americans: Protecting Minds at Risk*. Washington, DC: American Psychiatric Press, Inc., 1990.
Hazzard, W. R., R. Andres, E. L. Bierman, and J. P. Blass. *Principles of Geriatric Medicine and Gerontology*. New York: McGraw-Hill, 1990.
Sadavoy, J., L. W. Lazarus, and L. F. Jarvik. *Comprehensive Review of Geriatric Psychiatry*. Washington, DC: American Psychiatric Press, 1991.

Additional Reading

Abramson, Nancy, and others, eds. *The Elderly and Chronic Mental Illness: New Directions for Mental Health Services*. San Francisco, CA: Jossey-Bass, 1986.
American Association of Homes for the Aging (AAHA). *Guide to Caring for the Mentally Impaired Elderly*. Washington, DC: American Association of Homes for the Aging, 1985.
——. *The Nursing Home and You: Partners in Caring for a Relative with Alzheimer's Disease*. Washington, DC: American Association of Homes for the Aging, 1988.
American Journal of Alzheimer's Care and Related Disorders and Research. Boston Post Road, Weston, MA.
Becker, Robert, and Ezio Giacobini, eds. *Alzheimer's Disease: Current Research in Early Diagnosis*. Bristol, PA: Taylor & Francis, 1990.
Berman, Philip L., ed. *The Courage to Grow Old: Forty-one Prominent Men and Women Reflect on Growing Old*. New York: Ballantine, Del Rey, Fawcett, 1989.
Billig, Nathan. *To Be Old and Sad: Understanding Depression in the Elderly*. Lexington, MA: Lexington Books, 1987.
Binstock, Robert H. *Dementia and Aging: Ethics, Values, and Policy Choices*. Baltimore, MD: Johns Hopkins, 1992.
Butler, Robert N., ed. *Aging and Mental Health: Positive Social and Biomedical Approaches*. 4th ed. New York: Macmillan, 1991.
Cecil, C. *Never Too Late: A Message of Hope for Older Alcoholics, Their Families, and Friends*. Minneapolis, MN: CompCare Publishers, 1989.
Cohen, Donna, and Carl Eisdorfer. *The Loss of Self: A Family Resource for the Care of Alzheimer's Disease and Related Disorders*. New York: NAL Penguin, 1986.
Cohen, Gene D. *The Brain in Human Aging*. New York: Springer, 1988.
Colenda, C. C., R. B. Goos, and R. E. Lewis. *Medications Used for Mental Disorders in the Elderly: A Caregiver's Guide*. Burkeville, VA: Piedmont Geriatric Institute, 1991.
Dobrof, Rose, ed. "Social Work and Alzheimer's Disease: Practice Issues with Victims and Their Families." *Journal of Gerotological Social Work Studies* Vol. 9, no. 2 (1986): 126.
Fraser, Virginia, and Susan M. Thornton. *Understanding "Senility": A Layperson's Guide*. Buffalo, NY: Prometheus Books, 1987.
Gruetzner, Howard. *Alzheimer's: A Caregiver's Guide and Sourcebook*. New York: John Wiley & Sons, 1988.
Heckman-Owen, Carol. *Life with Charlie: Coping with an Alzheimer Spouse or Other Dementia Patient and Keeping Your Sanity*. Ventura, CA: Pathfinder, 1992.
Heston, Leonard, and June White. *The Vanishing Mind: A Practical Guide to Alzheimer's Disease and Other Dementias*. New York: W.H. Freeman, 1991.

Hinrichsen, Gregory. *Mental Health Problems and Older Adults*. Santa Barbara, CA: ABC-CLIO, 1990.

Jarvik, Lissy F., and Carol H. Winograd, eds. *Treatments for the Alzheimer Patient: The Long Haul*. New York: Springer, 1988.

Kemper, Donald W., and others, eds. *Growing Wiser: The Older Person's Guide to Mental Wellness*. Boise, ID: Healthwise, 1986.

Lieberman, Morton A., and Sheldon S. Tobin. *The Experience of Old Age: Stress, Coping, and Survival*. New York: Basic Books, 1983.

Lipton, Helen L., and Philip R. Lee. *Drugs and the Elderly: Clinical, Social, and Policy Perspectives*. Stanford, CA: Stanford University Press, 1988.

Mace, Nancy L. *Dementia Care: Patient, Family, and Community*. Baltimore, MD: Johns Hopkins University Press, 1990.

Mace, N. L., and P. V. Rabins. *The 36-Hour Day*. Baltimore, MD: Johns Hopkins University Press, 1981.

Maddox, George L., and others, eds. *Nature and the Extent of Alcohol Problems Among the Elderly*. New York: Springer Publishing, 1984.

Miller, Mary. *Suicide after Sixty: The Final Alternative*. (Vol. 2 of Springer Series on Death and Suicide). New York: Springer, 1979.

O'Connor, Kathleen, and Joyce Prothero. *The Alzheimer's Caregiver Strategies for Support*. Seattle, WA: University of Washington Press, 1987.

Osgood, Nancy J. *Suicide in the Elderly: A Practitioner's Guide to Diagnosis and Mental Health Intervention*. Rockville, MD: Aspen Systems Corp., 1985.

Powell, L. S., and K. Courtrice. *Alzheimer's Disease: A Guide for Families*. Reading, MA: Addison-Wesley, 1983.

Robinson, Anne, Beth Spencer, and Laurie White, eds. *Understanding Difficult Behaviors: Some Practical Suggestions for Coping with Alzheimer's Disease and Related Mental Illnesses*. Ypsilanti, MI: Geriatric Education Center of Michigan, 1989.

Roth, Marton. "The Psychiatric Disorder of Later Life." *Psychiatric Annals* Vol. 6, no. 9 (September 1976).

Sadavoy, Joel, M.D. and Molyn Leszcz, M.D. *Treating the Elderly With Psychotherapy*. Madison, CT: International Universities Press, 1986.

Safford, Florence. *Caring for the Mentally Impaired Elderly: A Family Guide*. New York: Henry Holt, 1989.

Sheridan, Carmel. *Failure-Free Activities for the Alzheimer's Patient: A Guidebook for Caregivers*. Oakland, CA: Cottage Books, 1987.

U.S. Congress, Office of Technology Assessment. *Confused Minds, Burdened Families: Finding Help for People With Alzheimer's Disease and Other Dementias*. Washington, DC: Government Printing Office, 1990.

———. *Losing a Million Minds: Confronting the Tragedy of Alzheimer's Disease and Other Dementias*. Washington, DC: Government Printing Office, 1987.

Zarit, Steven H. *Aging and Mental Disorders: Psychological Approaches to Assessment and Treatment*. New York: Free Press, 1983.

Zarit, Steven H., Nancy Orr, and Judy Zarit. *The Hidden Victims of Alzheimer's Disease: Families Under Stress*. New York: New York University Press, 1985.

Zgola, Jitka M. *Doing Things: A Guide to Programming Activities for Persons With Alzheimer's Disease and Related Disorders*. Baltimore, MD: Johns Hopkins University Press, 1987.

Stanley L. Smith, M.D., M.S.
Christopher C. Colenda, M.D., M.P.H.

25

Health Care Services

- Models of Health Care Delivery • Payment for Health Care Services • Patient Flow
- Health Care Providers • Alternative Health Care • Health Care Research • Health Care Reform

The American health care system potentially offers the best medical services in the world, but it is extremely complex. Health care delivery takes many different forms. Private practitioners, health maintenance organizations, and the Veteran's Administration all provide health care services, but in significantly different ways. Payment mechanisms are equally diverse. Fee-for-service was once the norm, but now more complex contractual arrangements are common. Patients used to pay directly for their own health care. Today, payments are more likely to be made indirectly through private insurance companies, employer insurance plans, or the government.

Patients interact with the health care system in many ways. Available services range from preventive health care, to intensive critical care, to hospice for a terminal illness. These services may be obtained in many different settings: hospitals, offices, special care facilities, or even the patient's own home. Health care providers may be generalists or specialists. Some are integrated into groups or teams that provide a particular type of care. However, most health care providers offer their services independently, allowing patients the freedom to pick and choose what they need or want.

The health care system is continually changing. As medical research increases our knowledge of how to provide better health care, the system evolves to improve care. The system is also changing, for better or for worse, in response to rapidly escalating health care costs.

Both health care providers and patients are confused by the bewildering array of health care insurance and payment plans. Patients who are informed consumers will be able to use the health care system much more effectively.

The diverse and changing nature of the American health care system is both an advantage and a disadvantage. There are services for almost every kind of problem. The latest technologic innovations are widely available. Alternative approaches are common. The elderly, through Medicare, are guaranteed payment of at least some of their health care costs. The disadvantage is that all the different programs have different eligibility criteria and different benefits. Even health care professionals seldom understand all facets of the system. Patients, the elderly in particular, are even less likely to be aware of all the available services. Both health care providers and patients are confused by the bewildering array of health care insurance and payment plans. Patients who are informed consumers will be able to use the health care system much more effectively.

• MODELS OF HEALTH CARE DELIVERY

Fee-for-Service

Traditionally health care in this country is provided on a fee-for-service basis. Health care

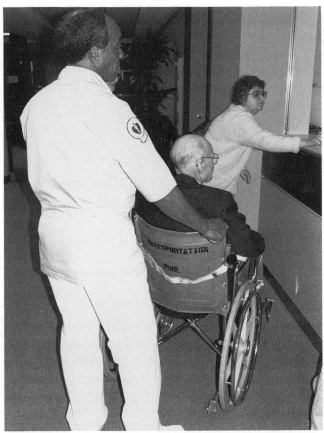

The health care system is changing, for better or for worse, in response to rapidly escalating health care costs. (Courtesy of Bowman Gray/Baptist Hospital Medical Center)

providers are licensed by the state to perform certain services. They work as independent contractors offering their services to patients in exchange for payment. A contract (usually unwritten) is made when a patient consults the provider about a particular problem. Health care providers who work on a fee-for-service basis include physicians, chiropractors, dentists, optometrists, podiatrists, and psychologists. Most are in private practice. Private practice means that the health care provider is self-employed, a member of a partnership or the owner of a small business that provides health care services.

Institutions that offer health care services also traditionally charge on a fee-for-service basis. Hospitals bill for daily room rates as well as charging separately for supplies and special procedures used by individual patients. Large clinics, whose health care providers are salaried employees, still frequently bill patients for the individual services they receive. Laboratories charge separately for each test performed. Long-term care facilities charge for rooms by the day or month.

Third-Party Payment

Although the health care contract is between the provider of the service and the patient, the payment is often made by a third party. Third-party payors include Blue Cross/Blue Shield, commercial insurance companies like Prudential or Aetna, employers, and the government. The third-party payment system in this country has evolved slowly over time. Initially, third-party payment mechanisms were designed to give financial stability to health care providers. Later, third-party payment plans were offered as a fringe benefit of employment. The federal government became involved in the health care system as a third-party payor to provide better health care to the medically underserved. Recent reforms in the third-party payment system have been devised to help contain rising health care costs. A brief history of the development of third-party payment mechanisms will help explain some of the complexities of our current health care delivery system.

Health care insurance in this country developed during the 1930s when hospitals had difficulty collecting payments because of economic effects of the Great Depression. Nonprofit prepayment programs for hospital care were developed under the auspices of the American Hospital Association. Special insurance legislation was enacted in each state to establish these plans, collectively called Blue Cross. Subsequently, state medical societies and the American Medical

The elderly, through Medicare, are guaranteed payment of at least some of their health care costs. (Courtesy of the American Association of Retired Persons)

Association encouraged the development of similar prepaid plans for physician fees referred to as Blue Shield.

The Blues, as Blue Cross/Blue Shield have come to be called, are nonprofit charitable organizations whose rates are regulated by the states. For-profit commercial insurance companies began entering the field when businesses started offering health care insurance as a fringe benefit. Commercial insurance companies are also regulated by the state to make sure that their premiums are high enough to cover the claims made under the insurance they sell.

Commercial insurers usually cover both hospital and physician services under one policy. They also offer cash-payment (hospital indemnity) policies which are sold directly to individuals and pay a flat sum of money per day of hospitalization to help defray the non-medical costs of an illness. Recently, many employers have developed self-insurance programs to cut their health care costs by decreasing the profits of the commercial insurers. The commercial insurance companies still usually manage these programs but provide administrative services only (ASO plans).

Medicare was implemented in 1966 to provide medical care for the elderly. Medicare is a federal government program modeled after Blue Cross/Blue Shield. Part A (similar to Blue Cross) covers allowable hospitalization, nursing home care and home care, and is financed by payroll taxes collected under the Social Security system. Part B (similar to Blue Shield) is a voluntary supplemental insurance program that covers some physician services and other medical expenses. Medicare Part B is financed largely by general tax revenues, but premiums paid by the elderly themselves pay for about 25 percent of the costs. In 1973, benefits were extended to the disabled, their dependents, and those suffering from chronic renal failure, in addition to the elderly. Current Medicare benefits are described in detail in the section Payment for Health Care Services.

The Blues, as Blue Cross/Blue Shield have come to be called, are nonprofit charitable organizations whose rates are regulated by the states.

In 1982, the federal government began encouraging HMOs (and similar competitive medical plans) to accept Medicare and enroll elderly patients. (Courtesy of Bowman Gray/Baptist Hospital Medical Center)

Medicaid was implemented in 1967 to provide medical care to the poor. Unlike Medicare, Medicaid is a joint program of the federal and state governments. The federal government requires that the states provide a certain minimum level of service. In exchange, federal funds are provided to the states on a cost-sharing basis according to the state's per capita income. Because exact eligibility criteria and level of service are determined by the individual states, Medicaid is really fifty different programs. All states, however, must provide coverage to the elderly poor, including nursing home care when needed.

The combination of third-party payment and fee-for-service is at least partially responsible for rapid increases in health care costs in the United States. Since patients do not directly pay for much of the health care they receive, they have little incentive to help contain health care costs by using fewer services, less costly services, or less costly providers. Health care providers, because they get paid for each service they provide, are strongly motivated to provide more services to patients whether or not they are truly needed. In order to place some checks on the unrestrained growth and costs of the fee-for-service health care system, third-party payors have begun to develop and implement new models of health care delivery.

Because exact eligibility criteria and level of service are determined by the individual states, Medicaid is really fifty different programs.

Preferred Provider Organizations

Preferred provider organizations (PPOs) are special arrangements between certain third-party payors and selected health care providers. Large self-insured employers and insurance companies can negotiate contracts with providers to accept discounted fees for services provided to their policyholders. The employer or insurance company then has lower overall costs. The health care provider also benefits if the increased volume of services generated by this arrangement is sufficient to compensate for the discounted fees. Patients retain free choice of health care providers under this system. If they use a health care provider who is not a member of the PPO, their benefits may be slightly limited or they may be charged higher deductibles and/or co-payments.

Because PPOs potentially benefit the patient, the provider, and the third-party payor, their numbers increased rapidly during the 1980s. A few private insurance companies have developed PPOs for Medicare supplemental insurance policyholders. Beginning in 1992, there is a three-year trial in fifteen states of Medicare supplemental insurance using PPOs. These Medicare *select* policies will become more widely available in the future if they are judged successful in holding down costs.

Health Maintenance Organizations

The first health maintenance organizations (HMOs) were formed in the 1930s. The success of a prepaid health care plan for construction workers building an aqueduct from the Colorado River to Los Angeles led to the development of the Kaiser Permanente Medical Care Program in the rural West. Federal employees of the Home Owners Loan Corporation in Washington, DC, formed another early HMO, the Group Health Association. In the late 1940s, Mayor Laguardia of New York helped develop the Health Insurance Plan of Greater New York for city employees. Despite the success of these early programs, physicians in private practice were resistant to the HMO concept, and HMOs disseminated slowly.

HMOs integrate health care delivery and health care insurance into one organization. In this system the health care providers are salaried employees of the HMO. The HMO then contracts with potential patients to provide a stated range of health care services including at least ambulatory care and hospitalization. Instead of fee-for-service, the HMO enrollee pays a fixed annual or monthly payment, whether or not services are used during that time period. A nominal charge (co-payment) may be made at the time of service in some HMOs to prevent excessive or frivolous use of services.

One of the great virtues of HMOs is that they have a strong incentive to provide preventive care. Traditional fee-for-service health care providers benefit financially from the illness of their patients. HMOs are financially at risk for the costs when enrollees develop illnesses. Another advantage is that HMOs emphasize ambulatory medical care. Unlike the original Blue Cross plans that only paid for services when the patient was hospitalized, HMOs save money by avoiding costly hospitalizations. Instead, they provide as much service as possible in the outpatient setting. Studies of HMOs show that they save 10 percent to 40 percent in overall costs over conventional insurance plans.

Because of their ability to cut overall health care costs as well as their emphasis on wellness and prevention, the federal government began to support the development of HMOs in the 1970s. Public Law 93-222 was passed in 1973, authorizing $325 million over five years for grants and loans to cover HMO start-up costs. The initial HMO Act provided for extremely comprehensive health benefits, making the program too costly to compete with existing plans like Blue Cross/Blue

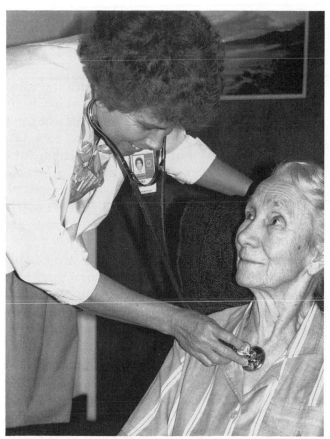

Medicare Part B, which is available to Part A beneficiaries for a small monthly premium, provides coverage for all physician services, and outpatient physical therapy, occupational therapy, and speech pathology services. (Courtesy of Bowman Gray/Baptist Hospital Medical Center)

Shield, even though the benefits were better. Amendments in 1976 loosened the requirements making HMOs more attractive to sponsors and participants. Employers were required to offer a choice of HMO benefits or conventional insurance plans if an HMO was available in their area. In 1982, the federal government began encouraging HMOs (and similar competitive medical plans) to accept Medicare and enroll elderly patients.

There are many benefits for the elderly who get their medical care through an HMO:

- HMOs provide more comprehensive services than traditional Medicare coverage.
- They are much more likely to offer preventive services.
- Services are often conveniently located in one building and can be arranged through one health care provider.
- Monthly out-of-pocket medical expenses can be more easily calculated, making bud-

geting easier for the elderly who live on fixed incomes.

There are also disadvantages to HMO enrollment:

- The patient has to give up established relationships with doctors and other health care providers who are not part of the HMO.
- There may be less continuity of care because of turnover among HMO health care providers.
- Waiting time for appointments under the HMO system is often longer.
- Choices of consultants and hospitals are restricted by the HMO.
- The patient does not get to decide what health care services are wanted; instead the HMO decides what health care services will be offered.
- Since non-emergency services are covered only when obtained from the HMO, the elderly who travel extensively will not have any coverage for minor or routine problems when they are away from home.

Independent Practice Associations

Independent Practice Associations (IPAs) combine features of private practice and HMOs. The IPA is an agency that enrolls physicians and other private practitioners who agree to a central billing mechanism, peer review of quality, and cost controls, including discounted fees. The IPA then contracts with employers, patient groups, or Medicare to provide a package of health care benefits to covered persons in exchange for a set payment.

IPA health care providers continue to work in their own offices providing care to both prepaid and fee-for-service patients. IPAs pay health care providers either on a fee-for-service basis (with careful monitoring by the IPA to prevent payment for unnecessary services) or on a capitation basis. Under capitation, a fixed payment per patient is made to cover all services for a set period of time. Capitation is commonly used to reimburse primary care physicians.

IPAs can expand faster than HMOs because they can draw on the services of the many existing private practitioners. There are none of the up front capital costs of HMOs to build facilities and hire staff. It is unclear, however, if IPAs provide the same benefits in cost-effectiveness as HMOs. Physicians in IPAs are less loyal to the arrangement than HMO physicians and may not emphasize prevention and health maintenance to the same degree. They also may not be as attuned to out-of-hospital care for acute or complex medical problems as their HMO counterparts.

Veteran's Administration

The United States Department of Veterans Affairs (VA) operates the single largest health care system in the country. Before World War II, the VA provided chronic care for a few veterans of World War I in isolated facilities run by the Civil Service Commission. After World War II, under the direction of General Omar Bradley, the system was expanded and affiliations between VA hospitals and medical schools were developed to provide care for the large number of postwar veterans. Currently, the VA operates 172 medical centers, 126 nursing homes, 32 domiciliary care units, and 46 independent or satellite clinics. In 1990, there were 983,000 hospital admissions and 22.6 million outpatient visits to VA facilities. In that year, VA health care facilities employed almost 220,000 people, including 12,241 physicians, and had an operating budget of $11.8 billion dollars.

There are approximately 30 million Americans who are potentially eligible for VA benefits by virtue of military service. In the 1980s, Congress restricted eligibility for hospitalization to veterans with service-connected disabilities, low-income veterans who might not otherwise be able to afford health care, and those who are recipients of VA pensions or support. Eligibility criteria for outpatient care and prescription drugs are more complex.

Roughly two million veterans who are eligible for Medicare choose to receive their medical care in the VA system. As the large pool of World War II veterans age, the VA system anticipates providing considerably more geriatric care. If out-of-pocket health care costs for the elderly continue to rise, the number of elderly obtaining their health care through the VA will likely further increase. In response to the need to care for an increasingly elderly patient population, the VA has developed a unique continuum of geriatric care services (see Table 25.1). The VA Geriatric

---

Voices of Creative Aging

Moe H., 71, uses his inventive skills to help Veterans Administration hospital patients with recovery. He talks about the rewards of his endeavors and enthusiasm for motorcycle riding.

I had a serious heart attack when I was 59 and had to leave my career in private aviation. I flew my own planes for more than thirty-five years. After my heart bypass surgery, I joined a cardiac rehabilitation program, because I wanted to start exercising again, and built a shop for my woodworking hobby. I also have been riding a motorcycle for some time—with the consent of my doctor.

Through the years I have gotten a great deal of satisfaction out of working with the Veterans Administration patients. I can share World War II memories with them and reassure the heart patients about their surgery, since I have gone through heart surgery.

With the help of the technicians, I make devices to assist patients dealing with a variety of problems in their recovery—some little tool. The technicians will explain the need to me, and we'll draw a diagram. Then I fashion the tool. Sometimes I work with the patients on how to use it.

One of the inventions that I made was for a man who had been in a very serious accident, had lost both arms up almost to his elbows. He wanted to do his own shaving. I asked him, "Why don't you just raise a beard?" He said, "Because I don't want to raise a beard. I don't want anybody shaving me; I want to do it myself." Well, the prostheses available were so limited that he couldn't operate an electric shaver or any kind of a shaver very well. So I invented a little holder for the razor. It manipulated on a universal joint. After practicing for a week or so, that elderly gentleman could shave himself just as well as anybody could.

If I can just be with people and be able to do them some good, have them do me some good, I think that will fulfill my desire at this go around.

Excerpt from Connie Goldman's "Late Bloomer" public radio series

Table 25.1
Geriatric Services Provided by the VA

Type of service	Availability
Hospice	5 VA hospitals
Adult day health care	15 VA hospitals
Respite care	128 VA hospitals
Geriatric research, education, and clinical centers (GRECCs)	12 VA hospitals
Nursing home care	30,000 patients/day (VA and community facility contracts)
Domiciliary care	30,000 patients/day (VA and community facility contracts)
Home health care	16,000 patients/year

Research, Education, and Clinical Centers (GRECCs) not only provide model geriatric patient care, they have also pioneered many innovations in geriatric care and trained many specialized geriatric health care providers.

Although the range of geriatric services available in the VA system is impressive, there are limitations. Not all services are available at all facilities. Many veterans do not qualify for full benefits. However, for eligible elderly veterans who live near a VA hospital with comprehensive geriatric services, the VA is an alternative health care delivery system that is well worth considering.

The United States Department of Veterans Affairs (VA) operates the single largest health care system in the country.

● PAYMENT FOR HEALTH CARE SERVICES

Medicare

Medicare is the federal health insurance program that pays part of the health care costs for almost everyone over the age of 65. The Social Security Administration handles enrollment and can also provide information about the Medicare eligibility and benefits. In general, anyone who is eligible for Social Security benefits is also eligible for Medicare. Otherwise ineligible older adults (certain public employees, non-U.S. citizens, certain convicted criminals) can receive Medicare by paying premiums.

The Health Care Financing Administration (HCFA) of the U.S. Department of Health and Human Services is responsible for the administration of Medicare. HCFA interprets Medicare laws and develops policies, rules, and regulations to implement the laws. HCFA contracts with regional intermediaries and carriers, usually private insurance companies, to do the day-to-day work of processing and paying claims. The intermediaries deal with claims from institutions and the carriers deal with claims from individual patients and their private practitioners. The *Medicare Handbook* is published by HCFA to explain Medicare benefits and can be obtained from Social Security offices. It includes a listing of the regional carriers with their names, addresses, and telephone numbers.

Medicare Part A covers hospitalization, posthospital skilled nursing facility care, home health care, hospice, and blood products. The service must be medically necessary and all eligibility criteria must be met. Some of the details of the coverage are provided in Table 25.2.

Beneficiaries should be aware that Medicare payments to hospitals for inpatient care are no longer directly related to hospital charges or costs. In 1983, HCFA adopted a Prospective Payment System (PPS) for hospitals. Under this new reimbursement scheme, the hospital payment for the care of a Medicare patient is based on the average costs in the past for patients with a similar diagnosis. The patient's principal diagnosis for the admission is classified into a Diagnostic Related Group (DRG). Medicare pays the hospital a predetermined amount according to the assigned DRG.

PPS was implemented to help contain costs. Many experts believed that hospitals and physicians were keeping patients in the hospital longer than necessary and performing too many tests and procedures. Under PPS, hospitals have a financial incentive not to provide unnecessary services and to discharge patients promptly.

Under PPS, there have been many allegations that hospitals are discharging patients "quicker

Table 25.2
Medicare Part A: Covered Services per Benefit Period[2]

Services	Time of Coverage	Medicare Pays[3]	Patient Pays[2]
Hospitalization[4] (Semi-private room and board, general nursing, and miscellaneous hospital services and supplies)	Days 1-60	All but $652	$652 deductible
	Days 61-90	All but $163/day	$163/day coinsurance
	Days 91-150[5]	All but $326/day	$326/day coinsurance
	Days 150+	Nothing	All charges
Post-hospital skilled nursing facility care (Medically necessary daily skilled nursing or rehabilitation within 30 days after a 3+ day hospitalization for same condition[6])	Days 1-20	100% approved amount	Nothing
	Days 21-100	All but $81.50/day	Up to $81.50/day
	Days 100+	Nothing	All charges
Home health care (Medically necessary skilled nursing or rehabilitation, home health aid, medical social worker, medical supplies, durable medical equipment)	As long as eligibility criteria are met	100% of approved amount for services; 80% of approved amount for equipment	Nothing for services; 20% of approved amount for equipment
Hospice care (Palliative medical and support services for terminally ill with less than 6 months to live according to their physician)	As long as eligibility criteria are met	All but some costs for drugs and respite care	Limited cost sharing for outpatient drugs and respite care
Blood	When medically necessary	All but charges for first 3 units/year	Charges for first 3 pints/year[7]

[1]Modified from *The Medicare Handbook.*
[2]A benefit period begins on the first inpatient day in a hospital and ends after the patient has been out of the hospital or skilled nursing facility for 60 days in a row or remains in a skilled nursing facility but does not receive skilled care there for 60 days in a row.
[3]These figures are for 1992 and subject to change each year.
[4]Coverage for care in a psychiatric hospital is limited to 190 lifetime days. Coverage for psychiatric care in a general hospital is the same as other hospitalizations.
[5]These 60 "reserve" days may be used only once.
[6]Most nursing homes admissions do not meet these criteria for coverage by Medicare.
[7]To the extent the blood deductible is met under one part of Medicare during the calendar year, it does not have to be met under the other part.

and sicker." In some cases, patients believe they are discharged before they are well enough to leave the hospital. Patients have the right to appeal discharge decisions. The first step is to ask for a review by the Peer Review Organization (PRO). PROs have nurses and physicians who review the quality of care provided by hospitals and attending physicians. PROs can also investigate other complaints or questions about the quality of care provided in a hospital. The names, addresses, and telephone numbers of all the PROs are listed in the *Medicare Handbook.*

Medicare Part B, which is available to Part A beneficiaries for a small monthly premium, provides coverage for all physician services, and outpatient physical therapy, occupational therapy, and speech pathology services. Also covered are Pap smears and mammograms to screen for cancer, and other laboratory tests and X-rays performed because of a medical problem. Outpatient hospital services and ambulance transportation are covered when medically necessary. Mental health services are partially covered. Patients who are eligible for home health care but do not

Table 25.3
Trends in Hospital Usage by People 65+: 1965–88

Year	Number of discharges (in thousands)	Discharge rate (discharges per 1,000 people)	Average length of stay per discharge (in days)
1988	10,146	334.1	8.9
1987	10,459	350.5	8.6
1986	10,716	367.3	8.5
1985	10,508	368.2	8.7
1984	11,226	401.3	8.9
1983	11,302	412.1	9.7
1982	10,697	398.8	10.1
1981	10,408	396.7	10.5
1980	9,864	383.8	10.7
1979	9,086	361.5	10.8
1978	8,708	355.4	11.0
1977	8,344	349.2	11.1
1976	7,912	339.9	11.5
1975	7,654	337.3	11.6
1974	7,185	325.7	11.9
1973	6,937	322.3	12.1
1972	6,634	315.6	12.2
1971	5,986	291.1	12.6
1970	5,897	293.3	12.6
1969	5,694	289.3	14.0
1968	5,529	285.5	14.2
1967	5,210	273.2	14.1
1966	4,909	261.7	13.4
1965	4,602	248.2	13.1

Sources: National Center for Health Statistics. "Trends in Hospital Utilization: United States, 1965–1986." *Vital and Health Statistics* Series 13, no. 101 (September 1989).

National Center for Health Statistics. "National Hospital Discharge Survey: Annual Summary, 1987." *Vital and Health Statistics* Series 13, no. 99 (April 1989).

National Center for Health Statistics. "1988 Summary: National Hospital Discharge Survey." *Advance Data* No. 185 (June 19, 1990).

have Medicare Part A benefits can be covered for these services under Part B. Details of Medicare Part B coverage are provided in Table 25.5.

Medicare Part B benefits do not take effect until the patient has paid a deductible. The deductible is the first $100 charged for services covered by Medicare Part B during the calendar year. Charges above the amounts normally allowed by Medicare do not count toward the deductible. After the patient pays the deductible, Medicare pays for 80 percent of approved charges for covered services for the rest of the year. Many

health care providers and suppliers charge more than the approved amount, and the patient is liable for the difference. This difference is called an excess charge or balance billing.

In 1992, a new federal policy on approved charges for physician services was adopted. Called the Resource Based Relative Value Scale (RBRVS), the new payment schedule assigns a dollar value to physician services based on the amount of work and time involved in providing the service, practice costs in the physician's area, and the cost of malpractice insurance. In the past,

Figure 25.1
Trends in Hospital Usage by People 65+: 1965–88

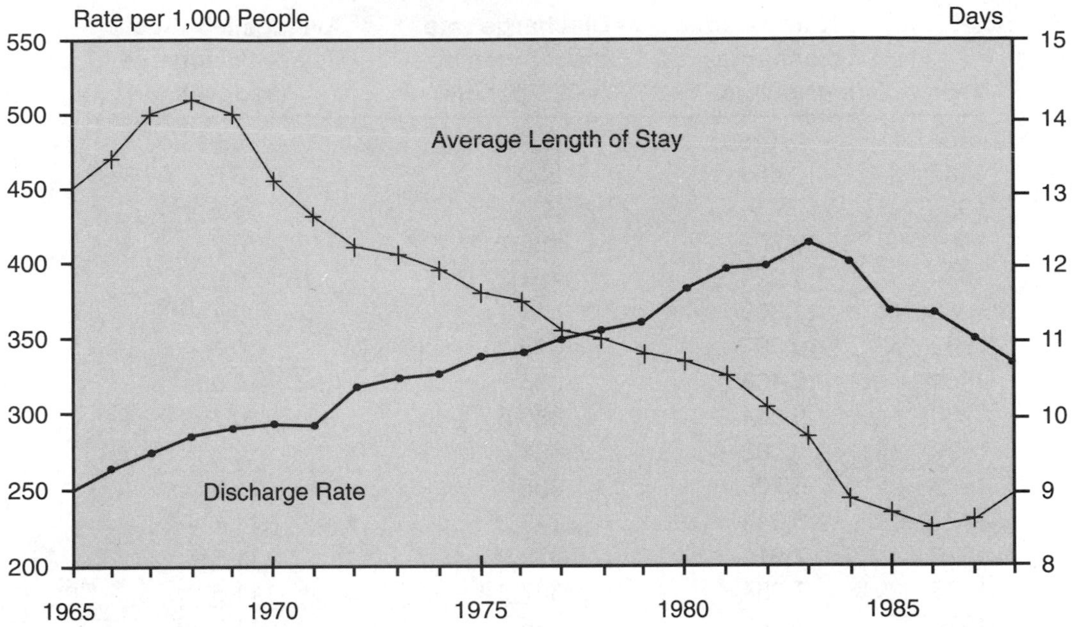

Sources: National Center for Health Statistics. "Trends in Hospital Utilization: United States, 1965–1986." *Vital and Health Statistics* Series 13, no. 101 (September 1989).

National Center for Health Statistics. "National Hospital Discharge Survey: Annual Summary, 1987." *Vital and Health Statistics* Series 13, no. 99 (April 1989).

National Center for Health Statistics. "1988 Summary: National Hospital Discharge Survey." *Advance Data* No. 185 (June 19, 1990).

physicians were paid more for performing medical procedures than for "cognitive services"—spending time talking with and examining the patient or thinking about the best way to handle a problem. RBRVS is designed to pay for cognitive services commensurate with procedural services.

Some physicians and suppliers have special participation agreements with Medicare. Participating physicians and suppliers agree to accept assignment. Accepting assignment on a Medicare claim means accepting the Medicare approved amount as payment in full. Claims for payment from a Medicare assignee are paid directly by Medicare. The patient is only responsible for paying the deductible and 20 percent co-payments.

The Medicare carriers can provide directories with the names and addresses of physicians and suppliers who accept assignment in their area. Many physicians who have not signed participation agreements will take assignment on a case-by-case basis, especially if the patient has a financial hardship. The patient usually needs to ask the physician or the office staff for this special consideration.

Physicians and suppliers who do not accept assignment file a claim with Medicare and then bill the patient directly for all charges. The patient is responsible for paying the total bill usually at the time of service. Medicare will reimburse the patient for its share of the approved amount.

Even when physicians do not accept assignment, there are several federal restrictions on what Medicare patients legally can be charged. (Some states impose additional restrictions as well.) In 1992, physicians could not charge more than 120 percent of the new fee schedule. In 1993, the maximum legal charge was 115 percent of the fee schedule. Physicians are also required to notify patients in writing if they anticipate Medicare will deny payment for a medical service because

Table 25.4
Hospital Discharges of People 65+ by First Listed and All Listed Diagnostic Categories: 1987

Major diagnostic category and selected sub-categories	First listed diagnosis			All listed diagnoses	
	Number (thousands)	Average Percent distribution	length of stay (days)	Number (thousands)	Percent distribution
All conditions	10,459	100.0	8.6	43,230	100.0
Infectious and parasitic diseases	172	1.6	11.2	1,046	2.4
Neoplasms	1,040	9.9	9.3	2,320	5.4
Malignant neoplasms	953	9.1	9.4	2,072	4.8
Endocrine, nutritional, and metabolic diseases, and immunity disorders	456	4.4	9.0	3,837	8.9
Diabetes mellitus	166	1.6	9.4	1,547	3.6
Diseases of the blood and blood-forming organs	125	1.2	7.6	1,153	2.7
Mental disorders	263	2.5	13.0	1,344	3.1
Diseases of nervous system and sense organs	303	2.9	6.9	1,558	3.6
Diseases of circulatory system	3,347	32.0	8.2	13,827	32.0
Heart disease	2,240	21.4	7.5	9,021	20.9
Cerebrovascular disease	665	6.4	10.1	1,484	3.4
Diseases of respiratory system	1,092	10.4	9.1	3,576	8.3
Pneumonia, all forms	445	4.3	10.0	751	1.7
Diseases of digestive system	1,270	12.1	8.0	3,486	8.1
Diseases of genitourinary system	733	7.0	7.0	2,852	6.6
Diseases of skin and subcutaneous tissue	152	1.5	11.2	517	1.2
Diseases of musculoskeletal system and connective tissue	554	5.3	9.1	2,086	4.8
Congenital anomalies	13	0.1	6.8	82	0.2
Symptoms, signs, and ill-defined conditions	65	0.6	4.6	2,176	5.0
Injury and poisoning	775	7.4	9.9	1,700	3.9
Fractures, all sites	404	3.9	11.8	564	1.3
Supplementary classifications	98	0.9	6.7	1,668	3.9

Source: National Center for Health Statistics. "National Hospital Discharge Survey: Annual Summary, 1987." *Vital and Health Statistics* Series 13, no. 99 (April 1989).

it is medically unnecessary. If written notice was not given and the patient did not know that Medicare would not pay, the patient cannot be held liable to pay for the service. Sometimes patients want health care services that Medicare may not consider medically necessary. The patient will be asked to sign a written agreement to pay for the service and will be financially liable, even if Medicare denies payment. Surgeons who do not accept assignment for elective surgery must provide a written estimate of the patient's costs if the total charge will be $500 or more. If a written estimate is not provided, the patient is entitled to a refund of any payment made in excess of the Medicare approved amount.

Gaps in Medicare Coverage

Medicare does not completely pay for services it covers, and many important services are not

Table 25.5
Medicare Part B: Covered Services per Calendar Year[1]

Services	Medicare pays	Patient pays
Physician services Diagnostic services Outpatient physical, occupational, and speech therapy[2] Ambulance services Durable medical equipment[3]	80% of approved amount (after $100 deductible[4])	$100 deductible[4], plus 20% of approved charge and all charges above approved amount[5]
Preventive medical care		
Pap smear every 3 years	80% of approved amount (after $100 deductible[3])	$100 deductible[4], plus 20% of approved charge
Mammogram every 2 years		
Pneumococcal pneumonia vaccine	100% of approved amount[6]	Nothing
Clinical laboratory services	100% of approved amount	Nothing
Outpatient hospital services	80% of approved amount (after $100 deductible[2])	$100 deductible[4], plus 20% of approved charge
Home health care	Same coverage as Medicare Part A for those who have Part B but not Part A	
Mental health services	50% of approved charges (after $100 deductible[2])	$100 deductible[4], plus 50% of approved charge
Blood	80% of approved amount (after $100 deductible[2] and payment for first 3 units)	$100 deductible[4], plus charges for first 3 units plus 20% of approved amounts for additional units[7]

[1]Modified from *The Medicare Handbook.*
[2]Medicare payments to independent physical and occupational therapists are limited to $600/year.
[3]The equipment must be used over and over again by the patient, must primarily serve a medical purpose, must be appropriate for home use and must not be useful to people who are not sick or injured. Medicare payment may be as a lump sum, lease purchase or rental.
[4]The $100 deductible only has to be paid once per calendar year and is then applied to any other claims made.
[5]The patient is responsible for paying charges higher than the approved rate unless the provider agrees to accept Medicare's approved amount as payment in full.
[6]Neither the $100 annual deductible or 20% co-insurance apply to this service.
[7]To the extent the blood deductible is met under one part of Medicare during the calendar year, it does not have to be met under the other part.

covered at all. Medicare does not pay for preventive health care like routine physical examinations. It does not pay for drugs except during hospitalizations or if they cannot be self-administered. Most nursing home care is not covered. Home health care services are not covered unless there is a skilled nursing or rehabilitation need.

> Patients have the right to appeal discharge decisions. The first step is to ask for a review by the Peer Review Organization (PRO).

Homemaker services, even if needed because of illness, are not covered. There is no coverage for routine eye examinations or eye glasses, routine hearing evaluations or hearing aids, dental care or dentures, routine foot care or orthotics (supportive devices). Medical care obtained outside the United States is not covered, except under limited circumstances in Canada and Mexico.

Private Supplemental Insurance

Because of the health care expenses Medicare does not cover, many older adults buy additional insurance coverage from private companies. Several different types of policies are available

Figure 25.2
Where the Medicare Dollar for the Elderly Goes: 1987

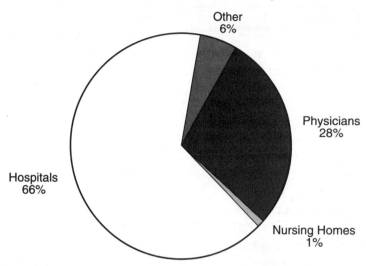

Other
6%

Physicians
28%

Hospitals
66%

Nursing Homes
1%

Note: Total exceeds 100 percent due to rounding.

Source: Waldo, Daniel R., Sally T. Sonnefeld, David R. McKusick, and Ross H. Arnett III. "Health Expenditures by Age Group, 1977 and 1987." *Health Care Financing Review* Vol. 10, no. 4 (Summer 1989).

(see Table 25.6). The costs, benefits, and rules and regulations for the different policies are variable. Some tips for obtaining good coverage at a good price are presented in Table 25.7.

Many elderly choose to purchase "Medigap" policies that are specifically designed to pay the patient's out-of-pocket expenses for covered Medicare services with or without additional benefits. Beginning in 1992, ten standard types of Medigap policies have been established to make it easier to understand the benefits and compare costs of policies offered by different companies.

Table 25.6
Private Health Insurance Policies That Help Pay Medical Expenses Not Completely Covered by Medicare

Type of Policy	Benefits
Medicare supplement	Payment of out-of-pocket expenses services covered by Medicare plus 9 standard additional benefit packages
Medicare select (limited availability)	Similar to standard Medicare supplements but uses PPOs to reduce costs
Continuation or conversion of policy held before age 65 (including employment-related group health plans)	Similar to Medicare supplements but benefits more variable
Coordinated care plan	Enrollment in an HMO or other similar pre-paid health care insurance plan
Long-term care	Cash payments for each day of covered nursing home care
Hospital indemnity	Cash amount for each day of inpatient hospital services
Specified disease	Usually pay set amount for treatment of disease specified by policy

Table 25.7
Health Insurance Shopping Tips

Shop carefully before you buy. Contact different insurance companies and compare premiums (what you have to pay) and benefits (what you get).

Look for an outline of coverage. You must be given a clearly worded summary of the policy. Read it carefully!

Don't buy more policies than you need. Duplicate coverage is expensive and unnecessary. A single comprehensive policy is better than several policies with overlapping coverage.

Consider your alternatives. Continuing existing coverage, joining a coordinated care plan, or buying a Medigap policy all may provide fairly comprehensive coverage. Consider long-term care insurance if you want complete coverage.

Check for pre-existing condition exclusions. Some policies limit or exclude coverage for medical problems the patient had before the policy went into effect.

Be careful when replacing existing policies. Only switch policies if you will get better benefits, better service, or a lower price. Do not cancel the old policy until the new one is in effect and you are sure you want to keep it.

Check your right to renew. Most states now require that policies be guaranteed renewable unless the premiums are not paid, health status is misrepresented on the application, or the company cancels all similar policies in that state. Premiums can be adjusted from time to time. Some old policies may be cancelled on an individual basis.

Know with whom you are dealing. Insurance agents and companies must be licensed by the state. Agents should be able to show you proof of licensure with their name and the company they work for. Write down the name, address, and telephone number of your agent and insurance company.

Complete the application carefully. If you do not provide complete and accurate medical information, the insurance company can deny claims or refuse payment for a period of time for medical problems that were not mentioned on the application. They can even cancel the policy.

Do not pay cash. Pay by check, money order, or bank draft made payable to the insurance company. Get a receipt.

Policy delivery or refunds should be prompt. Policies or refunds should be received within 30 days. If not, contact the company. If 60 days go by without a response, contact your state insurance department.

Use the free-look provision. Insurance companies must give you 30 days to review a Medigap policy. If you cancel the policy within 30 days, you are entitled to a full refund of any premiums paid.

Source: Modified from *1992 Guide to Health Insurance for People with Medicare.*

Existing policies and supplemental Medicare insurance offered by employers are not required to change to meet the new guidelines.

The new Medigap policies are designated by the letters A through J. All include five core benefits: (1) Part A coinsurance payment for days 61 through 90 of a hospital stay, (2) Part A coinsurance payments for the 60 lifetime reserve days of hospitalization, (3) 100 percent coverage of inpatient hospital care after Medicare benefits are exhausted, up to lifetime maximum of 365 days, (4) coverage for reasonable cost of the first three units of blood unders Part A or B, and (5) coverage for the 20 percent coinsurance payments under Part B after the $100 deductible is met.

There are also eight optional benefits that may be offered in different combinations. These include coinsurance payments for skilled nursing care and the Parts A and B deductibles. The five other additional benefits cover services not included under Medicare. Part B excess charges (those exceeding the Medicare approved amount) may be fully or partially covered. Foreign travel emergency coverage pays for medically necessary care in a foreign country. At-home recovery benefits pay up to $1,600 per year for short-term assistance with bathing, dressing, personal hygiene, etc., for those recovering from an illness, injury, or surgery. The prescription drug benefit may be basic or extended. Basic drug benefits have a $250 annual deductible, a 50 percent coinsurance payment, and a $1,250 annual maximum benefit. The extended drug benefit is the same, but has a $3,000 annual maximum benefit. The preventive medical care benefit pays up to $120 per year for a physical examination,

Table 25.8
Standard Medicare Supplement Benefit Plans A Through J

BENEFITS	A	B	C	D	E	F	G	H	I	J
Core benefits	X	X	X	X	X	X	X	X	X	X
Skilled nursing facility coinsurance (days 21–100)			X	X	X	X	X	X	X	X
Part A deductible		X	X	X	X	X	X	X	X	X
Part B deductible			X			X				X
Part B excess charges						100%	80%		100%	100%
Foreign travel emergency			X	X	X	X	X	X	X	X
At-home recovery				X			X		X	X
Prescription drugs								basic	basic	extended
Preventive medical care					X					X

Source: Modified from *1992 Guide to Health Insurance for People with Medicare.*

flu shot, hearing test, and screening tests for various diseases. The standard Medicare supplement benefit plans are summarized in Table 25.8. All plans may not be available from all insurance companies in all states.

Congress has recently passed legislation requiring a six month open enrollment period for people over the age of 65 to purchase Medigap policies. The open enrollment period begins on the effective date of Medicare Part B coverage. During the open enrollment period, insurance companies must offer the individual any policy they sell without delaying the effective date or increasing the premium because of medical conditions, large insurance claims in the past, or receipt of particular types of health care. The company can exclude payments for pre-existing conditions for the first six months after the policy takes effect. This law is designed to prevent people with serious health problems from being denied supplemental insurance.

An alternative to traditional Medigap insurance is to join a coordinated or managed care plan like an HMO or IPA that accepts Medicare enrollees. These plans usually charge a monthly premium and small co-payments for services. All Medicare benefits are preserved, and the patient does not have to pay the usual Medicare deductibles and coinsurance amounts. Services are usually more comprehensive than Medicare, and there is more of an emphasis on preventive care and ambulatory services. However, joining a coordinated care plan may result in loss of Medicare benefits for nonemergency services outside the plan. In other words, the patient is "locked in" to receiving their health care from the providers affiliated with the plan.

Long-Term Care Insurance

Long-term care is not usually covered by Medicare, supplemental insurance policies, or coordinated care plans. Some insurance companies are beginning to offer specific long-term care insurance. Long-term care insurance is expensive, and because it is new there has been little experience with the different policies. Special care should be taken in selecting policies.

Long-term care insurance covers care in a nursing home, but not all levels of care may be covered. A policy that only covers skilled care will exclude the majority of nursing home care. A policy that excludes custodial care also considerably limits benefits. Policies should not limit benefits to Medicare-certified nursing homes. Many nursing homes are not certified by Medicare, and those that are may have long waiting lists. A few policies cover long-term care at home. Benefits may be limited by requiring hospitalization or skilled care for the illness before coverage goes into effect. Policies with these clauses should be avoided, since acute care may not be needed before long-term care. Most policies have an elimination period or a waiting period before the benefits go into effect for a particular episode of long-term care.

Benefits are usually paid as a dollar amount for every day of long-term care. The actual amount varies widely. The benefit will typically

Table 25.9
Services Covered by Medicaid

Available in *Most* States	Available in *Some* States
Medicare deductibles and coinsurance payments	Private duty nursing
Prescription drugs	Personal care services
Medical transportation	Homemaker service
Eye examinations and eye glasses	Adult day care
Dental care and dentures	Home-delivered meals
Podiatric care	Emergency response systems
Chiropractic care	Respite services (to relieve caregivers)
Occupational therapy	Case management

be less than the actual daily charges for long-term care, and the patient will have to pay the difference. Most policies also have a maximum number of benefit days or dollars. Some policies have built in adjustments for inflation and increasing costs of long-term care. Policies that do not will gradually decrease in value over time (more of a problem for a 55 year old than a 75 year old).

Applicants for long-term care insurance will be screened to determine their medical condition. Insurance companies will charge higher premiums or deny coverage to people who have illnesses that increase their risk of needing long-term care. Waiting periods for coverage for pre-existing conditions (medical problems treated, diagnosed, or present prior to the effective date of the policy) can also be imposed. Some policies may exclude coverage for certain illnesses. Long-term care policies that exclude coverage for Alzheimer's disease and related disorders are probably not a good buy, since many nursing home patients have this problem.

Medicaid

Medicaid is a health insurance program for people of all ages who cannot otherwise afford to pay for their own health care. Older adults with limited financial resources may be eligible for Medicaid in addition to Medicare. Medicaid then pays the Medicare deductibles, coinsurance amounts, and Part B premiums, in addition to providing needed medical care not covered by Medicare. Medicaid is run by the states, so exact eligibility criteria and benefits vary from state to state. Information about Medicaid can be obtained from local Departments of Social Service.

In most states, all older adults who receive Supplemental Security Income (SSI) are automatically eligible for Medicaid. SSI is a cash assistance program for the elderly and disabled with very low incomes and limited assets. (SSI should not be confused with Social Security benefits received by most retired older adults.) The elderly may also "spend down" to Medicaid income and asset levels by paying for medical care and other necessities.

Medicaid provides many health care services that are not covered by Medicare. Medicaid pays for nursing home care in all states when it is medically necessary. Medicaid also pays for home health care services. In some states, the eligibility criteria for Medicaid home health services are less strict than the ones used by Medicare. Other Medicaid services are listed in Table 25.9.

Medicaid makes payment directly to the service providers. In each state, Medicaid determines the rate it will pay for services and contracts with providers who are willing to accept the established rate as full payment. Medicaid recipients can only obtain their health care from these providers that accept Medicaid.

Some low income older adults who are not eligible for full Medicaid benefits may still be able to receive some assistance from their state Medicaid office. All states have special programs for qualified Medicare beneficiaries. These programs pay the monthly Medicare Part B premiums and usually the Medicare deductibles and coinsurance payments as well.

Figure 25.3
Where the Medicaid Dollar for Elderly Goes: 1989

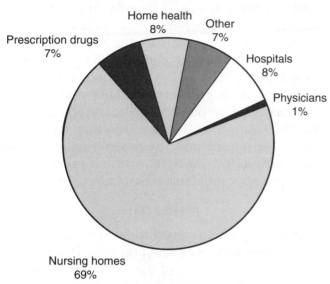

Home health 8%

Other 7%

Prescription drugs 7%

Hospitals 8%

Physicians 1%

Nursing homes 69%

Source: Reilly, Thomas W., Steven B. Clauser, and David K. Baugh. "Trends in Medicaid Payments and Utilization, 1975–89." *Health Care Financing Review* (1990 Annual Supplement).

● PATIENT FLOW

Ambulatory Care

Ambulatory care (also called outpatient care) refers to health care services that are provided outside of hospitals, long-term care institutions, and the patient's home. Ambulatory care accounts for most of the contacts that people have with the health care system.

The majority of ambulatory care services occur in the offices of private practitioners. Patients can often choose between solo, group, and multispecialty office practices. There are advantages and disadvantages to each. Solo practitioners generally provide very personal care with small friendly office staffs and a minimum of bureaucratic hassles. However, their patients may not have access to a covering physician when they are personally unavailable, they often don't have laboratory or X-ray facilities in their offices, their work is essentially unsupervised, and they have to devote considerable time to the administrative aspects of running a medical practice. Small single-specialty group practices have become more popular with physicians because they can share responsibility for patient calls at

night and on weekends and also divide the overhead costs and administrative duties required to run the office.

Many group practices now include multiple specialists. Large groups can be more economical by sharing staff and employing professional management. The different specialists can build their practices through referrals from other group members. Medical care for the patients may be more comprehensive if common medical records are used and the group is able to provide laboratory, X-ray, and/or pharmacy services. There is also usually more supervision of individual doctors who will be expected to perform in accordance with the standards of the group. However, as medical groups get larger, they can also become more impersonal. Another disadvantage of large multi-specialty fee-for-service groups is that they may encourage overutilization of services. All the providers benefit financially if they consult other members of the group or order more lab and X-ray tests.

The private practice fee-for-service system has been inadequate to promote the development of ambulatory care services in some areas. The federal government has financially supported the establishment of outpatient health centers in health manpower shortage areas. Ambulatory care programs that have received some federal support include community health centers and rural health clinics.

Local governments also provide some ambulatory care services through their health departments. Usually these services are in the form of categorical programs that care for a particular type of patient or disease. The services are typically ones that would not otherwise be available and are often offered for free or at low cost. Examples of these types of programs that might be used by the elderly include tuberculosis clinics, screening programs for chronic diseases, home health nursing, and homemaker services for the functionally impaired. The exact services available vary widely from community to community.

Hospitals are another source of ambulatory care, usually in the emergency room or a hospital clinic. Emergency rooms (ERs) are not a good place to get routine ambulatory care services. The focus of the ER is providing treatment for life-threatening emergencies. The patient with a minor problem will have to wait while more urgent problems are cared for. The staff generally has little interest or expertise in nonacute medical problems, and there is no continuity of care when follow-up visits are needed. Because of the need to provide high-tech services around the clock, ERs are much more expensive than other sources of outpatient care.

Hospitals clinics have historically been run by teaching hospitals to provide educational opportunities for medical students and physicians in training. In exchange, they provide care to indigent patients. The clinics are often overcrowded with less than optimal equipment and furnishings. Although patient care in these clinics is usually supervised by medical school faculty, there may be little continuity from visit to visit, and the focus may be on subspecialty issues rather than comprehensive primary health care.

Since Medicare and Medicaid have made reimbursement available for many previously uninsured patients, many teaching hospitals have developed group practice plans for their medical school faculty. The type of care patients receive in these clinics is usually similar to that in private offices. The physician is usually an expert in his or her field and may do research, in addition to seeing patients.

Some community hospitals are also developing clinics to provide care for patients who do not have a private physician. Many of these clinics function on a walk-in, urgent care basis and then refer patients to private physicians who have admitting privileges at the hospital. These clinics are often designed to help hospitals compete for patients.

In the 1980s there have been some innovations in ambulatory care. Free-standing urgent and emergent care facilities have been opened across the country by medical corporations and entrepreneurs. These centers emphasize convenience for the patient, are strategically located to maximize business, and are run on a walk-in basis. The patient may be expected to pay at the time of the service and file their insurance claims on their own. Physicians in these facilities often work on an hourly basis and there is little continuity of care. The quality of care provided in these facilities has not been well studied and is probably variable.

Another new development is the ambulatory surgery center. These facilities are often affiliated with hospitals or large group practices. In these centers, the patient is usually admitted, has surgery, and is discharged within four to eight hours. It has been estimated that about 40 percent of the surgical procedures traditionally performed in the hospital could be safely done on an outpatient basis with considerable cost savings. Patients need to be screened carefully prior to the procedure to make sure that they are at low risk for complications. In general, patients that have serious or poorly controlled chronic diseases are not candidates for ambulatory surgery.

Hospital Care

There are about seven thousand hospitals in this country with over a million beds. In any given year, about 20 percent of the elderly are hospitalized. In 1989, 55 percent of Medicare expenditures were for inpatient medical care.

The American Hospital Association classifies hospitals in several different ways. Short-term hospitals have an average length of stay less than thirty days, and in long-term hospitals the average length of stay is over thirty days. Hospitals can be (1) private nonprofit (voluntary or church-affiliated), (2) public (run by the government), or (3) proprietary (investor-owned and for-profit). Hospitals may be independent or part of a chain. Multihospital systems may be for-profit, like Hospital Corporation of America (HCA), or nonprofit, like the hospitals owned by Kaiser-Permanente.

Public hospitals are sponsored by federal, state, or local governments. Federal hospitals are usually designated for particular groups: Native Americans, merchant seamen, military personnel, or veterans. State hospitals often provide long-term care for patients with chronic or psychiatric diseases. A few states run hospitals that are affiliated with state-supported medical schools. In small cities and towns, the local governments often support community hospitals, which are used by private physicians and provide care to all patients, whether they have insurance or not. In large cities, public hospitals primarily provide care to the indigent. The physician staff often consists almost entirely of physicians in training. When these hospitals have strong medical school affiliations, the technical quality of the medical care is excellent. However, overall staffing, equip-

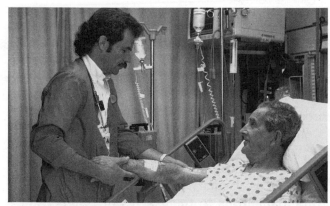

In teaching hospitals, the focus of care is very disease-oriented and may not be very personal. For routine, uncomplicated problems, patients may be better satisfied in a good community hospital. (Courtesy of Bowman Gray/Baptist Hospital Medical Center)

ment, buildings, and amenities are usually inferior to other hospitals. The patients may have special social problems (drug addictions, homelessness, prisoners from the local jail) and/or complex medical problems (AIDS, severe burns, premature babies, victims of trauma).

Hospitals can also be divided into teaching and nonteaching. Teaching hospitals are those that have postgraduate medical training programs called residencies. The physicians in training provide at least some of the care patients in the hospital receive and are referred to as house staff or house officers. The house staff are supervised by experienced physicians employed by the hospital and/or by the patient's private physician. Many teaching hospitals are affiliated with medical schools and also provide educational experiences for medical students.

Teaching hospitals usually have a very broad range of medical specialists on their staffs and can provide very complex, highly technical services like neonatal intensive care units for very premature babies, open heart surgery, organ transplants, and care for badly burned patients. Teaching hospitals are referred to as tertiary care centers, because they frequently receive referrals from other hospitals to provide care to patients who are very ill or have rare or undiagnosed conditions. In spite of (or perhaps because of) the ongoing educational process, teaching hospitals generally provide very high quality care. However, the patient is interviewed and examined by many different people and more tests are

done. The focus of care is very disease-oriented and may not be very personal. For routine, uncomplicated problems, patients may be better satisfied in a good community hospital.

Teaching hospitals are referred to as tertiary care centers, because they frequently receive referrals from other hospitals to provide care to patients who are very ill or have rare or undiagnosed conditions.

Emergency Medical Services

Emergency medical services (EMS) are those provided to victims of accidents and acute, catastrophic illnesses on an immediate basis. They are designed to preserve life and prevent or at least diminish the extent of permanent disability. EMS can be divided into prehospital care and emergency medical care provided at the hospital.

Historically, prehospital care consisted of ambulance services (essentially just rapid transportation services) run as a side line by funeral homes. Because ambulance services tend to be unprofitable, they were gradually abandoned by the funeral homes, leaving the communities with this responsibility. The quality of prehospital care is highly variable, depending on the resources that different communities have put into their programs. In some areas EMS is a government function, but in many rural areas EMS is staffed and coordinated by volunteers.

The prehospital care personnel are integral to EMS programs. They may be volunteers with special training or paid, full-time, highly trained professionals. Emergency Medical Technicians (EMTs) are certified by the states, and their activities are regulated according to the amount of training they have had. All EMTs can provide basic life support, including cardio-pulmonary resuscitation (CPR). Paramedics, who have hundreds of hours of advanced life support training, can treat patients with emergency drugs and perform some emergency medical procedures. Not all communities have paramedics to provide EMS.

A first-rate EMS program also requires adequate financing, high-quality equipment, and facilities. The cooperation of the involved professions, agencies, institutions, and local governments is required to coordinate services. A complex series of communication links between the victim, the dispatcher, the pre-hospital care personnel, and the hospital emergency room are also needed.

From the patient's point of view, access to EMS is paramount. Nationwide implementation of a uniform emergency telephone number, 911, is still ongoing. The elderly need to become familiar with the EMS program in their area so they know how to use it in case of emergency. In communities that don't have a 911 emergency system, the telephone numbers of emergency personnel need to be readily available at the telephone.

Definitive emergency care is usually provided in a hospital. Hospital emergency services are highly variable. Small rural hospital emergency rooms are often staffed with nurses, and the physician is on call but not necessarily in the hospital at all times. Most community hospitals have a physician on duty twenty-four hours a day. Medical centers usually have one or more physicians available in the hospital as well as a full range of specialists and subspecialists who are on call. Trauma centers have a surgeon available in the hospital at all times and surgical sub-specialists available on call.

Field EMS personnel know the capabilities of the hospital emergency rooms in their area, including how long patients are waiting to be treated. In life-threatening situations, patients are taken to the closest available facility *that can handle the problem*, bypassing hospitals that are geographically closer if necessary. When time is extremely critical or the hospital is far away, air transportation in specially equipped and staffed helicopters may be used.

Mental Health Care

The elderly seldom take advantage of formal mental health services. Mental illness is viewed as embarrassing and socially unacceptable. The mental health care delivery system is confusing with its many different options for care, most of which are not specifically for geriatric patients. Health care insurance programs, including Medicare, restrict benefits for mental illness.

Mental health care services are available on both an inpatient and outpatient basis, in public and private institutions. An increasingly large percentage of psychiatric services are provided by general hospitals. Federally funded community mental health centers provide a broad range of services to the residents of a specific geographic area. Fees are usually based on ability to pay.

In general patients have the right to refuse medical treatment, but all states permit involuntary treatment of mental illness under certain circumstances. Usually the patient must be judged to be dangerous to themselves or others. States also have provisions for guardianship for patients who are unable to think clearly enough to make health care or other decisions for themselves.

Rehabilitation

Rehabilitation is a multidisciplinary program of treatment designed to maximize the function of an individual with a disability or physical impairment. Early rehabilitation efforts were directed at war veterans with disabling injuries, workers injured on the job, and victims of crippling childhood illnesses like polio. Federal legislation in 1943 (Vocational Rehabilitation Law) prompted the development of state vocational rehabilitation programs. These programs were designed to help disabled individuals return to a normal functional state or acquire new job skills that they could perform despite their handicaps. In 1962, comprehensive research, rehabilitation, and training centers were created, which are now under the title of the National Institute on Disability and Rehabilitation Research (NIDRR). Because of a continuing emphasis on job skills and employability, the elderly were generally neglected by these programs established through federal legislation.

Although formal comprehensive rehabilitation programs have been geared towards younger individuals, the elderly frequently need and benefit from rehabilitation services. After an acute medical problem like a stroke or hip fracture, acute care hospitals initiate rehabilitation. Before the implementation of Medicare's prospective payment system, the elderly person often remained in the hospital through most of the rehabilitation process. Now, since PPS penalizes hospitals for lengthy patient stays and provision of "extra" services, patients are discharged as soon as their medical condition is stabilized.

Arrangements are made for rehabilitation after hospitalization.

Rarely, elderly patients are discharged to rehabilitation hospitals. Rehabilitation hospitals provide very intensive services and usually only accept patients who are relatively healthy aside from their disability, who are strongly motivated to improve and who have a good chance of becoming independently functional. The elderly frequently cannot meet all of these criteria. More commonly, the elderly receive rehabilitation services in a skilled nursing facility. If the patient's functional impairments are not too great and/or they have family or friends who can help provide care at home, the patient may receive rehabilitation services at home.

Medicare covers rehabilitation services in a rehabilitation hospital, skilled nursing facility, or at home. Medicare generally requires evidence of continual improvement to pay for rehabilitation services regardless of the setting. Services that help maintain function or prevent deterioration,

although they may be vitally important to the patient's well-being, are not covered.

Home Health Care

Home health care services are those that are delivered in the patient's own home. Home health services may be provided on a temporary basis, for an acute illness, or may be part of the long-term care plan for a chronic illness. Providers of home health care often require that the patient be homebound. Nurses are the primary providers of home health services, but other health care providers, like physical, speech, and occupational therapists, also often work in the home. Medicare pays for skilled nursing care and rehabilitative services in the home if they have been ordered by a physician, the patient is homebound, and the services are provided by a Medicare-certified home health agency (HHA).

House calls by physicians, once the standard for medical practice, are enjoying a resurgence in some areas. Many primary care physicians and

Due to the rapid increase in health care costs to care for elderly individuals with chronic illness, a great deal of effort and money is going into research on problems related to aging. (Copyright © Benjamin Porter)

geriatricians make at least some house calls to provide care to longtime patients who have difficulty getting into the office. In larger cities, where patients live close to each other and travel time is minimized, organized physician home care programs have developed. Some even use mobile vans to provide laboratory and X-ray services. One of the major impediments to further development of physician home care services is the low rate of Medicare reimbursement. Physician payments for home visits are based on usual and customary charges of a bygone era. Medicare currently pays far more for home visits by a nurse, because home health agencies receive cost-based reimbursement. Unless physicians receive reimbursement for house calls that is comparable to that for office visits, there will little incentive for them to provide more home health care.

Long-Term Care

Long-term care services are those that are provided on a sustained basis to enable people with chronic conditions resulting in functional impairments to maintain their maximum level of health and well-being. Long-term is defined as more than thirty days in the hospital setting and more than three months in other settings. Long-term care can be provided in many different settings: nursing homes, rest homes, assisted living housing, day care facilities, or the patient's own home. Life care communities are a relatively new concept in long-term care for the elderly. For a moderate to substantial entrance fee plus monthly fees, residents purchase a continuum of care. Depending on their functional status, they may reside in an independent living area (often with many leisure-time amenities), an assisted living area with meals, laundry, and housekeeping services provided, or a skilled nursing facility.

Until recently, long-term care for the elderly in this country was synonymous with nursing home care. There are roughly 19,000 nursing homes in this country, and about 75 percent of these are operated for profit. At any given time, about 5 percent of the elderly population is in a nursing home. About 20 percent of the elderly will spend some time in a nursing home. Most elderly dislike nursing home care because of the loss of independence and autonomy. There have also been many questions about the quality of institutional

long-term care. The high cost has been another major concern.

In the 1980s, the federal government and others sponsored several demonstration projects to try to substitute community-based long-term care programs for nursing home care. Although the clients of these programs and their caregivers often showed benefits from community-based long-term care, overall costs were no less than traditional nursing home care. Because of the failure to save money, the federal government is no longer strongly encouraging the development of community-based long-term care. However, many states run programs for the indigent through special Medicaid waivers from the federal government. The elderly who are not eligible for Medicaid may be able to pay for similar services through aging agencies or home health agencies.

Medicaid (not Medicare) is the primary public payor for long-term care; most Medicaid funds go to provide institutional care in nursing homes. When long-term care is provided in the community, much of the service is provided by informal caregivers like family and friends. When formal paid services are used, only about one-third of the costs are covered by federal programs. Medicare and Medicaid cover some of the costs of home health care, but they have strict eligibility criteria. Indirect federal funding through Title III of the Older Americans Act and Title XX of the Social Security Act is often used by the states to provide supportive social services for the chronically ill and home-bound elderly. These programs are also often targeted to the low-income elderly. Eligibility criteria and the range of services provided differ from state to state. Potentially available services are listed in Table 25.10.

Area Agencies on Aging (AAAs) are an important source of information about long-term care services for the elderly. An AAA is a public or private nonprofit agency that has been designated by the state to oversee services to meet the needs of Americans over 60 years of age in their geographic area. These organizations (1) serve as advocates for older adults, (2) identify the needs of the elderly in their area, and (3) administer funding for services provided under the Older Americans Act. The AAAs also monitor the quality of services for the elderly. The telephone number for the Information and Referral Service of the AAA in any area of the United

Table 25.10

Community Services for the Elderly Funded Through Title III of the Older Americans Act and Title XX of Social Security Act[1]

Information and referral: Provides information about available services and helps individuals contact service providers.	Home-delivered meals: Available to those unable to shop for and prepare food.
Transportation: May be through public transportation or volunteer programs.	Homemaker and chore services: Assistance with house work and home maintenance.
Case management: Assessment and care planning.	Telephone reassurance: Regular pre-scheduled calls to ensure personal safety.
Adult day care: A protective program to meet the needs of the functionally impaired who require assistance less than 24 hours a day.	Friendly visiting: Periodic visits to the home-bound to provide social contact and reassurance.
Congregate meals: Provide one-third of the Recommended Daily Allowance of nutrients in a group setting, e.g., senior center, church, or school.	Energy assistance and weatherization: Helps pay fuel bills and weatherization costs for low-income elderly.
Legal assistance: Wills, power of attorney, guardianship, "right to die" living wills, government benefits, consumer services, age discrimination, etc.	Emergency response systems: Electronic devices to link the individual with emergency services, usually just by pressing a button on the device.
Senior centers: Sites that support group activities for social, physical, religious, and recreational purposes.	Respite care: Allows family members to take a break from care-giving responsibilities.
Elder abuse prevention programs: Programs to reduce abuse, neglect, and self-neglect.	Pre-admission screening for long-term care: An evaluation to assess if nursing home placement is appropriate.
	Long-term care ombudsman: Investigates and helps resolve complaints about nursing home care.

[1]Not all services are available in all communities.

States can be obtained by calling Eldercare Locater at 1-800-677-1116. Eldercare Locater is a service of the National Association of Area Agencies on Aging.

There are roughly 19,000 nursing homes in this country, and about 75 percent of these are operated for profit. At any given time, about 5 percent of the elderly population is in a nursing home. About 20 percent of the elderly will spend some time in a nursing home.

Hospice

Hospice is a philosophy of care for the terminally ill that is comprehensive and holistic, emphasizing death with dignity rather than pro-

longing life at all costs. The principal goals of hospice care are to allow people who are dying to do so without pain, in peace, and in their own homes whenever possible. Pain and symptom control are a major focus of care, but psychological and spiritual needs are also addressed. Hospices extend their caring efforts to family and friends as well as the dying patient.

Hospice care is appropriate for patients who are expected to live less than six months when curative therapy is either not available or not desired by the patient. The patient and their family should be aware of the diagnosis and prognosis. Most hospices only accept patients who have a family member or friend willing to serve as the primary caregiver.

Most hospice patients are over the age of 65, partly because older people are more likely to have terminal illnesses and partly because they have different treatment preferences. Cancer is the most common diagnosis, but hospice care is appropriate for other terminal conditions, including severe congestive heart failure, chronic lung disease, renal failure, advanced neurologic diseases, and AIDS.

Hospices may be run by nonprofit volunteer organizations, home health agencies, or hospitals. Since 1983, services have been covered by Medicare when provided by a certified hospice. The patient must be willing to give up their other Medicare benefits for the terminal illness (except coverage for physician services), and the hospice must provide medical and nursing care, home health services including physical, occupational, and speech therapy, inpatient care when needed, medications, medical supplies and durable medical equipment, social work services, counseling, and have a nurse available twenty-four hours a day for emergencies.

Coordination of Care

The complexity of the current health care system has led to the development of case (or care) management programs to coordinate care for those who live in the community and have multiple medical, functional, and social problems resulting in high levels of service utilization. Case management is designed both to facilitate access to needed services and also help prevent inappropriate or excessive use of services resulting in increased costs. Case management, as it has been implemented with the elderly, is a process that includes assessment of needs, developing a plan of care, arrangement of services, and periodic reassessment. The case manager is usually a nurse or social worker. Case management programs may be run by community service agencies, hospitals, home health agencies, or even insurance companies and special Medicaid waiver programs. Some case management programs have financial resources and can pay for services that would otherwise not be covered by any third-party payor.

● HEALTH CARE PROVIDERS

Physicians

Physicians are an instrumental part of the health care system and traditionally head the health care team. Four years of postgraduate study after college are required to earn the M.D. degree. Before licensure, all physicians must also complete at least one postgraduate year of training called internship. Most physicians obtain additional years of training, called residency, in order to specialize. Residency, including the internship year, varies in length from three to five years. Some physicians choose to subspecialize and enter fellowship training for an additional one to three years. After completion of their training, physicians are board eligible, meaning they are eligible to take a special certifying examination to prove their competency in their field. After passing the examination, a physician is said to be board-certified. Some specialty boards now require periodic recertification examinations to insure that the specialists they certify keep up with new developments.

Although some older adults are still cared for by general practitioners, most will eventually receive some or even all of their medical care from a specialist. The specialists who most commonly provide care for the elderly are internists and family practitioners. Internists are physicians who specialize in internal medicine—the diagnosis and medical treatment of diseases of adults. (Internists are highly trained specialists and should not be confused with interns who are physicians just out of medical school in their first year of postgraduate training.) Family practitioners specialize in family medicine—providing comprehensive, continuous health care to all family members regardless of age or sex. Family practitioners and general internists (internists who do not have subspecialty training) provide primary care to the elderly. Primary care physicians perform routine preventive and health maintenance services like physical examinations, immunizations, and screening for cancer, diabetes, high blood pressure, and other diseases where early treatment is important. Primary care physicians also treat most common illnesses. When the care of a specialist or subspecialist is needed, the primary care physician makes a referral and helps coordinate the recommended care.

Many different specialists and subspecialists may participate in the care of an elderly person. Internal medicine subspecialists treat complicated medical diseases and/or perform highly technical diagnostic procedures. Surgeons treat diseases, injuries, and deformities of the body by operating on the body. Some of the specialists and subspecialists who are commonly involved in

Table 25.11
Specialists and Sub-Specialists Who Care for the Elderly

Type of Physician	Area of Expertise
Specialists	
Dermatologist	Skin diseases
Gynecologist	Disorders of the female reproductive system
Neurologist	Disorders of the nervous system
Physiatrist	Rehabilitation
Psychiatrist	Mental, emotional, and behavioral disorders
Internal Medicine Sub-specialists	
Cardiologist	Heart disease
Endocrinologist	Disorders of the glands of internal secretion, e.g., thyroid disease, diabetes
Gastroenterologist	Diseases of the digestive tract
Hematologist	Disorders of the blood
Nephrologist	Kidney diseases and kidney failure
Oncologist	Treatment of cancer
Pulmonologist	Diseases of the lung and chest
Rheumatologist	Treatment of arthritis and rheumatism
Surgical Sub-specialists	
Cardiothoracic surgeon	Surgery of the heart and chest
Neurosurgeon	Surgery of the spinal cord and brain
Ophthalmologist	Eye problems
Orthopedic surgeon	Surgery of the bones, joints, muscles, and tendons
Otolaryngologist	Diseases of the ear, nose, and throat
Urologist	Disorders of the urinary system in both sexes and the male reproductive system
Vascular surgeon	Surgery of the blood vessels

the care of the elderly are listed in Table 25.11, along with their area of expertise.

Geriatrics is emerging as a special area of expertise that extends across many traditional medical specialties. The American Board of Internal Medicine and the American Board of Family Practice jointly offer a qualifying examination to internal medicine and family medicine physicians who have extensive experience or fellowship training in geriatrics. Those who pass are awarded a Certificate of Added Qualifications in Geriatric Medicine. The American Board of Psychiatry and Neurology is establishing a similar certifying process for experts in geriatric psychiatry.

Because of the rapid growth in the elderly patient population, there will not be enough certified geriatricians to provide all the medical care for all older individuals in the foreseeable future.

For this reason, many fellowship-trained geriatricians concentrate their efforts on (1) teaching the important principles of geriatrics to primary care physicians in order to prepare them to provide the bulk of medical care for the elderly, and (2) doing research to find solutions to common geriatric medical problems.

Medical education in geriatrics is beginning to receive special emphasis from the medical school level on up. Ninety-seven percent of American medical schools now have geriatric curriculum requirements. Residency training programs, especially those in internal medicine and family medicine, are teaching geriatrics to prepare their graduates to care for the special needs of the elderly. However, physicians who trained prior to the last five to ten years may have had no formal training in geriatrics.

Government projections indicate that, overall, there will be an oversupply of physicians in the coming years. However, problems with physician maldistribution are expected to continue. Rural areas, where proportionately more elderly live, are expected to continue to have physician shortages. The number of physicians training to become primary care physicians is also expected to be inadequate compared to the demand for their services. Since training in geriatrics is being particularly directed at primary care physicians, the elderly may have trouble finding physicians who are well trained to meet their needs, particularly if they live in a rural area.

Ninety-seven percent of American medical schools now have geriatric curriculum requirements.

Osteopaths

Osteopathic physicians are graduates of schools of osteopathic medicine and have a D.O. degree. The curriculum of osteopathic schools is similar to other medical schools, except that their training has a more holistic emphasis and osteopaths are trained to use manipulation in the treatment of musculoskeletal disorders. Some osteopaths obtain specialty training in osteopathic residencies, but many enter residency programs for M.D.s.

Physician Assistants

Physician assistants (PAs) work in close association with doctors in hospitals, offices, and long-term care facilities. They perform some of the tasks traditionally done by doctors, such as taking medical histories, doing physical examinations, and treating uncomplicated medical problems. They can provide these medical services only under the supervision of a physician. New Jersey is the only state that does not license PAs, but even there PAs may practice in federal facilities.

Most PA training programs require a minimum of two years of college prior to admission, but about half of all PA students have college degrees. PA programs are usually two years in length and provide broad-based training in pri-

mary care medicine. The first year curriculum includes basic and behavioral medical sciences and an introduction to clinical medicine. The second year is typically spent in supervised clinical training. Some programs specialize in training surgeon assistants and emphasize clinical and technical skills related to surgical patient care. In recent years, specialized geriatric curricula have been added to many programs.

Like physicians, PAs can obtain specialized postgraduate training. However, most PAs work in primary care settings. Medicare pays the PA's employers on a discounted basis (relative to physicians) for the services of PAs working in hospitals and nursing homes. In rural areas, Medicare pays for PA services regardless of the setting. Consequently, PAs are in demand to provide services to the elderly in hospitals, nursing homes, and rural areas, as well as other areas where physician supply is inadequate to meet the need for services.

Nurses

Nursing is the backbone of the health care profession. Nurses have frequent patient care contacts and do much of the hands-on work of providing medical care. Nurses are involved in the entire spectrum of health care services from prevention to the care of the terminally ill. Nurses work in hospitals, in offices, in nursing homes, and in the community. In keeping with the many roles of nurses in the health care system, there are multiple educational pathways to become a nurse and several levels of certification and licensure.

The most basic nursing position is that of the nursing assistant or aide, which includes orderlies and home health aides. Traditionally the training for these ancillary nursing positions was provided on the job. Short educational courses to prepare for these positions are increasingly common, as nursing assistants work more independently in nursing homes and patients' homes. Certification for nursing assistants is now mandatory in the nursing home setting and usually requires completion of an eight-week course.

Licensed practical nurses (LPNs) commonly work in hospitals and nursing homes where they perform bedside nursing tasks. LPNs also work in settings where they assist a registered nurse or physician. They generally receive twelve months of formal training and then must pass their state certifying examination.

Registered nurses (RNs) can perform any type of nursing task and function independently in many settings. They must fulfill more extensive educational requirements than LPNs and also must pass a certifying examination. There are three different educational programs that qualify nurses to become RNs. These include diploma schools, associate degree programs, and baccalaureate degrees in nursing.

Diploma programs are usually sponsored by hospitals and require three years of training after high school. In 1960, 80 percent of RNs were prepared in diploma programs, but their popularity has declined markedly over the years. Currently, only 12 percent of nursing programs are in diploma schools.

Associate degree programs are offered by community colleges. They are rapidly proliferating, replacing both LPN programs and diploma schools. Eighteen to twenty-four months of course work are required, and college credits earned in these degree programs can often be applied to a baccalaureate degree in nursing, should the graduate desire to pursue additional training.

Baccalaureate programs, which confer a Bachelor of Science in Nursing (B.S.N.) degree are also increasing in number. These programs are run by colleges and universities and require a minimum of four years of training. The B.S.N. is the most comprehensive training program for RNs and includes a broad general education. The nursing training itself is also more comprehensive and emphasizes problem solving, critical thinking, and decision making, in addition to professional knowledge and technical skills.

Advanced training for nurses is offered by master's and doctoral degree programs, as well as programs that award certificates. Advanced training prepares nurses for (1) specialization in areas like geriatrics, midwifery, or anesthesia, (2) teaching nursing to others, (3) administration, and (4) research.

Nurses can also obtain training to become nurse practitioners to function as physician extenders in the primary care setting much like physician assistants. Some nurse practitioners specialize in geriatric care and have certification from the American Nurses' Association as Geriatric Nurse Practitioners. Medicare covers the services of nurse practitioners when they work in rural health clinics.

Dentists

Dentists not only take care of teeth but also treat oral conditions, including gum disease and jaw problems. They have three years of education after college to earn the D.D.S. or D.M.D. degree and become eligible for licensure as general dentists. About 16 percent of current dentists have also completed some postgraduate training and practice as dental specialists. The nature of dental practice is expected to change as the population ages. The increase in the number of elderly dental patients will result in an increased need for complex dental services, such as endodontics, fixed bridgework and partial dentures, more restoration of root caries, the need to maintain previously restored teeth, and treatment of periodontal disease and oral pathology. Dental schools have all adopted curriculum changes to train their students in geriatric dentistry. However, because there has been a decline in dental school enrollment since 1975, the demand for dental services is expected to increase more than the number of providers.

Optometrists

Optometrists are eye doctors who can examine the eyes and vision system. They may prescribe eyeglasses and contact lenses and other vision aids. They can diagnose some kinds of eye problems and may prescribe some topical eye medications, but they refer patients to ophthalmologists or other medical doctors if they need complex medical treatment or surgery. Optometrists usually have a bachelor's degree from a college and always have four years of graduate training in a School of Optometry to earn the O.D. degree. Some optometrists have postgraduate residency training. One of the areas of specialization is geriatric optometry. Medicare pays for only a limited number of optometry services.

Audiologists

Audiologists test and evaluate people who are suspected of having a hearing impairment. They recommend and sometimes dispense hearing aids. Most audiologists have a master's degree and are licensed by the state in which they practice. Medicare will cover diagnostic services by an audiologist but not routine hearing evaluations or hearing aid services.

Speech Pathologists

Speech pathologists diagnose and treat problems with speech and language. They often work with stroke victims or people who have had their vocal cords removed. Many patients with speech disorders also have trouble swallowing, and speech pathologists can treat these problems too. Speech pathologists usually have at least a master's degree and are licensed by the state where they work. Many of their services are paid for by Medicare.

Physical Therapists

Physical therapists (PTs) help people who have impairments of their strength, ability to move, or sensation. Physical therapy is commonly used in the treatment of strokes and other neurologic disorders, nerve or muscle injuries, fractures, arthritis, and to help patients recover from orthopedic surgery and amputations. Physical therapists employ a wide variety of treatment modalities, including exercise, heat, cold, and/or water therapy to help patients control pain, strengthen muscles, become more mobile, and improve coordination. They also instruct patients in the proper use of assistive devices like canes, walkers, and wheelchairs. All physical therapists have four years of college education, and some have further postgraduate training. Medicare pays for the services of a physical therapist in a hospital or skilled nursing facility and for some outpatient and home physical therapy services.

Occupational Therapists

Occupational therapists (OTs) work with patients whose ability to function has been impaired by accident, illness, or chronic disease. They use specialized activities and adaptive devices to help people feed, bathe, and dress themselves and perform basic homemaking tasks independently. OTs have either a bachelor's or master's degree with special training in occupational therapy. Medicare covers OT services in many cases.

Podiatrists

Podiatrists diagnose and treat diseases and injuries of the foot. They provide care for the toenails and can prescribe certain drugs. When indicated, they can perform surgery on the foot. They also make orthotics—devices to correct deformities or prevent foot problems. Podiatrists usually have four years of college education and then complete four years of professional school to earn the degree D.P.M.. Many podiatrists have one or more years of residency training after graduation. Medicare covers podiatric services except for routine foot care.

Registered Dietitians

Registered dietitians (RDs) provide dietary counseling in health and disease. They also supervise the nutritional services of hospitals and long-term care facilities. Some work in public health agencies or doctor's offices, and a few are in private practice. RDs have a bachelor's or graduate degree in dietetics and/or nutrition. They also complete an approved program in dietetic care. Nutritionist is a broad term that is used by some RDs but may also be used by practitioners with much less training or experience. Before seeking the advice of a nutritionist, it is a good idea to ask what kind of training and experience that person has. Medicare does not pay for dietary counseling services for individual patients.

Pharmacists and Clinical Pharmacologists

Pharmacists have extensive training in the correct use of medicines, including their chemical makeup, ingredients, side effects, appropriate uses, and potential interactions with other medicines. They have the legal authority to dispense prescription drugs according to the instructions of physicians and other health care providers who can prescribe drugs. They are also a good source of information about medications that are sold over the counter. Pharmacists must complete five years of college and have some practical experience to be licensed by the state as registered pharmacists (R.Ph.). Many pharmacists have postgraduate training to prepare them to work in particular settings. Nuclear pharmacy, pharmacotherapy, and nutrition support are three official recognized pharmacy specialties. Clinical pharmacologists have six years of training and a doctorate degree in pharmacy (Pharm.D.). Because of their additional expertise in pharmacology, they generally work in hospitals helping doctors plan and evaluate complicated or potentially toxic drug regimens.

Pharmacists and clinical pharmacologists can play a special role in the treatment of elderly patients. The elderly are especially vulnerable to the side effects of medications. They also take more medication than younger individuals making them at higher risk for drug interactions. Approximately one-fourth of all prescriptions are written for patients over 65 years of age, and the average elderly person receives thirteen prescription drugs in a year. Research has shown that when a pharmacist or clinical pharmacologist reviews drug regimens, consults with physicians about optimal drug regimens, and provides counseling to the patients, the elderly experience fewer problems with side effects and drug interactions. The elderly should not hesitate to consult their pharmacists when they have questions about their medications.

Psychologists and Counselors

Psychologists and counselors evaluate their clients for mental, emotional, or behavioral disorders and provide treatment for these problems through counseling. They do not prescribe psychoactive drugs. There are many different formal educational pathways to obtain the necessary skills, including master's and doctoral degree programs in psychology, nursing, social work, and counseling. Medicare does not pay for the services of psychologists and counselors except in certain situations where they are supervised by a physician.

Medical Social Workers

Medical social workers help coordinate supportive community services for patients. They are usually knowledgeable about community resources for the elderly and their eligibility criteria. They often can also help interpret Medicare and Medicaid rules and regulations. Many states do not have licensing requirements for social workers, so their training and educational background may vary. There are formal educational programs for social workers at the baccalaureate

(B.S.W.) and master's (M.S.W.) level. Medicare directly pays for social worker services is some settings, but often social worker services are part of more comprehensive services.

Approximately one-fourth of all prescriptions are written for patients over 65 years of age, and the average elderly person receives thirteen prescription drugs in a year.

Multidisciplinary Teams

Multidisciplinary (or interdisciplinary) teams are commonly used to provide more comprehensive geriatric services. Many older adults have complex medical problems, chronic functional impairments, and limited social support. The combination of all of these types of problems cannot be well handled by any single health care provider regardless of their background. Teams, usually consisting of at least a physician, nurse, and social worker, can approach the multiple problems of the elderly from different perspectives, often resulting in better outcomes.

● ALTERNATIVE HEALTH CARE

In addition to the traditional health care delivery system, there is a vast network of alternative approaches to health care. Some of these programs have merit, emphasizing wellness and preventive health care or mental and spiritual approaches to disease. Others are fraudulent schemes to make money by taking advantage of the worried well or incurably ill. Because there are so many different approaches with different practitioners, it is impossible to become knowledgeable about all of them. Some common alternative approaches to health care are listed in Table 25.12.

Little is known about the effectiveness of most alternative approaches to health care. Anecdotal evidence is usually all that is available, and it needs to be considered cautiously. Individuals often get better without any treatment. Many diseases wax and wane in severity, making it seem like treatments have had an effect. The placebo effect is a well-known, real phenomenon in which

Table 25.12
Alternative Approaches to Health Care

Acupuncture	Stimulation of particular points on the body to affect problems in other areas; usually used for pain control
Alexander technique	Coaching on posture and carriage to reduce muscle tension and stress
Aroma therapy	Use of certain odors to improve mood and reduce physical complaints
Biofeedback	Process of learning to control autonomic body functions (breathing, heart rate, blood pressure) through electronic monitoring; used to treat a wide range of problems like hypertension, migraine headaches, and chronic pain
Chiropractic	Manual manipulation of the spine; used for a wide variety of complaints; some evidence of effectiveness for low back pain
Hellerwork	Deep massage to decrease pain and tension in muscles and reduce injury
Homeopathy	The use of highly diluted toxic substances to cure syptoms caused by larger quantities
Hypnosis	Induction of a highly suggestible state to help reduce pain, promote healing, or change unhealthful behaviors
Naturopathy	The use of herbs, mega-doses of vitamins, homeopathy, imagery, physical therapies, and counseling to treat disease and promote health
Reflexology	Massage of specific areas of the foot to relieve stress on other body parts
Therapeutic touch	Touching the patient's body to unblock energy flow and boost natural healing powers

people feel better just because they believe they are receiving an effective treatment, and many traditional health care providers rely on it. Also some alternative approaches are truly beneficial. Many accepted drug therapies had their origins in herbal remedies.

Care should be taken when considering an alternative approach to health care. Proven conventional therapies should not be ignored. The credentials and training of the alternative practitioner should be investigated. Treatments that don't make any sense should be avoided. A prognosis should be obtained, and if the treatment does not produce the anticipated effects, it should be discontinued. The words natural and nontoxic are not synonymous. Many plants contain harmful substances, and large doses of some vitamins are toxic. Practitioners who claim to possess secret approaches should be regarded skeptically.

● HEALTH CARE RESEARCH

Research is an important part of our health care system. Basic scientists are continually trying to understand the intricacies of the human body. Clinical researchers build on what the basic scientists learn and strive to prevent and treat illness. Health services researchers want to figure out how to provide health care to everybody in the most timely and cost-effective way.

Until recently, the elderly were largely excluded from medical research for a variety of reasons. There were relatively few extremely old individuals in the population. The elderly are harder to study because they have multiple diseases. Premature morbidity and mortality were judged to be more important problems. But with the aging of our population and the rapid increase in health care costs to care for elderly individuals with chronic illness, a great deal of effort (and money) is going into research on problems related to aging.

Health care research is funded in a variety of ways. The four main sources of funding are: (1) the government, primarily through the National Institutes of Health, (2) private nonprofit institutions, including charitable foundations such as the Robert Wood Johnson Foundation or the Kellogg Foundation, (3) private profit-making corporations, especially drug companies and manufacturers of medical equipment, and (4) intramural support from the university with which an investigator is affiliated.

The government is the main sponsor of aging related health care research in terms of dollars spent. The National Institute on Aging (NIA) was established by Congress in 1974. As one of the thirteen institutes of the National Institutes of Health (NIH), the NIA is responsible for research on the aging process, the diseases and syndromes of the elderly, and some psychosocial problems of the aged. Training programs for both researchers and health care providers and dissemination of health information are also part of the work of the NIA.

Because of the increased emphasis on research related to aging, many more elderly will be asked to participate in scientific studies. Research cannot be conducted without the consent of the person involved, except in special situations where there is minimal risk to the individual. For example, exceptions to the informed consent rule might be made for the study of existing medical records if all identifying information like names and addresses is removed. The decision to participate in a research project is a personal one, but certain facts should be taken into consideration.

Until recently, the elderly were largely excluded from medical research for a variety of reasons.

All research involving human subjects is carefully reviewed by committees called institutional review boards (IRBs) at the institution where the research is going to take place. Research is not allowed if it is too risky for the subjects who participate or will not result in new understanding of the problem being studied. Informed consent for participation in a research study must be obtained in writing. The person must be advised what tests, procedures, or treatments they will undergo as part of the study and what alternatives are available if they do not wish to participate in the study. All the risks and benefits to the person being asked to participate in the study must be explained in terms that the person can understand. The person being asked to participate must be allowed to ask any questions they wish to help them make a decision. In general, individuals who are not competent to make their own decisions cannot be included in research although exceptions are sometimes made for the study of conditions such as Alzheimer's disease, where most affected individuals will be unable to give informed consent. Even in these situations where the subjects themselves cannot give consent, consent must still be obtained from the next of kin or legal guardian. There can be no coercion. Patients cannot be refused further medical care if they choose not to participate in the research projects being conducted by their physician or hospital. Even after agreeing to participate, study subjects can withdraw from a research project at any time without any penalty.

● HEALTH CARE REFORM

The United States spends a much larger percentage of its gross national product on health care than any other country. And costs are rapidly rising. Yet, year after year the United States ranks below many other developed countries in measure of overall health such as infant mortality and life expectancy. Large numbers of Americans have too little health care insurance or none at all. Health care benefits are tied to employment. People who choose to change jobs may be temporarily without insurance. Those who lose their jobs, even if it is through no fault of their own, also usually lose their health care coverage at a time when they can least afford to pay their medical bills themselves. Preexisting condition exclusionary clauses keep many from getting insurance coverage for needed medical care. The current system focuses too much on the treatment of disease and not enough on prevention. The complexities of the current system greatly increase administrative costs. Given these problems, health care reform is inevitable. The main question is whether change will occur in the form of the addition of new programs and modifications of existing programs or whether there will be major changes, such as national health care insurance for everyone.

Organizations

American Association of Retired Persons (AARP)
Health Advocacy Services
601 E St., NW
Washington, DC 20049

American Indian Health Care Association
245 East 6th St., Ste. 499
St. Paul, MN 55101
(612) 293-0233

American Managed Care and Review Association
1227 25th St., NW, Ste. 610
Washington, DC 20037
(202) 728-0506

National Alliance of Senior Citizens
1700 18th St., NW, Ste. 401
Washington, DC 20009
(202) 986-0117

National Coalition of Hispanic Health and Human Services Organizations
1501 16th St., NW
Washington, DC 20036
(202) 387-5000

National Hospice Organization
1901 North Moore St., Ste. 901
Arlington, VA 22202
(703) 525-5762

National Leadership Coalition for Health Care Reform
555 13th St., NW
Washington, DC 20004
(202) 637-6830

References

American Association of Retired Persons. *Before You Buy: A Guide to Long-Term Care Insurance.* Rev. ed. Washington, DC: American Association of Retired Persons, 1991.

American College of Physicians. "The Role of the Department of Veteran's Affairs in Geriatric Care." *Annals of Internal Medicine* Vol. 115 (1991): 896–900.

Begley, Sharon. "Alternative Medicine: A Cure for What Ails Us?" *American Health* (April 1992): 39–56.

Hollingsworth, J. W., and P. K. Bondy. "The Role of Veterans Affairs Hospitals in the Health Care System." *New England Journal of Medicine* Vol. 322 (1990): 1851–57.

Kovner, Anthony R., ed. *Health Care Delivery in the United States.* 4th ed. New York: Springer, 1986.

"Late Bloomer" audio cassette. Available from Connie Goldman Productions, 926 Second Street, Suite 201, Santa Barbara, CA 90403. (310) 393-6801.

The National Commission for the Protection of Human Subjects of Biomedical and Behavioral Research. "The Belmont Report: Ethical Principles and Guidelines for the Protection of Human Subjects of Research." *Department of Health, Education, and Welfare Publication No. (OS) 78-0012.* Washington, DC: U.S. Government Printing Office, 1978.

Torres-Gil, Fernando, and Lori L. Rosenquist. "Public Policy and Geriatric Rehabilitation." In *Geriatric Rehabilitation.* Eds. Bryan Kemp, Kenneth Brummel-Smith, and Joseph W. Ramsdell. Boston, MA: Little, Brown, 1990.

U.S. Department of Health and Human Services. "Guide to Health Insurance for People with Medicare." *HCFA Publication No. HCFA-02110.* Washington, DC: U.S. Government Printing Office, 1992.

———. "The Medicare 1991 Handbook." *HCFA Publication No. 10050.* Washington, DC: U.S. Government Printing Office, 1991.

———. "1990 HCFA Statistics." *HCFA Publication No. 03313.* Washington, DC: U.S. Government Printing Office, September 1990.

———. "Seventh Report to the President and Congress on the Status of Health Personnel in the United States." *USDHHS Publication No. HRS-P-OD-90-1.* Washington, DC: U.S. Government Printing Office, March 1990.

U.S. Department of Health and Human Services Rules and Regulations. "Protection of Human Subjects." *Title 45; Code of Federal Regulations; Part 46.* Washington, DC: U.S. Government Printing Office, Rev. ed. March 8, 1983.

Williams, Stephen J., and Sandra J. Guerra. *Health Care Services in the 1990s: A Consumer's Guide.* New York: Praeger, 1991.

Additional Reading

Abramson, Leonard. *Healing Our Health Care System.* New York: Grove Wiedenfeld, 1990.

Altman, Maya, and others. *How Do I Pay for My Long-Term Health Care? A Consumer Guidebook about Long-Term Care Insurance.* Berkeley, CA: Berkeley Planning Associates, 1988.

American Association of Retired Persons. *Knowing Your Rights: Medicare's Prospective Payment System.* Washington, DC: AARP Fulfillment.

Coleman, Daniel, ed. *Mind/Body Medicine.* Fairfield, OH: Consumer Reports Books, 1992.

Friedman, Jo-Ann. *Home Health Care.* New York: W. W. Norton, 1986.

Health Care Financing Administration. *Medicare and Medicaid Data Book.* Baltimore, MD: ORD Publications.

Hogue, Kathleen, Cheryl Jensen, and Kathleen M. Urban. *The Complete Guide to Health Insurance: How to Beat the High Cost of Being Sick.* New York: Walker, 1988.

Inlander, Charles B. *Medicare Made Easy (A People's Medical Society Book)* Reading, MA: Addison-Wesley, 1989.

Matthews, Joseph L. *Social Security, Medicare, and Pensions: A Sourcebook for Older Americans.* 3d ed. Berkeley, CA: Nolo Press, 1990.

Mills, Simon, and Steven J. Finando. *Alternatives in Healing: An Open Minded Approach to Finding the Best Treatment for Your Health Problems.* New York: New American Library, 1988.

Munley, Anne. *The Hospice Alternative: A New Context for Death and Dying.* New York: Basic Books, 1983.

Steinberg, Raymond M., and Genevieve W. Carter. *Case Management and the Elderly: A Handbook for Planning and Administering Programs.* Lexington, MA: Lexington Books, 1983.

Thomas, William W., ed. *All About Medicare.* 3d ed. Chicago, IL: National Underwriter Co. and Probus Publishing Co., 1990.

Catherine H. Messick, M.D., M.S.

26

Physicians, Medications, and Hospitalization

- Choosing a Doctor • Medications • Hospitalization and Surgery
- Patient Rights and Issues in Medical Care

The ideal old age would be to experience no debilitating or chronic illnesses and to lead an active and robust life until the very end. Life without serious illness until shortly before one expires, near the century mark, is called the compression of morbidity. There is considerable debate among researchers studying the aging process as to whether the combination of healthy life style and modern preventive medicine can offer this possibility to the majority of people. For the near future, most people will experience some degree of chronic illness in later life. Therefore, knowing how to choose a doctor, take medications properly, and interact with hospitals and other health care service agencies is an important part of taking care of oneself and loved ones.

● CHOOSING A DOCTOR

The choice of a primary care physician is one of the most important decisions made by older Americans. As people age, they do not necessarily develop illnesses or serious medical problems, but older Americans are more likely to develop medical problems and are therefore more likely to need a physician. The decision to choose a primary care physician should be thoughtful, reasoned and made when the individual is healthy—not when an emergency strikes and there is little time to consider the options. Faced with a stress-ful and frightening medical problem, a person will be comforted when he or she has carefully chosen and trusts the primary care physician, who, in turn, will be more effective once a relationship has been established with the patient. The intricacies of the health care system make the choice of a primary care physician a critical first step.

The primary care physician is an ally, an advocate, and a partner with the patient in negotiating an increasingly complex, expensive, and occasionally dangerous health care system. Years ago the health care system was simpler, with few choices available to physicians or patients. The discovery of penicillin, for example, means that patients who have died of disease might now survive. Decisions in health care are now much more complex: there are multiple choices in diagnosis and therapy; alternatives are numerous, frequently controversial, or even contradictory; the risks of diagnosis and therapy are more subtle and potentially more hazardous; and the information necessary to navigate the health care system is much more extensive. Health care is frequently a delicate balance of risks and benefits. The patient requires knowledgeable, concerned, and balanced guidance, and it is the primary care physician who is best able to fill these needs.

Forming a Partnership with a Primary Care Physician

A primary care physician provides continuing care, during both good and ill health, diagnosing

The decision to choose a primary care physician should be thoughtful, reasoned and made when the individual is healthy—not when an emergency strikes and there is little time to consider the options.

and treating the majority of medical conditions, mild or severe. This physician does not limit practice to a specific condition or a specific organ. He or she should be the first physician to consult for a medical problem. Even if an emergency visit is necessary, the primary care physician should be identified and notified as soon as possible. If a medical problem is chronic, the primary care physician monitors and treats the illness over time. When the condition requires intensive investigation or specialized treatment, the primary care physician knows which specialist to consult and coordinates the efforts of specialists in more complicated situations. At such times the large number of specialists can contribute to an already depersonalizing experience, and the primary care physician is responsible for establishing the patient, and not the disease, as the central focus of care.

The primary care physician manages more than just a health care crisis, however. Health care is a partnership. The physician makes recommendations on how to lead a healthy lifestyle, offers knowledge and advice on health-related questions, and recommends procedures to reduce the risk of developing health problems. The primary care physician also arranges and coordinates other health care and social services in the community, authorizing health-related ser-

When a relationship has been established, the primary physician will be an advocate for the patient, able to guide the patient through the maze of health care services. (Copyright © Marianne Gontarz)

vices, such as visiting nurse and home health workers, and justifing the need for home medical equipment.

The ongoing nature of the primary care physician's work is central to his or her effectiveness in advising patients when they need to make health care decisions, because this relationship causes the physician to know the patient's medical problems, medications, and allergies, as well as what was effective, what wasn't, and how the patient reacted. But more than just medical knowledge, the primary care physician learns the patient's attitudes toward health care and desires and fears about medical treatments. In other words, with an established relationship with the patient, the primary care physician is in the position to be an advocate, guiding the patient through the maze of health care services.

Choosing a primary care physician should be a thoughtful process. The considerations fall roughly into three domains:

1. the physician's qualifications and credentials
2. the physician's practice
3. the patient-physician relationship

Qualifications and Credentials of a Primary Care Physician

Medical education and training is a long and complex process, and the credentials and qualifications seem equally complex. Generally there are legal minimum requirements for a physician to practice medicine and additional educational and training requirements. Though not legally required, this latter training is necessary for the

Table 26.1
Definition of Primary Care

Primary care is coordinated, comprehensive and personal care, available on both a first contact and continuous basis. It incorporates several tasks: medical diagnosis and treatment, psychological assessment and management, personal support, communication of information about illness, prevention, and health maintenance.

Source: "Tasks of Primary Care." Primary Care Medicine (1988).

physician to be recognized by his or her peer organizations.

Each physician who provides patient care must be licensed by the state in which the practice takes place. Licensing is a legal requirement assuring that the physician has completed a minimum amount of training, usually four years of medical school and one year of additional training, frequently called an internship. This single year of training after medical school qualifies the physician to practice medicine as a general practitioner, or GP. Historically most physicians were general practitioners, but because of the complexity of modern medicine, few physicians now enter practice with this level of training. Most states also require a minimum of continuing education to maintain licensure, usually comprising attendance at conferences or seminars where the physician learns the most recent advances in medical knowledge.

The primary care physician for older Americans is usually trained in the specialties of internal medicine or family medicine. The internist tends to have more training in hospital-based medicine and generally restricts the practice to adults. The family practitioner spends more training time in the clinic and community and generally has pediatric and obstetric as well as adult patients. Both specialties require three or more years of training after medical school, and each specialty has a professional group that maintains high standards of medical knowledge and performance. These are the certifying "boards of examiners," groups of experts in the specialty that are charged with examining every physician to assure qualifications and competence in the specialty. To be "board eligible" the physician must have completed all the required specialty training at an institution recognized and certified by the specialty. To be "board certified" the physician must have completed the training and successfully passed the certifying examination for that specialty.

Both family medicine and internal medicine have a Certificate of Added Qualifications in Geriatrics, attesting to additional training or experience with older individuals; this certification requires successful completion of a written examination. Internal medicine has many additional subspecialties, each with additional training requirements and certifying boards, such as cardiology, pulmonary medicine, or gastroenterology. A subspecialist may treat patients only in the subspecialty who are referred by other physicians, or the subspecialist may provide primary care to patients as well.

Physician specialization continues to fuel often heated debate within the medical community, reflecting a national concern about the escalation of medical costs. The supply of physicians has been growing rapidly over the past decade, but the number of primary care physicians has increased only slightly. Most physicians graduating from medical school in recent years have chosen to specialize (Stimmel, 1992), a situation that many people believe contributes to the dramatic rate of increase in health care costs. Furthermore, the projected "glut" of physicians is dominated by specialists, generally clustered in large cities. While federal and state medical educators seek to remedy this imbalance with innovative financial and legislative initiatives, many older Americans, especially those living in rural areas, have difficulties finding a primary care physician.

Both family medicine and internal medicine have a Certificate of Added Qualifications in Geriatrics, attesting to additional training or experience with older individuals; this certification requires successful completion of a written examination.

The certifying boards of internal medicine, family medicine, and geriatrics now demand periodic recertification, generally requiring the physician to take and pass a written examination every seven to ten years. In this way the specialty organizations assure that physicians maintain their skills at a high level over their entire career. While these recertifying exams are voluntary, older Americans should know that recertification means their physician is committed to excellence and strives to provide state of the art health care to his or her patients.

In addition to licensing, education, and recertification, the primary care physician must maintain the privilege of admitting patients to a hospi-

Table 26.2
Some Necessary Credentials for a Primary Care Physician for Older Americans

- License to practice in the state
- Specialty training and board certification in internal medicine or family medicine
- Privileges to admit patients to the hospital
- Added qualification in geriatrics is desirable but rare

tal. Hospitals usually have a committee of physicians who review applications for "admitting privileges." This committee examines the training and practice experience of the physician and personally interviews each applicant. The committee is responsible for assuring that physicians are qualified to direct the care of patients in the hospital setting. The committee will also delineate the medical, diagnostic, and surgical procedures the physician is allowed to perform in the hospital, according to the physician's training and experience. Hospital admitting privileges are subject to periodic renewal, and even when granted, the primary care physician must continually keep credentials updated and level of performance high, since these are subject to ongoing review by the hospital credentials committee.

Which credentials are important to the patient? If one is available in their community, older Americans should seek a board eligible or board certified internal medicine specialist or family medicine as their primary care physician. This choice helps assure them that the physician has the knowledge and training to treat the frequently complex illnesses often experienced by older people. The physician should have hospital privileges to be able to maintain continuity of care during acute illness. In addition, it is often important to know if the primary care physician will continue to care for the patient if they enter a long term care facility or nursing home. The physician may occasionally see patients at home, although this option may be restricted to very disabled patients who otherwise cannot see a physician. But there are other factors also important to consider in choosing a primary care physician.

Physicians should be dedicated to a lifetime of learning: medicine changes very rapidly, and constant effort is required to maintain knowledge

and skills. Health care organizations strongly encourage ongoing study, states stipulate continuing education for renewal of license, specialty boards require periodic recertifying examinations, and hospitals review credentials for continued privileges. The older American needs commitment from the primary care physician, and choosing one requires thought. Careful consideration is not usually possible under the stress of acute illness. Patients can derive greater benefit from a learned, committed physician.

The Physician's Practice

The physician's office practice is a window into the attitudes and habits of the physician. A friendly courteous staff is important, and it should follow the philosophy of the practice. The first task on arriving at the office is to check in with the receptionist, who reviews the patient's address and phone number and checks insurance information. Generally the office staff can directly bill private insurers or Medicare (through the state Medicare carrier) for services provided in the office, greatly simplifying the patients' role in the process. If the physician "accepts Medicare assignment," this means that the doctor agrees to accept the Medicare-discounted amount, and the patient pays only the applicable deductible and any co-payment. If the patient has additional "Medigap" coverage, the office staff generally submits claims to these insurers as well. However, if the physician does not "accept assignment," then the patient is expected to pay all physician charges above the Medicare maximum allowable charge. These amounts are usually detailed in a periodic statement from the Medicare carrier called an "Explanation of Benefits," or EOB. When visiting each physician for the first time, the patient should clearly understand what visit charges the patient is responsible for, what the physician's practice billing policy is, and what bills to expect. (See Chapter 25 for a detailed discussion of health care finance.)

American physicians have a justified reputation for making patients wait and wait and wait! Nothing is more discouraging to a patient than to be obstructed or delayed when feeling ill or needing medical care. Everyone is aware that in a busy practice physicians are sometimes unavoidably detained by sudden emergencies, resulting in long waits and backed-up schedules. The sensitive office staff informs patients of unavoidable delays and estimates how long a wait to expect. However, long waits for appointments may also indicate poor scheduling practices, "overbooking," or an insensitive staff, about which the physician needs to know. A study conducted by the Socioeconomic Monitoring System in 1992 found that the average waiting time is 20 minutes. However, waiting times vary depending upon medical specialty and geographic region. The highest average waiting time of almost 25 minutes is found within the specialty of orthopedic surgeons, while those treating cardiovascular diseases have the lowest average time of 18.5 minutes (Gonzalez, 1992).

Many physicians now employ nurse practitioners and physician assistants to manage some routine aspects of patient care. These highly educated and trained individuals are directly supervised by the physician, and as with physicians, are required to register with the state in which they work. Physicians may delegate such duties as preliminary evaluation of patients during emergency visits, routine physical exams, or specific follow-up tasks to these individuals. However, the physician is ultimately responsible for the medical care provided.

The Patient-Physician Relationship

Physicians frequently request a complete history and physical exam for new patients, even if the patient has recently been seen by another doctor. Even though medical records may have been requested in advance (a good idea!), this initial visit allows the physician to learn about symptoms currently being experienced, chronic conditions, past illnesses and surgeries, as well as health habits and family history. The physician may then perform a complete physical exam, even though the patient may have had an exam recently. This extensive and time-consuming first visit serves a number of purposes: the physician can establish a baseline assessment of health, uncover risk factors that may lead to development of disease, and screen for conditions that may not have shown symptoms. And extremely important, the baseline visit allows the physician and patient to become familiar with each other and learn what to expect from each other.

The baseline visit allows the physician and patient to become familiar with and learn what to expect from each other. (Copyright © Marianne Gontarz)

Follow-up visits are generally briefer. Usually these visits follow specific conditions requiring intermittent attention, such as checking blood pressure or changing medication. Although the physician is aware of the medications taken by a patient, the patient should be sure to inform the physician when a prescription is near expiration and needs to be renewed.

During the visit the physician may request laboratory or X-ray studies, and the patient should discuss the reasons for doing them and how the results may change management of the condition. This is also a good time to find out whether or not the patient will be notified of the results. Important diagnostic studies (e.g., a mammo-

Table 26.3
Elements of a Complete Medical History

Current symptoms: Timing, duration, etc.
Past medical problems
Chronic conditions
Surgeries
Hospitalizations

Prescription medications
Over-the-counter medications

Allergies
Immunizations
Risk factors: social/occupational/environmental
Family history
Review of symptoms

Physical examination
Laboratory studies
X-rays, EKG, screening studies

Source: "Tasks of Primary Care." *Primary Care Medicine* (1988).

gram or pap smear) should generally be reported to the patient by the physician or staff, while more routine monitoring studies (such as many blood studies) may require notifying the patient only if results are abnormal or cause the patient's therapy to change.

Every visit is an opportunity to ask questions! The physicians should ask at the end of every visit if there are any specific questions, since a physician often interprets a lack of questions as meaning that the patient completely understands and agrees with the planned course. Questions signal the patient's need for clarification or further explanation. Questions should be written down and asked early in the visit, so the physician can adjust the history or physical exam to address these concerns. It is easier for the physician to answer questions with a patient's history and physical exam fresh in his or her mind. Even if a physician seems very busy, it is better to get an answer during the visit than to call later and perhaps wait hours (or days) for a return call.

Patient Autonomy and Advance Directives

An essential duty of the primary care physician is to discuss and clarify the patient's attitudes about health care. Individual patients have specific wishes and desires about their health care; some want "everything done"; some patients wish to limit some medical interventions for religious or other reasons. Advance directives (see also Chapter 27) specify the type and limits of health care when a patient has lost the ability to make decisions. Studies are suggesting that patients actually want less in the way of health care than previously thought, and despite concerns to the contrary, advance directives do not impact other health care outcomes (Schneiderman and others, 1992). The patient's wishes and advance directives should be made clear to family members, caretakers, and certainly the primary care physician. The patient's health care decisions must be respected by health care providers under the principle of patient autonomy: patients have the right to determine which treatments are accepted and which refused. The primary care provider is commonly the patient's advocate when such decisions are needed and endeavors to respect the patient's wishes.

Preventive Care and Screening

In recent years there has been increasing emphasis on disease prevention and early diagnosis in the form of screening for specific diseases. Traditionally trained in some aspects of preventive care, such as immunization to prevent pneumonia, influenza, and tetanus, physicians now agree that another goal of preventive care is to identify risk factors. Such behaviors may be habits or practices that may predispose a patient to develop disease or are associated with the eventual occurrence of a disease. One clear role for the primary care physician is the identification of patient risk factors by taking a thorough history, addressing ongoing or past exposures. Then the physician works with the patient to reduce or eliminate these factors.

However, even within the medical community, the most appropriate preventive care recommendations for older Americans are not always clear. Some risk factors, such as tobacco use or sedentary lifestyle, are clearly associated with disease—and eliminating these factors improves the quantity and quality of life at all ages. But other risk factors are more controversial. For example, it is clear that obesity, or grossly excessive

Table 26.4
Screening Recommendations of the U.S.
Preventive Services Task Force for Individuals
Age 65 and Over

History
  Diet
  Physical activity
  Tobacco, alcohol and drug use
  Functional status
  Symptoms of stroke
Physical exam
  Height and weight
  Blood pressure
  Visual activity
  Hearing and hearing aids
  Clinical breast exam (annually)
Diagnostic procedures
  Total cholesterol
  Urinalysis
  Mammogram (every 1-2 years at least to age 75)
  Thyroid function study (women)
Glaucoma testing by eye specialist

Source: U.S. Preventive Services Task Force. *Guide to Clinical Preventive Services: An Assessment of the Effectiveness of 169 Interventions.* Baltimore: Williams and Wilkins, 1989.

weight, is associated with heart disease. But while there are clear recommendations for younger individuals, such as ideal weight and height tables, there are no such standard tables for older Americans. It is also unclear what the ideal level of cholesterol should be for older persons in order to minimize the risk of heart attack. These problems highlight a clear deficiency in medical research: studies of younger adults have not been confirmed in older adults; and recommendations for the young, although frequently similar, may not always apply to older individuals. But recent government and private foundation initiatives have focused on the preventive care needs of older Americans, and studies are now being carried out to answer many of these questions.

Screening is the process of finding disease before the patient or physician have noticed symptoms or signs. The ultimate purpose of screening is to identify and treat a disease in the early stages when treatment is more likely to result in cure, or longer or more comfortable life. Several aspects of screening are important to consider, and concern both the test used for screening and the disease being sought. First, the disease for which screening is recommended must occur frequently in the population. The screening test must be safe, relatively inexpensive, easy to perform, and accurate. The disease must be serious and, if left untreated, cause suffering, disability, or premature death. Finally, the disease must be treatable, and the patient must be healthy enough and willing and able to undergo treatment if disease is found.

As with screening for preventive care, some screening guidelines for older individuals are well accepted by the medical community, and others are controversial. High-blood pressure is an excellent example of the benefits of screening.

Table 26.5

Immunizations Recommended by U.S. Preventive Services Task Force for Individuals 65 Years of Age and Older

- Tetanus-diphtheria (TD) booster every ten years on birthdays ending in 5 (65, 75, etc.)
- Influenza vaccine (annually)
- Pneumococcal vaccine (once)

Source: U.S. Preventive Services Task Force. *Guide to Clinical Preventive Services: An Assessment of the Effectiveness of 169 Interventions.* Baltimore: Williams and Wilkins, 1989.

Table 26.6

Counseling Recommendations of the U.S. Preventive Services Task Force for Individuals 65 Years of Age and Older

Diet and exercise
  Review daily intake of saturated fat, cholesterol, complex carbohydrates, fiber, sodium, and calcium intake
  Total calorie intake
  Selection and review of exercise program
Substance use
  Tobacco cessation
  Alcohol and other drugs:
    Limiting alcohol consumption
    Not driving while under the influence
  Treatment for substance abuse
Injury prevention
  Prevention of falls
  Automobile safety belts
  Smoke detectors
  Not smoking near bedding or upholstery
  Hot water heater temperature
  Safety helmets
Dental health
  Regular dental visits, tooth brushing, flossing

Source: U.S. Preventive Services Task Force. *Guide to Clinical Preventive Services: An Assessment of the Effectiveness of 169 Interventions.* Baltimore: Williams and Wilkins, 1989.

The disease is common in older individuals; left untreated, it causes stroke and heart disease. It is diagnosed with a safe, inexpensive, and accepted test (several blood pressure readings), and treatment is well accepted by patients. Given the safety and accuracy of clinical breast exam and mammography and the effectiveness of treatment, the same is true for breast cancer, even in the oldest women. However, exactly the opposite is true for lung cancer: screening is not effective and not recommended. There are many diseases for which the evidence may not be as clear-cut. Various organizations such as the U.S. Preventive Services Task Force (see Table 26.4), the American Cancer Society, the American College of Physicians, and several nationally recognized experts have proposed screening guidelines for older Americans, and frequently these experts disagree. There is no disagreement about the role of the primary care physician in issues of disease screening: the physician should present the screening options to the patient, advocate the use of safe and effective screening studies, avoid untested or ineffective studies (even when praised in the mass media), and judiciously balance the risk and costs of a test against the potential for benefit to the patient. Clearly both physician and patient must be well informed and knowledgeable to make these difficult decisions.

The Process of Diagnosis, Consultation, and Second Opinion

When a patient sees a physician for a medical problem, often the diagnosis is clear from the history of the problem and the physical examination. Other medical problems are more complex, and the physician may need to consider several possible diagnoses, called a *differential diagnosis*. The physician then may perform or recommend diagnostic tests to assess the likelihood of specific conditions. Many times these are simple, safe diagnostic studies like blood or urine studies. When more elaborate testing is required, other physicians may be consulted to perform or interpret diagnostic studies. The most common consultant is the radiologist, who reviews X-rays or other studies and reports back to the primary physician. Specialized diagnostic procedures may require the expertise of physicians with advanced training, using elaborate and expensive equipment or even surgical procedures like a biopsy.

There are no absolute rules for physicians to follow in the diagnostic approach to a problem, and as a result there is not always agreement among physicians that a procedure is necessary for a specific patient. To understand the controversy, one must understand the properties of diagnostic testing, diagnostic procedures, and the relationship of testing to the patient's outcome. One must further understand the motives for the performance of diagnostic procedures: satisfying patient expectations, reassuring physicians worried about malpractice suits for "failure to diagnose," and reconciling the financial incentives involved in performing high-priced diagnostic procedures.

Physicians almost never rely exclusively on test results to make a diagnosis. Diagnostic studies are not absolutely accurate: a negative X-ray *reduces the likelihood* that a fracture is present, but a fracture is not impossible even when an X-ray appears normal. Similarly, a positive diagnostic test *increases the likelihood*, but does not guarantee, that the diagnosis is correct. Since there are usually several ways to test for the presence of disease, physicians may order a number of tests, assuming that each positive test further increases the likelihood that the diagnosis is correct. Thus although many patients expect a test or study to "make the diagnosis," the diagnosis more resembles a combination of probabilities than an absolute certainty.

The threat of malpractice suits has been cited as an additional stimulus to the performance of diagnostic studies (Consumer Union, 1992). Physicians frequently fear "missing" an important diagnosis, especially serious but relatively unlikely or uncommon illnesses, and as a result, diagnostic tests with very little chance of contributing to the patient's care are performed. The amount of "defensive medicine" is difficult to measure, and the threat of malpractice is probably overestimated by physicians (Localio and others, 1991), but the intense fear of a malpractice suit and the potentially devastating consequences to the physician's career and livelihood are important issues to address in planning health care reform.

One must further understand the motives for the performance of diagnostic procedures: satisfying patient expectations, reassuring physicians worried about malpractice suits for "failure to diagnose," and reconciling the financial incentives involved in performing high-priced diagnostic procedures.

The process of diagnosis is not without risk to the patient, however. Major diagnostic procedures, such as a heart catheterization, may result in bleeding from the artery where the catheter was inserted or infection at the site, or irregular or extra heartbeats as the catheter enters the heart itself, for example. X-ray and other studies that require an injection of a "contrast" material may result in significant illness, such as reversible or irreversible kidney failure, shock, and, rarely, death. Therefore any diagnostic procedure having any risk of serious illness or death should not be undertaken without clear justification and due consideration to the risks involved. Diagnostic procedures may also be expensive and frequently require the expertise of physicians, nurses, and technicians and the use of complicated equipment. Most medical insurers place a high value on complex diagnostic procedures, and they reimburse physicians, clinics, and hospitals very well for such procedures. Given the patient and physician's desire to make a diagnosis, the fear of "missing the diagnosis" and possible malpractice charges, the value to the physician of performing the procedure (Hillman and others, 1992), and the relative safety of diagnostic studies, it is not surprising that authorities inside and outside the medical community are suggesting that too many tests and procedures are performed on patients (Consumers Union, 1992).

As patients, Americans have grown to expect an answer to the question "What is the diagnosis?" Moreover, physicians are trained to pursue the answer to that question with relentless enthusiasm. Given the climate of health care and the unrestricted resources of the past, this philosophy was uncritically accepted. However, with health care costs threatening the financial stability of many individuals, and some would say the nation, it is clearly time to reassess this philosophy.

The importance of a diagnosis most often relates to the impact it has on the patient: will the patient live longer or more comfortably as a result of the test or procedure? The answer to this question has become the driving force in health services research, which centers less on the dilemma of "diagnosis" and more on the final result, or "patient outcome." The Agency for Health Care Policy and Research (AHCPR), an agency of the federal government, is charged with reassessing many previously "accepted" health care practices. Medicare reimbursement mechanisms are slowly being restructured, and efforts are underway to financially reward physicians who spend time talking to patients (so-called "cognitive" specialties) and stabilize the fees for physicians who perform procedures. Clearly the process of diagnosis should be carefully considered by physician and patient, and the information gained must justify the costs and risk. Equally important, however, the procedure should be likely to have a positive impact on the health of the patient.

How can a patient determine if a procedure should be performed or is justified? The medical community, insurers, and the government are developing practice guidelines for physicians which, in the near future, may outline the accepted indications for many commonly performed procedures. At present, patients should consult reference books that outline these indications, highlighting when a procedure should be considered and for which symptoms (Arnot, 1992). Second opinions are as valuable for major diagnostic studies as they are for surgical interventions and may even be required by some health insurance plans. In a recent study of second opinions for coronary angiography, a procedure involving heart catheterization, the cardiologist rendering the second opinion judged that over 50 percent of the procedures could be put off or not performed at all. Subsequent review of patients' health and follow-up interviews with the patients and their physicians showed no difference in health outcome (Graboys and others, 1992).

Because communication between physicians is not perfect, it is important for the patient to discuss a specialist's recommendations with the primary care physician at the next visit. Specialists may be narrowly focused (e.g., kidney, liver, bones, etc.), restricting their practices to their areas of specialty. When a number of specialists are involved in the care of a patient, the patient may be easily confused by the various and even contradictory comments of the different practitioners. But the patient can do several things to minimize any confusion:

1. Always make the specialist aware of the name of the primary care physician.
2. Ask that copies of the specialist's reports be sent to the primary care doctor.
3. Bring all prescribed medications to every physician appointment.
4. Contact the primary care physician first when new symptoms occur.

This fourth recommendation deserves emphasis. The patient should always contact the primary care physician about consultations, procedures, and diagnostic testing, since this physician is the patient's advocate, having the knowledge and experience to advise the patient about a course of action and having the patient's best interests in mind. Many managed-care insurers even require that the primary care physician approve a consultation, referral, or procedure. There is growing evidence that this "gatekeeper" role also protects the patient from the risks of overtreatment and of undergoing procedures with limited proven benefit (Franks, Clancy, and Nutting, 1992). Given the potential harm from overtreatment and the special vulnerability of older Americans, the patient should contact the primary care physician before seeing any consulting physician or undergoing any but the most innocuous diagnostic studies and procedures.

In a recent study of second opinions for coronary angiography, a procedure involving heart catheterization, the cardiologist rendering the second opinion judged that over 50 percent of the procedures could be put off or not performed at all.

Who Needs a Geriatrician?

Physicians with geriatric training and certification are generally not in private practice in most communities. The majority remain in medical schools and affiliated hospitals. Currently, there is no consensus on what future role they may play in the American health care system—whether as specialists, community physicans, or academic physicans. Ongoing efforts are being made to increase the number of geriatricians trained each year, but years will pass before geriatricians become plentiful.

One innovative approach to care of older patients is the development of the multidisciplinary geriatric assessment team. A physician trained in geriatrics assembles a team that may include a clinical pharmacist, a nurse specializing in geriatrics, social workers, and physical and occupational therapists. In both inpatient and outpatient settings, the patient undergoes an extensive evaluation of medical history, medication history, social and environmental factors, mental and functional status, and detailed physical examination. The team then compiles a series of recommendations that may include medication changes, assistive devices, and community services necessary to maintaining independence.

But there is no agreement on which patients should seek out geriatric care. Very frail, elderly patients with a number of medical problems and those elderly who need a great deal of assistance to remain in the community might benefit from a geriatric evaluation. Many long term care facilities (nursing homes) could benefit from having a geriatric physician involved in decision-making, and their patients could gain from the geriatrician's expertise. For the moment, however, the scarcity of geriatricians remains a problem.

When Problems or Emergencies Arise

Physicians are generally available during office hours if problems arise. If the problem is not life-threatening, the patient should call the doctor's office. Primary care physicians usually have time in their schedule for urgent visits. If the problem is deemed too serious to be dealt with in the office, the patient may be asked to go to an emergency department. The physician may meet the patient at the emergency department or ask the physician on duty in the emergency department to evaluate the patient and call the primary care physician back. In either case, the primary care physician, who knows the most about the patient's condition, is directly involved in the evaluation, and unneeded tests or medications may be avoided.

At night and on weekends, physicians usually arrange some method for patients to have access to a physician. Many physicians share this responsibility, which means that the physician returning an emergency call may not be the patient's personal primary care physician. However, the problem will be addressed, after which the call will generally be referred to the primary care physician. The call to the covering physician may save the time and expense of an emergency room visit.

However, there are no easy guidelines to decide whether or not the condition warrants an emergency room visit or whether a call to the physician will suffice. Clearly if a threat to life exists, the call to the Emergency Medical Service (EMS) for an ambulance should not be delayed. However, many symptoms can be tolerated until office hours, and others may be addressed on the phone by the physician, though it is important to notify the primary care physician of serious occurrences at the first opportunity. Since communication between doctors is not always assured, it is wise for the patient to call the office to let the physician know what has occurred.

Which Physician Is for You?

One important consideration not yet mentioned: the patient must be comfortable with the manner, attitudes, and philosophy of their physician. Three models for the patient-physician relationship have been proposed (Brody, 1983). The dominant model in years past was the paternalistic relationship: the patient was passive and unquestioning, the physician made decisions and recommendations without consulting the patient. In the second model the patient cooperates with the physicians' recommendations to achieve a specific medical goal (such as treating an infection) but participates no further in making decisions about care. In the third model there is mutual participation between physician and patient, who are equal partners in health care. There is evidence that this latter model, which is most consistent with the consumer's approach to health care, is becoming the dominant philosophy of American patients (Haug and Lavin, 1981).

One approach to mutual participation in health care decisions is to view the relationship as a contract between two parties (Quill, 1983). The patient and physician agree that a problem exists and together select a course of action to address the needs of the patient. This process may require negotiation on the part of both the patient and the physician to achieve a solution satisfactory to both parties, but it is increasingly clear that patients who participate actively in their own health care achieve better results (e.g., they suffer fewer physical limitations) than patients who subscribe to the paternalistic model (Greenfield, Kaplan, and Ware, 1985). It is clearly in the best interest of both physician and patient to be equal participants in medical care.

The relationship with a physician is built on trust and mutual respect. The effectiveness of a patient-physician relationship depends on the ability of the patient to communicate signs, symptoms, and feelings, and the ability of the physician to effectively explain diagnostic and therapeutic options. Ultimately a course of action must be negotiated and completed. Patients should seek a therapeutic relationship that suits them, and they should not hesitate to change physicians to achieve such a relationship.

How do you find out if the physician is right for you? Clearly there are many factors to consider when choosing a physician or deciding to change physicians. Credentials and qualifications, hospital affiliation, office staff, and after-hours emergency coverage are all important. Sources for referral include state medical societies, medical schools, and hospitals, which can all provide patients with the names and qualifications of physicians. More medical practices are printing brochures describing office policies, and these can be requested by phone. For more subjective impressions, friends and neighbors are good sources for the name of local physicians. Friends may provide information not available from any other source about such considerations as waiting times in the office, ease of appointments, and attitudes and philosophy of the physicians. But ultimately only the individual can judge whether the relationship can be compatible, and the quickest and surest way to determine compatibility is to make an appointment for a "get acquainted" visit (be sure to make it clear on the phone that the visit is not an initial, complete physical). The impression left by such a visit allows the patient to make a more informed decision about choosing a doctor.

● MEDICATIONS

Medications are the most common form of medical treatment for older individuals, and the overwhelming majority of medications prescribed by physicians are for older Americans. Modern medications can prolong life, relieve symptoms, and greatly improve the quality of life for many individuals.

Prescription medications are very powerful compounds taken by patients to have a specific effect on a process or disease. This property of medications is called efficacy. In order to release and market medications, pharmaceutical companies must demonstrate their efficacy and safety by extensive testing and clinical trials prior to gaining approval by the Food and Drug Administration (FDA). But safety testing in older individuals has only recently become a priority for the FDA. After medications are available to the public, however, the physician, pharmacist, and patient have a role in monitoring the safety and efficacy of medications, a responsibility that

The pharmacist is an important resource for information about specific medications, the advisability of generic substitution, precautions, side effects, medication interactions, and instructions when a dose of medicine is missed. (Courtesy of the American Association of Retired Persons)

must be taken seriously to avoid unintended, adverse effects.

Adverse drug reactions are serious but unintentional effects of medications, commonly called side effects, drug reactions, or allergies. A recent study indicated that an astounding 10 percent of older Americans reported experiencing adverse medication reactions (Chrischilles, Segar, and Wallace, 1992). Three percent to ten percent of all hospital admissions of older Americans are the result of adverse reactions to medications, and one in four of the oldest patients experiences an adverse medication reaction while in the hospital (Kane, Ouslander, and Abrass, 1989). Clearly medications are a "two-edged sword," and the physician, pharmacist, patient, and caregiver should monitor them responsibly (Schulz and Brushwood, 1992).

Know Your Medications

Prescriptions are written in a standard format that includes the name of the medicine, its dosage and frequency, the total number of tablets or capsules dispensed, and sometimes the time length for the treatment. But this is only the bare minimum of information the patient needs to master. Patients need to remember all the medicines prescribed for them—or at least carry a list of them. Because there are many generic forms of prescriptions available, the color, shape, and size of a tablet or capsule no longer reliably identifies a particular prescription medicine. Furthermore, the names of many medicines sound alike when spoken aloud, which can easily confuse the patient. One pharmaceutical company recently changed the name of a product because its name sounded very similar to another company's commonly prescribed heart medicine.

Patients should be in the habit of taking all prescribed medicines with them when they go to see a physician. This "brown bag session" (Wolfe, Fugate, Hulstrand, Kamimoto, and PIRG, 1988) is especially important if the patient has seen a specialist or been hospitalized since the last office visit. The physician can then review the actual prescriptions and determine whether or not the medication is correct and being taken as the prescriber intended.

Three percent to ten percent of all hospital admissions of older Americans are the result of adverse reactions to medications, and one in four of the oldest patients experiences an adverse medication reaction while in the hospital.

When medications are absorbed into the body, they are rapidly removed from the bloodstream and excreted by the internal organs. As humans age, the efficiency of this removal is reduced, and as a result, the same amount of medication causing a certain effect in a younger person may cause a pronounced or prolonged effect in the older patient. Thus the dosage, the amount of active medicine in a tablet or capsule, may need to be reduced as the patient ages.

Equally important, some medications prescribed for one condition may make another condition get worse. For example, a commonly prescribed medicine for blood pressure control may worsen diabetes control. This is one of many good reasons for a person to take only medicines prescribed for him or her—and never anyone else's medicines!

Finally, the dosage of one medicine usually bears no relationship to the dosage of another medicine. The dosage of medicine is based on age, gender, weight, and other factors. A milligram (one thousandth of a gram) of one medicine may be appropriate for one condition, whereas a milligram of another medication may be toxic or cause death.

Know Your Medications: Why Take Them and For How Long?

Medicines are prescribed for specific reasons. Many, like those for blood pressure and diabetes, are taken on a regular basis. These daily medicines are prescribed to control the effects of a specific disease. When the medicine is taken, the blood pressure or blood sugar is reduced, preventing disease complications. This type of medicine may be taken for many years. The patient should make every effort to take the medicine as prescribed and not to skip doses.

Other medicines are prescribed for a course of treatment, should be taken regularly for a specified amount of time, and then stopped. For example, most antibiotic medicines are prescribed for seven to fourteen days, and are meant to be taken on a regular schedule until the course of treatment is completed, after which the medicine is discontinued.

Other medicines are prescribed to relieve symptoms. For example, the medicine prescribed for benign vertigo, a condition that causes a spinning sensation and nausea, relieves the symptom but does not cure the condition. Medicines prescribed to control symptoms are usually taken as "needed," and their labels clearly say so. It is extremely important, therefore, to know the purpose for which a medicine is prescribed, as well as the dosage, the dosing interval, and the duration of treatment. Patients should know how, why, and how long to take the medicine.

Know Your Medications: How to Take Them

A master list of medications is necessary for patients taking more than one or two medication dosages per day, and such a list is strongly encouraged for patients who take multiple medications. The name of the medicine and the time of day for each dose is listed and entered across the top of the sheet. The list should be placed in a prominent place in the house (e.g., refrigerator or cabinet) and a copy carried with the patient for reference.

It is a good habit to use *seven-day pill organizers* for daily medications. Usually small containers labeled with the days of the week, some daily pill organizers are further divided into two to four sections as needed for each dosing interval: once daily, twice daily, etc. In this way, if the patient does not remember whether he or she took the medicine for the day, the organizer will answer the question: for instance if the medicine in the Monday space is gone, the patient has taken the dose. Forming this simple habit will help to avoid taking two doses when only one dose was intended.

Know Your Medications: Side Effects?

All medications, both prescription and over the counter, have the potential to cause side effects

Table 26.7
Methods to Assist Patients in Complying with Medication Regimens

1. The medication regimen should be as simple as possible:
   - Medications should have the same dosing schedule
   - Medications should be timed with a daily routine (e.g., meals, bedtime)
2. Other people should know the patient's medication regimen:
   - Spouse, relative, caretaker
   - Home health nurse, health aide
3. The medications should be:
   - Affordable
   - Attainable from a pharmacy that is convenient
   - In a bottle that is not too difficult to open
4. Aids should be used (e.g., pill organizer, medication calendar)
5. Medication records should be kept up to date
6. Medications should be reviewed at every physician visit

(unintended, often undesirable results), and because older individuals do not eliminate medications as quickly as younger patients, side effects are more common in the elderly. Ideally physicians should review all potential side effects when prescribing medications, but in fact it is only practical to review the most common or serious ones. Although many side effects are reduced with continued therapy, the patient must report any unexpected reaction to the physician as soon as possible for advice on whether to continue the medication.

Older individuals do not tolerate side effects as well as young people, so that side effects may be more serious or harmful for older adults. For example, a brief episode of light-headedness may not be serious, but for an individual who has difficulty maintaining balance or has poor eyesight, such an episode may cause a fall and result in a hip fracture. Thus extreme care must be used with all medications: each may have side effects, which in turn may result in injury or illness. Be cautious!

Know Your Medications: Interactions?

Many medications interact when taken together. Interaction means that one medication may change the effectiveness of another. For example, one common heart medication can cause an increase in the blood level of another heart medication. Since the increase can be dangerous, the physician, patient, and pharmacist all must seek to avoid interactions or at least be aware of the potential for interactions.

Medications are often taken in some relationship to food. The patient should know whether a medication is to be taken before meals (generally thirty minutes before food), with meals, or after meals. Because some medicines interact with food, food can interfere with the absorption of a medicine from the stomach (e.g., certain antibiotics). On the other hand, other medicines can irritate the stomach (e.g., some pain medicines) and are better taken with food to reduce the chance of irritation. The older antibiotic tetracycline should not be taken with milk because milk interferes with absorption from the stomach, but milk does not effect the absorption of the newer

Table 26.8
Working with Your Doctor Toward Safer Medication Habits

1. Have "brown bag sessions" with your primary care doctor (bring along all prescribed medicines).
2. Find out if you are experiencing adverse reactions to medications.
3. Assume that any new symptom you develop after starting a new medication may be caused by the medication; call your doctor to report it.
4. Make sure a medication is really needed for your condition.
5. If a medication is needed, in most cases it is safer to start with a lower dose than the usual adult amount.
6. When adding a new medication, ask if it is possible to discontinue another medication.
7. Stopping a medication at the right time is as important as starting it.
8. Before leaving the doctor's office or the pharmacy, make sure the instructions for taking your medication are clear to you as well as a family member or friend.
9. Discard all old medications carefully.
10. Ask your primary care doctor to coordinate your care and medications.

Source: Wolfe, Sydney M., and others. Worst Pills, Best Pills. Washington, DC: Public Citizen Health Research Group, 1988.

tetracycline-type medicines. Thus the relationship of medication dosing to meals should be clear to the patient.

Medications commonly interact with alcohol (beer, wine, or spirits). The effects of sedative tranquilizers, blood thinners, and various heart medications may be dramatically increased by alcohol, and these changes can be dangerous. Other medications may interfere with absorption of prescription medicines. For example, a kaolin-containing medicine used for diarrhea may reduce the absorption of several heart medicines. Older persons should be sure to ask their physician or pharmacist about such effects.

Because medications are chemical compounds, the older tablets are less likely to work effectively. Generally, medicines more than one year old should be discarded, and certain medicines (like nitroglycerin, a heart tablet) should be discarded after six months. Discarding old prescription medications also reduces the temptation to take an old medication for the recurrence of a symptom, and the risk of taking an accidental dosage of the wrong medicine.

Medications commonly interact with alcohol (beer, wine, or spirits). The effects of sedative tranquilizers, blood thinners, and various heart medications may be dramatically increased by alcohol, and these changes can be dangerous.

Know Your Medications: Nonprescription Medicines

Many patients do not consider nonprescription medications as "real medications." This is an error! "Over-the-counter" medicines have similar properties to prescription medicines, and since the patient may choose these medicines without professional consultation, there is significant potential for adverse events.

The patient or caregiver should carefully read the educational material supplied with the medicine, with several considerations in mind. The medication must be appropriate for the symptom or condition to be treated, and this condition or symptom should be stated in the package insert under *Indications for Usage*. The dosage must be correct for the patient, keeping in mind the need

to reduce dosage for older individuals as well as the patient's medical conditions or other prescription medications. The minimum timing for each dose should be understood, and the patient should not exceed the maximum dosage in a twenty-four hour period. The duration of therapy should be defined, and any suggested limit for duration of therapy should be noted.

Labels often suggest that a physician be consulted if the symptom or condition does not resolve in a period of days or weeks. Interactions between readily available over-the-counter medicines and prescribed medicines are also common. Above all, side-effects must be clearly understood. Side effects of nonprescription medicines, seen commonly in young adults, may be more pronounced in older individuals, so even more caution is warranted. For example, many nonprescription medicines may reduce the level of alertness and predispose patients to falls or automobile accidents.

New problems or symptoms occurring after a nonprescription medicine is begun should alert the patient or caregiver to the possibility of side effects. The increasing difficulty in urination noted by an older man may signal a medication side effect and not necessarily a worsening prostate problem. Careful choice, thorough understanding of their use and effects, and continued surveillance for problems are all necessary to avoid problems with nonprescription medicines.

Medications and the Pharmacist

The pharmacist is taking a more active role in suggesting and monitoring medication use by patients. Although pharmacists have traditionally been an advocate for the physician, encouraging patient compliance, more recently the pharmacist has been endorsed as a patient advocate as well (Schulz and Brushwood, 1991). Changes in insurance regulations are now mandating an active role by pharmacists in patient education.

The pharmacist is an important resource for information about specific medications, the advisability of generic substitution, precautions, side effects, medication interactions, and instructions when a dose of medicine is missed. The pharmacist, frequently aided by a computer program, may also cross reference all the patient's prescription medicines to identify potentially harmful interactions. However, only if the patient purchases all medications at a single pharmacy can the pharmacist be aware of all medicines prescribed for the patient. The pharmacist should also be consulted when patients are selecting over-the-counter medications so potential interactions can be detected. The pharmacist is also a good source of techniques and helpful aids such as "pill organizers" that simplify compliance with complicated medication regimens.

The patient, pharmacist, and physician need to work together to avoid the potentially catastrophic consequences of medications taken improperly. As in other aspects of medical care, the best rule of thumb to guard against problems associated with medication use is to ask questions! The efforts of every professional involved in health care, as well as the patient and caregivers, must be directed toward maximizing the therapeutic effects of medications and reducing the alarming incidence of adverse medication reactions in older Americans.

The pharmacist is also a good source of techniques and helpful aids such as "pill organizers" that simplify compliance with complicated medication regimens.

● HOSPITALIZATION AND SURGERY

Hospitalization is almost invariably faced with apprehension, and surgery is equally feared by young and old alike. The reasons are multiple: the fear of pain, disability, or death, loss of control over one's individual liberty and autonomy, and the association of hospitalization with aging and the end of independent existence. These feelings are especially common in older Americans who may harbor many negative thoughts and memories about hospitals. Nevertheless, American hospitals are among the world's most sophisticated health care institutions, and Americans seem to highly value their hospitals.

Hospital costs are the largest segment of health care spending, which in 1992 exceeded $600 billion. Medicare, a federal program, is the largest single purchaser of health care services, and changes in Medicare regulations have drastically changed the hospital practice of medicine in the past several years: patients are discharged sooner, and more procedures and surgeries are accomplished in the outpatient setting. In addition, hospital physicians and services are undergoing intense scrutiny, and the findings have been somewhat alarming.

Hospitalization usually results in benefit to patients, but hospitalization can also entail significant risk. For patients 65 years of age and over staying in the hospital more than fifteen days, one study reported more than half the patients had some complication, the majority of which are considered "preventable" (LeFevre and others, 1992). A very large study of "adverse events" occurring to hospitalized patients indicated that almost 4 percent of the people admitted to hospitals suffer a disabling injury while hospitalized (Leape and others, 1991). The most common "adverse events" were related to medications, and the occurrence of adverse medication events increased with the age of the patient. In another study, medication-induced kidney injury occurred in 1 percent of the patients admitted to the hospital (more frequently in older adults), and resulted in death about 12 percent of the time (Morris and others, 1991).

For patients 65 years of age and over staying in the hospital more than fifteen days, one study reported more than half the patients had some complication, the majority of which are considered "preventable."

Hospital Quality

The majority of hospitals in the United States have agreed to periodic routine evaluation by an outside organization, the Joint Commission on Accreditation of Healthcare Organizations (JCAHO). The JCAHO inspects the hospital every two to three years, examining every aspect of care and recommending ways to improve patient care. If a hospital passes review, it is certified for an additional three years. If the JCAHO reviewers identify improper practices or problems, the organization will define specific remedies to allow certification. If the hospital does not comply

Hospitalization usually results in benefit to patients, but it can also entail significant risk. (Courtesy of Bowman Gray/Baptist Hospital Medical Center)

within a specific time interval, the hospital could lose certification, thus risking loss of all federal (Medicare, Medicaid) and other sources of reimbursement for services. Such an occurrence could threaten the continued existence of a hospital. Consequently JCAHO inspections are taken very seriously, and compliance with resulting recommendations is high. Although the system of inspection results in a high standard of care in American hospitals, the reviews do not truly reflect patient outcomes.

In the late 1980s, the federal government began releasing statistics on hospital performance and patient outcome, initially publishing mortality rates of individual hospitals. These rates however, had more to do with the severity of illness of the patients in the hospitals than the quality of hospital care. Many standardized quality measures have been developed that measure quality of care (Keeler and others, 1992), but generally these measures remain expensive and cannot be used for a patient to choose one hospital over another.

The federal government is attempting to improve quality of care through analysis of the Medicare billing system, applying computerized decision rules to transactions involving millions of patients (Jencks and Wilensky, 1992). No less importantly, innovative quality of care programs are being implemented at the hospital level, many of which parallel the industrial model of Continuous Quality Improvement (CQI). Nonetheless, there is no substitute for an assertive, questioning patient, a well-informed primary care and attending physician, and a meticulous professional staff.

Consent for Hospitalization and Procedures

With all the information and confusion surrounding admission to the hospital, it is not always clear: *"Who's in charge?"* Ultimately, the patient is in charge! Only under very specific circumstances, when the patient is too ill to make a decision, can treatment in a hospital be undertaken without the patient's permission. A prime example is the Patient Self-Determination Act, a federally mandated program to encourage the use of advance directives. Hospital personnel are required to ask each patient if he or she has completed an advance directive for health care, and these documents are included in the medical record as clear evidence of a patient's wishes. On admission to the hospital, the patient also signs a document called a "consent to treat," stating that the patient agrees to be treated in the hospital. Generally patients are not asked to agree to individual routine studies such as blood work, nor are they specifically asked to consent to routine, accepted low-risk therapies such as the administration of intravenous fluids. By signing the consent to treat, the patient does not give up the right to refuse treatment, nor does the patient yield any diagnostic or therapeutic decisions.

However, surgical and other procedures carrying more than minimal risk of complications and most types of anesthesia require a separate *informed consent.* Informed consent is an agreement between the patient and physician stating that the patient understands the procedure to be performed, the risks involved in accepting the procedure, any alternatives to the procedure, the expected benefit, and the potential for future complications. The essential component of informed consent is agreement: *The patient agrees to accept the risk of the test or procedure*

Table 26.9

Elements of Informed Consent for a Medical or Surgical Procedure

1. Explanation of the specific procedure to be performed
2. Explanation of any risk involved
3. Alternatives to the procedure (if any)
4. Expected results: Diagnose disease, relieve pain, return to normal function, etc.
5. Potential complications in the future

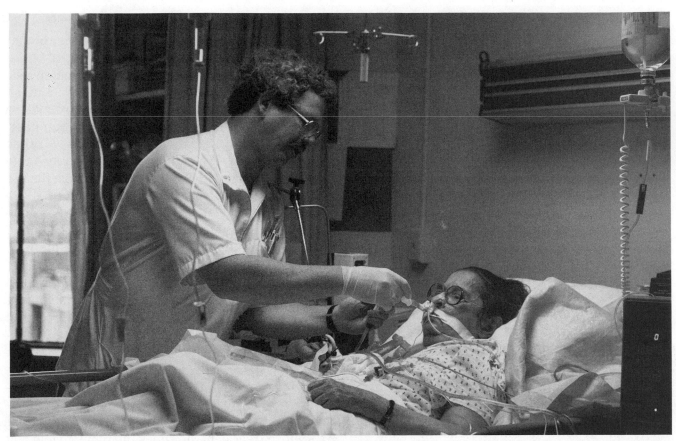

Patients may have a great number of physicians in the hospital: internist, family physician, consulting specialists, surgeon, resident physicians, physicians-in-training, etc. (Courtesy of Bowman Gray/Baptist Hospital Medical Center)

to gain the potential benefit. Signature of this agreement implies that the patient has received a satisfactory answer to all questions about the test or procedure and is capable of making an informed decision. If this is not the case, the patient has the right and responsibility to refuse consent until the risks and benefits are clear!

The Attending Physician or Surgeon

Patients may have a great number of physicians in the hospital: internist or family physician, consulting specialists, surgeon, resident physicians, physicians-in-training, etc. The physician who is ultimately responsible for the patient's medical care and who directs or coordinates this mass of medical manpower is the *attending physician or surgeon*, the physician who admitted the patient. The attending physician may be a specialist or subspecialist. His or her name appears as the physician of record on the patient's chart and is usually printed on the hospital bracelet. Questions about a specific surgical procedure should be directed to the surgeon, and

questions about anesthesia to the anesthesiologist. The attending physician remains responsible for presenting all the necessary information to the patient so he or she can weigh all risks and benefits, and will also make a recommendation to the patient.

Consulting Physicians or Surgeons

Many physicians may act as advisers to the attending physician and suggest specific diagnostic or therapeutic interventions. These physicians may then carry out their recommendations, if the patient and attending physician agree with the recommendation. These physicians may discuss their findings with the patient directly, or more often they present their findings to the attending physician. The attending physician will integrate the new information into an overall strategy for presentation to the patient.

Interns and Resident Physicians

At university and affiliated teaching hospitals, interns (first year of training) and residents (second through fifth year of training) are physicians who have completed medical school and are training in a hospital setting. Generally the interns and residents are an integral part of the health care team supervised either by the attending physician or the attending physician responsible for the ward (in the case of some teaching hospitals). They make nonemergency decisions regarding care after consultation with the attending physician.

Medical Students

Like interns and residents, medical students are frequently seen in university or affiliated hospitals and may visit patients to obtain historical information or perform a physical exam. Medical students are closely supervised and frequently have more time to discuss the medical history with patients than busy residents do. Medical students cannot make care decisions or order laboratory studies or medications for patients. Thus there is probably little reason for patients to discuss their condition with medical students. However, since the education and training of physicians in the United States is, at present, very dependent on the cooperation of hospitalized patients, patients lose a valuable opportunity to contribute to the education of future physicians if they refuse to be seen by medical students.

Preparing for Surgery

No matter how minor, surgery is both physically and psychologically stressful. Early active preparation is necessary to reduce the mental stress and minimize potential complications of surgery and the postoperative period. Although a generalized approach is outlined here, the individual's personal physician should be consulted for specific cases.

A *preoperative visit to a primary care physician* at least a month prior to the surgery is generally advisable. The purpose of the visit is to assure medical control of chronic diseases (e.g., asthma, heart disease, etc.) and maximize function. This visit allows the primary care physician an opportunity to complete necessary blood studies related to medication dosing and adjusting medications accordingly. The preoperative visit may not be necessary for many patients, but for those with medical problems, it may smooth the pre-operative course.

A preoperative visit to the *anesthesiologist* will generally be required prior to surgery. The anesthesiologist will review the history and physical exam and especially review the medication and allergy history, as well as any previous surgeries with anesthesia. The role of the anesthesiologist is to minimize the potential adverse effects of anesthesia and avoid any complications during the surgery (see next section). It is best for the patient to bring all medications for the preoperative visits so that the anesthesiologist may review them to advise which medicines should be continued up until surgery and when to discontinue others.

Admission to the hospital may occur the night before or more commonly early on the same day of surgery. Remaining paperwork may be completed first. Then an intravenous solution will be started and necessary monitors attached (most commonly heart, or EKG, monitor and a device that continuously measures blood pressure, oxygen, etc). The necessary premedications will be administered, and the anesthesia begun.

Anesthesia

The anesthesiologist is a physician who has trained for four or more years to anesthetize patients during surgery. *General anesthesia* involves both intravenous and inhaled medications, which render the patient unconscious for the duration of the surgery. As already mentioned, older patients may not tolerate medications as well as younger patients, and there may be a prolonged aftereffect resulting from the use of general anesthesia on older individuals. Older individuals may require lower doses of anesthesia and have prolonged recovery. In addition, a period of postoperative confusion is very common in the elderly, and this confusion may be worsened by preexisting cognitive difficulties. These problems have helped to stimulate interest in alternatives to general anesthesia, like *spinal and epidural anesthesia*. A small needle is inserted in the back to give medication for both of these techniques, and the patient will be pain free and may only be mildly sedated for the procedure. *Local and regional anesthesia* are alternatives in which only the part of the body requiring surgery (usually the eye, arm, or leg) is anesthetized, and the patient may be awake or mildly sedated during the surgery. The choice of anesthesia is commonly dictated by the type of surgery. However, the anesthesiologist has the safety of the patient uppermost in his or her mind, so the patient should not be biased about one technique of anesthesia or another. It is the job of the anesthesiologist to review the patient's history, medications, and medical conditions, then make a recommendation for anesthetic technique based on his or her best medical judgment in an effort to minimize the risk of the surgery.

Justification for Surgery and Possible Alternatives

Surgery is clearly not risk free, but most often the risk of the disease far outweighs the risk of an operation. In elderly patients, the operation to repair a hip fracture, for example, is far safer than the prolonged bedrest and traction used in the past. For other conditions, however, surgery may not result in an improvement that is worth the risk. As a case in point, hip replacement for arthritic conditions is only considered when there is great arthritic pain and the patient has lost much function. For other conditions, the potential for complications is high enough to weigh against surgical intervention. Even when surgery is clearly indicated, the procedure of choice may not be clear. The surgical procedure of choice for women with localized breast cancer may simply be excision of the tumor with follow-up therapy or removal of the entire breast, depending on the patient's preference for cosmetic result and the subsequent risk of recurrence.

How can a patient determine if the risk of surgery is worth the potential benefit? Analogous to diagnostic procedures (see Table 26.9), the decision to undergo surgery should be carefully considered, weighing the benefits against the risks. Reference books and national guidelines for physicians may be helpful under some circumstances. A second opinion is frequently invaluable, and may be required by some insurance carriers. As with other decisions about health care, however, the primary care physician is a critical resource for advice and should be consulted whenever possible prior to surgery.

Alternatives to surgery must be considered when a patient decides against having surgery, when the risk to the patient from surgery approaches the risk from the disease, or when the risk of surgery and disease are both very high. Newer procedures may be less effective but carry a much lower risk. For example, coronary bypass surgery, not possible twenty years ago, has prolonged and improved the lives of thousands of patients with heart disease. For those patients at high risk for complications of major heart surgery or those with limited disease, coronary balloon angioplasty provides an alternative. However, about 25 percent of arteries that undergo balloon angioplasty have narrowed again within one year, and the procedure needs to be repeated. Of course, in the future newer techniques employing lasers may replace angioplasty for patients who need or want an alternative to coronary bypass.

The Post-Operative Period

The recovery room and intensive care unit (ICU) may be the initial stops after the operation, especially for major surgical procedures. A large number of nurses and professional staff are available in these units. Equipped with complex machines and monitors to diagnose and treat potential postoperative complications, the ICU may appear to the patient to be a busy, noisy place, but the patient stay routinely is short and transfer to the regular hospital floor soon follows.

As with other decisions about health care, however, the primary care physician is a critical resource for advice and should be consulted whenever possible prior to surgery.

The focus of postoperative care is to restore normal function and mobility as quickly as possible. Even healthy older Americans can rapidly lose strength and mobility during hospitalization. Nurses, nursing assistants, and physical and respiratory therapists all work together to restore the patient to the preoperative condition. Postoperative recovery can be difficult, occasionally painful work for the patient, but studies of older patients show that prolonged immobility during hospitalization can result in complications such as pneumonia, skin problems, and infections. It is critical that the patient work toward restoring normal mobility.

Discharge Planning

The cost of medical care has resulted in dramatic decreases in the length of hospital stays and made discharge planning a high priority for hospitals. For minor surgical procedures, discharge from the hospital may occur the same day as the procedure. This shifts responsibility for much of the postoperative care to family members, which may be stressful for the relatives involved. It is very important to have adequate help and a clear plan for care when the patient is brought home. For questions that arise during the recuperation at home, the attending physician or surgeon should be contacted.

For major surgery and even routine medical admission to the hospital, discharge planning begins in the first few days. Frequently a nurse, a social worker, dietician, and other professionals will visit the patient to assess the home environment, family support, and the necessity and availability of community services after discharge. Visiting nurses, medical equipment, assistive devices, "meals on wheels," and even transportation for follow-up appointments should be arranged prior to discharge. Many older Americans may feel they are being "rushed" out of the hospital, but the home environment with adequate home services may be preferable to the risks, complications, and cost of longer hospital stays.

Some patients may not be discharged directly to home. They may need more support than can be arranged in the community and may need to enter retirement communities or other long-term care facilities, where more supportive services are available. A patient recovering from hip surgery, for example, may be transferred to a rehabilitation hospital, where teams of physical and occupational therapists with specialized equipment work intensively to restore function and mobility. In all cases, the patient must be

---

Visiting nurses, medical equipment, assistive devices, "meals on wheels," and even transportation for follow-up appointments should be arranged prior to discharge.

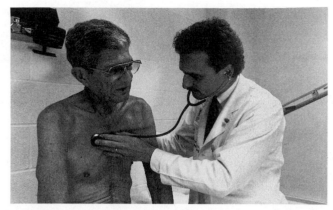

The patient must be knowledgeable and assertive in health care, and participate as an equal in the partnership. (Courtesy of Bowman Gray/Baptist Hospital Medical Center)

assured that the environment is safe and that adequate supportive services are available.

● PATIENT RIGHTS AND ISSUES IN MEDICAL CARE

The patient ultimately has the right and responsibility to make decisions about his or her health care. It is therefore imperative that the patient take an active role in health care. Asking questions, exploring alternatives, and synthesizing plans are the joint responsibility of the patient, physician, and other members of the health care team. A knowledgeable and assertive patient participates in the negotiations as an equal in the partnership.

Members of the health care team act as advisers and advocates for health care: they make recommendations based on their knowledge and experience. Although there is much known about diseases and treatments, there is also much still to learn. Medical research frequently raises as many questions as it answers, and although it may not be obvious from the patient's perspective, there are many areas in medicine where there are no clear answers. Physicians frequently find themselves forced to recommend decisions without adequate information or knowledge. It is here that the art of medicine and the need for clear communication are crucial. The physician and patient may not always agree, but, as in other human endeavors, this may be the sign of a healthy relationship, and the physician should continue to offer his or her best advice. The patient has the right to demand excellence in health care but also must, with the physician and other health care providers, accept responsibility for health care decisions.

Pamphlets

For Seniors Only: A Guide to Using Drugs in the Later Years and *Over-the-Counter Medications: A Guide for Older Adults.* Available from: SRx Regional Program, 1155 Market St., Suite 102, San Francisco, CA 94103.

Using Your Medicines Wisely: A Guide for the Elderly. Available from: National Clearinghouse for Alcohol and Drug Information, P.O. Box 2345, Rockville, MD 20852. DHHS publication no. 90–705.

References

Brody, David S. "The Patient's Role in Clinical Decision-Making." *Annals of Internal Medicine* Vol. 93 (1980): 718–22.

Chrischilles, Elizabeth A., Ellen T. Segar, and Robert B. Wallace. "Self-Reported Adverse Drug Reactions and Related Resource Use: A Study of Community-Dwelling Persons 65 Years of Age and Older." *Annals of Internal Medicine* Vol. 117 (1992): 634–40.

Consumers Union. "Health Care Dollars." *Consumer Reports* (July 1992): 435–49.

Davidman, Morris, Paul Olson, Jeffrey Kohen, Tom Leither, and Carl Kjellstrand. "Iatrogenic Renal Disease." *Archives of Internal Medicine* Vol. 151 (1991): 1809–12.

Franks, Peter, Carolyn M. Clancy, and Paul A. Nutting. "Gatekeeping Revisited: Protecting Patients from Overtreatment." *New England Journal of Medicine* Vol. 327 (1992): 424–29.

Gonzalez, Martin L., ed. *Physician Marketplace Statistics.* Chicago, IL: American Medical Association, 1992.

Gorell, Allan H., Lawrence A. May, and Albert G. Malley, eds. *Primary Care Medicine: Office Evaluation and Management of the Adult Patient.* Philadelphia: J. B. Lippincott, 1989.

Graboys, Thomas B., Beth Biegelsen, Steven Lampert, Charles M. Blatt, and Bernard Lown. "Results of a Second-Opinion Trial Among Patients Recommended for Coronary Angiography." *Journal of the American Medical Association* Vol. 268 (1992): 2537–40.

Greenfield, Sheldon, Sherrie Kaplan, and John E. Ware. "Expanding Patient Involvement in Care: Effects on Patient Outcomes." *Annals of Internal Medicine* Vol. 102 (1985): 520–28.

Haug, Marie, and Bebe Lavin. "Practitioner or Patient: Who's in Charge?" *Journal of Health and Social Behavior* Vol. 22 (1981): 212–29.

Hillman, Bruce J., George T. Olson, Patricia E. Griffith, Jonathan H. Sunshine, Catherine A. Joseph, Stephen D. Kennedy, William R. Nelson, and Lee B. Bernhardt. "Physicians' Utilization and Charges for Outpatient Diagnostic Imaging in the Medicare Population." *Journal of the American Medical Association* Vol. 268 (1992): 2050–54.

Jencks, Stephen F., and Gail R. Wilensky. "The Health Care Quality Improvement Initiative: A New Approach to Quality Assurance in Medicare." *Journal of the American Medical Association* Vol. 268 (1992): 900–3.

Kane, Robert L., Joseph G. Ouslander, and Itamar B. Abrass. *Essentials of Clinical Geriatrics.* 2d ed. New York: McGraw-Hill, 1989.

Keeler, Emmett B., Lisa V. Rubenstein, Katherine L. Kahn, David Draper, Ellen R. Harrison, Michael J. McGinty, William H. Rogers, and Robert H. Brook. "Hospital Characteristics and Quality of Care." *Journal of the American Medical Association* Vol 268 (1992): 1709–14.

Leape, Lucien L., Troyan A. Brennan, Nan Laird, and others. "The Nature of Adverse Events in Hospitalized Patients: Results of the Harvard Medical Practice Study II." *New England Journal of Medicine* Vol. 324 (1991): 377–84.

LeFevre, Frank, Joe Feinglass, Steven Potts, Lenore Soglin, Paul Yarnold, Gary J. Martin, and James R. Webster. "Iatrogenic Complications in High-Risk Elderly Patients." *Archives of Internal Medicine* Vol. 152 (1992): 2074–80.

Localio, A. Russell, Ann G. Lawthers, Troyan A. Brennan, and others. "Relation Between Malpractice Claims and Adverse Events Due to Negligence: Results of the Harvard Medical Practice Study III." *New England Journal of Medicine* Vol. 325 (1991): 245–51.

Quill, Timothy E. "Partnerships in Patient Care: A Contractual Approach." *Annals of Internal Medicine* Vol. 98 (1983): 228–34.

Schneiderman, Lawrence J., Richard Kronick, Robert M. Kaplan, John P. Anderson, and Robert D. Langer. "Effects of Offering Advance Directives on the Medical Treatments and Costs." *Annals of Internal Medicine* Vol. 117 (1992): 599–606.

Schulz, Richard M., and David B. Brushwood. "The Pharmacist's Role in Patient Care." *Hasting Center Report* (January-February 1991): 12–17.

Stimmel, Barry. "The Crisis in Primary Care and the Role of Medical Schools." *Journal of the American Medical Association* Vol. 268 (1992): 2060–65.

Additional Reading

American Heart Association. *The American Heart Association Heartbook: A Guide to Prevention and Treatment of Cardiovascular Diseases.* New York: E. P. Dutton, 1980.

Annas, George J. *The Rights of Hospital Patients.* New York: Avon Books, 1975.

Annas, George J, Leonard H. Glantz, and Barbara F. Katz. *The Rights of Doctors and Nurses and Allied Health Professionals.* New York: Avon Books, 1981.

Arnot, Robert, M.D. *The Best Medicine.* Reading, MA: Addison-Wesley, 1992.

Feltin, Marie. *A Woman's Guide to Good Health After Fifty.* Glenview, IL: American Association of Retired Persons and Scott, Foresman, 1987.

Inlander, Charles B. *Take This Book to the Hospital with You.* Allentown, PA: Peoples Medical Society, 1992.

Jones, J. Alfred, and Gerald M. Phillips. *Communicating with Your Doctor: Rx for Good Medical Care.* Carbondale, IL: Southern Illinois University Press, 1988.

Scheller, Mary Dale. *Building Partnerships in Hospital*

Care: Empowering Patients, Families, and Professionals. Palo Alto, CA: Bull Publishing, 1990.

Weiss, Robert J., and Genell J. Subak-Sharpe, eds. *Complete Guide to Health and Well-Being After Fifty.* Columbia University School of Public Health. New York: Times Books, 1988.

Wolfe, Sydney M., Lisa Fugate, Elizabeth P. Hulstrand, Laurie E. Kamimoto, and the Public Citizen Health Research Group. *Worst Pills, Best Pills: The Older Adult's Guide to Avoiding Drug-Induced Death or Illness.* Washington, DC: Public Citizen Health Research Group, 1988.

William P. Moran, M.D., M.S.
Ramon Velez, M.D., M.Sc.

Making Medical Care Decisions

● Informed Consent ● Informed Consent and Long-Term Care ● Truthtelling ● Advanced Directives
● Decisional Incapacity ● The Family, the Elder, and Medical Decision-Making ● Medical Futility
● Euthanasia and Physician-Assisted Suicide ● Summary

Traditionally, common law required that a physician obtain the patient's consent before carrying out medical tests, surgery, or other invasive procedures. Today, that general legal requirement, which rests on the individual's right to be left alone, has evolved into a complex ethical imperative. The contemporary view, simply stated, is that physicians are obligated to describe to patients the risks and benefits of medical procedures in sufficient detail to allow them to make an informed decision. Mentally competent patients may then consent to or refuse treatment, even if that refusal results in death. Great emphasis is now placed on active patient participation in making medical care decisions. While this is viewed as a firmly held right, the exercise of that right can be complicated, frustrating, and ambiguous for patients, their families, for physicians, and other health care professionals.

Patient participation in decision-making affects people of all ages. But, since older adults are now the age group likeliest to die of disease, likeliest to die in a hospital, and most frequently in need of complicated diagnostic and therapeutic procedures, they are often the central figures in discussions about health care decision-making. For some, the critical issue may be concern about being overtreated; for others, it may be an issue of being medically undertreated. In many instances, treatment of an older person involves others in the decision-making process, such as a spouse and other

family members who, in turn, have needs of their own. Added to the complexity is the issue of how medical professionals regard older people and whether they treat them differently from members of other age groups.

The following discussion traces the development of patient rights and examines the different paths that may be taken in making medical care decisions. How the process works for persons capable of making decisions, and for those who can no longer speak for themselves, is also explored. Following these sections is an examination of the ethical and practical challenges that remain.

● INFORMED CONSENT

Until mid-century, physicians usually made most medical care decisions. Few outsiders displayed any interest in the physician-patient relationship, and physicians maintained what Katz (1984) has described as a "stark silence"; consent meant only the right to refuse treatment. The doctors decided when a newborn's defects or an elderly person's prognosis were so grim that he or she would be better off untreated.

In the historical evolution of the new doctor-patient relationship, the doctrine of *informed consent*—the patient's right to make decisions based on information about risks and plausible alternative procedures—had its origins in law, not in ethics. Although tacit consent (without the requirement that one be informed) to surgical

527

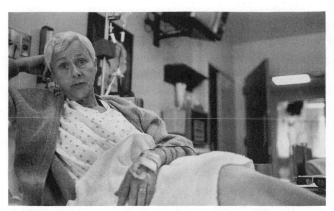

Great emphasis is now placed on active patient participation in making medical care decisions. (Copyright © Marianne Gontarz)

interventions is an ancient legal requirement, for generations this right to consent was exercised on a very limited basis.

The modern history of informed consent began in a California courtroom on October 22, 1957, the first step in the ongoing transformation of doctor-patient relationships. In *Salgo v. Leland Stanford Jr. University*, Justice Bray of the California Court of Appeals introduced the phrase *informed consent* in reversing a lower court ruling. Mr. Salgo, paralyzed after a diagnostic procedure, sued the hospital for not warning him of the risks attendant upon the procedure (for details, see Katz, 1984). The judge's ruling, though vague, held that the surgeons had not provided Mr. Salgo with sufficient information for an informed decision about the procedure. With Judge Bray's opening wedge, the discussion of what informed consent ought to mean in practice continues today.

In the historical evolution of the new doctor-patient relationship, the doctrine of *informed consent*—the patient's right to make decisions based on information about risks and plausible alternative procedures—had its origins in law, not in ethics.

If 1957 initiated the legal evolution of informed consent procedures, historian David Rothman (1991) pinpointed 1966 as the year that "outsider" ethics (i.e., ethics that did not originate in the codes of the professions) entered the medical arena. This new ethics is pivotal for the developing discussion about patient participation in decision-making.

In 1966, Harry Beecher, a noted Harvard anesthesiologist, published a powerful indictment of research ethics in the *New England Journal of Medicine* documenting what he considered abuse of human subjects in research. Most importantly, Beecher argued that the researchers had not actually obtained consent from their subjects. Secondly, Beecher reasoned that few of these patients, which included the elderly, would willingly put themselves in jeopardy. The public outrage that flowed from Beecher's revelations led finally to rewriting the rules for human experimentation. The new rules rested on the doctrine of informed consent (Rothman, 1991).

The Right to Refuse Treatment: Key Cases

In 1969, a baby with Down's Syndrome and a correctable intestinal blockage was moved to a corner of Johns Hopkins Hospital's neonatal nursery, where he died of starvation fifteen days later. His parents had refused permission for surgery, knowing their refusal meant their son's certain death. The physicians, deeply disturbed about the incident, which was not uncommon at the time, brought the case to professional and public attention, where it stimulated intense indignation and discussion. This case accelerated the involvement of non-physicians in determining procedural and substantive guidelines for medical care decision-making.

Seven years later, the parents of Karen Ann Quinlan, a young woman in a persistent vegetative state, asked her doctors to turn off the ventilator that helped her to breathe. In a landmark decision, the New Jersey Supreme Court supported the Quinlans' request. It took another sixteen years, again in a case involving a young woman, for the courts—this time the United States Supreme Court—to include the artificial provision of food and water as a treatment a surrogate (a substitute decision-maker who makes decisions for an incompetent person) can have withdrawn. Bioethicists, or individuals specializing in ethical problems that arise in health care, played key roles in both cases, which broadened surrogates' range of decision-making authority in making decisions for the incapacitated person.

That these cases came to public attention had much to do with their particular historical context. They reflected changes that were already occurring in the medical care setting. Influenced by accelerating technological innovations and the increasingly depersonalized tone of hospitals that provided care for the very sick, the relationship between physician and patient had lost much of its personal quality. As personal and professional distance increased, trust eroded. And as social challenges to expertise and authority, a legacy of the 1960s, entered the medical encounter, a new assertion of and protection for patient's rights emerged (Rothman, 1991). In particular, this took the form of the imposition of formal safeguards to govern the physician-patient relationship.

Informed Consent: Still Evolving

Informed consent procedures have become the ethical linchpin in this newly evolving medical setting. They have immediate significance as the primary vehicle available to assure patient participation in decision-making, but they also have longer range importance. As limited health care dollars constrain application of advanced medical technologies and therapeutic approaches, new kinds of consent procedures will need to emerge. If society, through its expression of social values, must limit treatment, how can this limitation be achieved without disregarding the patient's involvement in medical care decision-making (Scofield, 1991)?

Informed Consent for Competent Persons

As described above, both legal requirements and ethical standards now require that health care providers ask patients to give informed consent for diagnostic and therapeutic procedures. While that simple assertion may anchor a legal case, it provides insufficient guidance to either the physician who wants to take informed consent seriously or to the patient who wishes to share decision-making responsibilities with the physician. It fails to resolve how much information the physician must offer the patient to meet the informed criteria, how it is best offered, and what its goals are. In addition to these uncertainties, typical consent procedures often are particularly problematic (see discussion of negotiated consent under **Informed Consent and Long-**

Term Care) when, for example, the patient is a chronically impaired nursing home resident.

In practice, weak rather than strong notions of informed consent are often the rule. Two physician/ethicists, Jay Katz (1984) and Howard Brody (1992), insist that informed consent procedures, in most cases, have barely altered the formerly "silent world of doctor and patient" (Katz, 1984). Brody (1992) points out that physicians still see informed consent primarily in legal terms, not intrinsic to doing good medicine and, as such, not inherently valuable for the patient. Thus, the changes that lie ahead are less legal and ethical and more attitudinal. The patient's active participation as a questioning partner in the medical care setting is critical in facilitating such a shift.

Doctrine of Informed Consent Requirements

Patients or potential patients who understand the purposes, meanings, and complexities of informed consent will more easily assume an active role in making their medical care decisions. Minimally, the doctrine of informed consent requires the disclosure of the ailment, the nature of the proposed treatment, including risks, the probability of success, and the possible alternative treatments (Applebaum, Lidz, and Meisel, 1987). The requirements include disclosure, comprehension, and voluntary consent (Capron, 1987). By encouraging patients to exercise informed choice about the risks they are willing to assume, consent procedures encourage individual autonomy and partially redress the inevitably unequal relationship between the ill person and the medical experts.

In many states the courts have upheld a minimalist standard in which the physician determines what information to disclose. Ethically, however, the preferred standard is patient-oriented, as articulated in the 1972 landmark court case, *Canterbury v. Spence*. This case obligates

---

Minimally, the doctrine of informed consent requires the disclosure of the ailment, the nature of the proposed treatment, including risks, the probability of success, and the possible alternative treatments.

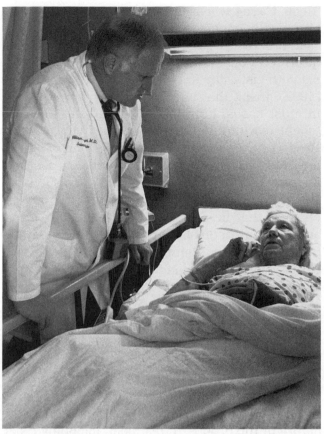

As the physician individualizes diagnostic and therapeutic procedures, so must he or she individualize the informing process. (Courtesy of Bowman Gray/Baptist Hospital Medical Center)

the physician to tell the patient, at a minimum, what any rational person would want to know about the proposed treatment prior to rendering a decision.

But even the rational patient standard, though richer than the physician-centered standard, is relatively impoverished. Because it is inadequately attentive to individual differences, it also can be blind to individual information needs. To a concert pianist the risk that a proposed treatment might result in slight hand tremors matters more than it might to an attorney handling wills and trusts. As the physician individualizes diagnostic and therapeutic procedures, so must he or she individualize the informing process (Capron, 1987).

Advances in Informed Consent Procedures

To address what they perceive as serious shortcomings in the actual operation of informed consent, Katz (1984), Brody (1992), and others advocate a conversational process, which uses primary care as its laboratory. In this process, the patient and the physician openly and freely discuss not only the patient's specific information needs for a single decision but the physician also solicits patient participation in setting broader treatment goals.

Developing this conversational approach, Brody (1989, 1992) introduces the transparency standard. He advises the physician to attend closely to what the patient wants to know; he recommends that the physician involve the patient in his or her thinking process—in a sense, to think aloud about treatment options—and he encourages the physician to give the patient ample opportunities to ask questions. This concept does not compel the physician to reveal everything to the patient, nor does it conceal a veiled reassertion of physician paternalism. Rather it urges the physician to communicate and listen sensitively—to converse authentically with the patient and to indicate that questions and active participation in decision-making are welcome. For this process of shared decision-making to work, the patient cannot abrogate his or her responsibilities.

Continuing Debates About Informed Consent

Many physicians still remain uncomfortable with the doctrine of informed consent, perceiving it either as an intrusion on their practice or a potential hindrance to providing what they define as optimal care. Thus, one problem physicians face is deciding just how much risk to disclose. A

Decision-making can be examined in the context of an entire life narrative that seeks to integrate the final chapter into the larger perspective. (Courtesy of The National Council on the Aging, Inc./Lauren Fyfe, photographer)

case will illustrate this point (adapted from Brody and Engelhardt, 1987):

> A 62-year-old woman is found to have carcinoma of the cervix. The cancer is in an early stage, confined to the cervix, with minor invasion of the tissue of the cervix. The tumor is still easily treatable with a simple hysterectomy and has the likelihood of a 90 percent cure. But Mrs. G is very apprehensive, and her physician, who has treated her for thirty years, knows that when she is nervous she procrastinates making a decision and worries about all the possible things that can go wrong. Therefore, he is concerned that if he describes all the risks of the surgery, then Mrs. G will postpone the surgery. Hence, he wonders if he should instead inform Mrs. G's husband of the usual risks and indicate to Mrs. G more generally that things will go well and that people are likely to return home after a few days.

Rarely (see below) would it be appropriate for the physician to bypass Mrs. G to obtain consent from her husband. In this case, however, the long and established relationship between the patient and the physician presumably implies sufficient trust for the physician to speak in general terms about rare risks while being prepared to answer Mrs. G's questions more explicitly if she requests further information.

> ### For this process of shared decision-making to work, the patient cannot abrogate his or her responsibilities.

In addition to uncertainty about disclosing remote risks, physicians fear that candor will induce patients to make choices less than medically optimal. Yet, honest regard for patients requires acknowledging that the medically optimal solution may be less than optimal for a specific patient living a specific life. Ethically responsible informed consent procedures recognize that different individuals may make different choices, based on their fundamental values and the role of this particular illness in their own biography. One case example, for which there is no one correct answer, will demonstrate the fundamental importance of values.

> Mrs. R is a 78-year-old resident of the Parklane Nursing Home. She has diabetes, hypertension, and severe rheumatoid arthritis. However, she is a cheerful person, visited often by her children and grandchildren. She recently developed a heart arrhythmia that can result in sudden death. Therefore her doctor recommends a pacemaker.

The value conflicts for a person in Mrs. R's condition revolve around her willingness to assume the immediate risks attendant upon inserting a pacemaker and the longer term complications that may develop. For her to decide, she would need to know, in sufficient detail, just what these risks are. Although her doctor's recommendation suggests her or his assessment of the pacemaker's value, Mrs. R may prefer the risk of sudden death to the possibility of further disability because of complications. Hence, her values (along with clear information) will help her decide whether or not to consent.

Comparable concerns arise when a 66-year-old woman, advised to have a radical mastectomy as the best treatment option for an invasive breast cancer, hesitates and finally refuses. The likelihood of good medical outcomes differs from her preferential, personal, and religious values. She may feel quite strongly that her physical wholeness is more important than what might appear to be the best medical outcome. Her stated preference does not mean the physician must refrain from thoughtfully probing the value basis of this choice. Respecting a person's autonomy does not mean abandoning him or her to that autonomy.

Informed consent procedures invite still other questions. For example, these procedures must account for the significant number of adults, including but not limited to the elderly, who would prefer to delegate responsibility for making some or all of their difficult decisions (Kapp, 1989). Although some commentators (e.g., Katz, 1984) believe that it is ethically unacceptable to permit a competent person to abdicate or waive the responsibility to make choices, others take a more subtle position. Kapp (1989) argues that "respect for persons necessarily entails respect for such conscious decisions not to decide personally." Such respect, however, requires that physicians make conscientious efforts to ascertain that this delegation is truly voluntary and based on adequate information about the treatment and its ramifications. Delegation cannot be treated casually.

● INFORMED CONSENT AND LONG-TERM CARE

Most discussions about informed consent center on acute care medicine. Yet some of the most problematic issues emerge in caring for a person who is chronically impaired. Two factors reveal the origins of these concerns. First, decisions about how to care for the impaired person inevitably involve others, often intimately. Second, some elders may wish to relinquish decision-making authority even though federal regulations and ethical considerations protect their right to participate in care planning. The first concern requires an assessment of how to think about consent procedures when others will be profoundly affected by the decisions rendered. The second requires an acknowledgement that mandating autonomy defeats its meaning and the underlying respect for people it is meant to convey.

Most discussions about informed consent center on acute care medicine. Yet some of the most problematic issues emerge in caring for a person who is chronically impaired.

To address the first concern, Moody (1988) considers a communal rather than an individual decision-making process. Instead of informed consent, he proposes a concept he labels negotiated consent "which is characterized by a clash and balancing of competing interests." Negotiation involves the patient, family, and the health care team. Unlike more traditional forms of ethical reasoning, negotiation depends on interpreting the situation from the perspective of each person involved. It relies less on formal codes of ethics than on discussion among all the people who will be influenced by the decision. It accepts suboptimal outcomes, because there may be no way of achieving the ideal outcome in the particular situation. Moody presents two cases as illustrations.

Mr. Allen, 81, was admitted two years ago to Our Lady of the Flowers Nursing Home after

suffering a stroke that left him partially paralyzed. As a result of successful rehabilitation therapy, he is now able to walk again and is eager to go home. But during the past two years his 55-year-old wife has rebuilt her own life, and now she is unwilling to take him back. She has visited her husband infrequently. But Mr. Allen demands to be released from the facility and asks staff members when he can "go home." Staff members evade his questions.

Miss Waters, 87 years old, has a single room and has been sitting alone there most of the day for a few weeks now. Most times she's called for meals she says she isn't hungry and refuses to go down to the dining hall. Nursing staff have charted an alarming weight loss and are unsure whether to look into the possibilities of compulsory feeding for her.

In the first case, the patient may not be able to exercise his autonomous choice because the day-to-day physical, financial, or emotional burden on his spouse may exceed her limits. In the actual setting, negotiations might explore the history of their relationship, possible means of assisting Mrs. Allen, or any other factors that might help to bridge the current chasm dividing Mr. and Mrs. Allen's wishes.

In the therapeutically uncertain long-term care environment, the patient, family members, physician, and other providers are likely to have conflicting interpretations and competing values about treatment (Tomlinson, 1986). For example, an 80-year-old competent nursing home patient may refuse treatment for metastatic breast cancer, affirming her readiness to die. Her physician and her daughter believe that she is making a terrible mistake. They try to persuade her but she is adamant. Her doctor requests a psychiatric consultation to determine if she has the capacity to make decisions.

Negotiation would go about resolving this disagreement differently, seeking to explore, through communication and clarification, why she has made this decision, if she grasps the consequences, and if she might have any wish to reconsider in the light of her daughter's deep concern. In such difficult and often ambiguous situations, negotiation will not always provide a clear, substantive direction, but it will encourage participants to keep talking and listening.

For informed consent to work in its fullest sense, the patient must share responsibility with the physician. (Courtesy of Bowman Gray/Baptist Hospital Medical Center)

In cases where the patient's choices deeply implicate others—practically as well as emotionally—negotiation will explicitly acknowledge the significant claims of others in the process of deciding, will highlight the interdependency and emotionally rich nature of relationships, and will critically question the single-minded focus of bioethics on narrowly conceived notions of autonomy (Collopy, 1988; Agrich, 1990).

Nursing home patients who are mentally alert but disabled also often have widely different wishes in regard to maintaining individual choice. Some impaired nursing home residents welcome participation in care planning; others resist, preferring to leave decisions to the physician, other caretakers, and family members (Wetle and others, 1988). As they become increasingly reliant upon their families, they may often want to delegate authority. In such cases, as emphasized above, the older persons should not be forced into a decision-making role they prefer to relinquish, and professionals and family members should not accept such refusals without probing.

Nursing homes, in particular, encourage posing the question: What shall be done, all things considered? The time frame of care in the nursing home offers unique opportunities to assess carefully patients' preferences about treatment long before a crisis occurs (Besdine, 1983). Rarely are the choices emergencies; residents often live in the facility long enough to develop new understandings with family members, friends, and health care providers. Thus, decision-making can be examined in the context of an entire life narrative that seeks to integrate the final chapter into the larger perspective. This luxurious approach to decision-making is rarely possible in the acute care setting; given the proper conditions, it can flourish in the nursing home.

These unique characteristics of decision-making in the nursing home encourage the testing of evolving feminist ideas about ethics. These concepts rest less on deducing decisions from abstract ethical theories than on observing how decisions are actually made, so that giving care and maintaining relationships (see Gilligan, 1982; Kittay and Meyers, 1987; Holmes and Purdy, 1992) can be encouraged. Such an ethic emphasizes a person's profound ties to others rather than his or her independence and rights-bearing characteristics. Arguably, the nursing home setting can mute the distinction between autonomy and paternalism by illustrating and emphasizing the "contextual basis of human relationships" (Moody, 1988).

The time frame of care in the nursing home offers unique opportunities to assess carefully patient's preferences about treatment long before a crisis occurs.

Informed Consent: A Summary

For informed consent to work in its fullest sense, the patient must share responsibility with the physician. One's willingness to engage in conversation, to request time to think, and to wean oneself from any remnants of the passive or good patient role are all essential. Although it may be difficult to overcome the inequality in the relationship between an ill person and a socially accepted expert, it is critical to assure the patient that he or she has the right to be as involved in decision-making as desired.

● TRUTH-TELLING

In much thinking about ethics, truth-telling grounds relations among people. It is also an important prerequisite for informed consent, which generally requires understanding of both diagnosis and prognosis.

Arguments For and Against Truth-telling

Yet even today, when the importance of truth-telling appears to be a settled issue, physicians and family members often argue against informing patients, particularly if the diagnosis is grim. They frequently rest their arguments on consequential grounds—the fear that something terrible will happen if the patient knows the worst. The most extreme version of this fear is the prediction, not supported by research, that the patient will become so depressed as to become suicidal.

In contrast, Veatch (1989) offers a strong argument that consequences will be worse when physicians deny information: "To many patients, the anxiety from not knowing their diagnoses accurately must be at least as great as that from knowing the terrible truth—at least if that information is revealed in a humane manner." Tolstoy expresses this dilemma forcefully in *The Death of Ivan Ilych:* "What tormented Ivan Ilych most was

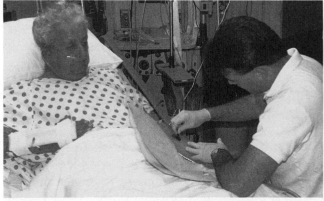

To many patients, the anxiety from not knowing their diagnoses accurately must be at least as great as that from knowing the terrible truth—at least if that information is revealed in a humane manner. (Courtesy of Bowman Gray/Baptist Hospital Medical Center)

the deception, the lie, which for some reason they all accepted, that he was not dying but simply ill.... This deception tortured him—their not wishing to admit what they all knew and what he knew, but wanting to lie to him concerning his terrible condition, and wishing and forcing him to participate in that lie.... Those lies ... were a terrible agony to Ivan Ilych."

But consequences are not the only way to think about truth-telling; a strong case for truth-telling rests on respect for individual autonomy and the virtue of fidelity. Among the arguments for disclosure is a simple one: patients have the right to know what is wrong with them. When a physician does not tell a patient the truth but rather tells his or her family, the physician is treating the patient as a child. This treatment simultaneously reduces one's freedom to choose desired treatment and one's status as a moral person (Green, 1981). For older people, especially older women, where the social desire to protect runs quite strongly, withholding truth reinforces other socially infantilizing tendencies.

> Yet even today, when the importance of truth-telling appears to be a settled issue, physicians and family members often argue against informing patients, particularly if the diagnosis is grim.

Truth-telling in the medical setting is not only an issue for individual physician-patient relationships but also has social ramifications. If people suspect that they are not going to be told the truth about their illness, the doctor-patient relationship becomes undermined, so that even patients with an optimistic prognosis distrust the information received. As a general principle, the burden of proof for lying must rest with those who support dishonesty (Bok, 1978). Honesty should be the prevailing position if trust in the medical community is to be maintained.

Practical Components of Truth-telling

A commitment to telling the truth still leaves open a series of questions about the extent, timing, and explicitness of the physician's communication with the patient. Many medical professionals rely on the patient's questions and demeanor to guide them in how, when, and to what degree they should disclose information. While, for reasons described above, complete honesty may be the best policy, at times a patient's resistance or denial would only be intensified by full disclosure of information. The physician has to trust that he or she can gradually convey all the information the patient needs to make well-informed decisions.

If people suspect that they are not going to be told the truth about their illness, the doctor-patient relationship becomes undermined, so that even patients with an optimistic prognosis distrust the information received.

By the physician not forcing information but responding sensitively to the patient's receptivity, a situation of trust will be fostered that can only add positively to the healing—or the dying—process.

External Factors and Truth-telling

A second caveat to the standard truth-telling requirement is the factor of cultural differences. Bioethics is only beginning to address the cultural variations in decision-making patterns, particularly what people wish to know.

A traditional view is that ethical principles are universal and transcend cultural differences. But respecting an elder's autonomy might call for different behavior when the elder identifies closely with a particular cultural heritage. For example, a Chinese American might interpret the directness of an American physician as a sign of disrespect—particularly if the diagnosis is terminal. The preliminary findings from a study conducted in 1990 by Stanford University and the Hastings Center suggested that first generation Chinese Americans had a strong bias against discussing death and viewed such discussions as fundamentally disrespectful.

This attitude is reflected in another example, the recent death of the Japanese emperor. Even as he lay dying of cancer, news reports surfaced that the emperor had not been informed of either the diagnosis or the immediacy of his impending death. While the emperor may have intuited his conditions, his culture required an indirect, unspoken attitude. The example should alert us to cultural norms that run contrary to more standard American practices.

Decision-Making and the Competent Patient

The variations in decision-making practices noted above are only one important reason why conversations, the heart of good decision-making, should become a routine part of health care. Respecting people is a fundamental ethical imperative; so, too, is seeking their well-being. But one must learn how to respect people, especially individuals whose cultural norms may differ from the predominant cultural ethos, and to understand what they perceive to be their well-being.

Most cases in medical ethics that make the textbooks and the six o'clock news take place in acute care hospitals and nursing homes and focus on decisions about terminal care. But in fact, most decisions are made in the context of day-to-day medical care in the offices of a primary care physician. For this reason, one must emphasize the mutual responsibilities of physician and patient to engage in interpretive conversations about medical care topics that either are emerging or might emerge in the future.

The older person who has a primary care physician should initiate a preliminary conversation—when healthy—with their primary care physician about their own wishes for family participation in decision-making or the kind of information they might want in the case of serious illness. For example, patients may be willing for the physician to tell family members about specific details of their medical condition but unwilling for the physician to reveal their concerns about sexual functioning. Such informal conversations, though not binding, can establish the basis for a conversational or relationship ethic. Patient and physician are working together to secure the patient's health and well-being. Patient autonomy need not mean protecting oneself from a paternalistic physician. Alternatively, the physician and the patient can work together over time to identify factors threatening autonomy and work to eliminate them (Brody, 1987).

These conversations and continuity of care become much more difficult when a person does not have or is unable to have a primary care physician; that lack is often a matter of cost which, in turn, is often deeply influenced by public policy and not individual choice.

The older person who has a primary care physician should initiate a preliminary conversation—when healthy—with their primary care physician about their own wishes for family participation in decision-making or the kind of information they might want in the case of serious illness.

● ADVANCE DIRECTIVES

A conversational beginning is particularly important should an individual reach the point when he or she cannot make decisions alone.

Mr. W, an 84-year-old widower living alone, was admitted to the hospital after his neighbors found him unconscious on the floor. The emergency team administered IV fluids and oxygen, then contacted the patient's only living family member, his daughter. Upon her arrival at the hospital, she was greeted by an unfamiliar physician in the hallway outside of her father's room. After a brief condition report, the physician asked if she wanted her father to have CPR and advanced life support if his condition deteriorated. Mr. W's daughter was alarmed and puzzled. She and her father had never discussed his wishes. How could she decide?

Although such a scenario, like many cases used for instructional purposes, omits details that can significantly influence decision-making, it focuses attention on issues concerning advance directives. The best way to assure that patients receive desired treatment or non-treatment is to plan ahead—to let others know one's preferences. Telling someone what we would like in case we cannot explain our own desires, and choosing someone to speak for us, are the two major principles underlying advance directives.

Advance directives can be any written or spoken declaration by patients of their treatment wishes. They are patients' freely made declara-

tions, when they are competent, about several matters: who they want to make decisions for them when they can no longer decide, and guidelines for how they want decisions to be made. As to the latter, patients may say they are unwilling to be fed artificially if there is no chance of regaining consciousness. Or, a nursing home patient might insist that she wants to be transferred to the hospital if she develops pneumonia, even if she has a number of other life-threatening medical conditions.

Advance directives can be any written or spoken declaration by patients of their treatment wishes.

The following are examples of formal, written advance directives. Each person should check with his or her physician, the local medical society, or the local bar association about the particular legal requirements in their state; these same sources should also have appropriate forms available.

The Living Will

The living will was the earliest form of advance directive developed. Although living wills allow individuals to describe, in advance, life-prolonging treatment they may wish to receive or reject, living wills are limited. Most importantly, they apply only when a decisionally incapacitated patient is terminally ill. Though living wills may appear to be clear statements, in practice they are often ambiguous. For example, should patients in the late stages of Alzheimer's disease, who still sit up, occasionally smile, but no longer swallow food, be considered terminal? Can their wish, outlined in their living will, that they do not want food and water to be provided artificially, be honored? Such treatment is particularly problematic since some states' living wills do not allow a person to use a living will to refuse, in advance, the artificial provision of food and water. This particular restriction may, however, be easing, following the Supreme Court's decision in the Cruzan case that ruled food and water to be comparable to other medical treatments such as antibiotics and respirators.

The living will has one other important restriction. It cannot legally authorize, in advance, the termination of life-prolonging treatment for non-terminal conditions—for example, pneumonia—even though the patient may have pre-existing metastatic cancer. The living will may be insufficient to impede the treatment for pneumonia. Hence, its limitations are important to note.

1. It goes into effect only when the particular illness or illnesses the person has are terminal; thus, the living will of a patient with last stage dementia may not allow a surrogate to refuse treatment for a new cancer.

2. It is unclear if a living will permits a surrogate to authorize withholding or withdrawing artificially provided food and water, even if the patient requested that such treatment not be given.

However, because states have different legislation that authorizes living wills, each person contemplating writing one should check the law in his or her own state.

The Durable Power of Attorney for Health Care

The essential characteristic that separates a durable power of attorney for health care (DPAHC) from a living will is the appointment of a proxy or surrogate decision-maker—a person authorized by the patient to make decisions if he or she can no longer do so. Although a DPAHC can be more or less specific in terms of instructions to the surrogate decision-maker, most people also prefer to add details to guide the choices of their agent or proxy. These instructions may accomplish some of the following:

1. Define the scope of the proxy's powers or limitations.

2. Provide guidelines for the proxy to follow.

3. Name successor proxies should something happen to the primary choice.

4. Include other directives aimed at ensuring the effectiveness of the document.

The instructions contained in a DPAHC are not limited to terminal conditions or to type of situation. They extend an individual's autonomy, the ability to be self-directing, into situations when one can no longer speak for oneself.

States vary in their legal requirements. For example, some states require two non-related wit-

nesses to the document, but even if the state does not have such a requirement, a witness can add force to the document and help assure its recognition in other states. In some states, for nursing home patients, one of the required witnesses must be an ombudsman.

The essential characteristic that separates a durable power of attorney for health care (DPAHC) from a living will is the appointment of a proxy or surrogate decision-maker—a person authorized by the patient to make decisions, if he or she can no longer do so.

The Importance of Advance Directives

There are ethical, legal, and personal reasons why planning for incapacity is so important. The ethical reason for planning ahead resides in the philosophical concept of autonomy, although autonomy is, in actual practice, far richer in meaning than self-direction. An advance directive extends autonomy beyond the point that one can exercise it for oneself. But it also can do much more. Recalling the idea of a conversational ethic noted earlier, an advance directive, if based on an extended conversation, helps loved ones to make decisions in what are often anguishing circumstances.

In terms of law, as noted in the introduction, all people have the right to assent to or refuse any treatment, not only life-extending treatment. The federal Patient Self Determination Act (PSDA) requires any hospitals, nursing homes, health maintenance organizations (HMOs), hospices, or home care agencies that accept Medicare and/or Medicaid reimbursement to: distribute written information about the new law to patients, develop policies about informing patients of their rights to assent to or refuse treatment and their right to execute an advance directive, and educate the staff and the general public about the law. Institutions must document in each individual's medical record whether he or she has an advance directive.

As the requirements of the PSDA become more institutionalized, nursing homes, in particular, should create opportunities to explore patient preferences with long-time residents who have lived in the institution prior to the implementation of the PSDA. Families can have a significant influence in assuring the documentation of patients' wishes, in particular about transfers to the hospital in the case of acute infections of unknown origin, pneumonia, breathing difficulties, or other emergency conditions.

But the existence of the PSDA also raises several problems. Although it facilitates patient awareness of the option to leave directions, it does not mandate that such a directive is required before treatment can be terminated. This protection could be very important. The problem of terminating treatment for the patient without an advance directive is particularly acute in nursing homes where regulations, monitoring, and enforcement by public agencies make administrators particularly leery of terminating treatment without express guidance. Although nursing homes cannot require a written advance directive to discontinue or forego treatment, in effect they may communicate a de facto requirement for such a directive prior to decision. However, neither a nursing home nor other institutions can make the provision of care contingent upon an executed advance directive (Johnson, 1991). As states develop their individual approaches to the PSDA, they should describe how state law approaches "continuing or withdrawing treatment from decisionally incapable patients who have *not* executed advance directives" (Rouse, 1991 [emphasis added]). A signed document must not be the only vehicle that people have to express their wishes. Verbal expressions are also significant and should be documented.

Advance directives offer individuals a unique sense of security that someone will act in their stead. In today's complex, bureaucratized, and often legalistic medical environment, many people fear overtreatment—being kept alive with tubes and machines—while others have the opposite fear, that their treatment will terminate too soon. Hence, thinking about, discussing, and documenting wishes enable people to be as secure as possible that their proxy will acknowledge their wishes and effectuate their treatment choices.

This positive result is less likely if the advance directive becomes simply a legally possible procedural device, a document signed in front of the admissions clerk upon admission to a hospital.

Responsibility to make it a significant document rests with all the parties—the signer, the surrogate, and the health care team. In all the legal discussions about compliance to the PSDA, this conversational component is often obscured. Its significance is that it reflects the central meaning of the advance directive—a conversation that encourages individuals to express their wishes, fears, and beliefs. Although planning for incapacity often involves legal instruments, at its heart it is something much more personal: the exploration of values as they relate to health care.

Probably as important as people's final treatment decision is understanding the reasons behind these choices. For example, an individual would want the proxy decision-maker to know that he or she would want no treatment in case of the permanent loss of his or her ability to relate to other people; however, one would also want the proxy to know of preference for treatment, like ventilator support for a trial period, if there was even a slight chance of recovery. The basic value—the ability to talk to, smile at, and, in general, relate to others—not the specific treatment, is the centerpiece of the advance directive.

In other cases, individuals might prefer to shorten their lives, even by a considerable amount of time, if they otherwise had to be bedridden. Although a person might tell their surrogate that they want no "life extending therapies," without grasping the values that frame that statement, a surrogate might not know if this requirement applied when the patient suffered a cardiac arrest as a result of a sudden allergic reaction to a drug used to treat an infection. Should the surrogate authorize CPR? Should the earlier declaration apply if there is every likelihood that CPR will restore spontaneous breathing?

A person might wish to protect their family from pain or financial hardship. What might appear to an outsider as family greed may instead be an authentic commitment to respecting the patient's wish not to waste resources on end-of-life treatment that might otherwise be directed at a grandson's education. Because neither a person nor a surrogate can fully anticipate what medical conditions and treatments might arise, the proxy, as noted above, will want to understand, in sufficient detail, what way of living is "worse than death." Thus, creating an advance directive is part of a process that includes preliminary communication about health care wishes, a revisiting of the questions, the execution of a DPAHC, and then revisiting the issues from time to time to be sure that the person retains the same basic values and beliefs. What seemed totally unacceptable may shift as a person accommodates to disability. Moreover, in a number of states, a DPAHC must be renewed, often after seven years.

Some people have used the values history (Gibson, 1990)—a detailed questionnaire that explores practical and value dimensions that support medical treatment choices—to open conversation with a patient or a family member about the values that support medical care choices. For decisionally incapacitated individuals who did not leave specific instructions, the surrogate may use a values history to reconstruct a profile or "voice" to guide decision-making. This instrument is also useful to guide decision-making for the person without a surrogate. Through interviews with friends and acquaintances based on the values history, details of the person's life choices that would otherwise be obscured can be revealed. In addition, knowing a person's values can be useful to the courts, in recommending a "substituted judgment" standard (i.e., deciding as the patient would have decided had wishes been expressed in advance). Hence, the values history can help with both competent and incapacitated patients.

Guidance for Using Advance Directives

The following guidelines summarize some factors to bear in mind when executing advance directives:

1. Obtain the commitment of the person who will serve as proxy.

2. Ask the physician for descriptions of the various treatment choices that most often occur in different circumstances.

3. Engage the proxy in conversation about values and any special ideas about treatment choices.

4. Stress the values—e.g., under what conditions would life be too much of a burden to continue?

5. Exercise caution in using terms such as ordinary and extraordinary care, since they are notoriously vague in application; instead describe feelings about different kinds of situations.

6. Execute the advance directive witnessed by two people not associated with one's care.

7. Let the proxy keep a copy of the directive and let others know where it is kept; give a copy to the doctor.

8. Let others know who the proxy is and what choices have been made.

9. Revisit the decisions from time to time, both in writing and in conversation.

Some people prefer to have someone other than a spouse or a child be the decision-maker. That option is perfectly acceptable. The important factor is the willingness of the selected person to serve as the proxy and his or her assurance about the key values that should govern decision-making.

● DECISIONAL INCAPACITY

Advance directives become applicable only when individuals are too sick or incapacitated to make decisions for themselves. Although incompetency is a legal status that must be decided by the courts, it is usually not required in cases of health care decision-making. But this fact in no way belittles the import of determining that a person cannot decide for him or herself, since it shifts ethical responsibilities away from the patient to someone else. In terms of power, the ability to decide that someone is decisionally incapacitated is significant; the obligation, then, is to use that power with due discretion and seriousness. In addition to setting the conditions to let another decide for an ill person, competency determinations play a major role in restricting the freedom of mentally ill individuals and hence have broad social consequences.

Caplan (1985) noted that if informed consent is the ethical linchpin of the professional-patient relationship, then knowing when a patient is competent is an essential element of patient care. The importance of capacity decisions escalates with the weight of the decision to be made. The President's Commission for the Study of Ethical Problems in Medicine and Biomedical and Behavioral Research (1982) accepted a person as technically competent if he or she possessed a set of values and goals, had the ability to communicate and understand information, and possessed the ability to reason and deliberate about choices.

Practitioners in the clinical setting often rely on a cognitive processes test, the Mini Mental State Exam (MMSE), for screening purposes. Yet, like many tests, it has its problems. Tancredi (1987) points out that it is frequently difficult to differentiate among Alzheimer's disease, profound depression, and feelings of aloneness and deprivation in the elderly. Any standardized test, particularly when its results can so overwhelmingly influence a person's life, requires confirmation from other methods of assessing competency.

While there is not full agreement on the meaning of decisional capacity and no single way to evaluate its status, the concept is used to "pinpoint those elements of physical, emotional, and cognitive ability requisite for participation in decisions concerning one's own medical care" (Caplan, 1985). A competent person can participate meaningfully in a particular health care decision (Brody, 1988). But what sounds straightforward often is not. Decisional capacity can be elusive, especially for older persons, since it may vary according to setting, time of day, or the influence of psychoactive drugs. Patients may be disoriented or behave differently on a test administered in a hospital or a nursing home than in their own home.

Making Competency Determinations

Every effort should be made to assure that competency determinations are part of a process in which several different health care providers and family members talk to the patient more than once. When a patient's choice differs from that of physician or a family member, it often becomes the proximate cause for challenging the patient's competency. It also sometimes becomes an informal decision that someone else should take over decision-making. Frequently, such disagreements result in a request for psychiatric consultation. These consultations must be used cautiously, for not only does the psychiatrist's ability to label a person incapacitated yield considerable power, but the psychiatrist's insights, though often important, rarely rest on substantial relationship with the patient. In many cases, nurses or other "hands-on" providers have a clearer sense of the patient's level of decisional capacity than other

more distant providers. In these difficult circumstances everyone is in a difficult dilemma. The fear of risk and the wish to protect a vulnerable patient can influence judgments.

Decisional Capacity: Conclusion

Because a decision that a person can no longer decide for him or herself may be critical, it requires caution, thoroughness, and sensitivity to fluctuations in mood and condition. As noted, one may be unable to decide to sell one's house, but one may know, with absolute certainty, that one does not want additional surgery for a cancer that is likely to be terminal. Thus, if health care providers and family members are to take patient choice seriously, except in certain instances, each decision that must be made should be viewed separately; that is, unless it is absolutely clear that the person can decide nothing, he or she should be encouraged to voice their wishes in each treatment decision that comes up.

Because a decision that a person can no longer decide for him or herself may be critical, it requires caution, thoroughness, and sensitivity to fluctuations in mood and condition.

Limitations to Formal Advance Directives

Emergency medical care. Many older people worry that their cherished plans to die at home will be defeated by a summons to emergency medical services. In the last moment, breathing or other difficulties frighten the caregiver and lead to a call (911) to emergency medical services. All advance preparations to forego treatment are obviated by the actions of the medics. There are several possible responses. The patient can be temporarily intubated, for example, and then the treatment withdrawn in time. Or, communities can work together to develop procedures that will honor pre-hospital "Do Not Resuscitate" (DNR) or other orders (Miles and Crimmins, 1985). Another approach is for family members and health care providers to work closely to make dying at home less frightening. Hospice is an important resource to make home deaths more comfortable for care-givers.

Many older people worry that their cherished plans to die at home will be defeated by a summons to emergency medical services.

Beyond advance directives. As advance directives become more common, another concern surfaces. Hospitals, nursing homes, and other medical care facilities may want to use them as the single source of authority about treatment choices. But they should not be the only means for determining treatment choices. Informally, physicians and health care providers have looked to family members to help make difficult decisions. These informal avenues are important to preserve, despite the availability of written instruments. For example, the family may be aware of the patient's treatment preferences. The advance directive statute does not reduce the legal force of other patient rights embedded in common or constitutional law (Wolfe, 1991).

Protection of informal decision-making may be essential for families whose cultural values differ from the prevailing American belief in individualism and the supporting legal protection. Advance directives may be particularly comfortable for the white, middle-class person who is at ease in this legalistic society but a repudiated intervention for people who more readily base relationships on implicit trust rather than on contract.

● THE FAMILY, THE ELDER, AND MEDICAL DECISION-MAKING

Family participation in decision-making predates the development of advance directives, and, as the last section indicated, families often play a particularly important role in the lives of incapacitated elders. There is both medical and ethical warrant for a strong family role in decision-making. Although procedurally the law has generally supported the common practice of turning to families to make decisions for those unable to decide, this recognition that family surrogacy has both moral and legal support is only the first step. Families and health professionals still need help in determining what considerations are morally appropriate as they struggle with decision-making. Bioethicists and the courts recognize three standards to guide decision-making for incapacitated persons:

1. Follow the patient's explicit directions as contained in a living will or some other written or oral advance directive.

2. Apply the patient's preferences and values in trying to choose what the patient would have wanted; that is, make a substituted judgment.

3. Act in the patient's "best interests" by choosing as a reasonable person in the patient's circumstances would have chosen.

If these procedural directions are emerging with relative clarity—that families are appropriate surrogate decision-makers with or without clear advance directives—some bioethicists raise more substantial concerns. They ask what considerations should count as families engage in the decision-making process, especially when no advance directive exists or it is unclear what the patient's real interests might be.

In considering this issue, some bioethicists suggest that involved and well-intentioned families should have broad discretionary authority to make decisions in whatever way they see fit. This notion rests on a concept of familial autonomy and the realm of privacy in which people who have shared a life have the moral authority to decide for one another. In many cases, as suggested in the section on negotiated consent and the competent patient, it may not only be the patient's interests that count in making decisions. What other considerations beyond the patient's well-being count?

This issue becomes particularly difficult, for example, when the patient has advanced Alzheimer's disease and the family has been providing care or attention for a number of years. Traditional ethics regards the doctor's relationship to each patient as paramount, and so, in making treatment decisions, the patient's well-being is the sole consideration. But with a disease like Alzheimer's when the burdens to family and society are so great—for such a long period of time—is this totally patient-centered ethic appropriate?

Most immediately, thinking about the family requires attention to the caregiver as well as the

Families should have broad discretion to make decisions unless it becomes clear that their intentions are specifically harmful to the patient. (Courtesy of Sanders-Brown Center on Aging, University of Kentucky/Tim Collins, photographer)

care receiver. Caregivers must temper mercy with justice, devotion, and beliefs about reciprocating care. Consideration must be given to how the constraints of our health care system compound this balancing act. What may be morally permissible—to consider fairness within the family, responsibility toward the self, and obligations toward others—may be practically impossible if caregivers have no available assistance. It is really hard to know what constitutes patient well-being and equally hard to know the power of other considerations.

In a seminal article, Nancy Rhoden (1988) suggested that when a proposed course of action falls into the gray area of uncertainty (i.e., it is hard to know what the patient might have wanted and equally difficult to know what might serve their best interests), then involved and well-intentioned family members should "have the discretion to act as they see fit."

Philosopher John Arras (1988) builds upon this position by encouraging families to summon values, religious affiliations, quality of life, and all those things which most competent people would consider. The decision may not be the only one possible, but it will be reasoned and considered.

At the other end of the continuum, still assuming that families are loving and involved, is the very narrow range of authority that the recent Supreme Court ruling in the Cruzan case would vest in families. The Court's ruling indicated a preference for a universal, state-imposed ranking of values (e.g., sanctity of life) rather than an individually determined ranking (e.g., respect for life, compassion for families, values of the patient) as selected by family surrogates. This decision, if adopted in other jurisdictions or health care facilities, would threaten family surrogacy in the absence of narrowly stated patient wishes.

Standing between these positions is the vast middle ground. In part, health professionals might argue for their traditional authority in decision-making, believing it is their duty to act in the patient's best interests while granting minimal authority to the family. Yet physician-ethicist Edmund Pellegrino and philosopher David Thomasma (1981) argue that a physician has a special obligation to act as a steward of the patient's right to have his or her wishes fulfilled. This beneficence-in-trust is neither an imposition of the physician's values or wishes, nor a slavish and uncritical submission to the surrogate's decisions, but dialogue with proxies and surrogates to interpret the patient's intent.

Given this continuum, how are families to decide? Can we reach any broad social consensus about the range of discretion that well-intentioned families should have in making decisions? Do families have to prove what standard they used in deciding? Do they have to construct a "case?" Or can they just say, this is what we think is right, given our family values and history? The nature of the relationship family members had with the patient—not abstract beneficence—is the touchstone of this decision. Families then can consider and weigh whatever seems appropriate to them. On the basis of the special value and moral significance of intimate others, philosopher Nancy Jecker (1990) argues for broad authority to transcend traditional autonomy models.

Older persons' dignity and self-respect may be intrinsically bound up with caring about their family as well as their individual well-being, and it may depend on recognition of responsibilities as well as rights. Recently and informally described as "distributive justice within families" (Brock, 1990), ethical obligations to loved ones who are dependent and in need of care should not override all other family concerns and needs. Families, according to this view, are an important social unit and deserve important responsibilities and discretionary authority. Ceding decision-making to families also can mean the inclusion of the interests and preferences of all.

Protecting the vulnerable is a very important social mission. Nonetheless, except in cases where families appear ill-intended or engage in harmful behavior toward the patient, "gray zone" decisions probably reside in the realm of privacy and are best left to the family. With adequate procedural safeguards for patients who do not have loving, non-conflictive families, families should have reasonably broad authority to act. The ideal of family autonomy is not meant to deflect attention from less than loving families. Based on the experience of the courts, individuals can enhance their security that decisions will reflect their wishes by informing more than one person about the contents of their DPAHC. We cannot trivialize the dangers that could occur if the chosen surrogate does not act in accordance with the patient's wishes or interests, especially if the patient chooses simply to designate a surrogate without providing any directions.

> Based on the experience of the courts, individuals can enhance their security that decisions will reflect their wishes by informing more than one person about the contents of their DPAHC.

The Family and Ethical Decision-Making: Conclusion

Families—in their traditional and shifting definitions—are keys to decision-making even if the patient has not executed an advance directive. Ideally, the family will act in ways that respect the patient's wishes—verbally expressed, written, or simply known from long years of close contact. In many cases, however, it is simply unclear what the best action might be. Families should have broad discretion to make decisions unless it becomes clear that their intentions are specifically harmful to the patient.

Older People's Attitudes Toward Advance Directives

As research by Dallas High (1988) suggests, many older people prefer to leave decisions up to their children. While that choice should be respected, it does not mean that there should be no discussion of treatment wishes. One might think that an older person, who has neither children nor spouse, is more likely to want to execute an advance directive, but there is a surprising hesitancy. A reluctance to execute an advance directive is often stated as "I just haven't gotten around to it."

> As research by Dallas High suggests, many older people prefer to leave decisions up to their children.

For the family member or the physician who hesitates to raise the topic of advance directives, older people generally are quite comfortable talking about treatment options. They have watched friends or spouses suffer and die and often find the process of dying more frightening than dying itself.

The Family Who Wants "Everything"

The life and death of the late Helga Wanglie exemplifies the confusion about limits. In this case, the medical team wished to discontinue treatment, but Mrs. Wanglie's husband and family insisted on its continuation. The unique features of the Wanglie case may be summarized as follows: "Because of her age, previously prolonged hospital stay . . . , multiple medical complications, and ultimately unsuccessful weaning from the ventilator, the medical staff caring for Mrs. Wanglie viewed her prognosis as extremely poor. They did not believe that the respirator could benefit her. However, the immediate family—her husband, daughter, and son—insisted that all forms of treatment be continued" (Cranford, 1991).

The medical care team consulted the hospital ethics committee, continued to talk to the Wanglie family, and sought another physician to

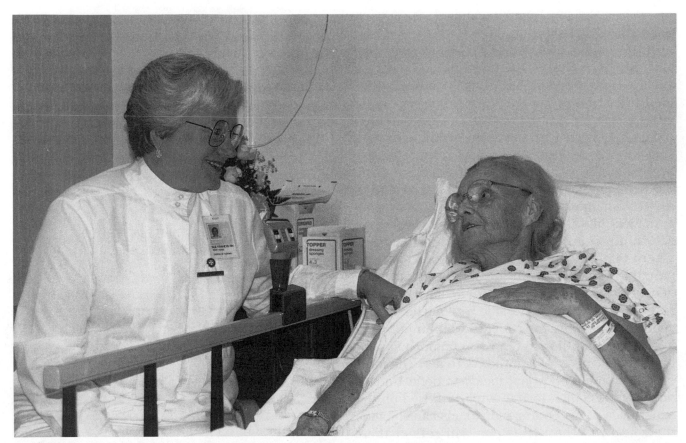

One might think that an older woman with neither children nor spouse is the person most likely to want to execute an advance directive. But even for this group there is a surprising hesitancy. (Courtesy of Bowman Gray/Baptist Hospital Medical Center)

assume responsibility for her care—all without result. When it became clear that the disagreement was unresolvable, the hospital filed papers with the court to have a conservator appointed to make decisions for Mrs. Wanglie. As summarized by the neurologist on the case, "The major point of the hospital's current position is that the family cannot *demand* that physicians continue to give treatment that is not in the patient's best *personal medical interest*" (Cranford, 1991). The disagreements among deeply thoughtful people abound. As a matter of fact, the court refused to appoint a conservator other than Mr. Wanglie. Mrs. Wanglie remained on the respirator until she died some months later. In considering patient participation in medical care decision-making, what is important about this case is the uncertainty that emerges when the patient or the family do not use their right to terminate treatment but rather decide to continue it. In this case, it is not entirely clear what Mrs. Wanglie might have wanted, since she was never asked; but the presumption must be that her husband most accu-

rately represented her wishes. And, it should be mentioned that cost is not a direct factor because Mrs. Wanglie's insurer did not question continued payment for her care. Indirectly, of course, it does affect others, since the result can easily be an increase in insurance rates. However, this case was chosen specifically as a test case because of the willingness of the insurer to continue payments.

● MEDICAL FUTILITY

The case of Mrs. Wanglie raises important questions about medical futility, a concept that appears clear until one tries to determine if, when, and how it should be applied. Because physicians are not obligated to provide "futile" treatments, this label shifts their ethical obligations to their patients. Common understandings about futility will have to be reached as the nation engages in a national dialogue about universal access to health care. What are reasonable boundaries to health care and who should decide

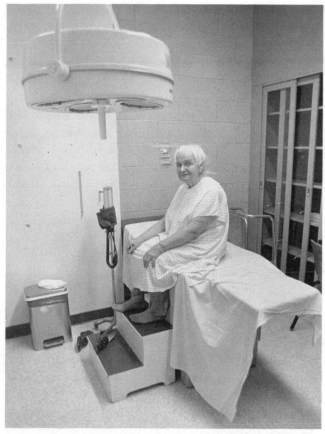

Older people generally are quite comfortable talking about treatment options. (Copyright © Marianne Gontarz)

tion of how much and which power society is willing to vest in the medical profession.

As medical interventions that cannot cure the patient but can prolong life, or, as some would say, prolong the dying process, become more common, the futility debate escalates. Most frequently, concerns about futility arise in the context of "Do Not Resuscitate" (DNR, or "no code") orders. Coding (determining how the medical staff will respond if a patient suffers a cardiac arrest) is a particularly compelling example. If a "no code" patient arrests, he or she will surely die.

To the public, resuscitation is a gripping effort to bring a presumed dead person back to life. It is not, however, a benign procedure. Designed initially for "otherwise healthy people who experience temporary but sudden cardiac arrhythmias [life threatening irregularities in the heart beat] who would die without resuscitation and who could be restored to a fully functioning state . . . in many instances" (Brody, 1992), it has become standardized procedure in many hospitals. Yet, the response rate is from 0 percent to 10 percent for chronically ill patients and those with major organ failures. Thus, the debate about cardio-pulmonary resuscitation has become an important focus for the futility debate.

these boundaries? In addition, the position adopted by the Wanglie family forces the question: Are there limits to what a person can request in their advance directive? Such directives were initially designed to permit the termination of treatment, but they can also be used to request treatment.

The positions of Mrs. Wanglie's physicians and her family also center on the fact/value debate. The disputants agreed that maintaining Mrs. Wanglie on the ventilator would prolong her life (fact); they disagreed about whether her life was worth prolonging (value) (Ackerman, 1991). Is the medical staff making a medical (factual) or moral (evaluative) judgment? Should decisions that have inescapable value components be in the hands of experts, or should they be decided in a more participatory way (Callahan, 1991)? Who should make these choices: the individual's family acting in a person's stead, the physicians, or society? As Brody (1992) and Callahan (1991) frame the debate about futility, it centers on the ques-

---

As medical interventions that cannot cure the patient but can prolong life, or, as some would say, prolong the dying process, become more common, the futility debate escalates.

The Wanglie case is a good example of the debate around issues of futility. It clearly questions the limits of the physician's obligation to respond to a patient's or family's request for treatment that, in the physician's judgment, offers no medical benefit to the patient. Physicians, not unlike patients or surrogates, are moral agents (Rie, 1991); as such, they must consider the limits of their obligations.

In part because this country is far from agreement about the limits of medical obligation, a recent article by Tomlinson and Brody (1990) suggests the path of social consensus. They recom-

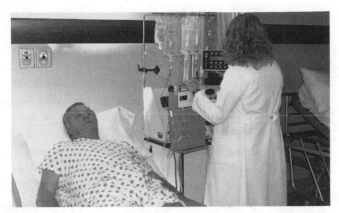

Common understandings about futility must be reached as the nation engages in a national dialogue about universal access to health care. (Courtesy of Bowman Gray/Baptist Hospital Medical Center)

mend the development of general social standards to make the necessary value judgments. In support, Callahan (1991) summarizes the debate, "There is no literature of any importance on the extent to which doctors should feel free to refuse to provide treatment they believe to be useless in the absence of common public standards for such refusal."

● EUTHANASIA AND PHYSICIAN-ASSISTED SUICIDE

Three different terms, bearing important distinctions, describe termination of life issues and the relationship of patients and physicians: passive euthanasia, voluntary or active euthanasia, and physician-assisted suicide.

Passive euthanasia is a term applied to choices patients and families make that a treatment, such as ventilator support, be withheld or withdrawn. Although emotionally these alternatives may feel different, legally and ethically there is no difference between withholding and withdrawing treatment. From a number of court cases, including the Supreme Court ruling in the case of Nancy Beth Cruzan, the artificial provision of food and water is included among treatments to which this rule applies.

> Passive euthanasia is a term applied to choices patients and families make that a treatment, such as ventilator support, be withheld or withdrawn.

Voluntary or active euthanasia implies more than the termination of treatment. Instead, patients have themselves decided they want to die and choose active means of doing so in which the physician may serve as the actual agent of death.

A third term, physician-assisted suicide, is different. The physician may make the means available (e.g., a prescription for a barbiturate which, when taken in sufficiently high dosage, will cause death), but does not directly participate in the patient's action of taking the drug.

While passive euthanasia has become generally accepted in the United States, there is no similar consensus for active euthanasia or physician-assisted suicide. Active euthanasia will continue to challenge society as is demonstrated with the publication and instant popularity of Derek Humphry's book on how to commit suicide, *Final Exit*, and the recent, though defeated, ballot proposition in Washington and other states to legalize active euthanasia or physician-assisted suicide in certain carefully documented cases.

Physician-assisted suicide has been in the headlines also because of the outspoken position and actions of Jack Kevorkian, the Michigan doctor who provided a "suicide machine" to individuals seeking a painless way to kill themselves. The machine enables people to press buttons that administer injections: first, a sedative, then a lethal drug. Kevorkian argues that patients with hopelessly terminal illnesses, who are capable of rational judgment, should be allowed to take these measures (Kevorkian, 1991). It is a doctor's obligation, he argues, to help patients in this situation of great need. Jailed and released in two counties several times for breaking a 1993 Michigan law against assisted suicide, Kevorkian eludes specific charges of being an accomplice to murder because of the unresolved nature surrounding the constitutionality of the law. Battles continue as a Wayne County circuit court judge ruled the law unconstitutional, while an Oakland County circuit judge moved forward with charges against Kevorkian.

A less aggressive, though no less dramatic, case for assisted suicide has been made by Timothy E. Quill, M.D., who added to the debate by revealing his participation in the suicide of his patient, Diane, a woman dying of acute leukemia

(Quill, 1991). Quill argues that compassion on the part of the physician is justification for responding to a competent patient's right and request to make his or her own decision about how his or her life will end. Quill, in fact, proposes certain guidelines and clinical criteria for physicians to follow (Quill, 1993). First, patients must be rational, fully understanding their situation; second, the patient's decision must not be caused by a reversible depression that could be treated if the patient were to change his or her mind. If these conditions hold, then the physician is advised to examine a set of clinical criteria: that the patient, of his or her own free will, clearly and repeatedly made requests to die; that the patient has an incurable disease associated with severe suffering, and so on.

Those arguing against physician-assisted suicide assert that compassion, while a commendable virtue, is not a sufficient basis for morally justifying what is, nevertheless, an act of intentional killing (Pellegrino, 1992). Edmund Pellegrino, a physician and ethicist, further argues that assisted suicide is a "violent remedy carried out in the name of beneficence" (doing good) which seriously distorts the healing purposes of medicine and lends indirect support and even encouragement to patient suicide.

Issues of euthanasia and physician-assisted suicide have particular relevance to older adults since modern medical technology has devised ways to prolong life while increasing the possibility to decide the time and circumstances of one's death. Moreover, while young adults account for the greatest number of suicides, it is the elderly who have the highest rate (i.e. percentage) of suicide, usually carried out during acute episodes of depression. How can one assure that depression is not a significant factor in an older person's choosing suicide? If voluntary or physician-assisted suicide becomes legal, will the small number of limited-situation cases begin to grow, possibly through misuse of the law? These and other questions are being hotly debated in both medical-professional circles and among voters.

● **SUMMARY**

An extraordinary change has occurred in just three decades. The recognition that patient participation in decision-making was an essential right came first, followed by the assertion that

such a right did not end when the patient lost the capacity to decide. As these new rights gained prominence, other voices were raised. These voices did not intend to silence the rights-based claims but only warned of their limits. Hence, in the past few years ethics has turned its attention to questions of the family, to a deeper understanding of what informed consent might mean, when it is understood as more than an intrusive legal requirement to limit physician paternalism. New ideas—conversational or relational ethics, negotiated consent—have grown alongside the traditional emphasis on autonomy. Many are suggesting that the single-minded focus on autonomy offered an impoverished view of how human beings actually functioned. Yet older people, especially those who are chronically impaired, still require notice of their autonomous status. Much thoughtful work remains ahead, but an excellent foundation now exists for better informed deliberations to continue. (For more information, see Chapter 29, **Long Term Care**.)

References

Ackerman, Felicia. "The Significance of A Wish." *Hastings Center Report* Vol. 21, no. 4 (1991): 27–29.

Agrich, George. "Reassessing Autonomy in Long-Term Care." *Hastings Center Report* Vol. 20, no. 6 (1990): 12–18.

Applebaum, Paul S., Charles Lidz, and Alan Meisel. *Informed Consent: Legal Theory and Clinical Practice.* New York: Oxford University Press, 1987.

Arras, John. "The Severely Demented, Minimally Functional Patient: An Ethical Analysis." *Journal of the American Geriatrics Society* Vol. 36 (1988): 938–44.

Besdine, Richard. "Decisions to Withhold Treatment from Nursing Home Residents." *Journal of the American Geriatrics Society* Vol. 31 (1983): 602–06.

Bok, Sissela. *Lying: Moral Choice in Public and Private Life.* New York: Pantheon Books, 1978.

Brock, Dan. Paper presented at The Hastings Center Fellows Meeting. Briarcliff Manor, NY, 1990.

Brody, Baruch. *Life and Death Decisionmaking.* New York: Oxford University Press, 1988.

Brody, Baruch, and H. T. Engelhardt. *Bioethics: Readings and Cases.* Englewood Cliffs, NJ: Prentice-Hall, 1987.

Brody, Howard. *The Healer's Power.* New Haven, CT: Yale University Press, 1992.

———. *Stories of Sickness.* New Haven, CT: Yale University Press, 1987.

———. "Transparency: Informed Consent in Primary Care." *Hastings Center Report* Vol. 19, no. 5 (1989): 5–9.

Callahan, Daniel. "Medical Futility, Medical Necessity: The Problem Without a Name." *Hastings Center Report* Vol. 21, no. 4 (1991): 30-35.

Caplan, Arthur. "Let Wisdom Find a Way." *Generations* Vol. 10, no. 2 (1985): 10–15.

Capron, Alexander M. "The Subjective Standard: Canterbury Can Require Too Little." In *Bioethics: Readings and Cases*. Eds. B. Brody and H. T. Engelhardt. Englewood Cliffs, NJ: Prentice-Hall, 1987.

Collopy, Bart. "Autonomy in Long-Term Care: Some Crucial Distinctions." *Gerontologist* Vol. 28, supplement (1988): 10–18.

Cranford, Ronald. "Helga Wanglie's Ventilator: Introduction." *Hastings Center Report* Vol. 21, no. 4 (1991): 23–24.

Gibson, Joan McIver. "National Values History Project." *Generations* supplement (1990): 51–64.

Gilligan, Carol. *In a Different Voice*. Cambridge, MA: Harvard University Press, 1982.

Green, R. M. "Truthtelling in Medical Care." In *Medical Ethics and the Law*. Ed. M. Hiller. Cambridge, MA: Ballinger, 1981.

High, Dallas. "All in the Family: Extended Autonomy and Expectations in Surrogate Health Care Decision-Making. *Gerontologist* Vol. 28 supplement (1988): 46–52.

Holmes, H. B., and L. M. Purdy. *Feminist Perspectives in Medical Ethics*. Bloomington, IN: Indiana University Press, 1992.

Jecker, Nancy. "The Role of Intimate Others in Medical Decision Making." *Gerontologist* Vol. 30, no. 1 (1990): pp. 51–65.

Johnson, Sandra. "PSDA in the Nursing Home." *Hastings Center Report* Vol. 21, no. 5 (special supplement: *Practicing the PSDA*, 1991): S3–S5.

Kapp, Marshall. "Medical Empowerment and the Elderly." *Hastings Center Report* Vol. 19, no. 4 (1989): 5–8.

Katz, Jay. *The Silent World of Doctor and Patient*. New York: The Free Press, 1984.

Kevorkian, Jack. *Prescription Medicine: The Goodness of Planned Death*. Buffalo, NY: Prometheus Books, 1991.

Kittay, Eva, and Diana Meyers, eds. *Women and Moral Theory*. Totowa, NJ: Rowman & Littlefield, 1987.

Miles, Steven, and Crimmins. "Orders to Limit Emergency Treatment." *Journal of the American Medical Association* Vol. 254 (1985): 525–27.

Moody, Harry R. "From Informed Consent to Negotiated Consent." *Gerontologist* Vol. 28, (supplement, 1988): 64–70.

Pellegrino, Edmund D. "Doctors Must Not Kill." *Journal of Clinical Ethics* Vol. 3 (1992): 95–102.

Pellegrino, Edmund, and David Thomasma. *A Philosophical Basis of Medical Practice*. New York: Oxford University Press, 1981.

President's Commission for the Study of Ethical Problems in Medicine and Biomedical and Behavioral Research. *Making Health Care Decisions*. Washington, DC: U.S. Government Printing Office, 1982.

Quill, Timothy E. "Death and Dignity: A Case of Individualized Decision Making." *New England Journal of Medicine* Vol. 324 (1991): 691–94.

———. "Doctor, I Want to Die. Will You Help Me?" *Journal of the American Medical Association (JAMA)* Vol. 270, no. 7 (1993): 870–73.

Rhoden, Nancy. "Litigating Life and Death." *Harvard Law Review* Vol. 102 (1988): 375–446.

Rie, Michael. "The Limits of a Wish." *Hastings Center Report* Vol. 21, no. 4 (1991): 24–27.

Rothman, David. *Strangers at the Bedside*. New York: Basic Books, 1991.

Rouse, Fenella. "Patients, Providers, and the PSDA." *Hastings Center Report* Vol. 21, no. 5 (special supplement: *Practicing the PSDA*, 1991): S2–S3.

Scofield, Giles. "Is Consent Useful When Resuscitation Isn't?" *Hastings Center Report* Vol. 21, no. 6 (1991): pp. 28–36.

Stanford University Center on Bioethics and The Hastings Center. "A Planning Study: Ethnic Ethics." Funded by the James Irvine Foundation: 1991.

Tancredi, Laurence. "The Mental Status Exam." *Generations* Vol. 11, no. 4 (1987): 24–31.

Tolstoy, L. *The Death of Ivan Ilych and Other Stories*. New York: New America Library, 1960.

Tomlinson, Tom. "The Physicians's Influence on Patient Choices." *Theoretical Medicine* Vol. 7 (1986): 127–46.

Tomlinson, Tom, and Howard Brody. "Futility and the Ethics of Resuscitation." *Journal of the American Medical Association* Vol. 264, no. 10 (1990): 1277.

Veatch, Robert M. *Death, Dying, and the Biological Revolution*. Rev. ed. New Haven, CT: Yale University Press, 1989.

Wetle, Terrie, and others. "Nursing Home Resident Participation in Medical Decisions: Perceptions and Preferences. *Gerontologist* Vol. 28 (supplement, 1988): 32–38.

Wolfe, Susan. "Honoring Broader Directives." *Hastings Center Report* Vol. 21, no. 5 (special supplement: *Practicing the PSDA*, 1991): S8-S9.

Additional Reading

Brown, Robert N. *The Rights of Older Persons*. Carbondale, IL: Southern Illinois University Press, 1989.

Callahan, Daniel. *Setting Limits*. New York: Simon & Schuster, 1987.

"Dying Well? A Colloquy on Euthanasia and Physician-Assisted Suicide." *Hastings Center Report* (March-April 1992). Entire issue is devoted to euthanasia and physician-assisted suicide.

Homer, Paul, and Martha Holstein, eds. *A Good Old Age? The Paradox of Setting Limits*. New York: Simon & Schuster, 1990.

Humphry, Derek. *Final Exit*. Eugene, OR: The Hemlock Society, 1992.

Kapp, Marshall B. *Legal Aspects of Health Care for the Elderly: An Annotated Bibliography*. Westport, CT: Greenwood Press, 1988.

Kapp, Marshall B., and others, eds. *Legal and Ethical Aspects of Health Care for the Elderly*. Ann Arbor, MI: Health Administration Press, 1985.

Moody, Harry R. *Ethics in an Aging Society*. Baltimore, MD: Johns Hopkins University Press, 1992.

Outerbridge, David, and Alan Hersh. *Easing the Passage: Medical and Legal Steps Including the Living Will to*

Guarantee a Tranquil and Pain-Free Death for Yourself and Loved Ones. New York: Harper Collins, 1991.

Soled, Alex J. *The Essential Guide to Wills, Estates, Trusts, and Death Taxes.* Washington, DC: American Association of Retired Persons and Scott, Foresman, 1986.

Waymack, Mark H., and George A. Taylor. *Medical Ethics and the Elderly: A Case Book.* Chicago, IL: Pluribus Press, 1988.

Winslow, Gerald R., ed. *Facing Limits: Ethics and Health Care for the Elderly.* Boulder, CO: Westview, 1993.

Martha Holstein M.A.

Section IX:

Elder Care

28

Caregiving

- What Is Caregiving? • Who Are the Caregivers of Impaired Older Americans?
- Caregiver Selection Process • Milestones in the Caregiving Career • The Stresses of Caregiving
- The Rewards of Caregiving • Resources for Caregivers • Overcoming Barriers to Service Use

As the world changes and becomes more complex, new words are invented to define and describe those changes. Terms such as "latch-key children," "yuppies," and "baby boomers" now are commonly used in conversation; twenty years ago, they didn't exist. "Caregiving" and the related term, "caregiver," also are new words. They didn't exist prior to the mid-1970s, and still are more common in scientific papers than in casual conversation. Although the words are new, the phenomenon is not. Caregiving is a fundamental human activity—and although it is difficult to date its historical appearance, it has clearly existed for a very long time.

● WHAT IS CAREGIVING?

Caregiving refers to the multiple ways that family and friends—informal associates rather than formal service providers—provide care to an impaired person. A caregiver is a relative or friend who provides care to an impaired individual. This chapter discusses caregiving for impaired older adults. Most knowledge about caregiving is based on studies of caregivers who help impaired older adults. Older persons also are at greater risk for the kinds of impairments that require caregiving assistance than their younger peers. Some younger persons also require caregiving (e.g., the developmentally disabled and the handicapped), but they are not the topic of discussion here.

Isn't it typical for friends and relatives to help

> Caregiving refers to the multiple ways that family and friends—informal associates rather than formal service providers—provide care to an impaired person.

each other in times of need? Is everyone a caregiver? It *is* typical to provide assistance to friends and family—and they need not be impaired to be offered assistance. But because they do not meet the criterion of providing help to an impaired person, these give-and-take relationships are not caregiving. The line between caregiving and other relationships in which help is given is not always clear-cut, but it is real. The best way to distinguish between caregiving and other close relationships is to understand how caregiving begins.

Caregiving usually emerges in long-term relationships between family members or friends. Examining the history of these relationships reveals many times that help was given and received. Changes begin when one member of the relationship experiences a long-term, chronic illness or permanent disability that impairs his or her ability to function independently. Caregiving does not apply to help given for a bout of the flu or other time-limited problems for which full recovery is expected. As in previous situations, family members and/or friends jump in to assist their loved one. But as time passes, (a) the dominant direction of assistance is to the impaired person from family and friends, and (b) it becomes clear that this unbalanced flow of assistance will continue indefinitely, or even increase if the impairment is progressive. This long-term, perhaps permanent, unbalanced flow of assistance is what distinguishes caregiving from other close relationships (George, 1986). At the point that caregiving begins, a subtle transformation occurs. Now the spouse is not only a spouse, but also a caregiver; a child is not only a child, but also a caregiver; and so forth. And this transformation is extremely consequential for both the caregiver and for the impaired older person, who becomes the care recipient.

As new words enter the language, one learns them at different rates. Many people are not yet acquainted with the term caregiver; indeed, many caregivers do not define themselves as such. Failure to identify oneself as a caregiver can have important implications. For example, some service agencies report that they advertised services to help caregivers with their responsibilities, but received few requests for assistance. When these agencies sought out caregivers and asked them

> This long-term, perhaps permanent, unbalanced flow of assistance is what distinguishes caregiving from other close relationships.

why they didn't use their services (or at least look into them), potential clients often reported that they didn't define themselves as caregivers or view the services as relevant to them. And yet, nearly everyone will be a caregiver or care recipient at some point. An important task for public education is to inform the public of what caregiving is and who caregivers are. It is very difficult for caregivers to receive appropriate services in a timely manner if they don't understand that those services are relevant to their lives.

● WHO ARE THE CAREGIVERS OF IMPAIRED OLDER AMERICANS?

The number of caregivers providing assistance to impaired older adults is determined primarily by the number of impaired older persons in the

Figure 28.1
People Age 65+ with Activities of Daily Living (ADL) Limitations, by Type of Limitation: 1987

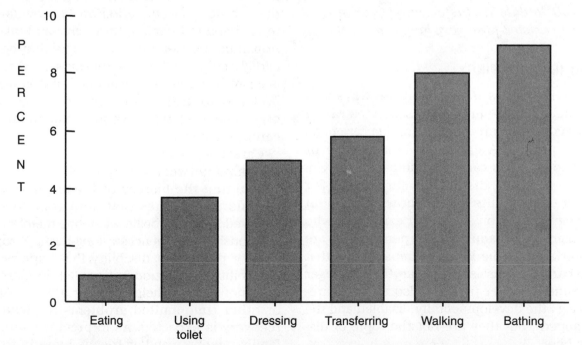

Source: Leon, J., and T. Lair. "Functional Status of the Noninstitutionalized Elderly: Estimates of ADL and IADL Difficulties." *National Medical Expenditure Survey Research Findings 4.* DHHS Pub. No. (PHS) 90-3462 (June 1990). Rockville, MD: Public Health Service, Agency for Health Care Policy and Research.

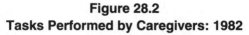

Figure 28.2
Tasks Performed by Caregivers: 1982

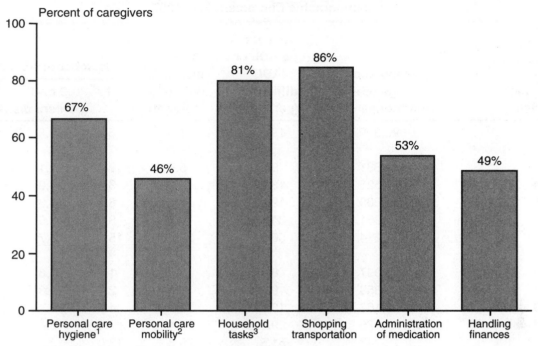

Notes: 1. One or more of: feeding, bathing, dressing, toileting. 2. One or more of: getting in and out of bed and/or getting around outside. 3. One or more of: meal preparation, housecleaning, laundry.

Source: "1982 Long-Term Care Survey/Informal Caregivers Survey." In *Exploding the Myths: Caregiving in America.* Select Committee on Aging, U.S. House of Representatives, January 1987.

population. Estimates of the population of impaired older adults, in turn, depend on how impairment is measured. For most purposes, including federal and state policies as well as the private sector (such as insurance firms), the level of disability is established by examining the older person's ability to perform self-care tasks, called activities of daily living (abbreviated as ADLs). ADLs are typically divided into two categories: instrumental and physical (Katz and others, 1963; Lawton and Brody, 1969). Instrumental ADLs (abbreviated IADLs) refer to self-care activities required to maintain a household. Major IADL tasks include meal preparation, taking medicine, performing light housework, shopping for groceries, and managing personal finances. Physical ADLs (abbreviated simply as ADLs) are very basic aspects of self-care, including eating, getting in and out of bed, toileting, dressing, and bathing.

Caregiver Surveys

The National Center for Health Statistics provides national estimates of the proportion of peo-

ple age 65 and older who suffer from ADL and IADL impairments. The best source of information of this kind is the 1984 National Long-Term Care Survey (Stone, Cafferata, and Stangl, 1987). Results of that survey indicate that in 1984 more than 2 million persons age 65 and older were unable to perform at least one physical ADL. If the inability to perform at least one IADL task is used to define disability, the number of disabled adults increased to more than 4 million. Obviously, how broadly or narrowly disability is defined greatly affects the size of the disabled population. All federal policies and most state programs define disability as impairment in two or more physical ADLs (Stone and Murtaugh, 1990). Using that definition, 1.35 million persons age 65 and older were disabled in 1984. The number of disabled older adults changes as the size of the older population grows. Thus, percentages may be more useful for depicting the size of the disabled older population. In 1984, 7.8 percent of the population age 65 and older were unable to perform at least one physical ADL. The percent-

Table 28.1
Estimates of ADL/IADL Difficulties of the Noninstitutionalized U.S. Population Age 65+, by Selected Demographic Characteristics: 1987

| Demographic characteristic | Population age 65+ (in thousands) | At least one ADL or IADL difficulty (percent) | At least one ADL difficulty (percent) | Number of ADL difficulties | | |
| | | | | 1 | 2 or 3 | 4 or more |
				(percent distribution)		
Total[1]	27,909	19.5	11.4	5.2	3.8	2.4
All						
65 to 69	9,361	9.9	5.9	2.4	2.1	1.3
70 to 74	7,525	13.2	7.9	3.4	3.0	1.5
75 to 79	5,389	19.9	11.5	6.2	3.3	2.0
80 to 84	3,361	34.1	18.6	8.0	7.5	3.2
85+	2,274	56.8	34.5	15.6	9.7	9.2
Men						
65 to 69	4,097	8.0	5.0	1.7	1.8	1.4
70 to 74	3,359	9.2	6.3	2.3	2.3	1.7
75 to 79	2,167	15.5	8.7	4.2	2.7[2]	1.8
80 to 84	1,175	29.5	17.4	7.4	6.6	3.4[2]
85+	743	51.5	26.3	13.0	9.2	4.1[2]
Women						
65 to 69	5,264	11.3	6.5	2.9	2.4	1.3
70 to 74	4,165	16.5	9.2	4.3	3.5	1.3
75 to 79	3,222	22.9	13.3	7.6	3.7	2.0
80 to 84	2,186	36.6	19.3	8.3	7.9	3.1
85+	1,531	59.3	38.4	16.9	9.9	11.7
Ethnic/racial background						
White	24,135	19.1	11.1	5.1	3.6	2.4
African-American	2,327	26.3	15.5	6.0	6.4	3.2
Hispanic	863	14.1	7.8	3.7[2]	4.1[2]	0.0[2]
Living arrangements						
Alone	8,985	25.5	13.3	6.5	5.2	1.5
With spouse only	12,744	13.1	7.9	3.5	2.4	1.9
With other relatives	5,631	23.1	15.6	6.7	4.8	4.1

Notes: 1. Includes people with other ethnic/racial background, unknown veteran and insurance status, and other living arrangements. 2. Relative standard error is greater than or equal to 30 percent.

Source: Leon, J., and T. Lair. "Functional Status of the Noninstitutionalized Elderly: Estimates of ADL and IADL Difficulties." *National Medical Expenditure Survey Research Findings 4*. DHHS Pub. No. (PHS) 90-3462 (June 1990). Rockville, MD: Public Health Service, Agency for Health Care Policy and Research.

ages of those unable to perform at least one IADL and those unable to perform two or more physical ADLs were 15.5 percent and 5.1 percent, respectively.

The National Long-Term Care Survey provides useful estimates of the size of the disabled older population. Unlike most studies, it is based on a national sample. But these data also have one important limitation: estimates are restricted to persons living *in the community*. Another important segment of the disabled older population lives in long-term care facilities—at any given time, about 5 percent of the older population (Comptroller General of the United States, 1977). It is reasonable to conclude that persons in long-term care facilities are unable to perform two or more physical ADL tasks. Thus, combining community and institutional residents, it appears that approximately 10 percent of the U.S. older population (2.7 million persons in 1984 and a larger number now) are disabled.

If at least 1.5 million severely disabled adults are living in the community, many people are providing care to that population. Moreover, although the definition of two or more physical ADL impairments is typically used for policy purposes, many other older adults need and receive informal care: those with one physical ADL impairment and those with one or more IADL impairments.

The National Center for Health Statistics performed a study in 1982 to estimate the number of informal caregivers serving impaired older Americans. This study, the Informal Caregivers Survey, also examined the characteristics of informal caregivers and the amounts and kinds of care they provided. Results of that survey suggest that in 1982, 2.2 million Americans were providing care to 1.6 million disabled older adults living in the community (Stone and others, 1987). In this study, an older adult was considered disabled if he or she had one or more physical ADL limitation. Because these estimates are dated, both the number of disabled older adults and the number of persons providing care to them are larger now.

Combining community and institutional residents, it appears that approximately 10 percent of the U.S. older population (2.7 million persons in 1984 and a larger number now) are disabled.

The Informal Caregivers Survey is important because it is the only national study of its kind. Nonetheless, two sizable groups of caregivers were omitted from this survey. First, the survey excluded relatives and friends providing care to older persons who had only IADL impairment. Although IADL tasks are less basic than ADL tasks, they are important for independent living, and many caregivers devote substantial periods of time to tasks such as money management, meal preparation, and providing transportation. Second, the survey excluded caregivers who were providing care to institutionalized older adults. There is strong evidence that family members continue to provide substantial care to their insti-

Figure 28.3
Caregivers and Their Relationship to the Elderly Care Recipient: 1982

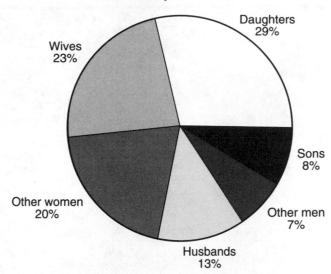

Note: Caregiver population includes primary and secondary caregivers.

Source: Exploding the Myths: Caregiving in America. Select Committee on Aging, U.S. House of Representatives, January 1987.

tutionalized older relatives (Bowers, 1988; Colerick and George, 1986; Stephens, Kinney, and Ogrocki, 1991). Levels of caregiving usually decrease after the care recipient is placed in an institution, but friends and relatives continue to provide important caregiving contributions. Thus, at least twice as many Americans provide some level of caregiving to impaired older adults than is estimated by the Informal Caregivers Survey.

An important contribution of the Informal Caregivers Survey is information about the characteristics of caregivers and the amounts and kinds of care that they provide. With regard to caregiver characteristics, most caregivers are women (72 percent), with wives and daughters comprising the majority of caregivers. Caregivers ranged in age from 14 to 99, with an average age of 57. The relatively high average age of caregivers reflects the predominance of spouse and adult child caregivers (most of the latter are age 45 or older; many are age 65 or older). Whites and non-whites were observed in the same proportions that they are found in the general population. The income distribution of caregivers was skewed to the low end, however, with nearly one-third living in or near poverty. The income distrib-

Gender does not affect spouse caregivers; husbands and wives are equally likely to take on caregiving responsibilities. (Copyright © Marianne Gontarz)

ution appears to reflect several factors: lower average incomes among older as compared to younger persons, increased likelihood of disability among poor older people, and the fact that disabled older adults with higher incomes are more likely to reside in institutions. Nearly three quarters of the caregivers lived with their care recipients. The proportion of adult children who resided with their impaired parents was much higher than the usual rate of shared residence (Soldo and Myelyluoma, 1983). Apparently, caregiving demands often result in shared residence of older parents and their adult children.

The Informal Caregivers Survey also highlighted the distinction between primary and secondary caregivers (George and Gwyther, 1986; Tennstedt, McKinlay, and Sullivan, 1989). Primary caregivers have the major responsibility for care of impaired older adults. In contrast, secondary caregivers provide assistance to primary caregivers. Both the amount of responsibility for the care recipient and the amount of time devoted to caregiving are substantially lower among secondary than primary caregivers. In the Informal Caregivers Survey, 70 percent of the caregivers reported having primary responsibility for the care recipient.

As detailed later, caregiving is generally more stressful if the caregiver has competing responsibilities, especially minor children at home and/or employment. In the Informal Caregivers Survey, 21 percent of the caregivers had minor children and 31 percent were employed. As would be expected, men were more likely than women to be working. Among employed caregivers, more than a third reported that they were working fewer hours, had rearranged their work schedules, or had taken time off without pay as a result of their caregiving responsibilities.

Caregivers in the Informal Caregivers Survey reported that caregiving duties require substantial time commitments. Eighty percent performed caregiving duties seven days a week, at an average of four hours per day. Overall, women reported spending more time caregiving than men. This sex difference is a bit misleading, however. Among non-spouse caregivers, women devoted considerably more time to caregiving than their male counterparts. Among spouse caregivers, however, husbands devoted somewhat more time to caregiving than wives did. Caregivers reported performing a wide variety of tasks. More than half of them reported helping with personal care and hygiene, administering medications, housework (including meal preparation), shopping, and transportation. Slightly smaller proportions provided assistance with mobility (46 percent) and handling finances (49 percent). As would be expected, primary caregivers reported greater time commitments and performance of a wider range of tasks than secondary caregivers.

As noted, a limitation of the Informal Caregivers Survey is its restricted definition of who is a caregiver—it ignores persons who provide care to older persons suffering only IADL impairment as well as those who provide assistance to institutionalized older adults. Despite this limitation, the profile of caregivers generated by the Informal Caregivers Survey appears to be quite accurate. There are now literally hundreds of research articles based on samples of caregivers. Compared to the Informal Caregivers Survey, these studies are disadvantaged because they are based on local samples and often involve only small numbers of caregivers. Many of these studies, however, have the strength of using a less restrictive definition of disability to identify informal caregivers. In general, the profile of caregivers generated by the Informal Caregivers Survey is similar to those described by other researchers (e.g., Cantor, 1983; George and Gwyther, 1986).

Monetary Value of Caregiving

Two important caregiving tasks that were not examined in the Informal Caregivers Survey deserve attention. First, financial assistance was not assessed, for understandable reasons. Measuring the financial transfers involved in caregiving is very difficult. Some caregivers pay for part or all of the living costs of their care recipients. Those direct transfers are potentially measurable, though it is doubtful that caregivers could easily provide the detailed documentation necessary to quantify those expenses. Other kinds of financial implications are much more difficult. The kinds of services that caregivers provide certainly are valuable. But how should one attach monetary value to caregiving tasks? Is the appropriate value that which one would pay in the open market for such services? Perhaps not; family members may provide better care than paid help because of their emotional attachment to the care recipient. Is the appropriate value that which the caregiver would earn on the job because, in theory, the caregiver could devote caregiving hours to employment if they were available? Again difficulties arise: Is the value of an hour of housecleaning increased because a lawyer rather than a sales clerk performs the work? Should a service be assigned a greater value if the caregiver could be employed, were it not for caregiving demands, than if the caregiver had retired prior to taking on caregiving responsibilities?

There have been attempts to attribute monetary values to caregiving tasks. The U.S. General Accounting Office, for example, computed monetary values based on what it would cost to provide the same service in an institutional setting (1977). But that strategy also has limitations. For example, in a nursing home, one nurse can supervise the administration of medications to thirty to forty residents. It would clearly cost much more to have a nurse supervise the medication use of thirty to forty impaired persons living in the community. Although it is difficult to attribute monetary values to caregiving contributions, they are of substantial value. Moreover, to the degree that disabled older adults are maintained in the community as a result of the efforts of informal caregivers, public expenditures for institutional care are substantially reduced.

Caregivers as Decision Makers

Second, the Informal Caregivers Survey did not inquire about caregivers' responsibilities for making care decisions. The process of caregiving can be usefully thought of as a decision-making process. Caregivers must decide what tasks they are willing to perform for their care recipients, the degree to which they will try to enlist the help of friends and family members, which relatives and friends they will turn to for help, whether to seek power of attorney for the care recipient, whether to supplement their care with community-based services, and whether and when to institutionalize the care recipient. Caregivers must determine the extent to which the care recipients themselves can and should be involved in decision-making. Primary caregivers must determine the extent to which secondary caregivers should have a say in care decisions. Substantial research suggests that decision-making is an important part of caregiving and that it can lead to interpersonal conflict and/or personal worry (George, 1986; Pratt and others, 1989). This important caregiving task was not addressed in the Informal Caregivers Survey.

Caregiving and Dementia

One other important issue was not addressed in the Informal Caregivers Survey. Although the survey obtained information about the functional impairments of care recipients, the diagnoses or specific medical conditions generating those impairments were ignored. In general, caregiving tasks are closely related to the specific ADL disabilities experienced by the care recipient. However, the illness experienced by the care recipient also is relevant. Diagnosis is important because illnesses differ in the specific caregiving demands they generate, the prognosis for full or partial recovery, the extent to which disability is expected to progress or remain stable, the complexity of the medical regimens prescribed by the care recipient's physician, and the course and outcome of the disease (including whether it is a terminal condition). Knowledge about the degree to which the illness of the care recipient affects the caregiving process over and above its effect on functioning is sparse. But one conclusion is compatible with available evidence: dementing illnesses that cause severe memory loss are more difficult for caregivers than other medical conditions (Scharlach, 1989; Schulz, Visintainer, and Williamson, 1990). Dementias are especially difficult for caregivers because the patient loses the ability to interact in a meaningful way, most dementias are progressive and terminal, late-stage dementia results in almost total functional incapacity, and dementia has no effective treatment. In addition, the time between diagnosis and death is often quite long (about eight years on average, with a range of from two to twenty years). There are no estimates of the proportions of caregivers whose care recipients suffer from specific medical conditions. However, dementia is the fourth leading cause of death among older adults. Thus, a substantial number of caregivers care for friends or family members with dementing illness.

The fact that caring for dementia patients is especially difficult has one additional implication for the understanding of caregiving more generally. A large and disproportionate amount of research on both caregiver stress and the effectiveness of programs designed to reduce caregiver burden and increase caregiver effectiveness is based on caregivers of dementia patients. Consequently, more is known about dementia caregiving than about caregiving in the context of other diseases common in later life. To the extent possible, the conclusions offered here are qualified in terms of the degree to which they are based primarily on the experiences of dementia caregivers.

● CAREGIVER SELECTION PROCESS

Caregiving responsibilities are not allocated at random. Choice of a caregiver, especially a primary caregiver, reflects a hierarchical process based on a combination of kinship and gender. This process has been variously described as "the principle of centrality" and a "substitution process" (Cantor, 1983; Shanas, 1979). The top of the caregiver hierarchy consists of the spouses of impaired older adults. If the impaired older adult is married, his or her spouse will serve as primary caregiver. Gender does not affect spouse caregivers; husbands and wives are equally likely to take on caregiving responsibilities. If the impaired older adult is not married, an adult child will serve as primary caregiver. At this stage of the hierarchy, gender becomes relevant. If the impaired older adult has children of both sexes, a daughter is more likely than a son to become the primary caregiver. If there is no daughter, the son will become the official primary caregiver, but the son's wife usually performs most caregiving tasks. If an impaired older adult lacks both spouse and children, caregiving responsibilities fall on more distant relatives. Siblings appear to be especially likely to take on caregiving tasks, but grandchildren and nieces or nephews also may become primary caregivers. The preference for women rather than men applies to this level of the caregiving hierarchy as well. Sisters are more likely to be caregivers than brothers, nieces are more likely to serve as caregivers than nephews, and so forth. The social preference for female caregivers appears to reflect sex-role expectations: housekeeping, personal care, and the other tasks frequently performed by caregivers are more compatible with traditional women's roles than with men's roles.

As the kinship basis of the caregiving relationship becomes more distant, caregivers are less willing to take on caregiving responsibilities and will perform those activities for shorter periods of time (Cantor, 1983; Diemling and others, 1989). The lower tolerance for long-term caregiving commitments among more distant relatives is one reason that women greatly outnumber men in long-term care facilities. In the typical scenario, the wife provides care to her husband for as long as possible, often until his death. Later, when the widow becomes disabled, she is less likely to have a caregiver who will provide long-term, community-based care.

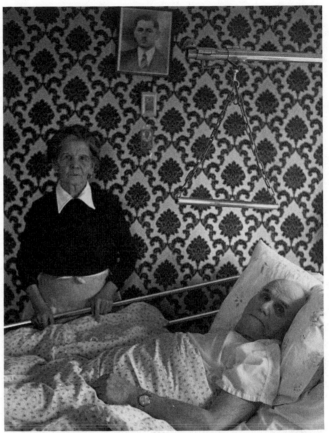

Typically the wife provides care to her husband for as long as possible, often until his death. Later, when the widow becomes disabled, she is less likely to have a caregiver who will provide long-term, community-based care. (Copyright © Marianne Gontarz)

If the impaired older adult has children of both sexes, a daughter is more likely than a son to become the primary caregiver.

Although kinship and gender explain most outcomes of the caregiver selection process, contingencies can alter the usual process. First, a small proportion of older persons lack family members. In such cases, friends or neighbors sometimes become caregivers, although the level and length of their commitments are typically less than those made by relatives. Second, a small number of older persons are estranged from their relatives. Thus, poor family relationships prevent some older persons from having family caregivers. Last, some older persons live at considerable distances from other family members. In such cases, "long-distance caregiving" is typical (Schoonover and others, 1985). Distant relatives do as much as they can for their impaired older relatives. Distance has its costs, however, and long-distance caregivers cannot provide help on a long-

term and/or daily basis. Although only a small proportion of older adults who have children live far away from all of them, this pattern is especially characteristic of families in which the children pursue professional or technical careers. This pattern is expected to increase in the future as larger proportions of adult children pursue careers in which geographic mobility is expected and desired.

● MILESTONES IN THE CAREGIVING CAREER

Caregiving careers typically emerge naturally as family members age and become the victims of chronic disease. Family members, apparently aware of the informal norms that govern caregiver selection, typically identify a primary caregiver without fanfare or conflict. Selection of secondary caregivers also is nonproblematic in most cases: adult children help one parent to care for the other, siblings contribute to the care of their sisters or brothers, and so forth. Although entry into the caregiver role typically occurs without fanfare or public recognition, it is a specific role that unfolds over time. The caregiving process as a whole can be usefully thought of as a career—a career that begins with the assumption of caregiving responsibility and ends with the death of the care recipient. The caregiving career is a career of contingency—that is, its flow and its dynamics are a result of the changing needs of the care recipient. As the care recipient's needs increase, caregiving involves a wider range of tasks and greater time commitments.

As is true of all careers, the caregiving career is typically punctuated by a series of milestones that represent times of sudden change or important events. Three milestones are commonly experienced by family caregivers and represent especially stressful events in the caregiving career. All of these milestones are experienced more directly by primary than secondary caregivers.

First, the care recipient's level of disability often reaches the point at which he or she is no longer able to make competent decisions and to handle legal and financial issues. At this point, it is often necessary or desirable for the caregiver to seek power of attorney on behalf of the care recipient. Power of attorney involves having another person legally appointed to handle business, legal, and financial matters. The decision to seek power of attorney is difficult and painful (Appolini and Cook, 1984). Sometimes care recipients understand that they are no longer competent to handle their own affairs and initiate this change in status. More frequently, however, family members must initiate this transition. Spouse caregivers often are able to simply "take over" legal and financial duties without a formal transfer of power of attorney, although some seek formal recognition of this act. For other family caregivers, formal power of attorney is usually necessary. Among non-spouse caregivers, power of attorney often is held by someone other than the primary caregiver. For example, an adult daughter may have primary responsibility for providing care to her impaired parent while power of attorney resides with an adult son.

Second, institutionalization of the care recipient is perhaps the most difficult milestone faced by family caregivers. Research evidence suggests

Caregivers usually spend considerable time with their care recipients in a nursing home, viewing themselves as the persons who must monitor the level and quality of care provided in the institution. (Copyright © Isabel Egglin)

that 30 percent to 40 percent of older adults will spend time in a long-term care facility (Liang and Tu, 1986; McConnell, 1984). Some older persons are placed in nursing homes only for recuperation and later are able to return to community living. The vast majority of institutional residents, however, reside in long-term care facilities for the rest of their lives. Thus the decision to institutionalize an older adult is important and typically permanent.

Several aspects of institutional care merit comment before discussing institutionalization in the context of caregiving. First, although the media frequently suggest that many nursing home patients do not require institutional care, research documents that this is not the case. Indeed, the truth is the opposite of this pervasive myth: for every severely impaired older adult residing in a nursing home, there are two to three equally impaired older adults living in the community (Comptroller General of the United States, 1977). Second, despite fears that the American family is weak, most institutional placements represent "last resort" tactics by family members who can no longer provide adequate care to their older relatives (Morycz, 1985). The reason that at least twice as many severely impaired older adults live in the community than in institutions is that family members provide the care that permits many disabled older persons to remain in the community. Of course some older adults do not have families; they will enter institutions earlier than those who have family caregivers.

Caregivers report that decisions about institutionalization are the most difficult ones that they face. For most caregivers, the decision-making process is a long one; certainly there is no evidence that family members rush to place their impaired relatives in long-term care facilities. Caregivers report that they experience regret and guilt when they place their relatives in institutional settings. Moreover, caregiving continues after the impaired person enters a long-term care facility. Although many personal care tasks are turned over to nursing home staff, caregivers typically spend considerable time with their care recipients, feel that they retain overall responsibility for their relatives, and view themselves as the person who must monitor the level and quality of care provided in the institution (Bowers, 1988; Colerick and George, 1986; Stephens and others, 1991).

The relationship between caregiver and care recipient also affects the timing of institutional placement. The more distant the relationship between caregiver and care recipient, the shorter the time between onset of disability and institutionalization. Thus, adult children institutionalize their parents earlier than husbands and wives institutionalize their spouses. Similarly, siblings, grandchildren, and other more distant relatives institutionalize their impaired care recipients earlier than adult children do.

The final milestone of the caregiving career is the death of the care recipient. The parameters of grief are well known. Loss of a loved one triggers a mourning process that varies for each individual, but also has a course which is, in broad brush, predictable (Schwartz-Borden, 1986). For several months, intense symptoms of grief—including sadness, crying spells, sleep problems, loss of appetite, and other symptoms—are typical. With time, symptoms become less intense and less frequent. After several months, bereaved persons typically begin to participate again in social activities. As time continues, although the pain of loss remains, individuals "recover" to the point that they again find meaning and pleasure in life and are no longer at excess risk of physical illness and intense psychological distress. For caregivers, bereavement triggers mourning, but also terminates the caregiving career. As is typical of other bereaved persons, after a period of mourning caregivers "recover" from their losses

It is often necessary or desirable for the caregiver to seek *power of attorney* on behalf of the care recipient when the care recipient is no longer able to make competent financial and legal decisions. (Courtesy of The National Council on the Aging, Inc./Jerry Hecht, photographer)

and from the demands of caregiving. Indeed, the well-being of caregivers often improves after bereavement, relative to what it was at the height of their caregiving responsibilities (Bass and Bowman, 1990; George and Gwyther, 1984).

● THE STRESSES OF CAREGIVING

Caregiving is stressful and places caregivers at increased risk of health and other problems. Caregiving is difficult and time-consuming. In addition, caregiving involves less tangible sources of stress. The most obvious of these is the pain and grief experienced as a loved one struggles with impairment and ultimately dies. Caregivers face other psychological battles as well. All caregivers have concerns about whether and how to set limits so that caregiving does not interfere with personal health and well-being. Many caregivers also face the problem of balancing caregiving demands against competing obligations to other family members or to employers. Psychologically, the course of caregiving is an odyssey in which self-interest is pitted against care for a loved one, a journey in which self-protection must be weighed against guilt and remorse.

Several dimensions of well-being are at risk as a result of the burdens of caregiving. Without question, the facet of well-being at greatest risk is mental health (Anthony-Bergstone, Zarit, and Gatz, 1988; George and Gwyther, 1986; Moritz, Kasl, and Berkman, 1989; Pruchno and others,

1990; Schulz and others, 1987). Caregivers average at least twice as many psychiatric symptoms as their age peers who are not caregivers. Common symptoms reported by caregivers include guilt, feeling overwhelmed by responsibilities, sleep problems, feeling sad or blue, bouts of restlessness and anxiety, and a variety of psychosomatic complaints including weakness, headaches, and diffuse pain. Some evidence suggests that caregivers of demented older adults experience more psychiatric symptoms than family members caring for older adults with other illnesses (Scharlach, 1989). Increased psychiatric symptoms do not always, or even typically, signal full-blown, diagnosable mental illness. Nonetheless, studies indicate that approximately 30 percent of the caregivers of demented older adults meet diagnostic criteria for a diagnosis of clinical depression (Cohen and Eisdorfer, 1988; Gallagher and others, 1989)—a much higher rate than the 2 percent to 3 percent observed in random samples of the population. Caregivers of demented older adults also use psychotropic drugs, especially antidepressants, at a much higher rate than the general population (approximately 30 percent versus 10 percent, respectively) (Clipp and George, 1990a). However, evidence is lacking concerning rates of psychiatric disorder and psychotropic medication use among caregivers of older adults with illnesses other than dementia.

Psychologically, the course of caregiving is an odyssey in which self-interest is pitted against care for a loved one, a journey in which self-protection must be weighed against guilt and remorse.

A second facet of well-being in which caregiving has widespread negative consequences is social and recreational activities. Research on the general population documents that contacts with friends and relatives and meaningful leisure activities are strongly associated with physical health and the sense that life is satisfying and meaningful. Many caregivers, however, have little or no time for social and recreational activities. Compared to their non-caregiving peers, family caregivers spend less time with friends and rela-

tives, pursuing hobbies, attending clubs, and participating in religious activities (George and Gwyther, 1986; Moritz and others, 1989). Consequently, most caregivers are dissatisfied with their social lives (George and Gwyther, 1986).

Many researchers believe that caregiving, especially intense levels of caregiving provided over a long period of time, can cause or exacerbate physical health problems. Evidence is ambiguous on this point, however. It appears that caregiving does not typically result in new physical illnesses (Schulz and others, 1987). However, like other stresses, caregiving is associated with reduced immune functioning, which places individuals at increased risk for illness (Kiecolt-Glaser and others, 1987). The stress of caregiving also can exacerbate existing illnesses, especially among spouse caregivers who are older and more likely to have pre-existing illnesses (Schulz and others, 1990). Many caregivers also neglect their own health habits, such as exercise and regular medical checkups, as a result of the time demands of caregiving.

However, researchers have ignored the question of whether caregiving is a risk factor for mortality. Two characteristics of previous research appear to explain this neglect: (a) small samples that make estimates of rare events such as mortality unstable, and (b) the lack of longitudinal data (i.e., following caregivers for long periods of time), which are required to predict outcomes such as mortality. Research at the Duke University Center for the Study of Aging suggests that the relationship between caregiving and mortality merits further investigation. In a longitudinal study of 510 family caregivers of demented older adults, George (1992) observed a death rate of 9 percent over a one-year period. In a longitudinal study of a random sample of more than 4,000 adults age 65 and older from the same geographic area, the Duke researchers observed an annual death rate of 4 percent. Thus, the death rate was more than twice as high among caregivers as among the representative sample despite the fact that, on average, members of the caregiver sample were seventeen years younger than members of the community sample.

As briefly noted earlier, caregiving also can have a negative impact on financial resources. Two scenarios are relatively common in terms of financial strain. For many caregivers, especially spouse caregivers, out-of-pocket costs for community-based and institutional care are the source of financial stress (Liu, Manton, and Liu, 1988). Limited third-party reimbursement for nursing home care, unless the care recipient is poor, causes many spouse caregivers to delay institutionalization of their impaired husbands and wives. Institutional placement often is delayed until after the caregiver has exceeded healthful limits on his or her own well-being. A second scenario is more typical of adult child and other non-spouse caregivers: wages are reduced or totally relinquished as a result of the demands of caregiving (Scharlach, 1989).

Another common consequence of caregiving is family conflict. Caregiving families are at risk of several kinds of conflict. One type concerns the relationship between the caregiver and care receiver (Litvin, 1992; Strawbridge and Wallhagen, 1991). Impaired older adults often feel guilty about the burdens they impose on family members and are understandably distressed about their disabilities. Sometimes those negative emotions create tensions in their relationships with the caregivers whom they depend upon for assistance. For caregivers, such conflicts are difficult—not only does the caregiver have the burden of providing care but also must deal with hostility or depression in the care recipient. Another common type of family conflict concerns the relationships between primary and secondary caregivers (George, 1986). Primary caregivers often feel isolated, sensing that secondary caregivers are providing less emotional and tangible support than they need. Conversely, secondary caregivers sometimes feel that their labor is welcome, but that they are left out of care decisions. For adult child caregivers, family conflict also can arise from the competing demands posed by their impaired parents and their own spouses and children (Brody, 1981; Matthews, Werkner, and Delaney, 1989; Stoller and Pugliesi, 1989). All caregivers grapple with the issue of balancing caregiving demands against their personal well-being. This is a family as well as a personal issue. One family member may set his or her boundary in a way that other family members find problematic, leading to debates about whether all family members are contributing to caregiving at an appropriate level (George, 1986). Thus, family

Impaired older adults often feel guilty about the burdens they impose on family members and are understandably distressed about their disabilities. (Copyright © Marianne Gontarz)

conflict can result from caregiving decisions in multiple ways.

Although all caregivers are at risk of negative outcomes, some caregivers are more likely than others to experience decreases in well-being. Several factors are associated with risk. First, women are more likely to experience negative outcomes than men. This sex difference holds true for mental health problems, physical health problems, dissatisfaction with social and recreational activities, and financial strain (Barusch and Spaid, 1984; George and Gwyther, 1986; Horowitz, 1985; Zarit, Todd, and Zarit, 1986). In addition, female caregivers are more likely than male caregivers to place their impaired relatives in nursing homes (Colerick and George, 1986). Reasons for these sex differences are unclear. Indeed, researchers initially expected caregiving to be more difficult for men than women because caregiving tasks are more compatible with women's traditional sex roles.

Second, caregivers who live in or near poverty are more likely to experience problems (Cantor, 1983; George and Gwyther, 1986). Caregivers who have good financial resources can pay for various kinds of assistance that are not within the reach of caregivers with limited finances. Third, the strongest predictor of decreased well-being among caregivers is lack of social support (George, 1987; George and Gwyther, 1986; Haley and others, 1987). Caregivers with strong networks of friends and relatives who provide both emotional support and tangible assistance are at lower risk of problems than caregivers who are socially isolated. Unfortunately, the limited longitudinal evidence available suggests that social support tends to decrease over time for caregivers (Clipp and George, 1990b). Early on and at times of crisis, friends and relatives are available to caregivers. But some caregivers report that levels of assistance with the day-to-day demands of caregiving decrease over time. One reason for this pattern may be the fact that caregivers do not have time to participate in the pleasurable activities and usual give-and-take of favors that are typical of most social relationships.

Spouse and non-spouse caregivers (the latter primarily consisting of adult children) are at differential risk of specific negative outcomes. Spouse caregivers tend to have higher rates of pre-existing illness and lower levels of financial resources, making those two areas especially problematic (George and Gwyther, 1986). Adult child caregivers typically face higher levels of competing demands, which limit the time available for caregiving; and they often must totally forego social and recreational activities when they add caregiving to their already hectic lives (George and Gwyther, 1986). Finally, caregiving intensity is related to the risk of negative outcomes. The more hours of caregiving provided and the more responsibility that the caregiver has, the greater the risk of problems (Enright, 1991). This is probably why most research suggests that caring for demented older adults is more stressful than caring for older persons with other impairments.

A final domain in which the costs of caregiving must be acknowledged concerns the care recipient. Although it is rare, elder abuse sometimes occurs in the context of caregiving (Quinn and Tomata, 1986). Caregivers are highly stressed and, if overly burdened, may use force or coercion in dealing with their impaired relatives. This phenomenon is rare; caregivers are much more likely to exceed the limits of their own health and well-being than to abuse their impaired relatives. Nonetheless, knowledge that caregiving can increase the risk of elder abuse provides a strong rationale for service programs that reduce caregiver burden.

● THE REWARDS OF CAREGIVING

Caregiving is a chronic stressor that places individuals at risk of negative health and social outcomes. These risks are the reason that federal agencies including the National Institute on Aging and the National Institute on Mental Health have made caregiver research a prominent part of their research agendas. However, to provide a balanced perspective on caregiving, the rewards of caregiving must be acknowledged.

Although no one looks forward to being a caregiver, family members report satisfactions and rewards associated with providing care to their impaired relatives. These rewards appear to fall in four primary areas (Farran and others, 1991; Kinney and Stephens, 1989; Montenko, 1989). First, caregivers often report that they derive satisfaction from providing care to a loved one. This satisfaction tends to be bittersweet in that it occurs when a loved one is suffering some degree of disability, but demonstrating in important and tangible ways that family bonds are strong provides a sense of accomplishment. Second, caregiving duties can provide a structure for use of time. Spouse caregivers, especially husbands, frequently draw analogies between caregiving and employment. The responsibility for performing useful tasks in an efficient manner helps some caregivers to feel that they continue to make contributions to society. Third, and at a more abstract level, some caregivers find meaning in life as a result of their caregiving careers. At one level this is similar to feelings of usefulness, but seems to be more than that. Caregivers' comments suggest that it is more of a sense of "calling," an answer to questions about the purpose of life. Finally, although some families experience conflict, other families become closer as a result of caregiving demands. Adult children sometimes view caregiving as a way of "returning" some of the benefits that they received from their parents. Spouses sometimes view loving caregiving as tangible proof of the seriousness with which they took their wedding vows. And some caregivers are touched and humbled by the extent to which other family members rally to their assistance

---

Although no one looks forward to being a caregiver, family members report satisfactions and rewards associated with providing care to their impaired relatives.

Adult children sometimes view caregiving as a way of "returning" some of the benefits that they received from their parents. (Copyright © Marianne Gontarz)

and go through the caregiving process together from beginning to end.

It is understandable for caregivers to report that caregiving produces rewards as well as costs. The capacity of the human spirit to grow despite (and, in some cases, because of) hardship is part of the gift of life. Moreover, acknowledging the rewards of caregiving does not dilute or weaken the need for programs to reduce the suffering that many caregivers experience.

● RESOURCES FOR CAREGIVERS

The willingness of family members to take primary responsibility for their impaired older relatives is of great benefit to older adults and to society. Family caregiving permits many impaired older adults to remain in the community, living with loved ones and experiencing higher quality of life than can be produced in institutional settings. Because of caregiving, public expenditures for long-term care are reduced substantially. However, caregivers often need or would benefit from assistance with their tasks. Both informal and formal resources can benefit caregivers and should be encouraged and strengthened.

Informal Resources

Caregivers are more likely to receive help from informal than formal sources. Informal assistance appears to be more strongly related to caregiver well-being than formal services (George, 1987). As used here, informal resources refer to all types of assistance received from non-paid and non-professional sources. Social support networks composed of family and friends are the major informal resources used by family caregivers, but other types of informal assistance also can be helpful.

Family and Friends. Family and friends are the front line of assistance for most family caregivers, although many caregivers receive less help than they desire. Family and friends are important for several reasons. First, building on long-term bonds of affection, family and friends offer emotional as well as instrumental assistance to caregivers. A paid sitter may be as capable of feeding or bathing an impaired older adult as a family member or friend, but the latter are better equipped to give the caregiver emotional rewards such as reassurance and pep talks. Moreover, care recipients often respond better to family and friends than to formal providers. Second, family and friends usually are willing to perform a variety of tasks, responding to the changing needs of the caregiver and care recipient. Formal providers often provide a narrower, more specialized range of tasks. Third, frequent contact with family and friends helps caregivers to feel less isolated. Visits from formal providers are not typically viewed by caregivers as meaningful social contacts. The importance of a network of supportive friends and relatives cannot be overemphasized. As noted above, lack of social support is the strongest single predictor of caregiver burden.

Caregiver Support Groups. During the last twenty to thirty years, support groups have been established to confront a wide variety of problems ranging from coping with widowhood to breaking addictions. Support groups for caregivers of older adults also have flourished. Many support groups focus on the problems of caregivers coping with specific illnesses, such as cancer or dementia. Support groups are typically informal and community-based. Both leadership and group activities are usually generated by caregivers themselves, although some groups turn to professionals for information or assistance with specific activities.

There are few estimates of the proportion of family caregivers who participate in support groups. Available estimates range from 5 percent to 25 percent (George and Gwyther, 1988) but are restricted to caregivers of demented older adults.

Both community and personal characteristics are related to support group participation. At the community level, support group availability, the degree to which groups emphasize outreach, and the type of programming offered all affect participation rates. With regard to individuals, participation rates are higher among female than male caregivers and among caregivers with higher levels of education and income (George and Gwyther, 1988; Jones and Vetter, 1984).

Support groups serve two primary functions for participants (George and Gwyther, 1988; Greene and Monahan, 1989). First, members experience a sense of mutual sharing and understanding. Support groups provide a forum in which people confronting similar stressors can share their experiences. Second, support groups provide information to participants. This educational function is usually served in two ways: informally, with members exchanging information about effective ways of handling problems, and formally, via professional sources. Evaluations of support groups for family caregivers of demented older adults document measurable benefits for support group members: members report feeling less isolated and misunderstood, know more about dementia, and are better informed about community services than non-members (George and Gwyther, 1988; Greene and Monahan, 1987 and 1989). Findings about use of services are mixed. Some investigators report that support group members use formal services at higher rates than non-members (Greene and Monahan, 1989); others report no differences between members and non-members (George and Gwyther, 1988).

Many caregivers who would profit from support groups are unable to participate because of their caregiving responsibilities. Finding someone to care for the impaired older adult while the caregiver is out is the largest obstacle to participation. Other barriers to participation include lack of availability, lack of knowledge about support groups, and caregiver fears that they will appear unable to cope if they seek comfort in a public setting.

Informal Organizations. Informal organizations such as clubs and churches sometimes provide assistance to caregivers. Examples of relevant activities include friendly visiting programs, pastoral counseling, sitting services offered by volunteers, and social activities at which impaired older adults are welcome and accommodated. With regard to the latter, some caregivers report that religious activities are the only ones in which they feel comfortable bringing severely impaired older adults. Although based in community organizations, these activities are not formal services because they are not expected to be financially self-supporting and are not provided by professionals.

Estimates of the proportion and characteristics of caregivers obtaining assistance from informal organizations are not available. Communities vary in the extent to which informal organizations provide services for caregivers. In addition, caregivers other than those with long-term ties to the organization are unlikely to use those services. When available, however, assistance offered by voluntary organizations can be of great benefit to caregivers.

Formal Resources

Research studies suggest that, with the exception of physician care for the impaired older adult, only 10 percent to 25 percent of family caregivers use formal services to help with caregiving tasks (Caserta and others, 1987; George, 1987; Nardone, 1990). Most researchers and service providers believe that fewer caregivers use community services than is appropriate and desirable. This section describes the kinds of formal services useful to family caregivers of impaired older adults. Obstacles to use of such services are discussed later.

The Family Physician. Family physicians are ideally positioned to help family caregivers obtain formal services appropriate to the needs of the impaired older adult and the intensity of caregiving required. However, physicians rarely refer their patients or patients' families to community-based service programs. This pattern may reflect, in part, physicians' lack of knowledge about service programs in their communities. Efforts to educate physicians about community services, however, have had little success in increasing referrals to service agencies. Persons who obtain their medical care in multidisciplinary settings, such as university clinics and HMOs, are somewhat better off in this regard. Although physicians in such settings rarely make referrals to local service programs, other staff members often make such referrals. Physicians are, however, the major source of referrals to medical specialists and institutional settings.

Information and Referral Services. A very useful service for impaired older adults and their families is a centralized location where information about and referral to the entire range of local services are provided. Communities vary in the extent to which information and referral are available, with many communities lacking such services. When offered, information and referral services are provided from a variety of agencies, with councils on aging and area agencies on aging being the most common. Information and referral services also vary in the degree to which they are aware of available services and the extent to which outreach is used to provide information to persons who need it.

Case management is an enriched form of information and referral. In addition to basic information and referral, case managers help clients to access services and monitor the needs of clients so that services can be added and dropped as needs change. Several studies have evaluated the cost-effectiveness of case management; findings are mixed (Applebaum and Christianson, 1988; Knight and Carter, 1990). Overall, case managers increase service use among impaired older adults, but costs of care increase as well. Case managers usually are available only on a fee-for-service basis, making them inaccessible to caregivers with limited financial resources.

Training Programs for Family Caregivers. Some community organizations offer programs to educate family caregivers. The focus of training programs varies, ranging from "tricks of the trade" to reduce caregiver burden, to information about specific service agencies, to more ambitious programs designed to train family members to serve as the "case managers" for their impaired older relatives (Seltzer, Irvy, and Litchfield, 1987). Formal evaluations have been performed for some training programs. Results of these evaluations are mixed (Haley, Brown, and Levine, 1987; Toseland and Rossiter, 1989; Whitlach, Zarit, and von Eye, 1991). Market forces tend to drive these programs. Programs that attract a critical mass of caregivers and that caregivers find useful are likely to survive; those that fail on these grounds disappear.

Finding out about training programs is often difficult for caregivers, who are relatively isolated and have limited time. The fact that training programs are offered by a variety of service agencies also makes it difficult to learn about them. In general, the best sources of information about caregiver training programs are area agencies on aging and local chapters of organizations such as the American Cancer Society or the Alzheimer's Association.

Assistance with Household Tasks. Caregivers often would benefit from help with household tasks such as cleaning, shopping, meal preparation, and household repairs. Assistance with household tasks reduces caregivers' overall levels of responsibilities without taking away from their caretaking activities. Household services can, of course, be purchased on the open market. Caregivers with limited financial resources cannot afford to pay for such services. Sometimes subsidized or reimbursed services are available. For example, Medicare will pay for chore workers under certain conditions, but only for a short time. Some local communities offer subsidized household services, with costs determined by ability to pay. There is little reason to expect increases in the availability of household services on a subsidized or reimbursed basis. Although such services are useful to family caregivers, they will continue to be available primarily to caregivers who can afford to pay for them out of pocket.

Respite Services for Caregivers. Respite care refers to assistance with caregiving tasks that frees the family caregiver for specified periods of time. Respite care workers provide impaired older adults with the supervision and assistance ordinarily performed by family caregivers. The many forms of respite care include in-home respite care programs, nurses aides hired from health care agencies, private arrangements for sitters or companions, adult day care, and institution-based respite, which can provide caregivers with relief overnight or for longer "vacations." The distinguishing characteristic of respite care is that it is specifically designed to provide relief to the caregiver. The care recipient is expected to obtain quality care, but there is no assumption that a more sophisticated level of care is needed than the family caregiver is able to provide.

Respite care is the type of formal service most

desired by family caregivers (Fortinsky and Hathaway, 1990; Jones and Vetter, 1984). In addition, caregivers strongly prefer in-home respite to other modes of supervised care, especially for care receivers with severe impairments. In-home respite care is preferred for several reasons: (a) the caregiver need not transport the care recipient to another location, (b) there is a one-to-one ratio of care provider to care recipient (which is not true for adult day care and institutional respite), and (c) caregivers believe that care recipients are most comfortable in their own homes.

Few formal respite care programs are available, but many caregivers obtain respite care by hiring sitters or companions from agencies or by other private arrangements. Many caregivers report problems in obtaining suitable respite care. Workers are difficult to locate; caregivers are concerned about the quality of respite care; and some respite workers are unreliable. Cost is a major obstacle to use of respite care. Many caregivers cannot afford to pay the full cost of respite care. Because respite care primarily serves the needs of caregivers rather than impaired older adults, third-party payment is rare.

Because respite care is the service modality most requested by family caregivers, a number of model programs have been developed and evaluated. Results of these evaluations suggest that (a) despite the stated desire for respite care, few caregivers make use of it when it is available, and (b) those who use respite care, use very few hours of it (Lawton, Brody, and Saperstein, 1989; Montgomery, 1980). These patterns hold true even when respite care is subsidized, though use increases somewhat when the service is free or partially subsidized. Available evidence suggests that respite care generates few measurable benefits for caregivers beyond more time to do things other than caregiving (Lawton and others, 1989; Miller, Gulle, and McCue, 1986; Montgomery, 1988). However, caregivers consistently report satisfaction with respite care services (Berry, Zarit, and Rabatin, 1991; Lawton and others, 1989). Some policy analysts have expressed disappointment that respite care does not alleviate caregiver burden in other ways, such as delaying institutionalization or reducing emotional distress. One might argue that respite care does what it intends to do—freeing time for care-

givers—and that it is unrealistic to expect a few hours of relief a week to have "spill over" effects into other dimensions of well-being. Moreover, most caregivers who receive respite care use the freed-up time to perform instrumental tasks (such as shopping or going to the doctor) rather than for recreation or relaxation (Berry and others, 1991). Thus, respite care is used for productive purposes.

Institutional and Terminal Care. When impaired older adults reach the point that intense levels of caregiving and/or professional medical management is needed, institutionalization is often required. Institutionalization is a "last resort" for caregivers (Morycz, 1985). Once the decision to institutionalize is made, other obstacles must be overcome. Family members often find it difficult to locate an acceptable nursing home and feel ill-equipped to evaluate the quality of institutional care. Many times impaired older adults must wait for a nursing home bed to become available (New York State Planning Commission, 1982), an increasing trend in states that have restricted the number of nursing home beds to control public expenditures on institutional care. Caregivers also must handle the guilt and regret that typically accompany the decision to institutionalize a loved one.

The cost of institutional care is of concern both to family members and to society more broadly. Tax dollars pay about 80 percent of the cost of institutional care in the United States, with Medicaid the primary form of reimbursement (Comptroller General of the United States, 1977). But Medicaid pays for care only for those in poverty. Many families delay or prevent institutionalization because of Medicaid rules that require individuals to "spend down" their assets until they are poor (Liu, Doty, and Manton, 1990). Medicaid spend-down rules are especially difficult for spouse caregivers who, in some states, must become paupers before their impaired spouses can obtain institutional care. These rules create "forced choice" situations in which either the needs of the impaired older adult or the financial needs of the spouse must be sacrificed. Financially advantaged impaired older persons fare better than their less advantaged peers. To use the analogy of airplane travel, those who can afford to pay for institutional care out-of-pocket can obtain "first class" institutional arrangements; those who must rely on public financing have "economy class" accommodations.

Terminal care often occurs in nursing homes, but it can take place in other settings as well. Many older persons are able to remain in the community until death or until shortly before death, at which point they are hospitalized. Hospice care provides a method of obtaining high-quality terminal care outside of a hospital or institution (Amenta, 1985). Third-party payers, including Medicare, are increasingly willing to reimburse hospice care. In addition to providing compassionate care for the terminally ill, many hospice programs provide counseling and services to family members.

Terminal care often imposes difficult decisions on caregivers. When the care recipient is severely impaired, family members must make decisions about use of life-sustaining technology, whether cardiac resuscitation should be attempted, and similar issues. These are difficult and painful decisions. Ideally, family members will have had conversations with their loved ones and thus be in a position to insure that the terminally ill person's wishes are followed. In some cases, the older person will have left a "living will" or advance directive to make his or her wishes known (Emanuel and Emanuel, 1989). More typically, however, these decisions are not made ahead of time, and the family is left with difficult decisions at a time when they are emotionally upset or drained.

Lifecare Communities. Increasing numbers of older adults live in lifecare communities, which offer a continuum of living arrangements and services. Initially, residents live in private dwellings where they care for themselves and live independently. When and if disability occurs, the community offers assisted living in which ADL impairments are compensated for by formal services (e.g., meal preparation, assistance with bathing). If a resident's level of impairment reaches the point that institutional placement is needed, such care is available in the lifecare community. In addition to a continuum of housing arrangements, most medical care is provided by the lifecare community, with hospitalization being the major exception.

Lifecare communities are affordable only to persons with substantial financial resources. In addition to monthly maintenance fees, residents typically must purchase their initial residences. These communities are frequently used by older individuals or couples without children or other close relatives. But many older persons who have children prefer to arrange for their own future needs, hoping to spare their children the responsibilities of caregiving as much as possible (Branch, 1987). Lifecare communities are based on a set of values and require levels of financial resources that are not suited to all older adults. However, they represent an increasingly popular method by which older adults anticipate their own needs and act to preclude family members from taking primary responsibility for their future care. Residents of lifecare communities continue to rely upon family and friends for emotional intimacy and social bonds, however.

The Interface Between Informal and Formal Services

In theory, the needs of most impaired older adults could best be met by an appropriate mix of services from informal and formal providers. Such a mix would help impaired older adults to retain as much independence as possible and to take advantage of caregivers' contributions without burdening them beyond healthful limits. Obviously the optimal mix of services would vary, depending upon the individual's ADL, physical, social, and psychological needs and resources. Research to date suggests that few impaired older adults and their family caregivers receive an optimal mix of formal and informal services (George, 1987; Litwak, 1985). The major impediment to obtaining this mix is the reluctance of many older people and their family caregivers to use formal services other than medical management (Nardone, 1990). Policy analysts have mistakenly made a different assumption—that if community-based services were available and affordable, family caregivers would reduce their levels of assistance and turn as much care as possible over to formal service providers.

If public policies are going to help impaired

Research to date suggests that few impaired older adults and their family caregivers receive an optimal mix of formal and informal services.

---

older adults to obtain appropriate mixes of formal and informal services, policy analysts must be made aware that caregivers continue their contributions when formal services are available. Research along these lines has examined three hypotheses about the ways that receipt of formal services is related to provision of care by family members. The first is referred to as the *substitution hypothesis*. It mirrors the fears of policy makers and suggests that increased use of formal services will reduce the contributions of informal providers (Bass and Noelker, 1987). The second hypothesis, called the *supplementation hypothesis*, predicts just the opposite—that caregivers will use formal services to supplement their own contributions and will be most likely to seek services that they are unable to provide (Bass and Noelker, 1987). The third hypothesis, referred to as the *linking hypothesis*, is a variant of the supplementation hypothesis and suggests that an important contribution of informal caregivers is to link their impaired older relatives with appropriate community services (George, 1987). Although the research base is small, most available evidence supports the supplementation hypothesis (Edelman and Hughes, 1990; Miller and McFall, 1991; Noelker and Bass, 1989; Penning, 1990). Family caregivers are reluctant to use formal services; when they do, they obtain help with tasks that they cannot perform or that are overwhelming in terms of the time required. Moreover, use of community services is associated with higher rather than lower levels of caregiver assistance (George, 1987; Stoller, 1989). Additional evidence supports the linking hypothesis: older persons who use community services are those with active networks of family caregivers who identify appropriate services and help their impaired relatives to access them (Chappell, 1985; Penning, 1990).

The topic here is caregiving; thus, the fate of older adults who lack family caregivers is tangential to this discussion. It is important to note, however, that impaired older adults without informal help enter institutions earlier than those who have family caregivers. Thus, community services obtained without additional help from family caregivers apparently do not delay institutional placement. This is a strong rationale for providing community services to impaired older adults with family caregivers; this is the only group for which

there can be realistic expectations of delayed institutionalization.

● OVERCOMING BARRIERS TO SERVICE USE

Reasons to encourage increased use of community services by family caregivers of impaired older adults are many. First, the burden borne by family caregivers is often high—so high that caregivers often push themselves beyond healthful limits. Second, if there is any realistic possibility of substituting less expensive community services for more expensive institutional care, those savings are most likely to be realized by providing services to impaired older adults with family caregivers. Third, although the knowledge base is small, mounting evidence indicates that use of community services can decrease caregiver burden and perhaps increase the functional capacity of impaired older adults.

Current low levels of service use reflect, in part, barriers that caregivers face in accessing services. These barriers can be overcome, although different barriers require different interventions. One barrier is *lack of information*. As noted previously, many caregivers do not define themselves as such and do not view community services as relevant to their needs. Public education has the greatest potential to overcome this barrier. Some public education can be targeted directly to caregivers. Public education also should be targeted at the family and friends of caregivers. Once sensitized to the risks of caregiving, friends and relatives can help to reduce caregivers' reluctance to use community services. Formal service providers also need to be proactive in recruiting caregivers as clients. Outreach is a critical component of effective service programs.

Financial barriers to using community services remain formidable. Most community services are not reimbursable under Medicare, Medicaid, and private health insurance, especially services designed to give respite to caregivers (as compared to services targeted toward improving the functioning of care receivers). As long as caregivers must pay the full cost of community services out of pocket, utilization rates will remain low and use will largely be restricted to the financially advantaged. In addition, many caregivers pay as little as possible for services, resulting in use of lower quality services. For example, most respite care programs utilize trained nurses aides as respite workers and have RNs or social workers who supervise the aides and develop care plans. To hire a "sitter" is usually much less expensive than to pay for agency-based respite care. But sitters may provide less adequate care than trained and supervised respite care workers. Advocacy efforts also are needed to apply pressure for increased third-party reimbursement for community services.

In addition to the obstacle posed by the absolute costs of community services, research suggests that caregivers are often more worried about future financial needs than about current financial strains. Caregivers are aware that their care recipients' needs for medical care (including institutionalization) may be greater in the future than at present. They also know that chronic conditions can continue for years. Thus, financial resources will be needed for the entire interval from disability onset to death of the care receiver. These are realistic concerns. Caregivers are, therefore, reluctant to invest *now* in services that would relieve their burdens. After all, those financial resources may be needed even more in the future. Service programs need to take into account not only the financial resources currently available to caregivers; they also need to be sensitive to caregivers' worries that financial resources will be exhausted before their caregiving careers are over. Many caregivers need to be convinced that use of community services is a worthwhile and cost-effective investment of their financial resources.

Psychological barriers are probably the greatest obstacles to appropriate use of community services. Those barriers take a variety of forms: the perception that no one can take care of a loved one as well as a family member; denial of caregiver burden, apparently used to sustain caregiving efforts; a "one day at a time" mentality that is useful for some purposes, but decreases long-term planning; and the perception that the care receiver will be uncomfortable with care providers who are not family members. Some of these psychological barriers are rooted in reality. For example, care receivers may be less comfortable being bathed or fed by an agency staff member than by their spouses or children. Nonetheless, it may be better to subject the care

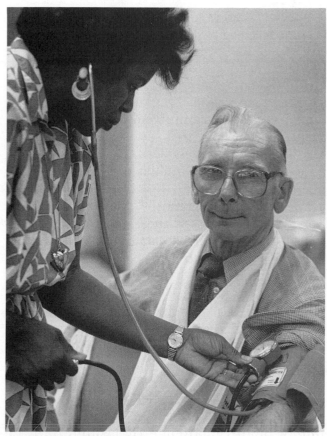

Many caregivers need to be convinced that use of community services is a worthwhile and cost-effective investment of their financial resources. (Courtesy of The National Council on the Aging, Inc./Jerry Hecht, photographer)

receiver to limited discomfort than to have the caregiver place his or her own health at risk. Both service providers and social support networks need to help caregivers to overcome psychological barriers to appropriate service use. Caregivers also need sustained encouragement to set appropriate boundaries on the levels of care they provide and to use appropriate services to the extent possible and practical. For example, caregivers may need to be reassured that a bad experience with one service provider does not mean that other programs should not be tried. Guilt and worry are often the dominant emotions of family caregivers. Supportive relatives and friends will help caregivers to keep those emotions from resulting in poor decisions about service use.

Some subgroups of caregivers face more obstacles to the use of community services than others. Because of the role that social support networks play in linking caregivers to services, socially isolated caregivers are disadvantaged.

Financial obstacles affect both low- and middle-income caregivers. For low-income families, paying for services may be impossible. In some communities, service programs are subsidized or free for low-income families, so caregivers should inquire about financial assistance. Middle-income caregivers also face problems, because they are ineligible for subsidized services and yet cannot pay the full costs of services out of pocket. Rural caregivers also face formidable obstacles because community services are less plentiful, and use of services involves significant transportation costs. Service programs need to be vigilant in identifying subgroups that face disproportionate barriers to service use and to help them overcome those barriers.

In summary, informal caregivers are the backbone of long-term care in the United States. They provide most of the care received by impaired older adults—and do so largely without assistance from service programs. Creating an environment in which family caregivers can provide the assistance that they clearly want to provide without excess risk to health and well-being is a public health challenge that should not be ignored.

References

Amenta, M. O. "Hospice in the United States: Multiple Programs and Varied Programs." *Nursing Clinic of North America* Vol. 20 (1985): 269–79.

Anthony-Bergstone, G. R., S. H. Zarit, and M. Gatz. "Symptoms of Psychological Distress Among Caregivers of Dementia Patients." *Psychology and Aging* Vol. 3 (1988): 245–48.

Apollini, T., and T. Cook. *A New Look at Guardianship.* Baltimore, MD: Paul H. Brookes, 1984.

Applebaum, R., and J. Christianson. "Using Case Management to Monitor Community-Based Long-Term Care." *Quarterly Research Bulletin* Vol. 14 (1988): 227–31.

Barusch, A. S., and W. M. Spaid. "Gender Differences in Caregiving: Why Do Wives Report Greater Burden?" *Gerontologist* Vol. 29 (1989): 667–76.

Bass, D. B., and L. S. Noelker. "The Influence of Family Caregivers on Elder's Use of In-Home Services." *Journal of Health and Social Behavior* Vol. 28 (1987): 184–96.

Bass, D. M., and K. Bowman. "The Transition from Caregiving to Bereavement: The Relationship of Care-Related Strain and Adjustment to Death." *Gerontologist* Vol. 30 (1990): 35–42.

Berry, G. L., S. H. Zarit, and V. X. Rabatin. "Caregiver Activity on Respite and Nonrespite Days: A Comparison of Two Service Approaches." *Gerontologist* Vol. 31 (1991): 830–35.

Bowers, B. J. "Family Perceptions of Care in a Nursing Home." *Gerontologist* Vol. 28 (1988): 361–68.

Branch, L. "Continuing Care Retirement Communities: Insuring for Long-Term Care." *Gerontologist* Vol. 27 (1987): 4–8.

Brody, E. M. "'Women in the Middle' and Family Help to Older People." *Gerontologist* Vol. 21 (1981): 471–80.

Cantor, M. "Strain Among Caregivers: A Study of Experience in the United States." *Gerontologist* Vol. 23 (1983): 597–604.

Caserta, M., D. Lund, S. Wright, and P. Redburn. "Caregivers to Dementia Patients: Use of Community Services." *Gerontologist* Vol. 27 (1987): 209–13.

Chappel, N. L. "Social Support and the Receipt of Home Care Services." *Gerontologist* Vol. 25 (1985): 47–54.

Clipp, E. C., and L. K. George. "Caregiver Needs and Patterns of Social Support." *Journal of Gerontology: Social Sciences* Vol. 45 (1990b): S102–S111.

——. "Psychotropic Drug Use Among Caregivers of Patients with Dementia." *Journal of the American Geriatrics Society* Vol. 38 (1990a): 227–35.

Cohen, D., and C. Eisdorfer. "Depression in Family Members Caring for a Relative with Alzheimer's Disease." *Journal of the American Geriatrics Society* Vol. 36 (1988): 885–89.

Colerick, E. J., and L. K. George. "Predictors of Institution-alization Among Caregivers of Alzheimer's Patients." *Journal of the American Geriatrics Society* Vol. 34 (1986): 493–98.

Comptroller General of the United States. *Home Health: The Need for a National Policy to Better Provide for the Elderly.* HRD78–79. Washington, DC: Government Printing Office, 1977.

Deimling, G. T., D. M. Bass, A. L. Townsend, and L. S. Noelker. "Care-Related Stress: A Comparison of Spouse and Adult Child Caregivers in Shared and Separate Households." *Journal of Aging and Health* Vol. 1 (1989): 67–82.

Edelman, P., and S. Hughes. "The Impact of Community Care on Provision of Informal Care to Homebound Elderly Persons." *Journal of Gerontology: Social Sciences* Vol. 45 (1990): S74–S84.

Emanuel, L. L., and E. J. Emanuel. "The Medical Directive: A New Comprehensive Advance Care Documentation." *Journal of the American Medical Association (JAMA)* Vol. 261 (1989): 3288–93.

Enright, R. B., Jr. "Time Spent Caregiving and Help Received by Spouses and Adult Children of Brain-Impaired Adults." *Gerontologist* Vol. 31 (1991): 375–83.

Farran, C. J., E. Keane-Hagerty, S. Salloway, S. Kupferer, and C. S. Wilken. "Finding Meaning: An Alternative Paradigm for Alzheimer's Disease Family Caregivers." *Gerontologist* Vol. 31 (1991): 483–89.

Fortinsky, R. H., and T. J. Hathaway. "Information and Service Needs Among Active and Former Family Caregivers of Persons with Alzheimer's Disease." *Gerontologist* Vol. 30 (1990): 604–9.

Gallagher, D., J. Rose, P. Rivera, S. Lovett, and L. W. Thompson. "Prevalence of Depression in Family Caregivers." *Gerontologist* Vol. 29 (1989): 449–56.

George, L. K. "Caregiver Burden: Conflict Between Norms of Reciprocity and Solidarity." In *Conflict and Abuse in Families of the Elderly: Theory, Research, and*

Intervention. Eds. K. Pillemer and R. Wolf. Boston, MA: Auburn House, 1986.

———. "Easing Caregiver Burden: The Role of Informal and Formal Supports." In *Health and Aging: Sociological Issues and Policy Directions.* Eds. R. A. Ward and S. S. Tobin. New York: Springer, 1987.

George, L. K., and L. P. Gwyther. "Caregiver Well-Being: A Multidimensional Examination of Family Caregivers of Demented Adults." *Gerontologist* Vol. 26 (1986): 253–59.

———. "The Dynamics of Caregiver Burden: Changes in Caregiver Well-Being Over Time" (abstract). *Gerontologist* Vol. 24 (1984): 249.

———. "Support Groups for Caregivers of Memory-Impaired Elderly: Easing Caregiver Burden." In *Families in Transition: Primary Prevention Programs That Work.* Eds. L. A. Bond and B. M. Wagner. Beverly Hills: Sage, 1988.

Greene, V. L., and D. J. Monahan. "The Effect of a Professionally Guided Caregiver Support and Education Group on Institutionalization of Care Receivers." *Gerontologist* Vol. 27 (1987): 716–21.

———. "The Effect of a Support and Education Program on Stress and Burden Among Family Caregivers to Frail Elderly Persons." *Gerontologist* Vol. 29 (1989): 472–77.

Haley, W. E., S. L. Brown, and E. G. Levine. "Experimental Evaluation of the Effectiveness of Group Intervention for Dementia Caregivers." *Gerontologist* Vol. 27 (1987): 376–82.

Haley, W. E., E. G. Levine, S. L. Brown, and A. A. Bartolucci. "Stress, Appraisal, Coping, and Social Support as Predictors of Adaptational Outcome Among Dementia Caregivers." *Psychology and Aging* Vol. 2 (1987): 23–30.

Horowitz, A. "Sons and Daughters as Caregivers to Older Parents: Differences in Role Performance and Consequences." *Gerontologist* Vol. 25 (1985): 612–18.

Jones, D. A., and N. J. Vetter. "A Survey of Those Who Care for the Elderly at Home: Their Problems and Their Needs." *Social Science and Medicine* Vol. 19 (1984): 511–14.

Katz, S., A. B. Ford, R. W. Moskowitz, B. A. Jackson, and M. W. Jaffe. "The Index of ADL: A Standardized Measure of Biological and Psychosocial Function." *Journal of the American Medical Association* Vol. 185 (1963): 94–99.

Kiecolt-Glaser, J. K., R. Glaser, E. C. Shuttleworth, C. S. Dyer, P. Ogrocki, and C. E. Speicher. "Chronic Stress and Immunity in Family Caregivers of Alzheimer's Disease Victims." *Psychosomatic Medicine* Vol. 49 (1987): 525–35.

Kinney, J. M., and M. A. Stephens. "Hassles and Uplifts of Giving Care to a Family Member with Dementia." *Psychology and Aging* Vol. 4 (1989): 402–8.

Knight, B. G., and P. M. Carter. "Reduction of Psychiatric Inpatient Stay for Older Adults by Intensive Case Management." *Gerontologist* Vol. 30 (1990): 510–15.

Lawton, M. P., and E. M. Brody. "Assessment of Older People: Self-Maintaining and Instrumental Activities of Daily Living." *Gerontologist* Vol. 9 (1969): 179–86.

Lawton, M. P., E. M. Brody, and A. R. Saperstein. "A Controlled Study of Respite Services for Caregivers of Alzheimer's Patients." *Gerontologist* Vol. 29 (1989): 8–16.

Liang, J., and E. S. Tu. "Estimating Lifetime Risk of Nursing Home Residency: A Further Note." *Gerontologist* Vol. 26 (1986): 560–63.

Litvin, S. J. "Status Transitions and Future Outlook as Determinants of Conflict: The Caregiver's and Care Receiver's Perspective." *Gerontologist* Vol. 32 (1992): 68–76.

Litwak, E. *Helping the Elderly: The Complementary Roles of Informal Networks and Formal Systems.* New York: Guilford, 1985.

Liu, K., P. Doty, and K. Manton. "Medicaid Spenddown in Nursing Homes." *Gerontologist* Vol. 30 (1990): 7–15.

Liu, K., K. Manton, and B. M. Liu. "Home Care Expenses for the Disabled Elderly." *Health Care Financing Review* Vol. 7 (1985): 51–58.

McConnel, C. E. "A Note on the Lifetime Risk of Nursing Home Residence." *Gerontologist* Vol. 24 (1984): 193–98.

Matthews, S., J. Werkner, and P. Delaney. "Relative Contributions of Help by Employed and Nonemployed Sisters to Their Elderly Parents." *Journal of Gerontology: Social Sciences* Vol. 44 (1989): S36–S44.

Miller, B., and S. McFall. "The Effect of Caregiver Burden on Changes in the Frail Person's Use of Formal Helpers." *Journal of Health and Social Behavior* Vol. 32 (1991): 165–79.

Miller, D. G., N. Gulle, and F. McCure. "The Realities of Respite for Families, Clients, and Sponsors." *Gerontologist* Vol. 26 (1986): 467–70.

Montenko, A. K. "The Frustrations, Gratifications, and Well-Being of Dementia Caregivers. *Gerontologist* Vol. 29 (1989): 166–72.

Montgomery, R. "Respite Care: Lessons From a Controlled Design Study." *Health Care Financing Review* Vol. 10 (1988): 133–38.

Moritz, D. J., S. V. Kasl, and L. F. Berkman. "The Health Impact of Living with a Cognitively Impaired Elderly Spouse: Depressive Symptoms and Social Functioning." *Journal of Gerontology: Social Sciences* Vol. 44 (1989): S17–S27.

Morycz, R. K. "Caregiving Strain and the Desire to Institutionalize Family Members with Alzheimer's Disease." *Research on Aging* Vol. 7 (1985): 329–61.

Nardone, M. "Characteristics Predicting Community Care for Mentally Impaired Older Persons." *Gerontologist* Vol. 20 (1980): 661–68.

New York State Health Planning Commission. *Patients Waiting for Alternate Care: Issues and Recommendations.* Albany, NY: New York State Health Planning Commission, 1982.

Newman, S. J., R. Struyk, P. Wright, and Michelle Rice. "Overwhelming Odds: Caregiving and the Risk of Institutionalization." *Journal of Gerontology: Social Sciences* Vol. 45 (1990): S173–S183.

Noelker, L. S., and D. M. Bass. "Home Care for Elderly Persons: Linkages Between Formal and Informal Caregivers." *Journal of Gerontology: Social Sciences* Vol. 44 (1989): S63–S70.

Penning, M. "Receipt of Assistance by Elderly People: Hierarchical Selection and Task Specificity." *Gerontologist* Vol. 30 (1990): 220–27.

Pratt, C. C., L. L. Jones, H. Y. Shin, and A. J. Walker. "Autonomy and Decision-Making Between Single Older Women and Their Caregiving Daughters." *Gerontologist* Vol. 29 (1989): 792–97.

Pruchno, R. A., M. H. Kleban, J. E. Michaels, and N. P. Dempsey. "Mental and Physical Health of Caregiving Spouses: Development of a Causal Model." *Journal of Gerontology: Psychological Sciences* Vol. 45 (1990): P192–P199.

Quinn, M., and S. Tomata. *Elder Abuse and Neglect.* New York: Springer, 1986.

Scharlach, A. E. "A Comparison of Employed Caregivers of Cognitively-Impaired and Physically-Impaired Elderly Persons." *Research on Aging* Vol. 11 (1989): 225–43.

Schoonover, C. B., E. M. Brody, C. Hoffman, and M. H. Kleban. "Parent Care and Geographically Distant Children." *Research on Aging* Vol. 10 (1988): 472–92.

Schulz, R., C. A. Tompkins, D. Wood, and S. Decker. "The Social Psychology of Caregiving: Physical and Psychological Costs to Providing Support to the Disabled." *Journal of Applied Social Psychology* Vol. 17 (1987): 401–28.

Schulz, R., P. Visintainer, and G. M. Williamson. "Psychiatric and Physical Morbidity Effects of Caregiving." *Journal of Gerontology: Psychological Sciences* Vol. 45 (1990): P181–P191.

Schwartz-Borden, G. "Grief Work: Prevention and Intervention." *Social Casework* Vol. 67 (1986): 499–505.

Seltzer, M. M., J. Irvy, and L. C. Litchfield. "Family Members as Case Managers: Partnership Between the Formal and Informal Support Networks." *Gerontologist* Vol. 27 (1987): 722–28.

Shanas, E. "The Family as a Social Support System in Old Age." *Gerontologist* Vol. 19 (1979): 169–74.

Soldo, B., and J. Myelyluoma. "Caregivers Who Live with Dependent Elderly." *Gerontologist* Vol. 23 (1983): 607–11.

Stephens, M. A. P., J. M. Kinney, and P. K. Ogrocki. "Stressors and Well-Being Among Caregivers to Older Adults with Dementia: The In-Home Versus Nursing Home Experience." *Gerontologist* Vol. 31 (1991): 217–23.

Stoller, E. "Exchange Patterns in the Informal Networks of the Elderly: The Impact on Morale." *Journal of Marriage and the Family* Vol. 47 (1985): 851–57.

Stoller, E. P. "Formal Services and Informal Helping: The Myth of Service Substitution." *Journal of Applied Gerontology* Vol. 8 (1989): 37–52.

Stoller, E. P., and Pugliesi. "Other Roles of Caregivers: Competing Responsibilities or Supportive Resources?" *Journal of Gerontology: Social Sciences* Vol. 44 (1989): S231–S238.

Stone, R., G. Cafferata, and Sangl. "Caregivers of the Frail Elderly: A National Profile." *Gerontologist* Vol. 27 (1987): 616–26.

Stone, R. I., and C. M. Murtaugh. "The Elderly Population with Chronic Functional Disability: Implications for Home Care Eligibility." *Gerontologist* Vol. 30 (1990): 491–96.

Strawbridge, W. J., and M. I. Wallhagen. "Impact of Family Conflict on Adult Child Caregivers." *Gerontologist* Vol. 31 (1991): 770–77.

Tennstedt, S., J. McKinlay, and L. Sullivan. "Informal Care for Frail Elders: The Role of Secondary Caregivers." *Gerontologist* Vol. 29 (1989): 677–83.

Toseland, R. W., and C. M. Rossiter. "Group Interventions to Support Family Caregivers: A Review and Analysis." *Gerontologist* Vol. 29 (1989): 438–48.

Whitlach, C. J., S. H. Zarit, and A. von Eye. "Efficacy of Interventions with Caregivers: A Reanalysis." *Gerontologist* Vol. 31 (1991): 9–14.

Zarit, S. H., P. A. Todd, and J. M. Zarit. "Subjective Burden of Husbands and Wives as Caregivers: A Longitudinal Study." *Gerontologist* Vol. 26 (1986): 260–66.

Additional Reading

Ball, Jane A. *Have I Done All I Can?* Buffalo, NY: Prometheus Books, 1992.

Brown, Dorothy S. *Handle With Care: A Question of Alzheimer's.* Buffalo, NY: Prometheus Books, 1992.

Chapman, Elwood N. *The Unfinished Business of Living: Helping Aging Parents Help Themselves.* Los Altos, CA: Crisp Publications, 1988.

Douglass, Richard L. *Domestic Mistreatment of the Elderly.* Washington, DC: American Association of Retired Persons, Criminal Justice Services, 1987.

Edinberg, Mark A. *Talking With Your Aging Parents.* Boston, MA: Shambhala Publications, 1987.

Greenberg, Vivian E. *Your Best Is Good Enough: Aging Parents and Your Emotions.* Lexington, MA: Lexington Books, 1989.

Hooyman, Nancy R., and Wendy Lustbader. *Taking Care: Supporting Older People and Their Families.* New York: Free Press, 1986.

Horne, Jo. *Caregiving: Helping an Aging Loved One.* Washington, DC: American Association of Retired Persons and Scott, Foresman, 1985.

How to Hire Helpers: A Guide for Elders and Their Families. Seattle, WA: Church Council of Greater Seattle, 1988.

Jarvik, Lissy, and Gary Small. *Parentcare: A Commonsense Guide for Adult Children.* New York: Crown Publishers, 1988.

Kenny, James, and Stephen Spicer. *Eldercare: Coping With Late-Life Crisis.* Buffalo, NY: Prometheus Books, 1992.

Kouri, Mary. *Keys to Survival for Caregivers.* Hauppauge, NY: Barron's, 1992.

Lustbader, Wendy. *Counting on Kindness: The Dilemmas of Dependency.* New York: Macmillan, 1991.

Mace, Nancy L., and Peter V. Rabins. *The Thirty-six Hour Day: A Family Guide to Caring for Persons with Alzheimer's Disease, Related Dementing Illness, and Memory Loss in Later Life.* New York: Warner Books, 1989.

Miles Away and Still Caring: A Guide for Long-Distance Caregivers. Washington, DC: American Association of Retired Persons, 1986.

Norris, Jane, ed. *Daughters of the Elderly: Building Partnerships in Caregiving.* Bloomington: Indiana University Press, 1988.

Shapiro, Barbara A. *The Big Squeeze: Balancing the Needs of Aging Parents, Dependent Children, and You.* Bedford, MA: Mills & Sanderson, 1991.

Shelley, Florence D. *When Your Parents Grow Old.* New York: Harper & Row, 1988.

Silverstone, Barbara, and Helen K. Hyman. *You and Your Aging Parent: The Modern Family's Guide to Emotional, Physical, and Financial Problems.* 3d ed. New York: Pantheon Books, 1989.

Sommers, Tish, and Laurie Shields. *Women Take Care: The Consequences of Caregiving in Today's Society.* Gainesville, FL: Triad Publishing Co., 1987.

Steinmeta, Suzanne K. *Duty Bound: Elder Abuse and Family Care.* Newbury Park, CA: Sage Publications, 1988.

Stephens, Susan A., and Jon B. Christianson. *Informal Care of the Elderly.* New York: Lexington Books, 1986.

Stone, Robyn. *Exploding the Myths: Caregiving in America; A Study.* Washington, DC: U.S. Congress, House Select Committee on Aging, 1987.

Tomb, David A. *Growing Old: A Handbook for You and Your Aging Parent.* New York: Viking, 1984.

Linda K. George, Ph.D.

29

Long-Term Care

- Public Policy and Historical Perspectives • Issues in Financing Health Care
- Long-Term Care as Part of the Health Care System • Institutional Long-Term Care
- Clinical Challenges in Long-Term Care • Long-Term Care Reforms
- Family Issues in Nursing Home Placement

*Many older adults cannot examine the subject of long-term care without emotion. The very idea of loss of independence and of being a burden on family members or others produces extreme anxiety. It is easier to envision death at the end of a long, active life than to consider a prolonged state of dependency. Some concerns, however, probably relate to the almost constant state of flux in which long-term care operates. This chapter examines historical perspectives and public policy influences on long-term care. It outlines the different types of long-term care available and the characteristics of providers and consumers of long-term care. The chapter also addresses financing of long-term care, the clinical challenges that exist in long-term care, and reforms recently implemented by the long-term care industry. Chapter 27, **Making Medical Care Decisions**, may also be consulted since it discusses some of the issues involved in a decision to place a loved one in long-term care.*

● PUBLIC POLICY AND HISTORICAL PERSPECTIVES

Since the turn of the century, public policy concerning older adults has been in a state of evolution. Current policy has resulted from major changes in the demographics of the population, changes in expectations for health care, struggles over the financing of health care, and exploration of alternatives to traditional health care systems.

Some observers have described these policies as "reactive," in contrast to policies planned in a proactive fashion to provide services along an expected continuum of needs.

Demographic shifts (see Chapter 2, **Growth, Distribution, and Characteristics of the Older Adult Population in the United States**) have been responsible for major reactive changes in health care policy. The most obvious change was caused by the large post-World War II increase in birth rate, resulting in the "baby boom." At about the same time, the nation began to experience a dramatic reduction in death rate, mainly as a result of improved survival from cardiovascular diseases. This survival trend resulted in a marked increase in the proportion of elderly people in the population. Improved survival also resulted in an increased proportion of the chronically disabled. Currently, the relative proportion of elderly people is larger than ever before. This phenomenon will continue until the middle of the twenty-first century. Since the period of the baby boom, the country has not experienced similar growth in the proportion of younger people in the population.

The customary retirement age of 65 has had major implications for health care policy. The tra-

---

It is easier to envision death at the end of a long, active life than to consider a prolonged state of dependency.

Table 29.1
Nursing Home Patient Mix by Type of Payer

| | Percentage of Set-up Beds Occupied by Patients Covered by | | | |
Type of owner	Medicare	Medicaid	Private pay/ private insurance	Veterans Administration
Government	6.2%	70.1%	25.0%	6.4%
Church-related	2.4	44.9	52.9	11.5
Secular not-for-profit	4.9	53.0	45.5	1.2
For-profit	6.1	64.7	29.5	2.7
Size (licensed beds)				
50–100 beds	5.4	61.2	38.0	3.3
101–150 beds	6.1	58.1	33.0	3.0
151–200 beds	5.5	64.7	28.8	2.9
201+ beds	6.2	65.8	22.6	1.3
Age of NH				
Under 5 years	5.6	60.6	28.2	2.5
5–10 years	9.2	67.6	24.3	1.7
11–15 years	5.9	64.3	33.2	3.4
16+ years	5.3	60.0	36.5	3.3
Overall avg.	**5.7%**	**61.1%**	**34.5%**	**3.0%**

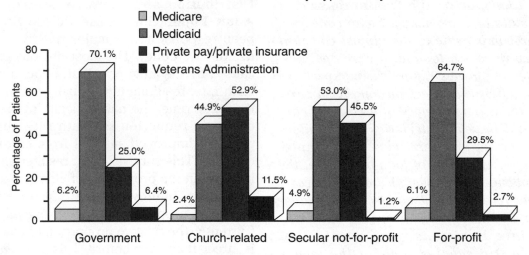

Nursing Home Patient Mix by Type of Payer

Note: In 1991, 61.1 percent of set-up beds in nursing homes were occupied by patients covered by Medicaid.

Source: Marion Merrell Dow. *Managed Care Digest: Long-Term Care Edition.* Kansas City, MO: Marion Merrell Dow, 1992.

ditional retirement age was tied to Social Security legislation and was appropriate during an earlier time when decline in health was more common in people reaching this age. The relatively long post-retirement life expectancy of most Americans has resulted in major societal and financial concerns for individuals and for the nation. Retirement benefits and pensions, as well as health care bud-

gets, may be inadequate to meet the needs of the elderly. Today's married older person can expect to remain part of a couple for a longer period of time after retirement and to depend on spouse and adult children for the bulk of care for chronic illness or disability. Profound changes in the family structure complicate these expected caregiving roles. Adult daughters, the traditional care-

Figure 29.1
Projected Nursing Home Expenditures for People Age 65+, by Source of Payment:
1990–2020

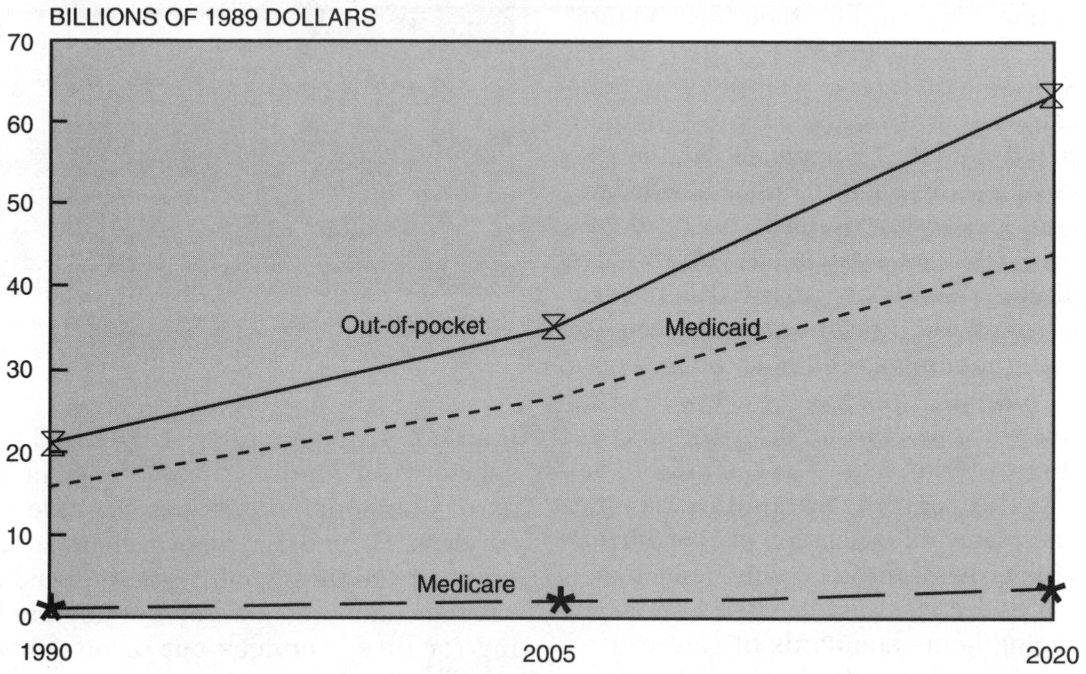

BILLIONS OF 1989 DOLLARS

Source: Brookings/OCF Long-Term Care Financing Model, *Aging America: Trends and Projections, 1991 Edition.*

givers for their parents, are no longer likely to be part of a nuclear family and are very likely to be in the work force. Because of decisions to delay childbearing, these women are often raising children at the time of their parents' greatest needs. Analysis of death certificates reveals that older people today are more likely to use institutional long-term care and to die in hospitals or nursing homes than ever before.

Today's elderly have experienced an astounding transition of the health care system during their lifetimes. During their formative years, many of these people received all their health care from a single practitioner. Much of the care was delivered outside hospital settings, most often in the home. Usually family members or friends carried out the care; and sophisticated technology was not involved. The availability of technology, the increase of medical specialization, changes in standards of care, and the complexity of Medicare paperwork have made interactions with the health care system perplexing for many older adults.

Services have moved away from a single provider system to a more disjointed series of acute health interventions, provided in a variety of settings by a large variety of practitioners. Partly because of the rapidity of changes in health care, the elderly may face some barriers in access to optimal care. Many older adults have an overwhelming fear of technology. This fear may be due in part to sensory impairment, such as hearing or vision loss, which impairs understanding of equipment or procedures and may limit an older person's participation in decision making. A person with intellectual impairment may have additional problems. Older adults may fear that technology will be used inappropriately to extend life when there is not much hope for recovery from dependency.

Another fear of many older adults is that they cannot pay for optimal medical care. Medicare has definite limits and bounds on the goods and services it covers (see Chapter 25, **Health Care Services**). Because of their financial barriers, older patients may not obtain eyeglasses, hearing aids, or dentures—necessary but relatively high cost items that Medicare does not cover. Older patients with Medicare as their only health insurance may be severely limited in their choice of physicians, since some physicians choose not to participate in the program. Medicare recipients may feel that they are being given second-rate medical treatment in return for their "second-rate" payment for medical services (Lyles, 1989). Sometimes older adults are very surprised to learn that Medicare covers institutional long-term care in only a small number of instances and is also limited in coverage of long-term home health care.

Throughout U.S. history publicly financed care of the elderly has been associated with the care of the destitute. This is particularly true of long-term care, where the historical precedent for today's nursing home was the alms house (poor house) of colonial America. The 1935 Social Security Act signified the birth of the nursing home industry. For the first time, older Americans had a guaranteed monthly income. Medicare and Medicaid legislation in 1965 further stimulated the growth of the nursing home industry. However, the concomitant legislative enactment of nursing home standards of care caused many small and substandard homes to close. Larger homes became the norm, and today most nursing homes are run as commercial enterprises.

Currently, support for long-term care for the elderly is provided under Titles XVIII, XIX, and XX of the Social Security Act and Title III of the Older Americans Act. The majority of public funding comes from Medicaid, a welfare program that supports care for the indigent. In 1991, Medicaid paid for the care of about 61 percent of patients in nursing homes (Marion, 1992). Medicaid is authorized under Title XIX of the Social Security Act and is jointly operated by federal and state governments. Consequently, the Medicaid program varies considerably from state to state. Federal guidelines, however, set

The majority of public funding comes from Medicaid, a welfare program that supports care for the indigent. (Copyright © Marianne Gontarz)

the minimum standards of care and mandatory services for Medicaid recipients in long-term care. Individual states may provide additional services. Many older Americans residing in long-term care settings qualify for Medicaid after they have accumulated a burden of poverty from paying for these services out of pocket for themselves. The Medicaid program spends a small proportion of its budget for long-term home health care.

● ISSUES IN FINANCING HEALTH CARE

Fiscal concerns have resulted in major dilemmas in health care for the elderly. Because the majority of health care dollars for medical care of older people comes from public funds, and because of the steady growth of expenditures for Medicare since the program's inception, control of these costs has become an important national concern. A closer look at Medicare expenditures reveals that their growth is due to several factors. A large part of total expenditure covers care for individuals in the last year of life. This expense is explained by increasing use of available technology and inherent labor costs associated with the technology. Often health care planners do not have clear information on the exact benefits of such technology; certainly patients have even less clear information on the personal benefits of technology. Physicians frequently employ technologies because they are easily available. Widespread public awareness of technology, such as the progress in organ transplantation seen on the nightly news, has fostered the belief that virtually any health problem should have a techno-

Nursing Home Facts

The nation's thirty largest nursing home chains operated 3,178 of the 15,324 nursing homes in operation during 1991. These chains accounted for 20.7 percent of all nursing homes and 367,732 licensed beds, or 22.6 percent of the nation's largest nursing home chains are ranked by the number of licensed beds.

logic "fix." This somewhat unrealistic view has equated the use of multiple technologies with the usual and customary standard of care, without regard to the actual benefit of such care for the frail elderly or dying patient.

Health planners have considered many mechanisms for more efficient financing of health care for the elderly. Suggested methods to control costs include reduction in the number, intensity, or duration of covered services (rationing). Another mechanism is to control payments to hospitals, long-term care facilities, and practitioners by establishing a fixed payment schedule, which is used regardless of actual costs or charges by providers. A third way to reduce costs is to impose a "needs test" on potential Medicare recipients, so that public funds would cover only those who could not cover their own expenses. Ways of increasing funds to pay for medical care include a higher rate of taxation on wages and the requirement of a larger co-payment for covered services by the recipients. Some of these methods are operative now. Especially since the advent of prospective payment to hospitals for the care of Medicare recipients, under diagnostic related groupings (DRGs), hospital stays have grown shorter. With patients discharged "quicker and sicker," long-term care facilities have experienced increased utilization and occupancy.

Attempts to control costs have resulted in the development of alternative health care systems. The best known is the health maintenance organization (HMO). Members of an HMO pay a set fee to receive all their health care from a selected group of providers. The care provided usually includes preventive services, often those that are not well reimbursed by commercial or government health insurance. Examples of covered services are well baby checkups, vaccinations, and routine Pap smears to screen for cervical cancer. Some HMOs do not open their enrollment to older adults, partly because of the increased consumption of services by this group, especially by the frail elderly. Recently some HMOs have been enrolling Medicare recipients in an attempt to see if they can provide services more efficiently to this group of patients. Social health maintenance organizations (SHMOs) are a type of HMO where a case management approach is used. Here a case manager acts as a broker for the patient, by determining the patient's needs for services, and by

contracting for the services to be provided in a cost effective manner.

● LONG-TERM CARE AS PART OF THE HEALTH CARE SYSTEM

Long-term care is best described as personal care and supervision on a continuing basis over time. Ideally it should be concerned with the preservation of an individual's maximum level of functioning. The distinction between acute care and long-term care is a source of confusion for patients and physicians, especially if a patient enters the long-term care system after a long hospital stay. The goals of hospital care include accurate diagnosis and treatment of acute conditions. The goals of long-term care include rehabilitation, restoration and maintenance of function, and supportive care when there is limited prospect for improving function. When discussing long-term care for the elderly, it is imperative to remember that the vast majority of such care occurs outside nursing homes. Most long-term care is non-institutional, informal, unpaid, and provided by family and friends. Community-based home health services are another large source of non-institutional long-term care. Only about 5 percent of older Americans over age 65 live in nursing homes (J.A. Brody, 1985). The lifetime risk for an individual's use of a nursing home was thought to be about 25 percent (E.M. Brody, 1985); but estimates based on the 1982–84 National Long-Term Care Survey suggest that the risk is over 40 percent (Murtaugh, 1990). Projections on the numbers of persons over 65 who will likely need long-term care show a steep rise from 1980 to 2040 (Manton and Soldo, 1985).

There are two distinct types of nursing home residents: residents who require a short period of care and those who require a long period. The short stay group is composed of patients with terminal illness, those who are medically unstable, and those who will require a period of convalescence or rehabilitation in preparation to return home. The long stay group is composed of those with chronic, relatively stable medical conditions, those with intellectual impairments (mainly dementia), and those with both. Most nursing home stays are less than three months, with about 40 percent lasting less than one month. About 20 percent of all stays exceed two years

When discussing long-term care for the elderly, it is imperative to remember that the vast majority of such care occurs outside nursing homes. (Copyright © Marianne Gontarz)

(Marion, 1992). In 1991, about 35 percent of patients in nursing homes had their stays paid by private insurance or out of pocket. The Veterans Administration (VA) covered about 3 percent of stays, Medicare about 6 percent, and Medicaid about 60 percent (Marion, 1992).

The most common situations in which Medicare will cover nursing home expenses are for a limited number of days following hospitalization, usually for a condition where skilled nursing care is expected to produce a measurable benefit. Examples include rehabilitation following a hip fracture, stroke, or amputation. Complex nursing care such as tube feeding or surgical dressing is another example. Long-term care under Medicare is often time-limited, with complete coverage of the first twenty days and the requirement for a substantial co-payment from the patient for days twenty-one through one hundred. Medicare will also cover some skilled nursing care for the terminally ill under a Medicare Hospice benefit. Medicare patient reim-

bursement to long-term care facilities is inclusive for room and board, supplies, and durable medical equipment. When the nursing home stay is no longer covered under Medicare, the patient may pay out of pocket or, if impoverished, have the remainder of long-term care funded by Medicaid. Medicaid patients in long-term care facilities adhere to some of the same limitations as non-institutionalized Medicaid patients. Some of these limitations include control over numbers and types of medications.

In 1991, about 35 percent of patients in nursing homes had their stays paid by private insurance or out of pocket. The Veterans Administration covered about 3 percent of stays, Medicare about 6 percent, and Medicaid about 60 percent.

As mentioned earlier, the Veterans Administration provides a small amount (about 3 percent) of long-term care. This is primarily provided for veterans whose care needs are related to service-connected illness or disability. The care may be provided in a VA-extended care facility (ECF) or a VA-skilled nursing facility (SNF). In areas of the country where VA nursing home beds are unavailable, the VA may contract with other facilities to provide long-term care for a veteran.

● **INSTITUTIONAL LONG-TERM CARE**

Institutional long-term care is a very large part of the U.S. health care system. At the time of the 1985 National Nursing Home Survey (DHHS, 1989), there were about 19,000 nursing homes in the United States, with a capacity of about 1.6 million beds, a capacity larger than that of acute care hospitals. The number of nursing home beds was estimated to be 1.65 million in 1990, and 1.63 million in 1991 (Marion, 1992). Nursing home beds are fully utilized with an overall occupancy rate of about 95 percent, with the highest occupancy being in church-related homes. More than half of all nursing homes are Medicare-certified. Most American nursing homes are proprietary for-profit homes; chain ownership is the rule. Beverly Enterprises and Hillhaven Corporation

Figure 29.2
People Age 65+ in Need of Long-Term Care: 1980–2040

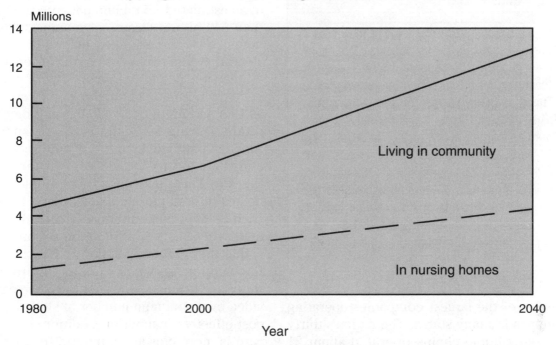

Source: Manton and Soldo. "Dynamics of Health Changes in the Oldest Old: New Perspectives and Evidence." *Milbank Memorial Fund Quarterly* Vol. 63, no. 2 (Spring 1985). Also published in *Aging America: Trends and Projections, 1991 Edition.*

Figure 29.3
The Aging Veteran Population: 1980–2040

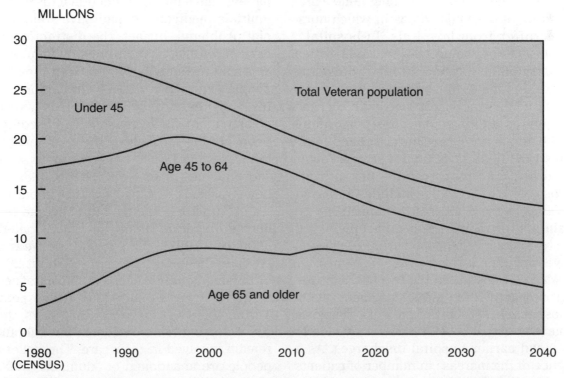

Source: Dept. of Veterans Affairs, 1990. Published in *Aging America: Trends and Projections, 1991 Edition.*

Nursing Home Facts

Ten states account for 52 percent of the nation's beds. Nursing homes in the ten leading states contained more than 50,000 beds per state. These ten states accounted for 52 percent of all nursing home beds. Three of these states reported more than 100,000 beds each. They were California, with 1,191 nursing homes and 116,032 beds; Illinois, with 936 nursing homes and 108,015 beds; and Texas, with 1,113 nursing homes and 118,586 beds. States having more than 80 nursing home beds per 1,000 people over the age of 65 included Indiana (82.7), Kansas (83.1), Oklahoma (80.3), and Wisconsin (86.3) (SMG Marketing Group, Inc., 1992).

are examples of the largest companies operating nursing homes in many states. The nation's thirty largest nursing home chains operated about 21 percent of homes and 23 percent of licensed beds in 1991 (Marion, 1992).

Staffing patterns in nursing homes vary widely and are the predominant factor in determining profits. The clear effects of staffing ratios on the quality of patient care have not been established in any well designed study of nursing home care. Staffing is one of the major areas in which nursing homes differ from hospitals. In hospitals, staffing is heavier on the professional side, with a larger proportion of registered nurses providing routine care. In long-term care, registered nurses often function in a supervisory role, with licensed practical nurses and nursing aides performing most of the hands-on care. Church-related nursing homes have less staff turnover, use fewer agency nurses, and tend to have better staff ratios. Possible explanations include increased funds available from church philanthropy to cover salaries, programs, and non-reimbursed patient care, and a more focused sense of mission in employees of church-related nursing homes.

When Medicare instituted the use of diagnostic related groupings (DRGs), a fixed payment schedule for hospitals based on the patient's diagnosis rather than the actual cost of care, many elderly patients faced earlier hospital discharges. As a consequence of the increase in number of patients needing convalescent care, nursing homes have become a more strategic part of the health care system. In spite of their importance, their service to an estimated 1.5 million patients and their more than $40 billion direct costs since 1985, nursing homes have experienced unique disadvantages. Two important examples are the absence of hospital technology and the limitations of staffing. The patients in American nursing homes are often just as sick and more dependent than patients in hospitals. During 1991 almost all (97 percent) of American nursing homes provided social services, and the majority (91 percent) offered physical therapy. Very few (about 7 percent) of nursing homes offered more complex medical treatments such as hyperalimentation (artificial feeding) or hemodialysis. The expectation of nursing homes is that they can provide comprehensive care with few support services such as laboratories and X-ray departments, and that this care can be provided by a minimum number of skilled nurses in a cost-effective manner. In addition, nursing home care is more closely monitored by governmental agencies.

About two-thirds of patients admitted to nursing homes are transferred there from acute care hospitals. Increasing numbers of patients with terminal illness are being shifted from hospitals to nursing homes. Most long-stay nursing home patients have multiple functional disabilities, take multiple medications, and have some psychosocial problems. In fact, the distinction of acute care and long-term care has become somewhat artificial, especially for the frail elderly. These people experience frequent transitions from one level of needs to another, often without any clearly identifiable reason. When compared to people of the same age in the community, nursing home residents use twice as many acute care (hospital-based) services (DHHS, 1989). Nursing home discharge data reveal that about one-quarter of nursing home patients become functional enough to return home, and about one-third die (Marion, 1992). The remainder experience repeated hospital admissions. About 20 percent of nursing home residents are hospitalized during their first year of nursing home residence. Throughout their long-term care stays, the majority of nursing home residents have families who remain involved in their care. The belief that old people are abandoned or "dumped" into nursing homes is a myth in most cases.

Table 29.2
The Nation's Largest Nursing Home Chains

Chain/headquarters	Tax Status	Total NHs[1]	Total Lic. Beds[1]	Avg Beds/NH	# of States
Beverly Enterprises, Fort Smith, AR	FP	832	88,575	106.5	40
Hillhaven Corp., Tacoma, WA	FP	367	45,066	122.8	38
ARA Living Centers, Houston, TX	FP	212	24,645	116.3	10
Manor Healthcare Inc., Silver Spring, MD	FP	163	22,551	138.4	28
National Heritage, Dallas, TX	FP	163	17,685	108.5	25
Life Care Centers of America, Cleveland, TN	FP	130	17,441	134.2	26
Health Care & Ret. Corp. (HCR Corp.), Toledo, OH	FP	137	16,954	123.8	20
Evangelical/Good Samaritan Society, North Sioux Falls, SD	NFP	184	15,163	82.4	26
Unicare Health Facilities, Milwaukee, WI	FP	131	14,885	113.6	17
Texas Health Enterprises Inc., Denton, TX	FP	88	10,308	117.1	4
National HealthCorp., Murfreesboro, TN	FP	78	9,349	119.9	11
Meritcare, Pittsburgh, PA	FP	57[2]	5,853	102.7	11
Horizon Healthcare Corp., Albuquerque, NM	FP	52	5,708	109.8	11
Diversified Health Services, Plymouth Meeting, PA	FP	24	5,595	233.1	4
Meridian Healthcare, Towson, MD	FP	38	5,432	143.0	6
Genesis Health Ventures Inc., Kennett Square, PA	FP	39	5,160	132.3	8
Carmelite Sisters Aged & Infirmed, Naperville, IL	NFP	25	5,057	202.3	10
GranCare Inc., Culver City, CA	FP	33	4,827	146.3	6
Care Enterprises, Tustin, CA	FP	44	4,631	105.3	3
Meadowbrook Healthcare Services, Clemmons, NC	FP	36	4,555	126.5	4
Brian Center Management Corp., Hickory, NC	FP	42	4,424	105.3	3
Integrated Health Systems, Hunt Valley, MD	FP	34	4,144	121.9	12
Geriatric & Medical Centers, Philadelphia, PA	FP	21	4,170	198.6	2
Diversicare Corp. of America, Franklin, TN	FP	40	4,148	103.7	5
Waverly Group/HCM Inc., Jackson, MS	FP	41	3,794	92.5	11
Medical Facilities of America, Roanoke, VA	FP	28	3,781	135.0	1
Care Initiative, Des Moines, IA	FP	41	3,511	85.6	1
Britthaven Inc., Kinston, NC	FP	33	3,504	106.2	14
Caremet Inc., Warsaw, IN	FP	32	3,441	107.5	1
VHA Long Term Care Inc., Memphis, TN	FP	33	3,375	102.3	3
Total U.S.		**3,178**	**367,732**	**115.7**	

Notes: 1. Effective September 1991; 2. 30 homes are 49% Meritcare-owned, 51% Bethesda-owned.

Source: Marion Merrell Dow. *Managed Care Digest: Long-Term Care Edition.* Kansas City, MO: Marion Merrell Dow, 1992.

Physicians who attend patients in long-term care provide medical care and quality assurance. Typically, a physician serves as the medical director of the nursing home, and this physician provides the primary medical care for some of the nursing home residents. Attending physician functions are constricted by a minimal frequency of reimbursed visits, specified by government regulations and by a low reimbursement rate. In addition, physicians perceive that the amount of required paperwork is intolerable. Thus, these reasons and others prompt many physicians to decline to care for long-term care patients. "Hospital models" of patient care, where physicians make rounds frequently and modify orders frequently, are rarely utilized, because they are not successful in the nursing home setting. In long-term care, a primary "nursing model" is the rule. Nurses carry out round-the-clock monitoring of chronic disease states in the residents. When acute changes in a resident's status are observed, the nurse notifies the attending physician. The physician often uses information obtained from the nurse to make clinical decisions. Physicians may be limited in their diagnostic and treatment options for nursing home residents. It may be impossible to obtain a blood test result in a timely fashion, unless the resident is sent to a hospital emergency department. It is often impossible to administer intravenous fluids or antibiotics.

● CLINICAL CHALLENGES IN LONG-TERM CARE

Within the nursing home, there are many clinical challenges. Some of the more common problems are falls and accidents, the use of restraints, weight loss, urinary incontinence, infectious diseases, abnormal mental states, and ethical dilemmas.

Accidents and Falls

Accidents and falls occur very frequently within nursing homes. Half of all nursing home residents fall at least once per year (Gryfe, 1977). These falls result in a variety of injuries. Repeated falls often lead to a "fear of falling" syndrome, where individuals progressively limit their activities and eventually become immobile. Regardless of whether or not restraints are used,

1 percent to 2 percent of falls in nursing homes result in hip fracture (Gryfe, 1977). Most falls are caused by a variety of factors, some of which are correctable. Common reasons for falls include impaired judgment, visual and hearing problems, impaired balance, weakness, urinary incontinence, obstacles in the environment, and poorly trained personnel. Restricting the mobility of handicapped persons results in fewer falls. However, this restriction also results in a reduced quality of life. This is a frequent area of conflict among patients, families, nurses, and nursing home administrators, who tend to view mobility and personal freedom from very different perspectives. Families often implicate lack of supervision by nursing home personnel as the sole reason for falls; administrators often view limiting mobility as the best way to minimize a facility's liability for falls; nurses have a more intermediate view. Environmental manipulations, such as improved lighting, installation of grab bars and wall railings, and the use of non-skid resilient floor surfaces, may reduce the frequency and severity of falls. Appropriate furniture may also be a help.

Restraints

Restraints are commonly used, sometimes misused, and currently highly regulated and monitored in nursing homes. There is a growing trend toward the creation of restraint-free environments. Physical restraints, such as bands around the wrists and vests, are thought to prevent self-inflicted injuries and to reduce the use of psychotropic (mind-altering) drugs, which may be a form of chemical restraint. Restraints may be used only upon a physician's order; their use must be reevaluated in a timely fashion. Orders for physical restraints must specify the type of restraint, the anatomical location, and the duration for use. The orders must also specify how to prevent complications from restraints, such as skin breakdown or the development of immobility. Patients, administrators, families, and nurses have divergent opinions on the use and value of restraints. For residents who tend to wander away, electronic alarms or monitors attached to wristbands, doorways, or beds are useful alternatives to restraints. However, the cost of these devices is often prohibitive.

Weight Loss

Weight loss in nursing homes is very common and is associated with a high risk for illness and for death. Just as with falls, the reasons for weight loss are usually multiple. Causes include medications, underlying disease—especially dementia and depression—disorders of taste and smell, and relative lack of variety and choice of foods. Strict therapeutic diets, such as those with severe salt or sugar restriction, may be unpalatable. Some patients who are served such diets simply refuse to eat; others with impaired judgment may steal or hoard food from other patients. Development of dehydration in nursing home patients is common and may reflect inadequate care, but often reflects a reduced sense of thirst and consequent inadequate fluid intake. Long-term tube feeding in the nursing home is complicated by major clinical and ethical dilemmas, especially when undertaken in demented patients (Ciocon, 1988; and Watts, 1986). The major clinical problems center around errors in tube placement, aspiration of the feedings into the lungs, and biochemical abnormalities. The lack of in-house X-ray and laboratories results in the reduced ability to monitor tube feeding for safety. In demented patients, the major problem is self-extubation. Usually after a number of attempts to replace the tube, the patient is restrained or sedated to maintain the tube in place.

Urinary Incontinence

Urinary incontinence is a condition that affects more than half of all nursing home residents (Resnick, 1989). Often there are several factors responsible for the patient's incontinence, some factors being reversible and others permanent. Reversible causes include potent diuretic medications, prostate enlargement in men, hormone loss in women after menopause, and slow gait caused by chronic diseases such as arthritis or Parkinson's disease. Dementia, with impairment of signal transmission from the brain to the nerves in the bladder, is a common cause of irreversible incontinence. Scheduled toileting, perhaps every two or three hours, helps to reduce incontinence accidents in patients with irreversible incontinence. Accessible toilets, even bedside commodes, and the discontinuation of restraints or offending medications are often very helpful.

Infections

Infections are a very common cause of illness in nursing home residents, afflicting about 15 percent of patients at any given time (Irvine, 1984). The most common infections are pneumonia, urinary tract infections, and infected pressure (bed) sores. Infection is the most frequent reason for hospital admission of nursing home patients. In nursing home residents, infections are often "masked" and hard to detect. Patients may lack the usual clinical clues to underlying infection. They may have life-threatening infections and yet not have fever, cough, sputum production, or pain on urination to help identify the nature of the infection. Indeed, in the nursing home the only clue to infection may be a change in level of alertness or the appearance of confusion or abnormal behavior. Infections may be obvious only when they have become far advanced and then are less likely to respond well to antibiotic treatment. Infection control programs are mandatory in nursing homes. The major thrusts of these programs are infection surveillance, tuberculosis screening, immunization, and education of personnel in techniques to minimize person-to-person spread of infections.

Abnormal Mental Status

Abnormal mental status of nursing home residents is an enormous problem. Fully three-fourths of nursing home residents have behavioral, intellectual, psychiatric, or sleep disorders, which produce abnormal mental status (Gurland, 1987). Common problems include depression, confusion, insomnia, delusions, hallucinations, agitation, and violence. Sometimes there are reversible causes for these abnormal mental states. Examples are unrecognized medical problems such as pain, adverse drug reactions, or severe psychosocial problems. Behavioral problems such as pacing, wandering, and hoarding food or objects are generally well tolerated. Violence, especially if it is repeated or directed at staff or defenseless residents, is intolerable and is often the reason for treatment with neuroleptic (major tranquilizing) drugs. The use of these drugs is very closely monitored. They cannot be used to treat behaviors that are merely a nuisance.

Ethical Dilemmas

Ethical dilemmas are everyday occurrences in the nursing home setting, not surprisingly. The majority of nursing home residents are frail, of advanced age, and have some intellectual impairment, which makes them dependent on others for help in decision-making. The most common situation is the determination of whether a treatment option is likely to be successful or futile in a person with terminal or progressive illness and impaired quality of life. An illustration of this situation is the patient with advanced Alzheimer's dementia who has lost the capacity to chew and swallow and who is requiring limb restraints to maintain a feeding tube in place. Major ethical decisions center around withholding or withdrawing treatments, whether or not to transfer to

hospital, and whether or not to resuscitate (Besdine, 1983). The most frequent decisions concern artificial feeding or hydration in demented nursing home residents. Certainly, instructions to physicians from their nursing home residents would help to clarify the types and intensity of treatments patients would prefer. The best time for outlining these instructions is during periods of mental clarity. However, by the time many elderly individuals reach the nursing home, they already have reduced ability to make any decisions. Then, proxy decisions by families become the norm, and occasionally a guardian will have to be appointed to serve as a decision maker for an incompetent patient.

Individuals have a right to specify their treatment preferences, although the specifics of these rights vary from state to state. The most common advance directives are the living will and the establishment of a durable power of attorney for health care. Decisions of nursing home residents to limit their treatment should not result in aban-

Requests and promises that an older person will never enter a nursing home are often unrealistic, when the actual care needs are honestly assessed. (Copyright © Marianne Gontarz)

donment by the physician or other health care personnel (Rango, 1985). Rather, treatment efforts should be intensified in the areas of pain relief, skin care, hygiene, and maintenance of dignity. Many nursing homes have established ethics committees to help their residents, residents' families, and staffs work through difficult ethical issues.

● LONG-TERM CARE REFORMS

Major long-term care reforms were mandated by the Omnibus Budget Reconciliation Act (OBRA) in 1987. Because of the magnitude and complexity of some of the regulations, implementation of most did not begin until after 1990. OBRA required facilities of one hundred or more beds to have a physician as medical director and to provide ninety hours of training for all nursing assistants. It broadened the scope of residents' rights. OBRA mandated the collection of clinical data on admission of each new resident, the minimum data set (MDS). This information is used to identify areas of patient care needs and serves as the basis for the interdisciplinary care plan, in which the resident and family may participate. Mandatory preadmission assessment for mental illness is required by OBRA. If an individual is found to be mentally ill and requires psychotropic (mind-altering) medications, that treatment must be monitored in a specific and timely fashion. OBRA also mandated quality assurance programs for all services provided in nursing homes. While the goal of this legislation is to assure appropriate attention to each resident's well-being, a disadvantage is that the marked increase in documentation requirements for OBRA has furthered physician disinterest in the nursing home and does remove some time from direct patient care. The requirement for more nursing documentation has resulted in reduction in other nursing services to patients in many nursing homes.

● FAMILY ISSUES IN NURSING HOME PLACEMENT

Families of impaired older persons are often called upon to arrange nursing home placement for a loved one. This process is never easy, and placement often results in family conflict. The older person may perceive that the family is conspiring against them. The family fears that if placement is postponed, a catastrophe may ensue. Requests and promises that an older person will never enter a nursing home are often unrealistic, when the actual care needs are honestly assessed. Nonetheless, the family member arranging the placement often has an overwhelming sense of guilt. Most families will seek advice from a health professional, usually their own physician, and will receive guidance from a social worker. One of the earliest decisions required for placement is to determine the level of care a patient will require. In general, the least restrictive level of care that will provide an adequate amount of supervision is best. Once the level of care is decided, the search for an appropriate facility can begin. Depending on the patient's situation, there may not be much opportunity for selection. A patient facing imminent hospital discharge may need to accept the first bed available. Patients in rural areas may not have many choices. Certain states have a critical shortage of nursing home beds, which affects all those waiting for beds (Marion, 1992). Patients who have the ability to pay for their own care, who reside in urban areas, and who require a level of care not in demand have the best chance for making choices.

Unannounced visits and visits during mealtime may provide valuable insights into the actual functioning of the nursing home.

In all cases, it is best to visit the facility before a decision is made. Ideally, the potential nursing home resident should visit. Unannounced visits and visits during mealtime may provide valuable insights into the actual functioning of the nursing home. Regardless of the ability of the older person to understand what is happening, he or she should always be told in advance of the placement. Once the nursing home move has occurred, the family should remain as close to the resident as feasible, but should not stifle the nursing home staff's attempt to meet and care for the new resident. The transition to a nursing home is slow and difficult and is characterized by a series of adjustments. Residents and their family members are most satisfied when they

Table 29.3
Number of Nursing Homes and Beds in Each State, by Facility Size

State	<50 Beds NHs	Beds	50-100 Beds NHs	Beds	101-150 Beds NHs	Beds	151-200 beds NHs	Beds	201+ Beds NHs	Beds	Total Beds	Beds/ 1,000*
Alabama	20	853	76	5,646	67	8,135	28	4,730	8	2,035	21,399	40.9
Alaska	6	241	5	342	1	101	_	_	1	224	908	41.3
Arizona	12	392	34	2,584	57	7,013	17	3,047	10	2,348	15,384	33.2
Arkansas	11	421	109	8,286	87	10,200	12	1,978	8	1,994	22,879	64.3
California	165	6,183	668	53,872	203	25,542	106	18,186	49	12,249	116,032	37.8
Colorado	18	669	74	5,316	58	6,871	24	4,151	7	1,663	18,670	57.6
Connecticut	29	1,033	81	6,027	89	11,214	29	5,117	19	5,102	28,493	64.6
Delaware	8	234	16	1,348	17	1,966	3	527	_	_	4,075	51.6
D.C.	4	147	2	113	_	_	5	882	6	1,988	3,130	41.2
Florida	31	1,069	171	12,207	273	32,986	66	11,535	34	8,804	66,601	29.2
Georgia	20	749	154	12,462	108	13,082	30	5,175	19	4,640	36,108	55.3
Hawaii	5	176	9	700	2	238	3	541	3	720	2,375	20.0
Idaho	10	362	23	1,662	17	2,051	4	700	1	216	4,991	41.2
Illinois	155	4,044	339	26,307	219	26,879	92	16,043	131	34,742	108,015	75.2
Indiana	109	4,186	203	15,359	134	16,322	64	11,109	39	10,421	57,397	82.7
Iowa	67	2,605	270	18,759	68	8,160	10	1,696	6	1,869	33,089	77.3
Kansas	51	2,069	248	16,894	61	7,227	8	1,387	4	935	28,512	83.1
Kentucky	25	782	134	10,023	63	7,757	15	2,609	4	1,077	22,248	47.1
Louisiana	7	281	89	7,111	127	15,505	49	8,456	21	4,771	36,124	74.2
Maine	40	1,279	72	5,111	18	2,141	3	539	2	483	9,553	58.3
Maryland	32	1,008	54	4,315	70	8,763	37	6,357	20	5,633	26,076	51.2
Massachusetts	129	4,353	178	13,376	174	21,121	50	8,633	16	3,866	51,349	63.2
Michigan	44	1,527	136	10,350	149	17,981	56	9,567	38	9,211	48,636	44.2
Minnesota	32	1,117	180	12,994	103	12,759	36	6,178	28	7,624	40,672	74.1
Mississippi	10	366	71	4,806	64	7,817	7	1,241	3	822	15,052	46.2
Missouri	80	2,667	220	15,910	168	20,316	44	7,534	27	7,264	53,691	74.7
Montana	20	743	32	2,352	11	1,257	5	868	3	735	5,955	56.2
Nebraska	28	1,149	130	8,867	31	3,665	15	2,548	3	950	17,179	76.7
Nevada	2	68	8	708	13	1,584	3	519	2	472	3,351	27.7
New Hampshire	19	401	34	2,417	19	2,164	2	344	6	1,608	6,934	55.0
New Jersey	44	1,316	58	4,332	105	12,624	59	10,479	56	16,402	45,153	44.2
New Mexico	9	241	32	2,289	26	3,076	2	355	2	619	6,580	40.9
New York	34	1,319	131	10,601	126	15,656	126	22,797	140	47,078	97,451	41.6
North Carolina	27	906	132	9,862	100	12,243	21	3,617	7	1,837	28,465	35.7
North Dakota	11	390	39	2,748	15	1,746	6	1,074	2	548	6,506	70.7
Ohio	247	7,314	489	38,153	174	21,420	65	11,342	55	13,435	91,664	65.5
Oklahoma	46	1,757	242	17,271	92	11,082	15	2,529	7	1,736	34,375	80.3
Oregon	28	1,057	86	6,384	46	5,378	12	2,059	_	_	14,878	38.0
Pennsylvania	83	2,762	157	11,347	240	29,631	88	15,525	80	26,079	85,344	46.9
Rhode Island	26	793	34	2,305	28	3,498	11	1,925	6	1,510	10,031	67.8
South Carolina	35	1,364	57	4,781	37	4,613	13	2,234	5	1,544	14,536	37.3
South Dakota	24	995	71	4,840	9	1,036	5	840	1	222	7,933	77.0
Tennessee	26	1,017	90	6,987	90	11,097	50	8,662	18	5,225	32,988	52.8
Texas	88	3,476	451	33,872	433	53,030	95	16,606	46	11,602	118,586	69.2
Utah	25	872	40	2,880	20	2,338	6	984	_	_	7,074	48.5
Vermont	15	421	20	1,381	8	924	5	831	_	_	3,557	52.3
Virginia	23	899	78	5,236	72	8,822	41	7,405	19	5,159	27,521	41.9
Washington	44	1,625	118	9,069	80	9,787	25	4,238	15	3,367	28,086	49.5
West Virginia	7	191	51	3,480	35	4,144	8	1,409	1	220	9,444	34.7
Wisconsin	55	1,808	159	12,003	105	12,646	41	7,138	51	14,888	48,483	86.3
Wyoming	1	32	14	967	7	870	2	330	1	204	2,403	52.2
Total U.S.	**2,087**	**71,729**	**6,369**	**477,012**	**4,319**	**526,478**	**1,519**	**264,576**	**1,030**	**286,141**	**1,625,936**	**52.6**

Source: Marion Merrell Dow. *Managed Care Digest: Long-Term Care Edition.* Kansas City, MO: Marion Merrell Dow, 1992.

take the time to form personal relationships with the staff and participate in advocacy and support groups.

References

Besdine, R. W. "Decisions to Withhold Treatment from Nursing Home Residents." *Journal of the American Geriatrics Society* Vol. 31 (1983): 602–6.

Brody, E. M. "Evaluation of the Social Setting." In *Principles of Geriatric Medicine*. Eds. R. Andres, E. L. Bierman, and W. R. Hazzard. New York: McGraw-Hill, 1985.

Brody, J. A., and D. J. Foley. "Epidemiologic Considerations." In *The Teaching Nursing Home*. Eds. E. L. Schneider, C. J. Wendland, A. W. Zimmer, N. List, and M. Ory. New York: Raven Press, 1985.

Ciocon, J. O., F. A. Silverstone, L. M. Graver, and C. J. Foley. "Tube Feedings in Elderly Patients: Indications, Benefits, and Complications." *Archives of Internal Medicine* Vol. 148 (1988): 429–33.

Department of Health and Human Services, Public Health Service. "The National Nursing Home Survey: 1985 Summary for the United States; Data from the National Health Survey. Vital and Health Statistics." DHHS Publication Series 13, no. 97; PHS Publication No. 89-1758. Washington, DC: Government Printing Office, 1989.

Department of Veterans Affairs. *Aging America: Trends and Projections, 1991 Edition.*

Gryfe, C. I., A. Mies, and M. J. Ashley. "A Longitudinal Study of Falls in an Elderly Population; 1: Incidence and Morbidity." *Age and Aging* Vol. 6 (1977): 201–10.

Gurland, B. J., L. J. Cote, P. S. Cross, and J. A. Toner. "The Assessment of Cognitive Function in the Elderly." *Clinics in Geriatric Medicine* Vol. 3 (1987): 53–63.

Irvine, P. W., N. Van Buren, and K. Crossley. "Causes for Hospitalization of Nursing Home Residents: The Role of Infection." *Journal of the American Geriatrics Society* Vol. 32 (1984): 103–7.

Lyles, M. F. "Public Policies and Issues." In *Manual of Geriatric Nursing*. Eds. A. S. Staab, and M. F. Lyles. Glenview, IL: Scott, Foresman/Little, Brown Higher Education, 1989.

Manton, and Soldo. "Dynamics of Health Changes in the Oldest Old: New Perspectives and Evidence." *Milbank Memorial Fund Quarterly* Vol. 63, no. 2 (1985): Also published in *Aging America: Trends and Projections; 1991 Edition.*

Marion Merrell Dow. *Managed Care Digest: Long-Term Care Edition*. Kansas City: Marion Merrell Dow, 1992.

Murtaugh, C. M., P. Kemper, and B. C. Spillman. "The Risk of Nursing Home Use in Later Life." *Medical Care* Vol. 28 (1990): 952–62.

Rango, N. "The Nursing Home Resident with Dementia: Clinical Care, Ethics, and Policy Implications." *Annals of Internal Medicine* Vol. 102 (1985): 835–41.

Resnick, N. M., S. V. Yalla, and E. Laurino. "The Pathophysiology of Urinary Incontinence Among Institutionalized Elderly Persons." *New England Journal of Medicine* Vol. 320 (1989): 1–7.

Watts, D. T., C. K. Cassel, and D. H. Hickam. "Nurses' and Physicians' Attitudes Toward Tube-Feeding Decisions in Long-Term Care." *Journal of the American Geriatrics Society* Vol. 34 (1986): 607–11.

Additional Reading

Contemporary Long-Term Care (periodical). P.O. Box 8391-44320, Akron, OH 44320.

Down, Ivy M., and Lorraine Schnurr. *Between Home and Nursing Home: The Board and Care Alternative*. New York: Prometheus Books, 1991.

Estes, Carroll L., Charlene Harrington, and Robert J. Newcomer. *Long-Term Care of the Elderly: Public Policy Issues*. Beverly Hills, CA: Sage, 1985.

Horne, J. *The Nursing Home Handbook: A Guide for Families*. Washington, DC: AARP Books, 1989.

Kane, Robert L., and Rosalie A. Kane. *A Will and a Way: What the United States Can Learn From Canada About Caring for the Elderly*. New York: Columbia University Press, 1985.

Kane, Rosalie A., and Robert L. Kane. *Long-Term Care: Principles, Programs, and Policies*. New York: Springer, 1987.

Karr, Katherine. *What Do I Do? How to Care for, Comfort, and Commune With Your Nursing Home Elder*. New York: Haworth Press, 1985.

Libow, L. S., and P. Starer. "Care of the Nursing Home Patient." *New England Journal of Medicine* Vol. 321 (1989): 93–96.

Mace, N., and L. Gwyther. "Selecting a Nursing Home with a Dedicated Dementia Care Unit." Chicago, IL: Alzheimer's Association, 1989.

Matthews, Joseph. *Elder Care: Choosing and Financing Long-Term Care*. Berkeley, CA: Nolo Press, 1991.

Mendleson, Mary A. *Tender Loving Greed: How the Incredibly Lucrative Nursing Home Industry Is Exploiting America's Old People and Defrauding Us All*. New York: Knopf, 1974.

Ness, David. *Keys to Planning for Long-Term Custodial Care*. Hauppauge, NY: Barron's, 1991.

Nursing Home Life: A Guide for Residents and Families. Washington, DC: American Association of Retired Persons (AARP), 1987.

Nursing Homes and Senior Citizen Care (periodical). Nursing Homes, 5615 West Cermak Road, Cicero, IL 60650.

Pelham, Anabel O., and William F. Clark, eds. *Managing Home Care for the Elderly: Lessons from Community Based Agencies*. New York: Springer, 1986.

Rabin, David L., and Patricia Stockton. *Long-Term Care for the Elderly: A Factbook*. New York: Oxford University Press, 1987.

Robhert, Eugene A., and James R. Daubert. *Horticultural Therapy for Nursing Homes, Senior Centers, Retirement Living*. Glencoe, IL: Chicago Horticultural Society, 1981.

Sandel, Susan L., and David R. Johnson. *Waiting at the Gate: Creativity and Hope in the Nursing Home*. New York: Haworth Press, 1987.

Tisdale, Sallie. *Harvest Moon: Portrait of Nursing Home*. New York: Henry Holt, 1987.

United Seniors Health Cooperative. 1988. *Long-Term Care: A Dollar and Sense Guide.* 1334 G St., NW, #500, Washington, DC 20005.

William, J. Winston, ed. *Marketing Long-Term and Senior Care Services.* New York: Haworth Press, 1984.

Zweibel, N. R., and C. K. Cassel, eds. "Clinical and Policy Issues in the Care of the Nursing Home Patient." *Clinics in Geriatric Medicine* Vol. 4 (1988): 471–697.

Mary Fennell Lyles, M.D.

30

End-of-Life Issues

● More Than One Issue; More Than One Solution ● What Decisions Are Ours to Make?
● Patient Self-Determination Options ● The Hospice Alternative ● Euthanasia ● Suicide
● Funerals and Memorials ● Surviving, Coping, and Contributing ● Communication Overview

Coming to terms with one's mortality, with the process of dying and death, is not unique to older adults. The fact that we tend to attribute end-of-life issues to the province of later life is a testimonial to the progress of public health measures, the overcoming of childhood diseases, and the applications of advanced medical technology. Indeed, the majority of people who die are elderly, and the majority of deaths occur in hospitals.

Older people and their families tend to have more advanced notice of impending death and of average time limits of irreversible diseases than any previous generation and certainly by contrast to those who die in accidents or by sudden acute illnesses. This means that questions and choices occur about how and where one might end life, whether medical interventions are to be restricted or engaged, what plans have been made for funeral ceremonies, burials, distribution of one's estate, or the bequeathal of one's ethical will—a testimonial of values and insights left as a legacy to surviving family members and friends.

● MORE THAN ONE ISSUE; MORE THAN ONE SOLUTION

Contemporary elders and their families are asked to take a relatively active part in decision-making about end-of-life issues, compared to earlier generations. But these issues are varied, and their resolutions may take many forms, as the following examples show.

● An active woman in her mid-eighties decides it is time to settle a few matters and to enjoy herself while doing so. Over the years Mrs. H. has accumulated a number of pieces of fine jewelry, each with sentimental as well as financial value. Now she meets with each of her daughters, and then with the granddaughter brigade. Each of these sessions is illuminated by shared reminiscences and sparked by humor. After a while, everybody has had the opportunity to select the piece or pieces they most admire, and to identify the items that should be saved for the robust crop of great-granddaughters as well.

● Two people widowed in midlife had created new lives together in an eventful and companionable second marriage. When Mr. W. experienced a "close call" with a heart attack, both recalled how they had felt unprepared for the deaths of their first spouses. They also were uneasy about what might happen should either of them become candidates for prolonged vegetative existence on a life-support system. Mrs. W. knew something about the living will option. Mr. W. had his doubts. Both felt anxious when a nurse of their acquaintance told them that there was now "a whole new ball game" that centered around a mandatory procedure called "the Patient Self Determination Act." "What's that all about?" Mr. W. asked. "Let's find out!" replied his wife, and they did.

- Friends and colleagues had long considered Mr. L. to be an exceptionally strong person. He was a rock of stability when things went wrong, the person who kept his head and helped others to cope with difficult situations. If these people had still been around and been admitted into Mr. L.'s private thoughts, they would have been astonished to learn that he was seriously considering self-destruction. He felt useless and adrift. The gun was now in his underwear and socks drawer.

- Mrs. E. was doing very well, everything considered. Without her late husband, life would never again be the same, but she still had the rest of the family, her home, and an income that should continue to suffice with careful management. Of no less importance was the fact that Mrs. E. could feel "right" about how she had met her husband's needs during his final illness. She was the one who had arranged for hospice care at home after looking into this new program ("Why didn't we have something like this years ago!" she wondered.) And she had herself taken on much of the responsibility for day-by-day care, rediscovering some of her own personal resources. Now Mrs. E. has been accepted as a hospice volunteer with the opportunity to give something back to the community that had come to her assistance not long ago.

All these people are dealing with end-of-life issues. The issues are numerous and so are the ways in which people cope with them. It would be unrealistic to expect the same solution to work equally well for everybody. Many years of developing one's own expectations, values, and preferences foster highly individual views of what issues are most significant and how they are best approached. Furthermore, people come to end-of-life considerations with many different kinds of strengths and sources of concern. For one person, financial anxieties may be dominant; for another, it may be anxiety about how a loved one will manage when he or she is gone. The belief that death is but a passage to an incomparably superior existence may comfort one person,

while another is apprehensive about the divine judgment that may be served upon his or her not-exactly-flawless life.

The objective of this chapter is to provide information and observations that individuals can use in their own ways. This objective requires attention to the communication process as well as to substantive topics. Consider the first real-life example given above. What was the substantive issue that Mrs. H. addressed? It is true that she was dealing with the issue of inheritance or, reduced to its essence, "who gets what." But there are different ways this substantive matter could have been handled. Mrs. H might have made all the decisions herself, and they could have been made fairly quickly, for nobody knew the jewelry collection better than Mrs. H. did. But she was also well tuned into the lives of all the younger women in the family. Had she merely decided whom to give the pieces to, the recipients would probably have felt grateful enough when the time came and cherished them as remembrances.

What Mrs. H. actually did, however, was far more effective. Through an adroit process of communication, she transformed the "who-gets-what" issue into a shared experience that was unique and memorable for everyone involved. Yes, the motivating circumstance involved some discomfort in the recognition of the prospect of death and parting. This recognition, however, contributed extra meaning and poignancy to the interactions. Moreover, by consulting members of her family, Mrs. H. affirmed her respect for what they thought and what they preferred. In the course of time, all would receive particular pieces of jewelry that they themselves had selected, thereby giving them a closer sense of involvement in the process. And some day, far into the future, Mrs. H.'s open circle of communication on an inheritance issue might well influence their own style of passing family treasures on to younger generations. *Communication* about end-of-life issues can be as significant as the particular decisions that are made. The various types of end-of-life issues often are interrelated: decisions made regarding one issue may exert a strong influence on the outcomes of other issues.

● WHAT DECISIONS ARE OURS TO MAKE?

People sometimes discover too late that they had the opportunity to influence the course of

Checklist 30.1
Some General Decisions Regarding Personal End-of-life Issues

Yes	No	
___	___	1. I feel ready to consider all the issues that are related to the end of my life.
___	___	2. I intend to discuss at least some of these issues thoroughly with at least one other person whose views matter to me.
___	___	3. I intend to require of my physicians that they provide me with all the information I need to guide my decision-making in a prompt, comprehensive, and honest manner.
___	___	4. I intend to select or create a document that clearly expresses my preferences regarding treatment during the terminal phase of life.
___	___	5. I intend to designate a person to represent my preferences and interests in the event that I become incapacitated.
___	___	6. I intend to review and, if appropriate, modify my will and other legal instruments to insure that they represent my final wishes in an effective way.
___	___	7. I intend to review my most significant relationships and take whatever steps are needed to resolve lingering problems and to renew and strengthen mutual ties.
___	___	8. I intend to do all that is possible to provide the opportunity for meaningful leave taking interactions with the people in my life.
___	___	9. I intend to convey my preferences regarding burial, cremation, and funeral services to those who will be responsible for making the arrangements.
___	___	10. I intend to review and reflect upon what is of most importance to me in life and to devote much of my remaining time and energies to these core values.

events. This situation is becoming increasingly common as more and more options emerge regarding end-of-life issues. Even health care professionals, insurance companies, attorneys, legislators, and educators have difficulty keeping up with these changes. Several basic rules govern the decisions that often are within one's power:

- Early decisions influence the kind of decisions that can be made later in the process.
- There is a crucial distinction between ordinary decisions and binding or nonreversible decisions.
- The opportunity for decision-making depends on the knowledge, competence, and goodwill of others as well as oneself: having the abstract "right" to make a decision does not guarantee that a person will actually be offered the opportunity to make that decision.
- Not making a decision is itself a decision—a decision to leave the decision to others.

Checklist 30.1 introduces some of the decisions that people may have the opportunity to make, if they so choose. It is presented from the standpoint of the individual whose own end-of-life issues are the focus of attention. Choosing yes or no answers is intended to stimulate and sharpen thinking on these matters, instead of getting off the hook with "that depends" and other noncommittal responses. Although "that depends" is a valid comment, such qualifiers are also a tactic to avoid facing up to issues in a prompt fashion. Responses should reflect the ideas and feelings of the moment. They are in no way binding; upon returning to the checklist on another occasion, one might make selections differently.

Each of these points requires attention to the specific life and circumstances. To reach the effective level of decision-making for a particular item, one would need to move from a "yes" answer to the operational details. It is not neces-

Communication about end-of-life issues can be as significant as the particular decisions that are made.

sary—and not really desirable—to rush through all these points just to complete them.

The information that follows will be useful in dealing with these decisions, especially with the new Patient Self-Determination option.

● PATIENT SELF-DETERMINATION OPTIONS

Living Will and the Patient Self-Determination Act

Not long ago, most people in the United States were just starting to hear about an unusual type of document known as the living will. Introduced in 1968, the living will was repugnant to some individuals, because it could not help but remind them that every life comes to an end. Nevertheless, within a relatively short period of time, the living will gathered widespread interest and support. Thirty-eight states and the District of Columbia have enacted legislation upholding the living will (Scofield, 1989). A major national survey (Times Mirror, 1990) found that most people know about the living will and support its objectives. Most adults in the United States (about 80 percent) now believe that terminally ill patients have the right to limit the types of treatment they receive. However, despite the development of a consensus favoring patient's rights and the living will, relatively few people (about 14 percent) report having actually signed such a document.

Events have now overtaken the public's own pattern of response to the living will. As recently as November 1991 one could choose to accept, postpone, or reject the opportunity to express one's preferences regarding medical care in the final phase of life. This situation has altered with the enactment of the Omnibus Reconciliation Act (1990). This congressional measure includes a provision known as the Patient Self-Determination Act (PSDA). Essentially, this measure lays a new requirement on every health care institution that receives either Medicare or Medicaid. Home care programs, hospices, hospitals, and nursing care facilities must ask all clients about their preferences in a terminal illness situation. It is the institution that must abide by this new regulation—but it is the individual who will be expected to have a firm and ready response.

Dealing with the PSDA challenge may be a lit-tle easier by recognizing the original purpose for this regulation and the attitude of many health care institutions. As potential clients, everyone could be caught in a kind of crossfire between the PSDA advocacy position and the institutional response.

Rouse (1991) offers a succinct background statement regarding the original purpose and the eventual disposition of the PSDA:

> The act's sponsors originally hoped to mandate passage of natural death or health care proxy legislation in every state. Constitutionally suspect, this was also strenuously opposed by groups such as the U.S. Catholic Conference who disfavored federal intervention and federal standards. Some groups representing institutional providers also challenged a federal role in requiring that information be provided to patients. Hospitals thought it would be inappropriate for them to give legal ... advice to their patients—a concern that was addressed in the final act by requiring the states themselves to develop the information institutions would hand out. To those who preferred that information be given to patients by physicians rather than institutions, the Health Care Financing Administration argued that the administrative burden of monitoring individual physicians for compliance would be enormous and practically impossible (Rouse, 1991, p. S2).

Despite the development of a consensus favoring patient's rights and the living will, relatively few people (about 14 percent) report having actually signed such a document.

Concerns such as these have every state and the District of Columbia engaged in developing specific guidelines for PSDA procedures, and virtually all health care institutions are also attempting to improvise some way of meeting the new requirements without having to expend a great deal of effort or "rock the boat." Some states and health care institutions are coming up with their own, somewhat different ways of obeying the law.

What does all this mean for individuals who might find themselves being admitted to a hospital or other health care system? First, they should be aware that they will be facing a situation that is somewhat new to the health care establishment and that is not entirely welcome to them because it (a) adds to the general burden of meeting local and federal regulations, (b) makes more work for admission personnel and generates more paper work, and (c) threatens to destabilize the institutional power structure. This final point refers to the fear among some health care professionals and administrators that patients will "interfere" too much with standard operating procedure by asking a lot of questions, making additional demands, and—most dangerously—striking a raw nerve in the health care system itself. The management and treatment of individuals with life threatening conditions has already become an issue that is fraught with controversy and discomfort among many health care professionals. The prospect of inviting—actually *inviting!*—patients to make their own needs and expectations known is one that not all physicians and hospital or nursing facility directors are facing with equanimity.

Second, people should be aware that the PSDA does in fact *empower* them with the right to tell health care providers what they will and will not accept in management and treatment when they are facing death. Third, they do not have to tolerate indifferent or unprofessional conduct on the part of health care personnel during the information exchange. The health care institution has the legal responsibility to provide adequate information so that patients, in turn, can tell them how they have decided to exercise their rights.

More specifically, people can be more informed and effective "health care consumers" if they have given attention to the following considerations, especially when they have the leisure to do so and are not experiencing the stress of acute discomfort:

- Recognize that they have the right but not the obligation to complete a living will type of document. Health care facilities cannot and generally would not require patients to present them with such a document, and the PSDA requires them only to give patients the opportunity to express their preferences if they choose to do so.
- Learn the current status of will-to-live (also known as "natural death") legislation

in their own state. If the state does have such legislation on its books, then consumers will want to obtain a copy of the specific living will form that is in use. This can be obtained from a state health department office or an attorney.

- Ask their attorney, physician, or librarian to provide examples of the *newest* types of advance directives. The living will is a document that belongs to a larger class of legal instruments known as advance directives. A popular version of the classic living will is presented here. But there is now an active process of revising and refining advance directives in order to provide more detailed and useful information to those who may be called upon to honor such intentions. It may be helpful to look at the basic living will document first and then read the following discussion of the specific points customarily added to an advance directive.

Most completed living wills are similar to this example. The absence of notarization does not necessarily invalidate the document; courts have repeatedly given opinions in which a clear and recoverable expression of an individual's wishes is considered acceptable. The specific circumstances under which a living will might come into action, including the identity of the service providers who happen to be present at the time, are difficult to predict. For this reason, notarizing the document reduces the possibility that it might be ignored or questioned at a critical moment.

After some years of experience with the living will in practical circumstances, however, a number of health care providers and other observers believe that greater specificity could improve the chances that an advance directive actually will be honored when the time comes. The standard living will has been criticized for being too ambiguous: precisely what is meant by "artificial means" or "heroic measures"? Competent service providers may differ in their interpretations, even within the same health care system. What seems like a "heroic measure" to a family physician or internist, for example, may be a routine procedure to an emergency room physician or other specialist.

A related criticism is that the living will too

The Living Will: Basic Version

My Living Will
To My Family, My Physician, My Lawyer, and
All Others Whom It May Concern

Death is as much a reality as birth, growth, maturity, and old age—it is the one certainty of life. If the time comes when I can no longer take part in decisions for my own future, let this statement stand as an expression of my wishes and directions while I am still of sound mind.

If at such a time the situation should arise in which there is no reasonable expectation of my recovery from extreme physical or mental disability, I direct that I be allowed to die and not be kept alive by medications, artificial means, or "heroic measures." I do, however, ask that medication be mercifully administered to me to alleviate suffering, even though this may shorten my remaining life.

This statement is made after careful consideration and is in accordance with my strong convictions and beliefs. I want the wishes and directions here expressed carried out to the extent permitted by law. Insofar as they are not legally enforceable, I hope that those to whom this Will is addressed will regard themselves morally bound by these provisions.

Durable Power of Attorney (Optional)

I hereby designate _____ to serve as my attorney-in-fact for the purpose of making medical treatment decisions. This power of attorney shall remain effective in the event that I shall become incompetent or otherwise unable to make such decisions for myself.

Signed_____Date_____

(Optional) Notarization: "Sworn and subscribed to

Witness_____ before me this _____ day

Address_____ of _____, 19___"

Witness_____

Notary Public Seal Address _____

Copies of this request have been given to

_____

_____

_____

often does not provide a sufficiently detailed guide to the individual's intentions. The living will makes it obvious that a person does not want his or her life prolonged needlessly, painfully, and expensively. However, the document may shed no light on the concrete decisions that can arise in the later phases of a terminal illness. For these reasons, people are now being encouraged to be more specific in their advance directives. To do so requires thought about the terminal phase of life in more detail. People who just can't bear to see themselves in the predicament of a dying person may recoil from this prospect—but many have been surprised to discover that they can think constructively about this challenge, once the initial reluctance is overcome.

An advance directive that gives clear answers to questions such as the following will be appreciated by the service providers who need to grasp the person's wishes clearly while in the midst of assessment, management, and treatment activities. Checklist 30.2 is based on suggestions made by a physician and a professor of philosophy (Culver and Gert, 1990). Although many of the items may appear to be similar, each in fact envisions a different situation.

These are not questions that most people think about very often; so the process of raising them for personal reflection and sharing with significant others can be quite educational. One may discover things about personal attitudes and values that had never before been put into words. In thinking about this set of treatment decisions, one should consider several key points:

- The advance directive would come into play only should one become incapacitated to the extent that he or she is unable to give personal expression to their wishes. If the person is alert and able to communicate when a critical decision is being made, the patient is free either to affirm or change the decision that had previously been put into writing: living wills and advance directives can be modified at any time, as long as one is competent to do so.
- The first three directives provide valuable guidance to health care providers by specifying that *all* life-sustaining treatments be discontinued under the particular condi-

**Checklist 30.2
Advance Directive Requests**

Yes	No	
____	____	1. I want all life-sustaining treatments to be discontinued if I become terminally ill and permanently incompetent.
____	____	2. I want all life-sustaining treatments to be discontinued if I become permanently unconscious, whether terminally ill or not.
____	____	3. I want all life-sustaining treatments to be discontinued if I become unconscious and have very little chance of ever recovering consciousness or avoiding permanent brain injury.
____	____	4. I want to be kept alive if I become gravely ill and have only a slight chance of recovery (5% or less), and would probably require weeks or months of further treatment before the outcome became clear.
____	____	5. I want to have fluids and nutrition discontinued if other life support measures are discontinued.

tions described. The doctors do not have to guess about what is meant.

- Whether or not to continue providing fluids and nutrition to a terminally ill person no longer able to speak is an extremely common problem that arises. It often provokes intense controversy at a time when understanding and consensus are what is really needed. A clear statement about one's wish to have fluids either continued or discontinued can reduce the anxiety of caregivers and family and improve the chances of having one's preferences honored.

Most of the points in Checklist 30.2 imply that the individual does not want to have measures taken to prolong life under the specified conditions (number 4 is the exception). Living wills and advance directives are almost always completed by people who definitely want to avoid being placed in a prolonged life support situation if there is little or no prospect for significant recovery. However, an advance directive could take the completely opposite approach by calling for service providers to do everything possible for as long as possible.

Advance Directive Cautions and Tips

Some hospitals and other health care facilities give serious attention to the information that is gathered in accordance with the PSDA. However, at this time many facilities have yet to put in place a system that will guarantee that one's stated preferences will actually be consulted when a decision must be made. Whether our preferences are expressed by a simple reply to one question asked by a member of the admissions team or provided to the facility in the form of a carefully designed and notarized advance directive, this information may be buried in hospital files, or personnel may not be adequately sensitized and educated to use this information properly. It is useful to ask questions and make a point of letting health care providers know that one expects them to consult and act in accordance with one's stated wishes, should the occasion arise.

It is wise to be on guard against attitudes and practices that may deprive one of adequate care. PSDA raises the possibility of inadvertently introducing a new source of discrimination. A person who has expressed the preference not to be put into a life support system if terminally ill or in a vegetative state might receive less attentive care, even when in a condition that could benefit from skillful management and treatment. Special educational and monitoring efforts may be needed if a pattern of subtle discrimination undermines the original purpose of the PSDA. A more familiar pattern of discrimination must also be acknowledged: ageism (Palmore, 1990). Some health care providers have transcended our society's general tendency to disvalue its older citizens; but one still encounters physicians, technicians, and administrators who characteristically give only perfunctory attention to older adults. No advance directive will automatically prevent or cure these biases; one must be vigilant and assertive at every opportunity to avoid situations in which a person is given less than adequate attention on the basis of age or advance directive preference.

Here is a scenario often faced by emergency medical technicians and paramedics. An elderly person with a life-threatening condition, such as severe congestive heart disease, suffers what to all intents and purposes is a fatal heart attack while at home or in some other community location. Somebody picks up the telephone and dials the emergency number. It soon becomes evident that the individual will not survive this episode— but the quickly-arriving emergency team *must* go through its drill. Bystanders, including family members, may be distressed to witness the emergency procedures, especially when they realize that "This is just what Joe didn't want to happen!" One cannot blame the paramedics for this kind of scene: they have no choice but to attempt resuscitative actions even if they know very well that these are doomed to failure. The lesson: do not call for emergency care if the stricken person has previously made known his or her wish to be allowed to die if another major episode occurs. In practice, however, it can be difficult to apply this lesson, either because of the emotional impact of the attack on the family members present or because, as lay people, they hesitate to make judgments about medical prognosis. Although each emergency situation is unique, it is helpful to think ahead and consider one's options.

● THE HOSPICE ALTERNATIVE

Another recent development, hospice care, has added a significant alternative to our end-of-life decisions. Hospice care programs are designed to provide physical, social, psychological, and spiritual comfort for terminally ill people. The guiding philosophy is to do all that is possible to protect the quality of the life that is remaining to the individual, rather than to pursue a more aggressive treatment course that seems more likely to increase distress than to extend life. Typically, one has already had the benefit of diagnostic and treatment procedures intended to arrest or reverse the illness and has come to the conclusion that further curative efforts would have no reasonable chance of success.

Modern hospice care programs, originating chiefly in England, Ireland, and Scotland (Gilmore, 1989) were introduced to the United States in 1974. The Connecticut Hospice (New Haven) resulted from a rare collaboration among health care specialists, community leaders, and lay people who shared the belief that care of the dying person should and could be improved. Today more than 1,700 hospice programs serve the American public. The growth of hospice programs is important not only for its contribution to the comfort of dying persons and their families, but also for its demonstration that other possibilities are available beyond the traditional model of medical and technological specialization. At its best, the hospice approach suggests that there is still a role for compassionate and community-spirited citizens to help each other directly rather than relying ever more heavily upon institutionalized programs.

"Should I select hospice care?" To answer this question, it is useful first to review the guiding principles and actual practices that characterize hospice care in the United States. This is followed by a consideration of how hospice has fared when subjected to evaluation research. One will then be ready to consider some specific points that are likely to influence the decision.

Hospice philosophy centers on the needs and strengths of the people who are most intimately involved: the dying person and his or her loved ones (Kastenbaum, 1989 and 1991). In other words, the person, not the disease, receives prime attention. Unlike the type of medical care that has become ingrained in our society, hospice invites—indeed, hospice expects—active participation by family members and friends in planning and carrying out a management plan that is designed to take the dying person's unique personality and life situation into account. When hospice achieves its objective, the individual ends his or her life in an individual way that is consistent with values of self and family.

Today more than 1,700 hospice programs serve the American public.

Differences between the conventional medical approach and the hospice approach to care of the dying person are highlighted in Table 30.1.

The health care system in the United States has distinguished itself in the treatment of acute diseases and traumatic emergency conditions. This system is generally more suited for responding to

Table 30.1
Two Approaches to Care of the Dying Person

	Conventional	Hospice
Goal	Remission or cure	Prevent suffering
Pain control	Secondary to treatment	A primary goal
Interventions	Aggressive treatment: Do all that can be done	Noninvasive: Do what aids patient's comfort
Site	Mostly in hospital	Mostly at home
Role of family	Follow doctor's orders	Active in planning and providing care
Volunteers	Little or no role	Major role
Dying and death are:	A disorder or failing; the enemy	A natural part of the human experience

acute medical difficulties than in managing situations in which people have long-term (or chronic) conditions. Furthermore, incentives and prestige for medical practitioners and facilities are much greater in the case of acute, and, especially, high-technology interventions. Doctors who devote themselves to the difficult and complex challenge of helping aging adults cope with several co-existing medical problems receive much less recognition and status than those who engage in dramatic (and expensive) state of the art procedures. Recent changes in the Medicare fee schedule have recognized this imbalance by increasing payments to family physicians and reducing those for certain types of surgical procedures.

The dying person poses a fundamental problem for the present health care establishment because he or she does not quite fit into either the acute or the chronic status model. There is a strong tendency to conceive of the terminally ill person as an acute case, thereby opening the way for the type of actions that are familiar and interesting to the health care system: a lot of testing, a lot of treatment, a lot of high tech equipment and procedures.

This standard procedure—converting the experience of dying into an acute episode—is rejected by those who favor the hospice approach. In fact, much of the motivation for introducing hospice care in both Europe and North America developed in reaction against the tendency to consider dying as an acute illness and death as an enemy who must be fought heroically every step of the way. The alternative has been less visible, but no less disturbing, to those in a position to observe.

Some people nearing the end of their lives have been treated in accordance with the chronic condition model: that is to say, not given very much attention from either the personal or professional standpoint. This type of situation develops all too frequently for elderly men and women who are institutional residents. To put it bluntly, altogether too many institutionalized elders have been treated as though they were dead for years by society in general and by their purported service providers (Gubrium, 1975; Kastenbaum, 1983).

Hospice philosophy envisions the end of a person's life as neither an acute nor a chronic situation, although there may be some specific features of both. Instead, those who endorse the hospice perspective conceive of the terminal phase as part of the natural course of the lifespan. The dying person is still, above all, a living person and a member of a family and a community. Every effort is made to provide support to the family as well as the dying person, so that the final weeks of life occur within the framework of familiarity, security, and caring. Volunteers play a significant role in this effort. It is not just what volunteers do; it is also what their involvement represents—the compassion of community and society. Generally speaking, hospice volunteers are people of outstanding character who know what it is like to go through difficult life challenges themselves and who have successfully completed a well-planned series of training sessions. It is not unusual for family members who have been helped by hospice later to become volunteers and do the same for others.

The dying person poses a fundamental problem for the present health care establishment because he or she does not quite fit into either the acute or the chronic status model.

Nevertheless, hospice care may not be appropriate or feasible for every person and family. Hospice is becoming an important option, a choice that one can make if so disposed. The following specifics should be considered when deciding whether to select the hospice alternative.

Knowing When to Select Hospice

This is the major decision regarding the course of management and treatment during the final illness. A major difficulty is knowing just when the point has been reached. Often a person has received diagnostic and treatment services for some time before it becomes clear that the life-threatening condition will not be halted or reversed. One cannot always rely on physicians to bring this point to one's attention. Some physicians are quite aware and supportive of hospice; others either are not well informed or not well disposed to having their patients favor hospice services. Patient, family, and friends are well advised to stay alert to the course of events, ask questions whenever necessary, and "push the pause button" before automatically consenting to the next round of diagnostic or treatment procedures.

Since it is terminal illness that is being discussed here, there often will be a point in conventional medical care in which the next procedure will exact a toll on the patient's energies, mobility, appearance, ability to communicate, or other vital aspect of his or her personhood. No red flag goes up automatically; no alarm sounds. One must depend on his or her own perceptions and judgment to either give the go ahead for another round of aggressive treatment, with life prolongation, not cure, as a goal, or choose instead the hospice course. The choice hinges on one's own judgment and preferences: either "I will go through anything and do whatever the doctors say to fight for my life," or "Enough is enough; I want to enjoy the time remaining as best I can with the people who are most important to me." This point is discussed again in the final section, when the focus is on communication. The key fact to keep in mind, however, is that one *does* have a choice; otherwise the opportunity to make an effective decision may be lost.

Hospice is intended for the care and comfort of people who have only a short time remaining to live. This time frame has been established as six months or less for official purposes. Most hospice clients, however, do not enroll themselves into the program until their life expectancy has been reduced to three months or less. How long a very sick person has to live is always a matter of guesswork because of individual differences and intangibles.

Controlling Pain and Symptoms

Hospice will offer expertise in the relief of pain and other symptoms as well as overall medical and nursing management. Hospice programs have earned respect for their leadership in controlling pain and other symptoms that might otherwise cause great distress for dying people and their families. A growing number of physicians and nurses associated with conventional hospice-based treatment programs have improved their own skills by learning from hospice contributions to symptom relief. Some medical centers now provide state of the art symptom relief, but one cannot assume that the local hospital or physicians will have versed and devoted themselves to the relief of suffering in terminally ill people. A strong symptom relief program is more likely to be in operation through a hospice program.

When the hospice movement was new, there was sometimes the misconception that the dying person's physical condition would be neglected. This erroneous idea arose because awareness of the high tech and aggressive side of medical practice has tended to obscure the possibility of alternatives. Hospice patients continue to receive medical and nursing services, along with auxiliary health care services, as required for their comfort and morale. The hospice movement developed in response to the total human needs of the dying person—physical, psychological, social, and spiritual—and all of these needs are carefully addressed by well-functioning hospice programs.

Earning the Approval of Health Policymakers

Hospice has lived up to its mission consistently enough to earn the approval of health policymakers and other critical observers. It has had to prove itself in the eyes of many tough-minded people, including those who control the purse strings for health care policies and programs and researchers from a variety of clinical and sociobehavioral disciplines. If hospice programs had turned out to be little different from conventional medical treatment of terminally ill people, harmful rather than helpful to patients, disturbing rather than comforting to families, or simply too expensive, then the whole movement might have disappeared from the scene by now. Studies of hospice care show that the participating patients spend more time at home, are not subjected to fatiguing tests or invasive procedures, and generally feel more secure (Mor, Greer, and Kastenbaum, 1988; Mor, 1987; Kastenbaum, 1992). One family member spoke for many others in reporting: "Dad's life was still Dad's life—and ours—right to the end. He was never taken away from us and separated by tubes and machines."

Hospice Is Not for Everyone

Hospice is not equally successful or appropriate for all dying people and their families. The limits, qualifiers, and negatives regarding the hospice alternative include the following:

1. *An available, competent, and committed next of kin is required.* Hospice is itself a kind of family or team approach that supports the caregiving efforts of the patient's own family. There must be at least one family member available who is willing and able to work with hospice (preferably more than one to help share the burden). Occasionally hospice and the local community are able to provide a "proxy next of kin." The availability of a person who is willing and able to function as primary family caregiver remains an important question to answer in considering the hospice alternative.

2. *Divided or dysfunctional families can undermine the hospice effort.* Because hospice care is essentially a person-to-person effort, it is vulnerable to situations in which the family is split by different opinions (e.g., favoring and opposing hospice). Serious problems may arise when a key person, such as the spouse, is psychotic or impaired by alcohol use. A fair degree of family mental health and unity is needed for the hospice approach to work effectively.

3. *Some types of illness are more suited to hospice care than others.* By far the greatest proportion of hospice patients have been people with some type of cancer-related condition. Hospice organizations do accept and serve people with a variety of other disorders as well. To take just one counter example, however, relatively few terminally ill people with heart disease have entered hospice programs, although heart disease is the leading cause of death among adults in the United States. Although hospice philosophy and principles seem applicable to people coping with all types of terminal disorders, the ability of a local hospice program to deal with illnesses that follow a markedly different course than those related to cancer requires examination.

4. *Hospice programs are not all alike.* To be eligible for federal reimbursement, a hospice must conform to a set of standards that includes the existence of a multi-disciplinary team, 24-hour availability, and many other requirements. Some hospices that have chosen not to participate in the federal program do offer all the specified services and features, but others do not meet these standards. Furthermore, like any other type of organization, a hospice program may itself be in varying degrees of health. The presence of many enthusiastic and competent volunteers is one useful indicator of a hospice that is doing its job well. However, some agencies have misled the public for a time by using the term "hospice" in reference to a program that lacks both the philosophy and the practice of the real thing. One is advised to inquire into the reputation of the available local hospice organizations as part of the decision-making process. It is also worth noting that elderly adults have not only predominated among hospice clients, but have also proven themselves compassionate and effective caregivers.

● EUTHANASIA

Few end-of-life issues have been as controversial as the question of euthanasia. Thoughtful people may agree in principle that there is a right to die but disagree on the methods by which this right should be exercised. Actually, there are several closely related questions here: Is there a right to die that can be exercised by (a) overdose, lethal injection, or some other form of active intervention, (b) discontinuation of treatment, or (c) not starting treatment of other life-supporting procedures? Surveys find that most Americans are supportive of the living will, which emphasizes that life-supporting procedures not be started in the first place when a person is close to death and/or in a vegetative state. There is more disagreement about the justification for discontinuing treatment (the "pulling the plug" scenario), and even more about hastening death through lethal injection or some other technique. Another dimension of this controversy centers on the specific circumstances under which euthanasia is justified. Some hold that only a dying person has this right; others would extend this right to people with multiple disabilities who are profoundly discouraged by their situation.

The term euthanasia itself is none too stable. Strictly speaking, *eu-thanasia* refers to a "good" or "happy" death, one that does not involve suffering or despair. However, it has come to mean the intentional foreshortening of life, the hastening of death. When interpreted in this manner, euthanasia runs afoul of two more clearly established concepts: suicide and murder. Indeed, opponents of "active euthanasia" often charge that self-administration of a lethal injection is simply a form of suicide, while a person who provides or facilitates active euthanasia is a murderer. Critics of "passive euthanasia" are apt to argue that it really does not matter whether death is brought about by doing something or by not doing something—the moral issue and the outcome are both the same and to suppose otherwise is to play a game with words. Furthermore, hovering over the entire discussion of euthanasia is the memory of the Nazi abuse of this concept (Lifton, 1986), as in killing some of their own citizens who were first classified as "unnecessary eaters" and then "euthanized" (killed by the doctors entrusted with their care). It is sometimes difficult to discuss today's euthanasia issues in a balanced manner when one can recall horrendous abuses of this concept in the past.

Currently the focus on euthanasia concerns the controversial Dr. Jack Kevorkian, inventor of a "suicide machine." This example illustrates the uneasy relationship between euthanasia, suicide, and murder (or manslaughter). Kevorkian himself (1991) has introduced still another term into the discussion, "medicide." This may not have been the best choice of words, because medicide implies the death of medicine or perhaps of physicians (*regicide* is the death of a king). As an advocate of "planned death" who has backed his views with daring action, Kevorkian's position statement is worth reading both by his supporters and his opponents.

The Hemlock Society has played a significant role in shaping opinion and supporting legislative initiatives since its establishment in 1980 (following the model of a London-based organization known popularly as EXIT). The Hemlock Society affirms the right of terminally ill people to end their lives in a planned manner, referring to this action as "active voluntary euthanasia" or "deliverance." Opponents tend to characterize the same actions as "suicide," "assisted suicide," or even "homicide." It is the official position of the Hemlock Society to withhold its support from active life-ending actions that are not associated with a terminal illness, and also to refrain from imposing its views on others. Classic statements of the Hemlock Society philosophy can be found in writings by Humphry and Wickett (1978 and 1986).

It is sometimes difficult to discuss today's euthanasia issues in a balanced manner when one can recall horrendous abuses of this concept in the past.

Although a significant topic for discussion, the euthanasia debate will not have the same practical implications for most people, as most will select PSDA methods and the hospice alternative. In fact, the decisions made in these spheres can go a long way toward protecting loved ones and oneself from having to face a situation in which euthanasia might seem to be the only way out. In general, the most effective approach is one that prepares everybody—family, friends, professional service providers, and, of course, oneself—well in advance through the following sequence of decisions:

- I decide to decide. I will think about end-of-life issues and make all the decisions that one can reasonably make in advance of the critical situations that might later arise.
- I will select or design an advance directive that expresses my values and responds to my needs and concerns. I will have this document ready to become part of my records, should I find myself being admitted to a health care facility. This document will place an obligation on the part of service providers to limit their interventions under the particular circumstances that I specify. This prevents the situation of having to discontinue unwanted interventions, and I do not then feel trapped and in despair because I am caught somewhere between life and death.
- I will communicate effectively with family, friends, and physician, so that everybody knows what I want and do not want to happen. This process of sharing and persuading will further protect me from being placed in a situation so unacceptable and distressful that I desire only to die quickly.
- After adequate inquiry, I decide to take the hospice option, should the time come when it is obvious that my life cannot be prolonged at an acceptable level of quality. The pain and symptom relief and sense of comfort and caring encouraged by hospice should go a long way toward protecting me from the need to give death a helping hand.

Some people do find themselves in desperate, unique, and unavoidable end-of-life situations. Within such contexts euthanasia does become a topic that must be given careful consideration by everybody involved. (For useful guidelines and bibliography, see Hastings Center, 1987.) However, by thinking ahead, exploring the options, discovering one's own preferences, and making these clearly known, it is possible to reduce substantially the likelihood of having to regard euthanasia as an end-of-life choice. (See also Chapter 27, **Making Medical Care Decisions.**)

● SUICIDE

Without benefit of Kevorkian's "suicide machine," each year more than 30,000 Americans (probably an underestimate) take their own lives. The suicide rate increases from the middle adult years onward for white males. Although old white men have the highest of all age/sex/race–specific suicide rates, this peak is something that has been steadily approached as the individual moves from his forties forward. Males have a higher suicide rate than females at every age level, and whites a higher rate than African Americans. Women become most vulnerable to suicide in their thirties, and Native Americans even earlier. Everything considered, there is no escaping the special connection between suicide and the aging white man.

From the statistical standpoint, some elderly white men are more at risk than others. Being single or divorced, living alone, and suffering from a depressive state of mind are among the factors that are associated with a higher risk of self-destruction in older men. All three of these circumstances tend to reduce the amount and quality of contact one has with other people (Kastenbaum, 1992). Financial and health difficulties as well as victimization by age discrimination can intensify this pattern. The elderly white man who kills himself often has had very little meaningful interaction with other people over a period of time—and therefore has had little opportunity to be cheered up, consoled, exposed to a different point of view, or reminded of his own ability to be interesting and useful to others. Several additional facts about suicide in the later adult years can help one to approach this issue realistically:

- Elderly people tend to use more lethal means (e.g., firearms) in their suicide attempts, resulting in a higher proportion of completed to attempted suicides than is the case with younger adults (McIntosh, 1992). Relatively few attempts can be classified as "gestures" intended to elicit attention; most often, the person really wants to die—at least at that moment.
- Use of alcohol contributes significantly to suicide among adults of all ages. Increased drinking is a warning sign that should be noticed. It is often an index of depression

and itself contributes to further loss of self-esteem.

- Many youth suicides occur when the individual is frustrated and overwhelmed, feeling unable to cope with a life situation. There is a sense of disorder, panic, and impulsive thinking. By contrast, many suicides by elderly adults are carefully planned attempts to end an existence that no longer seems useful or satisfying. Unlike the inexperienced youth, the suicidal older person has had a long track record of coping with challenges and developing a coherent lifestyle. Even the suicidal action itself reveals a sense of order and purpose.

- Illness, disability, and other adversities do not necessarily lead to suicidal behavior in later life. The great majority of elderly adults do *not* turn to suicide, but find compensations and satisfactions that keep life meaningful to them. The spirit of life often glows warmly, despite losses and limitations. However, the mistaken assumption that age somehow "causes" suicide can inhibit friends from providing the companionship and resources that could reduce the possibility of self-destructive actions. It is not unusual for a person to think passingly of suicide as an escape from increasing loss and stress. The older person with suicidal ideation seldom is a "crazy," "weak," or "immoral" individual. As already noted, usually this is a competent person who has survived many previous challenges and crises—otherwise he or she would not have made it this far. Older adults with suicidal thoughts or intentions often respond very well to counseling, as well as to enhanced companionship and social life and to opportunities to be useful to others.

● FUNERALS AND MEMORIALS

It can take some courage to open up discussion about end-of-life issues surrounding the body disposition, funeral, and memorialization process, because of fear that others do not want to hear about it. Most people are in the habit of assuming that life will just continue to go on and on; they

> **Males have a higher suicide rate than females at every age level, and whites a higher rate than African Americans.**

may at first feel anxious or resentful when reminded that all good things come to an end and some thought should be given to the particulars of that ending. Even those brothers, sisters, children, and grandchildren who seem most disconcerted by "funeral talk" do come around to recognize its usefulness and become interested participants in the discussion. The elderly adult who takes some initiative in bringing up the subject does more than contribute to working out his or her own future contingencies: he or she is also helping to prepare and instruct younger generations for the role they, too, eventually will play. There is nothing morbid in planning ahead and nothing peculiar about taking or sharing responsibility for events that so intimately concern the person.

Here is a brief check list of decisions that somebody will have to make sooner or later. It is realistic to recognize that even the best thought out plans may need to be modified somewhat when the situation actually arises, and that unforeseen circumstances can come about (e.g., sudden death in an accident while travelling abroad.) Nevertheless, it is useful to make one's wishes known to reduce the possibility of confusion and conflict among survivors who may not be quite sure what was really wanted.

These are but a few of the many points available, but they are sufficient to bring some useful issues to consideration. First, it is not unusual to encounter some enticements and pressures to make funeral (and, if desired, cemetery) arrangements in advance. Doing so can give some peace of mind ("Well, that takes care of that!"). One should be cautious, however, about prepayment plans. Funeral service establishments of the highest reputation will not pressure for advance payment. Another caution is similar to what might concern people in any advance contracting: between the time the arrangements are made and the time that the services are needed, there can be significant changes in the economic circumstances, the family situation, the community, or

Checklist 30.3
Some Funeral-Related Decisions

Yes	No	*"I would prefer ... "*
____	____	1. To have the basic funeral arrangements made in advance.
____	____	2. To have the observances and the disposition of my remains to take place in my present area of residence.
____	____	3. Cremation.
____	____	4. A funeral within a traditional religious framework.
____	____	5. A brief, simple, and inexpensive type of service.
____	____	6. A type of service that represents my distinctive way of life in a distinctive manner.
____	____	7. A memorial contribution in my name to a cause that is dear to my heart.

the funeral home. For this reason, a number of informed people choose to identify one or two funeral service establishments that would be satisfactory to them and to indicate the general nature of the arrangements they would prefer, but not to make hard and fast contractual arrangements.

Over the past three decades or so, many older adults have relocated to Sunbelt states, which has created some perplexing situations at the time of death. It is not always clear to the survivors whether or not the decedent wanted to have the funeral services and the burial or other final disposition take place in their current area, or "back home." Families have sometimes argued over this question (and the financial considerations involved), with funeral directors caught in the middle. This sort of confusion for others can be avoided by making and communicating the decision oneself—preferably after talking it over some with family and friends.

Cremation and traditional burial are almost equally popular choices among the general public. Too often neglected, however, is the question of what is to be done with the urn if cremation has been the choice. In some cases, funeral directors are faced with the awkward issue of wondering what to do with the "cremains" that have simply been left on their shelves by the survivors. In the ordinary course of events, nobody except the family survivors has the right or obligation to remove the cremains and see to their final disposition. There are as many choices as the imagination can conceive. The cremains can be buried in a traditional gravesite, preserved in an urn or other vessel, spread over a favorite pond or mountain top, and so forth. But somebody has to make this decision and somebody has to carry it out. If a person has preferences in this matter, it is a good idea to make these known.

Decisions about the preferred type of funeral arrangements have become more difficult in recent years. In a pluralistic society, a variety of ideas and preferences compete with each other. Today there are the extremes of expensive, public-oriented "mega" funerals and brief, simple, inexpensive funerals of the type endorsed by the Memorial Society and various humanist groups (Lamont, 1954; *Manual of Simple Burial*, 1964). This pluralism can affect decisions made within the same kinship group. For example, the older generations in the family may favor funeral arrangements that preserve some of the customs and values familiar to them in their own upbringing—while younger generations in the same family may prefer "something short and sweet."

Cremation and traditional burial are almost equally popular choices among the general public.

It is useful, then, to involve all generations in open and unpressured discussions. The first response sometimes proves to be only a stereotype with little substance behind it, so the young person who originally was turned off by the thought of a somewhat elaborate funeral later finds this to be a memorable and treasurable experience. Whatever the outcome, it generally proves rewarding to respect other people's viewpoints and develop something resembling a consensus.

Experts who have observed funeral attitudes and practices for many years believe that ritual is still important, even in today's fast-paced world that tends to ignore or belittle many traditional customs. Paul Irion (1991) offers both historical perspective and some good advice on the subject of modern funeral and memorial rituals. He sees a growing sensitivity on the part of many funeral directors and clergypersons and increasingly active participation on the part of family members and the community in general. His message is that there are more alternatives to the expensive, but empty, spectacle on the one hand and the quick "let's-get-it-over-with" prospect on the other. A ceremony that both respects death and celebrates life is likely to have enduring value for the survivors.

● SURVIVING, COPING, AND CONTRIBUTING

Older adults are themselves survivors. Their "age cohorts" (successive waves of individuals entering old age) through the lifespan have been reduced over the years with the deaths of family members, friends, and colleagues. In turn, there are also people who will survive them when their lives have come to an end.

When wondering how to cope with the death of other people, or how others will cope with one's own passing, it is useful to consider the following observations, all based on substantial clinical and research experience (e.g., Doka, 1989; Lund, 1989; Osterweis and others, 1984):

- Most people do recover from the intense feelings of loss, sorrow, and anxiety that comprise the grief experience. The emotional pain subsides—it does not continue forever, as the person sometimes fears it will, nor does the person "go crazy" with grief. The death of a loved person will leave a strong impact on others' lives, but most individuals show the resiliency to regain their hold on their own lives, fulfill their obligations to others, and find continuing meaning and satisfactions.
- Contrary to some assumptions, older adults often cope very well with the death of the spouse. This does not mean they are not touched by the loss, only that many years of successful coping with a variety of other crises have prepared them to deal resourcefully with this challenge as well. However, people who have not developed effective coping skills throughout their lives tend to have difficulties in later adulthood when a spouse or other key person dies.

- "Ups and downs" will occur during the grief and recovery process. There is no one, "normal" way to grieve. Each person has distinctive personal strengths and limitations and is moving from a unique past into an unique future. It does more harm than good to impose a schedule of recovery on other people—or on oneself for that matter—and to insist that one move quickly through real or imaginary stages.
- Wise and experienced friends can be extremely valuable to the bereaved person. Peer support groups are helpful to some, but not all, people. The peer support groups themselves differ widely in their style and sensitivity, just as individuals do. Whether individual or group interactions are chosen, grieving people need to express themselves and experience the support of others, especially in the first several months after bereavement.
- Self-esteem has been found to be a critical factor in recovery from grief. Researchers have found that some bereaved older adults feel that they deserve to be depressed, lonely, and incapacitated, an attitude that is sometimes intensified when the surviving partner is excluded from social occasions and interactions where couples are the rule. Helping people realize that they are still unique, attractive, and valuable can greatly enhance the recovery process.
- Recovery from grief can also be facilitated by providing practical assistance to the individual in coping with new demands and responsibilities. The bereaved older adult must adjust not only to the loss, but also to all the financial, legal, familial, and household responsibilities that once were shared with the spouse. Sometimes the survivor needs information about handling finances or resolving legal questions even more than he or she needs emotional support.

The ranks of fulfilled, productive, and creative older people include many who have survived the death of loved ones and gone on to take their own personal development to a higher level (Berman and Goldman, 1992). Some of the

Some of the strongest people in society are those who have loved, lost, and continued to live as intensely alive and sagacious human beings. (Courtesy of Sanders-Brown Center on Aging, University of Kentucky/Tim Collins, photographer)

strongest people in society are those who have loved, lost, and continued to live as intensely alive and sagacious human beings.

● COMMUNICATION OVERVIEW

Individuals differ in the way they cope with end-of-life issues. This diversity is not at all surprising, given the diversity of people's lives. Crucial to everybody, however, is the adequacy of communication techniques. Besides having a clear *idea* with regard to advance directives, terminal care, or funeral arrangements, one must successfully *communicate* these thoughts to others. Essentially, interpersonal communication is the art of exchanging messages with each other in a timely, accurate, and useful manner that also has the effect of affirming and strengthening the relationship. Failures in communication can have serious consequences when dealing with end-of-life issues. The physician who frowns, glances at

his or her watch, and backs off as the patient starts to ask a question may succeed in inhibiting the patient from asking an important question and, therefore, from making an important decision in a well-informed manner. The daughter-in-law or son-in-law whose opinion was never consulted may therefore never share a piece of information or an idea that could make all the difference in how one feels and what one decides.

Listening is a most important and most difficult facet of the interpersonal communication process. But people do not necessarily become better listeners as they grow older; in fact, there is a tendency to become less attentive to what others have to say (Strom and Strom, 1991). They often fall into the habit of concentrating on what they are going to say next, rather than on what the other person may be trying to share. Another habit that interferes with effective listening is assuming that one knows what the other person has in mind and therefore not registering all that is actually said. If such a pattern becomes firmly established, then eventually some people, who have the potential to inform, support, and delight, will instead "take their business elsewhere" and conclude that "There's no point in talking to him," or "She never really listens."

Besides having a clear *idea* with regard to advance directives, terminal care, or funeral arrangements, one must successfully *communicate* these thoughts to others.

"Really listening" is an active process. The effective listener is alert, attentive, and focused on the other person. Interest and receptivity are conveyed by the presence of some responses (e.g., eye contact, head nods, occasional "OK's") and the absence of others (e.g., fidgeting, turning away, apathetic posture). The effective listener neither attempts to rush the other person by completing his or her sentences, nor exercise control by disapproving frowns. Offering brief comments at appropriate times is also part of effective listening (Wolvin and Coakley, 1988). A personal interaction may either prove informative, and strengthen the relationship, or prove disappointing, and weaken the relationship, when one of the participants discovers that the other's mind is on something else and is simply waiting for the talking to stop. Two contrasting examples illustrate the differential consequences of "really listening" and an inattentive or passive response:

- A woman in her late sixties returns in an anxious state of mind from a medical appointment. Her son and his woman friend are waiting for her at home. She has preferred to keep her troubles to herself since the loss of her companionable husband, but she finds herself disclosing the bad news from the lab tests. Son and woman friend look at each other several times during this disclosure, but give little response to her. After about three minutes of intense communicational effort, she pauses, trying to regain control of her feelings and awaiting a response. There is a pause, then her son says: "Can I borrow your car, Mom?"

- A woman who now lives alone in a Sunbelt adult community almost declines an invitation to lunch with several women she knows through church activities. She hasn't felt much like going out lately and doesn't want to cloud other people's lives with her sorrow. The others, however, amaze her. "May I?" asks one woman, who hugs her warmly. As it turns out, they know that this is the first wedding anniversary since George's death, and two have been through that experience themselves. The bereaved woman then amazed herself by talking animatedly about George and their life together, with the obvious interest and encouragement of people who really cared about her. In leaving several hours later, she thought to herself, "I really have to get out more often and start to do something with my life."

Several principles of effective communication have been well documented by clinical research and observation in end-of-life situations. One set of principles concerns the challenge of "breaking the news" when the news is bad. Although the following suggestions are among those made by Howard G. Hogshead (1978) for use by other physicians and professional service providers, the concepts they embody can be useful to all:

1. *Keep it simple.* Don't go into too many details and technicalities.

2. Ask yourself, *"What does this diagnosis mean to this patient?"* The fact that a person has been told the diagnosis does not guarantee that this person has been able to attach a coherent meaning to it, especially at first hearing.

3. *Don't deliver all the news at once.* "People have a marvelous way of letting you know how much they are able to handle." The full disclosure may have to be spread out over several interactions.

4. *Wait for questions.* A long pause will provide the opportunity for a question or comment that suggests where the conversation should move.

5. *Do not argue with denial or evasion.* The person who is exposed to bad news will "hear" the message when he or she is ready to accept it.

6. *Do not destroy all hope.* It is possible to live with the prospect of death and not despair, as many people have demonstrated.

7. *Do not say anything that is not true.* "This would be the cruelest blow of all."

Another set of communication principles, derived from a variety of sources, applies to a broader range of situations:

1. *Unhurried interactions are more likely to prove valuable.* In the United States, both society and individuals tend to rush and overschedule. This bustling lifestyle can be challenging enough in everyday life (e.g., Schor, 1991), but it is likely to become oppressive and overwhelming when one is caught up in a crisis situation that is under the direction of busy professionals. When interacting with people who are trying to cope with terminal illness, bereavement, and other end-of-life situations, offering the gift of time can be most welcome and most effective.

2. *Touch and other nonverbal modes of communication can affirm the interpersonal bonds that enable people to be most helpful to each other in critical situations.* Individuals sometimes torment themselves, wondering exactly what they should say to someone who is dying or grieving. Usually, however, what matters is not so much what is said but what the overall quality of the interaction is. This fact is well appreciated by hospice workers,

who frequently touch in gestures of understanding and support when words do not seem sufficient. Obviously, the reassuring touch from a caring person must be genuine and in character with the existing relationship. Along with appropriate touching and active listening, communication in end-of-life situations is sometimes enhanced by singing or going through a photograph album together, as well as by any other shared activity in which what is said is secondary to conveying the sense of really being with the other person.

3. *Death need not be the primary topic of conversation.* People sometimes fear that they will be engulfed by "death talk" if they interact openly with a dying, grieving, or suicidal person. This is seldom the case in practice. A dying person, for example, is actually a living person who may continue to have a variety of interests, concerns, and enthusiasms. After all participants in the communicational network have established that they know that death is a pressing issue and are ready to deal with it when required by circumstances. Conversational topics may vary considerably over time, including the mundane and the lighthearted.

4. *Respect each person's individuality.* The anxieties associated with end-of-life issues often lead people to resort to thoughtless clichés, which come in many forms:

- "Children cannot understand death." (The research of Bluebond-Langner [1989], and many others, contradicts this concept.)
- "Old people are ready for death." (This statement is contested by the research of Weisman and Kastenbaum [1972] and many others.)
- "People die in stages and should be helped to reach the final stage." (The state of the art review of Corr [1991–92] and other researchers dispute this notion.)
- "Men are stronger than women in coping with the death of their spouse." (Stroebe, Stroebe, and Domittner [1988] and other researchers reject this theory.)

While such generalizations embody rough mixtures of fact, assumption, and fantasy, lay people or health care professionals reduce their opportunity to know, understand, and help others when they stereotype unique individuals.

Interacting with a dying person by voicing such fixed ideas is not authentic interaction but rather a playing out of a preexisting scenario. "Textbook cases" do not live and die: these adventures are reserved for unique men and women who are coping with unique circumstances.

References

Berman, P. L., and K. Goldman. *The Ageless Spirit.* New York: Ballantine, 1992.

Bluebond-Langner, M. "Children, Dying." In *Encyclopedia of Death.* Eds. R. Kastenbaum, and B. K. Kastenbaum. Phoenix, AZ: Oryx Press, 1989.

Corr, C. A. "A Task-Based Approach to Coping and Dying." *Omega: Journal of Death and Dying* Vol. 24 (1991–92): 81–94.

Culver, C. M., and B. Gert. "Beyond the Living Will: Making Advance Directives More Useful." *Omega: Journal of Death and Dying* Vol. 21 (1990): 253–58.

Doka, K. J., ed. *Disenfranchised Grief.* Lexington, MA: Lexington Books, 1989.

Gilmore, A. J. J. "Hospice Development in the United Kingdom." In *Encyclopedia of Death.* Eds. R. Kastenbaum, and B. K. Kastenbaum. Phoenix, AZ: Oryx Press, 1989.

Gubrium, J. F. *Living and Dying at Murray Manor.* New York: St. Martin's Press, 1975.

Hastings Center. *Guidelines on the Termination of Life-Sustaining Treatment and the Care of the Dying.* Bloomington: Indiana University Press, 1987.

Hogshead, H. P. "The Art of Delivering Bad News." In *Psychosocial Care of the Dying Patient.* Ed. C. Garfield. New York: McGraw-Hill, 1978.

Humphry, D., and A. Wickett. *Jean's Way.* New York: Quartet Books, 1978.

———. *The Right to Die.* New York: Harper & Row, 1986.

Irion, P. E. "Changing Patterns of Ritual Response to Death." *Omega: Journal of Death and Dying* Vol. 22 (1990–91): 159–72.

Kastenbaum, R. "Can the Clinical Milieu Be Therapeutic?" In *Aging and Milieu.* Eds. G. D. Rowles, and R. J. Ohta. New York: Academic Press, 1983.

———. *Death, Society, and Human Experience.* 4th ed. New York: Macmillan/Merrill, 1991.

———. "Death, Suicide, and the Older Adult." *Suicide and Life-Threatening Behavior* Vol. 22 (1992): 1–14.

Kevorkian, J. *Prescription: Medicide.* New York: Prometheus, 1991.

Lamont, C. *A Humanist Funeral Service.* New York: Horizon Press, 1954.

Lifton, R. J. *The Nazi Doctors.* New York: Basic Books, 1986.

Lund, D. A., ed. *Older Bereaved Spouses.* New York: Hemisphere, 1989.

McIntosh, J. "Epidemiology of Suicide in the Elderly." *Suicide and Life-Threatening Behavior* Vol. 22 (1992): 15–35.

Manual of Simple Burial. Burnsville, NC: Celo Press, 1964.

Mor, V. *Hospice Care Systems.* New York: Springer, 1987.

Mor, V., D. S. Greer, and R. Kastenbaum, eds. *The Hospice*

Experiment. Baltimore, MD: Johns Hopkins University Press, 1988.

Osterweis, M., F. Solomon, and M. Green, eds. *Bereavement: Reactions, Consequences, and Care.* Washington, DC: National Academy Press, 1984.

Reflections of the Times: The Right to Die. Washington, DC: Times Mirror Center for the People and the Press, 1990.

Rouse, F. "Patients, Providers, and the PSDA." *Hastings Center Report* Vol. 21, no. 5, Special Supplement (1991): S2–S3.

Schor, J. B. *The Overworked American.* New York: Basic Books, 1991.

Scofield, G. "The Living Will." In *Encyclopedia of Death.* Eds. R. Kastenbaum, and B. K. Kastenbaum. Phoenix, AZ: Oryx Press, 1989.

Stroebe, W., M. S. Stroebe, and G. Domittner. "Individual and Situational Differences in Recovery from Grief and Bereavement: A Risk Group Identified." *Journal of Social Issues* Vol. 44 (1988): 143–58.

Strom, R. D., and S. K. Strom. *Becoming a Better Grandparent.* Newbury Park, CA: Sage, 1991.

Weisman, A. D., and R. Kastenbaum. *The Psychological Autopsy: A Study of the Terminal Phase of Life.* New York: Behavioral Publications, 1972.

Wolvin, A., and C. Coakley. *Listening.* 3d ed. Dubuque, IA: W. C. Brown, 1988.

Additional Reading

I. Communication

Goodman, G. *The Talk Book: The Intimate Science of Communicating in Close Relationships.* Emmaus, PA: Rodale Press, 1988.

Tannen, D. *That's Not What I Meant! How Conversational Style Makes or Breaks Relationships.* New York: Ballantine, 1986.

———. *You Just Don't Understand: Women and Men in Conversation.* New York: William Morrow, 1990.

II. Family Caregiving and Relationships

Shelley, F. D. *When Your Parents Grow Old.* New York: Harper & Row, 1988.

Silverstone, B., and H. K. Hyman. *You and Your Aging Parent: The Modern Family's Guide to Emotional, Physical, and Financial Problems.* 3d ed. New York: Pantheon, 1989.

Sommers, R., and L. Shields. *Women Take Care: The Consequences of Caregiving in Today's Society.* Gainesville, FL: Triad, 1987.

Tomb, D. A. *Growing Old: A Handbook for You and Your Aging Parents.* New York: Viking, 1984.

III. Coping with Dying, Death, and Bereavement

Beresford, Larry. *The Hospice Handbook.* Boston, MA: Little, Brown & Co., 1992.

Bowman, Meg. *Memorial Services for Women.* San Jose, CA: Hot Flash Press, 1987.

Chase, D. *Dying at Home with Hospice.* St. Louis, MO: C. V. Mosby, 1986.

Coleman, B. *A Consumer Guide to Hospice Care.* Washington, DC: National Consumers League, 1990.

Collins, E. R., Jr., and D. Weber. *The Complete Guide to Living Wills.* New York: Bantam, 1992.

Dennis, C. *Plan Your Estate.* Berkeley, CA: Nolo Press, 1989.

Hill, T. Patrick, and David Shirley. *A Good Death: Taking More Control at the End of Your Life.* New York: Addison-Wesley, 1992.

Humphry, Derek. *Final Exit.* Eugene, OR: The Hemlock Society, 1992.

Kastenbaum, R. *The Psychology of Death.* Rev. ed. New York: Springer, 1992.

Leenaars, A. L., R. Maris, J. L. McIntosh, and J. Richman, eds. *Suicide and the Older Adult.* New York: Guilford Press, 1992.

Loewinsohn, R. J. *Survival Handbook for Widows (and for Relatives and Friends Who Want to Understand).* Washington, DC: American Association of Retired Persons (AARP), 1984.

Munley, A. *The Hospice Alternative.* New York: Basic Books, 1983.

Myers, E. *When Parents Die: A Guide for Adults.* New York: Viking, 1986.

Nelson, T. C. *It's Your Choice: The Practical Guide to Planning a Funeral.* Washington, DC: American Association of Retired Persons (AARP), 1987.

Norrgard, Lee E., and Jo DeMars. *Final Choices: Making End-of-Life Decisions.* Santa Barbara, CA: ABC-CLIO, 1992.

Osgood, N. J. *Suicide in the Elderly: A Practioner's Guide to Diagnosis and Mental Health Intervention.* Rockville, MD: Aspen Systems Corp., 1985.

Rando, T. A. *Grief, Dying, and Death: Clinical Interventions for Caregivers.* Champaign, IL: Research Press, 1984.

———. *Grieving: How to Go on Living When Someone You Love Dies.* Lexington, MA: Lexington Books, 1988.

Sanders, C. M. *Grief: The Mourning After.* New York: John Wiley & Sons, 1989.

Silverman, P. *Widow-to-Widow.* New York: Springer, 1986.

Soled, A. J. *The Essential Guide to Wills, Estates, Trusts, and Death Taxes.* Washington, DC: American Association of Retired Persons and Scott, Foresman, 1986.

Stoddard, S. *The Hospice Movement: A Better Way of Caring for the Dying.* Briarcliff Manor, NY: Stein & Day, 1978.

Tallmer, L., and D. Lester, eds. *Suicide in the Elderly: Counseling Needs and Management.* Boston: Charles Press, 1992.

Robert Kastenbaum, Ph.D.

Section X:

The Social Environment

31

Housing for Older Persons

- Housing Needs of an Aging Population ● Living Arrangements and Location of Older Americans
- Older Homeowners ● Home Modifications to Extend Independence
- Reverse Mortgages ● Neighborhood Environment and Alternative Housing Options
- Manufactured Housing ● Continuing Care Retirement Communities
- Older Renters and the Production of Rental Housing ● Trends

Housing is a critically important factor that determines whether older people experience old age as secure and meaningful or disabling and isolated. Although recent data helps to document important progress in meeting the housing needs of older persons, the rapidly growing number of older households will present new challenges to housing providers, policy makers, and, above all, older consumers and their families in the coming decades.

● HOUSING NEEDS OF AN AGING POPULATION

By 2020, the older population (aged 65 and over) will have grown to 52.1 million, a 65 percent increase from the 31.6 million in 1990. As a percentage of the total population, the older population will have grown from 12.6 percent to 17.7 percent (U.S. Congress, 1991). Yet important changes in the age structure of the older population are occuring. Between 1990 and 2000, as the older population grows by 3.3 million, 41 percent of the growth will be among those 85 years and older. In contrast, the population aged 65 to 74 will actually decline marginally during the same period, reflecting the "birth dearth" during the Great Depression.

Between 2000 and 2010, the older population will grow by 4.5 million, of which 33 percent of the growth will be among those 85 and older, while 62 percent of the growth will be among those 65 to 74, and a meager 4 percent of the growth will be among those 75 to 84. The decade of the 2010s will see explosive growth in the older population as the baby boomers begin to turn 65—12.8 million people aged 65 and older will be added during the decade. More than three-fourths (78 percent) of that growth will occur among the 65 to 74 years age group, with 18 percent growth among those 75 to 84, and a flat 4 percent growth rate among those 85 and older.

Successive waves of individuals entering old age, which gerontologists refer to as "age cohorts," will have very different experiences of aging due to differing historical experiences. For example, today's "old old" is made up of cohorts who generally came of age during the Great Depression. These oldest individuals and families generally have lower incomes and assets, both because they have outlived many of their

---

Between 1990 and 2000, as the older population grows by 3.3 million, 41 percent of the growth will be among those 85 years and older. In contrast, the population aged 65 to 74 will actually decline marginally during the same period, reflecting the "birth dearth" during the Great Depression.

---

resources and because their career patterns suffered at the outset from the timing of trying to get a job in the midst of the Depression.

The American Association of Retired Persons (AARP) Public Policy Institute recently commissioned the Urban Institute to develop a profile of the housing conditions of elders, (Mikelsons and Turner, 1992), comparing data from the 1980 and 1989 American Housing Surveys (AHS). These data indicate a dramatic increase in the poverty rate for those 75 and older, from 19.9 percent to 25 percent. In addition, the proportion of older households with incomes below $5,000 (in constant 1987 dollars) increased from 8.6 percent to 14.2 percent (1.38 million to 2.79 million households)—most of this increase is among the old old.

Also reflecting the unfavorable economic times for household formation and launching a family during the Great Depression, the cohorts that make up the old old during the 1990s have the highest rates of childlessness in American history. Among women who turned 85 before 1986, 22 percent never had any children, a rate that rises to 24 percent among women who became or will become 85 between 1986 and 1995. Thereafter the childlessness rate declines steadily for those cohorts turning 85 in the years 1996 to 2000 (23 percent), 2001 to 2005 (17 percent), 2006 to 2010 (14 percent), 2011 to 2015 (12 percent), and 2016 to 2020 (11 percent) (Congressional Budget Office, 1988).

These data indicate that a major demographic crunch is already facing the country. The 1990s will witness the most rapid growth in the oldest old, who are most likely to experience significant disabilities, who have lower incomes and fewer assets than any age group (save, perhaps, the very youngest families), and who have the weakest set of informal supports because of a high rate of childlessness. All of these factors increase the risk of nursing home use for long-term care needs.

Expanding housing options to accommodate an increasingly diverse range of needs among older persons and managing the transition between the cohorts of old old and young old will require foresight and planning on the part of developers, home builders, policy officials, and advocates. Meeting the challenge of a rapidly aging population will require increasing attention

Meeting the challenge of a rapidly aging population will require application of new technologies to improve the safety, convenience, efficiency, and affordability of housing for the span of a lifetime. (Copyright © Marianne Gontarz)

to promising new technologies to improve the safety, convenience, efficiency, and affordability of housing designed for a "life span" (Harootyan, 1992).

● LIVING ARRANGEMENTS AND LOCATION OF OLDER AMERICANS

The living arrangements of older people have changed dramatically over the past few decades, generally reflecting an improved ability to remain independent longer. Opinion surveys on the preferred living arrangements of older people have invariably documented a desire to live independently apart from children or others who might be inclined to take care of them. Changes in living arrangements since 1960 indicate that

Opinion surveys on the preferred living arrangements of older people have invariably documented a desire to live independently apart from children or others who might be inclined to take care of them. (Courtesy of Highland Farms Retirement Community, Black Mountain, North Carolina)

Figure 31.1
Living Arrangements of People Age 65+: 1989
(numbers in millions)

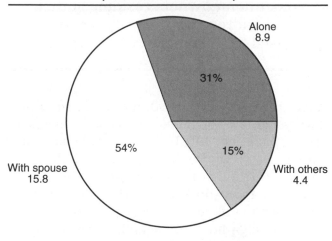

People Age 65+

Source: U.S. Bureau of the Census. "Marital Status and Living Arrangements: March 1989." *Current Population Reports Series P-20, no. 445* (June 1990).

increasing numbers of older people, especially women, are able to live independently. According to census data, 45 percent of all Americans aged 65 and over lived with people other than their spouses in 1960—a figure that declined dramatically to 15.2 percent by 1989 (Congressional Budget Office, 1988; U.S. Congress, 1991). The percentage of older people living only with a spouse rose from 37 percent to 54 percent during the same time period, while the percentage of those living alone rose from 19 percent to 31 percent.

Reflecting longer life spans, the tendency to marry older men, and the lower likelihood of remarriage after widowhood or divorce, older women are much more likely than men to live alone—41 percent for older women versus 16 percent of older men. Similarly, older women are much more likely than men to live with people other than their spouses—by a margin of 19 percent to 10 percent. Conversely, the vast majority of older men (74 percent) live with their spouses, versus only 40 percent of older women, a number that declines to only 9 percent for women over age 85.

Living arrangements also differ according to the ethnicity among the elderly, reflecting both economic and cultural differences. Older whites are only half as likely to live with relatives as older African Americans or Hispanics—12 percent for whites versus 24 percent for older African Americans and 26 percent for older Hispanics. Because of higher widowhood rates, only 39 percent of older African Americans live with a spouse compared to 50 percent of older Hispanics and 54 percent of older whites (U.S. Congress, 1991).

The stability of older households, always at a high level, is increasing. Between 1980 and 1989, the percentage of older homeowners residing at their current address for twenty years or more increased from 50.6 percent to 58 percent. In contrast, 40 percent of nonelderly homeowners had moved within the last five years. Even older renters tend to stay put—only 42 percent reported moving in the last five years compared

Figure 31.2
Distribution of the Elderly by Living Arrangements, 1960 and 1984

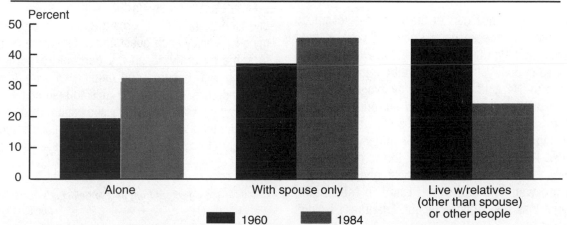

Source: Congressional Budget Office, 1988. (Prepared by AARP Public Policy Institute.)

to 82 percent of renters under 65 (Mikelsons and Turner, 1992).

During the 1980s, the older population tended to grow in small towns at the expense of rural areas. Between 1980 and 1989, the older population grew by an impressive 80 percent in small towns. Reflecting the move to suburban areas by the cohort that formed households in the post-World War II era, the great majority of this growth (59 percent) was among the young old—those aged 65 to 75.

The age profile of households in rural areas changed dramatically in the opposite direction. Between 1980 and 1989, the population over age 75 remained almost exactly the same—declining by 0.01 percent. On the other hand, the population aged 65 to 74 declined by a substantial 18 percent in rural areas. Major metropolitan areas were in between rural areas and small towns—with the population over 65 growing 22 percent. Most of the increase (57 percent) was among the older population over age 75 (Mikelsons and Turner, 1992).

● OLDER HOMEOWNERS

Of all age groups, older households have the highest rate of home ownership—78 percent own their homes, 84 percent own them mort-

---

Between 1980 and 1989, the percentage of older homeowners residing at their current address for twenty years or more increased from 50.6 percent to 58 percent.

---

gage-free. Between 1980 and 1989, the home ownership rate for those age 65 to 75 increased from 77 percent to 81 percent (Mikelsons and Turner, 1992). During the same period, the home ownership rate for households under age 65 declined from 65.2 percent to 62 percent. Accumulation of equity is a major source of savings, and high home ownership rates are a bulwark of financial security for older homeowners.

While the quality of housing of older persons generally improved during the 1980s (Mikelsons and Turner, 1992), problems persist among the following subgroups of older homeowners:

Minorities. In 1989, homes of older African-American owners were almost four times more likely (21.3 percent to 5.7 percent) to exhibit severe or moderate quality problems as the homes of older white owners (Mikelsons and Turner, 1992). In comparison, 13.4 percent of

---

Voices of Creative Aging

Colter H., a 77-year-old gentleman farmer and innkeeper, relates his belief that changing his lifestyle saved his life:

I have lived in this part of the world for seventeen years. When I came up here, I couldn't walk without crutches. I had high blood pressure and was supposed to be dead in about six months. I retired, thinking I had little time to live, and have fooled everybody including myself. I purchased the farm and surrounded myself with livestock, birds, and pets. This life was a lifelong dream and welcome change after thirty years in the American Foreign Service. I think the farm cured my ailments. I feel at home with animals, and I think that made me well. If I had them, I had to feed them, whether I was on crutches or not. Eventually I didn't

need my crutches, and eventually I didn't need much in the way of medicine for my blood pressure. It came down and stayed down pretty well.

After a time I opened my remodeled home as a bed and breakfast. I manage the fifteen-room house, cook everyone's breakfast, do the laundry, make the beds, and tend to the daily chores of feeding the animals on my own. I enjoy each guest and at times can be helpful to some by drawing on my personal experience of working with hospice and dealing with my loss of a wife and child. I have been able to help some men of my own age who are facing issues about death.

I don't think of myself as a very religious person, but I am grateful to the great I AM, whatever that great I AM is.

Excerpt from Connie Goldman's "Late Bloomer"
public radio series

older Hispanic households had a similar level of housing problems.

Single person households. Three-fifths of severe housing inadequacies occurred in single person households compared to less than one-quarter in married households (Alvarez and Gaberlavage, 1988).

Rural elders. According to the 1985 American Housing Survey (Lazere, et al., 1989), 57 percent of severe inadequacies among all elderly households occurred in rural areas. Older households in nonmetro areas were more than twice as likely as metropolitan households (13.1 percent to 6.4 percent) to experience housing inadequacies.

Central-city dwellers. Seventy-one percent of housing inadequacies in urban areas are concentrated in central cities (Alvarez and Gaberlavage, 1988).

Despite higher average incomes than renters, older homeowners represented 63 percent of older households with incomes $5,000 and below in 1989 (Mikelsons and Turner, 1992). Real estate taxes, utility costs, and insurance are often a substantial burden, even though the vast majority of poor elderly households own their homes free and clear (86 percent). According to the AHS, half of all poor elderly home owners spent at least 46 percent of their income on housing in 1989 (Apgar, 1989). Housing expenditures, when combined with the elderly's high out-of-pocket medical expenses, limit the cash resources available for maintenance, repairs, and modifications to assist with mobility problems.

Of all age groups, older households have the highest rate of home ownership—78 percent own their homes, 84 percent own them mortgage-free.

While most older people do not view themselves as functionally impaired, many experience problems with activities of daily living. Older homeowners overwhelmingly prefer to stay where they are as they grow older (AARP, 1990a). The ability to remain in their homes, however, often depends on the adaptability of the home environment. The location of the

home and its characteristics can aid in the provision of in-home, long-term care services—or make such services nearly impossible (Newman, 1985). Home modifications can diminish problems related to reductions in physical functioning (such as sight, hearing, mobility) and may reduce the incidence of withdrawal from activities, premature institutionalization, accidents, and fatal injuries (Pynoos and others, 1987).

Federal programs to deal with the maintenance, repair, and modification needs of older homeowners have been inadequate and badly coordinated. Only a tiny program run by the Farmers Home Administration (the Section 504 grant program) has focused on older homeowners. The Community Development Block Grant (CDBG) program and Title III of the Older Americans Act have funded some home repairs, though resources for both programs have stagnated in recent years. The National Affordable Housing Act of 1990 authorized home repairs for older and disabled homeowners under the newly created HOME block grant, though no funds have been spent under the program. No federal program authorizes the full range of repairs and modifications needed to address both substandard housing conditions and adaptations needed to promote mobility. Older homeowners, especially older minorities, are underserved by these programs relative to the extent of deficiencies in their housing. (Yurow, 1988)

Federal programs to deal with the maintenance, repair, and modification needs of older homeowners have been inadequate and badly coordinated. Only a tiny program run by the Farmers Home Administration (the Section 504 grant program) has focused on older homeowners.

● **HOME MODIFICATIONS TO EXTEND INDEPENDENCE**

Home modification refers to adaptations to the home environment that can assist older or functionally impaired individuals to maintain indepen-

Illustration 31.1. Ms. Benton in her kitchen—before modifications. (Courtesy of the American Association of Retired Persons from *The Perfect Fit: Creative Ideas for a Safe and Livable Home*)

dent living (Long Term Care National Resource Center, 1990). Modifications may range from structural changes, such as lowering cabinets and doorway thresholds, widening door frames, and installing ramps, to material adjustments like rearranging furniture and storage of essential items for easy access. Special equipment like grab bars, bath benches, and railings can prevent falls and other serious accidents (Pynoos and others, 1987).

A recent survey by AARP indicates that the most common home modifications undertaken by older persons are additional lighting (23 percent), confining living quarters to one floor to avoid stairs (18 percent), using lever faucets in place of knobs (18 percent), and installing additional hand rails or grab bars (17 percent). Modifications used less frequently are emergency response systems (9 percent), replacing door knobs with lever handles (5 percent), replacing stairs with ramps (4 percent), and widening doorways. Women, persons 75 and older, those with incomes under $20,000, and those with health limitations were

more likely to have added hand rails or grab bars (AARP, 1992).

Relatively simple modifications can reduce stress from routine activities of daily living and allow older occupants to continue to enjoy many activities such as bathing, cooking, and entertaining. By adjusting the home environment to more closely fit the physical capabilities and social needs of the older occupant, home modification is one option for fulfilling the desire of most older persons to remain in their current residence.

For instance, Illustration 31.1 shows Ms. Benton in her kitchen. She likes to have friends over in the late afternoon several times a week. She is well known in the neighborhood for her hot spiced-apple cider in the winter and iced mint tea in the summer as well as her special peach cobbler. She has found, however, that because of her arthritis, it is harder to prepare the food, serve her guests, and clean up.

Illustration 31.2 shows Ms. Benton after some modifications are made to her kitchen. The numbers correspond to recommended modifications.

Illustration 31.2. Ms. Benton in her kitchen—after modifications. (Courtesy of the American Association of Retired Persons from *The Perfect Fit: Creative Ideas for a Safe and Livable Home*)

1. Trays: Install roll-out trays to make base storage more accessible.

2. Faucet: Install a single lever-handled faucet that is easy to turn.

3. Reacher: Use a long-handled reacher for lightweight items on high shelves.

4. Additional shelves: Add additional shelves and hooks under cabinets to store objects used regularly, or use a wall rack.

5. Heavy objects lower: Keep heavy objects on bottom shelves or cabinet tops; put lightweight or least-used objects on top shelves.

6. Replace knobs: Replace knobs with lever or U-shaped pulls or handles.

7. Trolley cart: Use a trolley cart instead of a tray to transport food.

8. Stepstool: Obtain a solid stepladder with high railings to hold onto.

9. Objects over stove: Move objects over stove to another location to avoid potential burns.

10. Illumination: Install good ceiling illumi-nation and additional task lighting where food is prepared.

The preference among older households for staying in their current homes can be attributed to numerous factors. Respondents to an AARP survey most often mentioned location, comfort, the neighborhood, the size of their residence or property, the attractiveness of their property, and the floor plan or the lack of steps. (Dobkin, 1987) Present or expected lifestyle, health status, and financial resources are also key considerations. For many older persons, home ownership sym-bolizes independence and personal achievement. They are extremely reluctant to relinquish their present homes for less private or independent liv-ing arrangements (Golant, 1992). In addition, the prospective loss of familial contact and treasured possessions makes relocation difficult and emo-tionally traumatic (O'Bryant and McGloshen, 1987; Redfoot, 1987).

Diminishing physical abilities and chronic ill-nesses, however, often make it difficult for older

Illustration 31.3. Mrs. Klein in her bathroom—before modifications. (Courtesy of the American Association of Retired Persons from *The Perfect Fit: Creative Ideas for a Safe and Livable Home*)

persons to continue to live independently in their present environments. More than four out of five people age 65 and older have at least one chronic condition. Approximately 13 percent of older persons living in the community had difficulty with one or more activities of daily living such as walking, bathing, transferring, dressing, using the toilet, and eating. Instrumental activities of daily living posed difficulites for 17.5 percent. Such activities include doing light housework, preparing meals, use of the telephone, getting around the community, shopping, and handling money. A very high proportion of older persons who live alone suffer from chronic health problems and have difficulty performing daily activities. By the year 2020, this population is expected to increase by 57 percent (U.S. Congress, 1991).

Illustration 31.3 shows Mrs. Klein preparing for a bath. She has always enjoyed bathing—she finds it relaxing, therapeutic, and hygienic. But recently, she slipped getting out of the bathtub in her apartment. Luckily she didn't hurt herself, but it was a frightening experience. She has known several friends who have broken their hips in such falls and she doesn't want that to happen to her. At the same time, she wants to keep using the bathtub.

Illustration 31.4 shows Mrs. Klein after some modifications are made to her bathroom. The numbers correspond to recommended modifications.

1. Rug: Secure rug with nonskid tape or remove all loose rugs.
2. Grab bars: Add grab bars, either attached to studs in the wall or portable over bathtub ledge.
3. Bath mat: Add bath mat or nonskid strips to bottom of tub.
4. Toilet: Add grab bar by toilet.
5. Bath bench: Add bath bench in tub if necessary.
6. Shelf: Install small corner shelf over tub for bath supplies.
7. Shower: Install a hand-held shower.

Homes purchased when older occupants were

Illustration 31.4. Mrs. Klein in her bathroom—after modifications. (Courtesy of the American Association of Retired Persons from *The Perfect Fit: Creative Ideas for a Safe and Livable Home*)

raising families may now stress their physical abilities and financial resources. According to the latest American Housing Survey, 81 percent of older homeowners live in traditional single family detached homes, and almost two-thirds of these homes were built prior to 1960 (U.S. Dept. of Housing and Urban Development, 1991). These older homes can be more expensive to heat and maintain. In addition, very few have been modified to compensate for the increased frailty of their occupants (Golant, 1992).

A recent study notes that just 10 percent of older households with at least one member having a health or mobility limitation made any design modifications to their homes. The most common modification (6.6 percent) was the addition of hand rails and grab bars. Adjustments to sinks, cabinets, and light switches were found in little over 1 percent of the homes surveyed. Less than 1 percent of the households incorporated modifications to allow wheel chair access (Struyk and Katsura, 1987).

A high rate of fatal and disabling accidents

reflects the increasing imbalance between the demands of the home environment and physical abilities of older occupants. For example, falls make up two-thirds of all accidental fatalities among older persons (Pynoos and others, 1987). Approximately 85 percent of all stair-related deaths occur among persons age 65 and older (Pynoos and Cohen, 1992). Research indicates that two-thirds of these deaths could be prevented through home modifications or design changes (Pynoos and others, 1987).

Despite the fact that many modifications are relatively low cost and easy to accomplish, significant barriers exist to wider modification activity. For example, Medicare and Medicaid will not pay for nonmedical equipment such as grab bars (Golant, 1992). A confusing array of federal, state, and local programs provide some assistance for low-income homeowners, but the services offered vary considerably and funding has been inadequate (Yurow, 1988). Medical and other service providers often overlook home modifications that could assist older clients, and few communi-

Approximately 85 percent of all stair-related deaths occur among persons age 65 and older. Research indicates that two-thirds of these deaths could be prevented through home modifications or design changes. (Courtesy of the American Association of Retired Persons)

ties have programs to assist older persons or their families in assessing the home environment (Long Term Care National Resource Center, 1990). Finally, older persons may be reluctant to acknowledge that their capabilities have diminished, are unaware of how home modifications can improve their quality of life, or do not know where to obtain assistance in getting home modifications installed (Pynoos and others, 1987; Pynoos and Cohen, 1992).

According to the latest American Housing Survey, 81 percent of older homeowners live in traditional single family detached homes, and almost two-thirds of these homes were built prior to 1960.

A number of states have initiated programs using state monies to foster home repair and modification. For instance, Maine established a low-interest loan program for adaptive equipment, and Ohio included home modification as part of a $75 million aging services initiative. Much of this activity has been implemented through the network of area agencies on aging (Long Term Care National Resource Center, 1990 and 1991). These agencies can often provide information to consumers on available services and programs. Preliminary results from a demonstration program funded by the Robert Wood Johnson Foundation show the potential for a successful private pay market for home modifications using home health agencies. Under the demonstration, 45 percent of clients offered home repair services purchased them, and over half the revenues of participating agencies were derived from home maintenance and handyman services and installation of grab bars (Long Term Care National Resource Center, 1990).

Recent surveys by the AARP indicate that older persons are planning more for future housing needs and have become increasingly aware of the impact of health limitations on household activities (AARP, 1992). In response, the Association has published *The Do-Able Renewable Home: Making Your Home Fit Your Needs* and *The Perfect Fit: Creative Ideas for a Safe and Livable Home*. These booklets are available free and contain suggestions for home modifications; they list available assessment guides as well as sources of products and information. They also provide useful tips on hiring a contractor to complete repairs and modifications. (To order single copies, write: AARP Fulfillment, 601 E Street, NW, Washington, DC 20049. Indicate stock numbers D12470 and D14823.)

● REVERSE MORTGAGES

The National Affordable Housing Act of 1990 (NAHA) also contained a provision to expand a mortgage insurance demonstration for home equity conversion from 2,500 to 25,000 loans over five years. Home equity conversion allows older homeowners to use the equity in their homes to meet needs such as home repair and support services without having to move or sell the home.

At present, FHA-insured reverse mortgages are being offered by private lenders in at least thirty states. Eligible borrowers must be over 62, own and occupy a single family home with little or no mortgage balance, and maintain the home as a principal residence for the duration of the reverse mortgage. Counseling by an independent third party is required of every borrower prior to submitting a loan application. Four types of payment options are available under the FHA demonstration:

1. **Term:** Monthly payments to a homeowner for a fixed period

2. **Tenure:** Monthly payments to a home-owner for as long as at least one borrower remains in the home

3. **Line of Credit:** Draws permitted on an as needed up to the loan limit

4. **Combination:** A line of credit plus either form of monthly payment as described above

The FHA demonstration imposes a maximum loan amount limit that ranges from $67,500 to $101,250 depending on geographic area. Insurance premiums, which are 2 percent of the loan amount, paid by the borrower at closing and 0.5 percent annually on the increasing loan balance, insure the loan and provide protection to both the lender and the borrower. Repayment is not due until the borrower dies, sells, or permanently moves from the home.

The program is not without flaws. Consumers are often shocked by the cost of reverse mortgages, as high as $9,000 on a loan of $125,000. Lenders, on the other hand, feel the origination fee is not high enough to cover their costs. In addition, the availability and quality of the required counseling has been uneven (National Center for Home Equity Conversion, 1991b).

Recent data compiled from both public and private programs by the National Center for Home Equity Conversion indicates that the average reverse mortgage borrower is a single woman in her mid-seventies with an annual income of about $12,000. Almost all reverse mortgage borrowers use their loan advances to pay property taxes or repair their homes (National Center for Home Equity Conversion, 1991a). A recent survey of older homeowners by AARP found potential borrowers cite health needs and long-term care as the most likely reasons for considering a reverse mortgage (AARP, 1990a).

The potential for increased use of home equity conversion is considerable. Nearly 25 percent of low-income older homeowners have at least $50,000 equity in their homes. Research has indicated that almost 75 percent of poor single homeowners aged 75 and over could raise their incomes above the poverty line by converting home equity into spendable income (Jacobs, 1986).

Until recently, reverse mortgage lending has been mostly a public sector activity (National Center for Home Equity Conversion, 1991a).

These programs often place limits on the use of funds or the amount of the loans. For example, owners of high valued properties cannot receive as high a payment, either monthly or on a lump sum basis, from a FHA insured loan as they might from other private or public sector programs. However, the reverse mortgage industry is poised for major expansion. Private companies are now engaged in raising capital through public stock offerings, securitization of debt by institutional investors, and negotiation with major pension funds to finance reverse mortgages for their members. In addition, federally insured mortgages are expected to be offered shortly by multi-state lenders on both coasts and new regional lenders. AARP recently issued a model state statute on reverse mortgages to encourage additional lending by state housing finance agencies (AARP, 1990b).

Recent data compiled from both public and private programs by the National Center for Home Equity Conversion indicates that the average reverse mortgage borrower is a single woman in her mid-seventies with an annual income of about $12,000.

● **NEIGHBORHOOD ENVIRONMENT AND ALTERNATIVE HOUSING OPTIONS**

Most older households are choosing to reside in their current homes and are staying in these homes until late in life (AARP, 1990; Mikelsons and Turner, 1992). However, the housing stock and land use patterns of suburban communities, where most older people now live, were not intended for an aging population. Large single family homes can be difficult and expensive to maintain. Zoning ordinances and subdivision regulations often define as "incompatible" the small neighborhood retail and commercial establishments that older residents find convenient and reduce their dependence on the automobile. Further, these regulations tend to exclude multi-family housing and the use of alternative housing forms such as shared housing, accessory apartments, manufactured housing, and ECHO units (to be discussed later).

Diversity of housing options, accessibility to retail and social services, personal security, proximity to family members and close friends, and availability of assistance with household maintenance and repairs are characteristics of neighborhoods that work successfully for older residents (Warner, 1983). Fortunately, workable strategies are available for helping existing communities create a supportive environment for increasing numbers of older residents.

Regulatory Reform and Community Planning

Former HUD Secretary Jack Kemp appointed an Advisory Commission on Regulatory Barriers to Affordable Housing, which produced the report *Not in My Backyard*, and it has rekindled debate over the purpose and effect of local zoning and other land use regulations. Senior advocates have noted that the impact of zoning on senior housing options and community improvements is often a two-way street. Some "age inclusive zoning" permitting older homeowners to construct accessory apartments or establishing "retirement community districts" achieve a legitimate public purpose and have been upheld by the courts (Hopperton, 1986; Hedges, 1991; Pollak, 1991). Other restrictions such as those related to density and parking requirements, restrictions on mixed uses, housing types, or occupancy by unrelated persons can create obstacles. For example, parking requirements established when a neighborhood housed younger working couples or families with children who own more autos than older households, can add significantly to development costs of senior housing, since more land is needed to provide the required (and unnecessary) parking spaces. Similarly, density requirements can make construction of housing for the elderly economically infeasible. Research by the American Planning Association indicates that allowing developers greater flexibility in meeting local zoning and planning requirements can be important in reducing housing costs (Sanders, 1984).

An additional impediment is the narrow definition of family in many local ordinances, which tends to exclude nontraditional households and prevents the conversion of elderly owned single-family homes into shared residences and group homes. These ordinances often exclude group residences from residential neighborhoods most suitable for older persons. However, a number of landmark cases in both the U.S. Supreme Court and various state courts have undermined the legal basis for such restrictive definitions. In addition, the Fair Housing Act of 1988 has strengthened the rights of the disabled, including older disabled persons, to equal access to housing (Pollak, 1991).

Meeting the needs of a growing population of older residents is often a new activity for local governments (U.S. Conference of Mayors, 1985; Parker, Edmonds, and Robinson, 1991). Community planning activities such as revisions of local comprehensive land use plans and development of comprehensive housing affordability strategies (CHAS) can be one avenue for making needed changes in zoning, land use, and housing policies. Under the CHAS process, communities are required to assess regulatory barriers to affordable housing and develop action plans to remedy such barriers. The recent AARP report entitled *A Change for the Better* provides a number of recommendations for senior advocates to become involved in the community planning process (Parker, Edmonds, and Robinson, 1991). In addition, the AARP has published a model local ordinance for ECHO housing, a planning guide for local elected officials and housing advocates, and a number of zoning related reports dealing with shared residences, echo units, and accessory apartments.

Adaptive Reuse

Older structures such as schools closed due to a lack of students can often be refurbished to serve as housing and/or service centers for older persons. Such conversions are particularly useful in suburban jurisdictions, because they are centrally located in neighborhoods composed almost entirely of single-family residences. Abandoned factories, hotels, and hospitals in urban areas can often service a similar purpose. Historic structures have an additional advantage of being eligible for a number of federal and state tax credits (AARP, 1991). A survey by the U.S. Conference of Mayors (USCM) noted that nearly 150 cities had completed or started adaptive reuse projects for older persons (USCM, 1986).

Covering one square block in the residential area of the small town of Holdrege, Nebraska, these 16 independent living units are clustered around a central court that was conceived as a communal outdoor room. The court is anchored by a community building, which becomes the symbolic focus and entry gateway to this retirement "village." Each unit has a small entry court and rear patio, affording opportunities for social interaction and expressions of individuality while respecting resident's privacy. (Courtesy of the American Institute of Architects in cooperation with the American Association of Homes for the Aging/Gary Tarleton, photographer; Richard D. Nelson, Co., architect)

Accessory Apartments

Accessory apartments are independent living units built into or attached to an existing single-family home. At most they share an entrance, yard, and parking. Accessory apartments may be an appropriate housing option for an older person. Older homeowners may wish to continue living in their current residences but would benefit from having tenants to provide additional income and assistance with household maintenance, chores, and security. Accessory apartments promote independence, privacy, and extended family living by allowing homeowners to live adjacent to, but separate from, tenants who may be related.

At an average cost of $16,500, some older homeowners may not be able to afford construction of an accessory apartment. However, the major barrier to greater use of accessory apartments are restrictive zoning ordinances and covenants in deeds (Hedges, 1991). A number of localities are now permitting accessory units to be constructed by older homeowners.

Older persons own a considerable amount of underutilized housing. According to the latest American Housing Survey, over half of older homeowners lived in units with three or more bedrooms. (Mikelsons and Turner, 1992) A recent study indicated that accessory apartments could increase rental housing stock by 14 percent if units were legalized in all jurisdictions (Hedges, 1991).

Shared Housing

Shared housing refers to two or more unrelated persons living in the same housing unit, sharing living space and expenses. According to the National Shared Housing Resource Center, some 2 million persons are sharing homes. Approximately one-third of those sharing residences are older persons.

Elder Cottage Housing Opportunity (ECHO) units are small manufactured homes that can be installed in the back or side yard of an existing single family residence and removed when no longer needed. (Courtesy of the American Association of Retired Persons)

Home sharing has the advantage of allowing persons with limited incomes to remain in their home communities while making efficient use of the existing housing stock. According to the Shared Housing Resource Center, some 500 matching agencies now exist to assist homeowners and prospective tenants. A recent national survey of older households indicates that over one-fourth of older persons have shared a home with an unrelated adult, and nearly one-half would consider some form of home-sharing (AARP, 1990a). One difficulty with this living arrangement is finding a partner who is compatible. However, as mentioned earlier, the major obstacle to wider utilization of home sharing is local zoning regulations. AARP publishes *Consumer's Guide to Homesharing*, which provides guidelines for developing a home share lease.

ECHO Units

Elder Cottage Housing Opportunity (ECHO) units are small, manufactured homes that can be installed in the back or side yard of an existing single-family residence and removed when no longer needed. ECHO units are specially designed for older and disabled persons and are especially attractive to persons who wish to remain independent but live closer to supportive family members or friends. Such units are much less costly than traditional housing units and allow the owner to extend current financial assets, including equity in an existing home. However, the concept has only been attempted experimentally in the United States. ECHO units often encounter the same regulatory barriers placed on manufac-

A recent national survey of older households indicates that over one-fourth of older persons have shared a home with an unrelated adult, and nearly one-half would consider some form of home-sharing.

tured and modular housing. In 1985 AARP issued a model ordinance designed to assist localities in modifying their existing statutes to accommodate ECHO housing (Hare and Hollis, 1985).

The National Affordable Housing Act of 1990 included a provision to permit the use of section 202 funds to finance the purchase of ECHO units. However, the Department of Housing and Urban Development (HUD) has not issued regulations to implement the provision.

● MANUFACTURED HOUSING

Over 2 million older persons, 6 percent of older households, live in manufactured housing, more commonly referred to as "mobile homes." Older households account for 23 percent of all households (5.4 million) residing in this type of housing (U.S. Department of Housing and Urban Development, 1991). Between 1980 and 1989, the number of units occupied by older households rose 65 percent (Mikelsons and Turner, 1992).

An average retail price of $19,800 for a new single section and $36,600 for a new multisection home makes manufactured housing particularly attractive to retired persons (Manufactured Housing Institute, 1991). Many older persons also enjoy the close knit atmosphere and amenities of some manufactured home communities developed specifically for older persons. Forty percent of new home purchasers are age 50 and older (Hayes and others, 1991).

While over 90 percent of older mobile home households own their homes, over half rent a site in a mobile home park (U.S. Department of Housing and Urban Development, 1991). Park management practices have become a major political issue in state legislatures. Without oversight, the unique combination of home ownership and site tenancy can result in a number of unfair practices, including frequent and excessive rent increases, "tie-ins" between home sales and park rentals, excessive and unreasonable fees and park rules, and inadequate park maintenance (Sheldon and Simpson, 1991).

Older mobile home park residents are particularly vulnerable to increases in park rental fees and other costs associated with mobile home park living, because of their limited financial resources, increased medical costs, and the rising costs of maintaining an older home. According to

Even modestly priced manufactured homes are attractive in appearance and compatible with America's neighborhoods. (Courtesy of the American Association of Retired Persons)

the latest American Housing Survey (1989), 43 percent of older households residing in manufactured homes have annual incomes below $10,000, and 80 percent have incomes below $20,000.

At the heart of many of the problems faced by mobile home park residents is the prevalence of short-term rental agreements. An AARP-sponsored analysis of existing state mobile home park tenancy statutes by the National Consumer Law Center (NCLC), *Manufactured Home Park Tenants: Shifting the Balance of Power*, indicates that only thirteen states require that a lease of at least one year be offered.

Thirty-two states have enacted statutes that specifically regulate mobile home park tenancies. However, as shown in Table 31.1, even in states where statutes have been adopted, NCLC's analysis found that the extent of their protections varies widely.

At the request of AARP, NCLC developed a model statute to address the limitations of existing state legislation. The model statute, the Manufactured Home Owner's Bill of Rights, recognizes that mobile home owners are not "tenants" who can pack their bags and leave when a dispute arises with the park owner. Its key provision is a five-year renewable lease requirement that allows the parties to agree to rent levels, including increases, over the five-year term. The model legislation would also prohibit "tie-ins" and other unfair practices, remedy park maintenance problems by requiring a warrant of habitability, and require relocation assistance in the event of park closure.

Unlike site-built housing, manufactured homes

Profiles of Productive Aging

Esther Peterson
Consumer lobbyist

"(Retirement) never occured to me. I need to be active, doing something, feeling that I can make a difference, even as little as it might be. How could I retire? I wouldn't know what to do!"

Labor and consumer administrator Esther Peterson was born in 1906 in Provo, Utah, to a Mormon family, attended Brigham Young University, and majored in physical education. After two years of teaching in Utah, Peterson attended Columbia University for her master's degree. This is where she met her husband, Oliver Peterson, then a sociology student and a socialist.

Through him, Peterson became involved in the labor movement, volunteering for the YWCA's industrial department and the National Consumers' League in Boston and teaching at Bryn Mawr Summer School for Women Workers. From the early 1930s to 1961, Peterson worked for the International Ladies Garment Workers Union, was the assistant director of education for the Amalgamated Clothing Workers, and was the legislative representative for the industrial union department of the AFL-CIO. Nine years of this period she spent overseas with her husband, who was a foreign service labor attache, and raised four children.

As a lobbyist in Washington Peterson knew Senator John F. Kennedy. When Kennedy came to the White House, he appointed her director of the Women's Bureau of the Labor Department. She organized the President's Commission on the Status of Women and established Status of Women Commissions in every state in the country. Then Kennedy appointed Peterson assistant secretary of labor, a position she kept when Lyndon Johnson took office. He also made Peterson his special assistant for consumer affairs, but as her opinions on consumer issues were controversial, she resigned from the consumer post in 1967 to work at the Labor Department full time.

During the Nixon administration, Peterson worked for Giant Food Corp., a supermarket chain in the region around Washington, DC, where she established many reforms, including open dating, unit pricing, nutritional and ingredient labeling, and safety programs. When Jimmy Carter became president in 1976, he asked Peterson, at 70, to resume her previous office as special assistant for consumer affairs. She convinced Carter to re-authorize the Consumer Product Safety Commission and to sign an executive order restricting the export of hazardous products banned in the United States, which the Reagan administration revoked a few short weeks after its institution.

Out of the White House again, Peterson hosted television and radio shows on consumer issues for two years, then worked at the United Nations as a volunteer lobbyist. Once again at the forefront of the battle for consumer affairs, she hopes the fight will "go global." Peterson has predicted "The international consumer movement is going to be a new big force, just like the labor movement has been and the women's movement." Peterson's latest project is a Code of Conduct for multinational corporations. She also moderates between industry and consumer disputes, most recently the insurance industry and the manufactured housing business.

On the subject of growing older, Peterson revealed: "I didn't realize at a young enough age, how important the financial aspects were. If I had, I would have done certain things differently. Most women don't realize that their husbands may die earlier than they do. As a result they're less well-prepared than they should be to manage their own affairs."

Lydia Brontë

must be transported and installed at the intended site of consumer use. Many homes are improperly installed by dealers or subcontract installers. According to the National Conference of States on Building Codes and Standards (NCSBCS), improper installation is a significant problem and can lead to major structural failure. However, only thirty states have an installation standard,

and these are inadequately enforced. NCSBCS and the Manufactured Housing Institute recently formed a task force to develop a certification program for installers.

Local zoning commissions have often excluded or relegated manufactured housing to less desirable and nonresidential sites. Some local communities exclude manufactured housing by regulat-

Table 31.1
Summary of State Charts

Mobile homes statutes	
Prohibits tie-ins	13 states: AL, AZ, CO, IL, MA, NE, NV, NY, MI, OH, OR, VA, WI
Written lease required	18 states: MI, NJ, AZ, CA, CO, CT, DE, ID, MD, MA, MN, NH, NM, UT, VT, VA, WA, WI; must be offered in 6 states: IL, IA, NY, OH, OR, RI
1 year lease term	4 states: CT, FL, MD, OH; must be offered in 9 states: CA, DE, IL, IA, NY, OR, RI, WA, WI
Relocation expenses	9 states: AZ, CA, FL, ME, MN, NV, NH, OR, UT
Right of first refusal	6 states: CT, DE, FL, MA, NH, VT
Buyout at fair market value	2 states: FL, MI
Notice of change of use	20 states: AK, AZ, CA, CO, CT, DE, FL, ID, MD, MA, MN, NV, NM, OH, OR, PA, RI, UT, VT, WA
Outlines landlord's maintenance obligations	14 states: AZ, CT, DE, FL, IL, MD, NE, NV, NM, ND, OH, OR, VA, WA

Source: Sheldon, Jonathan, and Andrea Simpson. *Manufactured Housing Park Tenants: Shifting the Balance of Power.* Washington, DC: American Association of Retired Persons, 1991.

ing items not addressed by federal construction standards. Prohibitions on single siting of homes effectively exclude the less costly single-wide homes that might be suitable as elder cottage housing opportunity (ECHO) units for older persons (Wallis, 1991). Many states have attempted to eliminate such requirements by passing special legislation. As of 1989, twenty-two states have enacted statutes prohibiting discriminatory zoning practices.

Since 1976 the federal government has established construction and safety standards for manufactured housing. However, the states play an important role in implementing the program by acting as design and production inspection agencies and investigating consumer complaints. In 1990, Congress authorized a National Commission on Manufactured Housing to review the need for additional and revised standards and recommend improvements in the current system of inspection and enforcement. Issues before the commission are expected to include improved energy efficiency standards and strengthening warranty protections, warranty service, and installation requirements.

● CONTINUING CARE RETIREMENT COMMUNITIES

Continuing Care Retirement Communities (CCRC) offer a combination of residential, personal, and health care services. These services are secured by a contract usually requiring a substantial entrance fee and a monthly payment. In return, the facility guarantees fulfillment of the resident's housing and service needs for the term of the contract. The duration of the contract and extent of services may vary considerably. Some facilities extend life-time contracts and offer a full range of services, including nursing care. Others provide a much more limited menu of services. CCRCs are often attractive because they offer potential residents psychological and financial security and a wide range of services in a single location.

Approximately 700 CCRCs are in operation, and about 10 percent have been built since 1986 (Stearns and others, 1990). Fees and charges can be expensive, with entrance fees ranging from $40,000 to $200,000 and monthly charges from $400 to $1,500 (AARP, 1988). Because of the unpredictability of health care costs, many facilities are moving away from the total life care con-

Continuing Care Retirement Communities are often attractive because they offer potential residents psychological and financial security and a wide range of services in a single location. (Courtesy of Givens Estates United Methodist Retirement Community, Asheville, North Carolina)

cept toward a more limited array of services (National Consumer Law Center, 1986).

The CCRC concept does entail some risks for potential residents. More than 10 percent of all facilities have gone bankrupt or experienced extreme financial difficulties (AARP, 1986). A review of 1983 data from 109 facilities indicates that as many as one-third exhibited either a negative net income or negative net worth profile (Stearns and others, 1990).

Thirty states have enacted legislation to regulate the financial management of CCRCs (Stearns and others, 1990). Regulations generally address reserve requirements, refund policies, escrow accounts, marketing, audits, and financial procedures. Many of the statutes, however, rely primarily on consumer disclosure to regulate industry practices, and regulators often lack staff and oversight authority. Therefore, it is extremely important for prospective residents to carefully review

Table 31.2
Advantages and Disadvantages of Selected Alternative Housing Options

	Advantages	**Disadvantages**
Accessory apartments	• Provide additional income for elderly homeowners • Companionship and security • Increase supply of affordable rental housing • Personal support services may be provided	• Initial construction cost to homeowners • Neighborhood concern about lowered property values • Zoning restraints • Possible housing and building code violations

Table 31.2 (contd.)

	Advantages	**Disadvantages**
Board and care homes	• Homelike environment • Afford fragile, isolated elderly opportunity to interact with others • Economical	• Not licensed or concerned with standards and treatment of residents • Owner/operators often lack training • Few planned social activities
Congregate housing	• Provides basic support services that can extend independent living • Reduces social isolation • Provides physical and emotional security	• Tendency to oversee the needs of tenants, promoting dependency • Expensive to build and operate • Those without kitchen facilities restrict tenants' independence • Expensive for most elderly without subsidy
Elder cottages, granny flats	• Facilitate older persons receiving support from younger family members • Option to remain in individual home • Smaller housing unit, less expensive to operate	• Potential to lower property values • Attitude of and impact on neighborhood • Concerns about housing and building code violations
Home equity conversion	• Converts lifetime investment into usable income • Allows elderly with marginal incomes to remain in familiar surroundings • Can be used to finance housing expenses, e.g., make necessary repairs, utilities, taxes	• Risk that homeowner will live longer than term of loan • Homes of lower value (often type owned by elderly) may not provide monthly payments large enough to be worth cost of loan • Reluctance by homeowner to utilize due to lack of information, concern for lien on property, and/or impact on estate for heirs
Life care facilities	• Offer prepaid healthcare • Security and protection against inflation and financially draining illness • Wide range of social activities with health support systems	• Too expensive for many elderly • Questionable protections should the facility go out of business • Older person receives no deed to property • No guarantees that monthly payments will not rise • Location is usually rural, isolated from community services
Shared housing	• Less expensive due to shared costs for household operators • Companionship, security • Promotes intergenerational cooperation and understanding • More extensive use of existing housing • Program inexpensive to operate	• Problems with selection of individual to share home • Amount of privacy reduced • Does not meet medical and personal problems • Added income may mean owner is no longer eligible for public benefits • City zoning ordinances may prohibit

Source: Katz, Rosalyn, Ph.D. *A Manual of Housing Alternatives for the Elderly.* Vol. 1. Pittsburgh, PA: Health and Welfare Planning Association; American Association of Retired Persons, *Housing Choices for Older Homeowners.* West Virginia Commission on Aging. Reprinted with permission from *Generations* (American Society on Aging, 833 Market St., Suite 512, San Francisco, CA 94103: 1992).

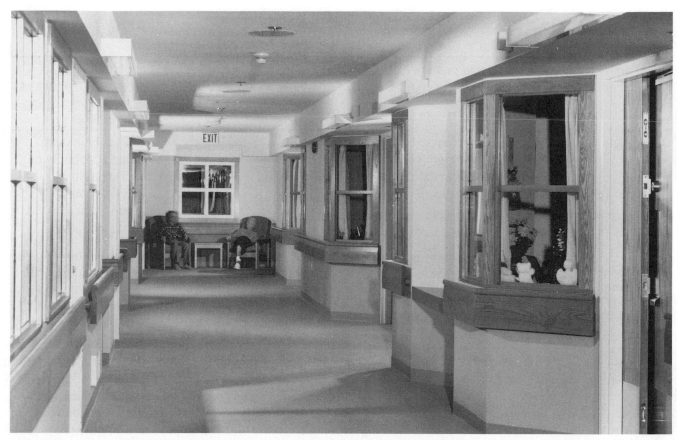

The architectural design of the Musquodoboit Valley Home for Special Care in Middle Musquodoboit, Nova Scotia, acknowledges the residents' need for privacy and command over their environment. Interior windows, uncommon in traditional configurations, help residents control their involvement with corridor activity. Doorway alcoves add a level of participation without interfering with corridor circulation. Residents are grouped into "neighborhoods" according to condition and need. (Courtesy of William Nycum Architects Ltd./David A. Steward Photography, photographer)

the contract prior to signing and seek the advice of a competent independent financial adviser.

CCRCs meeting strict national standards for financial practices and quality care can apply for accreditation by the Continuing Care Accreditation Commission (CCAC). Established by the American Association of Homes for the Aging, the CCAC maintains a list of accredited facilities.

● OLDER RENTERS AND THE PRODUCTION OF RENTAL HOUSING

As the demographic and economic profile of older Americans changes, the profile of older renters has changed significantly in recent years. According to data from the American Housing Survey, older renters became a great deal older and poorer over the decade of the 1980s. Between 1980 and 1989, the number of renters aged 65 to 74 actually declined by 4.6 percent, while the

number of renters aged 75 and over increased by 21.2 percent.

During the same period of time, older renters became dramatically poorer—the number of older renters with incomes under $5,000 (1987 dollars) rose by 86.7 percent, while the number of older renters with incomes over $5,000 declined by 5.8 percent. Older renters with incomes over $35,000 declined 41.5 percent during the decade. As a result, 60 percent of older renters (69 percent of older women renters living alone) spent more than 30 percent of their incomes—the federal standard for excessive rent—on rent (U.S. Congress, 1991). Older renters also tend to own fewer assets than younger renters—in 1989, the net worth of renters aged 65 and over was only $2,593, compared to $6,369 for renters aged 35 to 64 and $4,831 for renters under the age of 35 (Apgar and others, 1989).

The profile data on older renters indicates a high needs-driven market—largely concentrated

Older renters became a great deal older and poorer over the decade of the 1980s. (Courtesy of The National Council on the Aging, Inc./Jerry Hecht, photographer)

among the oldest, poorest, and frailest of the old, and the private market and federal housing programs have made some attempts to meet the needs of older renters.

Between 1980 and 1989, the number of renters aged 65 to 74 actually declined by 4.6 percent, while the number of renters aged 75 and over increased by 21.2 percent.

The Private Market

The production of any multifamily rental housing by the private market in the United States has been stymied in recent years by the combined effects of changing tax policy, earlier overproduction, wary credit markets, a slowly developing secondary market for multifamily mortgages, the withdrawal of federal credit enhancement, and the collapse of the financial institutions that have provided mortgages for multifamily housing. Tax advantages for investment in rental housing contributed to an overproduction of rental housing in the early 1980s—especially for rental housing geared to the relatively well-off. When those tax advantages were largely removed by the Tax Reform Act of 1986, investment in rental housing declined dramatically. Savings and loan associations, traditionally the major mortgage originators for multifamily housing, have decreased their loan activities—in no small part because of the enormous losses suffered by the industry during

the late 1980s. The federal government, which insured over 30 percent of multifamily mortgages at the beginning of the decade, retreated in the face of losses to the FHA mortgage insurance fund to insure only 6 percent of multifamily rental housing by the end of the decade (Guttentag, 1992).

The earlier overproduction may have moderated rent increases for renters with middle and upper incomes but did very little to ameliorate a precipitous decline in rental housing affordable to low-income renters in recent years. Between 1974 and 1985, the number of unsubsidized rental units in the private market that were affordable to a family with poverty-level income declined by one-third—a loss of 2.9 million such units. This loss can be explained in roughly equal measures by the deterioration of units no longer inhabitable and the upgrading of units that are no longer affordable to low-income families (Apgar, 1990).

The growth of rental housing among the oldest and poorest of the old indicates that the market is highly "needs" driven. When coupled with a widely expressed preference for staying put, the general experience with rental housing for older persons is that consumers are wary and move only when the need to move is driven by strong health or economic concerns. Combined with the factors just mentioned, which have dampened the production of all kinds of rental housing, the private market for rental housing for older persons has been very slow in recent years.

The experience of the Retirement Service

The earlier overproduction of multifamily rental housing may have moderated rent increases for renters with middle- and upper-level incomes but did very little to ease a sharp decline in rental housing affordable to low-income renters in recent years. (Courtesy of Highland Farms Retirement Community, Black Mountain, North Carolina)

Center (ReSC) program illustrates many of the problems with the private rental housing market for older persons. The program was initiated by the Reagan administration at the end of 1983 to provide mortgage insurance without other subsidies under the authority of the Section 221(d)4 program. The program suffered both from the general mismanagement of FHA mortgage insurance programs during that era and from a miscalculation of the elderly rental market. The procedures were revised in 1989, because:

- the renter clientele is older than originally thought (closer to 80 than 70)
- the more advanced age of the ReSC renter clientele means that these residents are, or soon become, more frail than originally anticipated
- in many cases, the decision to move to a ReSC or similar facility is not "demand driven" as with other rental housing, but "need-driven"

By the time these discoveries were made, however, the program was in deep trouble. Because the program provided only mortgage insurance without other subsidy, the market was restricted to those who could pay market rate rents—a dwindling market as documented above by the American Housing Survey data. Since the decision to move was "need-driven," the market was further limited to the very old. Since no public insurance exists for services in such facilities, the market was limited still further to those who could pay the full cost of needed supportive services. As a result, many of the ReSC projects had slow rent-up periods and high vacancy rates. Because of lax underwriting and low capitalization requirements, the default rate was roughly 30 percent and rising by the time the program was suspended by HUD secretary Jack Kemp in July 1989.

The lessons of the Retirement Service Center program are instructive to lenders and investors today. The market for rental housing for older persons is most likely to grow among the oldest and frailest of the old who have very modest means. Older people are likely to seek such housing only when driven by the need to address problems such as frailty, widowhood, and declining resources. Underwriters must recognize that such projects are likely to rent up slowly and must

offer realistic supportive services to attract renters.

In spite of all the obstacles and false starts in this market, the outlook is bright for housing facilities that understand the needs of older people and market accordingly. The increasing number of very old people who are seeking residential alternatives to nursing home care is growing rapidly. Succeeding cohorts are likely to have more resources with which to fund housing and services in an unsubsidized market. In its 1992 annual review of retirement housing, *Contemporary Long-Term Care* magazine documented substantial growth in "assisted living" facilities incorporating both housing and supportive services for frail older persons. An assisted living facility is typically a residential long-term-care environment in which residents have rooms, meals, help with activities of daily living, and some degree of protective supervision or 24-hour care (Porcino, 1993).

The market for rental housing for older persons is most likely to grow among the oldest and frailest of the old who have very modest means.

Federally Subsidized Rental Housing

In the face of dwindling rental housing resources affordable to low-income older persons on the private market, federally subsidized housing has played an increasingly important role. Over time, federal housing assistance has been increasingly targeted to older renters for three reasons: (1) elderly renters have had lower incomes, fewer assets, and poorer housing conditions than nonelderly renters; (2) long-term residents of subsidized housing programs "aged in place"; and (3) several new programs were created to serve older people, in part because older people have been viewed as the more "deserving" poor.

However, the range of federal housing programs serving older people is often bewildering for the average layperson seeking housing assistance. In any given market area, the consumer is likely to find federally subsidized elderly housing projects operated by for-profit developers, nonprofit sponsors, or public agencies—each with different facilities, services, and even eligibility criteria. The only way to understand the differences among the programs is to place them in historical context. Since housing projects typically operate under long-term contracts that define their amenities and eligibility standards, to understand programmatic differences requires understanding the evolution of American housing policy.

The first federal housing program to assist low-income renters was the public housing program. Created by the 1937 Housing Act, the public housing program provides housing owned and operated by local public housing authorities (PHAs). Federal grants to local PHAs finance construction and provide annual supplements for operating expenses and modernization. Single individuals were not eligible for public housing until 1956 (U.S. Congress, 1989a) when a definition of "elderly family" was enacted to include single older individuals as eligible residents of public housing.

No distinct program for the elderly has ever been authorized under the public housing program, but public housing authorities used the 1956 eligibility definition of "elderly family" to begin a major construction program of elderly projects (Council of Large Public Housing Authorities, 1991)—the first of which opened in 1962. The Department of Housing and Urban Development (HUD) estimates that 45 percent of the units of public housing—over 500,000 units— are currently occupied by the elderly, making public housing the largest single housing program serving older people in the United States (U.S. Congress, 1990).

In 1959 Congress created the first housing program specifically designed for the elderly, known widely by its section number in the National Housing Act, "Section 202." Section 202 originally provided direct, low interest loans to nonprofit sponsors (mostly religious) to provide housing targeted to moderate-income tenants who were ineligible for public housing. Under current financing arrangements, Section 202 sponsors receive construction grants and operating subsidies and must use the same very low-income eligibility standards as public housing. While Section 202 projects generally have more amenities, such as congregate spaces, than elderly pub-

lic housing, residents who have not been able to function independently have generally been expected to move on to more supportive settings such as nursing homes and board and care homes. The National Affordable Housing Act of 1990 (NAHA) clarified the ability of Section 202 to serve very frail older persons and authorized, for the first time, funding for a services coordinator and 15 percent of the cost of services to frail individuals. A total of over 240,000 units of Section 202 housing have been built to date.

Single individuals were not eligible for public housing until 1956 when a definition of "elderly family" was enacted to include single older individuals as eligible residents of public housing.

Mortgage insurance programs to stimulate the private production of multifamily housing were enacted during the 1950s and 1960s (especially Sections 221, 231, and 236). Though not specifically targeted to the elderly (except Section 231), each of these programs produced a disproportionate number of projects for older people. A rural counterpart to Section 202 was established by the Farmer's Home Administration's Section 515 program, a program that has since been expanded to all multifamily housing but continues to finance a large number of elderly projects.

The Housing Act of 1974 created the Section 8 rental assistance program, which originally could be used either as "tenant-based assistance" through certificates issued by PHAs to individual renters, or as "project-based assistance" to subsidize the construction or rehabilitation of multifamily projects. While the tenant-based assistance tended to be used by older people roughly in proportion to their numbers in the general population, as much as 70 percent of the project-based assistance may have been used for elderly projects.

The most recent approach to funding housing projects has been through the tax code. Enacted as part of the tax reform bill of 1986, the low-income housing tax credit (LIHTC) has produced over 100,000 units of low- and moderate-income housing per year for the past three years. How much of the tax credit has been used for elderly housing is unknown at this point. Finally, the National Affordable Housing Act of 1990 (NAHA) created the HOME program, a block grant to state and local governments to be used for a wide range of housing purposes, but the first funds from this program have yet to be awarded.

The sum of these programs represents a substantial investment in elderly housing. Though no government agency can give an accurate count, the number of federally funded elderly housing projects probably exceeds 20,000 nationwide. In all, over 1.5 million older Americans are served by federal housing subsidies. In 1988 older households represented 36 percent of the renter households receiving federal assistance, even though they made up only 27 per cent of the low-income renter households in the country, a significant targeting of housing subsidies to low-income older renters (Lazere and others, 1991).

● TRENDS

In general the housing situation of older people has markedly improved over the past few decades. This improvement is likely to continue for the immediate future as succeeding cohorts age with more resources at their disposal. Home repairs and adaptations are most likely to see substantial growth as older homeowners seek to "age in place." Older individuals and couples who move are most likely to do so out of substantial needs related to disabilities or declining financial resources. Housing facilities (such as assisted living) or types that promote caregiving in a residential environment (such as ECHO housing) are the most likely to see substantial growth.

Organizations

American Association of Homes for the Aging
901 E St., NW, Ste. 500
Washington, DC 20004-2837
(202) 783-2242

American Bar Association Commission on Legal Problems of the Elderly
1800 M St., NW
Washington, DC 20036
(202) 331-2299

Assisted Living Facilities Association of America
9401 Lee Hwy., Third Fl.
Fairfax, VA 22031-1802
(703) 691-8100

Congregate Housing Services Program
Housing for the Elderly and Handicapped People Division
Office of the Elderly and Assisted Housing
451 7th St., SW, Rm. 6122
Washington, DC 20410
(202) 708-3291

Emergency Community Services for the Homeless
Division of Community Services
Administration for Children and Families
370 L'Enfant Promenade, SW
Washington, DC 20447
(202) 401-9354

Housing and Urban Development Department
451 7th St., SW, Ste. 375
Washington, DC 20410
(202) 708-0417

Housing for the Elderly
Housing for the Elderly and Handicapped People Division
Office of Elderly and Assisted Housing
451 7th St., SW
Washington, DC 20410
(202) 708-2866

Mortgage Insurance for Cooperative Projects
Insurance Division
Office of Insured Multifamily Housing Development
451 7th St., SW, Rm. 2202
Washington, DC 20410
(202) 708-1223

National Association for Senior Living Industries
184 Duke of Gloucester St.
Annapolis, MD 21401-2523
(410) 263-0991

National Center for Home Equity Conversion
1210 East College Dr., Ste. 300
Marshall, MN 56258
(507) 532-3230

National Eldercare Institute on Housing and Supportive Services
University of Southern California
Andrus Gerontology Center
Los Angeles, CA 90089-9191
(213) 740-1364

National Shared Housing Resource Center
136½ Main St.
Montpelier, VT 05602
(802) 223-2627

North American Association of Jewish Homes and Housing for the Aging
10830 North Central Expy., Ste. 150
Dallas, TX 75231-1022
(214) 696-9838

Retirement Housing Foundation
401 East Ocean Blvd., Ste. 300
Long Beach, CA 90802
(213) 437-4330

References

Alvarez, D., and G. Gaberlavage. "Statistical Profile of Low-Income Older Homeowners: 1985 American Housing Survey." Washington, DC: American Association of Retired Persons (AARP) Public Policy Institute, 1988.

American Association of Retired Persons (AARP). "Historic Tax Credits Help Turn Old Buildings Into New Housing." *AARP Housing Report* (summer 1991).

———. *Housing Needs Survey*. Washington, DC: AARP Program Department, 1992.

———. "Life Care Pacts Create Woes for Some People." *AARP Bulletin* Vol. 29, no. 4 (1988).

———. *Model State Law on Reverse Mortgages.* Washington, DC: AARP Home Equity Information Center, Program Coordination and Development Department, 1990b.

———. *The Perfect Fit: Creative Ideas for a Safe and Livable Home*. Washington, DC: American Association of Retired Persons, 1992.

———. *Understanding Senior Housing for the 1990s*. Washington, DC: AARP Consumer Affairs, Program Coordination and Development Department, 1990a.

Apgar, W. C., Jr., D. DiPasquale, N. McArdle, and J. Olson. *The State of the Nation's Housing: 1989*. Cambridge, MA: Harvard University, 1989.

Congressional Budget Office. *Changes in the Living Arrangements of the Elderly, 1960–2030*. Washington, DC: Government Printing Office, 1988.

Council of Large Public Housing Authorities. *Applicant Screening and Nondiscrimination: Complying with HUD's Tenant Selection, 504, and Fair Housing Rules*. Washington, DC: Council of Large Public Housing Authorities, 1991.

Dobkin, L. "Retrofitting the American Dream." *Retirement Housing Report* Vol. 1, no. 8. (1987).

Golant, S. M. *Housing America's Elderly: Many Possibilities, Few Choices*. Newbury, CA: Sage Publications, 1992.

Guttentag, J. W. "When Will Residential Mortgage Underwriting Come of Age?" *Housing Policy Debate* Vol. 3, no. 1 (1992).

Hare, P. H., and L. E. Hollis. *A Model Ordinance for ECHO Housing*. Washington, DC: AARP Consumer Affairs, Program Coordination and Development Department, 1985.

Harootyan, R. A. "Life-Span Design of Residential Environments for an Aging Population." Conference proceedings. Washington, DC: AARP Forecasting and Environmental Scanning Department, 1992.

Hayes, E. J., and others. *Industry Study #365 Factory-Built Housing in the 1990s*. Cleveland, OH: Fredonia Group, 1991.

Hedges, H. *Key Issues in Accessory Apartments: Zoning and Covenants Restricting Land to Residential Uses*. Washington, DC: AARP Consumer Affairs, Program Coordination and Development Department, 1991.

Hopperton, R. "Land-Use Regulations for the Elderly." In *Housing an Aging Society: Issues, Alternatives, and Policy*. Eds. R. Newcomer, M. Lawton, and T. Byerts. New York: Van Nostrand, 1986.

Jacobs, B. J. "The National Potential of Home Equity Conversion." *Gerontologist* Vol. 26, no. 5 (1986).

"Late Bloomer" audio cassette. Available from Connie Goldman Productions, 926 Second Street, Suite 201, Santa Barbara, CA 90403. (301) 393-6801.

Lazere E. B., P. A. Leonard, C. N. Dolbeare, and B. Zigas. *A Place to Call Home: The Low-Income Housing Crisis Continues*. Washington, DC: Center on Budget and Policy Priorities, 1991.

Lazere, E. B., P. A. Leonard, and L. L. Kravitz. *The Other Housing Crisis: Sheltering the Poor in Rural America*. Washington, DC: Center on Budget and Policy Priorities, 1989.

Long Term Care National Resource Center. "Home Modifications and Repairs: An Emerging Need." *Linkages* (summer/fall 1990).

———. *State Units on Aging: Efforts In Housing for the Elderly*. Los Angeles, CA: Long Term Care National Resource Center at University of California, Los Angeles, and University of Southern California, 1991.

Manufactured Housing Institute. *Quick Facts* (1991).

Mikelsons, M., and M. A. Turner. "Housing Conditions of the Elderly in the 1980s." Volume II. Washington, DC: AARP Public Policy Institute, 1992.

National Center for Home Equity Conversion. *Home Equity Conversion in the United States: Programs and Data*. Washington, DC: AARP Public Policy Institute, 1991a.

———. *Reverse Mortgage Counseling: Preparing for the Next Stage of Market Development*. Washington, DC: AARP Consumer Affairs, Program Development and Coordination Department, 1991b.

National Consumer Law Center. *Senior Consumer Alert—Life-Care Contracts: Retirement Without Risk?* Washington, DC: AARP and National Association of Attorneys General, 1986.

Newman, S. J. "Housing and Long Term Care: The Suitability of the Elderly's Housing to the Provision of In-Home Services." *Gerontologist* Vol. 25, no. 1 (1985): 40.

O'Bryant, S. L., and C. I. Murray. "Attachment to Home and Other Factors Related to Widows' Relocation Decisions." *Journal of Housing for the Elderly* Vol. 4 (spring 1987).

Parker, V., S. Edmonds, and V. Robinson. *A Change for the Better: How to Make Communities More Responsive to Older Residents.* Washington, DC: AARP Consumer Affairs, Program Coordination and Development Department, 1991.

Pollak, P. B. *Key Zoning Issues for Shared Residences for Older Persons.* Washington, DC: AARP Consumer Affairs, Program Coordination and Development Department, 1991.

Porcino, Jane. "Designs for Living." *Modern Maturity.* (April-May 1993): 24–33.

Pynoos, J., and E. Cohen. *The Perfect Fit: Creative Ideas for a Safe and Liveable Home.* Washington, DC: AARP, 1992.

Pynoos, J., and others. "Home Modifications That Extend Independence." In *Housing for the Elderly: Design Directives and Policy.* Eds. V. Regnier and J. Pynoos. New York: Elsevier Science, 1987.

Redfoot, D. L. "On the Separatin' Place: Social Class and Relocation Among Older Women." *Social Forces* Vol. 66 (1987): 2.

Sanders, W. *Affordable Single Family Housing: A Review of Development Standards.* Chicago, IL: American Planning Association, Planning Advisory Service, 1984.

Sheldon, J., and A. Simpson. *Manufactured Housing Park Tenants: Shifting the Balance of Power.* Washington, DC: AARP Public Policy Institute and Program Coordination and Development Department, 1991.

Stearns, L. R., and others. "Lessons for the Implementation of CCRC Legislation." *Gerontologist* Vol. 30, no. 2 (1990).

Struyk, R. J., and H. M. Katsura. "Aging at Home: How the Elderly Adjust Their Housing Without Moving." *Journal of Housing for the Elderly* Vol. 4 (1987).

U.S. Conference of Mayors. *Adaptive Reuse of Elderly Housing.* Washington, DC: U.S. Conference of Mayors, 1986.

———. *Assessing Elderly Housing.* Washington, DC: U.S. Conference of Mayors, 1985.

U.S. Congress. *Developments in Aging: 1989.* 101st Cong., 2d sess., 1989a. S.Rept. 101–249.

U.S. Congress. Senate. Select Committee on Aging. *Aging America: Trends and Projections.* 102d Cong., 1991.

U.S. Department of Housing and Urban Development (HUD) and U.S. Department of Commerce. *American Housing Survey for the United States in 1989.* Washington, DC: Government Printing Office, 1991.

Wallis, A. D. *Wheel Estate.* New York: Oxford University Press, 1991.

Warner, K. P. "Neighborhoods as Housing Environments for Maturing People." In *Housing for a Maturing Population.* Eds. E. Smart and N. Stewart. Washington, DC: Urban Land Institute, 1983.

Yurow, J. H. "Federal Programs Providing Assistance With Repair and Rehabilitation to Low-Income Older Homeowners." Washington, DC: AARP Public Policy Institute, 1988.

Additional Reading

American Association of Retired Persons (AARP). *Your Home Your Choice: A Workbook for Older People and Their Families.* Washington, DC: AARP Consumer Affairs Program Coordination and Development Department, 1992.

American Institute of Architects (AIA). *Design for Aging: An Architect's Guide.* Washington, DC: AIA Press, 1985.

Carlin, Vivian F., and Ruth Mansberg. *If I Live to Be 100: A Creative Housing Solution for Older People.* Pennington, NJ: Princeton Book, 1989.

———. *Where Can Mom Live? A Family Guide to Living Arrangements for Elderly Parents.* Lexington, MA: Lexington Books, 1987.

Gillespie, Ann E., and Katrinka Smith Sloan. *Housing Options and Services for Older Adults.* Santa Barbara, CA: ABC-CLIO, 1990.

Hartford Insurance Group. *The Hartford House: How to Modify a Home to Accommodate the Needs of an Older Adult.* Hartford, CT: Hartford Plaza, 1990.

Hochschild, Arlie R. *The Unexpected Community: Portrait of an Old Age Subculture.* Englewood Cliffs, NJ: Prentice-Hall, 1975.

Horne, Jo. *Homesharing and Other Lifestyle Options.* Glenview, IL: AARP and Scott, Foresman, 1988.

Koncelik, Joseph A. *Aging and the Product Environment.* New York: Van Nostrand, 1982.

Lawton, M. Powell. *Environment and Aging.* 2d ed. Albany, NY: Center for the Study of Aging, 1986.

Porcino, Jane. *Living Longer, Living Better: Adventures in Community Housing for Those in the Second Half of Life.* New York: Continuum Publishing, 1991.

Raschko, Bettyann B. *Housing Interiors for the Disabled and Elderly.* New York: Van Nostrand, 1982.

Regnier, Victor, and Jon Pynoos, eds. *Housing the Aged: Design Directives and Policy Considerations.* New York: Elsevier Science, 1987.

George Gaberlavage, M. A.
Don Redfoot, Ph. D.

32

Transportation Issues

- The Mobility Continuum • Transportation Mandate • Trends
- How Transportation Services Are Delivered • How Services Are Financed
- How Aging Impacts Transportation Choices • Accidents • Driver Education • Driver Licensing
- Transit • Highway Improvements for Safety • Safety Through Vehicles • Summary

Fueled by congestion, energy costs, environmental concerns, and limited fiscal resources, the visibility of the transportation issue has risen dramatically in recent years. As the country's median age rises, the relationship between older transportation users and our transportation systems and services is also receiving increased attention. Moreover, demographic trends relating to population, longevity, place of residence, and personal safety suggest that new challenges will likely surface in the near future.

The personal mobility associated with transportation has a major impact on the basic quality of life of older people. As people age and eventually retire, most do not move into retirement communities, where compact development and the physical design promote easy circulation. Rather, most people age in the urban, suburban, and rural communities in which they worked and have lived for years. In these communities, they continue to depend on the automobile as the primary transportation (including rides from friends and family) and public transit as the secondary means.

● THE MOBILITY CONTINUUM

Transportation services which meet the mobility needs of older persons exist along a continuum. At one end, people enjoy the freedom and independence of unlimited and unrestricted driving in a private automobile. Over time, however, many are likely to experience difficulty with driving due to functional decline and will eventually discontinue driving. On the other end, consequently, people are totally dependent on public and private transit services.

An often cited problem with transportation services for the elderly is that movement along the mobility continuum does not occur very smoothly. For instance, current driver testing, screening, and licensing practices are based largely on chronological age rather than functional age. Few states offer a driver's license that is specially suited to the particular needs of a driver. Oftentimes, safe and capable drivers are tested more strenuously because they are older, while old and young drivers most at risk for accidents continue driving. In other words, the current system does not allow for the individual variability that occurs as people age, and tests, for the most part, do not accurately predict who will have accidents. Another often cited problem is that transit services for the non-work trips of older suburban dwellers are scarce. And many people are simply unaware of the transit services that are available (AARP, 1989).

Other problems exist: (1) the roadway system is inadequate to accommodate the changing functional capabilities of a growing number of road users; (2) transit services are uncoordinated and expensive to provide; and (3) transportation facilities, including vehicles and terminals, are not physically accessible to the mobility impaired. In many ways the transportation system has been developed to accommodate a young, working, auto-oriented society. Over time, an increasing median age of the population and the number of retirees will necessitate some change in this approach.

● TRANSPORTATION MANDATE

Most older people consider transportation to be one of their greatest needs. According to surveys of older people in states such as Oklahoma, Rhode Island, Pennsylvania, Alabama, and Colorado, transportation is the service most requested of social service providers by older people (Hasler, 1991). Transportation is a critical link to nutrition and health care facilities and shopping, as well as to social, work, recreation, community, and adult day care activities. Mobility is also critical to a person's independence, well-being, and overall quality of life. The isolation imposed by restricted mobility can adversely impact physical, mental, and spiritual health.

Other recent legislation and research demonstrates the increased importance of the transportation issue:

- 1988 landmark report by the National Academy of Sciences concerning the mobility of older Americans (Transportation in an Aging Society: Improving Mobility and Safety for Older Persons)
- 1990 passage of the Americans With Disabilities Act (ADA), a landmark civil rights law guaranteeing access to public facilities, including transportation
- 1991 establishment of the National Eldercare Institute on Transportation by the Administration on Aging to address the mobility needs of at-risk elders.

● TRENDS

Population

The absolute number and percentage of persons over 65 is growing. In 1900, only 4 percent of the U.S. population was 65 or older; in 1990, 12 percent of the population was in that age group; by 2020 it is projected that the percentage will

Most older people consider transportation to be one of their greatest needs. (Copyright © Thomas Hardin)

have grown to 17 percent—to over 51 million, compared with 32 million today. Moreover, people who reach 65 years of age can now expect to live into their eighties. The fastest growing group are those over 85—those most likely to experience difficulty with driving and to rely on transit services.

Transportation is a critical link to nutrition and health care facilities and shopping, as well as to social, work, recreation, community, and adult day care activities.

Drivers

In 1970, most older Americans lived in central cities. By 1980, the trend had changed; a majority of persons over 65 lived in suburban communities. By 1990, that majority as well as the proportion of the general population living in suburban communities had grown. The low densities and physical design of suburban communities promote the use of automobiles, not public transit. As older Americans continue to age in place, their transportation needs will move along the transportation continuum. Also in 1990, more than 22 million people over the age of 65 years were licensed to drive (Federal Highway Administration, 1991a). Over the coming decades, the number of drivers over 65 is expected to increase. On average, 85 percent of Americans eligible to drive do so. If present trends continue, it is estimated that as many 50 million persons over the age of 65 could be driving by 2020.

Transit Users

As an alternative to driving, transit provides mobility to many. It is estimated that more than 50 percent of those over 80 use transit services. It is also estimated that the number of nondrivers, or potential transit users, will grow to 14 million by 2020 (Rosenbloom, 1988). There are more than 5,000 transit service providers in the United States (APTA, 1991). In 1990, those systems provided over 9 billion passenger miles, 77 million of which were demand-responsive trips (a segment certain to grow if the transit-dependent, frail-elderly population increases as expected). In addition, human service (as opposed to transportation service) providers, such as area agencies on aging, provided more than 63 million trips (NAAAA, 1991).

If present trends continue, it is estimated that as many 50 million persons over the age of 65 could be driving by 2020.

Pedestrians and Cyclists

Another transportation option available to many older persons is walking. Most walking trips are for social, recreational, or health reasons. Americans over 65 years walk about 28 miles per year. Walking accounts for one-tenth of all trips taken (Rosenbloom, 1988). Generally, people with lower incomes who live in central cities make larger numbers of walking trips. Also, shopping trips constitute the vast majority

There are more than 5,000 transit service providers in the United States. (Courtesy of the American Public Transit Association)

of destinations for pedestrians, particularly those over 85 years. Far fewer people use bicycles as a primary means of transportation, and little information exists on the level of use. Nevertheless, to increase the availability and use of all modes of transportation, greater attention will need to be given to the environmental barriers, such as no sidewalks, inadequate curb cuts, rapid crosswalk signal timing, and driver awareness and consideration of pedestrians.

● HOW TRANSPORTATION SERVICES ARE DELIVERED

Historically, no highway trust fund appropriation has been earmarked to address the needs of older drivers. In recent years, states such as Pennsylvania, Florida, and New York have implemented, with federal assistance, pilot projects aimed at improving signs, pavement markings, lighting, and other roadway elements, but there has been no sustained national effort. Most public support for the transportation needs of older persons is for transit services. In 1991, the U.S. Congress passed into law the Intermodal Surface Transportation Efficiency Act (ISTEA), which authorized more than $151 billion to be invested over the next five years in highway, mass transit, and specialized transit and highway safety programs.

In the area of transit, federal, state, and local governments have instituted several programs aimed at meeting the needs of elderly riders. For example, the Federal Transit Act (Title III of ISTEA) contains several programs; the state of

Oregon designates a portion of the state tobacco tax; and many local governments have dedicated sources of revenue for transportation purposes. In addition, the Older Americans Act (OAA) authorized nearly $775 million for the fiscal year ending September 30, 1992, for elder supportive services. Funds from OAA, Medicaid, and Social Service Block Grant programs are the principle source of federal transportation funding in the human service sector. A recent study concluded that more than 50 percent of the operating funds for paratransit (defined under Transit Service heading) systems in area agencies on aging—a primary provider, contractor, and broker of local-level specialized transportation services—come from these federal human service programs (NAAAA, 1991).

In recent years, states such as Pennsylvania, Florida, and New York have implemented, with federal assistance, pilot projects aimed at improving signs, pavement markings, lighting, and other roadway elements, but there has been no sustained national effort.

But the multiple funding sources, differing eligibility requirements, geographic service area restrictions, and the costs of greater coordination are often cited as barriers to the more effective delivery of public transit services to the elderly. Perhaps the greatest fundamental problem is that human service providers are charged with, among others, insuring the provision of transportation services to those with the greatest economic need. The services are often incidental to the provision of such services as home health care or case management, whereas transportation service providers stress service to the general riding public. Consequently, mixing riders with varied trip purposes and various fare collection rules add to the inefficiency of service as well as frustration and confusion among users.

● HOW SERVICES ARE FINANCED

Public programs that fund transportation services are described in the following section.

However, some programs do not serve just the elderly or transportation needs for the elderly.

Social Security Act

Title XIX: Medical Assistance Program (Medicaid). Medicaid is a formula grant program available to states for the provision of medical services to older persons meeting certain income and resource requirements, providing for, among other things, transportation to and from medical facilities. The services are furnished by nonprofit and for-profit organizations. The program is administered by the Health Care Financing Administration in the U.S. Department of Health and Human Services (HHS).

Older Americans Act

Title III: Special Programs for the Aging and Congregate Nutrition Services. This program provides formula grants to state units on aging for distribution to local area agencies on aging, nonprofit, and for-profit organizations and government agencies to furnish transportation services to and from senior centers, medical facilities, congregate meal sites, and social and shopping trips. The target group are persons 60 and over with the greatest economic and social needs. The program is administered by the Office of Human Development Services, Administration on Aging, HHS.

Social Services Block Grant

This, too, is a formula grant program made available to states for the delivery of local-level transportation services. Unlike the others, however, the level, target group, and origin and destination of services are determined by each state unit on aging, with input from local area agencies on aging and community groups. The program is administered through the Administration for Children and Families, HHS.

Federal Transit Act

Section 9: Urban Mass Transportation Capital and Operating Assistance Program. Public transit agencies in urbanized areas receive these formula grants to provide fixed-route transit services. In addition, large metropolitan areas must offer elderly riders reduced fares during nonpeak travel times. The program is administered through the Federal Transit Administration (FTA), U.S. Department of Transportation.

Section 16(B)(2): Urban Mass Transit Capital Improvement Grants. The formula grant program provides capital purchase assistance to nonprofit organizations or to private operators contracting with nonprofit organizations to supply transportation services to elderly and persons with disabilities.

Section 18: Public Transportation for Nonurbanized Areas. This formula grant program addresses the transportation needs of people in nonurbanized areas. It specifies that a dedicated portion of the program funds will also be spent on providing intercity bus (Greyhound, Trailways, etc.) activities in nonurbanized areas.

State and Local Programs

Many state and local governments create programs to address needs particular to their jurisdictions. The target populations and funding sources of these programs vary.

The specific kinds of services funded by these

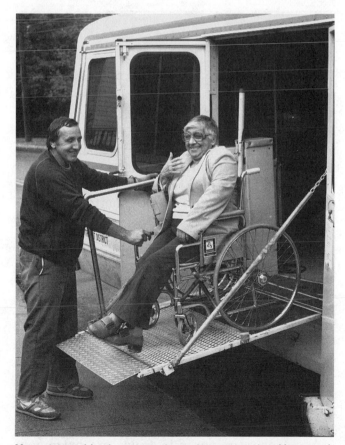

Many state and local governments create programs to address needs particular to their jurisdictions. (Copyright © Thomas Hardin)

programs are discussed in detail later. Services range from fare subsidies on buses to taxi cab vouchers and volunteer carpools. Generally speaking, ISTEA represents a major shift in policy away from building new roads to spending more money on transit, a move likely to benefit older persons in the future. In fact, the allocation for transit—including section 9, 16, and 18 programs—has doubled to $31.5 billion. Passage of the bill means more funds likely will be appropriated for services that meet part of the mobility needs of older persons. Most people, however, continue to drive. And more money does not necessarily address other problems described above, particularly the safety needs of older drivers and pedestrians.

● HOW AGING IMPACTS TRANSPORTATION CHOICES

As a process, aging is highly complex and varies tremendously among individuals. Very often, age-related changes are confused with signs of specific diseases, and, to the degree that changes occur, it is not easy to attribute the source. Factors such as general health, heredity, lifestyle, and environment tend to have a greater influence on how one ages than age itself. Nonetheless, as people age, functional limitations are more likely to appear, and these can impact transportation choices greatly. Yet, people who reach 65 years of age can now expect to live into their eighties. Those over 85 are most likely to experience difficulty with the driving task and to use public transportation services.

In fact, many older drivers also report having to work harder at the driving task than their younger counterparts. Some commonly reported problems include traffic sign legibility, reduced night vision, turning, reaching, merging, and exiting. At least some of these problems can be attributed to the effects of normal, healthy aging. Regardless of the source, however, perceptual, cognitive, and physical changes can cause problems with driving.

Vision

Studies of the visual abilities of bus travelers show that factors such as static, dynamic, and low-illumination acuity, motion in depth, contrast sensitivity, glare recovery, target detection, and

Many older drivers report having to work harder at driving than their younger counterparts, though chronological age alone is no predictor of driving performance. (Copyright © Alice A. Hardin)

depth perception have been linked to accidents and to problems with reading schedules and identifying landmarks during bus travel. But as to car drivers, driver license agencies do not test for and transit providers do not consider many of these factors.

Hearing

Generally, people first lose the ability to hear high-pitched sounds. So sounds such as sirens, horns, whistles, and announcements on buses may be obscured. There is also evidence that hearing is correlated with selected attention. However, no definitive research has linked these problems to driving performance. Further, no license agency screens or tests drivers on these factors.

Cognition

In the driving environment the ability to attend, recognize, and respond to stimuli is crucial. There is a growing body of knowledge on how to assess a person's visual and cognitive abilities as they relate to attention and reaction—the concept is generally known as useful field of view—in the driving environment. Research has shown that performance on a battery of tests measuring useful field of view is correlated with factors other than chronological age.

Physical

Physical agility tends to be limited as we age. The result can be slower, more cautious movements. Hence, the reported problems with reaching and turning, and boarding and exiting.

All of these aging factors having been considered, there is still great variability among older people, and none of these changes occur in the same ways or to the same degrees in everyone.

> Some commonly reported problems include traffic sign legibility, reduced night vision, turning, reaching, merging, and exiting.

● ACCIDENTS

Any reported or actual problems are tempered by several positive influences, which frequently include: increased behind-the-wheel experience and applied decision-making (exposure to and practice with driving's many circumstances); cautious approaches to driving situations (more fully recognizing the significance of the driving dynamic); and greater ability to control when driving must occur (less bondage to work-related timetables and destinations). The net result is a category of drivers with favorable overall accident frequency rates when compared to their younger counterparts (see Figure 32.1). This comparison indicates the value of experience, caution, and ability to limit exposure to accidents in high risk situations. However, older drivers' accident experience increases when exposure is considered. Persons 65 and older typically travel far shorter distance than others—an average of 12.2 miles per day as compared to 27.5 for those younger than 65 (USDOT, 1985).

Accident rates per-mile-driven are extremely high for very young drivers, lowest for young and

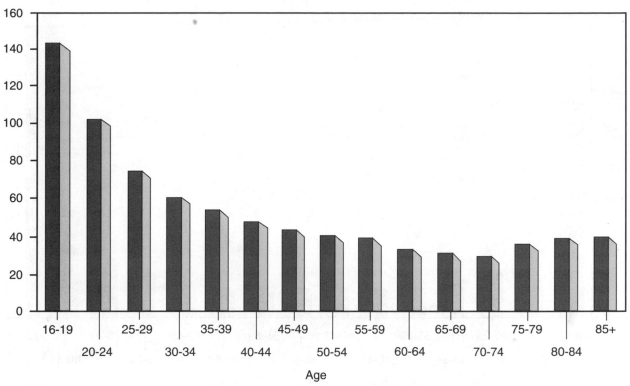

Figure 32.1
Accidents per One Thousand Drivers

Source: Federal Highway Administration, 1991a.

middle-aged adults, and climbing with age for older drivers (see Figure 32.2). Such data indicate that while sensory and cognitive changes vary considerably by individual, they do affect driving ability in aggregate. But there is no magic age at which all people experience these changes to the degree that they adversely impact driving. Raising self-awareness through education and improving highways and vehicles can be effective means for compensating for these age-related changes.

Injury

As a group, older drivers and pedestrians are more vulnerable to injury or death in traffic accidents than other age groups. For instance, older drivers have proportionately fewer car crashes than their younger counterparts but are more likely to be killed or seriously injured. Between 1980 and 1989, the number of people killed in auto accidents dropped more than 8 percent. At the same time, drivers over 65 years experienced a 43 percent increase in their death rate (Barr, 1991). Of the 8,000 annual pedestrian fatalities, more than 1,800—22.7 percent—are older per-

sons. Pedestrian accidents are exceeded only by falls and motor vehicle accidents as a cause of accidental death. As mentioned, older people represent 13 percent of the population, but are involved in only 7.7 percent of the 70,000 annual pedestrian accidents (FHWA, 1991b). Again, the higher rates among older drivers and pedestrians compared with their younger counterparts most likely reflects the higher susceptibility to injury and greater likelihood of complications following injuries.

● DRIVER EDUCATION

As people age, they need more information about how functional impairments can affect the driving task and how to compensate for any deficiencies. Through better self-awareness of abilities and limitations, they can more effectively regulate themselves and the circumstances in which they travel. In addition, older people and their families and caregivers need to understand whether the transportation system accommodates that change and how to insure that it is

Figure 32.2
Accidents per Mile Driven

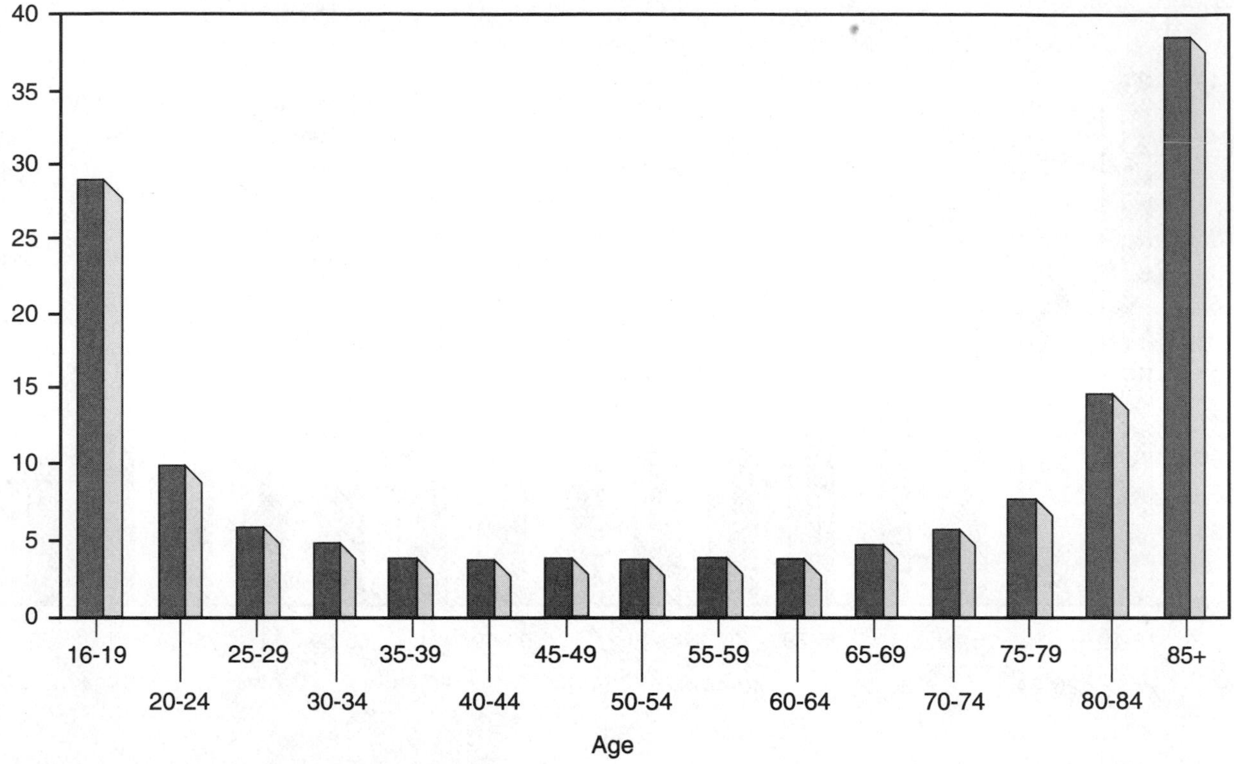

Source: Federal Highway Administration, 1991a.

responsive. Education efforts should also note that mobility is not always dependent on driving and should offer more information about public transportation options.

Many organizations are active in older driver education, and the hope is that many others will become involved as well. The American Association of Retired Persons (AARP), American Automobile Association, and National Safety Council each administer classroom refresher courses for drivers 50 and older. AARP's eight-hour defensive driving course, "55 Alive," reaches several hundred thousand older drivers each year with information about the aging process, interacting with traffic, safety restraints, accident prevention measures, other road users, and deciding about when not to drive.

The growing body of knowledge regarding medical conditions and pharmaceuticals and their impacts on mobility provides greater opportunity for the medical community to participate in older driver and pedestrian education. Select physicians currently serve on medical advisory boards for state licensing agencies. All practitioners

(doctors, nurses, pharmacists) have increasing information from which to recognize individual capabilities, diagnose conditions, and make recommendations to older people and their families and caregivers.

● DRIVER LICENSING

There is little consistency among state driver license policies regarding older drivers. A few states require older drivers to take added tests or to renew more frequently (Alaska, Arizona, California, District of Columbia, Hawaii, Illinois, Indiana, Iowa, Louisiana, Maine, Maryland, New Hampshire, New Mexico, Oregon, Pennsylvania, Rhode Island, and Utah), but most treat all drivers equally (AARP, 1992). For the most part, the ages designated by these policies are arbitrary. Chronological age alone is no predictor of driving performance.

Few states are prepared to assess meaningfully the abilities and needs of drivers as they age. At this juncture, there is no cost-effective and efficient battery of tests—states are already cutting costs and reducing lines at motor vehicle agencies. There is growing evidence that assessing functional age might be a better predictor of driver performance than chronological age. Some drivers at age 75 years or older are as capable as ever, making up in judgment and attitude whatever they may have lost in sensory abilities and reaction time (Malfetti and Winter, 1990). Others, however, may likely contribute to the increase in accidents that is well documented for those over 75. Between these two extremes are people who can safely drive, given a license that is compatible with their needs.

Graduated Driver Licensing

Greater use of accurate functional assessment tests could give rise to more flexible driver licenses, such as graduated licenses. A graduated license requires the holders to restrict their driving in some well-specified way, such as by type of vehicle, time of day, destination, or routes. A few states, such as Oregon and Washington, have developed effective graduated driver license programs. In these programs, problem drivers regardless of age are identified through police reports, insurance companies, personal physician, family, or others, and through accident and violation records or a report from an examiner at license renewal or re-examination.

Once identified, drivers can either take a regular re-examination or go through a special re-examination evaluation program. In the latter, medical history and medications are assessed; special reaction-time, vision, and road tests are administered. Once tests are completed, the driver could continue as an unrestricted driver; a driver improvement course or rehabilitation could be mandated; periodic medical examinations required; a graduated license issued; or driving privilege revoked. More and more states are looking seriously at functional assessments and graduated driver licenses.

● TRANSIT

As people age, drive less, and rely on (or choose to use) transit more, not only will systems need to be physically adapted to accommodate new users, but, more importantly, transit service providers will need to look at delivering new services that are more responsive to the mobility

needs of well and frail elderly. Furthermore, existing and potential transit users and the families, caregivers, and representatives must be empowered with information about public transportation options. Before a discussion of transit service can begin, it is important to consider the impact that the Americans With Disabilities Act (ADA) is having on service delivery.

Americans with Disabilities Act (ADA)

The ADA was signed into law July 26, 1990. Modeled after the Civil Rights Act and Title V of the Rehabilitation Act, the ADA prohibits discrimination against people with disabilities in employment, public services, public accommodations, transportation, and telecommunications. Disability under the ADA is defined as:

1) having a physical or mental impairment that substantially limits that person in some major life activity;

2) having a record of such an impairment that causes discrimination based upon a past disability; or

3) being regarded as having an impairment because of physical appearance.

Needless to say, many older persons are considered disabled under ADA, and this has many implications for transportation services. The ADA prohibits discrimination in transportation provided by public entities. Further, public entities that operate fixed route transportation systems are required to provide paratransit and other specialized transportation services; the intention is to furnish individuals with disabilities a level of service that is comparable to the level of transportation service provided to individuals without disabilities on the fixed route system.

ADA also requires that new transportation equipment (buses) and that special transportation services, such as paratransit, be made available for those who cannot use mainline transportation. New transportation facilities must be accessible, and existing facilities must be retrofitted. Intercity and commuter rail coaches and stations must also be made accessible or retrofitted.

As the ADA is implemented, many older persons with disabilities are entitled to new and better services. At the same time, those without a disability are being forced to mainstream onto fixed route systems so that limited dollars can

The Americans with Disabilities Act requires that special transportation services be made available for those who cannot use mainline transportation. (Courtesy of the American Public Transit Association)

fund more expensive special transportation services. Note that ADA is civil rights legislation and made no additional financial resources available for implementation. Although ADA presents improved access and opportunity for some, others may be adversely impacted.

Transit Service: Key Terms and Descriptors

The transit programs described earlier finance a number of different kinds of transit services. These are some key terms and descriptors common in transit service:

- **Traditional transit services:** include buses, rail, and commuter systems that primarily serve work trips in urban areas
- **Fixed-route service:** bus service that operates on a regular route at specified intervals between common stops
- **Paratransit:** a general term for transit service that includes smaller vehicles, which are usually accessible to people with mobility impairments, and provides

demand-responsive service to special populations, such as the elderly and people with disabilities
- **Demand responsive service:** transit services available on a limited basis to special populations, such as the elderly and disabled, which provide transit service at the request of the user; usually a telephone call and a reservation secures the service; also known as "dial-a-ride" service
- **Subscription services:** demand-responsive services provided to a user on a regular basis, at specified dates and time, for the same purpose or destination, such as dialysis or shopping
- **User-side subsidy:** reduced or free transit fares, provided through vouchers, tokens, or card systems, for use on taxis and paratransit service
- **Supply-side subsidy:** financial operating or capital assistance provided to a government or nonprofit transit service provider; usually occurs in areas, such as rural loca-

Paratransit is a transit service that includes smaller vehicles, providing demand-responsive service to populations such as the elderly and disabled. (Courtesy of the American Public Transit Association)

tions, where providers are scarce and service is expensive

- **Accessibility:** buses, vans, airplanes, trains, bus stops, transfer stations, airports, etc., which can accommodate a variety of sensory, cognitive, and physical impairments experienced by users

Transit Demand

The problems with transit are availability, affordability, and accessibility. The need for the most demand-responsive transit services far outweighs the supply. One study estimates that 5.6 million people over 65 years are without private transportation (Cutler and Coward, 1992). The implication is that they rely on, but don't necessarily have access to, public transportation. The deregulation of the intercity bus industry has made the problem of public transportation particularly acute in rural portions of this country.

Across the country more than 1,200 counties provided no transit services. Further, for every federal transit $1.00 spent on rural residents, $27.00 more are spent on their urban counterparts. Approximately $100 million from all sources are spent annually on rural transit services (CTAA, 1991). Because smaller populations do not support public transportation services, rural dwellers rely more heavily on their automobiles. Because of decreasing populations, other services are also decreasing, and rural people are being forced to travel longer distances to access medical care, shopping, and other activities.

Specialized Transit

Most communities deliver traditional specialized transit services, such as paratransit, demand-responsive, subscription, and taxi cabs. There is usually a combination of all in each community. Although specialized transportation operators use more than 50,000 vehicles to meet mobility needs of the transit dependent, many problems exist in urban areas. For instance, many services are located in places with no public transportation. Besides the rise in population of the transit-dependent, the low densities of most communities present a formidable barrier to greater transit use. Some communities are attempting to address this problem by creating new services.

Service Routes

One such form of transit are service routes. This service provides buses along regular routes, with specific stops and regular schedules—similar to fixed-route. But also it employs vehicles that are smaller than typical buses, fully accessible, routes planned to minimize walking, drivers sensitized to the needs of the riders, and travel to and from places of interest and need to older persons. The service is experiencing widespread use in Europe and is being piloted in the United States.

Given what is known about the population, housing patterns, and transportation opportunities, an increasing number of transportation planning decisions are made at the state, regional, and local levels. Participation in the decision-making process extends to those using the system. As the interests are broadened, meaningful community transportation must address needs-assessment for older transportation users, older persons with disabilities, and frail elderly. Hopefully, the elderly themselves can become stronger advocates for present and future service needs.

Across the country more than 1,200 counties provided no transit services. Further, for every federal transit $1.00 spent on rural residents, $27.00 more are spent on their urban counterparts.

● HIGHWAY IMPROVEMENTS FOR SAFETY

The design and operation of the roadway environment also needs to be more responsive to the changing functional capacity of the driving public. Public works officials are slowly but actively improving highways to accommodate these changes.

The most common approach taken by pubic works officials appears to be more conspicuous use of signs, markings, and signals. Generally, improvements to these traffic control devices occur through increased size, enhanced clarity, greater redundancy, and increased reflectivity. In other words, bigger and brighter is the rule of thumb. Other common strategies include reducing stopping sight distance times (how quickly a driver can stop once information is detected) and simplifying left turn intersections. Any of these strategies improve the traffic safety of the entire driving population, not just older drivers.

● SAFETY THROUGH VEHICLES

Features such as anti-lock brakes, air bags, and tinted windshields should become standard features on most cars. In addition, discussions related to the Intelligent Vehicle Highway System (IVHS) technology, so-called "smart car" technology, present an opportunity to improve safety for drivers in the future. It will be possible, for instance to provide the following.

- Information on road conditions to a driver through video displays and voice message. The system can advise drivers of optimum speeds and alternative routes.
- Head-up displays, which project information to a focal point near the front of the vehicle, allowing drivers to keep their eye on the road.
- Infrared night vision systems to enable drivers to look well beyond the range of their headlights.
- Crash avoidance systems, such as lane-change warning devices and rear-obstacle detectors that can alert drivers with visual and audio messages. The rear-obstacle detection system is activated when the vehicle is put in reverse. The lane-changing alarm prevents a driver from being surprised by another car in the driver's blind spot.
- Ultrasonic parking assistance that would allow a driver to maneuver safely in very tight parking spots or when near hidden objects. Ultrasonic converters measure the distance between a vehicle and an obstacle. The system audibly signals the driver.
- Headlight washing systems that could help compensate for the fact that dirty headlights can cut night vision up to 90 percent.
- Electrochromatic mirrors that automatically eliminate headlight glare from other vehicles and prevent the driver having to flip a day/night switch.
- Traction control systems that work with anti-lock brake systems to enable vehicles to stabilize acceleration in all types of road conditions.

Most of the features are now available, but the costs are too high and they are not standard options. Over time, increased consumer demand will undoubtedly encourage auto makers to make them widely available.

● SUMMARY

As we approach the twenty-first century, greater attention must be paid to the growing mobility needs of older Americans. It makes little sense to build a comprehensive care system, support continued suburbanization, and ignore the transportation implications of those decisions. More aggressive strategies are needed to improve the safety and mobility of all persons. For older persons, strategies such as graduated licenses and service routes provide a wider range of transportation choices. Such choices along a mobility continuum can keep older people active, independent, and empowered to meet their needs.

Organizations

American Association of Retired Persons
Transportation Section
601 E St., NW
Washington, DC 20049
(202) 434–6000
Driver education, licensing, safety, pedestrians, transit services.

American Automobile Association Foundation for Traffic Safety
1730 M St., NW, Ste. 401
Washington, DC 20036
(202) 775–1456
Driver education, licensing, safety.

American Public Transportation Association
1201 New York Ave., NW
Washington, DC 20005
(202) 898–4000
Transit services.

American Association of Motor Vehicle Administrators
4200 Wilson Blvd., Ste. 600
Arlington, VA 22203
Driver licensing.

Community Transportation Association of America
725 15th St., NW, Ste. 900
Washington, DC 20005
(202) 628–1480
Transit services.

National Eldercare Institute on Transportation
725 15th St., NW, Ste. 900
Washington, DC 20005
(202) 628–1480
Transit services.

National Highway Traffic Safety Administration
400 7th St., SW
Washington, DC 20590
(202) 366–0123
Driver and pedestrian safety.

U.S. Architectural and Transportation Barriers Compliance Board
1331 F St., NW, Ste. 1000
Washington, DC 20004
(202) 272–5434

Contact your local area agency on aging, public transit, or state driver license agency.

References

American Association of Retired Persons (AARP). *Eleventh Annual Survey of Middle-Age and Older Americans.* Washington, DC: AARP, 1989.

——. *Graduated Driver Licenses: Creating Mobility Choices.* Washington, DC: AARP, 1992.

American Public Transit Association (APTA). *Nineteen Ninety-one Transit Fact Book.* Washington, DC: APTA, 1991.

Barr, Robin. "Recent Changes in Driving Among Older Drivers." *Human Factors* Vol. 33, no. 5 (1991): 597–600.

Community Transportation Association of America (CTAA). *Public Transit in Rural America.* Washington, DC: CTAA, 1991.

Cutler, Stephen J., and Raymond T. Coward. "Availability of Personal Transportation in Households of Elders: Age, Gender, and Residence Differences." *Gerontologist* Vol. 32, no. 1 (1992): 77–81.

Federal Highway Administration (FHWA). *Highway Statistics, 1990.* Washington, DC: United States Government Printing Office, 1991a.

——. *Walking Through the Years: Pedestrian Safety for Older (65+) Adults.* Washington, DC: United States Government Printing Office, 1991b.

Gelfand, Donald E. *The Aging Network: Programs and Services.* 3d ed. New York: Springer, 1988.

Hasler, Bonnie S. *Barriers to Living Independently for Older Women with Disabilities: Transportation.* Washington, DC: AARP, 1991.

Huttman, Elizabeth D. *Social Services for the Elderly.* New York: Free Press, 1985.

Malfetti, James L., and Darlene J. Winter. *A Graded License for Special Older Drivers: Premise and Guidelines.* New York: Safety Research and Education Project, Columbia University, 1990.

National Association of Area Agencies on Aging and AARP. *Analysis of Area Agencies on Aging Transportation Survey.* Washington, DC: AARP, 1991.

Rosenbloom, Sandra. "The Mobility Needs of the Elderly." In *Transportation in an Aging Society: Improving Mobility and Safety for Older Persons.* Washington, DC: National Academy Press, 1988.

U.S. Department of Transportation. *Survey Data Tabulations, 1983–1984: Nationwide Personal Transportation Survey.* Washington, DC: United States Government Printing Office, 1985.

Steve Lee

33

Technology and Aging

● Types of Technology ● Older Adults and Technology
● Benefits and Limitations of Technology for the Aging Populace ● Medical Technologies
● Rehabilitation Technologies ● Assistive Technologies ● Communication Technologies
● Technologies for Caregivers

The word "technology" carries a variety of meanings. In the popular imagination it can denote a world of computers, robots, stainless steel, and panels of flashing lights. For others, technology is associated with scientific discovery or medical breakthroughs. Technology may include not only mechanisms and machines but techniques, procedures, and methods.

This chapter takes a comprehensive look at technology and aging, approaching the subject from the perspective that technology is: "the application of knowledge for practical ends, as in a particular field . . . and the sum of ways in which social groups provide themselves with the material objects of their civilization" (Random House Dictionary, 1968). The application of knowledge central to this section concerns the changes people undergo as they become older and how knowledge can benefit older adults and their families. The specific benefits discussed relate to four areas of technology: medical, rehabilitative, assistive, and communications.

● TYPES OF TECHNOLOGY

Technology for an aging society can be categorized by its degree of complexity and by application. Technology categorized by the degree of complexity is often referred to as high tech, low tech, hard tech, and soft tech. High technology may include advanced electronics, holograms, lasers, microprocessors, pacemakers, graphite

composites, and induction cooktops. Low technology may include simple tools such as canes, reachers, a buttoner, or an elongated shoe horn. Hard tech is tangible and can be felt and held. Soft tech is intangible, for example, a service or body of knowledge.

Technology categorized by application includes medical, rehabilitative, assistive, and communicative. Medical technologies can be subdivided into life-saving and life-sustaining types. Life-saving technologies have received the primary focus over the years and contribute to the reason people are living longer. Some medical technologies can now save the lives of people who, a few short years ago, would have died. These include magnetic resonance imaging (MRI) that allows a cancer to be detected at an earlier stage, medicines that counteract poisoning or dissolve blood clots, heart defibrillators, and the array of techniques and devices used by emergency personnel.

Life-sustaining technologies are drugs, medical devices, or procedures that can keep individuals alive who would otherwise die within a foreseeable, but usually uncertain, time period. These include mechanical ventilation to help a person breathe, renal dialysis to support kidney functions, nutritional support and hydration (sustaining the intake of nourishment and fluids), and antibiotics (Office of Technology Assessment, 1987).

Rehabilitation technologies include therapeutic regimens, prostheses (artificial limbs), and orthoses (braces or supports), focused on restoring the individual's capacities to former levels. Assistive technologies are products and systems that compensate for differences between the demands of a product or environment and the capabilities of an individual. Some assistive technologies (e.g., magnifying glass, step stool, safety pin) have been around for years and are used by everyone, while others are designed for individuals who have specific physical differences such as being shorter, weaker, nearsighted, or who have difficulty walking without support. Assistive technologies include aids for daily living that help with dressing, food preparation and eating, bathing and grooming, getting about, communicating, and augmenting vision.

Communication technologies are used to transfer information from one point to another. These technologies are likely to produce some of the most dramatic future changes in service delivery, education, and health care. They include telephone, facsimile transmission (FAX), remote monitoring and emergency alerting systems, and the multitude of media that store images and combine them with computing and playback systems. Computer and information systems are an integral part of the communication system, and as the capacity of these products continue to increase and their prices decrease, greater numbers of all segments of society will explore and adopt their use.

● OLDER ADULTS AND TECHNOLOGY

Many of our oldest Americans have lived through and well remember the advent of automobiles, discovery of nuclear energy, dropping of the atomic bomb on Hiroshima, launching of the first satellite in space, the first walk on the moon, and the multitude of space trips that have been taken since. They may recall when the transistor was developed and have watched computers change from requiring room-size space to fitting into a shirt pocket. When asked if the interactive video computer program she was using intimidated her, one research subject in her mid-eighties responded, "Honey, when you have lived as long as I have, and seen all the changes that I have seen, you aren't intimidated by something that plugs into the wall."

Many people unfamiliar with older consumers assume that they are intimidated by and won't adopt new technologies. This assumption is not true. Older adults are like young adults when purchasing a new product: they evaluate its appearance, what it will do for them, the ease of using it, and how much it costs. If it looks good, feels right, does the job well, and meets their expectations for price, they buy it. If it doesn't meet their expectations in any one of these criteria, it is likely they won't acquire it.

Bowe (1988) offered essentially these same conclusions and expanded on "the difference factor." Some seniors refuse to use a technology because they would rather endure inconvenience and occasional danger than use something that marks them as being old. Because most of the products for mature consumers are not used by the general population, many older people believe that using them calls attention to their need for special help.

Although there have been studies suggesting that older consumers are among "the last to adopt a product, service or idea innovation" (Gilly and Zeithaml, 1985), probably an equal number have documented that the mature consumer was the first to acquire a technology when its benefits were compatible with perceived needs. Frequently studies of older consumers' perceptions of "technology" have been completed "out of context." The studies have focused on this particular age group, asked its members what they thought about "technology," and then concluded that this age group was different from and more resistant to technologies than younger consumers.

Gilly and Zeithaml (1985) compared a sample of people 21 to 64 years of age with a group over age 65 regarding their knowledge of sources of information, implementation, and satisfaction with four technologies: scanner-equipped grocery stores, automated bank teller machines (ATMs), electronic funds transfer (EFT), and custom telephone calling services (CTCS). They found that older respondents' familiarity with the technologies was not different from that of the younger consumers; but with the exception of EFT, the older consumers had a lower rate of trial and adoption than the younger consumers. Although the authors suggested that the lack of adoption was related to age, it is more likely a function of lifestage. The older consumers were more likely not in the workforce full time and thus less apt to miss telephone calls or to have a sense of urgency about someone unable to reach them if the line were busy. Many of the older respondents' lack of ATM use may be less their lack of trust in the equipment than a desire to visit with someone (e.g., a bank teller).

Another study, completed by the American Association of Retired Persons (1984), concluded that older Americans who were receptive to technical innovations considered to have positive potential would probably have shown even stronger propensity if "technology" had been defined or put into context. Many of the questions in the survey were abstractly worded: "Machines are . . . ," "Improvements in technology make it . . . ," and "Machines make life . . . ." A study of women with limited experience using technology, who were older and who had lower incomes than the AARP sample but who had recently experienced using a high technology interactive video education program, revealed perceptions of technology more positive than those of the general AARP sample. Their frame of reference or context was the technology they had just used in the research study conducted by the Institute for Technology Development (1986).

Statements about knowledge, use, and adoption of technology by older adults must be put in context to both the lifestage of the individual and the definition of technology. Older consumers are not likely to balk at having cataract surgery because it is too "high tech." They may put it off for a variety of other reasons, but their concern would not be that it is too difficult, too impersonal, or too intimidating.

● BENEFITS AND LIMITATIONS OF TECHNOLOGY FOR THE AGING POPULACE

Technologies for an aging population are created to meet needs and demands of people who have outlived the benefits of the current generation of products, services, and techniques. In many ways, the products designed for the "general market" have failed to keep up with the changes among the consumers. For example, despite the fact that mature consumers comprise the largest percentage of their readers, little has been done to enhance the readability of newspapers. Some effort to increase the size of highway and street signs has been undertaken. Similarly, more than half the purchasers of American automobiles are people over age fifty, yet appropriate design modifications (e.g., to improve ease of reading dashboard instruments) are slow in coming.

Often technologies developed specifically for the mature consumer are designed from an ageist perspective. The designs focus singularly on compensating for the physical or sensory limitations of the individual and ignore the consumer's lifestyle and desire for an aesthetically pleasing product. Many technologies are developed by designers with limited experience or stereotypical image of the mature consumer. Most active designers are in the age range between 25 and 45 years. Thus the product designed by a young adult for an older adult, with advertising campaigns designed by young adults hoping to attract mature adults, often overcompensate and miss the mark. They sometimes seem designed for older and frailer persons than for those actually intended to use the product.

Barzel (1991) refers to the double-edged sword of technology and its effects in deconditioning the populace. He contends that "labor-saving devices" can prolong the independence of the frail elderly, but these same devices may have been the cause of their frailty through long-term deconditioning, exposing them to degeneration and weakness, potential harm, injury, and even premature death (Barzel, 1991). The automobile is a good example. Muscular strength diminishes without exercise. The convenience of an automobile has reduced the demand for walking. Lack of exercise reduces strength and stamina, which increases the need to use an automobile to travel a distance as short as one block. Using a technology can increase dependency on the technology.

The Stigma of Age

Technologies are too often dichotomized—presented as specifically intended for mature consumers, when the technology could actually be used and enjoyed by members of all generations. Devices are sometimes labeled for use by the handicapped, when in fact they are actually better designed products that happen to look different from ones that the general public has been using for years. Because designers and marketers have been directed to develop something for "the mature market," they box themselves into oppositional thinking: old versus young, able-bodied versus disabled. In truth, there is rarely a distinct threshold for attaining older adulthood or being physically disabled.

Our youth-oriented society tends to stigmatize anything specifically intended for use by older adults. The automobile industry has a saying, "You can sell an old man a young man's car, but you can't sell a young man an old man's car." Regardless of age, many people shun the idea that they are like older people. Consequently they may reject helpful technologies they associate with getting older.

Problems of Product Design

Many technologies for older consumers are developed to overcome a single limitation. The hearing aid is a good example. More than 30 percent of the population over age 65 has a hearing impairment. For years the hearing aid industry has been working to develop hearing aids that produce a sharper, clearer sound. However, in their zeal to satisfy the need to produce high quality sound, they have ignored other aspects related to successful use of a hearing aid, such as the manipulation and care of the device.

Countless numbers of older individuals who own hearing aids do not wear them because they find it difficult to correctly insert the devices into their ears, change the battery, or clean ear wax out of the sound channel. Thus research and development dollars have produced true innovations in hearing aid product technology, but the design of the product overlooks the multiplicity of changes that older persons experience. The hearing aid has been well designed to amplify sound but not to assist the person who has visual limitations, reduced manual dexterity, and limited range of shoulder motion. The hearing aid and hearing aid battery make significant demands on good vision, fine fingering, and wrist and shoulder rotation.

Technological devices for older consumers are often designed without attention to aesthetic considerations. Some products are so crudely designed as to be offensive—canes and walkers come to mind. A recent study completed for AARP found that a sizable proportion of cane users complained vehemently about the appearance of their canes. Many were using homemade canes, because they found them more attractive; others had made cloth covers for their canes that matched their clothing styles.

● MEDICAL TECHNOLOGIES

The development of new medical technologies has been both a burden and a blessing. Certainly the use of cardiopulmonary resuscitation (CPR), a simple yet highly effective life-saving procedure, must be considered a positive innovation. But machines that can prolong life almost indefinitely raise unprecedented issues about who decides when the quality of a person's life is acceptable or unacceptable. Increased interest in suicide, forms of euthanasia, and the notoriety of Dr. Kevorkian and his "suicide machines" dramatize the need for ethical guidelines and public debate.

Concern about life-sustaining technologies and "heroic" procedures has led to widespread use of living wills to help secure the patient's right to a death with dignity. The hospice movement, enabling a person to die at home with proper attention to pain control and family support, may be viewed as an example of a soft technology used to offset (or counter) a hard one.

Resuscitation

One of the primary lifesaving technologies is cardiopulmonary resuscitation (CPR), a method for restoring heartbeat and maintaining blood flow and breathing following cardiac or respiratory arrest. CPR techniques are taught through a variety of organizations—the Red Cross, schools, and many businesses. These courses focus on manual external cardiac massage and mouth-to-mouth ventilation. Advanced life-support measures include application of prescription drugs and devices such as an electrical defibrillator, temporary cardiac pacemaker, and mechanical ventilator. Resuscitation can be applied to anyone whose heart stops beating.

The Office of Technology Assessment (1987) reports that there are numerous instances in which elderly people who might benefit from life-sustaining treatments do not receive them. This results, in part, from the view that outcomes will not lead to an acceptable quality of life and that older people are readier to die than younger people. These two assumptions are often false and reflect ageist attitudes.

Profiles of Productive Aging

Gerard Piel
Magazine publisher

"That my career was going to be in science never occurred to me. But I discovered that very interesting people were engaged in working on deeply interesting questions, and that this was an ongoing, live enterprise of our civilization."

Gerard Piel founded the highly successful and critically acclaimed magazine *Scientific American.* He was born in 1915 on Long Island, the fourth of six children. Piel attended parochial school in Brooklyn before attending Andover then Harvard. Always an avid reader, he never had a particular aptitude for science; in fact, alienated by a boring and insensitive science teacher in school, he avoided taking science courses at all costs throughout the rest of his education.

His first career ambition was to be a journalist. One of his main role models was Ralph Ingersoll, a family friend and founder of *Life* magazine and a managing editor of the *New Yorker.* Piel, who had spent most of his extracurricular time at Andover and Harvard working on the school publications, admired Ingersoll's career. Upon graduation he moved to New York City "to be as close to where my hero was working as I could," he explained. Piel helped put out the first and only four issues of a picture magazine called *Picture,* as an office boy at Time Inc. and found another mentor, Alexander King. Piel worked closely with King at *Picture* and attributes to King much of his astute education in magazine publishing. King was the idea man and Piel the executor. With King, Piel learned the work ethic and formed his own ideology, which laid the groundwork for his own pioneering magazine.

By the early 1940s Piel was hired at *Life* as science editor, despite his lack of interest in the subject. The proposition was, "If you will learn about science and can explain it to me, then maybe you and I together can explain it to our readers." Learning that science was a whole other category of imagery, Piel began to use photographs to tell the story, providing "drama and interest" in addition to explaining the facts most vividly. Scientists also were among Piel's biggest readers. He gained their respect and trust by allowing them to review and correct his articles to "get the facts right."

By the end of World War II, Piel felt, "I didn't want to work for Henry Luce as science editor while there was an atomic bomb in the world. I had to be responsible for my own publication." By 1947 Piel and two partners bought the original and ailing *Scientific American* and relaunched it. Shrewd marketing tactics, frugal management, and Piel's fine reporting methods gained *Scientific American* a circulation of 100,000 by 1950. By 1957 the magazine was surviving, and by 1959 it was out of debt and making money.

Piel attributes *Scientific American*'s success to its unique style. "Blackie black, that was how science was supposed to look," he commented. "Well, we made it look like poetry and like art." *Scientific American* is now translated into ten different languages including Russian and has a worldwide circulation of over 1 million. Piel sold the magazine in the late 1980s, but continues to maintain an advisory position. And he has been deeply involved in the effort to implement and publicize the results of the 1992 U.N. Conference on the Environment.

Lydia Brontë

Mechanical Ventilation

Mechanical ventilation is the use of a machine to induce alternating inflation and deflation of the lungs to regulate the exchange of gases in the blood. It is used as an acute lifesaving technique and for individuals with chronic pulmonary difficulties. Estimates of the number of people requiring mechanical ventilation vary, but there are probably close to 7,000 ventilator-dependent persons in the United States, including approximately 2,200 persons over the age of 70 years (Make, Dayno, and Gertman, 1986).

Diagnostic Imaging

Diagnostic imaging is one of the most significant additions to lifesaving technologies and includes untrasound, X-ray computed tomography (CT), magnetic resonance imaging (MRI), positron emission tomography (PET), and single photon emission computed tomography (SPECT). These systems, used in all areas of medicine, help to detect, assess the severity of, and map the characteristics of pathology, including benign and malignant tumors and structural changes in soft tissue such as that seen in Alzheimer's Disease, other disorders of the brain, and virtually every other area of the body.

The practical considerations of imaging techniques are their resolution (how small an area they can look at), whether or not they expose the patient to radiation, where they are available (widely available or limited), and the cost. MRI has the least amount of risks associated with it, while CT, PET, and SPECT involve ionizing radiation, which carries some risk, although the doses are not considered excessive. CT and PET generally have the finest degree of resolution and are the most widely available (Margolin, 1990).

Renal Dialysis

Renal dialysis is an artificial method of maintaining the chemical balance of the blood when the kidneys have failed. There are approximately 100,000 renal dialysis patients in the United States. Approximately 31 percent of the patients in the Medicare dialysis program are over the age of 65 years (OTA, 1987). There are two primary types of dialysis, hemodialysis and peritoneal dialysis. In hemodialysis, blood is first pumped out of the patient's body into a dialyzer, where impurities are removed before the blood is returned to the patient's body. In peritoneal dialysis, the dialysis is performed inside the patient's body. A dialysis fluid that cleanses the blood through a semipermeable membrane surrounding the abdominal organs is placed in the patient's abdomen through a permanent catheter. The fluid is then drained out of the abdomen and replaced with new fluid. The process usually takes several hours.

Dialysis may occur in a hospital, a free-standing dialysis facility, or in a patient's home. Where the dialysis occurs depends to a great extent on the patient's condition and the support services available. Family members must be prepared for emergencies. Renal dialysis is problematic, since there is greater demand than can be met for this costly procedure.

Nutritional Support

Nutritional support refers to artificial methods of providing nourishment and fluids. Nutritional support has become highly controversial because of the many court cases involving decisions to continue or withdraw these support systems. Enteral, or tube, feeding involves providing the patient nutrients and water through a tube into the stomach or intestine. Parenteral feeding includes other methods, but usually involves providing nourishment through catheters into the patient's veins.

Most of the people receiving nutritional support are in hospitals (94 percent), a small proportion are in nursing homes (5 percent), and a few are at home (1 percent). In 1985 a marketing study completed by the Kline Company suggested that approximately 1.4 million persons were receiving nutritional support (American Society of Parenteral and Enteral Nutrition, 1985).

Medication

Growth in the development of new medications has been tremendous, especially in the areas of cardiovascular, gastrointestinal, psychotropic, rheumatological, and infectious diseases. Well known, for example, are the drugs used to control high blood pressure (hypertension) and irregular heart beat (arrhythmia). The development of antibiotics is another prominent area of the expanding drug industry.

Antibiotics are a large segment of the drugs used to cure or control bacterial, viral, and fungal infections. There are more than fifty antibiotics available in the United States that may be administered through application of a cream on the skin; through a tablet, capsule, or liquid form; through feeding tubes; and by injection in a muscle or a vein. Although available for more than fifty years, antibiotics are still considered wonder drugs, because people who appear near death one day can feel as if nothing had been wrong the next.

Older adults receive more antibiotics and are likely to have more infections than younger adults. One study suggested that older adults (Shapiro and others, 1979) represented approximately 20 percent of the census in hospitals but 40 percent of the patients receiving antibiotics. Other studies (OTA, 1987) suggest that between 8 percent and 16 percent of the patients in nursing homes are receiving antibiotic therapy.

Antibiotic therapy is controversial in the "right to die" milieu. Many physicians consider antibi-

Profiles of Productive Aging

Linus Pauling
Scientist

"I was so interested in scientific work that it was inconceivable that I would retire the way a businessman retires.... I was a productive researcher still in possession of his faculties. I could keep on doing scientific work."

Two-time winner of the Nobel Prize, Dr. Linus Pauling's prolific career indeed did not even slow down when he reached retirement age. At the age of 93, he continues to "publish more papers than ever before." During his lifetime, to date, Pauling has published some 800 scientific papers.

Pauling was born in Portland, Oregon in 1901. His father, a pharmacist, fostered his son's interests in books and the world around him at an early age. Pauling first became fascinated with chemical reactions by watching his father make pharmaceutical preparations. "As a boy I can remember that I was very curious about phenomena. . . . Ever since then I've continued to have much curiosity about the physical world."

Pauling left home at age sixteen to attend agricultural college, where he gained his bachelor's degree in chemical engineering. While at college he met a fellow student, Ava Helen Miller. They would later marry in 1923. Pauling moved to Pasadena in 1922 to study at the California Institute of Technology. "It was quite a revelation to go to Pasadena as a graduate student and to be taught a technique of X-ray defraction of crystals. This permitted me early on to begin answering some of the questions that I had been asking." He received his Ph.D. in chemistry and mathematical physics from the institute in 1925.

Pauling's work over the next twenty-two years dealt primarily with the nature of the chemical bond. His research included experimental studies of the structure of crystals, gas molecules, the magnetic properties of substances, and the structure of antibodies. His research in particular on the hemoglobin molecule led to the path-breaking discovery of numerous diseases caused by the malformation or malfunction of the red blood cell molecules known as hemoglobinopathies. Sickle-cell anemia is probably the best known of these diseases.

Pauling received his first Nobel Prize, in chemistry, in 1954 for his many years of research on the chemical bond. His contributions to chemistry would also be recognized by many other awards in the years to follow.

Inspired by his wife's interest in political and social issues, Pauling developed an interest in world peace in the mid-1940s, and devoted much energy to giving speeches around the world on the subject. It was these efforts that would earn him his second Nobel Prize, in 1963.

In the late 1960s Pauling became interested in the biochemistry of nutrition. After reading several papers that detailed the discovery that niacin (vitamin B3) could markedly improve the condition of some schizophrenics, he coined the term "orthomolecular medicine" to describe the use of substances normally present in the body itself—such as vitamins and minerals —to treat illness.

Pauling also discovered much to his surprise that an enormous amount of research—"thousands and thousands of papers"—had been published that showed that vitamin C had substantial positive effects on health in a number of respects: vitamin C was centrally involved in the manufacture of the basic building blocks of the body, collagen and elastin; a greater than normal intake of vitamin C could reduce the frequency of colds; and retardation of the growth of tumor cells in cancer also seemed linked to vitamin C. Pauling's findings were brought to the world's attention with the publication of the international bestseller *Vitamin C and the Common Cold,* in 1970.

Since then Pauling has continued his work in the field of biochemistry, concentrating on the role of vitamin C and other vitamins in the treatment of cancer. He is currently working on his second book on this subject. When not working he spends time with his large family. "I have four children, fifteen grandchildren, and approximately a dozen great-grandchildren," says Pauling. With a touch of pride, he adds "I stay in touch with all of them."

Lydia Brontë

otics a part of routine clinical procedure and do not consider them extraordinary lifesaving measures. Thus they administer them routinely even if a patient's condition is extremely debilitated and the chances for recovery are almost nonexistent. In other instances antibiotic therapy has been withheld from terminally ill patients who were near death from causes other than the infectious agent.

Medication Compliance

Reasons for people not receiving or taking needed medications include affordability, problems following required dosage frequency, side effects, and the perceived severity of illness. As to the latter, since patients suffering from hypertension do not feel any physical effects, they may ignore taking their medication. Compliance is highest when the person perceives the need of compliance as critical.

Several research studies have shown a high rate of noncompliance or refusal to taking medicines among older adults. Estimates of noncompliance range from 30 percent to 60 percent (Boczkowski and Zeichner, 1985; Burrel and Levy, 1984; Eve, 1986; Smith, 1984; Green, Mullen, and Stainbrook, 1984), and the cost of hospital admissions due to noncompliance was estimated in 1986 as $8.5 billion (Sullivan, Kreling, and Hazlet, 1990). Medication compliance is a life or death matter for many. Horwitz, Visoli, and Berkman, (1990) showed that the risk of dying within a year after a heart attack is 2.6 times greater for patients taking a beta blocker (propranolol) who did not carefully follow their treatment regimen, compared to those patients with good adherence. Poor adherence was defined as taking 75 percent or less of the prescribed medication.

Development of technologies to assist older persons in improving medication compliance present many problems. Many people do not think about keeping a record of the multiple drugs they may be taking, nor do they perceive over-the-counter medications as part of their medication program. Forgetfulness, visual impairment, inability to open medication packages, difficulty understanding cryptic directions, and color vision difficulties are just a few of the functional problems interfering with older persons' capabilities in dealing with medication packaging. Then, too, there is lack of coordination among physicians,

pharmacies, and other health care providers who should be monitoring the medication profile of persons for whom they prescribe and sell drugs. As of January 1, 1993, the federal government required pharmacists to provide oral and written directions with prescriptions to all Medicaid recipients.

Many technologies are being developed to help increase compliance with medication therapies. One of these is developing new methods of drug delivery, such as a transdermal controlled release system. These are medications that can penetrate the skin and be delivered through a patch that is adhered to the skin. Medications that are being used in this application include scopolamine for motion sickness, nitroglycerin for heart disease, clonidine for hypertension, and estradiol for menopause (Langer, 1990).

A host of electronic and non-electronic medication compliance devices have been developed. Among the non-electronic is a medication dispenser consisting of simple plastic box organizers that have compartments for time of day and each day of the week. Someone (the individual, a family member, or pharmacist) loads the box with the appropriate medications in each of the bins. The individual is responsible for opening the correct compartment, removing, and taking all of the pills at the appropriate times.

Other medication compliance devices are small alarm systems that can be worn as a wristwatch, carried in the pocket or purse, or adhered to the medication bottle. The alarms have a range of functions from sounding when the medication should be taken to providing a memo indicating the particular medication and amount that should be taken. Still others provide additional information about drug side effects, reminding people of appointments, or that prescriptions should be refilled. Each of these devices require programming by someone familiar with the system, the medication regimens, and the individual consumer. While these are helpful, their value rests on ease of programming, availability of someone to keep the system programmed, and ability to monitor correct use of the system.

Some sophisticated medication compliance devices on the market signal patients when it is time to take their medication, dispense the correct amount, and record the date and time at which the medication was taken from the dis-

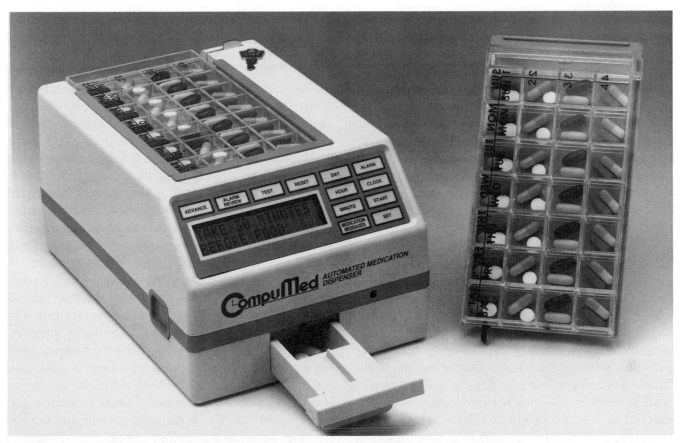

CompuMed Automated Medication Dispenser locks, reminds, and automatically dispenses the right medicine at the correct time and dose. A large display screen gives clear instructions for taking medication properly. An adjustable (pitch and volume) audio alarm sounds. For the hearing impaired, an optional flashing strobe is available. (Courtesy of CompuMed)

pensing bin. These devices are filled and programmed by family or pharmacist. If the patients are able to program these, they probably don't need the device. Sources for medication compliances devices are included in List 33.12 of the Manufacturers of Beneficial Products for the Aged section at the end of the chapter.

While these devices are of assistance to a great number of individuals, they do not solve all of the problems. For example, a woman who was provided the medication signaling device by her son-in-law would hear the alarm and would go to the device, but she could not remember where the small drawer holding the medications was located. The alarm would continue to signal, and she would become upset. While many of these devices seem to be well planned, many have design flaws that negate their usefulness.

● REHABILITATION TECHNOLOGIES

Rehabilitation of the older adult focuses on three levels: restoration of previous capabilities,

compensation for remaining impairments, and substitution of performance by human or technology proxies (Holm and Rogers, 1991). Technologies that compensate for remaining impairments or substitution of performance can be categorized as assistive, and those used to restore the individual's capabilities, as rehabilitative.

For several reasons, efforts to rehabilitate older persons are frequently inadequate. First, society may have low expectations about older persons' adaptive capacities and about what the level of functioning should actually be in old age. Second, the failure of older persons to return to former levels of function is considered acceptable. Thus society more readily accepts less effort in rehabilitating the older adult (Becker and Kaufman, 1988). Third, since rehabilitation is a two-way street, the older adult's attitude toward the need and prospective benefits of rehabilitation also plays an important role in its success. Lack of success with a rehabilitation technology may be as much the result of the person's attitude as the failure of the program or equipment to provide adequate support.

Rehabilitation for older persons is frequently provided for patients who have been admitted to hospitals for cardiovascular disorders, rheumatoid arthritis, stroke, and amputation. In a study of 67 consecutive patients admitted to a geriatric medical unit in a large teaching hospital, 67 percent were admitted for a cerebrovascular accident (CVA, or stroke), 21 percent were admitted for amputation, and the remaining were admitted with a variety of other diagnoses.

Cardiac Rehabilitation

The methodology of cardiac rehabilitation services has changed dramatically over the years. These services are designed for patients recovering from acute myocardial infarction (heart attack), coronary artery bypass graft surgery, or persons with chronic stable angina pectoris. These rehabilitation services are designed to restore certain patients with coronary heart disease to active and productive lives. The rehabilitation programs are divided into three phases: Phase I represents inpatient rehabilitation activities that begin while the patient is in the hospital and continue until discharge; Phase II is an ambulatory outpatient program and continues until the patient is capable of performing prescribed exercise and carrying out lifestyle changes; and Phase III is a lifetime maintenance phase accomplished in a minimally supervised regimen. Use of electrocardiographic monitoring of patients, via hardwired or telemetric equipment, is a common feature of rehabilitation services. Transtelephonic monitoring for patients exercising at home has also been used (Office of Health Technology Assessment Reports, 1987).

Orthopedic Rehabilitation

The technologies of prosthetics and orthotics are supplied to older adults in increasing number. A prosthesis is an artificial part to supply or replace a defect in the body. Older consumers are frequent recipients of replacement hips and knees as well as replacement limbs for amputations. Orthoses (e.g., braces and trusses) are used to help correct contractures and compensate for instability and misalignment of intact limbs by providing static support.

Orthopedic rehabilitation often involves use of medications. Bell (1989) reviewed the many practices in rehabilitation of individuals with rheumatoid arthritis and reported that medications are prescribed for patients in ascending order from least toxic to most aggressive. The progression is seen as a treatment pyramid beginning with nonsteriodal anti-inflamatory drugs (NSAIDs), such as aspirin and other salicylates, and progressing to secondary agents, such as hydroxycloroquine, gold, penicillamine, and methotrexate. The use of corticosteroids is reserved for patients waiting for a response from a slow-acting drug, who are in pain, and who have limited function (Bell, 1989).

When medication and physical therapy (aerobics, range of motion exercises, and mechanical therapies such as heat or ultrasound) fail, the physician may recommend orthopedic surgery. Orthopedic management of arthritic deterioration of joints was revolutionized by the introduction of total hip-joint replacement. Artificial joints are now available for most body joints (Parsons and Rappaport, 1977). Total joint arthroplasties for the hip, knee, and shoulder are effective in relieving pain and improving joint mobility (Bell, 1989).

Amputees, particularly young amputees, have been featured using some of today's most exciting prosthetics. Many have seen the television commercial showing the young man with two energy-storing prosthetic legs made by Dupont. According to Dudley Childress (Enders, 1990): "Today, specially designed prostheses are sophisticated and strong enough to withstand the pressures of running, skiing, boxing, and other activities. Their development was a direct response to veterans groups, handicapped athletic organizations and the desire of orthotists and prosthetists to better serve their patients."

While the application of "high tech" prosthetics has not been applied routinely to the older rehabilitation population, it is likely to occur. Attitudes relative to the abilities and expectations for an active life among the older segment of society are changing. Few are willing to accept the statement, "You are old—learn to live with it," and more are expecting advanced rehabilitation technologies to be available to them as well as to the younger population. At the age of 60 years, a person is likely to have at least one-third of his/her life ahead. With this knowledge,

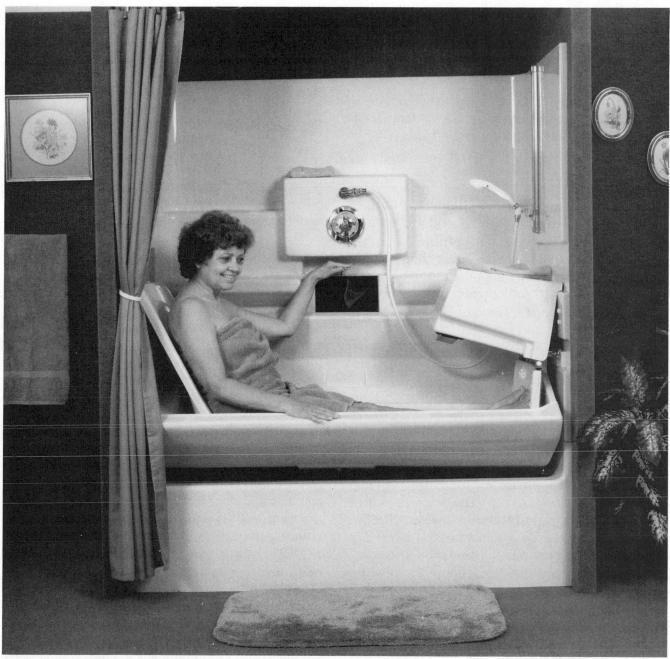

Comfort Care by Ferno Healthcare. (Courtesy of Ferno Healthcare)

few are going to want to accept learning to live with something that has the potential for correction.

● ASSISTIVE TECHNOLOGIES

Assistive technologies are required when there is a mismatch in the demands of the environment (product, service, or architectural) and the capabilities of the individual. In many instances, if the original product were better designed or designed differently, then an assistive device would be unnecessary.

It will be impossible to describe all of the assistive technologies that are available. Referenced here are those most frequently used and considered to be of benefit for older adults. Readers interested in additional technologies can consult many of the agencies that provide comprehensive information about products and services for individuals looking for assistive devices.

The basic activities of daily living include

bathing and grooming, dressing, toileting, and preparing food and eating. Multitudes of assistive products for activities of daily living can be located through several avenues (see Activities of Daily Living section of "Organizations"). Occupational therapists are an important source of expertise since they have specialized knowledge of assistive devices for self-care and aids to activities of daily living.

Bathing

Assistive technologies available for bathing range from accessible bathing systems to bath seats and back brushes. The problems people have using bathtubs include: losing their balance while getting in and out, slipping in the tub, lacking the strength to pull themselves up from a seated position on the floor of the tub, lack of strength, mobility and stamina to transfer in or out of the tub, and inability to regulate the water temperature and detect whether it is too hot before being burned.

Approximately 10 percent of the population over the age of 65 has difficulty bathing (Leon and Lair, 1990). This number increases to more than 50 percent of the people 85 years and older who live independently in the community. The estimates of those who bathe independently varies widely because of the way in which bathing has been defined on surveys. Bathing does not necessarily mean that the person is capable of taking a tub bath independently.

Assistive bathing systems attempt to solve the problems. Two systems, the Comfort Care System by Ferno Healthcare and the Safe-T-Bath by Safe-T-Bath, Inc., attempt to eliminate the potential of someone falling while in the tub by providing the bather a bathtub base at seat height (approximately 18 to 20 inches). Rather than standing and stepping into the tub, the bather sits on the floor of the tub and slides in. In the Comfort Care System, once the bather has lifted his legs onto the bath tray, a bathing tube (similar to a half barrel) rotates up around him. In the Safe-T-Bath tub, the bather opens a door in the side of the tub, sits on the floor of the tub and slides in. Once in, the bather closes the door and fills the tub with water.

Other bathing systems have doors in the sides of the bathtub so that the bather may walk into the tub without having to step over the side of the

Kohler Precedence with door by Kohler Co. (Courtesy of Kohler Co.)

tub. Two of these, a tub by BathEase, Inc., and The Precedence by Kohler look comparable to traditional bathtub/shower combinations except that they have doors mounted in the side of the tub and seats integrated in the construction of the tub that are higher than the floor of the tub, but low enough so that the bather will still be able to sit in the water. Other bathing systems use the door in the side but look slightly less conventional.

Two products, the Comfort Care System mentioned above and the Spa by Arjo use the technology of seating the bather, then rotating the bathtub around them. The Spa, which looks like an egg, has a seat suspended on an axis. The bather sits in the seat, and the egg rotates around the bather, encompassing the bather in the bath.

Many people attempt to solve the problems encountered by bathers by adding grab bars around the bathtub. While grab bars are important stabilizers and support systems, they still do not solve the problems many people encounter when trying to get in and out of the tub. Many people are still unable to use a conventional bathtub even with grab bars and bathseats installed according to ANSI 117.1 barrier-free design standards. Manufacturers of accessible bathing/showering systems are shown in List 33.1 of the Manufacturers of Beneficial Products for the Aged section at the end of the chapter.

Showers

There are not as many innovations in shower design, but many older persons find that they are more competent in a shower than climbing into and out of the tub. Shower units can be categorized into three types based on the threshold access. There are conventional units with a 3 to 6 inch threshold that the bather steps over to enter the shower. Ramped units allow someone to enter the shower in a shower wheelchair. Other showers have their sills flush with the floor. People may roll into these showers or walk into them without negotiating over the threshold.

Showers should have a sturdy seat that may be folded out of the way and grab bars mounted around the perimeter so that the bather has a handhold available regardless if standing or sitting.

Add-On Bathing Devices

Scores of products are available for assisting the bather to get in and out of the bathtub or shower. These include grab bars that clamp onto the side of the bathtub and transfer seats and bath seats that allow the individual to sit on the edge of the bathtub and scoot into a seat positioned at sill height in the tub. There are bathtub seats that position the bather out of the water, and others that allow the person to transfer onto the seat at the height of the bathtub edge, which then lowers the bather to be seated in the bath water. Other seats swivel the bather into the tub before lowering the person into the water.

Many bath seats do little to assist the bather into or out of the bathtub or provide solid support for that transfer. The purchaser needs to be certain that the bath seat will provide the necessary amount of support and security for the bather before investing in one of these products. Although many appear inexpensive, they may do little to assist the bather and may not protect the bather from a fall. It is also important for the bather to be taught the safe way to transfer onto the seat so that it can be used properly.

Grab Bars

Many companies offer grab bars. Those that have more innovating lines that are attractive and enhance the appearance of the bathroom include Normbau, Safe-Tek, and Universal Rundle (see List 33.8 of the Manufacturers of Beneficial Products for the Aged section at the end of the chapter). These grab bars come in a variety of colors and have other bathroom accessories that match.

Grab bars offer good support and solid handholds for people with the strength and mobility to move into and out of the bathtub or shower with-

out assistance. Grab bars may not be of assistance to people who are extremely frail or who have difficulty moving and transferring. Grab bars, nonetheless, should be installed in all bathrooms, in all homes, of people of all ages. They are tools that help prevent injury and should be added before an injury has occurred. They are not the only solution, but they are an important safety feature.

Criteria for the selection of appropriate grab bars include that they are capable of supporting a minimum of 250 pounds, they are between 1¼ and 1½ inches in diameter, and they are mounted into an area of the wall that has been prepared structurally for the grab bar. Also, they should be put at heights and angles appropriate to the user.

Grooming Aids

A few companies (ETAC, USA, and Lumex, Inc.) offer a nice assortment of grooming aids. These aids are a series of products that have long, angle-adjustable handles and include hair brushes and combs, back brushes, and devices that hold wash cloths, toilet paper, and other personal care

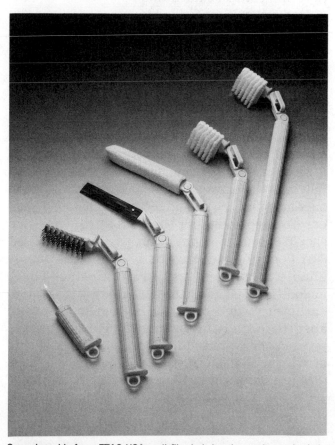

Grooming aids from ETAC USA: nail file, hair brush, comb, wash cloth, and back brushes. (Courtesy of ETAC USA)

items for those who have limited manual dexterity, range of motion, or mobility.

Normbau and others have a wall-mounted mirror that tilts so that shorter persons or people seated in wheelchairs can adjust the mirror. Sources for grooming aid products are shown in List 33.9 of the Manufacturers of Beneficial Products for the Aged section at the end of the chapter.

Toileting

Urinary incontinence (UI) affects approximately 10 million Americans, mostly elderly living both in the community and in institutional settings (Urinary Incontinence Guideline Panel, 1992). Urinary incontinence, loss of control over urination, is not a natural part of aging and can be caused by many physical conditions. There are three major categories of treatment for urinary incontinence: behavioral, pharmacologic (medication), and surgical. Behavioral includes bladder training, habit training, prompted voiding, and pelvic muscle exercises that may be used in conjunction with biofeedback, vaginal cone retention, or electrical stimulation.

Medication is prescribed to treat conditions that cause urinary incontinence, including infection, hormonal changes, abnormal bladder muscle contractions, or sphincter muscles. Surgery is used to return the bladder to its proper place in women with stress incontinence (urine loss when moving, sneezing, etc.), to remove tissue that may be blocking a channel, replacing or supporting weak pelvic muscles, or enlarging a bladder to hold more urine. In most cases urinary incontinence can be successfully treated or reversed. Persons experiencing urinary incontinence should recognize that many others are experiencing the same problems and should consult their physician.

A host of products are available for people unable to gain control of their urine. These include internal and external catheters, collection catheters, penile clamps, pessaries, and absorbent pads or garments. Although these products can be used independently, they should be used with medical guidance and management. (see Conditions That Cause Urinary Incontinence section in "Organizations").

Toilets

Several companies offer clamp-on elevated toilet seats for persons who need a higher seat sur-

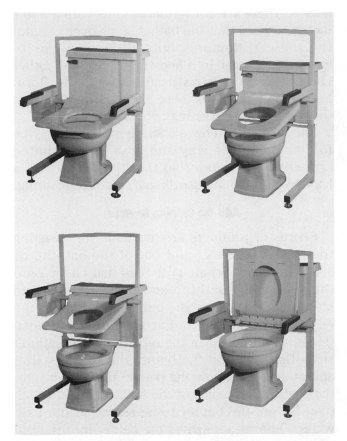

Power Toilet Elevator from Med/West. Switch in handle controls electric motor. Seat is driven easily and safely into position by rack and pinion gear set. Unit slips over standard or institutional toilet. (Courtesy of Med/West)

face to aid in getting on and off the commode. Some of the elevated toilet seats have grab bars mounted on them. The most important component of these products is the mechanism that clamps the seat onto the toilet. People using the seat-mounted grab bars for assistance in rising from the toilet may apply uneven pressure to the seat and, if it is not fastened securely, could tip the elevated seat off of the toilet. Whether or not the person can clamp the seat on independently should also be considered.

A few companies offer toilet seat systems that lower or lift the user onto the normal height seat. One of these, the Hydra Commode Lift, uses water pressure to automate hydraulic lifts that gently lower and raise the seat. The person using the toilet merely leans back against the raised toilet seat, flips a lever, and is slowly lowered onto the toilet. When the person is finished, the lever is reversed, and the water-pressured system brings the person to a standing position.

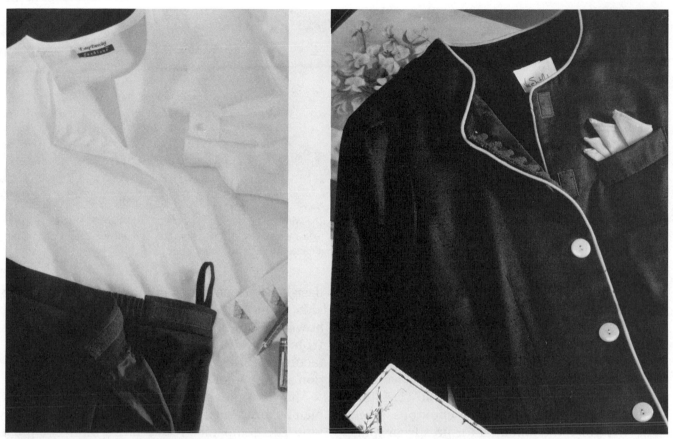

J. C. Penney's Easy Dressing Fashions have built-in features to make dressing easier and faster. Velcro Brand Wavelok® fasteners are concealed beneath decorative buttons. Sturdy pull loops are sewn inside the skirt's waistband to simplify dressing. (Courtesy of J. C. Penney)

The elevating toilet by Med/West of Marshalltown, Iowa, is an electrically powered system that bolts to the toilet in the holes normally used for the standard toilet seat. The elevating toilet lifts the user to a semi-standing height. The typical lift height is 23 inches in the front and 27 inches in the back. The elevating toilet is available in a 14-inch standard home model, an elongated model, and an institutional (18-inch) model. The suggested retail price for the home model is $695.

For people who have difficulty completing personal hygiene after toileting, the Showerlet provides a commode-mounted mini-shower that has a water spray nozzle, blow dryer, and push button controls. Sources for toileting aids and products are included in List 33.16 of the Manufacturers of Beneficial Products for the Aged section at the end of the chapter.

Dressing Aids

Many people have difficulty with fine fingering activities involved in buttoning their clothes or tying their shoes, while others cannot bend down to pull on their pantyhose, socks, or shoes. Simple low-tech devices such as buttoners, sock and stocking aids, and long-handled shoe horns are available to overcome these problems (see List 33.7 of the Manufacturers of Beneficial Products for the Aged section at the end of the chapter). Shoes with velcro fasteners, available for people of all ages, help eliminate the frustrations of trying to tie a bow.

J. C. Penney offers Easy Dressing Fashions, a selection of dressy or casual apparel that use a variety of easier to manipulate clothing fasteners including ring-pull zippers, Wavelok® designs, and Velcro closures. Clothing designed without back openings (and, hence, difficult to reach zippers), enlarged arm holes (easier to reach through), and elasticized waist bands are additional features. Others offering adaptive clothing include: Adaptawear, Inc., Adaptogs, Alimend, Designs for Comfort, Inc., Fashion-Able, Idea, Inc., Silver Lining Designs, Inc., and Wings Sewn products.

Food Preparation and Eating

Food preparation technologies are being enhanced in the general marketplace by the improvement of many precooked frozen and shelf packaged foods. Complete dinners that can be stored in the freezer or on the shelf are available for microwave cooking. Many of these do not require transfer to other cooking containers and thus enable the individual to prepare a meal by opening the container and adjusting the microwave to the appropriate time and temperature settings.

Microwave ovens are available that do all of the "thinking" for the user. The microwaves have sensor systems that sense the heat and amount of steam rising from a product being cooked and automatically adjust the length of time and power of the cooking process. Other home cooking devices, although they have changed in design, offer little to assist the older cook who may require assistance. Cooktops (ranges) have been improved by the introduction of solid glass tops which help in clean-up. These cooktops, while likely to reduce the potential for fires from spills, still get hot enough to burn someone. The manufacturer recommends that on these surfaces spills should be wiped up immediately, which is also a risk if the burner is hot. The Amana Insta-Glo range has a glowing red light under each burner that stays lit as long as the heat of the burner exceeds a specific temperature. Most of the others however, once they are turned off, do not indicate that the burner may still be hot. People who are more accustomed to the traditional coil burner may look at the solid glass top and not recognize that it may be hot.

The electro-magnetic induction cooktop, available from a variety of manufacturers, heats food in metal pans by inducing heat through an electro-magnetic force. These cooktops do not get hot, but transfer the heat to the contents of the food through the metal pan. The "burner" may be turned up to high but you would not get burned by placing your hand directly on it, because your hand is not electromagnetic. You would burn yourself on the hot metal pan, but not on the burner itself.

Several kitchen devices have ergonomic designs that help people with arthritis and other impairments. These products, many of them in

The Winsford Feeder, from Winsford Products, Inc., enables people to feed themselves at their own rate, without the use of their arms. (Courtesy of Winsford Products, Inc.)

designer lines, include preparation boards, slicing aids, bread slicers, cheese slicers, jar openers, bowl holders, and reachers. They are available from sources listed in List 33.5 of the Manufacturers of Beneficial Products for the Aged section at the end of the chapter.

Many people, too, have difficulty holding and manipulating small objects such as standard cutlery. The companies listed above offer complete lines of decorator cutlery with larger grips and easier-to-manipulate angles. Plates, glasses, and cups are available that aid people who have arthritis or decreased manual dexterity. The Winsford Personal Feeder or the Beeson Automaddak Feeder may be of benefit to people unable to feed themselves (see List 33.5 of the Manufacturers of Beneficial Products for the Aged section at the end of the chapter). These electric or battery-powered devices sit on the table and automatically scoop food into a spoon and lift it to the mouth of the eater when activated by a switch. It should be pointed out that these devices are very expensive. If people require assistance from their insurance to pay for these items, they are often denied if a caregiver is in the home who could feed the person.

Mobility

Among the U.S. civilian noninstitutionalized population, 6.4 million people use some kind of mobility technology, and 4.4 million use a cane or walking stick (LaPlante, Hendershot, and Moss, 1992). Sixty-seven percent of the people who use mobility devices are over the age of 75 years. Despite the fact that most of the mobility products are used by older adults, few companies have studied the full range of abilities of this market segment to ensure their products are compatible.

The majority of mobility products prescribed for the mature consumer are the "standard" or traditional product that is Medicare approved. These products are the basic, workhorse devices that are designated for the older person not because they better fit the older person's abilities, but because they are more durable.

Wheelchairs. Among the 645,000 persons in the noninstitutionalized population who use wheelchairs, 52 percent were 65 years old or older. More than half use them all of the time, and more than 40 percent have been using the wheelchair for more than five years. Almost all of the wheelchairs are used for chronic conditions.

The three primary types of manual wheelchairs are standard chairs, lightweight chairs, and ultralight, or custom, wheelchairs. Standard wheelchairs are usually the least expensive, are the most frequently prescribed under Medicare, and may weigh between 40 and 65 pounds (AARP, 1990). A lightweight chair weighs 20 to 30 pounds less than the standard chair but is similar in size, shape, and features to the standard chair. The differences are in the types of materials that the wheelchair frame and wheels are made of. Ultralight wheelchairs are lighter than most lightweight chairs, because they are made of lighter materials, and because they will often come without as much of the structural components (shorter seat backs, slimmer armrests, and foot rests that are slim bars) as the standard or lightweight chair. However, it may be difficult to get Medicare or other insurances to cover the cost of lightweight wheel chairs.

A study completed by the Institute for Technology Development for AARP learned that the older wheelchair users employed in "usage tests" of the wheelchairs felt as stable and secure in the ultralight chairs as they did in the heavier standard chairs. Without exception, the older wheelchair users were able to roll farther and faster with less effort using the ultralight chairs than using the lightweight or standard chairs.

Physical therapists are usually better informed than physicians or nurses to evaluate patients' needs for various types of wheelchairs. There is some tendency for doctors and nurses to think of ultralight wheel chairs as a more appropriate technology for younger generations than for older people. Persons in the market for a wheelchair should understand that there are dozens of choices on the market, and each choice of wheelchair comes in several sizes or colors and has a variety of options that make the chair more livable and usable. However, the healthcare delivery system has not offered choice, nor has it kept up with being informed about the various products on the markets. Many people receive new wheelchairs that are technologically obsolete.

Several new additions to the types of manual wheelchairs are available. Some have gigantic wheels, look like they should be on a "Fruit Loops" cereal commercial, and are used for getting around on the beach. One of the more recent innovations in wheelchairs allows the user to stand. While these products cannot be used by all persons who use wheelchairs, they help overcome one of the environmental barriers people in wheelchairs encounter, that of being too short. Some of these products can be moved while the person is in a standing position, while others are best used in a stationary position if they are standing. Many have gas cylinder or electrically assisted standing mechanisms. Manufacturers of these products are shown in List 33.18 of the Manufacturers of Beneficial Products for the Aged section at the end of the chapter.

Power Wheelchairs. Wheelchairs are also available with battery power. These products come in a variety of styles and dimensions that range from the traditional wheelchair with a motor and battery pack to a powered system that looks like a high tech captain's chair from a space set. The Love Lift system is a power wheelchair that is capable of acting as a lift for transferring someone into or out of the automobile. The chair seat raises and lowers and swivels and moves horizontally so that it can pick up someone from inside a car and move them onto the wheelchair base. The chair moves up and down to provide the rider access to higher levels. Manufacturers of power wheelchairs are shown in List 19 of the Manufacturers of Beneficial Products for the Aged section at the end of the chapter.

Power Scooters. Today's consumer may have more than fifty models to select from when looking for a motorized (battery-powered) scooter, but they have no readily available source of infor-

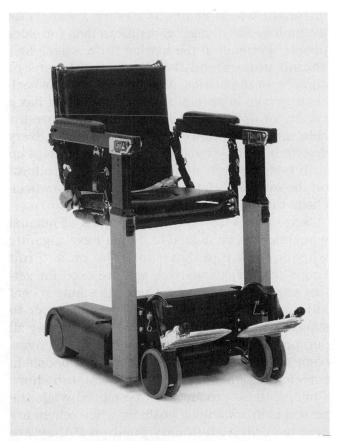

The Love Lift wheelchair functions as a normal wheelchair, yet has built-in power-lifting capabilities to aid the caregiver when lifting or transferring is required. (Courtesy of Love Lift)

mation to help them make the correct decision. However, many physical therapists are knowledgeable about power scooters and should be consulted.

An exhaustive search of the literature on scooters in professional and popular databases revealed fewer than fifteen publications on these products. Two publications (Waldman, 1991; Weisenberg, 1989) describe tips on marketing scooters to the consumer. Another article (Illinik, 1990) provides a humorous story about one woman who took a corner too fast in her scooter, and some helpful hints on how to avoid accidents. Another article (Sowell, 1992) describes one woman's viewpoint about using her scooter to conserve energy.

Three publications were identified that provide information relevant to selecting a scooter. One of these is a newsletter, *PAM Repeater*, published by PAM Assistance Center (1990). A second unpublished report (Denison, 1991) lists the results of a cursory evaluation of seventeen scooters. The final study, unavailable to the general public, is a comparative evaluation of forty-five different scooter models by the Rehabilitation Engineering Center at the National Rehabilitation Hospital. They provided comparative descriptions of each of the models of scooters and evaluated them relative to the ANSI/RESNA draft standard for the testing of manual and power wheelchairs. Their results provide an excellent reference for comparing specific models to each other.

The literature search failed to identify a single article that reported the results of research among scooter users to determine the features and performance characteristics important to use, control, maintenance, and transport, nor were there sources of information available to the consumer contemplating purchase of a scooter. The consumer, despite availability of many options, will be limited to the information offered by the sales organization and may not have the knowledge base to find and select the scooter best suited to personal abilities, needs, or lifestyle.

People who use scooters may have quite different abilities. Some may have physical weakness in all extremities or have sensory or cognitive limitations. Because of the weight of many components of the scooters, many users will be unable to maintain their scooters or transport them to places other than their immediate environment. Sources for power scooters are shown in List 33.14 of the Manufacturers of Beneficial Products for the Aged section at the end of the chapter.

Walkers. Of the more than 689,000 persons who use walkers, 80 percent are 65 years of age and older. More than half of them use walkers all of the time. Walker users include persons with recent amputations, persons in rehabilitation after knee or hip surgery, those with balance problems, and people with weak knees or ankles.

The hundreds of different walkers can be divided into four groups: (1) rigid walkers that are "pick up and put"; (2) pick up and put walkers that fold; (3) two-wheeled walkers; and (4) four-wheeled walkers. The folding and rigid pick up and put walkers are those seen most frequently. Two-wheeled walkers are usually the standard folding or rigid frame aluminum walker with wheels mounted on the front two legs and "glides" (plastic caps) placed on the back two legs. Four-wheeled walkers break down into two categories: (1) those that are the traditional rigid or folding walkers with small casters (3 to 4 inches in diameter) mounted on each leg; or (2) the newer walker that has larger wheels with pneumatic tires (6 to 12 inches in diameter) mounted on each of the four legs.

A study completed by the Institute for Technology Development for the American Association of Retired Persons found that older persons either were thrilled by the newer four-wheeled walkers or somewhat leery and frightened of them. Those who were excited by the newer walkers liked their increased maneuverability and the fact that most came equipped with a basket, seat, and handbrakes. The user could simply set the brakes and have a seat if walking somewhere and becoming fatigued. Those who were skeptical of the product felt that the walker "may get away" from them and that they would be unable to control it.

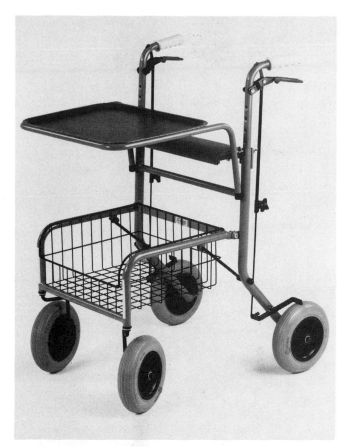

NextStep roller walker with tray from NobleMotion, Inc. Roller walkers are designed for in-home use and outdoor use. (Courtesy of Noble-Motion, Inc.)

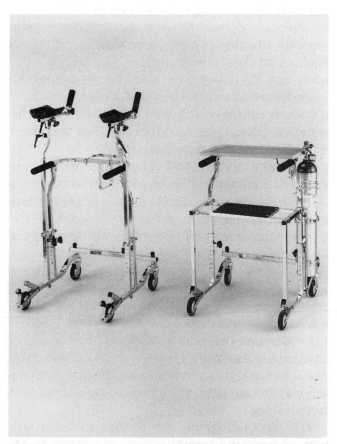

Wenzelite Safety Roller from Wenzelite Corp. offers full support at all times. The unique brakes are applied as the patient shifts his or her weight while walking. (Courtesy of Wenzelite Corp.)

The prices of the different walker technologies vary considerably. Prices of the pick up and put walkers ranged from $30 to $130, depending on the size of the walker and accessories. The two-wheeled walkers ranged in price from $63 to $180, again depending on the size and options. The four-wheeled walkers ranged in price from $260 to $465 (AARP, 1991).

As with the wheelchairs, most of the subjects who participated in the AARP study did not know that different types of walkers were available, and none knew about the four-wheeled walkers. When consumers are looking for a walker, they should be sure that they look at several different types of models and accessories available for them. They should "test drive" the walker and the walker should be fitted to them for height and width.

Manufacturers of walkers are shown in List 33.17 of the Manufacturers of Beneficial Products for the Aged section at the end of the chapter.

Canes. Almost 3 million people use canes in the United States, and three-fourths of them are

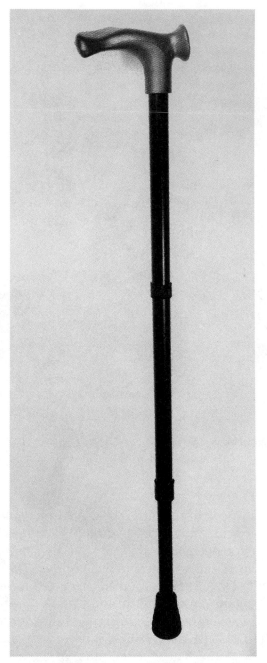

Stride-on cane from NobleMotion, Inc. (Courtesy of NobleMotion, Inc.)

65 years old and older. Almost half of the people using canes have been using them for more than one year but less than four years; 88 percent stated that the condition for which the cane was used was chronic.

Canes are walking aids designed to bear up to 25 percent of the user's weight. Some people use canes for balance and for orthopedic purposes (used on the side opposite the weakness). Canes have changed very little over the hundreds of years they have been in existence. The majority

of canes in use today (as reported by 1,000 letter writers to AARP) are made of aluminum (53 percent), while the rest were made of wood (44 percent), and a few were made of plastic or other materials (3 percent) (AARP, 1992).

Canes have four basic parts: a handle, a handle grip, a shaft, and the base. Most of the canes used have the C-curve or crook shaped handle, although pistol grips are becoming more prevalent. Most of the canes used have a single-tip base, as opposed to a four-pronged or quad base. Only a few companies manufacture canes with "ergonomic" grips. These grips are designed to distribute the individuals' weight over a greater portion of the hand to make using the cane more comfortable. Cane manufacturers are shown in List 33.3 of the Manufacturers of Beneficial Products for the Aged section at the end of the chapter.

Speech/Language Technologies

A variety of communication systems are being used by older persons who have difficulty speaking or understanding speech because of a speech or language deficit. Speech and language disorders of adulthood may result from conditions such as strokes, cerebral palsy, Lou Gehrig's disease, and Parkinson's disease, among others. All disorders relating to nerves and muscles can have a speech expression as well as a swallowing disorder element. Treatment for cancer of the larynx may also produce speech disorder.

Although a variety of technologies can help improve communication of people who are unintelligible, either because of speech and/or language problems, the systems employed most frequently for older adults tend to be more of the low-tech nature. The computer or microprocessor-based technologies have been developed and are employed more frequently for children with developmental disabilities. This lack of use of micro-processor based communication systems for older persons may reflect underlying ageist attitudes. Another factor is that Medicare, Medicaid, and many private insurers will not usually pay for alternative/augmentative communication devices.

High technology communication systems consist of portable communication aids that are manipulated through a touch-activated or light-activated display board. The display board is divided into a grid with pictures, words, or icons in each square of the grid. When a square is activated, the communication system "speaks" the word or phrase. Communication aids of this type may have anywhere from a few to more than 160 squares, each corresponding to a different thought or message.

Electronic communication devices are made with every conceivable access system. Keyboard entry and pressure-sensitive membrane boards are the obvious; switch access is frequently used—switches may be placed near any body part that has muscle control (there are eyebrow switches, bite switches, etc.). There are also infrared switches that detect eye movement to activate or access a device.

In addition, the capacity of computer based devices allows users to express anything a normal speaker can—including inflection and quality of voice. Some can even sing; it just takes longer to produce the expression.

Low technology communication aids consist of picture or word cards (depending on the cognitive level of the user) that can be pointed to or displayed to convey a thought. Some of the picture systems are printed on cardboard pages with many images or words on each page. Others are a series of photographs or drawings, one image per card. The cards can be arranged in an order to communicate a sequence of thoughts.

Manufacturers of augmentative communication aids are shown in List 33.4 of the Manufacturers of Beneficial Products for the Aged section at the end of the chapter.

Hearing

Although approximately 23.5 million individuals in the United States are hearing impaired (Kochkin, 1991), it is estimated that fewer than 4 million own hearing instruments (Christy, 1991). Fully 10.5 million acknowledge they have a problem hearing yet have not decided to obtain a hearing instrument (Christy, 1991).

Results of audiometric tests administered to individuals in an ongoing longitudinal health study conducted in the Framingham (Massachusetts) Cohort (Shock, 1984), confirmed a hearing problem prevalence rate of approximately 30 percent of the population over age 65 (Gates and others, 1990). This statistic is confirmed by other studies, though the rate of identified hearing

impairment in the over 65 population can vary, depending on the research criteria used to define significant hearing loss, the gender of those studied (more men have hearing impairment than women), and the age make-up of the group.

Despite a relatively high rate of hearing loss, the use of hearing aids among older adults, as well as younger individuals, is surprisingly low. Gates and others (1990) reported that among the hearing impaired members of the Framingham Cohort, 10.3 percent had purchased and used hearing aids, but 22 percent of that group reported they had discontinued using their hearing aid. Other studies (Stephens and others, 1991) confirm a low acceptance and usage rate of hearing aids, particularly without rehabilitative intervention. Adequate time spent by the hearing expert in helping the hearing aid wearer to understand how to insert and control the instrument can be a key determinant of successful usage.

There may be many reasons for the low rate of acceptance of hearing aids. Hearing care practitioners may be more enthusiastic about the benefits of amplification and more pessimistic about the communications abilities of older individuals than older individuals themselves (Kazunari and others, 1981). Older individuals may have other medical and economic demands that have a higher priority. Some have suggested that hearing aid usage may be low because hearing aid providers may have been unsuccessful reaching prospective users and their primary care physicians may fail to recommend further determination of need (HIA, Focus Group Research, 1991); others have suggested that users may be unsuccessful in using a hearing instrument because they are unable to manipulate the controls and components correctly (Stephens and Meredith, 1991; Upfold and others, 1990). For a small minority, certain forms of hearing loss do not benefit from amplification. Qualified and ethical dispensers of hearing aids will refuse to fit these types.

Traditionally hearing instruments have been divided into four categories: body-worn or pocket-type; eyeglass; behind-the-ear (BTE); and in-the-ear (ITE). The first two types are now practically obsolete. Additional important categories describe the variations of ITE aids: aids that generally fill the concha of the ear; in-the-canal (ITC)

Voices of Creative Aging

Harriet F., 70-year-old head of advertising agency, an advocate for hearings aids and adventures, cautions people not to isolate themselves due to hearing loss:

I'm the same way I always was. I'm just older, but I haven't changed. Inside I still feel 21. I have been dependent on a hearing aid since my early 20s. As a matter of fact, one of my soap boxes is to get people, as they age, to start wearing hearing aids so that they don't become isolated. People wait too long. They don't think they're hard enough of hearing or they won't get one because they think it makes them old. People begin to isolate themselves, and the longer they wait the harder it is to adjust. If you are hard of hearing, get a hearing aid. Nobody ever says if you can't see, don't wear glasses!

I work at my agency, and my life is full with community projects on the newspaper. I am also a member of the board of directors of my neighborhood organization. Another way I enjoy people is on annual outings with a group in the neighborhood. Our first activity was to go canoeing in the Okefenokee, and I canoed twenty-two miles. Every time I do these things, I think I'm going to die. Then I make it and am very proud of myself. Last year we went whitewater rafting—four hours in a raft. There were three of us in it—cold, freezing, soaked, and gratified that we did it.

I don't do things that I really think I'm going to get hurt doing. I just do the things that I think I can do with a bit of a challenge. I'm just so busy, and I don't want to retire. As long as I'm here, I don't want to quit. I want to just keep active and ignore the fact that the years are going.

Excerpt from Connie Goldman's "Late Bloomer" public radio series

---

aids that are encased in a small shell fitting almost entirely in the ear canal; and peri-tympanic, or deep canal, aids that are pushed deep into the ear canal almost to the tympanic membrane. Peri-tympanic instruments are virtually invisible unless you are looking directly into the individual's ear canal; they are also expensive and difficult to extract by the wearer. In addition to the categories based on the location in which the hearing instrument is worn, new electronics have added several parameters in the selection process.

The analog hearing aid is the traditional instrument, consisting of a microphone, amplifier, on/off switch (usually), volume control, and receiver. An analog hearing aid uses conventional electronic circuitry, i.e., electronic voltages to shape or develop the output signal. It can be supplied with adjustable frequency response circuity that permits the dispenser to change the amount of amplification the hearing aid provides at various frequency regions. Thus, if an instrument sounds too loud or gives the hearing aid wearer the impression that he is listening in a barrel, the dispenser can simply reduce the amount of amplification in the low frequencies. Or conversely, if the instrument seems to "hiss" or sound "tinny," the dispenser may reduce the amount of amplification in the high frequencies. Output limiting

variability allows the dispenser to adjust the maximum output (the loudest sound) of the hearing aid for greater listening comfort when loud sounds are present.

This circuitry is available in all types (ITE, ITC, and BTE) of hearing aids. It permits the dispenser to "fine-tune" the frequency response of the hearing aid, so that the instrument provides the user more or less gain in frequency regions and a sound quality that better meets the user's perceptions. A new and popular K-AMP compression circuit is available that amplifies *only* soft sounds, has the widest range of frequencies amplified, gets double battery life (one month), and has an audible low-battery warning signal. This wide dynamic range compression circuit has become enormously popular since its introduction several years ago. The K-AMP circuitry is $100 to $200 more costly than conventional hearing aids.

Recent technology includes digitally programmable, digitally controlled analog hearing aids offered by approximately twelve manufacturers (see List 33.6 of the Manufacturers of Beneficial Products for the Aged section at the end of the chapter). A digitally programmable hearing aid is actually a conventional hearing aid whose output filter is controlled by a discrete (on-off) digital function. These hearing aids add digital control and memory capacity to all of the traditional amplification, frequency response, and output-limiting circuitries (Radcliffe, 1991). They are not digitized amplification systems, but rather analog systems under digital control. The result is even greater and more refined flexibility for the dispenser in fitting the requirements of the user.

Some of the significant features (not available in a traditional analog system) are: multi-channel (multiple frequency bands) control of amplification and output limiting; amplification (gain) control in one decibel (a unit for expressing sound intensity) increments; multiple memories, each storing a variety of circuitry parameters so that a single hearing aid can have up to eight different hearing aid frequency response and output limiting settings; and, remote control of memory, volume, and on/off from a small hand-held device. Some combination of these features will be found in different instruments. Again, these hearing aids are rather costly ($1,200–$2,000).

An advantage of some programmable hearing aids is that the user can change, virtually instantaneously, the frequency response and output limiting characteristics of the hearing aid. With a conventional system, the dispenser adjusts the hearing aid to a single frequency response and output response setting. The programmable units, with up to eight memories, offer the user up to eight different frequency response and output limiting settings with the simple push of a button.

Assistive Listening Devices. Assistive listening devices include a variety of amplification systems used primarily for specific purposes,

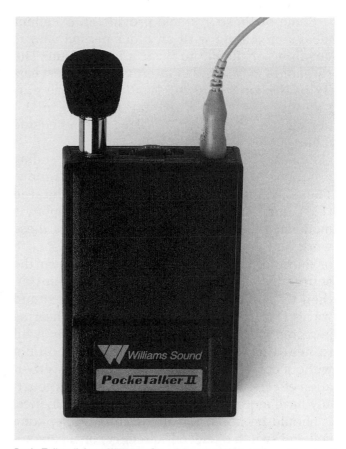

PockeTalker II from Williams Sound is a portable, high quality sound amplifier that can be used to boost TV sound without disturbing others or help overcome background noise in other difficult listening situations. (Courtesy of Williams Sound)

ReSound Personal Hearing System automatically separates incoming sounds into two bands, one for vowels and one for consonants, and processes each band independently. The electronically processed sounds are then matched to the precise size and shape of the user's impaired hearing range. (Courtesy of ReSound Corp.)

including personal, small room and large room amplification systems, television listening systems, telephone enhancement, and a variety of "sound signalling" devices that visually communicate the presence of sound.

Personal assistive listening devices have been available for more than twenty-five years, but they have not gained widespread use. These devices consist of a microphone, amplifier, and receiver (earphone) and operate in a manner identical to that of a hearing aid—except that these devices are larger and may have additional accessories such as an additional microphone. These range in price from $30 to approximately $500 and vary significantly in the quality of sound that they produce and their ease of use. In a study completed a few years ago, a panel of hearing impaired listeners rated the sound quality of the Pocket Talker by Williams Sound as being the best. Other types can be equally or more effective, depending on specific conditions.

Some of these systems provide an excellent means of talking with an older person who is unwilling or unable to wear a hearing aid. The earphones may be small insert types that rest easily in the ear canal, or "walkman" style earphones. The main unit may be worn in the pocket, on a belt loop, or placed on a bedside table.

Several technologies can aid people attending programs or activities in small or large rooms. These systems include frequency modulated (FM), infrared, and (though quite rare) amplitude modulated (AM) based technologies. All of these work on the same underlying principle—speech or music to be "broadcast" is picked up near the source by a microphone, fed to a transmitter, then transmitted via light (infrared) or sound waves (FM or AM) to receivers worn by hearing impaired individuals or people who simply want to hear the sounds from the stage or podium without competing background noise or reverberation effects. The FM and infrared systems generally have more uniform transmission capabilities. It should be noted that requesting a telephone coil and switch ("telecoil" circuitry) on a person's hearing aid may be useful for taking full advantage of some of the large area listening systems. An excellent article on "How to Buy a Hearing Aid" can be found in *Consumer Reports* (November 1992).

Television listening systems operate similarly to the small or large room assistive listening systems and differ only in their size and range of transmission. These work by placing the transmitting device on or near the television and connecting a microphone to the earphone jack of the television or placing a small microphone in front of the speaker. The sound from the television is fed into the transmitter, which transmits the signal to the individual wearing the receiver headset. The receiver headset has an individual volume control and on/off switch. The person who needs amplification can wear the headset and turn up the volume of the television at their ears rather than in the room; thus the remainder of the family can listen to the television at their comfortable listening level.

Sound signalling devices are activated by sound and alert the occupant through light or vibration that there is sound present. Some of these systems are attached to telephones and/or doorbells and flash a light or several lights in the house when the phone or doorbell rings.

Companies that produce assistive listening and sound signalling devices are shown in List 33.2 of the Manufacturers of Beneficial Products for the Aged section at the end of the chapter.

Vision Technologies

Almost 10 percent of the population over the age of 65 years has visual impairment (Elkind, 1990). Someone who is severely visually impaired would have difficulty reading newspaper print. They may be described as having "low vision," which means they have a severe degree of vision loss that interferes with the ease and safety of completing various aspects of daily activities. Approximately 70 percent of the totally blind and visually impaired population is over the age of 65 years (Orr and Piquera, 1991).

Persons with visual impairments use assistance, human and/or technological, in performing two classes of activity: (1) orientation and mobility, and (2) acquiring visually displayed information (Elkind, 1990). Schrier, Leventhal, and Uslan (1991) described four types of "access technology" for blind and visually impaired persons: enhanced image, braille, synthetic speech, and optical character recognition devices.

Orientation and Mobility Devices. Orientation and mobility devices are also called electronic travel aids. Among them is the laser cane, which emits pulses of infrared light to be reflected off obstacles and processed by the cane. Three beams of light oriented in different directions warn the user of objects below (stairs or curbs) with the emission of a low-pitched tone, of objects straight ahead by vibrating against the index finger, and of obstacles at head height by a high-pitched tone.

Kay Ultrasonic Spectacles radiate ultrasonic signals from both the right and left sides of the spectacles and code information about the location of objects in the user's pathway through the intensity of sound heard in both ears. The Mowat Sensor emits ultrasonic signals, which when bounced back to the receiver are translated into a vibratory response on the skin. Proximity is translated by the rate of vibration (Fish, 1985).

Many visually impaired persons rely upon the low-tech white cane, which provides feedback about obstacles and surface conditions of walkways by vibration and sound emitted when they tap the surface.

Visually Displayed Information. Enhanced image devices access printed material or personal computers. For personal computers the image is magnified through both software and hardware applications. Print information is magnified through exposing the printed document or package labels to a closed circuit television, which in turn illuminates and magnifies the material on a television screen. Optical character recognition systems convert print into an electronic form, such as synthetic speech. The person using the device scans the material to be read on a flatbed, page, or handheld scanner, which then "recognizes" the printed characters and "reads" the document. The Xerox Imaging System Kurzweil Personal Reader has nine optional reader "voices."

Another technology includes synthetic speech, with a synthesizer that does the speaking and a screen access program that tells the synthesizer what to say. The computer based systems can recognize grammatical markings in text and can speak, adhering to most of the grammatical rules of language. Although the synthetic speech is often difficult to understand at first, many become accustomed to it readily. Synthesized speech is also available on a variety of other devices including clocks, calculators, chess games, blood sugar screeners, and a money identifier that can identify American currency up to a $100 bill (Schrier and others, 1991).

Braille access devices include paperless devices and printers. Paperless devices generally interface with a computer and display the information on the computer screen on a 20, 40, or 80 character braille display. Braille notetakers are small, portable devices for entering information that can use either a speech synthesizer or braille display as an output. Braille printers convert text files into hard copy braille (Schrier and others, 1991).

Other Aids for Persons with Low-Vision. Probably some of the most common low vision aids are large print books, magnifying glasses, and tape recordings of books, magazines, and newspapers. A variety of other products include blood pressure monitoring kits, timers, needle threaders, watches (large print, braille, or talking), and writing guides.

Developed by Xerox Imaging Systems, the Kurzweil Personal Reader (KPR) was the first system to offer users immediate access to printed materials through high-quality, understandable speech. (Courtesy of Xerox Imaging Systems)

The National Library for the Blind provides free recorded books, magazines, and newspapers to subscribers. Other recordings may be available through public libraries and for sale through book stores and mail-order houses. Resources for technologies for the blind or persons with low-vision are shown in List 33.11 of the Manufacturers of Beneficial Products for the Aged section at the end of the chapter.

● COMMUNICATION TECHNOLOGIES

Communication technologies include telephone and emergency response systems. Many communication technologies that are of benefit to older persons are found in the general marketplace. These include remote and cellular telephones and programmable dialing systems. Remote and cellular phones offer the older consumer the opportunity to have the telephone within reach at all times.

Probably one of the most frequently used technologies is the telephone amplifier built into the handset of the phone. These assistive products are available through the regular telephone equipment companies and merely require plugging into the existing telephone set.

Many hearing aid wearers use hearing aids with electromagnetic induction coils. These require telephones that leak electromagnetic waves that may be picked up by the coils in the hearing aid. For a period of time many telephone sets were being sold and placed as public telephones that did not provide a sufficient amount of leakage. Recent legislation, however, requires

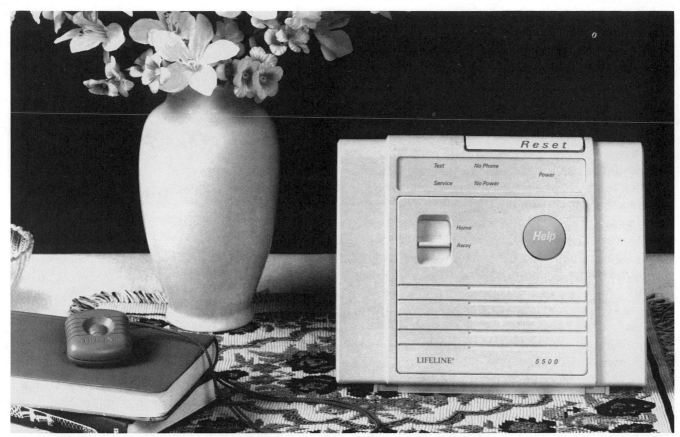

Personal Response System from Lifeline Systems Inc. Lifeline Systems pioneered and developed the personal response system in 1974. Systems such as the Lifeline L5500 (pictured) are communication devices that allow individuals at home to signal for emergency assistance by pushing a button. The button activates a communicator located in the home that immediately sends an emergency signal over a telephone line to a 24-hour monitoring center. The monitoring center determines the nature of the emergency and sends the appropriate "responder," usually a relative, neighbor, law enforcement official, or ambulance. (Courtesy of Lifeline Systems Inc.)

that all telephones must be "hearing aid compatible" by emitting the induction signal.

Emergency Response Systems

Emergency responses systems (ERS) are also known as personal response systems and personal emergency response systems. They became familiar to the general populace through some ill-conceived television commercials that showed older persons lying on the floor and proclaiming, "Help! I've fallen and I can't get up." Approximately 450,000 ERS systems are in use today, mostly by older adults (AARP, 1992).

The ERS consist of a portable "help button" with a radio transmitter mounted in it that communicates with a console response unit attached to the telephone or telephone line in the person's home. When the help button is activated, it sends a signal to the console, which automatically dials a preprogrammed number or numbers. The various systems operate around essentially the same principles but vary in their "response" technology. Some are preprogrammed to dial a national monitoring center, others dial a local monitoring center, and still others dial the home of a friend or relative.

While the basic help buttons are relatively small and easy to operate, they may differ in their effectiveness to transmit signals within a home. Prices of acquiring or being provided monitoring service vary widely and consumers are urged to shop around and test the systems in their homes before purchasing or renting a system (AARP, 1992). In the AARP study, 4,000 letters voluntarily sent by people who use emergency response systems were analyzed, and 96 percent of the letter writers were satisfied with the systems.

The companies providing emergency response systems in the United States that are available nationally are shown in List 33.13 of the

Manufacturers of Beneficial Products for the Aged section at the end of the chapter.

Computer and Information Systems

Although attitudes towards older adults' competence in learning to use computers may be biased negatively (Ryan, Szechtman, and Bodkin, 1992), many older adults acquire expertise, own several, and revel in the use of computer technology. Some investigations comparing younger non-computer users (18–30 years old) to older non-users (65–75 years) showed that the older adults were able to acquire expertise in the use of a computer word processor and to use that expertise to solve problems, although they did require more time to select and carry out the appropriate procedures than the younger age group. The older adults, however, were equivalent to the younger cohort in "transfer of training" activities and recall of training when they were matched with naive, age-matched control groups (Hartley and Hartley, 1984).

As with many other forms of technology, people are unlikely to seek out use of the equipment unless they perceive a need or benefits from the technology. For many persons, regardless of their age, a personal computer seems superfluous to their activities of daily living. They aren't interested in word processing, they have an accountant complete their income tax every year, and they enjoy going to the bank and stores to complete their shopping and business transactions. Still others have quickly adopted the technologies in order to follow their portfolio, enjoy a challenging game of chess, or write their memoirs.

Many older individuals have become involved in SeniorNet. SeniorNet is a nonprofit organization whose goal is to build an international community of computer-using older adults. Currently there are more than 35 SeniorNet sites operating across the United States and Canada. SeniorNet sites are places where computer classes specifically designed for older adults are offered, including classes on word processing, spreadsheets, and telecommunications. SeniorNet also offers an online bulletin board and conferencing service operating on the America On-Line telecommunication network. The network offers electronic mail, forums on a variety of topics, news from Washington about current legislation affecting older adults, and "live" conferences with other members and invited guests. There are special interest groups on subjects such as getting into computers, writing, and electronic citizenship. For more information about SeniorNet, contact SeniorNet, 399 Arguello Blvd., San Francisco, CA 94118; (415)750-5030.

● TECHNOLOGIES FOR CAREGIVERS

Increased attention will need to be paid to the development of technologies for caregivers. Many caregivers are older citizens themselves, caring for someone even older. It is not unusual any longer for someone in their seventies to be caring for a parent in their nineties, or for a spouse in her eighties to be caring for her husband. Additionally, the increasing number of persons with Alzheimer's disease will dictate greater needs for technologies to help care for these people who have a progressive loss of memory.

Technologies for caregivers include monitoring systems, lifting and moving equipment, and bathing equipment. A few home monitoring systems allow the caregiver to "keep an eye" on another individual—including the use of video systems. One technology is a room-to-room intercom system that allows the caregiver to listen to the activities of their family member without actually having to be present in the room with them. Another is a door monitoring system. In this system the doors are outfitted with "alarms" that signal when they have been opened. Some of these systems include an identification tag that is worn by the family member being monitored. Other family members may go in and out of the door without causing the alarm to be activated, but the person with the alarm activator will set off the alarm if they are in the proximity of the door. Thus, the caregiver doesn't have to keep an eye on the family member at all times, but is alerted (day or night) when the family member may be wandering outside of the home. Sources for the home wandering monitoring systems are shown in List 33.10 of the Manufacturers of Beneficial Products for the Aged section at the end of the chapter.

Lift Systems

A variety of lifting systems are available to help transfer someone from one place to another. These systems are intended to assist people

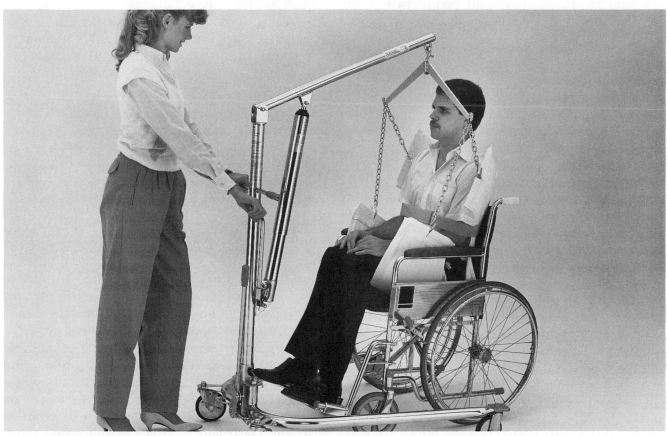

Hoyer Adjustable Base Patient Lifter by Ted Hoyer, Inc. (Courtesy of Ted Hoyer, Inc.)

unable to stand or slide from a bed to a wheelchair, or from the wheelchair to other locations. Lifts include portable lifts that are mounted on wheels. These lifts include a sling seat and a hydraulically operated lift that can pick up someone from bed, chair, toilet, or bathtub and move them to any of the other locations. The expense of lift systems may be prohibitive to many and are not covered by health care insurance.

Lifts are also available mounted on tracks on the ceiling that can help someone out of bed and transport them to another room. Some lifts stay in one location and assist the individual rising in or out of bed or on or off the commode. Many of the lifts can be operated independently by the individual requiring the assistance or with easy assistance from the caregiver. The important contributions that lifts make are that they may keep the caregiver from injuring him or herself; they also enable the individual to remain in the home.

Finally, although they aren't necessarily for caregiver use, several companies produce stairway lifts, home elevators, and platform lifts.

These are expensive and most homes may not be built to accommodate them. Sources for these products are shown in List 33.15 of the Manufacturers of Beneficial Products for the Aged section at the end of the chapter.

Organizations

General

Alliance for Technology Access
1128 Solano Ave.
Albany, CA 94706
(510) 578-0747

Centers for Disease Control
National Center for Health Statistics
Room 1064 Presidential Bldg.
6525 Belcrest Rd.
Hyattsville, MD 20782
(301) 436-8500

Closing the Gap
P.O. Box 68
Henderson, MN 56044
(612) 248-3294

Foundation for Hospice and Homecare
519 C St., NE
Washington, DC 20002
(800) 232-3442

Activities of Daily Living

ABLEDATA
8455 Colesville Rd., Ste. 935
Silver Spring, MD 20910-3319
(800) 346-2742

American Occupational Therapy Association
1383 Piccard Dr.
P.O. Box 1725
Rockville, MD 20849
(800) 729-2682

American Physical Therapy Association
1111 North Fairfax St.
Alexandria, VA 22314
(800) 999-APTA (2782)

Institute for Technology Development
Product Search Service
428 North Lamar
Oxford, MS 38655
(601) 234-0158

National Rehabilitation Information Center (NARIC)
8455 Colesville Rd., Ste. 935
Silver Spring, MD 20910-3319
(800) 346-2742

Trace Research and Development Center
University of Wisconsin
1500 Highland Ave.
Madison, WI 53705-2280
(608) 262-6966

Vision Foundation, Vision Information Center
818 Mt. Auburn St.
Watertown, MA 02172
(800) 852-3029

Cardiac Rehabilitation

American Heart Association
7272 Greenville Ave.
Dallas, TX 75231
(214) 373-6300

National Heart, Lung, and Blood Institute
Building 31, Rm. 4A21
Bethesda, MD 20892
(301) 496-4236

Low Vision

American Foundation for the Blind
15 West 16th St.
New York, NY 10011
(800) AFB-LIND

American Printing House for the Blind
1839 Frankfort Ave.
P.O. Box 6085
Louisville, KY 40206
(502) 895-2405

Recording for the Blind
20 Roszel Rd.
Princeton, NJ 08540
(800) 221-4792

Vision Foundation
818 Auburn St.
Watertown, MA 02172
(800) 852-3029

Mechanical Ventilation

National Association for Ventilator Dependent Individuals
3607 Poplar St.
P.O. Box 3666
Erie, PA 16508
(814) 455-6171

Renal Dialysis

National Kidney Foundation
30 East 33rd St., Ste. 1100
New York, NY 10016
(800) 622-9010

Speech, Language, Hearing

American Speech-Language-Hearing Association
Consumer HELPLINE: (800) 638-8255

National Hearing Aid Society
20361 Middlebelt Rd.
Livonia, MI 48152
(313) 478-4520

National Information Center on Deafness
Gallaudet University
800 Florida Ave., NE
Washington, DC 20002
(202) 651-5051

Urinary Incontinence

Continence Restored, Inc.
785 Park Ave.
New York, NY 10021
(212) 879-3131

Help for Incontinent People
P.O. Box 544
Union, SC 29739
(803) 579-7900

Simon Foundation
P.O. Box 815
Wilmette, IL 60091
(800) 237-4666

Manufacturers of Beneficial Products for the Aged

List 33.1: Accessible Bathing/Showering Systems and Accessories

Aqua Glass Corp.
P.O. Box 412
Industrial Park
Adamsville, TN 38310
(901) 632-0911

Aquarius Industries
6401 Centennial Blvd.
Nashville, TN 37209
(615) 297-3553

Bathcraft
1610 James P. Rodgers Rd.
Valdosta, GA 31601
(912) 333-0805

Bath-Ease
2537 Frisco Dr.
Clearwater, FL 34621
(813) 791-6656

Bradley Corp.
P.O. Box 309
1901 Fountain Blvd.
Menomonee Falls, WI 53051
(414) 251-6000

Braun Corp.
1014 South Monticello
P.O. Box 310
Winamic, IN 46996
(219) 946-6153

Concept Fiberglass Homes
US Army Ammo Plant
P.O. Box 1633
Grand Isle, NE 68802
(308) 381-1965

Dignified Products Corp.
P.O. Box 337
Manutua, NJ 08051
(609) 468-0316

Diversified Fiberglass Fab.
Hwy. 150 East
P.O. Box 670
Cherryville, NC 28021
(704) 435-9586

Electric Mobility
#1 Mobility Plaza
Sewell, NJ 08080
(800) 662-4548

ETAC USA
2325 Parklawn Dr., Ste. P
Waukesha, WI 53186
(800) 678-3822
(414) 796-4600

Ferno Healthcare
70 Weil Way
Wilmington, OH 45177
(513) 382-1451

Florestone Products Co.
P.O. Box 226
Union City, CA 94587
(209) 661-4171

Glastec
P.O. Box 1608
1625 James P. Rogers Rd.
Valdosta, GA 31603
(912) 247-2364

Kimstock
2200 Yale St.
Santa Ana, CA 92704
(213) 680-0470

Kohler Co.
444 Highland St.
Kohler, WI 53044
(414) 457-4441

National Fiber Glass Products
5 Greenwood Ave.
Romeoville, IL 60441
(708) 257-3300

Porta Shower of America
134D Route 111
Hampstead, NH 03841

Safe-T-Bath of New England
185 Millbury Ave.
Millbury, MA 01527
(617) 865-2361

Silcraft Corp.
528 Hughes Dr.
Traverse City, MI 49684
(616) 946-4221

Universal Rundle Corp.
303 North St.
P.O. Box 29
New Castle, PA 16103
(412) 658-6631

List 33.2: Assistive Listening Devices

AT&T Special Needs Center
2001 Route 46, Ste. 310
Parsippany, NJ 07054
(800) 233-1222

Audex
713 North 4th
P.O. Box 3263
Longview, TX 75606
(214) 753-7058

Audio Enhancement
8 Winfield Pointe Ln.
St. Louis, MO 63141
(314) 567-6141

Communication Products and Equipment Co.
R.R. 1 Box 406 Equipment Co.
Lawrenceville, IL 62439
(618) 943-2110

Comtek
357 West 2700 S
Salt Lake City, UT 84115
(801) 466-3463

Controlonics Corp.
5 Lyberty Way
Westford, MA 01886
(617) 692-3000

DYN-AURA Engineering Labs
8057 Vickers St.
San Diego, CA 92111
(619) 565-4922

General Technologies
7415 Winding Way
Fair Oaks, CA 95628
(916) 962-9225

Hal-Hen Company
25-53 24th St.
Long Island City, NY 11106
(800) 242-5436

HARC Mercantile
3130 Portage St.
P.O. Box 3055
Kalamazoo, MI 49003
(616)381-0177

Hear You Are
4 Musconetcong Ave.
Stanhope, NJ 07874
(201) 347-7662

Hearing Impaired Technologies
8205 Cass Ave., Ste. 109
Darien, IL 60559
(708) 963-5588

Heidico
P.O. Box 5665
Vancouver, WA 98668
(206) 694-0446

Let's Talk
915 Lloyd Bldg.
603 Stewart
Seattle, WA 98101
(206) 340-8255

National Catalog House of the Deaf
4300 North Kilpatrick Ave.
Chicago, IL 60641
(312) 283-2907

Oval Window Audio
251 Central St., Ste. 111
Natick, MA 01760
(508) 655-4049

Phonic Ear
250 Camino Atto
Mill Valley, CA 94941
(415) 383-4000

R & M Sales
9203 West Bluemound Rd.
Wauwatosa, WI 53226
(414) 475-7770

ReSound Corp.
220 Saginaw Dr.
Seaport Centre
Redwood City, CA 94063
(800) 248-HEAR

Sehas
533 Peachtree St., NE
Atlanta, GA 30308
(404) 876-2583

Sennheiser Electronic Corp.
6 Vista Dr.
P.O. Box 987
Old Lyme, CT 06371
(203) 434-9190

Sound Involvement
6529 Colerain Ave., Ste. A
Cincinnati, OH 54239
(800) 443-2353

Telex Communications
9600 Aldrich Ave. South
Minneapolis, MN 55420
(612) 884-4051

Williams Sound Corp.
10399 West 70th St.
Eden Prairie, MN 55344-3459
(612) 943-2252
(800) 328-6190

List 33.3: Canes

Activeaid
One Activeaid Rd.
P.O. Box 359
Redwood Falls, MN 56283-0359
(507) 644-2951
(800) 533-5330

Ambutech
Division of Melet Plastics
670 Golspie St.
Winnepeg, MB, Canada R2K 2V1
(204) 663-3340
(800) 561-3340

Autofold
208 Coleman St. Extension
P.O. Box 1063
Gardner, MA 01440-1063
(508) 632-0667

Carex Health Care Products
Division of Acorn Development
39 Thompkins Point Rd.
Newark, NJ 07114
(201) 824-7637
(800) 526-8051

CHADI
2191 North Cleveland Massilon Rd.
Akron, OH 44313
(216) 873-5342

Comfort Walking Cane Co.
115 Willow City Loop
Willow City, TX 78675
(512) 685-3396

Crescent Corp.
P.O. Box 610-987
Port Huron, MI 48060
(313) 982-2784
(800) 233-6506

Garelick Medical Products Division
Garelick Manufacturing Co.
644 Second St.
P.O. Box 8
St. Paul Park, MN 55071
(612) 459-9795
(800) 457-9795

Invacare Corp.
899 Cleveland St.
Elyria, OH 44033
(216) 329-6000
(800) 333-6900

Medline Industries
One Medline Pl.
Mundelein, IL 60060
(708) 949-5500

NobleMotion
5871 Centre Ave.
P.O. Box 5366
Pittsburgh, PA 15206
(800) 234-9255

PCP-Champion
300 Congress St.
P.O. Box 125
Ripley, OH 45167
(513) 392-4301
(800) 888-0867

Rock Ridge Cane
10503 Gateridge Rd.
Cockeysville, MD 21030
(410) 667-0277

Steve's Crazy Legs
3221 South Fillmore St.
Denver, CO 80210
(303) 758-1331

Tubular Fabricators Industry
600 W. Wythe St.
Petersburg, VA 23803
(804) 733-4000
(800) 526-0178

List 33.4: Communication Aids

Adaptive Communication Systems
P.O. Box 12440
Pittsburgh, PA 15231
(412) 264-2288

Canon U.S.A.
1 Canon Plaza
Lake Success, NY 11042
(516) 488-6700

Consultants for Communication
508 Bellevue Terrace
Pittsburgh, PA 15202
(412) 761-6062

Cybercom
P.O. Box 62
Bloomington, IL 47401
(812) 339-3009

Innocomp
33195 Wagon Wheel Dr.
Solon, OH 44139
(216) 248-6206

Jesana
P.O. Box 17
Irvington, NY 10533
(914) 591-5539

Luminaud
8688 Tyler Blvd.
Mentor, OH 44060
(216) 255-9082

Prentke Romich Co.
1022 Heyl Rd.
Wooster, OH 44691
(216) 262-1984

Sentient Systems Technology
5001 Baum Blvd.
Pittsburgh, PA 15213
(412) 682-0144

Venture Technologies
P.O. Box 821
Abingdon, MD
(301) 679-8847

Zygo Industries
P.O. Box 1008
Portland, OR 97207
(503) 684-6006

List 33.5: Cooking/Eating Aids

Adaptability
P.O. Box 515
Colchester, CT 06415
(800) 243-9232

Alimed
297 High St.
Dedham, MA 02026
(617) 329-2900
(800) 225-2610

Easier Living Products
580 Westbury Ave.
Carle Place, NY 11514
(516) 997-8679

Enrichments
145 Tower Dr.
P.O. Box 579
Hinsdale, IL 60521
(800) 323-5547

ETAC USA
2325 Parklawn Dr., Ste. P
Waukesha, WI 53186
(414) 796-4600
(800) 678-3822

Flaghouse
150 North Mac Questen Pkwy.
Mt. Vernon, NY 10550
(914) 699-1900
(800) 221-5185

Innovator of Disability Equipment and Adaptions
1393 Meadow Creek Dr., Ste. 2
Pewaukee, WI 53072
(414) 691-4248

Gladys E. Loeb Foundation
2002 Forest Hill Dr.
Silver Spring, MD 20903
(301) 434-7748

Maddak
6 Industrial Rd.
Pequannock, NJ 07440
(201) 694-0500
(800) 443-4926

Fred Sammons, Inc.
145 Tower Dr.
Bur Ridge, IL 60521
(312) 325-4602
(800) 323-5547

Winsford Products
179 Pennington-Harbourton Rd.
Pennington, NJ 08534
(609) 737-3313

List 33.6: Digital Aids

Audioscience
5420 Felti Rd.
Minnetonka, MN 55343
(612) 936-0200
(800) 545-2868

Beltone Electronics Corp.
4201 West Victoria St.
Chicago, IL 60646
(312) 583-3890
(800) 621-1275

Ensoniq Corp.
155 Great Valley Pky.
Malvern, PA 19355
(215) 647-3930
(800) 942-0096

GN Danavox
5600 Rowland Rd.
Minnetonka, MN 55343
(612) 930-0416
(800) 326-2689

Maico Hearing Instruments
7375 Bush Lake Rd.
Minneapolis, MN 55439-2029
(612) 835-4400
(800) 328-6366

Philips Hearing Instruments
601 Milner Ave.
Scarborough, ON, Canada M1B 1M8
(416) 754-6132
(800) 387-5271

Resound Corp.
220 Saginaw Dr.
Redwood City, CA 94063
(415) 780-7800
(800) 248-HEAR

Rexton
2415 Xenium Ln.
Plymouth, MA 55441
(612) 553-0787
(800) 876-1141

Siemens Hearing Instruments
10 Constitution Ave.
P.O. Box 1397
Piscataway, NJ 08855-1397
(908) 562-6600
(800) 766-4500

Starkey Labs
6700 Washington Ave. South
P.O. Box 9457
Eden Prairie, MN 55344
(612) 941-6401
(800) 328-8602

3M Hearing Health
3M Center Bldg. 270-4S-16
St. Paul, MN 55144-1000
(800) 882-3M3M

Widex Hearing Aid Co.
35-53 24th St.
Long Island City, NY 11106
(718) 392-6020
(800) 221-0188

List 33.7: Dressing Aids

Dixson
P.O. Box 1449
Grand Junction, CO 81502
(303) 242-8863
(800) 443-4926

Enrichments
145 Tower Dr.
P.O. Box 579
Hinsdale, IL 60521
(800) 323-5547

ETAC USA
2325 Parklawn Dr., Ste. P
Waukesha, WI 53186
(414) 796-4600
(800) 678-3822

Komak International
269-24L Grand Central Pkwy.
Floral Park, NY 11005
(718) 279-0550

North Coast Medical
187 Stauffer Blvd.
San Jose, CA 95125
(408) 283-1900
(800) 821-9319

List 33.8: Grab Bars

Normbau
Rt. 4 Branham Way
Mt. Washington, KY 40047
(502) 538-7386

SafeTek International
P.O. Box 23
Melbourne, FL 32902
(407) 952-1300

List 33.9: Grooming Aids

ETAC USA
2325 Parklawn Dr., Ste. P
Waukesha, WI 53186
(414) 796-4600
(800) 678-3822

Lumex
100 Spence St.
Bay Shore, NY 11706
(516) 273-2200
(800) 645-5272

List 33.10: Home Wandering Systems

RF Technologies
3720 N. 124th St.
Milwaukee, WI 53222
(414) 466-1771
(800) 669-9946

Tele Larm
Ashton Square
4020 Capital Blvd., Ste. 90
Raleigh, NC 27604
(919) 878-1105
(800) 835-5276

Wander Guard
P.O. Box 80238
941 O St., Ste. 325
Lincoln, NE 68501
(402) 475-4002
(800) 824-2996

List 33.11: Low Vision Aids

Access Unlimited
3535 Briarpark Dr., Ste. 102
Houston, TX 77042
(713) 781-7441

American Foundation for the Blind
100 Enterprise Pl.
P.O. Box 7044
Dover, DE 19903
(302) 677-0200
(800) 829-0500

American Printing House
1839 Frankfort Ave.
P.O. Box 6085
Louisville, KY 40206
(502) 895-2405
(800) 223-1839

Breyenton & Associates
Box 8823
Ottawa, ON, Canada K1G 3J2
(613) 727-5800

Henter-Joyce
10901-C Roosevelt Blvd., Ste. 1200
St. Petersburg, FL 33716
(813) 576-5658
(800) 336-5658

Johnston Developmental Equipment
P.O. Box 639
1000 North Rand Rd., Bldg. 115
Wauconda, IL 60084
(708) 526-2682
(800) 999-2682

Lighthouse Low Vision Service
111 East 59th St.
New York, NY 10022
(212) 355-2200

L. S. & S. Group
P.O. Box 673
Northbrook, IL 60065
(708) 498-9777

Massachusetts Association for the Blind
200 Ivy St.
Brookline, MA 02146
(617) 738-5110
(800) 682-9200

Resources for Rehabilitation
33 Bedford St., Ste. 19A
Lexington, MA 02173
(617) 862-6455

Science Products
P.O. Box 888
Southeastern, PA 19399
(215) 296-2114
(800) 888-7400

Sense-Sations
919 Walnut St.
Philadelphia, PA 19107
(800) 876-5456

Syntha-Voice Computers
125 Gailmont Dr.
Hamilton, ON, Canada L8K 4B8
(416) 578-0565
(800) 263-4540

Talking Signs
400 North Columbus, #42
Goldendale, WA 98620
(509) 773-5958

Technology Acesss Alliance
2100 Washington St.
Hanover, MA 02339
(617) 871-5396

Vis-Aids
102-09 Jamaica Ave.
P.O. Box 26
Richmond, NY 11418
(718) 847-4734
(800) 346-9579

Xerox Imaging Systems
Personal Reader Dept.
9 Centennial Dr.
Peabody, MA 01960
(508) 977-2000
(800) 248-6550

List 33.12: Medication Compliance Devices

Automated Medication Dispenser
CompuMed
1 Pitchfork Rd.
Meeteetse, WY 82433
(307) 868-2550
(800) 722-4417

Regimen 365 Medication Reminder
Namera Group
3-6685 Millcreek Dr.
Mississauga, ON, Canada L5N 5M5
(800) 387-8299

Timecal Pill Organizer
PaMed Medical Specialities
P.O. Box 189
Lincroft, NJ 07738
(201) 542-1511

List 33.13: Personal Emergency Response System Manufacturers

American Medical Alert
3265 Lawson Blvd.
Oceanside, NY 11572
(800) 645-3244

Colonial Medical Alert
22 Cotton Rd.
Nashua, NH 03063
(800) 323-6794

Communi-Call
2661 Whitney Ave.
Hamden, CT 05618
(800) 841-3800

Digital Designs
Subsidiary of JANKCO
3466 Progress Dr.
Bensalen, PA 19020
(800) 532-5276

Emergency Alert Systems
7820 South Holiday Dr., Ste. 300
Sarasota, FL 34321
(800) 765-8922

ERS
5777 West Century Blvd.
Los Angeles, CA 90045
(800) 833-2000

Home Technology Systems
722 Cycare Plaza
Dubuque, IA 52001
(800) 922-3555

Knight Protective Industries
7315 Lankershim Blvd.
Hollywood, CA 91605
(800) 356-4448

Lifecall Systems
1300 Admiral Wilson Blvd.
P.O. Box 5010
Camden, NJ 08101
(609) 963-5433

Lifeline Emergency Response System
Lifeline Systems
One Arsenal Marketplace
Watertown, MA 02172
(800) 642-0045

LifeWatch
P.O. Box 61331
Potomac, MD 20859
(301) 469-9564

Linear Corp.
2055 Corte del Nogal
Carlsbad, CA 92009
(619) 438-7000

Link to Life
1421-A Arnot Rd.
Horseheads, NY 14845
(800) 338-4176

Medic Alert Foundation International
2323 Colorado Ave.
Turlock, CA 95330
(209) 668-3333

Mytrex
Rescue Alert
7050 Union Park Ave.
Midvale, UT 84047
(800) 688-9567

PERSYS
Amcest Nationwide Emergency Monitoring
1017 Walnut St.
Roselle, NJ 07203
(800) 631-7370

Pioneer Medical
37 Washington St.
Melrose, MA 02176
(800) 338-2303

Protect ERS
100 Park Pl., Ste. 250
San Ramon, CA 94583
(800) 548-8805

TeleLarm
P.O. Box 98053
Raleigh, NC 27615
(800) 835-5276

Transcience
633 Hope St.
Stamford, CT 06907
(800) 243-3494

List 33.14: Power Scooters

Alpha Unlimited
1610 Northgate Blvd.
Sarasota, FL 34234
(813) 351-3488
(800) 237-6836

Amigo Mobility International
6693 Dixie Hwy.
Bridgeport, MI 48722
(517) 777-0910
(800) 248-9130

Braun Corp.
1014 S. Monticello
P.O. Box 310
Winamic, IN 46996
(219) 946-6153
(800) 873-5438

Bruno Independent Living Aids
430 Armor Ct.
P.O. Box 84
Oconomowoc, WI 53066
(414) 567-4990

Burke
P.O. Box 1064
Mission, KS 66222
(913) 722-5658
(800) 255-4147

Dignified Products Corp.
P.O. Box 337
Mantua, NJ 08051
(609) 468-3426
(800) 548-7905

Electric Mobility
#1 Mobility Plaza
Sewell, NJ 08080
(800) 662-4548

Golden Technologies
P.O. Box 357
Pittston, PA 18640
(717) 829-4119
(800) 624-6374

Jubilee Scooters
324 Lakeside Dr., Ste. A
Foster City, CA 94404
(415) 571-5029

Leisure-Lift
1800 Merriam Ln.
Kansas City, KS 66106
(800) 255-0285

Medical Concepts
10670 North Central Expy., Ste. 555
Dallas, TX 75231
(214) 227-0780
(800) 227-5349

Mobilectrics Co.
4311 Woodgate Ln.
Louisville, KY 40220
(800) 876-6846

Mobility Manufacturing
5555 Country Club Rd.
Tucson, AZ 85706
(602) 889-8655
(800) 767-2668

National Medical Industries
11440 W. Bannock St.
P.O. Box 3268
Boise, ID 83703
(208) 343-3639

Palmer Industries
P.O. Box 707
Endicott, NY 13760
(607) 754-1954
(800) 847-1304

Pride Health Care
71 South Main St.
Pittston, PA 18640
(717) 655-5574
(800) 457-5438

Ranger All Season Corp.
P.O. Box 132
George, IA 51237
(712) 475-2811
(800) 225-3811

Shoprider (Canada)
13880 Matfield Pl.
Richmond, BC, Canada V6V 2E4
(604) 273-5173

C. F. Struck Corp.
W51 N545 Struck Ln.
P.O. Box 307
Cedarburg, WI 53012
(414) 377-3300

Voyager
P.O. Box 1577
527 West Colfax
South Bend, IN 46634
(219) 288-0511
(800) 233-2682

List 33.15: Stair and Wheelchair Lifts

Aging Technologies
1329 Inverness
Lawrence, KS 66045
(913) 841-5036

Cheney Co.
2445 S. Calhoun Rd.
P.O. Box 188
New Berlin, WI 53151
(414) 782-1100

Flinchbaugh Co.
390 Eberts Ln.
York, PA 17403
(717) 848-2418

FlorLift of New Jersey
41 Lawrence St.
East Orange, NJ 07071
(201) 429-2200

Hiro Lift U.S.A.
510 North Bellevue Ave.
Cinnaminson, NJ 08077
(609) 829-4315

Hoyer Patient Lifter
Sunrise Medical Guardian Products
12800 Wentworth St.
Arleta, CA 91331
(800) 255-5022

Pick-a-Lift
2051 Edgewood Dr.
Lakeland, FL 33803
(813) 665-5355

Toce Brothers Manufacturing
P.O. Box 447
Broussard, LA 70518
(318) 856-7241

Vital Signs International
P.O. Box 27
Gays Mills, WI 54631
(608) 735-4718

List 33.16: Toileting Aids

Danmar Products
221 Jackson Industrial Dr.
Ann Arbor, MI 48103
(313) 761-1990
(800) 783-1998

Med/West
Division of Western Manufacturing Corp.
P.O. Box 130
Marshalltown, IA 50158
(515) 752-5446
(800) 247-7594

Sanlex International
P.O. Box 14717
Dayton, OH 45414
(513) 297-3011
(800) 424-1224

List 33.17: Walkers

Able-Walker
1122 Fir Ave.
Building C2
Blaine, WA 98230
(800) 663-1305

American Walker
797 Market St.
Oregon, WI 53575
(608) 835-9255

Arjo Hospital Equipment
6380 West Oakton St.
Morton Grove, Illinois 60053
(800) 323-1245
(708) 967-0360

E. F. Brewer Co.
13901 Main St.
Menomonee Falls, WI 53051
(414) 251-9530
(800) 558-8777

Carex Health Care Products
39 Tompkins Point Rd.
Newark, NJ 07101
(201) 824-7637
(800) 526-8051

ConvaQuip Industries
P.O. Box 3417
Abilene, TX 79604
(914) 677-4177

Crescent Corp.
P.O. Box 610987
Port Huron, MI 48061-0987
(313) 982-2784
(800) 726-6761

ETAC USA
2325 Parklawn Dr., Ste. P
Waukesha, WI 53186
(414) 796-4600
(800) 678-3822

Garelick Manufacturing Co.
644 Second St.
P.O. Box 8
St. Paul Park, MN 55071
(612) 459-9795
(800) 457-9795

Guardian Products
12800 Wentworth St.
Box C-4522
Arleta, CA 91331-4522
(818) 504-2820
(800) 255-5022

Invacare Corp.
899 Cleveland St.
Elyria, OH 44035
(216) 329-6000
(800) 468-2227

Kendall-Futuro Co.
5801 Mariemont Ave.
Cincinnati, OH 45227
(513) 271-3400
(800) 543-4452

Lumex
100 Spence St.
Bay Shore, NY 11706
(516) 273-2200
(800) 645-5272

NobleMotion, Inc.
P.O. Box 5366
Pittsburgh, PA 15206
(800) 234-WALK (9255)

PCP-Champion
300 Congress St.
Ripley, OH 45167
(513) 392-4301
(800) 888-0867

Products Finishing Corp.
350 Clarkson Ave.
Brooklyn, NY 11226
(715) 693-9700

Rajowalt Corp.
124 Industrial Pkwy.
Chardon, OH 44024
(216) 286-3336
(800) 348-2389

Stelmar Manufacturing Co.
950 Harbor Lake Ct.
Safety Harbor, FL 34695
(813) 726-2446

Wenzelite Corp.
261 Broadway
Huntington Station, NY 11746
(516) 673-7490
(800) 345-WALK (9255)

Winco
5516 S.W. First Lane
Ocala, FL 34474
(904) 854-2929
(800) 237-3377

List 33.18: Specialized Wheelchairs

ALTimate Medical
913 South Washington
Redwood Falls, MN 56283
(507) 637-3331
(800) 342-8968

Blatnik Enterprises
P.O. Box 753
Mira Loma, CA 91752
(714) 685-0204

Fortress
P.O. Box 489
Clovis, CA 93613
(209) 323-0292
(800) 866-4335

Hall's Wheels
11 Smith Pl.
Cambridge, MA 02138
(617) 547-5000

I.D.C. Medical Equipment
20 Independence Ct.
Folcroft, PA 19032
(215) 586-0986

Iron Horse Productions
2624 Conner St.
Port Huron, MI 48060
(313) 987-6700
(800) 426-0354

Levo
21050 Superior St.
Chatsworth, CA 91311
(818) 882-6944
(800) 882-6944

Love Lift
P.O. Box 2158
Holland, MI 49422-2158
(616) 393-8941

Luconex
3513 Arden Rd.
Hayward, CA 94545
(415) 783-5401
(800) 346-8447

Prime Engineering
4838 W. Jacquelyn #105
Fresno, CA 93722
(209) 276-0991
(800) 827-8262

Retec USA
10 Centre Dr.
Orchard Park, NY 14127
(716) 662-6815
(800) 877-3832

Stand Aid of Iowa
P.O. Box 386
Sheldon, IA 51201
(712) 324-2153
(800) 831-8580

Top End
6551 44th St.
Enterprise Pk. 5002
Pinellas Park, FL 34665
(813) 522-8677

List 33.19: Wheelchairs—Power

Damaco
14167 Meadow Dr.
Grass Valley, CA 95945
(916) 477-1234
(800) 432-2434

Everest & Jennings
3233 East Mission Oaks Blvd.
Camarillo, CA 93010
(805) 987-6911

Fortress
P.O. Box 489
Clovis, CA 93613
(209) 323-0292
(800) 866-4335

Love Lift
P.O. Box 2158
Holland, MI 49422-2158
(616) 393-8941

Quest Technologies
766 Palomar Ave.
Sunnyvale, CA 94086
(408) 739-3550

Quickie Designs
2842 Business Park Ave.
Fresno, CA 93727
(209) 294-2171

Redman Wheelchairs
3840 South Palo Verde
Tuscon, AZ 85714
(800) 727-6684

References

Adaptive Equipment Center. "Powered Scooters." *ABLE-DATA Fact Sheet 5.* Newington, CT: Newington Children's Hospital, 1989.

American Association of Retired Persons (AARP). *Product Report: Canes* Vol. 2, no. 3, AARP PF 4965 (1292), Product Fulfillment Number D1416. Washington, DC: AARP, 1992.

———. *Product Report: PERS—Personal Emergency Response Systems* Vol. 2, no. 1, PF3986(592), Product Fulfillment Number D12905. Washington, DC: AARP, 1992.

———. *Product Report: Walkers* Vol. 1, no. 7, AARP PF 4703(991), Product Fufillment Number D14390. Washington, DC: AARP, 1991.

———. *Product Report: Wheelchair* Vol. 1, no. 5, AARP PF 4584(1090), Product Fulfillment Number D14049, Washington, DC: AARP, 1990.

———. "Technology and Older Americans: Attitudes, Uses, and Needs." *Data Gram.* Washington, DC: AARP, 1984.

American Society of Parenteral and Enteral Nutrition. "1984 Nutritional Support Population Exceeds 6 Million." *Update* Vol. 8, no. 4 (1985): 8.

Barzel, U. S. "Modern Technology: A Double-Edged Sword." *International Journal of Technology and Aging* Vol. 4 (1991): 89–93.

Becker, G., and S. Kaufman. "Old Age, Rehabilitation, and Research: A Review of the Issues." *Gerontologist* Vol. 28, no. 4 (1988): 459–68.

Boczokowski, J. A., and A. Zeichner. "Medication Compliance and the Elderly." *Clinical Gerontologist* Vol. 4 (1985): 3–15.

Bowe, F. "Why Seniors Don't Use Technology." *Technology Review* (August/September 1988): 35–40.

Burrell, C. D., and R. A. Levy. "Therapeutic Consequences of Noncompliance." *Proceedings of a Symposium on Improving Medication Compliance.* Reston, VA: National Pharmaceutical Council, 1984: 7–16.

Christy, C.. "Today's Hearing Health Care Market." *Hearing Instruments* Vol. 42, no. 2, (1991): 6–10.

Davis, G. A., and T. W. Baggs. "Rehabilitation of Speech and Language Disorders." *Gerontology and Communication Disorders.* Rockville, MD: American Speech-Language-Hearing Association, 1984.

Denison, I. "Wheelchair Comparison Study." Unpublished report, 1989.

Elkind, J. "The Incidence of Disabilities in the United States." *Human Factors* Vol. 32, no. 4 (1990): 397–405.

Enders, A., and M. Hall. *Assistive Technology Sourcebook.* Washington, DC: Rehabilitation Engineering Society of America, 1990.

Ensign, A., ed. "The Selection of a Van Lift or a Scooter." *PAM Repeater.* 1990. Published at PAM Assistance Center, 601 West Maple St., Lansing, MI 48906.

Eve, S. B. "Self-Medication Among Older Adults in the United States." In *Self-Care and Health in Old Age: Health Behavior Implications for Policy and Practice.* Eds. K. Dean, T. Hickey, and B. E. Holstein. London: Croom Helm (1986): 204–29.

Fish, R. M. "Technology: Electronic Aids for the Blind." *Radio Electronics* (June 1985): 57–59.

Gates, G. A., and others. "Hearing in the Elderly: The Framingham Cohort, 1983–1985." *Ear and Hearing* Vol. 11, no. 4 (1990): 247–56.

Gilly, M. C., and V. A. Zeithaml. "The Elderly Consumer and Adoption of Technologies." *Journal of Consumer Research* Vol. 12 (1985): 353–56.

Green, L. W., P. D. Mullen, and G. L. Stainbrook. "Programs to Reduce Drug Errors in the Elderly: Direct and Indirect Evidence From Patient Education." *Proceedings of a Symposium on Improving Medication Compliance.* Reston, VA: National Pharmaceutical Council, (1984): 59–70.

Hartley, A. A., J. T. Hartley, and S. A. Johnson. "The Older Adult as Computer User." In *Aging and Technological Advances.* Eds. P. K. Robinson, J. Livingston, and J. E. Birren. New York: Plenum Press, (1984): 347–48.

Horwitz, R. I., C. M. Viscoli, and L. Berman. "Treatment Adherence and Risk of Death After a Myocardial Infarction." *Lancet* (1990): 542–45.

Illinik, M. L. "Playing It Safe, No Free-Wheeling While 3-Wheeling." *Accent on Living* (Winter 1990).

Kochkin, S. "MarkeTrak II: More MDs Give Hearing Tests, Yet Hearing Aid Sales Remain Flat." *The Hearing Journal* Vol. 44, no. 2 (1991).

Langer, R. "New Methods of Drug Delivery." *Science* (September 28, 1990): 1527–33.

LaPlante, M. P., G. E. Hendershot, and A. J. Moss. "Assistive Technology Devices and Home Accessibility Features:

Prevalence, Payment, Need, and Trends." *Advance Data No. 217.* U.S. Department of Health and Human Services, Vital and Health Statistics of the Centers for Disease Control, National Center for Health Statistics, 1992.

"Late Bloomer" audio cassette. Available from Connie Goldman Productions, 926 Second Street, Suite 201, Santa Barbara, CA 90403. (310) 393-6801.

Leon, J., and T. Lair. "Functional Status of the Noninstitutionalized Elderly: Estimates of ADL and IADL Difficulties." *DHHS Publication No. (PHS)90-3462.* National Medical Expenditure Survey Research Findings 4, Agency for Health Care Policy and Research. Rockville, MD: Public Health Service, 1990.

Make, B., S. Dayno, and P. Gertman. "Prevalence of Chronic Ventilator-Dependency." *American Review of Respiratory Diseases* Vol. 133, no. 4, part 2 (1986).

Margolin, R. A. "Computerized Brain-Imaging Devices, Aging, and Mental Health." *International Journal of Technology and Aging* Vol. 3 (1990): 7-17.

Office of Health Technology Assessment Reports. "Cardiac Rehabilitation Services." *Health Technology Assessment Series.* National Center for Health Services Research, Rockville, MD: U.S. Department of Health and Human Services (1987): 113-202.

Orr, A. L., and L. S. Piqueras. "Aging, Visual Impairment, and Technology." *Technology and Disability* Vol. 1, no. 1 (1991): 47-54.

Radcliffe, D. "Programmable Hearing Aids: Digital Control Comes to Analog Amplification." *Hearing Journal* Vol. 44, no. 5 (May 1991): 9-12.

Rehabilitation Engineering Center at the National Rehabilitation Hospital. "Product Comparison and Evaluation." *Scooters* (June 1991).

Ryan, E. B., B. Szechtman, and J. Bodkin. "Attitudes Toward Younger and Older Adults Learning to Use Computers." *Journal of Gerontology* Vol. 47, no. 2 (1992): 96-101.

Schrier, E. M., J. D. Leventhal, and M. M. Uslan. "Access Technology for Blind and Visually Impaired Persons." *Technology and Disability* Vol. 1, no. 1 (1991): 19-23.

Shock, N. W. "Normal Human Aging: The Baltimore Longitudinal Study of Aging." *NIH Publication No. 84-2450.* Washington, DC: U.S. Department of Health and Human Services, 1984.

Smith, M. "The Cost of Noncompliance and the Capacity of Improved Compliance to Reduce Health Care Expenditures." *Proceedings of a Symposium on Improving Medication Compliance.* Reston, VA: National Pharmaceutical Council (1984): 35-44.

Sowell, L. P. "Using a Scooter Saves Energy." *Accent on Living* (Spring 1992).

Stephens, S. D. G., and R. Meredith. "Physical Handling of Hearing Aids by the Elderly." *Acta Otolaryngology* Stockholm, Suppl. 476 (1991): 281-85.

Sullivan, S. D., D. H. Kreling, and T. K. Hazlet. "Noncompliance with Medication Regimens and Subsequent Hospitalizations: A Literature Analysis and Cost of Hospitalization Estimate." *Journal of Research in Pharmaceutical Economics* Vol. 2, no. 2 (1990): 19-33.

"Three Wheeling: A Scooter Comparison." *Mainstream* (April 1992): 13-17.

Upfold, L. J., A. E. May, and J. A. Battaglia. "Hearing Aid Manipulation Skills in an Elderly Population: A Comparison of ITE, BTE, and ITC Aids." *British Journal of Audiology* Vol. 24 (1990): 311-18.

Urinary Incontinence Guideline Panel. "Urinary Incontinence in Adults: Clinical Practice Guideline." *AHCPR Pub. No. 92-0038.* Rockville, MD: Agency for Health Care Policy and Research, Public Health Service, U.S. Department of Health and Human Services, 1992.

U.S. Congress. Office of Technology Assessment. "Life-Sustaining Technologies and the Elderly." *OTA-BA-306.* Washington, DC: Government Print Office, July 1987.

Waldman, A. "Customer Service Sparks Scooter Dealer's Success." *Homecare* (January 1991).

Weisenberg, L. "Scooter Sales Show Significant Cash Flow." *Homecare* (March 1989).

Additional Reading

Christenson, Margaret A. *Aging in the Designed Environment.* Binghamton, NY: Haworth Press, 1990.

Combs, Alec. *Hearing Loss Help.* San Luis Obispo, CA: Impact Publishers, 1991.

"How To Buy a Hearing Aid." *Consumer Reports.* (November 1992).

Koncelik, Joseph A. *Aging and the Product Environment.* New York: Van Nostrand, 1982.

McGuire, Francis A., ed. *Computer Technology and the Aged.* New York: Haworth Press, 1986.

Physical and Occupational Therapy in Geriatrics (subscriptions through Haworth Press, Binghampton, NY 13904-9980).

Regnier, Victor, and Jon Pynoos. *Housing the Aged: Design Directives and Policy Considerations.* New York: Elsevier Science, 1987.

U.S. Congress. Office of Technology Assessment. *Technology and Aging in America.* Washington, DC: Government Printing Office, 1985.

Margaret Wylde, Ph. D.

Section XI:

Lifestyles and Choices

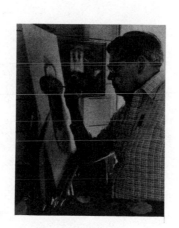

34

Spirituality and Religious Affiliation

- The Distinction Between Religion and Spirituality • Early Studies on Religion and Aging
- Religious Affiliation • Religious Participation and Activities
- Denominational Responses and Policies • Ministerial Training • Ecumenical Programs
- How Religions View the Aged • Wisdom and Creativity • Celebrations and Rituals on Aging
- Spiritual Practices • Expanding Study of Spirituality

The twentieth century has seen the rise of unprecedented secular societies that place great emphasis on progress through science. But as the century wanes, the expectation that science and technology will provide answers to all of life's questions is fading as well. As a cultural historian of aging has put it, human beings "are spiritual animals; we need love and meaning no less than food, clothing, shelter, and health care" (Cole, 1990). In their search for meaning, many people are turning to fields such as philosophy, ethics, religion, and the arts.

There is evidence that the rejection of materialism and the religious revival it is stimulating are worldwide phenomena. The collapse of the Eastern bloc and the new freedom of religion in those countries plays a part. A further influence is the coming of the year 2000, a second millennium associated in the Judeo-Christian tradition as a time of great change and great significance—perhaps the start of a Golden Age, perhaps the apocalypse. Since fear and insecurity accompany times of change, many are seeking security and comfort in spiritual belief (Naisbitt, 1990). While the need to find "something more" cuts across all age groups, it is

especially profound among the growing ranks of the elderly.

On the psychological level, fears about aging, coupled with its evident losses, have always drawn the elderly to reflect, in some degree, on life's purpose. There are two general themes in Western culture that have helped older people comprehend and cope with age as an integral part of life's wholeness: life conceived as a series of stages, and life viewed metaphorically as a journey (Cole, 1990). Several human development theories suggest that wisdom, personal wholeness, and spiritual insight are potential attainments of later life.

With advancing years, religious faith, belief in some form of divinity, and participation in a religious organization are commonly thought to become more important. While research to support this view is inconclusive, there is agreement that "religious feelings" or religiosity increases with age and that religious identification remains constant (Payne, 1981; Mindel and Vaughan, 1978; Blazer and Palmore, 1976; Ainlay and Smith, 1984; Ainlay, Singleton, and Swigert, 1992). If religion is meant to include the broader concept of spirituality, there is little doubt that its significance grows with age.

701

● THE DISTINCTION BETWEEN RELIGION AND SPIRITUALITY

One of the key issues in discussing aging and religion is the need to distinguish between religious affiliation and spirituality. They may, but do not automatically, correspond (Howe, 1983). The former concerns participation and membership in an organized religious community or institution and adherence to a body of beliefs, practices, and customs. Spirituality, while certainly overlapping with church or synagogue affiliation, refers to a psychological and personal inward experience that may be totally independent of institutional membership. For some, aspects of organized religion can even block such spiritual growth (Howe, 1983; McFadden and Gerl, 1990). Spirituality can be seen as an integrative force that "motivates us to search for meaning and purpose in life, to seek the supernatural or some meaning which transcends us, to wonder about our origins and our identities, to require morality and equity" (Ellison, 1983). It aims at unifying the self and others, along with the natural world of experience, providing individuals with a sense of connection to a power greater than themselves. It is this aspect of spirituality that is often associated with religion (McFadden and Gerl, 1990).

A growing body of literature on spirituality focuses on people's need to find meaning in late life, their quest for understanding the mystery of human experience, and their pursuit of a sense of the Holy (Bianchi, 1982).

Spirituality, while certainly overlapping with church or synagogue affiliation, refers to a psychological and personal inward experience that may be totally independent of institutional membership.

● EARLY STUDIES ON RELIGION AND AGING

The significance of religion in late life was observed by Edward Starbuck (1911) and G. Stanley Hall (1922), the first psychologists to study aging and the human spirit. Their opposing findings also mark the beginning of research differences related to religious beliefs and practices of older people. Starbuck reported that religious faith and belief in God grow in importance as the years advance, while Hall's early study of older peoples' religious beliefs (and fears of death) did not show an inevitable increase. Neither did it show that they became more fearful of death.

The eighth annual Southern Conference on Gerontology, sponsored by the University of Florida Institute of Gerontology, devoted its 1958 annual meeting to "Organized Religion and the Older Person." The meeting addressed such issues as the meaning of religion to the elderly, the responsibility of organized religion to contribute to the religious life of elders, facing loss, the nature and joy of fulfillment, and religious consciousness.

During the following decades, the role and significance of religion in the aging process received little attention from research gerontologists and service providers, who responded to government supported research on the biological, psychological, and sociological aspects of aging. A shift in emphasis from religion and religiosity to the broader umbrella of spiritual well-being was anticipated in 1971 by the name given the section on religion in the White House Conference on Aging: "spiritual well-being." This term circumvented policy problems involving the separation of church and state but also widened the research horizon. In 1975 the National Interfaith Coalition on Aging (NICA) offered a definition of spiritual well-being as "the affirmation of life in a relationship with God, self, community, and environment that nurtures and celebrates wholeness."

Civil rights advocates, feminists, and the youth counterculture captured the energies and attention of religious leaders, as well as the general public, through most of the 1960s and 1970s. The 1980s saw the first of the baby boomers approaching middle age. There was growing interest in the elderly—the present and coming generation—as a burgeoning demographic entity as well as in their religious and spiritual lives. Attempts were made to measure older persons' spiritual satisfaction and to correlate it with physical resilience and mental health (McSherry, 1983).

Further, the new topic of bioethics, with its thorny life-or-death medical questions, had inescapable religious implications. The bioethics (called a kind of applied philosophy) of such highly publicized cases as Nancy Cruzan and

Karen Quinlan underlined the link between aging and religion (Moody, 1992). Experts and the public began to debate such issues as whether human beings, young or old, terminally ill or simply depressed, have the right to time their own deaths or those of their loved ones.

Current Focus of Studies

More articles on spirituality and religion, from mainstream to esoteric groups, were appearing in the popular press and in professional publications, and gerontologists (belatedly) were featuring these subjects at their meetings. The focus shifted from religion/religiosity to spiritual well-being, and then to spirituality, a concept that is now expanding into a multidisciplinary approach that embraces the humanities (Payne, 1990; Achenbaum, 1992).

While such an encompassing overview is hard to categorize, there appear to be three major concerns at present: (1) the extent and nature of formal religious participation and involvement by the elderly; (2) the personal meaning of religion and the private devotional activities in the home, and (3) the influence of religious/spiritual practices, feelings, and beliefs on the attitudes of older people—especially as related to confrontation with death (Markides, 1987). How useful these practices and beliefs are in helping older people adjust to their changing lives was for years the thrust of inquiry (Payne, 1990) and the measure of "successful" aging. Now the quality of life up to its very end, frequently called "spiritual integration" or "spiritual well-being," is an object of study.

Appropriately, questions about the "endgame" of life, and about death, are being examined within organized religion. In the words of a Baptist minister, which apply to all faiths: "The religious community is the proper context for conversations about living and dying. . . . A dialogue is in order . . . Within the community of faith, one can discover important counsel on how to live as well as on how to die" (Gaddy, 1983). He suggests a further advocacy role for churches and synagogues—to help in dissipating the destructive, negative myths about old people that pervade our culture. Religious institutions "can model as well as proclaim truths about the aged—their reliability, mobility, productivity, and accountability."

A Spiritual Agenda for Later Life

1. Accepting one's own life story
   - Every life has meaning and is of value
   - Coming to grips with the past and the present with all sins and mistakes and accidents of fortune
   - Forgiving others and one's self
2. Dealing with loss
   - loss of others (friends, children, spouses, etc.)
   - loss of our bodies and mental functioning
3. Relocating personal dignity
   - Shifting toward being and away from possessions and prestige; we are more than what we own or do
4. Rediscovering God
   - The search may lead toward meditation, prayer, reflection
   - It may mean learning to expect not a God of consolation, but one who tries us
   - The casting away of earlier illusions can lead to a more genuine experience of the Spirit
5. Caring about the community
   - Genuine spiritual development leads toward concern for the common good rather than away from it
   - Disability may take us away from physical involvement in struggles for social welfare, but the good of society can remain a concern; passing on vital traditions to others has been seen as belonging to the responsibilities of old age

---

The spiritual needs and challenges of the elderly transcend denominational boundaries, but attempts to clarify them for different religious traditions have been made. Representing a Christian viewpoint, a former Jesuit priest and university chaplain, who later directed services for the aging in an East Coast City, developed an agenda of spiritual goals for older adults, which include discovering the meaning of their lives, both in broad terms and as a current, specific purpose; redefining the self, as the body and social network changes; dealing with loneliness and aloneness; and acceptance of death as the ultimate transcendence (Griffin, 1992).

● RELIGIOUS AFFILIATION

Today the major faith groups are acknowledging the graying of their congregations. This is reflected in their statements and policies, which respond to the aging membership in organizational structure and in programming of activities. Most American adults belong to a religious organization, and even more report they believe in God. More older adults are members of churches and synagogues than younger adults, and more than one-half attend services regularly (Gallup, 1985, 1987; Princeton Religious Research Center, 1991). There is no other social organization as acceptable to older adults as their church or synagogue (Palmore, 1987). Furthermore, church participation is the number one form of organizational activity among the elderly (Atchley, 1991). A higher proportion of persons over the age of 65 belong to a congregation of one of the three major faith groups than do younger persons, and they attend services more regularly. Moreover, the participation in church/synagogue worship for those over the age of 50 held steady for the quarter of a century ending in 1984 (Gallup, 1984). During this same time frame, membership and attendance of younger generations dropped substantially.

Researchers point out that these figures should be considered along with the sociological effect of various birth cohorts. In other words, different generations have unique profiles of religious participation; those who grew up in more religious times continue to be more devout than those, for example, who came of age during the 1960s. All generations, or cohorts, were more observant during the "religious revival" of the 1950s, and all registered some decline during the decade that followed (Markides, 1987).

While many younger people, especially on the east and west coasts, are drawn to alternative or New Age churches, others have become fundamentalists; the evangelical and charismatic movements are strong. Baby boomers are more likely to be returning to traditional churches and bringing their children, and the elderly are more com-

Most American adults belong to a religious organization, and even more report they believe in God. (Copyright © Paul Gilmore)

fortable in mainline churches and synagogues. Overall, the religious "growth areas" are on the extreme fringes. Mainline denominations are struggling to keep membership growth up to the level of the population growth (Naisbitt, 1990).

National denominational offices report a larger proportion of their membership over the age of 65 than the proportion of persons of the same age in the U.S. population. The majority of the faithful are still Protestant, 25 percent are Catholic, and about 3 percent are Jewish (Payne, 1988).

These major faith groups estimate that from 20 percent to 33 percent of their members are over 65, compared to 12 percent of the general population. It is not uncommon to find local congregations in urban, suburban, and rural congregations with 50 percent to 80 percent of the members over 65 years of age.

The most recent information from the Protestant and Catholic denominations (Table 34.1) reports the proportion of members over 65. It is projected that over 50 percent of their members will be in this group by the year 2000. The

Table 34.1
Members Over Age 65 of Selected Denominations (%)

Denomination	Percent
Baptist	22.0
Catholic	26.0
Episcopal	25.0
Methodist	26.0
Presbyterian (U.S.A.)	31.0
Lutheran	22.6

Source: Denominational Research Reports, June 1992.

aging of society will be highly visible in the houses of worship.

No precise breakdowns of synagogue/temple membership for Jews over 65 are available for the three main streams of Judaism: Orthodox, Conservative, and Reform. For all age groups, 45 percent of Jews report membership in a synagogue (Roof and McKinney, 1987). However, trends and countertrends exist in Jewish affiliation. The age pattern that emerges shows Jews over 65 more ritually observant and more likely to be members of a synagogue than their children—but *less* observant than their grandchildren (Silberman, 1985). One phenomenon noted since the 1970s is a sharp increase in Jewish Orthodoxy among young people, reversing the trend of past decades (Roof and McKinney, 1987; Jakobson, 1987). As young Jews are rediscovering religious ritual, older Jews are focusing more on the communal and ethnic aspects of Jewish identity than on religious ones. What this means in terms of actual membership in synagogue or temple by age group is not clear. Affiliation for Jews of any age is frequently an expression of a desire for community as it is a statement of faith (Silberman, 1985).

Further complicating the picture is the degree to which American Jews have assimilated following immigration. The majority of Jews over 85 were immigrants and are more apt to follow traditional religious practices than are the younger elderly in their sixties and seventies (Council of Jewish Federations, 1991).

Information about membership of older people in other religious groups such as Islam and Buddhism is minimal. Since the total membership in these groups has increased, it may be assumed

that there are many elderly members. In fact, reliable information about religious affiliation and participation is difficult to obtain. The U.S. Constitution provides for the separation of church and state, which limits the collection of data on religion by the government. Because the U.S. Government does not compile these data—and hasn't since 1956—information comes from two principal sources: denominations' annual reports submitted to the National Council of Churches (summarized in the *Yearbook of American and Canadian Churches*) and various public opinion polls. The most frequently cited information comes from Princeton Religious Research Center, Gallup International, National Opinion Research Center, and Survey Research Center of the University of Michigan.

The age pattern that emerges shows Jews over 65 more ritually observant and more likely to be members of a synagogue than their children—but *less* observant than their grandchildren.

Nevertheless, the data from the *Yearbook* should be used with caution, because church records go through many channels of church structure. Some churches, especially the smaller ones, do not keep records or do not report to the National Council of Churches. The information is also distorted by the variation in the definition of membership among the denominations. For example, some Protestant groups count all baptized persons, including children, as members, while most include only "adults" 13 years of age and older. Another factor limiting research on aging is that the age distribution of the membership is usually omitted (Payne, 1984).

The affiliations of Hispanics (including Mexican Americans), native Americans, and Asians are not usually reported separately. However, the Gallup Poll (1985) does include Hispanics (68 percent). Since most Hispanics are traditionally Catholic, it is most likely that they are included with denominational membership reports. Many of the Protestant denominations have community outreach programs for these ethnic groups. The Hispanic population over 65 years of age (5 percent) is expected to increase

395 percent by 2030 and could become the largest minority group in the United States (*Aging America*, 1991). The influence of Eastern religions will become one of the larger minority groups.

The U.S. Constitution provides for the separation of church and state, which limits the collection of data on religion by the government.

● RELIGIOUS PARTICIPATION AND ACTIVITIES

Attendance at a church or synagogue service may vary by age and denominational preference. Most but not all evidence points to an increase in participation—or at least, no sharp decline—as people age. When a decrease does occur, it is usually at a much older age than was formerly assumed. Some studies report a higher frequency of attendance even for the "oldest old" (over 80). Attendance seems to be a function of health status, social support, and lifetime practice.

The National Opinion Research Center (NORC) conducted a five-year study of attendance by age (1986–91) and confirmed that people attend church and synagogue more regularly as they get older. Sixty percent of adults 70 to 79 years of age attend regularly, and even at age 80 and up they attend more consistently than those under the age of 60 (Gallup, 1991). Factors normally thought to affect membership and participation are gender, marital status, and race. The infirmities of late life also limit participation for many who would choose to attend regularly if they were able.

Gender differences in church attendance have consistently existed among all age groups. Females maintain a higher church attendance than males. This trend persists into advanced old age. Even when regular attendance declines for those over 75, the decline is less for females than males. There is some evidence that male participation increases after retirement. This is offset by the disproportionate number of older women than men in the population. Studies show that older Jewish men increase their attendance at the synagogue (Kahana and Kahana, 1984).

More older adults are members of churches and synagogues than younger adults, and more than one-half attend services regularly. (Copyright © Marianne Gontarz)

Marital status is less likely to influence church participation of older adults than younger adults. The number of widowed persons is greatest in the age group over 65. More than half of all older women are widows; there are five times as many widows as widowers. The implication for church participation is that widowhood only has an adverse effect when it places a person in a position different from most of their age-sex peers. Older women, then, can be expected to be socially comfortable in continued church or synagogue participation.

The church plays a crucial role for racial and ethnic minorities, especially in the lives of elderly African Americans (Kyles, 1983; McSherry, 1983). They participate more in religious activities and are more likely to attend religious services weekly than are whites (Taylor, 1986). Regular church attendance is also a predictor of happiness among older African Americans, who are generally well regarded in their congregations (McSherry, 1983).

The National Opinion Research Center (NORC) conducted a five-year study of attendance by age (1986–91) and confirmed that people attend church and synagogue more regularly as they get older.

The increase in the Asian-American population due to immigration from the Middle East, India, and other parts of Asia is swelling the ranks of members of the Islamic faith. If the trend continues, Islam will become the second largest minority faith group in the United States, surpassing Judaism (Payne, 1988).

Regardless of race, gender, or national origin, relationship with a religious organization is usually a lifelong one for older people and a part of family practice. Religious roles increase in meaning with age and provide continuity and identity in the midst of physical, psychological, social, and cultural changes occurring in late life. Recent research indicates that social activity in religious groups rates high in importance for most elderly and contributes to their life satisfaction and personal adjustment (Blazer and Palmore, 1976). Churches and synagogues are located in neighborhoods and are the one non-kin organization that touches the lives of most older people, providing links to the community. Families of older people share this involvement and often receive support in caring for their older members from the church community.

One challenge for organized religions is to adapt their ministries and services so the elderly can continue to enjoy and participate. Transportation to services and programs can be provided for older members. Inability to follow rituals and practices of their faith can add depression and feelings of loss to the physical problems of old age (Carlson and Seicol, 1990). Various forms of outreach to the homebound can be helpful, but all denominations should make allowances in their regular worship services for people with failing hearing or eyesight. Large print worship aids can be offered, for example, and clergy can take pains to speak slowly and enunciate clearly.

Even older persons with dementias of various kinds have spiritual needs and can respond to appropriate religious stimuli (McFadden and Gerl, 1990; Richards, 1990). Caregivers too often ignore the spiritual aspects of a confused patient, thinking mistakenly that they no longer matter.

Private Religious Practices

In addition to participation in formal (public) religious services, private religious practices frequently increase with age (Blazer and Palmore, 1976). *Mature Market Report*'s survey found that 50 percent of those over 50 devote time to religion (1988). Many adults over 65 pray three times

a day or more and engage in Bible study and meditation. The most frequently read portions of the Bible are the Psalms and the New Testament. Older people pray for themselves and for others, for intervention and guidance in daily situations, for inspiration, to lift depression, and in thanksgiving (Payne, 1981).

In times of stress, older people with high educational and socioeconomic status rely more frequently on such religious practices as prayer and obtaining help and strength from God (Daniel Yankelovitch Group, 1987). There have been actual physical benefits documented as the result of deep meditative states such as prayer. Such states can release endogenous beta blockers into the system (McSherry, 1983).

A study called "If You Had Your Life to Live Over Again: What Would You Do Differently?" showed that many older people would devote more time to religious and spiritual concerns. Of the 200-some retirees in Lafayette, Indiana, who participated, roughly 44 percent claimed they would spend more time "in devotion to a religion," 42 percent "studying a religion," 41 percent "developing spirituality," and 49 percent in prayer. Less than 5 percent of those surveyed would spend less time in any of these pursuits (DeGenova, 1992).

● DENOMINATIONAL RESPONSES AND POLICIES

The needs of the increasing numbers of the aged are social and spiritual. Until recently, the mainline religious groups responded better to the social concerns of their members—health, food, shelter—than to their special spiritual needs (Deloff, 1983). Beginning in the 1950s, they operated homes for the aged, appointed staff in national offices responsible for programs for the elderly, and published booklets and manuals to guide local congregations in these activities. Many of the programs and services of these groups were incorporated in the Older Americans Act of 1965.

Catholic, Jewish, and most Protestant denominations issued position and policy statements on aging in 1980. They contain many similarities: (1) restoring dignity and a sense of worth to the elderly; (2) ending age discrimination in personal attitudes and institutions; (3) encouraging the elderly to use their skills and gifts; and (4) acknowledging older adults as full members of congregations (Elder and McCracken, 1980).

Today most national religious bodies have an office on aging to serve the national and local needs of aging congregations. These offices are developing age-relevant curricula, materials, and program books; they are holding area and national conferences for older adults and for training clergy. The policy direction is to develop ministry by, with, and for older adults as a part of the church program.

The Southern Baptists and the Presbyterians have developed the most comprehensive national and regional programs, publications, plans, and research on aging. The Southern Baptist church also conducts travel tours and twelve Chautauquas for seniors that combine education and entertainment. The Presbyterians (USA) adopted their newest policy statement on older adult ministries, priorities, and strategies at the 1992 General Assembly. In addition to the office for Older Adult Ministries in the Presbyterian Center (the national administrative headquarters), national programs include: (1) a national

Profiles of Productive Aging

Richard Bolles
Best-selling author

"As I look back over my life thus far, the motivating force seems to have been: 'What kind of person would you like to see more of in this world?'—and then trying hard to be that kind of person."

Former minister Richard Bolles is the author of the best-selling career-change manual of all time, *What Color Is Your Parachute?* Born in California in 1927, he grew up in Teaneck, New Jersey, served in the navy during World War II, and studied chemical engineering at Massachusetts Institute of Technology.

Interested in the ministry, Bolles enrolled at the Episcopal Church's General Seminary in New York. Ordained in 1953, he served in several New Jersey parishes, then worked at Grace Cathedral in San Francisco. In 1968 Bolles was unexpectedly laid off. The experience proved to be life-changing.

Though Bolles landed on his feet and got a job within six months—with United Ministries in Higher Education— the experience of suddenly being jobless made a profound impression on him. One of his new responsibilities was to oversee campus ministries in nine western states, where he encountered many others who were also losing their jobs. Bolles set out to pull together a little manual on career change. He read every book on job-hunting he could find (only eight existed at the time), and he made it his business to contact career experts in each city he visited.

Among the people Bolles encountered was John Crystal, who began sending Bolles, week in and week out, envelopes stuffed with notes and clippings about the whole career change process. This added material expanded Bolles's 'little manual' for campus ministers to a 160-page book, *What Color Is Your Parachute?*, self-published December 1, 1970. Two years later Berkeley, California, publisher Phil Wood of Ten Speed Press offered to publish it commercially. Bolles rewrote the book for a larger audience, and it first appeared under the Ten Speed imprint in November 1972. It has since sold well over 4.5 million copies and is published in seven other languages throughout the world.

Bolles explains *Parachute*'s popularity by saying, "I think it is a healing book masquerading as a job-hunting manual." He sees the search for a new job or career as inevitably a spiritual journey, and among the hundreds of job-hunting books that now exist as a consequence of *Parachute*, the spiritual aspect remains Bolles's unique perspective.

The book's success has changed Bolles's life completely, giving him a new career and freedom from worrying about how to support himself. Since 1976 he has revised *Parachute* every year, a task that sometimes involves, as in 1992, completely rewriting the book from cover to cover. In connection with the book, he has lectured extensively in the United States, Canada, and Great Britain, and now he teaches an annual two-week workshop on life/work planning with his European friend Daniel Porot, in Bend, Oregon, attended by people from all over the world. Bolles is also currently writing a book on relationships and a book on practical spirituality.

Lydia Brontë

network for resources in aging ministries; and (2) an Association of Older Adult Ministry Enablers, appointed by the regional organization to be trainers in Older Adult Ministries. A national conference is held annually to train new Enablers. There are two annual meetings for those involved in Older Adult Ministries and one for Older Adults.

The Episcopal Society for Ministry on Aging (ESMA) is the national agency of the Episcopal church responsible for the development and support of ministries on aging. Its stated purpose is to serve the spiritual, psychological, and physical needs of older persons and to maximize the use of their unique gifts and talents in contributing to church and society. ESMA's Board of Directors consists of designees appointed from the ninety-nine dioceses to develop the mission, programs, and resources for aging ministries. ESMA publishes a quarterly newsletter, *Aging Accent.*

The Methodists were one of the first denominations to make the aging a priority concern. In 1948 they assigned the first national staff member to work for the elderly (Palmore, 1987). In 1992 the United Methodist church recognized an unprecedented increase in members over 65 and established a Committee on Older Adult Ministries to serve as a forum for advocacy and program planning and related to the General Board of Discipleship (Smith, 1992). The General Conference of the United Methodist Church began its current programs on aging by establishing a four-year Task Force on Older Adult Ministries. The task force surveyed the needs and resources of older adults, gathering data from the Methodist retirement homes, general church agencies state and regional organizations, and holding hearings throughout the United States. The task force was replaced in 1988 by an Advisory-Coordinating Committee on Older Adult Ministries to facilitate cooperation among already existing boards and agencies and to advocate for civil and human rights for older adults. This committee was replaced in 1992 by a more permanent organizational form: the Methodist Committee on Older Adult Ministries, located in the General Board of Church and Society, and named a director of Education and Ministries for Older Adults.

Members of the Seventh-Day Adventists live long lives, on the average, due to the healthy lifestyle their faith dictates forbidding the use of

---

> **The Southern Baptists and the Presbyterians have developed the most comprehensive national and regional programs, publications, plans, and research on aging.**

---

alcohol and tobacco. Central to Adventist belief is rebirth in a life after death, according to the Scriptures. More than a decade ago they established an office for Retirees' Affairs that forms local clubs promoting fellowship, service, and social activities.

The social service work of the Catholic church is divided between two major organizations: Catholic Charities and the Third Age Center at Fordham University. The National Conference of Catholic Charities is a national membership organization of 633 agencies with locations in every diocese. Member agencies bear other names than Catholic Charities, such as Catholic Social Services or Catholic Family and Community Services. Aging services are located within these agencies and serve the local congregations. The focus usually is on health care, housing, and social services. Fordham's Third Age Center conducts research on health and social service issues. Another membership organization is the Catholic Golden Age movement which provides varied activities to its local club members and publishes a monthly magazine (Palmore, 1987).

Efforts within Judaism to help their aging members are extensive as well as diverse. An unusually large segment of the American Jewish population is over 65—an estimated 17 percent, compared to less than 13 percent of the total U.S. population in that age bracket. Many factors account for this, including low birth rate, intermarriage, and the Holocaust. As a consequence of this high percentage of elders, services for the elderly hold a high priority in Jewish organizations.

As with most Jewish activities, the organizations are decentralized and vary a great deal from one community to another. The coordinating body in any locality with a substantial number of Jews is the Jewish Federation, which, in turn, belongs to the New York-based Council of Jewish Federations. Among the constituent agencies within a federation are, typically, a Jewish Family Service Agency, offering counseling and aid of many kinds; a Jewish Community Center, providing social and educational activities; and a Jewish retirement and nursing home (or homes) for older Jews. Whether retirement homes or nursing homes, these generally include kosher kitchens that meet dietary requirements of traditional Judaism. Very large synagogues and temples often have their own elderly programs, services, or study groups. In addition, the major private Jewish organizations, such as Hadassah for women and B'nai B'rith for men, provide activities for the aged. Because there is no single, national committee within Judaism for the elderly, there is considerable overlapping of services within the organizations. Generally, however, the system is effective in meeting the needs of older Jews.

● MINISTERIAL TRAINING

Clergy of all faiths will be serving congregations with expanding memberships of the aged. Most of those currently serving in churches and synagogues received little or no gerontological education in their seminary training. Those currently in training are receiving a minimum of aging content in the required curriculum. A national survey of aging programs under religious auspices, including seminaries and schools of theology, was conducted by the National Interfaith Coalition on Aging (NICA) in 1974 and updated in 1987 by Georgia State University. Most of the training reported in both studies consisted of units within applied courses, such as congregational ministry and counseling. The Georgia State study found an increase in courses and types of curricula involving gerontology as well as heightened interest in the relevancy of aging issues in theological education (Payne and Brewer, 1989). Few of the seminaries are offering continuing education in gerontology for clergy on a regular basis. Most of the continuing education is through national denominational conferences or workshops.

Some recent developments in ministerial training include: (1) the creation of gerontology programs and centers at St. Paul Seminary, Boston University; Southwestern Baptist Seminary; Pittsburgh Presbyterian Seminary; Luther-Northwestern Theological Seminary; and the Presbyterian School of Christian Education; (2) the offering of joint certificate programs between a university gerontology center and a local seminary such as Baylor University and Southwest Baptist Seminary, Luther-Northwestern Theological Seminary, North Texas State University, Georgia State University, and the Candler School of Theology (Emory University).

● ECUMENICAL PROGRAMS

Interfaith efforts for the elderly have expanded in recent years. They can be effective as well as rewarding because, as one minister observed, aging is a "natural melting pot" where the barriers and differences in beliefs melt away.

The National Interfaith Coalition on Aging (NICA), organized in 1972 in response to recommendations of the 1971 White House Conference on Aging, directed attention of the religious sector toward meeting the spiritual well-being and needs of older Americans. It is by design a small organization made up of representatives of national religious bodies and related organizations for the purpose of maximizing collective efforts for the elderly. NICA prepared the 1981 White House Conference on Aging background and issue report, *An Age Integrated Society: Implications for Spiritual Well-Being* (Cook, 1981). Since 1991 NICA has been a unit of The National Council on the Aging, and together they hold meetings annually on ecumenical programs and responses to aging, and they publish research reports on congregational and national religious organizations' responses to aging. Their most recent project, National Clergy Leadership Project to Prepare for an Aging Society, produced the publication *Focus Group Report on Findings* (1992), which reports the findings of four focus groups about the challenges facing aging Americans and the current level of support offered to the aging from the churches. The major issues were health care and health care costs, financial resources, and deteriorating quality of life. At the national level, some denominations have joined to develop resources and to hold conferences on aging. The Episcopal Society for Ministry on Aging (ESMA) and the Presbyterian (USA) Office on Aging collaborated to produce and publish *Older Adult Ministry: A Resource for Program Development* (1987) and additional program guides.

Various ecumenical projects indicate that the traditional commitment of churches and synagogues to caring for the sick and needy is alive and well. The Interfaith Volunteer Caregivers, a project of the Robert Woods Johnson Foundation, is co-sponsored by NICA. The foundation has long been involved in efforts to aid the vulnerable—the frail elderly and disabled—within communities. In this effort, the interfaith aspect is paramount. The project began in the early 1980s with 25 funded church-synagogue coalitions comprised of 875 local congregations. From this beginning evolved an association of Interfaith Caregivers, holding annual meetings, and it grew into an organization for those operating caregivers programs (Lewis, 1989). The emphasis was filling the gaps in existing programs and becoming the "caregiver of last resort" (Johnson, 1983). Overburdened family caregivers are given relief through this effort.

The American Society on Aging (ASA) has a Forum on Religion and Aging with an ecumenical membership. The forum meets with the annual meeting of ASA and publishes a quarterly newsletter, *Aging and Spirituality.* Meetings include special topic seminars, networking sessions, and "how to" workshops on innovative programs.

In a cooperative effort with elderly groups in churches and synagogues, the city of Philadelphia has a multifaceted ecumenical program that avoids artificial church-state barriers. Called HEAD II (Help Elderly Adults Direct), it notes that the separation of church and state is not the real issue, but rather "the right of the aging to be served as a total person—mind, body and spirit" (Peralta, 1983). The emphasis is on self-help for older people, involving them in decisions on policies and programs affecting their total quality of life.

Probably the most widely known ecumenical program that has local and national organization is the Shepherd's Center. The purpose of a Shepherd's Center is to help older people remain independent in their own homes as long as they choose and to enrich the later years with opportunities for service to others, self-expression, meaningful work, and close friendships. The Shepherd's Center movement, begun in 1972 by twenty-five churches of various faiths in Kansas City, Missouri, has grown to more than ninety-two centers throughout the United States. All centers belong to the national organization, The Shepherd's Centers of America, and offer continued training, program and resource development, and networking.

On a global scale, the World Assembly of Aging (WAA) functions as a forum for discussion of religion and spirituality related to the aged. Under the auspices of the United Nations, WAA can recommend policies and courses of action, but not enforce them (Deloff, 1983).

● HOW RELIGIONS VIEW THE AGED

The three largest religions in the United States—Judaism, Christianity, Islam—have many common threads. All are monotheistic and see God as one whether he (or she) is called Yahweh, God, or Allah. All three are scriptural faiths, believing that divinity exists in and is revealed by the written word, and all trace their origins to Abraham (Peters, 1982). In addition, the elders hold an important position in each religion as custodians of the faith, who preserve traditions, laws, and wisdom handed down from the prophets to wise old men, and who are venerated and often given prominence in religious activities (Isenberg, 1992).

Then-U.S. Commissioner on Aging Dr. Joyce Berry launched the National Eldercare Campaign in 1991 to mobilize civic, business, religious organizations, and others on the behalf of vulnerable elderly. She recognized the vital role the religious community could play and held a National Roundtable on Religion and Aging in the fall of 1992 to acquaint selected religious leaders with the need to broaden the base of support and commitment to the vulnerable elderly. The Roundtable participants discussed the opportunities and difficulties for religious organizations in supporting the establishment of an eldercare agenda within a congregation or community, as well as the best ways to involve the religious establishment in disseminating information about the national Eldercare Campaign and other initiatives for the elderly. This ecumenical and collaborative effort on the part of the Administration on Aging heralds for the religious community the beginning of a new focus on the present and future needs of the elderly.

Judaism

The Jews are a historic people whose traditions date back some four thousand years, and have a distinctive culture above and beyond the religion of Judaism (Steinberg, 1947). In the tradition, the processes of learning have always been considered as sacred. Rabbis are teachers as well as spiritual leaders (Isenberg, 1992). While it is generally believed that wisdom is attained through obedience to God, as the books of Job, Ecclesiastes, and others proclaim, there is flexibility as to an individual's perception of, and relationship, to God. Study of the Torah—the Mosaic books or first five books of the Hebrew Bible (what Christians call the Old Testament)—has always been the way a pious Jew became a wise Jew (Torah derives from the Hebrew verb meaning "to teach"). The towering figures of Judaism are good men before they are wise, but they are usually wise as well as good (Steinberg, 1947).

Despite this ancient philosophical tradition of seeking knowledge, Judaism recognizes human limitations: God transcends man's comprehension, and man can know only in part. This idea of incomplete understanding is especially true concerning death. Judaism is not preoccupied with death, always preferring to affirm life here and now, and there is little speculation about an afterlife (Steinberg, 1947; Grollman, 1969). This contrasts sharply with the Christian belief that downplays life on earth and longs for glory in a world beyond death. Still, though emphasis differs between modern and traditional Jews, there is a general notion that virtue in this world will be rewarded somehow. Moreover, Jews believe that salvation is possible for any good man, not just a Jew. Returning again to the theme of wisdom, how individuals face death depends on how well they have understood the "riddle of life" (Seltzer, 1983; Grollman, 1969).

While old age was always seen realistically as a time of pain and frailty, age as a social problem was not a theme of historic Judaism. The elderly were cared for within the extended family and respected; Proverbs 16:31 refers to gray hair as a "crown of glory" (Isenberg, 1992). Long life used to be seen as a reward for fulfilling God's commandments, such as the fifth, which dictates

honor to one's parents. According to the Bible, the matriarchs and patriarchs lived astoundingly long lives. At the same time, the book of Job teaches that it is not that simple: goodness doesn't always lead to a long, happy life, and early death is not necessarily a punishment for evil. Jewish thinkers ever since have struggled with the complex mixture of suffering, pain, and fulfillment that characterizes old age (Seltzer, 1983; Isenberg, 1992).

In modern times, as Jews left Old World traditions and emigrated en masse, the status of the older person has changed. The transplanted elderly Jew is seen in part as rootless and obsolete but, at the same time, as symbolic of the lost purity and secure family values of the old religion (Isenberg, 1992).

Christianity

Because Christianity is the majority religion in America, its general beliefs and doctrines are familiar. Christian attitudes toward old age spring from the same sources as do Jewish attitudes: the elderly are to be respected and parents are to be honored. The appointment of elders (presbyteri) to administer the churches, in fact, grew out of Jewish methods of governing the synagogues (Durant, 1944).

Veneration of the aged continued within Christianity through the Middle Ages, fading somewhat toward the later period. Respect for age has always been less consistent in the West than in Eastern cultures. Stearns (1992) says that historically "respect for wisdom and a recognition of old age as a life stage equal in value to those that preceded it, was balanced by a tendency to scorn physical and mental decay and a persistent identification of selfishness and abuse of authority associated with the later years."

With modernization, the rise of the West, and increasing secularization, attitudes toward old people began to change; their authority dissipated, especially if they were without property. The hierarchy of the Christian church still favored older men for high priestly and scholarly functions (Stearns, 1992). But the advance in stature of the young, whose vigor and productivity spurred progress, continued and became the youth culture that has culminated in this century.

While affirming respect for the elderly, Christianity always acknowledged their infirmities and limitations. Like other major faiths, Christianity asserted that spiritual ascent could compensate for physical decline. Accepting Jesus as the son of God would transcend the losses of age and finally transcend death itself (Post, 1992). It was this basic question of salvation that would cause Jewish and Christian theology to part company. Christians accept Jesus' promise of eternal life; Jews reject the divinity of Jesus and admit they do not know what will happen after death. The Christian gospel—the "good news"—preaches that salvation is the key reason for the existence of the church (Cole, 1983).

While doctrinal differences abound in the various denominations, the central doctrine is that Christ's triumph over death assures eternal life in God's kingdom for all true believers. Elderly Christians can find meaning by continuing their lifelong growth toward the moral and spiritual perfection of a Christlike life. The same virtue is expected of the old as well as of all the faithful; in a life viewed as a spiritual journey, old people are just further along (Post, 1992).

Along with life everlasting, the hopeful theme of the Christian religion is that, in St. Augustine's words, it can "re-bind" the sinner to God. This is accomplished by living correctly in late life (as throughout life), that is, having faith in a merciful God, hope for eternal life, and love for one's neighbor. The faith is democratic and open to all, the simple and poor as well as the wealthy and wise. Christian love is not intellectual but is a matter of the heart.

With modernization, the rise of the West, and increasing secularization, attitudes toward old people began to change; their authority dissipated, especially if they were without property.

The darker side of Christianity is the orthodox view that the decay of age and eventual death are a punishment for original sin in the Garden of Eden (Post, 1992). The faithful of all ages must atone for that sin by repenting and living virtuously. The aged have an opportunity to detach themselves from worldly pursuits and pattern their actions after Christ's. While belief in original sin and its effects has undergone modification in

recent years in some denominations, it is still taken literally by fundamentalist churches. In contemporary Christian thinking, there is little need to delay death via sophisticated medical technology, since the faithful welcome death as the transition from a life of pain to glorious life everlasting (Post, 1992). Evangelical Christians view growing old as the time of fulfillment, of reaching the "better world" awaiting them after death. Age brings reassurance for devout evangelicals, and is a time of hope rather than of despair (Michael, 1983).

Christianity's benchmark contribution to great religious literature is the New Testament, the biblical account of the remarkable life and inspiring message of Jesus as interpreted by his disciples. Building on the moral framework of Old Testament teachings, Jesus outlined an ideal morality of revolutionary scope (Durant, 1944). Living up to its demands to love and serve others while purging oneself of lust, selfishness, and cruelty may not be easy, but the splendor of the vision has inspired Christians for 2,000 years.

Islam

Relatively recent among the major religions but growing rapidly, Islam today claims nearly one billion members (Islam is the name of the religion, and Muslim refers to an adherent of the religion). The divine will, according to Islam, will be revealed through the various prophets down to the last great messenger, the Prophet Muhammad (Thursby, 1992).

The message of Allah (God, in Arabic) is conveyed in the holy scriptures of the Qur'an (Koran), including the basic views on aging. One chapter meditates on old age as the afternoon of life, viewing it realistically as a time of loss and disintegration. But the difficulties of old age, considered a natural part of the life cycle, "are balanced by a potential for inner growth and development. Fulfillment is found only beyond death in the encounter with God" (Moody, 1990). Islam celebrates the family and family life and stresses filial respect more strongly than any religion except Confucianism. The nearness of death in old age reveals human dependency on God's mercy; acceptance of this brings religious maturity and transcendence. It is never too late to return to Allah (Moody, 1990).

While faith is seen as crucial to salvation, it co-exists within Islam with respect for rational thinking. Scholarship is important, and the Qur'an often addresses its readers as "those possessed of minds." Women traditionally occupy a subordinate role within Islam, though this is changing very slowly; they are viewed as complementary, but not equal, to men. This status continues even in widowhood (Thursby, 1992).

Hinduism

Interest in spirituality and the search for meaning in contemporary life has led to study of such Eastern religions as Hinduism and Buddhism.

Hinduism, the oldest of these religions, has multiple gods. It originated on the subcontinent of India, spread to southeast Asia, and is now making modest inroads in the West. Today there are approximately 700 million Hindus around the world.

Its conceptions of old age have changed over the centuries. Early beliefs were that life is good and therefore more life is better. However, this view evolved into a more somber outlook: man's lot was an endless cycle of pain and suffering with countless rebirths. Life, in fact, was a time of misery. Followers of Hinduism are provided with explicit plans for living under which withdrawal practices such as yoga and meditation can release them from pain. Though asceticism is a strong strain within the religion, family values are important as well; it is necessary to balance these concepts. Thus the life cycle is divided into four stages of appropriate activity. Old age is seen as the highest of these stages. While the first three stages are involved with life and family, the last stage portrays a homeless, solitary wanderer as the ideal. During this stage, human beings should turn inward and renounce the world and its values. While the ascetic life is still thought to be the ideal, in practice very few Hindus renounce the world.

The social structure of Hinduism, the caste system, envisions only males of the upper "twice-born" castes as following this developmental cycle. The Brahman class serves as the chief mediator of religious authority between the human and the divine. While the rigidity of this system is softening somewhat today, caste ideals persist ". . .because they are suffused with the traditional concern for spiritual liberation and diffused throughout the extended family system" (Thursby, 1992).

Buddhism

Buddhism, which grew out of Hinduism, claims some 300 million adherents worldwide. Like Hinduism, it is oriented toward casting off worldly values. The Buddhist ideal is renunciation of the world for a celibate, homeless, wandering existence. Gautama the Buddha, the founder of the religion, envisioned a monastic community at its core. A faith that actively recruits converts, Buddhism prescribes for them a disciplined life of selflessness (Thursby, 1992). Enlightenment, and progress toward release, or nirvana, comes through meditation and study of the Buddha's teachings. Buddhists portray old age with its "shattered body" and lost senses (mental control) as a miserable time that serves to motivate people to detach themselves from worldly values. So strict are the requirements of Buddhism that most devotees are lay, or popular, Buddhists, while the monastic tradition tends to be elite (Thursby, 1992).

● WISDOM AND CREATIVITY

Two large concepts that often merge with religious and spiritual orientation of the aged are wisdom and creativity. Each may, of course, be the subject of exhaustive separate treatises but they are noted here as they relate to aging.

Wisdom has for centuries been linked to mature age as one of the few gains that may offset some of its all too evident losses. It is the wisdom of the old that formerly justified their position of veneration in traditional societies. Only quite recently, in fact, as a by-product of the "youth culture" of the West, has the image of the foolish, useless, ineffectual elder (Gaddy, 1983) replaced that of the old person worthy of great respect. Sadly, even those cultures that honored their elders most strongly are now guilty of devaluing them, of finding their contributions irrelevant.

The powerful counter argument says that life's accumulated experiences can in fact add up to a contribution, that elder wisdom can be a great gift to society once it is transmitted. This gives the last stage of life intrinsic meaning beyond the spiritual integration that the older person may be

Profiles of Productive Aging

Rev. Norman Vincent Peale
Minister, author

"Don't look down, look straight ahead and think of God."

Inspirational lecturer and author of *The Power of Positive Thinking,* Dr. Norman Vincent Peale was born May 31, 1898, in Bowersville, Ohio. The son of a minister, Peale himself always wanted to be a newspaperman. He worked on the paper at Ohio Wesleyan University, followed by jobs with the *Findley Ohio Morning Republican* (now the *Courier*), then the *Detroit Journal.* "All that time," he recounted, "I was haunted by a feeling I couldn't escape that I was supposed to be a messenger of the Good News."

When he covered a fire in Detroit, a 12-year-old girl was trapped on the sixth floor. Though someone pushed a plank to her from a neighboring building, the girl was afraid to go across. Peale shouted up, "Honey, do you believe in God?" The girl nodded. "Do you believe he's right there with you?" he called to her. She nodded again. "Well, then he will guide you across that plank. Don't look down; look straight ahead and think of God." When the girl got halfway across the plank, he urged her on. As soon as she made it across, the sergeant in charge said to Peale, "Good job, boy. You ought to be a preacher." Peale protested, "I'm no preacher—I'm a reporter." "The hell you're not!" the sergeant countered him.

Peale graduated from Boston University with degrees in theology and ministry in 1924, then worked in Brooklyn and Syracuse, New York. After witnessing the hardships of the Depression, Peale believed individuals could overcome adversity and shape their own destinies if they had the right attitude. "I heard a man make a speech at the Rotary Club in Syracuse that this country would never prosper again. Never is a long time. And he was considered one of the greatest econ-omists of the day. I have taken a dim view of such people," Peale claimed. "The country can survive any disaster as long as we retain the honesty and spirit that have always activated us."

Peale began *The Power of Positive Thinking* in the 1940s, and it was, in part, a personal manifesto—Peale was trying to overcome his own shyness—but it was also about America's odyssey. "I always believed America could survive and come out unscathed in the long run," he stated. The first publisher he showed the manuscript to said it wouldn't sell more than 10,000 copies, so Peale put it away. When his wife, Ruth Stafford Peale, found it a year later, Peale told her to throw it away. Instead she showed it to Byron Borgman, who also liked it, but he wondered who the audience was? Church people? "No—to everybody, particulary the ones that don't go to church," Peale explained. Borgman told Peale, "You've got a phrase in there that would make a much better title—*The Power of Positive Thinking.*" Today the book has sold 18 million copies.

Other books followed, including *The Art of Living, A Guide to Confident Living,* and *You Can Win.* Peale started the inspirational magazine *Guideposts,* which has 4 million subscribers and has the fourth largest magazine circulation in the country today, hosted the nationally syndicated weekly TV program—"Positive Thinking with Norman Vincent Peale" and a weekly nationwide Sunday radio program, and wrote a news-paper column. He received numerous honorary degrees and awards, including the Freedom Foundation Award, the Horatio Alger Award, and the Presidential Medal of Freedom.

In his mid-nineties, Peale was busy writing two books and continuing to give speeches across the country until his death in December 1993.

Lydia Brontë

---

seeking. While white hair and wrinkles do not in themselves produce wisdom, still the simple fact of completing most of life's journey can be seen as an accomplishment. At this point, individuals can choose to move beyond chronological age to positive enhancement of their spiritual develop-ment. "Aging is not like a train one passively rides until one reaches the station called 'Wisdom'" (McFadden and Gerl, 1990).

Many older people describe their last years as a time when things seem to fall into place, when they can, with a little reflection, view problems of the past in a life span perspective. Of greater sig-nificance than the pursuit of things, or of success, are relationships to family and friends, and to some form of a divine being. As this kind of wisdom is closely akin to the spiritual (Howe, 1983), it may enhance spiritual well-being and inner peace for older adults.

Several themes have emerged from new scientific studies of wisdom over the past two decades. The first is that wisdom is the kind of knowledge that is both practical—as it sheds light on interpersonal affairs and everyday challenges—and deeply philosophical. Second, it can be expressed in judgments or in evaluating decisions. Finally, people who possess wisdom have particular distinguishing qualities—affective, interpersonal, and intellectual. Whether wisdom can be taught or nurtured or whether it depends totally on life experiences is another fascinating theme for study (Clayton, 1987).

An effort to promote wisdom in the elderly is the spiritual eldering program of Rabbi Zalman Schachter-Shalomi. Applicable to all religious traditions, his goal is to help older people "make the mind-moves from Aging to Saging" (Cole, 1991). Rabbi Schachter-Shalomi is presently developing a series of workshops and seminars to train people for work with elders in varied settings such as nursing homes, churches, and synagogues. Central to his project is the encouragement of mature wisdom as a philosophical outlook built out of people's experiences and insights. Asserting that "life is a sort of teaching machine," the rabbi believes older persons should pour back that hard-earned knowledge into a wisdom pool. In spiritual eldering, religion is revered but as "only one of the universe's teaching methods." A major focus of the program is helping people deal with "last things," resolve unfinished business, and prepare for dying (Cole, 1991).

Many older people describe their last years as a time when things seem to fall into place, when they can, with a little reflection, view problems of the past in a life span perspective.

Creativity

The "unfinished business" of the elderly may relate to past quarrels with individuals, or wrongs done them, that need resolution. But there is also the "business" of self-expression before death ends the opportunity. As John Keats put it:

"When I have fears that I may cease to be
Before my pen has glean'd my teeming brain."

Many older persons feel a strong need to glean—to fulfill—brain, soul, talent, whatever creative potential is still within them. "We may all truly be unfinished symphonies" (Kenyon, 1992) that cry out for finishing touches.

Creativity is not limited to the fine arts nor to youthful creators but exists in everyone. It has been called the older person's most profound response to the limits and uncertainties of late life (Kastenbaum, 1991). So intense, so transporting is the spark of inspiration that launches a creative act that many artists have likened it to a flash of religious fervor. The creator of any age, like the wise sage, can be a teacher, revealing meaning through a poem, a drawing, a concerto, a garden. . . .

The popular notion used to be that one's "creative juices" simply dried up in old age. Recent studies indicate that not only does individual creativity continue fairly steadily into late life, but that people frequently show a resurgence or second peak of creative intensity and output after their late sixties (Simonton, 1991). It is true that in some, but not all, artistic disciplines the number of creative products of an individual usually peaks in the late thirties or early forties. Exceptions abound, of course, from Picasso to Bach to Grandma Moses, and the age curve of productivity depends on when it began: there is such a thing as a "late bloomer."

As everyone knows, there is a tremendous variation in the creative potential and talent of people at all ages. Those who were creative as younger adults are most likely to be creative in old age. As with many abilities, creative skills that are "exercised" are most likely to be maintained into old age (Dohr and Portillo, 1990). Performance curves notwithstanding, individuals may produce their best work at any age.

How are the creative elderly identified? Whatever the age, the creative person is the one "most likely to score high on the personality dimension of being open to new experience" (Kastenbaum, 1991). He or she is "more reflective, contemplative, intense, resourceful, and adventurous" than the average, is essentially independent but is interdependent insofar as receiving and sharing ideas with others is involved (Dohr and Portillo, 1990).

Theorists of life span development point out that the final phase of life is often a time of phenomenal creativity (Simenton, 1991). The familiar—and apt—metaphor is that of the dying swan, whose song is incredibly sweet. Older people should be given every opportunity to sing their "swan song" regardless of obstacles. Neither failing eyesight, shaking hands, nor dwindling energy can cancel a creative spirit, if the will to express it is there.

● CELEBRATIONS AND RITUALS ON AGING

While most of life's milestones—birth, coming of age, marriage, death—have been marked by rituals of some kind as long as people have gathered in communities, the passage into middle/late adulthood has not generally been observed. Several denominations are now attempting to include some sort of celebration in their activities.

An unusual ritual available within Judaism for older Jewish men is a second bar mitzvah. This ritual of continued devotion and identity for elders repeats the ceremony when young Jews of 13 assume their obligations within the faith. Women can mark the attainment of the wisdom of age in a ceremony known as "croning."

In the Catholic church, a sister has recognized the need for rituals in which elderly members within the congregations can celebrate the passage into late adulthood. She has written a congregational missioning ceremony. While now used mainly by Christian groups, its wording and themes are designed to be ecumenical (Murphy, 1990).

Some of the religious groups and local congregations participate in services that celebrate and recognize their senior members during Older Americans Month each May. An example is a project of the Episcopal Church. The three-year program entitled "Age in Action" was begun by ESMA in May of 1992. Its focus is on aging and God relatedness. "Aging Is Becoming Aware of God's Grace" was the 1992 theme; "God's Gifts" will follow in 1993; and "God's Time" is projected for 1994. The program includes five sessions of intergenerational inquiry and discussion. The development of such rituals is in an informal and beginning stage. More formal rituals for older members may be expected from the major faith groups in this decade.

● SPIRITUAL PRACTICES

Programs within or outside of traditional religious bodies that help older adults focus on their spirituality vary in format. Some are workshops, seminars, or retreats; others may be study groups that require a daily commitment of time in reading religious texts such as the Bible or the Qur'an, reflection, and writing. While much of the content of these programs is Judeo-Christian, there is a growing interest in and study of the Eastern religions, in particular their emphasis on the use of the free time of retirement for prayer and meditation. From the positions of the various religions on old age summarized earlier, it is clear that one belief all of them share is that inward-looking reflection is highly appropriate for the last years of life.

Spiritual practice may be a private and/or a group experience. An example of the spirituality movement that combines these experiences is the work of Emma Lou Benignus, the coordinator of spiritual formation for the Episcopal Diocese of Pennsylvania. She conducts retreats that are not only for older adults, but may be intergenerational. The group deals with the older adult agenda items because they are concerns of all age groups. She is exploring the use of silence in groups, as well as urging them to share their experiences over a two- or three-day period.

The creative use of solitude is another spiritual development process for all ages, but especially for mature adults. The elderly who spend a great deal of time alone must often strive to keep loneliness at bay. The evolution of moving from loneliness to aloneness, to solitude, and ultimately to creative solitude may be a spiritual way to deal with this late-life experience. Nouwen (1986) has addressed this process as "the slow converting of loneliness into a deep solitude—a precious space where we can discover the voice telling us about our necessity, a movement toward a deeper engagement with the burning issues of our time."

Journaling

Journaling is another method of using solitude for expressing one's experiences and private feelings and chronicling one's spiritual journey (Bianchi, 1982). Journaling is different from keeping a diary; the focus is on one's inner life. It may or may not take an event as a starting point, but it explores in depth the feelings and reflections on the experience. The journals of the elderly can be seen as efforts to shape a coherent life story, to find and distill the meaning out of life's happenings (Berman, 1991).

While it is a means of thinking through how one feels and what one wants to say about it, journaling is both a spiritual and a creative discipline. It becomes spiritual when writing is used to strengthen one's faith. "Journaling can be used as a companion to prayer, Bible study, fasting, or any other spiritual discipline" that is already a part of one's spiritual life. "It can be a significant tool in deepening our spiritual lives as it leads to further understanding of who we are and who God is in our lives" (Broyles, 1988).

Historically, keeping a journal or diary has been an especially effective outlet for women. In the past when few creative avenues (other than creating a family) were open to women, writing down their innermost thoughts was often a refuge from the tedium of household tasks (Berman, 1991). Sensitive use of this literary form by women continues today, with such writers as May Sarton, Elizabeth Vining, and Florida Scott-Maxwell.

John Wesley, the founder of Methodism, used journaling as a discipline. His reflections on his own aging began on his fifty-first birthday and continued on every birthday until he was 83. His spiritual reflections and observations about his personal aging provide rare insight into the relationship of spiritual ascension and physical descent. If he had not used journaling this would have been lost.

● EXPANDING STUDY OF SPIRITUALITY

Attention to spirituality and aging within gerontology, and its new, wider focus on the humanities, coincides with the evident interest in the subject by all age groups. The attention being paid to the elderly within the denominations has been noted as well as the proliferation of published articles on the relationship of age and spirituality. Entire issues of such publications as *Generations*, the journal of the American Society on Aging, and *Aging and the Human Spirit*, newsletter of the Institute for the Medical Humanities (University of Texas, Galveston), have been devoted to the topic. New publications such as the *Journal of Religion and Aging* and *Aging and Spirituality* have made recent debuts, and there has been regular coverage in such long-standing journals as *Gerontologist* and the *Journal of Gerontology*.

On the popular level, such organizations as Elderhostel are including courses on spiritual subjects in their curricula. Wherever older adults turn for late-life education—community colleges, libraries, church or synagogue study groups, formal "learning in retirement" institutes—such courses now appear. Formerly taboo, topics such as "Death and Dying" have become popular subjects for study; so have discussion groups addressing such related bioethical issues as withholding care for the terminally ill.

In an address to the Theological Students Fellowship at Princeton Theological Seminary (December 10, 1990), George Gallup, Jr., observed that surveys have revealed much about the breadth of religion, but relatively little about the depth of an individual's inner life. He predicted that the new frontier of social research would be the inner life—the spiritual. He identified six basic spiritual needs of all Americans, regardless of age: (1) the need to believe that life is meaningful and has a purpose; (2) the need for a sense of community and deeper relationships with others; (3) the need to be appreciated and respected; (4) the need to be listened to—and heard; (5) the need to feel that one is growing in faith; and (6) the need for practical help in developing a mature faith (Gallup, 1990).

The exploration of the contribution of spirituality to the experience of aging has just begun, but as it expands and grows, information about this important connection can be expected to increase. For the growing legions of older Americans, the spiritual stakes are high, as a recent story in the *St. Petersburg Times* concluded (*Journey*, 1992): "Spirituality, whether it is manifested through religion or an understanding of a larger, more powerful life-force, helps the elderly find a meaning for their lives, overcome their regrets, make final amends with friends and family, and put their lives in perspective."

Organizations

American Association of Retired Persons (AARP)
Interreligious Liaison Office
601 E St., NW
Washington, DC 20049

American Society on Aging
Forum on Religion and Aging
833 Market St., Ste. 512
San Francisco, CA 94103

Association for Gerontology in Higher Education (AGHE)
1001 Connecticut Ave. NW, Ste. 410
Washington, DC 20036-5504.

Episcopal Society for Ministry on Aging (ESMA)
Sayre Hall
317 Wyandotte St.
Bethlehem, PA 18015

The National Council on Aging
National Interfaith Coalition on Aging (NICA)
409 Third St., SW
Washington, DC 20024

The Presbyterian Center
100 Witherspoon St.
Louisville, KY 40202

Shepherds Centers of America
6700 Troost, Ste. 616
Kansas City, MO

The Southern Baptist Convention
The Sunday School Board
Senior Adult Section
Family Ministry Department
127 Ninth Ave. N
Nashville, TN 37234

The Third Age Center (Catholic)
Fordham University
113 W. 60th St.
New York, NY 10023-7479

The United Methodist Church
General Board of Discipleship
Director: Education and Ministry for Older Adults
P.O. Box 840
Nashville, TN 37202-0840

Journals

Gerontologist
The Gerontological Society of America
1275 K St., NW, Ste. 350
Washington, DC 20005-4006

Journal of Aging and Judaism
Human Science Press
72 Fifth Ave.
New York, NY 10011

Journal of Religious Gerontology
(formerly *Journal of Religion and Aging*)
Haworth Press
10 Alice St.
Binghamton, NY 13904-1580

Newsletter

Aging and the Human Spirit
University of Texas, Medical Branch
Institute for the Medical Humanities, M-11
Galveston, TX 77555-1311

References

Achenbaum, W. Andrew. "Afterword: Integrating the Humanities into Gerontologic Research, Training, and Practice." In *Handbook of the Humanities and Aging.* Eds. Thomas R. Cole, David D. Van Tassel, and Robert Kastenbaum. New York: Springer, 1992.

Aging America: Trends and Projections, 1991 ed. Produced by U.S. Senate Special Committee on Aging, the American Association of Retired Persons, the Federal Council on Aging and the U.S. Administration on Aging, U.S. Department of Health and Human Services.

Ainlay, Stephen C., Royce Singleton, Jr., and Victoria L. Swigert. "Aging and Religious Participation: Reconsidering the Effects on Health." *Journal for the Scientific Study of Religion* Vol 31, no. 2 (1992).

Atchley, Robert. *Social Forces in Late Life.* Belmont, CA: Wadsworth, 1991.

Bianci, Eugene C. *Aging as a Spiritual Journey.* New York: Crossroads, 1982.

Blazer, Dan G., and Erdman Palmore. "Religion and Aging in a Longitudinal Panel." *Gerontologist* Vol. 16, no. 1 (1976): 82–85.

Broyles, Anne. "Journaling: A Spiritual Journey." *The Upper Room* (1987): 14.

Clayton, Vivian. "Wisdom." In *The Encyclopedia of Aging.* Ed. George L. Maddox. New York: Springer, 1987.

Cole, Thomas R. "Ministry of Spiritual Eldering." *Aging and the Human Spirit* (Fall 1991).

———. "Oedipus and the Meaning of Aging: Personal Reflections and Historical Perspectives." *Generations* (Fall 1990).

Cook, Thomas C., ed. *An Age Integrated Society: Implications for Spiritual Well-Being.* Washington, DC: White House Conference on Aging, 1981.

Council of Jewish Federations. *Jewish Environmental Scan: Toward the Year 2000.* New York: Council of Jewish Federations, 1991.

DeGenova, Mary Kay. "If You Had Your Life to Live Over Again: What Would You Do Differently?" *Aging and Human Development* Vol. 32, no. 2 (1992).

Delloff, Linda-Marie. "The WHCoA and WAA: Spiritual Well-Being Gets Lost." *Generations* (Fall 1983).

Dohr, Joy, and Margaret Portillo. "Creative Behavior and Education: An Avenue for Lifetime Development." In *Introduction to Educational Gerontology.* 3d ed. Eds. Ronald Sherron and Barry D. Lumsden. New York: Hemisphere, 1990.

Durant, Will. *Caesar and Christ.* New York: Simon & Schuster, 1944.

Elder, Harold G., and Patricia S. McCracken. "Position/Policy Statements on Aging of Representative Religious Bodies." In *U.S.A. Paper for the National Interfaith Coalition on Aging,* 1980.

Ellison, George W. "Spiritual Well-Being: Conceptualization and Measurement." *Journal of Psychology and Theology* Vol. 11, no. 4 (1983): 330–40.

Fischer, Kathleen. *Winter Grace: Spirituality for the Later Years.* New York: Paulist Press, 1985.

Gaddy, C. Welton. "Ethics in an Aging World: Rhetoric or Dynamic?" *Generations* (Fall 1983).

Gallup, George, Jr. *50 Years of Gallup Surveys on Religion 1935–1985.* Princeton, NJ: The Gallup Report, 1985.

———. *Religion in America* (Report No. 259). Princeton, NJ: The Gallup Report, 1987.

———. "What Every Pastor Should Know about the Average American." *Emerging Trends* Vol. 13, no. 3 (1991): 5.

Griffin, Richard. "Toward a Spiritual Agenda For Late Life." *Aging and the Human Spirit* Vol. 2, no. 2 (1992): 2–3.

Grollman, Earl A., ed. *Explaining Death to Children.* Boston, MA: Beacon Press, 1969.

Hall, G. Stanley. *Senescence: The Second Half of Life.* New York: Appleton, 1922.

Howe, Revel L. "Spiritual Dimensions of Aging." *Generations* (Fall 1983).

Jakobson, Cathryn. "The New Orthodox: A Jewish Revival on the Upper West Side." In *Religion in American Life: The Reference Shelf.* Ed. Janet Podell. New York: H. W. Wilson, 1987.

Johnson, Kenneth G. "The Robert Wood Johnson Foundation's Interfaith Volunteer Caregivers Program." *Generations* (Fall 1983).

Journey, Mark. "The Age of Discovery." *St. Petersburg Times* (January 28, 1992).

Kahana, Eva, and Boaz Kahana. "Jews." In *Handbook on the Aged in The United States.* Ed. Erdman B. Palmore. Westport, CT: Greenwood Press, 1984: 155–79.

Kyles, Josephine H. "The Black Elderly and the Church." *Generations* (Fall 1983).

Lewis, Mary Ann. *Religious Congregations and the Informal Supports of the Frail Elderly.* New York: The Third Age Center, Fordham University, 1989.

McFadden, Susan H., and Robert R. Gerl. "Approaches to Understanding Spirituality in the Second Half of Life." *Generations* (Fall 1990): 33–38.

McSherry, Elisabeth. "The Spiritual Dimension of Elder Health Care." *Generations* (Fall 1983).

Markides, Kyriakos S. "Religion." In *Encyclopedia of Aging.* Ed. George L. Maddox. New York: Springer, 1987.

Mature Market Report (July 1988): 7.

Michael, Stanley V. "Aging with the Paraclete: The Evangelical Tradition." *Generations* (Fall 1983).

Mindel, Charles, and C. Edwain Vaughn. "A Multi-Dimensional Approach to Religiosity and Disengagement. *Journal of Gerontology* Vol. 33, no. 1 (1978): 103–8.

Moody, H. R. "Bioethics and Aging." In *Handbook of the Humanities and Aging.* Eds. Thomas Cole, David D. Van Tassel, and Robert Kastenbaum. New York: Springer, 1992.

———. "The Islamic Vision of Aging and Death." *Generations* (Fall 1990).

Murphy, Patricia. "The Mission of Aging: Congregational Missioning Ceremony." *Generations* (1990): 67–68.

Naisbitt, John, and Patricia Aburdene. *Megatrends 2000.* New York: William Morrow, 1990.

National Interfaith Coalition on Aging (NICA), National Clergy Leadership Project to Prepare for an Aging Society. *Focus Group Report of Findings.* Washington, DC: The National Council on the Aging, 1992.

National Opinion Research Center (NORC). *Emerging Trends.* Princeton, NJ: Princeton Religion Research Center, 1991.

Nouwen, Henri J. M. *Reaching Out.* New York: Doubleday, 1986.

Older Adult Ministry: A Resource for Program Development. Episcopal Society for Ministry on Aging, Presbyterian Office on Aging, and United Church of Christ. Louisville, KY: Presbyterian Publishing House, 1987.

Palmore, Erdman. "Religious Organizations." In *Encyclopedia of Aging.* Ed. George Maddox. New York: Springer, 1987.

Payne, Barbara P. "Protestants." In *Handbook on the Aged in the United States.* Ed. Erdman B. Palmore. Westport, CT: Springer, 1984.

———. "Religion and the Elderly in Today's World." In *Ministry with the Aging.* Ed. William M. Clemments. New York: Harper & Row, 1981.

———. "Religious Patterns and Participation of Older Adults: A Sociological Perspective." In *Educational Gerontology* Vol. 14 (1988).

———. "Spirituality and Aging: Research and Theoretical Approaches." *Generations* (Fall 1990).

Payne, Barbara P., and Earl D. C. Brewer, eds. *Gerontology in Theological Education.* New York: Haworth Press, 1989.

Peralta, Victoria. "Project HEAD II: Public Sector Collaborates with Religious Sector." *Generations* (Fall 1983).

Peters, F. E. *Children of Abraham: Judaism, Christianity, Islam.* Princeton, NJ: Princeton University Press, 1982.

Post, Stephen G. "Aging and Meaning: The Christian Tradition." In *Handbook of the Humanities and Aging.*

Eds. Thomas R. Cole, David D. Van Tassel, and Robert Kastenbaum. New York: Springer, 1992.

Roof, Wade Clark, and William McKinney. "Denominational American and the New Religious Pluralism." In *Religion in American Life: The Reference Shelf.* Ed. Janet Podell. New York: H. W. Wilson, 1987.

Schachter-Shalomi, Z. "The Practice of Spiritual Eldering." *New Menorah: The P'nai; Journal of Jewish Renewal.* Second Series, no. 22 (1991): 9ff.

Seltzer, Sanford. "Some Jewish Perspectives on Aging and Society." *Generations* (Fall 1983).

Silberman, Charles E. *A Certain People: American Jews and Their Lives Today.* New York: Summit Books, 1985.

Smith, Alice M. "Mission Initiatives." *Wesleyan Christian Advocate* Vol. 156, no. 46 (1992): 2.

Starbuck, Edward D. *The Psychology of Religion: An Empirical Study of the Growth of Religious Consciousness.* New York: Walter Scott, 1911.

Stearns, Peter N. "Elders in World History." In *Handbook of the Humanities and Aging.* Eds. Thomas R. Cole, David D. Van Tassel, and Robert Kastenbaum. New York: Springer, 1992.

Taylor, Robert J. "Religious Participation Among Elderly Blacks." *Gerontologist* Vol. 29, no. 6 (1986): 630–38.

Thursby, Gene R. "Islamic, Hindu, and Buddhist Conceptions of Aging." In *Handbook of the Humanities and Aging.* Eds. Thomas R. Cole, David D. Van Tassel, and Robert Kastenbaum. New York: Springer, 1992.

Additional Reading

Clements, William M., ed. *Ministry With the Aging.* New York: Harper & Row, 1981.

LeFevre, Carol, and Perry LeFevre. *Aging and The Human Spirit.* Chicago, IL: Exploration Press, 1981

Maitland, David. *Aging as Counterculture.* New York: Pilgrim Press, 1991.

Maves, Paul B. *Faith for the Older Years: Making the Most of Life's Second Half.* Minneapolis, MN: Augsburg Press, 1986.

Nouwen, Henry J., and Walter J. Gaffney. *Aging: The Fulfillment of Life.* Garden City, NJ: Image Books, 1974.

Paul, Susanne, ed. *A Ministry to Match the Age.* New York: General Board of Global Ministries, United Methodist Church, 1991.

Peck, M. Scott, M.D. *The Road Less Traveled.* New York: Simon & Schuster, 1979.

Robb, Thomas B. *Growing Up: Pastoral Nurture for the Later Years.* New York: Haworth Press, 1991.

Roschen, John F. *Baby Boomers Face Midlife: Implications for the Faith Communities and in the 1990s and Beyond.* Minneapolis, MN: Adult Faith Resources, 1991.

Seeber, E. *Spiritual Maturity in the Later Years.* New York: Haworth Press, 1992.

Simmons, Henry G., and Vivienne S. Pierce. *Pastoral Response to Older Adults and Their Families: An Annotated Bibliography.* Westport, CT: Greenwood Press, 1992.

Barbara Payne Ph.D.

35

Lifelong Learning

- Emergence of Older Adult Education • National Policies and Older Adult Education
- Intellectual Functioning of Older Adults • Purpose of Education for Seniors
- Program Types and Learner's Motives • Institutions and Exemplary Programs
- Participation Rates and Public Policy

Adult educational opportunities in the United States date back to the 1700s when coffee houses functioned as adult educational institutions, mainly for disseminating political propaganda. The potential for influencing the thinking of a larger number of adults was recognized by political parties such as the Whigs, who oftentimes owned the coffee houses. Many of the coffee houses in New York City also provided writing and reading materials for their customers (Long, 1981).

The early colonial leaders believed that democracy depended on the educability of the citizenry, and that through widespread educational efforts, the public decision-making process could be improved. Benjamin Franklin, a great believer in this theory, established one of the first adult education activities in the colonies, called Junto. Established in 1727, Junto was a weekly study group of twelve people who met to discuss community and social issues and was responsible for the formation of the first local lending libraries. Junto lasted for thirty years. Almost one hundred years later a lecture series, given the name Lyceum (in ancient tradition, an association providing public lectures, concerts, and entertainment) was established. The Lyceum series introduced adult citizens residing in small towns and rural areas to scholarly knowledge. These lectures attempted to raise the educational levels of participants who had not completed an elementary level education. For well

over one hundred years the lecture series brought intellectual stimulation to many of the rural areas of the country (Peterson, 1983). Approximately fifty years later the Chautauqua movement began introducing adults to religious studies, liberal arts education, and the performing arts. Established at Lake Chautauqua, New York, in 1874 by the Methodist Episcopal Church, it was basically nondenominational and drew audiences from throughout the United States to the summer assembly tent performances. Similar "tent chautauquas" were held across the country. Still in existence today, Chautauqua attracts thousands of older adults each year. The program offerings have expanded to include vocational/personal education, and civic/community education (Peterson, 1983) as well as programming designed specifically for older adults (Chautauqua Institution, 1992).

Although the expression "lifelong learning" has been in use for many years, it is only recently that the concept has been applied to the older adult learner. As gerontology became an established field of practice and research, it influenced the adult education movement, and educators began to consider older adults as potential students of lifelong education (Lowy and O'Connor, 1986).

● EMERGENCE OF OLDER ADULT EDUCATION

In 1949, a Committee on Education for Aging was established under the Department of Adult

Education of the National Education Association (NEA). In 1951, this committee became a part of the Adult Education Association of the U.S.A. For the first time in history, a descriptive book on educational programming for older adult learners, *Education for Later Maturity: A Handbook*, was developed by this committee. Yet, until the early 1950s, a cultural bias toward youth exerted a detrimental effect upon the growth of educational programs for older adults. An emphasis on youth was prevalent in the majority of publications in the field of education. From 1950 to 1960 only a few educational administrators were considering offering educational programs for older adults. The very few programs that were in operation were experimental in nature with no research base. In the early 1960s, gerontological researchers devoted considerable energy to examining links between aging and intellectual functioning. The combined emphasis on the youth culture and research on age-related cognitive declines continued to have a negative impact upon attitudes toward older adult educational programs (Timmerman, 1979).

During this period, the trend that emerged for program planners was to segregate older learners because their integration in ongoing adult educational programs was deemed undesirable. Most practitioners pointed to the differences, not the similarities, between young and old (Timmerman, 1979).

By the mid-1960s small inroads were made in removing the educational bias toward the young while attitudes toward older adults began to change. For example, social workers trained during the 1940s and 1950s had been instructed to discourage reminiscing among older people because it was viewed as a form of pathology—the person denying or having lost contact with the present. However, between the late 1950s and early 1970s this view changed dramatically. The work of Butler (1963) and Erikson (1964) helped service providers and educators recognize a universal "life review" process occurring normally among the elderly and that this process could serve as the basis for therapies and educational programs building on older persons' life experiences and histories. Some researchers and educators went even further, recognizing elements of wisdom and creativity in the life review process (Manheimer, 1991).

Although the expression "lifelong learning" has been in use for many years, it is only recently that the concept has been applied to the older adult learner. (Copyright © Benjamin Porter)

Many educators have addressed the importance of past experiences in enhancing the older adult's learning experience. Education was defined by John Dewey (1971) as the "continuous reconstruction of experience." Adult educator Malcolm Knowles (1980) further contended that life experience distinguishes child learning from adult learning (Merriam, 1990).

A summary of the last forty years of older adult education can be found in Moody's view of the changing attitudes toward older adults and the value of education in their lives (Moody, 1988). He identified four stages, each with its own underlying presupposition about older adult education held by professionals and educators. The first presupposition (stage one) or attitude is *rejection* of older adults. This attitude contends that since older people are socially obsolete, it would be a waste of time and financial resources to provide educational programs for them. The second stage emphasizes the problems and needs of older adults and that these must be altered by a change in public policy. Education is regarded as one among many *social services* for the dependent elderly. With an emphasis on providing access and opportunity, older adults passively receive services rather than learning the necessary skills that will enable them to start their own programs. Many social service programs lead to the segregation of older adults, because such programs are designed to keep older adults busy, rather than providing them with opportunities that will assist them in improving their lives. All of this changes in stage three, in which the *participation* view maintains that older adults should be encouraged to actively continue in the mainstream of community life and to develop self-sufficiency. Their skills and abilities will be instrumental in helping them to overcome their problems as well as some of society's. *Self-actualization*, the fourth stage, emphasizes psychological growth and spiritual concerns as the major objective of educational programs for older adults. Based on Abraham Maslow's theory of the hierarchy of needs, self-actualization can only be realized through a combined psychological and spiritual quest for meaning and insight. Old age, being the last stage in the course of life, may be viewed as an attempt to explore the meaning of one's experiences and integrating an understanding of these experiences acquired throughout a lifetime. Many gerontologists and adult educators believe that self-actualization should be the ultimate goal of every older adult educational program (Peterson, 1990).

One can find elements of all four stages in current practice, though variations often depend on the situation and functional status of seniors. Hence, self-actualization may be the predominant goal in programs for and with the well, mobile elderly, while a more therapeutic, social work approach may prevail in a nursing home setting with frail elders. Nevertheless, poetry writing and creative dramatics courses are not uncommon in care centers.

● NATIONAL POLICIES AND OLDER ADULT EDUCATION

The change in societal attitudes has had significant impact on federal policies regarding the education of older adults. The first major development came with the creation of the Older Americans Act in 1965. This act established the Administration on Aging and provided needed funding for training and research at colleges and universities, which, in turn, opened the door for new educational opportunities for older adults and extended educational gerontology, workforce training, and multidisciplinary graduate programs as well as research in addressing the needs of older adult learners.

Another departure from prevailing attitudes occurred in 1971 when the White House Conference on Aging (WHCOA) advanced recommendations that paved the road for educational programming for older adults. The national event had significant impact on the attitudes of educators and gerontologists. Education received special attention at the conference, which called for increased funding and manpower to provide older adult educational programs in the private and public sector. The conference can best be summarized by the comments of educational gerontologist Howard Y. McCluskey: "Education is a basic right for all persons of all age groups. It is continuous and henceforth one of the ways of enabling older people to have a full and meaningful life and a means of helping them develop their potential as a resource for the betterment of society" (Timmerman, 1979). The 1971 White House Conference on Aging served as a benchmark in the history of older adult education.

Congress enacted the Older Americans Comprehensive Services Amendments of 1973 to strengthen the Older Americans Act. Under this act the Administration on Aging was reorganized under the U.S. Department of Health, Education, and Welfare (HEW), and the Federal Council on

---

Old age, being the last stage in the course of life, may be viewed as an attempt to explore the meaning of one's experiences and integrating an understanding of these experiences acquired throughout a lifetime. Many gerontologists and adult educators believe that self-actualization should be the ultimate goal of every older adult educational program.

Many library programs are available to older adults today. (Copyright © Benjamin Porter)

the Aging was created, as well as the National Information and Resource Clearinghouse for the Aging. Grants were awarded by the commissioner on aging to state governments for special library and education programs for older adults. Research in the field of aging and grants for training personnel to work with older adults was also encouraged by the commissioner on aging (Brahce and Hunter, 1990).

In addition to federal policies concerning older adult education, many states began to establish guidelines within their statutes to allow or require a waiver or reduction of tuition fees for older adults who are enrolled at a state-supported institution of higher education (Special Committee on Aging, U.S. Senate, 1991). This subject is discussed in the Support of Older Learners section later in this chapter.

The private sector also became involved in the educational pursuits of older adults during the 1970s. The private sector took the initiative to design projects that would enable older adults to become involved in new careers, to further their knowledge so that they might continue to contribute to society. Private sector programs established to meet the needs of the aging included those of the American Association of Retired Persons (AARP), National Retired Teachers Association, National Association of Retired Federal Employees, National Association for the Spanish Speaking Elderly, National Center on the Black Aged, The National Council on the Aging, National Council of Senior Citizens, National Farmers Union, and the National Indian Council on Aging. The Edna McConnell Clark Foundation funded many research projects to determine the

best utilization of services for older adults. One of their projects included a grant to the American Association of Community and Junior Colleges to extend the career opportunities to older adults by assisting them to prepare for further careers before and after retirement (Brahce and Hunter, 1990).

As older people comprise an increasingly large percent of the U.S. population, eventually every individual and institution will be affected (Pifer and Bronte, 1986). Education can no longer be associated exclusively with young people. In fact, the number of so-called traditional college students (18–22) continues to decline, while that of non-traditional students (over age 22) is increasing. Higher education institutions have expanded efforts toward establishing non-traditional learning programs, though opportunities for and impact on older adults is still modest (Moody, 1986).

● INTELLECTUAL FUNCTIONING OF OLDER ADULTS

Maintaining intellectual functioning and capacity is one purpose of education in later life. However, a popular stereotype still prevails that decline in intellectual functioning is usual with advancing age. This stereotype was supported by a body of literature generated in the 1960s and 1970s. However, K. Warner Schaie, has stressed the importance of analyzing the limitations of the research upon which these conclusions were based (Casey, 1984).

Schaie (1975) explains that often we make the observation that older people tend to function intellectually less well than younger people. If one draws the conclusion that the intellectual maximum peak is reached in the years of young adulthood, then it is not surprising that we assume there is a decline that accelerates during old age. In taking this point of view, one would need to explore whether the developmental change in intelligence is a uniform phenomenon. Intelligence is a construct that is measured by an intelligence, or I.Q. test. The intellectual behavior of an individual is based on an index number arrived at by examining various dimensions that are important for effective mental functioning. When examining the results of these studies, one must take into consideration that people who differ by age frequently differ by other characteristics. Differences in age mean differences in life experiences. Schaie contends that it does not follow that all older adults have declined intellectually. Individual differences must be taken into consideration. There may be two explanations for these individuals differences. People who have had a significant and chronic physical illness may be disadvantaged. Also, people who grow up or live in limited and static environments (substandard housing, lack of food and clothing, limited educational opportunities) will also likely show some decrement (Schaie, 1975).

Riley and Riley (1986) have explored a series of studies on intellectual functioning that shows improvement with age under certain conditions. The researchers have found that life situations must continue to be stimulating and challenging and people must use their skills. It is also important for the social environment to provide incentives as well as opportunities for learning. Experiments involving people with a mean age of 70 have focused on intellectual skills such as spatial orientation and inductive reasoning, in which older adults have been most likely to show declines in test performance. The results of these experiments have shown that intellectual performance does improve when the social environment has provided incentives and opportunities for learning. Test subjects in many studies have shown improvement following training (Riley and Riley, 1986). Some longitudinal studies have also shown that many remarkable individuals gained in level of performance from age 70 to age 84 (Schaie, 1975).

Swindell agrees that, based on a number of recent studies, no significant loss of intellectual functioning need be associated with older adults if they are cognitively stimulated throughout their lifetime. A report from the Panel on Behavioral and Social Sciences Research, National Advisory Council on the Aging in the U.S.A., explains that education may actually slow the onset of some consequences of old age (Swindell, 1991).

The standardized tests used to measure intellectual functioning have been designed for the young, primarily for use in the schools. Riley contends there may be other areas of intelligence that do not develop until middle or later in life. These areas would include experience-based decision making, interpersonal competence, and the wisdom to evaluate, set priorities, and take appropriate action. For years, the strengths and potentials of older learners have been grossly underestimated. Only now are researchers and educators beginning to understand the importance of providing productive and rewarding roles to older citizens (Riley and Riley, 1986).

Many leading adult educators and gerontologists believe that education plays an important role in helping older adults to solve problems. Some researchers contend that education can foster older adults' self-reliance and independence by increasing their self-esteem and strengthening their mental and physical health. Education enables the older adult to cope with many practical and psychological problems in a constantly changing world. Education also helps to strengthen their contribution to society. Many older people strive for expression and learning which is provided by education (Swindell, 1991).

● PURPOSE OF EDUCATION FOR SENIORS

Howard McClusky in his presentation to the 1971 White House Conference on Aging identified five categories of older adults' educational needs: coping, expressive, contribution, influence, and transcendence. McClusky describes *coping* needs as those enabling an older person to survive by adapting to changing social conditions. Educational programming that addresses coping needs will provide older adults with the skills necessary to deal with societal change, such as basic skills in reading, writing, and math, and nutrition, health care, and family adjustment. *Expressive* needs are those met by participating in an activity for the sheer value or enjoyment of the experience. Education can provide opportunities for meeting expressive needs when programming is fun, intellectually challenging, and interesting. Participation in the arts and humanities are examples of expressive needs that lead to creativity and improved self-image. *Contribution* needs include the desires of most people to assist others with their problems and concerns. D. O. Moberg (1962) asserts that people have a need to give something that is of value to others in order to become self-fulfilled. Education may be a means by which older adults realize their potential contribution in the most meaningful ways. For example, the American Association of Retired Persons (AARP) trains widowed persons

Participation in the arts and humanities are examples of expressive needs that lead to creativity and improved self-image. (Courtesy of Chautauqua Institution)

as peer counselors to help other widowed persons cope with grief, share experiences, and seek help (Lowy and O'Connor, 1986). *Influence* needs are not unique to older adults. People of all ages have a need to make a difference in the world. Educational programming can help in the fulfillment of these needs by helping older adults to identify appropriate roles, develop personal or group skills, and provide social support to assist them in having an impact on the issues and problems. *Transcendence* needs stem from the desire for a deeper understanding of life. These needs are experienced at all ages but become more acute in the later stages of life. Education can assist older adults in meeting these needs by providing insight into people of other ages and cultures and offering a supportive setting for life review. By meeting and talking with others, older adults may examine the insights of others and come to conclusions about their own life meanings (Peterson, 1983).

Rappole (1977) holds that educational pro-

grams for older adults increase self-esteem, feelings of personal worth, and renewed social participation. Rappole reports that sixteen community colleges across Texas taking part in the Community College Program for Elderly Texans have touched and perhaps changed the lives of many older adults residing in their service area through the imaginative presentation of academic

Voices of Creative Aging

Helen H., a graduate student at age 85, tells how her pursuit of learning on a college campus keeps her mentally alive and in contact with others:

When my husband retired, we moved into a retirement community that provided a life care plan. After he died, I moved to the Phoenix area and bought a house with my son, who was recently divorced. I gave up a secure lifestyle that provided complete medical coverage for the rest of my life and made a firm decision to keep learning. I did wonder what people would think of my going back to school at my age. And they do ask me if I am still taking classes and what am I going to use it for. I answer, "For me, for me."

I will take as many courses as my stamina will allow. My goal is not knowledge. My goal is increasing my awareness as I go along. I want to keep mentally alive for my own satisfaction. I like to go up on a campus and talk to anybody, everybody. Young people know me: There's that old lady with the umbrella, they say. People ask me if I am an instructor or on staff. I tell them that I am just here going to school because I like it.

When I began my course work, I attended classes five days a week. My biggest handicap now is arthritis. I cannot tell from one time to another if I will be able to make the walk to campus. I used to be able to walk there in ten or twelve minutes. Now it will take me at least twenty, sometimes thirty minutes, and I'll have to stop part way a get my breath a little bit. But I am still going. And you know what I am learning? The more you learn, the less you know. So, it will never end.

Excerpt from Connie Goldman's "Late Bloomer" public radio series

Table 35.1
Median Years of School for People 25+ and 65+: 1950–89

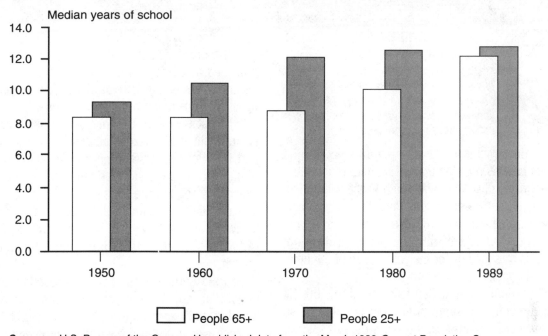

Median years of school

People 65+   People 25+

Sources: U.S. Bureau of the Census. Unpublished data from the March 1989 *Current Population Survey.*

U.S. Bureau of the Census. "Detailed Population Characteristics." *1980 Census of Population PC80-1-D1, United States Summary* (March 1984).

U.S. Bureau of the Census. "Detailed Characteristics." *1970 Census Population PC(1)-D1, United States Summary* (February 1973).

U.S. Bureau of the Census. "Characteristics of the Population." *1960 Census of Population Volume 1, Part 1, United States Summary, Chapter D* (1964).

courses, of methods and procedures in arts and crafts, and of needed social activities (Rappole, 1977).

Current U.S. elderly are the best educated and most prosperous generation of older adults in the nation's history. Older adults are mixing work, leisure, education, and personal growth in new ways. According to some experts, in the years ahead, older persons' accomplishments will be even more surprising (Thorson and Waskel, 1990).

● PROGRAM TYPES AND LEARNER'S MOTIVES

With the growing evidence that people can continue to learn at any age, one can expect the interest in lifelong learning to grow in the future. The educational attainment of the current population is changing. In the 1950s, the median years of school for people 65 and older was 9.0. By 1989, that level had reached 13.0 (U.S. Senate Special Committee on Aging and others, 1991). The rise in educational attainment is significant because

research has shown that individuals with higher levels of education are more inclined to enroll in educational programs upon retirement (Lowy and O'Connor, 1986) (see Table 35.1).

Harry Moody asserts that older adults are not necessarily interested in degree programs because tests, grades, and competition may hold little interest for them. Rather, most older adults prefer participative learning which allows them to be involved and active by drawing on their knowledge, life experiences, and interests. The most effective educational programs are those geared to the diverse interests of older learners (Moody, 1986). These programs may take many forms.

Theorists point to three types of learning that may be applied to older adult educational programs—instrumental, expressive, and adaptive. The source of the terms *instrumental* and *expressive* can be traced back to the 1951 work of Parsons, a leading sociologist of the structural-functional school of analysis. Parsons wrote of the gratification people receive when they partici-

Profiles of Productive Aging

John Gardner
Author, educator, founder

"I discovered that I like to fight! It was a big surprise. I enjoyed taking something on. It's very odd to discover that when you're in your mid-fifties. These are interesting things to learn about yourself."

Born in California in 1912, John Gardner read a great deal while he was growing up and wanted to be a novelist. During his childhood and youth in the 1920s and 1930s, there was a tremendous flowering of creativity in English-language fiction in the United States and Europe. The novelists of this era provided dashing, adventurous role models for the young men of the time, including Gardner.

At 16 Gardner entered Stanford University, but he found it difficult to engage in any of his courses, so after two years, he interrupted his studies to write. Being a novelist didn't suit him either. Enrolled again at Stanford, Gardner discovered that psychology seemed "more like the study of literature than anything else," so he "ettled" for psychology, taking his B.A. and M.A. at Stanford and his Ph.D. in the same subject at Berkeley, and then accepted a job teaching at Connecticut College, a small women's school in New London.

During World War II, Gardner worked Washington, D.C., for the Federal Communications Commission on propaganda analysis. Put in charge of six people, he began getting positive comments about his gift for management. Because he always thought of himself as a loner, he claimed: "No one could have been more surprised than I. I didn't even respect managers. It wasn't on my chart."

Later Gardner served in the Marine Corps and then in the OSS, ending up as executive officer of the OSS in Austria after the war. While in Austria he received a letter from Henry A. Murray, a professor at Harvard, saying that a job was waiting for him at Carnegie Corporation of New York. Gardner did not know anyone at Carnegie Corporation, and he thought the letter was a joke. On return to the United States, however, he met with Murray and discovered that it was *not* a joke. Gardner met the corporation's officers and took the job. He remained at Carnegie for nineteen years. For the last decade of his tenure he was Carnegie's president, and by all accounts an exceptionally fine one.

While at Carnegie, Gardner began using his writing ability again in an unexpected way: as a result of taking part in a Rockefeller Commission on the future of the nation, he wrote a slender book called *Excellence,* which has shaped the American debate about quality versus equality for almost thirty years. *Excellence* was followed within a few years by *Self-Renewal,* Gardner's reflections on the individual's need for continuing growth.

In 1965 Gardner was appointed secretary of Health, Education, and Welfare, which opened a period of learning and expansion in his life. "I didn't have the faintest inkling of the growth that lay ahead," Gardner said of his move to Washington. "I didn't know, for example, that I would enjoy politicians. I found that I was quite equal to handling myself. That there was very little likelihood that they would eat me alive. And I liked them! I found I liked journalists," Gardner added with a twinkle, "as much as you can like journalists. I understood why they have to do things that are irritating."

When Gardner stepped down from HEW, he founded an organization called Common Cause. Once it was established, Gardner saw another space in American life that needed to be filled: he created Independent Sector, an organization, for not-for-profit organizations, where those that fund and those that seek funds could come together under one umbrella and work toward the increased improvement of institutions. Both organizations are still running successfully.

Gardner left Washington for Stanford University Business School in 1990, where he was appointed Centennial Professor of Business. He continues to teach there and to write, and recently published another book, *Leadership.*

Lydia Brontë

pate in activities as they strive to meet their goals. Those activities that yield immediate gratification simply by participating in them are termed expressive. Those activities which provide delayed gratification upon completion of some future goal are termed instrumental. Adaptive learning involves acquisition of practical skills that help people to achieve what McCluskey has defined as coping needs. Basic skills in reading, writing, and computation, as well as education on good nutrition, health care, income security, and family adjustment (Lowy and O'Connor, 1986) assist older adults in adapting to an ever changing world. Instrumental and adaptive learning are overlapping concepts.

Londoner argues that instrumental educational activities should be given priority over expressive activities because they provide needed coping and growth skills (Londoner, 1990). Heimstra's earlier findings, in 1975, that older people actually prefer instrumental over expressive educational activities has strengthened Londoner's thesis, that instrumental activities provide the essential skills for survival and growth when interacting with the social environment (Londoner, 1991). The goal of instrumental education for older adults is to enhance life. Under instrumental education four types of skills may be taught: (1) financial, (2) health care, (3) work, and (4) familial (Graney and Hays, 1976).

> The rise in educational attainment is significant because research has shown that individuals with higher levels of education are more inclined to enroll in educational programs upon retirement.

Havighurst describes education as the tool for changing the learner's situation. Expressive activities provide learning in which the goal lies within the act of learning itself. In his research, Heimstra has found that a person's occupation prior to retirement, educational attainment, and previous participation in adult education programs will determine whether instrumental or expressive educational activities are preferred (Ventura and Worthy, 1982). Wirtz and Charner describe expressive motivators as the desire for general knowledge or to become more well-rounded. Instrumental motivations include a desire to learn skills for hobbies, to meet new people, to better understand community and political issues, to improve family life, to learn skills for a new job, to improve ability to read, write, speak, or do math, to help plan retirement, and to get a high school diploma, GED, or college degree.

Education may be a means by which older adults realize their potential contributions and help them implement those contributions in the most meaningful ways. (Copyright © Benjamin Porter)

In 1981, the National Center for Education Statistics reported that reasons for taking adult education courses were either job-related (suggesting instrumental inclinations) or non-job-related (more likely to include expressive inclinations). Males, 55–64, showed preference for job-related activities, and females, 55–64 and 65 and older, showed preference for non-job-related educational activities. Londoner argues that both types of educational activity, expressive and instrumental, are important to older adults and should be used in assessing how best to meet the needs of the older adult learner (Lowy and O'Connor, 1986).

● INSTITUTIONS AND EXEMPLARY PROGRAMS

Colleges, Universities, and Community Colleges

In the 1990s institutions of higher education are confronted with difficult economic challenges. Since the 1970s there has been a significant decline in the proportion of full-time, traditional-aged students (18–22 years of age). Along with this decline in the traditional-aged students, costs for providing education continue to rise (Romaniuk, 1983). In the 1980s educators predicted that the decline in enrollment of traditional-aged students would also have an impact on the use of facilities, need for faculty, and the relevance of curriculum (Peterson, 1981). Today, institutions of higher education may not be having as many problems in terms of enrollment as once expected. Non-traditional-aged students in their thirties and forties are making up for the decline in enrollment of traditional-aged students.

Older students are welcomed in the regular academic programs, but the 30- and 40-year-old students have outnumbered them considerably (Thorson and Waskell, 1991).

Fischer has found that until the past ten to fifteen years, older adult education was an issue of speculative discussion rather than practice. Currently, higher education institutions have begun to recognize that the college campus is no longer just for the traditional-aged student. Fischer contends that there is a new, creative, and innovative spirit at work in higher education focusing on adults 55 and older, as well as students in their twenties to fifties (Fischer, 1992).

Degree and Non-Degree Programs

In a 1976 survey conducted by the Academy for Educational Development (AED) of a selected sample of 814 colleges and universities believed to be offering programs for older adults throughout the United States, researchers found that colleges and universities offering educational programs for older adults fell into three categories: (1) courses specifically designed for older adults; (2) regular or continuing education courses either for credit or on an auditing basis provided free or reduced tuition to older adults; and (3) courses of special interest to older adults offered through a continuing education program (Scanlon, 1978).

In 1981, a Louis Harris survey sponsored by The National Council on the Aging (NCOA) found that adults 65 and over are most often enrolled in older adult educational programs at colleges and universities as opposed to their place of business, high school, community or senior center, church, library, museum, or by correspondence. In another survey conducted by the National Center for Education Statistics (NCES) in 1981 concerning the location preferred by older adults, NCES reported that 32 percent of the courses taken by persons 65 and over were taken in educational settings: elementary or high schools, two- and four-year colleges, business, trade or vocational schools, and particularly at community colleges (Ventura and Worthy, 1982).

The National Center for Education Statistics reported in fall 1987 that 238,029 students 50 to 64 years of age, and 94,875 students 65 and older, were enrolled in undergraduate credit programs at higher education institutions throughout the United States. At the same time 2,078 students 50 to 64 years of age, and 272 students 65 and older, were enrolled in first-professional programs at higher education institutions. Additionally, 51,591 students 50 to 64 years of age, and 7,494 students 65 and older, were enrolled in graduate programs at higher education institutions (National Center for Education Statistics, 1991) (see Table 35.2).

In 1989, the League for Innovation in the Community College and the American Association of Retired Persons (AARP), conducted a national survey of league member institutions (community colleges). From the approximately 600 community colleges responding to the survey (Doucette and Ventura-Merkel, 1991) the researchers found: (1) most older adult educational programs come under organizational units such as community services, adult education, or short courses; (2) the majority of the colleges conduct non-credit courses with fees ranging between $25 and $50 per course; (3) some colleges allow students 60 and older to audit credit courses with fees waived; (4) half of the League colleges have a special program and/or center for older adults at their college; (5) three-fourths of the colleges reported offering non-credit classes to older adults; and (6) full-term credit courses are often taught at off-campus sites (Charles and Bartunek, 1989).

Catherine Ventura-Merkel, senior education specialist in the special projects section of AARP, and Don Doucette, associate director of the League for Innovation in the Community College, reported that the types of courses offered in the community colleges were the traditional classes in exercise and nutrition, avocational arts, crafts, hobbies, and trips; and financial management programs on retirement and estate planning. The courses least likely to be offered were, in fact, the ones demographers and other analysts contended were most needed by the older adult population. These courses included skills training for second and third occupations, personal development courses, and health care programs. Ventura-Merkel and Doucette concluded that only a small number of community colleges now offer programs and services designed for retired groups of seniors. Colleges reported that lack of funding was a major obstacle in offering more programs and services for older adults. Ventura-Merkel and Doucette proposed that the most logical explanation for the few programs offered for older adults by community colleges was that this particular population did not realize what community colleges could offer to them. Older adults were only likely to demand such programs when they began to realize their need for new skills, which would assist them in adapting to a fast-changing world and to the personal changes of aging and retirement (Doucette and Ventura-Merkel, 1991).

Charles and Bartunek identified several community colleges that provide outstanding programs and services designed specifically for older adults. One example was Cuyahoga Community College in Warrensville Township, Ohio, which provides a comprehensive range of educational services, including seminars, workshops, and special events; courses in the humanities, social, behavioral, and biological sciences; and courses on a variety of special interest topics related to health and well-being in the later years. The program, designed for adults 55 and older and offered in forty locations throughout the county where older adults live or meet, is held in cooperation with the Office on Aging, Title III nutrition sites, and community and senior centers and residences. A special program, Elder's Campus, is a day-long, weekly program held on the eastern and western campuses of the college. The participants in that program assist in planning and implementation, serve as the advisory committee, and function as teaching faculty (Charles and Bartunek, 1989).

Overcoming Barriers to Participation in College and University Programs

Many kinds of barriers, real or perceived, may prevent older adults from participating in educational opportunities. These barriers may be categorized as situational, dispositional, and institutional. Situational barriers may include a lack of mobility or knowledge about available educational opportunities or the cost of programs. These barriers pertain to one's situation at the time of the educational offering. The dispositional barriers include how the person views himself or herself as a learner. For example, many adults believe they are simply too old to learn. Some older adults have limited educational backgrounds. As a result of this limitation the older adult may have a lack of interest in further education, feelings of insecurity concerning the ability

to learn, and lack of ability to see the need for education at this time in his or her life. Institutional barriers are practices or procedures within an institution that may discourage participation. Inflexible schedules, expensive fees, inappropriate course offerings, complicated application and registration procedures, inaccessible buildings, and lack of communication concerning what educational opportunities are available are all examples of institutional barriers (Cross, 1981).

Ruth Weinstock believes institutions can remove many barriers to education for older adults. For example, admissions procedures and registration for college credit courses is a difficult experience for all students and should be modified specifically for the older adult learner. When an applicant has to request permission to audit a course from a professor, the professor's office location, telephone number, and office hours should be readily available. Weinstock suggests other modifications for the older adult learner such as campus orientation and publication of an older student handbook (Weinstock, 1978).

John Scanlon cited Fordham University's College at Sixty as an example of a college reaching out to older adults to enroll them in credit classes. College at Sixty's enrollment is open to college and non-college graduates alike who express an interest in reading and demonstrate the ability to undertake college-level work. Upon successful completion of four seminars offered by the College at Sixty program, a student is awarded a certificate entitling him or her to enter Fordham's College of Liberal Arts without having to meet any of the other admission requirements (Scanlon, 1976).

There are many other strategies that may be used by educational programs for increasing older adult's participation: reduced or waived tuition, courses designed specifically for older adults, support services (orientation workshops and counseling), and outreach strategies to include older adults.

As the need for educational programs for older adults continues to grow, educational institutions and community organizations are attempting to meet these demands by developing programs to serve this special population. At many institutions these barriers are simply not understood; there-

Table 35.2
Total Enrollment in Institutions of Higher Education, by Level, Sex, Age, and Attendance Status of Student: Fall 1987

Attendance status and age of student	All levels			Undergraduate		
	Total	Men	Women	Total	Men	Women
1	2	3	4	5	6	7
All students	12,766,642	5,932,056	6,834,586	11,046,235	5,068,457	5,977,778
Under 18	207,085	87,168	119,917	206,271	86,732	119,539
18 and 19	2,696,652	1,253,984	1,442,568	2,695,892	1,253,615	1,442,277
20 and 21	2,392,038	1,168,820	1,223,218	2,375,398	1,160,289	1,215,109
22 to 24	2,025,725	1,078,235	947,490	1,724,576	915,014	809,562
25 to 29	1,839,916	926,756	913,160	1,327,828	639,577	688,251
30 to 34	1,242,344	558,441	683,903	921,165	386,317	534,848
35 to 39	882,763	337,774	544,989	647,596	231,380	416,216
40 to 49	872,120	288,231	583,889	654,007	209,118	444,889
50 to 64	291,698	98,263	193,435	239,029	80,086	157,943
65 and over	102,641	38,507	54,134	94,875	33,904	60,971
Age unkonwn	213,660	95,877	117,783	160,598	72,425	88,173
Full-time	7,231,085	3,610,888	3,620,197	6,462,549	3,163,676	3,298,873
Under 18	113,938	48,513	65,425	113,659	48,348	65,311
18 and 19	2,331,202	1,088,972	1,242,220	2,330,703	1,088,703	1,242,000
20 and 21	1,919,332	948,534	970,798	1,905,791	941,234	964,557
22 to 24	1,251,794	716,088	535,706	1,034,268	590,066	444,202
25 to 29	727,279	412,056	315,223	462,354	246,357	215,997
30 to 34	371,825	181,798	190,027	248,644	107,274	141,370
35 to 39	217,470	90,852	126,618	148,050	53,779	94,271
40 to 49	170,162	62,796	107,366	119,511	41,946	77,565
50 to 64	38,224	14,556	23,668	27,116	10,122	16,994
65 and over	9,330	5,463	3,867	6,565	3,209	3,356
Age unknown	30,529	41,250	39,269	65,888	32,638	33,250
Part-time	5,535,557	2,321,168	3,214,389	4,583,686	1,904,781	2,678,905
Under 18	93,147	38,655	54,492	92,512	38,384	54,228
18 and 19	365,450	165,012	200,438	365,189	164,912	200,277
20 and 21	472,706	220,286	252,420	469,607	219,055	250,552
22 to 24	773,931	362,147	411,784	690,308	324,948	365,360
25 to 29	1,112,637	514,700	597,937	865,474	393,220	472,254
30 to 34	870,519	376,643	493,876	672,521	279,043	393,478
35 to 39	665,293	246,922	418,371	499,546	177,601	321,945
40 to 49	701,958	225,435	476,523	534,496	167,172	367,324
50 to 64	253,474	83,707	169,767	210,913	69,964	140,949
65 and over	93,311	33,044	60,297	88,310	30,695	57,515
Age unknown	133,131	54,617	78,514	94,710	39,787	54,923

First-professional			Graduate		
Total	Men	Women	Total	Men	Women
8	9	10	11	12	13
258,332	170,129	98,203	1,452,075	693,470	758,605
47	33	14	767	403	364
194	106	88	566	263	303
7,269	4,102	3,167	9,371	4,429	4,942
99,604	53,181	36,463	201,505	100,040	101,465
95,381	63,701	31,680	416,707	223,478	193,229
33,065	20,691	12,374	288,114	151,433	136,681
16,159	9,368	5,791	219,008	97,026	121,982
9,898	4,959	4,939	208,215	74,154	134,061
2,078	1,114	964	51,591	17,063	34,522
272	156	116	7,494	4,447	3,047
4,325	2,718	1,607	48,737	20,734	28,003
241,807	153,668	88,139	526,729	293,544	233,185
45	31	44	234	134	100
190	103	87	309	166	143
7,170	4,037	3,133	6,371	3,263	3,108
96,885	61,446	35,439	120,641	64,576	56,065
86,390	57,807	28,583	178,535	107,892	70,643
26,779	16,682	10,097	96,402	57,842	38,560
12,130	6,968	5,162	57,290	30,105	27,185
6,737	3,296	3,441	43,914	17,554	26,360
1,261	683	578	9,847	3,751	6,096
197	113	84	2,568	2,141	427
4,023	2,502	1,521	10,618	6,120	4,498
26,525	16,461	10,064	925,346	399,926	525,420
2	2	0	533	269	264
4	3	1	257	97	180
99	65	34	3,000	1,166	1,334
2,759	1,735	1,024	80,864	35,464	45,400
8,991	5,894	3,097	238,172	115,586	122,586
6,286	4,009	2,377	191,712	93,591	98,121
4,029	2,400	1,629	161,718	66,921	94,797
3,161	1,663	1,498	164,301	56,600	107,701
817	431	386	41,744	13,312	28,432
75	43	32	4,926	2,306	2,520
302	216	86	38,119	14,614	22,505

Source: U.S. Department of Education, National Center for Education Statistics. Integrated Postsecondary Education Data System. "Fall Enrollment, 1987" survey. (This table was prepared in March 1990).

Education can provide opportunities for meeting expressive needs when programming is fun, challenging, and interesting. (Copyright © Benjamin Porter)

fore, efforts to overcome them are not universal (Peterson, 1983).

Elderhostel

Elderhostel is an international educational network providing opportunities for adults over 60 to live with other students and participate in noncredit educational activities on college campuses and in other educational settings (Gelfand, 1988).

Founded in 1975 by Martin Knowlton as a short term residential college program, Elderhostel originally operated under the auspices of the Center for Continuing Education at the University of New Hampshire in Durham. The first elder-hostel programs in 1975 were run by a small group of colleges and universities in New Hampshire, with 220 older adults participating in course offerings. In 1977, Elderhostel became an independent, nonprofit organization with the full support of the University. A national office was established in Boston to coordinate all Elderhostel activities. In 1979, a computerized national mailing list system

was installed, and the national office began registering participants for any Elderhostel program anywhere in the country by phone or mail (O'Donnell and Berkeley, 1980).

Since 1986 Elderhostel has grown at a rate of 15 percent to 25 percent. The program is operating in more than 1,800 sites in the United States and Canada and in 45 countries worldwide. The enrollment averages 250,000 annually (U.S. Senate Committee on Aging, 1991). The sponsoring institutions are largely four-year colleges and universities, but environmental study centers, scientific research stations, and conference centers also host programs. Variations in programming also allow the participants to bring their recreational vehicles to programs offered in state and national parks in the United States (Goggin, 1991).

Elderhostel's international activity provides opportunities for Elderhostelers to study abroad. The catalogue of courses for studying abroad is published three times a year. Catalogues of the courses in Canada and the United States are published four times annually (Special Committee on Aging, U.S. Senate, 1991).

Participants are responsible for their room and board, transportation, and course fees. The cost of an average one-week stay is $275 in the United States, which includes a campus dorm room, cafeteria meals, three college-level courses, and extracurricular activities (Goggin, 1991).

AARP's Institute of Lifetime Learning grants two hundred scholarship awards annually for attendance at Elderhostel programs in the United States. Applicants must be 60 years or older, a member of AARP, and have given a significant amount of volunteer time in their communities. Special consideration is given to those who could have difficulty paying the Elderhostel fee. Applications are available from the AARP Fulfillment, Elderhostel Application Form D 12309, P.O. Box 2400, Long Beach, CA 90801.

A notable aspect of Elderhostel is that none of the courses offered take old age as the subject matter. This is based on the view that courses that deal with aging teach people to be old (Peterson, 1983). The program mainly focuses on the expressive needs of students, using a liberal arts curriculum that is preselected by the institution's administration (Lowy and O'Connor, 1986). The courses are generally designed for a one-week period. Three courses are offered in each of the one week programs (Gelfand, 1988). The courses do not require homework, grades, or a prior knowledge of the subject matter. The noncredit course offerings enable students to participate for the sheer enjoyment of learning (Goggin, 1991).

Elderhostel programs range from exploring the Alaska mountain range to studying the culture and society of China. At Denali National Park, location of Mt. McKinley, Elderhostel class sessions include lectures, slide presentations, and guided tours of the wildlife, natural history, history and management, and glaciers and glacial geology of Denali. Participants are housed in two-room cabins on the banks of the Nenana River.

Since 1986 Elderhostel has grown at a rate of 15 percent to 25 percent. The program is operating in more than 1,800 sites in the United States and Canada and in 45 countries worldwide. The enrollment averages 250,000 annually.

The Elderhostel program in China is organized in cooperation with the Chinese American Educational Exchange (CAEE) based at the City University of New York. The "Chinese Culture and Society" program is designed so participants may achieve a deeper understanding of the Chinese people, their lives, and their cultures as reflected in the differences dictated by the history and traditions of the various geographical areas in which they live. The programs are offered in the provinces of Hebei and Shandong. Each program is three weeks long and held in university settings. All programs offer the opportunity for observing both rural and city life and for studying a large, "modern" city and a smaller, ancient city, as well as the chance to view various aspects of country life through visits to agricultural villages.

An example of Elderhostel programming in the continental United States is the "Colorado's Colorful History: Peaks, Poems, and Pokes" program located at Colorado Mountain College Springwood Valley Center in Glenwood Springs. Participants explore the history of Aspen, Redstone, Markie, and Glenwood Springs through art, cowboy poetry, old photographs, and field trips.

These programs are just a few of the examples of diverse and stimulating educational opportunities available through Elderhostel.

Learning in Retirement Institutes (LRIs)

A learning in retirement institute (LRI) is an organization of retirement-age learners dedicated to meeting the educational needs of its members. LRIs generally fall into one of two general program categories: institution-driven or member-driven. Francis A. Meyers of the Association of Learning in Retirement Organizations in the Western Region (ALIROW), a consortium of LRIs, defines the institution-driven model as an educational offering traditionally designed by professional staff and taught by the regular higher education faculty. The member-driven model is developed, designed, and taught by the members with the cooperative sponsorship of a higher education institution. The members also take an active role in governing the organization, with elected directors and officers (Meyers, 1987).

A set of common characteristics has been identified in LRIs: (1) LRIs are typically designed to meet the educational needs of older adults that live within commuting distance of the program; (2) the offerings are varied and cover a broad spectrum, with the majority consisting of college-level material; (3) LRIs are sponsored by accredited colleges or universities, by institutions or organizations working in collaboration with an accredited higher education institution, or by an organization or institution sponsoring a comparable college- or university-level program; (4) the institutes are nonprofit organizations charging a modest tuition or membership fee; (5) a needs-based scholarship program is available; (6) affirmative action goals are of utmost importance; (7) members often serve as volunteer teachers or course leaders; (8) social, cultural, and physical experience are a part of the offerings; and (9) participants are encouraged to be involved in planning, evaluating, teaching, and (when appropriate) administering the program (Fischer, 1992).

The New School for Social Research in New York City is often cited as the beginning the LRI movement in 1962 when it established the Institute for Retired Professionals (IRP). During the 1960s and 1970s colleges and universities began replicating or adapting the IRP model. Many national conferences have been devoted to the institute concept, and the number of LRIs is steadily increasing (Elderhostel Institute Network, 1992).

In 1989, Elderhostel established the Institute Network to advance and promote LRIs (Goggin, 1991). This voluntary association of independent institutes is dedicated to extending the institute concept to new people in new institutions and strengthening and supporting the effectiveness of established institutes. In 1992, there were over 130 LRIs in existence in the United States (Elderhostel Institute Network, 1992).

The LRI programs include core courses and classes in the humanities and liberal arts. Literature, history, public affairs, and music and art appreciation have proven to be most popular among participants. Many times the core curriculum is supplemented by classes in computer science, foreign languages, painting, and writing. Recreational and physical fitness programs are also offered. Classes are not limited to the traditional classroom setting. Cultural events and field trips, including one-day or overnight travel to museums and historical sites, are part of the LRI's offerings (Lipman, 1992).

During the past few years the Institute Network began offering national study/travel opportunities. These programs include such opportunities as exploration of the myriad aspects of Rome; a naturalist's study in Costa Rica, a naturalist's paradise; architectural studies in London and Dublin; the study of European unification, focusing on the position of smaller countries like Belgium and Holland; and numerous other ventures (Elderhostel Institute Network, 1992).

The New School for Social Research in New York City is often cited as the beginning the LRI movement in 1962 when it established the Institute for Retired Professionals (IRP).

There are many outstanding LRIs in the United States and Canada today. One example is the College for Seniors, established in 1988 at the North Carolina Center for Creative Retirement, University of North Carolina at Asheville (UNCA). This member-driven institute provides life enrichment courses to anyone 55 and over who pays the required membership fee (some scholarships are available when needed). There are no educational prerequisites and no exams or grades. The program was founded on the desire of adults to pursue learning for pleasure and stimulation, and to do so in the company of others similarly motivated. Participants are involved in more than taking classes. From teaching to working on a newsletter, from registering participants to designing curriculum, there is much to become involved in. The curriculum provides a variety of exciting courses in almost every field—music, literature, history, fitness and wellness, art, religion, environmental issues, psychology, philosophy, computer science, political science, foreign language, and current events of interest to the older adult population. The College for Seniors is an organization that welcomes participant involvement in the shaping and creating of its offerings and thus is able to offer a full and varied program because of its members, people who give freely of their time and knowledge.

In addition to the College for Seniors, the Center for Creative Retirement conducts programs in leadership, intergenerational collaboration, research, volunteerism, wellness, and retirement planning. The Senior Academy for Intergenerational Learning (SAIL) matches retired civic and professional leaders with undergraduate students and UNCA faculty to work together on learning projects. The SAIL "Senior Fellows" volunteers share their time and expertise with students. For example, senior adults work with university athletes sharing career interests, and retired physicians serve as mentors for premedical students. The SAIL program provides an opportunity for retirees to continue their contributions to their professions and community (Special Committee on Aging, U.S. Senate, 1991).

The Leadership Asheville Seniors (LAS) program provides an intensive learning experience for its older adult participants. Local political leaders, agency directors, and civic leaders share information about community issues through lectures and problem-solving sessions, enabling the LAS participants to improve their leadership skills and to contribute meaningfully to the community.

The life journey program provides outreach humanities programming through reading and group discussion led by trained volunteers at churches, community centers, and other sites in the rural areas of western North Carolina. In cooperation with the National Endowment for the Humanities, the center provides other humanities programs led by paid, trained scholars, including a program entitled "The Carolina Special: Railroads Through the Carolinas and Beyond as Reflected in Literature and History," cosponsored with public libraries in North Carolina, South Carolina, Tennessee, and Viriginia.

The center's retirement planning program offers corporations and individuals retirement seminars. The research institute has studied the economic and social impact of in-migrating retirees in the western North Carolina and conducted a national survey of older adult educational programs. The latter study provides a national perspective on certain forms of educational programs for older adults in the United States, examining critical variables in the success of these programs and highlighting organizational features that might lend themselves to replication in other programs, whether already existing, in the planning process, or simply as ideas in the minds of senior leaders, college administrators, or administrators of community organization.

The center serves as a laboratory for North Carolina and the nation by designing, implementing, and evaluating innovative educational programs, and its long-range mission is to encourage an age-integrated society.

In addition to the College for Seniors, the Center for Creative Retirement conducts programs in leadership, intergenerational collaboration, research, volunteerism, wellness, and retirement planning.

Duke University's Institute for Learning in Retirement (DILR), established in 1977, is another good example of programming for people aged 50 and older. Older adults participate in peer-taught academic classes in a year-round program. Numerous benefits are available to students enrolled in the program including use of the library, swimming pool, language labs, and the faculty dining room. The class offerings range from drama to religion to literature to science. Approximately forty courses are offered each semester. These classes meet once a week for ninety minutes over a twelve-week period. The class offerings are determined by faculty availability, student interest, and variety. Membership in the program is $100 per semester, entitling students to enroll in as many as five classes. These students volunteer in such activities as teaching some of the courses, leading study groups, acting as teaching assistants, and assisting with administrative tasks (Fischer, 1991).

Another example is the Renaissance Society at California State University, Sacramento. Established in 1986, the program provides a number of study discussion groups on life-enrichment topics where each member, or a team of members, is encouraged to investigate the topic under study and participate in an informal discussion, with a coordinator presiding. There is a writer's group meeting in the homes of members, a group studying the opportunities of aging in today's society, and field trips enhancing the learning taking place in the classroom. Various study groups are led by member volunteers. Each semester opens with a free public forum featuring a speaker and the opportunity to learn more about the purposes of the Renaissance Society, the curriculum for the next semester, and procedures for joining. No educational background is required for admission, and an annual membership fee covers the courses offered during the year, as well as a campus parking permit (The Renaissance Society, 1992).

Each LRI has many similar and many unique characteristics, reflecting the creativity of its participants.

Certification

While LRI participants are pursuing educational courses for the sheer enjoyment of learning, some older adults require programs to retrain them for second and even third careers. Certification programs provide this type of training.

As noted frequently in this almanac, the demographic profile of the United States is changing.

Fewer younger workers are projected to be available, and many employees may increasingly hire older workers to meet their labor requirements (Gelfand, 1988). Many of these positions require employees to have specific skills and certification in order to meet job challenges.

Many colleges and universities are establishing special programs and making the older learner's transition back into the educational environment more appealing as well as preparing them for new careers or new job challenges. One such program is Kingsborough Community College's "My Turn." This special tuition-free college education program has waived all admission requirements with the exception that students must be residents of New York State and 65 years of age by the first day of class. Many students are working toward a general equivalency diploma (GED) while others are working toward an associate degree (Special Committee on Aging, 1991).

The University of Massachusetts, Boston campus, offers a program to qualified students over 60 who are preparing to serve as professionals in the fields of gerontology. The educational backgrounds of the students vary. Not all have high school diplomas, and only one-third have college degrees. The university has sought diversity in the backgrounds of the students as well as age and ethnicity. Classes are scheduled during daytime hours and are held in easily accessible buildings. Tutoring services and administrative assistance is provided to students when needed. Upon completion of two terms of intensive study, an equivalent of thirty undergraduate hours, students receive a State Certificate in Gerontology. Graduates of the program have found job opportunities in government agencies serving the aging, nursing homes, working for political candidates, and administering programs for the aging (Special Committee on Aging, U.S. Senate, 1991). These programs all facilitate job-market competitiveness for older adults.

The Role of Public Libraries

Many older adults find themselves with increased leisure time, reduced income, and declining health at a time when their information needs are increasing. As they become more socially isolated, older adults have fewer opportunities to seek answers from daily communication with other people and other traditional sources (Hales, 1985). The public library is a community service that may fill this void.

The older adult is one of many publics that the library serves on a regular basis. Established to serve the community as a whole, from preschoolers to the oldest citizens, public libraries purpose to facilitate informal self-education of all people in the community; to enhance the subjects being undertaken in formal education; to meet the informational needs of the total population; to support education, civic, and cultural activities of groups; and to encourage recreation and constructive use of leisure time (Hendrickson, 1976).

Library services for older adults is not a new concept. The movement to provide direct library services to the older adult began in the 1950s, when the Adult Education Department of the Cleveland Public Library established its "Live Long and Like It Library Club" for adults over 60. A study and discussion group, the club began with a mailing list of 50 and grew to 1,600 participants. As a result of Cleveland's success, similar programs were established across the country. In 1956 Congress passed the first Library Services Act (LSA), which recognized the need for libraries to expand their community service. Preparations for the 1961 White House Conference on Aging spurred an intense effort by libraries to serve older adults. Between 1957 and 1961, the American Library Association (ALA) established the Adult Services Division and appointed a permanent Committee on Library Services to the Aging (renamed Library Service to an Aging Population in the 1970s). In 1957, the Office of Education funded the committee to conduct a survey of library services to older adults. The study revealed many libraries offering special services to older adults, such as (1) supplying books, (2) publicizing materials for the older adult, (3) providing services to home-bound, and (4) working with other agencies serving older adults (Turock, 1982).

In 1964 Congress approved amendments to the Library Services and Construction Act (LSCA), formerly called the Library Services Act (LSA), which provided funding for the construction of libraries. This legislation and funding enabled libraries to alter their physical structure to meet the needs of the physically disabled and older adults. Title I of the LSCA also became the primary funding source for the initiation of library programs for older adults. LSCA was also responsible for funding large-print collections and services. In 1966 the thirty-year-old Pratt-Smoot Act was amended to provide a wider range of large-print materials and to make more persons eligible to participate including older adults who were unable to use conventional books (Turock, 1982).

Title III of the Older Americans Act increased library services to the homebound and institutionalized older adult. Even though library services for older adults were being developed and implemented across the United States, many librarians did not have the educational background and training to provide these services. In 1965 Title II-B of the Higher Education Act provided funding for workshops, institutes, and research programs to provide the special training needed (Turock, 1982).

In preparation for the 1971 White House Conference on Aging, the U.S. Office of Education and the Cleveland Public Library conducted an extensive study of library services, "National Survey of Library Services to the Aging," which revealed that library services for older adults had not increased at a pace consistent with the increase in the older adult population. The researchers concluded that development had been inhibited by a lack of recognition of services to older adults in federal, state, and local library plans. As a result of the survey findings, an amendment was added to LSCA through Title IV, Older Readers Service, passed into law in 1973. This title provided a federal program of grants to the states for older readers' services, but it has never been funded. There are several factors contributing to the miscarriage of the program, including the failure of the library community to instigate its resolution or push its appropriations (Turock, 1982).

The 1981 White House Conference on Aging was nonproductive in terms of library service to the aging. Conference coordinators denied the American Library Association's request for an official delegate and would not permit the association to distribute its literature. Even though the 1981 White House Conference was disappointing, some progress has been made in library services for older adults (Turock, 1982).

For many years special programs from public and state libraries have provided library services to the aging via bookmobiles, cable TV, and

---

Preparations for the 1961 White House Conference on Aging spurred an intense effort by libraries to serve older adults. Between 1957 and 1961, the American Library Association (ALA) established the Adult Services Division and appointed a permanent Committee on Library Services to the Aging (renamed Library Service to an Aging Population in the 1970s).

---

books-by-mail delivery. Many bookmobiles are more user-friendly, with hydraulic lifts to raise patrons into the bookmobile. Books-by-Mail connects the older learner to selected readings, including large print materials, by way of free, prepaid mailings. Regular, on-site library programs enable older adults to participate in discussions, films, videos, arts and crafts demonstrations, exhibits of older adults' hobbies, concerts or forums on consumer issues and health concerns, and life enrichment programs. Many of the library programs are brought directly to retirement and senior centers, while transportation is provided to the library for other programs (Casey, 1984).

A service available from The National Council on the Aging is an outstanding packaged educational program for older adults offered through public libraries, "Discovery Through the Humanities," described in the humanities program section of this chapter.

Librarians and volunteers make visits to the homebound, to residents of nursing homes, and to other institutional settings to provide reading materials and many times to read to their audience. Talking books and closed-captioned video tapes are also provided by public libraries. These materials are excellent resources for the visually- and hearing-impaired older adult (Institute of Lifetime Learning, 1991).

Public libraries also serve as an information and referral service for educational opportunities. Older adults may acquire information on where to learn a specific skill, who teaches desired courses, where to get a specific type of educational program, and what the eligibility requirements are for the program (Turock, 1982).

Many library programs are available to older adults today. The Brooklyn Public Library's Service to the Aging (SAGE) program for older adults is a nationally recognized example of what can be accomplished (Hales-Mabry, 1990). The SAGE project's older adult volunteer program sends older people into the community to establish library-based senior groups, organize educational programs using films, lectures, and television, oversee trips to cultural events, and expand the homebound service. These volunteers recruit older adults to teach minicourses on crafts, art, music, and photography. They also organize intergenerational projects that bring older adults in touch with young children (Turock, 1982).

The Monroe County Library System (MCLS) in Rochester, New York, provides a program of live entertainment for and by older adults. Older adult performers include magicians, pianists, and collectors. MCLS also helps older adults learn advocacy skills on their own behalf. The older adult advocates present their views to local, state, and federal offices on various issues. MCLS publishes a directory of services for older adults, nursing homes, and housing for seniors and a newsletter, *Sunburst*, written by older adult MCLS patrons (Turock, 1982).

As the older adult population grows, so does the emphasis to educate librarians to provide library and information services for older adults to meet the needs of the aging as well as the needs of their service providers (Turock, 1982).

In 1987, the American Library Association's Library Services to an Aging Population Committee of its Reference and Adult Services Division prepared "Guidelines of a Library Service to Older Adults," emphasizing the growing importance of designing library services for older adults as this population grows in numbers. Libraries can meet those needs by exhibiting and promoting a positive attitude toward older adults. Information and resources on aging and its implications must be promoted to older adults, their family members, professionals in gerontology, and persons interested in the aging process. The library services provided must reflect cultural, ethnic, and economic differences. The potential of older adults (paid or volunteers) as liaisons should be utilized in reaching other older adults and as a resource in intergenerational programming. Older adults should be employed at profes-

sional and support staff levels for general library work and older adult programs. Older adults should be involved in the planning and design of library services and programs for the entire community as well as older adults. A good working relationship should be promoted and developed with other agencies serving older adults. Preretirement and later-life career alternatives programs, services, and information should be made available. Library design improvements and access to transportation should be implemented to facilitate library use by older adults. The library's planning and evaluation process should incorporate the changing needs of older adults. An aggressive funding effort should be implemented and a portion of the library budget committed to older adult programs and services (American Library Association, 1987).

Humanities Programs

Humanities programs are learning experiences based on the study of history, literature, philosophy, and criticism of the arts. "Lifelong Learning for an Aging Society," prepared by the U.S. Senate's Special Committee on Aging (1991) cited David Shuldiner's definition of humanities programs as educational programs that explore and interpret the human experience. Shuldiner contended that good humanities programs involve participants in lively discussion, critical thinking, and life review, all of which add information and insight to the topics at hand.

A major development in this direction took place in 1976 with the establishment of the "Senior Center Humanities Program" by The National Council on the Aging (NCOA) with a grant from the National Endowment for the Humanities (NEH). The program was designed to provide life enrichment and self-discovery through the humanities (Lowy and O'Connor, 1986). The program became known as "Discovery Through the Humanities" in 1984 and is organized around informal discussion groups initiated in local communities.

NCOA lends their "Discovery" materials on literature, history, philosophy, and the arts to any group or organization that serves older adults. Anthologies are used as a basis for discussion, inviting participants to explore the works of distinguished writers and artists, to relate what they read and hear to their own experiences, and to consider issues of profound meaning for every generation. At the local community level, older adults meet on a regular basis to reflect on the readings and to share their responses with the guidance of discussion leaders. Today, the NCOA humanities program is offered free of charge at libraries, community colleges, retirement communities, senior centers, nutrition sites, nursing homes, adult day care centers, housing complexes, churches, and synagogues. For a small fee to organizations, NCOA provides the program materials, discussion leader guides, publicity materials, and audiotapes for conducting the program (The National Council on the Aging, 1991).

Organization of the program requires a volunteer discussion group leader, a place for up to twenty people to meet, eight to twelve weekly meetings, and a promotional program to recruit participants. The humanities program encourages new interest in cultural, educational, and social activities that translate into expanded participation in community events (The National Council on the Aging, 1991). The "Discovery Through the Humanities" programs develop several themes: (1) We Got There on the Train, (2) A Family Album, (3) Americans and the Land, (4) The Remembered Past: 1914–1945, (5) Work and Life, (6) The Search for Meaning, (7) In the Old Ways, (8) The Heritage of the Future, (9) Words and Music, (10) Exploring Values, (11) Portraits and Pathways, (12) Art in Life, (13) The Family, the Courts, and the Constitution, and (14) Roll On, River.

With the Federation of State Humanities Councils, Esther Mackintosh compiled *Humanities Programming for Older Adults*, which reported that many state humanities councils have begun to recruit older adults into humanities programs. Mackintosh contended that older adults are a ready and growing audience for these programs; they have the time to devote to humanities activities as participants and volunteers, and they are a responsive and interested audience because they seek out intellectual stimulation. The lifetime of experience that older adults bring to these programs enriches and enlivens them. No other age group can provide the oral history as older adults may. Older individuals have political influence, but as a large group that political influence becomes magnified. Homebound or institutionalized older adults may also benefit

from the intellectual and social qualities these humanities programs offer (Mackintosh, 1988).

In New York City, for the past twenty-three years, Hospital Audiences, Inc. (HAI) has brought arts and humanities programming to over 7 million people including the frail elderly. HAI is supported by city, state, and federal agencies as well as the private sector. HAI has three components: (1) community oriented, (2) institution oriented, and 3) advocacy. The institutional component brings live music, dance, and theater by professional artists into institutions. Its Senior Composers Program enables composers to share their talents and experiences as performers for the aged, and its community-oriented access program provides an opportunity for thousands of homebound frail elderly to attend cultural events throughout the year. These events include the New York Philharmonic and Metropolitan Opera concerts in the parks, the Delacorte Theater, and Macy's Fourth of July Fireworks and Thanksgiving Day Parade. Daytime appearances of renowned artists at auditoriums selected for accessibility are also available. In its advocacy role, HAI has formed the Arts Access Task Force, a consortium between HAI, the Arts and Business Council, and the New York Foundation for the Arts. The mission of the task force is to make the arts more accessible to people with disabilities. A guide to neighborhood restaurants, movies, and other leisure sites for and by consumers with disabilities, *Access NY*, is available from the HAI office (HAI, 1992).

Another unique program is Museum One, offering arts and humanities programming to thousands of older adults 60 years of age and older in the Washington, D.C., area, at more than one hundred facilities, including nursing homes, retirement communities, senior centers, adult day care centers, and senior apartment complexes. Programming includes courses on impressionism, American heritage and traditions, Renaissance artists, modern art, Afro-American art, art and aging, American women artists, and Latin-American art. Special courses and workshops are designed for intense geriatric rehabilitation of the mentally ill, hearing impaired, and the blind and visually impaired older adults in hospitals, senior centers, and retirement communities.

For professionals working with older adults, Museum One has developed educational and

Profiles of Productive Aging

J. William Fulbright
Senator

"I never had any idea of being a politician."

J. William Fulbright, senator from Arkansas for thirty years, was born in Missouri on April 9, 1905, and moved with his family to Fayetteville, AK. During his senior year at the University of Arkansas, Fulbright won a Rhodes scholarship to study at Oxford University in England for three years.

Fulbright returned to Arkansas and worked briefly in his father's business, then studied law at George Washington University, completing his degree in 1934. During his law school days, he married Elizabeth Williams. He spent a year as a special attorney for the U.S. Department of Justice, taught law for a year at George Washington, followed by three years of teaching law at the University of Arkansas.

Then in 1939, at the age of 35, Fulbright became the youngest man ever elected to be president of the University of Arkansas, but was fired two years later by the newly elected governor, whom Fulbright's mother's newspaper had opposed. He ran for U.S. Congress from Arkansas's Third District in 1942, won unexpectedly and served for a single term, then ran for the Senate against the governor who had fired him from the university presidency. Despite a difficult race, Fulbright won by a reasonable majority, and held the Senate seat

for the next thirty years. During his years of political service, Fulbright pushed to revitalize the concept of the League of Nations, which ultimately led to the creation of the United Nations. In 1954, he served as a delegate to the 9th General Assembly of his realized dream, the United Nations Organization.

Another of Fulbright's most notable contributions was legislation authorizing the construction of the Kennedy Center for the Performing Arts in Washington, D.C. Money for its construction was raised through private contributions, and Edward Durrell Store, an architect from Fulbright's hometown of Fayetteville, designed the center.

The achievement for which Fulbright is known throughout the world is the Fulbright scholarship for American students, initially funded by loan repayments made to the United States by foreign countries after World War II. Made in foreign currency, the payments provided for travel and tuition of American students overseas. Although the loans have long since been repaid, the scholarship still exists, with funds appropriated from the U.S. budget and the contributions of thirty foreign countries.

Since leaving the Senate in 1974, Fulbright has been associated with Hogan & Hartson, a Washington, DC, law firm, and is the honorary chairman of the Fulbright Alumni Association, with thousands of members all over the world.

Lydia Brontë

---

training materials, "Enriching Life Through the Humanities: Workshops for Practitioners in Aging," focusing on how staff can utilize the arts to better communicate with their groups and clients (Hart, 1992).

Senior Centers

A senior center is a physical facility, resulting from a community planning process, that offers a wide variety of services and activities for older adults (Krout, 1989). They are an outgrowth of senior clubs that can be traced back to 1870, which served as associations of peers providing social support for their members (Gelfand, 1988). The first senior center, William Hodson Community Center, was established in 1943 for low-

income elderly in New York City, by the Public Welfare Department under the direction of Harry Levine and Gertrude Landau. Social workers in the community have been credited with the idea of senior centers because they recognized the need for human contact and communication required by their older clientele. These social workers concluded that older adults could benefit from a setting that would enable them to socialize and participate in activities with other older adults. Since Hodson's founding, other centers opened in San Francisco (1947), Philadelphia (1948), and Bridgeport (1951) (Lowy and O'Connor, 1986). By the late 1950s there were approximately 200 senior centers nationwide, established by local resources and sponsored by nonprofit organizations and/or local government agencies (e.g., departments of social service or recreation). No federal or state legislation existed yet to fund the senior center concept (Krout, 1989). The first state senior center association was organized in Ohio in 1959.

In 1962 The National Council on the Aging (NCOA) published "Centers for Older People: Guide for Programs and Facilities," an overview of the concept and operation of senior centers. This was the first national attempt to provide a comprehensive overview of senior centers. In 1963, the NCOA held its first annual conference of senior centers (Leanse, 1978).

During the following decade the multiservice senior center concept began to flourish. Activities and services available at these centers included nutrition, health, employment, transportation, social work, education, creative arts, recreation, leadership, and volunteer opportunities (Lowy and O'Connor, 1986). In the 1970s, federal legislation funded development of senior centers. Title V, Section 501 of the Older Americans Act was amended to include the new "Multipurpose Senior Centers" title and provided funds to renovate or construct senior centers. Title III of the Act then made operational monies available to develop and deliver specific services (Gelfand, 1988).

In 1970 the NCOA sponsored the National Institute of Senior Centers (NISC), a network of 1,200 centers in all parts of the country. By the late 1980s the NCOA reported 9,000 senior centers in existence nationwide (Krout, 1989). In 1991 NISC reported approximately 8 million older adults participating in senior centers (Special Committee on Aging, U.S. Senate, 1991). The NISC classifies senior center services into individual, group, and community categories. The individual services include counseling, employment, and health maintenance. Group services involve recreational, nutritional, and educational activities, as well as group social work. The participants in the senior centers provide services to the local community through volunteer work in community institutions or organizations (Krout, 1989). Services available through senior centers depend on their resources, facilities, and community supports; many are provided by the center staff, by appropriate agency staff assigned to the center, or by agencies on rotation through the center (Gelfand, 1984).

A senior center is a physical facility, resulting from a community planning process, that offers a wide variety of services and activities for older adults.

While some senior centers provide a wide range of offerings, many provide mainly recreational and educational activities (Krout, 1989). The recreation-education component of senior center programming varies with availability of community resources and participant interest. Some of the more common activities include arts and crafts, nature, science and outdoor life, drama, physical activity, music, dance, table games, special social activities, literary activities, excursions, hobby or special interest grouping, speakers, lectures, movies, forums, round tables, and community service projects (Gelfand, 1988). As mentioned earlier, one of the most popular educational programs used by senior centers is the NCOA's "Discovery Through the Humanities Program."

At one senior center in Brooklyn, New York, off-campus instruction in the liberal arts has been conducted under the auspices of the Institute of Study for Older Adults. Under institute direction, members of local senior centers help design courses, and the local community colleges provide faculty to teach them at the senior centers. Liberal arts courses and self-help instruction are popular among the clientele that attend these centers (Moody, 1988). The Iowa City/Johnson County Senior Center in Iowa City, Iowa, recorded serving 75,000 older adults in 1991. Educational offerings included applied arts, performing arts, art appreciation, crafts, exercise, and computers. Special workshops also featured topics varying from medication to chair caning.

In the 1970s at the Siouxland Senior Center, Sioux City, a program called "Talk Show" provided opportunities for older adults to meet newsmakers, discuss current events, or talk with a doctor or lawyer. Although the program has made many changes over the years, it is still held weekly, from 10:30 A.M. to 12:00 P.M., with approximately 65 older adults meeting to hear about and discuss the day's topic (Special Committee on Aging, U.S. Senate, 1991).

Older Adult Service and Information System (OASIS)

The Older Adult Service and Information System (OASIS) is a consortium between business and not-for-profit organizations designed to challenge and enrich the lives of adults 55 and older. Educational, cultural, health, and volunteer outreach programs are offered at OASIS Institutes, providing participants opportunities to remain independent and active in community affairs (OASIS, 1991). Marylen Mann, executive director of OASIS National, and Margie Wolcott May established OASIS in St. Louis, Missouri, in 1982. The May Department Stores Company, the major national sponsor, furnishes the meeting and activity space in many of its stores. Initial support for the program came from the Administration on Aging (OASIS, 1991). The program is administered nationally from St. Louis. The national office establishes program-quality requirements and overall management and operations guidelines; it also supplies management training, new programs and materials, and ongoing support to local program directors.

Currently there are OASIS Institutes in Portland, Los Angeles (2), Long Beach, San Diego, Escondido, Phoenix (2), Tucson, Denver (2), Houston, San Antonio, St. Louis (3), Chicago, Indianapolis, Akron, Cleveland (2), Rochester, Buffalo, Pittsburgh, Hyattsville, Boston, Enfield, and Waterbury, with over 129,000 members participating. Each institute has permanent and specially designed space for offices, student lounges, and meeting rooms. In addition to May Company support, in many cities, local hospitals and not-for-profit community agencies sponsor institutes. People from all socio-economic, cultural, and educational backgrounds are invited to participate. OASIS membership is free, and the programs have minimal or no charge. Courses, which last from one to twelve weeks, are scheduled by calendar quarters or trimesters, and classes are held once a week during daytime hours. Course offerings include visual arts, music, drama, creative writing, contemporary issues, history, science, exercise, and health. The collaboration of local cultural and educational institutions benefits many courses (OASIS, 1991).

Volunteer outreach is an important component of the OASIS program. The Older Adult Peer Leadership (OAPL) program, trains participants to teach classes in the community and to work in intergenerational programs helping young children. In 1990 more than 2,000 volunteers gave over 110,000 hours of their time to run OASIS sites (OASIS, 1991).

The OASIS Institutes in St. Louis are housed in Famous-Barr Department Stores and other area locations. The programs are sponsored by Famous-Barr and its parent company, the May Department Stores Company, by Jewish Hospital of St. Louis, and Washington University School of Medicine. Volunteers are on duty from 10:00 A.M. to 3:00 P.M., Monday through Friday, to enroll students 60 years of age and older in the classes. All health-related classes are free of charge, and most other programs require a nominal fee of $1. The courses include wellness, liberal arts, and vocational training. OASIS/OAPL are provided to older adults throughout the St. Louis Metro area by the OAPL Outreach program. Volunteers are trained in subject matter and leadership skills and conduct these classes at libraries, churches, residential and senior centers, and other sites (OASIS, 1991). In 1990 the St. Louis OASIS Institutes established the OASIS award to recognize outstanding volunteer contributions to the St. Louis community made by the area's older adults.

Special events and travel programs are also an integral part of the OASIS Institutes in St. Louis. Special events, such as the Opera Theatre St. Louis, Picnic at the St. Louis Zoo, and an Evening at Queeny Pops, provide OASIS participants an opportunity to participate in local cultural activities free or at a nominal charge. Travel programs to the Winston Churchill Memorial, Inn of the Ozarks, McDonnell-Douglas Aerospace Center, a cruise on the *Belle of St. Louis;* and other places of interest provide adventure and new learning experiences for OASIS members (OASIS, 1991).

The OASIS Institute is the central gathering point for classes, seminars, and special events offered throughout the year. OASIS strives to empower adults, 55 and older, to live independently and continue to expand their knowledge and remain productive individuals (OASIS, 1992).

Chautauqua

The Chautauqua Institution is a 750–acre complex on the shores of Chautauqua Lake in southwestern New York state. Established over a century ago, the institution provides educational, religious, recreational, and cultural opportunities for persons of all ages from all parts of the United States and abroad (Chautauqua Institution, 1992).

Chautauqua Institution's "55 Plus" Weekend, established eighteen years ago, is an important component of the multifaceted Chautauqua experience. Each weekend program presents topics through discussion, workshops, lectures, films, cassette tapes, or any other appropriate means. Cultural programs are scheduled for Saturday evenings. Weekend themes and discussions have included topics on socialism to capitalism and the presidential campaign and election year. Housing and meals are available on site. The registration fee covers all programs and accommodations. In addition to the weekend programs, a special one week program, "The Chautauqua Experience," introduces older adults to lectures, music, recreation, drama, and group fellowship (Chautauqua Institution, 1992).

Shepherd's Centers

A Shepherd's Center is a nonprofit community organization sponsored by a coalition of religious congregations committed to the delivery of services and programs for older adults. In 1972, the first Shepherd's Center was founded by Dr. Elbert C. Cole in Kansas City, Missouri. Twenty-three churches and synagogues joined in an interfaith effort to provide a ministry by, with, and for older adults. In 1972 the original center began with only six volunteers. Today, 87 Shepherd's centers in 25 states comprise a network of 15,000 volunteers serving over 175,000 older adults. The services and programs of the Shepherd's Center are designed to empower older adults to lead creative, productive, meaningful, and dependent lives. The Shepherd's Centers are controlled and operated by older adults. Dr. Cole reports that Shepherd's Centers are an expression of congregations in a defined area. By working together the congregations may accomplish what can not be done alone. The Shepherd's Centers focus on neighborhoods or specifically defined territories. The participants develop an attitude of ownership, empowering them to take responsibility for their well being. Governed by a self-perpetuating board of trustees appropriately representative and ecumenical, with age-relevant skills and interests, the board is committed to the overall concept of the centers. Church and synagogue

property is used for office space and major programs and services. Duplication of services is a problem that Shepherd's Centers seek to avoid. The center encourages partnerships with other agencies serving older adults, always giving credit and recognition where due. Congregations, participants, friends, businesses, civic organizations and clubs, United Way, public funds, and foundations are the funding sources for the centers. The Shepherd's Center concept is a new social model with a healthy view of life after retirement. The idea is applicable to any ethnic, economic, or cultural group of older adults (Maves and Bock, 1990).

One of the many offerings of the Shepherd's Centers is the "Adventures in Learning" educational program, utilizing older adults as both teachers and students, as planners and participants. Classes are normally held weekly, biweekly, or monthly and provide an environment where older adults may share their knowledge, talents, skills, and new interests with their peers.

A committee of volunteers makes the program decisions regarding curriculum, faculty, marketing, and evaluating. This committee is composed of faculty and students with background experience in education, public relations, administration, the arts, health, and clerical services. Most of the teachers are older adults who volunteer their time, knowledge, and skills. The educational program allows students to choose their own subjects. If the student finds a course that does not meet his or her needs, the student may then try a different class. Many classes may require advanced registration due to space limitations (Maves and Bock, 1990).

A Shepherd's Center is a nonprofit community organization sponsored by a coalition of religious congregations committed to the delivery of services and programs for older adults.

"Adventures in Learning" program students participate for the joy of learning without the pressures of tests, grades, and academic credits. Courses are organized on an academic semester or quarter basis with classes being held during

Table 35.3
Civilian Labor Force and Participation Rates by Race, Hispanic Origin, Sex, and Age, 1970 to 1989, and Projections, 2000

For civilian noninstitutional population 16 years old and over. Annual averages of monthly figures. Rates are based on annual average civilian noninstitutional population of each specified group and represent proportion of each specified group in the civilian labor force. Based on *Current Population Survey*.

Race, sex and age	Civilian Labor Force (millions)						
	1970	1975	1980	1985	1988	1989	2000
Total[1]	82.8	93.8	106.9	115.5	121.7	123.9	141.1
White	73.6	82.8	93.6	99.9	104.8	106.4	119.0
Male	46.0	50.3	54.5	36.5	58.3	59.0	63.3
Female	27.5	32.5	39.1	43.5	46.4	47.4	55.7
Black[2]	9.2	9.3	10.9	12.4	13.2	13.5	16.5
Male	5.2	5.0	5.6	6.2	5.5	5.7	8.0
Female	4.0	4.2	5.3	5.1	6.6	6.8	8.5
Hispanic[3]	(NA)	(NA)	6.1	7.7	9.0	9.3	14.3
Male	(NA)	(NA)	3.8	4.7	5.4	5.6	8.3
Female	(NA)	(NA)	2.3	3.0	3.6	3.7	6.0
Male	51.2	56.3	61.5	64.4	66.9	67.8	74.3
16-19 years	4.0	4.8	5.0	4.1	4.2	4.1	4.4
16 and 17 years	1.8	2.1	2.1	1.7	1.7	1.6	1.9
18 and 19 years	2.2	2.7	2.9	2.5	2.4	2.5	2.5
20-24 years	5.7	7.5	8.6	8.3	7.6	7.5	6.9
25-34 years	11.3	14.2	17.0	18.8	19.7	19.9	16.6
35-44 years	10.5	10.4	11.8	14.5	16.1	16.6	20.2
45-54 years	10.4	10.4	9.9	9.9	10.6	10.9	16.4
55-64 years	7.1	7.0	7.2	7.1	6.8	6.8	7.8
65 years and over	2.2	1.9	1.9	1.8	2.0	2.0	2.0
Female	31.5	37.5	45.5	51.1	54.7	56.0	66.8
16-19 years	3.2	4.1	4.4	3.8	3.9	3.8	4.4
16 and 17 years	1.3	1.7	1.8	1.5	1.6	1.5	1.8
18 and 19 years	1.9	2.4	2.5	2.3	2.3	2.3	2.6
20-24 years	4.9	6.2	7.3	7.4	6.9	6.7	6.7
25-34 years	5.7	8.7	12.3	14.7	15.8	16.0	15.1
35-44 years	6.0	6.5	8.6	11.6	13.4	14.0	18.6
45-54 years	6.5	6.7	7.0	7.5	8.5	9.0	14.4
55-64 years	4.2	4.3	4.7	4.9	5.0	5.1	6.1
65 years and over	1.1	1.0	1.2	1.2	1.3	1.4	1.4

Race, sex and age	Participation Rate (percent)						
	1970	**1975**	**1980**	**1985**	**1988**	**1989**	**2000**
Total[1]	60.4	61.2	63.8	64.8	65.9	66.5	69.0
White	50.2	61.5	64.1	65.0	66.2	66.7	69.5
Male	90.0	78.7	78.2	77.0	76.9	77.1	76.6
Female	42.5	45.9	51.2	54.1	56.4	57.2	62.9
Black[2]	61.8	58.8	61.0	62.9	63.8	64.2	66.5
Male	76.5	71.0	70.6	70.8	71.0	71.0	71.4
Female	49.5	48.9	53.2	56.5	58.0	58.7	62.5
Hispanic[3]	(NA)	(NA)	64.0	64.6	67.4	67.6	69.9
Male	(NA)	(NA)	81.4	80.3	81.9	82.0	90.3
Female	(NA)	(NA)	47.4	49.3	53.2	53.5	59.4
Male	79.7	77.9	77.4	76.3	76.2	76.4	75.9
16-19 years	56.1	59.1	60.5	56.8	56.9	57.9	59.0
16 and 17 years	47.0	48.6	50.1	45.1	46.1	46.3	48.9
18 and 19 years	66.7	70.6	71.3	68.9	68.1	69.2	69.7
20-24 years	83.3	84.5	85.9	85.0	85.0	85.3	86.5
25-34 years	96.4	95.2	95.2	94.7	94.3	94.4	94.1
35-44 years	96.9	95.6	95.5	95.0	94.5	94.5	94.3
45-54 years	94.3	92.1	91.2	91.0	90.9	91.1	90.5
55-64 years	83.0	75.6	72.1	67.9	67.0	67.2	68.1
65 years and over	26.8	21.6	19.0	15.8	16.5	16.6	14.7
Female	43.3	46.3	51.5	54.5	56.5	57.4	52.5
16-19 years	44.0	49.1	52.9	52.1	53.6	53.9	59.5
16 and 17 years	34.9	40.2	43.6	42.1	44.0	44.5	49.8
18 and 19 years	153.5	58.1	61.9	61.7	62.9	62.5	69.0
20-24 years	57.7	64.1	68.9	71.8	72.7	72.4	77.9
25-34 years	45.0	54.9	65.5	70.9	72.7	73.5	82.4
35-44 years	51.1	55.8	65.5	71.8	75.2	76.0	84.9
45-54 years	54.4	54.6	59.9	54.4	69.0	70.5	76.5
55-64 years	43.0	40.9	41.3	42.0	43.5	45.0	49.0
65 years and over	9.7	8.2	8.1	7.3	7.9	8.4	7.6

Notes: NA: Not available; 1. Beginning 1975, includes other races not shown separately; 2. For 1970, African-American and other; 3. Persons of Hispanic origin may be of any race.

Source: U.S. Bureau of Labor Statistics. *Employment and Earnings,* monthly; *Monthly Labor Review* (November 1989); and unpublished data.

the daylight hours. Some centers close during August and between sessions. During the long breaks some centers offer alternative programs, such as short-term classes, picnics, trips, or fairs to provide an opportunity for those who count on the friendship and stimulation of the center's activities. Registration fees are kept low with a maximum of $15 for a full quarter of classes. All classes are held on one day of the week in the same location, usually a church or synagogue. Every hour courses are offered in intellectual pursuits, current events, or history; philosophy, humanities, religion, or art; needlework, crafts, or painting; exercise, yoga, nutrition, or health information; and travelogues.

Noontime fellowship is a very important part of the "Adventures in Learning" program. Students, teachers, and volunteers share a meal and friendship, at which time the program coordinator makes announcements, recognizes teachers, celebrates accomplishments, and welcomes and introduces new participants in the program. Musical entertainment, a theater presentation, an address by a community leader, or a guest speaker on a topic of interest to the students rounds out the program. The planning committee of the "Adventures in Learning" program has Protestant, Catholic, and Jewish persons serving on the committee (Maves and Bock, 1990).

Workplace Education

Workplace education or training programs are not new. For years, pre-service and in-service training for workers has taken place in the private and public sectors. Traditionally these programs were reserved for the younger worker, because the older worker was forced to retire at or before the age of 65. Social policy has promoted retirement instead of employment for older adults. Yet, over the past twenty-six years a new policy has evolved, encouraging older adults to stay in the labor force rather than retire early. The current belief is that working beyond "traditional" retirement age will help older adults feel better while they continue contributing to society (Moody, 1988).

These trends are evident in recent legislation concerning age and the workplace. In 1967 Congress passed laws prohibiting age discrimination in employment. By 1978 the mandatory retirement age for older workers was pushed back to 70, and in 1986, mandatory retirement at any age was abolished for almost all workers (Long, 1990).

The U.S. Bureau of Labor Statistics reported in 1989, males in the civilian workforce, 55 to 64 years of age, totaled 6.8 million or 67.2 percent; and males, 65 and older, totaled 2.0 million or 16.6 percent. Females in the civilian labor force, 55 to 64 years old, totaled 5.1 million or 45.0 percent; and females, 65 and older, totaled 1.4 million or 8.4 percent. By the year 2000, males in the civilian labor force, 55 to 64 years of age is expected to total 7.8 million or 68.1 percent; and males, 65 and older will total 2.0 million or 14.7 percent. Females in the civilian labor force, 55 to 64 years of age, will total 6.1 million or 49.0 percent; and females, 65 years and older, will total 1.4 million or 7.6 percent (U.S. Bureau of Census, 1991) (See Table 35.3).

The U.S. Bureau of the Census (1980) reported 4.2 percent of the labor force, 85 years and older, were white males, and 1.5 percent of the labor force, 85 years and older, were white females. The same report found that 4.3 percent of the labor force, 85 years and older, were nonwhite males, and 3.0 percent of the labor force, 85 years and older, were nonwhite females (Rosenwaike, 1985) (See Table 35.4).

Today employers are facing new problems. The Committee for Economic Development, a private, nonprofit, and nonpartisan research and education organization made up of 250 top business executives and university presidents, has stated that the nation has now entered a time when there are fewer young job entrants into the workforce and an increasing older adult population. It urged business and policymakers to develop qualified workers to fill the increasing number of knowledge- and technology-driven jobs (Special Committee on Aging, U.S. Senate, 1991). The tight labor market could provide incentives for employees to encourage older workers to remain in the workforce. By the year 2000, over 50 percent of the workforce will be 35 to 55 years of age (Moody, 1986). One trend that is contributing to this projection is the number of women having children after age 35. Parents, in their sixties with college-aged young adults, may remain in the workforce longer to pay college costs and other expenses of their young children (Long, 1990).

With the changes in laws regarding age and employment, higher costs of living, reduced labor market of younger workers, and an increasing

Table 35.4
Labor Force Participation Rates of Persons 85
Years and Over, by Race and Sex: 1950 to 1980
(Percent of Extreme Aged in Labor Force)

Race and sex	1950	1960	1970[a]	1980
White				
Male	6.6	6.9	6.6	4.2
Female	1.2	1.9	3.2	1.5
Nonwhite				
Male	9.8	8.0	8.8	4.3
Female	2.1	3.1	5.7	3.0

Note: [a] Ages 85 to 99 years only.

Sources: U.S. Bureau of the Census, 1953a: table 118; 1964: table 194; 1970 Census Public Use Sample; 1980 Census Public Use Microdata Sample.

elderly population, many corporations are implementing programs to bring in older workers. McDonald's Corporation has the "McMasters" program, which provides skills training and job placement for persons 55 and older. Annually 80 to 100 employees are trained in each McMasters program. General Electric has a special "Technical Renewal Program" in its Aerospace Electronic System Department, which provides training to engineers to update their skills and stay current with new technology. The public sector also has to train its older workers. One program on a local level has been established in Union City, New Jersey, training older adults to take care of children in training centers. The program has been accredited by the National Association for the Education of Young Children, an organization responsible for accrediting childcare programs. In Boston, Massachusetts, Operation ABLE (Ability Based on Long Experience), is a consortium effort between industry, government, and private foundations, which provides computer training to older workers for competing successfully in the workplace (Special Committee on Aging, U.S. Senate, 1991).

Many older workers are still choosing to retire before the age of 70, but for those who wish to remain in the workforce, business and industry have major responsibilities to train these older workers (Peterson, 1990). For older workers who wish to remain in the workforce, AARP has developed the booklet *Using the Experience of a Lifetime*, which provides an in-depth look at cre-

ative programs and opportunities for older workers (Special Committee on Aging, U.S. Senate, 1991).

● PARTICIPATION RATES AND PUBLIC POLICY

Statistics on Older Learners

There have been few studies on the actual participation rates of older adults in educational programs, leaving a dearth of data on educational statistics for this particular population. Most studies tend to group people over 35 or over 55 into one category, leaving no room for the interpretation of data on older adults (55 and older).

In her *Factbook on Aging*, Elizabeth Vierck used data on older adults from various studies in the 1980s. In October 1986, there were 159,000 persons 55 and older; 124,000 age 55 to 64; and 35,000 65 and older enrolled in high school or college courses. In 1987, 30 percent of adults age 50 and older said they give high priority to continuing education lectures or courses (Vierck, 1990).

Older adults are increasingly participating in education. However, the optimistic picture must be qualified by recognizing the variation among different groups of older adults. For example, the median years of school completed for white people age 65 and older in 1989 was 12.2 years, while for older African Americans it was 8.5 years, and for Hispanics it was 8.0 years. Fifty-eight percent of whites age 65 and older are high school graduates, while only 25 percent of older African Americans and 28 percent of Hispanics are high school graduates (U.S. Department of Health and Human Services, 1991) (See Table 35.5).

With the increasing educational opportunities for older adults, continued research is needed on the older adult learner.

Support of Older Learners

In the 1990s, there is no central system supporting or monitoring educational activities for older adults. Programs have developed around the preferences of administrators and/or the needs of the local community. This process has responded to the immediate needs of the older adult learner but has not provided program categories or models that could be easily described or replicated in other sites. The federal government has encouraged public and private sector employers and community organizations to offer educational opportunities to assist older adults in hold-

Table 35.5

Measures of Educational Attainment, by Age Group, Sex, Race, and Hispanic Origin: March 1989 (Excludes People in Institutions)

Measure of educational attainment and age	Sex			Race and Hispanic origin								
				White			African-American			Hispanic origin*		
	Total	Men	Women	Total	Men	Women	Total	Men	Women	Total	Men	Women
Median years of school completed:												
25+	12.7	12.8	12.6	12.7	12.8	12.7	12.4	12.4	12.4	12.0	12.0	12.0
60 to 64	12.4	12.5	12.4	12.5	12.5	12.4	10.7	10.6	10.7	9.3	9.6	8.9
65+	12.1	12.1	12.2	12.2	12.2	12.2	8.5	8.1	8.7	8.0	8.1	8.0
65 to 69	12.3	12.3	12.3	12.4	12.4	12.4	9.5	9.1	9.8	8.4	8.5	8.3
70 to 74	12.2	12.2	12.2	12.3	12.3	12.3	8.4	8.2	8.6	8.0	8.1	7.9
75+	10.9	10.5	11.3	11.6	11.1	11.9	7.8	7.0	8.2	7.1	7.0	7.1
Percent with a high school education:												
25+	77	77	77	78	79	78	65	64	65	51	51	51
60 to 64	66	65	67	69	68	71	39	43	37	34	37	31
65+	55	54	56	58	57	59	25	22	26	28	26	29
65 to 69	63	61	65	67	65	68	31	28	33	33	31	35
70 to 74	57	56	58	60	59	62	21	20	22	25	21	29
75+	46	44	48	49	47	50	21	18	23	23	21	24
Percent with four or more years of college:												
25+	21	25	18	22	25	19	12	12	12	10	11	9
60 to 64	14	19	10	15	21	10	5	7	4	6	5	7
65+	11	14	9	12	15	10	5	4	5	6	7	5
65 to 69	13	16	10	13	17	10	5	3	6	9	9	9
70 to 74	11	13	9	11	13	10	3	3	3	3	3	3
75+	10	12	9	11	13	9	4	4	6	4	7	3

*People of Hispanic origin may be of any race.

Source: U.S. Bureau of the Census. Unpublished data from the March 1989 *Current Population Survey.*

ing or gaining contributive roles in society (Peterson, 1987).

A number of major federal statutes currently authorize provision of federal assistance for adult and continuing education. Much federal assistance is channeled through appropriate state agencies which in turn disperse the funds at the local level. The following is a brief description of a few of the programs available.

The Older Americans Act authorizes state agencies on aging to provide education and training to adults 60 and older in the areas of consumer education, continuing education, health education, pre-retirement education, financial planning; and other education and training services. The Adult Education Act provides a means by which all adults (young and old) may obtain basic educational skills (Special Committees on Aging, U.S. Senate, 1991).

There are federal as well as state policies to waive tuition fees of older adults, and researchers have conducted many studies of these tuition waiver programs. The minimum age requirement varies from 60 to 65. Many institutions offer credit, others specify audit only, and many limit enrollment on a space-available basis only. According to Moyer and Lago, cost is neither a barrier nor an incentive to older adults participating in education programs (Leptak, 1987). Twenty-nine states have established some guidelines on this subject of tuition waiver programs. Nine additional states have state policies to waive or reduce tuition mostly on a space-available basis. However, Alabama, Arizona, Colorado, District of Columbia, Iowa, Maine, Mississippi, Missouri, Nebraska, Pennsylvania, Vermont, West Virginia, and Wyoming have remained silent both in their statutes and in their written state policies (Special Committee on Aging, U.S. Senate, 1991).

More information about the older learner is needed to assist government and institutions of higher education in meeting future needs appropriately, as more older adults demonstrate increasing interest in educational pursuits.

Organizations

Academy for Educational Development (AED)
1255 23rd St., NW
Washington, DC 20037
(202) 862-1900

American Association for Adult and Continuing Education (AAACE) (formerly Adult Education Association)
1112 16th St., NW, Ste. 420
Washington, D.C. 20036
(202) 463-6333

American Association of Retired Persons (AARP)
Institute of Lifetime Learning
601 E St., NW
Washington, DC 20049
(202) 434-2277

Association of Learning in Retirement Organizations in the Western Region (ALIROW)
1607 Angelus Ave.
Los Angeles, CA 90026

Chautauqua Programs for Older Adults
Program Center for Older Adults
P.O. Box 1095
Chautauqua, NY 14722
(716) 357-6200

Discovery Through the Humanities Program
The National Council on the Aging, Inc.
409 Third St., SW, Ste. 200
Washington, DC 20024
(202) 479-1200

Elderhostel
75 Federal St.
Boston, MA 02110-1941
(617) 426-7788
FAX (617) 426-8351

Elderhostel Institute Network
15 Garrison Ave.
Durham, NH 03824
(603) 862-3642
FAX (603) 862-3390

Federation of State Humanities Councils
1012 Fourteenth St., NW, Ste. 1007
Washington, DC 20005
(202) 393-5400

The Gerontological Society of America
1275 K St., NW, Ste. 350
Washington, DC 20005-4006
(202) 842-1275

Institute for Learning in Retirement
Duke University—OCE
The Bishop's House
Durham, NC 27708
(919) 684-6259

League for Innovation in the Community College
25431 Cabot Rd., Ste. 204
Laguna Hills, CA 92653
(714) 855-0710
FAX (714) 855-6293

Museum One
P.O. Box 11535
Washington, DC 20008-0735

National Center for Education Statistics (NCES)
Office of Educational Research and Improvement
U.S. Department of Education
Capitol Place 555
New Jersey Ave., NW
Washington, DC 20208

National Endowment for the Humanities
1100 Pennsylvania Ave., NW
Washington, DC 20506
(202) 786-0373

National Institute of Senior Centers
409 Third St., SW
Washington, DC 20024
(202) 479-6683

National University Continuing Education Association (NUCEA)
1 Dupont Circle, Ste. 615
Washington, DC 20036
(202) 659-3130

North Carolina Center for Creative Retirement
The University of North Carolina at Asheville
Asheville, NC 28804-3299
(704) 251-6140
FAX (704) 251-6803

Older Adult Service and Information System (OASIS)
National Headquarters
7710 Carondelet Ave., Ste. 125
St. Louis, MO 63105
(314) 862-2933

The Renaissance Society
California State University at Sacramento
Student Service Center, Rm. 111H
6000 J St.
Sacramento, CA 95819

Shepherd's Centers of America
6700 Troost, Ste. 616
Kansas City, MO 64131
(816) 523-1080
FAX (816) 523-5790

References

American Library Association. "Guidelines for Library Service to Older Adults." *RQ* Vol. 26, no. 4 (Summer 1987): 444–47.

Baum, M., and B. M. Rich. *The Aging: A Guide to Public Policy.* Pittsburgh, PA: University of Pittsburgh Press, 1984.

Bove, R. "Retraining the Older Worker: Interest Rises in Keeping the Older Worker in the Workplace." *Training and Development Journal* Vol. 41B (March 1987): 77–78.

Brahce, C. I., and W. W. Hunter. "Leadership Training for Retirement Education." In *Introduction to Educational Gerontology.* Eds. R. H. Sherron and D. B. Lumsden. New York: Hemisphere Publishing, 1990.

Casey, G. M. "Library Services for the Aging." *Library Professionals Publications* Vol. 33 (1984).

Charles, R. R., and C. Bartunek, eds. *Community College Programs for the Older Adult Learner.* ERIC Document Reproduction Service Service No. ED 322 977, 1989.

Chautauqua Institution. *"55 Plus" Program for Older Adults* (brochure). Chautauqua Institution, 1992.

The Chronicle of Higher Education. "Colleges to Provide Programs for Older People." *The Chronicle of Higher Education* Vol. 18, no. 15 (May 1979).

Cross, K. P. *Adults as Learners.* San Francisco: Jossey-Bass, 1981.

Cross, K. P., and A. McCartan. "Adult Learning: State Policies and Institutional Practices." *ASHE-ERIC Higher Education Research Report.* ERIC Document Reproduction Service No. ED 246 831, 1984.

Doucette, D., and C. Ventura-Merkel. *Community College Programs for Older Adults: A Status Report.* League for Innovation in the Community College, 1991.

Elderhostel Institute Network. *The Institute Movement and Elderhostel: A National Overview.* Elderhostel Institute Network, 1991.

Engle, M. "Little Old Ladies are Much Maligned: Diversity Reconsidered." *Educational Gerontology* Vol. 16 (1990): 339–46.

Fischer, R. B. "Higher Education Confronts the Age Wave." *Educational Record* Vol. 15 (Winter 1991).

Fischer, R. B., M. L. Blazey, and H.T. Lipman. *Students of the Third Age—University College Programs for Retired Adults.* New York: Macmillan, 1992.

Gelfand, D. *The Aging Network: Programs and Services.* New York: Springer, 1984.

Gelwicks, L. E., and R. Weinstock. "Managing the Environment for Older Students." *New Directions for Higher Education* Vol. 30 (1980): 67–79.

Goggin, J.M. "Elderhostel: The Next Generation." *Aging Today* (February/March 1991).

Graney, M. J., and W. C. Hays. "Senior Students: Higher Education After Age 62." *Educational Gerontology* Vol. 1 (1976): 345–48.

Gross, R. *Lifelong Learner*. New York: Simon and Schuster, 1977.

Hales, C. "How Should the Information Needs of the Aging Be Met? A Delphi Response" *The Gerontologist* Vol. 25, no. 2 (April 1985).

Hales-Mabry, C. "Serving the Older Adult." *Special Populations in the Library*. New York: Haworth Press, 1990.

Hart, J. *Beyond the Tunnel: The Arts and Aging in America*. Washington, DC: Museum One, 1992.

Henderson, C. "Old Glory: America Comes of Age." *The Futurist* (March-April 1988): 36–40.

Hendrickson, A. *A Manual on Planning Educational Programs for Older Adults*. Tallahassee, FL: Department of Adult Education, 1973.

Hospital Audiences, Inc. *HAI News* (Spring 1992).

Krout, J. A. *Senior Centers in America*. New York: Greenwood Press, 1989.

Lammers, W. W. *Public Policy and the Aging*. Washington, DC: CQ Press, 1983.

"Late Bloomer" audio cassette. Available from Connie Goldman Productions, 926 Second Street, Suite 201, Santa Barbara, CA 90403. (310) 393-6801.

Leanse, J. "A Blend of Multi-Dimensional Activities." *Perspective on Aging* Vol. 7 (March-April 1978): 8–13.

Leptak, J. "Older Adults in Higher Education: A Review of the Literature." ERIC Document Reproduction Service No. ED 283 021, 1987.

Links, Marjorie. *The Renaissance Society* (brochure). Sacramento: California State University, 1992.

Londoner, C. A. "Instrumental and Expressive Education: From Needs to Goals Assessment for Educational Planning." In *Introduction to Educational Gerontology*. Eds. R. H. Sherron and D. B. Lumsden. New York: Hemisphere Publishing, 1990.

Long, H. "Educational Gerontology: Trends and Developments in 2000–2010." *Educational Gerontology* Vol. 16 (1990): 317–26.

Long, H. B. "Taverns and Coffee Houses: Adult Educational Institutions in Colonial America." *Lifelong Learning: The Adult Years* (1981): 14–16.

Lowy, L., and D. O'Connor. *Why Education in the Later Years?* Lexington, MA: D. C. Heath, 1986.

Mackintosh, E. *Humanities Programming for Older Adults*. Federation of State Humanities Councils, 1988.

Manheimer, R. J. "Creative Retirement in an Aging Society." In *Students of the Third Age-University/College Programs for Retired Adults*. Eds. R. B. Fischer, M. L. Blazey, and H. T. Lipman. New York: Macmillan, 1992.

———. "Developing Arts and Humanities Programming with the Elderly." *Adult Services in Action* Vol. 2 (1984).

———. "The Politics and Promise of Cultural Enrichment Programs." *Generations* (Winter 1987–88): 26–30.

Maves, P. B., and Bock, K., eds. *Organizational Manual for Shepherd's Center*. Shepherd's Center of America, 1990.

Meyers, F. *The Handbook for Learning in Retirement Organizations*. Los Angeles, CA: The Association for Learning in Retirement Organizations, 1987.

Moody, H. R. *Abundance of Life*. New York: Columbia University Press, 1988.

———. "Education as a Lifelong Process." In *Our Aging Society: Paradox and Promise*. Eds. A. Pifer and L. Brontë. New York: W. W. Norton, 1987.

National Center for Educational Statistics. *Digest of Education Statistics, 1991*. Washington, DC: U.S. Government Printing Office, 1991.

National Council on the Aging. *Discovery Through the Humanities Introductory Handbook*. National Council on the Aging, 1991.

———. *Discovery Through the Humanities Program Brochure*. Washington, DC: National Council on the Aging, 1991.

OASIS, Older Adult Service and Information System: OASIS Fact Sheet and Brochure. St. Louis, MO: OASIS, 1991.

OASIS Summer Brochure. St. Louis, MO: OASIS, 1992.

O'Donnell, K. M., and W. D. Berkeley. "Elderhostel: A National Program." *New Directions for Higher Education* Vol. 29 (1980).

Peterson, D. A. "Adult Education." In *The Encyclopedia of Aging*. Ed. G. L. Maddox. New York: Springer, 1987.

———. "Education for the Aging." *Lifelong Learning: The Adult Years* (1981): 16–18.

———. *Facilitating Education for Older Learners*. San Francisco: Jossey-Bass, 1983.

Pifer, A., and L. Brontë. *Our Aging Society: Paradox and Promise*. New York: W. W. Norton and Company, 1987.

Rappole, G. "An Overview of Community College Programs for Elderly Texans." *Educational Gerontology* Vol. 3, no. 1 (January-February 1977): 363–83.

Riley, M. W., and J. W. Riley. "Changing Meanings of Age in the Aging Society." In *Our Aging Society: Paradox and Promise*. Eds. A. Pifer and L. Brontë. New York: W. W. Norton, 1987.

Romaniuk, J. G., "Development of Educational Programs for Older Adult Learners: A State Perspective." *The Gerontologist* Vol. 23, no. 3 (1983): 313.

Rosenwaike, I. *The Extreme Aged in America: A Portrait of an Expanding Population*. Westport, CT: Greenwood Press, 1985.

Scanlon, J. *How to Plan a College Program for Older People*. Academy for Educational Development, 1978.

Schaie, K. W. "Age Changes in Adult Intelligence." In *Aging: Scientific Perspectives and Social Issues*. Eds. D. S. Woodruff and J. E. Birren. New York: D. Van Nostrand, 1975.

Shepherd's Centers of America. *Meeting the Challenge and Opportunity of an Aging Society*. Shepherd's Centers of America, 1991.

Sherron, R. H., and D. B. Lumsden. *Introduction to Educational Gerontology.* 3d ed. New York: Hemisphere Publishing, 1989.

Special Committee on Aging: U.S. Senate. *Lifelong Learning for an Aging Society: An Information Paper* Washington, DC: U.S. Government Printing Office, 1991.

Swindell, R. F. "Educational Opportunities for Older Persons in Australia: A Rationale for Future Development." *Educational Gerontology* Vol. 35, no. 2 (1991): 176–77.

Thorson, J. A., and S. A. Waskel. "Educational Gerontology and the Future." In *Introduction to Educational Gerontology.* Eds. R. N. Sherron and D. B. Lumsden. New York: Hemisphere Publishing, 1990.

Timmerman, S. "Older Learners in an Aging Nation: Projections and Guidelines for Planners and Policymakers." *Dissertation Abstracts International* (1979).

Turock, B. *Serving the Older Adult: A Guide to Library Programs and Information Sources* New York: R. R. Bowker, 1982.

U.S. Bureau of the Census. *Statistical Abstract of the United States 1991.* Washington, DC: U.S. Department of Commerce, 1991.

U.S. Senate Special Committee on Aging, the American Association of Retired Persons, the Federal Council on the Aging, and the U.S. Administration on Aging. *Aging in America: Trends and Projections.* Washington, DC: U.S. Department of Health and Human Services, 1991.

Ventura, C., and E. H. Worthy. *Education for Older Adults: A Synthesis of Significant Data.* ERIC Document Reproduction Service No. ED 303 607, 1982.

Vierck, E. *Factbook on Aging.* Santa Barbara, CA: ABC-CLIO, 1990.

Weinstock, R. *The Graying of the Campus.* Educational Facilities Laboratories, 1978.

Wirtz, P. W., and I. Charner. "Motivations for Educational Participation by Retirees: The Expressive-Instrumental Continuum Revisited." *Educational Gerontologist* Vol. 15 (1989): 275–84.

Woodruff, D. S., and J. E. Berrin, eds. *Aging: Scientific Perspectives and Social Issues.* New York: D. Van Nostrand, 1975.

Woolf, L. "How Senior Centers Grew Through Three WHCOAs." *Perspective on Aging* Vol. 11 (1982): 13–17.

Additional Reading

American Association of Retired Persons (AARP). *Using the Experience of a Lifetime.* Washington, DC: AARP.

Mackintosh, Esther. *Humanities Programming for Older Adults.* Washington, DC: Federation of State Humanities Councils, 1990.

Diane Moskow-McKenzie, M.A.

③⑥

Volunteerism

● How Many Volunteers? ● Types of Volunteer Work ● Service Exchange Programs
● Who Volunteers: A Demographic Profile ● Who Volunteers: The Personality Factor
● Religion and Volunteering ● Does Volunteering Make Older People Healthier and Happier?
● Why Volunteer? ● The Good That Volunteers Do ● Older Volunteers ● An Untapped Potential?

Older citizens, working as volunteers, make enormous contributions to their communities, to charitable and cultural organizations, and to individuals who depend on their help. Older volunteers provide loving care to children who are starved for attention; they provide transportation, homemaking, caregiving, and a whole range of other kinds of help to frail elderly; they run cultural programs at museums, theaters, and music centers; they are mentors for university students; they repair leaky faucets for poor people—and the list goes on.

Millions of elderly persons in this country serve as volunteers; even many people who are in their eighties and nineties continue to volunteer. According to a national estimate, older volunteers contribute about 3.6 billion hours of voluntary service to organizations every year (Marriott, 1991). If valued at the minimum wage, this amounts to a contribution to American society of about $15.3 billion. And this does not even count all of the hours that older people spend in "informal" services, helping their neighbors, friends, and relatives.

In the last twenty years or so, volunteer programs for seniors—both public and private—have developed and flourished. Locally and nationally, there are now thousands of senior volunteer programs organized through church and interfaith groups, health care institutions, and a broad range of cultural and social service organizations. The Retired Senior Volunteer

Program (RSVP), the Senior Companion Program, and the Foster Grandparent Program, which are partially funded by the federal government, were initiated in the 1960s. Many other programs are even newer, including experimental programs to integrate education and volunteering for retirees, to link nurturing older persons with troubled teenagers, to offer caregiving to isolated and frail elderly, to provide mentors for children in inner city schools, to serve as companions for homeless children, and so forth.

The development of these programs has meant that there has been a tremendous increase in opportunities for older persons to volunteer, as well as in services provided by older volunteers. Even so, many successful programs are found in only a few local areas, while elsewhere older persons with comparable interests and skills have no such volunteer opportunities. Moreover, many fine programs have very small budgets, which constrict their services and limit their ability to recruit and work with older volunteers.

(Portions of this chapter are taken from Older Volunteers: A Guide to Research and Practice. *Lucy Rose Fischer and Kay Schaffer. Newbury Park, CA: Sage Publications, 1993.)*

● HOW MANY VOLUNTEERS?

It may be surprising to learn that older people seem to be *less* likely to volunteer than other

Newer experimental programs link nurturing older persons with troubled teenagers. (Courtesy of the American Association of Retired Persons)

adults. A number of surveys have found a U-shaped curve for the relationship between volunteering and age: People in their thirties and forties are the most likely to volunteer. Both younger people and older people have lower rates of volunteering.

But studies of volunteering have been based on differing definitions, and the wording of questions has varied from one survey to the next. There is enormous variability in estimates of how many Americans volunteer. Even surveys conducted in the same year report different numbers of volunteers. Among people ages 18 to 64, somewhere between 14 percent and 55 percent volunteer. For older adults, the estimates range from 11 percent to 52 percent.

Table 36.1 summarizes findings from a number of studies on rates of volunteering, with the studies listed chronologically. The differences can be accounted for, at least in part, by variation among samples and by a lack of standard questions on volunteering. However, there does appear to be a consistent trend: *rates of volunteering have been increasing over time, for both younger and older volunteers.*

The various studies are also consistent in another way—that older people do *not* volunteer more than working age adults. An important rationale for recruiting older volunteers is that retirees ought to have more time to do volunteer work than younger people, who are in the paid work force. Retirees, it would seem, should be more likely to volunteer than younger people. But this does not seem to be true. If anything, older people volunteer less. Moreover, studies have shown that

most elderly volunteers do not spend large amounts of time in their volunteer work. One study, for example, found that only 5 percent of older adult volunteers worked more than six hours a week (see Worthy and Ventura-Merkel, 1982).

There are a number of significant barriers to volunteering by older people. The elderly are much more likely than others to give the following two reasons for not volunteering: poor health and lack of transportation. Another problem is income level. Low income is likely to restrict a person's ability to volunteer time, as well as to give money to charity.

According to national surveys, older people are much more likely than working-age adults to have only enough money for basic necessities. However, most elderly are healthy and capable of volunteering. Moreover, people age 65 and over give the highest proportion of their income to charity. A recent report on charitable giving in the United States noted: "Among the 56 percent of contributors who worried about having enough

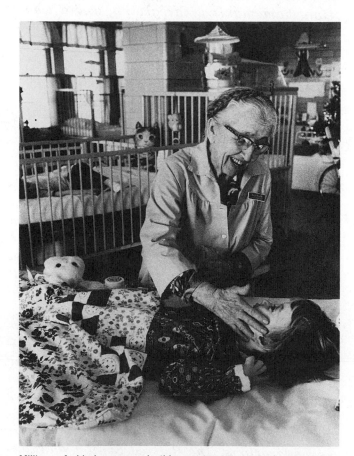

Millions of elderly persons in this country serve as volunteers; even many people who are in their 80s and 90s continue to volunteer. (Courtesy of the American Association of Retired Persons)

Table 36.1
How Many Adults and How Many Older Adults Volunteer?

Date	Organization Conducting the Study	Percent of Adults Volunteering	Percent of Older Adults Volunteering
1965	Gallup[2,3]	18%	11% (65+)
1974	The National Council on Aging[7]	35%	28% (65–69)
			20% (70–79)
			12% (80+)
1974	Gallup[2,3]	25%	14% (65+)
1981	The National Council on Aging[6]	55%	28% (65–69)
			23% (70–79)
			12% (80+)
1981	AARP[5]	——	28% (60–64)
			29% (65–69)
			33% (70–79)
			13% (80+)
1981	Independent Sector[10]	52%	37% (65+)
1985	Independent Sector[11]	48%	38% (65+)
1985	Gallup[3]	47%	36% (65+)
1988	AARP[4]	——	41% (65–69)
			37% (70+)
1988	Independent Sector[12]	45%	40% (65–74)
			29% (75+)
1988	Gerontologist[1]	——	52% (60+)
1989	Monthly Labor Review[8]	20%	17% (65+)
1989	Generations[9]	45%	40% (65–74)
			26% (75+)
1989	Independent Sector[13]	54%	47% (65–74)
			32% (75+)
1991	Marriott Seniors Living Services[14]	——	42% (60–64)
			46% (65–69)
			45% (70–74)
			39% (75–79)
			27% (80+)

Notes/Sources:

1. Fischer, L. R., D. P. Mueller, and P. W. Cooper, "Older Volunteers: A Discussion of the Minnesota Senior Study." *Gerontologist* Vol. 31 (1991): 183–94.
2. Gallup Organization. *Americans Volunteer.* Princeton, NJ: Gallup Organization, 1981.
3. Gallup Organization. *Americans Volunteer.* Princeton, NJ: Gallup Organization, 1986.
4. Hamilton, Frederick, and Schneiders Co. *Attitudes of Americans Over Forty-five Years of Age on Volunteerism.* Washington, DC: AARP, 1988.
5. ———. *A Survey of Older Americans.* Washington, DC: AARP, 1981.
6. L. Harris & Associates. *Aging in the Eighties.* Washington, DC: National Council on the Aging, 1982.
7. ———. *Myth and Reality of Aging in America.* Washington, DC: National Council on the Aging, 1975.
8. Hayghe, H. V. "Volunteers in the United States: Who Donates the Time?" *Monthly Labor Review* (February 1991): 17–23.
9. Herzog, A. R., and J. S. House. "Productive Activities and Aging Well," *Generations* Vol. 15 (Winter 1991): 49–54.
10. Independent Sector. *The Charitable Behavior of Americans.* Hodgkinson, V. A., and M. S. Weitzman. Washington, DC: Yankelovich, Skelly & White, 1981.
11. Independent Sector. *The Charitable Behavior of Americans.* Hodgkinson, V. A., and M. S. Weitzman. Washington, DC: Yankelovich, Skelly & White, 1985.
12. Independent Sector. *The Charitable Behavior of Americans.* Hodgkinson, V. A., and M. S. Weitzman. Washington, DC: Gallup Organization, 1988.
13. Independent Sector. *The Charitable Behavior of Americans.* Hodgkinson, V. A., and M. S. Weitzman. Washington, DC: Gallup Organization, 1990.
14. *Marriott Seniors Volunteerism Study.* Washington, DC: Marriott Seniors Living Services and U.S. Administration on Aging, 1991.

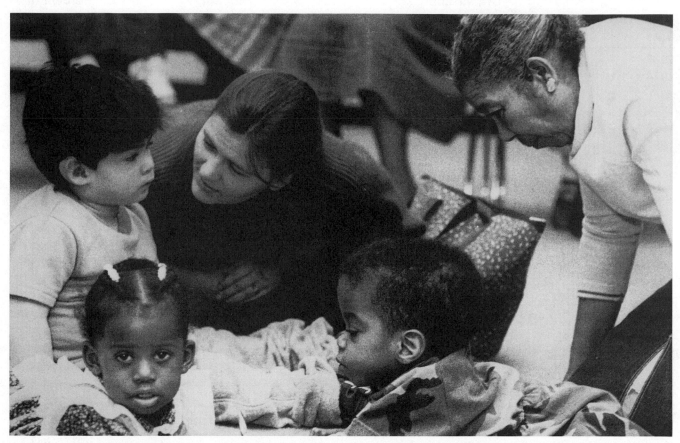

Among people ages 18–64, somewhere between 14 percent and 55 percent volunteer. (Courtesy of The National Council on the Aging, Inc.)

money in the future, *only respondents 65 years of age or older gave an average of 2 percent or more of their household income to charity*" [emphasis added] (Independent Sector, 1988). Even if rates of volunteering decline with age, there are still substantial numbers of elderly, even among the very old, who continue to volunteer. About an eighth of Americans over age 80 are volunteers (Worthy and Ventura-Merkel, 1982; see also Fischer and others, 1989, 1991).

However, the age curve may be changing so that the decline in volunteering occurs at much later ages. Previous surveys indicated that there was a substantial decline in volunteering at around age 60. In more recent surveys, the drop-off in rates of volunteering seems to happen much later—*after* age 75 or 80.

This suggests that post-retirement "careers" (including volunteer careers) may last for many years, suggesting the following implications:

- that there is ample time for "career development" among retired volunteers;
- that periodic re-training may be important;

- that retiree volunteers may need opportunities for growth and advancement to sustain a long-term involvement in volunteering; and
- there may need to be provisions made for "retiring" older volunteers.

● TYPES OF VOLUNTEER WORK

The types of activities included under the term volunteering are extraordinarily diverse. A volunteer might be the president or chair of a charitable foundation, an usher for a church function, a campaign worker who stuffs envelopes for a political candidate, a driver who delivers "meals-on-wheels," or a friendly visitor at a hospital. People who do any of these types of jobs might be called volunteers, and this is just a small sample of types of volunteer jobs or positions. There is also "informal" volunteering—that is, helping neighbors and friends, as individuals, but not through an organization. If a volunteer for a church, for example, gives rides

Table 36.2
Classifying Volunteer Roles

| | Formal volunteer work | | Informal volunteer work | |
| | Time commitment | | | |
Type of service activity:	Regular[1]	Occasional[2]	Regular	Occasional
Serving the public	Permanent volunteer in public role. *Examples:* Officer of charitable organization; unpaid editor of newsletter for nonprofit organization.	Temporary volunteer in public role. *Examples:* Chairperson of ad hoc committee; unpaid usher for cultural event.	_____	_____
Working with objects	Core volunteer for general services to organizations. *Examples:* Envelope stuffer for political campaign; church handy-person.	Recruit for general services to organizations. *Examples:* Cake baker for church bazaar; decoration-maker for fund-raising event.	Permanent helper for general tasks for neighbors or friends. *Examples:* Bookkeeper for neighbor or friend; person who regularly shovels neighbor's driveway for no pay.	Temporary helper for general tasks for neighbors or friends. *Examples:* House-watcher for traveling neighbor; person who fixes neighbor's broken window.
Helping individuals	Core volunteer for personal service work. *Examples:* Driver for a senior center; language tutor; personal companion, sent by church-group.	Recruit for personal service work. *Examples:* Red Cross volunteer who helps victims during a natural disaster.	Permanent helper for personal care. *Examples:* Caregiver for someone who is disabled; person who drives neighbor to church weekly.	Temporary helper for personal care. *Examples:* Caregiver for someone with the flu; person who drives neighbor on one or two errands.

Heading Notes:
1. Refers to an on-going commitment;
2. Refers to a voluntary service which is done once or twice, associated with an episode or event.

Sources: Fischer, L. R., and others. "Older Volunteers: A Discussion of the Minnesota Senior Study." *Gerontologist* Vol. 31 (1991): 183–94; Fischer, L. R., and K. B. Schaffer. *Older Volunteers: A Guide to Research and Practice.* Newbury Park, CA: Sage, 1993.

to her neighbor as part of a church-sponsored transportation program, why should the same type of service (giving a ride) not be counted as volunteering if this service is offered without any organization?

A list of all the different types of voluntary ser-

Profiles of Productive Aging

Shirley Brussell
Job agency founder

"The trend of older people working past the age of 65 is only going to keep growing. We don't have to sell older workers anymore. Our problem is matching them to the right job. We have far more jobs than we can fill—the demand is so great."

Chicagoan Shirley Brussell started Operation Able, an employment agency for persons over 45, in the summer of 1977. Since then, Able has grown into a nationally acclaimed program that has found jobs for more than 60,000 Chicagoans over 45. Born in Chicago in 1920, Brussell earned a college degree and did graduate work at the University of Chicago. After an internship in the Secretary of War's office in Washington, DC, Brussell became civilian personnel officer in Detroit, where 2,300 engineers were preparing military vehicles for the invasion of North Africa. After a transfer to the War Labor Board, she served as director of personnel in Detroit and Washington.

After the war she returned to Chicago and went into private industry, becoming the personnel manager of a mini-conglomerate food and restaurant chain with 2,200 employees. Three years later she married Judge Abraham Brussell. Though Brussell left work to have a family, she still managed to run a staggering list of volunteer projects.

When the children left home twenty-four years later, Brussell finished a master's degree in community organization. Volunteer work at the university involved her in creating employment programs for older people, and in 1974 she created the first temporary agency for older people, Re-Entry. By 1977 the Chicago Community Trust asked Brussell to direct a program called Life Options which was the start of Operation Able.

"There was nothing at 'Able' when I started," Brussell remembered. "There were some by-laws. The Metropolitan Welfare Council had given it some space. There were three of us: I had an assistant who was a gerontologist ex-nun with a Ph.D. who had left the church a few years ago, and I had a secretary. And a lot of good advice from the Trust; and a very supportive and involved board."

Brussell has built Operation Able into an organization with a staff of 346 people, including 70 permanent staff, 125 temps, and 100 independent career counselors, and a yearly budget of over $4 million. The tightening economy and increasing use of early retirement by large corporations has only increased Able's clientele and usefulness. Able offshoots have formed in seven American cities; in 1990 Sears asked Able to go into five additional communities and create "baby Ables" there.

Brussell has advised the International Labor Organization of the United Nations as well as countless older worker programs throughout the United States. In 1991 she received the YWCA's Outstanding Achievement Award for Community Leadership.

"I didn't retire at 65 because I thought I was only getting started," explained Brussell. "I don't think of retirement; I think of what other area would I like to help in or grow in. It's corny, but it's fun as you get older to grow. If you can feel growth and development, you don't feel old. It's when you feel you can't learn anything or do anything new that it's the end of the road."

Lydia Brontë

---

vices would be long and quite varied. One way to think about the different types of volunteering is to group volunteer jobs or roles according to the following criteria (see Table 36.2):

- Is the voluntary service "formal" (arranged through an organization) or "informal" (arranged by individuals)?
- Does the activity require a regular (ongoing) time commitment or an occasional (once or twice) commitment?

- What is the nature of the activity—working with the public? working with objects? or helping individual people?

Formal Versus Informal Volunteering

Formal volunteering refers to services arranged through or for organizations—churches, social welfare agencies, museums, hospitals, and so forth. In informal voluntary service, there is no organizational affiliation. Informal helping

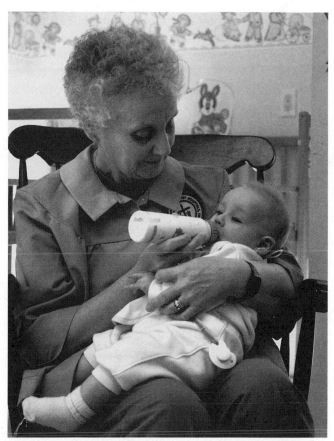

Formal volunteering refers to services arranged through or for organizations—churches, social welfare agencies, museums, hospitals, and so forth. (Courtesy of the American Association of Retired Persons)

includes services for friends, neighbors, and other individuals in the community. As Table 36.2 shows, many of the same activities may be arranged either formally or informally.

Time

The time-commitment issue is important because there are fundamental differences between regular and occasional volunteering. In formal volunteer organizations, volunteers who have on-going responsibilities have jobs that are often very similar to paid jobs. In informal volunteering, regular voluntary service is similar to responsibilities typically done in families.

Serving the Public

Some kinds of volunteering require interactions with the "community" or with large organizations or groups of people. Leadership roles such as the president or treasurer of a charitable organization fit this type. But there are also other volunteer jobs that largely entail contacts with people in the community—for example, an usher at a cultural event, the editor of a newsletter, the salesperson at a hospitality shop, or a performer at a charity concert. Public roles, almost by definition, involve formal rather than informal arrangements.

Working with Objects

In some kinds of volunteering, although the service is intended to help a person or group, the actual work centers on manipulating objects. This type of work includes stuffing envelopes for a charitable organization or political campaigns, bookkeeping, baking a cake for a bake sale, housecleaning for a church or neighbor, fixing a car, or mowing a lawn. The service may or may not lead to contact with others (one can stuff envelopes alone or with others), but the performance of the work is oriented toward contact with objects rather than people.

Helping Individuals

Some types of volunteering require private and face-to-face involvement with other people. This type of service work may be arranged on an informal basis or may be organized through a church or other organization. One obvious example of this type of service is caregiving, which can be formal or informal, regular or occasional. Other person-to-person services, not necessarily as intimate as caregiving, include personal services such as providing transportation, serving food, babysitting, and tutoring.

For a person who is considering volunteering, it is useful to think how each of these types

Volunteers in Action

In a large Midwestern community, retired executives work as volunteer mentors with high school students. One mentor was assigned to work with a high school student who is very talented in art. Her parents had told her that there was no way of making a living through art. But her mentor took some of her artwork to a local art institute, and the institute director said that hers was the best artwork for that age he had ever seen! Through this initiative she received a scholarship at a well-known arts academy.

Some types of volunteering require private and face-to-face involvement with other people. (Copyright © Benjamin Porter)

matches his or her individual preferences. People who like to spend their time interacting with people are not likely to be very satisfied with jobs that mainly involve working with objects—or vice versa. Someone who is unwilling to make a regular commitment for a volunteer job can volunteer for occasional events. Conversely, a retiree who wants an on-going commitment needs to look for regular volunteer opportunities.

● SERVICE EXCHANGE PROGRAMS

There is a special type of volunteering that needs its own explanation and discussion—a service exchange program. The incentive system for this type of program is rather different from most other volunteer activities. A few such experimental programs have been tried. For example, there is a program in Missouri in which volunteers earn "service credits" by providing respite care and other services, primarily to the elderly (Cahn, 1988). In an intergenerational neighborhood exchange program in a suburb of Los Angeles, older neighbors offer babysitting services in exchange for help with transportation (Pynoos and others, 1984).

Cahn (1988), a major proponent of the service credit system, asserts that an exchange program can generate a considerable amount of service for a modest set of administrative costs and is attractive to legislators, who can satisfy service needs without having to raise large revenues. He estimates that service credits cost about $1.50 per hour of service. Four states have enacted service credit laws, and nine other states are considering such legislation.

The service credit concept is especially interesting as a way to provide long-term care at home for frail elderly who are at risk of institutionalization. Long-term care is expensive and does not necessarily require a high level of skill. The use of volunteers through a service credit program or through other types of volunteer programs both serves the needs of the elderly, who usually want to continue living in their own homes, and also potentially can reduce public expenditures on long-term care.

But administrating service exchange programs can be complicated. An exchange program is only valuable *if* there is an adequate tracking system and *if* the program continues. Otherwise a donor risks getting no payback for time volunteered. An exchange program becomes increasingly valuable as the range of services grows. The larger the program, the more complex it is to administer and the greater the administrative costs.

> The service credit concept is especially interesting as a way to provide long-term care at home for frail elderly who are at risk of institutionalization.

Cahn (1988) notes that until service credits establish a track record, their extrinsic value will be regarded with skepticism, making it a catch-22 type of problem: An exchange program has little value unless it is functioning; but it can only attract participants—volunteers, clients, and stable sources of funding—if it has value!

● WHO VOLUNTEERS: A DEMOGRAPHIC PROFILE

Demographic factors seem to influence who volunteers. For example, people with more education, higher incomes, a higher occupational status, and better health are more likely to volunteer than other people. However, research findings on demographic characteristics of volunteers are not entirely consistent across studies.

Social Class

Among demographic factors that are associated with rates of volunteering, social class seems to be the most significant. People with higher incomes, with more education, and with professional types of occupations not only are more likely to give money to charity, they also are more likely to volunteer their time to organizations. Moreover, among volunteers, the more affluent and the better educated are the most active and give the most time. One researcher observed, "We also know from an earlier study asking about all volunteer work—for organizations or relatives—that income dominated the explanations, so much so that, surprisingly, the single best predictor was the number of modern appliances in the home" (Morgan, 1986).

Among the elderly, income and education also affect the amount of volunteering. Various studies suggest, in fact, that social class has much more of an impact on volunteering than age. It is possible that older persons are less likely to volunteer than working age adults, in large part, *because* the elderly tend to have less education and lower incomes (see, for example, Chambre, 1984; Fischer and others, 1989, 1991; Independent Sector, 1988; Kieffer, 1986; J. C. Penney, 1987; Romero, 1986).

People with higher incomes, with more education, and with professional types of occupations not only are more likely to give money to charity, they also are more likely to volunteer their time to organizations.

Gender

Do women volunteer more than men? Certainly there is the perception that volunteering is an avocation for women who are housewives. In fact, a major reason for rising concern about the supply of volunteers and the need to recruit older volunteers is that women have been entering the paid labor force in increasing numbers. Research findings on the effect of gender on volunteering, however, are somewhat mixed. Some studies have found that women volunteer more. Others have found no gender difference in rates of volunteering but have reported that women spend somewhat more hours volunteering than men. According to some research, women *no longer* do more volunteering than men—thus much of the growth in volunteering has come from increased participation by men. Whether men or women are

more likely to volunteer, it is quite clear that volunteering, like the paid labor force, tends to be gender related—that is, men and women often do different kinds of jobs as volunteers—with the differences largely conforming to gender role expectations (see, for example, Chambre, 1984; Fischer and others, 1991; Herzog and others, 1989; Morgan, 1986).

Marital Status

Married people are more likely to volunteer than unmarried persons. This has been found both in general populations and in studies of the elderly. Married people tend to have more income than unmarried people, and the gap in income level may be enough to explain the difference in volunteering by marital status (see Fischer and others, 1991; Hayghe, 1991; Independent Sector, 1988).

Health

Poor health is a significant barrier to volunteering. This has been reported in a number of studies of volunteering among the elderly. In fact, when non-volunteers are asked why they do not volunteer, poor health is given as one of the two most common reasons; lack of time is the other (see Cohen-Mansfield, 1989; Fischer and others, 1989, 1991; Independent Sector, 1988; Ozawa and Morrow-Howell, 1988).

Work and Retirement

An important rationale for recruiting older volunteers is that retirees ought to have more time to do volunteer work than workers, raising expectations that older retirees would be more likely to volunteer than older adults who are still working. In fact, the reverse appears to be true—that is, the elderly who remain in the labor force are more likely to volunteer than retired elderly. Surveys have found that older persons who are working part-time are more likely to volunteer than either full-time workers or those who have retired completely. But studies also show that, among older volunteers, those who are retired spend somewhat more time in volunteering than those still in the paid work force. Comparisons between retirees and older workers point out the substantial age and health differences between these groups. Older workers, on average, are considerably younger than retirees, and they are much less likely to have health and functional problems (see Chambre, 1984; Fischer and others, 1989, 1991; Hayghe, 1991; Morgan, 1986).

Religion

A very large proportion of volunteering and charitable giving in the United States is through religious organizations. Church members are considerably more likely to give to charity and to volunteer than non-members. Furthermore, among church members, those who are the most active—that is, those who attend services at least once a week—are the most likely to volunteer their time. Survey findings are mixed, however, on how specific religious affiliation affects volunteering (see Hamilton and others, 1988; Hodgkinson and Weitzman, 1989; Hodgkinson and others, 1990).

Race and Ethnicity

The research on how racial and ethnic factors affect volunteering is very limited, and the conclusions are controversial. Some data show that certain minority groups have substantially lower rates of volunteering than the white majority. Other studies, however, have found no difference or even the converse of these trends. It is clear that income and education are confounding factors in assessing the relationship between volunteering and race or ethnicity. In fact, middle and upper income African Americans are more likely to volunteer than poorer African Americans (see Carson, 1990; Chambre, 1987; Hayghe, 1991; Height, 1989; Independent Sector, 1985, 1988, 1990; Sundeen, 1988).

Why and how do these demographic factors determine whether or not someone volunteers? It

Volunteers in Aging

Retired engineers, from a very successful corporate volunteer program, work as a team at a residential facility for disabled persons. They design and manufacture mechanical devices for people with handicaps. Most of the people they have helped never could have afforded such devices without their donation of talent and time.

seems that the most logical explanation is that virtually all of these demographic determinants are resources of various types. Income and health are obvious resources. Education is another kind of resource—in terms of knowledge and skills (education also is connected to status, which is another resource). Marital status is a personal resource, in that being married means having a spouse—that is, having a roommate, a financial partner, a confidant, and a companion in leisure activities. Being employed means having an income and also having regular contact with other people. These various resources affect both the costs and the opportunities for volunteering in a variety of ways.

An absence of these resources raises the cost of volunteering. For example, a volunteer who does not have good health must expend a much larger portion of his or her available energy on volunteering tasks than would otherwise be required. For a person whose income is very low, the direct and indirect expenditures associated with volunteering (such as transportation or foregone wages) might be an insurmountable obstacle.

Conversely, having resources expands opportunities for volunteering in many ways. For example, having many social contacts increases the likelihood that a person will be invited to volunteer. Thus, for example, being employed (in contrast to being retired or being a housewife) exposes an individual to many relationships and opens up possibilities for a variety of activities, including volunteering.

Education is a particularly important resource. It is likely that well-educated persons have the most interesting and attractive volunteer opportunities. Among older volunteers, retired executives and other professionals may be in a uniquely advantageous volunteer position. Their skills and expertise are valued, and they are able to offer volunteer services that are both useful to others and meaningful to themselves.

To what extent do these demographic factors "determine" whether or not someone volunteers? A recent survey on volunteering (J. C. Penney, 1988) found that "volunteers and nonvolunteers are very similar with respect to sex, age, marital status, annual household income, the presence of children under the age of 18 in the household, and region of the country in which they live." From the research evidence to-date, it is apparent that demographic factors operate as predispositions in volunteering. But demography, by itself, cannot explain who volunteers—or why.

● WHO VOLUNTEERS: THE PERSONALITY FACTOR

There are some people who are helpers—women and men who seem to have a natural talent for doing good. Everyone knows such a person. There is the man who cleans driveways for all his neighbors with his snow blower; he never allows them to pay him, and he is embarrassed when they bring him Christmas gifts as a way of saying "thank you." There is the woman who has been cooking for her church for years and years; whenever there is a special event, she is in charge of the kitchen. There are the people who volunteer for a dozen worthy causes and who always say yes when they are asked to make a charitable donation.

Why do some people help and volunteer more than others? Research suggests that there is an altruistic personality. That is, some people are inclined to be helpers because of their moral character, their capacity for empathy, and their particular configuration of personality traits. Laboratory experiments reveal that people with altruistic or "other-oriented" personality traits, according to psychological test scores, are more likely to help others, if presented with opportunities.

An important component of the altruistic personality is the capacity for empathy. People behave altruistically when they feel empathy for the person in need of help. People who are inclined to volunteer seem to have a high emotional IQ—that is, a well-developed capacity for empathy (see Salovey and others, 1991).

It also appears that when people *believe* that they are altruistic, they develop an altruistic identity and are more likely to behave generously. This has been found in research with both children and adults. A study of blood donating found that people who give blood begin to identify themselves as donors, and this identity motivates future donations, year after year. Conversely, being rejected as a blood-donor affects the potential giver's self-image negatively. People who are rejected, for whatever reason, develop an identity as non-donors and tend not to try again (Piliavin and Charng, 1990; see also Grusec, 1991).

> Research suggests that there is an altruistic personality. That is, some people are inclined to be helpers because of their moral character, their capacity for empathy, and their particular configuration of personality traits.

A number of studies have revealed an association between doing good and good feelings. Optimism, positive mood, self-esteem, and extroversion all seem to increase altruism and volunteering. Thus, people who feel good about themselves are more likely to help and give to others. Furthermore, people are more likely to help others when they are in a good mood than when they are in a bad mood. Potentially there is a positive reinforcement loop: good feelings create a positive identity—which is both created and reinforced by altruistic behavior.

Older people who volunteer tend to be joiners. Older volunteers, most commonly, have volunteered in the past and have high levels of activity in most other areas of their lives as well. It may be that volunteers are people who are energized by contact with other people. They have recreational activities, spend time with and care for their families, do things with their neighbors and friends, and attend church regularly. In other words, there tends to be a "general activity syndrome"—so that volunteering is one type of activity for generally active people.

● RELIGION AND VOLUNTEERING

A very large proportion of volunteering is through religious organizations. This is particularly true for older volunteers, who have high rates of church membership. Thus, a large portion of volunteering by older persons is church work.

Religion is very strong in this country. Most Americans say they belong to a church or synagogue and the great majority (about 90 percent) say they believe in God. Scarcely any American is more than a few miles away from a house of worship. In an essay on "Religion and the Voluntary Spirit," Robert Wuthnow (1990) asserts that "despite changes in the nature of faith and in the wider society, religious organizations remain one of the most effective mechanisms in our society for motivating, organizing, and disseminating charitable giving."

Why is it that churches are so important in fostering volunteer work? One reason may be that volunteer work is simply a part of everyday church work. Churches, as nonprofit organizations, are bound to rely heavily on unpaid labor. Thus, it ought not to be surprising that a large portion of church members say that they are volunteers. But there may be other factors as well. Religions are likely to encourage altruistic values and behavior. Religious values also tend to foster a sense of community responsibility. This may be why church members are more likely to volunteer, in general, not just for church-sponsored activities (see Hodgkinson and Weitzman, 1989).

It is also possible that churches offer another indirect impetus to volunteer work—that is, they provide a way to organize volunteers. Religious organizations are in a particularly advantageous position to locate and recruit older volunteers. They can provide potential volunteers with a spiritual rationale for their services. They can offer recognition within their congregational community. Churches also can help to develop a lay leadership among older volunteers. For all these reasons, church work has important implications for volunteering that go well beyond services provided to or through individual churches or particular religious organizations.

● DOES VOLUNTEERING MAKE OLDER PEOPLE HEALTHIER AND HAPPIER?

What do people get from volunteering? Some research and many personal anecdotes have suggested that people who volunteer enjoy certain benefits—like better health, more positive self-

Volunteers in Action

A 100-year-old woman, living in a residential facility in a small town in New York state, started doing volunteer work about six years ago. Although she needs help herself, she offers telephone-outreach to other elderly people who are homebound and isolated.

esteem, and having more friends. In *The Healing Power of Doing Good*, Allan Luks with Peggy Payne argue that volunteering brings a "helper's high," which comes from the release of endorphins into the bloodstream and actually makes people feel healthier.

It may be that the potential benefits from volunteering are especially important for older persons confronting the hazards of old age. Some studies have suggested that people are healthier and happier in old age if they remain socially involved and participate in productive and meaningful activities. An older volunteer, who helps a child from a troubled family, says:

"I get out more. I have lost weight. I have played games and rode a bicycle since I started visiting Johnny, and I had not done much outside for a long time until me and Johnny started visiting each other. We take walks, play ball, ride bicycles, swim and go fishing. We also go out to eat a lot. Johnny is a wonderful friend. . . . I think this program is what every child and old person needs. It gets your time clock started again. I think it gives new meaning to my life, also to Johnny" (adapted from Landmann, 1991).

But it is difficult to get convincing evidence that volunteer work *causes* older people to be healthier and happier—because healthier and more active persons are the most likely to choose to be involved in volunteer work, as well as other activities. Although some research indicates associations between volunteering and good health, greater life satisfaction, better friendships, and so forth, other studies have not shown these effects. In any case, *causality is extremely difficult to prove.* Possibly volunteering does make people healthier and happier. But these benefits have not yet been adequately demonstrated.

Much of the research in volunteerism—especially on older volunteers—suggests that the most important benefits are intangible, or "spiritual." In his theory of life span development, social psychologist Erik Erikson argues that a central theme in later life is generativity—the human need to be productive and creative, to have meaning in one's life, and to be connected to others, across generations. If an individual does not have meaning and a sense of connection with others, his or her life may seem empty and purposeless. Without a sense of purpose, Erikson

By giving to others, individuals connect themselves to society and become part of something that is much larger than their individual lives. (Copyright © Benjamin Porter)

says, adults will have a "pervading sense of stagnation and personal impoverishment" (Erikson, 1963). Erikson points out that in later stages of life, people become increasingly aware of their own mortality. The great fact of human life is death. Young people may deny, ignore, and even disbelieve mortality. The old, however, struggle to find meaning in life—especially when confronting the fact of death.

> It is difficult to get convincing evidence that volunteer work *causes* older people to be healthier and happier—because healthier and more active persons are the most likely to choose to be involved in volunteer work, as well as other activities.

By giving to others, people connect to society and become part of something much larger than their individual lives. People's "spiritual wealth,"

however, allows them to confront death with some prospect of immortality. Robert Wuthnow writes in *Acts of Compassion:*

> "When someone shows compassion to a stranger, it does set in motion a series of relationships that spreads throughout the entire society. Even if the chain is broken at some point so that no direct benefits come back to us as individuals, the whole society is affected, just as an entire lake is affected when someone pours in a bucket of water."

● WHY VOLUNTEER?

When people are asked why they volunteer, they often say something about wanting to help, wanting to be useful, having a sense of social responsibility, or wanting to do good. Virtually every study of volunteer motivation has found that most volunteers give such altruistic responses. In a recent national survey (J. C. Penney, 1988), 97 percent of volunteers gave "I want to help others" as a reason for volunteering.

Voices of Creative Aging

Samuel A., A retired attorney and literature teacher, at 68 years he volunteers his time and scholarship to teach public school children.

I don't feel that I am fully retired; I feel that I am engaged as much as I ever was. When I look back, I wonder how I found time to go to work. When I retired I joined the Reading Aloud program as a volunteer in the Boston School system. I talk to the students about outstanding figures in black history: Harriet Tubman, Frederick Douglass, and a number of others. I find there is a great deal of interest in this subject among the kids. I also enjoy reading poetry to them—some pieces I have written. One I often read to them is about the great baseball player Satchel Paige: "Sometimes I feel like I will never stop, just go on forever till one fine morning I'm gonna to reach up and grab me a handful of stars, swing out my long lean leg, and whip three hot strikes burning down the heavens and look over at God and say, 'How about that.'"

A marvelous aspect of being older and free of some of the responsibilities you had before is to contemplate, to meditate, to reflect upon things. I think that's an important part of aging. One reason that I rejoice is that I have this time to involve myself in those things.

Excerpt from Connie Goldman's "Late Bloomer"
public radio series

Altruism—just doing good—is rarely the only motivation; most people give multiple reasons for volunteering.

Some volunteering is for personal, materialistic, or "selfish" reasons. For example, some people volunteer in order to expand their career opportunities, with the ultimate goal of paid employment; a business executive may donate time and money to a charitable or arts organization to benefit his or her business through publicity, public good will, and opportunities to network with other influential persons in the community; a person who volunteers in a cooperative neighborhood group or for the Parent Teacher Association at his or her child's school is providing a service to the family, in addition to serving others. Of course, the fact that individuals receive personal benefits from volunteering does not entirely answer the question about why these particular people—and not others —have chosen to volunteer.

Retired volunteers tend to have little interest in volunteering for the sake of enhancing or developing their careers. In this sense, older people tend to be less motivated by the possibility of material benefits. Conversely, older volunteers are more attracted to volunteering as an opportunity for socialization, learning, and personal growth.

A noted authority on volunteerism has suggested that it may be futile to try to understand motivations for volunteering. Jone Pearce (1985) writes, "Perhaps we should accept the inherent mystery of volunteer motivation—recognizing its benefits as well as its costs—rather than searching for an 'explanation' that will never really fit." Apparently there are certain topics—e.g., love and religious belief—for which scientific research can only nip around the edges. It does not yet fully convey why humans love one another or why humans help one another.

● THE GOOD THAT VOLUNTEERS DO

Certain circumstances encourage and inspire helping behavior. In effect, the more favorable the social conditions, the larger the numbers of people who would be inclined to help and volunteer. Imagine the following scene:

It is evening and you are taking a walk in your neighborhood. You look up and see a woman lying in the road. She seems to have been hit by a car. In the moonlight, you think you notice blood staining the road, and she seems to be moaning in pain. It is a quiet neighborhood and, although there are lights on in some of the houses, you see no one else on the street. What do you do?

And here is another scene:

In the early evening, you are walking along a city street. The street glitters with neon lights, and there are many restaurants and a few shops open. You pass a woman and a child, squatting in the doorway of a shop. They are both dirty and shabbily dressed. An old blanket and a pair of adult-sized crutches are lying on the cement sidewalk beside them. The woman, looking up at you, asks for money. "We need money to eat," she says. What do you do?

These are both situations in which an individual may help someone in need. But they seem quite different. Emotionally, morally, and legally they elicit different levels of responsibility. It is not likely that the two situations would provoke identical responses.

In the first situation it is hard to imagine not helping. In fact, to simply notice and walk on might be considered, morally if not legally, as negligence—since there is no assurance that someone else would help, and the woman could die. Yet the woman and child in the second vignette may also be in peril. They seem to be lacking a basic necessity—food—without which they also could die. Even so, many people who pass them probably will turn away and give nothing.

Experts on altruism contrast two kinds of conditions that elicit helping behavior: strong versus weak situations. In "strong situations," the following conditions apply:

- There is a pressing need
- There no alternative source of help
- There is a strong likelihood of a direct and positive impact

All of these conditions are met by the first scenario; they are arguable in the second. In the case of the woman lying injured on a lonely street, the vulnerability is clear: there is an ostensible risk of immediate death. Since the street seems to be empty, there is no one else to take responsibility for this woman's life. There is also a strong probability that intervention by a passerby will be useful—at the very least, an ambulance can be called. Moreover, what is called for is a one-time service. The passerby has no reason to suppose that, after this one act, he or she will be called upon for any on-going responsibility or rescue service. A quick and spontaneous "altruistic calculus" will show that the cost (to the helper) is relatively modest, while the benefit (to the woman on the street) is substantial.

With the situation of the woman begging on the street, the first condition is partially met: the woman asking for help is vulnerable and in need.

Even so, the need is not so immediate that she would actually die if the passerby does not help her. In fact, one of the most critical factors here is the presence of other alternative sources of help. Numerous studies of the "bystander effect" have shown that the number of people nearby strongly affects the choice to help or not. In this case, a passerby can rationalize that there are many others on the street to give her money, and/or there are other sources of help (government funds and private charities), and/or perhaps she could help herself (get a job). There is, finally, the issue of the impact of help. At best, the benefit will be temporary. In a short while, this same woman and child will again need money for food. Moreover, donating to these two people will make virtually no dent in the overwhelming problem of hungry and homeless people in our cities. There is a risk, in fact, that a passerby who gives to one person with a tin cup will be seen as a "mark" by others on the street, and the demands could be limitless. Therefore, the cost-benefit assessment in this case is very different from the first situation.

Regular volunteer work for organizations is more likely to approximate a "weak" than a "strong" helping condition. In regular volunteering, there is more likely to be a muted than a critical need for help. In many kinds of volunteer work, the impact is subtle rather than obvious. And, most important, it is very rare for a potential volunteer to believe that he or she is indispensable for the service to be provided.

Studies of natural and human-caused disasters have found that in such situations there are often more volunteers than needed. These are situations with obvious vulnerability and a clear benefit to those in need. When a situation is viewed as a crisis, then there is inherently a *perceived shortage of volunteers*, since there is little time to recruit helpers. Similarly, personal crises also

---

Volunteers in Action

A West Coast museum has 300 or so paid staff and over 600 volunteers. About half of them are seniors who serve as guides and teachers, working in every department. About 8,000 people visit the museum each day.

function as strong helping situations. Kidney donors are more likely to volunteer if there are no other possible donors. Moreover, donors, particularly if they are relatives, tend to decide instantaneously, without having to think about the decision (Simmons, 1991). Such situations meet all the conditions of strong helping situations: there is immediate vulnerability (risk of kidney failure), no alternative helpers (the relative has, by far, the best tissue match); and there is a direct, positive impact (the probability of saving a life).

Even if regular volunteering constitutes a relatively "weak" helping situation, there are still matters of degree. For example, sometimes potential volunteers offer unique contributions, so that alternative sources of help either are not available or could not be nearly as effective. Often, there are immediate and critical needs for help (e.g., for AIDS patients, teenagers using drugs, elderly at risk of losing their independence, and so forth).

A very important factor is the probable impact of a volunteer's efforts. A number of studies have shown that people are more likely to help if they feel competent and effective. The "warm afterglow of success" reinforces helping behavior, while failure and frustration make people want to quit (Organ, 1988). As one researcher notes: "people do not volunteer if they perceive that their time and efforts will be wasted" (Wheeler, 1986–87).

A number of studies have shown that people are more likely to help if they feel competent and effective.

● OLDER VOLUNTEERS

In many ways, the factors affecting who volunteers and why are essentially the same for younger and older volunteers. And yet, there are several special issues for older volunteers. First, there are aging related concerns. Second, there are access issues, because of changes in work and family life. Third, there are scheduling issues related to the time frame of postretirement lives. Finally, there is the experience factor—that is, older persons have accumulated many years worth of experiences that potentially affect their

interest in volunteering and the value of their contributed time.

Older persons, especially if they are retired, are likely to have more time to offer as volunteers than people who are working-age—but there are also more barriers. Older people have more health and functional problems; their incomes tend to be somewhat lower; and access to transportation is more likely to be a problem. Volunteers may become frail or, even without serious health problems, they may simply have less energy as they enter older and older ages. Their eyesight may become impaired, and they may no longer be able to safely drive a car. Not all or even most older volunteers are incapacitated, but, quite simply, there are more risks of health and functional problems with older volunteers, which present special challenges for organizations that have many volunteers in their late seventies and over.

Age affects access to volunteering in a paradoxical way: Older people potentially are more accessible as volunteers because they have diminished responsibilities in work and family roles and therefore have more time for volunteering. But without these roles, older persons are less accessible for recruitment, because they are not associated with the institutions and organizations from which volunteers are commonly recruited. Many volunteer programs are associated, directly or indirectly, with careers and occupations. Two of the most common types of voluntary associations to which individuals contribute their time are trade groups and civic organizations; both of these tend to attract memberships through their occupations and professions. There are also many programs associated with family roles. Parent-teacher associations, Boy Scouts, Girl Scouts, and church youth programs are several obvious examples of organizations that recruit volunteers primarily because of parental ties. According to a survey by Gallup, almost a quarter of volunteers indicated that they were motivated to contribute their time because they had a "child, relative or friend who was involved in the activity or would benefit from it" (Gallup, 1981). Corporate and executive retiree programs are *unusual* in attempting to recruit older volunteers because of their special affiliations and past work experience. There are also a few experimental programs that recruit grandparents to volunteer in school and other youth programs because of commitments to their own grandchildren. But such programs are exceptions. Most older volunteers are recruited despite their lack of such ties through family or work. There is one notable exception to this lack of institutional affiliation: large proportions of older persons are members of religious organizations. Church work has a unique place in volunteerism, particularly for older persons, in part because it offers communal affiliations outside of work and family roles (see earlier discussion on Religion and Volunteering).

Access to older volunteers is also related to scheduling issues. Retirees are potentially more accessible because they do not have work commitments during daytime hours. On the other hand, many older volunteers are unable or unwilling to volunteer after dark, either because of problems with night driving or fear of crime. The implication is that not only are many older volunteers available during the day but they may be available *only* during the day. In the winter months this may cause some scheduling problems for volunteer programs. There is also another winter problem: in January and February, volunteer programs in cold-climate states sometimes lose many of their regular volunteers who go as "snowbirds" to Florida, California, Arizona, and other states with warmer winter climates. Older persons are able to be snowbirds because they lack time commitments imposed by work or school schedules. It is their relative freedom from such schedules that makes retirees both accessible and, in some ways, irregular, as volunteers.

There is at least one other age factor: Persons in later life have accumulated many years of experience and, in a number of ways, these past experiences affect the recruitment of older volunteers. For example, consider the issue of whether or not a person has previously volunteered. At age 20, it would not be unusual for a person to have had no experience as a volunteer; yet this person is more likely to be considered as not-yet-a-volunteer rather than a non-volunteer. Conversely, if by age 70 an individual has never volunteered, he or she has missed various opportunities for volunteering in middle age, for whatever reason. Surveys have shown that both young persons and the elderly have relatively lower rates of volunteering than people in their middle

years. But these patterns have different meaning—because past experience is a more significant factor for older persons. Similarly, older persons have had many experiences over their lives—in family, work, friendship, and so forth. Older volunteers are especially valuable to volunteer programs when they are given opportunities to use the particular skills and abilities that they have gained over their lives.

● AN UNTAPPED POTENTIAL?

"When a society has vast unmet needs at the same time that there are large numbers of healthy, energetic, productive human beings for whom the society can find no use—even though they would like to be useful—then something is wrong" (Cahn, 1988).

Does our society give adequate opportunities for older persons to continue in productive activities? Is there an untapped potential for recruiting older persons as volunteers? Many older people who do not currently volunteer say they would like to. Many current volunteers say that they would be willing to spend more time volunteering. Is this evidence that many more elderly would or could volunteer?

Actually, it is not easy to extrapolate based on what people say they might or should do. Motivations for volunteering are complex. When people say that they might or they should volunteer, it is hard to know what this means. Moreover, it is unrealistic to expect that all elderly will volunteer. Many older persons either are not interested in volunteering or have health and physical limitations that seriously limit what they can do. When elderly non-volunteers are asked why they are not volunteering, by far the most common reasons they give are health problems and their age (Independent Sector, 1990).

It is also clear that an elder volunteer force

Older volunteers are especially valuable to volunteer programs when they are given opportunities to use the particular skills and abilities that they have gained over their lives.

does not offer a cure for shortages in public funding for human services. Even if it were possible to recruit millions more elderly as volunteers, their work would largely complement rather than supplant other health and social services. An older volunteer force, by itself, cannot be expected to solve serious social problems confronting American society today—like poverty, drug abuse, crime, and teenage pregnancy.

Nonetheless, *much more could be done.* Many volunteer programs—especially service-oriented programs—are small because their funds are very limited. When public and/or private monies are available to support volunteer programs, these programs thrive and grow. The implication is clear: *To the extent that more opportunities are developed and more funds are invested in programs for older volunteers, the "pay-off" should be more older volunteers and increased services by older volunteers.*

Studies have found that a major reason that many older people give for not volunteering is that *no one asked them.* Volunteer organizations rely heavily on word-of-mouth recruitment, in part because this is an effective method of recruitment but also because they do not have the funds to develop larger programs. Volunteers tend to be recruited from closed networks, and many people who are different from the people in these networks are simply never asked to volunteer. Again the implication is intriguing: *With systematic recruitment efforts, many more elderly persons, from diverse backgrounds and experiences, could be recruited as volunteers.*

There is also both theory and research to support the importance of "productive aging"—that older persons are interested in and can benefit from opportunities for productive activities, including volunteerism. According to theorists like Erik Erikson, the human need to be productive and to have meaning in life becomes increasingly poignant as people age. Most older people believe strongly that "life is not worth living if you can't contribute to the well-being of others" (Herzog and House, 1991). Even so, older people spend much of the extra time that they have gained through retirement in passive activities, such as watching television. There is, thus, the implication that: *There are many older people who could be attracted to enhanced opportunities for productive activities through volunteerism.*

Older persons, over their lifetimes, have developed and accumulated knowledge, skills, experience, abilities, and talents. Much of their knowledge is practical—how to soothe a child, how to drive nails into a corner beam, how to make chicken soup, how to adjust a pair of eyeglasses, how to teach someone to read. What structures or opportunities are readily available for older persons to make use of the full range of their accumulated talents and skills? Since the investment in volunteerism has been rather limited, the conclusion seems obvious: *The accumulated life experiences and skills of older persons are not being as well utilized as they might be.*

Volunteers tend to be recruited from closed networks, and many people who are different from the people in these networks are simply never asked to volunteer. Again the implication is intriguing: *With systematic recruitment efforts, many more elderly persons, from diverse backgrounds and experiences, could be recruited as volunteers.*

This century has witnessed a miracle of survival, as life expectancy has increased by as much as 50 percent in the last fifty years or so. Of all the revolutions in recent times, the age revolution is in some ways the most miraculous, the most dramatic, and possibly the most significant in its impact on everyday lives. But, according to many gerontologists, current social policies are out-of-step with the "age revolution." Matilda White Riley and John Riley (1989) argue that, while about twenty-eight years have been added to the life span, there is a problem of "structural lag, because the age structure of social opportunities has not kept pace with the rapid changes in the ways people grow old." In *Productive Aging*, Robert Butler writes (1985): "No government or private institution within society has addressed effectively and comprehensively the multiple challenges posed by societal aging."

Current social policies and most public expenditures on aging focus on old age as a terminal stage. The problems of old age—frailty and sickness—cost hundreds of billions of dollars. The

Older persons, over their lifetimes, have developed and accumulated knowledge, skills, experience, abilities and talents. (Copyright © Benjamin Porter)

lion's share of the aging budget, both federal and state, is for health and long-term care. While there are some publicly supported programs to provide activities for senior citizens, the budget for these projects is almost negligible.

It may be time to refocus—to develop social definitions and public policies that are future-focused, that offer meaningful futures to older citizens, and that use their capacities to help shape a better future world for everyone. This will require broadening social visions, expanding public-private investments in programs for older volunteers, and developing social policies that redefine the meaning of the last third of life.

Organizations

For readers who are interested in learning more about volunteer opportunities, here is a list of organizations that serve as resource centers on volunteering. Most of these organizations are national, but many have local affiliates that should be listed in telephone directories. Since there are many different types of volunteer pro-

grams, this list is not comprehensive but rather is intended as a representative sample of places to contact.

For a retiree, a good place to begin looking for volunteer work is to contact the local office of the Retired Senior Volunteer Program (RSVP) whose mission is to find placements for older volunteers in many different agencies. Churches, synagogues, and other religious organizations also usually offer programs for volunteers. A number of large corporations also have volunteer programs for their retirees.

ACTION
1110 Vermont Ave., NW
Washington, DC 20525
(202) 634-9108

ACTION is the federal agency for volunteer service. Its purpose is to stimulate volunteerism in general and, in particular, to demonstrate the effectiveness of volunteers in problem solving. Its major programs include Foster Grandparents (FGP), Retired Senior Volunteers (RSVP), Senior

Companions (SCP) for elders, Volunteers in Service to America (VISTA), and a variety of programs for youth. Periodical: *Action Update.*

American Association for Museum Volunteers
1225 Eye St., NW, Ste. 200
Washington, DC 20005
(202) 289-6575

Formerly the United States Association of Museum Volunteers, this membership organization holds its annual training conference in conjunction with the American Association of Museums. Periodicals: *Museum News; AVISO.*

American Association of Retired Persons (AARP)
601 E St., NW
Washington, DC 20049
(202) 434-3200

Non-profit, non-partisan organization whose members are all 50 years of age and over. AARP offers a wide range of membership benefits and services, and education and advocacy materials. The AARP Volunteer Talent Bank matches volunteers age 50 or older with suitable volunteer positions nation-wide, in both AARP programs and other organizations. Periodicals: *Prime Time, Modern Maturity; AARP News Bulletin* (monthly), and *Legislative Report.*

American Red Cross
National Headquarters
17th and D Sts., NW
Washington, DC 20006

The Red Cross brings together trained volunteers and paid staff to help prevent, prepare for, and cope with emergencies. The ARC is chartered by the U.S. Congress to provide disaster relief at home and abroad. It collects, processes, and distributes voluntarily donated blood and involves 1.4 million volunteers.

Habitat for Humanity International
Habitat and Church Sts.
Americus, GA 31709-3498
(912) 924-6935

Habitat for Humanity is an ecumenical Christian housing ministry whose objective is to eliminate poverty housing from the world and to make decent shelter a matter of conscience.

Over 40,000 volunteers have helped build or rehabilitate over 2,000 homes for low-income families in the United States and in developing countries.

Independent Sector (IS)
1828 L St., NW
Washington, DC 20036
(202) 223-8100

IS is a national membership organization formed through the merger of the Coalition of National Voluntary Organizations (CONVO) and the National Council of Philanthropy (NCOP). It works to preserve and enhance the national traditions of giving, volunteering, and not-for-profit initiative. Periodical: *Update.*

International Association for Volunteer Effort (IAVE)
c/o Ruth March
P.O. Box 27095
Los Angeles, CA 90027
(213) 467-6443

Membership in IAVE is open to volunteers everywhere who share the desire to encourage and promote worldwide volunteer action dedicated to improving the quality of life. Membership fee is $30 for individuals and $60 for organizations. Periodical: *LIVE Newsletter.*

Minnesota Office on Volunteer Services (MOVS)
117 University Ave.
St. Paul, MN 55155
(612) 296-4731

The Minnesota Office of Volunteer Services, Department of Administration, strives to improve the quality of life in Minnesota through voluntary action. It works with both public and private organizations. MOVS is involved in the following activities: advocacy for volunteers and volunteer service; publishing a bi-monthly newsletter; operation of a resource library; technical assistance and information; research on special volunteer issues and projects; convening meetings of volunteer groups and leaders and providing training opportunities. Membership is not required for MOVS services. Periodical: *Volunteers Move Minnesota.*

Habitat for Humanity is part of a global effort to provide decent housing for "God's people in need." (Copyright © Susan Granados)

National Assembly of National Voluntary Health and Social Welfare Organizations
1319 F St., NW, Ste. 601
Washington, DC 20004
(202) 347-2080

The National Assembly is an organizational membership association formed to facilitate cooperation and communication among voluntary organizations and to pursue mutual goals and convictions. It also acts as a clearinghouse and resource center.

National Association of Partners in Education (NAPE)
209 Madison St., Ste. 401
Alexandria, VA 22314
(703) 836-4880

NAPE (formerly National School Volunteer Program - NSVP) is a membership organization comprised of those involved in or interested in school volunteer programs. It functions as a resource for its members and as an advocate activity within the educational field. Periodicals: *School Volunteering; Partners in Education.*

National Casa Association (CASA)
2722 Eastlake Ave. E, Ste. 220
Seattle, WA 98102
(206) 328-8588

Membership organization for court appointed special advocates formed in 1982 to provide coordination, technical training and assistance to CASA/guardian and listen programs nationwide. CASA is a nationwide movement of community volunteers who speak for abused or neglected children in court. The National CASA Association represents more than 377 CASA programs and 13,000 CASA volunteers in 47 states. Periodical: *CASA Connection.*

National Council on Corporate Volunteerism (NCCV)
c/o The Points of Light Foundation
1737 H St., NW
Washington, DC 20006
(202) 223-9186

NCCV, a corporate membership organization promotes volunteerism by serving as a national resource for the development and expansion of corporate employee volunteer programs. The council also serves as a clearinghouse for the exchange of information on corporate volunteerism and produces a quarterly newsletter as part of VOLUNTEER's "Volunteers from the Workplace" service. NCCV President is Jill Ragatz who is manager of corporate volunteer programs, Honeywell, Inc., Minneapolis, MN. Periodical: *Corporate Newsletter.*

The National Council on the Aging
P.O. Box 7227
Ben Franklin Station
Washington, DC 20044
(202) 479-1200

The NCOA is a resource for information, training, technical assistance, advocacy, publications and research on every aspect of aging. The membership organization offers various networking opportunities and sponsors an annual conference.

National Executive Service Corps (NESC)
257 Park Ave., S
New York, NY 10010
(212) 867-5010

NESC uses senior, unpaid business executive retirees to counsel national nonprofits in the fields of education, health, religion, social services and the arts for periods of three to six months. They also coordinate the efforts of a network of local Executive Service Corps which work with local nonprofit organizations.

National Retiree Volunteer Center (NRVC)
905 Fourth Ave., S
Minneapolis, MN 55404
(612) 341-2689

The National Retiree Volunteer Center is the catalyst that empowers retirees to be a contributing force in their communities through the investment of their skills and expertise. It initiates, develops and expands retiree volunteer programs, for community benefit, in cooperation with corporations, government, educational institutions and professional associations.

National Volunteer Center (VOLUNTEER)
1737 H St., NW
Washington, DC 20006
(202) 223-9186

VOLUNTEER was created in 1979 through the merger of the National Center for Voluntary Action and the National Information Center on Volunteerism. It serves as the only national voluntary organization whose sole purpose is to encourage the more effective use of volunteers in community problem solving. VOLUNTEER helps to improve the effectiveness of volunteer management skills by providing information sharing, training and technical assistance services; operates special projects to demonstrate new, unique and innovative ways to get people involved; and serves as a national advocate for volunteering and citizen involvement. Periodicals: *Voluntary Action Leadership; Volunteering; Volunteer Readership Catalog.*

Points of Light Foundation
1737 H St., NW
Washington, DC 20006
(202) 223-9186

The mission of the newly created POL Foundation is to make community service aimed at serious social problems central to the life of every American. The Foundation will work to stimulate new initiatives and build on and enhance the efforts of existing organizations in addressing its goals. These goals include: enlisting the media in making people aware of the benefits of engaging in service; persuading businesses, unions, schools, civic groups, religious institutions and other organizations to mobilize all of their members for community service; and identifying and disseminating community service ideas that work.

Service Corps of Retired Executives (SCORE)
409 Third St., NW
Washington, DC 20024
(202) 205-6762

SCORE is sponsored by the Small Business Administration, but it is an independent nonprofit organization. SCORE's primary purpose is to render a community service by providing, without charge, the expert assistance of its volunteer counselors in solving the problems encountered by small businesses.

United Way of America (UWA)
701 North Fairfax
Alexandria, VA 22314
(703) 836-7100

UWA provides leadership and service to over 2,200 local United Ways in fundraising, fiscal and program management. It is also engaged in research and liaison activities with other national organizations and the government. Periodical: *Community.*

Volunteers in Prevention and Probation (VIP)
527 North Main St.
Royal Oak, MI 48067
(810) 398-8550

An organization to support and promote citizen involvement in court and correction programs. Periodical: *VIP Examiner.*

References

Americans Volunteer. Manpower Research Monograph No. 10. Washington, DC: U.S. Department of Labor, 1965.

Americans Volunteer. Washington, DC: ACTION, 1974.

Butler, R. N., and H. P. Gleason. *Productive Aging: Enhancing Vitality in Later Life.* New York: Springer, 1985.

Cahn, E. S. "Service Credits: A Market Strategy for Redefining Elders as Producers." In *Retirement Reconsidered: Economic and Social Roles for Older People.* Eds. R. Morris and S. Bass. New York: Springer, 1988.

Carson, E. D. "Black Volunteers as Givers and Fundraisers." *Working Papers: Center for the Study of Philanthropy* (1990).

Cohen-Mansfield, J. "Employment and Volunteering Roles for the Elderly: Characteristics, Attributions, and Strategies." *Journal of Leisure Research* Vol. 21 (1989): 214–27.

Erikson, E. *Childhood and Society.* New York: Norton, 1963.

Fischer, L. R., D. P. Mueller, and P. W. Cooper. "Older Volunteers: A Discussion of the Minnesota Senior Study." *Gerontologist* Vol. 31 (1991): 183–94.

Fischer, L. R., D. P. Mueller, P. W. Cooper, and A. Chase. *Older Minnesotans: What Do They Need? How Do They Contribute?* Amherst H. Wilder Foundation: Wilder Research Center, 1989.

Gallup Organization. *Americans Volunteer.* Princeton, NJ: Gallup Organization, 1981.

Grusec, J. E. "The Socialization of Altruism." In *Prosocial Behavior.* Ed. Margaret Clark. Newbury Park, CA: Sage Publications, 1991.

Hamilton, Frederick, and Schneiders Co. *Attitudes of Americans Over Forty-five Years of Age on Volunteerism.* Washington, DC: AARP, 1988.

———. *A Survey of Older Americans.* Washington, DC: AARP, 1981.

Harris, L., and associates. *Aging in the Eighties.* Washington, DC: National Council on the Aging, 1981.

———. *Myth and Reality of Aging in America.* Washington, DC: National Council on the Aging, 1974.

Hayghe, H. V. "Volunteers in the United States: Who Donates the Time?" *Monthly Labor Review* (February 1991): 17–23.

Height, D. "Self Help: A Black Tradition." *Nation* (July 24, 1989): 136–38.

Herzog, A. R., and J. S. House. "Productive Activities and Aging Well." *Generations* Vol. 15 (Winter 1991): 49–54.

Herzog, A. R., R. L. Kahn, J. N. Morgan, J. S. Jackson, and T. C. Antonucci. "Age Differences in Productive Activities." *Journal of Gerontology* Vol. 44 (1989): S129–S138.

Hodgkinson, V. A., and M. S. Weitzman. "From Commitment to Action: Religious Belief, Congregational Activities, and Philanthropy." Paper Presented at Independent Sector Spring Research Forum, Chicago, IL (March 10–11, 1989).

Hodgkinson, V. A., M. S. Weitzman, and A. D. Kirsch. "From Commitment to Action: How Religious Involvement Affects Giving and Volunteering." *Faith and Philanthropy in America: Exploring the Role of Religions in America's Voluntary Sector.* 1990.

Independent Sector. *The Charitable Behavior of Americans.* V. A. Hodgkinson and M. S. Weitzman. Washington, DC: Yankelovich, Skelly & White, 1985.

———. *Giving and Volunteering in the United States.* V. A. Hodgkinson and M. S. Weitzman. Washington, DC: Gallup Organization, 1988.

———. *Giving and Volunteering in the United States.* V. A. Hodgkinson and M. S. Weitzman. Washington, DC: Gallup Organization, 1990.

J. C. Penney Co. *Study on Volunteerism.* 1988.

Kieffer, J. "The Older Volunteer Resource." In *Productive Roles in an Older Society.* Committee on an Aging Society. Washington, DC: National Academy Press, 1986.

Landmann, R. *West Virginia Rural Family Friends Project: Evaluation Report.* Washington, DC: National Council on Aging, 1991.

"Late Bloomer" audio cassette. Available from Connie Goldman Productions, 926 Second Street, Suite 201, Santa Barbara, CA 90403. (310) 393-6801.

Luks, A., with P. Payne. *The Healing Power of Doing Good.* New York: Fawcett Columbine, 1991.

Marriott Seniors Volunteerism Study. Washington, DC: Marriott Senior Living Services and U.S. Administration on Aging, 1991.

Morgan, J. N. "Unpaid Productive Activity Over the Life Course." In *Productive Roles in an Older Society.* Committee on an Aging Society. Washington, DC: National Academy Press, 1986.

Organ, D. W. *Organizational Citizenship Behavior: The Good Soldier Syndrome.* Lexington, MA: Lexington Books, 1988.

Ozawa, M. N., and N. Morrow-Howell. "Services Provided by Elderly Volunteers: An Empirical Study." *Journal of Gerontological Social Work* Vol. 13 (1988): 65–80.

Pearce, J. "Insufficient Justification and Motivation to Volunteer." In *Motivating Volunteers.* Ed. L. Moore. Vancouver, BC: Vancouver Volunteers Center, 1985.

Piliavin, J. A., and H. W. Charng. "Altruism: A Review of Recent Theory and Research." *Annual Review of Sociology* Vol. 16 (1990): 27–65.

Pynoos, J., B. Hade-Kaplan, and D. Fleisher. "Intergenerational Neighborhood Networks." *Gerontologist* Vol. 24 (1984): 266–69.

Riley, M. W., and J. W. Riley. "The Lives of Older People and Changing Social Roles." *Annals of the American Academy of Political and Social Science* (1989).

Romero, C. J. "The Economics of Volunteerism: A Review." In *Productive Roles in an Older Society.* Committee on an Aging Society. Washington, DC: National Academy Press, 1986.

Salovey, P., J. D. Mayer, and D. L. Rosenhan. "Mood and Helping: Mood as a Motivator of Helping and Helping as a Regulator of Mood." In *Prosocial Behavior.* Ed. M. S. Clark. Newbury Park, CA: Sage Publications, 1991.

Simmons, R. G. "Presidential Address on Altruism and Sociology." *Sociological Quarterly* Vol. 32 (1991): 1–22.

Sundeen, R. A. "Explaining Participation on Coproduction: A Study of Volunteers." *Social Science Quarterly* Vol. 69 (1988): 547–68.

Wheeler, C. M. "Facing Realities: The Need to Develop a Political Agenda for Volunteerism." *Journal of Volunteer Administration* (Winter 1986–87): 1–12.

Worthy, E. H., and C. Ventura-Merkel. *Older Volunteers: A National Survey.* Washington, DC: National Council on the Aging, 1982.

Wuthnow, R. *Acts of Compassion: Caring for Others and Helping Ourselves.* Princeton, NJ: Princeton University Press, 1991.

———. "Religion and the Voluntary Spirit in the United States: Mapping the Terrain." In *Faith and Philanthropy in America: Exploring the Role of Religions in America's Voluntary Sector,* 1990.

Additional Reading

Chambre, Susan. *Good Deeds in Old Age: Volunteering by the New Leisure Class.* Lexington, MA: Lexington Books, 1987.

Fischer, Lucy Rose, and Kay Schaffer. *Older Volunteers: A Guide to Research and Practice.* Newbury Park, CA: Sage Publications, 1993.

Freedman, Marc. *The Kindness of Strangers: Adult Mentors, Urban Youth, and the New Voluntarism.* San Francisco, CA: Jossey-Bass, 1993.

Isley, Paul J. *Enhancing the Volunteer Experience.* San Francisco, CA: Jossey-Bass, 1990.

Lucy Rose Fischer, Ph.D.

37

The Meaning and Uses of Leisure

- Changing Attitudes Toward Leisure • The Meaning of Leisure • Retirement Planning
- Limits on Leisure • Time and Older Americans • Continuing to Work • Hobbies
- Social and Religious Participation • Minorities and Leisure • Housing and Activities
- Sports and Fitness for Seniors • Entertainment: The Performing Arts and the Media • Travel
- Trends in Leisure and Retirement

Most Americans now entering later life can expect to become members of a "new leisure class," due to the massive social and demographic changes over the twentieth century. Because leisure looms so large in the lives of all but the poorest older Americans, it deserves more than a cursory examination. Free time is important not only because retirement provides so much of it, and so suddenly, but because aging well depends in large part on making this time meaningful.

Living longer, fuller, and healthier lives, most Americans now look forward to a post-work time span of approximately nineteen to twenty-five years. The French call the period the Troisième Age, *or* Third Age, *in the life cycle, following the broad stages of learning (youth) and working (adulthood).*

As a people, Americans have decidedly mixed feelings about what, for most, will constitute the Third Age: leisure and retirement. On the one hand, after leading busy lives raising and supporting a family, the prospect of finally having plenty of time seems like a gift. On the other hand, our cultural conditioning carries with it guilt feelings about leisure that may diminish its pleasures. Writing about retirement, Paul Fremont Brown (1988) explained: "When I relaxed, I felt guilty.... Some of us have spent our whole lives thinking of idleness as a vice." Unless he was busy accomplishing something, his conscience hounded him.*

● CHANGING ATTITUDES TOWARD LEISURE

Ancient cultures—chiefly the Greeks and Romans—elevated leisure to the highest status. Aristotle rated it "better than work and its end." But since the Reformation, the work ethic, also called the Protestant ethic, has dominated and shaped the attitudes toward work (and play) of all Western societies, including the United States (Havighurst, 1961; Osgood, 1982). Leisure, according to the Puritans who settled this land, was the work of the devil. Making a living, being productive, was the accepted goal.

The generation now facing retirement grew up believing that recreation and leisure were highly marginal—fine for kids but to be taken in small doses by adults. It was only the "idle rich" who possessed limitless leisure.

Sometime in the middle of the twentieth century, thanks to industrialization coupled with hard work, Western societies were producing more goods than they could consume. The relationship between the job and leisure time began to change. If work was the seed of progress, its fruits included the shorter work week, the paid vacation, the pension, and the long period of retirement.

It has been said that a measure of civilization

781

may be the degree that people perceive the use of time to be a problem (Havighurst, 1961). The problem, typically, doesn't emerge the morning after retirement. To most new retirees, still fit and energetic, the first few months are euphoric, full of the delight of children just sprung from school for summer vacation. Eventually, however, many experience a down side to the freedom that has replaced alarm clocks, commutes, and rigid schedules: the challenge of how to fill it.

Thus the "honeymoon" phase of retirement is usually followed by a "disenchantment" phase (Palmore, 1985). In fact, a large AARP survey of the elderly in 1980 found that disposing of leisure was their third most significant problem—after health and finances.

People with guilt feelings about retirement sometimes compensate by cramming their calendars with a multitude of projects. In effect, they exchange the work ethic for the "busy ethic." Cautioning against this, behaviorist B.F. Skinner (1983) advised: "To keep busy just because you feel you should . . . is not likely to be of much help. You must get more out of what you do than an escape from feeling guilty because you are idle. Instead of trying hard to enjoy what you are doing, try hard to find something that you like better."

Other older adults accept late-life leisure as an earned privilege (Atchley, 1987), as "bonus time" to which their labor has entitled them. This more relaxed approach reflects a fairly recent trend in theory that views leisure as an avenue to self-realization and, as such, as an end in itself—not only for seniors but for all Americans. Writing of leisure's current role, French theorist Dumazedier (1974) observed, "Part of what used to be considered sinful by religious institutions is now recognized as the art of living."

Regardless of how leisure is perceived by older people, the exchange of the routines and rituals of work for leisure is one of life's most abrupt transitions. Retirees must deal with the suddenness of the change along with the feelings of emptiness and disorientation that often accompany a major life transition (Bridges, 1980). Some find that time stretches before them "like the open sea"; this can be frightening or exhilarating.

What people fear in retirement, as well as the challenge of filling time, is the sense of diminished self-respect and purpose. Other losses—

> A large AARP survey of the elderly in 1980 found that disposing of leisure was their third most significant problem—after health and finances.

real or perceived—include loss of income, status and recognition, the "perks" of the job, a sense of accomplishment, and—perhaps most crucial—social contacts. "Work, since time immemorial, has been the means to satisfy man's need for belonging to a group and for a meaningful relationship to others of his kind" (Drucker, 1973). The challenge of retirement is replacing these losses with meaningful leisure activities (Osgood, 1987). Cutler (1990) assigns an even loftier role to leisure, proposing that "it is through leisure that new and renewed selves may be produced."

● THE MEANING OF LEISURE

How, then, to define the multi-faceted condition that is leisure? A good, working definition by the late A. Bartlett Giamatti (1989), university president and commissioner of major league baseball, called leisure "that form of non-work activity felt to be chosen, not imposed." He maintained that the use of freely chosen leisure reveals more about an individual—or a culture—than does its labor, for "to pursue leisure is to use freedom, our most precious possession."

More simply, leisure is the time left over after life's necessities have been attended to. It is uncommitted time.

In one sense the notion of leisure is subjective, for the attitude toward the activity, not the activity itself, defines its nature. Making ceramic pots or analyzing the stock market, for example, may be leisure-time hobbies for some but businesses for others (Cutler, 1990).

Leisure time and recreation are closely related but not identical concepts. Leisure refers to time availability, while recreation is the use of that time to refresh one's mind or body. In her autobiography, actress Helen Hayes (1984) summed up the positive outlook an older person needs in dealing with both of them: "To feel refreshed and ready for the next plateau, there must be some genuine eagerness to get there—a plan, a reason, a goal, a commitment . . . enthusiasm, productiveness, stimulating activities, intellectual progress—these are the ingredients for avoiding an enervating retirement routine."

All human activity, including leisure, may be classified broadly into physical action, social action, and mental action (Havighurst, 1961). Whatever the type of leisure, researchers have found that retired persons tend to seek the same values and satisfactions from these pursuits as they once did from their work.

It is the quality of leisure that lends it meaning, not the type. To realize the potential for late-life growth in free time, it must be used "meaningfully." Buhler (1961) defines meaningful use of time as that which contributes to the fulfillment of life. Such fulfillment is highly individual, and may be found in active or contemplative pursuits. (Social scientists often use the terms "developmental" and "disengaged.") Active leisure runs the gamut from home-centered projects such as gardening, needlework, and refinishing furniture, to taking part in countless organizations and volunteer projects, working part time or perfecting a golf game. Each of these activities provides some meaning to the participant. Contemplative use of time is equally valid. Seeking self-knowledge through meditation or prayer, selective reading, corresponding with old friends, writing one's memoirs, conducting a "life review"—are all quiet but highly meaningful pastimes. They form a common pattern especially among the "oldest-old" (Buhler, 1961).

> Whatever the type of leisure, researchers
> have found that retired persons tend to
> seek the same values and satisfactions
> from these pursuits as they once did from
> their work.

In the Third Age of life, many people feel a strong desire to give something back (Dychtwald, 1989). The reflections of the elderly can enrich their lives but may also enrich society. Their insights and experiences are uniquely able to build a bridge from the past to the present. In a culture that has been called "throw-away," it is particularly important to re-cycle the wisdom of the elderly and preserve it in some form.

Table 37.1
The Meaning of Activity

The same activity can mean quite different things to different people. The following is an incomplete list of some of the meanings activities can have:

- A source of personal identity—I am what I do
- A way to make money
- A way to be with people
- A way to get the "vital juices" flowing
- A source of personal development
- A way to focus creativity
- A source of sensory experience
- A source of prestige or status
- A source of new experience
- A way to be of service to others
- A way of passing time
- Something to look forward to
- A way to exercise competence
- A source of peace and quiet
- A means of escape
- A source of joy and fun
- A source of feelings of accomplishment

Source: Atchley, Robert C. *Aging: Continuity and Change.* 2d ed. Belmont, CA: Wadsworth, 1987.

Interestingly, the values and meanings people seek from their leisure do not appear much affected by age, by social class, or by gender. They do vary, however, according to the personality of the individual (Havighurst, 1961).

Some gerontologists note that retirees, often unconsciously, divide their leisure time between self-chosen projects or "assignments" leading to a goal, and "R & R" activities that are pure relaxation. This helps maintain the rhythm of alternate work and play that has characterized one's earlier years and appears to promote a positive adjustment to retirement (Buhler, 1961; Havighurst, 1961). In "Henry IV, Part I," Shakespeare alluded to this human need for rhythm and balance when Prince Hal mused: "If every day were holiday, to sport would be as tedious as to work."

Every day *is* holiday for retirees, hence the need to redefine some of one's activities. Linked to the work ethic again, it is a major reason why so many seniors spend so much time in goal-oriented volunteer work. (For more discussion of this topic, see Chapter 36, **Volunteerism.**) Even after they retire, most Americans still struggle to fit into a culture shaped by industrialization; they

The reflections of the elderly can enrich their lives but may also enrich society. Their insights and experiences are uniquely able to build a bridge from the past to the present. (Copyright © Marianne Gontarz)

are what Hannah Arendt (1959) called "a society of laborers without labor."

● RETIREMENT PLANNING

Only a minority of Americans make detailed, thoughtful plans about retirement before it is upon them, despite the growing field of leisure counseling and the fact that many large companies, as well as government employers, offer some form of pre-retirement advice, workshop, or seminar. Much of this counseling, however, is financial and doesn't help seniors deal with leisure.

The best preparation for retirement, of course, is lifelong. If during youth and middle age people considered how to make old age both active and meaningful, it would be more likely to happen (Dychtwald, 1989). Studies show that most people who have had active non-work interests before retirement continue to enjoy them afterward. The level of middle-aged involvement is generally an accurate predictor of involvement after retirement (Cutler, 1990).

People fall into three main categories at retirement age (Havighurst, 1961):

1. Those who do not retire: the self-employed, artists, professors, housewives, who

---

Voices of Creative Aging

Adele D., age 81, speaks about self-reliance and looking on life as a creative adventure:

If I put up a sign in front of my house, it would say: Herb plants for sale, lectures given, groups welcomed, palms read on Thursday between 1:15 and 2:45, Tarot card fortunes, figure drawing classes on Tuesday nights.

I don't feel 81. I don't even know what 81 is supposed to feel like. One of the real hazards of aging is not aging itself, it's believing what people tell you about old age. I think the main thing to remember is don't believe a word anybody tells you, even me.

I believe your life is what you expect. I think we are co-creators of our lives, and if we think things are going to happen that we like, they will. If we think bad things are going to happen, they will. I know lots of miserable people who are famous and lots of miserable people

who are very rich. You see, they talk about acquiring money and fame for security. There's no security in that. Who knows what's going to happen next? There's only one security and that's a feeling you have inside yourself that whatever comes up, you can handle it. It doesn't take money for that. I have very little money and mainly exist on my Social Security income.

Every year at the end of summer I rent my house and am off to see the world. I've traveled to Japan, China, Mexico, Guatemala, Spain, France—all over. You've got everything in the world to do, all the things you always wanted to do and didn't have time because you had to do other things. Do them now, and enjoy them.

Every day, when I get up, I think of millions of projects I want to undertake. I'm so happy to have the chance to take them on.

Excerpt from Connie Goldman's "Late Bloomer"
public radio series

may scale down their work, and those who keep working out of financial necessity or choice

2. Those who retire to a new life fully anticipated and planned for

3. Those who leave the work force with little or no advance planning

For the first group, use of leisure is not a problem. It is the third group—the largest category—whose adjustment may be difficult. Without some game plan for their lives, retirees may wonder whether "a Sunday evening is robbed of its pleasure if there is no anticipation of work on Monday" (Kaplan, 1961). There is little doubt that planning eases the adjustment, but those whose work was especially rewarding or was closely linked to their self-image are likely to miss it more than those whose jobs were physically demanding or boring.

The level of middle-aged involvement is generally an accurate predictor of involvement after retirement.

Just how much leisure time does retirement in the 1990s deliver to the American retiree? Table 37.2 indicates it is a great deal.

In all likelihood the number of hours of freedom will be between 2,000 and 2,500 hours a year. Converting this freedom windfall into hours of satisfaction is the business of later life. There should be room within the hours of freedom for pure relaxation, for activities where pleasure is an end in itself. Dr. Joyce Brothers (1992) said that fun should be savored: "When we are truly having fun, we briefly drop out of time, focus on the moment and lose ourselves in it. . . . so long as we abandon ourselves to the possibility of delight of what is around us right now . . . we look past the serious problems; they'll still be there. . . . We are left refreshed and relaxed with a new perspective and a sharper focus."

● **LIMITS ON LEISURE**

While the scope of leisure is broad for most older Americans, they are still limited by a number of factors: their health, economic resources,

Table 37.2
Work Hours Inventory

To determine the number of new free hours you will have in retirement, complete the following on the basis of an average work week.

	M	T	W	Th	F	Sa	Su	Total
Daily work hours away from home—leave/return								
Average business trip hours per week in excess of above								
Hours spent at home on company work								
Hours spent at work-related social functions each week								

Total work-related
hours in week   (1) _____
Number of weeks in year   52
Convert yearly vacation
and holidays to weeks,
subtract (–) from 52   (–) _____
Total yearly work weeks   (2) _____
Total work-related
hours in week   (1) _____
Total yearly work
weeks (multiply)   ×(2) _____
New free hours in retirement each year   _____

Source: Fred E. Lee and Associates, Inc. *New Horizons in Retirement Seminar.*

family situation, location (urban versus rural), climate, living arrangement, transportation access, even by their socioeconomic status and ethnic background (Kaplan, 1961; Buhler, 1961; Cutler, 1990).

Health is of course the most important factor limiting leisure choices. Energy and physical vigor vary widely among individuals and inevitably decline with age. Most recent research shows, however, that mental alertness is far more stable than was previously thought. Serious mental impairment among Americans over 65 is less than 5 percent (Dychtwald, 1989). And that decrement is found chiefly in those over 85.

Evidence indicates that those who achieved competence in various mental occupations in

In all likelihood the number of hours of freedom will be between 2,000 and 2,500 hours a year. Converting this freedom windfall into hours of satisfaction is the business of later life.

---

early life can maintain it as they age, though speed for learning new things declines somewhat (Atchley, 1987). The motivation to learn is strong well into the Third Age, and extending intellectual growth is one of its most hopeful aspects. (See Chapter 35, **Lifelong Learning,** "Educational Opportunities.")

The financial limit on free-time activities is less important than in the past because leisure has been democratized. Many types of leisure are publicly provided or low in cost, such as activities at community and senior centers, parks, libraries, local AARP chapters, etc. Seniors of all economic classes attend the same movies and sports events, for example, at relatively low prices.

● TIME AND OLDER AMERICANS

Both personal experience and research reveal that time is subjective. The elderly perceive it differently; it seems to pass more quickly for them than for the young (Havighurst, 1961). Some seniors report spending half a morning on ordinary activities they used to rush through—balancing a checkbook, buying groceries, etc. (Atchley, 1987). This is partly because they can afford to be prodigal with time. A widow can bake "from scratch" and lavishly decorate a birthday cake for her granddaughter. An elderly woodcarver crafts an entire zoo of miniature animals. Each task can be given the time it deserves; time no longer equals money.

Some moments in time are much more significant than others. Time studies of how people allocate their leisure, which began in the 1930s and continue today, are only partially instructive (Cutler, 1990), because they can't measure "quality time." A six-minute long-distance call from an old high school pal has far more meaning to an older man than three hours of watching television—but both are leisure.

The pace of life slows for physical reasons as people move from the "young-old" (ages 55 to 69) through the "old" (70 to 84) to the "oldest-old" (85 and over). Chosen activities become less strenuous and often more introspective. Arthritis in the shoulders might dictate a change from playing tennis to taking nature hikes. If vision fails, perhaps gardening can replace needlepoint. Satisfying uses for leisure can yet be found.

Older Americans recognize that most of their lives are past and the future is limited. Nevertheless, late life can include expansion and growth for seniors who have basic economic security and reasonably good health. The first generation to enjoy both for extended periods, today's elderly are also the first to enjoy the potential in old age. They practice a broader spectrum of lifestyles than any other age group (Dychtwald, 1989).

● CONTINUING TO WORK

Those whose lifestyles change the least with aging are the many seniors who continue to work

Table 37.3
Life Expectancy in Years

Age in 1988	White		African American	
	Male	**Female**	**Male**	**Female**
60	18.4	22.6	16.2	20.3
65	14.9	18.7	13.4	16.9
70	11.8	15.0	10.9	13.8
75	9.1	11.7	8.6	10.9
80	6.8	8.7	6.8	8.4

Source: U.S. National Center for Health Statistics. *Vital Statistics of the United States* (annual); *Statistical Abstract of the United States,* 1991.

Figure 37.1
Percent of Persons 65 and Older Reporting Specific Leisure-Time Activities, 1980

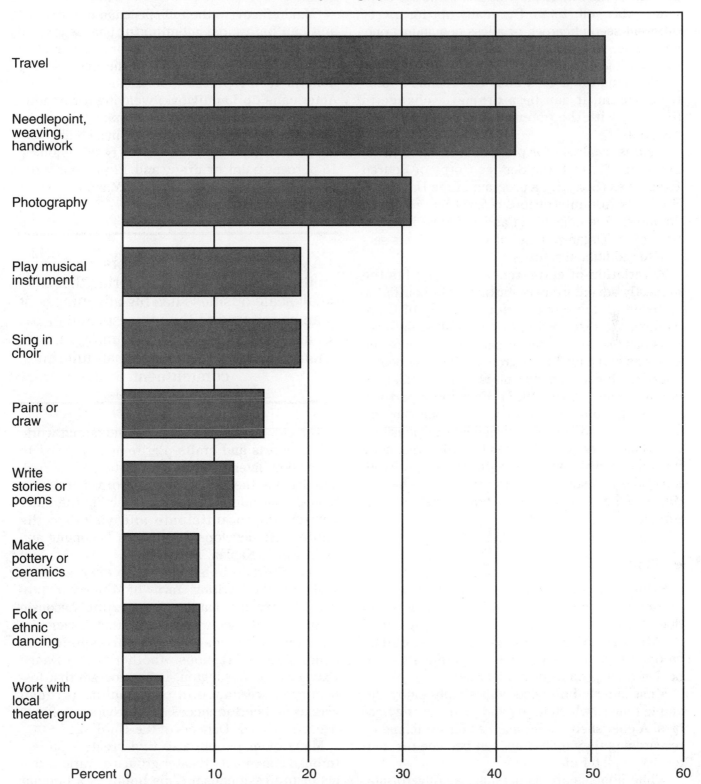

Source: Harris, Lewis & Associates. *Aging in the 80s: America in Transition.* Washington, DC: The National Council on the Aging, 1981. In *Statistical Handbook on Aging Americans.* Ed. Frank K. Schick. Phoenix, AZ: Oryx Press, 1986.

at their regular jobs, at least part time. In 1989, 12 percent of the American workforce was age 65 or older (Maxwell, 1992). But many opt for a very different second career, or a less demanding one, and some, with expertise in a specific area, turn to teaching. Others start their own businesses. While being one's own boss can realize a long-time dream, it can be a dramatic change in lifestyle, with the potential both for risks and rewards.

Help is available for prospective senior entrepreneurs. Through the Service Corps of Retired Executives (SCORE), a program of the U.S. Small Business Administration, retired businessmen volunteer free counseling and practical information. (See "Organizations" at the end of this section for additional sources.)

A variation of entrepreneurship that fits the modestly adventurous is starting a mini-business. A growing number of seniors, many of them women, are discovering that a small-scale business has big advantages: it can be tailored to the interests and pace of a retiree, it often can be run out of the home, and it requires less than full-time commitment (Olsen, 1988). Forming a partnership for a mini-business or a larger one can bolster morale and spread management responsibilities. Small service businesses that fill a real need but require little initial investment are probably most likely to succeed. These range from pet-sitting to resume writing to a telephone wake-up service.

● HOBBIES

Sometimes a favorite hobby can be metamorphosed into a business, though this entails a risk that "going commercial" may take the joy out of it. All sorts of craft items—jewelry, quilts, wooden toys, pottery, T-shirts, table mats—can be designed, produced, and marketed.

Most elderly hobbyists will simply enjoy the ample time in which to expand their lifelong hobbies. A cherished hobby, such as birdwatching or researching the family tree, can become the centerpiece of later life.

While hobbies are as personal as fingerprints, there are three main types: the doing, making, and collecting hobbies (Mulac, 1959). "Doing" is the broadest category, including such diverse activities as going fishing, visiting Civil War bat-

tlefields, playing cards, and learning to square dance.

"Making" covers the full spectrum of creativity and can be a most meaningful use of leisure hours. Seniors in great numbers practice creative hobbies. A National Council on the Aging survey done in 1980 reported that 42 percent of older Americans do handiwork, weaving, or needlepoint; 31 percent enjoy photography; 38 percent play a musical instrument or sing in a choir (making music); 8 percent make pottery or ceramics; 15 percent paint or draw, and 12 percent write stories or poetry (Schick, 1986). Many do two or three of these things.

A growing number of seniors, many of them women, are discovering that a small-scale business has big advantages: it can be tailored to the interests and pace of a retiree, it often can be run out of the home, and it requires less than full-time commitment.

The elderly also take lessons and attend workshops in arts and crafts. Retirement appears to foster both latent and active artistic ability. Such activity has the power to transform because it "can go on indefinitely, thus directing the older participant to anticipate and visualize the future.... He develops a feeling of becoming and of growing" (Kaplan, 1961).

One effort to bolster creative expression in seniors is the "Writing: Yarns of Yesteryear" project, headquartered at the University of Wisconsin at Madison. It encourages the writing of memoirs and reminiscences through correspondence courses and workshops. Another is The Dance Exchange, a Washington, D.C., program that fosters creative dance in older adults through classes and performances of its troupe of elderly dancers, named "Dancers of the Third Age."

Many older people also find creative outlets through community theater groups at various levels of professionalism. This hobby is a popular one, whether it is considered "doing" something or "making" a performance.

Collecting things continues to fill time constructively for seniors, according to hobby maga-

Profiles of Productive Aging

Will Barnet
Artist

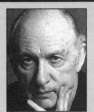

"For painters, maturity is more important than being young ... if you study the history of art, you will find the greatest painters were those who were trying to understand their language and develop it as they grew older. That's what it's all about. Maturing and then letting it flourish into a wonderful painting."

Born in Beverly, Massachusetts, in 1911, Will Barnet remembers from early childhood going to the library. When he was about 6, he picked up a book filled with fantastic, wonderful colored drawings. He was entranced by these illustrations and declared, "That's what I want to do." With exceptional determination for someone so young, he set about shaping his education so that he could become an artist. His parents had very little money and knew nothing about art, and there was no art instruction in Beverly, so, at 15, Barnet won a fellowship to the School of Fine Arts at the Boston Museum to begin his formal artistic training and complete his high school degree.

After three years of study in Boston, Barnet grew restless. He had become a young revolutionary artist, no longer wanting to be limited to classical techniques. "We used to have fist fights over art!" Barnet said about his group of classmates at the art school. He had been studying modern artists such as Gauguin and Modigliani and decided to move to New York to better explore his avant-garde interests. So he wrote to the Art Students League and was awarded a fellowship. To support himself during the Depression, Barnet drew cartoons for the *New Yorker* magazine, worked as a librarian, and became a lithograph printer. The Art Students League hired him as the school's printer for students, outside professionals, and the graphics instructors.

Within two years, he became the youngest instructor ever at the Art Students League, teaching both printing and graphics. The Art Students League was the focal point of the art world in America at the time; the most famous artists came to the League to exhibit, to work,

and to teach. And the students were top-notch as well: young Jackson Pollock was studying at the League in this period. The League also acted as a meeting place for the artists, who were deeply concerned with the social and political issues of the day.

By the early 1940s, Barnet was developing his own work and showing in galleries around New York. Most of his work consisted of oil paintings; but in 1939 he did a woodcut called "Early Morning," one of his most important prints of the period. "That was the beginning of the development of my work towards a more abstract concept," explained Barnet. "I was always seeking to break away, to become more contemporary on the way I handled my language and form. So 'Early Morning' became a symbol."

During the war he was recruited to work in a lithograph company, printing secret war documents at night, while continuing to teach during the daytime. When the war ended, veterans flooded his classroom, and Barnet began to shape the younger generation of artists. Throughout his career Barnet made mentoring other artists a priority, and many of his former students have gone on to achieve world fame. He also continued making both prints and oil paintings, showing and selling some of both.

In the 1950s, Barnet began to do more representational work that was still heavily influenced by his understanding of abstract forms, a style which Barnet calls "figurative abstraction." He became known for this style, and by the 1960s, he had achieved recognition within the art world as one of the most accomplished contemporary painters. But it was in the 1970s that a renaissance in prints gave him much wider recognition. He continues to paint and teach in New York. Barnet has had major exhibits in museums and galleries across the country. His works are exhibited in public collections at our nation's greatest museums and can also be seen at the Library of Congress and the New York Public Library.

Lydia Brontë

zines. The number of different items considered to be collectibles is nearly 3,000, and there are publications and clubs for almost all of them

(Rinker, 1992). Displaying, mounting, and cataloguing a collection extends the hobby beyond simple acquisition.

Retirement appears to foster both latent and active artistic ability. (Copyright © Benjamin Porter)

● SOCIAL AND RELIGIOUS PARTICIPATION

While many hobbies are home-centered, others lead to social interaction through clubs, hobby fairs, and conventions. Seniors also build social contacts by joining fraternal organizations, civic groups, clubs, and religious bodies.

Participation in job-related organizations predictably drops after retirement, but membership in other associations holds up fairly well until late age. The AARP, founded in 1958, is undoubtedly the most popular senior organization, claiming 33 million Americans 50 years and over as members in 1992.

Overall, those with higher education levels who live in cities participate more in clubs and organizations than do rural and blue-collar Americans. Elderly lower-income individuals tend to concentrate leisure pursuits around home and family; higher incomes correlate with wider interests (Lipman and Osgood, 1982). Those who need social contacts the most—solitary older people—

tend to be less active in communal activities than those with companions, a spouse, family member, or close friend (Cutler, 1990). Transportation problems are often the biggest barrier to participation by the elderly in organizations of all sorts (Atchley, 1987).

Several studies over the past few decades have attempted to determine the life satisfaction of retired Americans. It appears that a sense of well-being correlates strongly with health, with financial security, and with marital status, but also with the level of participation in social events outside the family (Palmore, 1985).

Attendance at churches and synagogues peaks somewhere around age 60 (Atchley, 1987). Older people are often leaders in church-related activities and, in general, hold more memberships in church or synagogue than other generations. Studies on aging and religious activity tend to be inconclusive; some show a rise in attendance at services while others find participation drops slightly with age but religious feelings increase.

According to a 1981 Gallup poll of seniors over 65 (Schick, 1986), 82 percent said religion was the most important influence in their lives. Clearly, participation in church- or synagogue-related activities does not decline with age as sharply as does participation in other groups and organizations.

Elderly lower-income individuals tend to concentrate leisure pursuits around home and family; higher incomes correlate with wider interests.

Older Americans who regularly attend senior centers—currently less than 5 percent of those over 65—typically are middle class, with a strong attachment to the community. In addition to social services, such centers offer varied educational and recreational programs and informal companionship (Atchley, 1987). Their purpose is to support both independence and community involvement among older adults (Teaff, 1985).

Following the Older Americans Act of 1965, the senior center movement spread rapidly. Today

Profiles of Productive Aging

Françoise Gilot
Artist and writer

"Being an artist is a continuous ascent, rather like mountain climbing. There can be particular moments of achievement in the art itself. Outward recognition always follows much later, so it is not felt as strongly as a breakthrough in the work itself."

Painter and author Françoise Gilot was born in Paris in 1922. Exposed to literature and art from an early age, she recalls having her portrait painted in oils on a commission from her grandmother and being fascinated by the colors, smells, and processes of painting. On New Year's Day after her fifth birthday, she woke up bursting with the knowledge that she wanted to be an artist; shortly afterwards her mother enrolled her in her first drawing class.

But in time Gilot's father decided she should acquire a practical skill that would enable her to earn a living: she should go to law school. Though she enrolled in law school, she left after two years, determined to live her own life and become an artist. Gilot was selling and exhibiting her work by the age of 21. "I could not conceive of a woman not living through the fruits of her own efforts. For an artist it is the way to become a professional artist," Gilot said.

Gilot met artist Pablo Picasso, and they began living together and had two children, Claude and Paloma. Meanwhile Gilot continued to draw and paint, receiving favorable critical attention and mounting several shows. As her career bloomed, Picasso became more jealous because it distracted her from him, and he began to be unfaithful.

In 1954, feeling the situation was hopeless, Gilot left Picasso. She is the only one of Picasso's companions to leave him; in every other case—except for his last companion, Jaqueline Roque, whom he married—Picasso was the one who left.

In Paris Gilot tried to reestablish herself alone but discovered that Picasso, in his fury at her departure, had told every dealer he knew that if they handled her work he would never give them any of his. The technique was partly effective, although she was able to work around it over time and largely diminish it. Seeking a wider geographical range, Gilot attended the Tamarind Workshop in Los Angeles several times. On one such visit, mutual friends introduced her to Dr. Jonas Salk, and they were married some six months later. They live in La Jolla, California, not far from the Salk Institute, and periodically travel to New York and Paris.

Always a writer, Gilot published *Life With Picasso* in 1964, which became an international best-seller. Author of two versions of the book, Gilot actually wrote the book twice: once in English, once in French. She has published a number of other books, including several volumes of poems and the recent memoir *Matisse and Picasso: A Friendship in Art*.

Gilot also continues to paint, write, lecture, and exhibit widely. When asked about retiring, she declared, "Art is not a career, it's a lifetime calling."

Lydia Brontë

there are well over 9,000 centers in the United States, offering services ranging from income tax counseling to bridge tournaments to courses in defensive driving.

Activities for the elderly are also offered through Golden Age clubs, community and neighborhood centers, and parks and recreation departments. However, in a 1981 survey (Schick, 1986), only 9 percent of people over 65 said they had attended any of these within the past two weeks. But a larger percentage (27 percent) said they would like to attend such a facility; the most interest was reflected among elderly African Americans.

● MINORITIES AND LEISURE

Retirement—in the conventional sense of abundant leisure supported by adequate income—does not apply to most ethnic minorities (Markides, 1987). Many continue to work, or to look for work, and many live in real poverty. Overall, poorer educational opportunities and discrimination have yielded smaller retirement incomes than whites enjoy. Few African Americans, Chicanos, or Native Americans have pensions, and fewer own their own homes than do whites. But because their jobs were less rewarding, some research indicates they miss

Figure 37.2
Spiritual Commitment of Older and Younger Persons, 1981

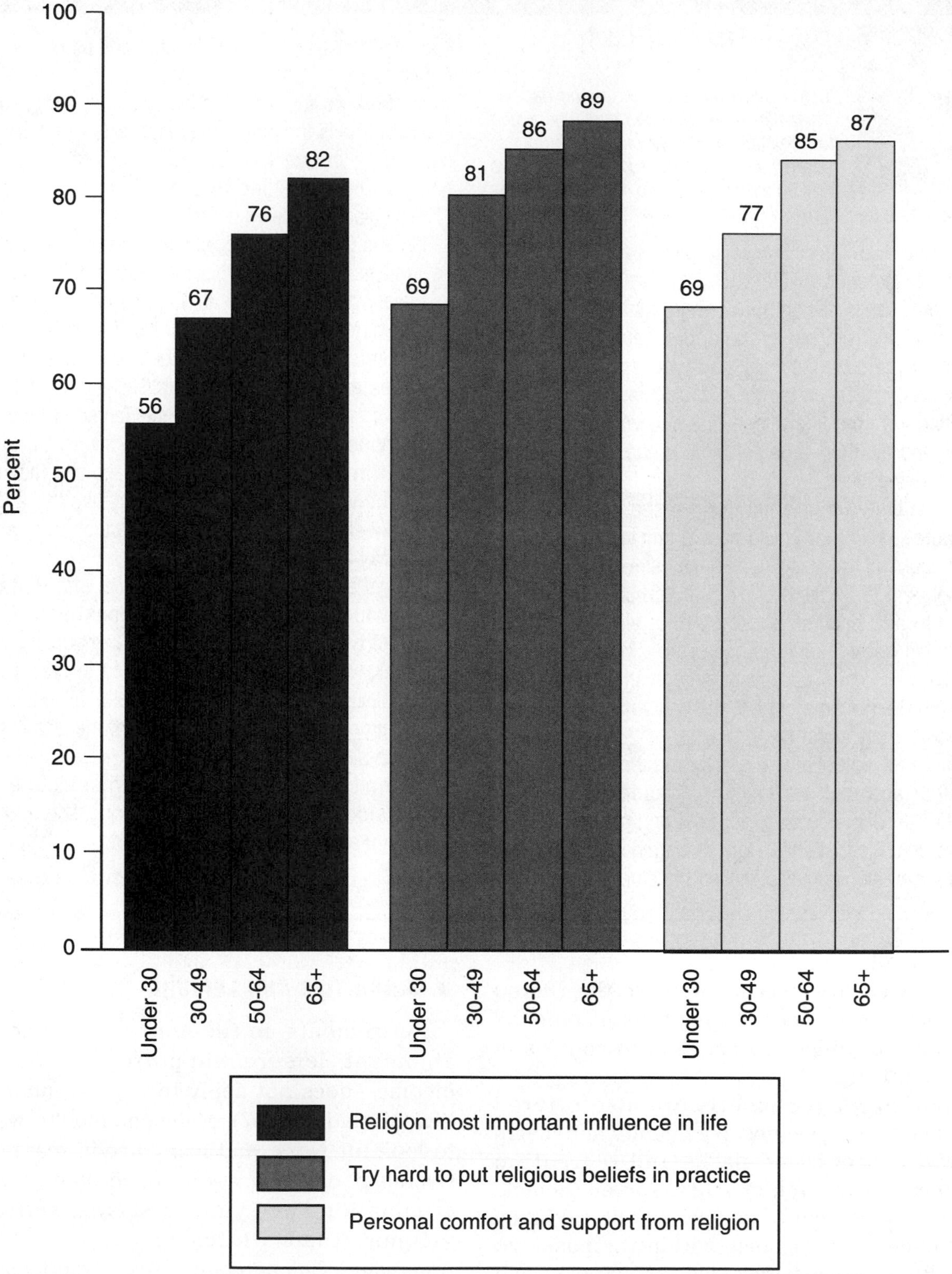

Religion most important influence in life

Try hard to put religious beliefs in practice

Personal comfort and support from religion

Source: "Religion in America." *The Gallup Report.* Report nos. 201–2 (June-July 1982). In *Statistical Handbook on Aging Americans.* Ed. Frank K. Schick. Phoenix, AZ: Oryx Press, 1986.

Informal networks such as the family, the extended family, and friends are the chief source of social support for elderly minorities. (Copyright © Isabel Egglin, 1993)

them less at retirement. This easier adjustment is usually only temporary, and later on they report greater disappointment with retirement (Watson, 1982).

Life expectancy is less for most minority groups than for whites. Minority elderly have less access to health services and generally inferior health conditions than their white counterparts. Older African Americans are less likely than whites to have cultivated hobbies. They take part in fewer activities outside the home. The little research done in this area shows, not surprisingly, that their morale, or life satisfaction, also tends to be lower (Palmore, 1985).

Ethnic minorities generally take pride in caring for their own ill or aging members, and very few live in planned retirement communities. Informal networks such as the family, the extended family, and friends are the chief source of social support for elderly minorities.

Because discriminatory barriers to participation in certain sports and access to travel accommodations have now been lowered for African Americans, these leisure activities have increased slightly (Watson, 1982). Church-related activities are important, though African Americans also attend movies, sporting events, classes, and club meetings (Bryant, 1992). Historically the church has been a strong support for African Americans, but while the elderly attend church in high numbers, they are not necessarily more religious than the elderly in other ethnic groups.

One recent study (Bryant, 1992) focused on predictors of mortality among older African Americans. It found a higher risk of death among those with little family contact who did not take part in activities or attend church.

Elderly Japanese Americans are far less secure financially than their offspring; some 20 percent live below the poverty level. The older generation, having grown up in highly structured families where the elders were revered, now must struggle with changing attitudes of filial piety. Their expectations of total support and respect from their children are often disappointed. Most older Japanese Americans cling to religious observances for stability as well as for social interaction (Kii, 1982).

● HOUSING AND ACTIVITIES

Where older Americans live affects their leisure lifestyles. Most seniors choose to live in independent households, but multiple living arrangements are on the rise. The activity levels of elderly people living in multiple unit housing are higher than those who live in dispersed housing (Cutler, 1990).

Age-congregated living features a potpourri of activities and recreation as part of the expected lifestyle. Housing arrangements vary from small retirement homes to senior apartments to huge retirement complexes such as Leisure World and Sun City.

The planned retirement community (RC) offering safe, attractive, communal living is a post–World War II, largely white phenomenon. By 1984 there were approximately 2,300 RCs, mostly in the Sunbelt. An RC offers flexible living, from small apartments in a central lodge to townhouses and cluster homes.

Two of the oldest and largest RCs are Sun City and Sun City West, near Phoenix, which together house some 75,000 people. Facilities include several recreation centers, multiple golf courses, pools, bowling alleys, and tennis courts, chapters of national service organizations (Rotary, Lions, etc.), and activity clubs in mind-boggling variety. Table 37.4 lists the leisure choices of one RC.

The activity levels of elderly people living in multiple unit housing are higher than those who live in dispersed housing.

● SPORTS AND FITNESS FOR SENIORS

As Americans advance in age, their participation in sports decreases. This will be less true of future generations who have been taught to view physical fitness as a major goal. Still, seniors in the 1990s have heard, loud and clear, the repeated warning that Americans in general do not get enough exercise. Unlike younger working people, retirees cannot use the excuse of insufficient

time. Further, longevity and better physical condition are decidedly linked.

How are they responding? Particularly among the "young-old," taking part in sports and exercise is an escalating trend. They are keeping pace with other Americans in purchase of home gym equipment, exercise videotapes, and jogging shoes. They are flocking to classes in aerobics and water aerobics. Probably still not as active as optimum fitness dictates, the elderly are moving in the right direction. In sports as gentle as croquet or as demanding as parachute jumping, there are seniors, somewhere, who are participating.

The importance of exercise for older adults is underscored by copious research. Demonstrated benefits are both physiological—increased flexibility, strength, endurance, bone mass, cardiovascular fitness—and psychological (Teaff, 1985). Numerous studies show that participating in exercise programs can improve memory, reduce anxiety and fatigue, and even alleviate depression. Becoming more proficient in a sport or exercise can also lift seniors' self-esteem.

Which sports do older Americans prefer? A survey taken in 1989 by the National Sporting Goods Association (Statistical Abstract of the United States, 1991) ranked these as the favorite sports activities for those over 65: (1) exercise walking, (2) swimming, (3) fishing, (4) bicycle riding, and (5) golf. Bowling followed closely in sixth place.

Older Americans play an estimated one-third of all rounds of golf; the National Golf Association says about 3.2 million people over 60 enjoy the game. Some 14 percent of seniors go fishing or hunting (*Statistical Abstract*, 1989).

In sports as gentle as croquet or as demanding as parachute jumping, there are seniors, somewhere, who are participating.

Special organizations to encourage sports participation among the elderly abound (many are listed in the "Organizations" section). One of the most successful programs is the Senior Games, sponsored by the U.S. National Senior Olympics. Held every other year in participating states (currently in thirty-five states), the games classify par-

Table 37.4
Sun City West Chartered Club Activities
(Number after a club indicates more than one club)

Art	Golf (10)	Quilters
Astronomy	Greenhouse	
	Horseshoes	Rhythm tappers
Ballet	Knitting (machine)	Rock-hounds
Basketeers	Knitting and macrame	Rosemaling
Bicycle riders		RV club
Billiards	Lapidary	
Bocce	Laugh-in club	Saddle club
Book review	Lawn bowling (3)	Sewing
Bowling (10)	Leathercarvers	Shuffleboard
	Library friends	Silk flowers
Calligraphy		Silver craft
Card clubs (13)	Mah jongg	Singles social club
Ceramics	Mini golfers	Softball (2)
Chess	Metal-craft	Sportsmen (5)
China painting	Misc. chartered activities (20)	Stained glass
Chorus (Westernaires)	Model railroad	
Clay-craft	Musicians club	Tennis (court, platform and
Coin and stamp		table)
Computers (4)	Needle and craft	Theater (drama)
Copper-craft	Newcomers coffee	Tole-Craft
Dance clubs	Organ and keyboard	Weavers
		Women's social club
Espanol club	Photography	Woodworking
Exercise clubs (10)	Prides (street cleaners)	Writers club
Garden clubs (2)		

Source: Sun City West Chartered Club.

ticipants in five-year age brackets. Standards for judging are professional but appropriate to older abilities.

Among the games are tennis, swimming, golf, table tennis, bowling, shuffleboard, horseshoes, badminton, and track and field events. They provide a formal structure for participation and recognition of fitness in older adults (Gandee, 1989). In 1989, 200,000 senior athletes took part in the local qualifying games for the Second Biennial National Senior Olympics. Roughly half that number participated in the National Senior Olympics member game events. More than one-third of all participants were women.

The success of these programs is helping to shatter the myth that seniors are too frail for fitness.

Many other frameworks for senior competition exist. The Senior Softball World Series, with five age divisions beginning at 50, has held annual tournaments since 1989. To promote tennis as a lifetime sport, the Senior Games Development Council launched a "Condo Tennis" program in south Florida. Geared to the area's large retired population living in condos with tennis courts, the program offers free tennis lessons to participants.

There are organizations for seniors built around virtually every sport, from skiing (the Over the Hill Gang International and the 70 + Ski Club) to mall walking. Older swimmers join associations such as San Francisco's Dolphin Club, whose members take a four-mile swim in the bay every New Year's Day. Many YMCAs, park and recreation departments, community centers, etc., have sports and exercise programs for seniors, at different skill levels—and more are being organized all the time.

Numerous studies show that participating in exercise programs can improve memory, reduce anxiety and fatigue, and even alleviate depression. (Copyright © Marianne Gontarz)

Whether or not they participate, older Americans are frequent spectators at sporting events of all kinds. Following favorite teams and studying the players and statistics can consume quantities of free time.

Watching one's team, whether it's the Yankees, the Bulls, or the grandson's Little League, can be ᵃ ery special experience, offering a shared

In 1989, 200,000 senior athletes took part in the local qualifying games for the Second Biennial National Senior Olympics.

moment of leisure (Giamatti, 1989). The communal aspect adds to the pleasure when, reacting together to some play or triumph, the crowd becomes a community.

For sports fans who also like to travel, the National Senior Sports Association organizes trips, usually off season to keep prices down, to senior tournaments in golf, tennis, bowling, etc., at elegant resorts.

● ENTERTAINMENT: THE PERFORMING ARTS AND THE MEDIA

Not only are older people pursuing the arts as participants, they are increasingly rating cultural institutions as important to the quality of

One of the most successful programs is the Senior Games, sponsored by the U.S. National Senior Olympics. (Copyright © Phil Kukelhan)

Profiles of Productive Aging

John Forsythe
Actor

Dynasty stars were the same ages as their characters.

Born in 1918 in Penn's Grove, New Jersey, actor John Forsythe grew up wanting to be a baseball player, then a sports writer and play-by-play announcer. He attended the University of North Carolina at Chapel Hill, majoring in writing, but in his junior year he dropped out of college to be the announcer for baseball games at Ebbets Field.

But baseball announcing had one disadvantage Forsythe had not anticipated: It was only a summertime occupation! Looking for an off-season job, he auditioned to do radio dramas for WNYC radio in New York. He found he loved this job more than sports announcing. He went on to a job with a children's theater in Chappaqua and then worked with a Shakespearean company for a year. This led to Broadway appearances in *Vickie* and *Yankee Point* and a contract with Warner Brothers, debuting in *Destination Tokyo* with Cary Grant.

While serving in the army during World War II, Forsythe acted in *Winged Victory,* Moss Hart's stage musical using only servicemen. Other stage roles followed, including the Pulitzer Prize-winning *Teahouse of the August Moon.* Forsythe worked in early live television, including *Studio One, Philco Playhouse, Kraft Theater,* and *World of Survival,* a national wildlife series.

Movies occupied Forsythe as well, among them *Captive City, The Trouble With Harry, Topaz, And Justice For All,* and most recently in *Scrooged.*

But the TV series *Dynasty* made Forsythe a major star. A sensation when it first aired, *Dynasty* kept millions of Americans enthralled with its high-powered portrayal of the life and business dealings of Forsythe's hard-driving but attractive character, Denver oil magnate Blake Carrington. One of the series' greatest accomplishments was that it depicted mature adults whose lives were eventful, glamorous, and exciting—and the stars who played the roles were the same ages as their characters. *Dynasty* broke age barriers in television, an industry that until then created few attractive and interesting roles for women over forty or men over fifty. Forsythe, a happily married man in his sixties, became a sex symbol for millions of women.

In 1991 Forsythe became Senator Powers in a new comedy series called *The Powers That Be,* a satire on American political life in the 1990s. He has also completed a romantic comedy for NBC, entitled *Opposites Attract,* and has directed, produced, and narrated a documentary on the life and career of jockey Bill Shoemaker, called "Nice Guys Finish First."

Forsythe was honored with two Golden Globe Awards as best actor in a dramatic television series and an Emmy nomination for his performance on *Dynasty.*

Lydia Brontë

life (Moody, 1988). They continue to attend cultural events as they age, and the over-65 contingent reflects greater gains in attendance than do other groups. Ten percent of this group attend a play at least once a year, and 13 percent attend a musical. Classical music performances attract 13 percent of the group, and art museums and galleries draw 16 percent (*Statistical Abstract,* 1989). These figures are based on a 1985 survey for the National Endowment for the Arts. The Endowment in recent years has made major strides in extending access to cultural programs. Its outreach initiatives both bring arts programs to people in nursing homes, senior centers, and rural areas, and facilitate bringing people to programs (Moody, 1988) through sub-

sidized transportation and special tickets for seniors.

Older people go to movies for entertainment and rent them on videotape to enjoy at home. They read all kinds of periodicals, they both read and subscribe to daily newspapers in higher numbers than younger people (Schick, 1986). They particularly enjoy the more than 200 publications geared to elderly audiences (Dychtwald, 1989). Having grown up with radio, they still listen to it. "Mature Focus Radio," produced by AARP for the Mutual Broadcasting System, is especially popular. More than 160 radio stations carry it in English and 170 stations in Spanish (Maxwell, 1992).

It is television, however, that accounts for a

huge bite out of seniors' free time. Among those over 65, surveys show that from 92 to 95 percent watch TV regularly. As a segment of the total viewing audience, seniors watch more than 40 hours a week, more than any other age group (Bell, 1992).

Both a curse and a blessing to the aging, TV is always readily available, requires no physical effort or special transportation, and is inexpensive. It entertains—or at least distracts. It can simulate companionship for the lonely and provide a link to the larger world. Further, it offers structure in an existence that often lacks it.

Occasionally, TV presents fine fare in drama, music, nature, news, and public affairs. Its critics, however, say that for older people it threatens "the domination of late-life leisure through one-way communication that reduces the last stage of life to silence" (Moody, 1988).

Prior to the 1980s, the images of older people presented on TV were too often inaccurate or inappropriate. For the past ten years, the situation has improved: there were many more portrayals of seniors, and they were far more positive than in the past (Bell, 1992). Credit goes to such innovative shows as *The Golden Girls*, *Mr. Belvedere*, *Matlock*, and *Murder, She Wrote*.

Among those over 65, surveys show that from 92 to 95 percent watch TV regularly. As a segment of the total viewing audience, seniors watch more than 40 hours a week, more than any other age group.

● **TRAVEL**

One of the most popular pastimes for retirees is travel. Seniors take all kinds of trips, from a short drive to a neighboring town to visit their children to ambitious round-the-world voyages. Of all passport holders, 44 percent are over age 55. Seniors represent 22 percent of all travelers and 30 percent of domestic travelers (Vierck, 1990).

A market survey of older travelers revealed their five favorite vacation choices: national parks, historic sites, beaches (and other warm weather spots), fall foliage trips, and special events or festivals (Vierck, 1990).

Cruises are enjoyed by the elderly, whether by luxury ocean liner, freighter, barge, or paddleboat steamer; seniors make up 30 percent of all cruise passengers. They are also getting hands-on sailing experiences via sailing schools and windjammer cruises (St. Claire, 1991).

Countless older couples travel, and many seniors travel alone, but the largest segment of the elderly sign on for some type of group package tour.

One of the appealing features of travel, for people of all ages, is the element of adventure. This comprises the joys of exploring and learning, common to any new experience, and the excitement of taking risks. While the majority of elderly travelers insist on comfortable beds and confirmed reservations, others are anything but timid travelers. Those who have traveled extensively in earlier years are particularly apt to seek such exotic forms of travel as camel expeditions, river rafting, balloon flights, and wildlife safaris.

Of all passport holders, 44 percent are over age 55. Seniors represent 22 percent of all travelers and 30 percent of domestic travelers.

Consider these challenging trips, all undertaken by people over 60:

- A 5,000-mile expedition by canoe and kayak, starting at the mouth of the Mackenzie River in Canada and ending thirty-three months later at Cape Horn, Chile. The couple who made this trip had to cope with snakes, black bears, and killer bees along the way.
- A trek up Tanzania's Mt. Kilimanjaro—the especially rugged Machame Trail—by an 85-year-old woman.
- An 8,000-mile flight following the Alcan Highway in a home-built biplane. A World War II bomber pilot built the plane in his Kansas garage, then made the trip to Fairbanks, Alaska, with a 71-year-old buddy as co-pilot.

- A river rafting trip down the Colorado by a group of grandmothers.
- A leisurely camping trip through Alaska—not by lavish RV, but by four-wheel-drive pick-up truck. A resourceful husband and wife built a deck on their truck to fit their tent; this gave them flexibility at rock-bottom cost.
- A solo round-the-world flight in a small Cessna. The pilot, age 74, got his pilot's license ten years earlier and made some fifteen flights, including one to Australia, before attempting the worldwide trip.

Special interest, or theme travel, is a rapidly growing part of the travel market for all travelers. Trips built around such interests as archaeology, gardening, or birdwatching are popular with older adults who have had enough of conventional travel. Almost any interest can be the centerpiece for such a trip, either planned by a travel agent or by the travelers themselves. Seniors with plenty of time often relish the fun of researching and planning a trip, down to the last detail, on their own.

Because the older market is such a fertile one for the travel industry, in recent years a number of organizations have focused on tours specifically for seniors. The pace is a bit more relaxed, and comfortable accommodations can be counted on. Two of the larger companies geared to foreign trips for the elderly are Grand Circle Travel and Saga International Holidays. Another is the AARP Travel Service, which arranges both foreign and domestic escorted tours for its members.

Some special tours emphasize international understanding as one of the pleasures of the trip. Seniors Abroad arranges three-week home visits in one of six foreign countries for those over 50. The Friendship Force, another organization emphasizing the people-to-people aspect of travel, places travelers of all ages in homes in some forty countries, then arranges exchange visits that bring foreigners into American homes.

Also noteworthy is Grandtravel, an organization that plans domestic and foreign tours for grandparents and their grandchildren.

Trips that mix learning with travel, both in the United States and abroad, are growing in importance for seniors. The largest and oldest organiza-tion is Elderhostel, which began in 1975 and has been hugely successful; another is Interhostel (see Chapter 35, **Lifelong Learning** for more information).

Research expeditions, such as Earthwatch, offer the chance to take part in scientific research along with travel. Some of these unusual trips carry academic credit for participants.

Discounts for older adults are available in virtually every facet of travel, from transportation to accommodations to services. Not only are they too wide-ranging and numerous to list here, they also are changing constantly in response to the needs of the industry. Older Americans considering any sort of trip are well advised to investigate such bargains either through a travel agent or by individual research well in advance of the departure date. Newspaper advertisements, for example, sometimes list last-minute travel clubs, or travel clearinghouses, that offer big discounts on unsold accommodations. Some are legitimate, others are not, but the reliable operators may be ideal for retirees who can be flexible about timing their trips.

There is a wealth of information catering to wanderlust: travel magazines and newsletters, including several slanted to the elderly, as well as practical guidebooks and books by travel writers that accurately convey the atmosphere of a destination. Libraries and bookstores have many shelves of literature on travel. State departments of tourism, Chambers of Commerce, travel agents, private tour companies, and even the U.S. Government are valuable sources of information (see "Organizations").

There are also video and audio tapes that highlight various travel destinations. Public libraries usually have some; others can be obtained free from travel agents or rented from video stores (St. Claire, 1991).

Older Americans travel by car 80 percent of the time, and they make 72 percent of all trips made in recreational vehicles (RVs) (Vierck, 1990). Whether the RV is a motor home, trailer, truck camper, van conversion, or folding camper trailer, its appeal to seniors is that it combines transportation and overnight accommodation in one. One favorite RV owners' motto is "home is where we park it." Many are in the young-old age group and represent all economic backgrounds (Micheli, 1987). What they have in common is a

Staying in one of the growing number of RV parks gives seniors valuable social contacts and the opportunity to network about travel destinations. (Courtesy of the Recreation Vehicle Industry Association)

desire to see the country and to do so in a more flexible way than conventional trips allow.

Some RV owners travel and live full time in their vehicle. Others become nomads for a few weeks or a season. RVs can also be rented so people can test the lifestyle before making a big purchase. Living expenses for full-time RVers are usually lower than for those making home mortgage payments, but costs for health care, food, and services may be higher because they are less familiar with the community (St. Claire, 1991).

Staying in one of the growing number of RV parks gives seniors valuable social contacts and the opportunity to network about travel destinations. Some belong to RV singles groups such as Loners on Wheels and Loners of America. In addition there are countless clubs for RV owners that sponsor caravans, campouts, and state, regional, and international rallies.

Camping is a leisure activity related to travel that counts some 5 million Americans over 55 among its devotees (Statistical Abstract, 1991).

Some 39 percent of campers prefer RV camping, and 20,000 campgrounds in the United States will accommodate RVs (St. Claire, 1991). Many large campgrounds cater to older campers, especially in the Sunbelt states. Retired campers can often utilize camp facilities off season when they are not in demand by younger campers.

While most elderly campers camped in their younger days and still enjoy the outdoor setting, the chance to develop their skills, and the simple living that camping provides (Hupp, 1987), others are recent converts to camping.

Living expenses for full-time RVers are usually lower than for those making home mortgage payments, but costs for health care, food, and services may be higher because they are less familiar with the community.

● TRENDS IN LEISURE AND RETIREMENT

The focus on how to spend leisure time, while it has captured the public eye, ignores a countertrend to that of early retirement. This is the large proportion of the elderly who, according to several recent polls, still work or would prefer to be working. Some demographers believe that today's trend toward early retirement may have peaked, or soon will peak. They speculate that the burgeoning older population may have to stay longer in the labor force to relieve the strain on the Social Security system. At the same time, there would probably be greater flexibility during the working years, such as sabbaticals for study or leisure, to offset later retirement (Teaff, 1985; Dychtwald, 1989). The result could be a better balance between work and leisure over the entire life span.

The present concern with leisure, however, is so widespread that the United Nations has a global project on Leisure and Aging. The U.N. World Leisure and Recreation Association holds periodic symposia, where representatives from many countries discuss leisure opportunities for the elderly.

Some social scientists say it is not only the old who are focusing on leisure, that in fact Western society is in the process of replacing the work ethic of five centuries with a new leisure ethic (Osgood, 1982). If so, older Americans may be its most expert practitioners.

While no survey of leisure time can be fully comprehensive, the chief ways older Americans spend their time have been discussed. Their leisure choices will dictate whether they are, to paraphrase a Middle Eastern proverb, heading into the winter of their lives—or into the harvest.

Organizations

AARP Travel Service
4801 110th St.
Overland Park, KS 66207–9976

ACCESS AMTRAK
National Railroad Passenger Corp.
400 North Capitol St., NW
Washington, DC 20001

Brochure on special train services for seniors.

American Society of Travel Agents
(703) 739–2782
Consumer Affairs Dept.

For complaints about travel service providers.

BritRailPass
c/o Brit Rail Travel International, Inc.
630 Third Ave.
New York, NY 10017

Earthwatch
680 Mt. Auburn St.
Box 403
Watertown, MA 02272

Matches volunteers with worldwide scientific expeditions.

Elderhostel
80 Boylston St., Ste. 400
Boston, MA 02116

Escapees, Inc.
Route 5, Box 310
Livingston, TX 77351

Organization for RV owners.

Eurailpass
Box 10383
Stamford, CT 06904-2383

Pass good for low-cost travel throughout Europe; must be bought before leaving the United States.

Foster Grandparent Program
c/o ACTION
1100 Vermont Ave., NW
Washington, DC 20525

Friendship Force
575 South Omni International
Atlanta, GA 30303

Golden Age Passport
c/o Information Office
U.S. Department of Interior
18th and C Sts., NW
Washington, DC 20240

Information on the passport, which entitles those over 62 to free lifetime entrance to national parks, historic sites, monuments, etc.

Grand Circle Travel
347 Congress St.
Boston, MA 02210

Grandtravel
6900 Wisconsin Ave.
Chevy Chase, MD 20815

Tours for grandparents and grandchildren.

Interhostel
University of New Hampshire
6 Garrison Ave.
Durham, NH 03824-3529

Literate Traveler
8306 Wilshire Blvd., Ste. 591
Beverly Hills, CA 90211

Catalog of unique travel books, $1.

National Genealogical Society
4527 North 17th St.
Arlington, VA 22207-2399

National Senior Sports Association
10560 Main St., Ste. 205
Fairfax, VA 22030

Purina Pets for People Program
Ralston Purina Co.
Checkerboard Square, OCA
St. Louis, MO 63164

Helps those over 60 adopt cats and dogs, aiding in visits to the vet, and securing pet supplies.

Recreational Vehicle Industry Association
1896 Preston White Dr.
Reston, VA 22090

Request information for mature RV-ers.

Saga International Holidays
120 Boylston St.
Boston, MA 02116-9804

Senior Companions
c/o ACTION
1100 Vermont Ave., NW
Washington, DC 20525

Senior Games Development Council
200 Castlewood Dr.
North Palm Beach, FL 33408

Organizes Condo Tennis and Senior Softball World Series.

Seniors Abroad
12533 Pacato Circle, N
San Diego, CA 92128

Service Corps of Retired Executives (SCORE)
1441 L St., NW
Washington, DC 20416

Superintendent of Documents
U.S. Government Printing Office
Washington, DC 20402

"Health Information for International Travel," information on health and immunizations, $2.

U.S. Customs Department
P.O. BOX 7407
Washington, DC 20044

"Travel Abroad," free booklet on customs and related legal matters for travelers.

References

American Association of Retired Persons. "Rank Order of Retirement Problems." Unpublished report. Los Angeles: Andrus Gerontology Center, 1980.

Arendt, Hannah. *The Human Condition.* Garden City, NY: Doubleday, 1959.

Atchley, Robert C. *Aging: Continuity and Change.* 2d ed. Belmont, CA: Wadsworth, 1987.

Bell, John. "In Search of a Discourse on Aging: The Elderly on Television." *Gerontologist* Vol. 32, no. 3 (1992).

Bridges, William. *Transitions.* Reading, MA: Addison-Wesley, 1980.

Brothers, Joyce. "Are You Afraid to Have Fun?" *Parade Magazine* (February 2, 1992).

Brown, Paul F. *From Here to Retirement.* Irving, TX: Word, Inc., 1988.

Bryant, Sharon, and William Rakowski. "Predictors of Mortality Among Elderly African-Americans." *Research on Aging* (March 1992).

Buhler, Charlotte. "Meaningful Living in the Mature Years." In *Aging and Leisure.* Ed. R. W. Kleemeier. New York: Oxford University Press, 1961.

Cutler, Stephen J., and Jon Hendricks. "Leisure and Time Use Across the Life Course." In *Handbook of Aging and the Social Sciences.* 3d ed. Eds. Robert H. Binstock and Linda K. George. San Diego, CA: Academic Press, 1990.

Drucker, Peter F. *Management.* New York: Harper, 1973.

Dychtwald, Ken. *Age Wave.* Los Angeles, CA: Jeremy P. Tarcher, 1989.

Gandee, Robert N., Thomas Campbell, Helen Knierim, and others. "Senior Olympic Games." *Journal of Physical Education, Recreation, and Dance* (March 1989).

Giamatti, A. Bartlett. *Take Time for Paradise.* New York: Summit Books, 1989.

Havighurst, Robert J. "The Nature and Values of Meaningful Free-Time Activity." In *Aging and Leisure.* Ed. R. W. Kleemeier. New York: Oxford University Press, 1961.

Hayes, Helen. *Our Best Years.* Garden City, NY: Doubleday, 1984.

Hupp, Sandra. "Camping in the Third Age." *Camping Magazine* (January 1987).

Kaplan, Max. "Toward a Theory of Leisure for Social Gerontology." In *Aging and Leisure*. Ed. R. W. Kleemeier. New York: Oxford University Press, 1961.

Kii, Toshii. "Japanese-American Elderly." In *Life After Work: Retirement, Leisure, Recreation, and the Elderly*. Ed. Nancy J. Osgood. New York: Praeger, 1982.

"Late Bloomer" audio cassette. Available from Connie Goldman Productions, 926 Second Street, Suite 201, Santa Barbara, CA 90403. (310) 393-6801.

Lipman, Aaron, and Nancy J. Osgood. "Retirement: The Emerging Social Institution." In *Life After Work*. Ed. Nancy J. Osgood. New York: Praeger, 1982.

Markides, Kyriakos S., and Charles H. Mindel. *Aging and Ethnicity*. Newbury Park, CA: Sage, 1987.

Maxwell, Robert B. "Our Opinion." *Modern Maturity* (March 1992).

Micheli, Robin. *Money Magazine* (September 1987).

Moody, Harry R. *Abundance of Life*. New York: Columbia University Press, 1988.

Mulac, Margaret. *Hobbies: The Creative Use of Leisure*. New York: Harper, 1959.

Olsen, Nancy. *Starting A Mini-Business: A Guide Book for Seniors*. Sunnyvale, CA: Fair Oaks, 1988.

Osgood, Nancy J. "Introduction." *Life After Work*. New York: Praeger, 1982.

———. "Leisure Programs." In *The Encyclopedia of Aging*. Ed. George L. Maddox. New York: Springer, 1987.

Palmore, Erdman, Bruce Burchett, Gerda Fillenbaum, and others. *Retirement: Causes and Consequences*. New York: Springer, 1985.

Rinker, Harry L. "Column." *Antiques and Collecting* (February 1992).

St. Claire, Allison. *Travel and Older Adults*. Santa Barbara, CA: ABC-CLIO, 1991.

Schick, Frank K., ed. *Statistical Handbook on Aging Americans*. Phoenix, AZ: Oryx, 1986.

Skinner, B. F., and Margaret Vaughan. *Enjoy Old Age: Living Fully in Your Later Years*. New York: Warner Books, 1985.

Solomon, David H., Elyse Salend, Anna Nolen Rahman, and others. *A Consumer's Guide to Aging*. Baltimore, MD: Johns Hopkins University Press, 1992.

Teaff, Joseph D. *Leisure Services with the Elderly*. St. Louis, MO: Times Mirror/Mosby College Publishing, 1985.

U.S. Department of Commerce, Bureau of the Census. *Statistical Abstract of the United States*. 111th ed. Washington, DC: U.S. Government Printing Office, 1991.

Vierck, Elizabeth. *Fact Book on Aging*. Oxford, England: Clio Press, 1990.

Watson, Wilbur H. "Retirement and Leisure Among Older Blacks: A Comparative Analysis." In *Life After Work*. Ed. Nancy J. Osgood. New York: Praeger, 1982.

Additional Reading

Coberly, Lenore M., et al. *Writers Have No Age: Creative Writing with Older Adults*. Binghamton, NY: Haworth Press, 1985.

Deland, Antoinette. *Fielding's Worldwide Cruises*. New York: William Morrow, 1989.

Friedman, R., and A. Nussbaum. *Coping with Your Husband's Retirement*. New York: Simon & Schuster, 1986.

Harris, Robert W. *Gypsying after 40: A Guide to Adventure and Self-Discovery*. Santa Fe, NM: John Muir Publications, 1987.

Hayes, Greg, and Joan Wright. *Going Places: The Guide to Travel Guides*. Boston, MA: Harvard Common Press, 1988.

Kamoroff, Bernard. *Small Time Operator: How to Start Your Own Small Business, Keep Your Books, Pay Your Taxes, and Stay Out of Trouble*. Laytonville, CA: Bell Springs Publishing, revised annually.

Lee, Alice. *A Field Guide to Retirement: Fourteen Lifestyle Options for a Successful Retirement*. New York: Doubleday, 1991.

Liebers, Arthur. *How to Start A Profitable Retirement Business*. Babylon, NY: Pilot Books, 1987.

Mature Traveler (newsletter). Reno, NV.

Palder, Edward L. *The Retirement Sourcebook*. Kensington, MD: Woodbine House, 1989.

Selden, Ina Lee. *Going Into Business for Yourself: New Beginnings After 50*. Des Plaines, IL: AARP Books and Scott Foresman, 1988.

Travel 50 & Beyond (periodical). Houston, TX: Vacation Publications, Inc.

Vorenberg, Bonnie L., ed. *New Plays for Mature Actors: An Anthology*. Morton Grove: IL: Coach House Press, 1987.

Webster, Harriett. *Trips for Those Over 50*. Dublin, NH: Yankee Books, 1988.

Weintz, Carolyn, and Walter Weintz. *The Discount Guide for Travelers Over 55*. 4th ed. New York: Dutton, 1988.

Lyn Teven, Fred Lee, and Alice Lee

38

Productive Aging in the 1990s and Beyond

- The Expansion of Longevity • The Failure Model of Aging • The Concept of Productive Aging
- Physical Aging and the Capacity to Contribute • The Appearance of the Second Middle Age
- Retirement and Beyond • Toward the Twenty-first Century

By the year 2030, 20 percent to 25 percent of the U.S. population will be 65 and older. The conventional population pyramid—broad at the base (higher percentages of youth) and narrower at the top (lower percentages of living elderly)—is becoming square-shaped as the huge birth cohort of post–World War II baby boomers moves up the life course (see Figures 38.1 through 38.5). Victory over once-fatal diseases of infancy and childhood and improvements in sanitation and hygiene have contributed to adding almost forty years to the at-birth life expectancy of Americans from 1900 to the end of this century. Advances in medical knowledge and technology have then added years to the middle and later portions of the life course. Consequently, populations of the United States, Western Europe, and Japan are experiencing a lengthening of lifetimes. Not only is it common for most people to reach the later years (75+), but other portions of the life course, such as middle age (40-64), are being lengthened— that is, health and life activity patterns established in middle-adulthood are now extended into the 65+ period.

*The new population patterns present a picture of aging that seems to defy earlier biological and medical views that linked aging with decline and death: over-the-hill graphs of sharply rising and falling functional curves. Attitudes toward and experiences of aging have correspondingly changed (see Chapter 1, **The History of Aging in America**). Today the United States is described as an "aging society" in which the average age is 33 and will climb to 40 by the year 2010. Middle-aged and older U.S. society is being challenged to adapt to an unprecedented demographic make up. Businesses are beginning to recognize the economic importance of people over 50, middle-aged and older people are dressing differently than their age-peers of twenty years ago, and older adults are appearing in advertising and are playing positive roles in television and movie dramas. Retirement, itself a new portion of the life course, is being reinvented with each new wave of retirement-age individuals.*

What is to be learned about the new patterns of aging and what do they imply for the future? The answers lie, in part, in the complex factors of the evolution of aging during the twentieth century. This chapter examines the expansion of longevity, emerging late-twentieth-century views of aging, new models of physical aging, the expansion of middle age, changing views of retirement, and prospects for the twenty-first century.

● THE EXPANSION OF LONGEVITY

As life expectancy has increased during the twentieth century, from 47.3 years for someone

Figure 38.1
Population, by Sex and Age: 1955 (in millions)

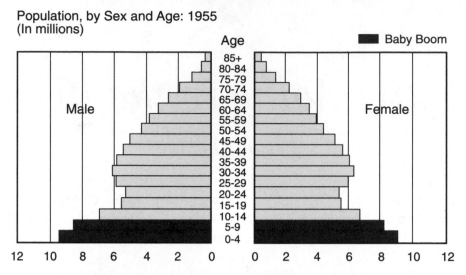

Population, by Sex and Age: 1955
(In millions)

Source: U.S. Bureau of the Census. "Estimates of the Population of the United States, by Single Years of Age, Color, and Sex: 1900 to 1959." *Current Population Reports. Series P-25, no. 311.* Washington, DC: Government Printing Office, 1965.

born in 1900, to 75 years for someone born in 1987, both the experience of growing older and people's ideas about aging have changed. The social adjustments associated with the advent of longevity have been more turbulent and more problematic than the purely physical or biological changes. In order to assess current views of aging and project future developments, one must be aware of the radical fluctuations in images of aging and definitions of the life course that have taken place just within the narrow time band of the twentieth century.

Extension of life expectancy has far exceeded projections made earlier in the century, and it continues to generate controversy as some researchers predict much longer average life-

Figure 38.2
Population, by Sex and Age: 1975 (in millions)

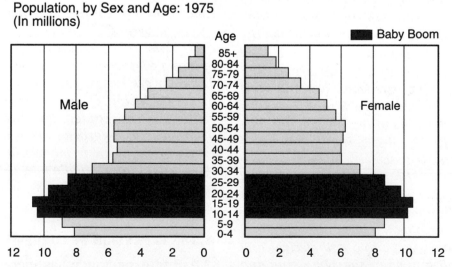

Population, by Sex and Age: 1975
(In millions)

Source: U.S. Bureau of the Census. "Estimates of the Population of the United States, by Single Years of Age, Color, and Sex: 1970 to 1981." *Current Population Reports. Series P-25, no. 917.* Washington, DC: Government Printing Office, 1982.

Figure 38.3
Population, by Sex and Age: 2010 (in millions)

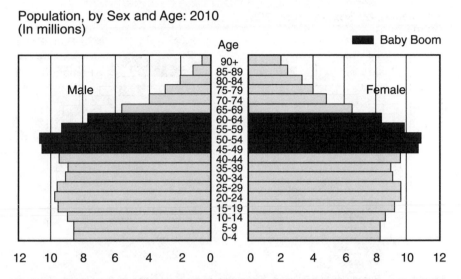

Population, by Sex and Age: 2010
(In millions)

Source: U.S. Bureau of the Census. "Estimates of the Population of the United States, by Single Years of Age, Color, and Sex: 1980 to 2080." Gregory Spencer. *Current Population Reports. Series P-25, no. 1018.* Washington, DC: Government Printing Office, 1989 (middle series projections).

times occurring sooner than those predicted by the U.S. Bureau of the Census. The greatest gains in longevity were made during the first half of the twentieth century, largely due to dramatic reduction in infant and childhood deaths from infectious diseases. But most of the increases in longevity since 1970 are due to declines in mortality among middle-aged and elderly populations. Drugs and hi-tech medicine do not completely account for this lengthening of lifetimes. It is relatively easy to see that new lifesaving technologies, such as coronary bypass and organ transplant operations, have had a profound affect on how long some Americans live, but these tech-

Figure 38.4
Population, by Sex and Age: 2030 (in millions)

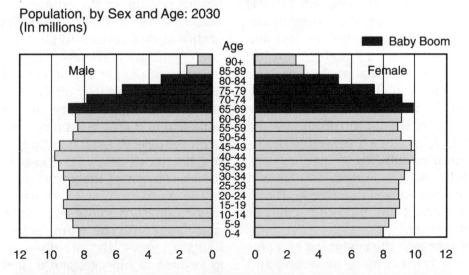

Population, by Sex and Age: 2030
(In millions)

Source: U.S. Bureau of the Census. "Estimates of the Population of the United States, by Single Years of Age, Color, and Sex: 1988 to 2080." Gregory Spencer. *Current Population Reports. Series P-25, no. 1018.* Washington, DC: Government Printing Office, 1989 (middle series projections).

Figure 38.5
Population, by Sex and Age: 2050 (in millions)

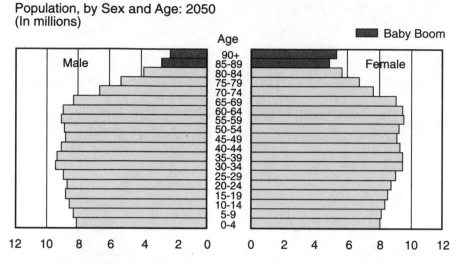

Population, by Sex and Age: 2050
(In millions)

Source: U.S. Bureau of the Census. "Estimates of the Population of the United States, by Single Years of Age, Color, and Sex: 1980 to 2080." Gregory Spencer. *Current Population Reports. Series P-25, no. 1018.* Washington, DC: Government Printing Office, 1989 (middle series projections).

nologies alone do not account for the tremendous increase in life expectancy. As community medicine expert Myrna Lewis has pointed out, in a time period that is 2 percent of human history to date, we have gained more in average life expectancy than in the other 98 percent of human time on earth.

This new longevity has generated a societal reshuffling of customs, priorities, values, and concepts throughout the entire life course. For example, the percentage of U.S. traditional age (18–24) college students has been almost eclipsed by the 25 and over population (47 percent of college students in 1989). The so-called "modernized life course," a product of industrial society with its sequence of education (childhood), work (adulthood), and leisure (old age), is changing as people periodically reenter school for retraining and personal enrichment, as women delay the timing of childbearing until established in their careers, and as older adults, once exhorted to relax and withdraw, are now encouraged to exercise, travel, take courses, volunteer, and pursue second or third "retirement careers."

As Americans approach the beginning of a new millennium, there remain many tensions and imbalances between the new experience of longevity on the one hand and out-of-date images of aging on the other. The clash of popular image

and self-image is exemplified in a recent *American Demographics* essay, "The World According to AARP." The author, Ross K. Baker, recounted the shock he experienced on his fiftieth birthday when he received an invitation from AARP to join the ranks of its 33 million members. The invitation, he wrote, hit him like "the combined force of a draft notice, an IRS audit notification, and a bank overdraft slip" (Baker, 1992). Baker may be reacting to his own fears of aging, but his critique of the articles and ads in AARP's magazine, *Modern Maturity*, reflects age and generational differences likely to occur whenever one organization attempts to span the needs and interests of people aged 50 to 100. To Baker, the products and services offered in *Modern Maturity* appear inappropriate and unattractive to a person in mid-life and mid-career. Apart from certain health services, Baker finds it hard to believe that his future desires and needs will correspond to these images of longevity.

The word "longevity" is used deliberately in this chapter to avoid presumed connotations associated with the word "aging." For example, living a longer lifetime does not simply imply more time in old age, and it does not inevitably mean more disability and longer periods of illness—as many Americans assume. Evidence accumulated since 1980 indicates that the period

Figure 38.6
Life-Span Distribution of Education, Work, and Leisure

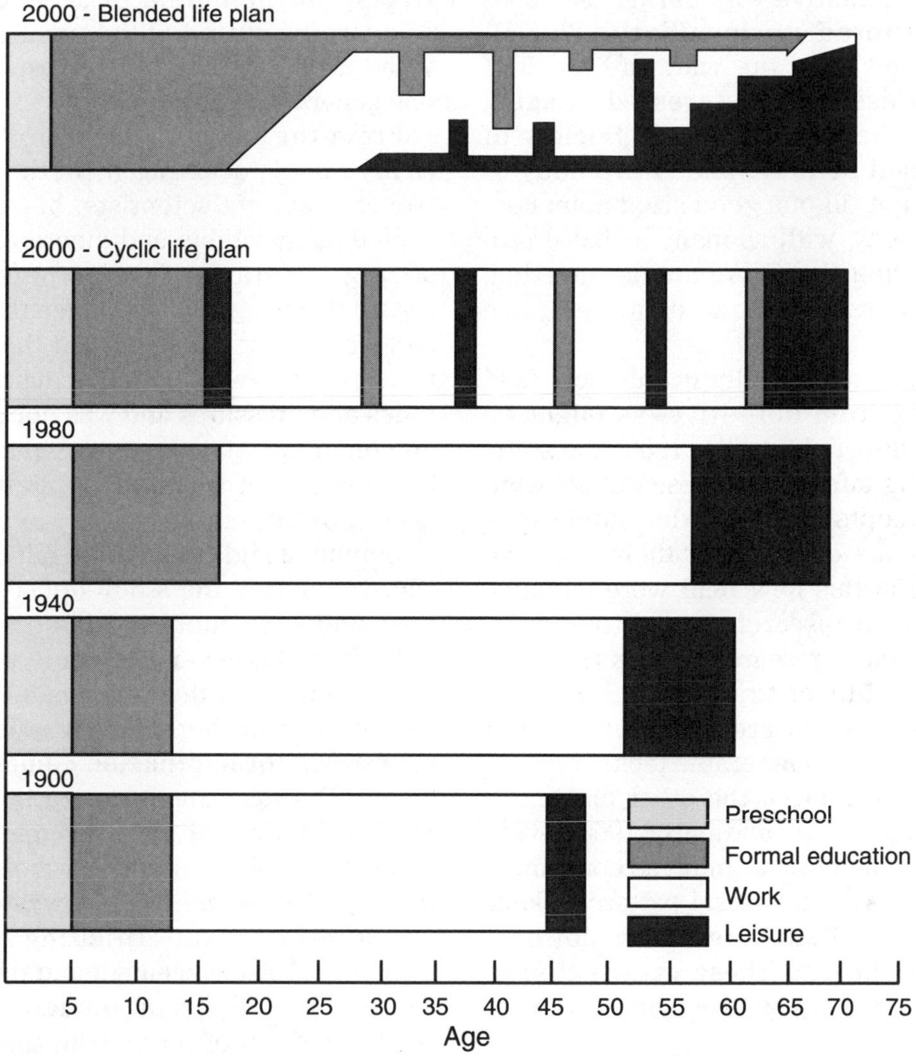

2000 - Blended life plan

2000 - Cyclic life plan

1980

1940

1900

Preschool

Formal education

Work

Leisure

5　10　15　20　25　30　35　40　45　50　55　60　65　70　75
Age

Source: Work in America Institute. *The Future of Older Workers in America.* Scarsdale, NY: Work in America Institute, 1980.

of illness at the end of life, and the age of death, are being pushed higher on the age scale as longevity increases (Atchley, 1991). Moreover, evidence is accumulating from research in a variety of fields that some of the illnesses and debilities traditionally ascribed to old age turn out to be the product of disuse, malnutrition, and lack of stimulation. Human beings retain the potential for increased physical fitness far later in life than previously supposed: in several landmark experiments at the Tufts University USDA Center on Aging, older people—even frail 90-year-olds—who participated in a weight-training program gained strength and demonstrated muscle fiber

growth at the same rate as would be true for younger people (Frontera and others, 1990; Fiatarone and others, 1990).

Not enough is known about contemporary longevity to fully understand its implications. But it is apparent that certain historically rooted ideas about aging, which persist because of their familiarity, no longer fit the generalized experience of many individuals.

● **THE FAILURE MODEL OF AGING**

Many of the negative views of aging current in our society were given tremendous momentum by the research of biological and social scientists shortly after World War II. The scientific study of aging began in a tentative way during the 1930s but was interrupted during World War II. Research resumed after the war, and the first meeting of professionals interested in aging occurred when the Gerontological Society of America convened in 1947. The entire body of participants did not fill one good-sized hotel conference room. Today, with as many as 5,000 professionals attending the GSA's annual meeting, the participants easily fill one or more entire hotels.

Research performed initially in this new field of study was far from definitive, as might be expected in any new field. In the 1950s the study of aging was in its infancy, and researchers were groping for concepts and data that could give them a basis for the direction of their research. That discoveries in this new field were tentative was clear neither to researchers nor to journalists, who treated early research results as definitive findings not subject to later modification. These early concepts entered the public mind with the forcefulness of inalterable fact.

Two concepts, one social the other biological, reported in the late 1950s and early 1960s, were linked together in the popular mind as confirming what was taken to be a universal pattern of later life: social withdrawal and a relentless downhill slope in physical health. These contributed to what later became known as "the failure model of aging."

Disengagement Theory

The first of these midcentury studies, conducted by sociologists Elaine Cumming and William Henry in the 1950s, examined 275 older adults between the ages of 50 and 90 living in Kansas City.

The study found a pattern of gradual withdrawal from normal adult activity as the participants aged. The book written from the study's results, *Growing Old: The Process of Disengagement* (Cumming and Henry, 1961), proposed an idea that became the first major theory in the social study of aging: an "inevitable mutual withdrawal or disengagement" between the older person and other members of the society. From a psychological perspective, this theory matched the analytic view then popular that sexual energy,

what Freud called libido, begins to wane in older people and as it does there is a simultaneous narrowing in their field of activity. This unconsciously motivated withdrawal supposedly provided a smooth transfer of responsibilities from one generation to the next.

From the first publication of Cumming and Henry's book, disengagement theory created controversy among scientists, because it was presented as inevitable and inherent. It encountered strong resistance from experts who did not regard disengagement as a healthy social pattern, and from those who believed that the disengagement process was actually caused by social attitudes and pressures and was not a biological phenomenon. Moreover, some experts regarded the conclusions of the study as indications of bias against older people.

Cumming and Henry did a fair amount of backtracking during the study's postpublication hubbub, and each modified his or her position in some way. However, the study received tremendous attention at the time, made a strong impression on researchers, and was infused into the mainstream of information communicated to the public. Disengagement theory fit neatly with the idea of a universal age retirement by giving it a presumed biological and psychological basis. On the everyday social level, it was often translated into a rationale for criticizing non-conforming behavior: if disengagement and retirement are the "norm," and a person deviates from the prescribed pattern of retirement, then there must be something wrong with that person.

Cumulative Decline

In 1958, Dr. Nathan Shock, a pioneer in gerontology and then head of the newly established Gerontology Research Center in Baltimore, met with a retired Public Health Service officer, Dr. W. W. Peter, who believed that knowledge about aging was crucial to the future development of public health programs and that studies on healthy, productive people living in the community were essential. A skilled organizer with a great deal of drive and enthusiasm, Peter recruited a number of friends and acquaintances into a research project set up to make repeated measurements on the same subjects as they aged. This was the birth of the often-cited Baltimore Longitudinal Study of Aging (BLSA).

In the early 1960s Dr. Shock published a series of charts describing many different kinds of physical functioning—breathing, heart rate, kidney function, and so on—throughout the life course. In each chart there was a peak of functioning during the twenties and early thirties and then a long, gradual downhill slope. The apparent message of these charts, partly because of the way they were drawn, was that after one's twenties, organ system functioning goes into marked decline. The charts were much used in the medical community and were incorporated into medical school textbooks. For decades every fledgling physician saw these charts and understood them to be a factual depiction of continually deteriorating physical functions during and after the thirties. However, there are four elements in these early charts that were unintentionally misleading.

First, they were made from stress test results, not from ordinary functioning. Performance on stress tests falls much more sharply as one ages than ordinary performance does. Older people (indeed, Americans as a whole) in the 1950s and 1960s often didn't exercise regularly; lack of *consistent* exercise can also cause a steep decline on stress test performance, which does not show up in ordinary life. In other words, stress test performance is not necessarily an index of how well the person functions on an everyday basis. One can do poorly on a stress test and still get along quite well in everyday terms.

Second, an average does not describe—and cannot predict—the experience of any given individual. The Shock charts were averages and were subject to the same weakness later found by other researchers in longitudinal studies, notably psychologist Dr. K. Warner Schaie, who has extensively studied the functioning of mental processes throughout adult life (Birren and Schaie, 1990). When a group's scores are averaged together, perhaps 90 percent of the group may be essentially stable in performance, for another 5 percent performance has begun to deteriorate, and of the remaining 5 percent performance is deteriorating rapidly and catastrophically. The moderately and severely deteriorating 10 percent will pull down the performance curve for the whole group. As a result, it will appear that there is a steady decline in performance for every member of the group, whereas 90 percent of the group is really performing at the same level.

Third, whatever decline does occur in physical functioning is in reality quite gradual. The charts from the Shock study compressed a long period of time into a small amount of visual space. As a result, the lines appeared much steeper than the group's decline really was. If, for instance, the chart had been twelve inches long instead of three, the visual impression of the slope would have more accurately characterized the data, as it would have reflected a much more gradual decline.

Fourth, the assumptions drawn from the original Shock charts were premature. The results could not have been accurately judged so soon after the study began. The results of the Baltimore study as they are assessed today, after thirty-four years of continuing research, are precisely the opposite of the impression given by Shock's early charts. In a revised view, Shock and others (1989) argue that the study has shown that aging does not necessitate a general decline in all physical and psychological functions; "some abilities decline, but some remain stable. Others actually improve."

The cumulative decline model is a medical model, and medical models are formed from the observation of illness, not health. Dr. James Birren believes that this model has been heavily influenced by physicians themselves, who are in contact mostly with the sick and who often see a continuous decline in their older patients. Any model that is predominantly medical is potentially biased, in that it presents a picture of the experience of sick persons rather than those who are healthy. In a similar fashion, there are other professions with built-in distortions of perspective as, for example, social workers—who constantly see the indigent elderly and assume that a much higher proportion of older people live in poverty than may be the case.

Some illnesses *do* lead to a process of cumulative decline, even in young people. Multiple sclerosis, for example, can occur at any age and produces a cumulative deterioration of functions that ends in death. But human aging, although it can follow this pattern, does not *necessarily* do so.

One other qualifying factor is that researchers are unsure how much life-style figures into these studies. The number of variables is enormous and complex, so that this question is not likely to be resolved quickly or easily. Earlier generations of Americans, by and large, did not exercise frequently nor systematically once they were out of their twenties, and exercise is extremely important in maintaining good functioning. Older generations of Americans are more likely to have held jobs requiring hard physical exertion, which may break down the body's structure faster than jobs with physically less grueling requirements. Nutrition may or may not have improved, but contemporary Americans do get a much wider variety of fresh foods year around than was true for earlier generations. They no longer have to stockpile apples and potatoes in root cellars to get enough Vitamin C to survive through the winter. It is impossible to speculate how much impact these aspects of life might have had on the Schock studies.

The question of the relationship between aging and disability is important to the future of aging. If growing old incapacitates a large part of a population, then the future of "productive aging" is a very limited one. Larger numbers and percentages of older people will mean correspondingly greater numbers and percentages of despondent and disabled elders, unable to contribute to others let alone take care of themselves. On the other hand, if disability can be linked to specific causes, some of which are avoidable or remediable—and if disability can be prevented or diminished for future generations of older people—then the older years of life take on the role of a different stage of normal adulthood.

Toward the end of his life, Shock concluded that the three decades of the Baltimore Longitudinal Study favored healthy aging. "The BLSA has provided substantive evidence showing that age changes take place rather slowly," he wrote, "and that most individuals adapt to these changes as they occur. The disabilities seen in old people are primarily the results of disease rather than age itself. . . . Changes in intellectual performance, such as the ability to solve problems, show very little change until after age 70. Intellectual deterioration and severe memory loss is more apt to be the result of disease rather than aging" (Shock, 1983).

● THE CONCEPT OF PRODUCTIVE AGING

The phrase "productive aging" captures a paradoxical rethinking of later life generated by the clash between fluid, lived experience and fixed, historically rooted ideas. Coined in the early 1980s by Dr. Robert Butler, the first director of the National Institute on Aging and now chairman of the Department of Geriatric Medicine at Mt. Sinai Medical Center in New York City, the term "productive aging" was meant to imply a type of old age not characterized by dependency and decline, but instead as a period of continued growth and contribution to the society. Butler's first published use of the term was in the title of a volume of papers presented at a Salzburg Seminar on "productive aging," which he organized in summer 1983 (Butler, 1985).

Butler created the term because he saw a need to detach the image of aging from its rigid association with weakness, disability, passivity, and dependency. He recognized that, in post–World War II America, "productivity" had become the preeminent measure of personal worth. Individuals reaching their mid-sixties were then caught in a paradox. They were encouraged or required to retire—they had earned their retirement, to be sure, but they were also forced to take it at 65 whether they wanted to or not. Once retired, they were exiled from the core processes of society because they were no longer "productive" and were now viewed as socially irrelevant, if not a burden to society.

Many older people had the capacity to be "productive" in the ordinary sense of continuing to do work or take part in other activities they loved and were good at, and they could continue contributing to the collective good of society. If they were not productive in this sense, it was due in large part to the practice of retirement, which was dictated by corporate and government policies and not the personal choice of older people. But Butler also understood that many older people actually *were* productive, in ways that economists did not count: mentoring children and grandchildren, helping to put them through schools, buffering them from the effects of life's temporary setbacks, doing volunteer work, mentoring younger friends, and creating works of art, literature, and music. Older people provided a historical continuity that reassured and stabilized the lives of other people around them, despite the negative societal view of the older person's value.

Butler was also frustrated with the pervasive

age bias present in American society at the time. Being older in itself did not necessarily make one better or worse than one was at a younger age, yet it was universally regarded as a clear detriment. Creating a more positive term to describe the older years of life was Butler's effort to focus attention on the positive aspects to getting older.

Butler's bid to reorient the nation's perspective on aging by adding a new term to the dialogue has been successful. Other experts have added additional refinements of the concept, such as "successful aging" by Dr. John H. Rowe (now president of Mt. Sinai Medical Center), who heads the MacArthur Foundation Research network on Successful Aging; and "resourceful aging," a title used for a conference given by the New Roles in Society Program of the American Association of Retired Persons (AARP) and Cornell University in October 1990. While the term productive aging will itself gradually fade from use, it denotes the changing perspectives on later life and the turn toward new conceptions, attitudes, and social policies.

● PHYSICAL AGING AND THE CAPACITY TO CONTRIBUTE

There are other, substantial indications that aging in itself does not mean decrepitude, or a long period of illness and decline. The 1989 Health Interview Survey conducted by the National Center for Health Statistics found that 71 percent of Americans 65 and older report that their health is good and even excellent compared to others their own age. "Cumulative decline" does not reflect the general experience of aging.

The Long Careers Study

A study conducted from 1987 to 1992 of 150 older people who continued working past the traditional retirement age of 65, the Long Careers study (Bronte, 1993) indicates much greater variety in patterns of physical aging than previously thought. Of the 21 participants from the study who have died as of April 1993, 50 percent did not experience a "cumulative decline." Instead they followed a very different pattern, the "Plateau of Vitality" model, first observed and named by Dr. James E. Birren. The second largest number, 35 percent, experienced "cumulative decline," while two smaller groups had patterns described as

"episodic health and illness" (10 percent) and "ill but functional" (5 percent).

The Plateau of Vitality Pattern of Aging

There have always been some older people who remained healthy and active consistently until very old age and who died with no period of illness or only an extremely brief one. Dr. Birren became aware of this when he received an unexpected visit one day at the Andrus Center from a woman who told his receptionist that she was 102 and she had just dropped in because she was curious to see what a gerontology center did.

Birren said that the woman appeared to be about 70. "You couldn't tell how old she was. She didn't use a cane, she wasn't enfeebled in her walking or in her manner. You reacted to her as if she were Mrs. Everyday or Mrs. Everyperson, not as if she were a fragile hundred-and-two-year-old woman," claimed Birren. He was even more astonished when she told him that to reach the Andrus Center she had taken the bus—a heroic feat in Los Angeles at any age. She had come, she said, because she was curious to see what a university gerontology center did; Birren took note of this because according to gerontological thinking in the late 1970s when this incident occurred, older people were widely believed neither to be curious about new ideas nor interested in the external world.

The woman returned several more times over the next few years, developing a very cordial and interested relationship with Birren and his staff. Then Birren received a letter from one of the woman's friends telling him that she had died in her 104th year, without any trauma or apparent illness. She just simply "faded out" over a period of a few months.

The incident piqued Birren's interest, and he began to collect anecdotes of lives similar to this woman's. In many of the examples he has found so far, the lifetime extended past 100, often to 104 or 105, without any significant change in the person's abilities right up to the end of life. No formal study of the phenomenon has been initiated, but it bears further exploration. Birren observed that some people seem to reach a "plateau of healthy aging" in their late sixties or early seventies, after which they maintain the same level of functioning until the very end of their lives— sometimes for thirty years or more. For them there is no slow decline, no long period of ill health, and no real impairment in functioning.

Several of the Long Careers Study participants had relatives whose lives followed this pattern. Interviewee Ollie Thompson told about his grandmother, who at 103 could thread a needle without glasses and did all her own housework. One day, for no particular reason, she called Thompson's mother, Martha, and told her to bring all the grandchildren over for dinner, because she felt a bit weak. She took everyone out to a movie and then for ice cream before returning to her home for dinner. About 9:30 she went upstairs to bed. When Martha checked an hour later, she found her mother was dead. "She wasn't sick at all," Thompson remembers, "she just slept away."

Ninety-two-year-old Dr. Irving Wright told a similar story about his father, who died at 88. An inventor and a machinery patternmaker, Wright's father at the age of 72 had helped to design the B-29 bomber, which carried the atom bomb during World War II. After the war he continued to be active and kept up his pace of invention. Then, in 1950, Dr. Wright said, "my father was presiding at our annual Thanksgiving dinner, when suddenly he said, 'I think I'll take a nap.' Nobody had ever heard of Perry Wright taking a nap in the afternoon and they all commented on it. He went up and went to sleep and was dead three days later. It was as simple as that."

Regardless of scientific controversies, these anecdotal examples demonstrate that some people have a long, healthy older adulthood, without cumulative decline and with little or no illness at the end of life. This is echoed by the pattern of the Long Careers Study participants to date, although since the group is not in any sense representative, one cannot know to what extent a scientifically selected group would echo these results.

Because of the cumulative decline model's fifty year dominance, researchers know comparatively little about the plateau model: How prevalent is it in comparison with cumulative decline? How large or small a percentage of older people are healthy and functioning until a short time before death compared with those who experience cumulative decline? Because people who stayed healthy throughout their old age have been regarded as exceptions, the question hasn't been pursued. Perhaps when researchers know more

about these alternative patterns they may find that, without the intervention of specific diseases, the plateau model represents the normal progression of late life.

The Episodic Health and Illness Pattern of Aging

A third model of the physical aging process is a kind of halfway point between the first two. It is suggested by the experiences of several participants in the Long Careers Study, most strikingly by the life of the late Norman Cousins (Bronte, 1993). In it, the person does experience episodes of specific illness but recovers completely from each episode and regains the same level of functioning as before the illness. The person's health does not go gradually downhill, and there is no long period of illness at the end of life. Instead there is a zigzag pattern of periods of good health, interspersed with periods of illness.

Cousins experienced and recovered from two bouts with potentially fatal illness after the age of fifty. The first was a degenerative disease of the connective tissue, ankylosing spondylitis, which he contracted in the early 1970s and from which he recovered completely. An article he wrote about the experience for the *New England Journal of Medicine*, (Cousins, 1976) received such favorable comment that he expanded it into a book, *Anatomy of an Illness* (1979). The book revolutionized Americans' attitude toward actively participating in their own health care, and it did so without alienating the medical profession.

About ten years later, Cousins suffered a heart attack. He and his wife, Ellen, had just moved to southern California, where he was an adjunct professor at the UCLA Medical School, designing and taking part in research that documented the effect that the mind has on physical health via brain hormones. Again, Cousins recovered from this illness so completely that he returned to all his regular activities, including playing tennis and golf. His research at UCLA lasted for almost a decade and yielded major advances in understanding the mind's role in physical illness. After ten years of vigorous health, with no preliminary warning signs and no indication that anything was wrong, Cousins died suddenly of cardiac arrest at the age of 75. The day before he died Cousins had played eighteen holes of golf. An interesting sequel to this story suggests a genetic element in Cousin's pattern of healthy longevity. His sister, Sophie Cousins Silberberg, was remarkably like him in appearance, stature, and personality. Six months after Cousins's death, Sophie Silberberg suddenly died—likewise with no warning whatsoever—of full cardiac arrest.

The episodic model may be a product of modern medicine: the people in this category might have succumbed earlier if they had lived in previous eras. Is their complete recovery due to advances in medical technology? The Episodic Pattern illustrates the astonishing power of the physical body to recover its functioning, even at older ages and from major illnesses.

The "Ill but Functional" Pattern of Aging

A fourth pattern of aging was suggested at the very end of the Long Careers Study by the experience of Alberta Jacoby, a filmmaker who taught at Yale University until her death in mid-1992. In a long interview Jacoby extensively described her varied career, which included being a professional dancer, playing Olympic-caliber golf, being a civil servant during World War II, and subsequently becoming a filmmaker. After Jacoby's death it was learned that she had suffered from leukemia for many years. But her leukemia was under control; she had found and followed a regimen that enabled her to maintain a stable condition. The result was that there was essentially no difference in her life or activities, although technically she had a serious illness.

This balance was abruptly altered in February 1992, when Jacoby was injured in a car accident while driving with a longtime friend. The friend was killed, Jacoby's wrist was broken, and she was severely traumatized by the whole event. In the following months she failed to recover her energy and zest fully. Late in the spring it became clear that she had contracted a rapidly progressing form of cancer, different from leukemia. She died in June 1992, her leukemia still stabilized, but her body ravaged by the post-accident second form of cancer.

Several other Long Careers Study participants with serious disabilities or continuing illnesses have nevertheless continued to function apparently as well as they might have without the illness. One is Westport, Connecticut, attorney Virginia Boyd, who suffered a stroke at the age of 59 which left her permanently unable to walk

unaided. She has continued her practice of law and gets around with the aid of a walker, crutches, or wheelchair depending on the circumstances. She has traveled internationally for vacations during this period, and while she acknowledged that it takes more effort, she leads a life that is essentially like that of other people still working in their seventies.

In summary, at present one can identify at least four models of physical functioning in old age. There is no set chronological age at which physical functioning begins to "go downhill" for human beings. For an undetermined number of older people, once they enter their sixties and early seventies, physical and mental functioning shows little decline. There are some who have episodes of illness, with periods of recovery and undiminished functioning in between. And there are some who become ill in some respect, but like Alberta Jacoby and Virginia Boyd, continue being productive and creative. Clearly a more complex view of older people and the physical aging process is needed. Older people are not a monolithic group; rather people seem to become increasingly differentiated as they age. While older people are not universally poor, sick, and frail, neither are they all glowingly healthy and out playing tennis. There are people in each category, and in between. The image of the frail, sick older person shouldn't be replaced with the image of what Mary Catherine Bateson terms a super-elder, who leaps tall buildings at a single bound. It is as oppressive to expect all older people to be super-achievers as it is to expect them to be helpless and incompetent. Neither image truthfully represents all older people as a group.

● THE APPEARANCE OF THE SECOND MIDDLE AGE

Most Americans probably believe that the increase in longevity means that we will all spend much more time being old, based on our longstanding assumption that increased longevity period officially begins at the fixed chronological age of sixty-five. If one adds years to this age, then the calculation appears very straightforward: we have many more years of "old age" to look forward to, instead of the five to ten we might otherwise have expected. Since old age is the period people generally find least attractive, it goes almost without saying that increased longevity is not an appealing prospect. However, as lifetimes have grown longer, the process of physical aging has gradually and rather mysteriously slowed down. People are not only living longer, they are entering physiological old age later in life. In effect, there has been a postponement of the physical aging process, and most are feeling its effect to some degree.

This postponement of old age is responsible for the most surprising effect of the longevity factor. The extra twenty or thirty years of life gained have been added to the middle of life—the prime of adulthood—as well as to its end. Like a rubber band pulled by giant hands, the whole length of the life course has stretched evenly, not just one end or the other. The result is not just a simple addition of time to the end of our lives, but transformation of the entire life course, especially of adulthood. The period between what was formerly the end of middle age (about age 50) and what is now the beginning of real, physical old age (at some point after age 75) forms a new second middle age of adult life—one that has never

before existed as a generalized experience for large numbers of people. In lifetimes that may reach close to 100 years for many, especially the baby boomers, this new stage occupies the third quarter of life.

Extension of the period of vitality in the middle of adult life radically alters many existing beliefs about the life course and the aging process. Many things once thought inevitable may not really be inevitable at all. As an example, consider current attitudes toward reaching the fifth decade of life. The conventional perspective is that the age of 50 is the beginning of a long, downhill slide. A fiftieth birthday is often treated, albeit humorously, as if it is the end of life's potential. One doesn't need to engage in sophisticated research to find evidence that this depressing idea is very much alive in the American consciousness, on the level of everyday events. If one goes into any greeting card store and reads the messages on the cards for fiftieth birthdays, one finds that they describe a grim landscape of "downhill slides" for people who are "over the hill" and worse.

Many of the Long Careers Study participants

Profiles of Productive Aging

Frances Lear
Former magazine editor

"I'm the latest bloomer…I started my career at 62! I think that, although I hate to chart anything by chronology, I've had more growth from 55 on than during all the rest of my life put together."

Frances Lear, founder of *Lear's* magazine and the woman who worked to revolutionize the attitude of a nation toward women who "weren't born yesterday," overcame many obstacles before beginning her real career at the age of 62.

An adopted child, she reported being neglected by her mother and abused by her stepfather. She ran away from home at 16, graduated from Sarah Lawrence College, and by age 34, Lear speculated that she must have had "fifteen different careers, because I was forever hating what I was doing and wanting to be something better, and use my head more."

In 1957, she married television writer/producer Norman Lear. The marriage lasted twenty-eight years

and produced two children. Though Lear worked closely with her husband, she was dissatisfied with the subordinate role assigned to women in Los Angeles. During the late 1960s, Lear founded The Women's Place Inc., a consulting firm for women that engaged in government-funded work projects. When the need for qualified women in industry became apparent, Lear established Lear, Purvis, Walker & Co., the first U.S. executive search firm specializing in the placement of women executives.

When Lear relocated to New York, she decided to start a magazine for "women like me"—educated, affluent women 35 and over. *Lear's* became "an early road map to much of the second half of life." She was named Editor of the Year by *Advertising Age* in 1989. Lear folded the magazine in March 1994 to form her own television company and to make videos that tell women how to manage their money.

Lydia Brontë

referred to this belief as one they had discarded because their experience contradicted it. "When I was fifty," 77-year-old Washington psychotherapist Evelyn Nef said, "I thought my life was over. I was recently widowed; my job had been phased out because of my husband's death; and I was moving to a new city to start all over again. Little did I know that the best years of my life were still ahead of me" (Bronte, 1993).

In the interviews conducted for the Long Careers Study, many of the participants described a sequence of experiences very different from the stereotypes one might expect. In their early fifties, these people felt that they were just beginning to come into their own. They had accomplished or were nearing the end of most of the family tasks of early adulthood—marriage, childrearing, and putting children through college. They had served their apprenticeship at work; they knew how to get things done and had a firm grasp of the responsibilities of their job or profession. With these major tasks accomplished, they were beginning to reach out for greater creativity in their work, for broader impact, for solutions that hadn't yet been found. In short, they were poised for flight. Their real stage of professional development bore no resemblance to the conventional idea of what people do at age 50.

Because this isn't the image that our culture normally associates with turning 50, one can ask whether these experiences are atypical or perhaps even rare. In a scientific sense, that question hasn't been definitively asked or answered. Because the stereotypes have been solidly planted, and because in the past society has focused almost exclusively on the negative aspects of aging—illness, frailty, the need for health care and nursing home care—we simply have not seen the positive shifts that have taken place. We can hope that in the future more research will be devoted to positive aspects of aging, and that more answers will emerge.

● RETIREMENT AND BEYOND

According to government population statistics, there has been a sharp decline since the 1950s in the number of people over 55 who remain in the work force. In themselves, the figures are convincing: in 1950, 65 percent of all men 55 and over were still employed; by 1990, there were only 38

percent in this category. Women's work force participation curve has been somewhat different from that of men, because more women joined the work force during those forty years: in 1950, 18 percent of women over 55 were employed; by 1990, the figure had risen to 22 percent. But with women and men combined, the percentage of people employed over 55 fell from 41 percent in 1950 to 29 percent in 1990.

Looking at work force figures for those 55 and older does not give us a complete picture, however; we must also look at figures for those between 45 and 54. The traditional boundaries of retirement began to expand in the 1970s and 1980s, when a trend toward early retirement—the practice of allowing or encouraging employees to retire before they reached age 65—appeared in corporations and businesses. Early retirement offers have been extended to people as young as 50; in a few well-publicized instances, companies like Atlantic Richfield and CBS offered early retirement packages to thousands of 50-year-old employees at one time. The percentage of employed men aged 45 to 54 has also been falling—from 91.9 percent in 1950, to 87.4 percent in 1990.

To a large degree, early retirement trends can be linked to economic issues. From the 1960s to the 1980s, characterized by high unemployment and a surplus of labor, it seemed to be in the short-term interest of many companies to offer attractive retirement plans to their older employees, who were drawing the largest salaries. However, this kind of short-term planning overlooked the dramatic—and ultimately costly—loss of human capital any business suffers when losing experienced employees. The same trend, now in response to corporate downsizing, is occurring in the 1990s. Also, the long-term expense of supporting an ever-growing percentage of the population that is not working will certainly impact public policy planning, particularly as employee shortages due to the declined birth rate of the 1960s and 1970s, the baby bust, begin to affect the U.S. labor force and economy.

This trend towards early retirement could slow down in the next few decades, if recent changes in Social Security law persuade workers to retire at older ages. In the first twenty-five years of the next century, the retirement age at which a worker will be eligible to collect full Social

Security benefits will rise from 65 to 67. Nevertheless, the retirement figures show that participation in work is steadily declining in both of these age categories. Older people may stay in the work force because they need the money; they can't afford to retire. The social environment of everyday experience can be expected to reflect this statistical profile, showing few older people who are still working. But the level of everyday experience shows something different: many older people are continuing some form of work, for one reason or another. This is borne out by a major national survey of 3,000 older Americans 55 and older, conducted in 1991 by Louis Harris and Associates for the Commonwealth Fund. In this study Harris employed the term "productive activity," rather than the strict definition of work used in national statistical reports. Harris's investigations included paid and unpaid work, as well as volunteering, helping children and grandchildren, and helping the sick and disabled. This survey revealed that almost 75 percent of the participants were involved in one or more of the activities designated as productive activity, with almost 50 percent giving twenty or more hours a week to that activity. Although the percentage of older people with full-time employment declined sharply after age 75, the percentage of those doing unpaid, volunteer, or community/family work dropped only slightly with age.

According to Bass and Caro (1993), productive aging is a concept that "has evolved from the convergence of four elements: (1) the recognition of unused physical and mental capacities of the current group of older people; (2) the expanded window of time between formal retirement and frailty; (3) a desire among some older people to remain engaged and active in society; and (4) a social and economic need for independent and productive older people" (Bass and Caro, 1993). The dramatic results of this survey indicate that today's older people are clearly committed to continuing non-leisure activities after retirement. In fact, 31 percent of those not working were eager to obtain jobs. Even more of the respondents were willing and able to do volunteer work, but were not doing so. These figures demonstrate the tremendous untapped resource these people represent to society.

Although some aging experts worry that older persons' opportunities for work could become obligations in the future or might provide a rationale to cut much-needed spending on long-term care and other aging programs, it seems overly cautious not to encourage the millions of older people who want to be more active. No one is suggesting an end to the concept of retirement, which many Americans continue to cherish, but studies like that of the Commonwealth Fund indicate that it is time to reevaluate assumptions about the kinds of contributions older people can make to society.

The Commonwealth Fund findings are echoed by those of the Long Careers Study. The study participants were active older people at every economic and social level, working at an enormous variety of pursuits and in many different circumstances, apparently enjoying what they were doing. Most of them said they were working by choice because they had too much energy "just to sit at home" or because they were so interested in what they were doing.

That there were so many people who continue to work—by choice, not just because they needed the income—gave rise to a variety of questions. Why were they still working if they didn't need the money? Were they just workaholics who couldn't give up their way of life? Were they afraid of retirement, classic cases of people who couldn't adjust? Or were they exceptions, able to continue their work because of unusual circumstances?

Researchers in the field of aging have speculated about the effect of having so many increasingly vigorous older people and so few ways for them to participate in the society as a whole. Traditional retirement has been called a "roleless role": although it is treated as if it gives the retiree a role, it offers few models and no real way of staying involved in the life of society. Many retirees do find a creative outlet for their energies in individual pursuits or in organizations geared to "seniors." But not all retirees have creative outlets, and as the number of older people increases, the need for more alternatives is becoming greater.

Aging researchers John Riley and Matilda White Riley point out that in American society there is a serious lag in finding new roles for healthy older people. "As members of successive cohorts retire at young ages and are better educated and perhaps healthier than their predecessors," the Rileys observed, "it seems predictable that pressures from old people and from the public at large will modify the existing work and retirement roles" (Riley and Riley, 1986). Study after study suggests that the need for involvement and participation in the larger society does not end with formal retirement. Yet the needs still outstrip the incipient opportunities.

In other words, older people may choose to continue to work, and this impulse would be generated by individuals, since institutions and organizations were doing very little to deal with the lack of roles. "One inference seems inescapable," noted the Rileys: "The presence of increasing numbers of capable people living in a society that offers them few meaningful roles is bound to bring about changes. Capable people and empty role structures cannot co-exist for long."

It is worth noting that the Rileys are justifiably experts on this phenomenon, not solely on the basis of their academic credentials. Born in 1908 (John Riley) and 1911 (Matilda White Riley), they have been active in the field of aging since it was inaugurated in 1947. And both are still working: he as a consultant for the Equitable Life Insurance Society and the International Association on Aging, and she with the Behavioral and Social Science Research Section of the National Institute on Aging, first as its director and, since 1992, as a senior scholar. It seems reasonable to conclude that working older people may be doing just what the Rileys themselves predict and exemplify: creating new roles where no other satisfactory roles existed.

● TOWARD THE TWENTY-FIRST CENTURY

"Productive aging" has already begun to affect every sector of U.S. society. Older Americans are having a tremendous economic impact both as consumers and as potential workers. Businesses that deal with aging-related services are among the fastest growing in the country. Political discussions on issues like long-term health care, Medicare, Social Security law, and social programs continue to dominate the media. The social contributions of older Americans through volunteer work is increasingly being recognized as vital to the existence of thousands of organizations and communities. These indications represent the first stages of the radical impact that the rising

number of older people, and their unprecedented vitality and engagement, will continue to have throughout the twenty-first century.

Currently it is difficult to see beyond the dilemmas posed by the longer lifetime and the demographics of aging societies. Public and scholarly debate continues to focus on the issue of longevity versus quality of life. While the "plateau of vitality" health pattern may be expanding, the optimistic view that healthy life-styles and modern medicine will combine to produce a "compression of morbidity" (Fries, 1988), that most people will live free of chronic or acute illness until just before death, is not supported by studies showing that while onset of some diseases may in fact be delayed, long periods of chronic illness and disability remain a major factor of old age (Gerhard and Cristofalo, 1992).

Are we moving toward a future society in which the designation "old" will simply be shifted forward to encompass people over 80 or 85, while those younger are considered to be in the second half of middle age? Will radical medical interventions such as gene therapy so alter the concept of "natural death" that individuals will be responsible for deciding when they have lived enough life, or will economic factors determine when people are to be excluded from further life extending therapies (Cassell, 1992)?

Can one imagine a society of the future in which length of life and quality of life are not in inverse relationship? An intimation of this is found in a recent segment of the popular science fiction television series "Star Trek: The Next Generation." The spaceship's commander, Captain Jean Luc Picard, rebukes a just thawed out cryogenic survivor of some 300 years who continues to be obsessed with money and power. Material and health concerns have been solved, Picard tells the disbelieving earthling. What motivates people now is self-improvement and service to others. Somewhere between our aging society and the starship *Enterprise* lies the future.

References

American Association of Retired Persons. *Resourceful Aging: Today and Tomorrow.* Conference Proceedings, October 9–10, 1990. Washington, DC: AARP, 1991.

Atchley, Robert C. *Social Forces and Aging: An Introduction to Social Gerontology.* Belmont, CA: Wadsworth, 1991.

Baker, Ross K. "The World According to AARP." *American Demographics* (1992): 23.

Bass, Scott A., and Francis G. Caro. "The New Politics of Productive Aging." *In Depth: A Journal for Values and Public Policy on "Revisioning the Aging Society"* Vol. 2, no. 3 (Fall 1993): 59–79.

Birren, James E., and K. Warner Schaie. *Handbook of the Psychology of Aging.* 3d ed. San Diego, CA: Academic Press, 1990.

Brontë, Lydia. *The Longevity Factor.* New York: Harper Collins, 1993.

Butler, Robert. *Productive Aging: Enhancing Vitality in Later Life.* New York: Springer, 1985.

Cassel, Christine. "Ethics and the Future of Aging Research: Promises and Problems." *Generations* Vol. 16, no. 4 (Winter/spring 1992): 61–65.

Cousins, Norman. *Anatomy of an Illness.* New York: W. W. Norton, 1979.

———. "Anatomy of an Illness: As Perceived by the Patient." *New England Journal of Medicine* Vol. 295 (1976): 1458–63.

Cumming, Elaine, and William H. Henry. *Growing Old: The Process of Disengagement.* New York: Basic Books, 1961.

Fiatarone, M. A., and others. "High-Intensity Strength Training in Nonagenarians: Effect on Skeletal Muscle." *Journal of the American Medical Association* Vol. 263 (1990): 3029–34.

Fries, J. "Aging, Illness, and Health Policy: Implications of the Compression of Morbidity." *Perspectives in Biology and Medicine* Vol. 31, no. 3 (1988): 407–28.

Frontera, W. R., and others. "Strength Conditioning in Older Men: Skeletal Muscle Hypertrophy and Improved Function." *Journal of Applied Physiology* Vol. 64 (1988): 1038–44.

Gerhard, Glenn S., and Vincent J. Cristofalo. "The Limits of Biogerontology." *Generations* Vol. 16, no. 4 (Winter/spring 1992): 55–59.

Lerner, Max. *Wrestling With the Angel: A Memoir of My Triumph Over Illness.* New York: W. W. Norton, 1990.

National Center for Health Statistics. "Current Estimates from the National Health Interview Survey." *Vital and Health Statistics* Series 10, no. 176. Washington, DC: Government Printing Office, 1989.

Riley, Matilda White, and John W. Riley, Jr. "Longevity and Social Structure: The Potential of the Added Years." In *Our Aging Society.* Eds. Alan Pifer and Lydia Brontë. New York: W. W. Norton, 1986.

Shock, Nathan W., T. Franklin Williams, and James L. Fozard. "Historical Origins of the Study." BLSA Silver Anniversary Symposium, September 10, 1983.

———. *Older and Wiser.* NIH Publication 89-27987. Washington, DC: Government Printing Office, 1989.

U.S. Bureau of the Census. "Estimates of the Population of the United States, by Single Years of Age, Color, and Sex: 1900 to 1959." *Current Population Reports.* Series P-25, no. 311. Washington, DC: Government Printing Office, 1965.

———. "Estimates of the Population of the United States, by Single Years of Age, Color, and Sex: 1970 to 1981." *Current Population Reports.* Series P-25, no. 917. Washington, DC: Government Printing Office, 1982.

———. "Estimates of the Population of the United States, by Single Years of Age, Color, and Sex: 1980 to 2080." Gregory Spencer. *Current Population Reports.* Series P-25, no. 1018. Washington, DC: Government Printing Office, 1989 (middle series projections).

———. "Estimates of the Population of the United States, by Single Years of Age, Color, and Sex: 1988 to 2080." Gregory Spencer. *Current Population Reports.* Series P-25, no. 1018. Washington, DC: Government Printing Office, 1989 (middle series projections).

Work in America Institute. *The Future of Older Workers in America.* Scarsdale, NY: Work in America Institute, 1980.

Additional Reading

Bruntland, G. *Our Common Future: World Commission on Environment and Development.* New York: Oxford University Press, 1987.

Callahan, D. *Setting Limits: Medical Goals in an Aging Society.* New York: Simon & Schuster.

Cassel, C., and B. Neugarten. "The Goals of Medicine in an Aging Society." In *"Too Old" for Health Care? Controversies in Medicine, Law, Economics and Ethics.* Eds. R. Binstock and S. Post. Baltimore, MD: Johns Hopkins University Press, 1991.

Cole, T. *The Journey of Life: A Cultural History of Aging in America.* New York: Cambridge University Press, 1992.

Ehrlich, P., and A. Ehrlich. *The Population Explosion.* New York: Simon & Schuster, 1990.

Freeman, J. T. *Aging: Its History and Literature.* New York: Humana Science Press, 1979.

Rose, M. R. *Evolutionary Biology of Aging.* Boston: Oxford University Press, 1989.

Warner, H. R., and others. *Modern Biological Theories of Aging.* New York: Raven Press, 1987.

Lydia Brontë, Ph. D.

General Bibliography

A

Abramson, Leonard. *Healing Our Health Care System.* New York: Grove Wiedenfeld, 1990.

Achenbaum, W. A. *Old Age in the New Land.* Baltimore, MD: Johns Hopkins University Press, 1978.

———. *Shades of Gray.* Boston, MA: Little, Brown, 1983.

———. *Social Security: Visions and Revisions.* New York: Cambridge University Press, 1986.

Adams, R. G., and R. Blieszner, eds. *Older Adult Friendship: Structure and Process.* Newbury Park, CA: Sage, 1989.

Aday, Ron H. *Crime and the Elderly: An Annotated Bibliography.* Westport, CT: Greenwood Press, 1988.

Ainlay, Stephen C., Royce Singleton, Jr., and Victoria L. Swigert. "Aging and Religious Participation: Reconsidering the Effects on Health." *Journal for the Scientific Study of Religion* Vol 31, no. 2 (1992).

Alexander, Jo, Jr., et al., eds. *Women and Aging: An Anthology by Women.* Corvallis, OR: Calyx Books, 1986.

Altman, Maya, and others. *How Do I Pay for My Long-Term Health Care? A Consumer Guidebook about Long-Term Care Insurance.* Berkeley, CA: Berkeley Planning Associates, 1988.

American Association of Homes for the Aging (AAHA). *Guide to Caring for the Mentally Impaired Elderly.* Washington, DC: AAHA, 1985.

———. *The Nursing Home and You: Partners in Caring for a Relative with Alzheimer's Disease.* Washington, DC: AAHA, 1988.

American Association of Retired Persons (AARP). *The Age Discrimination in Employment Act Guarantees You Certain Rights: Here's How . . . .* Washington, DC: AARP, 1987.

———. *Before You Buy: A Guide to Long-Term Care Insurance.* Rev. ed. Washington, DC: AARP, 1991.

———. *Business and Older Workers: Current Perceptions and New Directions for the 1990s.* Washington, DC: AARP, 1989.

———. *Eleventh Annual Survey of Middle-Age and Older Americans.* Washington, DC: AARP, 1989.

———. *Graduated Driver Licenses: Creating Mobility Choices.* Washington, DC: AARP, 1992.

———. *A Guide to Understanding Your Pension Plan.* Washington, DC: AARP.

———. "Historic Tax Credits Help Turn Old Buildings Into New Housing." *AARP Housing Report* (summer 1991).

———. *Housing Needs Survey.* Washington, DC: AARP Program Department, 1992.

———. *How to Manage Older Workers.* Washington, DC: AARP, Worker Equity Department, 1988.

———. *How to Recruit Older Workers.* Washington, DC: AARP, Worker Equity Department, 1988.

———. *How to Train Older Persons.* Washington, DC: AARP, Worker Equity Department, n.d.

———. *Ideas for Helping a Friend in Crisis.* Washington, DC: AARP, Social Outreach and Support Program Department, 1989.

———. *Knowing Your Rights: Medicare's Prospective Payment System.* Washington, DC: AARP Fulfillment.

———. *Look Before You Leap: A Guide to Early Retirement Incentive Programs.* Washington, DC: AARP Worker Equity, 1988.

———. *Miles Away and Still Caring: A Guide for Long-Distance Caregivers.* Washington, DC: AARP, 1986.

———. *Model State Law on Reverse Mortgages.* Washington, DC: AARP Home Equity Information Center, Program Coordination and Development Department, 1990.

———. *The Perfect Fit: Creative Ideas for a Safe and Livable Home.* Washington, DC: AARP, 1992.

———. *Resourceful Aging: Today and Tomorrow.* Conference Proceedings, October 9–10, 1990. Washington, DC: AARP, 1991.

———. *Understanding Senior Housing for the 1990s.* Washington, DC: AARP Consumer Affairs, Program Coordination and Development Department, 1990.

———. *Work and Retirement: Employees Over Forty and Their Views.* Washington, DC: AARP, 1986.

———. *Workers Over 50: Old Myths, New Realities.* Washington, DC: AARP, n.d.

———. *Your Home Your Choice: A Workbook for Older People and Their Families.* Washington, DC: AARP Consumer Affairs Program Coordination and Development Department, 1992.

American Bar Association. *Attorney's Guide to Home Equity Conversion.* Washington, DC: American Bar Association Commission on Legal Problems for the Elderly, 1992.

American Bar Association Commissions on Legal Problems of the Elderly and the Mentally Disabled. *An Agenda for Reform.* Washington, DC: American Bar Association, 1989.

———. *Court Related Needs of Elderly Persons with Disabilities.* Washington, DC: American Bar Association, 1991.

The American Cancer Society Cancer Book: Prevention, Detection, Diagnosis, Treatment, Rehabilitation, Cure. New York: Doubleday, 1986.

American Heart Association (AHA). *The American Heart Association Heartbook: A Guide to Prevention and Treatment of Cardiovascular Diseases.* New York: E. P. Dutton, 1980.

———. *Sex and Heart Disease.* Dallas: AHA.

American Institute of Architects (AIA). *Design for Aging: An Architect's Guide.* Washington, DC: AIA Press, 1985.

American Journal of Alzheimer's Care and Related Disorders and Research. Weston, MA.

American Library Association. "Guidelines for Library Service to Older Adults." *RQ* Vol. 26, no. 4 (Summer 1987): 444–47.

American Society on Aging. "Progress and Prospects in Mental Health." *Generations* Vol. XVII, No. 1 (Winter/Spring 1993).

Atchley, Robert C. *Aging: Continuity and Change.* 2d ed. Belmont, CA: Wadsworth, 1987.

———. "Continuity Theory of Normal Aging." *Gerontologist* Vol. 29 (1989): 183–90.

———. "The Meaning of Retirement." *Journal of Communications* Vol. 24 (1974): 97–101.

———. *Social Forces and Aging.* 6th ed. Belmont, CA: Wadsworth, 1991.

Axel, Helen. "Job Banks for Retirees." *Research Report No. 929.* New York: Conference Board, 1989.

Axel, Helen, ed. *Employing Older Americans: Opportunities and Constraints.* New York: Conference Board, 1988.

B

Babchuk, N., and T. B. Anderson. "Older Widows and Married Women: Their Intimates and Confidants." *International Journal of Aging and Human Development* Vol. 28 (1989): 21–35.

Baker, Ross K. "The World According to AARP." *American Demographics* (1992): 23.

Barusch, A. S., and W. M. Spaid. "Gender Differences in Caregiving: Why Do Wives Report Greater Burden?" *Gerontologist* Vol. 29 (1989): 667–76.

Barzel, U. S. "Modern Technology: A Double-Edged Sword." *International Journal of Technology and Aging* Vol. 4 (1991): 89–93.

Bass, D. B., and L. S. Noelker. "The Influence of Family Caregivers on Elder's Use of In-Home Services." *Journal of Health and Social Behavior* Vol. 28 (1987): 184–96.

Bass, D. M., and K. Bowman. "The Transition from Caregiving to Bereavement: The Relationship of Care-Related Strain and Adjustment to Death." *Gerontologist* Vol. 30 (1990): 35–42.

Bass, Scott A., and Francis G. Caro. "The New Politics of Productive Aging." *In Depth: A Journal for Values and Public Policy on "Revisioning the Aging Society"* Vol. 2, no. 3 (Fall 1993): 59–79.

Bass, Scott A., Elizabeth A. Kutza, and Fernando M. Torres-Gil, eds. *Diversity in Aging: Challenges Facing Planners and Policymakers in the 1990s.* Glenview, IL: Scott, Foresman, 1989.

Baum, M., and B. M. Rich. *The Aging: A Guide to Public Policy.* Pittsburgh, PA: University of Pittsburgh Press, 1984.

Beauvoir, Simone de. *The Coming of Age.* New York: Warner, 1973.

Becerra, Rosina M. *The Hispanic Elderly: A Research Reference Guide.* Lanham, MD: University Press of America, 1984.

Becker, G., and S. Kaufman. "Old Age, Rehabilitation, and Research: A Review of the Issues." *Gerontologist* Vol. 28, no. 4 (1988): 459–68.

Becker, Gaylene. *Growing Old in Silence.* Berkeley, CA: University of California Press, 1980.

Becker, Robert, and Ezio Giacobini, eds. *Alzheimer's Disease: Current Research in Early Diagnosis.* Bristol, PA: Taylor & Francis, 1990.

Belgrave, Linda Liska. "The Effects of Race Differences in Work History, Work Attitudes, Economic Resources, and Health in Women's Retirement." *Research on Aging* Vol. 10, no. 3 (1988): 383–98.

Bell, John. "In Search of a Discourse on Aging: The Elderly on Television." *Gerontologist* Vol. 32, no. 3 (1992).

Bengtson, V. L., and J. F. Robertson eds. *Grandparenthood.* Beverly Hills, CA: Sage, 1985.

Beresford, Larry. *The Hospice Handbook.* Boston, MA: Little, Brown & Co., 1992.

Berg, Robert L., and Joseph S. Cassells, eds. *The Second Fifty Years: Promoting Health and Preventing Disability.* Washington, DC: Institute of Medicine, National Academy Press, 1990.

Berger, R. M. "Realities of Gay and Lesbian Aging." *Social Work* Vol. 29 (1984): 57–62.

Berger, R. M., and J. Kelley. "Working with Homosexuals of the Older Population." *Social Casework* Vol. 67 (1986): 203–10.

Berman, P. L., and K. Goldman. *The Ageless Spirit.* New York: Ballantine, 1992.

Berman, Philip L., ed. *The Courage to Grow Old: Forty-one Prominent Men and Women Reflect on Growing Old.* New York: Ballantine, Del Rey, Fawcett, 1989.

Bernstein, Merton C., and Joan B. Bernstein. *Social Security: The System That Works.* New York: Basic Books, 1988.

Berry, G. L., S. H. Zarit, and V. X. Rabatin. "Caregiver Activity on Respite and Nonrespite Days: A Comparison of Two Service Approaches." *Gerontologist* Vol. 31 (1991): 830–35.

Bianci, Eugene C. *Aging as a Spiritual Journey.* New York: Crossroads, 1982.

Biegel, D. E., and A. Blum, eds. *Aging and Caregiving: Theory, Research, and Policy.* Newbury Park, CA: Sage, 1990.

Billig, Nathan. *To Be Old and Sad: Understanding Depression in the Elderly.* Lexington, MA: Lexington Books, 1987.

Binstock, R., and S. Post, eds. *"Too Old" for Health Care? Controversies in Medicine, Law, Economics and Ethics.* Baltimore, MD: Johns Hopkins University Press, 1991.

Binstock, R. H., and L. K. George, eds. *Handbook of Aging and the Social Sciences.* 3d ed. San Diego: Academic Press, 1990.

Binstock, Robert H. *Dementia and Aging: Ethics, Values, and Policy Choices.* Baltimore, MD: Johns Hopkins, 1992.

Biracree, Tom, and Nancy Biracree. *Over Fifty: The Resource Book for the Better Half of Your Life.* New York: HarperCollins, 1991.

Bird, Carolina. *Second Careers. New Ways to Work After 50.* Boston, MA: Little, Brown, 1992.

Birren, James E., and K. Warner Schaie, eds.

Handbook of the Psychology of Aging. 3d ed. New York: Harcourt Brace, 1990.

Birren, James E., Bruce Sloane, and Gene D. Cohen. *Handbook of Aging and Mental Health.* 2d ed. New York: Academic Press, 1992.

Blau, Z. S. *Old Age in a Changing Society.* New York: New Viewpoints, 1973.

Board of Trustees, Federal Old-Age and Survivors Insurance and Disability Insurance Trust Funds. *Annual Report of the Board of Trustees of the Federal Old-Age and Survivors Insurance and Disability Insurance Trust Funds, 1992.* Washington, DC: U.S. Government Printing Office, April, 1992.

Board of Trustees, Federal Supplementary Medical Insurance Trust Fund. *Annual Report of the Board of Trustees of the Federal Supplementary Medical Insurance Trust Fund, 1992.* Washington, DC: U.S. Government Printing Office, April, 1992.

Booth, A., ed. *Contemporary Families: Looking Forward, Looking Back.* Minneapolis, MN: National Council on Family Relations, 1991.

Botwinick, Jack. *Aging and Behavior.* 3d ed. New York: Springer, 1984.

Bove, R. "Retraining the Older Worker: Interest Rises in Keeping the Older Worker in the Workplace." *Training and Development Journal* Vol. 41B (March 1987): 77–78.

Bowe, F. "Why Seniors Don't Use Technology." *Technology Review* (August/September 1988): 35–40.

Bowers, B. J. "Family Perceptions of Care in a Nursing Home." *Gerontologist* Vol. 28 (1988): 361–68.

Bowman, Meg. *Memorial Services for Women.* San Jose, CA: Hot Flash Press, 1987.

Branch, L. "Continuing Care Retirement Communities: Insuring for Long-Term Care." *Gerontologist* Vol. 27 (1987): 4–8.

Braun, K. L., and C. L. Rose. "Geriatric Patient Outcomes and Costs in Three Settings: Nursing Home, Foster Family, and Own Home." *Journal of the American Geriatrics Society* Vol. 35 (1987): 387–97.

Brecher, Edward M., and the editors of Consumer Reports Books. *Love, Sex and Aging.* Boston, MA: Little, Brown, 1984.

Brody, Baruch. *Life and Death Decisionmaking.* New York: Oxford University Press, 1988.

Brody, Baruch, and H. T. Engelhardt. *Bioethics: Readings and Cases.* Englewood Cliffs, NJ: Prentice-Hall, 1987.

Brody, David S. "The Patient's Role in Clinical Decision-Making." *Annals of Internal Medicine* Vol. 93 (1980): 718–22.

Brody, E. *Women in the Middle: Their Parent-Care Years.* New York: Springer, 1990.

Brody, Howard. *The Healer's Power.* New Haven, CT: Yale University Press, 1992.

———. *Stories of Sickness.* New Haven, CT: Yale University Press, 1987.

———. "Transparency: Informed Consent in Primary Care." *Hastings Center Report* Vol. 19, no. 5 (1989): 5–9.

Brontë, Lydia. *The Longevity Factor.* New York: Harper Collins, 1993.

Brown, Arnold S. *The Social Processes of Aging and Old Age.* Englewood Cliffs, NJ: Prentice-Hall, 1990.

Brown, Dorothy S. *Handle With Care: A Questions of Alzheimer's.* Buffalo, NY: Prometheus Books, 1992.

Brown, Judith N., and Christina Baldwin. *A Second Start: A Widow's Guide to Financial Survival at a Time of Emotional Crisis.* New York: Simon & Schuster, 1987.

Brown, Robert N. *The Rights of Older Persons.* Carbondale, IL: Southern Illinois University Press, 1989.

Brubaker, Timothy H. *Family Relationships in Later Life.* Newbury Park, CA: Sage Publications, 1990.

Bryant, Sharon, and William Rakowski. "Predictors of Mortality Among Elderly African-Americans." *Research on Aging* (March 1992).

Bureau of National Affairs. *Flexible Workstyles: A Look at Contingent Labor.* Washington, DC: U.S. Department of Labor, Women's Bureau, 1988.

———. *Older Americans in the Workforce: Challenges and Solutions.* Washington, DC: Bureau of National Affairs, 1987.

Burgio, Kathryn, and others. *Staying Dry: A Practical Guide to Bladder Control.* Johns Hopkins University Press, 1989.

Burkhauser, R. V. "The Early Acceptance of Social Security: An Asset Maximization Approach." *Industrial and Labor Relations Review* Vol. 33 (1980): 484–92.

Burnside, Irene M., ed. *Nursing and the Aged.* New York: McGraw-Hill, 1981.

Butler, R. N., and H. P. Gleason. *Productive Aging: Enhancing Vitality in Later Life*. New York: Springer, 1985.

Butler, Robert N. "The Life Review: An Unrecognized Bonanza." *International Journal of Aging and Human Development* Vol. 12 (1980–81): 35–38.

———. *Why Survive? Being Old in America*. New York: Harper & Row, 1975.

Butler, Robert N., and Myrna L. Lewis. *Aging and Mental Health: Positive Psychosocial and Biomedical Approaches*. New York: Merrill, 1991.

———. *Love and Sex after 60*. New York: Harper and Row, 1988.

C

Callahan, D. *Setting Limits: Medical Goals in an Aging Society*. New York: Simon & Schuster.

Callahan, Daniel. "Medical Futility, Medical Necessity: The Problem Without a Name." *Hastings Center Report* Vol. 21, no. 4 (1991): 30-35.

Callahan, David P., and Peter J. Strauss. *Estate and Financial Planning for the Aging or Incapacitated Client*. New York: Practicing Law Institute, 1990.

Campbell, Scott, and Phyllis R. Silverman. *Widower*. New York: Prentice-Hall, 1987.

Campione, Wendy A. "Predicting Participation in Retirement Preparation Programs." *Journal of Gerontology: Social Sciences* Vol. 43, no. 3 (1988): S91–95.

Carlin, Vivian F., and Ruth Mansberg. *If I Live to Be 100: A Creative Housing Solution for Older People*. Pennington, NJ: Princeton Book, 1989.

———. *Where Can Mom Live? A Family Guide to Living Arrangements for Elderly Parents*. Lexington, MA: Lexington Books, 1987.

Carlsen, M. Baird. *Creative Aging: A Meaning-Making Perspective*. New York: Norton, 1991.

Caserta, M., D. Lund, S. Wright, and P. Redburn. "Caregivers to Dementia Patients: Use of Community Services." *Gerontologist* Vol. 27 (1987): 209–13.

Casey, G. M. "Library Services for the Aging." *Library Professionals Publications* Vol. 33 (1984).

Cassel, Christine. "Ethics and the Future of Aging Research: Promises and Problems." *Generations* Vol. 16, no. 4 (Winter/spring 1992): 61–65.

Cecil, C. *Never Too Late: A Message of Hope for Older Alcoholics, Their Families, and Friends*. Minneapolis, MN: CompCare Publishers, 1989.

Chalker, Rebecca, and Kristene Whitmore, M.D. *Overcoming Bladder Disorders*. New York: Harper & Row, 1990.

Chambre, Susan. *Good Deeds in Old Age: Volunteering by the New Leisure Class*. Lexington, MA: Lexington Books, 1987.

Chapman, Elwood N. *Comfort Zones: A Practical Guide for Retirement Planning*. Los Altos, CA: Crisp Publications, 1987.

Charles, R. R., and C. Bartunek, eds. *Community College Programs for the Older Adult Learner*. ERIC Document Reproduction Service Service No. ED 322 977, 1989.

Chase, D. *Dying at Home with Hospice*. St. Louis, MO: C. V. Mosby, 1986.

Cherlin, Andrew J., and Frank F. Furstenberg. *The New American Grandparent: A Place in the Family, A Life Apart*. New York: Basic Books, 1988.

Chinen, A. B. *In the Ever After: Fairy Tales and the Second Half of Life*. Wilmette, IL: Chiron Publications, 1989.

———. *Once Upon a Midlife: Classic Stories and Mythic Tales to Illuminate the Middle Years*. Los Angeles: Jeremy P. Tarcher, 1992.

Christensen, Alice, and David Rankins. *Easy Does It Yoga for Older People*. San Francisco: Harper & Row, 1979.

Christenson, Margaret A. *Aging in the Designed Environment*. Binghamton, NY: Haworth Press, 1990.

Chudacoff, H. *How Old Are You?* Princeton, NJ: Princeton University Press, 1990.

Clark, Etta. *Growing Old Is Not For Sissies: Portraits of Senior Athletes*. Corte Madera, CA: Pomegranate Books, 1986.

Clements, William M., ed. *Ministry With the Aging*. New York: Harper & Row, 1981.

Clipp, E. C., and L. K. George. "Caregiver Needs and Patterns of Social Support." *Journal of Gerontology: Social Sciences* Vol. 45 (1990): S102–S111.

———. "Psychotropic Drug Use Among Caregivers of Patients with Dementia." *Journal of the American Geriatrics Society* Vol. 38 (1990): 227–35.

Coberly, Lenore M., et al. *Writers Have No Age:*

Creative Writing with Older Adults. Binghamton, NY: Haworth Press, 1985.

Cohen, Donna, and Carl Eisdorfer. "Depression in Family Members Caring for a Relative with Alzheimer's Disease." *Journal of the American Geriatrics Society* Vol. 36 (1988): 885–89.

———. *The Loss of Self: A Family Resource for the Care of Alzheimer's Disease and Related Disorders*. New York: NAL Penguin, 1986.

Cohen, Gene D. *The Brain in Human Aging*. New York: Springer, 1988.

Cohen-Mansfield, J. "Employment and Volunteering Roles for the Elderly: Characteristics, Attributions, and Strategies." *Journal of Leisure Research* Vol. 21 (1989): 214–27.

Cohler, B. J., and H. U. Grunebaum. *Mothers, Grandmothers, and Daughters: Personality and Childcare in Three-Generation Families*. New York: Wiley, 1981.

Cole, T. R. *The Journey of Life*. New York: Cambridge University Press, 1992.

Cole, Thomas R., David D. Van Tassel, and Robert Kastenbaum, eds. *Handbook of the Humanities and Aging*. New York: Springer, 1992.

Coleman, B. *A Consumer Guide to Hospice Care*. Washington, DC: National Consumers League, 1990.

Colenda, C. C., R. B. Goos, and R. E. Lewis. *Medications Used for Mental Disorders in the Elderly: A Caregiver's Guide*. Burkeville, VA: Piedmont Geriatric Institute, 1991.

Collin, F. J., J. Lombard, Jr., A. L. Moses, and H. J. Spitler. *Drafting the Durable Power of Attorney: A Systems Approach*. 2d ed. New York: Shepard's McGraw-Hill, 1991.

Collins, E. R., Jr., and D. Weber. *The Complete Guide to Living Wills*. New York: Bantam, 1992.

Commerce Clearing House, Inc. *Social Security Benefits*. Chicago. Commerce Clearing House, 1992.

Connor, J. Robert. *Cracking the Over-50 Job Market*. New York: Plume, 1992.

"Consensus Conference: Osteoporosis 1984." *Journal of the American Medical Association (JAMA)* Vol. 252 (1984): 799.

Cook, Thomas C., ed. *An Age Integrated Society: Implications for Spiritual Well-Being*. Washington, DC: White House Conference on Aging, 1981.

Cousins, Norman. *Anatomy of an Illness*. New York: W. W. Norton, 1979.

Coyle, Jean M. *Women and Aging: A Selected Annotated Bibliography*. No. 9 of *Bibliographies and Indexes in Gerontology*. New York: Greenwood Press, 1989.

Cross, K. P. *Adults as Learners*. San Francisco: Jossey-Bass, 1981.

Crown, William H., Phyllis H. Mutschler, and Thomas D. Leavitt. *Beyond Retirement: Characteristics of Older Workers and the Implications for Employment Policy*. Waltham, MA: Policy Center on Aging, Heller School, Brandeis University, 1987.

Culver, C. M., and B. Gert. "Beyond the Living Will: Making Advance Directives More Useful." *Omega: Journal of Death and Dying* Vol. 21 (1990): 253–58.

Cumming, E., and W. H. Henry. *Growing Old: The Process of Disengagement*. New York: Basic Books, 1961.

D

Day, Christine L. *What Older Americans Think: Interest Groups and Aging Policy*. Princeton, NJ: Princeton University Press, 1990.

Dean, K., T. Hickey, and B. E. Holstein, eds. *Self-Care and Health in Old Age: Health Behavior Implications for Policy and Practice*. London: Croom Helm (1986): 204–29.

Deevey, S. "Older Lesbian Women: An Invisible Minority." *Journal of Gerontological Nursing* Vol. 16 (1990): 35–39.

Dennis, Helen, ed. *Fourteen Steps in Managing an Older Workforce*. Lexington, MA: Lexington, 1988.

Dobkin, L. "Retrofitting the American Dream." *Retirement Housing Report* Vol. 1, no. 8. (1987).

Dobrof, Rose, ed. "Social Work and Alzheimer's Disease: Practice Issues with Victims and Their Families." *Journal of Gerontological Social Work Studies* Vol. 9, no. 2 (1986): 126.

Doka, K. J., and M. E. Mertz. "The Meaning and Significance of Great-Grandparenthood." *Gerontologist* Vol. 28 (1988): 192–97.

Donow, H. S. "Two Approaches to the Care of an Elder Parent." *Gerontologist* Vol. 30 (1990): 486–90.

Doress, Paula Brown, Diana L. Siegal, and the Midlife and Older Women Book Project. *Our-*

selves, Growing Older. New York: Simon and Schuster, 1987.

Doucette, D., and C. Ventura-Merkel. *Community College Programs for Older Adults: A Status Report.* League for Innovation in the Community College, 1991.

Douglass, Richard L. *Domestic Mistreatment of the Elderly—Towards Prevention.* Washington, DC: American Association of Retired Persons, 1987.

Down, Ivy M., and Lorraine Schnurr. *Between Home and Nursing Home: The Board and Care Alternative.* New York: Prometheus Books, 1991.

Driedger, L., and N. Chappell. *Aging and Ethnicity: Towards an Interface.* Toronto, Canada: Butterworths, 1987.

Dychtwald, Ken. *Age Wave.* Los Angeles, CA: Jeremy P. Tarcher, 1989.

"Dying Well? A Colloquy on Euthanasia and Physician-Assisted Suicide." *Hastings Center Report* (March-April 1992). Entire issue is devoted to euthanasia and physician-assisted suicide.

E

Edinberg, Mark A. *Talking with Your Aging Parents.* Boston, MA: Shambhala Publications, 1987.

Ekerdt, David J. "Why the Notion Persists that Retirement Harms Health." *Gerontologist* Vol. 27 (1987): 454–57.

Elderhostel Institute Network. *The Institute Movement and Elderhostel: A National Overview.* Elderhostel Institute Network, 1991.

Erikson, E. H. *The Life Cycle Completed: A Review.* New York: Norton, 1982.

Erikson, E. H., J. M. Erikson, and H. Q. Kivnick. *Vital Involvement in Old Age.* New York: Norton, 1987.

F

Fairlie, Henry. "Talkin' 'bout My Generation." *New Republic* (March 28, 1988): 18–22.

FannieMae Customer Education Group. *Money from Home: A Consumer's Guide to Home Equity Conversion Mortgages.* Washington, DC: Federal Publications, 1992.

Federal Highway Administration (FHWA). *Walking Through the Years: Pedestrian Safety for Older (65+) Adults.* Washington, DC: United States Government Printing Office, 1991.

Feltin, Marie. *A Woman's Guide to Good Health After Fifty.* Glenview, IL: American Association of Retired Persons and Scott, Foresman, 1987.

Ferraro, K. F., ed. *Gerontology Perspectives and Issues.* New York: Springer Publishing Company, 1990.

Fischer, D. H. *Growing Old in America.* Expanded ed. New York: Oxford University Press, 1977.

Fischer, Kathleen. *Winter Grace: Spirituality for the Later Years.* New York: Paulist Press, 1985.

Fischer, L. R., D. P. Mueller, and P. W. Cooper. "Older Volunteers: A Discussion of the Minnesota Senior Study." *Gerontologist* Vol. 31 (1991): 183–94.

Fischer, Lucy Rose. *Linked Lives: Adult Daughters and Their Mothers.* New York: Harper & Row, 1986.

Fischer, Lucy Rose, and Kay Schaffer. *Older Volunteers: A Guide to Research and Practice.* Newbury Park, CA: Sage Publications, 1993.

Fischer, R. B., M. L. Blazey, and H. T. Lipman, eds. *Students of the Third Age—University/College Programs for Retired Adults.* New York: Macmillan, 1992.

Fowler, M., and P. McCutcheon, eds. *Songs of Experience.* New York: Ballantine, 1991.

Freeman, J. T. *Aging: Its History and Literature.* New York: Humana Science Press, 1979.

Friedman, R., and A. Nussbaum. *Coping with Your Husband's Retirement.* New York: Simon & Schuster, 1986.

Friend, R. A. "The Individual and Social Psychology of Aging: Clinical Implications for Lesbians and Gay Men." *Journal of Homosexuality* Vol. 4 (1987): 307–31.

Fries J. F., and L. M. Crapo. *Vitality and Aging.* San Francisco, CA: W.H. Freeman, 1981.

Fries, James. *Aging Well.* Menlo Park, CA: Addison-Wesley, 1989.

G

Gaudio, Peter, and Virginia Nicols. *Your Retirement Benefits.* New York: Wiley, 1992.

Gelfand, Donald E. *The Aging Network, Programs & Services.* 3d ed. New York: Springer Publishing Co., 1988.

Gelfand, Donald E., and Charles M. Barresi, eds.

Ethnic Dimensions of Aging. New York: Springer, 1987.

George, L. K., and L. P. Gwyther. "Caregiver Well-Being: A Multidimensional Examination of Family Caregivers of Demented Adults." *Gerontologist* Vol. 26 (1986): 253–59.

Gibson, Joan McIver. "National Values History Project." *Generations* supplement (1990): 51–64.

Gillespie, Ann E., and Katrinka Smith Sloan. *Housing Options and Services for Older Adults*. Santa Barbara, CA: ABC-CLIO, 1990.

Glasse, L., and J. Hendricks, eds. *Gender and Aging*. Amityville, NY: Baywood, 1992.

Goggin, J. M. "Elderhostel: The Next Generation." *Aging Today* (February/March 1991).

Golant, S. M. *Housing America's Elderly: Many Possibilities, Few Choices*. Newbury, CA: Sage Publications, 1992.

Gold, D. T. "Generational Solidarity: Conceptual Antecedants and Consequences." *American Behavioral Scientist* Vol. 33 (1989): 19–32.

———. "Sibling Relations in Old Age: A Typology." *International Journal of Aging and Human Development* Vol. 28, no. 1 (1989): 37–51.

Gordon, Michael. *Old Enough to Feel Better: A Medical Guide for Seniors*. Rev. ed. Baltimore, MD: John Hopkins University Press, 1989.

Grad, Susan. "Earnings Replacement Rates of New Retired Workers." *Social Security Bulletin 53*. Washington, DC: U.S. Social Security Administration, October 1990.

Graebner, W. *A History of Retirement*. New Haven, CT: Yale University Press, 1980.

Gratton, B. *Urban Elders*. Philadelphia, PA: Temple University Press, 1985.

Greenberg, Vivian E. *Your Best Is Good Enough: Aging Parents and Your Emotions*. Lexington, MA: Lexington Books, 1989.

Griffin, Richard. "Toward a Spiritual Agenda For Late Life." *Aging and the Human Spirit* Vol. 2, no. 2 (1992): 2–3.

Gruetzner, Howard. *Alzheimer's: A Caregiver's Guide and Sourcebook*. New York: John Wiley & Sons, 1988.

Gruman, G. *A History of Ideas About the Prolongation of Life*. Philadelphia, PA: Transactions of the American Philosophical Society, 1966.

Gubrium, J. F. *Living and Dying at Murray Manor*. New York: St. Martin's Press, 1975.

Gutmann, D. L. *Reclaimed Powers: Toward a New Psychology of Men and Women in Later Life*. New York: Basic Books, 1987.

H

Haber, C. *Beyond Sixty-Five*. New York: Cambridge University Press, 1983.

Hales-Mabry, C. "Serving the Older Adult." *Special Populations in the Library*. New York: Haworth Press, 1990.

Hall, G. Stanley. *Senescence: The Second Half of Life*. New York: Appleton, 1922.

Halpern, James. *Helping Your Aging Parents: A Practical Guide for Adult Children*. New York: Crown, 1988.

Hamilton, Dana. "Selected Legislation Affecting the Elderly in the 102nd Congress." Congressional Research Service 91–624 EPW. Washington, DC: The Library of Congress, August 9, 1991.

Harootyan, R. A. "Life-Span Design of Residential Environments for an Aging Population." Conference proceedings. Washington, DC: AARP Forecasting and Environmental Scanning Department, 1992.

Harris, Richard J. "Recent Trends in the Relative Economic Status of Older Adults." *Journal of Gerontology* Vol. 41, no. 3 (1986): 401–7.

Hart, J. *Beyond the Tunnel: The Arts and Aging in America*. Washington, DC: Museum One, 1992.

Hartford Insurance Group. *The Hartford House: How to Modify a Home to Accommodate the Needs of an Older Adult*. Hartford, CT: Hartford Plaza, 1990.

Hasler, Bonnie S. *Barriers to Living Independently for Older Women with Disabilities: Transportation*. Washington, DC: AARP, 1991.

Hastings Center. *Guidelines on the Termination of Life-Sustaining Treatment and the Care of the Dying*. Bloomington: Indiana University Press, 1987.

Hatch, Laurie Russell. "Effects of Work and Family on Women's Later-Life Resources." *Research on Aging* Vol. 12, no. 3 (1990): 311–38.

Havighurst, R. J. *Developmental Tasks and Education*. New York: David McKay, 1972.

Hayes, E. J., and others. *Industry Study #365*

Factory-Built Housing in the 1990s. Cleveland, OH: Fredonia Group, 1991.

Hayflick, L. "The Cell Biology of Human Aging." *Scientific American* Vol. 242 (1980): 58–65.

Hazzard, W. R., R. Andres, E. L. Bierman, and J. P. Blass. *Principles of Geriatric Medicine and Gerontology.* New York: McGraw-Hill, 1990.

Hazzard, W. R., and others, eds. *Principles of Geriatric Medicine.* New York: McGraw-Hill, 1991.

Health Care Financing Administration. *Medicare and Medicaid Data Book.* Baltimore, MD: ORD Publications.

Heckman-Owen, Carol. *Life with Charlie: Coping with an Alzheimer Spouse or Other Dementia Patient and Keeping Your Sanity.* Ventura, CA: Pathfinder, 1992.

Hedges, H. *Key Issues in Accessory Apartments: Zoning and Covenants Restricting Land to Residential Uses.* Washington, DC: AARP Consumer Affairs, Program Coordination and Development Department, 1991.

Hertzog, A. R., K. C. Holden, and M. M. Seltzer, eds. *Health and Economic Status of Older Women.* Amityville, NY: Baywood, 1989.

Hill, T. Patrick, and David Shirley. *A Good Death: Taking More Control at the End of Your Life.* New York: Addison-Wesley, 1992.

Hinrichsen, Gregory. *Mental Health Problems and Older Adults.* Santa Barbara, CA: ABC-CLIO, 1990.

Hodgson, L. G. "Adult Grandchildren and Their Grandparents: The Enduring Bond." *International Journal of Aging and Human Development* Vol. 34 (1992): 209–25.

Holahan, C. "Marital Attitudes over Forty Years: A Longitudinal and Cohort Analysis." *Journal of Gerontology* Vol. 39 (1984): 49–57.

Homer, Paul, and Martha Holstein, eds. *The Good Old Age? The Paradox of Setting Limits.* New York: Simon & Schuster, 1990.

Hooyman, N. R., and H. A. Kiyak. *Social Gerontology: A Multidisciplinary Perspective.* Boston, MA: Allyn & Bacon, 1988.

Hooyman, N. R., and W. Lustbaden. *Taking Care: Supporting Older People and Their Families.* New York: Free Press, 1986.

Horne, Jo. *Caregiving: Helping an Aging Loved One.* Washington, DC: American Association of Retired Persons and Scott, Foresman, 1985.

———. *Homesharing and Other Lifestyle Options.* Glenview, IL: AARP and Scott, Foresman, 1988.

———. *The Nursing Home Handbook: A Guide for Families.* Washington, DC: AARP Books, 1989.

"How To Buy a Hearing Aid." *Consumer Reports* (November 1992).

Humphrey, James H. *Health and Fitness for Older Persons.* New York: AMS Press, 1992.

I

ICF. *The Impact of Increased Employment of Older Workers on the National Economy* (report prepared for the Commonwealth Fund). Fairfax, VA: ICF Inc., 1989.

———. *Why Workers Retire Early* (report prepared for the Commonwealth Fund). Fairfax, VA: ICF Inc., 1989.

Inlander, Charles B. *Medicare Made Easy (A People's Medical Society Book)* Reading, MA: Addison-Wesley, 1989.

———. *Take This Book to the Hospital with You.* Allentown, PA: Peoples Medical Society, 1992.

J

Jackson, J. S., ed. *The Black American Elderly: Research on Physical and Psychosocial Health.* New York: Springer, 1988.

Jacobs, Ruth. *Be An Outrageous Older Woman.* Manchester, CT: Knowledge, Ideas, and Trends, Inc.

Jarvik, Lissy, and Gary Small. *Parentcare: A Commonsense Guide for Adult Children.* New York: Crown Publishers, 1988.

Jarvik, Lissy F., and Carol H. Winograd, eds. *Treatments for the Alzheimer Patient: The Long Haul.* New York: Springer, 1988.

Jecker, Nancy. "The Role of Intimate Others in Medical Decision Making." *Gerontologist* Vol. 30, no. 1 (1990): 51–65.

Jencks, Stephen F., and Gail R. Wilensky. "The Health Care Quality Improvement Initiative: A New Approach to Quality Assurance in Medicare." *Journal of the American Medical Association* Vol. 268 (1992): 900–3.

Johns Hopkins Medical Letter, Health After 50. Baltimore, MD: Johns Hopkins University.

Johnson, Sandra. "PSDA in the Nursing Home." *Hastings Center Report* Vol. 21, no. 5 (special supplement: *Practicing the PSDA*, 1991): S3–S5.

Johnson, Tanya F., et al. *Elder Neglect & Abuse: An Annotated Bibliography.* Westport, CT: Greenwood Press, 1985.

Jones, Reginald L., ed. *Black Adult Development and Aging.* Berkeley, CA: Cobb & Henry, 1989.

K

Kalish, R. A. *Death, Grief, and Caring Relationships.* Monterey, CA: Brooks/Cole, 1985.

Kane, Robert L., and Rosalie A. Kane. *A Will and a Way: What the United States Can Learn from Canada About Caring for the Elderly.* New York: Columbia University Press, 1985.

Kane, Robert L., Joseph G. Ouslander, and Itamar B. Abrass. *Essentials of Clinical Geriatrics.* 2d ed. New York: McGraw-Hill, 1989.

Kane, Rosalie A., and Robert L. Kane. *Assessing the Elderly: A Practical Guide to Measurement.* Lexington, MA: Lexington Books, 1981.

——. *Long-Term Care: Principles, Programs, and Policies.* New York: Springer, 1987.

Kapp, Marshall. "Medical Empowerment and the Elderly." *Hastings Center Report* Vol. 19, no. 4 (1989): 5–8.

Kapp, Marshall B., and others, eds. *Legal and Ethical Aspects of Health Care for the Elderly.* Ann Arbor, MI: Health Administration Press, 1985.

Karp, N., and B. Brewer. "Medigap Insurance." *Clearinghouse Review* Vol. 25 (1991): 670–77.

Karr, Katherine. *What Do I Do? How to Care for, Comfort, and Commune with Your Nursing Home Elder.* New York: Haworth Press, 1985.

Kastenbaum, R. "Death, Suicide, and the Older Adult." *Suicide and Life-Threatening Behavior* Vol. 22 (1992): 1–14.

Kastenbaum, R., and B. K. Kastenbaum, eds. *Encyclopedia of Death.* Phoenix, AZ: Oryx Press, 1989, 175–76.

Katz, Jay. *The Silent World of Doctor and Patient.* New York: The Free Press, 1984.

Kaufman, S. R. *The Ageless Self.* New York: New American Library, 1986.

Kehoe, M. *Lesbians over Sixty Speak for Themselves.* New York: Harrington Park Press, 1989.

Kemper, D. W., M. Mettler, J. Giuffre, and B. Matzek. *Growing Wiser: The Older Person's Guide to Mental Wellness.* Boise, ID: Healthwise, 1986.

Kemper, Donald, and Molly Mettler. *Healthwise for Life: Medical Self-Care for Healthy Aging.* Boise, ID: Healthwise, 1992.

Kenny, James, and Stephen Spicer. *Eldercare: Coping with Late-Life Crisis.* Buffalo, NY: Prometheus Books, 1992.

Kenyon, G. M., J. E. Birren, and J. Schroots, eds. *Metaphors of Aging in Science and the Humanities.* New York: Springer, 1991.

Kirk, Juanda. *Multiple Family Responsibilities, Caregiving, and Related Concerns: An Annotated Bibliography.* Washington, DC: American Association of Retired Persons, 1991.

Kivnick, H. Q. *The Meaning of Grandparenthood.* Ann Arbor, MI: University of Michigan Press, 1982.

Kleemeier, R. W., ed. *Aging and Leisure.* New York: Oxford University Press, 1961.

Kollman, Geoffrey. "Social Security: Proposed Modifications to the Earnings/Test." Congressional Research Service Order Code 1B89114. Washington, DC: The Library of Congress, December 18, 1991.

Kouri, Mark K. *Volunteerism and Older Adults.* Santa Barbara, CA: ABC-CLIO, 1992.

Krout, J. A. *Senior Centers in America.* New York: Greenwood Press, 1989.

Kushner, Irving, ed. *Understanding Arthritis.* New York: Charles Scribner's Sons, 1984.

Kyles, Josephine H. "The Black Elderly and the Church." *Generations* (Fall 1983).

L

LaLanne, Elaine. *Fitness After 50.* Hauppauge, NY: Barron's, 1991.

Lammers, W. W. *Public Policy and the Aging.* Washington, DC: CQ Press, 1983.

Laslett, P. *Household and Family in Past Time.* Cambridge, Eng.: Cambridge University Press, 1972.

"Late Bloomer" audio cassette. Available from Connie Goldman Productions, 926 Second Street, Suite 201, Santa Monica, CA 90403. (310) 393-6801.

Lawton, M. Powell. *Environment and Aging.* 2d ed. Albany, NY: Center for the Study of Aging, 1986.

Lee, Alice. *A Field Guide to Retirement: Fourteen Lifestyle Options for a Successful Retirement.* New York: Doubleday, 1991.

Lee, J. A. "What Can Homosexual Aging Studies

Contribute to Theories of Aging." *Journal of Homosexuality* Vol. 13 (1987): 43–71.

Leenaars, A. L., R. Maris, J. L. McIntosh, and J. Richman, eds. *Suicide and the Older Adult.* New York: Guilford Press, 1992.

Legal Counsel for the Elderly. *Decision-Making, Incapacity, and the Elderly.* Washington, DC: Legal Counsel for the Elderly, 1987.

———. *Medicare Practice Manual.* Washington, DC: Legal Counsel for the Elderly, 1991.

———. *Organizing Your Future: A Guide to Decision-Making in Your Later Years.* Washington, DC: Legal Counsel for the Elderly, 1991.

Levitan, Sara A., and Elizabeth A. Conway. *Part-Time Employment: Living on Half Rations.* Washington, DC: George Washington University, Center for Social Policy Studies, 1988.

Lewis, Mary Ann. *Religious Congregations and the Informal Supports of the Frail Elderly.* New York: The Third Age Center, Fordham University, 1989.

Lipton, Helen L., and Philip R. Lee. *Drugs and the Elderly: Clinical, Social, and Policy Perspectives.* Stanford, CA: Stanford University Press, 1988.

Litwak, E. *Helping the Elderly: The Complementary Roles of Informal Networks and Formal Systems.* New York: Guilford, 1985.

Litwak, E., and C. F. Longino, Jr. "Migration Patterns among the Elderly: A Developmental Perspective." *Gerontologist* Vol. 27 (1987): 266–72.

Liu, K., P. Doty, and K. Manton. "Medicaid Spend-down in Nursing Homes." *Gerontologist* Vol. 30 (1990): 7–15.

Loewinsohn, R. J. *Survival Handbook for Widows (and for Relatives and Friends Who Want to Understand).* Washington, DC: American Association of Retired Persons (AARP), 1984.

Long, H. B. "Educational Gerontology: Trends and Developments in 2000-2010." *Educational Gerontology* Vol. 16 (1990): 317–26.

Long Term Care National Resource Center. *State Units on Aging: Efforts in Housing for the Elderly.* Los Angeles, CA: Long Term Care National Resource Center at University of California, Los Angeles, and University of Southern California, 1991.

Longino, Charles F., Jr., and William H. Crown. "Older Americans: Rich or Poor?" *American Demographics* Vol. 13, no. 8 (1991): 48–52.

Longman, P. *Born to Pay.* Boston, MA: Houghton Mifflin, 1978.

Lopata, H. and D. R. Maines, eds. *Friendship in Context.* Greenwich, CT: JAI Press, 1990.

Lowy, L., and D. O'Connor. *Why Education in the Later Years?* Lexington, MA: D. C. Heath, 1986.

Lund, D. A., ed. *Older Bereaved Spouses.* New York: Hemisphere, 1989.

M

Mace, Nancy L., and Peter V. Rabins. *The Thirty-six Hour Day: A Family Guide to Caring for Persons with Alzheimer's Disease, Related Dementing Illness, and Memory Loss in Later Life.* New York: Warner Books, 1989.

Mace, Nancy L. *Dementia Care: Patient, Family, and Community.* Baltimore, MD: Johns Hopkins University Press, 1990.

McFadden, Susan H., and Robert R. Gerl. "Approaches to Understanding Spirituality in the Second Half of Life." *Generations* (Fall 1990): 33–38.

McGuire, Francis A., ed. *Computer Technology and the Aged.* New York: Haworth Press, 1986.

Maddox, George L., ed. *The Encyclopedia of Aging.* New York: Springer, 1987.

Maddox, George L., and others, eds. *Nature and the Extent of Alcohol Problems among the Elderly.* New York: Springer Publishing, 1984.

Maitland, David. *Aging as Counterculture.* New York: Pilgrim Press, 1991.

Manheimer, R. J. "The Politics and Promise of Cultural Enrichment Programs." *Generations* (Winter 1987–88): 26–30.

Margolis, Simeon, M.D., and Hamilton Moses, M.D., eds. *The Johns Hopkins Medical Handbook: The 100 Major Medical Disorders of People Over 50.* New York: Rebus, 1992.

Marion Merrell Dow. *Managed Care Digest: Long-Term Care Edition.* Kansas City: Marion Merrell Dow, 1992.

Markides, K. S., and C. L. Cooper, eds. *Aging, Stress, and Health.* Chichester, Eng.: Wiley, 1989.

Markides, K. S., and C. Mindel. *Aging and Ethnicity.* Newbury Park, CA: Sage, 1987.

Marriott Seniors Volunteerism Study. Washington, DC: Marriott Senior Living Services and U.S. Administration on Aging, 1991.

Marshall, V., ed. *Aging in Canada.* 2d ed. Markham, Ont.: Fitzhenry & Whiteside, 1987.

Matthews, Joseph L. *Elder Care: Choosing and Financing Long-Term Care.* Berkeley, CA: Nolo Press, 1991.

——. *Social Security, Medicare and Pensions: A Sourcebook for Older Americans.* 3rd ed. Berkeley, CA: Nolo Press, 1990.

Mayes, Kathleen. *Osteoporosis: Brittle Bones and the Calcium Crisis.* Santa Barbara, CA: Pennant Books, 1986.

Mercer, William M. *1993 Guide to Social Security and Medicare.* Louisville, KY: William M. Mercer, Inc., 1992.

Meyers, F. *The Handbook for Learning in Retirement Organizations.* Los Angeles, CA: The Association for Learning in Retirement Organizations, 1987.

Miller, Mary. *Suicide after Sixty: The Final Alternative.* Vol. 2 of Springer Series on Death and Suicide. New York: Springer, 1979.

Millman, Linda J. *Legal Issues and Older Adults.* Santa Barbara, CA: ABC-CLIO, 1992.

Minois, G. *History of Old Age from Antiquity to the Renaissance.* Trans. by S. H. Tenison. Chicago: University of Chicago Press, 1989.

Mirkin, Barry. "Early Retirement as a Labor Force Policy: An International Overview." *Monthly Labor Review* (March 1987): 19-33.

Mockenhaupt, Robin, and Kathleen Boyle. *Healthy Aging.* Santa Barbara, CA: ABC-CLIO, 1992.

Moody, Harry R. *Abundance of Life.* New York: Columbia University Press, 1988.

——. *Ethics in an Aging Society.* Baltimore, MD: Johns Hopkins University Press, 1992.

Moon, Marilyn. "Impact of the Reagan Years on the Distribution of Income of the Elderly." *Gerontologist* Vol. 26, no. 1 (1986): 32–37.

——. "The Rise and Fall of the Medicare Catastrophic Coverage Act." *National Tax Journal* Vol. 43 (1991): 371–81.

Mor, V., D. S. Greer, and R. Kastenbaum, eds. *The Hospice Experiment.* Baltimore, MD: Johns Hopkins University Press, 1988.

Morris, Robert, and Scott A. Bass, eds. *Retirement Reconsidered: Economic and Social Roles for Older People.* New York: Springer, 1988.

N

National Association of Area Agencies on Aging and the American Association of Retired Persons (AARP). *Analysis of Area Agencies on Aging Transportation Survey.* Washington, DC: AARP, 1991.

National Center for Home Equity Conversion. *Home Equity Conversion in the United States: Programs and Data.* Washington, DC: AARP Public Policy Institute, 1991.

National Council on the Aging (NCOA). *Aging in the Eighties.* Washington, DC: NCOA, 1981.

National Institute on Aging. *Resource Directory for Older People.* Bethesda, MD: National Institute on Aging, 1989.

National Senior Citizens Law Center. *Representing Older Persons: An Advocates Manual.* Washington, DC: National Senior Citizens Law Center, 1990.

Neugarten, B. L. *Age or Need in Public Policies for Older People.* Beverly Hills, CA: Sage, 1982.

Norrgard, Lee E., and Jo DeMars. *Final Choices: Making End-of-Life Decisions.* Santa Barbara, CA: ABC-CLIO, 1992.

Norris, Jane, ed. *Daughters of the Elderly: Building Partnerships in Caregiving.* Bloomington: Indiana University Press, 1988.

O

O'Connor, Kathleen, and Joyce Prothero. *The Alzheimer's Caregiver Strategies for Support.* Seattle, WA: University of Washington Press, 1987.

O'Shaughnessy, Carol. "Older Americans Act: 1991 Reauthorization and FY 1992 Budget Issues." Congressional Research Service, Order Code 1391002. Washington, DC: The Library of Congress, November 27, 1991.

Olsen, Nancy. *Starting a Mini-Business: A Guide Book for Seniors.* Sunnyvale, CA: Fair Oaks, 1988.

Osgood, Nancy J. *Suicide in the Elderly: A Practitioner's Guide to Diagnosis and Mental Health Intervention.* Rockville, MD: Aspen Systems Corp., 1985.

Osgood, Nancy J., ed. *Life After Work: Retirement, Leisure, Recreation, and the Elderly.* New York: Praeger, 1982.

P

Palmore, Erdman, B. M. Burchett, G. G. Fillenbaum, L. K. George, and L. M. Wallman. *Retirement: Causes and Consequences.* New York: Springer, 1985.

Papas, A. S., ed. *Geriatric Dentistry.* St. Louis, MO: Mosby Year Book, 1991.

Parker, V., S. Edmonds, and V. Robinson. *A Change for the Better: How to Make Communities More Responsive to Older Residents.* Washington, DC: AARP Consumer Affairs, Program Coordination and Development Department, 1991.

Payne, Barbara P., and Earl D. C. Brewer, eds. *Gerontology in Theological Education.* New York: Haworth Press, 1989.

Perspectives in Health Promotion and Aging. Quarterly. National Eldercare Institute on Health and Aging, AARP, 601 E Street N.W., 5th floor-B, Washington, DC 20049.

Petersen, M. D., and D. L. White, eds. *Health Care for the Elderly: An Information Source Book.* Newbury Park, CA: Sage, 1989.

Peterson, D. A. *Facilitating Education for Older Learners.* San Francisco: Jossey-Bass, 1983.

Petras, Kathryn, and Ross Petras. *The Only Retirement Guide You'll Ever Need.* New York: Poseidon Press, 1991.

Pifer, A., and L. Brontë, eds. *Our Aging Society: Paradox and Promise.* New York: W. W. Norton, 1987.

Pillemer, K., and R. Wolf, eds. *Conflict and Abuse in Families of the Elderly: Theory, Research, and Intervention.* Boston, MA: Auburn House, 1986.

Polniaszek, S., and J. Firman. *Long-Term Care Insurance.* Washington, DC: United Seniors Health Cooperative, 1991.

Porcino, Jane. *Living Longer, Living Better: Adventures in Community Housing for Those in the Second Half of Life.* New York: Continuum Publishing, 1991.

Pratt, H. J. *The Gray Lobby.* Chicago, IL: University of Chicago Press, 1977.

Pynoos, J., and E. Cohen. *The Perfect Fit: Creative Ideas for a Safe and Liveable Home.* Washington, DC: AARP, 1992.

Q

Quadagno, J. *The Transformation of Old Age Security.* Chicago, IL: University of Chicago Press, 1988.

Quinn, M., and S. Tomata. *Elder Abuse and Neglect.* New York: Springer, 1986.

R

Raschko, Bettyann B. *Housing Interiors for the Disabled and Elderly.* New York: Van Nostrand, 1982.

Regnier, Victor, and Jon Pynoos, eds. *Housing for the Elderly: Design Directives and Policy.* New York: Elsevier Science, 1987.

————. *Housing the Aged: Design Directives and Policy Considerations.* New York: Elsevier Science, 1987.

Riegel, Klaus F. "The Dialectics of Human Development." *The American Psychologist* Vol. 31 (1976): 689–700.

Rix, Sara E. *Older Workers: Choices and Challenges.* Santa Barbara, CA: ABC-CLIO, 1990.

Robinson, P. K., J. Livingston, and J. E. Birren, eds. *Aging and Technological Advances.* New York: Plenum Press, (1984).

Ruberstein, Robert L. *Singular Paths: Old Men Living Alone.* New York: Columbia University Press, 1986.

S

Sabatino, C. *Health Care Powers of Attorney.* Washington, DC: American Bar Association, 1990.

Sadavoy, J., L. W. Lazarus, and L. F. Jarvik. *Comprehensive Review of Geriatric Psychiatry.* Washington, DC: American Psychiatric Press, 1991.

Safford, Florence. *Caring for the Mentally Impaired Elderly: A Family Guide.* New York: Henry Holt, 1989.

St. Claire, Allison. *Travel and Older Adults.* Santa Barbara, CA: ABC-CLIO, 1991.

Sandell, S. H., ed. *The Problem Isn't Age: Work and Older Americans.* New York: Praeger, 1987.

Schaie, Warner. "Perceptual Speed in Adulthood: Cross-Sectional and Longitudinal Studies." *Psychology and Aging* (1989).

Schneider, Edward L., and John W. Rowe, eds. *Handbook of the Biology of Aging.* 3d ed. New York: Harcourt Brace, 1989.

Schulz, James H. *The Economics of Aging.* 5th ed. Westport, CT: Auburn House, 1992.

Schulz, Richard M., and David B. Brushwood. "The Pharmacist's Role in Patient Care."

Hasting Center Report (January-February 1991): 12–17.

Schwenk, F. N. "Women Sixty-five Years or Older: A Comparison of Economic Well-Being by Living Arrangement." *Family Economic Review* Vol. 4, no. 3 (1991): 2–8.

Scott-Maxwell, Florida. *The Measure of My Days.* New York: Knopf, 1968.

Seeber, E. *Spiritual Maturity in the Later Years.* New York: Haworth Press, 1992.

Selden, Ina Lee. *Going into Business for Yourself: New Beginnings after 50.* Glenview, IL: Scott, Foresman, 1989.

Seltzer, M. M., J. Irvy, and L. C. Litchfield. "Family Members as Case Managers: Partnership Between the Formal and Informal Support Networks." *Gerontologist* Vol. 27 (1987): 722–28.

Sennett, D., ed. *Full Measure: Modern Short Stories on Aging.* Saint Paul, MN: Graywolf Press, 1988.

Sennett, D., and A. Czarniecki, eds. *Vital Signs: International Stories on Aging.* Saint Paul, MN: Graywolf Press, 1991.

Serow, W. J., D. F. Sly, and J. M. Wrigley. *Population Aging in the United States.* New York: Greenwood Press, 1990.

Seskin, Jane. *Alone—Not Lonely: Independent Living for Women Over Fifty.* Washington, DC: American Association of Retired Persons and Scott, Foresman, 1985.

Sexon, Sue V., and Mary Jean Etten. *Physical Change and Aging: A Guide for the Helping Professions.* New York: Tiresias Press, 1987.

Shanas, Ethel, P. Townsend, D. Wedderburn, H. Friis, P. Milhoj, and J. Stehouwer. *Older People in Three Industrial Societies.* New York: Atherton Press, 1968.

Shapiro, Barbara A. *The Big Squeeze: Balancing the Needs of Aging Parents, Dependent Children, and You.* Bedford, MA: Mills & Sanderson, 1991.

Shea, Edward J. *Swimming for Seniors.* Champaign, IL: Leisure Press, 1986.

Shelley, F. D. *When Your Parents Grow Old.* New York: Harper & Row, 1988.

Sherman, E. *Reminiscence and the Self in Old Age.* New York: Springer, 1991.

Sherron, R. H., and D. B. Lumsden, eds. *Introduction to Educational Gerontology.* 3d ed. New York: Hemisphere Publishing, 1989.

Shock, N. W. "Normal Human Aging: The Baltimore Longitudinal Study of Aging." *NIH Publication No. 84-2450.* Washington, DC: U.S. Department of Health and Human Services, 1984.

Shock, Nathan W., T. Franklin Williams, and James L. Fozard. *Older and Wiser.* NIH Publication 89-27987. Washington, DC: Government Printing Office, 1989.

Silverstone, B., and H. Kandel Hyman. *You and Your Aging Parent.* New York: Pantheon, 1989.

Simmons, Henry G., and Vivienne S. Pierce. *Pastoral Response to Older Adults and Their Families: An Annotated Bibliography.* Westport, CT: Greenwood Press, 1992.

Snyder, Harry. *Medicare/Medigap: The Essential Guide for Older Americans and Their Families.* New York: Consumer Report Books, 1990.

Soled, Alex J. *The Essential Guide To Wills, Estates, Trusts, and Death Taxes.* Glenview, IL: Scott, Foresman, 1988.

Solomon, David H., Elyse Salend, Anna Nolen Rahman, and others. *A Consumer's Guide to Aging.* Baltimore, MD: Johns Hopkins University Press, 1992.

Sommers, T. *Til Death Do Us Part: Caregiving Wives of Disabled Husbands.* Washington, DC: Older Women's League, 1982.

Sommers, Tish, and Laurie Shields. *Women Take Care: The Consequences of Caregiving in Today's Society.* Gainesville, FL: Triad Publishing Co., 1987.

Stearns, L. R., and others. "Lessons for the Implementation of CCRC Legislation." *Gerontologist* Vol. 30, no. 2 (1990).

Stearns, P. *Old Age in Preindustrial Society.* New York: Holmes and Meier, 1982.

Stegner, W. S. *Crossing to Safety.* New York: Random House, 1987.

Steinmeta, Suzanne K. *Duty Bound: Elder Abuse and Family Care.* Newbury Park, CA: Sage Publications, 1988.

Stiegel, L. *Alternatives to Guardianship.* Washington, DC: American Bar Association, 1992.

Stoller, E. P. "Males as Helpers: The Role of Sons, Relatives and Friends." *Gerontologist* Vol. 30 (1990): 228–35.

Stone, R., G. Cafferata, and J. Sangl. *Caregivers of the Frail Elderly: A National Profile.*

Washington, DC: U.S. Department of Health and Human Services, 1986.

Stone, Robyn. *Exploding the Myths: Caregiving in America; A Study*. Washington, DC: U.S. Congress, House Select Committee on Aging, 1987.

Streib, Gordon F., and C. J. Schneider. *Retirement in American Society: Impact and Process*. Ithaca, NY: Cornell University Press, 1971.

Strom, R. D., and S. K. Strom. *Becoming a Better Grandparent*. Newbury Park, CA: Sage, 1991.

Szinovacz, M., ed. *Women's Retirement*. Beverly Hills, CA: Sage, 1982.

T

Tallmer, L., and D. Lester, eds. *Suicide in the Elderly: Counseling Needs and Management*. Boston: Charles Press, 1992.

Taylor, R. J., and L. M. Chatters. "Extended Family Networks of Older Black Adults." *Journal of Gerontology* Vol. 46 (1991): S210–S217.

Taylor, Robert J. "Religious Participation Among Elderly Blacks." *Gerontologist* Vol. 29, no. 6 (1986): 630–38.

Tideiksaar, Rein. *Falling in Old Age: Its Prevention and Treatment*. New York: Springer, 1989.

Torres-Gil, Fernando M. *The New Aging: Politics and Change in America*. New York: Auburn House, 1992.

Troll, Lillian E. *Continuations: Adult Development and Aging*. Monterey, CA: Brooks/Cole, 1982.

Troyansky, D. *Old Age in the Ancien Regime*. Ithaca, NY: Cornell University Press, 1989.

Turner, John A., and Daniel J. Beller, eds. *Trends in Pensions, 1992*. Washington, DC: U.S. Government Printing Office, 1992.

Turock, B. *Serving the Older Adult: A Guide to Library Programs and Information Sources* New York: R. R. Bowker, 1982.

U

U.S. Bureau of the Census. Current Population Reports, Special Studies, 23–178, *Sixty-Five Plus in America*. Washington, DC: United States Government Printing Office, 1992.

———. *Employment Discrimination Against Older Women: A Handbook on Litigating Age and Sex Discrimination Cases*. Washington, DC: Older Women's League, 1989.

———. *Labor Market Problems of Older Workers*. Report of the Secretary of Labor, prepared by Philip L. Rones and Diane E. Herz. Washington, DC: Department of Labor, 1989.

U.S. Congress. Office of Technology Assessment. *Life-Sustaining Technologies and the Elderly*. OTA-BA-306. Washington, DC: Office of Technology Assessment, July 1987.

U.S. Congress. Senate. Special Committee on Aging. *Aging America: Trends and Projections, 1991*. Washington, DC: U.S. Department of Health and Human Services.

———. *Lifelong Learning for an Aging Society: An Information Paper* Washington, DC: U.S. Government Printing Office, 1991.

U.S. Congress. Senate. Special Committee on Aging; American Association of Retired Persons; Federal Council on Aging; and U.S. Administration on Aging, U.S. Department of Health and Human Services. *Aging America: Trends and Projections*. 1991 ed.

U.S. Department of Health and Human Services. "Guide to Health Insurance for People with Medicare." *HCFA Publication No. HCFA-02110*. Washington, DC: U.S. Government Printing Office, 1992.

U.S. Department of Health and Human Services. Public Health Service. "The National Nursing Home Survey: 1985 Summary for the United States; Data From the National Health Survey. Vital and Health Statistics." DHHS Publication Series 13, no. 97; PHS Publication No. 89–1758. Washington, DC: Government Printing Office, 1989.

U.S. Department of Labor. *Labor Market Problems of Older Workers: Report to the Secretary of Labor*. Washington, DC: U. S. Department of Labor, 1989.

V

Vacha, Keith. *Quiet Fire: Memoirs of Older Gay Men*. Trumansburg, NY: Crossing Press, 1985.

Ventura, C., and E. H. Worthy. *Education for Older Adults: A Synthesis of Significant Data*. ERIC Document Reproduction Service No. ED 303 607, 1982.

Vierck, E. *Factbook on Aging*. Santa Barbara, CA: ABC-CLIO, 1990.

Villers Foundation. *On the Other Side of Easy Street: Myths and Facts about the Economics of Old Age*. Washington, DC: Villers Foundation, 1987.

W

Ward, R. A., and S. S. Tobin, eds. *Health and Aging: Sociological Issues and Policy Directions*. New York: Springer, 1987.

Weaver, Peter, and Annette Buchanan. *What to Do with What You've Got: The Practical Guide to Money Management in Retirement*. Washington, DC: American Association of Retired Persons and Scott, Foresman, 1984.

Wetle, Terrie, and others. "Nursing Home Resident Participation in Medical Decisions: Perceptions and Preferences. *Gerontologist* Vol. 28 (supplement, 1988): 32–38.

Winslow, Gerald R., ed. *Facing Limits: Ethics and Health Care for the Elderly*. Boulder, CO: Westview, 1993.

Z

Zarit, Steven H., Nancy Orr, and Judy Zarit. *The Hidden Victims of Alzheimer's Disease: Families under Stress*. New York: New York University Press, 1985.

Index

An 'f' appearing next to a page number denotes figure; a 't' appearing next to a page number denotes table; italicized page numbers refer to illustrations.

creation of, 114
legal services through, 170
administrative law, and government benefits, 188
adult child(ren)
    as caregivers, 560, 565, 566, 580–81
    as legal client, 169
    proximity to aging parents, 326, 362t, 362–63
    relationships with, 325–27
    residing with impaired parents, 558
    as social support, 327–28, 339, 361–64, 362t
adult day care, 368, 569
adult development, 90, 92–93, 106
adult education, 204, 723–26
adult grandchild(ren), and grandparents, 330
adult identity, 93–94
adulthood, 91, 397
    stages of, 90–94
advance directive(s), 177, 519, 536–39, 599, 600–601, 601f, 607. *See also* durable power of attorney (DPOA); living will(s)
    cautions and tips, 601–2
    checklist for level of care, 601
    guidelines for using, 539
    importance of, 537–39
    individual considerations, 538–39
    limitations of, 540–41
    medical, 232
    older people's attitudes toward, 543
    patient autonomy and, 508
    terminating treatment without, 538
advance planning. *See* advance directive(s); durable power of attorney (DPOA); estate planning; living will(s)
advance planning directives. *See* advance directive(s)
Adventists. *See* Seventh-day Adventists
adventure, during travel, 798–99
adverse drug reactions, 514
Advisory Commission on Regulatory Barriers to Affordable Housing, 628
advocacy
    by Area Agencies on Aging, 127–28
    organizations, 160–61
    in Social Security appeals process, 188
    by state units on aging, 126–27
AED. *See* Academy for Educational Development (AED)
aerobic exercise, 375, 378
affectual solidarity, 61
affluence, elderly in age of, 18–21

African Americans, 61, 62, 101–2, 103
    adult children, 326
    church attendance, 706, 793
    economic status, 57
    income, 229, 262t, 262–63
    labor force participation (male), 217
    leisure activities, 793
    life expectancy of, 3–4, 34, 408–9, 409t, 786t
    living arrangements, 44t
    marital status, 58t
    slavery of, 12
    support for parents, 327, 363–64
age
    and absenteeism, 201
    and activity limitations, 409–10
    chronological, 97, 97t, 200
    classifications, 40, 40t, 41t
    and driving performance, 650–51
    employment statistics and, 196t
    median income and, 262t
    of older population, 41t
    of retirement, 238–39
    stigma of, 659–60
age cohort. *See* cohort
age-condensed family, 322
age-congregated living arrangements, 794
age discrimination, 101
Age Discrimination in Employment Act (ADEA), 193, 234–35
age disqualification, 96
age-gapped family, 321
An Age Integrated Society: Implications for Spiritual Well-Being (National Interfaith Coalition on Aging), 710
age-linked fields, 98
age norms, 97–98, 107
age peers, siblings as, 364
age-segregated housing, 355
age-similar friends, 365–66
aged. *See* older adult(s)
ageism, 601
Agency for Health Care Policy and Research (AHCPR), 511
AGHE. *See* Association for Gerontology in Higher Education (AGHE)
aging
    acute and chronic illness during, 81
    adult development and, 90–94
    attitudes toward, 6, 10–13
    biological, 73

21   36

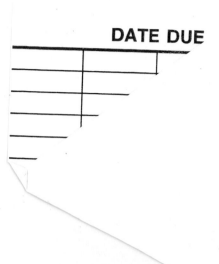

DATE DUE